THE BIOGRAPHICAL DICTIONARY OF SCIENTISTS

THE BIOGRAPHICAL DICTIONARY OF SCIENTISTS

THIRD EDITION

Volume II

(Lebedev to Zworykin)

Consultant Editors
Roy Porter
Marilyn Ogilvie

OXFORD UNIVERSITY PRESS
New York   2000

Copyright © 2000 Helicon Publishing Ltd
Illustrations © 2000 Helicon Publishing Ltd

First published in Great Britain in six volumes as
The Biographical Dictionary of Scientists:
Biologists (1983), *Chemists* (1983),
Astronomers (1984), *Physicists* (1984),
Engineers and Inventors (1985),
Mathematicians (1985)

Second edition published 1994

Third edition published 2000 in Great Britain
by Helicon Publishing Limited
Third edition published 2000 in the United States of America
by Oxford University Press, Inc.,
198 Madison Avenue, New York, NY 10016
www.oup.com

Oxford is a registered trademark of Oxford University Press

Library of Congress Cataloging-in-Publication Data is available.

ISBN 0–19–521663–6 (2v. set)
ISBN 0–19–521664–4 (v. 1)
ISBN 0–19–521665–2 (v. 2)

1 3 5 7 9 8 6 4 2

CONTENTS

CONTRIBUTORS

Neil Ardley, Gareth Ashurst, Jim Bailey, Mary Basham, Alan
Bishop, Anthony Burton, William Cooksey, Christopher
Cooper, David Cowey, Michael Darton, Keld Fenwick, Lorraine
Ferguson, Judy Garlick, Richard Gulliver, Ian Harvey, Maggy
Hendry, Keith Hutton, Nicholas Law, Lloyd Lindo, Robert
Matthews, Nigel Morrison, Robert Mortimer, Patricia Nash,
Valarie Neal, Jon and Lucia Osborne, Adam Ostaszewski,
Caroline Overy, David Pimm, Roy Porter, Helen Rapson, Peter
Rodgers, Mary Sanders, Martin Sherwood, Robert Smith,
Robert Stewart, E. M. Tansey, Fred Taylor, Christopher Tunney,
Martin Walters, Zusa Vrbova, David Ward, Edward Young

EDITORS

Consultant Editors
Roy Porter
Marilyn Ogilvie

Editorial Director
Hilary McGlynn

Managing Editor
Elena Softley

Technical Editor
Tracey Auden

Project Editor
Catherine Thompson

Researcher and Contributor
Maggy Hendry

Text Editors
Malgorzata Colquhoun
Sara Jenkins-Jones
Karen Lines

Bibliographies
Andrew Colquhoun

Production Director
Tony Ballsdon

Page Make-up
TechType

Art and Design Manager
Terence Caven

Biographies

(Lebedev to Zworykin)

Lebedev, Pyotr Nikolayevich (1866–1912) Russian physicist whose most important contribution to science was the detection and measurement of the pressure that light exerts on bodies, an effect that had been predicted by James Clerk ◊Maxwell in his electromagnetic theory of light.

Lebedev was born in Moscow on 8 March 1866. He initially received training in business and engineering in Moscow but decided that he would rather be a physicist and so went to the University of Strasbourg to study physics under August ◊Kundt. His teacher moved to Berlin in 1888 and Lebedev tried to follow him but found that he did not possess the qualifications necessary to enrol in Berlin University, and so he returned to Russia in 1891. On his return he joined the physics department of Moscow Univeristy – at the invitation of the head of the department, A G Stoletov – and became professor of physics there in the following year, although he did not obtain his PhD until 1900. In 1911 government interference in university affairs caused a storm of protest, which led to the resignation of many of the university's staff, including Lebedev. Although he was subsequently offered numerous prestigious positions at other universities, both in Russia and elsewhere, the shock of the upheaval precipitated a collapse of his health and he died shortly afterwards in Moscow, on 14 March 1912.

Lebedev began studying light pressure (now called radiation pressure) in the late 1890s but did not complete his investigations until 1910. Working first with solid bodies and later with gases, he not only observed the minute physical effects caused by the infinitesimal pressure exerted by light on matter but also measured this pressure using extremely lightweight apparatus in an evacuated chamber. His findings provided substantial supportive evidence for Maxwell's theory of electromagnetic radiation, which had predicted the phenomenon of light pressure. Also, Lebedev suggested that the force of the light pressure emanating from the Sun could balance the gravitational force attracting cosmic dust particles towards it, and that this was the reason why comets' tails point away from the Sun. Later, however, it was discovered that comets' tails point away from the Sun because of the much greater effect of the solar wind. The Swedish chemist Svante ◊Arrhenius took up the idea of light pressure to explain how primordial spores might have travelled through space in his theory of the extraterrestrial origin of life. This model has not become widely accepted because it does not explain how the spores themselves originated nor how the travelling spores could endure the intense cosmic radiation in outer space.

Lebedev also investigated (while working for his doctorate) the effects of electromagnetic, acoustic, and hydrodynamic waves on resonators; demonstrated the behavioural similarities between light and (as they are now known to be) other electromagnetic radiations; detected electromagnetic waves of higher frequency than the radio waves that had been studied by Heinrich ◊Hertz and Augusto Righi; and researched into the Earth's magnetic field.

Lebesgue, Henri Léon (1875–1941) French mathematician who is known chiefly for the development of a new theory of integration named after him.

Lebesgue was born in Beauvais on 28 June 1875 and educated at the Ecole Normale Supérieure in Paris 1894–97. From 1899 to 1902 he worked on his doctoral thesis while teaching mathematical science at the lycée in Nancy. He received his doctorate from the Sorbonne in 1902 and in the same year was appointed a lecturer in the faculty of sciences at the University of Rennes. He left there to become a professor at the University of Poitiers in 1906, remaining at Poitiers until 1910, when he was appointed lecturer in mathematics at the Sorbonne. In 1920 he was promoted to the chair of the application of geometry to analysis, but he left the Sorbonne in the following year to take up his final academic post as professor of mathematics at the Collège de France. He died in Paris on 26 July 1941.

Lebesgue was awarded many honours, including the Prix Houllevique in 1912, the Prix Poncelet in 1914, and the Prix Saintour in 1917. He was elected to the French Academy of Sciences in 1922 and to the Royal Society in 1934.

Lebesgue made contributions to several branches of mathematics, including set theory, the calculus of variation, and function theory. With Emile ◊Borel he laid the foundations of the modern theory of the functions of a real variable. His chief work, however, was his creation of a new approach to the theory of integration.

From an early stage in his mathematicial career, Lebesgue was intrigued by problems associated with Riemannian integration and he began to get results in this field in 1902. His introduction of the Lebesgue integral was not only an impressive piece of mathematical creativity in itself, but quickly proved itself to be of great importance in the development of several branches of mathematics, especially calculus, curve rectification, and the theory of trigonometric series. Later the integral was also discovered to be of fundamental significance for the development of measure theory.

Leblanc, Nicolas (1742–1806) French industrial chemist who devised the first commercial process for the manufacture of soda (sodium carbonate), which became the general method of making the chemical for a hundred years.

Leblanc was probably born in Ivoy-le-Pré, Indre, on 6 December 1742, although there is some doubt as to the exact place and date. His father was an ironmaster and paid for his son's education as an apothecary's apprentice; he went on to study medicine, qualifying as a doctor. In 1780 he became physician and assistant to the future duc d'Orléans, Philippe Egalité. Leblanc invented his famous process in the 1780s and in 1791, using capital supplied by the duke, he built a factory for making soda at St Denis, near Paris. But the duc d'Orléans was guillotined in 1793 during the French Revolution and Leblanc was forced to run the factory at no profit, giving all the output to the state. He had no money left to re-establish the process when the factory was handed back to him by Napoleon in 1802. He became a pauper and committed suicide at St Denis on 16 January or February 1806.

Soda was an important industrial chemical in the second half of the 18th century for making glass, soap, and paper. It was made by calcining wood, seaweed, and other vegetable matter, hence its common name soda ash. Common salt (sodium chloride) was, however, plentiful and in 1775 the French Academy of Sciences offered a cash prize for the first person to devise a commercially practical way of making soda from salt. Leblanc invented his process in 1783 (although he never received the prize money).

In the Leblanc process, salt (sodium chloride) was dissolved in sulphuric acid to form sodium sulphate:

$$2NaCl + H_2SO_4 \rightarrow Na_2SO_4 + 2HCl$$

The large amounts of hydrogen chloride generated in this reaction were released into the atmosphere. The sodium sulphate (called salt cake) was then roasted with powdered coal and crushed chalk or limestone (calcium carbonate) to yield a dark residue ('black ash') which was made up mainly of sodium carbonate and calcium sulphide:

$$2Na_2SO_4 + 2CaCO_3 + 4C \rightarrow 2Na_2CO_3 + 2CaS + 4CO_2$$

The sodium carbonate was dissolved out of the residue with water and recrystallized by heating the solution. The waste calcium sulphide that remained was known as 'galligu'.

Leblanc patented the process in 1791, and at his first factory produced 350 tonnes of soda a year. But the patent was rendered useless by the activities of the Revolutionary government, which confiscated the factory. The process was adopted and used throughout Europe, particularly in England, and earned large amounts of money for the soda manufacturers (who by the 1860s were making 180,000 tonnes of soda a year using the Leblanc process) and for the makers of sulphuric acid, one of the starting materials.

After the development of the ammonia–soda process by Ernest ◊Solvay in the 1860s, the Leblanc process gradually fell into disuse, although from time to time it was given a new lease of life by modifications. In the 1850s the British industrial chemists Henry Deacon (1822–1876) and Ferdinand Hurter (1844–1898) introduced the improvement of catalytically oxidizing the waste hydrogen chloride to chlorine, which was absorbed by lime to make bleaching powder, then much in demand by the Lancashire textile industry. In the late 1880s Alexander Chance (1844–1917), of the Birmingham glassmaking family, turned his attention to calcium sulphide, the other main waste product of the Leblanc process. He used carbon doxide to react with an aqueous slurry of the noxious waste to produce hydrogen sulphide gas (and leave calcium carbonate), which he then oxidized to sulphur in a Claus kiln. By the 1890s in the UK alone the Chance process, as it came to be known, was producing 35,000 tonnes of sulphur each year. Eighty years after Leblanc's death, his process and its adaptations were still providing chemical industry with some of its most important basic raw materials. The last Leblanc plant (in Bolton, Lancashire) did not close until 1938.

Lebon, Phillipe (1767–1804) French engineer who was the first person successfully to use 'artificial' gas as a means of illumination on a large scale.

Lebon was born in the charcoal-burning town of Bruchay, near Jonville. He received a sound scientific education, first at Chalon-sur-Saône and later at the Ecole des Ponts et Chaussées, a famous school for engineers. He graduated in 1792 and received the rank of major, serving as a highway engineer. After a short while in Angouleme, near Bordeaux, he was recalled to Paris to teach mechanics at the Ecole des Ponts et Chaussées.

In about 1797, Lebon became interested in using 'artificial' gas, produced from wood, for heating and lighting purposes. He also made some attempts at perfecting the steam engine and received a national prize of 2,000 livres for the improvements he accomplished. In 1799 he read a paper on his experiments with gas to the Institut de France and was granted a patent on his invention later that year. Further patents were granted in 1801. Lebon's work was, however, cut short by his sudden death on 2 December 1804. He was attacked and stabbed on the Champs Elyssée in Paris, and died of his wounds.

Lighting on a large scale was demonstrated when the streets of Paris were first lit in 1667 using large lanterns containing candles and metal reflectors. An oil lantern was developed in 1744 and, in 1786, Argand completed his invention of an oil lamp with a glass chimney. Carcel introduced an oil pump and such oil lamps continued to be popular for lighting streets and houses.

Lebon was the first person to consider using gas as a lighting medium.

In 1797, at Bruchay, he became interested in the extraction of gas from wood for this purpose and began experimenting with sawdust. He placed some sawdust in a glass tube and held it over a flame. The gas given off caught alight as it emerged from the tube – but it smoked badly and emitted a strong resinous smell. On his return to Paris, Lebon discussed his work with several scientists, including Antoine Fourcroy (1755–1809). They encouraged him and, in 1799, he read a paper on the subject before the Institut de France. He patented his invention in that year and called his new lamp the Thermolampe (heat lamp) because he intended to use it for heating as well as lighting purposes.

Approaches to the government to interest them in using his invention for public heating and lighting proved of no avail. To publicize his Thermolampe, Lebon leased the Hotel Seignelay in Paris in 1801 and, for several months, he exhibited a large version of the lamp, which attracted huge crowds. But, although they admired Lebon's successful attempt to illuminate a fountain in the hotel, because he had been unable to eliminate the repulsive odour given off by the gas, the public decided that his invention was not a practical one.

Further work by Lebon was curtailed by his early death and it was left to William ◊Murdock (working independently at about the same time in Scotland) to succeed where Lebon had failed, and it is Murdock who has received the credit for the invention of gas lighting.

Le Châtelier, Henri Louis (1850–1936) French physical chemist, best known for the principle named after him which states that if any constraint is applied to a system in chemical equilibrium, the system tends to adjust itself to counteract or oppose the constraint.

Le Châtelier was born in Paris on 8 October 1850, the son of France's inspector general of mines. He was educated at the Collège Rollin in Paris and went to study science and engineering at the Ecole Polytechnique, although his studies were interrupted by the Franco-Prussian War 1870–71. He graduated in 1875, then, after working for two years as a mining engineer, he took up an appointment as professor of chemistry at the Ecole des Mines in 1877. In 1898 he moved to the Collège de France as professor of mineral chemistry, before finally settling at the Sorbonne in 1908 as professor of chemistry in succession to Henri Moissan (1852–1907). He worked for the Ministry of Armaments during World War I and retired in 1919. He died in Miribel-les-Echelles, Isère, on 17 September 1936.

Le Châtelier's first major contribution was to temperature measurement, a subject that followed naturally from his high-temperature studies of metals, alloys, glass, cement, and ceramics. In 1887 he devised a platinum–rhodium thermocouple for measuring high temperatures by making use of the Seebeck effect (the generation of a current in a circuit made up of two dissimilar metals with the junctions at different temperatures; the magnitude of the current is proportional to the difference in temperature). Le Châtelier also made an optical pyrometer that measures temperature by comparing the light emitted by a high-temperature object with a standard light source.

This work involving flames and thermometry led him to thermodynamics, and in 1884 Le Châtelier put forward the first version of his principle, in which he stated that a change in pressure on an equilibrium system results in a movement of the equilibrium in the direction that opposes the pressure change. By 1888 he had generalized the principle as the *Loi de stabilité de l'équilibre chimique* and applied it to any change that affects chemical equilibrium. In its general form Le Châtelier's principle is all-embracing, and includes the law of mass action, as formulated by Cato Guldberg (1836–1902) and Peter Waage (1833–1900) in 1864. It is particularly relevant in predicting the effects of changes in temperature and pressure on chemical reactions: for example, it predicts that a rise in temperature or an increase in pressure should facilitate or accelerate a reaction that is reluctant to take place at normal temperatures and pressures. Industrial chemists, such as Fritz ◊Haber and his process for synthesizing ammonia, were soon to make good use of the principle. It also agreed with the new thermodynamics being worked out in the USA by Willard ◊Gibbs. Le Châtelier was largely responsible for making Gibbs's researches known in Europe, translating his papers into French and performing experiments to test the phase rule. He also wrote extensively about labour relations and efficiency in industry. In 1895 he put forward the idea of the oxyacetylene torch for cutting and welding steel.

Leclanché, Georges (1839–1882) French engineer who invented the Leclanché battery, or dry cell, in 1866. This is the kind of battery used today in torches, calculators, portable radios, and so on.

Leclanché was born in Paris in 1839. Educated at the Ecole Centrale des Arts et Manufactures, he joined the Compagnie du Chemin de l'Est as an engineer in 1860. Six years later, he developed his electric cell, which consisted of a zinc anode and a carbon cathode separated by a solution of ammonium chloride. The following year, in 1867, he gave up his job as a railway engineer to devote all his time to the improvement of the cell's design. He was successful in having it adopted by the Belgian Telegraphic Service in 1868.

The Leclanché cell rapidly came into general use whenever an intermittent supply of electricity was needed and it was later developed into the familiar dry battery in use today. Towards the end of his life, Leclanché diversified his researches and worked for a while on electrical methods of time measurement. He died in Paris on 14 September 1882.

Almost any electrolytic cell with electrodes of different materials can act as a battery. The first cells to be invented were wet cells made by Alessandro ◊Volta in 1800. They were made of tin or copper and zinc or silver separated by pasteboard or hide soaked in water, vinegar, or salt solution. These first electric batteries, although cumbersome, caused a revolution by making comparatively large amounts of electric current available for the first time. The revolution was carried even further when Leclanché produced the first dry cell, which facilitated both handling and mobility. Leclanché's investigations into new kinds of electrodes and electrolyte enabled him to make the advance that he did. Volta's cell prompted several other types of cell, among them a design by Robert ◊Bunsen for a battery containing carbon and zinc electrodes and an acid such as chromic acid as the electrolyte. Leclanché produced the most useful design of all by having zinc for the negative pole, carbon for the positive pole and a solution of ammonium chloride as the electrolyte. This first cell was the forerunner of all subsequent dry cells in that it was sealed so that the outside stayed dry.

Although there are other types of dry cells in existence today, such as those using mercury, the Leclanché cell is still the only one produced on a large scale. In the modern dry Leclanché cell, zinc serves both as the container and anode, the cathode is formed from graphite, and the electrolyte is a paste of ammonium chloride, zinc chloride, manganese dioxide, and carbon particles. The cell produces 1.5 volts.

Lederberg, Joshua US geneticist; see ◊Beadle, Tatum, and Lederberg.

Lee, Tsung Dao Chinese physicist; see ◊Yang and Lee.

Leeuwenhoek, Anton van (1632–1723) Dutch microscopist, famous for the numerous detailed observations he made using his single-lens microscopes. He was not the first of the many well-known early microscopists, being preceded by Marcello ◊Malpighi for example, nor did he make notable innovations to the microscope itself (the forerunner of the modern compound microscope was developed in Leeuwenhoek's lifetime by Robert ◊Hooke, an English physicist and microscopist). But such was the dramatic nature of Leeuwenhoek's discoveries that he became – and remains – world renowned.

Leeuwenhoek was born on 24 October 1632 in Delft, Holland. Relatively little is known of his early life but it seems that he received scant schooling. His stepfather died when Leeuwenhoek was 16 years old and he was apprenticed to a cloth merchant in Amsterdam. He returned to Delft four years later in 1652 and opened a drapery shop. In 1660 he obtained the sinecure of chamberlain to the sheriffs of Delft. Having guaranteed his financial security, Leeuwenhoek devoted much of his time to his hobbies of lens grinding and microscopy. From 1672–23 he described and illustrated his observations in a total of more than 350 letters to the Royal Society of London, which elected him a fellow in 1680. Leeuwenhoek continued his work almost until he died, aged 90 years, on 26 August 1723. After his death several of his microscopes were sent to the Royal Society, in accordance with his will.

Leeuwenhoek ground more than 400 lenses, which he mounted in various ways. Most of them were very small (some were about the size of a pinhead) and had magnifying powers of between 50 and about 300 times; but each was meticulously made and the optical excellence of these lenses – combined with Leeuwenhoek's careful observations – undoubtedly helped him to make so many important discoveries. In 1674 he discovered protozoa, which he called 'animalicules', and calculated their sizes. He was also probably the first to observe bacteria, when he saw tiny structures in tooth scrapings; the first known drawing of bacteria was made by Leeuwenhoek and appeared in the Royal Society's *Philosophical Transactions* in 1683. He made many other important observations: he was the first to describe spermatozoa (1677) and also studied the structure of the lens in the eye, muscle striations, insects' mouthparts, the fine structure of plants, and discovered parthenogenesis in aphids. In 1684 he gave the first accurate description of red blood corpuscles, also noticing that they can have different shapes in different animal species.

Leeuwenhoek became world famous during his lifetime and was visited by several reigning monarchs, including Frederick I of Prussia and Tsar Peter the Great. Many of Leeuwenhoek's observations remained unsurpassed for more than a century – partly because his microscopes were of very high optical quality and partly because he kept secret the details of the techniques he used.

Further Reading

Ford, Brian, *Leeuwenhoek Legacy,* Biopress Ltd, 1991.
Palm, L C (ed), *The Collected Letters of Antoni van Leeuwenhoek,* Swets and Zeitlinger, 1996.
Yount, Lisa, *Antoni van Leeuwenhoek: First to See Microscopic Life,* Great Minds of Science series, Enslow Publishers, 1996.

Legendre, Adrien-Marie (1752–1833) French mathematician who was particularly interested in number theory, celestial mechanics, and elliptic functions.

Legendre was born in Paris on 18 September 1752, studied mathematics and natural science at the Collège Mazarin in Paris, and – despite having a private income to sustain him in independent research – took employment as a lecturer in mathematics at the Ecole Militaire in 1775. He taught there until 1780 without making any impression on the mathematical world. His fortunes began to rise in 1882, when he won the prize awarded by the Berlin Academy for an essay on the path of projectiles travelling through resistant media. A year later he was elected to the French Academy of Sciences and from 1783 began to publish important papers. He was appointed professor of mathematics at the Institut de Marat in Paris in 1794, the same year in which he became head of the government department established to standardize French weights and measures. From 1799 to 1815 he served as an examiner of students of artillery and in 1813 he succeeded Pierre ◊Laplace as chief of the Bureau de Longitudes. He remained at that post until his death, in Paris, on 10 January 1833.

Legendre's first published work, a paper on mechanics, appeared in 1774, but a decade passed before his real talent showed itself. In several papers of 1783–84 he introduced to celestial mechanics what are now known as Legendre polynomials. These are solutions to the second-order differential equation (still important in applied mathematics):

$$(1 - x^2) \frac{d^2y}{dx^2} - 2x \frac{dy}{dx} + n(n + 1)y = 0$$

Where n is a non-negative integer. The functions that satisfy this equation are called Legendre functions.

During the 1780s Legendre worked on a number of other topics, including indeterminate analysis and the calculus of variations, but at the end of the decade his research was interrupted for a time by the outbreak of the French Revolution and the suppression, in 1793, of the French Academy of Sciences. He placed himself at the service of the revolutionary government, however, to direct the project that altered the system for the measurement of angles and other decimalization projects.

His two most important contributions to mathematics were made in the 1790s, although he had begun work on both – number theory and elliptical functions – in the mid-1780s. In number theory his significant result was the law of reciprocity of quadratic residues, although the credit for establishing the law rigorously belongs to Karl ◊Gauss in 1801. It was Legendre alone, however, who in 1798 gave the law of the distribution of prime numbers; and very late in his

career, in 1823, he proved that there was no solution in integers for the equation:

$$x^5 + y^5 = z^5$$

Of even more use to fellow mathematicians was Legendre's long and painstaking work on elliptical functions. In 1786 he made a tentative start on the subject with a paper on the integration of elliptical curves and in 1792 he touched on the theory of elliptical transcendentals in a paper to the academy. His great achievement, however, was the two-volume textbook on elliptical functions which he published in 1825 and 1826, in which he gave the tables of elliptical functions which he had laboriously compiled.

One other accomplishment of Legendre, of a more mundane character, ought not to be forgotten. In 1794 he published his *Eléments de géometrie*, a re-working and a clarification of ◊Euclid's *Elements*. Among its delights was the single proof of the irrationality of π and the first proof of the irrationality of π^2. The text was translated into several languages and in many parts of the world stood as the basic school text in geometry for the next hundred years.

Leibniz, Gottfried Wilhelm (1646–1716) German philosopher and mathematician who was one of the founders of the differential calculus and symbolic logic.

Leibniz was born on 1 July 1646 in Leipzig, where his father was professor of moral philosophy at the university. Although he attended the Nicolai School at Leipzig, most of his early education came from his own reading, especially in the classics and the early Christian writers, in his father's library. At the age of 15 he entered the University of Leipzig, where his formal training was chiefly in jurisprudence and philosophy. Privately, he read all the important scientific texts – of Francis ◊Bacon, ◊Galileo, Johannes ◊Kepler, René ◊Descartes, and others. In 1663 he went to the University of Jena, where he was taught Euclidean geometry by Erhard Weigel (1625–1699). He then returned to Leipzig and after three years more study of law applied for the degree of Doctor of Law in 1666. It was refused on the ground that he was too young. He therefore went to Altdorf, where his thesis 'De casibus per plexis in jure' was accepted and the doctorate awarded.

Leibniz turned down the offer of a professorship at Altdorf and decided to travel about Europe. At the end of 1666 he entered the service of the elector and archbishop of Mainz; he was employed chiefly in foreign affairs, his special task being to devise plans to preserve the peace of Europe, just then emerging from the Thirty Years' War. He was invited to France by Louis XIV, to present to him his plan for a French invasion of

Egypt (and so transfer war from European to African soil) and although, in the event, he never met the king, he remained in Paris for about three years. It was in Paris that his serious work in mathematics began. He met leading scientists, including Christiaan ◊Huygens, made a thorough study of Cartesianism, and began work on his calculating machine. The machine was completed in about 1672 and was a marked improvement on Blaise ◊Pascal's machine, in that it was able to multiply, divide, and extract roots.

The death of the elector of Mainz in 1673 left Leibniz without an official position. He was offered the post of librarian to the Duke of Brunswick at Hannover, but went instead to London. The visit marked a Turning point in his mathematical life, for it was in London in 1673 that he became acquainted with the work of Isaac ◊Newton and Isaac ◊Barrow and began to work on problems that led to his independent discovery of differential and integral calculus.

In 1676 Leibniz at last took up the appointment as librarian to the house of Brunswick. He remained in that service for the rest of his life and much of his time was spent in conducting research into the genealogy and history of the Brunswick line.

He also continued to be charged with diplomatic missions and on one of his visits to Berlin he succeeded in persuading the local elector to establish an academy of science. It was founded in 1700 and Leibniz was appointed president for life. From 1712 to 1714 he was an imperial privy councillor at Vienna. In 1714 the elector of Hanover, Georg Ludwig, duke of Brunswick, acceded to the English throne as George I. Leibniz asked to be allowed to accompany him to London, but the request was denied. He therefore spent the last two years of his life engaged in genealogical work, embittered by the dispute with Newton over the invention of the calculus and suffering from gout. He died a neglected man – neither the Royal Society nor the Berlin Academy took any notice of the event – on 14 November 1716 in Hannover.

The imaginary number is a fine and wonderful recourse of the divine spirit, almost an amphibian between being and not being.

GOTTFRIED LEIBNIZ ATTRIBUTED REMARK

Just as much of his service to princes consisted in the search for a balance of power and international cooperation in Europe, and as he sought to reconcile in much of his philosophical writing Protestantism and Roman Catholicism, so did Leibniz dream of an international community of scholars, served by academies like that of Berlin, freely sharing their discoveries and continually exchanging their ideas. To this end he worked intermittently throughout his life at devising what he called a Universal Characteristic, a universal language accessible to everyone. It is therefore a matter of some sorrow that he became embroiled in a long and acrimonious dispute about the authorship of the calculus, a dispute that darkened the last 15 years of his life. In 1699 the Swiss mathematician and fellow of the Royal Society, Fatio de Duillier, accused Leibniz of stealing the idea from Newton, a charge that the Royal Society formally upheld in 1711. Leibniz himself never sought to conceal that it was after his 1673 visit to London, by which time Newton had worked out his calculus of fluxions, that he began his investigations into tangents and quadratures, the research that eventually led to his discovery of the calculus. But Newton's discovery, probably made in 1665, was not published for many years and there is no doubt that Leibniz arrived at his calculus independently. As he put it, he, Newton, and Barrow were 'contemporaries in these discoveries'. Leibniz always communicated his findings to fellow mathematicians; most mathematicians of the time were working on the same problems and they all knew the work that had been done on infinitesimal quantities. At any rate, to Leibniz is due the credit for first using the infinitesimals as differences. To him also is due the credit for working out, like Newton, a complete algorithm and for devising a notation so much more convenient than Newton's that it remains in standard use today.

The idea of the calculus was in the mathematical air. It was Leibniz who expressed its fundamental notions in the most effective manner. That should not be surprising, for Leibniz will always be remembered chiefly as the founder of symbolic logic. Centuries later, it has become clear that his logic, free from all concepts of space and number and hence in his lifetime not recognized as mathematical at all, was the prototype of future abstract mathematics.

Further Reading

Adams, Robert, *Leibniz: Determinist, Theist, Idealist*, Oxford University Press, 1998.

Cristin, Renato, *Heidegger and Leibniz: Reason and the Path*, Contributions to Phenomenology series, Kluwer Academic Publishers, 1998.

Jolley, Nicholas, *The Light of the Soul: Theories of Ideas in Leibniz, Malebranche, and Descartes*, Oxford University Press, 1998.

McCullough, Lawrence B, *Leibniz on Individuals and Individuation: The Persistence of Premodern Ideas in Modern Philosophy*, Philosophical Studies in Contemporary Culture series, Kluwer Academic Publishers, 1996, v 3.

Rescher, Nicholas, *Leibniz: An Introduction to His Philosophy,* Modern Revivals in Philosophy series, Gregg Revivals, 1994.

Rutherford, Donald, *Leibniz and the Rational Order of Nature,* Cambridge University Press, 1995.

Savage, Reginald O, *Real Alternatives: Leibniz Metaphysics of Choice,* Philosophical Studies, Kluwer Academic Publishers, 1998.

Woolhouse, R S and Francks, Richard (eds), *Leibniz's 'New System' and Associated Contemporary Texts,* Oxford University Press, 1997.

Leishman, William Boog (1865–1926) Scottish army physician who discovered the protozoan parasite that causes kala-azar, a relatively common and potentially fatal infectious disease endemic to the tropics and subtropics that affects the reticulo-endothelial system (particularly the liver, spleen, and bone marrow). The genus to which the causative microorganism belongs is called *Leishmania,* after Leishman. He received many honours for his work, including a knighthood in 1909.

Leishman was born on 6 November 1865 in Glasgow, a son of the regius professor of midwifery at Glasgow University. He was educated at Westminster School, London, then studied medicine at Glasgow University, from which he graduated in 1886. After graduation he obtained a commission in the Royal Army Medical Corps, in which he remained for the rest of his life. He was posted to India 1890–97, after which he returned to England to the Army Medical School at Netley, Hampshire, where he was soon appointed assistant professor of pathology under Almroth ◊Wright. After Wright resigned, Leishman succeeded him as professor in 1903; in the same year the medical school was transferred to London and Leishman moved with it. In 1914 he became a member of the Army Medical Advisory Board, advising the War Office on tropical diseases then, with the outbreak of World War I, he joined the British Expeditionary Force as advisor in pathology. After the war ended he became the first director of pathology at the War Office in 1919. In 1923 he was appointed director general of the Army Medical Service, a position he held until his death on 2 June 1926 in London.

Leishman discovered the protozoan parasite that causes kala-azar in 1900, using his modified form of the Romanowsky stain for protozoa and blood cells (this modified stain is now called Leishman's stain) to examine cells from the spleen of a soldier who had died of kala-azar at Netley. He published his findings in 1903 but in the same year Charles Donovan of the Indian Medical Service independently made the same discovery, as a result of which the causative protozoan was called the Leishman–Donovan body. Other workers later discovered that species related to the kala-azar-causing protozoan were responsible for various other diseases; all such similar protozoans were therefore classified as members of the same genus, named *Leishmania* – the protozoan causing kala-azar being called *Leishmania donovani* – and the diseases they cause were grouped under the term leishmaniasis.

Leishman also assisted Wright in developing an effective antityphoid inoculation, and helped to elucidate the life cycle of the spirochaete *Spirochaeta duttoni,* which causes African tick fever.

Lemaître, Georges Edouard (1894–1966) Belgian cosmologist who – perhaps because he was also a priest – was fascinated by the Creation, the beginning of the universe, for which he devised what later became known as the 'Big Bang' theory.

Lemaître was born in Charleroi on 17 July 1894. Trained as a civil engineer, he served as an artillery officer with the Belgian army during World War I. After the war he entered a seminary, where he was ordained a priest in 1923. He nevertheless maintained an unwavering interest in science, and he visited the University of Cambridge 1923–24, where he studied solar physics and met Arthur ◊Eddington. Afterwards he spent two years at the Massachusetts Institute of Technology in the USA, and it was while he was there that he became influenced by the theories of Edwin ◊Hubble and the Harvard astronomer Harlow ◊Shapley concerning the likelihood of an expanding universe.

Having returned to his native country with better insight into the thinking of his contemporaries, Lemaître was made professor of astrophysics at the University of Louvain from 1927. In 1933 he published his *Discussion on the Evolution of the Universe,* which stated the theory of the Big Bang, and he followed this in 1946 with his *Hypothesis of the Primal Atom.* He died in Louvain on 20 June 1966.

The main feature of Lemaître's theory of the beginning of the universe stemmed from his belief in the 'primal atom', formulated first in 1931. He visualized this atom as a single unit, an incredibly dense 'egg' containing all the material for the universe within a sphere about 30 times larger than the Sun. Somewhere between 20,000 and 60,000 million years ago, in his view, this atom exploded, sending out its matter in all directions. There then took place a balancing act between expansion and contraction. Ultimately expansion won, since when (around 9,000 million years ago) the galaxies have been drifting away from each other. The significance of this theory is not so much its affirmation of the expansion of the universe as its positing of an event to begin the expansion.

In 1946 George ◊Gamow improved on Lemaître's basic theory, considering the Big Bang from just before the event to just after, thus giving the Big Bang itself a definite beginning and a definite end (and a scientific existence in between). However, Lemaître's and Gamow's solutions were for a time somewhat overshadowed by the invention of the radio telescope, which began to reveal aspects of the universe previously unknown. Hermann ◊Bondi, Thomas ◊Gold, and Fred ◊Hoyle, working at Cambridge, put forward their 'steady-state' theory, in which they saw the universe as having no beginning and no end: stars and galaxies were created, went through a life-cycle, and died, to be replaced by new matter being created out of 'nothingness' (possibly hydrogen atoms).

For a time during the late 1940s and early 1950s the steady-state theory was a serious rival to Lemaître and Gamow's Big Bang, but more recently the steady-state theory has been virtually abandoned. Research by Martin ◊Ryle and others has shown that the universe may simply undergo periods of total expansion and total contraction that will go on indefinitely.

Further Reading

Berger, A (ed), *The Big Bang and George Lemaître,* Reidel Pub Co, 1984.

Godart, Odon and Heller, M, *Cosmology of LeMaître,* History of Astronomy series, Pachart, 1985, v 3.

Heller, Michael, *Lemaître, Bing Bang, and the Quantum Universe: With His Original Manuscript,* History of Astronomy series, Pachart Publishing House, 1996, v 10.

Kraghe, Helge, *The Beginning of the World: Georges Lemaître and the Expanding Universe,* Centaurus, 1987, v 30, pp 114–139.

Lenard, Philipp Eduard Anton (1862–1947)

Hungarian-born German physicist who devised a way of producing beams of cathode rays (electrons) in air, enabling electrons to be studied. This led him to the first conclusion that an atom is mostly empty space, and Lenard was awarded the 1905 Nobel Prize for Physics as a result. He also did pioneering research on the photoelectric effect.

Lenard was born on 7 June 1862 at Pozsony, Hungary (now Bratislava in the Slovak Republic), but spent most of his life in Germany. He studied physics at Heidelberg under Robert ◊Bunsen and at Berlin under Hermann von ◊Helmholtz, receiving a doctorate in 1886 from Heidelberg. He spent a further three years as an assistant at Heidelberg and in 1891 became assistant to Heinrich ◊Hertz at Bonn, assuming command of Hertz's laboratory on his early death in 1894. He took an associate professorship at Breslau the same year, then moved in turn to Aachen in 1895, Heidelberg in 1896, and Kiel, where he was appointed professor of experimental physics in 1898. He then held the same post at Heidelberg 1907–31. Lenard became a follower of Hitler, the only eminent scientist to do so, in 1924 and spent his later years reviling Jewish scientists such as Albert ◊Einstein. He was antagonistic by nature and in his book *Great Men of Science* (1934), he omitted Wilhelm ◊Röntgen and several other eminent modern scientists who had had priority disputes with him, who had criticized Lenard's work, or whose work Lenard considered inferior to his own. Lenard died in Messelhausen, Germany, on 20 May 1947.

Lenard's initial studies were in mechanics investigating the oscillation of precipitated water drops, work no doubt stimulated by his regard for the studies of Hertz. In his youth Lenard had been fascinated by the phenomena of luminescence and later with his knowledge of science he returned to the topic. He studied the luminosity of pyrogallic acid in the presence of alkali and sodium hydrogen sulphite, establishing that the crucial factor was the oxidation of the acid. He continued to look at luminescent compounds for 20 years along with his main field of study.

Lenard's principal contribution to physics can be traced back to work begun in 1892. Inspired by William ◊Crookes, who in 1879 had published a paper on the movement of cathode rays in discharge tubes, Lenard conceived an experiment to examine these rays outside the tube. He was then assistant to Hertz, who had shown that a piece of uranium glass covered with aluminium foil and put inside the discharge tube became luminescent when struck by cathode rays. Lenard developed a technique using aluminium foil as a window in a discharge tube, and showed that the cathode rays could move about 8 cm/3 in through the air after passing through the thin aluminium window. Since the cathode rays were able to pass through the foil, he suggested that the atoms in the metal must consist of a large proportion of empty space. A further conclusion of greater significance to later work was that the part of the atom where the mass was concentrated consisted of neutral doublets or 'dynamids' of negative and positive electricity. This proposal preceded by ten years the classic model of the atom proposed by Ernest ◊Rutherford in 1911.

Lenard had at his fingertips a great knowledge of electricity. He devised the grid in the thermionic valve that controls electron flow. He also showed that an electron must have a certain minimum energy before it can produce ionization in a gas. From 1902 onwards, Lenard studied photoelectricity and discovered several fundamental effects. He showed that negative electricity can be released from metals by exposure to ultraviolet light and later found that this electricity was identical in properties to cathode rays (electrons). He also discovered that the energy of the electrons produced depends on the wavelength of the light incident on the metal. He explained that the release of electrons was caused by a resonance effect intensified by vibrations induced by the ultraviolet light. Einstein in 1905 provided a correct explanation of photoelectricity by using the quantum theory, which Lenard rejected.

Philipp Lenard was a gifted experimental physicist who was able to build on the earlier work of other scientists, enabling theoretical physicists to use his results to delve deeper into the structure of matter. Many of his discoveries are fundamental to our understanding of atomic physics.

Lenoir, Jean Joseph Etienne (1822–1900) Belgian-born French engineer and inventor who in the early 1860s produced the first practical internal-combustion engine and a car powered by it. He also developed a white enamel in 1847, an electric brake in 1853, and an automatic telegraph in 1865. Lenoir was born in Mussy-la-Ville, Belgium, on 12 January 1822; he died in Varenne-St-Hilaire, France, on 4 August 1900.

The first self-propelled road vehicles were steam cars – using an external-combustion steam engine. The French army captain Nicolas ◊Cugnot built a three-wheeled steam tractor for hauling cannon as early as 1769, and a passenger-carrying vehicle was constructed in England in about 1801. By 1830, steam carriages were in regular use but they were noisy and dirty, and the smoke and hot coals often caused fires along the route, making them unpopular with farmers who feared for their crops.

Several people had claimed to have invented an internal-combustion engine before Lenoir. The Reverend W Cecil read a paper to Cambridge University in 1829 about his experiments, and William Barnett in 1838 also laid claims, but not until Lenoir in 1859 did a practical model become a reality. His engine consisted of a single cylinder with a storage battery (accumulator) for the electric ignition system. Its two-stroke cycle was provided by slide valves, and it was fuelled by coal gas, as used then for domestic purposes and street lighting. Lenoir built a small car around one of his prototypes in 1863, but it had an efficiency of less than 4% and although he claimed it was silent, this was only true when the vehicle was not under load.

The real value of his engine was for powering small items of machinery, and by 1865 more than 400 were in use in the Paris district driving printing presses, lathes, and water pumps. Its use for vehicles was restricted by its size and it was not until some 20 years later, when Gottlieb ◊Daimler and Karl ◊Benz independently devised the four-cycle engine, that internal-combustion engines were successful in vehicles.

Lenz, Heinrich Friedrich Emil (1804–1865) Russian physicist, known for Lenz's law, which is a fundamental law of electromagnetism.

Lenz was born in Dorpat (now Tartu, Estonia) on 12 February 1804. He graduated from secondary education in 1820 and entered the University of Dorpat, where he studied chemistry and physics. His physics teacher recommended Lenz for the post of geophysical scientist to accompany Otto von Kotzebue (1787–1846) on his third expedition around the world 1823–26. Upon his return, Lenz was appointed scientific assistant at the St Petersburg Academy of Science, later becoming associate academician in 1830 and full academician in 1834. From 1840 to 1863, Lenz was dean of mathematics and physics at the University of St Petersburg, where he was also elected rector. He was also the author of a number of very successful books which ran to many editions. Lenz died after suffering a stroke while on holiday in Rome on 10 February 1865.

Lenz's major fields of study were geophysics and electromagnetism. While on his voyage with Kotzebue, he studied climatic conditions such as barometric pressure, finding the areas of maximum and minimum pressure that exist in the tropics and determine the overall climatic pattern. Lenz also made a careful investigation of water salinity, discovering areas of maximum salinity either side of the Equator in the Atlantic and Pacific Oceans and establishing the differences in salinity between these oceans and the Indian Ocean. Lenz also made extremely accurate measurements of the temperature and specific gravity of sea water. His geophysical observations of the oceans were not bettered until the following century.

In 1829 Lenz went on a mountaineering expedition to the Caucasus in southern Russia, where he made a study of some of the natural resources of the area as well as making measurements of mountain heights and of the level of the Caspian Sea.

Lenz's studies of electromagnetism date from 1831, following the discovery in that year of electromagnetic induction by Michael ◊Faraday and Joseph ◊Henry. Lenz's first major discovery was that the direction of a current induced by an electromagnetic force always opposes the direction of the electromagnetic force that produces it. This law was published in 1833 and it is known as Lenz's law. When a moving magnet or coil produces a current by induction in a conductor, the induced current flows in such a direction that it in turn produces a magnetic field that opposes the motion of the magnet or coil inducing the current. This means that work has to be done by the magnet or coil to produce current, and Lenz's law is in fact a special case of the law of conservation of energy. If the induced current were to flow in the opposite direction, it would assist the motion of the magnet or coil and a perpetual-motion machine would result because energy would increase without any work being done, which is impossible. Lenz's law later helped Hermann von ◊Helmholtz to formulate the law of conservation of energy, and it is applied today in electrical machines such as generators and electric motors.

Around the same time, Lenz also began to study the relationship between heat and current and discovered, independently of James ◊Joule, the law now known as Joule's law, which describes the proportional relationship between the production of heat and the square of the current. Lenz also found that the strength of a magnetic field is proportional to the strength of the magnetic induction. He also worked on the application of certain theoretical principles to engineering design, on formulating programmes for geographical expeditions, and on establishing the unit for the measurement of electrical resistance. A final major area of study was electrochemistry, where in the 1840s he made a series of investigations into additivity laws.

Leonardo da Vinci (1452–1519) Italian artist, inventor, and scientist, regarded as one of the greatest figures of the Italian Renaissance for the universality of his genius.

Leonardo was born on his father's estate in Vinci, Tuscany. The illegitimate son of the Tuscan landowner Ser Piero and a peasant woman, he was taken into his father's household in Florence, where he was the only child. He received an elementary education and in about 1467 was apprenticed to the artist Andrea del Verrocchio. There he trained in artistic as well as technical and mechanical subjects. He left the workshop in about 1477 and worked on his own until 1481. He went to Milan the following year and was employed by Ludovico Sforza, the Duke of Milan, as 'painter and engineer of the duke'. In this capacity he advised the duke on the architecture of proposed cathedrals in Milan and nearby Pavia, and was involve in hydraulic and mechanical engineering. After Milan fell to the French in 1499, he fled and began a long period of wandering. In 1500 he visited Mantua and then Venice, where he was consulted on the reconstruction and fortification of the church San Francesco al Monte. Two years later he went into the service of Cesare Borgia as a military architect involved in the designing and development of fortifications. In 1503 he returned to Florence to investigate, on Cesare Borgia's behalf, the possibility of re-routing the River Arno so that the besieged city of Pisa would lose its access to the sea. It was at about this time that he painted his internationally renowned portrait the *Mona Lisa*. He was invited that year by the governor of France in Milan, Charles d'Amboise, to work for the French in Milan, and in 1506 he took up the offer. There he devised plans for a

castle for the governor and for the Adda Canal to connect Milan to Lake Como. In 1513 the French were defeated and forced to leave Milan; Leonardo left with them and went to Rome to look for work. He stayed with Cardinal Giuliano de' Medici, the brother of Pope Leo X, but there was little for him to do (although both Michelangelo and Raphael were working there at that time) other than to advise on the proposed reclamation of the Pontine marshes. Three years later he left Italy for France on the invitation of King François I, and he lived in the castle of Cloux, near the king's summer residence at Amboise. Leonardo spent the rest of his life there, sorting and editing his notes. He died on 2 May 1519.

Leonardo's training in Verrocchio's workshop developed his practical perception, which served him well as a technical scientist, a creative engineer, and as an artist. In the years of his first visit to Milan, principally between 1490 and 1495, he produced his well-known notebooks, in mirror-writing. The illustrated treatises deal with painting, architecture, anatomy, and the elementary theory of mechanics. The last was produced in the late 1490s and is now in the Biblioteca Nacional, Madrid. In it Leonardo proposes his theory of mechanics – illustrated with sketches of machines and tools such as gear, hydraulic jacks and screw-cutting machines, with explanations of their functions and mechanical principles and of the concepts of friction and resistance.

Wisdom is the daughter of Experience,
Truth is only the daughter of Time.
LEONARDO DA VINCI QUOTED IN J HUXLEY
ESSAYS IN POPULAR SCIENCE *1926*

Leonardo's interest in mechanics developed as he realized how the laws of mechanics, motion, and force operate everywhere in the natural world. He studied the flight of birds in connection with these laws and, as a result, designed the prototypes of a parachute and of a flying machine.

During this time, he also developed his ideas about the Renaissance Church Plan, which later were considered favourably by the architect Bramante in connection with the building of the new St Peter's in Rome.

In about 1503, when Cesare Borgia's plan for the diversion of the River Arno failed, Leonardo also devised a project to construct a canal, wide and deep enough to carry ships, which would bypass the narrow portion of the Arno so that Florence would be linked to the sea. His hydrological studies on the properties of water were carried out at this time.

The variety of Leonardo's inventions reflect his passionate absorption in biological and mechanical details and ranged from complex cranes to pulley systems, lathes, drilling machines, a paddlewheel boat, an underwater breathing apparatus, and a clock that registered minutes as well as hours. As a military engineer he was responsible for the construction of assault machines, pontoons, a steam cannon, and a tortoise-shaped tank. For a castle in Milan he create a forced-air central heating system and also a water-pumping mechanism. His notes and diagrams established him, beyond dispute, as the greatest descriptive engineer and scientist of his age. Despite these achievements, he remains most famous as an artist, unique in the history of the world's greatest painters.

Further Reading

Brown, David A, *Leonardo da Vinci: Origins of a Genius,* Yale University Press, 1998.

Clark, Kenneth, *Leonardo da Vinci,* Viking Penguin, 1989.

Doeser, Linda, *Life and Works of Leonardo Da Vinci,* Life and Works series, Smithmark Publishers, 1996.

Romei, Francesca, *Leonardo da Vinci: Artist, Inventor and Scientist of the Renaissance,* Masters of Art series, Peter Bedrick Books, 1994.

Vezzosi, Alessandro, *Leonardo da Vinci: The Mind of the Renaissance,* Discoveries series, Thames & Hudson, 1997.

Whiting, J R S, *Leonardo: A Portrait of the Renaissance Man,* Knickerbocker Press, 1998.

Lesseps, Ferdinand, Vicomte de (1805–1894)

French civil engineer who is remembered as the designer and builder of the Suez Canal, the strategic importance of which, as a trade route between Europe and the East, remains until the present day.

Lesseps had the distinction of being born in the Palace of Versailles, being a cousin of the Empress Eugénie. As befitted his noble birth (he was a Vicomte), he was brought up to regard diplomatic service as the natural choice for a career and from 1825 he held posts in various capitals including Lisbon, Tunis, and Cairo.

He also had other interests, and these centred around engineering and construction, especially where canal-building was concerned. When it was suggested in 1854 that a passage be cut to link the Mediterranean with the Red Sea, Lesseps was the ideal person to take charge of the work.

In 1856 permission was granted by the viceroy of Egypt, Muhammad Said, and the actual canal was begun in 1860, financed mainly with money put up by the French Government and Ottoman Empire. Ten years later the canal opened for traffic.

Lesseps received many honours for his achievement, an English knighthood, the Grand Cross of the Legion of Honour, and election to the French Academy of Science being chief among them. Unfortunately, all these were rather overshadowed by the disaster of the Panama Canal, the construction of which he reluctantly undertook in 1881. The project met with failure and bankruptcy. Lesseps was sentenced to five years' imprisonment for breach of trust, but was too ill to leave his house. A broken and sick old man, he was allowed to remain there and died on 7 December 1894.

Since Roman times, thoughts of cutting across the isthmus of Suez had been discussed at various intervals. Napoleon I, on his visit to Egypt in 1799, saw the possibilities and advantages of a canal, but no practical steps were taken until 1854 when the Suez Canal scheme was conceived. A technical commission met in 1855 and mapped out a suitable route. It then remained for permission to be granted by the viceroy and for a company to be formed to finance the operation. All this was achieved by 1860 when work began in earnest.

As there was no great difference in the levels of the two seas at either end of the isthmus, locks were unnecessary and the construction, although long – more than 160 km/100 mi – was relatively simple. It linked the cities of Port Said and Suez, and was initially 8 m/26 ft deep, 22 m/72 ft wide at the bottom, and 70 m/230 ft across at the surface. When it was finished on 17 November 1869 it reduced the journey from the Mediterranean to the Indian Ocean by thousands of miles and removed the necessity for weeks at sea traversing the Cape of Good Hope.

Originally the UK owned none of the shares in the Suez Company, but in 1875 the khedive of Egypt, Ismail Pasha (who succeeded Muhammad Said in 1863) sold his stock to the British government. From then on the company was mainly controlled by the British and the French, and in 1888 it was agreed that the canal should be opened to all nations, at all times. Constructed in the beginning as a one-lane canal, it has been widened and deepened in recent years to accommodate the increase of traffic, particularly from the oil fields of the Arab countries. At one time, tankers made up 70% of shipping recorded as passing through the canal.

The Suez Canal was a brilliant piece of engineering carried out efficiently under the watchful eye of Lesseps. The advantages to trade were obvious to the Victorians, and in the modern world that narrow strip of artificial waterway has proved vital to the Western economy.

Leverrier, Urbain Jean Joseph (1811–1877)

French astronomer who, as well as being a trained chemist, became an authority in France on many aspects of astronomy and is chiefly remembered for his contribution to the discovery of the planet Neptune. Leverrier was also instrumental in the establishment of the meteorological network across continental Europe.

He was born in St Lô, Normandy, on 11 March 1811, and went first to local schools before attending the Collège de Caen 1828–30 and then the Collège de St Louis in Paris. There, in 1831, he won a prize in mathematics and entered the Ecole Polytechnique. After a short time doing research in chemistry under the direction of Joseph ◊Gay-Lussac at Administration Tobaccos, he began teaching, both privately and at the Collège Stanislas in Paris. He applied for the post of demonstrator in chemistry at the Ecole Polytechnique in 1837, but was instead offered a post in astronomy, which, having already published some work in this subject, he accepted. Leverrier was soon recognized as an astronomer of distinction. After the discovery of Neptune, he was elected to the Academy of Sciences in Paris in 1846 and made a fellow of the Royal Society in London in 1847 (which also awarded him the Copley Medal). A new chair of astronomy was created for him at the Faculty of Science in 1847, and in 1849 the chair of celestial mechanics was established for him at the Sorbonne. He was politically active in the revolution of 1848, serving as a member of the legislative assembly in 1849, and later in 1852 as a senator. In 1854 Leverrier took over the directorship of the Paris Observatory after the death of his friend and colleague François ◊Arago. He was not a popular administrator (evidently he kept a tight rein on both the direction of research and its funding) and he was eventually dismissed from the post in 1870. The untimely death of his successor (Charles Delaunay), however, brought him back to the observatory, albeit with some restrictions imposed. Thereafter, during the last few years of his life, Leverrier was plagued with a progressive deterioration in his health. He died in Paris on 23 September 1877.

Leverrier's first paper in astronomy, which dealt with shooting stars, was published in 1832. At the Ecole Polytechnique his first major investigation 1838–40 was into the stability of the Solar System. He made calculations based on minor variations in the planetary orbits and extended them to cover a period of more than 200,000 years, intending to demonstrate how little variation over time does actually occur. Through this exercise, however, he became fascinated by the notion of tracing the cause of the perturbations he had recorded, and he immediately began a study designed to identify the periodic comets and other bodies within the Solar System whose gravitational pulls might affect the planets in their orbits.

It was already known that the point of the planet Mercury's orbit closest to the Sun was progressively 38 seconds per century greater than would be predicted on the basis of Newtonian mechanics. In 1845 Leverrier attempted to resolve this by proposing the existence of a planet – which he named Vulcan – lying 30 million km/19 million mi from the Sun, *inside* the orbit of Mercury. (Leverrier was by no means the only astronomer of the time, or since, to be seeking an 'intramercurial' planet. Samuel ◊Schwabe, for instance, also had the idea. However, all attempts optically to detect a planet in this location have failed – and in any case, the anomaly in Mercury's orbit was later used by Karl ◊Schwarzschild in 1916 to support Einstein's general theory of relativity, which predicted such an advance in Mercury's perihelion.)

In the same year Arago pointed out to Leverrier that there was another discrepancy between the predicted and the observed behaviour of a planet, in the Solar System. Alexis Bouvard (1767–1843) had produced tables on the planet Uranus in 1821, and fewer than 25 years later they were already grossly inaccurate. This suggested to Leverrier that some planet outside Uranus's orbit was having a profound influence (although the possibility that another planet might exist beyond Uranus had in fact already been suggested by William ◊Herschel and by Friedrich ◊Bessel). Accordingly, Leverrier published three papers on the subject during 1846, in the last of which he gave a prediction for the position and apparent diameter of the hypothetical planet.

Unknown to Leverrier, a young English astronomer, John Couch ◊Adams, had carried out virtually identical calculations a year earlier at Cambridge and had sent them to the Astronomer Royal, George ◊Airy. For various reasons, Airy had left Adams's communication unread – until he perused Leverrier's second publication on the matter. By that time Leverrier had written to a number of observatories, asking them to test the prediction contained in his third paper. It happened that Johann ◊Galle and Louis d'Arrest at the Berlin Observatory had just received a new and accurate star map of the relevant sector, and in order to test it, were glad to oblige. On the very first night of observation the new planet was found within 1° of Leverrier's coordinates.

The argument that then ensued over who should receive the credit for the planet's discovery was aggravated by somewhat chauvinistic debate in the popular presses of both France and the UK. It extended to the question of naming the new planet. Arago wanted it to be named after Leverrier, but (perhaps because of its optically greenish hue) he finally proposed that it should be called Neptune.

Thereafter, at the Paris Observatory, Leverrier saw it as his life's work to compile a comprehensive analysis of the masses and the orbits of the planets of the Solar System, taking special note of their mutual influences. The work on Mercury, Venus, the Earth, and Mars was carried out during the 1850s; that on Jupiter, Saturn, Uranus, and Neptune during the 1870s. The whole was published only after Leverrier's death, in the *Annals* of the Paris Observatory.

Levi-Civita, Tullio (1873–1941) Italian mathematician skilled in both pure and applied mathematics whose greatest achievement was his development, in collaboration with Gregorio ◊Ricci-Curbastro, of the absolute differential calculus.

Levi-Civita was born in Padua on 29 March 1873 and received his secondary education there before entering the University of Padua to study mathematics in 1890. There he came strongly under the influence of Ricci-Curbastro, one of his teachers. He was awarded his BA in 1894 and took up employment as a lecturer at the teacher-training college at Pavia. In 1897 he was appointed professor of mechanics at the Engineering School at Padua. In 1918 he left Padua to become professor of higher analysis at the University of Rome; in 1920 he was made professor of rational mechanics. He remained there until 1938, when the anti-Jewish laws promulgated by the Fascist government forced him to leave the university; he was also expelled from all Italian scientific societies. His health began to deteriorate rapidly and he died of a stroke, at Rome, on 29 December 1941.

Although Levi-Civita began to publish while he was still an undergraduate, his first important results – the fruit of several years' labour – were first published, with Ricci-Curbastro, in 1900. Together they presented to the mathematical world a completely new calculus, which became known as absolute differential calculus. One of the most important features of this new system was its remarkable flexibility – applicable, as it was, to both Euclidean and non-Euclidean spaces. Most significantly, it could be applied to Riemannian curved spaces, and the tensor system which the paper outlined was fundamental to Albert ◊Einstein's development of the general theory of relativity. Levi-Civita's own most important contribution to the absolute differential calculus was the publication in 1917 of a paper in which he postulated a law of parallel translation of a vector in a Riemannian curved space. This introduction of the concept of parallelism in curved space was Levi-Civita's most brilliant contribution to the history of mathematics. The discussions to which it gave rise eventually allowed absolute differential calculus to develop into tensor calculus, a tool of immense usefulness to mathematicians attempting to derive a unified theory of gravitation and electromagnetism. The idea of parallel displacement has also been of great importance in the field of the geometry of paths.

In addition to this central work, Levi-Civita also published interesting papers on celestial mechanics and hydrodynamics, and in general it may be said that his achievements in both pure and applied mathematics

established him as one of the foremost mathematicians of his age.

Levi-Montalcini, Rita (1909–   ) Italian neuroscientist whose work has principally been on chemical factors that control the growth and development of cells. In particular she isolated a substance called nerve growth factor that promoted the development of nerve cells. For this she shared the 1986 Nobel Prize for Physiology or Medicine with Stanley Cohen (1922–   ).

Levi-Montalcini was born and educated in Turin, graduating in medicine from the city's university in 1936. She immediately began studying the mechanisms of nerve growth. From 1939 she was unable to hold an academic position in an Italian university because she was Jewish. She constructed a home laboratory for herself, making microsurgical instruments out of cutlery, and also served as a volunteer physician towards the end of World War II. In 1947 she moved to the USA, to the Washington University in St Louis, where she remained until 1977. From 1969 to 1978 she was also director of the Institute of Cell Biology in Rome, and from 1979 to 1989 was guest professor there.

It was while in St Louis that she had discovered nerve growth factor in the salivary glands of developing mouse embryos. She continued to try to find further sources of this factor and established that it was chemically a protein. She also analysed the mechanism of its action in isolated tissues and then in whole neonatal and adult animals. She showed that nerve growth factor could be identified in many tissues, including mouse cancer cells and snake venom glands; and that it was most effective on cells when they were in the early stages of differentiation. Her work has stimulated important new work into understanding processes of some neurological diseases and possible repair mechanisms; into tissue regeneration; and into cancer mechanisms.

Lewis, Gilbert Newton (1875–1946) US theoretical chemist who made important contributions to thermodynamics and the electronic theory of valency. He is best known for his explanation of the behaviour of acids and bases.

Lewis was born in Weymouth, Massachusetts, on 23 October 1875. He was educated at the preparatory school of the University of Nebraska and Harvard, from which he graduated in 1896, gaining his MA in 1898 and his PhD a year later for a thesis on the electrochemical and thermochemical relations of zinc and cadmium amalgams. He remained at Harvard for a year as an instructor, before going to Europe on a travelling scholarship to study under Friedrich ◊Ostwald at Leipzig and Hermann ◊Nernst at Göttingen. He then went to the Philippines for a year as superintendent of weights and measures and chemist at the Bureau of

Lewis A molecule of chlorine with a covalent bond involving the sharing of a pair of electrons by the two atoms, and two hybrid forms of a molecule of nitric oxide (nitrogen monoxide), each with an odd (unpaired) electron.

Science in Manila. He returned to the USA in 1905 to join the research team of A A Noyes at the Massachusetts Institute of Technology (MIT). In 1912 he became chairman of the chemistry department at the University of California, where he remained until his death. He died in his laboratory at Berkeley on 23 March 1946.

During his seven years at MIT Lewis published more than 30 papers, including fundamental work on chemical thermodynamics and free energies. At Berkeley he set about reorganizing and rejuvenating the department, appointing staff with a broad chemical knowledge rather than specialists.

In 1916 Lewis began his pioneering work on valency. He postulated that the atoms of elements whose atomic mass is higher then helium's have inner shells of electrons with the structure of the preceding inert gas. The valency electrons lie outside these shells and may be lost or added to comparatively easily to form ionic bonds. He went on to state that bonding electrons prefer to pair up – the idea of the covalent bond. Much of this work involved the building of bridges between inorganic and organic chemists, who had often considered that polar (predominantly ionic) and non-polar (predominantly covalent) substances bore little relation to each other. Lewis also drew attention to the unusual properties of molecules that have an odd number of electrons, such as nitric oxide (nitrogen monoxide, NO).

In 1923 Lewis and M Randall published *Thermodynamics and the Free Energy of Chemical Substances,* which was the culmination of 20 years' research in compiling data on free energies (ΔG). Until the early years of this century it was considered that the heat of reaction (ΔH) could be taken as a measure of chemical affinity and that changes in enthalpy could be used to predict the direction of the reaction. It was

later realized that free energy is the correct basis for such predictions. Lewis's treatise listed the free energies of 143 important substances, which could be used to evaluate the outcome of several hundred reactions. This work was linked to the determination of the electrode potentials of more than a dozen elements.

Also in 1923 Lewis published his highly influential book *Valence and the Structure of Atoms and Molecules.* In it he put forward a new definition of a base as a substance that has a lone pair of electrons which may be used to complete the stable group of another atom, and defined an acid as a substance that can use a lone pair from another molecule in completing the stable group of one of its own atoms. In other words, a base supplies a pair of electrons for a chemical bond, and an acid accepts such a pair. This definition, which has stood the test of time, was remarkable because it was the first to suggest that bases include substances that do not produce hydroxyl ions.

Previously, according to the Brönsted–Lowry theory, it was thought that an acid is a substance capable of donating a proton (hydrogen ion) to an acceptor substance, a base. Lewis proved his theory by carrying out acid–base reactions, detected by colour changes to indicators, in non-aqueous, hydrogen-free solvents such as tetrachloromethane (carbon tetrachloride) in which proton transfer was not possible.

For several years during the mid-1930s Lewis's research team carried out investigations on heavy water and deuterium (which had been discovered in 1932 by Harold ◊Urey, one of Lewis's former students). In his later years he carried out studies on the excited electron states of organic molecules, contributing to the understanding of the colour of organic substances and the complex phenomena of phosphorescence and fluorescence. Lewis died in his laboratory while performing experiments on fluorescence.

Li, Choh Hao (1913–) Chinese-born US biochemist who is best known for his work on the hormones secreted by the pituitary gland.

Li was born in Canton on 21 April 1913 and educated at the University of Nanking, from which he graduated in 1933. He was an instructor in chemistry at Nanking University 1933–35 and then in 1935 he emigrated to the USA, where he took up postgraduate studies at the University of California at Berkeley. After obtaining his PhD in 1938, Li joined the staff of the university, becoming in 1950 professor of biochemistry and professor of experimental endocrinology and director of the Hormone Research Laboratory. In 1955 he was granted US citizenship.

Li spent his entire academic career studying the pituitary gland hormones. In collaboration with various co-workers, he isolated several protein hormones

Lewis The neutralization of an acid and a base, during which the base supplies a pair of electrons to form a chemical bond.

from the pituitary gland, including adreno-corti-cotrophic hormone (ACTH), which stimulates the adrenal cortex to increase its secretion of corticoids. In 1956 Li and his group showed that ACTH consists of 39 amino acids arranged in a specific order, and that the whole chain of the natural hormone is not necessary for its action. He isolated another pituitary hormone called melanocyte-stimulating hormone (MSH) and found that not only does this hormone produce some effects similar to those produced by ACTH, but also that part of the amino-acid chain of MSH is the same as that of ACTH. Li has also studied pituitary growth hormones, finding that they are effective only in the species that produces them – that is, growth hormone from cattle, for example, is ineffective in humans. Continuing this line of research, he discovered in 1966 that human pituitary growth hormone (somatotropin) consists of a chain of 256 amino acids, and in 1970 he succeeded in synthesizing this hormone, thereby setting a record for the largest protein molecule synthesized up to that time.

Libby, Willard Frank (1908–1980) US chemist best known for developing the technique of radiocarbon dating, for which he was awarded the 1960 Nobel Prize for Chemistry.

Libby was born in Grand Valley, Colorado, on 17 December 1908, the son of a farmer. He received his university education at the University of California, Berkeley, from which he graduated in 1931 and gained his PhD in 1933. He then took a teaching appointment at Berkeley and in 1941, soon after the outbreak of World War II, moved to Columbia University, New York, to work on the development of the atomic bomb (the Manhattan Project). After the war, in 1945, he became professor of chemistry at the University of Chicago's Institute for Nuclear Studies. From 1954 to 1959 he was a member of the US Atomic Energy Commission, then in 1959 he returned to the University of California to become director of the Institute of Geophysics. He died in Los Angeles on 8 September 1980.

During the early 1940s at Columbia Libby worked on the separation of uranium isotopes for producing fissionable uranium-238 for the atomic bomb. Back in Chicago after the war he turned his attention to carbon-14, a radioactive isotope of carbon that had been discovered in 1940 by Serge Korff. It occurs as a small constant percentage of the carbon in the carbon dioxide in the atmosphere – resulting from cosmic-ray bombardment – and in the carbon in the tissues of all living plants and animals. Carbon-14 has an extremely long half-life (5,730 years) but when the plant or animal dies, it accumulates no more of the radioactive isotope, which steadily decays and changes into

nitrogen. Libby reasoned that a determination of the carbon-14 content of anything derived from plant or animal tissue – such as wood, bones, cotton or woollen cloth, hair, or leather – gives a measure of its age (or the time that has elapsed since the plant or animal died). He and his co-workers accurately dated ancient Egyptian relics by measuring the amount of radiocarbon they contained using a sensitive Geiger counter. By 1947 they had developed the technique so that it could date objects up to 50,000 years old. It has proved to be extremely useful in geology, anthropology, and archaeology. In 1946 Libby showed that tritium (a radioactive isotope of hydrogen of mass 3) is formed by the action of cosmic rays and devised a method of dating based on the amount of tritium in the water in an archaeological specimen. Later workers extended the method using other isotopes, such as potassium-40.

Lie, (Marius) Sophus (1842–1899) Norwegian mathematician who made valuable contributions to the theory of algebraic invariants and who is remembered for the Lie theorem and the Lie groups.

Lie was born in Nordfjordeid, near Bergen, on 17 December 1842. He received his primary and secondary schooling in Moss and then in 1859, at the age of 17, entered the University at Christiania (now Oslo) to study mathematics and science. He graduated in 1865 without, it appears, having formed a determination to become a mathematician. But in the next two or three years, while he earned money by giving private lessons, he read the works of Jean ◊Poncelet and Julius ◊Plücker and his imagination was fired by the latter's idea for creating new geometries by using figures, not points, as elements of space. This idea stayed with Lie to influence him throughout his career.

In 1869 Lie was awarded a scholarship to study abroad and he went to Berlin, where he worked under Felix ◊Klein, and then to Paris. In 1870 he was arrested for spying – a false charge – but was released within a month and made his way to Italy just before the German blockade of Paris in the Franco-German war of that year. In 1871 the University of Christiania awarded him a scholarship to do doctoral research and he returned there in 1872. By the end of the year he had gained his doctorate and had a chair of mathematics created for him. He remained there until 1886, when he travelled to Leipzig to succeed Klein in the chair of mathematics at the university. His years at Leipzig, which lasted until 1898, were broken by a year in a mental hospital, caused by a kind of nervous breakdown (which was then called neurasthenia) in 1889. His last year was spent at Christiania, where another chair of mathematics was specially created for him. He died there of pernicious anaemia on 18 February 1899.

Lie shares with Klein the distinction of being the first mathematician to emphasize the importance of the notion of groups in geometry. By using group theory they were able to show that it was possible to decide to which kind of geometry a particular notion belonged. It was also possible to establish the relationships between different kinds of geometry, for instance of non-Euclidean geometry to projective geometry.

Lie's first great discovery, made while he was in Paris in 1870, was that of his contact transformation, which mapped straight lines with spheres and which mapped principal tangent curves into curvature lines. In his theory of tangential transformations occurs the particular transformation that makes a sphere correspond to a straight line. By 1873 Lie had turned away from contact transformation to investigate transformation groups. In this work on group theory he chose a new space element, the contact element, which is an incidence pair of point and line or of point and hyperplane. This led him to his greatest achievement, the discovery of transformation groups known as Lie groups, one of the basic notions of which is that of infinitesimal transformation.

The Lie groups provided the means to deduce from the structure the type of auxiliary equations needed for their integration, and the integration theorem which he developed (and which goes by his name) made it possible to classify partial differential equations in such a way as to make most of the classical methods of solving such equations reducible to a single principle. Moreover, the theorem led to a geometric interpretation of Cauchy's solution to partial differential equations.

The general effect of Lie's discoveries was to reduce the amount of work required in integration, although Lie's own papers on integration in the last 20 years of his life were clumsily presented and repetitive. His chief contribution to mathematics was to provide, in the Lie groups, the foundations of the modern science of topology.

Liebig, Justus von (1803–1873) German organic chemist, one of the greatest influences on 19th-century chemistry. Through his researches and those of his ex-students, he had a profound influence on the science for nearly a hundred years. To the schoolchild of today he is best known for the piece of chemical apparatus that he made popular and which still bears his name (the Liebig condenser). A better measure of his status is the fact that his students, assistants and co-workers included such famous chemists as Edward Frankland, Joseph ◊Gay-Lussac, August von ◊Hofmann, Friedrich ◊Kekulé von Stradonitz, Friedrich ◊Wöhler, and Charles ◊Wurtz.

Liebig was born in Darmstadt, Hesse, on 12 May 1803. His father sold drugs, dyes, pigments, and other chemicals and carried out his own chemical experiments, to which Liebig was introduced as a boy. When he was 15 years old he was apprenticed to an apothecary and first went to university to study under Karl Kastner at Bonn (where Liebig was arrested for his liberalist political activity) and then he accompanied Kastner to Erlangen University, where he gained his PhD in 1822 when he was still only 19 years old. Financed by the Grand Duke of Hesse, Liebig went to Paris for two years where Alexander von ◊Humboldt obtained a position for him in Joseph Gay-Lussac's laboratory at the Arsenal. He also made the acquaintance of Louis Thénard, who with von Humboldt recommended the 21-year-old Liebig for the chair of chemistry at the small University of Giessen. He stayed there for 27 years, 1825–52, building up a prestigious teaching laboratory. In 1840 he founded the journal *Annalen der Chemie* and was made a baron in 1845. Then in 1852 he moved to the University of Munich but, because of failing health, did less active research himself and concentrated on lecturing and writing. He remained there for the rest of his life and died in Munich on 18 April 1873.

In the early 1820s Liebig investigated fulminates, at the same time that Wöhler was independently working with cyanates. In 1826 Liebig prepared silver fulminate (modern formula AgCNO) and Wöhler made silver cyanate (AgNCO). When they reported their results they assigned the same formula to the two different compounds, which stimulated Jöns ◊Berzelius's work that led to the concept of isomers.

Liebig and Wöhler became friends and continued their researches together. In 1832, from a study of oil of bitter almonds (benzaldehyde; phenylmethanal), they discovered the benzoyl radical (C_6H_5CO-). They showed that benzaldehyde can be converted to benzoic acid and made a number of other related compounds, such as benzyl alcohol and benzoyl chloride. The benzene ring had, in fact, conferred unusual stability to the benzoyl grouping, allowing it to persist in the various reactions. Liebig and Wöhler introduced the idea of compound radicals in organic chemistry, although they found no other radicals that as convincingly supported their theory and found themselves in an acrimonius dispute over the matter with Berzelius and Jean Baptiste ◊Dumas. They had, however, tried to introduce a degree of systematization into the confused field of organic chemistry. To facilitate this work, many new methods of organic analysis were introduced by Liebig, and he devised ways of determining hydrogen, carbon, and halogens in organic compounds.

From 1838 Liebig's work centred on what we would now call biochemistry. He studied fermentation (but would not acknowledge that yeast is a living substance, a view to which Berzelius also subscribed, and which brought them both into contention with Louis ◊Pasteur) and analysed various body fluids and urine. He calculated the calorific values of foods, emphasizing the role of fats as a source of dietary energy, and even developed a beef extract – long marketed as Liebig extract. Liebig also applied his chemical knowledge to agriculture. He demonstrated that plants absorb minerals (and water) from the soil and postulated that the carbon used by plants comes from carbon dioxide in the air rather than from humus in the soil. He also thought, incorrectly, that ammonia in rainwater passed into the soil and provided plants with their sole source of nitrogen. He thus advocated the use of artificial fertilizers in agriculture instead of animal manure, although his original formulation omitted essential nitrogen compounds.

In later life his rather rigid views made Liebig even more dogmatic in his statements – often labelled as arrogance by both his friends and his antagonists – but by then he was an established authority and his opinions were seldom questioned.

It is said that he could be grossly unfair, stimulating controversy and admitting an error only when it no longer mattered; only his lifelong friend Wöhler seems to have continued to have survived Liebig's irascibility.

Further Reading

Brock, William, *Justus von Liebig: The Chemical Gatekeeper,* Cambridge University Press, 1997.

Holmes, Frederic L, 'Justus Liebig and the construction of organic chemistry' in: Mauskopf, Seymour H (ed), *Chemical Sciences in the Modern World,* University of Philadelphia Press, 1993, pp 119–134.

Lilienthal, Otto (1848–1896) German engineer whose experiments with gliders helped to found the science of aeronautics. But for his premature death in a flying accident, he might well have beaten Orville and Wilbur ◊Wright to the achievement of powered flight.

Lilienthal was born in Pomerania (then part of Prussia), and trained as an engineer just before the outbreak of the Franco-Prussian War in 1870. He made exhaustive studies of the flight of birds, especially of the stock, but was aware that it was 'not enough to acquire the art of the bird' it was also necessary to put the whole problem of flight on a scientific basis. From these studies he learnt that curved wings allow horizontal flight without an angle of incidence to the wind, and that soaring is related to air thermals. In 1889 he published his famous book *Der Vogelflug als Grundlage der Fliegekunst/Bird Flight as a Basis for Aviation,* which was to have a great influence on the work of the pioneers of the next vitally important years. He was one of the few who showed conclusively that birds produce

thrust by the action of their outer primary feathers. It was perhaps this that kept Lilienthal on the path of the ornithopter – a machine which simulated the winged flight of a bird as the ultimate means of powered flight.

Lilienthal flew the first of his famous series of gliders in 1891, and continued, until his final fatal glide in 1896, to hold to his fundamental conviction that the key to eventual powered flight was in glider-flying, in which pilots could master the elements of control and design. Its relative safety – sadly not safe enough for Lilienthal – allowed the pioneers of flying to come to terms with problems of movement and airflow. The step to powered flight was a straightforward progression from advanced gliding. The Wrights' breakthrough was a simple extension of their own work with gliders, which in turn was greatly helped by Lilienthal's many glides and careful observations. Among other things, he had demonstrated the superiority of cambered wings over flat wings – the principle of the aerofoil.

By 1893 he was flying a cambered-wing monoplane from a springboard near his home. It had a wingspan of 7 m/23 ft and a surface area of about 13 sq m/140 sq ft; its wings folded for transport. Other gliders included two biplanes, with tailplanes in front of the vertical tail fin (the first gliders were tail-less). His 1894 model (Number 11 in the offical biographies) became his standard machine. With a wing surface of 14 sq m/150 sq ft this glider had the tailplane integral with the fin and achieved glides of more than 300 m/1,000 ft. By this time his activities had given a boost to gliding as a sport, and enthusiasts began 'sailing' in many countries.

1894 also saw the introduction of a shock-absorbing hoop, which, on 9 November, certainly helped to save his life in a crash. A detailed description of this incident caused other workers, including the Wrights, to build elevators in front of their machines, the idea being to prevent damage in the event of a nose-dive. By 1889 Lilienthal had introduced leading-edge flaps to counteract the tendency to nose-dive. Also in that year he introduced the biplanes referred to above, which were found to possess increased stability with reduced wingspan, but he did not develop these machines. (The Wrights' successful flights were with biplanes.) Lilienthal's later machines were flown from an artificial earthwork which he had constructed outside Berlin. These gave a launching height of about 15 m/50 ft and, being conical, allowed independence of wind direction. In 1895 Lilienthal resumed some earlier work on the idea of a powered machine with moving wing-tips, using a carbon dioxide motor despite the fact that petrol engines had been made by that time. The machine was not tested. Only in that year did he consider means of control other than body swinging. Up to then the 'pilot' was suspended by his arms – like a modern hang-glider – the rest of him dangling free after the running take-off. Movement was produced by swinging the body, thus altering the centre of gravity. The idea of the body harness was introduced, an echo of something ◊Leonardo da Vinci had sketched some 500 years previously.

The influence of Lilienthal, both before and after his death, was enormous, helped greatly by the developments in photography and printing of that period – the dry-plate negative and the half-tone printing process. These advances allowed a magnificent series of pictures to be given worldwide circulation. They had a tremendous and important impact at a time when even a scientist like Lord ◊Kelvin was saying that he had 'not the smallest molecule of faith' in flying, other than in balloons!

On a fine summer's day in 1896, after several trouble-free glides, an unexpected gust caused Lilienthal's Number 11 to stall and fall to the ground. His spine was broken and he died the following day. His gravestone carries a favourite saying of his: 'Sacrifices have to be made'.

Lindblad, Bertil (1895–1965) Swedish expert on stellar dynamics whose chief contribution to astronomy lay in his use of the work of Jacobus ◊Kapteyn and Harlow ◊Shapley to demonstrate the rotation of our Galaxy.

Lindblad was born in Örebro in southern central Sweden on 26 November 1895. He completed his education at Uppsala University, where he studied mathematics, astronomy, and physics. He graduated in 1920, having earned his PhD for research on radiative transfer in the solar atmosphere. He spent a two-year postdoctoral research period in the USA, visiting the Lick, Harvard, and Mount Wilson observatories. Lindblad returned to Sweden in 1922, and continued his work first in Uppsala and, from 1927, in Stockholm. He was appointed director of the new Stockholm Observatory in 1927, and made professor of astronomy at the Royal Swedish Academy of Sciences.

Lindblad's original research earned him international recognition, and he was accorded many professional honours, including the Gold Medal of the Royal Astronomical Society. He died in Stockholm on 26 June 1965.

Lindblad's early research was concentrated in the field of spectroscopy, but he soon became interested in stellar dynamics. At that time there was a vigorous astronomical debate on the subject of the structure of the galaxy. Jacobus Kapteyn had proposed a model based on his observations on stellar motion, which suggested to him that the Solar System lay near the centre of the Galaxy. Harlow Shapley alternatively proposed that the centre of the Galaxy was some 50,000 light years away in the direction of the constellation Sagittarius.

Lindblad analysed Kapteyn's results and suggested that the two streams of stars that Kapteyn had observed could in fact represent the rotation of all the stars in our Galaxy in the same direction, around a distant centre; he thus confirmed Shapley's hypothesis that the centre lay in the direction of Sagittarius. But he also went on to stipulate that the speed of rotation of the stars in the Galaxy was a function of their distance from the centre (the 'differential rotation theory').

Such an interpretation of Kapteyn's work was supported by an analysis put forward by Jan ◊Oort, published shortly thereafter.

Stellar motion continued to be the dominant theme in Lindblad's research. He inspired many other Swedish astronomers, including his son, P Lindblad, who succeeded him as director of the Stockholm Observatory.

Lindemann, (Carl Louis) Ferdinand von (1852–1939) German mathematician who is famous for one result, his discussion of the nature of π, which laid to rest the old question of 'squaring the circle'.

Lindemann was born in Hanover on 12 April 1852, did his undergraduate work at Göttingen and Munich, and received his doctorate from the university at Erlangen (where he studied under Felix ◊Klein) in 1873. He then spent a couple of years travelling in England and France, meeting leading mathematicians and carrying on private research. In 1877 he was appointed a lecturer at Würzburg and in 1879 he was promoted to professor. From 1883 to 1893 he was a professor at Königsberg (now Kaliningrad); from 1893 until his death, he taught at Munich. He died on 6 March 1939.

Lindemann published papers on a number of subjects, including spectrum theory, invariant theory, and theoretical mechanics (his doctoral dissertation was on the infinitely small movements of rigid bodies). He was also a highly acclaimed teacher, supervising more than 60 doctoral candidates during his career and being more than anyone else responsible for introducing the seminar method of teaching into German universities. He also translated and edited the works of Henri ◊Poincaré and made his mathematics known in Germany.

His fame, nevertheless, rests almost entirely on the paper that he published in 1882 on the nature of π as a transcendental number. Since the time of the Greeks, mathematicians had known of irrational numbers and wondered if they were algebraic: or, in other words, was it possible to define an algebraic equation with rational coefficients in which irrational numbers were the roots? In 1844 Joseph ◊Liouville had shown, by the use of continued fractions, that a host of numbers exist that are non-algebraic. These are known as transcendental numbers. Then in 1872 Charles ◊Hermite proved a rigorous demonstration that e, the base of 'natural' logarithms, was a transcendental number. The highly interesting question, whether π was also a transcendental number, had still, however, not received a satisfactory answer.

It was Lindemann who provided, in his 1882 paper, the proof. He demonstrated that, except in trivial cases, every expression of the form:

$$\sum_{i=1}^{n} A_i e^{a_i}$$

Where A and a are algebraic numbers, must be nonzero. Therefore, since i is a root of $x^2 + 1 = 0$, and since it was known that:

$$1^{i\pi} + 1^0 = 0$$

$$\text{(that is } 1^{i\pi} = -1\text{)}$$

Then iπ and therefore π (since i is algebraic) must be transcendental. If π cannot be the root of an equation, it cannot be constructed. Therefore the 'squaring of a circle' is impossible. Lindemann had brought an end to one of the oldest puzzles in mathematics.

Lindemann, Frederick Alexander (1886–1957)

Viscount Cherwell. British physicist who was involved with Hermann ◊Nernst in advancing the quantum theory. He later became Lord Cherwell and played an important role in the administration of British science during and after World War II.

Lindemann was born in Baden-Baden, Germany, on 5 April 1886. He went to school in Scotland and Germany, and attended the University of Berlin, where he gained his PhD in 1910. Lindemann remained at Berlin until 1914, when he returned to the UK and during World War I became director of the RAF Physical Laboratory, where he was concerned with aircraft stability. In 1919, Lindemann became professor of experimental philosophy at Oxford, building up the Clarendon Laboratory into an important scientific institution. In 1941, he was granted a peerage and took the title of Lord Cherwell. Lindemann was paymaster general 1942–45 and again 1951–53. In this position he gave valuable advice to the British government, helping to direct scientific research during World War II and to create the Atomic Energy Authority afterwards. Lindemann returned to Oxford 1945–51 and 1953–56, after which he retired. He was then instrumental in founding Churchill College, Cambridge, to promote the study of technology. Lindemann was awarded the Hughes Medal of the Royal Society in 1956, and died in Oxford on 3 July 1957.

Lindemann's main contributions to physics were made in his early years at Berlin, where he studied with and later assisted Nernst. Nernst and Lindemann together made an important advance in quantum theory in 1911 by constructing a special calorimeter and measuring specific heats at very low temperatures. They confirmed the specific heat equation proposed by Albert ◊Einstein in 1907, in which he used the quantum theory to predict that the specific heats of solids would become zero at absolute zero. Lindemann also derived a formula that relates the melting point of a crystalline solid to the amplitude of vibration of its atoms.

In World War I, Lindemann developed a theory to explain why the aircraft of that time were liable to spin out of control. He then worked out a way of recovering from a spin and successfully tested it himself.

Linnaeus, Carolus (1707–1778)

Latinized form of Carl von Linné. Swedish botanist who became famous for introducing the binomial system of biological nomenclature (which is named after him and is universally used today), and for formulating basic principles for classification.

Linnaeus was born on 27 May 1707 in South Råshult, Sweden, the son of a clergyman. He was

Linnaeus Swedish botanist Carolus Linnaeus who in the mid-18th century devised the system of plant classification that forms the basis of the nomenclature used today. Linneaus' family surname was Ingemarsson, but he named himself after a plant, the linden tree, that grew in his family garden. *Mary Evans Picture Library*

interested in plants even as a child, but his father sent him to study medicine, first at the University of Lund in 1727 and then at Uppsala University.

In 1730 Linnaeus was appointed lecturer in botany at Uppsala and two years later explored Lapland for the Uppsala Academy of Sciences. In 1735 Linnaeus left Sweden for Holland to obtain his MD at the University of Harderwijk. On his return to Sweden in 1738 Linnaeus practised as a physician, with considerable success, and in the following year he married Sara Moraea, a physician's daughter. In 1741 he was appointed professor of medicine at Uppsala University but changed this position in 1742 for the chair of botany, which he retained for the rest of his life. In 1761 Linnaeus was granted a patent of nobility – antedated to 1757 – by which he was entitled to call himself Carl von Linné. He suffered a stroke in 1774, which impaired his health, and he died on 10 January 1778 in Uppsala Cathedral, where he was buried.

Linnaeus's best-known work is probably *Systema naturae* (1735). In this book he introduced a simple yet methodical system of classifying plants according to the number of stamens and pistils in their flowers. This system overshadowed the earlier work of John ◊Ray and was so convenient that it was a long time before it was replaced by a more natural system – despite the fact that Linnaeus himself recognized its artificiality.

Linnaeus made his most important contribution – the introduction of the binomial system of nomenclature, by which every species is identified by a generic name and a specific name – in 1753, with the publication of *Species plantarum*. Even today the starting point in the nomenclature of all flowering plants and ferns is internationally agreed to be the first edition of *Species plantarum*, together with the fifth edition of *Genera plantarum* (1754; first edition 1737). In these works he became the first person to formulate the principles for defining genera and species and to adhere to a uniform use of specific names. In 1758 he applied his binomial system to animal classification. With the rapid discovery of previously unknown plants and animals that was occurring in the 18th century, the value of Linnaeus' system was soon recognized and it had become almost universally adopted by the end of his life. The survival of the system to the present day is probably due to its great flexibility; Linnaeus himself believed that species were immutable and that he was classifying Creation (although he later modified this viewpoint slightly), but so adaptable was his system that it was able to accommodate modifications that later resulted from the introduction of evolutionary principles to taxonomy.

In addition to his books on classification, Linnaeus wrote many other works, including *Flora Laponica*

(1737), the results of his journey to Lapland; *Hortus Cliffortianus* (1738), a description of the plants in the garden of George Clifford, a merchant with whom Linnaeus stayed during much of his time in Holland; and *Flora Sueccia* (1745) and *Fauna Sueccia* (1746), accounts of his biological observations during his travels in Sweden. After Linnaeus' death, his widow sold his manuscripts and natural history collection to James Edward Smith (1759–1828), the first president of the Linnean Society (founded in 1788), who took them to England. When Smith died the society purchased Linnaeus' manuscripts and specimens and they are now preserved by the society in Burlington House, London.

Linnaeus: classification of modern humans

Kingdom Animalia
Phylum Chordata
Sub-phylum Vertebrata
Class Mammalia
Order Primates
Family Hominidae
Genus Homo
Species sapiens

Further Reading

Frängsmyr, Tore, Lindroth, Sten, *Linnaeus, the Man and His Work*, Uppsala Studies in History of Science, Science History Publications (USA), 1994, v 18.

Linné, Carl von; Black, David; and Lee, Stephen (eds), *Travels*, Nature Classics series, Paul Elek, 1979.

Linnett, John Wilfred (1913–1975) English chemist of wide-ranging interests, from spectroscopy to reaction kinetics and molecular structure.

Linnett was born in Coventry on 3 August 1913. He was educated locally at the King Henry VIII School and in 1931 won a scholarship to read chemistry at St John's College, Oxford, from which he graduated in 1934. He was awarded his doctorate three years later for a thesis on the spectroscopy and photochemistry of the metal alkyls; he continued this work in 1938 during a visit to Harvard. From 1938 to 1965 Linnett was at Oxford, becoming a reader in 1962. In 1965 he was appointed professor of physical chemistry at Emmanuel College, Cambridge, where he remained for the rest of his research life. He became master of Sidney Sussex College, Cambridge, in 1970, deputy vice chancellor of Cambridge University in 1971, and vice chancellor 1973–75. He died on 7 November 1975.

The beginning of Linnett's career coincided with the outbreak of World War II in 1939. During that period he participated in a broad project aimed at providing methods of protection from gas attacks, such as developing catalysts that would oxidize carbon monoxide. After the war he studied molecular force fields, the measurement of burning velocities in gases, the recombination of atoms at surfaces, and theories of chemical bonding.

His work on explosion limits concentrated on the reaction between carbon monoxide, hydrogen, and oxygen, which led to the study of atomic reactions on surfaces, such as the efficiency of the surface recombination of hydrogen atoms on palladium/gold, palladium/silver, and copper/nickel alloys. In the early 1960s he was using mass spectroscopy for the direct sampling of reacting systems. In 1967, using this technique, he discovered that the HCO radical attracts the hydrogen from the methyl group of acetaldehyde (ethanal):

$$\cdot HCO + CH_3CHO \rightarrow CO + H_2 + \cdot CH_2CHO$$

The following year he extended the method to study the pyrolysis of mixtures of methyl iodide (iodomethane, CH_3I) and nitric oxide (nitrogen monoxide, NO), and attempted to account for the formation of N–N bonds in the reaction of methyl radicals with excess nitric oxide.

In 1960, while visiting Berkeley on a Cherwell Memorial Fellowship, Linnett originated his important modification to the Lewis–Langmuir octet rule concerning valency electrons. He proposed that the octet should be considered as a double quartet of electrons rather than as four pairs, and in this way he was able to explain the stability of 'odd electron' molecules such as nitric oxide.

nitric oxide
(nitrogen monoxide)

combination
NO

dimer
N_2O_2

Nitrogen has five valence electrons and oxygen has six; there are $2^1/_2$ bonds (or electron pairs) linking the two atoms. In the dimer N_2O_2, however, there are five bonds with two sets of coincident electrons, whereas in the five bonds of 2NO the quartets of each spin do not have the same orientation. The 2NO version should therefore have the lower electron–electron repulsion energy. Linnett and his co-worker Hirst described this analysis as the non-pairing method to distinguish it from the valence-bond and molecular-orbital methods.

Linnett published more than 250 scientific papers and two textbooks, in one of which (*Wave Mechanics and Valency*) he explains to the experimental chemist

the processes and techniques involved in the application of wave mechanics to the electronic structures of atoms and molecules.

Liouville, Joseph (1809–1882) French mathematician who wrote prolifically on problems of analysis, but who is famous chiefly as the founder and first editor of the learned journal popularly known as the *Journal de Liouville*.

Liouville was born in St Omer, Pas-de-Calais, on 24 March 1809 and studied at Commery and Toul before entering the Ecole Polytechnique in Paris in 1825. In 1827 he transferred to the Ecole des Ponts et Chaussées, where he received his baccalaureate in 1830. For the next 50 years, beginning with his appointment to the Ecole Polytechnique in 1831, Liouville taught mathematics at all the leading institutions of higher learning in Paris. While he was lecturing at the Ecole Centrale des Arts et Manufactures 1833–38, he received his doctorate in 1836 for a thesis on Fourier series.

In 1838 he was elected to the chair of analysis at the Ecole Polytechnique, where he remained until 1851, when he became a professor at the Collège de France. He stayed at the Collège until 1879, although in the years 1857–74 he held concurrently the post of professor of rational mechanics at the Sorbonne. He was also for a time the director of the Bureau de Longitudes. Quite unexpectedly, having shown no political ambition previously, he became infected by the revolution of 1848 and was elected as a moderate republican to the constituent assembly in April 1848. A year later he was defeated in the elections to the new Legislative Assembly and his political career closed as suddenly as it had opened. He died in Paris on 8 September 1882. Although Liouville's early interest lay in problems associated with the study of electricity and heat, and although he was elected to the Academy of Sciences in 1839 as a member of the astronomy section, the chief mathematical interest of his career was in analysis. In that field he published more than a hundred papers 1832–57. In collaboration with Charles-François Sturm (1803–1855) he published papers in 1836 on vibration, which were of considerable importance in laying the foundations of the theory of linear differential equations. He also provided the first proof of the existence of transcendental functions and in a paper of 1844 laid down that the irrational numbers, e and e^2 were transcendental, since they could not be used to solve any second-degree polynomial equation. The proof of this, however, had to await Charles ◊Hermite's demonstration in 1873.

More important than his research was Liouville's founding of the *Journal des mathématiques pures et appliqués* in 1836. Since the demise of Gergonne's *Annales de mathématiques* in 1831 French mathematicians had been deprived of a receptacle for their research papers. Liouville's journal filled the gap. He edited it from the issue of the first number in 1836 down to the 39th number in 1874. When he retired from the editorship, the mathematical spark died in him and he produced nothing more of importance.

Further Reading

Lutzen, Jesper, *Joseph Liouville, 1809–1882: Master of Pure and Applied Mathematics,* Studies in the History of Mathematics and Physical Sciences series, Springer-Verlag, 1990, v 15.

Lutzen, Jesper, 'The geometrization of analytical mechanics: a pioneering contribution by J Liouville (ca 1850)' in: Rowe, David E and McCleary, John (eds), *The History of Modern Mathematics,* Academic Press, 1989, v 2, pp 77–97.

Lipschitz, Rudolf Otto Sigismund (1832–1903)

German mathematician of wide-ranging interests who is remembered for the so-called Lipschitz algebra and the Lipschitz condition.

Lipschitz was born in Königsberg (now Kaliningrad in Russia) on 14 May 1832. He does not appear to have become seriously interested in mathematics until, in 1847, he entered the University of Königsberg, where one of his teachers was Franz Neumann. After graduating from Königsberg he continued his studies at the University of Berlin, chiefly under Lejeune ◊Dirichlet. He was awarded his doctorate in 1853. For the next few years he taught at schools in Königsberg and Elbinc, before becoming a lecturer at the University of Berlin in 1857. He moved to Breslau (now Wrocław in Poland) in 1862, but was there for only two years. In 1864 he was appointed professor of mathematics at the University of Bonn. He remained there for the rest of his career, so contented with his work and life there that he turned down an invitation to become a professor at the more prestigious University of Göttingen in 1873. He died in Bonn on 7 October 1903.

Lipschitz did extensive work in number theory, Fourier series, the theory of Bessel functions, differential equations, the calculus of variations, geometry, and mechanics. He was also much interested in the fundamental questions concerned with the nature of mathematics and of mathematical research, and German higher education was much indebted to him for his two-volume *Grundlagen der Analysis* (1877–80), a synthetic presentation of the foundations of mathematics and their applications. The work provided a comprehensive survey of what was then known of the theory of rational integers, differential equations, and function theory.

Among his more specific contributions to mathematical knowledge, several stand out. His work in basic analysis provided a condition now known as the Lipschitz condition, subsequently of great importance in proofs of existence and uniqueness, as well as in approximation theory and constructive function theory. He has a place in the history of number theory, too, as the developer of a hyper-complex system which became known as Lipschitz algebra. In investigating the sums of arbitrarily many squares, Lipschitz derived computational rules for certain symbolic expressions from real transformations. Even more important were the investigations he began in 1869 into forms of n differentials, for these led to his most valuable contribution to mathematics – the Cauchy–Lipschitz method of approximation of differentials. Finally, there was his work on co-gradient differentiation, which he conducted parallel to, but independently of, similar research by Elwin ◊Christoffel. Lipschitz showed that the vanishing of a certain expression is a necessary and sufficient condition for a Riemannian manifold to be Euclidean, and further research into Bernhard ◊Riemann's mathematics enabled him to produce what is now the chief theorem concerning mean curvature vectors. Lipschitz's two papers on this subject, taken together with one written by Christoffel, formed a vital ingredient of what became the tensor calculus of Gregorio ◊Ricci-Curbastro and Tullio ◊Levi-Civita.

Partly because he spread himself so wide, Lipschitz's star does not shine as brightly as some others in the mathematical firmament; but he was one of the most industrious and most technically proficient of 19th-century mathematicians.

Lipscomb, William Nunn (1919–   )

US chemist whose main interest is in the relationships between the geometric and electronic structures of molecules and their chemical and physical behaviour. He was awarded the 1976 Nobel Prize for Chemistry for his work on the structure of boron hydrides (boranes).

Lipscomb was born in Cleveland, Ohio, on 9 December 1919. He graduated from the University of Kentucky in 1941 and gained his PhD from the California Institute of Technology in 1946. During World War II he was associated with the Office of Scientific Research and Development Projects. He taught at the University of Minnesota 1946–59, and at the University of Harvard after 1959. He became Abbott and James Lawrence Professor at Harvard in 1971 (emeritus from 1990).

Lipscomb studied the boron hydrides and their derivatives to elucidate problems about electron-deficient compounds in general. He developed low-temperature X-ray diffraction methods to study simple crystals and established the structures of these compounds, which are not readily described using the usual electron-pair-bonding method. He and other research workers related them to the polyhedral structures of borides. Using the simpler members of the series, they developed bonding theories that account for filled electron shells in terms of three-centre two-electron bonds. They also proposed molecular orbital descriptions in which the bonding electrons are delocalized over the whole molecule. Much of this work was summarized in Lipscomb's book *Boron Hydrides*, published in 1963.

Lipscomb went on to investigate the carboranes, $C_2B_{10}H_{12}$, and the sites of electrophilic attack on these compounds using nuclear magnetic resonance (NMR) spectroscopy. This work led to the theory of chemical shifts. The calculations provided the first accurate values for the constants that describe the behaviour of several types of molecules in magnetic or electric fields. They also gave a theoretical basis for applying quantum mechanics to complex molecules, with wide potential for both inorganic and organic chemical problems. Lipscomb and his co-workers developed the idea of transferability of atomic properties, by which approximate theories for complex molecules are developed from more exact calculations for simpler but chemically related molecules, using high-speed computers. With Pitzer, Lipscomb made the first accurate calculation of the barrier to internal rotation about the carbon–carbon bond in ethane.

Lipscomb's team developed X-ray diffraction techniques for studying simple crystals of nitrogen, oxygen, fluorine, and other substances that are solid only below liquid nitrogen temperatures. They also determined the molecular structure of cyclo-octatetraene iron and the tricarbonyl complexes of natural products. One of these, leurocristine, is used in leukaemia therapy. Lipscomb also elucidated the three-dimensional structure of carboxypeptidase A, one of the largest globular proteins, with a molecular mass of 34,400.

Lissajous, Jules Antoine (1822–1880) French physicist who developed Lissajous figures for demonstrating wave motion.

Lissajous was born in Versailles on 4 March 1822. He was educated at the Ecole Normale Supérieure 1841–47, when he became professor of physics at the Lycée Saint-Louis. He became rector of the Academy of Chambéry in 1874, and then took up the same position at Besançon in 1875. In 1879 Lissajous was elected a member of the Paris Academy, and he died in Plombières on 24 June 1880.

Lissajous was interested in acoustics and from 1855 developed Lissajous figures as a means of visually demonstrating the vibrations that produce sound waves. He first reflected a light beam from a mirror attached to a vibrating object such as a tuning fork to another mirror that rotated. The light was then reflected onto a screen, where the spot traced out a curve whose shape depended on the amplitude and frequency of the vibration. Lissajous then refined this method by using two mirrors mounted on vibrating tuning forks at right angles, and produced a wider variety of figures. By making one of the forks a standard, the acoustic characteristics of the other fork could be determined by the shape of the Lissajous figure produced.

Lissajous figures can now be demonstrated on the screen of an oscilloscope by applying alternating currents of different frequencies to the deflection plates. The curves produced depend on the ratio of the frequencies, enabling signals to be compared with each other.

Lister, Joseph (1827–1912) English surgeon with a great interest in histology and bacteriology. He introduced the concept of antiseptic surgery and was a pioneer, in the UK, of preventive medicine.

Lister was born on 5 April 1827, in Upton, Essex, the son of the physicist Joseph Jackson Lister (1786–1869). He was educated at various Quaker schools and at University College, London, the only university then open to dissenters. He first studied arts and after graduation took up medicine at University College, where he was taught by the eminent physiologist William Sharpey and graduated in 1852. In 1856 he was a surgeon at the Edinburgh Royal Infirmary as assistant to James Syme, and three years later was appointed regius professor of surgery at the University of Glasgow. In 1861 he took charge of the surgical wards at the Royal Infirmary, Glasgow, and in 1869 became professor of clinical surgery at Edinburgh. Eight years later he took up the chair in clinical surgery at King's College, London. He was knighted in 1883 and was made a peer in 1897. Nearing retirement in 1891, he became chairman of the newly formed British Institute of Preventive Medicine (later the Lister Institute) and served as president of the Royal Society 1895–1900. He died on 10 February 1912 in Walmer, Kent.

Nearly half the patients who underwent major surgery at that time died as the result of post-operative septic infection. Sepsis was thought to be a kind of combustion caused by exposing moist body tissues to oxygen – an assertion put forward by the German chemist Justus von ◊Liebig in 1839. Great care was therefore taken to keep air from wounds, by means of plasters, collodion, or resins. Lister doubted the explanation and these methods; he regarded wound sepsis as a form of decomposition.

In 1865 Louis ◊Pasteur suggested that decay is caused by living organisms in the air, which enter matter and cause it to ferment. Lister immediately saw the connection with wound sepsis. In addition, the previous year he had heard that carbolic acid (phenol) was being used to treat sewage in Carlisle, and that fields irrigated with the final effluent were freed of a parasite that was causing disease in cattle. Lister began to use a solution of carbolic acid for wound cleansing and dressings, and also experimented with operating under a spray of carbolic acid solution. In 1867 he announced to a British Medical Association meeting that his wards in the Glasgow Royal Infirmary had remained clear of sepsis for nine months. At first his new methods met with hostility or indifference, but gradually doctors began to support his antiseptic techniques.

Continuing his studies in histology and bacteriology Lister became interested in Robert ◊Koch's work, carried out 1876–78, on wound infections. In Germany, Koch was demonstrating that steam was a useful sterilizer for surgical instruments and dressings, and German surgeons were beginning to practise aseptic surgery, keeping wounds free from microorganisms by using only sterilized instruments and materials. Lister realized that both methods relied on destroying pathogenic microorganisms, and believed that, in the future, more emphasis would be placed on preventive medicine. He strove for the establishment of an institute of preventive medicine, which he saw opened in 1891.

Further Reading

Fisher, Richard B, *Joseph Lister, 1827–1912*, Macdonald and Jane's, 1977.

Rains, Antony J Harding, *Joseph Lister and Antisepsis*, Pioneers of Science and Discovery series, Priory Press, 1977.

Truax, Rhoda, *Joseph Lister, Father of Modern Surgery*, G G Harrap, 1947.

Lobachevsky, Nikolai Ivanovich (1792–1856)

Russian mathematician, one of the founders of non-Euclidean geometry, whose system is sometimes called Lobachevskian geometry.

Lobachevsky was born in Nizhniy-Novgorod on 2 November 1792. About eight years later, when his father died, he moved with his family to Kazan in Tatarstan, where he was educated at the local school. In 1807 he entered the University of Kazan to study mathematics and in 1814 he was appointed to the teaching staff there. In 1822 he was made a full professor and in 1827 he was elected rector of the university. He also took on administrative work for the government, serving as assistant trustee for the Kazan educational district 1846–55. For reasons that remain obscure (perhaps to compel him to devote himself to his government work), the government relieved him of his posts as professor and rector in 1847. Earlier it had recognized his talent by raising him to the hereditary nobility in 1837. In his later days Lobachevsky suffered

from cataracts in both his eyes, and he was nearly blind when he died in Kazan on 24 February 1856.

Lobachevsky's whole importance rests on the system of non-Euclidean geometry which he developed 1826–56. Karl ◊Gauss and János ◊Bolyai were working on ◊Euclid's fifth postulate and formulating their own non-Euclidean geometries at the same time; but in 1826, when Lobachevsky first gave the outline of his system to a meeting of colleagues at Kazan, neither Gauss nor Bolyai had uttered a public word, and Lobachevsky's first published paper on the subject appeared in 1829, three years before Bolyai's appendix to his father's *Tentatem*. The clearest statement of his geometry was made in the book *Geometrische Untersuchungen zur Theorie der Parallellinien*, which he published in Berlin in 1840. His last work on the subject, the *Pangéométrie*, was published just before his death.

Ever since the time of Euclid it had been believed that no geometry could be constructed without his fifth postulate – or, in other words, that any set of axioms other than Euclid's must, in the course of the geometry's development, produce contradictory consequences that would invalidate the geometry. Like Gauss and Bolyai, Lobachevsky abandoned the fruitless search for a proof to the fifth postulate. He came to see – this was the starting-point of his invention – that it was not contradictory to speak of a geometry in which all of Euclid's postulates *except* the fifth held true. His new geometry, by analogy with imaginary numbers, he called 'imaginary geometry'. By including imaginary numbers geometry became more general, and Euclid's geometry took on the appearance of a special case of a more general system.

Non-Euclidean geometry might find application in the intimate sphere of molecular attraction.

NICKOLAI LOBACHEVSKY COMPLETE GEOMETRICAL WORKS 1883–1886

The chief difference between the geometry of Euclid and that of Lobachevsky may be pointed up by the fact that, in Euclid's system, two parallel lines will (as a consequence of the fifth postulate) remain equidistant from each other, whereas in Lobachevskian geometry, the two lines will approach zero in one direction and infinity in the other. Another example of the difference is that in Euclidean geometry the sum of the angles of a triangle is always equal to the sum of two right angles; in Lobachevskian geometry, the sum of the angles is always less than the sum of two right angles. Lobachevskian space is such a different concept from that of Euclid's, that in the former triangles can be defined as functions of their angles, which determine the length of the sides. In Lobachevskian space, also, two geometric figures cannot have the same shape but different sizes.

The work of Lobachevsky, as of Gauss and Bolyai, demonstrated that it was useless to attempt to prove Euclid's fifth postulate by showing all other alternatives to be impossible. It demonstrated that different geometries, self-contained and self-consistent, were logically possible. The notion, prevalent since the time of Euclid, that geometry offered *a priori* knowledge of the physical world was destroyed (somewhat ironically it is the Lobachevskian model, not the Euclidean, which today seems closer to the actual world of space). Non-Euclidean geometry destroyed, once and for all, the notion of empirical mathematics. It represented, William ◊Clifford has said, a revolution in the history of human thought as radical as the revolution begun by ◊Copernicus. Largely unrecognized in his lifetime, Lobachevsky and his fellow revolutionaries are still, outside the highest mathematical circles, too little recognized today.

Locke, Joseph (1805–1860) English railway engineer, a contemporary and associate of Isambard Kingdom ◊Brunel and the Stephensons.

Locke was born on 9 August 1805, the youngest of four sons of a colliery manager at Attacliffe Common, Sheffield. Yorkshire. His father was a man of strong views and for various reasons changed employers several times while Joseph was still a child. He did, however, receive a 'sort of an education' at the grammar school in Barnsley and left at the age of 13 knowing a little but, as he said, 'knowing that little well'.

Locke found employment carrying letters at Pelaw, County Durham, under the watchful eye of William Stobart, colliery viewer for the Duke of Norfolk, but after two years he returned to Barnsley. He was then sent to Rochdale to work for a land surveyor named Hampson. The situation looked promising until he was asked to look after the Hampson baby. He gave up the job and once again returned home – this time after only a fortnight.

His family resigned themselves to the fact that he was rather idle and left him to find work for himself. He might well have remained unsettled had not luck interceded. His father's old friend from the Attacliffe colliery called to see them – George ◊Stephenson, the civil engineer. When he saw the plight of his friend's young son he suggested Joseph should be sent to work for him, and this began what was to prove a fortunate career as a railwayman.

From 1823 to 1826 Locke learnt much about surveying, railway engineering, and construction. He loved the life and learnt with enthusiasm, something which had been lacking in his earlier attempts at a career. After three years he was to emerge as one of the foremost engineers of the railway era.

Locke's first task undertaken alone was the construction of a railway line from the Black Fell colliery to the River Tyne. This he managed so successfully that Stephenson confessed to have 'complete confidence' in Locke's ability. He was immediately asked to begin surveys for lines running between Leeds and Hull, Manchester and Bolton, and Canterbury and Whitstable.

The hectic era of railway expansion was underway when George Stephenson (now joined by his son Robert ◊Stephenson), Brunel, and Locke were in great demand. By 1842 more than 2,900 km/1,800 mi of track had been laid and Locke had made a reputation for himself as a man who built as straight as possible, used the terrain, and avoided the expense of tunnels whenever he could. He was asked to tackle the London to Southampton line and although others favoured tunnelling through the chalk Downs, he chose to cut through them, leaving steep embankments on either side of the line. His method proved successful and gave few problems after the line was opened on 11 May 1840.

Locke took over part of the construction of the Grand Junction railway from Stephenson and the Sheffield-to-Manchester route from Vignoles. The latter was a complicated operation that cut a 4,850-m/15,900-ft bore through the millstone grit of the Pennines. In 1841 he began work as chief engineer on the Paris to Rouen line and completed it on schedule in May 1843. This was to be the first of several contracts in France and it added even more prestige to his name.

Turning once more to work in the UK, he carried out construction of lines on behalf of the Lancaster and Carlisle Railway and the Caledonian Railway, but during 1846 he made some important decisions regarding his own life. He bought the manor of Honiton in Devon and fulfilled a boyhood ambition to enter Parliament. Many accused him of buying his way in, although he did in fact stand for election in 1847 and remained Liberal member for Honiton until his death 13 years later.

All three of the railway 'giants' spent their remaining years in well-earned comfort while yet being fully employed. The construction of new railways continued relentlessly, and their skills were always in great demand. Contemporaries to the point of all being born within the same three-year period, strangely they all died within the same space of time: Brunel on 14 September 1859, Robert Stephenson, his friend of long-standing, on 12 October 1859, and Locke himself on 18 September 1860.

Lockyer, (Joseph) Norman (1836–1920) English scientist whose interests and studies were wide-ranging, but who is remembered mainly for his pioneering work in spectroscopy, through which he discovered the existence of helium, although it was not to be isolated in the laboratory until nearly 30 years later.

Lockyer was born in Rugby on 17 May 1836. After his schooling in the Midlands he worked briefly as a civil servant in the War Office. The high reputation he was meanwhile gaining as an amateur astronomer led to his becoming (temporarily) secretary to the Duke of Devonshire's commission on scientific instruction. He was then appointed to a permanent post in the Science and Art Department and in 1890 he became director of the Solar Physics Observatory in South Kensington. He remained in this post until 1911, when he resigned rather than move with the observatory to Cambridge.

Elected to the Royal Society in 1869 – the year in which he founded the scientific journal *Nature,* which he was to edit for 50 years – he was awarded its Rumford Medal in 1874. He was knighted in 1897, after the element he had named helium so many years before had finally been isolated in the laboratory by William ◊Ramsay. Lockyer died in Salcombe Regis, Devon, on 16 August 1920.

A primary influence on Lockyer's researches was the newly discovered science of spectroscopy initiated in 1859 when Gustav ◊Kirchhoff, together with his colleague Robert ◊Bunsen, showed how the lines in the spectrum of a substance could indicate the actual composition of that substance. Throughout his life Lockyer was especially interested in solar phenomena. In 1868 he attached a spectroscope to a 15-cm/6-in telescope and made a major breakthrough by observing solar prominences at times other than during a total solar eclipse. The success of Lockyer's experiment was ensured by his use of an instrument that could breach the spectrum of the diffused sunlight in the atmosphere, and thereby make visible the bright lines of the prominence spectrum. Although Lockyer had been the first to think of it, the same idea had occurred to Jules César ◊Janssen – then working in India – and both men, in mutual ignorance, decided to put their theory to the test during the same eclipse. Accordingly, the French Academy of Sciences experienced the surprising coincidence of receiving a message from each man confirming the success of their experiments within minutes of each other. This remarkable event was duly commemorated with the issuing of a medal by the French government that bore the likenesses of both astronomers.

Almost simultaneously with their recording of prominence spectra, Lockyer and Janssen (this time working together) announced a more momentous discovery. While studying the spectrum of the Sun during the eclipse, Janssen had noticed a line he had not seen before. He forwarded his observations to Lockyer, who,

after comparing the reported position of the line with that of the known elements, concluded that it originated in some previously unknown element that possibly did not exist on Earth. This idea did not receive widespread support among the chemists of the day. Spectroscopy was a new science, which in the opinion of many had still to prove the bold claims that were being made for it. Lockyer's claim, however, was to prove an exception to the general record of contemporary illusory 'discoveries'. He named the unknown element 'helium', after the Greek word for the Sun.

In 1881 Lockyer declared that certain lines produced in a laboratory became broader when an element was strongly heated. It was his belief that at very high temperatures atoms disintegrated into yet more elementary forms. The truth was not so simple, but in the next 20 years it was discovered that the atom has a complex internal structure and that it can acquire an electrical charge through the systematic removal of electrons. Lockyer was also the first astronomer to study the spectra of sunspots.

Further subjects of Lockyer's interest and investigation were the mysterious megalithic monuments that occur in Brittany and Britain, the most celebrated being those at Carnac and Stonehenge. It had long been believed that these erections were primarily of religious significance, but Lockyer noticed that the geometrical axis of Stonehenge is oriented towards the northeast, the direction in which the Sun rises at the time of the summer solstice. In the case of Stonehenge the central 'altar stone' seemed out of alignment by some 1° 12'. Lockyer believed, however, that the original builders had not been guilty of any inaccuracy but that the apparent error could be explained by a gradual change in position of the solstitial sunrise. And because the only possible source of change was the minute but regular variation in the progress of the Sun's ecliptic, it would be possible to calculate how many years were needed to have achieved a difference of 1° 12'. By this means Lockyer dated Stonehenge from the year 1840 BC (plus or minus 200 years) – a reckoning that was virtually confirmed in 1952 when, by radiocarbon dating of charred wood found in post-holes, a date of 1848 BC (plus or minus 275 years) was indicated.

Lodge, Oliver Joseph (1851–1940) English physicist who was among the pioneers of radio. He also proved that the ether does not exist, a discovery that proved fundamental to the development of relativity.

Lodge was born in Penkhull, Staffordshire, on 12 June 1851, where his father supplied clay and other materials for the pottery industry. As the eldest son, Lodge entered his father's firm at the age of 14 and worked there for six years. In 1871 he began to study science at London University, at first while still working part-time for his father. He obtained his BSc in 1873 followed by a DSc on electrical topics in 1877.

Lodge became the first professor of physics at the University of Liverpool on its founding in 1881, and there carried out his most important experimental work. In 1900 he moved to the University of Birmingham to become its first principal. Among many subsequent honours were a knighthood in 1902 and the presidency of the British Association for the Advancement of Science in 1913. Lodge retired in 1919. Following the death of his son in World War I, he became interested in psychic phenomena and devoted much of his later life to psychical research. Lodge died in Lake near Salisbury on 22 August 1940.

Lodge's first significant paper concerned the shape of lines of force and equipotential lines between two electrodes applied to conducting surfaces. He also proposed how a Daniell Cell could be modified in order that it might be used as a standard for measurements of electromotive force (emf). During the 1880s, Lodge devoted a great deal of time to experiments involving the discharge of electricity from Leyden jars. Two of his sons extended this work, which was then used as the basis of the high-tension electric ignition system used in early internal-combustion engines.

Lodge also began work on the production of electromagnetic waves, following the prediction by James Clerk ◊Maxwell that such waves must exist. He came close to achieving Maxwell's prediction, but was just anticipated by Heinrich ◊Hertz in 1888. Lodge then turned to methods of detecting the waves and invented a coherer, a device consisting of a container packed with metal granules whose electrical resistance varies with the passage of electromagnetic radiation. This was developed into a detector of radio waves in the early investigations of radio communication, with which Lodge was closely involved.

Lodge's other major contribution to science was made in 1893 following the classic Michelson–Morley experiments of 1881 and 1887. These had failed to detect the ether that was postulated as a medium for the propagation of light waves. This result could be explained by the ether moving with the Earth, but Lodge disproved this unlikely cause in a clever experiment in which light rays were passed between two rotating discs. The resulting interference effects showed the ether does not exist, providing one of postulates – that all motion is relative – on which Albert ◊Einstein built the special theory of relativity.

Further Reading

Hunt, Bruce, 'Experimenting on the ether: Oliver J Lodge and the great whirling machine', *Hist Stud Phys Biol Sci,* 1986, v 16, pp 111–134.

Rowlands, Peter, *Oliver Lodge and the Liverpool Physical Society,* Liverpool Historical Studies series, Liverpool University Press, 1990, v 4.

Rowlands, Peter and Wilson, J Patrick (eds), *Oliver Lodge and the Invention of Radio,* PD Publications, 1994.

Longuet-Higgins, Hugh Christopher (1923–)

English theoretical chemist whose main contributions have involved the application of precise mathematical analyses, particularly statistical mechanics, to chemical problems. He has also researched extensively into perception and cognition.

Longuet-Higgins was born in Lenham, Kent, on 11 April 1923. He was educated at Winchester College and won a scholarship to Balliol College, Oxford, where he worked under Charles ◊Coulson and obtained his doctorate in 1947. He continued at Oxford as a research fellow, before spending a year studying molecular spectroscopy with Robert Mulliken (1896–1986) in Chicago. On his return to the UK in 1949 Longuet-Higgins was appointed a lecturer and reader in theoretical chemistry at the University of Manchester, and it was there that he turned his attention to statistical mechanics, work that he pursued further while he was professor of theoretical physics at King's College, London, 1952–54. In that year he became professor of theoretical chemistry at Cambridge, where he stayed for 13 years. In 1967 he took a Royal Society Research Fellowship at Edinburgh University to study artificial intelligence and information-processing systems, which he thought had a closer bearing on true biology than purely physio-chemical studies. Then in 1974 he moved to Sussex University as Royal Society Research Professor, where he expanded this field into studies of the mechanisms of language and the perception of music. In 1989 he became professor emeritus at Sussex.

Longuet-Higgins made his first contribution to theoretical chemistry when he was only 20 years old and still an undergraduate. He overthrew the previously held views about the structures of the boron hydrides, the simplest of which, diborane (B_2H_6), was thought structurally to resemble ethane. Longuet-Higgins pointed out that spectroscopic evidence suggested a bridged structure:

ethane   diborane

This hypothesis later proved to be correct, but not before he had also predicted the structures of other boranes and the then-unknown beryllium hydride. He returned to this work after 23 years and predicted the existence of the ion $(B_{12}H_{12})^{2-}$, whose stability was strikingly verified several years later.

For his doctorate in 1947 Longuet-Higgins developed, with Coulson, the orbital theory of conjugated organic molecules, deriving theoretically results that had been known experimentally for decades. He continued this work in Chicago, showing how the properties of conjugated systems can be derived by combining into molecular orbital theory a study of 'non-bonding' orbitals. This work led directly to Michael Dewar's linear combination of molecular orbital theory. A later collaboration between Dewar and Longuet-Higgins resulted in the discovery of a system (biphenylene) in which the molecular orbital theory and the then more fashionable resonance theory gave contrary predictions. They published their findings in 1957 and several years later experimental results confirmed the molecular orbital predictions.

The work in statistical mechanics which Longuet-Higgins began at Manchester in 1949 made important contributions to many fields. He formulated a theory to describe the thermodynamic properties of mixtures, which he later extended to polymer solutions. He also investigated the optical properties of helical molecules and continued his work on electronic spectra.

At Cambridge, from 1954, he used mathematical techniques to make theoretical chemical predictions. He predicted, for example, that cyclobutadiene (which had defeated all attempts to prepare it) should exist as a ligand attached to an atom of a transition metal; such a compound was successfully prepared three years later.

In a larger piece of work, he applied group theory to define the elements of symmetry of non-rigid molecules, such as hydrazine (N_2H_4), and thus was able to classify the individual quantum levels of the molecule. This, in turn, allowed analysis of the spectra of such molecules and the evaluation of their molecular characteristics.

Other work of this nature involved the study of a group of important organic reactions known as electrocyclic rearrangements, of which the best known is the Diels–Alder reaction. With W Abrahamson, Longuet-Higgins discovered symmetry principles in combination with molecular orbital theory that permit clear predictions to be made about the outcomes of such reactions, some of which seem to be quite contrary to others. In this and his other contributions Longuet-Higgins demonstrated the large part he has played in advancing chemistry from a science of largely practical experiment to one of predictive theory.

Lonsdale, Kathleen, born Kathleen Yardley (1903–1971) Irish-born British X-ray crystallographer who rose from the most humble background to become one of the best-known workers in her field, being among the first to determine the structures of organic molecules. She also paved the way in a male-dominated world for the many women who followed in her footsteps.

Lonsdale was born in Newbridge, Ireland, on 28 January 1903, the youngest of the ten children of the local postmaster. The family was desperately poor – her father drank heavily – and four of her brothers died in infancy. An elder brother, unable to take up a scholarship to secondary school because he had to work to help to support the family, later became one of the first wireless operators and founded a school of wireless telegraphy in the north of England.

The family moved to England in 1908 and settled in Seven Kings, Essex. Kathleen went to the local elementary school until 1914, when she won a scholarship to the county high school for girls in nearby Ilford. For her last two years there she had to attend classes at the boys' school as the only girl to study chemistry, physics, and higher mathematics. At the age of 16 she went to Bedford College for Women in London, switching from mathematics to physics after one year. She graduated as top student in the University in 1922 and William ◊Bragg immediately offered her a place in his research team at University College, London, and then later at the Royal Institution.

In 1927 she married Thomas Lonsdale and moved to Leeds. There she had three children and worked in the physics department of Leeds University. She moved back to London in 1931 and carried out research for 15 years at the Royal Institution, first under Bragg and then with Henry ◊Dale. In May 1945 she and Marjory Stephenson became the first women to be elected to the Royal Society. In 1946, after World War II, Lonsdale became professor of chemistry and head of the department of crystallography at University College, London, and only then (at the age of 43) did she start university teaching and developing her own research school. She was made a dame in 1956 and in 1968 became the first woman president of the British Association for the Advancement of Science. She died in Bexhill-on-Sea, Sussex, on 1 April 1971.

In her first post under Bragg she worked with W T Astbury, trying to relate space group theory to the phenomenon of X-ray diffraction by crystals. She assembled her own apparatus and the first organic crystal she measured was succinic acid (butanedioic acid). At Leeds she used a grant from the Royal Society to buy an ionization spectrometer and electroscope and correctly solved the structure of crystals of hexamethylbenzene provided by Christopher ◊Ingold, who was then professor of chemistry at Leeds. Her solution for hexachlorobenzene was less complete, but was important as the first investigation using Fourier analysis. Lonsdale was a competent mathematician and did all her own calculations, aided only by logarithm tables. When she returned to work with Bragg in London she derived the structure factor formulae for all space groups.

At the Royal Institution she researched many subjects. She was interested in X-ray work at various temperatures and thermal motion in crystals. She also used divergent beam X-ray photography to investigate the textures of crystals. Lonsdale continued this work at University College, while also studying solid-state reactions, the pharmacological properties and crystal structures of methonium compounds, and the composition of bladder and kidney stones.

Lonsdale's attitudes were influenced by the Society of Friends (Quakers) and at the outbreak of World War II in 1939 she did not register for employment, regarding all war as evil. On being fined £2 she refused to pay and was sent to prison at Holloway for one month. One result of this experience was an even stronger commitment to pacifism and a lifelong interest in prison visiting.

Further Reading

Hodgkin, Dorothy, *Kathleen Londsdale: A Biographical Memoir,* Royal Society, 1976.

Lonsdale, Kathleen, *The Christian Life Lived Experimentally: An Anthology of the Writing of Kathleen Lonsdale,* Friends Home Service Committee, 1976.

Mason, Joan, The admission of the first woman to the Royal Society of London, *Notes Rec Roy Soc Lond,* 1992, v 46, pp 279–300.

Lorentz, Hendrik Antoon (1853–1928) Dutch physicist who helped to develop the theory of electromagnetism, which was recognized by the award (jointly with his pupil Pieter ◊Zeeman) of the 1902 Nobel Prize for Physics.

Lorentz was born in Arnhem, the Netherlands, on 18 July 1853. He was educated at local schools and at the University of Leyden, which he left at the age of 19 to return to Arnhem as a teacher while writing his PhD thesis on the theory of light reflection and refraction. By the time he was 24 he was professor of theoretical physics at Leyden. He remained there for 39 years, before taking up the directorship of the Teyler Institute in Haarlem, where he was able to use the museum's laboratory facilities. He died in Haarlem on 4 February 1928.

Much of Lorentz's work was concerned with James Clerk ◊Maxwell's theory of electromagnetism, and his development of it became fundamental to Albert ◊Einstein's special theory of relativity. Lorentz attributed the generation of light by atoms to oscillations of charged particles (electrons) within them. This theory was confirmed in 1896 by the discovery of the Zeeman effect, in which a magnetic field splits spectral lines.

In 1904 Lorentz extended the work of George ◊FitzGerald to account for the negative result of the Michelson–Morley experiment and produced the so-called Lorentz transformations, which mathematically predict the changes to mass, length, and time for an object travelling at near the speed of light.

Lorenz, Konrad Zacharias (1903–1989) Austrian zoologist who is generally considered to be the founder of modern ethology. He is best known for his studies of the relationships between instinct and behaviour, particularly in birds, although he also applied his ideas to aspects of human behaviour, notably aggression. He received many honours for his work, including the 1973 Nobel Prize for Physiology or Medicine, which he was awarded jointly with Karl von ◊Frisch and Niko ◊Tinbergen.

Lorenz was born in Vienna on 7 November 1903, the son of an orthopaedic surgeon. From an early age he collected and cared for various animals, and kept a detailed record of his bird observations. He was educated at the high school in Vienna, then in 1922, following his father's wishes, went to the USA to Columbia University and studied medicine. After two years he returned to Austria and continued his medical studies at the University of Vienna, from which he graduated in 1928. In the previous year he had married Margarethe Gebhardt, and they later had a son and two daughters. After graduation he studied comparative anatomy as an assistant in the anatomy department of Vienna University, where he remained until 1935 – having gained his doctorate in 1933. In 1936 the German Society for Animal Psychology was founded and in the following year Lorenz was appointed co-editor in chief of the society's new journal *Zeitschrift für Tierpsychologie,* which became one of the world's leading ethology journals; he held the post for many years. Also in 1937 he became lecturer in comparative anatomy and animal psychology at Vienna University, remaining there until 1940, when he was appointed professor and head of the department of general psychology at the Albertus University in Königsberg. From 1942–44 he was a physician in the German army, but was captured in the Soviet Union and spent four years as a prisoner of war there. He returned to Austria in 1948 and in the following year was appointed head of the Institute of Comparative Ethology at Altenberg. In 1951 he established the comparative ethology department in the Max Planck Institute at Buldern, becoming its co-director in 1954. He then worked at the Max Planck Institute of Behavioural Physiology in Seewiesen 1958–73 (as its director after 1961), when he was appointed director of the department for animal sociology at the Austrian Academy of Sciences' Institute for Comparative Ethology.

Lorenz made most of his observations and basic discoveries during the late 1930s and early 1940s. From 1935 to 1938 he carried out intensive studies on bird colonies he had established, including those of jackdaws and greylag geese, and published a series of papers on his observations, which gained him worldwide recognition. In 1935 he described the phenomenon for which he is perhaps best known: imprinting. He discovered that many birds do not instinctively recognize members of their own species but that they do possess an innate ability to acquire this capacity. He observed that during a brief period after hatching a young bird treats the first reasonably large object it sees as representative of its species – the object becomes imprinted. Normally this object is the bird's parent but Lorenz found that it is possible to substitute almost any other reasonably sized object, such as a balloon or a human being, in which case the bird does not respond in the usual manner to other members of its species. There has since been evidence that imprinting may also occur in human children, although this is still a matter of controversy because it is extremely difficult to differentiate between innate and learned responses, especially in humans and other higher animals.

After this research, Lorenz collaborated with Niko Tinbergen on further studies of bird behaviour. They showed that the reactions of many birds to birds of prey depend on attitudes or gestures made by the predators and on a particular feature of their shapes – the shortness of their necks, which is common to all birds of prey. Lorenz and Tinbergen found that the sight of any bird with a short neck – or even a dummy bird with this feature – causes other birds to fly away.

On the subject of instinct and behaviour, Lorenz hypothesized that every instinct builds up a specific type of 'desire' in the central nervous system. If there is no appropriate environment that helps to release the behaviour pattern corresponding to the desire, then tension gradually increases, eventually reaching such a level that instincts take control, even when the correct stimulus is lacking. For example, a pregnant ewe acts in a maternal manner towards a new-born lamb, although the ewe herself has not yet given birth.

In his later work Lorenz supplied his ideas to human behaviour, most notably in his book *On Aggression* (1966), in which he argued that aggressive behaviour in human beings has an innate basis but, with a proper understanding of instinctual human needs, society can be changed to accommodate these needs and so aggression may be diverted into socially useful behaviour.

Lorenz, Ludwig Valentin (1829–1891) Danish mathematician and physicist who made important contributions to our knowledge of heat, electricity, and optics. He is, however, relatively little known, partly because he published most of his work in Danish and partly because of his idiosyncratic mathematical style.

Lorenz was born in Elsinore on 18 January 1829. He graduated in civil engineering from the Technical University in Copenhagen. He then taught at a teacher-training college and at the Military Academy in Copenhagen, becoming professor of physics at the latter in 1876. After 1887, however, he received sufficient financial support from the Carlsberg Foundation to be able to devote himself entirely to research. He died in Copenhagen on 9 June 1891.

Lorenz is perhaps best known for his work on optics and electromagnetic theory. Early in his investigations he found that the theoretical models describing the nature of light were contradictory and incompatible, and he therefore concentrated his efforts on studying the transmission of light rather than its nature. He investigated the mathematical description for light propagation through a single homogeneous medium and also described the passage of light between different mediums. His most famous discovery was the mathematical relationship between the refractive index and the density of a medium. This formula was published by Lorenz in 1869 and by Hendrick ◊Lorentz (who discovered it independently) in 1870 and is therefore called the Lorentz–Lorenz formula. Today it is usually given as

$$R = \frac{(n^2 - 1)}{(n^2 + 2)} \times \frac{M}{\rho}$$

Where R is the molecular refractivity, n is the refractive index, M is the molecular mass, and ρ is the density. Also in 1869 Lorenz published an experimental verification (for water) of the formula. In addition, he studied birefringence (double refraction) and wrote a paper on the electromagnetic theory of light in 1867 – after James Clerk ◊Maxwell's theory had been published in the UK but at a time when it was almost unknown elsewhere in Europe. Lorenz's approach was different from that of Maxwell and he was able to derive a correct value for the velocity of light using his theories.

Lorenz's other main major contribution to science was his discovery of what is now called Lorenz's law. Relating a metal's thermal conductivity (λ) and its electrical conductivity (σ) to its absolute temperature (T), the law is usually stated mathematically as:

$$(\lambda/\sigma)\propto$$

A believer in combining theory and experiment, he performed a series of experiments to test his law and thereby confirmed its validity.

Lorenz also did basic work on the development of the continuous loading method for reducing current losses along cables, and helped to establish the ohm as the internationally accepted unit of electrical resistance. His work in pure mathematics included studies of prime numbers and Bessel functions, which are widely used in mathematical physics.

Lovelace, (Augusta) Ada Byron, Countess of Lovelace (1815–1852)

English mathematician and writer who created the first program for Charles ◊Babbage's analytical engine – she is known as the first computer programmer.

Ada, Lady Byron, was born on 10 December 1815 in Piccadilly Terrace, Middlesex (now in London), the daughter of a brief marriage between the Romantic poet Lord Byron and Anne Isabel Millbanke. She never met her father because her parents separated when she was a month old and he left England shortly afterwards. Her mother was determined that Ada should not grow up a poet and encouraged her by engaging tutors in mathematics and music to counteract any poetic tendencies. Ada taught herself geometry and was educated by private tutors including Augustus ◊De Morgan, London University's first professor of mathematics, who taught her advanced mathematics. She was also instructed in astronomy and mathematics by William Frend. At the age of 13 she produced a design for a flying machine.

Ada and her mother moved in elite circles, in which they were likely to meet the 'gentlemen scientists' of the day. In 1833, at the age of 17, Ada met and became a lifelong friend of Charles Babbage, Lucasian Professor of Mathematics at Cambridge and inventor of the difference engine. They corresponded on mathematics, logic, and life. In 1934 Babbage planned a new kind of calculating machine, the analytical engine, and in 1842 Ada produced an annotated translation of the Italian mathematician Menabrae's *Notions sur la machine analytique de Charles Babbage.* In her annotations she described how the analytical engine could be programmed to compute Bernoulli numbers, showing her understanding of the programmed computer. Her notes also anticipated further developments, including the possibility of computer-generated music. This article was the source of her relatively recent reputation as the first computer programmer. She also had a good grasp of symbolic logic, which was thought to produce dangerous tensions in the mind of a woman. She later used her mathematical skills to devise a secret gambling system.

In 1835 she had married William King, eighth Baron King and ten years her senior, becoming Countess of Lovelace in 1838 when he became earl. They had three children – their daughter, Anne Blunt, becoming a famous traveller. Dogged by ill-health throughout her life, the countess died of cancer on 27 November 1852 at the age of 36, and was buried beside her father. The high-level computer-programming language Ada was named in her honour in 1977 by the US Department of Defense.

Lovell, (Alfred Charles) Bernard (1913–)

English radio astronomer and author. His experience with radar during World War II led to his applying radar to the detection of meteors and to his energetic instigation of the construction of the radio telescope at Jodrell Bank Experimental Station (now the Nuffield Radio Astronomy Laboratories) in Cheshire, where he was director 1951–81.

Lovell was born in Oldland Common, Gloucestershire, on 31 August 1913, the son of a lay preacher. Educated at the Kingswood Grammar School, Bristol, he then attended Bristol University, where he read physics, graduating in 1933. Three years later he became assistant lecturer in physics at Manchester University. During World War II he was in the Air Ministry Research Establishment in Malvern where, under his guidance, centimetric airborne radar was developed for use on 'blind bombing' air raids and submarine defence. At the end of the war, Lovell returned to Manchester as lecturer in physics and immediately began pressing the authorities to set up a radio astronomy station at Jodrell Bank (about 32 km/ 20 mi south of Manchester). He was appointed senior lecturer in 1947 and reader in 1949, all the while agitating for his dream of a radio telescope at Jodrell Bank to be made a reality. Finally, in 1951, Manchester University created a special chair of radio astronomy for him and, with the government guaranteeing part of the financing of his radio telescope, made the directorship of Jodrell Bank an official post. In 1980 he became professor emeritus at Manchester. He was elected a fellow of the Royal Society in 1955 and received the Royal Medal of the Society in 1960. He was knighted in 1961.

His books include *Radio Astronomy* (1951), *The Individual and the Universe* (1958), *The Exploration of Space by Radio* (1957; with Robert Hanbury ◊Brown), *The Exploration of Outer Space* (1961), *Discovering the Universe* (1963), *The Story of Jodrell Bank* (1968), and *Out of the Zenith* (1973).

Lovell's first postwar research used radar to show that echoes could be obtained from daylight meteor showers invisible to the naked eye. Significantly, he proved the worth of such radio techniques by observing the meteor shower as the Earth passed through the tail of a comet in 1946 – a meteor shower that was visible to the naked eye. Having established the value of radio in this way, he showed by further studies that it was possible to make determinations of the orbits and radiants of meteors and thus prove that all meteors originate within the Solar System. With the same equipment, Lovell investigated the loud solar radio outburst in 1946, and in 1947 began to examine the aurora borealis.

In 1950, Lovell discovered that galactic radio sources emitted at a constant wavelength (frequency) and that the fluctuations ('scintillation') recorded on the Earth's surface (the subject of considerable scientific speculation) were introduced only as the radio waves met and crossed the ionosphere.

The year 1951 saw the beginning of the construction of the Jodrell Bank radio telescope. Taking six years to build, under Lovell's close personal supervision, the gigantic dish has an alt-azimuth mounting with a parabolic surface of sheet steel; it remains the largest completely steerable radio telescope in existence. It was completed just in time to track the Soviet *Sputnik 1* (the first artificial satellite), thus confounding the criticism that too much money had been spent on the project. The Jodrell Bank radio telescope (now part of the Nuffield Radio Astronomy Laboratories) is still probably the most useful instrument in the world for tracking satellites.

From 1958 Lovell became interested in radio emission from flare stars. After two years at work, when his results were still inconclusive, he began a collaboration with Fred ◊Whipple of the Smithsonian Astrophysical Observatory in the USA. A joint programme was arranged for simultaneous radio and optical observations of flare stars using Baker Nunn cameras from the Smithsonian satellite tracking network. The first results were published in *Nature* in 1963; they opened up new avenues for the study of large-scale processes occurring in a stellar atmosphere. It was also shown at that time that the integrated radio emission from the flare stars may account for a fraction of the overall emission from our Galaxy. These combined optical and radio observations have also led to the establishing of a new value for the constancy of the relative velocity of light and radio waves in space.

Lovelock, James Ephraim (1919–   ) English scientist, specializing in the atmospheric sciences, who began the study of chlorofluorocarbons (CFCs) in the 1960s and who invented the concept of the Earth as a single organism – the Gaia hypothesis.

Born in London on 26 July 1919, Lovelock was educated at London and Manchester Universities in the early years of the World War II. Graduating in 1941 he worked at the National Institute for Medical Research (NIMR) in London on wartime problems such as the measurement of blood pressure under water, the freezing of viable cells and the design of an acoustic anemometer. Twenty years later, feeling stifled by the security of his position at the National Institute, Lovelock gave up his job and worked briefly for NASA on the first lunar *Surveyor* mission in California.

Determined not to become part of an institution – a government department, university, or multinational company – which, he believes compromises the freedom of scientists to express themselves, he left NASA in 1964. Income from his inventions especially from Hewlett Packard helped him to support himself and his family while he developed his Gaia hypothesis. In 1966 he discovered chlorofluorocarbons (CFCs) by monitoring what had been thought to be clean Atlantic air on the west coast of Ireland, using the electron capture detector he had invented at NIMR (which measures minute traces of atmospheric gases). However, it was not until he accumulated the money to travel to the Antarctic in 1971 that he was able to corroborate this finding by detecting more CFCs. His discovery sparked off research by US chemist F Sherwood Rowland (1927–   ) and Mexican chemist Mario Molina (1943–   ) who predicted the destruction of the ozone layer by human use of CFCs in 1974.

As an independent scientist working from home, Lovelock found himself free from what he calls the 'tribal rules' of each discipline that inhibit the passage of ideas from one branch of science to the other. His first thoughts on what was to become known as Gaia came when he was invited by NASA in the early 1960s to work in the biosciences department of a jet propulsion laboratory, sending out probes to detect signs of life on other planets, especially Mars. He predicted the absence of life on Mars based on the consideration that the Martian atmosphere is in a state of 'dead equilibrium' in contrast to the Earth's atmosphere which is in a state that is 'far from equilibrium' with an unlikely balance of atmospheric gases unique in the Solar System. This led him to question the processes at work on Earth allowing an 'equilibrium which was far from equilibrium', especially in terms of the percentage ratio of nitrogen to oxygen (77:21). The Earth seemed to him to be a uniquely self-evolving and self-regulating living system. He put forward his first ideas on this phenomenon at a meeting of the American Astronautical Society in 1968 and in a letter to *Atmospheric Environment* in 1971. Shortly after this he began a collaboration with US microbiologist, Lynn ◊Margulis that put flesh on the bones of the Gaia hypothesis. Margulis, according to Lovelock, is unique in the breadth of her vision at a time when biology is fragmenting into smaller and smaller more specialized areas.

Lovelock presented his Gaia hypothesis in print first in *Gaia: A New Look at Life on Earth* (1979). Dismissed by some scientists as pseudoscientific but seen as a workable hypothesis by others, it has been widely accepted by conservationists, ecologists, greens and 'New Age' thinkers. (The name Gaia was suggested by English novelist William Golding, Lovelock's neighbour in Wiltshire, after the Greek Earth goddess who drew the living world forth from Chaos.) Existing theories held that the evolution of plants and animals is distinct from the evolution of the inanimate planet.

According to Lovelock's theory, life and the environment are inextricably linked and mutually dependent. The rocks, oceans and atmosphere, and all living things are part of one great organism that has evolved through the aeons. Life regulates the atmosphere and the atmosphere provides the conditions necessary for life. Thus the Earth has maintained a more or less constant temperature (unlike stars which get hotter as they age). The theory has not been properly accepted in the formal traditional sciences but has provoked debate and also speculation on the planet's reaction to the greenhouse effect – will it be able to look after itself and adapt to these new conditions? In *The Ages of Gaia: A Biography of Our Living Earth* (1988) Lovelock evolves and refines the nature of Gaia and discusses the greenhouse effect, acid rain, the depletion of the ozone layer, and other topics in detail, demonstrating the geophysical interaction of atmosphere, oceans, climate, and the Earth's crust that are comfortably regulated by the use of the Sun's energy by living organisms.

Lovelock is president of the British Marine Biology Association, a fellow of the Royal Society and visiting professor of cybernetics at Reading University, England.

Lowell, Percival (1855–1916) US astronomer and mathematician, the founder of an important observatory in the USA, whose main field of research was the planets of the Solar System. Responsible for the popularization in his time of the theory of intelligent life on Mars, he also predicted the existence of a planet beyond Neptune, which was later discovered and named Pluto.

Lowell was born in Boston, Massachusetts, on 13 March 1855. His interest in astronomy began to develop during his early school years. In 1876 he graduated from Harvard University, where he had concentrated on mathematics, and then travelled for a year before entering his father's cotton business. Six years later, Lowell left the business and went to Japan. He spent most of the next ten years travelling around the Far East, partly for pleasure, partly to serve business interests, but also holding a number of minor diplomatic posts.

Lowell returned to the USA in 1893 and soon afterwards decided to concentrate on astronomy. He set up an observatory at Flagstaff, Arizona, at an altitude more than 2,000 m/6,600 ft above sea level, on a site chosen for the clarity of its air and its favourable atmospheric conditions. He first used borrowed telescopes with diameters of 30 cm/12 in and 45 cm/18 in to study Mars, which at that time was in a particularly suitable position. In 1896 he acquired a larger telescope and studied Mars by night and Mercury and Venus during the day. Overwork led to a deterioration in Lowell's health, and he could do little research 1897–1901, although he was able to participate in an expedition to Tripoli in 1900 to study a solar eclipse.

He was made non-resident professor of astronomy at the Massachusetts Institute of Technology in 1902, and gave several lecture series in that capacity. He led an expedition to the Chilean Andes in 1907, which produced the first high-quality photographs of Mars. The author of many books and the holder of several honorary degrees, Lowell died in Flagstaff on 12 November 1916.

The planet Mars was a source of fascination for Lowell. Influenced strongly by the work of Giovanni ◊Schiaparelli – and possibly misled by the English translation of 'canals' for the Italian *canali* ('channels') – Lowell set up his observatory at Flagstaff originally with the sole intention of confirming the presence of advanced life forms on the planet. Thirteen years later the expedition to South America was devoted to the study and photography of Mars. Lowell 'observed' a complex and regular network of canals and believed that he detected regular seasonal variations that strongly indicated agricultural activity. He found darker waves that seemed to flow from the poles to the equator and suggested that the polar caps were made of frozen water. (The waves were later attributed to dust storms and the polar caps are now known to consist not of ice but mainly of frozen carbon dioxide. Lowell's canal system also seems to have arisen mostly out of wishful thinking; part of the system does indeed exist, but it is not artificial and is apparent only because of the chance apposition of dark patches on the Martian surface.)

Lowell also made observations at Flagstaff of all the other planets of the Solar System. He studied Saturn's rings, Jupiter's atmosphere, and Uranus's rotation period. Finding that the perturbations in the orbit of Uranus were not fully accounted for by the presence of Neptune, Lowell predicted the position and brightness of a planet that he called Planet X, but was unable to discover. (Nearly 14 years after Lowell's death Clyde ◊Tombaugh found the planet – Pluto – on 12 March 1930; the discovery was made at Lowell's observatory and announced on the 75th anniversary of Lowell's birth.)

Lowell is remembered as a scientist of great patience and originality. He contributed to the advancement of astronomy through his observations and his establishment of a fine research centre and he did much to bring the excitement of the subject to the general public.

Ludwig, Karl Friedrich Wilhelm (1816–1895)

German physiologist – one of the great teachers and experimenters in the history of physiology.

Ludwig was born in Witzenhausen, Hesse, on 29 December 1816. He completed his schooling at Hanau Gymnasium and then went to Marburg University in 1834. He was compelled to leave the university as a result of his political activities, but after studying at Erlangen and at the surgical school in Bamberg, was allowed to return to Marburg to complete his studies. After graduating with a medical degree in 1840, he became professor of anatomy there. As extraordinary associate professor at Marburg from 1846, he continued teaching and carrying out research here until 1849, when he moved to Zürich to became professor of physiology and anatomy. Six years later he took up the professorship of anatomy and physiology at the Viennese military medical academy, the Josephinum, which had been founded in 1854. In 1865 he accepted the newly created chair of physiology at Leipzig and set out to develop it into an important teaching centre for physiology. He held this post until his death in Leipzig on 23 April 1895.

While studying at Marburg, Ludwig investigated the mechanism of secretion. In 1844 he was studying renal secretion and, on examining the structure of the kidney tubules (glomeruli), he recognized that during the first stage of secretion the surface membrane of the glomeruli acts as a filter. Liquid diffuses through it as a result of the pressure difference on either side of the membrane. Ludwig also devised a system of measuring the level of nitrogen in urine to quantify the rate of protein metabolism in the human body. Continuing his research on secretion, he showed that it is not the blood supply that enables secretion from the salivary glands but stimulation by the secretory nerve.

Following William ◊Harvey's findings on the circulation of blood it was believed that blood was moved by an unseen vital force. Ludwig was against this idea and in 1847 developed the kymograph (an instrument that continuously records changes in blood pressure and respiration). Ludwig could thus prove that blood is moved by a mechanical force.

In 1856, when studying the effects of certain drugs on the heart, Ludwig discovered that a frog's heart, removed after the death of the animal, could be revived and that organs could be kept alive in vitro. This was the first time this operation had been performed successfully and was done by perfusing the coronary arteries under pressure with blood or a salt solution that resembles the salinity of the blood plasma.

Ludwig was also the first to discover the depressor and accelerator nerves of the heart, and in 1871, working with Henry Bowditch, a US physiologist, he formulated the 'all-or-none' law of cardiac muscle action. This law postulates that when a stimulus is applied to a few fibres of heart muscle, the whole heart muscle contracts to the extent that with increased stimulation there is no further increase in the contraction. The 'all-or-none' law is most evident in cardiac muscle although it can occur elsewhere.

In 1859, in a paper published by his student Sechenov, Ludwig described his invention of the mercurial blood-gas pump, which enabled him to separate gases from a given quantity of blood taken directly in vivo. This invention led to later understanding of the part played by oxygen in the purification of the blood. Ludwig also invented the *stromuhr*, a flowmeter that measures the rate of the flow of blood in the veins.

Ludwig's ingenuity and inventiveness, combined with a good knowledge of physics and chemistry, made him important in the development of modern physiology. The kymograph with its subsequent modifications has become the standard tool for the recording of experimental results, and much of what is now known about the mechanism of cardiac activity is based on his work. Ludwig published a textbook for his students, *Das Lehrbuch der Physiologie* (A Physiology Textbook), the first volume in 1852 and the second in 1856, which was the first modern text on physiology.

Lumière, Auguste Marie Louis Nicolas (1862–1954) and Louis Jean (1864–1948)

French brothers who pioneered cinematography.

Louis Lumière, the younger of the two and ultimately the one who spent his whole career in photography, was born on 5 October 1864; Auguste was born on 19 October 1862. Both brothers were born at Besançon in eastern France. The family owned and operated a photographic firm in Lyon. When the brothers were old enough to join the business they did so with enthusiasm and contributed several minor improvements to the developing process, including in 1880 the invention of a better type of dry plate.

In 1894 their father purchased an Edison kinetoscope (a cine viewer), which impressed them greatly, although more for the potential it represented than for itself. They borrowed some of the ideas and developed a new all-in-one machine – camera and projector – which they patented in 1895, calling it a cinematograph. To advertise their success they filmed delegates arriving at a French photographic congress and 48 hours later projected the developed film to a large audience.

When the brothers ultimately separated, Auguste went on to do medical research, leaving Louis to

Lumière French pioneer of cinematography Louis Jean Lumière. Together with his elder brother Auguste, Louis constructed the first cine camera. They also presented a photorama, a 360-degree panoramic projector at the International Exhibition in Paris in 1900. *Mary Evans Picture Library*

continue in the photographic industry. Louis was associated with several other improvements, among them a photorama for panoramic shots and in 1907 a colour-printing process using dyed starch grains. During World War I he worked on aircraft equipment and afterwards carried on with photography, branching out into stereoscopy and three-dimensional films. He died in Bandol, France, on 6 June 1948. Auguste died in Lyons on 10 April 1954.

Thomas ◊Edison had patented his design for the kinetograph in 1888, after persuading George ◊Eastman to make suitable celluloid film. Unfortunately the pictures could be viewed only through a peep-hole and, although Edison had seen the possibility of projecting them so they could be viewed by a large audience, he had omitted this from his patent, which was for him a rare error.

The Lumière brothers took the best of Edison's ideas and developed them further, inventing a combined camera and projector that weighed much less than the Edison model. The film passed through the camera at a rate of 16 frames per second, slower than the modern equivalent, while a semicircular shutter cut off the light

between the lens and the film. By the end of 1895 the brothers had opened their first cinema in Paris, attracting large crowds to see the real-life films. Other establishments soon followed and a whole new industry was founded, bringing cinema entertainment within the reach of the average person.

In the USA, Edison had seen how the error in his patent had been exploited and had resumed his interest in the moving-picture phenomenon, joining forces with Thomas Armat who had devised a projector. To the Lumières in France and Edison in the USA can be attributed the honours for the origin of the motion-picture industry.

Lummer, Otto Richard (1860–1925) German physicist who specialized in optics and is particularly remembered for his work on thermal radiation. His investigations led directly to the radiation formula of Max ◊Planck, which marked the beginning of quantum theory.

Lummer was born in Jena, Saxony, on 17 July 1860. He attended a number of different German universities, which was a common practice at the time, and in 1884 wrote his doctoral dissertation at Berlin on work conducted in the department of Hermann von ◊Helmholtz. Lummer then became an assistant to Helmholtz and moved with him to the newly established Physikalische Technische Reichsanstalt in Berlin in 1887. Lummer became a member of this research institute in his own right in 1889, and in 1894 was made professor there. In 1904, he was appointed professor of physics at Breslau (now Wrocław, Poland), and he died there on 5 July 1925.

Lummer's early research was on interference fringes produced by internal reflection in mica plates. These fringes had in fact been noted before, but were nevertheless named Lummer fringes. His next area of study concerned the establishment of an international standard of luminosity. This work was done in collaboration with Eugen Brodhun, and they designed a photometer named the Lummer–Brodhun cube. This represented a considerable improvement on the grease-spot photometer, which Robert ◊Bunsen had originated.

The study of radiant heat then attracted Lummer's attention. As a black body is a perfect heat absorber, a black-body radiator was believed to be the most efficient transmitter of thermal radiation. However, until that time, it was considered to be merely a theoretical object. Lummer and Wilhelm Wien (1864–1928) made a practical black-body radiator by making a small aperture in a hollow sphere. When heated to a particular temperature, it behaved like an ideal black body.

In 1898 Lummer and Ernst ◊Pringsheim began a quantitative study on emission from black bodies. They were able to confirm Wien's displacement law, which is used to determine the temperature of a black body spectroscopically and has been applied to stellar temperature determinations, but found an anomaly in Wien's radiation law. Their result was confirmed by another research group headed by Heinrich Rubens (1865–1922) and Ferdinand Kurlbaum (1857–1927), who extended the work. These studies were of critical significance in the development of Planck's radiation formula, which was presented to the Berlin Physical Society on 19 October 1900 and marks the beginning of quantum theory.

Lummer's early work on interference fringes led him in 1902 to the design of a high-resolution spectroscope. Ernst Gehrcke improved it by adding a prism, and the Lummer–Gehrcke interference spectroscope was a great advance on its predecessor, the interferometer designed by Charles ◊Fabry and Alfred Perot (1863–1925).

Other areas that interested Lummer were the subject of solar radiation and the problem of obtaining a source of monochromatic illumination. In the former area, he managed to obtain an estimate for the temperature of the Sun, and in the latter he designed a mercury vapour lamp, which is still used when monochromatic light is required – for instance, in fluorescence microscopy.

Lwoff, André Michael (1902–1994)

French microbiologist who was awarded the 1965 Nobel Prize for Physiology or Medicine for his research into the genetic control of enzyme activity. He shared the prize with his fellow researcher Jacques Lucien ◊Monod and François ◊Jacob.

Lwoff, of Russian-Polish descent, was born in Ainy-le-Château, Allier on 8 May 1902. He studied natural sciences, graduating in 1921 and taking a post at the Pasteur Institute; in 1927 he received doctorates in medicine and science. During World War II he was an active member of the French Resistance movement, for which his country awarded him the Legion of Honour. From 1959–68 he was professor of microbiology at the University of Paris and from 1968 to 1972 he was head of the Cancer Research Institute at Villejuif. He died on 30 September 1994.

In his early research carried out in the 1920s, Lwoff demonstrated the coenzyme nature of vitamins. He also discovered the extranuclear genetic control of some characteristics of protozoa. In the early 1940s the US geneticist George Beadle (see ◊Beadle, Tatum, and Ledergerg) had done important work that showed that genes are responsible for the production of the enzymes that moderate biochemical processes. Towards the end of the decade Lwoff and his coworkers proved that enzymes produced by some genes regulate the functions of other genes.

He worked out the mechanism of lysogeny in bacteria, in which the DNA of a virus becomes attached to the DNA within the chromosome of a bacterium, behaving almost like a bacterial gene. It is therefore replicated as part of the host's DNA and so multiplies at the same time. But certain agents (such as ultraviolet radiation) can turn the 'latent' viral DNA, called the prophage, into a vegetative form that multiplies, destroys its host, and is released to infect other bacteria.

Lyell, Charles (1797–1875)

Scottish geologist who succeeded in turning the opinion of his time away from the theory that the Earth was produced literally along the lines expounded in the Old Testament book of Genesis towards the principle of an unlimited, gradual effect of natural forces. His beliefs became known in geology as 'uniformitarianism'.

Lyell was born in Kinnordy, Forfarshire, Scotland, on 14 November 1797, the son of a lawyer and amateur botanist. When he was still a child the family moved to Hampshire. Lyell always had an interest in natural history; he was a keen lepidopterist, and his interest in geology was stimulated by Bakewell's book on the

Lyell Engraving of Scottish geologist Charles Lyell who established the principle that geological processes act in a uniformly regular way to shape the Earth over long periods of time, rather than by a series of catastrophic events. He suggested that the Earth was as much as 240 million years old: much older than the 6,000 years that was thought in the early 19th-century. *Mary Evans Picture Library*

subject. Lyell went to Oxford University to study classics, but also attended lectures given by William ◊Buckland, the professor of geology. Buckland was of the opinion that the different strata in rocks result from silt being laid down under water over a long period of time: he was a 'neptunist'. Lyell made his first tentative geological observations during family holidays in Britain and from 1818 on the Continent, and he began to believe more fully in the principles of uniformitarianism. (In fact the geologist James ◊Hutton had postulated similar theories 50 years earlier, but Lyell formed his conclusions independently; it was only when he later read Hutton's work that he realized that their views were similar.)

Lyell continued his education by studying law, was called to the Bar in 1822, and started to practise in 1825. In 1823 he became involved in the running of the Geological Society as its secretary and later as foreign secretary; he was twice its president some 15 years later. He also set up the finance for the Lyell Medal and the Lyell Fund. He made a trip to Paris in 1823 and met Georges ◊Cuvier, the eminent French anatomist who had stuck rigidly to the geological theories of 'catastrophism', despite his brilliant understanding in other fields. Lyell also met Alexander von ◊Humboldt, the German naturalist; both men influenced his eventual ideas. In 1831 he became professor of geology at King's College, London, and a year later he married the daughter of the geologist Leonard Horner. Lyell was knighted in 1848 and created a baronet in 1864. He died in London on 22 February 1875.

A scientific hypothesis is elegant and exciting insofar as it contradicts common sense.

CHARLES LYELL ATTRIBUTED REMARK, QUOTED IN
S J GOULD EVER SINCE DARWIN 1978

Lyell did not originate much material, but he expounded the theories of Hutton and organized them into a popular and coherent form. His masterpiece, *The Principles of Geology*, was published in three volumes 1830–33 and was revised regularly until 1875. It laid out evidence to support the theory that the Earth's geological structure evolved slowly through the continuous action of forces still at work today, including the erosive action of the wind and weather. Lyell conceded very little to catastrophism, although modern geologists accept that some 'catastrophies' must have occurred – for instance, at the time of the disappearance of the dinosaurs. Lyell classified some geological eras – subdividing the Tertiary into the Eocene, Miocene, Pliocene, and Pleistocene – and suggested that some of the oldest

rocks might be as much as 240 million years old. People were astonished by such a time scale, even though present-day geologists think that ten times that number may be nearer the probable truth.

The conservative scientists were alarmed by Lyell's theories, but his book was popular and stimulated other geologists to investigate along similar lines. Charles ◊Darwin, a colleague and friend of Lyell's, was deeply impressed, and Lyell in turn eventually embraced the theory of evolution as outlined in Darwin's *On the Origin of Species* (1859) – it was Lyell and Joseph ◊Hooker who in 1858 presented to the Linnaean Society the original papers on natural selection by Darwin and Alfred Russel ◊Wallace. Lyell then went further than Darwin had been prepared to do in an attempt to trace human origins, and used archaeological findings as the key to his book *The Geological Evidence of the Antiquity of Man with Remarks on Theories of the Origin of Species by Variation* (1863).

Further Reading

Lyell, Charles; Lyell, Katharine M (ed), *Life, Letters, and Journals*, Darwin series, AMS Press, 1983, 2 vols.

Lyell, Charles; Wilson, Leonard G (ed), *Sir Charles Lyell*, Yale Studies in the History of Science and Medicine, Yale University Press, v 5.

Wilson, Leonard G, *Lyell in America: The Transatlantic Years, 1841–1853*, Johns Hopkins University Press, 1998.

Lyman, Theodore (1874–1954) US physicist famous for his spectroscopic work in the ultraviolet region.

Lyman was born in Boston on 23 November 1874. His father was a marine biologist devoted to the interests of Harvard College, where Lyman also spent his scientific career. Lyman came from a wealthy family and after 1885 lived at the ancestral mansion built by his grandfather at Brookline, Massachusetts. Lyman entered Harvard in 1893 with tastes leaning towards physical sciences. In his first year, he took and passed a course in physics. In his second and third years, he worked hard at electrical engineering and might well have gone on to make a career of it had it not been for the influence of Wallace Sabine (1868–1919), who lectured Lyman in optics. Lyman was offered an assistantship in physics and gained a BA in 1897 followed by a PhD in 1900. During the winter of 1901–1902 he studied under J J ◊Thomson at Cambridge University in the UK and then spent the summer of 1902 in Göttingen, Germany. On his return to Harvard he became an instructor, progressing to assistant professor in 1907. In 1921, he became Hollis Professor of Mathematics and Natural Philosophy. He held this position for five years and then retired emeritus in 1925, some 15 years before the official age of retirement. It was generally thought that he retired to have more freedom. From 1910 to 1947, he also held the position of director of the Jefferson Physical Laboratory. Lyman received many honours, among them the presidencies of the American Physical Society 1921–22 and the American Academy of Arts and Sciences 1924–27. He died after a long illness at Brookline on 11 October 1954.

Lyman's scientific work was confined to the spectroscopy of the extreme ultraviolet region. When he was commencing his research, the observable spectrum had been extended into the ultraviolet as far as 1,260 Å (1 Å = 10^{-10} m) by Victor Schumann (1841–1913), who enclosed the entire spectroscope in an evacuated chamber to eliminate absorption by air and used fluorite for windows, lenses, and prisms. Although Schumann had obtained a wealth of new spectroscopic lines beyond 2,000 Å, the wavelengths could not be exactly determined without knowledge of the index of refraction of the fluorite of his prism.

Sabine suggested that Lyman should try a concave ruled grating instead of a fluorite prism. Success took seven years. False lines of a new kind were found in the Schumann range due to light in the visible region. These came to be called Lyman ghosts and gave Lyman the subject for his PhD thesis. By 1906, he had published reports of more than 300 lines due to hydrogen in the 1,675–1,228 Å region and another 50 probably due to hydrogen in the 1,228–1,030 Å region. He established the limit of transparency of fluorite to be 1,260 Å and looked at the absorbency of other suitable solids but found none better. He also examined the absorption of various gases.

At the beginning of the century, spectroscopic analysis had received an enormous boost because of the discovery of the mathematical regularities shown by many spectra. This was very important in substantiating the quantum theory of atomic structure proposed by Niels ◊Bohr in 1913. Two series of hydrogen spectra had been found, the Paschen series and the Balmer series. The wave number v of each line in these series is given by the expression:

$$v = R(\frac{1}{m^2} - \frac{1}{n^2})$$

Where R is the Rydberg constant and n is an integer greater than m, which has the value 3 for the Paschen series and 2 for the Balmer series. Johann ◊Balmer, who discovered this relationship, had predicted the existence of a series of lines in the ultraviolet in which m would be equal to 1. Lyman announced the discovery of the first three members of this series in 1914, and it was named the Lyman series. He predicted that the first line, the Lyman alpha, would be present in the Sun's spectrum but absorption by the Earth's atmosphere prevented Lyman from observing it. The line was eventually photographed by a rocket five years after

Lyman's death, and ultraviolet observation of the Sun by satellite has since become very important in solar research.

By 1917, Lyman had extended the spectrum to 500 Å. War service and then college administration subsequently reduced his scientific output, and others continued to extend the spectrum further. Lyman turned to spectroscopic examination of elements other than hydrogen, the first being helium. In 1924, seven lines were tabulated in the principal series of helium and Lyman made the rare observation of the continuous spectra beyond the limit of this series due to the recapture of free electrons of different kinetic energies. Papers followed on a series of spectra in the ultraviolet region of aluminium, magnesium, and neon. Lyman's last paper was published in 1935 on the transparency of air between 1,100 and 1,300 Å. Towards the end of his life, Lyman suffered a very sore hand from excess exposure to ultraviolet radiation, and impaired eyesight.

Lyman was also a keen traveller and collector. His most important trip was to the Altai Mountains of China and Mongolia. He brought back the first specimen of a gazelle that became named *Procapra altaica* and also 13 previously unknown smaller mammalian species. A stoat became known as Lyman's stoat, *Mustela lymani*.

Lynden-Bell, Donald (1935–) English astrophysicist particularly interested in the structure and dynamics of galaxies.

Lynden-Bell was born the son of an army officer on 5 April 1935. Educated at Marlborough College, he went to Cambridge University, where he graduated from Clare College. In 1960, having completed his PhD, he was elected Harkness Fellow of the Commonwealth Fund and joined the California Institute of Technology (Caltech) to work with Allan Sandage (1926–), at the Hale Observatory, on the dynamics of galaxies. Two years later he returned to Cambridge to take up an appointment as assistant lecturer in applied mathematics. Afterwards he became fellow and director of studies in mathematics at Clare College. In 1972 he became professor of astrophysics at the Institute of Astronomy in Cambridge, and served as its director 1972–77, 1982–87, and 1992–94. The author of a number of significant papers, he is a fellow of the Royal Astronomical Society.

During his second period at Caltech, Lynden-Bell published a paper on 'Galactic nuclei as collapsed old quasars' (1969), which proposed that quasars were powered by massive black holes. Later, continuing this line of thought, he postulated the existence of black holes of various masses in the nuclei of individual galaxies. The presence of these black holes – objects optically invisible because their light is 'imprisoned' by the object's own tremendously strong gravitational attraction – as power centres of galaxies would account for the large amounts of infrared energy that emanate from a galactic centre. Lynden-Bell further argued that in the dynamic evolution of star clusters the core of globular star clusters evolves independently of outer parts, and that it is necessary to postulate a dissipative collapse of gas to account for that evolution. This is certainly compatible with the presence of a central black hole within a stellar system.

Lynen, Feodor (1911–1979) German biochemist known for his research into the synthesis of cholesterol in the human body and into the metabolism of fatty acids. For this work he shared the 1964 Nobel Prize for Physiology or Medicine with the US biochemist Konrad ◊Bloch.

Lynen was born in Munich, Bavaria, on 6 April 1911. He studied at the University of Munich, gaining his doctorate in 1937. In the same year he married the daughter of his professor, Heinrich ◊Wieland. He remained on the academic staff at Munich as a lecturer 1942–46, associate professor 1947–53, and professor of biochemistry from 1953. Between 1954 and 1972 he was director of the Max Planck Institute for Cell Chemistry in Munich, and from 1972 director of the Max Planck Institute for Biochemistry.

Cholesterol is a key substance in the body, the starting material for adrenal cortical hormones, sex hormones, and other steroids. Lynen in Munich and Konrad ◊Bloch in the USA studied the complicated mechanism by which cholesterol is formed. Bloch found that the basic unit for cholesterol synthesis is the simple acetate (ethanoate) ion, a chemical fragment containing only two carbon atoms. Fritz Lipmann postulated that the substance known as coenzyme A, which he isolated in 1947, might be the carrier of the fragment. In 1951 Lynen isolated 'active acetate' from yeast and found it to be identical to acetyl coenzyme A, a combination of coenzyme A and a two-carbon fragment, thus confirming Lipmann's hypothesis. Bloch then found an intermediate compound, squalene – a long hydrocarbon containing 30 carbon atoms. Lynen and Bloch corresponded and worked out the 36 steps involved in the synthesis of cholesterol. The final stage was found to be the transformation of the carbon chain of squalene ($C_{30}H_{50}$) into the four-ring molecule of cholesterol.

Lynen also worked on the biosynthesis of fatty acids, isolating from yeast an enzyme complex that acts as a catalyst in the synthesis of long-chain fatty acids from acetyl coenzyme A and malonyl coenzyme A. His study of fatty acids also elucidated a series of energy-generating reactions that occur when fatty acids from food are respired to form carbon dioxide and water. From this research has resulted the more general conclusion that repeated condensation of two carbon fragments originating from acetate is the basis of the synthesis of many natural substances.

Lyot, Bernard Ferdinand (1897–1952) French astronomer and an exceptionally talented designer and constructor of optical instruments. He concentrated on the study of the solar corona, for which he devised the coronagraph and the photoelectric polarimeter, and he proved that some of the Fraunhofer lines in the solar spectrum represent ionized forms of known metals rather than undiscovered elements.

Lyot was born in Paris on 27 February 1897. He graduated from the Ecole Supérieure d'Electricité in 1917 and in 1918 he was awarded a diploma in engineering. He worked under Alfred Pérot at the Ecole Polytechnique in Paris as a demonstrator in physics 1918–29, and from 1920 he held the post of assistant astronomer at the Meudon Observatory. In 1930 Lyot was made joint astronomer at the observatory, where he began to work full-time. Lyot's advances in the study of polarized and monochromatic light soon earned him an international reputation. He was elected to the French Academy of Sciences in 1939 and in the same year was awarded the Gold Medal of the Royal Astronomical Society in London. He published several books that outlined his discoveries and innovations. Having become chief astronomer at the Meudon Observatory in 1943, Lyot travelled to the Sudan in 1952 to observe a total eclipse of the Sun. He suffered a heart attack on the train journey home and died near Cairo, Egypt, on 2 April 1952.

Most of Lyot's research during the 1920s was devoted to the study of polarized light reflected to the Earth from the Moon and from other planets. In addition to designing a polariscope of greatly improved sensitivity, Lyot made a number of observations about the surfaces and atmospheric conditions on other planets. In 1924 he reported that the Moon was probably covered by a layer of volcanic ash and that duststorms were a common feature of the Martian surface. (He also claimed to have detected water vapour on the surface of Venus, but it was later demonstrated that the tiny amount of water vapour present could not have been seen using Lyot's instruments.)

For centuries, astronomers wishing to study the solar corona had been restricted to the rare and brief occasions of total eclipses of the Sun. The main problem involved in using optical instruments at other times had always been the 'scattering' of light – by even the slightest particle of dust or the minutest fault in the object lens – so that the corona, which has only one-millionth of the brilliance of the solar disc, was totally obscured. In 1930 Lyot designed a 'coronagraph', which included three lenses. The object lens was as perfect as he could make it, with a diameter of 8 cm/3 in and a focal length of 2 m/6.5 ft. He took the instrument to the clear air of the Pic du Midi Observatory in the Pyrenees, at an altitude of 2,870 m/9,420 ft, and for the first time in the history of astronomy was able to observe the corona in broad daylight.

During the 1930s Lyot improved upon his coronagraph: he increased the size and focal length of the object lens and fitted the device with a sophisticated monochromatic filter designed to enable him to concentrate on the most important wavelengths in the coronal light. By increasing the length of time during which the solar corona could be observed, the coronagraph also permitted the observation of continuous changes in the corona. This meant that the corona could be filmed, as Lyot demonstrated for the first time in 1935. Lyot also reported the rotation of the corona in synchrony with the Sun.

The coronagraph was also essential to Lyot's realization that some of the lines in the solar spectrum, believed to represent the unknown elements 'coronium', 'geocoronium', and others, did in fact represent the highly ionized forms of elements well-known on Earth.

Lyot's later work included the construction of the photoelectric polarimeter, which facilitated further research on the solar corona.

Lysenko, Trofim Denisovich (1898–1976)

Ukrainian botanist who dominated biology in the Soviet Union from about the mid-1930s to 1965. During this period he was virtual dictator of biology in the Soviet Union and his theories, although largely rejected outside his own country, were officially adopted within the Soviet Union. He actually contributed very little to scientific knowledge and his importance has been attributed to his friendship with the Soviet political leaders Josef Stalin and Nikita Khrushchev, who awarded Lysenko many honours: he was made a Hero of Socialist Labour, and received the Order of Lenin eight times and the Stalin Prize three times.

Lysenko was born on 29 September 1898 in Karlovka in the Russian Ukraine, the son of a peasant, and was educated at the Uman School of Horticulture. After graduating in 1921, he went to the Belaya Tserkov Selection Station then to the Kiev Agricultural Institute to study for his doctorate, which he gained in 1925. He was stationed at the Gandzha (now Kirovabad) Experimental Station 1925–29, when he became the senior specialist in the department of physiology at the Ukrainian All-Union Institute of Selection and Genetics in Odessa. In 1935 he became scientific director of this institute and in the following year he was promoted to director, a post he held until 1938. With the increase of his political influence, Lysenko rose rapidly to the top of the scientific hierarchy, becoming director of the

Institute of Genetics of the USSR Academy of Sciences in 1940. As a result of Khrushchev's fall from power in 1964, Lysenko's influence diminished considerably and in 1965 he was removed from his post and stripped of all authority. He died on 20 November 1976, his ideas discredited both within the Soviet Union and by the Western world.

Lysenko rose to prominence as a result of his advocating vernalization to increase crop yields. In vernalization – a practice well known since the 19th century – seeds are moistened just sufficiently to allow germination to begin, then, when the radicles start to emerge, the seeds are cooled to slightly above 0 °C/32 °F, thereby halting further growth. When the seeds are planted in spring, they mature quickly; this is particularly useful in the Soviet Union because large areas of the country have only a very short growing season. Using this method Lysenko achieved considerable increases in crop yields, which gained him substantial political support. A succession of important appointments followed, and by 1935 Lysenko had become a powerful influence in Soviet science.

As Lysenko's influence increased, so he enlarged the scope of his theories, using his authority to remove any opposition. He innovated the doctrine of the phasic development of plants, claiming that all plants develop in recessive phases, each with different requirements. He stated that by altering any stage of development, changes could be caused in successive stages. This doctrine was opposed by Nikolai Vavilov (1887–1942/3), an internationally respected Soviet geneticist, but Lysenko used his political influence to have Vavilov arrested and banished to Siberia, where he died in exile in 1942 or 1943.

Expanding his theories still further, Lysenko defined heredity as the capacity of an organism to require specific conditions for its life and development, and to respond in different ways to various conditions. Moreover, he believed that when an organism is subjected to abnormal environmental conditions, it develops in such a way as to take advantage of these conditions and that the offspring of this organism also tend to develop in the same way as the parent. This idea was, in fact, a restatement of the Lamarckian doctrine of the inheritance of acquired characteristics.

As leader of the Soviet scientific world, Lysenko encouraged the defence of mechanistic views about the nature of heredity and speciation. These views – termed Michurin biology after the prominent Soviet scientist I V Michurin – became an integral part of Soviet scientific thought and created an environment conducive to the spread of unverified facts and theories, such as the doctrine of the non-cellular 'living' substance and the transformation of viruses into bacteria. To many people, this period represented the dark ages of Soviet science and research in several areas of biology came to a halt.

Although Lysenko's views were imposed on Soviet scientists, his ideas were widely criticized by many European and US scientists and, encouraged by this external support, the struggle to counteract Lysenkoism gained strength.

Further Reading

Joravsky, David, *The Lysenko Affair*, University of Chicago Press, 1986.

Roll-Hansen, Nils, 'A new perspective on Lysenko?', *Ann Sci*, 1985, v 42, pp 261–278.

Soyfer, Valery N; Gruliow, Leo and Gruliow, Rebecca (transl), *Lysenko and the Tragedy of the Soviet Science*, Rutgers University Press, 1994.

Lyttleton, Raymond Arthur (1911–1995) English astronomer and theoretical physicist whose main interest was stellar evolution and composition, although he extended this in order to investigate the nature of the Solar System.

Lyttleton was born in Warley Woods, near Birmingham. Educated at King Edward School, Birmingham, he then went to Clare College, Cambridge. As a visiting fellow at Princeton University in the USA 1935–1937, Lyttleton worked with Henry ◊Russell (one of the originators of the Hertzsprung–Russell diagram) and was inspired while there to propose a theory of planetary formation that at the time received some critical acclaim. Upon his return to Cambridge in 1937, Lyttleton was awarded his PhD and appointed research fellow of St John's College; together with Fred ◊Hoyle he established an active research school there in theoretical astronomy. During World War II he served as an experimental officer with the Ministry of Supply 1940–42 and as a technical assistant to Sydney Chapman as scientific adviser to the Army Council War Office 1942–45. Lyttleton was then appointed lecturer in mathematics at Cambridge University, becoming Stokes Lecturer in Mathematics in 1954, reader in theoretical astronomy in 1959, and

professor of theoretical astronomy in 1969 (emeritus from 1978). In 1967 he was an original member of the Institute of Astronomy at Cambridge. Lyttleton was the author of many papers and several books on astronomical subjects and a member of leading scientific societies. He was elected fellow of the Royal Society in 1955, from whom he received a Royal Medal in 1965. He died on 16 May 1995.

Lyttleton's research has spanned most areas of theoretical astronomy. His earliest work in the subject, his theory of planetary formation, was formulated at Princeton. It involved the possibility of a binary companion star to the Sun, dealt with the rotation of the planets and their satellites, and showed that Pluto may be an escaped satellite of Neptune.

Upon his return to Cambridge, Lyttleton began his long and fruitful association with Fred Hoyle, with whom he contributed to the growing knowledge of stellar evolution. In the early 1940s they applied the new advances in nuclear physics, as developed by Hans ◊Bethe and others, to the problem of energy generation in stars. They also published, in 1939, a paper that demonstrated the presence of interstellar hydrogen on a large scale, at a time when most astronomers believed space to be devoid of interstellar gas.

In 1953 Lyttleton published a book on cometary formation and evolution, based upon the accretion theory. In the same year he published an important monograph on the stability of rotating liquid masses.

Lyttleton also made important contributions to geophysics. He postulated that the Earth's liquid core was produced by a phase-change resulting from the combined effects of intense pressure and temperature. This is of great significance in the determination of the rate of change of Earth's volume, and would be of considerable relevance to the mechanics of mountain-formation. Lyttleton also stressed the hydrodynamic significance of the liquid core in the processes of precession and nutation.

M

McAdam, John Loudon (1756–1836) Scottish civil engineer whose system of road-building – and particularly, surfacing – made a major contribution to the improvement of road transport during the 19th century. Indeed, his methods continued to be used after the development of motorized road vehicles, well into the 20th century.

McAdam was born in Ayr, Scotland, on 21 September 1756. At the age of 14 he emigrated to the USA, where he settled in New York City. He went to work for his uncle, and eventually became a successful businessman in his own right. McAdam returned to Ayrshire in 1783, and 15 years later moved to Falmouth in Devon. He was appointed surveyor general of the roads in Bristol in 1816, and of all the roads in Britain in 1827. He died on 26 November 1836.

McAdam's success came not so much from his making wide, straight roads but for his technique – which came to be known as 'macadamizing' – for creating excellent road surfaces. He also drew up basic rules for highway management. Before McAdam's time there was some organization of roads repairs in Britain, but it seldom worked well. Each parish was responsible for its own repairs, but the parishes were small (and sometimes poor) and often not particularly interested in maintaining roads largely for the use of travellers from outside the parish. Also there

McAdam Scottish civil engineer John Loudon McAdam who, in the mid-19th century, pioneered the technique of building roads from layers of graded building material that is still used today. *Mary Evans Picture Library*

was little skill and experience among either the labourers or the supervisors.

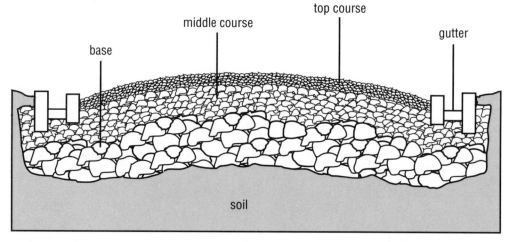

McAdam McAdam raised the road above the surrounding terrain, compounding a surface of small stones bound with gravel on a firm base of large stones. A camber, making the road slightly convex in section, ensured that rainwater rapidly drained off the road and did not penetrate the foundation.

Towards the end of the 18th century the usual method of making a road was to plough the area, smooth the surface, and put down loose sand, gravel, or pebbles. McAdam raised the road above the surrounding terrain, compounding a surface of small stones bound with gravel on a firm base of large stones. A camber, making the road slightly convex in section, ensured that rainwater rapidly drained off the road and did not penetrate the foundation. By the end of the 19th century, most of the main roads in Europe were using this method.

McAdam was also responsible for reforms in road administration that were as important as his innovatory road surfacings. He encouraged people to enter the profession of road-making by offering them suitable salaries, thus ensuring that more able and intelligent workers would be attracted to the task. He was in a better position to wield such influence after he was appointed surveyor general of metropolitan roads in 1827.

It was, in fact, many years before this that McAdam began to take an interest in road construction – indeed it became almost an obsession with him. In the ten years from 1810 he had spent his fortune on his 'hobby' and he petitioned Parliament for reward. The roads he had made in Bristol and other areas, and the three books he had written on road-making, had ensured that his name was very well known. At the time of his appointment as surveyor general he was also granted £10,000 by a grateful government.

Prior to the ultimate job in highways maintenance, McAdam became, in 1816, surveyor to the Bristol Turnpike Trust; he re-made the roads there and his advice was widely sought. Further to his belief in the importance of good road administration, he recommended the strengthening of turnpike trusts – but under the control of Parliament – and was advisor to many of these trusts. Turnpike roads were introduced in the late 17th century to provide better roads, but the costs were transferred to the road-users. McAdam ensured that public roads became the responsibility of the government, financed (out of taxes) for the benefit of everyone.

MacArthur, Robert Helmer (1930–1972) Canadian-born US ecologist who did much to change ecology from a descriptive discipline to a quantitative, predictive science.

MacArthur was born on 7 April 1930 in Toronto, Canada. He studied mathematics at Marlboro College, Vermont, graduating in 1951, and at Brown University, Providence, from which he gained his master's degree in 1953. He then went to Yale University to do his doctorate in mathematics but changed to zoology at the end of his second year and began to study ecology under G Evelyn Hutchinson, one of the leading US ecologists of the time. MacArthur's studies were interrupted by a two-year period of military service, after which he returned to Yale to complete his doctoral dissertation, which won him the Mercer Award for the best ecology paper of 1957–58. He then joined the staff of the University of Pennsylvania, first as assistant professor of zoology 1958–61, then as associate professor of zoology 1961–64. In 1965 he was appointed professor of biology at Princeton University, where he remained until he died of cancer on 1 November 1972, only 42 years old.

In his doctoral thesis, MacArthur studied the relationship between five species of warbler that coexist in the New England forests; these species (now known as MacArthur's warblers) are ecologically very similar and it was suspected that they violated the competitive exclusion principle. MacArthur discovered, however, that there are subtle differences in the foraging strategies used by each species.

During the remainder of his life, MacArthur devoted himself to investigating population biology. He examined how the diversity and relative abundance of species fluctuate over time and how species evolve – particularly the evolution of communities – and the strategies that coexisting species evolve under the pressures of competition and natural selection. In these studies he attempted to interrelate several important factors: the structure of the environment, the morphology of the species, the economics of species' behaviour, and the dynamics of population change. But perhaps his most important contribution was to quantify some of the many factors involved in the ecological relationships between species. For example, complex habitats such as forests support more species of birds than do grasslands, but it was only after MacArthur had devised his index of vegetational complexity (called foliage height diversity) in 1961 that it became possible to translate the observation about bird species' diversity into a definite equation whereby habitat structures can be compared and their bird species' diversity predicted.

McBain, James William (1882–1953) Canadian physical chemist whose main researches were concerned with colloidal solutions, particularly soap solutions.

McBain was born in Chatham, New Brunswick, and entered the University of Toronto at the age of 17, graduating in chemistry and mineralogy. He spent the winter of 1904–05 at the University of Leipzig, which at that time was at the height of its academic activity in physical chemistry. His first academic appointment was as a lecturer at the University of Bristol in 1906, a post he held until he became the first Leverhulme Professor of Chemistry there in 1919. In 1926 he went to the USA to become professor of chemistry at the

University of Stanford, California; he became emeritus professor in 1947, six years before he died.

McBain's first research concerned the rate of oxidation of ferrous (iron (II)) salts on exposure to air. But he was soon attracted to colloid chemistry and a study of simple soaps. As early as 1910 he showed that aqueous solutions of soaps such as sodium palmitate are good electrolytic conductors. He discovered the interesting anomaly that there are maxima and minima in the conductivity–concentration curves. In his next investigation he examined the degrees of hydrolysis for various concentrations of soap. He postulated the existence of highly mobile carriers of negative electricity with mobilities similar to that of the citrate ion. This led to the concept of the 'association ion' or 'ionic micelle', which has since proved invaluable in elucidating the properties of a large class of colloidal systems, including soaps, detergents, and dyes.

McBain and his co-workers also developed new apparatus for their studies. They improved on the method of Northrop and Anson for determining the diffusion constants of substances in solution by passing them through discs of sintered glass. They developed a simple and elegant transparent air-driven ultra-centrifuge. McBain pointed out that in the sedimentation of an equilibrium system such as that which exists in soap solutions above the micelle point, the rapidly moving micelles dissociate as they leave their normal environment of the equilibrium concentration of monomer, but as the material collects at the periphery of the centrifuge rotor, micelles naturally reform. To determine the thermodynamic properties of soap solutions he examined the possibility of using various methods: osmotic pressures, lowering of vapour pressure, and lowering of freezing point. Ultimately he developed his own method based on the lowering of the dew point.

In aqueous solution the micelle (association particle) encloses the non-polar or chain portions of the molecules, with the carboxyl or hydrophilic portions on the outside of the sphere. McBain pointed out that invert micelles should exist, with the polar heads clustered together at the centre, and these should be capable of dissolving substances that are usually insoluble. Such micelles in aqueous solutions should be able, for example, to dissolve hydrocarbons. He gave the name 'solubilization' to this phenomenon and spent much time and energy to experiments in this field. He also introduced the term 'cosolvency' to describe the process of effecting solution by means of a mixture of liquid solvents.

McBain also questioned the idea that the surface phase in simple solutions was only one monolayer thick (as implied by the experimental work of Frederick Donnan and the theoretical proposals of Irving ◊Langmuir). Above the micelle point there are several distinct species of potentially active materials (anions, undissociated molecules, and micelles), all of which could accumulate at the surface. McBain proved that oriented underlayers do exist beneath the monolayers of soap, and he devised an ingenious apparatus for determining their actual composition. William Hardy came to a similar conclusion: that molecular orientation is not confined to a monolayer of liquid in contact with a solid surface, but that long-range forces give rise to cybotactic layers of considerable thickness (cybotactics are regions of 'order' for molecules within the structure of a liquid).

Another phenomenon studied by McBain was the adsorption of gases and vapours by solids. Various processes can take place simultaneously: physical sorption, chemisorption, and – by 'activating' the solid or forming it into a skeletonized structure – permeation of the solid by the gas or vapour. McBain introduced the generalized term 'sorption' to include all such cases. He devised the McBain–Bakr spring balance, which provides a continuous record of the quantities and rate of sorption by direct weighing.

McClintock, Barbara (1902–1992) US geneticist who discovered jumping genes (genes that can change their position on a chromosome from generation to generation), thereby offering an explanation of how originally identical cells take on specialized functions as skin, muscle, bone, and nerve, and also how evolution can give rise to the multiplicity of species. For this she was awarded a Nobel Prize for Physiology or Medicine in 1983. Unusually the award was not shared with another scientist.

She was born on 16 June 1902 in Hartford, Connecticut, but grew up in Brooklyn, New York. She developed an interest in science while still at school and went to Cornell University in 1919. She achieved her PhD in 1927 for work on the genetics of maize. She moved from Cornell in 1931 to the California Institute of Technology and then to the University of Missouri but failed to achieve tenure at any of these institutes, and in 1941 moved to the Cold Spring Harbour Laboratory where she remained until her formal retirement in 1967, although she continued to work in the laboratory almost until her death at Long Island on 2 September 1992.

As an undergraduate at Cornell, and from 1941, she studied maize chromosomes. She observed that the patterns on twin sectors of maize seedlings were the inverse of one another, and that pigmentation of certain kernels did not correspond to their genetic makeup. Realizing that as a single cell divided into sister cells, one gained what the other had lost, she deduced that not all genes behave in the same way: some genes can switch others on and off, moving from one place to another on one chromosome, or even 'jumping' from one chromosome to another. These jumping genes acted as regulators and were later discovered in bacteria and in fruit flies.

McClintock's discovery that genes are not stable overturned one of the main tenets of heredity laid down by Gregor ◊Mendel in the 19th century. It had enormous implications and explained, for example, how resistance to antibiotic drugs can be transmitted between entirely different bacterial types.

She utilized X-rays to induce chromosomal aberrations and rearrangements and examined the ways in which chromosomes repair such damage. This information helped other scientists understand the problems of radiation sickness after the explosion of the atomic bomb at Hiroshima, Japan.

McCollum, Elmer Verner (1879–1967) US biochemist and nutritionist best known for his work on vitamins, and for originating the letter system of naming them.

McCollum was born on 3 March 1879 in Fort Scott, Kansas, the fourth child of an initially prosperous farming family. But his father became ill when McCollum was still very young and he had to take a succession of jobs while at school and university to pay for his education and to help to support his parents. McCollum studied at the University of Kansas, graduating in 1903, then gained a postgraduate scholarship to Yale University, from which he obtained his doctorate in 1906. In the following year he joined the faculty of the University of Wisconsin, where he remained for ten years. In 1917 he was appointed professor of biochemistry in the School of Hygiene and Public Health at Johns Hopkins University, a post he held until his retirement in 1944. McCollum died in Baltimore on 15 November 1967.

In his first years at Wisconsin University, McCollum worked on analysing the food and excreta of cattle. He soon decided, however, that it would be much easier to perform this work using a more convenient laboratory animal, and he chose the albino rat. This led to the establishment of the first rat colony for nutrition experiments, and it is largely through McCollum's efforts that albino rats have today become one of the most used animals for research. Investigating the nutritional requirements of his albino rats, McCollum discovered in the early 1910s that growth retardation results from a diet deficient in certain fats and that such deficiencies can be compensated for by providing a specific extract from either butter or eggs. He called this essential component 'fat-soluble A', because it dissolves in lipids. This was the start of the alphabetical naming system for vitamins. McCollum then showed that there is another essential dietary component that is not found in lipids but which is water soluble; he called this component

'water-soluble B'. Initially he thought that the two essential components were single compounds, but he later showed that they are in fact complexes.

McCollum continued his nutritional research at Johns Hopkins University, where he collaborated in the discovery of vitamin D. He also investigated the way in which sunlight prevents rickets, but it was not shown until later that the anti-rickets effect of sunlight is caused by the conversion of fats in the skin to vitamin D by the ultraviolet component of sunlight. In addition to his work on vitamins, McCollum also researched into the role of minerals in the diet.

McCormick, Cyrus Hall (1809–1884) US inventor best known for developing the first successful mechanical reaper.

The son of the inventor Robert McCormick, Cyrus McCormick was born in Virginia on 15 February 1809. Under the guiding influence of his father, he was encouraged to use the talents of his own inventive mind, and in 1831 produced a hillside plough, the first of several agricultural implements with which he was associated. In the same year he invented the prototype for his reaping machine, and although it was another nine years before it was perfected, when the machine was put into production a ready market existed.

With the Midwest opening up there was a need for mechanization to cope with the huge acreages involved. McCormick was invited to Chicago to demonstrate his machine and, as a result, began manufacturing there in 1847. But in 1848, when his patent expired, he had to face strong competition and only his good business sense kept him from being overwhelmed by other manufacturers who had been waiting to encroach on his markets. He survived and prospered, introduced his reaping machine into Europe and opened up an entirely new market, winning several prizes (including one at the Great Exhibition in London in 1851).

An inventor first and foremost, he also had the intelligence to spread his interests in other directions, including mining, railways, and newspaper publishing. He died in Chicago on 13 May 1884.

McCormick's reaping machine consisted of seven basic mechanisms that were principally the same as in its modern equivalent: the divider, reel, straight reciprocating knife, guards, platform, main wheel and gearing, and side-draft propulsion. The working was simple. A pulley at the side of the one road-driving wheel was connected by a band to another pulley above, turning the circular wooden frame. The blades of this were slightly twisted so that they gradually bent the corn down. Bevelled gears turned a small cranked shaft, which gave the movement to the cutting knife, working it backwards and forwards. The machine was designed purely as a reaper, and it left the corn lying flat, ready to be raked up and tied into sheaves. In the original machine the raker had to walk backwards while raking to avoid standing on the corn; in later models a seat was incorporated into the machine so that the raker could sit.

It was estimated that a McCormick reaper operated by a two-person crew and drawn by a single horse could cut as much corn as could 12–16 people with reap hooks. In a nation like the USA, with a rapidly expanding population (from 13 million to 60 million in 40 years) needing to be fed, it was essential that agriculture should be lifted from the manual to the mechanical wherever possible. McCormick's invention was the first of many that were to increase the production of cereals and guarantee enough food for all.

McCoy, Elijah (1843–1929) US engineer and the inventor of a device that allowed machines to be lubricated while they were in use. His invention is thought to have originated the expression 'the real McCoy'.

McCoy was born on 2 May 1844 in Colchester, Ontario, Canada. His parents were escaped slaves who had taken the underground railroad from Kentucky. The family moved back to the USA when he was a child to settle in Ypsilanti, Michigan, where his father worked in the logging industry. There are conflicting versions of McCoy's education. One is that he attended a local school until his parents saved enough money to send him to Scotland, at the age of 15, to study in Edinburgh. While he was there he served an apprenticeship in mechanical engineering. Returning to the USA as a fully qualified engineer and one of the most educated African-Americans of his day, he could not find a job because of his colour. For lack of better offers he took a job as a fireman on the Michigan Central Railroad, which entailed shovelling coal and oiling all the moving parts. Another version is that as a youth he was fascinated by machines and tools and learned all he could by observation and by asking questions.

At the time, many new machines were being invented with numerous moving parts, but the problem of lubrication had not been tackled. McCoy had seen young 'grease monkeys' in factories and mills crawling around among machinery that was kept moving to avoid the cost of regularly turning them off. These children risked serious injury or death. Trains had to stop every few miles for lubrication. McCoy developed his idea for an automatic lubricating device with an adjustable stopcock that could oil machinery while it was still in motion by allowing small amounts of oil to drip slowly onto the moving parts. He called it the 'lubricator cup'.

The lubricator cup won a patent in 1872 and McCoy then established his own firm, the Elijah McCoy Manufacturing Company, in Detroit, Michigan, which was responsible for a further 57 patents. McCoy's other inventions included the ironing board and the lawn sprinkler. The lubricator cup was a life-saving, labour-saving, money-saving revolution. Railway engines no longer had to be stopped every few miles for oiling, and factory machinery could safely be kept moving day and night to keep up with the demands of the industrial revolution. The lubricator cup was so reliable that buyers of machinery would ask whether it contained 'the real McCoy', popularizing the US expression meaning the real thing.

McCoy died on 10 October 1929 in Eloise, Michigan, and was buried in Detroit.

McCrea, William Hunter (1904–   ) Irish theoretical astrophysicist and mathematician whose main interest has been the evolution of galaxies and planetary systems. He has proposed several theories that have aroused considerable scientific speculation.

McCrea was born in Dublin on 13 December 1904. He was educated in England, first at Chesterfield Grammar School, Derbyshire, and then at Trinity College, Cambridge. Graduating in 1926, McCrea then travelled to the University of Göttingen as part of his postgraduate research programme, before returning to receive his PhD at Cambridge in 1929. From 1930 to 1932 he lectured in mathematics at Edinburgh University, then moved to London to take up the position of reader and assistant professor in the department of mathematics at Imperial College.

In 1936 McCrea became professor of mathematics at Queen's University, Belfast. Although he formally held this post until 1944, McCrea was a temporary principal experimental officer with the operational research section of the Admiralty 1943–45. After World War II McCrea became professor of mathematics at the Royal Holloway College of the University of London, a post he held – with some visiting professorships – until 1966, when he was appointed research professor of theoretical astronomy at the University of Sussex. He became emeritus professor there in 1972, but remained active and travelled widely. A fellow of the Royal Society, and a recipient of the Gold Medal of the Royal Astronomical Society, McCrea wrote several influential books on physics.

In pursuit of his investigations into the evolution of galaxies, McCrea had studied the factors that would influence the earliest stages of this evolution, when 'protostars' condense out of the primordial gas cloud (formed predominantly of hydrogen, but with some helium) and then disintegrate to form globular clusters that in turn disperse as older (or 'Population II') stars, located mainly in dust-free zones of space. He particularly focused his attention on what might happen to this process if it encountered interstellar matter that was itself in a state of turbulence. Such an encounter would be critical in regulating the instability of the condensing material. McCrea also analysed the effect of angular momentum, since the spinning of the interstellar matter would tend to counter the gravitational forces that promote condensation. Magnetic forces may also be of significance in this process. As a corollary of this research, McCrea has proposed a theory for the mechanism by which planets and other satellites may form.

Together with Edward ◊Milne, McCrea was the founder of modern 'Newtonian' cosmology. Milne had devoted much effort to investigating alternatives to relativistic cosmology, and with McCrea he found that Newtonian dynamics could be advantageously applied to the analysis of the primordial gas cloud. The model relied on the assumption that the gas cloud would be 'very large' rather than of infinite size, although for the purposes of observation it would be 'infinite'.

McCrea has also contributed to discussion of Paul ◊Dirac's 'large number hypothesis', which deals – among other things – with the ratio of the electrical and gravitational forces between an electron and a proton. This number comes to 10^{39}, which is – strikingly – the age of the universe in terms of atomic units. This may suggest some meaningful connection between the age of the universe (which is always increasing) and either the (hitherto presumed to be constant) electrical or gravitational forces – or it may be coincidental.

Other areas of interest to McCrea include the formation of molecules in interstellar matter (the formation of clouds of hydrogen in a gas cloud originally made up predominantly of monoatomic hydrogen), and the composition of stellar atmospheres. He has also investigated the fact that the emission of neutrinos from the Sun appears to be less than would be expected on the basis of predictions about the nuclear reactions taking place inside. This may simply mean, however, that thermal conditions in the Sun's interior are different from what has been so far deduced.

In physics the most notable of McCrea's contributions has been his work on forbidden (low-probability) transitions of electrons between energy states, analyses of penetration of potential barriers (for instance by 'tunnelling'), and his writings on relativity theory.

McCrea's work has covered many scientific fields, including mathematics, quantum mechanics, stellar astronomy, and cosmology. He has made fundamental contributions to all of these fields and is an important figure in contemporary science.

Mach, Ernst (1838–1916) Austrian physicist whose name was given to the Mach number, the velocity of a body in a medium relative to the speed of sound in that medium. Mach also made an important contribution to science in a fundamental reappraisal of scientific thought. He sought to understand knowledge in the context of the physiological, sensory, and psychological processes that govern and limit its acquisition. This led him to question mechanical explanations of matter and the universe that could not be adequately observed, and to favour more conceptual or mathematical explanations. This approach to science had a profound influence on Albert ◊Einstein in the formulation of the general theory of relativity.

Mach was born in Turas, then in Austria-Hungary but now in the Czech Republic, on 18 February 1838. His family moved to Unter Siebenbrunn near Vienna in 1840. He was almost entirely educated at home by his parents until the age of 15, when he entered the local Gymnasium. He was most impressed by the study of natural science and, in particular, enjoyed the lessons of his teacher of natural history, a man named F X Wessely. Mach began his studies at the University of Vienna in 1855 and was awarded his PhD in 1860 for a thesis on electricity. While in Vienna he was influenced by Gustav Fechner (1801–1887), who worked on 'psychophysics' or the physiology of perception.

Mach lectured at the university, and also earned extra money by giving popular lectures on a variety of scientific topics. He published two books in 1863, one on physics for medical students and the other on psychophysics. He moved to Graz in 1864 where he became professor of mathematics and, in 1866, professor of physics. He then went to the University of Prague in 1867, where he was appointed professor of experimental physics.

Mach remained in Prague for 28 years, conducting many research projects and publishing many books and lectures. He served as rector to the university 1882–84. In 1895 he became professor of history and theory of inductive sciences at the University of Vienna. He suffered a stroke in 1897, which paralysed his right side and from which he made only a slow recovery. He retired from the university in 1901, and was appointed to the upper chamber of the Austrian parliament, a post he held for 12 years. In 1913, Mach moved to his son's home in Vaterstetten, near Munich, Germany. He continued to write books and died there on 19 February 1916.

Mach's early work in Vienna was in the department of Andreas von Ettingshausen, who had succeeded Christian ◊Doppler as professor of experimental physics. Accordingly, Mach's research was aimed at investigating Doppler's then controversial law describing the relationship between the perceived frequency of sound and light and the motion of the observer relative to that of the source. Mach also investigated vibration and resonance. His interest in subjects that his colleagues saw as being only of peripheral interest, such as perception, was active even in these early days. His book on psychophysics, published in 1863, examined the complex physiological problems associated with vision and Mach concluded that the reductionist mechanistic approach had not given satisfactory explanations of phenomena.

At Graz, Mach was forced to fund his research out of his own pocket and, lacking equipment for investigations into physics, he continued to study subjects such as vision, hearing, and our sense of time. He investigated stimulation of the retinal field with spatial patterns and discovered a strange visual effect called Mach bands. This was subsequently forgotten, and was rediscovered in the 1950s.

In Prague, Mach was able to turn to issues of a more physical nature. He made a long theoretical study of mechanics and thermodynamics. He did not, however, abandon his other interests. Among his projects were a study of the kinesthetic sense and how it responds to body movements, more work on Mach bands, investigations of hearing and vision, various aspects of optics, and wave phenomena of mechanical, electrical, and optical kinds. One of Mach's most important contributions arose from his work, published in 1887, on the photography of projectiles in flight, which showed the shock wave produced by the gas around the tip of the projectile. The Mach angle describes the angle between the direction of motion and the shock wave, and Mach found that it varies with the speed of the projectile, the flow of gas changing its character when the projectile reaches the speed of sound. This came to be very important in aerodynamics and particularly in supersonic flight, and in 1929 the term 'Mach number' came into use to describe the ratio of the velocity of an object to the speed of sound in the medium in which the object is moving. An aircraft flying at Mach 2 is therefore flying at twice the speed of sound in air at that particular height.

Mach's philosophy of science – although he would never have described it in those terms, feeling himself to be a scientist and not a philosopher – included an investigation of modern science based on an analysis of the sequence of previous developments. He felt that the very order in which discoveries had been made altered their content and that this was an important factor to bear in mind when assessing their value and meaning. Mach was very suspicious of any model that could not be tested in at least an indirect fashion. Because they could not be observed, he was forced to reject the theory of atoms (which was in his day quite inaccurate, but became less crude towards the end of his life) as being merely a hypothesis that had got out of hand. He was considered quite eccentric by many of his colleagues for whom atomism was an exciting development.

However, it subsequently became increasingly difficult to explain atoms as concrete objects, and theoretical physicists turned to mathematical and statistical treatments of the energies and positions of atomic particles to obtain more valid descriptions of the atom; Mach can, therefore, be said to be vindicated in his approach and his views did in fact aid the development of quantum mechanics.

One of Mach's most important books was *Die Mechanik* (1863). This gave rise to an enduring debate on Mach's principle, which states that a body could have no inertia in a universe devoid of all other mass as inertia depends on the reciprocal interaction of bodies, however distant. This principle influenced Einstein who tried to find a mathematical formulation to describe it, and it played a role in Einstein's thinking that culminated in his explanation of gravity in the general theory of relativity.

Mach was greatly displeased to find that he was being hailed as a predecessor of relativity, a model he rejected. He intended to write a book criticizing Einstein's theory, but died before this was possible.

Mach postulated that all knowledge is mediated by perception, and believed that the greatest scientific advances would only arise through a deeper understanding of this process. His stubborn scepticism forced him into a somewhat isolated position, but he was subsequently respected by scientists as great as Einstein. Mach is remembered as a scientist skilled not only at experimental design, execution, and interpretation but also at thinking about the wider implications of his work – a rare quality.

Further Reading

Blackmore, John (ed), *Ernst Mach, A Deeper Look: Documents and New Perspectives*, Boston Studies in the Philosophy of Science series, Kluwer Academic, 1992, v 143.

Blackmore, John T, *Ernst Mach: His Work, Life, and Influence*, University of California Press, 1972.

Bradley, John, *Mach's Philosophy of Science*, Athlone Press, 1971.

Cohen, Robert Sonné and Seeger, Raymond John, *Ernst Mach: Physicist and Philosopher*, Synthese Library series; Boston Studies in the Philosophy of Science series, Reidel, 1970, v 6.

Maclaurin, Colin (1698–1746) Scottish mathematician who first presented the correct theory for distinguishing between the maximum and minimum values of a function and who played a leading part in establishing the hegemony of the Newtonian calculus in 18th-century Britain.

Maclaurin was born in Kilmoden in February 1698. His father died when he was six weeks old and his mother before he was ten, and he was raised by his uncle, the incumbent in the parish of Kilfinnan, in Argyllshire. In 1709 he entered the University of Glasgow to study divinity, but within a year – influenced largely by Robert Simson, the professor of mathematics – he abandoned divinity for mathematics. In 1713 he presented a paper entitled 'On the power of gravity' and received his MA. Four years later, aged 19, he was appointed professor of mathematics at the Marischal College of Aberdeen.

On a visit to London during the vacation in 1719 Maclaurin met Isaac ◊Newton and was elected to the Royal Academy. He visited Newton again in 1721 and a year later left Aberdeen, without official leave, to become travelling tutor to the eldest son of the English diplomat Lord Polwarth. The next three years were spent chiefly in France and Maclaurin's paper on 'The percussion of bodies' (later included in substance in his treatise on fluxions) won him a prize from the French Academy of Sciences. When his pupil died in the autumn of 1724 Maclaurin returned to Scotland, but having forfeited the goodwill of his colleagues at Aberdeen, moved to Edinburgh. Thanks to the kindness of Newton, who wrote a letter on his behalf and promised to provide £20 annually towards the stipend, he was appointed deputy professor of mathematics at the university there. A few months later he succeeded to the chair.

Although Maclaurin's chief work for the next 20 years was on fluxions, he was a popular lecturer on many subjects and won the admiration of Edinburgh society for his public lectures and demonstrations in experimental physics and astronomy. He also wrote a paper on the gravitational theory of tides, which won a prize in 1740 from the French Academy. In 1745, during the Jacobite rebellion, he organized the defence of Edinburgh, and the exertions and exposure to cold that the effort entailed ruined his health. He died of oedema at Edinburgh on 14 June 1746.

Maclaurin's reputation rests on his great *Treatise of Fluxions,* published in 1742. It was an attempt to prove Newton's doctrine of prime and ultimate ratios and to provide a geometrical framework to support Newton's fluxional calculus. Indeed, so highly praised and so influential was the treatise, that it may be accounted, one of the major contributions to the ascendancy of Newtonian mathematics that cut Britain off from developments on the continent and left it to the continental mathematicians, for the next three generations, to make the running in the establishment of those methods of analysis that are the foundation of modern mathematical analysis.

The treatise did also include, however, important solutions in geometry and in the theory of attractions. It contained Maclaurin's development of his paper on the gravitational influence on tides, and proved that an ellipsoid of evolution is formed whenever a homogeneous fluid mass under the action of gravity revolves uniformly about an axis. The treatise also included the method of defining the maximum and minimum points on a curve.

The specific theorem for which Maclaurin is most famous, and which is named after him, is a special case of the Taylor theorem. It can be used to find the series for functions such as $\log_e$, $(1 + x)$, e^x, $\sin x$, $\cos x$, $\tan x$, and so on, where e is the base of natural logarithms. The theorem, however, is of minor significance in the history of mathematics. Maclaurin's real distinction lies in being the first to publish a logical and systematic exposition of the methods and principles of Newtonian mathematics.

McNaught, William (1813–1881)

Scottish mechanical engineer who invented the compound steam engine. This type of engine extracts the maximum energy from the hot steam by effectively using it twice – once in a high-pressure cylinder (or cylinders) and then, when exhausted from this, in a second low-pressure cylinder.

He was born in Paisley on 29 May 1813, the son of an engineer. He was apprenticed at the age of 14 and at 19 went to India to manage a mill there. He returned three years later to join his father in manufacturing steam engines. The evolution of the steam engine had been taking place for nearly a hundred years when McNaught developed his method of compounding at his Glasgow works in 1845. The technique became known as 'McNaughting', and was to prove to be a valuable energy-saving system for many years to come. The firm of J and W McNaught was eventually established in 1860, and in 1862 acquired premises at St George's Foundry, Rochdale, Lancashire, where they set about manufacturing small steam engines. Later the business branched out into the construction of larger types and moved to a bigger building, where it remained in operation until 1914. William died in Manchester on 8 January 1881.

In all the McNaughts were responsible for making of some 95 engines, many of which were for used in the northern textile industry. At least two of the engines have been preserved as fine examples of their type, one at the Glasgow Kelvingrove Museum and the other at the Bradford Industrial Museum.

The forerunner of the steam engine was invented by Thomas ◊Savery, an English military engineer, in 1698. The idea was taken up in 1712 by Thomas ◊Newcomen, a blacksmith, and became known as an atmospheric engine. But the first real 'steam engine' is credited to James ◊Watt, a Scottish instrumentmaker, in 1765. Watt unfortunately met with various technical problems after his initial success and, faced by lack of resources, was about to give up when he met Matthew ◊Boulton. Together they formed the partnership of Boulton and Watt and were concerned with the making of more than 500 engines, which supplied power to all manner of equipment during the crucial years of the Industrial Revolution.

Many steam engines were used to power the textile mills of the cotton and wool trade in the north of England. By 1845, the majority of these mills found that even by the introduction of higher steam pressures, their engines (most of which were of the Boulton and Watt design) could no longer keep up with the increasing demand for more power. This meant that the mill owners faced the costly business of replacing the engines, but naturally they were reluctant to do so. It was at this point that McNaught supplied a very acceptable answer, by offering a conversion to compound action.

His conversion consisted of a high-pressure cylinder exhausting into the original low-pressure cylinder. The new cylinder was connected to the opposite end of the 'beam', halfway between its pivot and the connecting-rod end, making it necessary for the stroke to be shorter than on the original cylinder. Three types of new engine were to emerge using McNaught's principle. The first used cylinders mounted side by side, the second had cylinders in a line (a tandem compound), and the third and rarer type had the high-pressure cylinder enclosed by the low-pressure one. As a measure of the success of the McNaught's design, the last beam engine made for use in a mill in 1904 was partly based on his principles. It can be said, therefore, that he was responsible for a vast and enduring improvement in the performance of the factory 'steam giants'.

Magendie, François (1783–1855) French doctor who pioneered modern experimental physiology.

Born in Bordeaux on 6 October 1783, Magendie graduated in medicine in Paris in 1808, subsequently practising and teaching medicine in Paris, and becoming physician to the Hôtel Dieu. Elected a member of the Académie des Sciences in 1821, he became its president in 1837. In 1831, he was appointed professor of anatomy at the Collège de France. Magendie died in Sannois on 7 October 1855.

He was a distinguished pioneer of scientific pharmacology. Using extensive vivisection and a certain amount of self-experimentation, he conducted trials on plant poisons, deploying animals to track precise physiological effects. He demonstrated that the stomach's role in vomiting was essentially passive, and analysed emetics. Through such researches, he helped to introduce into medicine the range of plant-derived compounds now known as alkaloids, many of which possess outstanding pharmacological properties.

Magendie demonstrated the medicinal uses of strychnine (derived from the Indian vomit nut), morphine and codeine (derived from opium), and quinine (obtained from cinchona bark).

Magendie's studies were remarkably comprehensive. He investigated the role of proteins in human diet; he was interested in olfaction; and he studied the white blood cells. He worked protractedly on the nerves of the skull – a canal leading from the fourth ventricle is now known as the 'foramen of Magendie'. His demonstration of the separate pathways of the spinal nerves extended the findings of Pierre Flourens and Charles ◊Bell. His numerous works include the *Elements of Physiology* (1816–17). Magendie's style of investigation avoided speculation and stuck to data.

He has a good claim to be called the founder of experimental physiology.

Maiman, Theodore Harold (1927–   ) US physicist who is best known for constructing, in 1960, the first working laser.

Maiman was born in Los Angeles on 11 July 1927, the son of an electrical engineer. After a period of military service 1945–46 in the navy, he studied engineering and physics at Columbia University, obtaining his BS degree in 1949. He then moved to Stanford University to do postgraduate work, gaining his MS in electrical engineering in 1951 and his PhD in physics in 1955. From 1955 to 1961 – the period in which he built the first laser – he worked at the Hughes Research Laboratories. In 1962 he founded his first company, the Korad Corporation (of which he was the president until 1968), which became a leading developer and manufacturer of lasers. In 1968 he founded Maiman Associates, a laser and optics consultancy, and four years later he cofounded the Laser Video Corporation, of which he was vice president until 1975. In that year he joined the TRW Electronics Company, Los Angeles, as director of advanced technology.

On moving to the Hughes Research Laboratories in 1955, Maiman began working on the maser, the first working model of which had been built in 1953 by Charles ◊Townes. Maiman made a number of design improvements that increased the practicability of the solid-state maser, then set out to develop an optical maser, or laser (an acronym for *light amplification by stimulated emission of radiation*). Although Townes and Arthur Schawlow (1921–1999) published a paper in which they demonstrated the theoretical possibility of constructing a laser and started to build one themselves, it was Maiman who actually constructed the first working laser in 1960. His laser consisted of a cylindrical, synthetic ruby crystal with parallel, mirror-coated ends, the mirror coating at one end being semi-transparent to allow the emission of the laser beam. A 'flash lamp' provided a burst of intense white light, part of which was absorbed by the chromium atoms in the ruby, which, as a result, were stimulated to emit noncoherent red light. This red light was then reflected back and forth by the mirrored ends of the ruby until eventually some of the light emerged through the semi-transparent end as an intense beam of coherent, monochromatic red light – laser light. Maiman's apparatus produced pulses of laser light; the first continuous-beam laser was made in 1961 by Ali Javan at the Bell Telephone Laboratories.

Since its original development, numerous improvements have been made to the laser and, using materials other than synthetic ruby (gases, for example), it is now possible to generate laser light of almost any frequency; even tunable lasers have been constructed. Moreover, the laser has found many practical applications – as a 'light scalpel' in microsurgery, and in astronomy, spectroscopy, holography (a type of three-dimensional photography), and communications, to give but a few examples.

Malpighi, Marcello (1628–1694) Italian physician who discovered, among other things, blood capillaries, and pioneered the use of the microscope in the study of tissues.

Malpighi was born in Crevalcore, Italy, on 10 March 1628. He attended the University of Bologna 1646–53 and graduated as doctor of medicine and philosophy. He first lectured in logic at Bologna, and then accepted the chair in theoretical medicine at the University of Pisa in 1656. There he met and befriended the mathematician Giovanni Borelli. Malpighi found that the climate in Pisa did not suit his health and he returned to Bologna after three years, to lecture in theoretical and practical medicine. In 1662 he took up the offer of the chair in medicine at the University of Messina, but four years later was back in Bologna. In 1667 the Royal Society invited him to submit his research findings to them and made him an honorary member – the first Italian to be thus elected – and also supervised the printing of his later works. In 1691 Malpighi moved to Rome and retired there as chief physician to Pope Innocent XII. He died in Rome on 30 November 1694.

In Malpighi's time the microscope was a new invention and he became absorbed in using it to study animal and insect tissue, as did Anton van ◊Leeuwenhoek. One of Malpighi's early investigations, in 1661, concerned the lungs of a frog. These organs were previously thought to have been fleshy structures, but Malpighi found them to consist of thin membranes containing fine blood vessels covering vast numbers of small air sacs. This discovery made it easier to explain how air (oxygen) seeps from the lungs to the blood vessels and is carried around the body. Malpighi traced the network of capillaries and found that they provide the means of blood travelling from the small arteries to the small veins. These findings filled the gap in the theory of blood circulation proposed by William ◊Harvey.

Malpighi also investigated the anatomy of insects and found the tracheae, the branching tubes that open to the outside in the abdomen and supply the insect with oxygen for respiration. Turning to the dissection of plants, Malpighi found what he took to be tracheae in the stem – long tubes with rings of thickening. In fact he was looking at young vessels in the xylem. He also discovered the stomata in leaves but had no idea of their function.

Malpighi included the various structures and organs of the human body in his examinations. He indentified the sensory receptors (papillae) of the tongue, which he thought could be nerve endings. He also investigated the spinal cord and nerves and found them to be composed of the same fibres, but did not put forward a correct theory of their function. He proved that bile was uniform in colour, not yellow and black (as had been believed), and also indentified the urinary tubules in the kidney.

Chick embryos also fascinated Malpighi and in his microscope studies he recorded their neural folds and neural tube, the aortic arches, the optic vesicles, and feather follicles.

Malpighi was a pioneer in the field of microscopy, and studied such a wide range of material that the curiosity of many scientists was aroused. Their combined efforts laid the foundations for further studies in a number of directions including histology, embryology, and the anatomy of organisms until then too small to observe.

Malthus, Thomas Robert (1766–1834) English economist who made the first serious study of human population trends, although his views of the future of the human race enraged many thinkers of his day.

Malthus was born near Dorking, Surrey, on or about 14 February 1766. He went to Cambridge University, was ordained in 1788, and in 1796 became a curate in Albury, Surrey. In 1805 he was invited to accept a professorial post at Haileybury College, where he became professor of history and political economy. During this time Malthus produced his major books on economics: *An Inquiry into the Nature and Progress of Rent* (1815) and *Principles of Political Economy* (1820). His work was acknowledged by many foreign academies, and he became a fellow of the Royal Society in 1819. He died near Bath, Somerset (now Avon), on 23 December 1834.

Malthus's most controversial work was *An Essay on the Principle of Population*, which was published anonymously in 1798. In it he set out his reasons for believing that the human population of the world will increase at such a rate that it will eventually outstrip the Earth's resources. He postulated, that the situation will ultimately become resolved as the numbers are whittled away by starvation and disease, or war. In a later revision of the work Malthus conceded that moral constraints on sexual intercourse and marriage could stabilize population growth.

Malthus's theories brought a storm of protest at the time, which only slightly abated with publication of the revised work. Now it is accepted that Malthus was probably correct up to a point. Populations throughout the plant and animal kingdoms also tend to increase faster than the resources to support them until some check builds up sufficiently. After reading Malthus's work, Charles ◊Darwin postulated that the transformation or extinction of species depends on their response (a function of variability) to changing environmental factors.

Further Reading

Dupaquier, J and Fauve-Chamoux, A, *Malthus Past and Present*, Advances in Historical Demography series, Academic Press, 1983.

Gilbert, Geoffrey, *Malthus: Critical Responses*, Routledge, 1997.

Petersen, William, *Malthus: Founder of Modern Demography*, Transaction Publishers, 1998.

Raphael, D D; Winch, Donald; and Skidelsky, Robert, *Great Economists: Smith, Malthus, Keynes*, Past Masters series, Oxford University Press, 1997.

Winch, Donald, *Malthus*, Past Masters series, Oxford University Press, 1987.

Wood, John C (ed), *Thomas Robert Malthus: Critical Assessments*, Critical Assessments of Leading Economists series, Routledge, 1993, v 14.

Malus, Etienne Louis (1775–1812) French physicist who discovered polarized light. He found that light is not only polarized on passing through a double-refracting crystal but also on reflection from a surface.

Malus was born in Paris on 23 June 1775. He received private instruction in the classics and mathematics until the age of 18. After a year in military service, he became one of the first students to enter the Ecole Polytechnique in Paris. He studied there for only two years without receiving any diplomas, and then became a sublieutenant in the engineers' corps in 1796. Malus was sent on Napoleon's campaign in Egypt and Syria in 1798, but contracted a serious infection and was sent home to Marseille in 1801. He then undertook postings to Lille in 1802, Anvers in 1804, and Strasbourg in 1806. During this period, Malus was able to resume his scientific activities. He

became an examiner for the Ecole Polytechnique in geometry, analysis, and physics, which caused him to make frequent visits to Paris. This allowed him to renew his contacts with many other scientists.

Malus was recalled to Paris permanently in 1808, and in 1810 was elevated to the rank of major. His scientific career reached its peak in the same year with the award of a prize from the Institut de France and his election to its first class. In addition Malus was awarded the Rumford Medal by the Royal Society in 1811. However, his health had been seriously undermined by the illness he suffered abroad and he died of tuberculosis in Paris on 23 February 1812 at the early age of 37.

Malus's research in the field of optics may be traced as far back as his period in Egypt under Napoleon, when he found the time to work on the nature of light. His first important publication appeared in 1807. It was entitled *Traité d'optique,* and was notable for its mathematical style. In it he put forward the equation that was later known as the Malus theorem, which described some of the differences in the properties of light following a second reflection or refraction as distinct from its properties following the first reflection or refraction. This theorem was given a full mathematical proof by William Rowan ◊Hamilton in 1824, who also extended the work.

Malus began doing experiments on double refraction in 1807. This phenomenon, which was first found in 1669 by Erasmus Bartholin (1625–1698), causes a light beam to split in two on passing through Iceland spar and certain other crystals. The Institut de France offered a prize in 1808 for an experimental and theoretical explanation of double refraction, and this encouraged Malus to continue his work in this area. Christiaan ◊Huygens had found empirical laws to describe double refraction, but they were based on the assumption that light is wavelike in character, a theory that was not popular with those scientists who held with Isaac ◊Newton's belief in its particulate nature. However, Malus's results confirmed Huygens's laws, and in 1810 he was awarded the Institut de France's prize for his experiments and also for his theoretical deduction of the laws. The method he used in his analysis was the same as that which Pierre ◊Laplace had applied to the same problem a year previously.

A more important result of Malus's investigations was announced soon after its discovery in 1808. Malus held a piece of Iceland spar up to some light reflecting off the windows of the Luxembourg Palace in Paris. To his surprise, the light beam emanating from the crystal was single, not double. He further noted that of the two beams that normally emerge from the crystal, only one was reflected from a water surface if the crystal was held at a certain angle. The other passed into the water and was refracted. If the crystal was turned perpendicular, the second beam was reflected and the first refracted. The effect was most intense at an angle of reflection that varied from one medium to another. Malus concluded that light reflected from a surface behaves in the same way as the beams of light emerging after double refraction in a crystal. Although he had confirmed Huygens's laws of double refraction, Malus still believed that light consisted of particles which have sides or poles, and he thought that in the two refracted beams, the particles were lined up in planes perpendicular to each other. He described the light as being 'polarized' in perpendicular directions and thus concluded that light is also polarized on reflection from surfaces. He found too that the reflected ray is polarized in one plane while the refracted ray that passes into the surface is polarized in the perpendicular plane. Malus also discovered the law of polarization that relates the intensity of the polarized beam to the angle of reflection.

Malus's work on polarization was continued by David ◊Brewster, Jean Biot (1774–1862), and François ◊Arago after his untimely death. His explanation of polarization was rationalized by Augustin ◊Fresnel, who, in 1821, concluded that light exists as transverse waves.

Malus was a talented scientist who made a major discovery but whose research was curbed by his devotion to his military duties and by his poor health and early death.

Mandelbrot, Benoit B (1924–   ) Polish-born French mathematician who coined the term 'fractal' to describe geometrical figures in which an identical motif repeats itself on an ever-diminishing scale. The concept is associated with chaos theory. Another way of describing a fractal is as a curve or surface generated by the repeated subdivision of a mathematical pattern.

He was born in Warsaw, Poland, on 20 November 1924, and was educated at the Ecole Polytechnique, Paris, graduating in 1947. He went on to the California Institute of Technology, receiving an MS in 1948 and returned to Paris where he was awarded his PhD from the Sorbonne in 1952. Between 1949 and 1957 he was a staff member at the Centre National de la Recherche Scientifique, Paris, during which time he spent a year at the Institute of Advanced Study, New Jersey 1953–54 and two years at the University of Geneva as assistant professor of mathematics 1955–57. Mandelbrot then went as junior professor of applied mathematics to Lille University and of mathematical analysis at the Ecole Polytechnique, Paris. In 1958 he was appointed a research staff member at the IBM Thomas J Watson

Research Centre in New York and was made an IBM fellow in 1974. In 1987 he became the Abraham Robinson Professor of Mathematical Sciences at Yale University, New Haven.

Mandelbrot's research has provided mathematical theories for erratic chance phenomena and self-similarity methods in probability. He has also carried out research on sporadic processes, thermodynamics, natural languages, astronomy, geomorphology, computer art and graphics, fractals, and the fractal geometry of nature. His books include *Logique, langage et théorie de l'information* (1957; with L Apostel and A Morf), *Fractals: Form, Chance, and Dimension* (1977), and *The Fractal Geometry of Nature* (1982); he has also published numerous scientific papers, and is on the editorial boards of several journals. For his research, Mandelbrot has received honorary degrees from several universities and numerous awards and medals, including that of Chevalier of the Legion of Honour in 1989.

Mannesman, Reinhard (1856–1922) German iron-founder who invented a method of making seamless steel tubes.

Mannesman was born on 13 May 1856 in Remscheid. Both he and his brother Max were iron-masters and, like other inventors in the second half of the 19th century, they increasingly turned their attentions from machine tools to heavy equipment for the production of metals. They perfected a way of making a seamless tube, which was much more accurate than the welded tube. Reinhard died in Remscheid on 22 February 1922. The idea behind the invention had been conceived by their father in 1860, while he was working at Remscheid.

The Mannesman process, as it was later to be called, involved the passing of a furnace-heated bar between two rotating rolls. Because of their geometrical configuration, the rolls drew the bar forward and at the same time produced tensions in the hot metal that caused it to tear apart at the centre. A stationary, pointed mandrel caused the ingot of metal to open out and form a tube. The tubes were later forged to size – again on mandrels in rolling mills with grooved rolls that varied in diameter like cams. Between the compression phases, in which the tube is advanced by the rolls, the activating mechanism rotates and then partially returns the tubes. Thus the process is intermittent, taking place in a series of short steps. This later technique involved the tube stock being fed to pilger mills from the Mannesman machines; thus the process was called pilgering.

The first Mannesman plant and pilger mills were installed in Swansea, south Wales, in 1887 and operated by the Landore Siemens Steel Company of Swansea. The plant consisted of six Mannesman machines, the largest being capable of piercing solid billets of up to 25 cm/10 in in diameter. In 1891 the process was granted a patent. It was this invention that most impressed the US inventor Thomas ◊Edison during his visit to the World Exhibition in Chicago in 1893.

The Landore Siemens Steel Company remained the major manufacturer of seamless steel tubes until near the end of the 19th century. Then a plant designed and created at Youngstown, Ohio, took over as the most important manufacturer in the world.

Manson, Patrick (1844–1922) Scottish physician who showed that insects are responsible for the spread of diseases like elephantiasis and malaria.

Born at Old Meldrum, Aberdeenshire, on 3 October 1844, the son of a bank manager, Manson qualified in medicine at Aberdeen in 1865. He travelled to eastern Asia, becoming medical officer in Formosa (now Taiwan), and later moving to Hong Kong. In all, he worked in the region for 23 years, being – among other things – active in the introduction of vaccination. Manson addressed himself to the problems of tropical diseases; focusing, after 1876, on filarial infection in humans. Having gained a clear idea of the life history of the invading parasite, he correctly conjectured that the disease was transmitted by an insect, a common brown mosquito, setting out his views of the crucial importance of the insect vector in *The Filaria Sanguinis Hominis and Certain New Forms of Parasitic Diseases* (1883). Manson went on to study other parasitic infections, for instance, the fluke parasite, ringworm, and Guinea worm. But he is best remembered for his part in the discovery of the life history of the malarial parasite – work begun in the Far East and continued after his return to the UK. By analogy with his work on filaria, he developed in 1894 the thesis that malaria was also spread by a mosquito. Manson and Ronald ◊Ross between them developed the work that proved this (later they wrangled fiercely). It became axiomatic for Manson that the key to understanding and controlling many tropical diseases involved an arthropod vector that was indispensable as a host to the life cycle of the parasite.

After his return to the UK in 1892, Manson delivered at the Seaman's Hospital Society in London's dockland the first courses of lectures in tropical medicine given in England. It was largely through his initiatives, supported by Joseph Chamberlain at the Colonial Office, that the London School of Tropical Medicine was founded in 1899; he taught there till his retirement in 1914. He was knighted in 1903 and died in London on 9 April 1922.

Marconi, Guglielmo (1874–1937) Italian electrical engineer who saw the possiblity of using radio waves – long-wavelength electromagnetic radiation – for the

Marconi Italian electrical engineer Guglielmo Marconi who pioneered the invention of the radio. His first transmissions were made from the roof of the General Post Office in London, and the first transatlantic signals were sent in 1901 from Cornwall, England, to Newfoundland, Canada. *Mary Evans Picture Library*

transmission of information. He was the first to put such a service into operation on a commercial scale, and was responsible for many of the developments that made radio and telegraph services into major industries.

Marconi was born in Bologna into a wealthy family on 25 April 1874. His education consisted largely of private tutoring, although he was sent for a brief period to the Technical Institute in Livorno where he received instruction in physics. He studied under a number of prominent Italian professors but never enrolled for a university course.

His studies of radio transmission began on his father's estate in the 1890s. By 1897 he had established a commercial enterprise in London, based on developments from his early work. He became famous in 1901 when he succeeded in sending a transatlantic coded message.

In 1909 he was awarded, jointly with Karl Ferdinand ◊Braun, the Nobel Prize for Physics, and was honoured by the receipt of the Albert Medal from the Royal Society of Arts in 1929. He was also being made a Knight Grand Cross of the Royal Victorian Order, and was given the title of Marchese by the Italian government. From 1921 he lived aboard his yacht *Elettra*, which served as a home, laboratory, and receiving station. Marconi was given a state funeral after his death in Rome on 20 July 1937.

Marconi's researches began in 1894, the year of Heinrich ◊Hertz's death, when he read a paper on the possible technical applications of the electromagnetic waves discovered by Hertz in 1886. Marconi realized that the waves could be used in signalling and began experiments with Augusto Righi of the University of Bologna to determine how far the waves would travel.

Marconi based his apparatus on that used by Hertz, but used a coherer to detect the waves. (The coherer was designed to convert the radio waves into electric current.) Marconi improved Hertz's design by earthing the transmitter and receiver, and found that an insulated aerial enabled him to increase the distance of transmission. During 1895 he slowly increased the distance over which he was able to transmit a signal, first from the house into the garden and eventually to about 2.5 km/1.5 mi – the length of the family estate.

The Italian government was not interested in the device, so Marconi travelled to London, where he enlisted the help of relatives to enable him to obtain a patent and to introduce his discovery to the British government. He obtained his patent in June 1896 for the use of waves similar to those discovered by Hertz but of longer wavelength, for the purpose of wireless telegraphy. Marconi enabled Queen Victoria to send a message to the Prince of Wales aboard the royal yacht, and increased his transmission distance to 15 km/9 mi, then to 30 km/18 mi. The first commercial 'Marconigram' was sent by Lord ◊Kelvin.

The Wireless Telegraph Company was founded in London in 1897, and later became the Marconi Wireless Telegraph Company Ltd in Chelmsford in 1900. In 1899 Marconi went to the USA and sent reports about the presidential election taking place there. On 12 December 1901, after many hold-ups, Marconi succeeded in sending a radio signal in Morse across the Atlantic Ocean from Pondhu in Cornwall to St Johns in Newfoundland, Canada.

Marconi became increasingly involved with the management of his companies from 1902, but he attracted many distinguished scientists to work with him. Some of the most important developments were the magnetic detector in 1902, horizontal direction telegraphy in 1905, and the continuous wave system in 1912.

During World War I Marconi worked on the development of very short wavelength beams, which could be used for many purposes including enabling a pilot to fly an aircraft 'blind'. After the war these short wavelength beams contributed to communication over long distances. In 1932 Marconi discovered that he could detect microwave radiation – that is, waves with very high frequencies. These wavelengths were soon to form the basis of radar.

Further Reading

Baker, W J, *History of the Marconi Company 1874–1965,* Routledge, 1998.

Birch, Beverley, *Marconi's Battle for Radio,* Science Stories series, Barron's Educational Series, Inc, 1996.

Masini, Giancarlo, *Marconi,* Marsilio Publishers, 1998.

Tedeschi, Enrico, *Guglielmo Marconi in London,* Hove Books, 1998.

Margulis, Lynn (1938–) US biologist who made a major contribution to microbial evolution and organelle heredity through the study of serial endosymbiosis (one cell living beneficially within another) and has had a long collaboration with English scientist, James ◊Lovelock, the originator of the Gaia hypothesis. She is well known as a popularizer of science and a spokeswoman on environmental issues.

Born in Chicago, Illinois, on 5 March 1938, Margulis was educated at the University of Chicago graduating in 1957 with an AB in Liberal Arts. She gained an MS from the University of Wisconsin in 1960, and a PhD from Berkeley, California in 1963. From 1966 to 1988 she taught and did research at Boston University before becoming Distinguished University Professor in the botany department at the University of Massachusetts, Amherst (UMASS). In 1997 she transferred to the department of geosciences at UMASS, as she feels academically happiest amongst geologists. Married twice – first to astronomer Carl Sagan, then to T N Margulis, she has a daughter and three sons.

Margulis's contribution to microbial evolution was in the introduction of the serial endosymbiosis theory in which she noted the resemblance of mitochondria in cells to certain primitive bacteria and suggested that a unique cooperation took place between them at an early stage of the evolution of life and that eukaryotic cells (cells with nuclei) evolved through the symbiotic relationships of prokaryotes (cells without nuclei) which ultimately evolved into animal cells. She published her findings in *Origin of Eukaryotic Cells* (1970). It is now commonly acknowledged that the components of cells – such as chloroplasts and mitochondria – were once separate organisms and that they evolved into the eukaryotic cells over time. Her notion of the interdependency of all living things led to a collaboration with Lovelock, whose Gaia hypothesis, first proposed in his book *Gaia* (1979), considers the Earth as a single living self-sustaining entity, or ecosystem, to which life provides a feedback system, leading to a stabilization in temperature, atmospheric chemistry, and the other factors necessary to sustain itself.

Margulis has been the recipient of numerous honours and awards. She held a Sherman Fairchild Fellowship in the geological and planetary sciences department at the California Institute of Technology in 1977. From 1977 to 1980 she was chair of the National Academy of Science's Space Science Board Committee on Planetary Biology and Chemical Evolution which helped to develop research strategies for NASA. She was the recipient a Guggenheim Fellowship in 1979 for her work on microbial mats and was elected to the membership of the US National Academy of Sciences in 1983. She was awarded the 1999 Sigma Xi William Proctor Prize for Scientific Achievement in Minneapolis, an annual award made to scientists who have made outstanding contributions to research and have demonstrated their ability to communicate the significance of their work to scientists in other disciplines.

Margulis's books cover a wide range of topics and include *Origins of Life* (1970) and work undertaken with her son, Dorion Sagan, including *Microcosmos: Four Billion Years of Evolution from our Microbial Ancestors* and *Slanted Truths: Essays on Gaia Symbiosis and Evolution*. As well as her academic work, Margulis is a vigorous popularizer of science and has contributed to popular magazines, educational journals, and produced a number of videos. She has worked on the development of science-teaching materials from elementary school to postgraduate level and continues teaching courses mostly to advanced undergraduates and postgraduates.

Margulis's later research includes the study of Archaean and Proterozoic evolution, and concerns closure of the serial endosymbiotic theory of the origin of cells, the study of life cycles and sediment impact of the inhabitants of microbial mats, and the theory of Lovelock's Gaia hypothesis.

Markov, Andrei Andreevich (1856–1922) Russian mathematician, famous for his work on the probability calculus and for the Markov chains.

Markov was born into the minor gentry class at Ryazan on 14 June 1856, a somewhat sickly child who was dependent upon crutches until the age of ten. He studied mathematics at the University of St Petersburg, where he was fortunate to have Pafnuty Tchebychev as a teacher 1874–78. His BA dissertation of 1878, on the integration of differential equations by means of continued fractions (a special interest of Tchebychev), was awarded a gold medal. He began to tutor at the university in 1880 and four years later was awarded a doctorate for his thesis on continued fractions and the problem of moments.

For the next 25 years Markov continued his research and teaching at St Petersburg, where he became an extraordinary professor at the age of 30 and a full professor in 1893. At the same time he became involved in liberal political movements and perhaps only his academic eminence saved him from punitive government measures when he protested against the tsar's refusal to accept Maxim Gorky's election to the St Petersburg Academy in 1902. He also refused to accept tsarist decorations and in 1907 renounced his membership of the electorate when the government dissolved the fledgling representative Duma, or parliament. In the harsh winter famine months of 1917 he worked, at his own request and without pay, teaching mathematics in a secondary school in Zaraisk, deep in the Russian interior. Shortly afterwards his health began to fail, and he died in St Petersburg (then named Petrograd) on 20 May 1922.

Markov's early work was devoted primarily to number theory – continued fractions, approximation theory, differential equations, and integration in elementary equations – and to the problem of moments and probability theory. Throughout he used the method of continued fractions, most notably applying it to evaluate as precisely as possible the upper and lower boundaries of quantities such as quadratic forms.

In the latter 1890s he began to concentrate upon the probability calculus. During the middle years of the century there had been considerable development of the law of large numbers and of the central limit theorem invented by Pierre ◊Laplace and Abraham ◊de Moivre. But there were still no proofs with satisfactorily wide assumptions; nor had the limits of their applicability been discovered. Together, Tchebychev, Alexander Lyapunov (1857–1918), and Markov explored these problems far enough to bring about what amounted to the modernization of probability theory. Tchebychev's argument was extended by Markov in a paper of 1898 entitled 'The law of large numbers and the method of least squares' (written, in fact, as a series of letters to Alexander Vassilyev). Two years later he published his book *Probability Calculus*, which was based on the method of moments. Markov's method was less flexible than Lyapunov's, who a year later published his proof of limit theorems using a method of characteristic functions; and although Markov attempted over the next eight years to establish the superiority of his method, and did succeed in proving Lyapunov's conclusions by means of it, the method of moments remains cumbersome, more complex, and less general than the method of characteristic functions.

The chief fruit of Markov's endeavours to justify his method was the discovery of the important sequence of random variables named after him, the Markov chains. Put in informal language, a Markov chain may be described as a chance process that possesses a special property, so that its future may be predicted from the present state of affairs just as accurately as if the whole of its past history were known. Markov seems to have believed that the only real examples of his chains were to be found in literary texts, and he illustrated his discovery by calculating the alteration of vowels and consonants in Pushkin's *Eugene Onegin*. Markov chains are now used, however, in the social sciences, in atomic physics, in quantum theory, and in genetics. They have proved to be his most valuable contribution to 20th-century thought.

Martin, Archer John Porter (1910–)

English biochemist who shared the 1952 Nobel Prize for Chemistry with his co-worker Richard ◊Synge for their development of paper chromatography.

Martin was born in London on 1 March 1910, the son of a doctor of medicine. He was educated at Bedford School and then went to Cambridge University, where he graduated in 1932 and gained his PhD three years later, having been influenced by J B S ◊Haldane. He worked at the Dunn Nutritional Laboratories for two years, leaving in 1938 to join the Wool Industries Research Association at Leeds. In 1946 he became head of the biochemistry division in the research department of the Boots Pure Drug Company in Nottingham, and he held this position until 1948 when he was appointed to the staff of the Medical Research Council. He worked first at the Lister Institute of Preventive Medicine and then at the National Institute for Medical Research, where he was head of the division of physical chemistry 1952–56 and chemical consultant 1956–59. He became director of the Abbotsbury Laboratory 1959–70, consultant to Wellcome Research Laboratories 1970–73, professor at the University of Sussex 1973–78, and invited professor of chemistry at the Ecole Polytechnique at Lausanne, Switzerland 1980–84.

In his first researches, at the Dunn Nutritional Laboratory, Martin investigated problems relating to vitamin E. After 1938, at Leeds, he was involved in a study of the felting of wool. The work for which he was to become famous began in 1941, when he and Synge began the development of partition chromatography for separating the components of complex mixtures (of amino acids). In their method a drop of the solution to be analysed is placed at one end of a strip of filter paper and allowed to dry. That end of the strip is then immersed in a solvent, which as it moves along the strip carries with it, at different rates, the various components of the mixture, which thus become separated and spread out along the strip of paper. Their positions are revealed by spraying the dried strip with a reagent that produces a colour change with the

components; Martin and Synge used ninhydrin to record the positions of amino acids. The 'developed' strip is called a chromatogram.

The technique combines two different principles, adsorption chromatography (devised by the Russian botanist Mikhail ◊Tswett in 1903 and later revived by Richard ◊Willstätter) and counter-current solvent extraction for partitioning components between solvents – hence the name partition chromatography. It also has the advantage of requiring only a small sample of material and has proved to be a powerful tool in analytical chemistry, particularly for complex biochemicals.

In 1953 Martin and A T James began working on gas chromatography, which separates chemical vapours by differential adsorption on a porous solid. The versatility of both techniques has been extended by using radioactive tracers in the mixture to be analysed, when the positions of components in the resulting chromatogram can be found by using a counter.

Martin, James (1893–1981)

Northern Irish aeronautical engineer whose pioneering work in the design and manufacture of ejection seats has saved the lives of thousands of military jet aircrew since 1949.

Martin was born on 11 September 1893 at Crossgar, County Down. The son of a farmer, he had designed, made, and sold various machines while still a teenager. He scorned conventional education, but by practical work and study he had become an accomplished engineer before the age of 20. In his early 20s he designed a three-wheeled enclosed car as a cheap runabout. Small oil engines and specialized vehicles were among his first products when he set up in business in Acton, London. In 1929 Martin established the works at Denham, Middlesex, that became his company's permanent home. His first aircraft, a two-seater monoplane, which had the engine mounted amidships, driving a propeller through an extension shaft, did not reach completion.

In the early 1930s he designed and built a small, cheap, two-seater monoplane that used an ingenious construction – round-section, thin-gauge steel tubing throughout. The design of this machine, Martin–Baker MB1, marked the start of the partnership between Martin and Captain Valentine Henry Baker, the company's chief test pilot. During the next ten years to 1944 Martin was to design three significant fighter aircraft, each of which could have been developed into an outstanding machine for the Royal Air Force (RAF) – but no orders were forthcoming.

Martin is remembered best for his devices that help to save the lives of aircrew. The first of these devices was a barrage-balloon cable cutter, designed before World War II, which was produced in large quantities and employed with great success by most RAF Bomber Command aircraft.

Martin's quick response to an urgent need during the Battle of Britain heralded his pioneering work on ejection seats. This was to make it possible to jettison the cockpit canopy of the Spitfire to improve the pilot's chances of escape by parachute. In 1943 increased aircraft speeds, and the prospect of even greater speeds with the jet engine, led to considerable interest in means for improving the chances of escape for aircrew.

Martin's first response was demonstrated in model form in 1944. Using a powerful spring and a swinging arm to lift the pilot from the aircraft, this scheme generated sufficient official interest to enable Martin to pursue the much more elegant solution of the seat and its occupant being forceably ejected from the aircraft by means of an explosive charge.

The first successful dummy ejections took place in May 1945 and Martin developed his seat until it reached the level of sophistication, reliability, and universal application that it has today. Most notable landmarks were the first live ejection on 24 July 1946, the first live ground-level ejection on 3 September 1955, ejection from an aircraft with rear-facing seats on 1 July 1960, and a zero-speed–zero-altitude ejection on 1 April 1961.

Martin was appointed a Commander of the British Empire in 1957 and knighted in 1965. He continued to develop the ejection seat for use at higher speeds, greater altitudes, vertical take-off, multiple crew escape, and underwater ejection.

When he died in January 1981 he was managing director and chief designer of the company he had founded. About 50,000 seats had been delivered and, in February 1983, the 5,000th life was saved.

Martin's MB2 fighter of 1938 had a performance as good as that of contemporary fighters. It could be produced quickly and cheaply, because of the simplicity of its structure and easy assembly – features not shared by the Spitfire. The MB5, developed at the war's end, attained the highest standards in piston-engined fighter aircraft. Despite the praise it attracted from fighter pilots, it is thought to have been viewed officially as 'decadent', and was never put into production.

Martin's development of the ejection seat was pioneering because there was no previous knowledge of the effects on the human body of violent acceleration. He experimented first with sandbags and then human volunteers, firing them up test rigs. So successful and significant was this work that the decision was taken to install Martin–Baker seats in new British military jet aircraft as early as June 1947. The experience from their service pointed the way for the numerous improvements, such as automatic separation of pilot from seat and automatic parachute deployment.

In the mid 1950s, when most US carrier-borne aircraft were fitted with US ejection seats, ejection at take-off was usually fatal. So convinced was the US Navy that the Martin–Baker seat would increase the chances of pilot survival that, against great opposition from politicians and industrialists, it took Martin and a team to the USA in August 1957 to demonstrate conclusively the efficiency of the ground-level ejection system.

Martin–Baker seats were then fitted retrospectively to the whole inventory of US carrier-borne aircraft. Similarly, Martin–Baker was called in to fit its seat to existing NATO aircraft, including the F-86 Sabre, RF Thunderstreak, and F-100 Super Sabre.

With Rolls-Royce, Martin–Baker's is one of the few British companies to leave its mark on the US aerospace industry. At the time of his death it was reckoned that about 35,000 ejection seats were in service with the air forces and navies of 50 countries.

Maskelyne, Nevil (1732–1811) English astronomer, physicist, and – like so many others of his time – priest. He was the founder of the *Nautical Almanac* and he became Astronomer Royal at the age of 32.

Maskelyne was born in London on 6 October 1732. Educated at Westminster School, he studied divinity at Trinity College, Cambridge, where he received his bachelor's degree in 1754. He was ordained a year later, but instead of taking up a living, he went to the Greenwich Observatory as an assistant to James ◊Bradley. He was awarded his master's degree by Trinity College in 1757 and elected a fellow of the college. In the following year he was made a fellow of the Royal Society, which sent him, with R Waddington, to the island of St Helena to observe the 1761 transit of Venus. Four years later he was appointed director of the Greenwich Observatory and (the fifth) Astronomer Royal, although he continued to carry out his clerical duties in such parishes as Shrawardine, Shropshire, and North Runcton, Norfolk. Awarded the Royal Society's Copley Medal in 1775, he received a doctorate in divinity from Cambridge University in 1777 and was elected to the French Academy of Sciences in 1802. He died in Greenwich on 9 February 1811.

It was probably his early interest in solar eclipses that led Maskelyne into his career as an astronomer. His first major project in observational astronomy was the excursion to St Helena, under the auspices of the Royal Society, in order to study the solar parallax during the 1761 transit of Venus and thereby determine accurately the distance of the Earth from the Sun. At the appropriate moment, however, the weather turned bad and, in any case, he had lost confidence in the instruments he had brought with him. (It was not until 1772 that Maskelyne perfected his technique for observing transits – by which time another transit of Venus had occurred, in 1769.) Nevertheless, on the sea journey to and from St Helena, he developed an interest in marine navigation by astronomical methods (an interest that was to colour most of what he later achieved), and spent a considerable amount of effort trying to devise a better means of determining longitude at sea.

Maskelyne's interests were perfectly represented by his foundation, in 1767, of the *Nautical Almanac*. This comprised a compendium of astronomical tables and navigational aids and included many of the results of Maskelyne's studies of the Sun, the Moon, the planets, and the stars. His observations of the proper motions of several of the brighter stars were used by William ◊Herschel to demonstrate the movement of the Sun, which until 1783 had been presumed stationary.

Maskelyne's experiment on plumb-line deflection in 1774 aroused great interest among fellow geodeticists, although it was one of many attempts to determine the gravitational constant, solve Isaac ◊Newton's gravitational equation, and thus deduce the density of the Earth. To measure the gravitational effect an isolated mountain might exert, he travelled to Mount Schiehallion in Perthshire, and determined the latitude both north and south of the mountain both by using a plumb line and by direct survey. He found that the mass of the mountain between the two points of measurement caused the plumb line to be deflected, so that the separation of the points was 27% greater than was found by direct geographical measurement. Making certain assumptions about the mass and volume of the mountain, Maskelyne deduced from the magnitude of the plumb line's deflection a gravitational constant and came to the conclusion that the Earth had a density of between 4.56 and 4.87 times that of water. This was reasonably close to the value now accepted (approximately 5.52 times that of water).

Maskelyne's work in astronomy contributed to a number of fields of study, but perhaps his most enduring contribution was the establishment of the *Nautical Almanac*.

Mästlin, Michael (1550–1631) German scholar, author, and teacher who was one of the first influential people to accept the theories of Polish astronomer Nicolaus ◊Copernicus, and to transmit them. One of Mästlin's pupils was Johannes ◊Kepler.

Mästlin was born on 30 September 1550 in Goppengin, Germany. He attended the University of Tübingen and gained both a bachelor's and a master's degree there before joining a theological course. While still a student Mästlin compiled astronomical tables and wrote learned essays that were read by influential scientists of the age; he also began to put together the

information for a popular textbook. His education completed, Mästlin became assistant to Apian, the professor of mathematics at Tübingen. When Apian went on extended leave in 1575, Mästlin took over his duties. But the arrangement proved unsatisfactory and after only a year he became a local pastor instead. In 1580, however, he was appointed professor of mathematics at Heidelberg and when, four years later, Apian was dismissed from Tübingen for refusing to sign the oath of Protestant allegiance, Mästlin was reinstated there. The religious oath did not present Mästlin with a problem: never a fervent believer, his religious views were compatible enough with those required for professorship. He had already advised Protestant governments against accepting the Gregorian calendar because it seemed to him a papal scheme to regain power over lost territories. Consequently, all of Mästlin's books and writings appeared on Pope Sixtus V's index of prohibited books in 1590.

Mästlin taught at Tübingen for 47 years, during which period he was elected rector of the College of Arts and Sciences no fewer than eight times. He remained at Tübingen until his death in 1631.

In 1573 Mästlin published an essay concerning the nova that had appeared the previous year. He had taken some care to establish the position of the nova, and its location in relation to known stars convinced him that the nova was a new star – which implied, contrary to traditional belief, that things could come into being in the spheres beyond the Moon. Mästlin's essay made ingenious use of relatively simple observations and it impressed his contemporary Tycho ◊Brahe enough for him to incorporate it into his own *Progymnasmata*.

Mästlin's great popular work, the *Epitome of Astronomy*, represented the fruits of his researches as a student. A general introduction to the subject for the layperson, it ran quickly through seven editions after its publication in 1582. Yet it propounded a severely traditional cosmology based on the ancient system of ◊Aristotle (because this was easier to teach) despite the fact that Mästlin's own research had convinced him that Aristotle was wrong.

Later, Mästlin was explicitly to argue against the ideas of Aristotle, on the basis of his own observations, not only of the 1572 nova, but also of the 1577 and 1580 comets. Traditionally it was supposed that comets were merely meteorological phenomena, existing between the Moon and the Earth. Observation of the comet of 1577, however, showed no perceptible parallax: changes in observational position should have resulted in a particular and apparent displacement of the comet. Together with other observations, this led Mästlin to the conclusion that the comet was located beyond the Moon, probably in the sphere of Venus. These conclusions, in turn, seemed to Mästlin to be better explained on the basis of Copernicus' cosmology of 1513 than on the basis of the one propounded by ◊Ptolemy in the 2nd century AD. Mästlin's subsequent expositions of the superiority of Copernican cosmology were delivered as lectures at Tübingen. Kepler attended these lectures as a young man, was deeply influenced by them, and, while Mästlin remained cautious in his acceptance, went on to embrace and develop the new cosmology quite fully. As a result the teacher–pupil relation between Mästlin and Kepler matured into a lifelong, affectionate friendship.

Masursky, Harold (1922–1990) US geologist who conducted research into the surface of the Moon and the other planets of the Solar System. From the early years of the US space programme, Masursky was a senior member of the team at the National Aeronautics and Space Administration (NASA), responsible for the surveying of lunar and planetary surfaces, particularly in regard to the choice of landing sites. He and his colleagues – it is a field in which teamwork is especially important – participated from the very first in the Ranger, Apollo, Viking, Pioneer, and Voyager programmes.

Masursky was born on 23 December 1922 at Fort Wayne, Indiana. He graduated from Yale University in 1943 and gained his master's degree in geology there in 1951. At the end of that year, he joined the US Geological Survey, working in its fuels branch in the search for petroleum. Eleven years later, still with the survey, he transferred to the branch for astrogeological studies and began work at NASA. He received four medals from NASA for exceptional scientific achievement, and in 1979 was made a member of the space-science advisory committee of NASA's advisory council. An associate editor of a popular astronomical journal, he also published more than a hundred technical papers and edited books for NASA on the Apollo missions.

As early as 1964, Masursky was a member of the *Ranger 9* site-selection programme and coordinated the *Ranger 8* and *9* science reports published a year later. His interest in the lunar surface led him, two years afterwards, to become a member of the Lunar Orbiter site-selection working group and of the Apollo group that monitored and guided the Moon landing. The results gained from *Apollo 8* and *10* about the chemical and geological composition of the Moon were studied by the lunar-science working group under Masursky's chairmanship. His work on *Apollo 14, 15, 16,* and *17* was soon followed by involvement with teams exploring Mars and Venus.

Masursky participated in the *Mariner 9* and Viking explorations of Mars in 1971 and 1975, respectively. He led the team that selected and monitored the observa-tions of Mars made by the Mariner orbital craft, then selected sites on Mars for the *Viking 1* and 2 landings. Contrary to expectation, their observations showed the existence of craters and very high mountains (Nix Olympia rising 27 km/17 mi above the mean surface level of Mars, compared with Mount Everest's 9 km/5.5 mi). A more surprising discovery concerned thousands of small channels on the planet's surface. These were not the 'canals' observed by Giovanni ◊Schiaparelli, but something new. They were mostly a few kilometres wide; themselves sinuous and twisting, they also had tributary systems and, in some photographs, were almost indistinguishable from orbital observations of rivers on Earth. According to Masursky, only the assumption that rainfall occurred on Mars can adequately account for the observed nature of these channels. Some of the tributaries are reckoned to be as young as a few hundred million years, suggesting further to Masursky that the process of their creation occurred repeatedly.

In 1978 Masursky joined the imaging working group for the Pioneer Venus orbiters. The surface of Venus, hidden from visual or televisual observation by its thick layer of cloud, was mapped on the basis of radar readings taken by these.

The pictures gained from the Voyager space probes' passage past Saturn provided data for which geological interpretation has continued for a number of years.

Mauchly, John William (1907–1980) US electronics engineer who, with Presper ◊Eckert, became co-inventor of one of the first electronic computers (the ENIAC). He played an active role in the development of more advanced machines (EDVAC, BINAC, and UNIVAC) and in encouraging the appreciation of their enormous potential for government, military, scientific, and business purposes.

Mauchly was born in Cincinnati, Ohio, on 30 August 1907. He attended Johns Hopkins University, entering as an engineering student but transferring into the physics department. He was awarded his PhD in physics in 1932 and went into teaching, becoming professor of physics at Ursinus College in Collegeville, Pennsylvania. He attended a course in electronics at the Moore School of Electrical Engineering of the University of Pennsylvania in the summer of 1941. The faculty there requested him to stay on as an instructor. He learnt of the work being done at the Moore School under contract from the Ballistics Research Laboratory as part of the war effort. He submitted a memorandum in 1942 on the design of a computing machine, and the Moore School was awarded a contract for its construction. The project lasted from 1943 to 1946, with Mauchly as principal consultant and Eckert as chief engineer.

A W Burks, T K Sharpless, and R Shaw were three of the many other scientists involved in the project.

The ENIAC (Electrical Numerical Integrator and Computer) was announced in 1946 and put into operational service a year later. A dispute over patent policy with the Moore School caused Mauchly and Eckert to leave the institute, although they had been in the middle of the development of the EDVAC (Electronic Discrete Variable Automatic Computer). Their departure greatly hindered the development of this machine, which did not make its debut until 1951. Mauchly and Eckert set up a partnership, which became incorporated in 1948 (as the Eckart–Mauchly Computer Corporation). An unfortunate accident in 1949 meant that they lost their financial backing, so in 1950 they sold the company to Remington Rand, which merged with the Sperry Corporation in 1955. From 1950 to 1959 Mauchly served as director of UNIVAC (Universal Automatic Computer) applications research. He left the Sperry Rand Corporation in 1959 in order to set up a consulting company called Mauchly Associates, and set up a second consulting organization (Dynatrend) in 1967. Mauchly returned to the Sperry Rand Corporation as a consultant in 1973.

The importance of Mauchly's work is so great that it is all the more surprising that he is not better known outside the ranks of his own profession. He received many awards and honours, but was not famous with the general public. He died during surgery for a heart ailment in Abington, Pennsylvania, on 8 January 1980.

Mauchly's early research, at Collegeville, was on meteorology. It involved many laborious calculations, so he was deeply interested in finding methods of speeding up the process. He realized the possibility of using an electronic apparatus, constructed with vacuum tubes (valves), and it was in order to improve his understanding of electronics that he attended the course in 1941 at the Moore School.

The US Army found that new battle conditions and new types of weapons required that its artillery range tables (which enabled the gunners to aim and fire effectively) needed to be recalculated. This was a mammoth task, and so Mauchly and the army had a community of interest: both needed methods for rapid calculation. Mauchly's 1942 memorandum on computer design initiated the project that culminated in 1946 with the ENIAC. (It was first tested in 1947 at the Aberdeen Proving Ground in Maryland, for ballistics purposes.)

The ENIAC was one of the first electronic computers. It could perform addition in 200 microseconds and multiplication in 300 microseconds. Although it was primarily designed for trajectory calculation, it could also be used for other purposes, including the solution of partial differential equations. Its drawbacks were that it was huge, and had vast power requirements and running costs. Its input and output consisted of punched cards; it had limited storage, and no memory.

Work on the EDVAC began in 1944, with John ◊Von Neumann working to improve the design of the storage system. In 1947 Mauchly and Eckert obtained a contract from the Northrop Aircraft Company to design a small-scale binary computer. The BINAC (Binary Automatic Computer) was completed in 1949, and was more economical to use as well as being faster and more compact. A new feature was the replacement of punch cards with magnetic tape, and the computer's capacity to use internally stored programs. The UNIVAC was designed during the early 1950s, and was first tried out in 1951 by the US Bureau of Census; it was designed to serve the business community. Mauchly's role in its development was primarily in the design of the software.

Maudslay, Henry (1771–1831) English engineer and toolmaker who, in an age when mechanical engineering lagged behind other crafts, improved the metal-working lathe to the point that it could be employed for precise screw cutting. He also desiged a bench micrometer, which became the forerunner of the modern instrument.

Maudslay was born on 22 August 1771 at Woolwich, London, where his father was a joiner at the Royal Arsenal. He had little formal education and at the age of 12 went to work at the arsenal, filling cartridges at first but then, after two years, moving to the joiner's shop and then to the metalworking shop as an apprentice. By the time he was 18 his skill as a craftsman was renowned. He joined the firm of Joseph ◊Bramah, the pioneer of hydraulics and the inventor of the Bramah press and lock. Maudslay eventually became manager of the workshop but after a disagreement over pay he left to start his own business.

In his works, just off Oxford Street, London, he developed a method of cutting screw threads on a lathe. Previously large threads had been forged and filed, and small threads had been cut by hand by the most skilled of craftsmen. Maudslay's new screw-cutting lathe gave such precision as to allow previously unknown interchangeability of nuts and bolts and standardization of screw threads. He was also able to produce sets of taps and dies.

Using his new device he cut a long screw with 50 threads per inch (about 20 per cm) and made this the basis of a micrometer, which came into daily use as an instrument to check the standard of the work he produced. In the period 1801–08, in conjunction with Marc ◊Brunel, he constructed a series of machines for making wooden pulley blocks at Portsmouth dockyard. The A3 special-purpose power-driven machines, operated by ten unskilled workers, did the work formerly done by 110 skilled workers using hand methods.

Maudslay's firm, with him as its chief working craftsman, went on to produce marine steam engines. The first was a 13 kW/17 hp model: later, engines of 42 kW/56 hp were built. In 1838, after Maudslay's death, the company built the engines for the first successful transatlantic steamship, Isambard Kingdom ◊Brunel's *Great Western,* which developed 560 kW/750 hp. Early in 1831 Maudslay caught a chill on his return to the UK after a trip to France and he died on 15 February that year. He was buried in a cast-iron tomb at Woolwich.

Maury, Antonia Caetana de Paiva Pereira (1866–1952)
US expert in stellar spectroscopy who specialized in the detection of binary stars. She also formulated a classification system to categorize the appearance of spectral lines, a system that was later seen to relate to the appearance of the stars themselves.

Maury was born on 21 March 1866, into a family that had already produced several prominent scientists. Educated at Vassar, she became an assistant at the Harvard College Observatory even before she graduated in 1887. Working under the direction of Edward ◊Pickering she rapidly mastered spectroscopy, to the extent that within four years she had devised her new classification scheme for spectral lines, and in 1896 published the results of her work, based on the examination of nearly 5,000 photographs and covering nearly 700 bright stars in the northern sky. For many years following the publication of her scheme, Maury lectured in astronomy in various US cities. She accepted private pupils and occasionally also took on teaching jobs. At the age of 42 she returned to Harvard as a research associate to study the complex spectrum of Beta Lyrae. Following her retirement in 1935, Maury became curator of the Draper Park Museum at Hasting on Hudson while continuing her study of Beta Lyrae. She died in Dobbs Ferry, New York, on 8 January 1952.

Maury's first spectroscopic work was to assist Pickering in establishing that the star Mizar (Zeta Ursae Majoris) was in fact a binary star, with two distinct spectra. That successfully accomplished, Maury was the first to calculate the 104-day period of this star. In 1889 she discovered a second such star, Beta Aurigae, and established that it had a period of only four days. During the next year she was engaged in a project studying the spectra of bright stars. Previously the great variety in types of star, as judged by their spectra, had been classified according to the mere absence or presence of the Fraunhofer lines. Maury now found this system inadequate for representing all the characteristics she observed: it was also possible to make classifications according to the appearance of the lines – their intensity, distinctions, and width, for example. Maury assumed the existence of three major divisions among spectra, depending upon the width and distinctness of the spectral lines. She defined class A as having normal lines; class B had hazy or blurred lines; and class C had exceptionally distinct lines. These divisions and their combinations represented in many ways a better classification of stellar spectra than both the system previously used, and the 'improved' version proposed – also at Harvard – by Annie ◊Cannon almost simultaneously.

Maury's system enabled Ejnar ◊Hertzsprung, co-originator of the Hertzsprung–Russell diagram, to verify his discovery of two distinct varieties of star: dwarfs, which in Maury's scheme fall under A and B, and giants (C).

Maury, Matthew Fontaine (1806–1873)
US naval officer and pioneer of oceanography.

Matthew Maury was born near Fredericksville, Virginia, on 14 January 1806, the seventh child of Richard Maury, a small planter of Huguenot descent whose family had come to Virginia from Ireland in 1718, and Diana Minor who was of Dutch and English descent. The family moved to Williamson County, Tennessee, in 1810 where Matthew grew up. He graduated from Harpeth Academy in 1925 and joined the US Navy as a midshipman. In 1836 he published a *Treatise on Navigation,* was promoted to lieutenant, and had a promising career ahead of him. However, three years later he sustained a leg injury in a stagecoach accident that left him unfit for service at sea. He remained a naval officer serving in Washington, DC, and writing on the cause of naval reform.

In 1842 he was appointed superintendent of the Depot of Charts and Instruments at Washington and in 1844 he was chosen as head of the new National Observatory and Hydrographical Office. In spite of his lack of astronomical qualifications he remained in charge of what was one of the world's best equipped and funded observatories for 17 years, publishing very few papers and incurring hostility in the astronomical community.

Maury's main interest was in improving maritime technology and thereby improving maritime commerce, and in 1847 he published his *Wind and Current Chart of the North Atlantic,* issued free to mariners in return for a copy of their logs of winds and currents. He published a series of charts and such time-saving sailing directions for all the oceans that sailors happily supplied him with data. Faced with the growth of steam ships, he became one of the leading developers of the technology of sail.

He claimed that his charts cut the journey from New York to California from 183 to 135 days and from England to Australia from 124 to 97 days.

Many scientists in the mid 19th century were charting physical phenomena and in 1853 Maury organized a conference in Brussels on meteorological observations that was to be the first of several such conferences. He was hoping to coordinate land and sea meteorology but British and US governments insisted that this conference dealt only with the sea. It was only after Maury's death that his uniform system of weather reporting at sea was extended to land.

Maury had many critics in the scientific community. His writings were couched in a religious language that had largely been abandoned by his colleagues and while his articles and books were enthusiastically taken up by general and religious journals, they were treated with suspicion in the scientific press. His best known articles were compiled into *Explanation and Sailing Directions to Accompany the Wind and Current Charts* (1850) and *Physical Geography of the Sea* (1855), the first textbook of modern oceanography. Maury defended his theories against their critics and refused to modify them. The popularity of his books forced other more meticulous scientists to improve on his interpretations.

Maury's idea, based on Michael ◊Faraday's work on the paramagnetism of oxygen, that changes in wind direction were caused by the Earth's magnetism, and his explanations for this were not accepted in the scientific community. His dogmatic beliefs, which he insisted on promoting in Congress, brought him into increasing conflict with colleagues and this opposition closed doors to him. He was not appointed, for example, when a committee was set up to organize the land meteorology of North America, and this opposition was also responsible for the restrictions on his 1853 Brussels conference. His critics felt that his insistence that knowledge of one subject should be an excuse for claiming knowledge in others was damaging to US science, but Maury claimed that his aims were purely to improve the life of farmers as he had the lives of sailors.

In the American Civil War Maury became a commander in the Confederate Navy and in 1865 took the post of Imperial commissioner for immigration to Emperor Maximilian of Mexico, with the aim of establishing a confederate colony. After the collapse of the Mexican empire he could not return home having represented a defeated cause in a foreign country, so he went to England where he received a public subscription and wrote textbooks for two years. He was awarded a doctorate of law by Cambridge University. For the last four years of his life he was professor of meteorology at the Virginia Military Institute. He died in Lexington, Virginia, on 1 February 1873.

In spite of his unpopularity and the professional jealousy that met many of his ideas, Maury was honoured for many of his achievements. He received honorary degrees from Columbian College in 1853 and North Carolina University in 1852, as well as from Cambridge University in 1868. He was a member of several scientific academies and societies and was decorated by the sovereigns of Russia, Portugal, and Denmark. Maury married a distant cousin, Ann Herndon, in 1834 and they had five daughters and three sons. One of his daughters, D F M Corbin, wrote a biography, *Life of Matthew Maury* (1888).

Maxim, Hiram Stevens (1840–1916) US-born British inventor, chiefly remembered for the Maxim gun, the first fully automatic, rapid-firing machine gun.

Maxim was born on 5 February 1840 in Sangerville, Maine, the son of a farmer and wood-turner. He spent his early life in various apprentiships before exhibiting his talent for invention at the age of 26 with a patent for a curling iron in 1866. More significant ideas followed, and in 1878 he was appointed chief engineer to the United States Electric Lighting Company. While working for this company he came up with a way of manufacturing carbon-coated filaments for the early light bulbs that ensured that each filament was evenly coated.

It was during a trip to the Paris Exhibition of 1881 that Maxim made the statement that was to change his life. He declared that work on armaments would prove the most profitable sector of invention. Taking his own advice, he left the USA to settle in the UK, where he thought the most opportunity for his work existed. He set up a small laboratory at Hatton Garden, London, and set to work on improving the design of current guns.

In 1884 he had produced the first fully automatic machine gun, which used the recoil from the shots to extract, eject, load, and fire cartridges. With a water-cooled barrel, the Maxim gun used a 250-round ammunition belt to produce a rate of fire of ten rounds per second. Its efficiency was further improved by Maxim's development of a cordlike propellant explosive, cordite. His own company, set up on the unveiling of the Maxim gun, became absorbed into Vickers Limited. By 1889 the British Army had adopted the gun for use, and not until the appearance of tanks on the battlefront was the power of the Maxim weapon eclipsed significantly. Maxim became a naturalized British subject in 1900, was knighted by Queen Victoria in 1901, and later also became a Chevalier of the Legion of Honour of France.

Although chiefly remembered for the gun, Maxim is responsible for many other, lesser, inventions, having taken out well over a hundred patents in both the

USA and the UK for devices ranging from mouse-traps to gas-powered engines. He was particularly interested in powered flight, his experiments being described in his book *Artificial and Natural Flight*. In 1889 he started investigations into the relative efficiencies of aerofoils and airscrews driven by steampowered engines. Five years later he had produced a steam-driven machine whose engine produced 4.5 kW/6 hp for every mass of 0.4 kg/1 lb weight. After three trials the aircraft succeeded in leaving the tracks along which it ran. Although impressive, it was clear that the massive amount of feed-water needed for longer flights would add an impossible weight burden to the craft.

Maxim wrote an autobiography in 1915, a year before his death in Streatham, south London, on 24 November 1916. He was survived by his inventor son, Hiram Percy Maxim (1869–1936), who developed a 'silencer' for rifles.

Further Reading

Goldsmith, Dolf, *Devil's Paintbrush: Sir Hiram Maxim's Gun*, Collector Grade Publications, 1993.

Hamilton, James and Holmes, Phil, *Chronic Inventor: Life and Work of Hiram Stevens Maxim, 1840–1916*, Bexley Libraries and Museums, 1991.

Schumacher, Alice C, *Hiram Percy Maxim*, Electric Radio Press, 1998.

Maxwell, James Clerk (1831–1879) Scottish physicist who discovered that light consists of electromagnetic waves and established the kinetic theory of gases. He also proved the nature of Saturn's rings and demonstrated the principles governing colour vision.

Maxwell was born in Edinburgh on 13 November 1831. He was educated at Edinburgh Academy 1841–47, when he entered the University of Edinburgh. He then went on to study at Cambridge in 1850, graduating in 1854. He became professor of natural philosophy at Marischal College, Aberdeen, in 1856 and moved to London in 1860 to take up the post of professor of natural philosophy and astronomy at King's College. On the death of his father in 1865, Maxwell returned to his family home in Scotland and devoted himself to research. However in 1871 he was persuaded to move to Cambridge, where he became the first professor of experimental physics and set up the Cavendish Laboratory, which opened in 1874. Maxwell continued in this position until 1879, when he contracted cancer. He died in Cambridge on 5 November 1879, at the early age of 48.

Maxwell demonstrated his great analytical ability at the age of 15, when he discovered an original method for drawing a perfect oval. His first important contribution to science was made from 1849 onwards, when

Maxwell Scottish physicist James Clerk Maxwell who proposed the electromagnetic theory of light. Maxwell also made important contributions to the kinetic theory of gases. *Mary Evans Picture Library*

Maxwell applied himself to colour vision. He revived the three-colour theory of Thomas ◊Young and extended the work of Hermann von ◊Helmholtz on colour vision. Maxwell showed how colours could be built up from mixtures of the primary colours red, green, and blue, by spinning discs containing sectors of these colours in various sizes. In the 1850s, he refined this approach by inventing a colour box in which the three primary colours could be selected from the Sun's spectrum and combined together. Maxwell confirmed Young's theory that the eye has three kinds of receptors sensitive to the primary colours and showed that colour blindness is due to defects in the receptors. He also explained fully how the addition and subtraction of primary colours produces all other colours, and crowned this achievement in 1861 by producing the first colour photograph to use a three-colour process. This picture, the ancestor of all colour photography, printing, and television, was taken of a tartan ribbon by using red, green, and blue filters to photograph the tartan and to project a coloured image.

Maxwell worked on several areas of enquiry at the same time, and from 1855 to 1859 took up the problem of Saturn's rings. No-one could give a satisfactory explanation for the rings that would result in a stable structure. Maxwell proved that a solid ring would collapse and a fluid ring would break up, but found that a ring composed of concentric circles of satellites could achieve stability, arriving at the correct conclusion that the rings are composed of many small bodies in orbit around Saturn.

Maxwell's development of the electromagnetic theory of light took many years. It began with the paper 'On Faraday's lines of force' (1855–56), in which Maxwell built on the views of Michael ◊Faraday that electric and magnetic effects result from fields of lines of force that surround conductors and magnets. Maxwell drew an analogy between the behaviour of the lines of force and the flow of an incompressible liquid, thereby deriving equations that represented known electric and magnetic effects. The next step towards the electromagnetic theory took place with the publication of the paper 'On physical lines of force' (1861–62). Here Maxwell developed a model for the medium in which electric and magnetic effects could occur (which might throw some light on the nature of lines of force). He devised a hypothetical medium consisting of an incompressible fluid containing rotating vortices responding to magnetic intensity, separated by cells responding to electric current.

By considering how the motion of the vortices and cells could produce magnetic and electric effects, Maxwell was successful in explaining all known effects of electromagnetism, showing that the lines of force must behave in a similar way. However Maxwell went further, and considered what effects would be caused if the medium were elastic. It turned out that the movement of a charge would set up a disturbance in the medium, forming transverse waves that would be propagated through the medium. The velocity of these waves would be equal to the ratio of the value for a current when measured in electrostatic units and electromagnetic units. This had been determined by Friedrich Kohlrausch (1840–1910) and Wilhelm ◊Weber, and it was equal to the velocity of light. Maxwell thus inferred that light consists of transverse waves in the same medium that causes electric and magnetic phenomena.

Maxwell was reinforced in this opinion by work undertaken to make basic definitions of electric and magnetic quantities in terms of mass, length, and time. In *On the Elementary Regulations of Electric Quantities* (1863), he found that the ratio of the two definitions of any quantity based on electric and magnetic forces is always equal to the velocity of light. He considered that light must consist of electromagnetic waves, but first needed to prove this by abandoning the vortex analogy and arriving at an explanation based purely on dynamic principles. This he achieved in *A Dynamical Theory of the Electromagnetic Field* (1864), in which he developed the fundamental equations that describe the electromagnetic field. These showed that light is propagated in two waves, one magnetic and the other electric, which vibrate perpendicular to each other and to the direction of propagation. This was confirmed in Maxwell's 'Note on the electromagnetic theory of light' (1868), which used an electrical derivation of the theory instead of the dynamical formulation, and Maxwell's whole work on the subject was summed up in *Treatise on Electricity and Magnetism* (1873).

The treatise also established that light has a radiation pressure, and suggested that a whole family of electromagnetic radiations must exist, of which light was only one. This was confirmed in 1888 with the sensational discovery of radio waves by Heinrich ◊Hertz. Sadly, Maxwell did not live long enough to see this triumphant vindication of his work. He also did not live to see the ether (the medium in which light waves were said to be propagated) disproved with the classic experiments of Albert ◊Michelson and Edward ◊Morley in 1881 and 1887, which Maxwell himself had suggested in the last year of his life. However this did not discredit Maxwell as his equations and description of electromagnetic waves remain valid even though the waves require no medium.

Maxwell's other major contribution to physics was to provide a mathematical basis for the kinetic theory of gases. Here he built on the achievements of Rudolf ◊Clausius, who in 1857–58 had shown that a gas must consist of molecules in constant motion colliding with each other and the walls of the container. Clausius developed the idea of the mean free path, which is the average distance that a molecule travels between collisions. As the molecules have a high velocity, the mean free path must be very small, otherwise gases would diffuse much faster than they do, and would have greater thermal conductivities.

Maxwell's development of the kinetic theory was stimulated by his success in the similar problem of Saturn's rings. It dates from 1860, when he used a statistical treatment to express the wide range of velocities that the molecules in a quantity of gas must inevitably possess. He arrived at a formula to express the distribution of velocity in gas molecules, relating it to temperature and thus finally showing that heat resides in the motion of molecules – a view that had been suspected for some time. Maxwell then applied it with some success to viscosity, diffusion, and other properties of gases that depend on the nature of the motion of their molecules.

The only laws of matter are those which our minds must fabricate, and the only laws of mind are fabricated by matter.
JAMES CLERK MAXWELL *ATTRIBUTED REMARK*

However, in 1865, Maxwell and his wife carried out exacting experiments to measure the viscosity of gases over a wide range of pressure and temperature. They found that the viscosity is independent of the pressure and that it is very nearly proportional to the absolute temperature. This later finding conflicted with the previous distribution law and Maxwell modified his conception of the kinetic theory by assuming that molecules do not undergo elastic collisions as had been thought but are subject to a repulsive force that varies inversely with the fifth power of the distance between them. This led to new equations that satisfied the viscosity–temperature relationship, as well as the laws of partial pressures and diffusion.

Maxwell's kinetic theory did not fully explain heat conduction, however, and it was modified by Ludwig ◊Boltzmann in 1868, resulting in the Maxwell–Boltzmann distribution law. Both men thereafter contributed to successive refinements of the kinetic theory and it proved fully applicable to all properties of gases. It also led Maxwell to an accurate estimate of the size of molecules and to a method of separating gases in a centrifuge. The kinetic theory, being a statistical derivation, also revised opinions on the validity of the second law of thermodynamics, which states that heat cannot of its own accord flow from a colder to a hotter body. In the case of two connected containers of gases at the same temperature, it is statistically possible for the molecules to diffuse so that the faster-moving molecules all concentrate in one container while the slower molecules gather in the other, making the first container hotter and the second colder. Maxwell conceived this hypothesis, which is known as Maxwell's demon. Even though this is very unlikely, it is not impossible and the second law can therefore be considered to be not absolute but only highly probable.

Maxwell is generally considered to be the greatest theoretical physicist of the 1800s, as his forebear Faraday was the greatest experimental physicist. His rigorous mathematical ability was combined with great insight to enable him to achieve brilliant syntheses of knowledge in the two most important areas of physics at that time. In building on Faraday's work to discover the electromagnetic nature of light, Maxwell not only explained electromagnetism, but paved the way for the discovery and application of the whole spectrum of electromagnetic radiation that has characterized modern physics. In developing the kinetic theory of gases, Maxwell gave the final proof that the nature of heat resides in the motion of molecules.

Further Reading

Forbes, Eric G, *James Clerk Maxwell, FRSE, FRS (1831–1879)*, Scottish Men of Science series, History of Medicine and Science Unit, University of Edinburgh, 1982.

Harman, P M, *The Natural Philosophy of James Clerk Maxwell*, Cambridge University Press, 1998.

Hendry, John, *James Clerk Maxwell and the Theory of the Electromagnetic Field*, Hilger, 1986.

Maxwell, James Clerk; Garber, Elizabeth, Brush, Stephen George, and Everitt, C W Francis (eds), *Maxwell on Molecules and Gases*, MIT Press, 1986.

Maxwell, James Clerk; Garber, Elizabeth, Brush, Stephen George, and Everitt, C W Francis (eds), *Maxwell on Heat and Statistical Mechanics: On 'Avoiding All Personal Enquiries' on Molecules*, Associated University Presses, 1995.

May, Charles Paul, *James Clerk Maxwell and Electromagnetism*, Immortals of Science series, Chatto & Windus, 1964.

Maybach, Wilhelm (1847–1929) German engineer and inventor who worked with Gottlieb ◊Daimler on the development of early motorcars. He is particularly remembered for his invention of the float-feed carburettor, which allowed petrol (gasoline) to be used as a fuel for internal-combustion engines – most of which up to that time had been fuelled by gas.

Maybach was born in Heilbronn, Württemberg, on 9 February 1846, and raised in an orphanage from the age of ten. From 1862, when Maybach was still a teenager, he was a great friend and associate of Daimler. In 1882 they went into partnership at Cannstatt, where they produced one of the first petrol engines. In 1895, Maybach became technical director of the Daimler Motor Company. While working with Daimler, in 1901, Maybach designed the first Mercedes car – named after Mercedes Jellinec, the daughter of their influencial associate, the Austro-Hungarian consul in Nice. He died in Constaff, near Stuttgart, in December 1929.

Maybach invented the spray-nozzle, or float-feed, carburettor in 1893. An adjusting screw controlled the rate of maximum fuel flow and a second screw varied the area of the choke. When the inlet valve was opened, air sent along the choke passage caused a drop in pressure, making the fuel enter through a jet as a fine spray. The vaporized fuel mixed with air to produce a combustible mixture for the engine's cylinders.

Maybach's other inventions included the honeycomb radiator – still used in some Mercedes cars – an internal expanding brake in 1901 and an axle-locating system for use with independent suspensions. He left Daimler in 1907 to set up his own factory making engines for Ferdinand von ◊Zeppelin's airships.

Mayer, Christian (1719–1783) Austrian astronomer, mathematician, physicist, and Jesuit priest. His work was seriously interrupted by the pope's dissolution of the Jesuit order in 1773, although he managed to continue his astronomical studies, researching particularly into double stars.

Mayer was born on 20 August 1719 in Moravia, in a district now known as Mederizenlin, in the Czech Republic. Various sources suggest that he was educated in many centres of learning around Europe and that he excelled in Greek, Latin, philosophy, theology, and mathematics, but all that is definitely known is that he left home in his early twenties because his father disapproved strongly of his determination to become a Jesuit. Mayer entered the novitiate in Mannheim, Germany, and by the age of 33 he had had such success in his chosen career that he was appointed professor of mathematics and physics at Heidelberg, although his main interest remained astronomy. Consequently, when the elector palatine, Karl Theodor, built an observatory first at Schwetzingen, then another larger one at Mannheim, Mayer was appointed court astronomer and given responsibility for equipping both with the best available instruments. The effects of Pope Clement XIV's dissolution of his order, however, rendered Mayer's court position untenable and he was relieved of his duties before he had completed the furnishing of the observatories. He managed to continue his own astronomical work and became well known in Europe – and even in the USA – for the careful presentation of his discoveries and observations in international journals. He died in Heidelberg on 12 April 1783.

Mayer carried out important astronomical research before, during, and after Karl Theodor's patronage. His studies included measurement of the degree of the meridian, based on work conducted in Paris and in the Rhenish palatinate, and observations of the transits of Venus in 1761 and 1769. (The latter observation was conducted in Russia at the invitation of Catherine II.)

Mayer also studied double stars. His equipment was unable to distinguish true binary stars (in orbit round each other) from separate stars seen together only by the coincidence of Earth's viewpoint, but Mayer was the first to investigate and catalogue stars according to their apparent 'binary' nature. Later work was more critical and therefore more successful, but Mayer's pioneering contribution is important to the history of astronomy.

In the late 1770s Mayer turned his attention to observing the companions of fixed stars, mistakenly thinking that he had discovered more than a hundred planets of other stars. The controversy arising from this claim marks the inauguration of a period of methodologically more sound observation in the study of stars.

Mayer, Johann Tobias (1723–1762) German cartographer, astronomer, and physicist who in his short life did much to improve standards of observation and navigation, although a considerable amount of his research was superseded shortly after his death.

Mayer was born in Marbach, near Stuttgart, on 17 February 1723, the son of a cartwright and the youngest of six children. Shortly after his birth, his family moved to Esslingen, where he grew up. When he was six both his parents died and Mayer went to live in an orphanage. He developed some skill in architectural drawing and surveying and, under the direction of a local artillery officer, in 1739 produced plans and drawings of military installations. Mayer's map of Esslingen and its surroundings – the oldest such map still extant – was made in the same year. Having taught himself mathematics (a subject not studied at his Latin school), he published his first book two years later, on the application of analytical methods to the solution of geometrical problems; he was 18 years old. Within the next few years he also acquired some knowledge of French, Italian, and English. In 1746 he began work for the Homann Cartographic Bureau, in Nürnberg, devoting much of his time to collating geographical and astronomical facts contained in Homann's archives. He became so interested in the astronomical side of his work that in 1750 he published a compilation called *Kosmographische Nachrichten und Sammlungen auf das Jahr 1748.* His reputation both as cartographer and astronomer earned him an invitation to take up the post of professor at the Georg August Academy in Göttingen, which he accepted. He contracted gangrene, and died on 20 February 1762. At the Homann Cartographic Bureau, Mayer's most important work was the construction of some 30 maps of Germany. These established exacting new standards for using geographical data in conjunction with accurate astronomical details to determine latitudes and longitudes on Earth. To obtain some of the astronomical details, he observed lunar oscillations and eclipses using a telescope of his own design. But it was in Göttingen that he decided to produce a map of the Moon's surface, which entailed both theoretical and practical work never undertaken previously. By observing the Moon he concluded that it had no atmosphere, and continuous observations with his repeating (or reflecting) circle produced Mayer's *Lunar Tables* in 1753, the accuracy of which (correct to one minute of arc) gained him international fame. After 1755 he used a superior instrument, a 1.8-m/6-ft radius mural quadrant made by John Bird, with which he made improvements on his earlier stellar observations, enabling him to introduce correction formulae for meridian transits of stars.

Mayer also invented a simple and accurate method for calculating solar eclipses, compiled a catalogue of zodiacal stars, and studied stellar proper motion. In the process of devising a method for finding geographical coordinates without using astronomical observations, he arrived at a new theory of the magnet, which provided a convincing demonstration of the validity of the inverse-square law of magnetic attraction and repulsion.

Acting upon one of his last requests, shortly after Mayer died, his widow submitted to the British Admiralty a method for computing longitude at sea. Although the tables resulting from this method were superseded not long after by more accurate data being compiled by James ◊Bradley at Greenwich, Mayer's widow was awarded £3,000 by the British government for her husband's claim to a prize offered for such a venture.

Mayer, Julius Robert (1814–1878)

German physicist who was the first to formulate the principle of conservation of energy and determine the mechanical equivalent of heat.

Mayer was born in Heilbronn on 25 November 1814 and received a classical and theological education there. In 1832 he went to the University of Tübingen to study and in spite of being expelled in 1837 for membership of a student secret society, he managed to qualify as a doctor with distinction in the following year. In 1840, he took a position as a ship's physician and sailed to the East Indies for a year. He then settled in his native city and built up a prosperous medical practice. In 1842, Justus von ◊Liebig published Mayer's classic paper on the conservation of energy in his *Annalen der Chemie*. This was followed by two papers that Mayer himself published. In 1845, he extended his ideas into the world of living things and in 1848 to the Sun, Moon, and Earth. Disappointed at the lack of recognition and despairing because others were making the same discoveries independently and gaining priority, Mayer tried to kill himself in 1850. He was then confined to mental institutions during the 1850s, but from 1858 he at last began to gain the credit he deserved, principally by the efforts of Hermann von ◊Helmholtz, Rudolf ◊Clausius, and John ◊Tyndall. As a result, Mayer was recognized by the scientific world, receiving the Royal Society's Copley Medal in 1871. Mayer died in Heilbronn on 20 March 1878.

Mayer's conviction that the various forms of energy are interconvertible arose from an observation made during his voyage to the East. He found while bloodletting that the venous blood of the European sailors was much redder in the tropics than at home. Mayer put this down to a greater concentration of oxygen in the blood caused by the body using less oxygen, as less heat was required in the tropics to keep the body warm. From this, Mayer made a conceptual leap to the idea that work such as muscular force, heat such as body heat, and other forms of energy such as chemical

energy produced by the oxidation of food in the body are all interconvertible. The amount of work or heat produced by the body must be balanced by the oxidation of a certain amount of food, and therefore work or energy is not created but only transformed from one form to another.

This in essence is the principle of conservation of energy, which Mayer conceived as an idea but without any evidence to prove it in 1840. On returning to his home, he set about learning physics in order to prove his conviction. In fact, other scientists had been working towards the same conclusions but no one had yet formulated them so widely as Mayer. In 1839, Marc ◊Seguin had made a rough estimate of the mechanical equivalent of heat, assuming that the loss of heat represented by the fall in temperature of steam on expanding was equivalent to the mechanical work produced by the expansion. He also remarked that it was absurd to suppose that 'a finite quantity of heat could produce an indefinite quantity of mechanical action and that it was more natural to assume that a certain quantity of heat disappeared in the very act of producing motive power'.

In 1842, Mayer stated the equivalence of heat and work more definitely. He published an attempt to determine the mechanical equivalent of heat from the heat produced when air is compressed. He made the assumption that the whole of the work done in compressing the air was converted into heat, and by using the specific heats of air at constant volume and constant pressure, he was able to reach a value for the mechanical equivalent solely on theoretical grounds. He concluded that the heat required to raise the temperature of 1 kg/2.2 lb of water by 1 °C/1.8 °F would be equivalent to the work done by a mass of 1 kg/2.2 lb in falling 365 m/1,200 ft. This result is about 15% too low, but this was mainly due to the inaccuracy of the values for specific heats that Mayer had to use. James ◊Joule made the first accurate derivation experimentally in 1847, and credit for the determination of the mechanical equivalent of heat goes to him. But Mayer had clearly demonstrated the validity of the principle of conservation of energy and is generally regarded as its founder, though Helmholtz expressed it in a much clearer and more specific way in 1847.

In 1845, Mayer extended the principle of the interconvertibility and conservation of energy to magnetism, electricity, and chemical energy and to the living world. He described the energy conversions that take place in living organisms, realizing that plants convert the Sun's energy into food that is consumed by animals to provide a source of energy to power their muscles and provide body heat. By insisting that living things are powered solely by physical processes utilizing solar energy and not by any kind of innate vital force, Mayer took a daring step forward and laid the foundations of modern physiology.

Mayer's paper of 1848 was concerned with astronomy. He realized correctly that chemical reactions could not provide enough energy to power the Sun, and proposed incorrectly that the Sun produces heat by meteoric bombardment. But he also calculated that tidal friction caused by the Moon's gravitation gradually slows the Earth's rotation, an effect now known to exist. However, like most of Mayer's ideas, this was later proposed independently by others.

Mayer was a very bold thinker and it is unfortunate that his lack of experimental ability and his position outside the scientific community prevented him from securing the proofs and immediate recognition that his ideas deserved. However in conceiving the principle of conservation of energy and applying it to all processes in the universe both living and nonliving, he made a discovery of fundamental importance to science.

Further Reading

Caneva, Kenneth L, *Robert Mayer and the Conservation of Energy*, Princeton University Press, 1993.

Caneva, Kenneth L, *Bull Hist Chem*, 'Robert Mayer and the conservation of matter', 1992–93, v 13–14, pp 27–29.

Mechnikov, Ilya (Elie) Ilich (1845–1916) Russian-born French zoologist who discovered phagocytes, amoebalike blood cells that engulf foreign bodies. For this discovery he was awarded (jointly with Paul ◊Ehrlich) the 1908 Nobel Prize for Physiology or Medicine.

Mechnikov was born on 15 May 1845 in Kharkov, Russia, the son of an officer of the Imperial Guard. He was educated at the University of Kharkov, from which he graduated in 1864. He then travelled to Germany to pursue his studies but returned to Russia in 1867, becoming professor of zoology and comparative anatomy at the University of Odessa. In 1882 he inherited sufficient money to make him financially independent and moved to Messina in Italy to continue his research. In 1886 he accepted the post of director of the Bacteriological Institute in Odessa but remained there only a short time, being invited to join the Pasteur Institute, where he remained for the rest of his life, becoming director on Louis ◊Pasteur's death in 1895. Mechnikov died in Paris on 16 July 1916.

Mechnikov first noticed phagocytes while he was in Messina studying the transparent larvae of starfish; he observed that certain cells surrounded and engulfed foreign particles that had entered the bodies of the larvae. He then deliberately introduced bacteria into starfish larvae and fungal spores into water fleas (*Daphnia*) and again observed that special amoebalike cells moved to where these foreign bodies were and

engulfed them. Mechnikov continued this line of research at Odessa and later at the Pasteur Institute, where he demonstrated that phagocytes exist in higher animals. In humans about 75% of the white blood cells, or leucocytes, are phagocytic, and they form the first line of defence against acute infections, moving to the site of infection and engulfing the invading bacteria. This work opposed the theory of the time, which postulated that leucocytes actually helped the growth of bacteria, but it is now accepted that leucocytes are one of the body's basic defence mechanisms against disease.

In his later years Mechnikov became interested in longevity, and he spent the last decade of his life trying to demonstrate that lactic-acid-producing bacteria in the intestine increased a person's lifespan.

Medawar, Peter Brian (1915–1987) British zoologist best known for his contributions to immunology, for which he shared the 1960 Nobel Prize for Physiology or Medicine with Frank Macfarlane ◊Burnet. He also received many other honours for his work, including a knighthood in 1965.

Medawar was born on 28 February 1915 in Rio de Janeiro, Brazil. He was educated at Magdalen College, Oxford, from which he graduated in 1939. From 1938–44 and 1946–47 he was a fellow of Magdalen College; and from 1944 to 1946 he also held a fellowship at St John's College, Oxford. In 1947 he was appointed Mason Professor of Zoology at Birmingham University and he held this position until 1951, when he became Jodrell Professor of Zoology and Comparative Anatomy at University College, London. Medawar remained at University College until 1962, when he was appointed director of the National Institute for Medical Research at Mill Hill in London, becoming director emeritus in 1975. In 1977 he was appointed professor of experimental medicine at the Royal Institution.

If politics is the art of the possible,
research is surely the art of the soluble.
Peter Medawar Art of the Soluble

Medawar began his Nobel prizewinning research in the early 1950s. Acting on Burnet's hypothesis that an animal's ability to produce a specific antibody is not inherited, Medawar inoculated mouse embryos of one strain (strain A) with cells from mice of another strain (strain B). He found that the strain A embryos did not produce antibodies against the strain B cells. When the strain A embryos had developed sufficiently to be capable of independent existence, he grafted onto them skin from strain B mice. Again he found that the strain A embryos did not produce antibodies against the strain B tissue. Thus Medawar confirmed Burnet's hypothesis that the ability of an animal to produce a specific antibody develops during the animal's lifetime and is not inherited. This finding suggests that an animal's immune system can be influenced by external factors, which may have significant implications in the field of transplant techniques.

Meitner, Lise (1878–1968) Austrian-born Swedish physicist who was one of the first scientists to study radioactive decay and the radiations emitted during this process. Her most famous work was done in 1938, in collaboration with her nephew Otto ◊Frisch, describing for the first time the splitting or fission of the uranium nucleus under neutron bombardment. This publication provoked a flurry of research activity and was of pivotal importance in the development of nuclear physics.

Meitner was born in Vienna on 7 November 1878. She became interested in science at an early age, but before studying physics, her parents insisted that she should first qualify as a French teacher in order to be certain of supporting herself. She passed the examination in French and then entered the University of Vienna in 1901. She obtained her PhD from that university in 1905, becoming only the second woman to do so, her thesis work on thermal conduction having been supervised by Ludwig ◊Boltzmann.

In 1907, Meitner entered the University of Berlin to continue her studies under Max ◊Planck. She met Otto ◊Hahn soon after arriving in Berlin. He was seeking a physicist to work with him on radioactivity at the Kaiser-Wilhelm Institute for Chemistry. Meitner joined Hahn, but their supervisor Emil ◊Fischer would not allow Meitner to work in his laboratory because she was a woman, and they had to set up a small laboratory in a carpenter's workroom. Despite this inauspicious start, Meitner became a member of the Kaiser-Wilhelm Institute in 1912, and in 1917 was made joint director of the institute with Hahn and was also appointed head of the physics department.

In 1912 Meitner had also become an assistant to Planck at the Berlin Institute of Theoretical Physics. She was appointed docent at the University of Berlin in 1922, and then made extraordinary professor of physics in 1926. Meitner, who was Jewish, remained in Berlin when the Nazis came to power in 1933 because she was protected by her Austrian citizenship. However the German annexation of Austria in 1938 deprived her of this citizenship and placed her life in danger. With the aid of Dutch scientists, she escaped to Holland and soon moved to Denmark as the guest of Niels ◊Bohr. She was then offered a post at the Nobel

Physical Institute in Stockholm, where a cyclotron was being built, and Meitner accepted. It was shortly after her arrival in Sweden that Meitner and Frisch, who was working at Bohr's Institute in Copenhagen, made the discovery of nuclear fission.

During World War II, Meitner was invited to participate in the development programme for the construction of the nuclear bomb, but she refused in the hope that such a weapon would not be feasible. In 1947, a laboratory was established for her by the Swedish Atomic Energy Commission at the Royal Institute of Technology, and she later moved to the Royal Swedish Academy of Engineering Science to work on an experimental nuclear reactor. In 1949, she became a Swedish citizen. In 1960 she retired from her post in Sweden and settled in Cambridge, England. The Fermi Award was given jointly to Meitner, Hahn, and Fritz Strassmann (1902–1980) in 1966, Meitner being the first woman to be so honoured. She died in Cambridge on 27 October 1968.

Meitner's early work in Berlin with Hahn concerned the analysis of physical properties of radioactive substances. Hahn's primary interest lay in the discovery of new elements, but Meitner's work was concerned with examining radiation emissions. They were able to determine the beta line spectra of numerous isotopes, leading to the discovery of protactinium in 1918. During the 1920s, Meitner studied the relationship between beta and gamma radiation. She examined the basis for the continuous beta spectrum, her results leading Wolfgang ◊Pauli to postulate the existence of the neutrino. She was the first to describe the emission of Auger electrons, which occurs when an electron rather than a photon is emitted after one electron drops from a higher to a lower electron shell in the atom.

The rapid developments in physics during the 1930s, such as the discovery of the neutron, artificial radioactivity, and the positron, did not leave Meitner behind. In 1933 she used a Wilson cloud chamber to photograph positron production by gamma radiation and in the following year, she began to study the effects of neutron bombardment on uranium with Hahn. They were interested in confirming the results of Enrico ◊Fermi that suggested the production of transuranic elements – that is, elements with atomic numbers higher than that of uranium (92). In 1935 Meitner and Hahn used a hydrogen sulphide precipitation method to remove elements with atomic numbers between 84 and 92 from their neutron-irradiated sample of uranium. They thought that they had found evidence for elements with atomic numbers of 93, 94, 95, and 96. Then in 1938, after Meitner was forced to flee from Germany, Hahn and Strassmann found that the radioactive elements produced by neutron bombardment of uranium had properties like radium. From Sweden, Meitner requested firm chemical evidence for the identities of the products. Hahn and Strassmann were surprised to find that the neutron bombardment had produced not transuranic elements but three isotopes of barium, which has an atomic number of 56.

Meitner and Frisch realized that these results indicated that the uranium nucleus had been split into smaller fragments. They predicted correctly that krypton would also be found among the products of this splitting process, which they named fission. A paper describing their analysis appeared in January 1939, and immediately set in motion a series of discoveries leading to the first nuclear reactor in 1942 and the first atomic bomb in 1945.

Meitner had also found evidence for the production of uranium-239 by the capture of a neutron by uranium-238. Beta decay of this new, heavy isotope would yield a transuranic element with the atomic number 93. This element was found by Edwin McMillan (1907–1991) and Philip Abelson (1913–   ) in 1940 and named neptunium.

Meitner continued to study the nature of fission products and contributed to the design of an experiment whereby fission products of uranium could be collected. Her later research concerned the production of new radioactive species using the cyclotron, and also the development of the shell model of the nucleus.

Meitner was a distinguished scientist who made important contributions to nuclear physics despite having to overcome both sexual and racial discrimination.

Further Reading

Rife, Patricia, *Lise Meitner and the Dawn of the Nuclear Age*, Birkhauser, 1997.

Sime, Ruth Lewin, *Lise Meitner: A Life in Physics*, California Studies in the History of Science, University of California Press, 1997, v 13.

Sime, Ruth Lewin, 'Lise Meitner's escape from Germany', *Amer J Phys*, 1990, v 58, pp 262–267.

Sime, Ruth Lewin, 'Lise Meitner in Sweden 1938–1960: exile from physics', *Amer J Phys*, 1994, v 62, pp 695–701.

Mellanby, Kenneth (1908–1993) English entomologist and ecologist best known for his work on the environmental effects of pollution.

Mellanby was born in West Hartlepool, County Durham, on 26 March 1908 and was educated at the Barnard Castle School. He gained a scholarship to read natural sciences at London University and graduated in 1929. In the following year he became a research worker at the London School of Hygiene and Tropical Medicine, from which he gained his doctorate in 1933, and remained a member of staff there until 1945.

During this period he went to east Africa to study the tsetse fly and, while doing his World War II military service, investigated scrub typhus in Burma (now Myanmar) and New Guinea. In 1945 he was appointed reader in medical entomology at London University, and in 1947 became the principal of University College, Ibadan – Nigeria's first university, which Mellanby played a substantial part in creating. He was then appointed head of the entomology department at Rothamsted Experimental Station in 1955, a position he held until 1961, when he founded and became the director of the Monks Wood Research Station (now called the Institute of Terrestrial Ecology) at Huntingdon in Cambridgeshire. He remained in this post until he officially retired in 1974. In 1978 he visited Australia to advise the newly established Association for the Protection of Rural Australia, and in 1979 he went to Peru to advise on the ecological effects of the Montaro Transfer Scheme, a plan to divert water from the Montaro River to Lima. He died on 23 December 1993.

Mellanby's early career was spent in entomological research but his most important contributions are probably his pioneering investigations into the effects of pollution, particularly by pesticides. Shortly after he had established the Monks Wood Research Station, he drew attention to the deleterious effects of pesticides – before Rachel ◊Carson had published her famous book on this theme, *Silent Spring*. Continuing his research, Mellanby undertook a comprehensive study of pesticides, concluding that although these chemicals damage the environment, pests destroy huge amounts of food and other essential materials and must therefore be controlled. Instead of pesticides, however, Mellanby advocated the use of biological control methods, such as introducing animals that feed on pests.

He wrote several books about entomology, ecology, and pollution, and was the editor of *Environmental Pollution*, one of the main research journals in this subject area.

Mendel, Gregor Johann (1822–1884) Austrian botanist and monk who discovered the basic laws of heredity, thereby laying the foundation of modern genetics – although the importance of his work was not recognized until after his death.

Mendel was born Johann Mendel on 22 July 1822 in Heinzendorf, Austria (now Hyncíce in the Czech Republic), the son of a peasant farmer. He studied for two years at the Philosophical Institute in Olmütz (now Olomouc), after which, in 1843, he entered the Augustinian monastery in Brünn, Moravia (now Brno), taking the name Gregor. In 1847 he was ordained a priest. During his religious training, Mendel taught himself a certain amount of science and for a short time

Mendel Austrian botanist Gregor Johann Mendel whose work on hybrid pea plants laid the foundations of genetics. Little is known of his later work, and his work on peas did not become widely known until the 20th century. *Mary Evans Picture Library*

With tall plants, however, he found that both tall and dwarf offspring were produced and that only about one-third of the tall plants bred true, from which he concluded that there were two types of tall plants, those that bred true and those that did not. Next he cross-bred dwarf plants with true-breeding tall plants, planted the resulting seeds and then self-pollinated each plant from this second generation. He found that all the offspring in the first generation were tall but that the offspring from the self-pollination of this first generation were a mixture of about one-quarter true-breeding dwarf plants, one-quarter true-breeding tall plants and one-half non-true-breeding tall plants. Mendel also studied other characteristics in pea plants, such as flower colour, seed shape, and flower position, finding that, as with height, simple laws governed the inheritance of these traits. From his findings Mendel concluded that each parent plant contributes a factor that determines a particular trait and that the pairs of factors in the offspring do not give rise to an amalgamation of traits. These conclusions, in turn, led him to formulate his famous law of segregation and law of independent assortment of characters, which are now recognized as two of the fundamental laws of heredity.

Mendel reported his findings to the Brünn Society for the Study of Natural Science in 1865 and in the

he was a teacher of Greek and mathematics at the secondary school in Znaim (now Znojmo) near Brünn. In 1850 he tried to pass an examination to obtain a teaching licence but failed, and in 1851 he was sent by his abbot to the University of Vienna to study physics, chemistry, mathematics, zoology, and botany. Mendel left the university in 1853 and returned to the monastery in Brünn in 1854. He then taught natural science in the local technical high school until 1868, during which period he again tried, and failed, to gain a teaching certificate that would have enabled him to teach in more advanced institutions. It was also in the period 1854–68 that Mendel performed most of his scientific work on heredity. He was elected abbot of his monastery at Brünn in 1868, and the administrative duties involved left him little time for further scientific investigations. Mendel remained abbot at Brünn until his death on 6 January 1884.

Mendel began the experiments that led to his discovery of the basic laws of heredity in 1856. Much of his work was performed on the edible pea (*Pisum*), which he grew in the monastery garden. He carefully self-pollinated and wrapped (to prevent accidental pollination by insects) each individual plant, collected the seeds produced by the plants, and studied the offspring of these seeds. He found that dwarf plants produced only dwarf offspring and that the seeds produced by this second generation also produced only dwarf offspring.

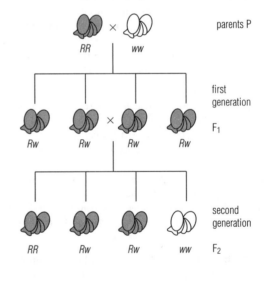

Mendel Mendel's law of independent assortment applied to an initial cross between pea plants with smooth yellow seeds and pea plants with green wrinkled seeds. The second generation includes four visibly different types of seeds – yellow smooth, yellow wrinkled, green smooth and green wrinkled to the ratio 9;3;3;1.

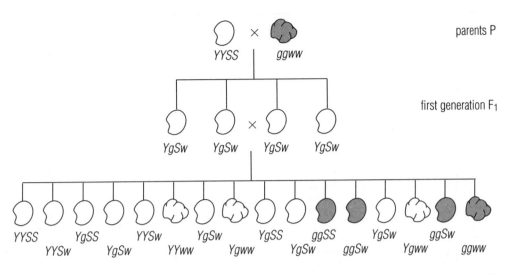

Y = dominant yellow S = dominant smooth g = recessive green w = recessive wrinkled

Mendel Mendel's law of segregation applied to an initial cross between pea plants with red flowers and pea plants with white flowers. The second generation had red-flowered plants to white-coloured plants in the ratio 3;1.

following year he published 'Experiments with plant hybrids', a paper that summarized his results. But the importance of his work was not recognized at the time, even by the eminent botanist Karl Wilhelm von Nägeli, to whom Mendel sent a copy of his paper. It was not until 1900, when his work was rediscovered by Hugo de Vries, Carl Erich Correns, and Erich Tschermak von Seysenegg, that Mendel achieved fame – 16 years after his death.

Further Reading

Edelson, Edward; Gingerich, Owen (ed), *Gregor Mendel,* Oxford Portraits in Science series, Oxford University Press, 1999.

George, Wilma B, *Gregor Mendel and Heredity,* Pioneers of Science and Discovery series, Priory Press, 1975.

Gribbin, John R, *Mendel (1822–1884) in 90 minutes,* Constable, 1997.

Klare, Roger, *Gregor Mendel: Father of Genetics,* Great Minds of Science series, Enslow Publishers, 1997.

Orel, Vitezslav, *Gregor Mendel: The First Geneticist,* Oxford University Press, 1996.

Sootin, Harry, *Gregor Mendel, Father of the Science of Genetics,* Blackie, 1961.

Mendeleyev, Dmitri Ivanovich (1834–1907)

Russian chemist whose name will always be linked with his outstanding achievement, the development of

Mendeleyev Russian chemist Dmitri Ivanovich Mendeleyev who formulated the periodic law that forms the basis of the Periodic Table of elements. The law was first described in a lecture to the Russian Chemical Society in 1868, but Mendeleyev himself was unable to present it due to illness. *Mary Evans Picture Library*

H= 1			Ti= 50	Zr= 90	?= 180
			V= 51	Nb= 94	Ta= 182
			Cr= 52	Mo= 96	W= 186
			Mn= 55	Rh= 104.4	Pt= 197.4
			Fe= 56	Ru= 104.4	Ir= 198
			Ni= Co	Pd= 106.6	Os= 198
			= 59		
	Be= 9.4	Mg= 24	Cu= 63.4	Ag= 108	Hg= 200
	B= 11	Al= 27.4	Zn= 65.2	Cd= 112	
	C= 12	Si= 28	?= 68	Ur= 116	Au= 197?
	N= 14	P= 31	?= 70	Sn= 118	
	O= 16	S= 32	As= 75	Sb= 122	Bi= 210?
	F= 19	Cl= 35.5	Se= 79.4	Te= 128?	
Li= 7	Na= 23	K= 39	Br= 80	I= 127	
		Ca= 40	Rb= 85.4	Cs= 133	Te= 204
		?= 45	Sr= 87.6	Ba= 137	Pb= 207
		?Er= 56	Ce= 92		
		?Yt= 60	La= 94?		
		?In= 75.6	Di= 95		
			Th= 118?		

Mendeleyev Mendeleyev's original (1869) periodic table, with similar elements on the same horizontal line.

the periodic table. He was the first chemist to understand that all elements are related members of a single ordered system. He converted what had hitherto been a highly fragmented and speculative branch of chemistry into a true, logical science.

Mendeleyev was born in Tobol'sk, Siberia, on 7 February 1834, the youngest of the 17 children of the head of the local high school. His father went blind when Mendeleyev was still a child, and the family had to rely increasingly on their mother for support. He was educated locally but could not gain admission to any Russian university (despite his mother's attempts on his behalf with the authorities at Moscow) because of the supposedly backward attainments of those educated in the provinces. In 1855 he finally qualified as a teacher at the Pedagogical Institute in St Petersburg. He took an advanced degree course in chemistry, and in 1857 obtained his first university appointment.

In 1859 he was sent by the government for further study at the University of Heidelberg in Germany, where he made valuable contact with the Italian chemist Stanislao ◊Cannizzaro, whose insistence on a proper distinction between atomic and molecular masses influenced Mendeleyev greatly. In 1861 he returned to St Petersburg and became professor of general chemistry at the Technical Institute there in 1864. He could find no textbook adequate for his students' needs and so he decided to produce his own. The resulting *Principles of Chemistry* (1868–70) won him international renown; it was translated into English in 1891 and 1897.

Mendeleyev began work on his periodic law in the late 1860s, and he went on to conduct research in various other fields. Then in 1890 he chose to be a spokesman for students who were protesting against unjust conditions. For these allegedly improper activities he was retired from the university and became controller of the Bureau for Weights and Measures, although from 1893 he received no other professorial appointment. He died in St Petersburg on 2 February 1907, five days before his 73rd birthday. His nomination for the 1906 Nobel Prize for Chemistry failed by one vote – the award went to the French chemist Henri Moissan (1852–1907) – but his name became recorded in perpetuity 50 years later when element number 101 was called mendelevium.

Before Mendeleyev produced his periodic law, understanding of the chemical elements had long been an elusive and frustrating task. The attempts by various chemists to put the whole field into some intelligible reference system had acted rather like the progressively stronger lenses of a microscope in bringing a sensed but unseen object into clear vision. According to Mendeleyev the properties of the elements, as well as those of their compounds, are periodic functions of their atomic weights (relative atomic masses). In 1869 he stated that 'the elements arranged according to the magnitude of atomic weights show a periodic change of properties'. Other chemists, notably Lothar ◊Meyer in Germany, had meanwhile come to similar conclusions, Meyer publishing his findings independently.

Mendeleyev compiled the first true periodic table, listing all the 63 elements then known. Not all elements would 'fit' properly using the atomic masses of the time, so he altered indium from 76 to 114 (modern value 114.8) and beryllium from 13.8 to 9.2 (modern value 9.013). In 1871 he produced a revisionary paper showing the correct repositioning of 17 elements.

Also in order to make the table work Mendeleyev had to leave gaps, and he predicted that further elements would eventually be discovered to fill them. These predictions provided the strongest endorsement of the periodic law. Three were discovered in Mendeleyev's lifetime: gallium in 1871, scandium in 1879, and germanium in 1886, all with properties that tallied closely with those he had assigned to them.

There will come a time, when the world will be filled with one science, one truth, one industry, one brotherhood, one friendship with nature ... this is my belief, it progresses, it grows stronger, this is worth living for, this is worth waiting for.
DIMITRI MENDELEYEV *IN Y A URMANTSEV*
THE SYMMETRY OF NATURE
AND THE NATURE OF SYMMETRY *1974*

Far-sighted though Mendeleyev was, he had no notion that the periodic recurrences of similar properties in the list of elements reflect anything in the structures of their atoms. It was not until the 1920s that it was realized that the key parameter in the periodic system is not the atomic mass but the atomic number of the elements – a measure of the number of nuclear protons or electrons in the stable atom. Since then great progress has been made in explaining the periodic law in terms of the electronic structures of atoms and molecules.

Among Mendeleyev's other investigations were the specific volumes of gases and the conditions that are necessary for their liquefaction. Following visits to the oilfields of the Caucasus and in the USA he examined the origins of petroleum. He was convinced that the future held great possibilities for human flight, and in 1887 he made an ascent in a balloon to observe an eclipse of the Sun. He farmed a small estate and applied his scientific knowledge to improve the yield and quality of crops, an endeavour invaluable for Russia's predominantly agricultural economy.

Further Reading

Bensaude-Vincent, Bernadette, 'Mendeleev's periodic system of chemical elements', *Brit J Hist Sci*, 1986, v 19, pp 3–17.
Petrianov-Sokolov, I V, *Elementary Order: Mendeleev's Periodic System*, Mir, 1985.

Menzel, Donald Howard (1901–1976) US physicist and astronomer whose work on the spectrum of the solar chromosphere revolutionized much of solar astronomy. He was one of the first scientists to combine astronomy with atomic physics and, as a teacher and writer he had a considerable influence on the development of astrophysics during the 20th century.

Menzel was born on 11 April 1901 in Florence, Colorado, where his father was a railroad agent. When Menzel was four his father moved to Leadville, a remote mining centre where Menzel then lived until the age of 16, when he enrolled at the University of Denver. After graduation, he joined the staff of Princeton University as a graduate assistant and came under the benign influence of Henry ◊Russell, the co-originator of the Hertzsprung–Russell diagram, who taught a course on basic astrophysics there. Menzel soon became fascinated by the combination of atomic physics, mathematics, and relativity theory. Nevertheless, to gain more practical astronomical experience, he became assistant astronomer at the Lick Observatory in California in 1924. There, priority was given to measuring visual binary stars and stellar radial velocity, but of more interest to Menzel was William ◊Campbell's collection of solar chromospheric spectra and he took the opportunity to develop a quantitative spectroscopy using recently gained knowledge of the spectra of complex atoms and wave mechanics.

In 1932 Menzel joined Harvard University Observatory (where he was to become director some 30 years later). After four years he began experimental work to study the solar corona outside eclipses. The coronagraph he constructed for this purpose was the beginning of the High Altitude Observatory, which has since been developed into one of the leading institutions participating in solar physics research. At Harvard, Menzel established a course that included study of radiative transfer, the formation of spectra in stellar atmospheres and gaseous nebulae, and atomic physics and statistical mechanics, together with the study of dynamics, classical electromagnetic theory, and relativity. (This comprehensive syllabus was later published as *Mathematical Physics*.)

During World War II Menzel served with the US Navy, advising on the effect of solar activity on radio communication and radar propagation. After the war, he became involved in raising funds for a number of observatories. The war had shown the value of radio communication, and the need for information about solar activity led the US Air Force to construct a solar observatory in New Mexico. Menzel supervised the design of several instruments for the laboratory, using the results obtained to further study solar prominences, low temperatures in sunspots, and the origin of solar flares. Menzel was also chairman of the National

Radio Astronomy Observatory Advisory Committee; he participated in setting up the Kitt Peak National Observatory in Arizona; he was instrumental in bringing the Smithsonian Astrophysics Observatory from Washington to Cambridge; and he was a key figure in finding independent funding for the Solar Observatory in South Africa.

Menzel retired from Harvard in 1971 to become scientific director of a company manufacturing antennae for communications and radio astronomy. He died on 14 December 1976 after a prolonged illness.

At Princeton, Menzel and Henry Russell held a virtual monopoly on theoretrical astrophysics. But that was by no means Menzel's sole interest. He devised a technique for computing the temperature of planets from measurements of water cell transmissions and he made important contributions to atmospheric geophysics, radio propagation, and even lunar nomenclature. He also held patents on the use of gallium in liquid ball bearings and on heat transfer in atomic plants. Further work included the development of a fluid clutch and the investigation of solar energy conversion into electricity.

In his early days at Harvard, Menzel returned to his favourite subject, the Sun. In observing eclipses he developed a means of taking photographs with very good height resolution. Examining more than 800 spectra, he then established a wholly new theoretical approach to the structure of the gaseous envelope surrounding the Sun and other stars. With Perkins, Menzel also calculated the theoretical intensities of atomic hydrogen's spectral lines – a work that became a standard reference on the subject. It was followed by a series of papers on 'Physical processes in gaseous nebulae', which provided a framework for the quantitative analysis of nebular spectra.

Mercator, Gerardus (1512–1594) Latinized name of Gerard de Cremere or Gerhard Kremer. Flemish mathematician, geographer, instrumentmaker, and cartographer. He is primarily remembered for the map projection that bears his name, in which the globe is projected onto a cylinder, the meridian and parallels appearing as straight lines crossing at right angles. Mercator's projection is still widely used for navigation. In 1585 he was the first to use the word 'atlas' to describe his book of maps (completed by his son in 1594), which had a drawing of Atlas holding the globe on his shoulders on the cover.

Born in Rupelmonde, Flanders (now Roermonde, Netherlands) on 5 March 1512, Gerard de Cremere was educated at 's-Hertogenbosch in the Netherlands and entered the University of Louvain in 1530 at which time he Latinized his name. He graduated with an MA in 1532.

Philosophy and theology had been his principle subjects at Louvain and after his graduation he underwent a personal philosophical and religious crisis, being unable to reconcile the Bible's version of the universe with that of ◊Aristotle. He travelled at this time, visiting Mechelen and Antwerp, and returned with his doubts unresolved but with a growing interest in geography. On his return to Louvain he studied mathematics under Dutch mathematician, astronomer, and geographer Gemma Frisius (1508–1555), learning also to apply mathematics to astronomy and geography. By the age of 24 he was also a proficient engraver, calligrapher, and scientific instrumentmaker, having studied with Gaspar a Myrica. His contributions to calligraphy and engraving were very influential among artisans.

In 1534, Mercator founded a centre for the study of geography at Louvain, from which he made a series of maps. Working with Frisius and Myrica, he constructed a terrestrial globe in 1536, and in 1537 they constructed a celestial globe. He also made a map of Palestine and scientific instruments, and became a reputable surveyor during his time in Louvain, making two sets of surveying instruments for Charles V.

As a Protestant, Mercator suffered persecution. Suspicions were also aroused by the travels he made collecting information for his maps and he was imprisoned in 1544 on charges of heresy. The charges could not be proved for lack of evidence and with the help of the University of Louvain he was released after seven months. In 1552, to escape continued persecution, he emigrated to Duisberg in Germany, where he opened a cartographer's workshop. In Duisberg he published the first modern maps of Europe in 1554 and of Britain and Lorraine in 1564. He taught mathematics from 1559 to 1562, in which year he was appointed court cosmographer to Duke Wilhelm of Cleve.

In 1568 Mercator published his chronology of the world from the creation onwards, based on astronomical records, especially those of eclipses. His cylindrical chart of the world using what is now known as Mercator's projection appeared in 1569. It was designed for seafarers and provided a line of constant bearing for navigators using parallel lines that crossed all the meridians at the same angle. On the surface of a globe these lines are curved and converge at the poles. Flattening the map out and making the lines parallel produced distortions in east–west distances and towards the poles. Twentieth-century attempts to reduce this distortion (such as the Peters projection) have shown that it is geometrically impossible to produce a totally accurate map of the spherical world on a cylinder or a flat piece of paper. Mercator's projection, which was modified by Wright and Molyneux at the end of the 16th century, has endured and is still used as a navigational tool.

In later years, Mercator designed, engraved, and published the collection of maps that he called an atlas. He made a important break away from ◊Ptolemy's methods of mapmaking and produced updated and improved versions of Ptolemy's maps (1578) as the first part of his atlas, adding a series of detailed and accurate maps of France, Germany, and the Netherlands in 1585. He published a further series, in 1889, of maps of the Balkans and Greece. After his death in Duisberg on 2 December 1594, Mercator's son, Rumold, completed the work and published it under the name *Atlas – or Cosmographic Meditations on the Structure of the World.*

Mergenthaler, Ottmar (1854–1899) German-born US inventor who devised the Linotype machine, which greatly speeded typesetting and revolutionized the world of printing and publishing.

Mergenthaler was born in Germany on 11 May 1854 and was apprenticed to a watchmaker before emigrating to the USA in 1872. He settled in Washington, DC and found employment in a factory manufacturing scientific instruments. In 1876 he moved to Baltimore and began working for James O Clephane, remedying faults in a recently invented prototype of a writing machine. Although a full-sized machine was constructed, it was not a success and the two men abandoned the idea. They combined their talents and in 1884 produced what was to become known as the Linotype machine.

By 1886, the first machines were in use and a company was formed to spearhead their production with Mergenthaler as one of the directors. He resigned from the position in 1888 but continued to show an interest in the firm, contributing over the years as many as 50 new modifications to the original design. He died in Baltimore on 28 October 1899.

Before Linotype, printing was carried out by hand-setting, a long and laborious process. Mergenthaler's invention speeded this operation and made printed matter, from books to penny news sheets, cheaper to produce. The design of the machine enabled a line of type (hence the name) to be composed at one time and cast as a single piece of metal. The machine was rather like a large typewriter, about two metres high, with a store of matrices (moulds) at the top. The operator selected the letters by means of rods controlled by the 'typewriter' keys, and these letters fell through tiny trap-doors to drop into position in a line setting. As each line was completed it was passed on to the 'metal pot' area where a cast was made to form a 'slug' with the letters in relief on one side. This then fitted into a page of type ready for printing, while the matrices were returned to the store at the top of the machine for re-use.

A person operating one of Mergenthaler's keyboards could set type up to three or four times faster than by hand-setting, cutting the labour cost of production to a fraction of before. The machine heralded a new age for printing in which books became affordable, and newspapers could really claim to carry up-to-the-minute information, for the Linotype made it possible to change and re-set copy to within minutes of going to press.

Further Reading

Schlesinger, Carl, *Biography of Ottmar Mergenthaler, Inventor of the Linotype,* History of the Book series, Oak Knoll Press, 1988, v 4.
Schlesinger, Carl (ed), *The Biography of Ottmar Mergenthaler,* Oak Knoll Press, 1993.

Meselson and Stahl, Matthew Stanley Meselson (1930–) and Franklin William Stahl (1929–) US molecular biologists who are best known for their collaborative work that confirmed the theory of Francis ◊Crick and James ◊Watson that DNA replication is semi-conservative (that is, that the daughter cells each receive one strand of DNA from the original parent cell and one newly replicated strand, in contrast to conservative replication in which one daughter cell would receive both of the parental DNA strands and the other daughter would receive both the newly replicated strands).

Meselson was born on 24 May 1930 in Denver, Colorado. He studied liberal arts at the University of Chicago, gaining his doctorate in 1951, then physical chemistry at the California Institute of Technology (Caltech), obtaining a second doctorate in 1957. He remained at Caltech until 1976 – as assistant professor of chemistry 1958–60, as associate professor of chemistry 1958–60, then as associate professor and later professor of biology. In 1976 he became Cabot Professor of Natural Sciences at Harvard University. Since 1963 he has also been a consultant to the US Arms Control and Disarmament Agency.

Stahl was born on 8 October 1929 in Boston, Massachusetts. He was educated at Harvard University, from which he graduated in 1951, and at the University of Rochester, from which he gained his doctorate in biology in 1956. He was a research fellow in biology at Calafornia Institute of Technology 1955–58, when he moved to the University of Missouri, where he was associate professor of zoology 1958–59, then associate professor until 1970. Since 1970 he has been professor of biology at the University of Oregon and a research associate of the Institute of Molecular Biology.

Meselson and Stahl began their research that demonstrated the semi-conservative nature of DNA replication in 1957. After unsuccessfully experimenting with viruses, they turned their attention to the bacterium

Escherichia coli. They grew the bacteria on a culture medium containing nitrogen-15 (a heavy isotope of nitrogen) as the only nitrogen source, so that the nitrogen-15 would become incorporated into the nitrogenous bases of the bacterial DNA. They then transferred the bacteria to a medium containing nitrogen-14 (the normal nitrogen isotope) as the only nitrogen source. After the bacteria had reproduced several times, they were centrifuged to extract their DNA, and the density of the DNA was determined by equilibrium density gradient centrifugation, in which samples of different densities separate into discrete bands; the concentration of DNA in each band can then be determined by ultraviolet absorption spectrography.

From these processes Meselson and Stahl obtained three different types of DNA; one containing only nitrogen-14, one containing only nitrogen-15 and a hybrid containing both nitrogen isotopes. On heating, the hybrid separated into two halves, one from the parental DNA and one that had been newly synthesized. These findings demonstrated that the double helix of DNA splits into two strands when the DNA replicates, with each of the single strands acting as a template for the synthesis of a complementary strand; the final result is two DNA molecules, each comprising one strand from the parent molecule and one newly synthesized strand. Thus Meselson and Stahl confirmed the hypothesis of semi-conservative DNA replication, one of the most important concepts in modern molecular biology.

In 1961, working with Sydney ◊Brenner and François ◊Jacob, Meselson and Stahl demonstrated that ribosomes require instructions in order to be able to manufacture proteins, and that ribosomes can make proteins that are different from those normally produced by a particular cell. They also showed that messenger RNA supplies the instructions to the ribosomes.

In addition to their collaborative work, Stahl has researched into the genetics of bacteriophages and has written a book on the mechanism of inheritance; and Meselson has investigated the molecular biology of nucleic acids, the mechanisms of DNA recombination and repair, and the processes of gene control and evolution.

Messerschmitt, Willy (Wilhelm Emil) (1898–1978) German aircraft designer and industrialist, the foremost of only a handful of people who shaped the development of the aircraft industry in his country from the early 1920s to the early 1980s.

Messerschmitt was born in Frankfurt am Main on 26 June 1898. In Bamberg, in 1909, he attended the Realschule, a secondary school with a scientific bias. He was fascinated by the fast-developing world of aviation, and in 1912 met the architect and gliding pioneer Friedrich Harth. It was their experimentation with primitive canard (tail-first) gliders that decided Messerschmitt on his future career.

As a student at the Oberealschule in Nürnberg during 1915, Messerschmitt undertook the detailed design and construction of his first glider. Given a military discharge on medical grounds in 1917, he continued his education at the Technische Hochschule in Munich.

A glider he designed with Harth achieved an unofficial world duration record in 1921. The following year they set up a flying school and in 1923, while still a student, Messerschmitt formed his own company in Bamberg. Its first product, the S-14 cantilever monoplane glider, formed the subject of the thesis for his diploma.

After experiments with gliders powered by auxiliary engines, he produced his first powered aircraft in 1925, the ultra-light sports two-seater Me-17. In 1926 came the flight of the Me-18 small transport, the production version of which was adapted to largely metal construction.

Working in a country in which the manufacture of military aircraft was forbidden under the Treaty of Versailles, Messerschmitt pursued designs for light sporting aircraft, none of which attracted many orders. When the Nazis came to power in 1933, however, the German air ministry gave great stimulus to aviation, and an order to Messerschmitt to develop a new touring aircraft.

The resulting design, the Me-37 (or Bf-108 in production) became the archetypal low-wing, four-seater, cabin monoplane, with retractable landing gear and flaps. It was the success of this aircraft that kept Messerschmitt in the industry, for in 1934 he had given serious thought to taking up a professorship in Danzig Technical College.

In taking part in the German air ministry's 1934 design competition for a fighter aircraft to equip the 'secret' Luftwaffe, Messerschmitt risked all by building a machine of advanced concept and employing the most modern techniques. The resulting Bf-109 was to become the standard fighter of the Luftwaffe and several other air forces. It was to be equated with the legendary Spitfire.

By 1938, firmly established as a designer of advanced fighter aircraft, Messerschmitt was appointed chairman and general director of the company manufacturing his designs – Bayerische Flugzeugwerke – which was then renamed Messerschmitt Aktiengesellschaft. He and his company went on to produce numerous designs for fighter, bomber, and transport aircraft, many of which served the Luftwaffe in large numbers throughout World War II.

At the war's end Messerschmitt was taken prisoner by the British, who with the French and Americans, asked him to work for them as an adviser, but he declined all proposals. On his return to Germany he was arrested by US troops and held in custody for two years. Banned from manufacturing aircraft in Germany, Messerschmitt went on to design and produce components for prefabricated houses, sewing machines, and a two-seater 'bubble' car.

He took up aircraft design again in 1952 under an advisory contract with the Spanish manufacturer Hispano, which was already building his '109' fighter under licence. His HA-200 Saeta, first flown in 1955, served in the early 1980s as the standard advanced trainer of the Spanish Air Force.

Between 1956 and 1964 Messerschmitt worked in association with the German Bolkow and Heinkel companies and developed the VJ-101 supersonic V/STOL (vertical/short take-off and landing) combat aircraft. His company merged with Bolkow in 1963 and they were later joined by Hamburger Flugzengbau. In 1969 Messerschmitt became chairman of the supervisory board of the resulting Messerschmitt Bolkow Blohm (MBB) group.

MBB is identified today with the Tornado multi-role combat aircraft being built for NATO countries, and the A300 Airbus airliner, both designs being initiated before Messerschmitt's death on 15 September 1978, when he was honorary chairman.

Many of the great names in aircraft manufacture were from the generation before Messerschmitt's. They built their companies on the sales of vast numbers of military biplanes for World War I. Messerschmitt, however, never willingly designed biplanes. To him they were a retrograde step. The efficient cantilever monoplanes he designed from the early 1920s failed to secure large sales mainly because they were launched on to a market convinced of the need for visible struts and bracing wires.

The Me-18 small transport and the Me-19 sporting aircraft, both of the mid-1920s, embodied characteristics to be found in any aircraft designed or supervised by him. These were: simple concept, minimum weight and aerodynamic drag, and the possibility of continued development.

The last-mentioned characteristic was taken to the extreme in his '109' fighter, which, in 20 years and more than 35,000 examples (making the second largest production of any aircraft), was developed in more than 50 variants. Messerschmitt's devotion to innovation in construction was exemplified by the hundreds of personal patents that were used throughout his designs.

Many of Messerschmitt's aircraft, when first flown, were the most advanced of their kind, having considerable performance advantage over competitors. Performance, coupled with elegance, characterizing his earlier designs, was to be seen also during World War II in the Me-262 twinjet fighter. In operation at the same time as the Gloster Meteor jet, Messerschmitt's machine featured a triangular minimal-cross-section fuselage, high-aspect-ratio swept wings, heavier armament and a 210-kph/130-mph speed advantage over the staid British design.

Messerschmitt's '109' fighter, which gave employment to (or forced it upon) as many as 81,000 people in 25 plants, was the backbone of the Luftwaffe fighter force for the whole of the war. Production topped an incredible 2,000 per month by the end of 1944. Messerschmitt's name and work live on in what is today Germany's largest aerospace enterprise, Messerschmitt Bolkow Blohm. Employing more than 20,000 people, MBB makes satellites, helicopters, missiles, and transport systems, as well as the Tornado and Airbus aircraft.

Messier, Charles (1730–1817) French astronomer whose work on the discovery of comets led to a compilation of the locations of nebulae and star clusters – the Messier catalogue – that is still of some relevance 200 years later.

Messier was born on 26 June 1730 in Badonviller, in the province of Lorraine. Little is known about his life until he joined the Paris Observatory as a draughtsman and astronomical recorder under the duration of one of the most famous men of the time, Joseph-Nicolas Delisle (1688–1768). Later he searched the night sky for comets, but he was continually hampered by encountering other rather obscure forms that he came to recognize as nebulae. During the period 1760–84, therefore, Messier set about compiling a list of these nebulae and star clusters in order that he and other astronomers could more easily pinpoint (and thus ignore) these celestial features, in this way not only saving time but reducing the risk of any confusion with possible new comets.

At an early stage in Messier's career, his work was already being acknowledged for its importance and thoroughness, and in 1764 he was elected to the Royal Society in London. Six years later, in 1770, he was duly honoured by his own country and made a member of the prestigious Academy of Sciences in Paris. He died in Paris on 12 April 1817.

Initially, Messier's interest in comets stemmed from the predicted return of Halley's comet; before he died (in 1740), Edmond ◊Halley had calculated that the comet's reappearance would take place in around 1758–59. Messier duly sighted its return on 21 January 1759, an experience that was to inspire him with the desire to go on discovering new comets for the rest of his life. (Although he is attributed with being the first person to resight the Halley comet from French soil, a German amateur astronomer is believed to have been the first actually to see it, on Christmas Day, 1758.)

Messier certainly earned his nickname, the 'Comet Ferret', from Louis XV. He spent long hours, over many years, to discover ultimately between 15 and 21 new comets. (The actual numbers vary according to the source of information, but it is thought not to be less than 15.) In the beginning, he was frustrated by nebulae and star clusters, which were, on occasions, readily confused with comets and had to be investigated continuously, a process that was also time-consuming. Messier decided that the most sensible idea was to compile a list identifying each of these permanent objects, numbering them, and noting their position.

The task he undertook was an extremely difficult one, given the equipment available at that time. Although a vast improvement had then recently been achieved with the development (during the first half of the 1700s) of the compound lens, the range and capability of the telescope was still in its infancy. Nevertheless, Messier began this work in earnest in 1760, and by 1771 he had completed a preliminary list of 45 nebulae and galaxies, giving each one an identifying M number. Within ten years he had compiled the

majority of his catalogue, and by 1784 the list consisted of 103 numbers.

Basically, Messier's original catalogue is still relevant today with some additions – Pierre Méchain (1744–1804) added six more during Messier's lifetime – although doubts inevitably exist as to the reality of some he registered. But none can doubt the presence of such famous astronomical features as the Crab nebula M1, Andromeda M31, and the Pleiades M45.

Meyer, (Julius) Lothar (1830–1895) German chemist who, independently of Dmitri ◊Mendeleyev, produced a periodic law describing the properties of the chemical elements.

Meyer was born in Varel, Oldenburg, on 19 August 1830, the son of a doctor of medicine. He began his university career by studying medicine at Zürich in Switzerland. He then took courses in chemistry at Heidelberg (under Robert ◊Bunsen), in physics at Königsberg, and in pathology at Würzburg, where he qualified as a physician in 1854. Four years later he gained his PhD from the University of Breslau (now Wrocław in Poland). On the basis of this wide combination of interests he began his career as a science educator in 1859, holding various appointments until he became professor of chemistry at Karlsruhe

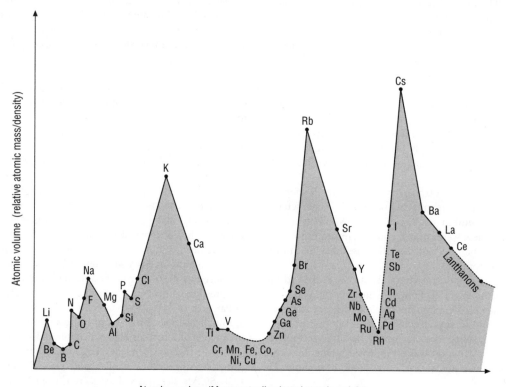

Meyer Part of the Lothar Meyer curve (with modern additions).

Polytechnic in 1868. In 1876 he was appointed the first professor of chemistry at Tübingen University, where he remained for the rest of his life. He died in Tübingen on 11 April 1895.

In his book *Modern Chemical Theory* (1864), a lucid exposition of the contemporary principles of the science of chemistry, Meyer drew up a table which presented all the elements according to their atomic weights (relative atomic masses), relating the weights to chemical properties. In 1870 he published the results of his further researches in the form of a graph of atomic volume (atomic weight divided by density) against atomic weight, which demonstrated the periodicity in the variation of the elements' properties. He showed that each element will not combine with the same numbers of hydrogen or chlorine atoms, establishing the concept of valency. He coined the terms univalent, bivalent, trivalent, and so on, according to the number involved. Consequently it became customary to divide the elements into groups defined by the number of hydrogen atoms with which a given element can combine (or displace).

Despite the fact that Meyer had reached his conclusions quite independently of Mendeleyev, he never claimed priority for his findings. And unlike Mendeleyev, he made no predictions about the composition and properties of any elements still to be discovered.

Meyer, Viktor (1848–1897) German organic chemist best known for the method of determining vapour densities (and hence molecular masses) named after him. He was also the discoverer of the heterocyclic compound thiophene.

Meyer was born in Berlin on 8 September 1848. His undergraduate studies were carried out partly at Heidelberg (under Robert ◊Bunsen), at Berlin (under Johann von ◊Baeyer), and at Würtemberg. He gained his PhD at Heidelberg in 1867 while only 19 years old and three years later was appointed professor of chemistry at Stuttgart Polytechnic. In 1872 he progressed to the Technische Hochschule at Zürich in Switzerland and in 1885 he became a professor at Göttingen. When Bunsen died in 1889, Meyer succeeded to his professorship at Heidelberg. A long period of working with iodine and bromine at high temperatures undermined his health and, in a fit of depression, he committed suicide by taking cyanide on 8 August 1897.

Meyer's discovery about the nature of vapour densities was based largely on previous work in this field, notably that of the Italian physical chemist Amedeo ◊Avogadro, who as early as 1811 had indicated the difference between atoms and molecules. Later, in his celebrated law, Avogadro maintained that equal volumes of two gases contain the same numbers of

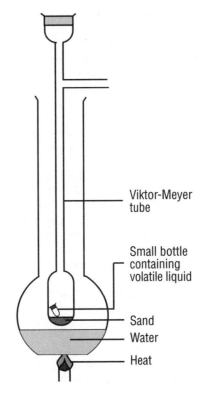

Meyer Viktor Meyer's apparatus for measuring vapour density.

molecules (when the temperatures and pressures are also equal). When the two volumes of gas combine chemically, the individual atoms join to form molecules, whose volume depends on the proportion in which the atoms combine.

This welcomingly straightforward definition of one of the key processes in experimental chemistry met with little acceptance from the leading chemists of the day until, in 1871, Meyer gave an incontestable demonstration of its validity. He determined the molecular weights of volatile substances formed in this way by measuring their vapour densities (molecular weight, or relative molecular mass, is twice the vapour density).

He went on to a series of pyrotechnical studies in which he determined the vapour densities of inorganic substances at high temperatures. The results of this work, undertaken with his brother Karl, were published in 1885 in their book *Pyrotechnical Research*. At about the same time, Meyer described his organic vapour density studies in his *Textbook of Organic Chemistry* (published in two volumes, 1883–96).

In 1883, in the course of a lecture demonstration on the nature of benzene, Meyer was surprised to discover that the substance did not react in the way he had predicted. Benzene obtained from petroleum reacted as expected, whereas a purer sample synthesized from benzoic acid did not. From the impure benzene Meyer isolated thiophene, a heterocyclic compound containing sulphur, which much later was to become an important component of various synthetic drugs.

In the Viktor Meyer method for determining vapour density (and hence molecular mass), the apparatus shown is used. A known mass of a volatile liquid is rapidly vaporized by raising its temperature well above the boiling point and the volume occupied by the resulting vapour is determined by measuring the volume of air it displaces. The inner tube (Viktor-Meyer, or V-M tube) contains a little sand to break the fall of the small bottle of liquid introduced at the top (after removing the stopper) and the heating jacket causes the liquid to boil, pushing off the ground-glass stopper of the small bottle. The heavy vapour remains at the bottom of the V-M tube and an equal volume of air is displaced and collected 'over water'. This volume is converted to standard temperature and pressure and, by using the fact that the relative molecular mass in grams occupies 22.4 l/ 39.4 pt at standard temperature and pressure (or the vapour density in grams occupies 11.2 l/19.7 pt), these values can be found.

The Viktor Meyer method is simple to carry out and adaptable, only small amounts of the volatile liquid being needed, and the method can be used over a wide temperature range.

Meyerhof, Otto Fritz (1884–1951) German-born

US biochemist who shared (with Archibald ◊Hill) the 1922 Nobel Prize for Physiology or Medicine for his research into the metabolic processes involved in the action of muscles.

Meyerhof was born on 12 April 1884 in Hanover, the son of a merchant. He attended school in Berlin but was often absent because of a kidney disorder, as a result of which he received much of his early education at home. Later he became a medical student at the universities of Freiburg, Berlin, Strasbourg, and Heidelberg. In 1909 he graduated from Heidelberg and worked in a medical laboratory there until 1912, when he moved to the University of Kiel as an assistant in the department of physiology, becoming a professor at the university in 1918. Shortly after receiving his Nobel prize, he was offered a chair in biochemistry in the USA. To keep him in Germany, Meyerhof was appointed the head of a new department specially created for him at the Kaiser-Wilhelm Institute for Biology in Berlin-Dahlem; he held this position 1924–29, when he became head of the department of physiology in a new institute for medical research at the University of Heidelberg. As a result of Adolf Hitler's rise to power in the 1930s, Meyerhof left Germany in 1938 and went to Paris, where he became director of research at the Institut de Biologie Physiochimique. In 1940, when France fell to Germany in the early part of World War II, he fled to the USA, where he was appointed research professor of physiological chemistry at the University of Pennsylvania, Philadelphia, a position he held for the rest of his life. Meyerhof became a US citizen in 1948, and died three years later on 6 October 1951.

Meyerhof's early work concerned energy exchanges in nitrifying bacteria, about which he published three papers 1916–17. He then became interested in the mechanism by which energy from food is released and utilized by living cells. In 1920 he showed that, in anaerobic conditions, the amounts of glycogen metabolized and of lactic acid produced in a contracting muscle are proportional to the tension in the muscle. He also demonstrated that 20–25% of the lactic acid is oxidized during the muscle's recovery period and that energy produced by this oxidation is used to convert the remainder of the lactic acid back to glycogen. Meyerhof introduced the term 'glycolysis' to describe the anaerobic degradation of glycogen to lactic acid, and showed the cyclic nature of energy transformations in living cells. The complete metabolic pathway of glycolysis – known as the Embden–Meyerhof pathway (after Meyerhof and a co-worker) – was later worked out by Carl and Gerty ◊Cori. Despite these and later revisions, Meyerhof's work remains the basic contribution to our knowledge of the very complex processes involved in muscular action.

Continuing his research on intracellular energy metabolism, between 1926 and 1927 Meyerhof demonstrated that glycolysis is not the result of bacterial activity, and in 1928, working with Lohmann, discovered that 50,000 joules per gram molecule of phosphate are liberated during the hydrolysis of creatine phosphate. In the following year Lohmann discovered adenosine triphosphate (ATP) in muscle and, with Meyerhof, began to study the new concept of oxidative phosphorylation. In the 1940s Meyerhof found in the microsomes in muscle cells a new ATPase enzyme that is magnesium activated.

Michelson, Albert Abraham (1852–1931) German-

born US physicist who, in association with Edward ◊Morley, performed the classic Michelson–Morley experiment for light waves. Michelson also made very precise determinations of the velocity of light. This work entailed the development of extremely sensitive optical equipment, and in recognition of his achievements in optics and measurement, Michelson was awarded the 1907 Nobel Prize for Physics, becoming the first US citizen to gain a Nobel prize.

Michelson was born in Strelno in Germany (now Strzelno in Poland) on 19 December 1852. His family emigrated to the USA while he was a young child, and eventually settled in Nevada. Michelson went to school in San Francisco and then tried unsuccessfully to enter the US Naval Academy at Annapolis. However, he was allowed to plead his case with the US president, Ulysses S Grant, who directed that Michelson be admitted in 1869. After graduating in 1873, Michelson spent two years at sea and was then appointed as an instructor in physics and chemistry at the academy. From 1880–82, Michelson undertook postgraduate study at Berlin under Hermann von ◊Helmholtz and at Paris. On returning to the USA, he left the navy and was appointed professor of physics at the Case School of Applied Science in Cleveland, Ohio. In 1889 Michelson moved to Clark University at Worcester, Massachusetts, and then in 1892 became professor of physics at the University of Chicago, a position he held until 1929. Among his honours were the presidency of the American Physical Society 1901–03 and the award of the Royal Society's Copley Medal in 1907. Michelson died on 9 May 1931.

Michelson began his scientific career in 1878, when he improved the rotating-mirror method of Léon ◊Foucault to determine the velocity of light. This led to the construction of an interferometer to detect any difference in the velocity of light in two directions at right angles. In this instrument, a beam was split into two beams at right angles. Each was sent to a mirror and the reflected beams were made to interfere with each other. The interference pattern produced was recorded and the interferometer turned through a right angle. If there was any difference in the velocity of light, it would cause the light to take different times to traverse the same paths and a change would occur in the interference pattern produced. Michelson built the interferometer to make an experiment suggested by James Clerk ◊Maxwell to detect the motion of the Earth through the ether, which was believed to exist as the medium in which light waves were propagated. If the Earth were moving through the ether, light would travel slower in the direction of the Earth's motion than at right angles to it. The amount of change in the interference pattern produced in the interferometer would indicate how fast the Earth was moving through the ether.

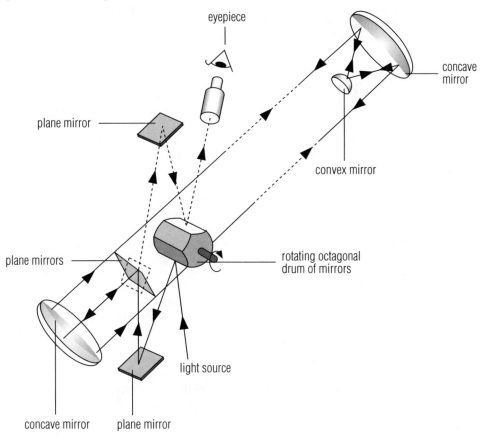

Michelson In 1926 US physicist Albert Michelson measured the speed of light precisely by using an octagonal drum of mirrors spun at 550 revolutions per second to time a light beam over a distance of more than 70 km/43 mi.

Michelson first undertook this experiment at Berlin in 1881. He could detect no change in the interference pattern and so later set about constructing a much more sensitive interferometer in collaboration with Morley, with whom Michelson began to work in 1885. The experiment was repeated in 1887 and still no effect due to the ether was found. This was a disappointment to Michelson, and he set about finding other uses for the interferometer. However, the experiment, which is now known as the Michelson–Morley experiment, marked a turning point in theoretical physics, for its negative result demonstrated that the velocity of light is constant whatever the motion of the observer. Two explanations could account for this. One was that the ether does exist but moves with the Earth; this was disproved by Oliver ◊Lodge in 1893. The other was that the ether does not exist but that moving objects contract slightly in the direction of their motion. This was put forward by George ◊FitzGerald and became part of the special theory of relativity proposed by Albert ◊Einstein in 1905. Thus the Michelson–Morley experiment was of crucial importance in the formulation of relativity, though Michelson himself remained sceptical.

Michelson's other achievements were concerned with extremely precise measurement. In 1892 and 1893, he and Morley redefined the length of the standard metre kept at Paris in terms of a certain number of wavelengths of monochromatic light, using a red line in the cadmium spectrum. This method of defining the standard unit of length was finally adopted in 1960, and a krypton line is now used.

Michelson also developed his interferometer into a precision instrument for measuring the diameters of heavenly bodies and in 1920 announced the size of the giant star Betelgeuse, the first star to be measured. Michelson then undertook extremely precise determinations of the velocity of light, measuring it over a 35-km/22-mi path between two mountain peaks in California. In 1926, he obtained the value 299,796 ± 4 km per second, a range that includes the present value of 299,792.5 km/186,291 mi per second.

Michelson later returned to the Michelson–Morley experiment and repeated it yet again to try and produce a positive result. He did not succeed a third time, and this helped to verify Einstein's theories. No one else has succeeded since.

Michelson's gift for extremely precise experimental work enabled him to make one of the most important discoveries in physics. It is ironic that only such ability could yield the negative result that was required for a new understanding of the nature of the universe.

Midgley, Thomas (1889–1944) US industrial chemist and engineer who discovered that tetraethyl lead is an efficient antiknock additive to petrol (pre-

venting pre-ignition in car engines) and introduced Freons (a group of chlorofluorocarbons) as the working gases in domestic refrigerators. Today the most commonly used is Freon 12, which is difluorodichloromethane, CF_2Cl_2.

Midgley was born in Beaver Falls, Pennsylvania, on 18 May 1889, the son of an engineer and inventor. He studied mechanical engineering at Cornell University, graduating in 1911. Early in World War I he worked on torpedo control systems. In 1916 he went to Ohio to work in the research department of an engineering firm, the Dayton Engineering Laboratories Company. He became a vice president of the Ethyl Corporation in 1923 and ten years later was a director of the Ethyl–Dow Chemical Company. In 1940 he contracted poliomyelitis and became paralysed. He died in Worthington, Ohio, on 2 November 1944.

While working for the Dayton Engineering Company, Midgley discovered empirically that ethyl iodide (iodoethane) prevents pre-ignition in car engines using low-octane fuel. He spent several years teaching himself the relevant chemistry and looking for a less expensive additive. In 1921 he experimented with tetraethyl lead, showing it to be an efficient antiknock agent. It became a standard additive, but its use was questioned from the 1970s because of the hazardous effects of airborne lead compounds emitted in exhaust fumes, and from the 1980s unleaded petrol became increasingly common.

Midgley used ethyl bromide (bromoethane) in his research, which led him to investigate the bromine in sea water and demonstrate a method for its extraction. Dayton Engineering was taken over by General Motors and he continued to work in their research laboratories.

In 1930 Midgley introduced Freon (CF_2Cl_2) as a non-inflammable, non-toxic refrigerant, which rapidly replaced ammonia, methyl chloride (chloromethane), and sulphur dioxide as the volatile but liquefiable gas in the mechanisms of domestic refrigerators. This gas and closely related compounds are still used universally for this purpose in freezers, fridges, and air-conditioning units. For many years after World War II, Freons were also extensively used as propellants in aerosol containers. A hypothesis that continued release of these compounds into the atmosphere could damage the Earth's ozone layer (which acts as a filter to prevent excessive ultraviolet radiation reaching the surface of the Earth) led to restrictions or bans on the use of Freon propellants in the 1970s.

Miller, Stanley Lloyd (1930–) US chemist who carried out a key experiment that demonstrated how amino acids, the building blocks of life, might have arisen in the primeval oceans of the primitive Earth.

Miller was born in Oakland, California, on 7 March 1930. He graduated from the University of California in 1951 and three years later gained his PhD from the University of Chicago. From 1954 to 1955 he was a postdoctoral Jewett Fellow at the California Institute of Technology; he then worked for five years in the department of biochemistry at the Columbia College of Physicians and Surgeons, first as an instructor in biochemistry and then as assistant professor. From 1960 he held appointments at the University of California in San Diego as assistant professor, associate professor, and finally professor of chemistry.

While working for his PhD under Harold ◊Urey, Miller set himself the task of trying to account for the origin of life on Earth. He chose as his experimental substances the components that had been proposed for the Earth's primitive atmosphere by Urey and the Russian biochemist Alexandr ◊Oparin. He used sterilized and purified water under an 'atmosphere' of methane, ammonia, and hydrogen, which he circulated for a week past an electric discharge (to simulate the likely type of energy source). He then analysed the mixture and, surprisingly, after such a relatively short experimental period, found organic compounds such as simple amino acids. These were of great significance because of their ability to combine together to form proteins.

It is important when assessing the significance of the results (which have been duplicated by various other workers since) to bear in mind the time scale of the experiment in comparison with that for the origination of life on Earth. If the conditions of Miller's experiment had been continued for millions of years (instead of just seven days) and other plausible prebiotic syntheses added in, the oceans of the primordial Earth – analogous to the water used in the experiment – would have become rich with a whole range of different types of organic molecules: the so-called prebiotic soup.

There are many other steps that are needed to develop a system that is capable of self-replication. Some of these have also been worked out in the laboratory, such as the prebiotic syntheses of purines, pyrimidines, and sugars needed to make up RNA or DNA. And we still do not know how the nucleic acids first began to self-replicate.

Millikan, Robert Andrews (1868–1953) US physicist who made the first determination of the charge of the electron and of Planck's constant. For these achievements, he was awarded the 1923 Nobel Prize for Physics.

Millikan was born in Morrison, Illinois, on 22 March 1868. He showed no interest in science as a child and became interested in physics only after entering

Oberlin College in 1886, where he obtained his BA in 1891 and MA in 1893. Millikan then went to Columbia University to continue his studies in physics, gaining his PhD in 1895. He then went to Germany to study with Max ◊Planck at Berlin and Hermann ◊Nernst at Göttingen before taking up an assistantship in physics at the University of Chicago in 1896.

Millikan remained at Chicago until 1921. At first he concentrated on teaching but from 1907, when he became associate professor of physics, he took more interest in research and began his experiments to find the electronic charge, completing this work in 1913. In 1910, Millikan became professor of physics at Chicago and during World War I was director of research for the National Research Council, which was concerned with defence research. In 1921, Millikan moved to Pasadena to become director of the Norman Bridge Laboratory at the California Institute of Technology. He retained this position until 1945, when he retired. In addition to the 1923 Nobel Prize for Physics, Millikan received many honours, including the award of the Royal Society's Hughes Medal in 1923 and the presidency of the American Physical Society 1916–18. Millikan died in Pasadena on 19 December 1953.

Millikan employed a method to determine the electronic charge that was simple in concept but difficult in practice, and a satisfactory result took him the five years, 1908–13, to achieve. He began by studying the rate of fall of water droplets under the influence of an electric field. Millikan conjectured correctly that the droplets would take up integral multiples of the electronic charge, which he would be able to compute from the strength of field required to counteract the gravitational force on the droplets. By 1909, Millikan had arrived at an approximate value for the electronic charge. However, the droplets evaporated too quickly to make precise determination possible and Millikan switched to oil droplets. These were far less volatile and furthermore Millikan was able to irradiate the suspended droplets to vary their charge. In 1913, Millikan finally announced a highly accurate value for the electronic charge that was not bettered for many years.

Millikan also worked on a study of the photoelectric effect during this period, investigating the interpretation of Albert ◊Einstein that the kinetic energy of an electron emitted by incident radiation is proportional to the frequency of the radiation multiplied by Planck's constant. Millikan took great pains to improve the sensitivity of his apparatus and announced in 1916 that Einstein's equation was valid, thereby obtaining an accurate value for Planck's constant.

After World War I, Millikan moved into two new areas of research. In the 1920s, he investigated the ultraviolet spectra of many elements, extending the frequency range and identifying many new lines.

Millikan also undertook a thorough programme of research into cosmic rays, a term that he coined in 1925, when he proved that the rays do come from space. Millikan did this by comparing the intensity of ionization in two lakes at different altitudes. He found that the intensity was the same at different depths, the absorptive power of the difference in the depth of water being equal to the absorptive power of the depth of atmosphere between the two altitudes. This proved that the rays producing the ionization must have passed through the atmosphere from above and could not have a terrestrial origin.

Millikan went on to assert that cosmic rays were electromagnetic waves, a theory disproved by Arthur ◊Compton in 1934, when he demonstrated that they consist of charged particles. However, in the course of his research, Millikan directed Carl ◊Anderson to study cosmic rays in a cloud chamber and, as a result, Anderson discovered the positron.

Millikan's achievements are of fundamental value in the history of science. His determination of the charge on the electron was very important because it proved experimentally that electrons are particles of electricity, while the determination of Planck's constant was vital to the development of quantum theory.

Mills, William Hobson (1873–1959) English organic chemist famous for his work on stereochemistry and on the synthesis of cyanine dyes.

Mills was born in London on 6 July 1873, although his family came from Lincolnshire and he was educated at Spalding Grammar School. He then went to Uppingham School and Jesus College, Cambridge, where he began research under Thomas Easterfield and became a fellow of the college in 1899. Also in 1899 he went for two years to Tübingen in Germany to work under Hans von Pechmann; while there he met the English inorganic chemist Nevil ◊Sidgwick, who was to become his lifelong friend. He returned to England in 1902 as head of chemistry at the Northern Polytechnic Institute, London, and ten years later he was appointed professor of natural philosophy at Jesus College. In 1919 he became a university lecturer and in 1931 the university created for him a readership in stereochemistry, a post he held until he retired in 1938. He died in Cambridge on 22 February 1959.

Mills's early research concerned stereochemistry, particularly optical isomerism – the phenomenon in which pairs of (usually organic) compounds differ only in the arrangements of their atoms in space. Certain oximes (derivatives of aldehydes and ketones) were known to exist in two or more isomeric forms. In 1931, with B C Saunders, Mills prepared the *ortho*-carboxyphenylhydrazone of ß-methyl-trimethyl-enedithiolcarbonate and resolved it into two optically

active forms. This work confirmed the theory of Arthur Hantzsch and Alfred ◊Werner that optical isomerism of oximes is caused by the non-planar orientation of the nitrogen atom valencies.

It had also been recognized that a spirocyclic compound consisting of two carbon rings linked together by a common carbon atom should show optical activity if the rings possessed appropriate substituents to ensure molecular dissymmetry. In 1921 Mills and C R Nodder synthesized and resolved the first compound of this kind, the ketodilactone of benzophenone-2,4,2′,4′-tetracarboxylic acid.

Chemists had realized that a suitably substituted compound of allene (propadiene) would also be disymmetric, but had been unable to synthesize any such compound with acidic or basic groups for resolution. After six years of patient research Mills and Maitland synthesized an allene derivative with two phenyl and two naphthyl substitutents.

$$H_2C = C = CH_2$$
allene

pair of isomers with 'large' substituents A and B

αγ-biphenyl-αγ-di-α-naphthyl allene

By extending these general methods, they went on to show that the nitrogen atom of a quaternary ammonium salt has a tetrahedral configuration (like a carbon atom), and is not situated at the centre of a square-based pyramid. On the other hand, in 1935 Mills and his co-workers produced stereochemical evidence that a four-coordinated platinum atom has a planar as opposed to a tetrahedral configuration.

Other workers were puzzled by the fact that a biphenyl molecule shows optical activity if there are suitable substituents in the 2, 2′, 6, and 6′ positions. In 1926 Mills was the first to point out that the size of the substituents can prevent the free rotation of the two phenyl groups about their common axis. He then became interested in the general problem of restricted rotation and investigated substituted derivatives of naphthalene, quinolene, and benzene.

Mills's other field of research was into the synthesis of cyanine dyes. In 1905 German chemists had synthesized pinacyanol, which, when added to photographic emulsions, extended their sensitivity into the red region of the spectrum, as well as into the blue, violet, and ultraviolet regions. Mills and his co-workers investigated similar dyestuffs for preparing photographic emulsions, mainly for use by the military in World War I.

After his retirement Mills had more time to devote to his interest in natural history, especially to the British bramble plant *Rubus fructiosus*. His collection of 2,200 specimens of 320 of the 389 'microspecies' of this plant is arranged in systematic order and is now housed in the botany department of Cambridge University.

Milne, Edward Arthur (1896–1950) English astrophysicist, mathematician, and theoreticist, most famous for his formulation of a theory of relativity parallel to Albert ◊Einstein's general theory which he called kinematic relativity.

Milne was born in Hull, Yorkshire, on 14 February 1896. After attending local schools, he won scholarships to Hymer's College, Hull (where he showed exceptional talent in mathematics), and then to Trinity College, Cambridge, which he entered in 1914. Poor eyesight prevented him from taking up active service on the outbreak of World War I, but in 1916 he began work at the Anti-Aircraft Experimental Section of the Munitions Inventions Department, and carried out important research there, surrounded by many of the country's leading mathematicians and physicists. It was during these years that Milne became interested in atmospheric theory. His research contributions during the war years were later recognized in the award of an MBE.

Milne returned to Cambridge in 1919 and wrote three papers derived, in part, from the work he had been engaged in during the war. On the strength of these papers he was elected prize fellow of Trinity College in 1919 (a post he held until 1925). He was offered the post of assistant director of the Solar Physics Observatory at Cambridge in the same year, but deferred acceptance for a year while he made additional studies of the subject. From 1921 to 1924 he served as lecturer in astrophysics and from 1924 to 1925 as lecturer in mathematics at Cambridge. Milne then moved to Manchester University to take up the chair of applied mathematics. He was elected fellow of the Royal Society in 1926, at the age of 30. Three years later, he accepted the Rouse Ball Chair of Mathematics at Oxford University, where he was elected a fellow of Wadham College. He held both of these posts until his death.

From 1939 to 1944, during World War II, Milne served as a member of the Ordnance Board at Chislehurst, part of the Ministry of Supply. There he carried out research very similar to the sort he had done during World War I. His later years were affected by deteriorating health and he died suddenly while at a conference in Dublin on 21 September 1950.

Milne received many honours in recognition for the contributions he made to astrophysics and to cosmology, including the Royal Medal from the Royal Society in 1941. A member of many prominent international scientific organizations, he was also the author of several books.

There were three main phases in the development of Milne's work: his research on stellar spectra and radiative equilibrium at Cambridge and Manchester; his study of stellar structure during his early years at Oxford; and his formulation and development of kinematic relativity during the later years at Oxford.

At Cambridge Milne collaborated with Ralph Fowler to extend earlier theoretical work by Meghnad Saha (1894–1956) on thermal ionization. Together they developed a temperature scale for stellar spectra that has been used to improve the understanding of stellar surface conditions. It was then recommended to Milne that he investigate stellar atmospheres, and he turned to the primary work done by Karl ◊Schwarzschild and Arthur Schuster (1851–1935) on radiative equilibrium. Interested in the balance between radiation pressure and gravity in the Sun's chromosphere, Milne found that under certain conditions there would be great instability, and that such instability could lead to the emission of atoms from the Sun at speeds as high as 1,000 km/600 mi per second. Milne derived a mathematical method to describe the net amount of radiation passing through the atmosphere.

He continued to investigate the structure of stellar atmospheres and he was able to relate the optical depth (or opacity) to observations on spectral frequency. At the time of his move to Oxford, Milne began to re-examine some of the work done by Arthur ◊Eddington on stellar structure. His proposals for a number of changes to the theory were not generally accepted, but his critical approach to the subject prompted serious scientific reappraisal. It was at about this time that Milne suggested that a decrease in luminosity might cause the collapse of a star, and that this would be associated with nova formation.

In 1932 Milne began the development of his theory of kinematic relativity. He felt that kinematics could be used to explain the properties of the universe, thus providing at least an equivalent, a parallel rendering, of Einstein's general theory of relativity. Basing his theory on Euclidean space and on Einstein's special theory of relativity alone, Milne was able to formulate a system of theoretical cosmology (in which he was also able to derive a gravitational theory) and systems of dynamics and electrodynamics. Furthermore, he provided a more acceptable estimate for the overall age of the universe (10,000 million years) than that provided by the general theory of relativity.

Kinematic relativity has not in fact replaced the general theory, largely because it cannot be used to resolve detailed issues. Nor does it provide any genuinely new insights into the physical nature of the universe. Its approach to the problem of time and space–time did, however, stimulate considerable and creative interest.

Milstein, César (1927–) Argentine-born British molecular biologist who has performed important research on the genetics, biosynthesis, and chemistry of immunoglobulins (antibody proteins), developing a technique for preparing chemically pure monoclonal antibodies. For this he shared the 1984 Nobel Prize for Physiology or Medicine with Georges Köhler (1946–1995) and Niels Jerne (1911–1994).

Milstein was born on 8 October 1927 in Bahia Blanca, Argentina. From 1939 to 1944 he was educated at the Collegio Nacional, Bahia Blanca, from which he gained his Bachiller; in 1945 he went to the University of Buenos Aires, from which he graduated in 1952. He remained at Buenos Aires University until 1963, initially to study for his doctorate (which he obtained in 1957), then as a member of the staff of the Institute of Microbiology. During a period of leave of absence, Milstein worked in the department of biochemistry at Cambridge University, from which he gained his second doctorate in 1960. He returned to Cambridge in 1963 as a member of the staff of the Medical Research Council's Laboratory of Molecular Biology and went on to become joint head (with Frederick ◊Sanger) of its Protein and Nucleic Acid Chemistry Division 1983–95, and deputy director of the laboratory 1988–95.

Milstein and his colleagues were among the first to determine the complete sequence of the short, low-molecular-mass part of the immunoglobulin molecule (known as the light chain). He then determined the nucleotide sequence of a large portion of the messenger RNA for the light chain and found that there is only one type of messenger RNA for both domains within that chain. The separate domains within the heavy (high-molecular-mass) and light chains are called constant and variable, and Milstein deduced that although the genes for the constant and variable domains may be separate in the germ line, these genes must have come together in the antibody-producing cells. This finding led Milstein to develop his technique for preparing chemically pure monoclonal antibodies. Working with German biochemist Georges Köhler in 1975, Milstein succeeded in fusing myeloma cells (which are easily cultured but produce only their own predetermined immunoglobulin) with spleen cells (which cannot be cultured but can produce immunoglobulin against any antigen with which an animal has been injected) to produce hybrid cells that can be cultured and that can produce antibodies against a wide range of antigens. Moreover, by selecting clones Milstein and Köhler obtained cell lines that secreted only one chemically homogenous antibody. This was a revolutionary piece of research, because the permanent cultures derived from one clone can be propagated indefinitely and can therefore provide an unlimited supply of a specific immunoglobulin. The technique was later extended to human cells and can also be used to prepare purified antibodies against impure antigens.

Minkowski, Hermann (1864–1909) Lithuanian-born German mathematician whose introduction of the concept of space–time was essential to the genesis of the general theory of relativity.

Minkowski was born in Alexotas, near Kaunas, on 22 June 1864, but moved to Germany with his family in 1872 and settled in Königsberg (now Kaliningrad in Russia). There he was educated, receiving his doctorate from the University of Königsberg in 1885. He lectured at the University of Bonn 1885–94, when he returned to Königsberg as associate professor of mathematics. After only two years there, he accepted the post of professor of mathematics at the Federal Institute of Technology in Zürich, Switzerland. His last years were spent at Göttingen University, where he held the chair created for him by David ◊Hilbert from 1902 until his death on 12 January 1909.

Minkowski's genius first declared itself when, at the age of 19, he shared the French Academy's Grand Prix for a paper on the theory of quadratic forms with integral coefficients. Quadratic forms remained his chief interest, although he failed to find a method, like many before and after him, of generalizing Karl ◊Gauss's work on binary quadratic forms so as to describe '*n*-ary' forms. His passion for pure mathematics led him also into problems in number theory, to which his concept of the geometry of numbers constituted an important addition. This was achieved by his use of the lattice in algebraic theory, and it was his research into that topic that led him to consider certain geometric properties in a space of *n* dimensions and so to hit upon his notion of the space–time continuum. The principle of relativity, already put forward by Henri ◊Poincaré and Albert ◊Einstein, led Minkowski to the view that space and time were interlinked. He proposed a four-dimensional manifold in which space and time became inseparable, a model that has not received much acceptance; but the central idea – contained in his *Raum und Zeit* (1909) – was, as Einstein allowed, necessary for the working out of the general theory of relativity.

So, in a manner not uncommon in the history of science, Minkowski, who was moved chiefly by a love of pure mathematics, made his most brilliant discovery in the field of mathematical physics.

Minkowski, Rudolph Leo (1895–1976) German-born US astrophysicist, responsible for the compilation of the incomparably valuable set of photographs found in every astronomical library, the National Geographic Society Palomar Observatory Sky Survey. A leading authority on novae and so-called planetary novae, he was a pioneer in the science of radio astronomy.

Minkowski was born in Strasbourg (then in Germany, now in France) on 28 May 1895. His family was of Polish extraction, and after he had been educated in local schools, he attended the University of Breslau (now Wrocław in Poland) and gained a PhD in optics in 1921. After a year on the physics teaching staff at Göttingen, he became professor of physics at Hamburg University. Increasing oppression because of his racial background in Germany in 1935, however, caused him to emigrate to the USA, where he joined his friend and former colleague, Walter ◊Baade, at Pasadena. Shortly afterwards, he found a position as research assistant at the Mount Wilson Observatory, California, and, comfortably settled into a regular staff position, he remained there for more than 20 years before transferring to the Palomar Observatory. Minkowski retired twice, first from the Mount Wilson and Palomar observatories in 1959, then, after spending a year at the University of Wisconsin and another five at the University of California at Berkeley, again in 1965. He continued his observations and investigations, publishing scientific papers until well into the 1970s. He died on 4 January 1976.

Minkowski became one of the world's leading investigators of the universe's more violent phenomena.

One of his central interests during a long career was the examination of supernovae. He quickly distinguished between the two principal types of supernovae and studied the spectra of many individual types in other galaxies. In collaboration with Walter Baade he studied the remnants of the few supernovae known to have appeared in our own Galaxy. The Crab nebula was the subject of a particularly stringent examination. Its importance in astrophysics has increased as it has been discovered successively to be a radio source, an X-ray source, and a pulsar.

It was the collaboration between Minkowski and Baade that first identified a 'discrete radio source', Cygnus A, in 1951 – the first time that an extragalactic radio source was optically identified, albeit as an extremely distant object. But because of the distance, the radio emission was seen to be of immense power. It was Baade's view (in which Minkowski, at least at the beginning, concurred) that Cygnus A represented the collision of two galaxies; the fact that two apparent nuclei were identifiable by their radio signals seemed evidence enough. (Later investigation, however, has failed to find the expected corroborative evidence and the theory of colliding galaxies is at the moment discredited.)

The nature of planetary nebulae (dense stars in the process of becoming white dwarfs and shedding mass to do so) was another of Minkowski's long-term interests. In addition to his analysis of these objects he set up a survey, using a 25-cm/10-in telescope, that more than doubled the number of planetary nebulae then known. It was at this time that he took over supervision of the National Geographic Society Palomar Observatory Sky Survey.

During Minkowski's study of supernovae and disturbed galaxies, his investigation into the internal motions within elliptical galaxies was important; but it was superseded only 12 years later when new and improved observing equipment became available. Minkowski determined the optical red shift of the radio source 3C 295 (which remained the farthest point on the velocity–distance diagram of cosmology for 15 years) in his last observing run at the Palomar 500-cm/200-in telescope.

Mises, Richard von (1883–1953) Austrian-born US mathematician and aerodynamicist who made valuable contributions to statistics and the theory of probability.

Mises was born on 19 April 1883 at Lemberg (now Lvov, Ukraine). He was educated at the University of Vienna, where he received his doctorate in 1907, and was professor of applied mathematics at the University of Strassburg (now Strasbourg, in France) 1909–18. In 1920 he was appointed professor of applied mathematics and director of the Institute for Applied Mathematics at the University of Berlin. With the coming to power of Adolf Hitler in 1933, he emigrated to Turkey and taught at the University of Istanbul until 1939. In that year he went to the USA to join the faculty of Harvard University. He was made Gordon McKay Professor of Aerodynamics and Applied Mathematics in 1944, the chair he held until his death, in Boston, on 14 July 1953.

Mises looked upon himself principally as an applied mathematician and was especially proud of having founded in 1921, and edited until 1933, the journal *Zeitschrift für angewandte Mathematik und Mechanik.* His first interest was fluid mechanics, especially in relation to the new and exciting field of aerodynamics and aeronautics. In the summer of 1913, after learning to fly aircraft, he organized what is now upheld as the first university course in the mechanics of powered flight. In the next year or so he made significant improvements in boundary-layer-flow theory and aerofoil design and, in 1915, built a 440-kW/600-hp aeroplane for the Austrian military. During World War I he served as a pilot and in 1916 published a book on flight that formed the basis of his later book, *Theory of Flight,* published with scientists in the UK towards the end of World War II.

Mises's chief contribution to pure mathematics was in the field of probability theory and statistics. He was drawn into this subject by his association from 1907 until the 1920s with the Viennese school of logical positivism. The development of the frequency theory of probability had proceeded slowly, in opposition to the classical theory of Pierre Laplace, during the second half of the 18th and the first half of the 19th century. It then took a leap forward with John ◊Venn's imaginative stroke when he equated the notion of probability with the comparative frequency of the event 'in the long run'. Venn introduced the concept of a mathematical limit and the infinite set, but Mises came to the conclusion that a probability cannot be simply the limiting value of a relative frequency. He added the proviso that any event should be irregularly or randomly distributed in the series of occasions in which its probability is measured. This emphasis on the idea of random distribution, in other words bringing the notion of the Venn limit and that of a random sequence of events together, was Mises's outstanding contribution to the frequency theory of probability.

Mises's ideas were contained in two papers that he published in 1919. Little noticed at the time, they have come to influence all modern statisticians. The consistency of the mathematics of Mises's theory has been called into question by a number of mathematicians, but it seems doubtful that any of the proposed alternatives will prove to be more satisfactory. After 1919

Mises achieved very little of a highly creative or original nature, but his *Probability, Statistics and Truth* (1928) is both historically sound and, for the lay reader, stimulating.

Mitchell, Maria (1818–1889) US astronomer and one of the most famous US scientists of the 19th century. She was the first woman to become professor of astronomy in the USA and the first woman appointed to the American Academy of Arts and Sciences.

Mitchell US astronomer Maria Mitchell. *Mary Evans Picture Library*

Born on the island of Nantucket, Massachusetts, in 1818, Maria Mitchell was the third of ten children in a Quaker family. She and all her siblings were educated chiefly by their father, William Mitchell, a schoolteacher and distinguished amateur astronomer. He taught astronomy and navigation to boys and girls alike. Women in Nantucket followed a tradition of independence, as local men were often absent on long whaling voyages and Lydia Coleman instilled independence in her daughters and encouraged them to learn occupations.

As a child, Maria helped her father with his work in regulating the chronometers for whaling ships and, in 1831, during an eclipse of the Sun, she helped him determine the longitude of their home town. At the age of 18 Maria became a librarian at the Nantucket Athenaeum, giving her access to books through which she continued to educate herself. In the same year, 1836, the US coastal survey equipped an observatory at their home for her father. This gave her ample opportunity to study astronomy in her spare time.

On 1 October 1847 Mitchell achieved international fame by discovering a telescopic comet (Comet Mitshel 1847IV), which earned her a gold medal from the king of Denmark in 1848 and election as the first woman fellow of the American Academy of Arts and Sciences. Her first professional appointment in 1849 was to compute the ephemerides of Venus for the US Nautical Almanac Office, a duty she performed for the next 20 years. In 1853 she was awarded the first advanced degree given to a woman by Indiana Hanover College.

In 1865 Mitchell was appointed to the American Philosophical Society and also became professor of astronomy (first woman faculty member) and director of the observatory at the newly founded Vassar College at Poughkeepsie. She proved to be a devoted and inspiring teacher and nurtured a generation of Vassar graduates. She was also a keen suffragist, abolitionist, and promoter of higher education for women and she was elected president of the American Association for the Advancement of Women in 1875.

In 1888, when her health began to fail her, Mitchell retired to Nantucket, and died in Lynn on 28 June 1889. Her family's home there is now a museum and she was inducted into the US National Women's Hall of Fame in 1994.

Mitchell, Peter Dennis (1920–1992) English biochemist who performed important research into the processes involved in the transfer of biological energy. He received many honours for his work, including the award of the 1978 Nobel Prize for Chemistry.

Mitchell was born on 29 September 1920 in Mitcham, Surrey. He was educated at Queen's College, Taunton, and then at Jesus College, Cambridge, from which he graduated in 1943 and gained his doctorate in 1950. He worked in the biochemistry department of Cambridge University 1943–55, becoming a demonstrator in 1950. In 1955 he was appointed director of the chemical biology unit in the department of zoology at Edinburgh; he was later promoted to senior lecturer and then, in 1962, to reader. In the following year he established and became director of the privately run Glynn Research Institute in Bodmin, Cornwall. In the early 1960s the way in which the synthesis of ATP (adenosine triphosphate) is linked with the transfer of electrons was still unknown. At the intracellular level, metabolic energy is stored in the form of ATP, produced by phosphorylating the diphosphate ADP (in effect the metabolic energy is stored in ATP's extra chemical bond). The energy needed for this reaction is produced by the transfer of electrons

along a chain of proteins attached to the double membrane of mitochondria within the cell.

In 1961 Mitchell postulated that, simultaneously with this electron transfer, protons are expelled from the outer surface of the inner mitochondrial membrane and are transmitted through the outer membrane by osmosis, thus setting up an ion-concentration gradient (and therefore a potential difference). He further suggested that this potential difference is the form in which the energy needed to convert ADP to ATP is stored. It has since been shown that other cellular processes that require energy make use of the mechanism proposed by Mitchell and that the chemical equilibrium in the phosphorylation of ADP to ATP is highly sensitive to the concentration of ions, which is controlled by the mitochondrial membrane.

Although greeted with great scepticism at first, Mitchell's theory is now considered to be correct and it has been established as the basic principle in the science of bioenergetics.

Mitchell, R(eginald) J(oseph) (1895–1937) English aeronautical engineer who, in the UK at least, was largely responsible for the development of the high-speed monoplane. His early work on the design of seaplanes for the Schneider Trophy competition led to ideas for the construction of a single-engined fighter, which became the Spitfire.

Mitchell was born in Talke, near Stoke-on-Trent, on 20 May 1895. His father was a school teacher and later a printer. His early childhood was spent at Longton, a few miles from his birthplace, and he went first to the village school and later to Hanley High School. On leaving school he became apprenticed to a firm of locomotive builders in Stoke. Mitchell realized the importance of sound scientific principles in engineering, and continued his education in the evenings at technical colleges. It was not an easy way to get the scientific and practical expertise needed to become a design engineer, but he succeeded. He soon passed from the workbench to the drawing office, and in 1916 he moved to the Supermarine Aviation Company at Southampton. He had always had an interest in aeroplanes and had built models to test his own theories. Now he was able to test his ideas on a larger scale.

Aviation was still in its infancy, but was rapidly developing. Jacques Schneider, the son of a wealthy armaments manufacturer, was impressed by the flights of Wilbur Wright (see Orville and Wilbur ◊Wright) in France in 1908, and decided at the Aero Club of France in 1912 to offer a trophy (Le Coupe d'Aviation Maritime Jacques Schneider) to the national aero club of the country that produced the fastest seaplane. If a country won the trophy three times within five years, then it was to retain it.

Mitchell first became involved with producing aeroplanes for the trophy for the 1919 race (the third contest). Partly under his direction, the Supermarine Sea Lion (G-EALP) was adapted from a standard design. No aeroplane completely finished the course, Mitchell's Sea Lion having retired during the first lap.

A year later Mitchell became chief engineer for Supermarine. The firm at that time specialized in flying boats, and later models of the Sea Lion flew with distinction in the 1922 race, when Sea Lion II came first with a speed of 234.4 kph/45.7 mph and in 1923 when Sea Lion III came third at 252.9 kph/157.2 mph. For the next contest, in 1924, Mitchell was allowed to design his own aeroplane. This was the Supermarine S-4. It was a monoplane and the whole wing section was made in one piece. The radiator for the engine was on the underside of the wing and the fuel was carried in the floats. The S-4 looked fast and elegant and, was probably too fast for its design for it crashed during the trial before the race, previously having captured the world seaplane speed record at 365.055 kph/226.752 mph. In the 1927, 1929, and 1931 contests, Mitchell's S-5, S-6, and S-6B – the direct descendants of the ill-fated S-4 – took the trophy with speeds finally increased to 547.30 kph/340.08 mph. The Schneider Trophy was won forever for the UK and it now has a place of honour in the Science Museum, London. This was not quite the end of the story: the S-6B S1585 set a speed record of 668.19 kph/415.2 mph on 29 September 1931 with George Stainforth at the controls.

To fulfil an Air Ministry contract for a single-engined fighter, Mitchell used and extended the ideas that had been embodied in the Schneider Trophy winners. This was not a simple task because he had to develop a reliable aeroplane that could fly time and again carrying a heavy load of fuel and ammunition at high speeds. His first aeroplane built directly to the specifications is said to have been mediocre, but when he was allowed full rein for his own ideas he produced the prototype of the Spitfire (K-5054). This was first flown by Captain J Summers on 5 March 1936.

The Spitfire came into being when the storm clouds of war were gathering and it proved to be the UK's most important, but by no means only, fighter aeroplane. The early Spitfires had a top speed of 557 kph/346 mph, but the later ones were capable of about 740 kph/460 mph. More than 19,000 Spitfires were built, adapted to every role and circumstance appropriate to a high-speed single-engined aeroplane. Although faster single-engined fighters were eventually built, the manoeuverability and all-round adaptability of the Spitfire made it one of the most successful aeroplanes ever.

Mitchell saw very little of his greatest creation after its first flight. When it took to the air he was already seriously ill with tuberculosis. He died on 11 June 1937, aged 42 years.

Mitscherlich, Eilhard (1794–1863) German chemist, famous for his discovery of isomorphism (the phenomenon in which substances of analogous chemical composition crystallize in the same crystal form). He also synthesized many organic compounds for the first time.

Mitscherlich was born in Neuende, Jever (now part of Wilhelmshaven), on 17 January 1794, the son of a minister. He was educated at Jever and in 1811 entered Heidelberg University to study Oriental languages, later continuing this study at Paris, with the intention of becoming a diplomat. The fall of Napoleon ended that prospect and he returned to Germany, enrolling at Göttingen to read science and medicine. He thought that he might reach the Orient as a ship's doctor (since he could not do so as a diplomat) but became increasingly interested in chemistry and in 1818 went to Berlin to work in the laboratory of the botanist Heinrich Link. There he began his study of crystallography.

In 1819 Mitscherlich met Jöns ◊Berzelius while he was visiting Berlin, and when the Prussian Minister of Education offered Berzelius the professorship of chemistry at Berlin University following the death of Martin ◊Klaproth, he declined but recommended Mitscherlich for the appointment. But at only 25 years old Mitscherlich was thought to be too young and as a compromise he was sent to Stockholm to work with Berzelius for two years, to widen his knowledge of chemistry. He returned to Berlin in 1822 as assistant professor of chemistry, becoming professor three years later (finally succeeding Klaproth) and retaining the appointment until his death. He died in Berlin on 28 August 1863.

Mitscherlich began studying crystals in Link's laboratory in 1818. He observed the near-identical form of the crystals of both potassium phosphate and potassium arsenate. Securing the support of mineralogist Gustav Rose (1798–1873), who instructed him in exact crystallographic methods to facilitate precise measurements, Mitscherlich then used spherical trigonometry on the collected data. In his first publication he announced that the same amounts of water of crystallization result in the sulphates of various metals, as well as the double sulphates of potassium and ammonium, crystallizing in like forms. The book also expressed his expectation that 'through crystallographic examination the composition of bodies will be determined with the same certainty and exactness as through chemical analysis'.

Berzelius immediately recognized the importance of Mitscherlich's work and applied it to his determinations of atomic weights (relative atomic masses); he was later able to correct the atomic weights of 27 elements. While he was in Stockholm, Mitscherlich extended his researches to phosphates, arsenates, and carbonates, publishing the results in 1822 and introducing the term 'isomorphism'. He continued the work after his return to Berlin, refining his isomorphism law and establishing more and more classes of compounds to which it applies. In 1827, during the course of this work, he discovered selenic acid.

In 1834 Mitscherlich synthesized benzene (introducing the name, which he termed *Benzin)* by heating calcium benzoate (the calcium salt of benzene carboxylic acid, or benzoic acid). Two years earlier he had synthesized nitrobenzene, and he went on to prepare azobenzene, benzophenone, and benzene sulphonic acid. He recognized that the part played by the oxides of nitrogen in the chamber process for making sulphuric acid is that of a catalyst, and showed that yeast (which in 1842 he identified as a microorganism) can invert sugar in solution. He maintained his early interest in geology and mineralogy, and was particularly concerned with the production of artificial minerals, achieving valuable experimental results in this area.

In 1829 Mitscherlich published his influential *Lehrbuch der Chemie,* which in less than 20 years had run to four further new editions in German as well as two in French and one in English. Continuing Mitscherlich's comprehensive lectures on pure and applied chemistry (and including a significant proportion of physics), this work reflected Mitscherlich's exemplary clarity and ingenious approach to scientific experimentation.

Mitscherlich's youngest son also became a chemist and, with help from his father, developed the Mitscherlich process for extracting cellulose from wood pulp by boiling it with calcium bisulphite (calcium hydrogen sulphite), which became the basis of the German cellulose industry.

Further Reading

Barkan, Diana, 'Simply a matter of chemistry? The Nobel Prize for 1920', *Perspect Sci,* 1994, v 2, p 357–395.

Barkan, Diana, 'Walther Nernst and quantum theory' in: Woodward, William R and Cohen, Robert S (eds), *World Views and Scientific Discipline Formation,* Kluwer, 1991, pp 151–162.

Schutt, Hans-Werner (ed); Russwy, William E (transl), *Eilhard Mitscherlich: Prince of Prussian Chemistry,* History of Modern Chemical Sciences series, American Chemical Society, 1996.

Möbius, August Ferdinand (1790–1868) German mathematician and theoretical astronomer, whose name is attached to several discoveries, most notably the 'barycentric calculus'.

Möbius was born in Schulpforta, near Naumburg, on 17 November 1790. His father was a dancing master and his mother a descendant of Martin Luther. Until the age of 13 he was educated at home by his father and, after his father died in 1798, by his uncle. Although he showed a talent for mathematics at school 1803–09, he went to the University of Leipzig in 1809 to study law. He soon abandoned law for mathematics and astronomy and in 1813 he went to Göttingen University to receive two semester's instruction from Karl ◊Gauss. He received his doctorate from Leipzig in 1814 and in the following year was appointed an instructor in astronomy there. In 1816 he was promoted to extraordinary professor of astronomy and was appointed as an observer at the Leipzig Observatory. He spent time in the next few years visiting observatories throughout Germany and his recommendations for the refurbishing and reconstruction of the Leipzig Observatory were carried out in 1821. In 1844 he was made a full professor of astronomy and higher mechanics and in 1848 director of the observatory. He died in Leipzig on 26 September 1868.

Möbius made important contributions to both astronomy and mathematics. His chief astronomical work was *Die Elemente der Mechanik des Himmels* (1843), a somewhat novel book, in that it provided a thorough mathematical discussion of celestial mechanics without resort to higher mathematics. His most important mathematical work, now regarded as something of a classic, was *Der barycentrische Calkul* (1827). Möbius had formulated his idea of the barycentric calculus in 1818. The word 'barycentric', formed from the Greek *barys* for 'heavy', means 'pertaining to the centre of gravity'. Möbius began with the well-known law of mechanics that several weights positioned along a beam can be replaced by a single weight, equal to the sum of the other weights, at the centre of the beam's gravity. From that law he constructed a mathematical system in which numerical coefficients were assigned to points. The position of any point in the system could be expressed by varying the numerical coefficients of any four or more non-coplanar points. This calculus proved helpful in a number of geometrical problems.

The treatise also introduced the principle of duality and gave a thorough treatment to the cross ratio; in addition, it included a discussion of the 'Möbius net', a concept later of great value in the development of projective geometry. A number of other discoveries bear his name: the Möbius tetrahedrons – two tetrahedrons that mutually circumscribe and inscribe each other – which he described in 1828; the Möbius function in number theory, published in 1832; and the Möbius strip.

The Möbius strip, presented in a paper discovered only after his death, was devised by him to illustrate the

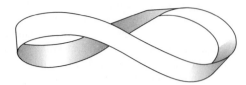

Möbius The Möbius strip has only one side and one edge. It consists of a strip of paper connected at its ends with a half-twist in the middle.

properties of one-sided surfaces, and consists of a length of paper connected at its ends with a half-twist in the middle. Credit for its discovery is shared with Johann Benedict Listing, a 19th-century German mathematician who is now known to have discovered it independently at the same time. The strip is one of Möbius's two contributions to the pre-natal stage of the history of topology. The other is his five-colour problem, given as a poser during a lecture of 1840. The problem he set was to find the least number of colours required on a plane map to distinguish political regions, given that each boundary line should separate two differently coloured regions. He drew maps requiring at least two, three, or four colours. Neither Möbius nor anyone else has ever found a five-colour solution (though on a torus five-colour maps are easily drawn). Recently, it has been proved by computer analysis that four colours will always suffice.

Mohs, Friedrich (1773–1839) German mineralogist who devised the Mohs scale, by which minerals are classified in order of relative hardness.

Born at Gernrode in the Saxon Hartz Mountains on 29 January 1773, Mohs studied at Halle and at the Freiberg Mining Academy under the great teacher, Abraham Gottlob ◊Werner. After almost obtaining a post at a proposed mining school in Dublin (the undertaking fell through), he was appointed professor of mineralogy at Graz in 1812, and later at Freiberg – though by then he had abandoned Werner's doctrines. He finally occupied a chair in Vienna from 1826. Mohs died in Agordo, South Tyrol, Austria, on 29 September 1839.

During his lifetime, Mohs achieved eminence for his system of the classification of minerals, dividing these into genera and species in the manner of ◊Linnaeus. Though recognized as useful, the strategy was widely criticized on account of its failing to take sufficient account of chemical composition.

Mohs is chiefly remembered for having given his name to a scale of relative hardness. The Mohs scale extends from talc (1) to diamond (10). Higher numbered minerals will scratch anything beneath them or equal to them in hardness. Despite first appearances,

the scale is not linear (the simple unit differences on the scale do not correspond straightforwardly to differences in hardness) and it possesses only limited applicability to crystals (the hardness of crystals tends to differ in separate crystal directions). The main use of the scale has been in field mineralogy.

Mond, Ludwig (1839–1909) German-born British chemist who established many industrial chemical processes in the UK. He gave his name to a method of extracting nickel from nickel carbonyl, one of its volatile organic compounds.

Mond was born in Kassel on 7 March 1839, the son of a well-to-do Jewish merchant. He studied chemistry at Marburg (under Hermann ◊Kolbe) and Heidelberg (under Robert ◊Bunsen) but did not proceed to a doctorate, instead embarking in 1858 on a career of short-term employment in the chemical industry. In 1859 he was working in a small soda works at Ringkuhl, near Kassel, where he initiated a new process for the recovery of sulphur. This attitude, that of making good commercial use of hitherto wasted by-products, was to help to shape his career as an industrial chemist. In 1862 he accepted an invitation from a Lancashire industrial chemist to apply his idea for the recovery of sulphur from the alkali waste from the Leblanc process (see Nicolas ◊Leblanc) for making soda (sodium carbonate). For several years, Mond travelled regularly between John Hutchinson's works in Widnes and Utrecht in Holland, where another Leblanc soda works was being constructed. He died in London of heart disease on 11 December 1909.

From 1867 Mond made his home in the UK and increased his involvement in the alkali industry, to meet the ever-growing needs of textile manufacturers. Then in 1872 he met Ernest ◊Solvay, the Belgian industrial chemist who had devised the ammonia–soda (Solvay) process for making sodium carbonate from ammonia and salt. Using the royalties from his sulphur-recovery process, Mond and his partner John Brunner became the sole British licensees of the Solvay process. His works at Winnington, near Northwich in Cheshire, eventually superseded those still using the now outdated Leblanc process, although it was several years before it came into full production. The Brunner, Mond Company became the most successful in its field, employing more than 4,000 people by the end of the century, with the world's largest output of alkali.

In 1879 Mond became interested in the production of ammonia, an intermediate in the Solvay process, which was increasingly being used as an artificial fertilizer. One outcome was the development of the Mond producer gas process, in which carbon monoxide and hydrogen are produced by alternately passing air and steam over heated coal or coke (the hydrogen being used to convert nitrogen into ammonia). By the early 1900s, Mond's Dudley Port plant in Staffordshire was using 3 million tonnes of coal each year to make producer gas (Mond gas). An interesting extension of this work was the attempt, with the assistance of K Langer, to turn the energy of the fuel directly into electrical energy. This early fuel cell, which used porous plates moistened with sulphuric acid, was not developed further at that time. Mond also hoped to recover the chlorine from the waste calcium chloride from the Solvay process, but this endeavour was also largely unsuccessful.

One unexpected result of the producer gas process came from Mond's observation that nickel is corroded by gases containing carbon monoxide. This led in 1889 to the discovery of nickel carbonyl, $Ni(CO)_4$, one of the first organometallic compounds. After two years' work, with Langer and Quincke, he had developed a new extraction process for nickel. The Mond Nickel Company was founded at Clydach, near Swansea in south Wales, to produce nickel from Canadian ores by the thermal decomposition of nickel carbonyl; it later became the British manufacturing plant of Imperial Nickel Limited.

Mond became a rich man. He was generous with his wealth during his lifetime, and among various trusts he founded was one for the building of the Davy Faraday Laboratory at the Royal Institution, London. He lived in Italy towards the end of his life, and bequeathed a valuable collection of paintings to the British National Gallery. His son Robert (1867–1938) became a scientist and Egyptologist and was knighted, and his other son Alfred, 1st Baron Melchett (1868–1930), was a successful politician and the first chairman of Imperial Chemical Industries (ICI) when it was founded in the 1920s. Mond's great-grandson Julian Mond, 3rd Baron Melchett, became the first chairman of the British Steel Corporation in 1967.

Monge, Gaspard (1746–1818) French mathematician and chemist who was famous for his work in descriptive and analytical geometry and is generally regarded as the founder of descriptive geometry.

Monge was born in Beaune, into a merchant family, on 9 May 1746, and received his first education at the local oratory. From 1762 to 1764 he studied at the Collège de la Trinité at Lyon, where he displayed such advanced scientific knowledge and such instinctive skill that he was placed in charge of the physics course. He returned to Beaune in 1764 and never again received formal scientific education. In the summer of 1764 he made a graphic sketch of his native town, the excellence of which won the praise of an officer at the Ecole Royale du Génie at Mézières and gained Monge his first appointment, as a draughtsman and tech-

nician, at the school. His official duties were to prepare plans of fortifications and other architectural models, but in his spare time he devoted himself to geometrical research. It was in these years, 1766–71, that he made his most fruitful insights into the nature of descriptive geometry.

In 1769 Monge succeeded the professor of mathematics at the Ecole Royale, although he was not given the title of professor. A year later he was also appointed an instructor in experimental physics. In 1771 he met Jean ◊d'Alembert, by whom he was drawn into the scientific circle attached to the Academy of Sciences in Paris. In that year he submitted four papers to the Academy, of which the most significant was the 'Mémoire sur les développées des rayons de courbure et différents genres d'inflexions des courbes à double courbure', which was read to the Academy in 1771, but was not published until 1785. That paper was Monge's first important original work; it was followed in 1776 by another paper in infinitesimal geometry in which Monge introduced lines of curvature and the congruences of straight lines.

In 1780 Monge was elected to the Academy of Sciences and was given official duties as assistant geometer to the academy. By then he was showing as much interest in the physical sciences as in mathematics. In 1783, independently of Antoine ◊Lavoisier, he synthesized water. He also collaborated with J F Clouet to liquefy sulphur dioxide. In 1785 he was appointed examiner of naval cadets by the French government, an appointment that marked the beginning of his long participation in French public life. The burdens of the job, added to his duties at the academy, forced him to resign his professorship at Mézières in 1784. For the next eight years Monge divided his time between inspecting naval schools throughout the country and participating in the activities of the academy.

By the time the French Revolution broke out in 1789, Monge was one of the most celebrated of French scientists. He was an earnest supporter of the radicals and joined several revolutionary clubs and societies. In 1792 he was appointed Minister of the Navy, but as the revolution took its speedy course towards the Terror, he was discovered (despite his association with the left-wing Jacobins) to be a moderate and he resigned his post in April 1793. Thereafter he held no overt political position, although he was a member of the Committee on Arms 1793–94 and did important work in supervising the Paris armaments workshops and in helping to develop military balloons. He also served on the commission established to standardize French weights and measures. In March 1794 he was appointed to the commission set up to establish the Ecole Centrale des Travaux Publics and was its instructor in descriptive geometry when the new school opened in 1795. It soon changed its name to the Ecole Polytechnique.

In 1796 Monge's friendship with Napoleon began. Having conquered Italy, the revolutionary French government decided to plunder the country of its artistic and scientific treasures and Monge was sent, as a member of the Commission des Sciences et des Arts en Italie, to assist in the selection of objects to be removed to France. He met Napoleon briefly, but was then recalled to France in 1797 to take up a new appointment as director of the Ecole Polytechnique. He then went back to Italy in 1798, this time as a member of a mission to inquire into the country's political organization. While he was there he was invited by Napoleon to assist in the preparation for the Egyptian campaign; he then accompanied Napoleon on the expedition to Egypt and was appointed president of the Institut d'Egypte established at Cairo in 1798. Monge also went with Napoleon on the expeditions to the Suez region and Syria in 1799, before returning to Paris at the end of the year.

He had scarcely begun to resume his duties as director of the Ecole Polytechnique when the *coup d'état* of 18 Brumaire placed Napoleon in control of the French government. Two months later Napoleon appointed him a senator for life and he resigned the directorship of the Ecole Polytechnique. For the rest of Napoleon's ascendancy Monge assumed the role of the foremost scientific supporter of the imperial regime. He was rewarded by being made a Grand Officer of the Legion of Honour in 1804, president of the senate in 1806, and the Count of Péluse in 1808. His creative scientific life was now a thing of the past, but in the leisure that freedom from onerous official appointments allowed, Monge brought together his life's work in a number of publications: the *Géométrie descriptive* (1799), the *Feuilles d'analyse appliquées à la géométrie* (1801), its expanded version *Application de l'analyse à la géométrie* (1807), and several smaller works on infinitesimal and analytical geometry.

In the last decade of his life Monge was painfully afflicted by arthritis, which forced him to abandon his teaching at the Ecole Polytechnique in 1809. Thereafter he lived in semi-retirement, although he went to the district of Liège in 1813 to organize the defence of the region against the allied armies then making their final victorious penetration into France. When Napoleon was finally overthrown in 1815, Monge was discredited. In 1816 he was expelled from the Institut de France (the renamed Academy of Sciences) and on 28 July 1818 he died in Paris.

Monge was one of the most wide-ranging scientists and mathematicians of his age. In the years between 1785 and 1789, for example, he submitted to the Academy of Sciences papers or notes on an astonishing variety of subjects: the composition of nitrous acid, the generation of curved surfaces, finite difference equations and partial differential equations (1785); double refraction, the composition of iron and steel and the action of electric sparks on carbon dioxide (1786); capillary phenomena (1787); and the physiological aspects of optics (1789). He holds an honoured place in the history of chemistry, not simply for his independent synthesis of water, but also for working with Lavoisier in 1785 in the epoch-making experiments on the synthesis and analysis of water. Although his own research had not led him to break entirely with the phlogiston theory, he was readily converted to the new chemistry by Lavoisier and played an energetic part in getting it accepted. Such was his standing as a chemist that he was one of the founders of the *Annales de chimie*.

It is, nevertheless, as a geometer that Monge gains his place in the scientific pantheon. Probably because he began his career as a draughtsman, he was always able to combine the practical, analytical, and geometrical aspects of a problem. It was from his work on fortifications and architecture that he developed the basic principles of his descriptive geometry. The *Géometrie descriptive* was based on lectures given at the Ecole Polytechnique in 1795. Its achievement was to translate the practical graphic procedures used by draughtsmen into a generalized technique, elegantly ordered and based upon rigorous geometrical reasoning. So popular was the book that it was quickly being used throughout Europe. It established Monge as the founder of descriptive geometry and, more, made a vital contribution to the 19th-century renaissance in geometry.

Throughout his life Monge's principal interest was infinitesimal geometry, especially in so far as it provided him with the opportunity to improve the rigour and enhance the status of analytical geometry. Monge broke with Cartesian tradition and asserted the autonomy of analytical geometry as a separate branch of mathematics. In particular he devoted himself to two subjects: the families of surfaces as defined by their mode of generation (which he studied in relation to their corresponding partial differential equations); and the properties of surfaces and space curves. Much of this work was a development of the theory of developable surfaces outlined by Leonhard ◊Euler in 1772, although as early as 1769 Monge had defined the evolutes of a space curve and demonstrated that such curves are the geodesics of the developable envelope of the family of planes normal to a given curve. Monge established the distinction between ruled surfaces and developable surfaces and he provided a simple method of determining, from its equation, whether a surface is developable. His work in analysis was less original and less rigorous, but he made valuable contributions to the theory of both partial differential equations and ordinary differential equations. He introduced the notions, fundamental to later work, of the characteristic curve, the integral curve, the characteristic developable, and the characteristic cone. He also created the theory of equations of the type $Ar + Bs + Ct + D = 0$, which are now known as 'Monge equations'.

He also introduced contact transformations, which were to be generalized by Sophus ◊Lie a century later.

By his development of descriptive geometry and his application of analysis to infinitesimal geometry Monge not only paved the way for much of the geometrical flowering of the 19th century; he also proved himself to be one of the most original mathematicians of his time.

Monod, Jacques Lucien (1910–1976) French biochemist who is best known for his research into the way in which genes regulate intracellular activities. For this research Monod and his co-workers André ◊Lwoff and François ◊Jacob were jointly awarded the 1965 Nobel Prize for Physiology or Medicine.

Monod was born in Paris on 9 February 1910 and was educated at the university there. He graduated in 1931 and carried out research on the origins of life on Earth. He became assistant professor of zoology at the University of Paris in 1934, and gained his doctorate in 1941. He worked for the French Resistance during World War II. From 1945 to 1953 he was laboratory chief at the Pasteur Institute, and it was during this period that he collaborated with Lwoff and Jacob on the work that was to gain them their Nobel prize. In 1953 Monod became director of the department of cellular biochemistry at the Pasteur Institute and also a professor in the faculty of sciences at the University of Paris. In 1971 he was appointed director of the entire Pasteur Institute. Monod died in Cannes on 31 May 1976.

Working on the way in which genes control intracellular metabolism in microorganisms, Monod and his colleagues postulated the existence of a class of genes (which they called operons) that regulate the activities of the genes that actually control the synthesis of enzymes within the cell. They further hypothesized that the operons suppress the activities of the enzyme-synthesizing genes by affecting the synthesis of messenger RNA (mRNA). This theory has since been proved generally correct for many types of microorganisms but there is some doubt as to whether or not it applies in more complex plants and animals.

In 1971 Monod published his well-known book *Chance and Necessity,* a wide-ranging biological and philosophical work in which he summoned contemporary biochemical discoveries to support the idea that all forms of life result from random mutation (chance) and Darwinian selection (necessity). In the conclusion to this book, Monod stated his belief that there is no overall plan to human existence and that the human race must choose its own values in a vast and indifferent universe.

Montgolfier, Joseph Michel (1740–1810) and Jacques Etiènne (1745–1799) French brothers whose hot-air balloon, on 21 November 1783, was used for the first successful human flight.

The Montgolfier brothers were sons of a paper manufacturer from Annonay, near Lyon, France. The eldest, Joseph, was born on 26 August 1740 and although he was given to playing truant from school, he developed a strong interest in chemistry, mathematics, and natural science, even to the point of setting up his own small laboratory. Jacques, the younger by nearly five years, was born at Vidalon on 7 January 1745. He became a successful architect before joining his father's company, but, once involved, invented the first vellum paper.

Both brothers were fascinated by the views and theories on the possibility of flight by early scholars like the 14th-century Augustinian monk Albert of Saxony and the 17th-century Jesuit priest Father Francesco de Lana de Terzi, who designed a 'ship of the air' supported by evacuated copper spheres. But neither made any attempt at invention until 1782.

It was then, purely by chance, that they noticed the effects of rising smoke on particles of unburnt paper. Using this as a basis for their work, they progressed within two years from inflating paper bags to the first crewed free balloon flight in history.

Their success story really began in June 1783, when the brothers demonstrated their invention to an admiring crowd in the marketplace of Annonay. A large fire of straw and wood was built and the brothers placed over it a sphere of their own design made of paper and linen, allowing the heat to lift it gently into the air. Encouraged by their achievement, they took their invention to Versailles and in the grounds of the palace before a large audience (which included Louis XVI and Marie Antionette) their balloon ascended, carrying a sheep, a cock, and a duck, and made an eight-minute flight of approximately 3 km/2 mi.

A month later, on 15 October 1783, the first crewed ascent was made by François Pilâtre de Rozier (1757–1785) in a tethered balloon, paving the way for the first crewed free balloon flight on 21 November of that year. The crew of two, Pilâtre de Rozier and the Marquis d'Arlandes, ascended from the gardens of the Château la Muette, near Paris, and travelled over the city, completing a journey of 9 km/12 mi.

Originally the brothers thought they might have discovered a new gas, but this was obviously not so and they discarded the idea. The success of their invention could not be denied, however, and other people were quick to set up in competition, the main rivals being the Robert brothers, who used hydrogen to inflate their balloon under the instructions of the French scientist Jacques ◊Charles. The first crewed flight in this type of balloon took place on 1 December 1783.

Jacques Montgolfier died in Servières on 2 August 1799 and, after his death, his brother Joseph devoted himself entirely to scientific research with varying degrees of success. He developed a type of parachute, a calorimeter, and a hydraulic ram and press. He was elected to the French Academy of Science and honoured by Napoleon when he was created Chevalier of the Legion of Honour. Outliving his brother by 11 years, he died in Balaruc-les-Bains on 26 June 1810.

Further Reading

Clancy, Judith, et al, *Paris Alive,* Synergistic Press, 1986.

Gillespie, Charles Coulston, *The Montgolfier Brothers and the Invention of Aviation, 1783–1784, with a Word on the Importance of Ballooning for the Science of Heat and the Art of Building Railroads,* Princeton University Press, 1983.

Remington, Preston, 'A monument honouring the invention of the balloon', *Bull Metrop Mus Art, new series,* April 1944, pp 241–248.

Moore, Patrick (1923–) English broadcaster, writer, and popularizer of astronomy. An extrovert character, Moore has presented the BBC Television series *The Sky At Night* since 1968, as a result of which he has become a national celebrity, in constant demand as a speaker and raconteur.

Moore was born on 4 March 1923. Privately educated because of his poor health, he nevertheless served with the Royal Air Force during World War II, and for seven years after the war he assisted at a training school for pilots. After 1952 his interest in astronomy and his talent for communication inspired him to become a freelance author, although for three years, beginning in 1965, he was director of the Armagh Planetarium in Northern Ireland. He was awarded the OBE in 1968 and the Royal Astronomical Society's Jackson-Gwilt Medal in 1977. He has also received many honours from abroad, such as honorary membership of the Astronomic-Geodetic Society of the Soviet Union (1971).

To Moore, astronomy was once merely an exciting hobby for the evenings and other times off work. Part of his immense appeal today is the fact that he has managed to retain the air of the enthusiastic amateur, while at the same time boldly entering areas of study and research that to most lay people are fraught with complexities. He has never himself been employed as an astronomer, but it is very evident from his books and his broadcasts that he is consistently up to date with all modern facets of astronomy and that he understands his subject so thoroughly as to be able to make even the most difficult concepts clear to ordinary people.

His many books include *Moon Flight Atlas* (1969), *Space* (1970), *The Amateur Astronomer* (1970), *Atlas of the Universe* (1970), *Guide to the Planets* (1976), *Guide to the Moon* (1976), *Can You Speak Venusian?* (1977), *Guide to the Stars* (1977), and *Guide to Mars* (1977).

Morgagni, Giovanni Battista (1682–1771) Italian anatomist, generally seen as the founder of pathology.

Born in Forli on 20 February 1682, and graduating in Bologna, Morgagni taught anatomy there and later in Padua. Active throughout his life in anatomical research, his great work *De sedibus et causis morborum per anatomen indagatis* (1761) was not published until he was 80. It was grounded on over 600 post mortems and was written in the form of 70 letters to an anonymous medical confrère. Case by case, Morgagni described the clinical aspects of the illness during the patient's lifetime, before proceeding to detail the post-mortem findings. His goal was to relate the illness to the lesions established at autopsy. Morgagni did not use a microscope and he regarded each organ of the body as a composite of minute mechanisms. His book may be seen as a crucial stimulus to the rise of morbid anatomy, especially if physicians also availed themselves of the techniques of percussion, developed by Auenbrugger, and auscultation, pioneered by René Laênnec.

Morgagni himself made significant discoveries. He was the first to delineate syphilitic tumours of the brain and tuberculosis of the kidney. He grasped that where only one side of the body is stricken with paralysis, the lesion lies on the opposite side of the brain. His explorations of the female genitals, of the glands of the trachea, and of the male urethra also broke new ground. Judged the founder of pathological anatomy, his work was later developed by Xavier ◊Bichat and others. He died in Padua on 6 December 1771.

Morgan, Ann Haven (1882–1966) US zoologist and ecologist.

Morgan was born on 6 May 1882 in Waterford, Connecticut, and entered Wellesley College, Massachusetts, in 1902 to study biology. She later transferred to Cornell University and graduated in 1906. After a brief period as an instructor in zoology at Mount Holyoke College, Massachusetts, she returned to Cornell and received her PhD in zoology in 1912 for a dissertation on mayflies. She returned to Mount Holyoke in that year as an instructor in zoology, became an associate professor in 1914, and a full professor in 1918; she served as chair of the department of zoology from 1914 until her formal retirement in 1947. She died on 5 June 1966 at her home in South Hadley, Massachusetts.

Her research interests covered a broad range of biological problems, including the zoology of aquatic insects, the comparative physiology of hibernation, and conservation and ecology, and she spent her summers at a variety of research laboratories, including the Marine Biological Laboratory at Woods Hole in Massachusetts, and also worked at the Tropical Research Laboratory of British Guiana (now Guyana). She was a keen communicator of her subject, and her *Field Book of Ponds and Streams: An Introduction to the Life of Fresh Water* (1930) was an important book in attracting and encouraging amateur naturalists, as well as providing an authoritative taxonomic guide for professional collectors and zoologists. Further books on hibernation and animal behaviour, and an educational film brought her work and interests to a wide audience, and after her retirement she devoted a considerable amount of energy to reform of the scientific curriculum, especially in promoting the study of ecology and conservation. She was a member of the National Committee on Policies in Conservation Education and produced annual summer schools for teachers. She remained active in science education and local conservation movements until the end of her life.

Morgan, Garrett A (1875–1963) US inventor who patented the safety hood, later known as the gas mask, and the automatic three-way traffic signal.

Garrett Morgan was born in Paris, Kentucky, on 4 March 1875. He received only elementary school education and at the age of 14 he left home to work as a handyman in Cincinnati, Ohio. In 1895 he moved to Cleveland as a sewing-machine adjuster. He remained in Cleveland, where he patented his inventions until his death on 27 July 1963. Morgan married in 1908 and had three sons. After opening his own shop selling and repairing sewing machines in 1907 and a tailoring shop in 1909, Morgan went on to establish the G A Morgan Hair Refining Company in 1913 as a result of discovering a human hair-straightening process. He is best known, however, for his invention of his safety hood, for which he obtained a patent in 1914. After rescuing men trapped in a tunnel following an explosion at Cleveland Water Works in 1916, requests came from fire and police departments and mining companies for demonstrations of the hood; Morgan then set up a company to manufacture and sell them. During World War I the design was improved and it became part of the standard field equipment of US soldiers. Morgan is not only known for his invention of the gas mask: in 1923 he obtained the patent for his invention of the three-way automatic traffic signal (he was also awarded the British and Canadian patents). He sold the right to the traffic signal to the General Electric Corporation for $40,000. Morgan also invented a woman's hat fastener, a round belt fastener, and a friction drive clutch.

Morgan was very much concerned with black welfare, and in 1920 he started his own newspaper, the *Cleveland Call,* later the *Call and Post.* He served as treasurer of the Cleveland Association of Colored Men from 1914 until it merged with the National Association for the Advancement of Colored People of which he remained an active member all his life. In 1931 he ran as an independent candidate for the city council in Cleveland but was unsuccessful.

Morgan received several awards for his inventions: he was awarded the First Grand Prize Golden Medal by the National Safety Device Company at the Second International Exposition of Safety and Sanitation in 1914, and following the rescue in 1916 he was awarded the Carnegie Medal, a medal for bravery by the city of Cleveland, and honorary membership of the International Association of Fire Engineers. In 1976 a public school in Harlem, New York City, was named after him.

Morgan, Thomas Hunt (1866–1945) US geneticist and embryologist famous for his pioneering work on the genetics of the fruit fly *Drosophila melanogaster* – now extensively used in genetic research – and for establishing the chromosome theory of heredity. He received many honours for his work, including the 1933 Nobel Prize for Physiology or Medicine.

Morgan was born on 25 September 1866 in Lexington, Kentucky, the son of a diplomat. He was educated at the State College of Kentucky, graduating in 1886, and then at Johns Hopkins University, from which he gained his PhD in 1890. In the following year he joined the staff of Bryn Mawr College, near Philadelphia, as associate professor of zoology and remained there until 1904, when he became professor of experimental zoology at Columbia University. In 1928 he was appointed director of the Laboratory of Biological Sciences at the California Institute of Technology, a post he held until his death in Pasadena on 4 December 1945.

Morgan's early work was in the field of embryology, investigating such phenomena as fertilization in nucleated and unnucleated egg fragments, the development of embryos from separated blastomeres, and the effect of salt concentration on the development of unfertilized and fertilized eggs. In about 1907, however, his interest turned to the mechanisms involved in heredity (following the rediscovery of Gregor ◊Mendel's work), and in 1908 he began his famous research on the genetics of *Drosophila* – initially to test Mendel's laws, about which Morgan was sceptical. After breeding several generations of *Drosophila,* Morgan noticed many small phenotypic variations, some of which could not be accounted for by Mendel's law of independent assortment – he discovered, for example, that the

Drosophila variant now known as white eye is confined almost entirely to males. From his findings he postulated that certain characteristics are sex-linked, that the X chromosome carries several discrete hereditary units (genes), and that the genes are linearly arranged on chromosomes. Morgan also demonstrated that sex-linked characters are not invariably inherited together, from which he developed the concept of crossing-over and the associated idea that the extent of crossing-over is a measure of the spatial separation of genes on chromosomes. (From these ideas A H Sturtevant – one of Morgan's student collaborators – drew up in 1911 the first chromosome map, which showed the positions of five sex-linked genes.) Morgan realized that his findings proved that Mendel's 'factors' have a physical basis in chromosomes and revised his earlier scepticism of Mendelian genetics. In 1915, in collaboration with Sturtevant and his other students A B Bridges, and Hermann ◊Muller, Morgan published a summary of his work in *The Mechanism of Mendelian Heredity,* which had a profound influence in genetic research and evolutionary theory.

In the following years Morgan and various co-workers continued to elaborate the chromosome theory of heredity. Towards the end of his life, however, he returned to embryological investigations, trying to support with experimental evidence the theoretical links between embryological development and genetic theory. But it is his early work that is the most important, providing one of the cornerstones of modern genetic theory. Moreover, largely as a result of Morgan's experimentation, *Drosophila* became one of the principal experimental animals used for genetic investigations.

Morley, Edward Williams (1838–1923) US physicist and chemist who is best known for his collaboration with Albert ◊Michelson in the classic Michelson–Morley experiment that disproved the existence of the ether as a medium that propagates light waves.

Morley was born in Newark, New Jersey, on 29 January 1838. He was taught at home by his parents until 1857, when he entered Williams College. He obtained a bachelor's degree from there in 1860, and then began theological training at the Andover Seminary, intending to become a Congregational minister like his father. At the same time he continued his studies at Williams College, which awarded him a master's degree in 1863.

Morley completed his theological training in 1864, and worked for a year with the Sanitary Commission in Fort Monroe in Virginia, before returning to the Andover Academy for another year of study. In 1866 he got a teaching job at the South Berkshire Academy in Marlboro, Massachusetts.

In 1868 Morley was offered a ministry in Twinsburg, Ohio, and a teaching post in the chemistry department of Western Reserve College in Hudson, Ohio. He accepted the latter, but only on the condition that he be permitted to preach at the university chapel. Morley remained at Western Reserve College, later called Adelbert College when the college moved to Cleveland, Ohio, for the rest of his career. He became professor of chemistry there in 1869 and retired in 1906. From 1873 to 1888, he simultaneously held the post of professor of chemistry and toxicology at Cleveland Medical College. Morley's contributions to the fields of physics and chemistry were recognized with the award of several distinguished honours, including the Davy Medal of the Royal Society in 1907, and the presidency of the American Association for the Advancement of Sciences 1895–96. Morley died in West Hartford, Connecticut, on 24 February 1923.

All of Morley's research involved the use of precision instruments. During the early part of his scientific career, he was involved with the design of such equipment. One of his instruments was a eudiometer, which he applied to test a theory concerning the origin of cold waves of air. Using the eudiometer, which was accurate to within 0.0025%, Morley was able to confirm on the basis of the oxygen content of the air and meteorological data that, under certain conditions, cold air derives from the downward movement of air from high altitudes rather than from the southward movement of northerly cold air.

Morley's most important contribution to science came with his collaboration with Michelson, which began in 1885. Michelson too was concerned with precision measurement, and the two men improved the interferometer that Michelson had first used in 1881 in an unsuccessful attempt to detect the motion of the Earth through the ether. The confirmation of this negative result in 1887 by Michelson and Morley led to the conclusion that the velocity of light is constant irrespective of the motion of the observer, which is one of the postulates of the special theory of relativity.

Morley also achieved wide recognition with the publication in 1895 of his accurate determinations of the densities of hydrogen and oxygen, and the ratios for their combination. Morley also investigated a controversial and long-standing theory known as Prout's hypothesis (proposed by William ◊Prout in 1815), which suggested that all the elements of the periodic table are multiples of the hydrogen atom. Morley decided to test this theory by taking the atomic mass of hydrogen to equal one, and then determining the relative atomic mass of oxygen by chemical means. He found that the ratio of their atomic weights was 1:15.879, not 16 as expected if oxygen was an integral multiple of hydrogen. Morley felt that he had finally disproved Prout's hypothesis. However the discovery of isotopes later led scientists to realize that chemical methods of determining atomic mass provide only an average result for the masses of all the different isotopes present in the sample. Prout's idea was essentially correct and he was honoured in 1920 when Ernest ◊Rutherford suggested that the subatomic particle that forms the hydrogen nucleus be named the *pro*ton.

Morley continued doing analytical research after his retirement. His constant preoccupation with precision and accuracy produced a rich yield of results during the course of his career, and their importance was quickly recognized.

Morris, Desmond John (1928–) English zoologist and writer and broadcaster on animal and human behaviour.

Morris was born on 21 January 1928 and was educated at Birmingham University where he gained as BSc in zoology. He then went to Magdalen College, Oxford, to read for a PhD, working on animal behaviour under Niko ◊Tinbergen. From 1954 he worked in the department of zoology at Oxford before becoming head of the Granada Television and Film Unit at the Zoological Society in London in 1956. Three years later he was appointed curator of mammals at the Zoological Society of London and from 1967 to 1968 served as director of the Institute of Contemporary Arts in London.

Morris has been a prolific writer, as well as having made several films and presented television programes on social behaviour. Probably the best known of his books are *The Naked Ape* (1967), in which he examines the human animal in a brutally objective way, and *The Human Zoo* (1969), which follows on in that he scrutinizes the society that the naked ape has created for itself. Morris compares civilized humans with their captive animal counterparts and shows how confined animals seem to demonstrate the same neurotic behaviour patterns as human beings often do in crowded cities. He believes the urban environment of the cities to be the human zoo.

He has done much to popularize sociology and zoology, and is an entertaining presenter of programmes with some social influence.

Morse, Samuel Finley Breese (1791–1872) US artist who invented an electric telegraph and gave his name to Morse code.

Morse was born on 27 April 1791, in Charlestown, Massachusetts, the eldest son of a clergyman. Brought up to appreciate all forms of culture, he chose to devote himself to art, and after studying at Yale University, from which he graduated in 1810, he studied at the Royal Academy in London.

Morse US inventor Samuel Morse who pioneered the telegraph and devised the Morse code which was first used in 1844. This method of communication was used widely during World War II, and is still used today. *Mary Evans Picture Library*

On returning to the USA he achieved a fair amount of success, particularly in sculpture and in the painting of miniatures on ivory. Unfortunately the financial rewards brought him no more than a bare living, and in 1829 he returned once more to Europe in the hope of establishing a firm artistic reputation. From 1829 to 1832 he travelled widely, but after three years he once more set sail for home aboard the ship *Sully*. It was on this voyage that fate took a turn in the shape of fellow passenger Charles Jackson, who had recently attended lectures on electricity in Paris. He had with him an elctromagnet and Morse, having made his acquaintance, became fascinated with the talk of electricity and the possiblities of this new idea.

For the remainder of the voyage he spent hours making notes and became fired with the concept of communication by electric current 'telegraph'. As soon as he landed he set about turning his theories into working models and became so obsessed with the invention that he more or less abandoned his art career, relying for means of support on his appointment as professor of the art of design, at the University of New York.

By 1836 he had devised a simple relay system and having enlisted the help of Professor Gale, a chemist, and Alfred Vail, he improved his apparatus to the point where it became a commercial proposition.

After a further four years of political wrangling, his invention was finally given the backing of Congress and with a salary to give him freedom from money problems, Morse undertook the superintending of the first line between Baltimore and Washington. A trial run was telegraphed on 23 May 1843 and the line was eventually opened for public use on 1 April 1845. Morse died in New York on 2 April 1872.

Morse's idea hinged on the idea that an electric current could be made to convey messages. The signal current would be sent in an intermittent coded pattern and would cause an elctromagnet to attract intermittently to the same pattern on a piece of soft iron to which a pencil or pen would be attached and which in turn would make marks on a moving strip of paper. Once a suitable code had been worked out and batteries with sufficient power located, the technical problems mainly concerned the conductors, which on the first line were carried above ground on poles. Although underground conductors were envisaged, telegraph poles became a familiar feature of the countryside for the next 100 years.

The original receiver recorded signals by indentation. The Morse inker was a later innovation, invented mainly because Morse disliked the operators 'reading' the messages by ear (they became so adept they could identify letters from the sound of the clicks made by the machine), and also because he felt a written proof of receipt by the machine was a necessity.

Further Reading

Mabee, Carleton, *The American Leonardo: A Life of Samuel F B Morse*, Alfred A Knopf, 1943.

Prime, Samuel Irenaeaus, *The Life of Samuel F B Morse, Inventor of the Electromagnetic Recording Telegraph*, D Appleton, 1875.

Staiti, Paul J, *Samuel F B Morse*, Cambridge University Press, 1989.

Morton, William Thomas Green (1819–1868) US

dentist who in 1846 gave the first public demonstration of ether anaesthesia during surgery. Although he was neither the discoverer of the painkilling effects of ether nor the first to use it during a surgical operation, it was largely as a result of his efforts that anaesthesia became quickly and widely adopted by surgeons and dentists.

Little is known about Morton's early years. He was born in Charlton City, Massachusetts, on 9 August 1819, the son of a smallholder and shopkeeper, and is reputed to have graduated from the Baltimore College of Dentistry, although this is uncertain. After a brief period in partnership with Horace ◊Wells, another pioneer in the use of anaesthesia, Morton set up his own dental practice in Boston in 1844 and began investigating ways of deadening pain during dental surgery. After numerous unsuccessful attempts, he consulted the chemist and former physician Charles Jackson (1805–1880), who advised him to try ether as an anaesthetic. (This was not a new idea: Crawford Long (1815–1878) had in 1842 successfully used ether anaesthesia during an operation to remove a tumour from a patient's neck, although he did not publish this work until 1849 – by which time he had been preempted by Morton. In addition, Wells used nitrous oxide anaesthesia in a public demonstration – attended and partly arranged by Morton – in 1845, but had failed to convince his spectators of the gas's effectiveness as an anaesthetic.) In 1846 Morton successfully extracted a tooth from a patient under ether and later in the same year staged a public demonstration of ether anaesthesia in an operation (also successful) to remove a facial tumour; this operation was performed at the Massachusetts General Hospital – where Wells had earlier failed in his demonstration. So successful was Morton's demonstration that ether anaesthesia was rapidly adopted by surgeons and dentists in the USA and Europe.

Morton derived no financial benefits from his work. Morton and Jackson had jointly patented the process of ether anaesthesia but Morton attempted to claim sole credit as its discoverer. Jackson strongly contested this claim and Morton spent the rest of his life in costly litigation with him. A large fund was raised for Morton in the UK as an award for his discovery of anaesthesia but the offer was withdrawn in the face of strong opposition from Jackson. The French Academy of Medicine offered another monetary award to both men jointly, but Morton refused to accept it. Likewise, a bill to award Morton $100,000 in recognition of his work failed to pass in the US Congress in 1852, 1853, and again in 1854. Meanwhile, official recognition of priority had been accorded to Wells (for discovering nitrous oxide anaesthesia) and Long (for discovering ether anaesthesia). Finally Morton died, bitter and poor, on 15 July 1868 in New York City. Eventually, however, his role in the development of anaesthesia was recognized when he was elected in 1920 to the American Hall of Fame.

Moseley, Henry Gwyn Jeffreys (1887–1915)

English physicist who first established the atomic numbers of the elements by studying their X-ray spectra. This led to a complete classification of the elements, and also provided an experimental basis for an understanding of the structure of the atom.

Moseley was born in Weymouth on 23 November 1887. He came from a family of prestigious scientists, his father being professor of anatomy at Oxford and a member of the great *Challenger* expedition that surveyed the world's oceans 1872–76. Moseley was educated at Eton and in 1906 entered Trinity College,

Oxford, where he obtained a degree in physics in 1910. Immediately after graduation, he was appointed lecturer in physics in the laboratory of Ernest ◊Rutherford at Manchester, becoming a research fellow in 1912. Moseley remained with Rutherford until 1913. He then worked privately at Oxford with a view to obtaining a professorship there, and in 1914 he visited Australia. On the outbreak of World War I, he returned home and immediately enlisted in the army. Fearing for his safety, Rutherford endeavoured unsuccessfully to secure him scientific duties. Moseley was sent to the Dardanelles and was killed at Gallipoli on 10 August 1915.

Moseley was a researcher only from 1910 to 1914, and yet he made discoveries that were of fundamental importance to the development of both physics and chemistry. When he joined Rutherford's group in 1910, Rutherford was researching the phenomena associated with natural radioactivity. Moseley at first helped Rutherford in this work, but when reports of the diffraction of X-rays by Max von ◊Laue reached him in 1912, Moseley persuaded Rutherford to allow him to study X-ray spectra. He received instruction in X-ray diffraction from Lawrence Bragg (see William and Lawrence ◊Bragg) and in 1913 Moseley introduced X-ray spectroscopy to determine the X-ray spectra of the elements.

In a series of brilliant investigations, Moseley allowed the X-rays produced from various substances used as a target in an X-ray tube to be diffracted by a crystal of potassium ferrocyanide. The glancing angles were measured accurately and the position of the diffracted beams determined to obtain the wavelengths and frequencies of the X-rays emitted. Moseley examined metals from aluminium to gold and he found that their X-ray spectra were similar but with a deviation that changed regularly through the series. He found that a graph of the square root of the frequency of each radiation against the number representing the element's position in the periodic table gave a straight line. He called this number the atomic number of the element, which has since been shown to be the positive charge on the nucleus and thus the number of protons in the nucleus. Since the atom is electrically neutral, the atomic number is also the number of electrons surrounding the nucleus.

It was as a direct result of this work that atomic numbers were placed on a sound experimental foundation. Moseley found that when the elements are arranged in the periodic table according to their atomic numbers, all irregularity caused in the older system of grouping elements by their atomic weight (relative atomic mass) disappeared. Now that the elements were numbered, the rare earth elements could be sorted out, a process that Moseley began at Oxford towards the end of his life. The numbering system also

enabled Moseley to predict that several more elements would be discovered, namely those with atomic numbers of 43, 61, 72, 75, 87, and 91. These were all found in due course.

Although the number of elements that Moseley was able to examine was limited, the equation relating the square root of the frequency to the atomic number has been found to hold in all cases. The equation is known as Moseley's law. It has enabled scientists to identify a total of 105 elements in a continuous series of atomic numbers. Any further elements that might be produced by nuclear reactions can only have greater atomic numbers.

In 1913 and 1914, the young physicist published his findings in two remarkable papers in the *Philosophical Magazine* and entitled them 'The high-frequency spectra of the elements'. Moseley's discovery told how many electrons were present in any element, and tied in nicely with the quantum theory of the hydrogen atom that was published in 1913 by Niels ◊Bohr.

Moseley's fundamental discovery was a milestone in our knowledge of the constitution of the atom, and we are left to ponder on what this great brain might have discovered had he not been so tragically killed at so young an age.

Mössbauer, Rudolf Ludwig (1929–) German physicist who was awarded (with Robert ◊Hofstadter) the 1961 Nobel Prize for Physics for his discovery of the Mössbauer effect. The effect, which involves the recoil-free absorption of gamma radiation by an atomic nucleus, provided experimental verification for Albert ◊Einstein's theory of relativity.

Mössbauer was born in Munich on 31 January 1929, and was educated there. He graduated from the Munich Institute of Technology in 1952 and was awarded his PhD in 1958, the same year that he announced the Mössbauer effect, which he discovered during his postgraduate research in Heidelberg at the Max-Planck Institute for Medical Research. In 1960 he went to the USA and a year later became professor of physics at the California Institute of Technology, Pasadena. From 1964 to 1972 and again from 1977 he was professor of experimental physics at the Technical University of Munich. Mössbauer began research into the effects of gamma rays on matter in 1953. The absorption of a gamma ray by an atomic nucleus usually causes it to recoil, so affecting the wavelength of the re-emitted ray. Mössbauer found that at low temperatures crystals will absorb gamma rays of a specific wavelength and resonate, so that the crystal as a whole recoils while the nuclei do not. This recoil-less nuclear resonance absorption became known as the Mössbauer effect. A lengthening of the gamma-ray wavelength in a gravitational field, as predicted by the general theory of relativity, was observed experimentally in 1960.

Mott, Nevill Francis (1905–1996) English physicist whose work on semiconductors won him the 1977 Nobel Prize for Physics. He shared the prize with Philip ◊Anderson, who has also worked on crystalline materials, and John ◊Van Vleck, who played a central role in the development of the laser.

Mott was born on 30 September 1905. He was educated at Clifton College and then at St John's College, Cambridge. He became a lecturer at Manchester University in 1929 and at Gonville and Caius College, Cambridge, in 1930. In 1933, he moved to Bristol to become Melville Wills Professor of Theoretical Physics and held this position until 1948, when he became director of the Henry Herbert Wills Physical Laboratories at Bristol. From 1954 to 1971, he was Cavendish Professor of Physics at Cambridge University (later emeritus) and then senior research fellow at Imperial College, London, 1971–73. His honours included a knighthood in 1972 and the award of the Royal Society's Copley Medal also in 1972. He died on 8 August 1996.

Mott was a leading authority on solid-state physics, particularly on the theory of electrons in metals and on dislocations and other defects in the crystalline structure. He was the first, with R W Gurney, to put forward a comprehensive theory of the process involved when a photographic film is exposed to light. They postulated that the incident light produces free electrons and holes that wander about the crystal. The electrons become trapped at imperfections, which might be dislocations or possibly foreign atoms, and attract interstitial silver ions to form silver atoms and make the latent image. When a developer is present, the entire grain may be catalysed into free silver by the initially formed specks of silver.

Mott's work on semiconductors, which won him the Nobel prize, showed how a cheap and reliable material can be used to improve the performance of electronic circuits, increasing the memory capacity of computers by several times. More efficient photovoltaic cells, capable of converting solar energy into electricity, can now be produced.

Mottelson, Ben Roy (1926–) US physicist; see ◊Bohr, Mottelson, and Rainwater.

Muir, Thomas (1844–1934) Scottish mathematician, famous for his monumental and pioneering work in unravelling the history of determinants.

Muir was born in Stonebrye, Lanarkshire, on 25 August 1844 and grew up in the nearby town of Biggar, where his father was a shoemaker. He was educated at

Wishaw Public School and Glasgow University, where he excelled at Greek and mathematics. He then spent some time in Berlin, studying and book-collecting, before returning to Scotland in 1868 to take up a post as mathematics tutor at College Hall, St Andrews. From 1871 to 1874 he was assistant professor of mathematics at Glasgow and from 1874 to 1891 head of the mathematics and science department at the Glasgow High School. That he chose to leave university life for secondary-school teaching revealed the deep interest he took in the general educational standards of the community. In 1891 his wife, who suffered poor health, was advised to move to a warmer climate and together they emigrated to South Africa, where, in 1892, Muir accepted the post of superintendent general of education in the colony. He held the post until his retirement in 1915. From 1892 to 1901 he was also vice chancellor of the University of Cape Town. In addition to his mathematical work, Muir took a keen interest in geography and he was elected a fellow of the Royal Geographical Society in 1892 and of the Royal Scottish Geographical Society in 1899. He was knighted in 1915. In 1916 he received the Gunning-Victoria Prize for his contribution to science. He died in Cape Town on 21 March 1934.

Muir earned the gratitude of South Africans for the part that he played – by far the most important part – in raising educational standards in the country and securing a proper place for science in the curriculum. In the history of mathematics he is remembered for his work on determinants, first discovered by Gottfried ◊Leibniz in 1693. In all he published 307 papers, most of them on determinants and allied subjects, in addition to his books, *A Treatise on the Theory of Determinants* (1882), *The Theory of Determinants in its Historical Order of Development* (1890), and, above all, the magisterial five-volume treatise on the history of determinants. The first volume appeared in 1906, the last in 1930, and when it was completed it was widely acclaimed as one of the most thorough treatments of the history of any branch of theoretical knowledge. Muir's work made the results of Pierre ◊Laplace, Augustin ◊Cauchy, and a host of other mathematicians accessible to scholars. Muir himself was not a creative mathematician but his book lay behind many an algebraic discovery.

Further Reading
Leadbetter, Russell, *Thomas Muir: A Passion for Liberty*, Neil Wilson Publishing, 1999.

Muller, Hermann Joseph (1890–1967) US geneticist famous for his discovery that genetic mutations can be artificially induced by means of X-rays, for which he was awarded the 1946 Nobel Prize for Physiology or Medicine.

Muller was born on 21 December 1890 in New York City and was educated at Morris High School in the Bronx district of the city. In 1907 he won a scholarship to Columbia University, from which he graduated in 1910. He remained at Columbia to do postgraduate research on genetics – under Thomas Hunt ◊Morgan – and gained his PhD in 1916. Muller then spent three years at the Rice Institute in Houston, Texas, at the invitation of Julian Huxley (1887–1975), followed by a brief period as an instructor at Columbia University. Then in 1920 he joined the University of Texas, Austin, initially as associate professor of zoology and later as professor of zoology. The next 12 years at the University of Texas were the most scientifically productive in Muller's life but eventually the pressure of work, the ending of his marriage to the mathematician Jessie Marie Jacob (whom he had married in 1923), and the constraints on his freedom to express his socialist political views all combined to produce a nervous breakdown, and in 1932 Muller left the USA to work at the Kaiser-Wilhelm Institute in Berlin. In 1933 he moved to Leningrad (now St Petersburg) to become – at the invitation of Nikolai Vavilov – senior geneticist at the Institute of Genetics; the institute was transferred to Moscow in the following year and Muller moved with it. But in the mid-1930s the false ideas of Trofim ◊Lysenko began to dominate Soviet biological research; Muller openly criticized Lysenkoism but so great was Lysenko's political influence that Muller was forced to leave the Soviet Union in 1937. After serving in the Spanish Civil War he worked at the Institute of Animal Genetics in Edinburgh, where in 1939 he met and married Dorothea Kantorowitz, a German refugee. Muller returned to the USA in 1940. He held various posts at Amherst College, Massachusetts, 1941–45, when he was appointed professor of zoology at Indiana University. He remained there and died on 5 April 1967 in Bloomington, Indiana.

Muller began his research on genetics while working for his doctorate under Morgan, in the course of which he made several important contributions to the understanding of the arrangements and recombinations of genes. During this period he became particularly interested in mutations, and when he began independent research he attempted to find techniques for accelerating mutation rates. In 1919 he found that the mutation rate was increased by heat, and that heat did not always affect both of the chromosomes in a chromosome pair. From this he concluded that mutations involved changes at the molecular or sub-molecular level. Next Muller experimented with X-rays as a means of inducing mutations, and by 1926 he had proved the method successful. This was an important finding because it meant that geneticists could induce mutations when

required, rather than having to wait for the considerably slower process of natural mutation, and it also showed that mutations are nothing more than chemical changes.

Muller's research had convinced him that almost all mutations are deleterious. He realized that in the normal course of evolution deleterious mutants die out and the few advantageous ones survive but he also believed that if the mutation rate is too high, the number of imperfect individuals may become too large for the species as a whole to survive. Consequently, he began to concern himself with the social effects of genetic mutations. He campaigned against the needless use of X-rays in diagnosis and treatment, and pressed for safety regulations to ensure that people who were regularly exposed to X-rays were adequately protected. He also opposed nuclear bomb tests, arguing that the radioactive fallout could burden future generations with an excessive number of deleterious mutations. Furthermore, he advocated the establishment of sperm banks, in which the sperm of gifted men could be preserved for use by later generations so that the human gene pool would be improved.

Müller, Johannes (1436–1476) Also known as Regiomontanus. German astronomer who compiled astronomical tables, translated ◊Ptolemy's *Almagest* from Greek into Latin, and assisted in the reform of the Julian Calendar.

Müller was born in Königsberg (now Kaliningrad in Russia) on 6 June 1436, the son of a miller. Nothing is known of him until he enrolled at the University of Vienna on 14 April 1450, under the name of 'Johannes Molitoris de Künigsberg'. The name Regiomontanus is derived from a latinization of his birth place: Regio Monte, meaning 'king's mountain'. At the age of 15 he was awarded his bachelor's degree and, in 1457, was appointed to the faculty of astronomy at the University of Vienna. He died, probably of the plague, in Rome in 1476.

At Vienna Regiomontanus (as he was called by then) became a close friend and colleague of G von Peuerbach, under whom he had studied astronomy. The course of their lives was deeply affected in 1460 by the arrival in Vienna of Cardinal Bessarion, who, as part of his campaign to bring ancient Greek authors to the attention of intellectuals in the Latin west, persuaded Peuerbach to translate Ptolemy's *Almagest* from Greek into Latin. But Peuerbach failed to finish this mammoth task and his last wish before dying in April 1461, was that Regiomontanus should complete the project. Regiomontanus complied and, in addition to translating the work, he added more recent observations, revised some computations and added his own criticisms. Regiomontanus named the complete translation *Epitome,* but it was not printed until 20 years after his death. Nicolaus ◊Copernicus had been aware of many of the inaccuracies in Ptolemy's system (which nevertheless remained prevalent) and it was the critical reflections in the *Epitome* that led to Copernicus' rejection of the Ptolemaic system, so paving the way for modern astronomy.

In 1467 Regiomontanus started compiling trigonometric and astronomical tables. He began computing his *Tables of Directions,* which gave the longitudinal positions of celestial bodies relative to the apparent rotation of the heavens on a daily basis, and whose listings applied to observations made from points on the Earth as far north as 60° (although the finished work was not published until 1490). In 1468 he completed his sine tables, which facilitated the making of astronomical observations prior to the advent of logarithms, but these too were not published until more than 50 years after his death.

In 1471 Regiomontanus moved to Nürnberg, and became one of the first publishers of astronomical and scientific literature, which he produced on a printing press at his house. Among his first publications were Peuerbach's *New Theory of the Planets* and his own *Ephemerides,* which was issued in 1474. This was the first publication of its kind to be printed, listing the predicted daily positions of the heavenly bodies for the years 1475–1506. It acquired some historical interest when it was used by Christopher Columbus in Jamaica to predict a lunar eclipse that frightened the hostile Indians into submission.

The *Nuremberg Chronicle* records Regiomontanus as accepting a papal invitation in 1475 to assist in amending the ecclesiastical calendar, which was riddled with inaccuracies. Arriving in Rome in 1475, he unfortunately died within a year of leaving Nürnberg, probably struck down by the plague epidemic that engulfed Rome when the Tiber flooded the city in 1476.

After Regiomontanus' death, the statement 'the motion of the stars must vary a tiny bit on account of the motion of the Earth' was found to be written in his handwriting. This fact has led some people to believe that Regiomontanus propounded 'Copernican' views before Copernicus. It has also been suggested that Regiomontanus sent the letter containing this statement to Novara (who was Copernicus' teacher), who in turn communicated it to Copernicus. Thus some people infer that the revolutionary geocentric doctrine was first conceived by Regiomontanus.

Müller, Paul Hermann (1899–1965) Swiss chemist, known for his development of DDT as an insecticide, for which he was awarded the 1948 Nobel Prize for Physiology or Medicine.

Müller was born in Olten, Solothurn, on 12 January 1899. He received his early education in Basel and worked in the electrical and chemical laboratories of several industrial firms before continuing his academic studies. He gained his doctorate in chemistry at Basel in 1925 and then went to work for J R Geigy, researching principally into dyestuffs and tanning agents; he subsequently joined the staff of Basel University. He died in Basel on 12 October 1965.

In 1935 Müller started work on a research project designed to discover a substance that would kill insects quickly but have little or no poisonous effect on plants and animals, unlike the arsenical compounds then in use. He concentrated his search on chlorine compounds and in 1939 synthesized dichlorodiphenyl trichloroethane (DDT) – which had first been prepared 65 years earlier by the German chemist Othmar Zeidler, who had not been aware of its insecticidal properties.

The Swiss government successfully tested DDT against the Colorado beetle, a potato pest, in 1939 and by 1942 it was in commercial production. Its first important use was in Naples, where a typhus epidemic broke out soon after the city had been captured by US forces in 1943; in January of the following year the population of Naples was sprayed with DDT to kill the body lice that are the carriers of typhus. A similar potential epidemic was arrested in Japan in late 1945 after the US occupation of the country.

For the following 20 years the use of DDT was to have a profound effect on the health of the world, both by killing insect vectors such as the mosquitoes that spread malaria and yellow fever and by combating insect pests that feed on food crops. Gradually the uses of DDT in public hygiene and in agriculture became limited by increasing DDT-resistance in insect species, and it has been supplanted by new synthetic insecticides. Also DDT is a very stable chemical compound; it does not break down and tends to accumulate in the environment, disrupting food chains and presenting a hazard to animal life. By the 1970s its use had been banned in several countries.

Murchison, Roderick Impey (1792–1871) and Charlotte née Hugonin (1788–1869) Scottish geologists who were two of the most prolific British geologists of the 19th century.

Born into an ancient Scottish Highland family in Tarradale on 19 February 1792, Roderick Murchison's father died when he was four years old and the family moved to England. He was educated at the military college at Great Marlow becoming an officer in the Dragoons, an excellent horseman and keen foxhunter. He briefly saw active service in the Peninsular War in 1908, resigning his commission in 1814. He and

Charlotte, the daughter of General Francis and Mrs Charlotte Hugonin met on the Isle of Wight and married in August 1815. The first winter of their marriage the couple stayed in Hampshire where Roderick learned about natural history from Charlotte and her family. On a tour in France, the Alps, and Italy the following spring, Charlotte introduced him to wild flowers, rocks and mountains. The couple travelled in Europe from 1816 to 1818, studying art and natural sciences and on their return Murchison sold his family estate. They settled for a short time in Charlotte's late grandfather's house in County Durham where Roderick devoted himself to foxhunting. Charlotte meanwhile was studying mineralogy and conchology and was trying to influence him to pursue a more intellectual lifestyle himself. A chance meeting with Humphry ◊Davy inspired him to further his interest in science and in 1924 he sold most of his horses and they moved to London. Encouraged by Charlotte, he focused his attentions on geology, presenting his first paper to the Geological Society in 1825 which described the fieldwork he and Charlotte had jointly undertaken in the land surrounding Charlotte's home in Hampshire. Through the influence of William Buckland (1784–1856) he was elected fellow of the Geological Society in London in 1825 and of the Royal Society in 1826. Murchison soon embarked upon a series of arduous geological field explorations, often accompanied by Adam ◊Sedgwick or Charles ◊Lyell, and always by Charlotte, who was by this time an excellent fossil hunter and geological artist and who tirelessly labelled and sketched specimens. They explored Scotland, France, and the Alps. In 1839, Murchison produced his major book, *The Silurian System,* on the basis of their study and classification of the 'greywackes' (old slatey rocks) of south Wales. It was illustrated with Charlotte's sketches and drawings. (A follow-up work, *Siluria,* came 15 years later.) The Silurian system (that is, those strata of the lower Palaeozoic beneath old red sandstone) contained, in Murchison's view, remains of the earliest life forms, though no fossils of vertebrates or land plants were to be expected. Following controversy with Henry ◊De la Beche, Murchison, with Sedgwick's cooperation, also established the Devonian system in southwest England. An expedition to Russia in 1841 led him to define yet another worldwide system, the Permian, named after the strata of the Perm region.

In spite of the ill health which had dogged her since she caught a fever in Rome in 1817, Charlotte was always on hand to give scientific advice to her husband and it can be concluded that many of his views were actually hers. Her considerable collection of fossils was useful to Roderick and others. James de Carle Sowerby,

author of the six volume *Mineral Conchology of Great Britain* (1827), named an ammonite in her honour – *Ammonites murchinsoniae*. William Buckland also used her specimens to illustrate one of his books.

In 1831 Charlotte and her friend Mary Somerville (1780–1872) were involved in persuading Lyell, who had just been appointed first professor of geology at King's College, London, to open his lectures to women. A number of women had asked to be admitted but his response had been that it would be 'unacademical' to allow women to attend. The number of interested women, plus the fact that they considerably swelled his audiences, made it ultimately impossible for him to refuse. This was a first move towards the admission of female students to British universities, although admission to lectures was later cancelled again.

Charlotte's considerable inheritance at her mother's death allowed Roderick to buy a house in Belgravia at which they laid on lavish dinners and soirees where scientists could mingle with politicians, dignitaries and literary figures. Murchison's biographer, Geikie (1875) put the purpose of these soirees down to maintaining and improving 'the social status of scientists, particularly geologists and especially Murchison himself'.

Roderick became increasingly rigid and more and more full of his own importance as a geologist. It is not clear what Charlotte's reaction to this was but as Disraeli described them in 1838: 'Murchison is a stiff geological prig, and his wife silent.'

Murchison had a distinct philosophy of geology. He believed in a universal order of the deposition of strata, indicated by fossils rather than solely by lithological features. Fossils showed a clear progression in complexity from azoic (pre-life) times to invertebrates, and thence up to vertebrate forms, with humans being created last of all: this progression was seen in respect of the Earth's cooling.

Knighted in 1846, Murchison became a 'professional' in 1855, succeeding De la Beche as director of the Geological Survey. He was one of the founders of the British Association. An ardent imperialist, for many years he was also president of the Royal Geographical Society, encouraging African exploration and annexation. In fact, in his later years he was better known as a geographer and for his support of the missionary activity of Scottish missionary explorer David Livingstone (1813–1873) in Africa. The Murchison Falls in Uganda are named after him. A haughty, dogmatic, and increasingly tetchy man, Murchison quarrelled sooner or later with most leading geologists. A catastrophist, he opposed the glacial theory of Louis Agassiz and his noisy campaign against Lyell's uniformitarianism turned into a rigid denial of Darwinian evolution. Roderick Murchison died in London on 22 October 1871.

Murdock, William (1754–1839) Scottish engineer who introduced gas lighting and was a pioneer in the development of steam engines and their application.

Murdock was born in Auchinleck, Ayrshire on 21 August 1754. In 1777 he entered the engineering firm of Matthew ◊Boulton and James ◊Watt at their Soho works in Birmingham, and two years later was sent to Cornwall to supervise the fitting of Watt's engines in mines. He lived in Redruth and proved an invaluable help to Watt, and references to him are numerous in the Soho correspondence. According to documents at Soho he signed an agreement on 30 March 1800 to act as an engineer and superintendent of the Soho foundry for a period of five years. He was, however, constantly despatched to various parts of the country, and he frequently visited Cornwall after he had ceased to reside there permanently. His connection with Boulton and Watt's firm continued until 1830, when he virtually retired. He died in 1839 at his house at Sycamore Hill, within sight of the Soho foundry.

An industrious but modest man, Murdock's subsequent fame has been somewhat overshadwed by that of his employers, Boulton and Watt. In about 1782, while residing in Cornwall, he began experiments on the illuminating properties of gases produced by distilling coal, wood, peat, and so on. He lit his house at Redruth by these means, and in 1892 the centenary of gas lighting was duly celebrated, but on the evidence now available it appears that the decisive breakthrough came several years later than 1792. Murdock succeeded in producing coal gas in large iron retorts and conveying it 21 m/70 ft through metal pipes. After returning to Birmingam in about 1799 he perfected further methods for making, storing, and purifying gas.

In 1802, in celebration of the Peace of Amiens with France, part of the exterior of the Soho factory was illuminated by gas, and a year later the factory interior was similiarly lit. Thereafter apparatus was erected ensuring that a part of the Soho foundry was regularly lit in this way, and the manufacture of gas-making plant seems to have been commenced about this period, probably in connection with apparatus for producing oxygen and hydrogen for medical purposes. In 1804, George Lee of the firm of Phillips and Lee, cotton-spinners of Manchester, ordered an apparatus for lighting his house with gas. Subsequently Phillips and Lee decided to light their mills. On 1 January 1806, Murdock wrote informing Boulton and Watt that 'fifty lamps of the different kinds' were lighted that night with satisfactory results. There was, Murdock added, 'no Soho Stink' – an expression that seems to show that the method of purification used at the foundry was somewhat primitive.

In February 1808 Murdock read a paper before the Royal Society in which he gave a full account of his investigations, and also of the saving effected by the adoption of gas lighting at Phillip and Lee's mill. The paper is the earliest practical essay on the subject. The Rumford Gold Medal, bearing the inscription *Ex fume clare lucem,* was awarded to Murdock for his paper, which concludes with these words: 'I believe I may, without presuming too much, claim both the first idea of applying and the first actual application of the gas to economical purposes.'

Murdock also made important improvements to the steam engine. He was the first to devise an oscillating engine, of which he made a model about 1784. In 1786 he was bringing to the attention of Boulton and Watt, who both remained highly sceptical of such possibilities, the idea of a steam carriage or road locomotive, an enterprise that was not successful. In 1799 he invented the long-D slide valve. He is generally credited with inventing the so-called Sun and planet motion, a means of making a steam engine give continuous revolving motion to a shaft provided with a fly wheel. Watt, however, patented this motion in 1781. Murdock also experimented with compressed air, and in 1803 constructed a steam gun. He died in Birmingham on 15 November 1839.

N

Nagell, Trygve (1895–1988) Norwegian mathematician whose most important work was in the fields of abstract algebra and number theory.

Nagell was born in Oslo on 13 July 1895 and was educated at the University of Oslo, where he received his MA in mathematics in 1920. He was appointed to the mathematics faculty of the university in that year and was awarded his PhD in 1926. He was promoted to the rank of associate professor in 1930, but a year later left Oslo to become professor of mathematics at the University of Uppsala, in Sweden, where he remained until his retirement in 1962. For his work in mathematics he was awarded the Norwegian Order of St Olav and made Knight Commander in the Swedish Order of the North Star.

Nagell first made his name with a series of papers in the early 1920s on indeterminate equations, investigations into which led to the publication of a treatise on indeterminate analysis in 1929. He also published papers and books, in Swedish and English, on number theory. From the late 1920s onwards his chief interest was the study of algebraic numbers, and his 1931 study of algebraic rings was perhaps his most important contribution to abstract algebra.

Napier, John (8th Laird of Merchiston) (1550–1617) Scottish mathematician who invented logarithmic tables.

Napier was born in Merchiston Castle, near Edinburgh, in 1550, into a family of influential landed nobility and statesmen who were staunchly attached to the Protestant cause. As a young boy he was educated chiefly at home, although he may have spent some time at the Edinburgh High School and, less probably, studying in France. At the age of 13 he was sent to St Salvator's College, in the University of St Andrews. There he studied mainly theology and philosophy, gained a reputation for his quick temper, and left without taking his degree. He may then have passed a few years studying on the continent. He was, at any rate, in Scotland in 1571. He built a castle at Gartnes, on the banks of the Endrick, and lived there with his wife, whom he married in 1572, until the death of his father in 1608 brought him the inheritance of Merchiston.

Napier was an aristocratic scientific and literary amateur. He never occupied any professional post in his life. But he became known as the 'Marvellous Merchiston'

Napier Engraving of Scottish mathematician John Napier, inventor of logarithms. The 8th Laird of Merchiston, Napier inherited the family estates near Edinburgh, Scotland in 1608, and devoted his time to mathematics, religious controversy, and the invention of weapons. *Mary Evans Picture Library*

for his varied accomplishments. He made advances in scientific farming, especially by the use of salt as a fertilizer; he invented a hydraulic screw and revolving axle by means of which water could be removed from flooded coalpits and obtained the patent for its sole manufacture and use in 1597; he also published, in 1593, a violent denunciation of the Roman Catholic Church entitled *A Plaine Discovery of the Whole Revelation of St John*, a popular work that ran through several editions and was translated into French, Dutch, and German. He had scarcely a moment of idleness, and overwork – combined with the gout from which he suffered in his later years – brought him to his death, at Merchiston, on 4 April 1617.

Napier's favourite intellectual pursuit was astronomy, and it was via astronomy that he was led to make his great invention. He performed many calculations in the course of his observations and research. He found the lengthy calculations, involving the use of trigonometric functions (especially sines) a tiresome burden, and over the course of about 20 years the idea of logarithmic tables slowly gestated in his mind. In 1614 he explained his new invention and printed the first logarithmic table in the *Mirifici logarithmorum canonis descriptio*. The word 'logarithm' he formed from the Greek *logos* for 'expression' and *arithmos* for 'number'. The best statement of his invention, however, was given in the posthumously published *Constructio* (1619).

Napier's publication was immediately recognized by mathematicians for the great advance that it was. In particular, it excited the English mathematician Henry ◊Briggs, who went to Edinburgh in 1616 (and a couple of times thereafter) to discuss the new tables with Napier. Together they worked out improvements – such as the idea of using the base ten – and the result, Briggs's tables of 1617, was the production of the standard form of logarithmic tables in use until the advent of cheap electronic calculators.

Napier himself has a claim as the inventor of the first mechanical calculator, albeit one of a wholly primitive kind. His last work, *Rabdologia* ('numeration by little rods'), he published in 1617. In it he explained his system of multiplying and dividing by the use of rods –

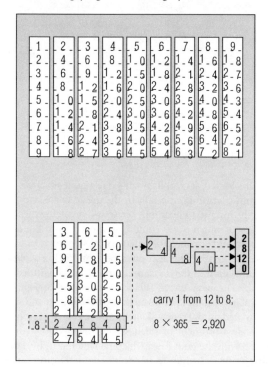

Napier In 1617 Scottish mathematician John Napier published his description of what was arguably the first mechanical calculator – a set of numbered rods, usually made of bone or ivory and therefore known as Napier's bones. Using them, multiplication became merely a process of reading off the appropriate figures and making simple additions.

usually made of bones or ivory, and hence known as Napier's bones – and showed also how square roots could be extracted by the manipulation of counters on a chessboard.

As a footnote, and a testament to the splendid practical inventiveness of the man, it should be remembered that it was Napier, too, who first used and then popularized the decimal point to separate the whole-number part from the fractional part of a number.

Nasmyth, James (1808–1890) Scottish engineer who contributed greatly to the design and production of tools. He is particularly known for his invention of the steam hammer and powered milling, shaping, slotting, and planing machines. One of his lesser-known inventions, which he did not choose to patent, is the flexible drive shaft for drilling and other machines.

Nasmyth was born in Edinburgh on 19 August 1808; his father was a well-known Scottish painter and amateur engineer. He attended Edinburgh High School, and on leaving there at the age of 12 he devoted his time to building engines and other mechanical devices. His success was such that he attempted to build a steam road carriage. When he was 21 he travelled to London with his father, and there met Henry ◊Maudslay, himself famous for work in tool and engine construction. Nasmyth showed Maudslay a model steam engine he had built, and so impressed him that he was taken on as his assistant. Over the next two years he learned Maudslay's techniques and developed his own accurate and rapid means of producing hexagonal-heading nuts. Also during this period he devised a flexible shaft of coiled spring steel for drilling holes in awkward places. (Later in life, during a visit to his dentist, he was told that this was the latest US invention.) Shortly after the death of Maudslay in 1831 he returned to Edinburgh and built his own small workshop, which included a Maudslay lathe and a number of other machine tools.

On seeing better prospects for an engineer in Manchester, he moved there in 1834 to a small workshop in which power was available. With the success of his machine-tool business he moved to a site on the Bridgwater Canal at Patricroft. In his Bridgwater foundry Nasmyth continued to manufacture machine tools and began to build railway locomotives and other machinery. His famous steam hammer was invented there in 1839, initially to forge the driving shaft of the steam ship *Great Britain*. This device speeded up the production of large forgings without the loss of accuracy. It was a very successful tool in the great age of machine building.

Nasmyth devised many other tools, including a vertical cylinder-boring machine that speeded up the production of steam engines, and all sorts of milling, shaping, slotting, and planing machines. Apart from the obvious effect these had on the accurate repetition of old techniques at an increased rate, they handled metal in new ways: all manner of lateral, transverse, and rotating cutting machines were devised. His shaping machines in particular were a financial success. Generally these devices speeded up the rate of production in the engineering industry in an unprecedented manner. Even with his hand-held tools, such as taps, he devised means of producing more accurate work with increased ease.

As the building of locomotives, and other heavy engineering projects, overshadowed the machine-tool aspect of his business, his personal interest declined and in 1856, at the age of 48, he retired from engineering. This was not the end of his scientific curiosity, for he devoted more time to astronomy, a hobby he pursued in a serious way. At his foundry he had built a number of telescopes, the largest being a reflector with a 50-cm/20-in mirror. During his retirement he lived at Penshurst in Kent, and used this instrument to make an extensive study of the Sun and Moon. In the course of his solar observations he was particularly concerned with sunspots. He chartered the lunar surface and developed his own volcanic theory of the origin of the craters. In 1851 his maps of the Moon received a prize at the Great Exhibition in London. Later he wrote a book about his lunar discoveries and theories. He died in London on 7 May 1890.

Nathans and Smith, Daniel Nathans (1928–) and Hamilton Othanel Smith (1931–) US microbiologists who shared, with Swiss microbiologist Werner Arber (1929–), the 1978 Nobel Prize for Physiology or Medicine for their work on restriction enzymes, which are special enzymes that can cleave genes into fragments.

Nathans was born on 30 October 1928 in Wilmington, Delaware. He was educated at the University of Delaware, from which he graduated in 1950, and at Washington University, St Louis, from which he gained his medical degree in 1954. He then worked as a clinical associate at the National Cancer Institute until 1957, when he became a resident physician at the Columbia-Presby Medical Center. From 1959 to 1962 he was a guest investigator at the Rockefeller University, New York City, after which he held several positions at the Johns Hopkins University, Baltimore: assistant professor then professor of microbiology at the school of medicine there 1962–76, director of the department of microbiology 1972–82, and Boury Professor of Microbiology 1976–82. In 1982 he became professor of molecular biology and genetics.

Smith was born on 23 August 1931 in New York City. He was educated at the University of California,

Berkeley, from which he graduated in mathematics in 1952, and at the Johns Hopkins University, from which he obtained his medical degree in 1956. From 1956 to 1957 he was a junior resident physician at Barnes Hospital, then carried out research at the Henry Ford Hospital, Detroit, 1959–62, when he became a research fellow in microbial genetics at the University of Michigan. Since 1964 he has been at Johns Hopkins University, becoming professor of microbiology 1973–81 and professor of molecular biology and genetics from 1981. He was also Guggenheim Fellow there 1975–76.

Arber discovered restriction enzymes in the bacterium *Escherichia coli* in the 1960s. These enzymes cleave genes at specific sites on the DNA molecules and thus enable the order of genes on the chromosomes to be determined. The gene fragments can also be used to analyse the chemical structure of genes as well as to create new gene combinations. Smith, working at the Johns Hopkins University independently of Arber, verified Arber's findings and was also able to identify the gene fragments. Smith collaborated with Nathans on some of his work, but Nathans also performed much original research of his own in this field. Using the carcinogenic SV40 virus, he showed in 1971 that it could be cleaved into 11 specific fragments, and in the following year he determined the order of these fragments.

As a result of the work of Nathans, Smith and Arber, it is now possible to determine the chemical formulae of the genes in animal viruses, to map these genes and to study the organization and expression of genes in higher animals.

Natta, Giulio (1903–1979) Italian chemist who shared the 1963 Nobel Prize for Chemistry with Karl ◊Ziegler for his work on the production of polymers.

Natta was born in Imperia, near Genoa, on 26 February 1903, the son of a judge. He obtained his doctorate in chemical engineering from the Polytechnic Institute in Milan in 1924 and then held professorships in general chemistry at the University of Pavia, in physical chemistry at Rome, and in industrial chemistry at Turin. In 1938 he returned to Milan Polytechnic as professor of chemistry and director of the Industrial Chemistry Research Institute. There he was charged by the government to investigate the problems of producing artificial rubber, because the supply of natural rubber had ceased with the imminence of World War II.

In 1953 Natta began intensive studies of macromolecular chemistry. These investigations were initiated by knowledge obtained through a licence arrangement between Ziegler and the Italian company of Montecatini, of which Natta was a consultant. Ziegler had discovered how to synthesize linear polythene of high molecular mass at low pressures using as a catalyst a resin containing ions of titanium or aluminium. Because the polymer was made up of unbranched chains it was tougher and had a higher melting point than previous types of polythene.

Natta used these catalysts to polymerize propylene (propene, $CH_3CH=CH_2$). Early in 1954 he found that part of the polymer is highly crystalline and realized that it must have an ordered structure. He confirmed this using X-ray crystallography and coined the term 'isotactic' to describe the polymer's symmetrical structure. He also postulated that the surface of the catalyst must be highly regular to give rise to isotactic polymers.

After 1954 he continued to study the mechanism of the reaction and its stereo-specific aspects. He made other similar catalysts and produced new polymers, such as *cis*-buta-1,4-diene and copolymers of ethylene (ethene) and propylene (propene), both potentially important synthetic rubbers. He died in Bergamo on 1 May 1979.

Natta's early work on heterogeneous catalysts formed the basis for modern industrial syntheses of methyl alcohol (methanol); of formaldehyde (methanal) from methyl alcohol (methanol); of propionaldehyde (butanal) from propylene (propene) and carbon monoxide; and of succinic acid (butandioic acid) from acetylene (ethyne), carbon monoxide and synthetic gas.

The isotactic polymers he discovered after 1954 showed remarkable and unexpected properties of commercial importance, such as high melting point, high strength, and an ability to form films and fibres. It was realized that a new type of polymerization, called coordination polymerization, was involved. The growth of the polymer chain occurs by insertion of monomer between the existing chain and the solid surface of the catalyst, which controls the geometry of the reaction. (In other types of polymerization the catalyst remains remote from the growing end of the chain and therefore has no effect on the reaction geometry.)

Needham, Joseph (1900–1995) English biochemist, science historian and Orientalist whose most important scientific contribution was in the field of biochemical embryology. In the later part of his career his interests turned to the history of science, particularly the development of science in China.

Needham was born in London in December 1900, the son of one of the first Harley Street specialists in anaesthesia. He attended Oundle School and during the school holidays assisted in military hospitals, which were greatly understaffed due to the influx of casualties from World War I. From Oundle he went on to study natural sciences at Gonville and Caius College, Cambridge. On graduation in 1921 he was offered a place in the research laboratory of Frederick Gowland

◊Hopkins, and subsequently gained his doctorate and was elected a fellow of Gonville and Caius College. In the same year he married Dorothy Moyle, a fellow student at Hopkins's laboratory; she was a talented scientist and her work on the biochemistry of muscles led to her election as a fellow of the Royal Society in 1948 (Needham himself had become a member in 1941).

In 1928 Needham was appointed university demonstrator in biochemistry at Cambridge, then in 1933 he became Dunn Reader in Biochemistry (also at Cambridge), a post he held until 1966. It was during this latter period that he progressively reduced his scientific work and became increasingly devoted to studying Chinese science and culture. He learned Chinese, and in 1942 accepted an invitation to head the British Scientific Mission to China; he spent the next four years travelling through the country. From 1946 to 1948 he was head of the Division of Natural Sciences at the United Nations, after which he returned to Cambridge. He was elected master of Gonville and Caius College in 1966 and held this post until 1976, when he retired in order to pursue his Oriental studies at the East Asian History of Science Library in Cambridge. Needham travelled extensively throughout his career, visiting and lecturing in numerous universities in the USA, Europe, and Asia. He died on 24 March 1995.

Needham's principal scientific contributions were made in the first half of his academic career. Initially he worked on the biochemistry of embryonic development, trying to discover the processes underlying the development of a fertilized egg from a mass of undifferentiated cells into a highly differentiated complex organism. In his three-volume *Chemical Embryology* (1931) Needham surveyed the morphogenetic changes and the various attempts to explain them, concluding that embryonic development is controlled chemically – in contrast to the traditional vitalistic view of Hans ◊Driesch and others, which held that some indefinite principle (called entelechy) caused embryonic changes. The discovery of morphogenetic hormones that control embryonic development confirmed Needham's mechanistic view, and he proceeded – in collaboration with Conrad Waddington (1905–1975) – to hypothesize (before the discovery of DNA) that only structural chemistry could fully explain the complex changes that occur during an organism's development. In *Order and Life* (1935) Needham foresaw the importance of organelles, anticipating some of the discoveries about the microstructure of living cells that later resulted from electron microscopy.

From about the mid-1930s Needham became increasingly interested in the history of science, particularly of Chinese science, and he progressively reduced his scientific investigations in order to devote himself to a comprehensive study of the development of

Chinese science and culture. The first volume of *Science and Civilization in China* was published in 1954 and was followed by several more volumes in this huge synthesis of history, science, and culture in China.

Further Reading

UNESCO, *Joseph Needham: 20th-Century Renaissance Man,* UNESCO, 1995.

Nernst, (Walther) Hermann (1864–1941)

Nernst, (Walther) Hermann (1864–1941) German physical chemist who made basic contributions to electrochemistry and is probably best known as the discoverer of the third law of thermodynamics. He was awarded the 1920 Nobel Prize for Chemistry.

Nernst German physical chemist Hermann Nernst who proposed the third law of thermodynamics in 1906 while working in Berlin. Nernst retired from the chair of physical chemistry in Berlin in 1933, when he fell out of favour with the Nazi government. *Mary Evans Picture Library*

Nernst was born in Briessen, East Prussia (now Wabreźno, Poland), on 25 June 1864, the son of a civil servant and judge. He was educated at Grandenz Gymnasium, and went on to read natural sciences at university. He continued his studies with Albert von Ettinghausen at Graz, took a PhD degree under Friedrich Kohlrausch at Würzburg in 1886, and became an assistant to Wilhelm ◊Ostwald at Leipzig in the following year. Under their influence his interests narrowed into aspects of physical chemistry. In 1891 he

became a reader in physics at Göttingen University and three years later, after a new laboratory had been built, the first professor of physical chemistry. In 1905 he moved to a similar position in Berlin as successor to Hans Landolt (1831–1910), and remained there until 1922. Nernst then became president of the Physikalisch-Technische Reichsanstalt for two years, but relinquished this post to return to Berlin University as professor of physics and director of the Physical Laboratory, where he stayed until he retired in 1934. No subscriber to the politics of Nazi Germany (two of his daughters married Jews), he spent his latter years in farming and agriculture on his country estate at Zibelle near the Polish border. He had a heart attack on 18 November 1941 and died in Muskan, near Berlin; his body was later re-interred in Göttingen, where his academic career began.

Nernst's first publication (1886) described his work with von Ettinghausen at Graz. What became known as the Ettinghausen–Nernst effect concerns the establishment of a potential difference across a metal plate along which there is a temperature gradient and a magnetic field. These experiments were significant in the development of the electronic theory of metals, according to which both thermal and electrical conduction are caused by the motion of electrons.

Working with Kohlrausch, an expert in electrochemistry, Nernst studied solution chemistry. Theories presented in the late 1880s are still in use today; every pH measurement depends on them, as does the use and theory of indicators and buffer solutions.

Nernst's theory concerning solids in contact with a liquid developed from the supposition that metals go into solution only as positive ions, the driving force being a 'solution pressure', which is opposed by the osmotic pressure of its ions in solution. The solution acquires a positive charge and the metal a negative one, if the metal is high in the electrochemical series. (A metal low in the electrochemical series has a low solution pressure and collects metal ions to become positively charged.) The Nernst equation relates ionic concentration c and electrode potential E:

$$E = E_0 \pm \frac{RT}{zF} \log_e c$$

Where R is the gas constant, T the temperature, z the valency of the ion, F Faraday's constant, and E_0 the standard electrode potential. Nernst was also the first to advocate that the electrochemical standard be based on the hydrogen electrode. This work led, in 1890, to the theory of solubility product, which had been initiated by Ostwald who had shown that it could be used as the basis for a system of qualitative and quantitative analysis.

The work on thermodynamics was carried out in Berlin 1905–1906. Developing the theories of

Hermann von ◊Helmholtz, Nernst formulated the third law of thermodynamics. It may be stated in various ways, one expression being:

If the entropy of each element in a crystalline state be taken as zero at the absolute zero of temperature, then every substance has a finite positive entropy but at absolute zero the entropy may become zero and does so in the case of a perfect crystalline substance.

Nernst and his students collected accurate thermodynamic data to substantiate the law. In 1911, with Frederick ◊Lindemann (later Lord Cherwell), Nernst constructed a special calorimeter for measuring specific heats at low temperatures.

Knowledge is the death of research.

HERMANN NERNST ON EXAMINATIONS, IN
C G GILLESPIE (ED) THE DICTIONARY OF
SCIENTIFIC BIOGRAPHY *1981*

Two other significant contributions to physical chemistry concerned chemical equilibria and photochemistry. With Fritz ◊Haber he studied equilibria in commercially important gas reactions, such as the reversible reaction between hydrogen and carbon dioxide to form water and carbon monoxide. He also examined the hydrogen–nitrogen reaction at high pressures (the basis of the Haber process). In 1918 Nernst investigated reactions that are initiated by light. He proposed that the fast reaction between chlorine and hydrogen begins when light causes chlorine molecules to dissociate into atoms:

$$Cl_2 + h\nu \rightarrow 2Cl\cdot$$

A chlorine atom then reacts with a hydrogen molecule to form hydrogen chloride and a hydrogen atom:

$$Cl\cdot + H_2 \rightarrow HCl + H\cdot$$

The hydrogen atom reacts with a chlorine molecule to produce another chlorine atom, and the process continues as a chain reaction:

$$H\cdot + Cl_2 \rightarrow HCl + Cl\cdot$$

Like many great scientists of the time, Nernst did not restrict himself to one narrow field. In 1897 he invented an electric lamp that, instead of a carbon filament, had a 'glower' made from zirconium oxide and some rare earth oxides. It was a good source of infrared and highly successful until superseded ten years later by the tungsten filament lamp. Even so, Nernst sold his patent for a million marks, and used the money to become a pioneer motorist. Many early motor cars had difficulty climbing hills, but Nernst devised a method of injecting nitrous oxide (dinitrogen oxide) into the cylinders when the engine got into difficulties. In the 1920s he invented a 'neo-Bechstein' piano, which amplified sounds produced at low amplitudes. Although acoustically correct, it did not find favour with musicians or concert audiences.

During an academic career of about 50 years, Nernst published 157 papers and 14 books, one of which, *Theoretische Chemie* (1895), became the recommended text for a generation of physical chemists throughout the world.

Neugebauer, Gerry (Gerald) (1932–) US astronomer whose work has been crucial in establishing infrared astronomy.

Neugebauer was born on 3 September 1932 and was educated at Cornell University. He received his PhD from the California Institute of Technology in 1960. Having completed his education, he served in the US Army 1960–62 and was stationed at the Jet Propulsion Laboratory. In 1962 he accepted a post as assistant professor of physics at the California Institute of Technology (Caltech), being promoted to associate professor in 1965. In 1965 he was also appointed a staff associate of Mount Wilson and Palomar observatories. Since 1970 he has been professor of physics at Caltech.

During his professional career. Neugebauer has been closely involved with NASA's interplanetary missions and the design of new infrared telescopes. From April 1969 to July 1970 he was a member of the NASA Astronomy Missions Board and from 1970 to 1973 he was as the principal investigator of the infrared radiometers carried aboard the Mariner missions to Mars and the Infrared Explorer Satellite. He was also the team leader of the infrared radiometer for the Large Space Telescope Definition Study. Since 1976 he has been the US principal scientist on the Infrared Astronomical Satellite.

During the mid-1960s Neugebauer and his colleagues began to establish the first infrared map of the sky. As their telescope was designed to pick up radiation of in the region of 2.2 μm (2.2×10^{-6} m), this project became known as the 'two micron survey'. The results of this survey were astounding; from the part of the sky that can be mapped from the top of Mount Wilson, some 20,000 new infrared sources were detected and most of these did not coincide with known optical sources. The survey also highlighted a large number of curious objects that demanded further study, among the most interesting of which are cool objects that are immersed in thick warm dust. These are thought to be stars that are in the process of formation. Among the brightest and strangest of these sources is an object known as the Becklin–Neugebauer object, named after its discoverers. It is located in the Orion nebula, but it cannot be seen in photographs taken in visible light. Carbon monoxide, detected as being associated with this object, is blowing outward from it at a high velocity. This phenomenon is being interpreted as a strong stellar wind blowing from a young star that only began the process of nuclear fusion as recently as 10,000 or 20,000 years ago.

Newcomb, Simon (1835–1909) Canadian-born US mathematician and astronomer who compiled charts and tables of astronomical data with phenomenal accuracy. His calculations of the motions of the bodies in the Solar System were in use as daily reference all over the world for more than 50 years, and the system of astronomical constants for which he was most responsible is still the standard.

Newcomb was born in Wallace, Nova Scotia, on 12 March 1835. He had little or no formal education, although his father later claimed he was a mathematical prodigy. At the age of 16 he was apprenticed to a quack doctor in Salisbury, New Brunswick, but after two or three years he ran away and settled in Maryland, USA, as a country schoolteacher. Deciding that his talents lay in mathematics, he became a 'computer' at Cambridge, Massachusetts, in 1857. He enrolled in the Lawrence Scientific School of Harvard University and received a degree in 1858. In 1861 he applied for, and received, a commission in the corps of professors of mathematics in the US Navy, where he was assigned to the US Naval Observatory at Washington, DC. Sixteen years later he was put in charge of the American Nautical Almanac office, then also in Washington. In 1884 he obtained the additional appointment of professor of mathematics and astronomy at Johns Hopkins University, Baltimore, but continued to live in Washington. When he reached the compulsory retiring age for captains in 1897, he received the unusual distinction of retirement with the rank of rear admiral.

For many years the editor of the *American Journal of Mathematics,* Newcomb was also one of the founders of the American Astronomical Society and its first president 1899–1905. He received honorary degrees from 17 universities and was a member of 45 foreign societies; he was awarded the Gold Medal of the Royal Astronomical Society in 1874, the Copley Medal of the Royal Society in 1890, and the Schubert Prize of the Imperial Academy of Sciences, St Petersburg, in 1897. He wrote several popular books on astronomy, one or two on finance and economics, and even published some fiction. Altogether his books and papers totalled an amazing 541 titles. Newcomb died on 11 July 1909 and was buried in Arlington National Cemetery.

Assigned to the US Naval Observatory in Washington, DC, in 1861, Newcomb worked for more than ten years determining the positions of celestial bodies with the meridian instruments, and for two years with the new 66-cm/26-in refractor. When he was put in charge of the American Nautical Almanac office, he started the great work that was to occupy most of his time for the rest of his life: the calculation of the motions of the bodies in the Solar System. His most important work appeared in *Astronomical Papers Prepared for the Use of the American Ephemeris and Nautical Almanac,* a series of memoirs that he founded in 1879. Newcomb was the principal author of 25 of 37 articles in the first nine volumes. Among them were his tables of data concerning the Sun, Mercury, Venus, Mars, Uranus, and Neptune, together with Hill's tables concerning Jupiter and Saturn. This series of papers is of a virtually unsurpassable standard; hardly a figure or statement in them has been found to be incorrect, and they are still widely used to calculate daily positions of celestial objects.

Newcomb's most far-reaching contribution, however, was his establishment, jointly with Arthur Matthew Weld Downing (1850–1917), superintendent of the British Nautical Almanac office, of a universal standard system of astronomical constants. Until then there had been a considerable diversity in the fundamental data used by astronomers of different countries and institutions. In May 1896 a conference was held in Paris for the directors of the astronomical almanacs of the USA, UK, France, and Germany. They came to the resolution that after 1901 a single set of constants, mainly Newcomb's, should be used by each country. Although some of Newcomb's work was not complete then, time has proved the decision to have been a wise one. A similar conference held in 1950 decided that the system of constants that had been adopted in 1896 was still preferable to any other for practical use.

Further Reading

Archibald, Raymond Clare, 'Simon Newcomb', *Science,* 1916, v 44, pp 871–878.

Brasch, Frederick E, 'Einstein's appreciation of Simon Newcomb', *Science,* 1929, v 49, p 248.

Moyer, Albert E, *A Scientist's Voice in American Culture: Simon Newcomb and the Rhetoric of Scientific Method,* University of California Press, 1992.

Newcomen, Thomas (1663–1729) English blacksmith who developed the first really practical steam engine, which was principally to power pumps in the tin mines of Cornwall and the coal mines of northern England.

Newcomen was born in Dartmouth in 1663, and christened there on 24 February of that year. His family were probably merchants. His education was probably obtained from a Noncomformist called John Favell. It is thought that he was eventually apprenticed to an ironmonger in Exeter, and on completion of his training went to Lower Street, Dartmouth, where he established his own business as a blacksmith and ironmonger. Newcomen is known to have been an ardent Baptist and a lay preacher.

In his trade Newcomen was assisted by a plumber called John Calley. It is not known exactly when they built the first steam engine. The first authenticated Newcomen engine was erected in 1712 near Dudley Castle, Wolverhampton. This engine was, however, much more than a prototype and it is believed that a number of earlier machines must have been operated to develop the engine to this point. The whole situation is confused by a patent granted to Thomas ◊Savery to 'raise water by the force of fire' and most steam machines of the time were referred to as 'Saverys'. Also Newcomen may have infringed Savery's patent and deliberately not advertised the fact. In later years Newcomen paid royalties to Savery and, after his death, to a syndicate that had bought up the patent.

The Newcomen engine was used to draw water from mines and so operated a pump. The engine consisted of a boiler and cylinder, with the cylinder mounted above the boiler. In the cylinder was a piston, sealed as closely as possible to the wall with a leather flap. The piston was, in turn, attached to one end of a large wooden beam, the other end being attached to the water pump. Steam from the boiler entered the cylinder at little more than atmospheric pressure when the piston had been pulled to the top of the cylinder by the weight of the beam. The steam valve was shut and water injected into the cylinder to condense the steam. As the steam condensed a vacuum was created, and the pressure of the atmosphere pushed the piston to the bottom of the cylinder, thus operating the pump. Gravity operating on the beam again raised the piston ready for the next stroke.

Newcomen's engine consumed an enormous amount of coal because fresh hot steam had to be raised for each stroke. This made the machine more popular in the coal mines. The early engines were very expensive because the cylinder was made of brass, which could be founded and machined more accurately than iron. Later, iron cylinders were produced, but they were thick-walled and consequently much less efficient in terms of coal consumed. This was, of course, of little importance as long as they were used in coal mines. As mining operations changed, the pumps were moved to new locations and sometimes modified. The practical success and usefulness of the Newcomen engine was such that after later refinements, several of which were introduced by James ◊Watt in the 1800s, they became popular for adoption anywhere water was to be raised. Some are known to have remained in operation until the early part of the 20th century when they were superceded by the electric pump.

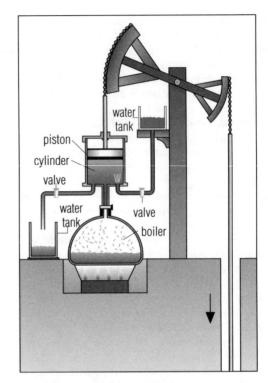

Newcomen Thomas Newcomen's steam engine, invented in 1712, was the first practical steam engine and was used to power pumps in the tin mines of Cornwall and the coal mines of northern England. Steam from the boiler entered the cylinder as the piston moved up (pulled by the weight of a wooden beam). Water from a tank was then sprayed into the cylinder, condensing the steam and creating a vacuum so that air pressure forced down the piston and activated the pump.

It was with the Newcomen engine that the art and science of steam was begun. Tables were drawn up in 1717 by Henry Beighton to show the size of cylinder required to raise a particular quantity of water through a particular height. For water drawn from great depths several lifts could be used in series, one raising through the first level and then another taking it from there upwards, and so on.

Thomas Newcomen did not live to see the widespread adoption of his long-serving engine or its effect on developing British industry. He died of a fever in Southwark, London, on 5 August 1729.

Further Reading

Rolt, L T C and Allen, J S, *Steam Engine of Thomas Newcomen*, Landmark Publishing, 1998.

Smart, I H, 'The Dartmouth residences of Thomas Newcomen and his family', *Trans Newcomen Soc*, 1988–89, v 60, pp 145–160.

Smith, Edgar C, 'Thomas Newcomen: two hundred years of steam power', *Trans Newcomen Soc*, 1928–29, v 9, pp 102–104.

Newlands, John Alexander Reina (1837–1898)

English chemist who preceded Dmitri ◊Mendeleyev in formulating the concept of periodicity in the properties of chemical elements, although his ideas were not accepted at the time.

Newlands was born in Southwark, London, on 26 November 1837, the second son of a Presbyterian minister; his mother, born Maria Reina, was of Italian descent. He was educated by his father and in 1856 entered the Royal College of Chemistry, London, where he studied for a year under August ◊Hofmann. He then became assistant to J T Way, the Royal Agricultural Society's chemist. He remained with Way for eight years – except for a brief time in 1860 when he served as a volunteer under Giuseppe Garibaldi in Italy – until he set up in practice as an analytical chemist in 1864, at the same time teaching chemistry as a way of supplementing his income. His strong interest in sugar in chemistry, and his special study of this, led to his appointment in 1868 as chief chemist in a sugar refinery belonging to James Duncan. With Duncan he pioneered a new method for cleaning sugar as well as introducing improved techniques for processing. When the business foundered under the pressure of foreign competition, Newlands formed a partnership with his brother B E R Newlands, again setting up a practice in analytical chemistry. The Newlands brothers revised an established treatise on sugar-growing and refining, in collaboration with C G W Lock, one of the original authors. John Newlands died in London on 29 July 1898.

Newlands's first published paper on organic compounds suggested a new nomenclature, and the second proposed the compilation of tables to show the relationships between compounds. Both were hampered by the absence of any clear ideas about structure and valency. But they did show his inclination towards systematization. His first submitted article to *Chemical News* in February 1863 on the numerical relationships between atomic weights (relative atomic masses) of similar elements mainly summarized the observations of others, of whom he credited only Jean Baptiste ◊Dumas. The first of two key phenomena to be observed was the existence of groups of three elements (the 'triads' of Johann Döbereiner) of similar properties, the atomic weight of the middle one being the mean of those of the other two. The second phenomenon outlined was the frequent incidence of the difference between atomic weights of analogous elements in multiples of eight.

Newlands originally employed the terms 'equivalent weight' and 'atomic weight' without establishing any distinction in meaning, and in this first paper he used the values accepted by his predecessors and most of his contemporaries. Then in 1864 he employed Alexander

◊Williamson's values (based on the system of Stanislao ◊Cannizzaro) in a table of the 61 then known elements in order of their 'new' atomic weights. A subsequent table grouped 37 elements into ten classes, the majority of which contained one or more triads. He attributed the incompleteness of the table to a lack of knowledge of the properties of some elements only recently discovered, and to the possibility that other elements were still to be recognized. For example he considered that silicon (atomic weight 28) and tin (atomic weight 118) constituted a triad of which the middle member was an unknown quantity. Thus his later claim to have predicted the existence of germanium (atomic weight 73, the mean of 28 and 118) before Mendeleyev can be ascertained to be a valid one.

He went on to number the elements in the order of their atomic weights, giving the same number to any two having the same atomic weight and observed that elements with consecutive numbers frequently either belonged to the same group or occupied similar positions in other groups. He set the list out as a table.

Group		No.		No.		No.		No.		No.
a	N	6	P	13	As	26	Sb	40	Bi	54
b	O	7	S	14	Se	27	Te	42	Os	50
c	F	8	Cl	15	Br	28	I	41	–	–
d	Na	9	K	16	Rb	29	Cs	43	Tl	52
e	Mg	10	Ca	17	Sr	30	Ba	44	Pb	53

The difference in number between the first and second members of a group was seven. In Newlands's words: 'The eighth element starting from a given one is a kind of repetition of the first, like the eighth note in an octave of music.' To achieve acceptable groupings, minor reshuffling was carried out; mercury (which would have been number 51) was omitted because it could obviously not be grouped with the halogens.

In 1865 he tabled all 62 elements (including indium, which was newly discovered), again emphasizing the difference of seven (or multiples of seven) between the numbers of the elements in the same group, and termed the relationship the law of octaves.

H	1	F	8	Co, Ni	22	Br	29	Pd	36	I	42	Pt, Ir	50	Cl	15
Li	2	Na	9	Cu	23	Rb	30	Ad	37	Cs	44	Tl	53	K	16
Be	3	Mg	10	Zn	25	Sr	31	Cd	38	Ba, V	45	Pb	54	Ca	17
B	4	Al	11	Y	24	Ce, La	33	U	40	Ta	46	Th	56	Cr	19
C	5	Si	12	In	26	Zr	32	Sn	39	W	47	Hg	52	Ti	18
N	6	P	13	As	27	Di, Mo	34	Sb	41	Nb	48	Bi	55	Mn	21
O	7	S	14	Se	28	Rh, Ru	35	Te	43	Au	49	Os	51	Fe	21

It was considered that he had forced the elements into too rigid a framework and this hindered his case, precluding the possibility that the filling of gaps in the sequence would result in a more acceptable grouping. When he read his paper to the Chemical

Society in 1866 he was severely criticized and even ridiculed – G C Foster, professor of physics at University College, London, is reputed to have asked Newlands if he had ever examined the elements when listed in alphabetical order. More seriously, Foster pointed out the unacceptability of any system that did not group together chromium and manganese, and iron with cobalt and nickel.

Discouraged, Newlands did no more work on his theories until Mendeleyev's periodic table appeared in 1869. Newlands claimed priority, particularly after the award of the Davy Medal of the Royal Society to Mendeleyev and Lothar ◊Meyer in 1882. Newlands's dogged tenacity was finally rewarded in 1887, when he received the medal in acknowledgement of his work – nearly 25 years after its first published appearance.

Newton, Isaac (1642–1727) English physicist and mathematician who is regarded as one of the greatest scientists ever to have lived. In physics, he discovered the three laws of motion that bear his name and was the first to explain gravitation, clearly defining the nature of mass, weight, force, inertia, and acceleration. In his honour, the SI unit of force is called the newton. Newton also made fundamental discoveries in optics, finding that white light is composed of a spectrum of

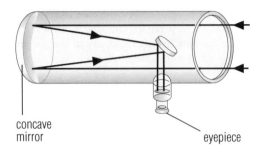

Newton In about 1670 Isaac Newton constructed the first reflecting telescope, which uses a concave mirror to collect and focus incoming light.

colours and inventing the reflecting telescope. In mathematics, Newton's principal contribution was to formulate calculus and the binomial theorem.

Newton was born in Woolsthorpe, Lincolnshire, on 25 December 1642 by the old Julian calendar, but on 4 January 1643 by modern reckoning. His birthplace, Woolsthorpe Manor, is now preserved. Newton's was an inauspicious beginning for he was a premature, sickly baby born after his father's death, and his survival was not expected. When he was three, his mother remarried and the young Newton was left in his grandmother's care. He soon began to take refuge in things mechanical, reputedly making water clocks, kites bearing fiery lanterns aloft, and a model mill powered by a mouse, as well as innumerable drawings and diagrams. When Newton was 12, he began to attend the King's School, Grantham, but his schooling was not to last. His mother, widowed again, returned to Woolsthorpe in 1658 and withdrew him from school with the intention of making him into a farmer. Fortunately, his uncle recognized Newton's ability and managed to get him back to school to prepare for university entrance. This Newton achieved in 1661, when he went to Trinity College, Cambridge, and began to delve widely and deeply into the scholarship of the day.

In 1665, the year that he became a BA, the university was closed because of the plague and Newton spent 18 months at Woolsthorpe, with only the occasional visit to Cambridge. Such seclusion was a prominent feature of Newton's creative life and, during this period, he laid the foundations of his work in mathematics, optics, dynamics, and celestial mechanics, performing his first prism experiments and reflecting on motion and gravitation.

Newton returned to Cambridge in 1666 and became a minor fellow of Trinity in 1667 and a major fellow the following year. He also received his MA in 1668 and became Lucasian Professor of Mathematics – at the age of only 26. It is said that the previous incumbent, Isaac

Newton English physicist and mathematician Isaac Newton, who aside from his prolific work on dynamics, optics, and mathematics, exerted a profound influence on 18th-century scientific method and philosophy. He developed the three standard laws of motion and the universal law of gravitation. *Mary Evans Picture Library*

◊Barrow, resigned the post to make way for Newton. Newton remained at Cambridge almost 30 years, studying alone for the most part, though in frequent contact with other leading scientists by letter and through the Royal Society in London, which elected him a fellow in 1672. These were Newton's most fertile years. He laboured day and night in his chemical laboratory, at his calculations, or immersed in theological and mystical speculations. In Cambridge, he completed what may be described as his greatest single work, the *Philosophae naturalis principia mathematica/ Mathematical Principles of Natural Philosophy*. This was presented to the Royal Society in 1686, who subsequently withdrew from publishing it through shortage of funds. The astronomer Edmond ◊Halley, a wealthy man and friend of Newton, paid for the publication of the *Principia* in 1687. In it, Newton revealed his laws of motion and the law of universal gravitation.

After the *Principia* appeared, Newton appeared to become bored with Cambridge and his scientific professorship. In 1689, he was elected a member of Parliament for the university and in London he encountered many other eminent minds, notably Christiaan ◊Huygens. The excessive strain of Newton's studies and the attendant disputes caused him to suffer severe depression in 1692, when he was described as having 'lost his reason'. Four years later he accepted the appointment of warden of the London Mint, becoming master in 1699. He took these new, well-paid duties very seriously, revising the coinage and taking severe measures against forgers. Although his scientific work continued, it was greatly diminished.

... and I feign no hypotheses [hypotheses non fingo] *for whatever is not deduced from the phenomena is to be called an hypothesis; and hypotheses, whether metaphysical or physical, whether of occult qualities or mechanical, have no place in experimental philosophy.*

ISAAC NEWTON PRINCIPIA *1687*

Newton was elected president of the Royal Society in 1703, an office he held until his death, and in 1704, he summed up his life's work on light in *Opticks*. The following year, Newton was knighted by Queen Anne. Although he had turned grey at 30, Newton's constitution remained strong and it is said he had sharp sight and hearing, as well as all his teeth, at the age of 80. His later years were given to revisions of the *Principia,* and he died on 20 March 1727. Newton was accorded a

state funeral and buried in Westminster Abbey, an occasion that prompted Voltaire to remark that England honoured a mathematician as other nations honoured a king.

Any consideration of Newton must take account of the imperfections of his character, for the size of his genius was matched by his ambition. A hypersensitivity to criticism and possessiveness about his work made conflicts with other scientists a prominent feature of his later life. This negative side of Newton's nature may be well illustrated by his dispute with Gottfried ◊Leibniz. These two great mathematicians worked independently on the development of a differential calculus, both making significant advances. No one today would seriously question Leibniz's originality and true mathematical genius, but Newton branded him a plagiarist and claimed sole invention of calculus. When Leibniz appealed to the Royal Society for a fair hearing, Newton appointed a committee of his own supporters and even wrote their, supposedly impartial, report himself. He then further proceeded to review this report anonymously, later remarking that 'he had broken Leibniz's heart with his reply to him'. The partisan and 'patriotic' views that resulted from this controversy served to isolate English mathematics and to set it back many years, for it was Leibniz's terminology that came to be used.

A similar dispute arose between Newton and Robert ◊Hooke, one of the more brilliant and versatile members of the Royal Society, who supported Huygens's wave theory of light. Although, in the past, he had collaborated with Hooke, Newton published results without giving credit to their originator. Hooke, however, was notably disputatious and better able to stand up for himself than Leibniz. On the other hand, Newton remained faithful to those he regarded as friends, appointing several to positions in the Mint after he took charge, and part of his quarrel with the Astronomer Royal, John ◊Flamsteed, was that Flamsteed had fallen out with Newton's friend Halley.

Newton's work itself must be considered in many parts: he was a brilliant mathematician and an equally exceptional optical physicist; he revolutionized our understanding of gravity and, throughout his life, studied chemistry and alchemy, and wrote millions of words on theological speculation and mysticism.

As a mathematician, Newton developed unusually late, being well through his university career when he studied the work of Pierre de ◊Fermat, René ◊Descartes and others, before returning to ◊Euclid, whom he had previously dismissed. However, in those two plague years of 1665 and 1666, Newton more than made up for this delay, and much of his later work can be seen as a revision and extension of the creativity of that period. To quote one of his own notebooks: 'In the beginning of the year 1665 I found the method for approximating series and the binomial theorem. The same year I found the method for tangents of Gregory and in November had the direct method of fluxions [differential calculus] and in January [1666] had the theory of colours [of light] and in May following I had entrance into the inverse method of fluxions [integral calculus] and in the same year I began to think of gravity extending to the orb of the moon ...'

The zenith of his mathematics was the *Principia*, and after this Newton did little mathematics, though his genius remained sharp and when Leibniz composed problems with the specific intention of defeating him, Newton solved each one the first day he saw it. Both in his own day and afterwards, Newton influenced mathematics 'following his own wish' by 'his creation of the fluxional calculus and the theory of infinite series', which together made up his analytic technique. But he was also active in algebra and number theory, classical and analytical geometry, computation and approximation, and even probability. For three centuries, most of his papers lay buried in the Portsmouth Collection of his manuscripts and only now are scholars examining his complete mathematics for the first time.

Newton's work in dynamics also began in those two years of enforced isolation at Woolsthorpe. He had already considered the motion of colliding bodies and circular motion, and had arrived at ideas of how force and inertia affect motion and of centrifugal force. Newton was now inspired to consider the problem of gravity by seeing an apple fall from a tree – a story that, according to Newton himself, is true. He wondered if the force that pulled the apple to the ground could also extend into space and pull the Moon into an orbit around the Earth. Newton assumed that the rate of fall is proportional to the force of gravity and that this force is inversely proportional to the square of the distance from the centre of the Earth. He then worked out what the motion of the Moon should be if these assumptions were correct, but obtained a figure that was too low. Disappointed, Newton set aside his considerations on gravity and did not return to them until 1679.

Newton was then able to satisfy himself that his assumptions were indeed true and he also had a better radius of the Earth than was available in the plague years. He then set to recalculating the Moon's motion on the basis of his theory of gravity and obtained a correct result. Newton also found that his theory explained the laws of planetary motion that had been derived earlier that century by Johannes ◊Kepler on the basis of observations of the planets.

Newton presented his conclusions on dynamics in the *Principia*. Although he had already developed calculus, he did not use it in the *Principia*, preferring to prove all his results geometrically. In this great work, Newton's plan was first to develop the subject of general dynamics from a mathematical point of view and then to apply the results in the solution of important astronomical and physical problems. It included a synthesis of Kepler's laws of planetary motion and ◊Galileo's laws of falling bodies, developing the system of mechanics we know today, including the three famous laws of motion. The first law states that every body remains at rest or in constant motion in a straight line unless it is acted upon by a force. This defines inertia, finally disproving the idea, which had been prevalent since ◊Aristotle had mooted it in the 4th century BC, that force is required to keep anything moving. The second law states that a force accelerates a body by an amount proportional to its mass. This was the first clear definition of force and it also distinguished mass from weight. The third law states that action and reaction are equal and opposite, which showed how things could be made to move.

Newton also developed his general theory of gravitation as a universal law of attraction between any two objects, stating that the force of gravity is proportional to the masses of the objects and decreases in proportion to the square of the distance between the two bodies. Though, in the years before, there had been considerable correspondence between Newton, Hooke, Halley and Kepler on the mathematical formulation of these laws, Newton did not complete the work until the writing of the *Principia*.

'I was in the prime of my age for invention' said Newton of those two years 1665 and 1666, and it was in that period that he performed his fundamental work in optics. Again it should be pointed out that the study of Newton's optics has been limited to his published letters and the *Opticks* of 1704, its publication delayed until after Hooke's death to avoid yet another controversy over originality. No adequate edition or full translation of the voluminous *Lectiones opticae* exists. Newton began those first, crucial experiments by passing sunlight through a prism, finding that it dispersed the white light into a spectrum of colours. He then took a second prism and showed that it could combine the colours in the spectrum and form white light again. In this way, Newton proved that the colours are a property of light and not of the prism. An interesting by-product of these early speculations was the development of the reflecting telescope. Newton held the erroneous opinion that optical dispersion was independent of the medium through which the light was refracted and, therefore, that nothing could be done to correct the chromatic aberration caused by lenses. He therefore set about building a telescope in which the objective lens is replaced by a curved mirror, in which aberration could not occur. In 1668 Newton succeeded in making the first reflecting telescope, a tiny instrument only 15 cm/6 in long, but the direct ancestor of today's huge astronomical reflecting telescopes. In this invention, Newton was anticipated to some degree by James Gregory (1638–1675) who had produced a design for a reflecting telescope five years earlier but had not succeeded in constructing one.

Other scientists, Hooke especially, were critical of Newton's early reports, seeing too little connection between experimental result and theory, so that, in the course of a debate lasting several years, Newton was forced to refine his theories with considerable subtlety. He performed further experiments in which he investigated many other optical phenomena, including thin-film interference effects, one of which, 'Newton's rings', is named after him.

The *Opticks* presented a highly systematized and organized account of Newton's work and his theory of the nature of light and the effects that light produces. In fact, although he held that light rays were corpuscular in nature, he integrated into his ideas the concept of periodicity, holding that 'ether waves' were associated with light corpuscles, a remarkable conceptual leap, for Hooke and Huygens, the founder of the wave theory, both denied periodicity to light waves. The corpuscle concept lent itself to an analysis by forces and established an analogy between the action of gross bodies and that of light, reinforcing the universalizing tendency of the *Principia*. However, Newton's prestige was such that the corpuscular theory held sway for much longer than it deserved, not being finally overthrown until early in the 1800s. Ironically, it was the investigation of interference effects by Thomas ◊Young that led to the establishment of the wave theory of light.

Although comparatively little is known of the bulk of Newton's complete writings in chemistry and physics, we know even less about his chemistry and alchemy, chronology, prophecy, and theology. The vast number of documents he wrote on these matters have yet to be properly analysed, but what is certain is that he took great interest in alchemy, performing many chemical experiments in his own laboratory and being in contact with Robert ◊Boyle. He also wrote much on ancient chronology and the authenticity of certain biblical texts.

Newton's greatest achievement was to demonstrate that scientific principles are of universal application. In the *Principia mathematica,* he built logically and analytically from mathematical premises and the evidence of experiment and observation to develop a model of the universe that is still of general validity. 'If I have seen further than other men,' he once said with perhaps assumed modesty, 'it is because I have stood on the shoulders of giants'; and Newton was certainly able to bring together the knowledge of his forebears in a brilliant synthesis. Newton's life marked the first great flowering of the scientific method, which had been evolving in fits and starts since the time of the ancient Greeks. But Newton really established it, completing a scientific revolution in Europe that had begun with Nicolaus ◊Copernicus and ushering in the Age of Reason, in which the scientific method was expected to yield complete knowledge by the elucidation of the basic laws that govern the universe. No knowledge can ever be total, but Newton's example brought about an explosion of investigation and discovery that has never really abated. He perhaps foresaw this when he remarked 'To myself, I seem to have been only like a boy playing on the seashore, and diverting myself in now and then finding a smoother pebble or a prettier shell than ordinary, whilst the great ocean of truth lay all undiscovered before me.'

With his extraordinary insight into the workings of nature and rare tenacity in wresting its secrets and revealing them in as fundamental and concise a way as possible, Newton stands as a colossus of science. In physics, only ◊Archimedes and Albert ◊Einstein, who also possessed these qualities, may be compared to him.

Further Reading

Barry, James, *Measures of Science: Theological and Technological Impulses in Early Modern Thought,* Northwestern University Studies in Phenomenology and Existential Philosophy series, Northwestern University Press, 1996.

Chandrasekhar, Subrahmanyan, *Newton's Principia for the Common Reader,* Clarendon Press, 1995.

Christianson, Gale E, *Isaac Newton and the Scientific Revolution,* Oxford Portraits in Science series, Oxford University Press, 1998.

Debrock, Guy and Scheurer, Paul B, *Newton's Scientific and Philosophical Legacy,* Archives Internationales d'Histoire des Idées series, Kluwer Academic, 1988, v 123.

Gribbin, John and Gribbin, Mary, *Newton in 90 Minutes,* Scientists in 90 Minutes series, Constable, 1997.

Hall, Alfred Rupert, *Isaac Newton: Adventurer in Thought,* Cambridge Science Biographies series, Cambridge University Press, 1996.

Parker, Steve, *Isaac Newton and Gravity,* Science Discoveries series, Belitha, 1993.

Westfall, Richard Samuel, *The Life of Isaac Newton,* Cambridge University Press, 1993.

White, Michael, *Isaac Newton: The Last Sorcerer,* Fourth Estate, 1997.

Nice, Margaret Morse (1883–1974) US biologist and ornithologist.

Margaret Morse was born on 6 December 1883 in Amherst, Massachusetts, the fourth of seven children of an intellectual family. In 1901 she entered Mount

Holyoke College to study languages, but then switched to natural sciences. She graduated in 1906 and moved to Clark University in Worcester, Massachusetts, to study biology. In 1909 she married a fellow graduate student at Clark, Leonard Blaine Nice, who studied medicine at Harvard University before moving to the University of Oklahoma where he was head of the department of physiology. While bringing up five daughters, born between 1910 and 1923, Margaret Nice undertook ornithological research relying on close observation, a technique she later applied to studying child psychology in which she graduated from Clark in 1915, writing several papers on the subject from observations on her own children. However her interests in bird behaviour continued and she devoted herself to a detailed study of the birds of Oklahoma. In 1927 her husband moved to Ohio State University, and Margaret Nice began an extensive study of the life history of the sparrow, recording the behaviour of individual birds over a long period of time, which established her as one of the leading ornithologists in the world. A further family move to Chicago provided fewer opportunities for Margaret Nice to study living birds, and she spent more of her time writing, and became particularly involved in conservation issues, such as campaigning against the indiscriminate use of pesticides. Despite never having a faculty appointment she achieved a unique position in US ornithology, and received several honours and an honorary doctorate from Mount Holyoke. She died in Chicago on 26 June 1974, shortly after her husband.

Nicol, William (1768–1851) Scottish physicist and geologist who is best known for inventing the first device for obtaining plane-polarized light – the Nicol prism.

Very little is known of Nicol's life. He was born in Scotland in 1768 and seems to have spent most of his career lecturing at the University of Edinburgh, where James Clerk ◊Maxwell may have been one of his students. Nicol did not publish any of his research findings until 1826, when he was 58 years old, with the result that his work made relatively little impact during his lifetime. He died in Edinburgh on 2 September 1851.

Nicol invented the Nicol prism, as it is now called, in 1828. Consisting of Iceland spar (a naturally occurring, transparent crystalline form of calcium carbonate), it utilized the phenomenon of double refraction discovered by Erasmus Bartholin in 1699. Nicol made his prism by bisecting a parallelepiped of Iceland spar along its shortest diagonal then cementing the two halves back in their original position with Canada balsam, which has a refractive index between the two indices of the double-refracting Iceland spar. Light

entering the prism is refracted into two rays, one of which is reflected by the Canada balsam (an example of total internal reflection) out of the side of the prism, the other ray being transmitted, with very little deviation, through the prism and emerging as plane-polarized light. This second, plane-polarized ray can then be passed through another Nicol prism aligned parallel to the first. Rotating the second prism causes the amount of light transmitted through it to decrease, reaching a minimum (with no light transmitted) when the second prism has been rotated through 90°, then increasing again to a maximum when the second prism has been rotated through 180°. Furthemore, if a solution of an organic substance is placed between the two prisms, the second prism must be turned through a specific angle to allow maximum light transmission; this angle represents the degree of refraction of the polarized light. Nicol prisms greatly facilitated the study of refraction and polarization, and later played an essential part in the development of polarimetry, especially in the use of this technique to investigate molecular structures and optical activity of organic compounds.

In 1815 Nicol, who was primarily a geologist, developed a method of preparing extremely thin sections of crystals and rocks for microscopical study. His technique (which involved cementing the specimen to a glass slide and then carefully grinding until it was extremely thin) made it possible to view mineral samples by transmitted rather than reflected light and therefore enabled the minerals' internal structures to be seen. Nicol also used this technique to examine the cell structure of fossil woods, and the information he obtained from these studies was later used as a basis for identification and classification. But because of his reluctance to publish his work, Nicol's slide-preparation technique did not become widely used until after 1853, when Henry ◊Sorby demonstrated its usefulness for studying mineral structures.

Nirenberg, Marshall Warren US biochemist; see ◊Holley and Nirenberg.

Nobel, Alfred Bernhard (1833–1896) Swedish industrial chemist and philanthropist who invented dynamite and endowed the Nobel Foundation, which after 1901 awarded the annual Nobel prizes.

Nobel was born in Stockholm, Sweden, on 21 October 1833, the son of a builder and industrialist. His father, Immanuel Nobel, was also something of an inventor, and his grandfather had been one of the most important Swedish scientists of the 17th century. Alfred Nobel attended St Jakob's Higher Apologist School in Stockholm before the family moved to St Petersburg, Russia, where he and his brothers were

Nobel Swedish chemist and philanthropist Alfred Nobel photographed in 1885. Nobel made a fortune from manufacturing explosives, and in his will established the Nobel prizes for chemistry, physics, physiology or medicine, literature, and peace. *Mary Evans Picture Library*

taught privately by Russian and Swedish tutors, always being encouraged to be inventive by their father. From 1850 to 1852 Nobel made a study trip to Germany, France, Italy, and North America, improving his knowledge of chemistry and mastering all the necessary languages.

During the years of the Crimean War 1853–56, Nobel worked in St Petersburg for his father's munitions company, which produced large quantities of munitions. After the war, his father went bankrupt, and in 1859 the family returned to Sweden. During the next few years Nobel developed several new explosives and factories for making them, and became rich. He spent the latter years of his life in San Remo, Italy, and died there on 10 December 1896.

Guncotton, a more powerful explosive than gunpowder, had been discovered in 1846 by the German chemist Christian Schönbein. It was made by nitrating cotton fibre with a mixture of concentrated nitric and sulphuric acids. A year later the Italian Ascanio Sobrero discovered nitroglycerine, made by nitrating glycerine (glycerol). This extremely powerful explosive gives off 1,200 times its own volume of gas when it explodes, but for many years it was too dangerous to use because it can be set off much too easily by rough handling or shaking. Alfred and his father worked independently on both explosives when they returned to Sweden, and

in 1862 Immanuel Nobel devised a comparatively simple way of manufacturing nitroglycerine on a factory scale. In 1863 Alfred Nobel invented a mercury fulminate detonator for use with nitroglycerine in blasting.

In 1864 the nitroglycerine factory blew up, killing Nobel's younger brother and four other people. Nobel turned his attention to devising a safer method of handling this sensitive liquid. After many experiments he patented dynamite (in Sweden, the UK, and the USA) in 1867. Consisting of nitroglycerine absorbed by keiselguhr, a porous diatomite mineral, this is an easily handled, solid, ductile material. However, Guhr dynamite, as it was known, had certain technical weaknesses. Continuing his research, Nobel in 1875 created blasting gelatine, or gelignite, a colloidal solution of nitrocellulose (guncotton) in nitroglycerine, which in many ways proved to be an ideal explosive. Its power was somewhat greater than that of pure nitroglycerine, and it was easier to work with because less sensitive to shock, and it was strongly resistant to moisture.

The Nobels had long been trying to improve blasting powder. In 1887 the younger Nobel produced a nearly smokeless blasting powder called ballistite, a mixture of nitroglycerine and nitrocellulose with camphor and other additives. Upon ignition it burned with almost mathematical precision in concentric layers. Nobel's last development was progressive smokeless powder, a further product of ballistite devised in his San Remo laboratory.

Nobel's interests as an inventor were not confined to explosives. He worked in electrochemistry, optics, biology, and physiology and helped to solve many problems in the manufacture of artificial silk, leather, and rubber and of artificial semiprecious stones from fused alumina. In his will, made in 1895, he left almost all his fortune to a foundation that would bestow annual awards on 'those who, during the preceding year, shall have conferred the greatest benefit on mankind'. In 1958 the new element number 102 was named nobelium in his honour.

Further Reading

Bergengren, Erik; Blair, Alan (transl), *Alfred Nobel, the Man and His Work, with a Supplement on the Nobel Institutions and the Nobel Prizes by Nils K Stahle*, Thomas Nelson, 1962.

Fant, Kene; Ruuth, Marianne (transl), *Alfred Nobel: A Biography*, Arcade Publishing, 1996.

Henriksson, Fritz, *The Nobel Prizes and Their Founder, Alfred Nobel*, Bonnier, 1938.

Nobel Foundation (ed), *Nobel: the Man and His Prizes*, Elsevier, 1962.

Nobili, Leopoldo (1784–1835) Italian physicist who carried out early research into electrochemistry and thermoelectricity.

Nobili was born in Trassilico in 1784. After leaving university he joined the artillery as a captain, and then became professor of physics at the Florence Museum. He died in Florence on 5 August 1835.

In 1828 Nobili published the results of his electrochemical research, in which he made simple cells by immersing platinum electrodes in various solutions of mixed salts and alkalis. Later, in 1825, he measured the currents produced by them, using a moving-magnet astatic galvanometer of his own invention. Four years later he made use of the Seebeck effect to construct a thermocouple for measuring radiant heat (by calibrating the current it generated), employing a series of six antimony–bismuth bimetallic junctions.

Noether, Emmy (Amalie) (1882–1935) German mathematician who became one of the leading figures in modern abstract algebra.

Noether was born in Erlangen on 23 March 1882, the eldest child of the mathematician Max ◊Noether, professor of mathematics at the University of Erlangen. After completing her secondary education, she came up against the rule then prevailing in Germany that barred women from becoming fully fledged students at a university. She was, however, allowed to attend lectures in languages and mathematics without student status for two years 1900 to 1902; eventually she was accepted as a student and awarded a doctorate in 1907 for a thesis on algebraic invariants.

Once more the rules blocked her way, this time barring her from a post in the university faculty. She nevertheless persisted with her research independently and at the request of David ◊Hilbert was invited to give lectures at Göttingen University 1915–16. There she worked with Hilbert and Felix ◊Klein on problems arising from Albert ◊Einstein's theory of relativity, and thanks to Hilbert's constant nagging the university eventually, in 1919, gave her the status of 'unofficial associate professor'. In 1922 her position was made official, and she remained at Göttingen until the Nazi purge of Jewish university staff in 1933. The rest of her life was spent as professor of mathematics at Bryn Mawr College in Pennsylvania, where she died from a post-surgical infection on 14 April 1935.

Noether first made her mark as a mathematician with a paper on non-commutative fields which she published in collaboration with Schmeidler in 1920. For the next few years she worked on the establishment, and systematization, of a general theory of ideals. It was in this field that she produced her most important result, a generalization of Richard ◊Dedekind's prime ideals and the introduction of the concept of primary ideals. Modern work in this field dates from her papers of the early 1920s. After 1927 she returned to the subject of non-commutative algebras

(in which the order in which numbers are multiplied affects the result), her chief investigations being conducted into linear transformations of non-commutative algebras and their structure.

Further Reading

Dick, Auguste, *Emmy Noether, 1882–1935*, Birkhauser, 1980.
Srinivasan, B and Sally, J (eds), *Emmy Noether in Bryn Mawr: Proceedings of a Symposium Sponsored by the Association of Women in Mathematics in Honor of Emily Noether's 100th Birthday*, Springer-Verlag, 1983.

Noether, Max (1844–1921) German mathematician who contributed to the development of 19th-century algebraic geometry and the theory of algebraic functions.

Noether was born in Mannheim on 24 September 1844 and educated locally until the age of 14, when he contracted polio, which left him permanently handicapped and for two years deprived him of the use of his legs. He was tutored at home until he entered the University of Heidelberg in 1865 to study mathematics. He was awarded his doctorate in 1868 and was appointed to the Heidelberg faculty. In 1874 he became an associate professor, but a year later he moved to the University of Erlangen, where he was promoted to a professorship in 1888. He retired, with an emeritus professorship, in 1919 and died in Erlangen on 13 December 1921. His daughter Emmy ◊Noether also became a famous mathematician.

Noether published books on algebraic curves, in 1882, and algebraic functions in 1894, as well as several biographies of mathematicians, but his reputation rests principally on his work in the early 1870s. Much of his initial inspiration came from the work of Luigi Cremona (1830–1903). In 1871 he published a proof (independently found at about the same time by William ◊Clifford and J Rosanes) that a Cremona transformation can be constructed from quadratic transformations. Then, two years later in 1873, he published his one outstanding result, the theorem concerning algebraic curves that contains the 'Noether conditions'. The theorem runs as follows. Given two algebraic curves, $\varphi(x, y) = 0$ and $\psi(x, y) = 0$, which intersect at a finite number of isolated points, the equation of an algebraic curve that passes through all the points of intersection may be expressed as:

$$A\Phi + B\Psi = 0$$

Where A and B are polynomials in x and y if, and only if, certain conditions (the 'Noether conditions') are satisfied.

Noether said that his result could be extended to surfaces and hypersurfaces, but he never succeeded in demonstrating this. It was left to Julius König to generalize the theorem to n dimensions in 1903.

Norrish, Ronald George Wreyford (1897–1978)

English physical chemist who studied fast chemical reactions, particularly those initiated by light. For his achievements in this area, he shared the 1967 Nobel Prize for Chemistry with his co-worker George ◊Porter and the German chemist Manfred ◊Eigen.

Norrish was born in Cambridge on 9 November 1897. He was educated at Perse School, Cambridge, and won a scholarship to the university. His studies where interrupted by World War I, during which he was an officer in the artillery. He graduated from Cambridge two years after returning in 1919, gaining his PhD in 1924. He was made a fellow of Emmanuel College, Cambridge, in 1925 and became professor of physical chemistry in 1937. He retired in 1965 and died, in Cambridge, on 7 June 1978.

Norrish began working in photochemistry in 1923 with E K Rideal, studying the reactions of potassium permanganate solution. For the next few years he investigated the photochemistry of nitrogen dioxide. Then in 1928 his paper on the photochemistry of glyoxal (ethan-1,2-dial, $(CHO)_2$) announced his studies of various aldehydes and ketones. This led to the recognition of what became known as the Norrish type I and type II reactions, which may be generalized as:

$$\text{Type I} \left\{ \begin{array}{l} R^1COR^2 + h\nu \rightarrow \bullet R^1 + \bullet COR^2 \\ \qquad\qquad\quad \rightarrow \bullet R^1 + \bullet R^2 + \bullet CO \end{array} \right.$$

$$\text{Type II} \quad R^1COCH_2CH_2CH_2R^2 + h\nu \rightarrow R^1COCH_3 + \\ CH_2 = CHR^2$$

in which the alkyl radicals R^1 and R^2 contribute one or two carbon atoms.

Up to the mid-1930s, Norrish studied the correlation between photodecomposition and physical phenomena such as spectral character and phosphorescence. Then his studies were again interrupted, this time by World War II. During this period his department contributed to the war effort, investigating methods of suppressing the flash from guns and developing incendiary materials.

Norrish's interest in using intense flashes of light to initiate photochemical reactions seems to have been stimulated by his work during the war with his student George Porter. Flash photolysis makes use of a powerful 'photoflash' to bring about the rapid dissociation of a compound into radicals or ions. A second spectroscopic flash triggered at a precise time interval after the first allows the transient species to be observed. By varying the time delay between the two flashes,

Norrish was able to study the kinetics of the formation and decay of such short-lived entities, even if they existed only for microseconds.

Norrish went on to apply these techniques to the study of chain reactions. He established, for example, that the retarding effect of hydrogen chloride in a pure system and one containing oxygen can be attributed to the process:

$$\bullet H + HCl \rightarrow H_2 + \bullet Cl$$

In his investigation of the combustion of hydrocarbons, he studied the transition between slow reactions and ignition, demonstrating the existence of degenerate or delayed branching. He also made pioneering studies of the kinetics of polymerization. He and his co-workers discovered the gel-effect, which occurs in the later stages of free-radical polymerization and results from the steadily decreasing rate of chain termination that sets in when the viscosity becomes high. He also correlated the photolysis of certain polymers with his type I and II reactions.

Norrish was largely responsible for the advance of reaction kinetics to a distinct discipline within physical chemistry. He was one of the first to realize the power of absorption spectroscopy for identifying intermediates and products of thermal and photochemical gas reactions and to introduce high vacuum techniques for handling gases.

Nüsslein-Volhard, Christiane (1942–)

German geneticist who shared the Nobel Prize for Physiology

Nüsslein-Volhard German geneticist Christiane Nüsslein-Volhard. *AKG*

or Medicine in 1995 with US geneticists Edward Lewis (1918–) and Eric Wieschaus (1947–) for her work on genes controlling the early embryonic development of *Drosophila melanogaster,* the fruit fly. She examined 40,000 random genuine mutations for their effect on the fly's development and identified 150 genes. She subsequently cloned many of those genes and worked out their interactions.

Nüsslein-Volhard was born in Magdeburg on 20 October 1942, the daughter of an architect. She developed an interest in biology as a child through visits to her grandparents' farm. Beginning her university career in Frankfurt, Nüsslein-Volhard was disappointed and bored with her course and moved to Tübingen in 1964 to study biochemistry. This gave her a solid training in the basics of physical chemistry, thermodynamics, and stereochemistry, and she passed her exams for the diploma in biochemistry in 1969.

Influenced by Friedrich Bonhoffer, who was working with genetic mutations, Nüsslein-Volhard became convinced of the power of genetics in analysing complex processes. Looking for an organism in which genetics could be applied to developmental problems, she came across descriptions of the early *Drosophila* mutants in a review by Ted Wright (1971) and the 1972 description of the first rescue experiments of a maternal mutant by Swiss geneticist Walter Gehring (1939–). In 1975 she joined Gehring's laboratory in Basel.

Nüsslein-Volhard became fascinated by flies and at this time met Eric Wieschaus and Edward Lewis, whose pioneering work she found inspiring. Lewis had identified the transformations in the fruit fly that cause the substitution of one segment of the body for another. These transformations were found to be the result of mutations in a gene family called the bithorax complex. Genes at the beginning of the complex were found to control anterior body segments while genes further down the genetic map controlled more posterior body segments. This work was shown to be of particular importance when it was demonstrated that the gene ordering of this complex is observed in humans.

With a fellowship from the DFG Nüsslein-Volhard worked for a year in the laboratory of German insect embryologist Klaus Sander in Freiburg. She worked with Margit Schardin on the segmental pattern of *Drosophila* larvae, presenting the results of their research in the USA and in 1978 was offered a job in the European Molecular Biology Laboratory in Heidelberg where she shared a laboratory for three years with Eric Wieschaus. They worked together on several joint projects, amongst them running a successful screening for embryonic mutants. They also fed adult flies with chemicals that cause mutations in the genetic DNA, subsequently breeding the flies and looking for abnormal embryos. Checking back to the parent flies, they could pinpoint the genes responsible for different mutations. By 1980 they had identified 139 developmental genes falling into several classes. One class caused whole body segments to be missing, and another caused defects in every second body segment. Their paper was published in *Nature* in 1980.

In 1981 Nüsslein-Volhard took up the offer of a position at the Max Planck Society in Tübingen where she continued to work on *Drosophila* with colleagues, conducting a large-scale screen for maternal mutants in 1982, and publishing three papers with Eric Wieschaus in 1984. In 1986, she became director of developmental biology and since 1990 she has been director of the department of genetics of the Max Planck Institute for Developmental Biology in Tübingen. In the 1990s she has worked on a large-scale project using zebra fish instead of fruit flies to generate and classify genetic variations, in the belief that the combination of several approaches in one laboratory provides a powerful basis for further understanding. Work continues in her laboratory on the investigation of the molecular mechanisms involved in the establishment of polarity in the *Drosophila* embryo, as well as the exploration of the zebra fish as a model for the study of vertebrate specific features.

Nüsslein-Volhard has advocated more support for women in science, believing that women need much more encouragement from the state to 'dare to be scientists'. She has backed and partly funded a daycare centre at the Max Planck Institute, using money from a scientific prize she had won.

Nüsslein-Volhard has won a number of prizes and awards as well as the Nobel prize. In 1991 she won the Albert Lasker Award, and in 1992 the Louis Jeantet Prize. She was also awarded the Albert P Sloan Jr Prize, the Franz-Vogt Prize, the Liebnizpreiz of the Deutschen Forschungsgemeinschaft, and the Rosenthal Medal from Brandeis University in 1993.

Nyholm, Ronald Sydney (1917–1971) Australian inorganic chemist famous for his work on the coordination compounds (complexes) of the transition metals. He was also interested in science education, and was responsible for many of the changes in chemistry-teaching methods in British schools.

Nyholm was born in Broken Hill, New South Wales, on 29 January 1917, the fourth of the six children of a railway employee whose father had emigrated to Australia from Finland. He was educated at local schools and in 1934 won a scholarship to study natural sciences at Sydney University. He worked for a short time as a research chemist with the Ever Ready Battery Company near Sydney and in 1940 became a member of the staff of Sydney Technical College, where he worked on the coordination compound of rhodium.

In 1947, after World War II, he was awarded an ICI Fellowship to University College, London, where he studied under Christopher ◊Ingold and became a lecturer. He returned to Australia in 1951 as associate professor of inorganic chemistry at the University of New South Wales, Sydney. Four years later he again went to the UK to take up a professorship at University College, and in 1963 he was made head of the chemistry department. He was granted a knighthood in 1967 for his services to science. He was killed in a car accident on the outskirts of Cambridge on 4 December 1971.

Nyholm was introduced to coordination chemistry during his final undergraduate year at Sydney by George Burrows, with whom he worked on the reactions between ferric (iron(III)) chloride and the simple arsines. Then Nyholm and F P J Dwyer studied the coordination compounds of rhodium, again using arsines as ligands.

Diarsine had been synthesized in 1937 by Chatt and Mann, and Nyholm met Chatt in London in 1948 and realized that the arsenic compound might help with his own work. He prepared the complex formed between diarsine and palladium chloride, and went on to use the same ligand to prepare stable compounds of transition metals in valence states that previously had been thought to be unstable. For example, he prepared an octahedral complex of nickel(III), in which the nickel has a coordination number of six.

He also made the diarsine complexes of the tetrachloride and tetrabromide of titanium(IV), the first example of an 8-coordination compound of a first-row transition metal.

Nyholm also systematically exploited physical methods to study the structures and properties of coordination compounds. He used potentiometric titrations to determine oxidation states, and electrical conductivity measurements to discover the nature of the charged species in which the coordinated transition metal was contained. He also employed X-ray crystallography and nuclear magnetic resonance (NMR) spectroscopy, and found that magnetic moment seemed to give the closest connection between electronic structure, chemical structure, and stereochemistry. He always insisted that the three main branches of chemistry – physical, inorganic, and organic – are closely interwoven and that methods from one could often be used to solve problems in another.

Nyholm maintained his interest in the teaching side of chemistry, and was a member of the Science Research Council 1967–71. It was partly as a result of his influence that the Nuffield Foundation set up the Science Teaching Project. He was a strong advocate of an integrated approach to the teaching of chemistry, particularly at the introductory levels.

Ochoa, Severo (1905–1993) Spanish-born US bio-chemist who reproduced in the laboratory the way in which cells synthesize nucleic acids by their use of enzymes. For this achievement, he shared the 1959 Nobel Prize for Physiology or Medicine with Arthur ◊Kornberg.

Ochoa was born in Luarca on 24 September 1905, the youngest son of a lawyer. He graduated from the University of Málaga in 1921 and obtained a degree in medicine from the University of Madrid eight years later. He lectured at Madrid 1931–36. He spent a year in Germany at the University of Heidelberg in 1936 before going to the UK for three years at Oxford University. He then went to the USA in 1940 and was an instructor and research associate at Washington University 1941–42. Ochao moved to New York University, first as a research associate in the College of Medicine and then from 1954 to 1975 as a professor in the department of biochem-istry. He joined the Roche Institute of Molecular Biology in 1975. Ochoa became a US citizen in 1956. He died in Madrid on 1 November 1993.

Ochoa's early work concerned biochemical path-ways in the human body, especially those involving carbon dioxide. But his main research was into nucleic acids and the way in which their nucleotide units are linked together, either singly (as in RNA) or to form two helically wound strands (as in DNA).

In 1955 Ochoa obtained an enzyme from bacteria that was capable of joining together similar nucleotide units to form a nucleic acid, a type of artificial RNA. (Nucleic acids containing exactly similar nucleotide units do not occur naturally, but the method of syn-thesis used by Ochoa was the same as that employed by a living cell.) He also found that strands of similar nucleotides form random small fibres, but when mixed with a similar preparation made from a different nucleotide, two-stranded helixes form, one strand from each preparation.

Ochoa's synthesis of an RNA was the result of out-standing experimental work. Research by other workers soon yielded further important results. For example Arthur Kornberg, working independently, isolated an enzyme that will link different nucleotides to form nucleic acids that closely resemble natural ones.

Oersted, Hans Christian (1777–1851) Danish physicist who discovered that an electric current pro-duces a magnetic field.

Oersted was born in Rudkøbing, Langeland, on 14 August 1777. He had little formal education as a child, but on moving to Copenhagen in 1794, Oersted entered the university and gained a degree in phar-macy in 1797, proceeding to a doctorate in 1799. He then worked as a pharmacist before making a tour of Europe 1801–03 to complete his studies in science. On his return, Oersted gave public lectures with great suc-cess, for he was a very good teacher, and then in 1806 became professor of physics at Copenhagen. He retained this position until 1829, when he became director of the Polytechnic Institute in Copenhagen. As a teacher and writer, Oersted was instrumental in rais-ing science in Denmark to an international standard, founding the Danish Society for the Promotion of Natural Science in 1824. Oersted remained at the Polytechnic Institute until his death, which occurred in Copenhagen on 9 March 1851.

Oersted made his historic discovery of electromag-netism in 1820, but he had been seeking the effect since 1813 when he predicted that an electric current would produce magnetism when it flowed through a wire just as it produced heat and light. Oersted made this prediction on philosophical grounds, believing that all forces must be interconvertible. Others were also seeking the electromagnetic effect, but consid-ered that the magnetic field would lie in the direction of the current and had not been able to detect it. Oersted reasoned that the effect must be a lateral one and early in 1820, he set up an experiment with a compass needle placed beneath a wire connected to a battery. A lecture intervened before he could perform the experiment and, unable to wait, Oersted decided to try it out before his students. The needle moved feebly, making no great impression on the audience but thrilling Oersted. Because the effect was so small, Oersted delayed publication and investigated it more fully, finding that a circular magnetic field is pro-duced around a wire carrying a current. He communicated this momentous discovery to the major scientific journals of Europe in July 1820.

In 1822, Oersted turned to the compressibility of gases and liquids, devising a useful apparatus to determine compressibility. He also investigated ther-moelectricity, in 1823. Oersted may have wanted to continue work on electromagnetism, but his sensa-tional discovery resulted in an explosion of activity by other scientists and Oersted possibly felt unable to compete. Major theoretical and practical advances were made by André ◊Ampère and Michael ◊Faraday soon afterwards, Oersted thereby providing the basis for the main thrust of physics in the 1800s.

Ohm, Georg Simon (1789–1854) German physicist who is remembered for Ohm's law, which relates the current flowing through a conductor to the potential difference and the resistance.

Ohm German physicist Georg Simon Ohm, who established Ohm's law of electricity in 1826. Ohm also carried out research on hearing, and on interference in crystals. *Mary Evans Picture Library*

Ohm was born in Erlangen, Bavaria, on 16 March 1789. He received a basic education in science from his father, who was a master locksmith, and in 1805 he entered the University of Erlangen. However, he left after a year and until 1811 was a school teacher and private tutor in Switzerland. He then returned to Erlangen and gained his PhD in the same year. Ohm then became a *Privatdozent* (unpaid lecturer) in mathematics at Erlangen, but after a year was forced to take up a post as a schoolteacher in Bamberg. In 1817, Ohm moved to Cologne to teach at the Jesuit Gymnasium and in 1825 he decided to pursue original research in physics. He obtained leave in 1826 and went to Berlin, where he produced his great work on electricity, *Die galvanische Kette,* in 1827.

Ohm hoped to obtain an academic post on the strength of his achievements, but found that his work was little appreciated, mainly because of its mathematical rigour, which few German physicists understood at that time. He stayed in Berlin as a schoolteacher, and then in 1833 moved to Nürnberg where he became professor of physics at the Polytechnic Institute, which was not the prestigious university appointment that Ohm both desired and deserved. However, Ohm's work began to achieve recognition, especially in the UK where he was awarded the Royal Society's Copley Medal in 1841. His ability eventually also made its mark in Germany and in 1849 he became extraordinary professor of physics at Munich, acceding to the chair of physics proper in 1852. Ohm thus achieved his ambition but had little time left to savour his success. He died in Munich on 6 July 1854.

Ohm began the work that led him to his law of electricity in 1825. He investigated the amount of electromagnetic force produced in a wire carrying a current, expecting it to decrease with the length of the wire in the circuit. He used a voltaic pile to produce a current and connected varying lengths of wire to it, measuring the electromagnetic force with the magnetic needle of a galvanometer. Ohm found that a longer wire produced a greater loss in electromagnetic force.

Ohm continued these investigations in 1826 using a thermocouple as the source of current because it produced a constant electric current unlike the voltaic pile, which fluctuated. He found that the electromagnetic force (emf), which is in fact a measure of the current, was equal to the electromotive force produced by the thermocouple divided by the length of the conductor being tested plus a quantity that Ohm called the resistance of the remainder of the circuit, including the thermocouple itself. From this, Ohm reached the more general statement that the current is equal to the tension (emf or potential difference) divided by the overall resistance of the circuit, thus expressing the law in the form known as Ohm's law.

Ohm went on to use an electroscope to measure how the tension varied at different points along a conductor to verify his law, and presented his arguments in mathematical form in his great work of 1827. He made a useful analogy with the flow of heat through a conductor, pointing out that an electric current flows through a conductor of varying resistance from one tension or potential to another to produce a potential difference, just as heat flows through a conductor of varying conductivity from one temperature to another to produce a temperature difference. Ohm used the analytical theory of heat published by Joseph ◊Fourier in 1822 to justify this approach, believing partly from his use of thermocouples that there was an intimate link between heat and electricity.

Ohm's derivation of a basic law of nature from experiment was a classic piece of scientific deduction. Together with the laws of electrodynamics discovered by André ◊Ampère at about the same time, Ohm's law marks the first theoretical investigation of electricity. It is fitting that his name is remembered in both the unit of resistance, the ohm, and the unit of conductivity, the mho (ohm spelt backwards).

Olbers, Heinrich Wilhelm Matthäus (1758–1840)

German doctor, mathematician, and astronomer who is now chiefly remembered for his work on the discovery of asteroids and the formulation of Olbers's method for calculating the orbits of comets. He also caused considerable scientific controversy by asking the basic question, why is the night dark?

Olbers was born near Bremen on 11 October 1758. He attended the local school where, at the age of 16, his mathematical and astronomical interests were so advanced that he computed the time of a solar eclipse. In 1777 he went to Göttingen to study medicine, but attended lectures also in physics and mathematics, coming under the influence of Kästner, the director of the small observatory there. Olbers's pursuit of the phenomenon of comets began two years later (and was to last the rest of his life), when he applied his findings from observing Bode's comet to determine its orbit following a method devised by ◊Euclid. In 1781 he received his degree in medicine and, moving to Bremen, he quickly established a successful medical practice from which he retired only at the age of 64, in 1823. Astronomy had in the meantime become a consuming hobby, to satisfy which he had early on installed all the equipment for a full observatory on the second floor of his house – refractors, a reflector, a heliometer, and three comet-seekers. He collected the finest private library of literature on comets (now part of the Pulkovo collection). Olbers died in Bremen on 2 March 1840.

Discovering a new comet in 1796, Olbers devised a new method to compute its parabolic orbit. The new system was less complicated than that used by Pierre ◊Laplace at an earlier date. Laplace had given formulae for the computation of a parabola through successive approximations, but the procedure was cumbersome and unsatisfactory. It had been assumed that when three observations of a comet had been obtained within a short period of time, the radius vector of the middle observation would divide the chord of the orbit of the comet from the first to the last observation in relation to the traversed time. Olbers's contribution was to establish that this assumption could be applied with equal advantage to the three positions of the Earth in its orbit. His treatise was read by Baron von Zach who used it to calculate the orbit the 1779 comet. Through the publication of the baron's work, Olbers was established as one of the leading astronomers of the day and Olbers's method was universally adopted throughout the 1800s.

For some years astronomers had searched the apparent 'gap' in the Solar System between the planets Mars and Jupiter – a gap emphasized by the formulation of Bode's law (see Johann Elert ◊Bode). Then the first asteroid was discovered in 1801 by Giuseppe ◊Piazzi, who noticed a celestial object that changed position over a period of successive days. News of the sighting was passed on to other astronomers, and it was quickly deduced that a new (minor) planet had been discovered, which Piazzi named Ceres. However, before further deductions could be carried out, the asteroid disappeared from view – astronomers of the time could not calculate the orbit of such a small planet without having to make assumptions about the eccentricity. However, the young mathematician and astronomer Karl ◊Gauss determined the orbit and Olbers, in January 1802, rediscovered the new planet close to the position predicted by Gauss. This was the beginning of a lifelong friendship and collaboration between the two men.

While following Ceres, Olbers discovered a second asteroid, Pallas, in 1802; a third, Juno, was discovered by Karl Harding (1765–1834) at Lilienthal in 1804. The orbits of these small planets suggested to Olbers that they had a common point of origin and might have originated from one large planet. For years, Olbers searched the sky where the orbits of Ceres, Pallas, and Juno approached each other; this resulted in his discovery of Vesta in March 1807.

Olbers's main interest remained the search for comets, however, and his efforts were rewarded with the discovery of four more. Of particular interest is the comet that he discovered in March 1815, which has an orbit of 72 years, like Halley's. Olbers also calculated the orbits of 18 other comets. Noticing that comets consist of a starlike nucleus and a parabolic cloud of matter, he suggested that this matter was expelled by the nucleus and repelled by the Sun.

In a publication of 1823 Olbers discussed the paradox that now bears his name, that if we accept an infinite, uniform universe, the whole sky should be covered by stars shining as brightly as our Sun. Olbers explained the darkness of the night sky by assuming that space is not absolutely transparent and that some interstellar matter absorbs a minute percentage of starlight. This effect is sufficient to dim the light of the stars, so that they are seen as points against the dark sky. (In fact, darkness is now generally accepted as a by-product of the red shift caused by stellar recession.)

Although interested in the study of comets, Olbers was also interested in the influence of the Moon on the weather, the origin of meteorite showers, and the history of astronomy. A very modest man, he encouraged many young astronomers and claimed that his greatest contribution to astronomy had been to lead Friedrich

◊Bessel to become a professional astronomer, after Bessel had approached him in 1804 with his calculation of the orbit of Halley's comet.

Further Reading

Jaki, Stanley L, *Olbers Studies: With Three Unpublished Manuscripts by Olbers*, History of Astronomy series, Pachart Publishing House, 1990, v 8.

Struve, Otto, 'Some thoughts on Olbers' Paradox', *Sky Telesc*, 1963, v 25, pp 140–142.

Onsager, Lars (1903–1976) Norwegian-born US theoretical chemist who was awarded the 1968 Nobel Prize for Chemistry for his work on reversible processes.

Onsager was born in Oslo on 27 November 1903. He was educated at the local high school and then at the Norges Tekniske Høgskole in Trondheim, where he studied chemical engineering. During the five years at Trondheim he acquired the mathematical skills he was to use later on, and developed an interest in electrolytes. After qualifying in 1925 he went to Zürich to work as a research assistant to Peter ◊Debye. He emigrated to the USA in 1928 and was appointed an associate in chemistry at Johns Hopkins University, Baltimore. He was not, however, a success as a lecturer (because his course did not attract a sufficient number of students) and he soon moved to Brown University, where he was a research instructor 1928–33.

In 1933 he went to Europe to visit the Austrian electrochemist Falkenhagen, and while there met and married Falkenhagen's sister. His lectures at Brown University were no more comprehensible to the students, who named his course 'Sadistical Mechanics'. Also in 1933 he took up an appointment at Yale, becoming assistant professor in chemistry a year later. The university authorities were disconcerted to have a plain 'Mr' as a professor, and urged Onsager to submit one of his published papers as a PhD thesis. Onsager chose 'Solutions to the Mathieu equation of period 4π and certain related functions'. The chemistry department were unable to make anything of it so they passed it to the physics department, which in turn passed it to the mathematics department. The final outcome was an award of a PhD by the bemused chemists. It is little wonder that the students at Yale were no kinder than those at Brown and described Onsager's lectures as 'Advanced Norwegian I and II'. His almost total failure as a lecturer probably came from the fact that he could not appreciate that others were unable to understand the topics that interested him. He did, however, remain at Yale for the rest of his career.

Onsager was not required to do military service during World War II because he had not yet become a US citizen and his wife was Austrian; he adopted US nationality in 1945. After retirement he bought a farm at Tilton, New Hampshire, and grew his own crops. He died in Coral Gables, Florida, on 5 October 1976.

In 1925 Peter Debye and Erich ◊Hückel had put forward a new theory of electrolytes based on the idea that the electrostatic field of a dissolved ion is effectively screened by surrounding ions of opposite charge. They were able to calculate the activity coefficient for any ion in dilute solution although the calculated values for conductivity differed considerably from experimental values, particularly for strong electrolytes. When Onsager went to Zürich in 1925 he told Debye that he thought the electrolyte theory was incorrect – and was offered a research assistantship. Debye had assumed that one particular ion should be thought of as moving uniformly in a straight line, while all other ions undergo Brownian motion. Onsager showed that this constraint should be lifted and the result, known as the Onsager limiting law, gave better agreement between calculated and actual conductivities. He went on to investigate dielectric constants of polar liquids and solutions of polar molecules.

At Brown University Onsager submitted a PhD thesis on what is now a classic work on reversible processes, but the authorities turned it down. It was published in 1931 but ignored until the late 1940s; in 1968 it earned Onsager a Nobel prize. He then turned his attention to the equilibrium states in the mutarotation (change in optical rotation) of sugars. Riiber had shown in 1922 that galactose exists in at least three tautomeric forms (interconvertible stereoisomers). Onsager proposed that the equilibrium states between these forms must conform to the principle of 'detailed balancing', as conceived by Gilbert ◊Lewis, and showed that this idea is thermodynamically equivalent to the principle of 'least dissipation' used by Hermann von ◊Helmholtz in his theory of galvanic diffusion cells and by Lord ◊Kelvin in his theories about thermoelectric phenomena.

Onsager also looked at the connection between microscopic reversibility and transport processes. He found that the key to the problem is the distribution of molecules and energy caused by random thermal motion. Ludwig ◊Boltzmann had shown that the nature of thermal equilibrium is statistical and that the statistics of the spontaneous deviation is determined by the entropy. Using this principle Onsager derived a set of equations known as Onsager's law of reciprocal relations, sometimes called the fourth law of thermodynamics. It has many applications to cross-coefficients for the diffusion of pairs of solutes in the same solution, and for the various interactions that can occur between thermal conduction, diffusion, and electrical conduction. He announced these ideas in the late 1930s, but not until 1960 did the theory receive experimental confirmation.

During and after World War II Onsager made calculations concerning the two-dimensional Ising lattice (an assembly of particles or 'spin' located at the vertices of an infinite space lattice; the simplest case is a two-dimensional planar square lattice). It can be used as a model to describe ferromagnetism and anti-ferromagnetism of gaseous condensations, phase separations in fluid mixtures, and metallic alloys. Onsager's treatment showed that the specific heat approaches infinity at the transition point. In 1949 he published a paper that established a firm statistical basis for the theory of liquid crystals, and at Cambridge 1951–1952 he put forward a theory concerned with diamagnetism in metals.

Further Reading

Hemmer, P C; Holden, H; and Kjelstrup Ratkje, S, *The Collected Works of Lars Onsager: With Commentary,* Series in Twentieth-Century Physics, World Scientific Publishing Co, 1996, v 17.

Longuet-Higgins, H Christopher and Fisher, Michael E, 'Lars Onsager, November 27, 1903–October 5, 1976', *Biogr Mem Nat Acad Sci,* 1989, v 58, p 407–423.

Onsager, Lars, *The Collected Works of Lars Onsager,* World Scientific Publishing Co, 1996.

Oort, Jan Hendrik (1900–1992) Dutch astrophysicist whose main area of research was the composition of galaxies. In his investigation of our own Galaxy, he used data provided by other scientists to demonstrate the position of the Sun within the rotating Galaxy, and through the use of the radio telescope, he traced our Galaxy's spiral arms by the detection of interstellar residual hydrogen.

Oort was born in Franeker, the Netherlands, on 28 April 1900, the son of a doctor. Completing his education at the University of Groningen, he studied under Jacobus ◊Kapteyn, from whom, perhaps, he derived his great interest in galactic structure and movement. In 1926 he received his PhD at Gröningen and went immediately (for a short time) to work at Yale University in the USA. He then returned to join the staff of Leiden University, in the Netherlands, where he became professor of astronomy in 1935. Ten years later he was made director of the Leiden Observatory, retiring finally in 1970. He died in Leiden on 5 November 1992.

Kapteyn, only four years after Oort was born, had published in 1904 the results of an investigation to find the centre of our Galaxy. He preferred to believe that the Sun itself was at or very near the middle, but he was puzzled by two definite 'streams' of galactic stars apparently moving in a linear sequence in two opposing directions; moreover, a line connecting the streams would follow the Milky Way. The Swedish astronomer Bertil ◊Lindblad, using these data in the year that Oort was receiving his PhD, suggested that if the Sun were not at the centre, the two streams could represent stars going to the centre and stars returning, and on this basis he worked out that the centre of the Galaxy was somewhere in the direction of the constellation Sagittarius – incidentally agreeing with independent calculations by US astronomer Harlow ◊Shapley. Oort's major success was to provide confirmation for Lindblad and Shapley, although he located the centre of the Galaxy at a distance of 30,000 light years rather than at Shapley's 50,000.

Oort went on to show that the streams of stars were not in fact linear, but very much like the planets revolving round a sun, in that the stars nearer the centre of the Galaxy revolved faster round the centre than those farther out. Noting the Sun's position in the Galaxy, and calculating its period of revolution as slightly more than 200 million years, Oort derived a calculation also of the mass of the Galaxy: about 100,000 million (10^{11}) times that of the Sun.

The beginning of radio astronomy during and just after World War II was of great assistance to Oort's investigations. After considerable theoretical work on the structure of the hydrogen atom, over the passage of time and under different circumstances, he and Hendrik van de Hulst (1918–   ) discovered in 1951 the radio emission at a wavelength of 21 cm/8 in of interstellar neutral hydrogen. The fact that hydrogen occurs between galactic stars, not in open space (so to speak), meant that the shape of the Galaxy could now be traced by the shape of the hydrogen between the stars. For the first time it was possible accurately to chart the spiral arms of our Galaxy. It was also possible to study the centre of the Galaxy in detail, by monitoring its radio waves.

At about the same time, Oort put forward an ingenious theory concerning the origin of comets. He suggested that at a great distance from the Sun – a light year, say – there was an enormous 'reservoir' of comets in the form of a cloud of particles. Gravitational perturbations by passing stars could, he suggested, every now and then cause one of them to be hurled into the Solar System and become a comet.

In 1956, Oort and Theodore Walraven studied the radiation emitted from the Crab nebula and found it to be polarized, indicating synchrotron radiation produced by high-speed electrons in a magnetic field.

Oparin, Alexandr Ivanovich (1894–1980) Russian biochemist who made important contributions to evolutionary biochemistry, developing one of the first of the modern theories about the origin of life on Earth.

He received many honours for his work, particularly from the Soviet Union.

Oparin was born on 3 March 1894 in the small village of Uglich, north of Moscow, the youngest of three children. When he was nine years old, his family moved to Moscow because Uglich had no secondary school. He studied plant physiology at Moscow State University, where he was influenced by K A Timiryazev, a plant physiologist who had known Charles Darwin. After graduating in 1917, Oparin researched in biochemistry under A N Bakh, a botanist, then in 1929 became professor of plant biochemistry at Moscow State University. In 1935 he helped to found, and began working at, the Bakh Institute of Biochemistry in Moscow, which had been established in honour of his former teacher. Oparin became director of the Bakh Institute in 1946 and held this post until his death in April 1980.

Oparin first put forward his ideas about the origin of life in 1922 at a meeting of the Russian Botanical Society. His theory contained three basic premises: that the first organisms arose in the ancient seas, which contained many already formed organic compounds that the organisms used as nutriment (thus his hypothetical first organisms did not synthesize their own organic nutrients but took them in ready-made from the surrounding water); that there was a constant, virtually limitless supply of external energy in the form of sunlight (thus conditions in which the first forms of life arose did not constitute a closed system and were not limited by the second law of thermodynamics); and that true life was characterized by a high degree of structural and functional organization, an idea that was contrary to the prevailing view that life was basically molecular.

Oparin's theory did not explain how complex molecules could have arisen in the primordial seas, nor how his primitive organisms could reproduce. Later research, however, suggested that a degree of order in the structure of proteins might have occurred as a result of the restrictions imposed on the coupling of amino acids due to their different shapes and distributions of electric charge. Regarding reproduction, later experiments with microscopic coacervate droplets of gelatine and gum arabic demonstrated that these droplets repeatedly grow and reproduce by budding. Oparin then showed that enzymes function more efficiently inside such synthetic cells than they do in ordinary aqueous solution.

Oparin's theory (which was first published in 1924, although it reached its widest audience after 1936, when he published *The Origin of Life on Earth*) stimulated much research into the origin of life, perhaps the most famous of which is Stanley ◊Miller's attempt in 1953 to reproduce primordial conditions in the laboratory. In his experiment, Miller put sterile water, methane, ammonia, and hydrogen (simulating the primordial atmosphere) in a sealed container and subjected the mixture to electrical discharges (simulating lightning). After one week he found that the solution contained simple organic compounds, including amino acids. In addition, C Ponnamperuma, using slightly different experimental conditions, demonstrated that nucleotides, dinucleotides, and ATP can be formed from simple ingredients.

Although best known for his pioneering work on the origins of life, Oparin also researched into enzymology and did much to provide a technical basis for industrial biochemistry in the Soviet Union.

Öpik, Ernst Julius (1893–1985) Estonian astronomer whose work on the nature of meteors and comets was instrumental in the development of heat-deflective surfaces for spacecraft on their re-entry into the Earth's atmosphere.

Öpik was born in Kunda, a coastal village 15 km/9 mi north of Rakvere, Estonia, on 23 October 1893. He completed his education at the Tartu State University, and in 1916 began working at the Tashkent Observatory in Uzbekistan; he then moved in 1918 to the observatory at the University of Moscow, where he worked as an assistant and instructor. From 1920 to 1921 he served as a lecturer at Turkistan University, before returning to Tartu University as a lecturer in astronomy. Apart from four years as a research associate and visiting lecturer at the Harvard College Observatory, in the USA, Öpik remained at Tartu University until 1944. He was then appointed research associate at the University of Hamburg in Germany; he became professor and Estonian rector at the German Baltic University in 1945. Three years later, Öpik moved to Northern Ireland where, initially appointed as a research associate, he eventually became director of the Armagh Observatory. From 1956 onwards he held a concurrent post as a visiting professor (and later associate professor) at the University of Maryland, in the USA, where in 1968 he was appointed to the chair of physics and astronomy. Öpik received several awards, including the Gold Medal of the Royal Astronomical Society (1975).

Öpik's early research was devoted to the study of meteors; he was the originator of the 'double-count' method for counting meteors, a method that requires two astronomers to scan simultaneously. His theories on surface events in meteors upon entering the Earth's atmosphere at high speed (the ablation, or progressive erosion, of the outer layers) proved to be extremely important in the development of heat shields and other protective devices to enable a spacecraft to withstand the friction and the resulting intense heat upon re-entry.

Much of Öpik's other work was directed at the analysis of comets that orbit the Sun. He postulated that the orbit of some of these comets may take them as far away as one light year. He also made studies of double stars, cosmic radiation, and stellar photometry. His interests and contributions thus covered a broad range of astronomical disciplines.

Oppenheimer, J(ulius) Robert (1904–1967) US physicist who contributed significantly to the growth of quantum mechanics and played a critical role in the rapid development of the first atomic bombs. In his later years, he was a prominent advocate of international control of nuclear technology and of a cautious approach to the escalation of the military applications of that knowledge.

Oppenheimer was born in New York on 22 April 1904. He attended the Ethical Culture School and was a very serious, studious child. His interest in minerals and geology led to his admission to the Minerological Club of New York at the mere age of 11. In 1922, he went to Harvard University, graduating after only three of the usual four years in 1925. He spent the next year in Cambridge with Ernest ◊Rutherford, Werner ◊Heisenberg, and Paul ◊Dirac, and in 1926 at the invitation of Max ◊Born he went to Göttingen where he worked on quantum theory of molecules and *bremsstrahlung* (continuous radiation emission). He received his PhD from Göttingen in 1927. Oppenheimer then returned to the USA and became a national research fellow, and in 1929 he was appointed assistant professor at both the California Institute of Technology (Caltech) and the University of California at Berkeley. He spent the next 13 years commuting between these two campuses, becoming associate professor in 1931 and professor in 1936.

From 1943 to 1945, Oppenheimer was director of the Los Alamos Scientific Laboratories in New Mexico, where he headed the research team that produced the first atomic bombs. After World War II he returned briefly to California and then in 1947 was made director of the Institute of Advanced Study at Princeton University. Oppenheimer also served as chairman of the General Advisory Committee to the Atomic Energy Commission 1946–52. He retired as director of the Institute of Advanced Study in 1966, but continued as professor there until his death at Princeton on 18 February 1967.

Oppenheimer's most important research was to investigate the equations describing the energy states of the atom that Dirac had formulated in 1928. In 1930, Oppenheimer was instrumental in showing that the equations indicated that a positively charged particle with the mass of an electron could exist. This particle was detected in 1932 and called the positron.

During the 1930s at California, Oppenheimer built up a formidable research group around him. Theoretical physics had never before been studied with such intensity in the USA. When World War II broke out in 1939 in Europe, it was immediately apparent to Oppenheimer that the newly discovered phenomenon of nuclear fission could have great military significance. Work on the various aspects of bomb construction began in many places, one of them being Berkeley. The Manhattan Project, the code name for the programme aimed at the production of the atomic bomb, was formally initiated in 1942. Oppenheimer suggested that the work on the various related projects be brought together to one site and proposed a remote location in the Pecos Valley, New Mexico. The Los Alamos research centre was set up there in 1943 with Oppenheimer as director.

> *The atomic bomb ... made the prospect of future war unendurable. It has led us up those last few steps to the mountain pass; and beyond there is different country.*
> **J ROBERT OPPENHEIMER** QUOTED IN R RHODES THE MAKING OF THE ATOMIC BOMB *1987*

Oppenheimer did not take on personal responsibility for the development of any single aspect of the bomb programme, but concentrated first on gathering together the finest scientists he could find and secondly on instilling in the whole team a sense of urgency and intense excitement. The success of the Los Alamos project in so quickly overcoming the enormous number of new problems is in no small measure attributable to his efforts. Oppenheimer also served as one of the four scientists consulted on the decision of how to deploy the bomb, the scientists recommending that a populated 'military target' be selected.

Oppenheimer was also involved in the decision to develop the hydrogen bomb after the war. The majority of the AEC Advisory Committee, of which Oppenheimer was chairman, was opposed to this but the unexpected explosion of a nuclear device by the Soviet Union in the summer of 1949 led to President Truman overriding this advice. Oppenheimer's offer of resignation from the committee was not accepted, but in 1953, at the height of the McCarthy era, Oppenheimer was informed that President Eisenhower had ordered that his security clearance (permission for access to secret information) was to be withdrawn on the basis of suspicions concerning his loyalty. Oppenheimer opposed this and underwent a gruelling quasi-judicial procedure which did not lead to his clearance being restored. There is little doubt that those who had disagreed with Oppenheimer's position regarding the H-bomb were at least partly responsible for this.

In 1963 President Johnson publicly awarded Oppenheimer the Enrico Fermi Prize, the highest award the AEC can confer, as an attempt to make amends for the unjust treatment he had received.

Further Reading

Driemen, J E, *Robert Oppenheimer: Atomic Dawn: A Biography of Robert Oppenheimer,* People in Focus series, Silver Burdett Press, 1988.

Goodchild, Peter, *J Robert Openheimer: Shatterer of Worlds,* Fromm International Publishing Corporation, 1985.

Holloway, Rachel L, *In the Matter of J Robert Oppenheimer: Politics, Rhetoric, and Self-Defense,* Praeger Publishers, 1993.

Rummel, Jack, *Robert Oppenheimer: Dark Prince,* Makers of Modern Science series, Facts on File, 1992.

York, Herbert F, *The Advisors: Oppenheimer, Teller, and the Superbomb,* Nuclear Age series, Stanford University Press, 1989.

Oppolzer, Theodor Egon Ritter von (1841–1886)

Austrian mathematician and astronomer whose interest in asteroids and comets and eclipses led to his compiling meticulous lists of such bodies and events for the use of other astronomers.

Oppolzer was born in Prague (then in the Austrian Empire, now in the Czech Republic) on 26 October 1841. He displayed keen mathematical abilities from an early age and was a top student at the Piaristen Gymnasium in Vienna 1851–59. Although he followed his father's wishes and studied to qualify as a doctor – he was awarded his medical degree in 1865 – Oppolzer devoted most of his spare time to carrying out astronomical observations. In 1866 he became lecturer in astronomy at the University of Vienna. He was promoted to associate professor in 1870, made director of the Austrian Geodetic Survey in 1873, and in 1875 became professor of geodesy and astronomy at Vienna. In addition to his teaching and research activities, Oppolzer was active in many European scientific societies. He was elected to the presidency of the International Geodetic Association in 1886, shortly before his death in Vienna on 26 December 1886.

Oppolzer was fortunate to possess a private observatory, which permitted him to make accurate and thorough investigations of the behaviour of comets and asteroids. (Asteroids were in fact only discovered by Giuseppe ◊Piazzi in 1801, and the details of their orbits were of considerable interest to astronomers.) Oppolzer methodically sought, by observation and calculation, to confirm and amend, where necessary, the putative orbits of these bodies. He was the originator of a novel technique for correcting orbits he found to be inaccurate. His two-volume text on the subject 1870–80 provides a clear description of this work.

In 1868 Oppolzer participated in an expedition to study a total eclipse of the Sun and his interest in eclipses dates from that time. He decided to calculate the time and path of every eclipse of the Sun and every eclipse of the Moon for as long a period as possible. The resulting *Canon der Finsternisse* was published posthumously in 1887. It covered the period 1207 BC–AD 2163, an astonishing total of 3,370 years.

Oppolzer's contributions to astronomy were characterized by their great thoroughness and by the accuracy of his mathematical procedures.

Ore, Oystein (1899–1968)

Norwegian mathematician whose studies, researches, and publications concentrated on the fields of abstract algebra, number theory, and the theory of graphs.

Ore was born on 7 October 1899 in Oslo, where he grew up and was educated, entering Oslo University in 1918; he received his BA in 1922. He then paid a fleeting visit to the University of Göttingen – that great centre of mathematics – where he met the influential mathematician Emmy ◊Noether who was at that time building up an active research group in abstract algebra. The work being done at Göttingen undoubtedly exercised a strong influence over Ore.

Returning to Scandinavia, he worked from 1923 to 1924 at the Mittag-Leffler Mathematical Institute in Djursholm, Sweden, at the end of which time he was awarded his PhD in mathematics by the University of Oslo. Two years later (and after another short visit to Göttingen), Ore was appointed professor of mathematics at Oslo University. Only 12 months later, however, he moved to take up an equivalent position at Yale University in the USA; there, he was rapidly promoted to associate, in 1928, and then to full professor in 1929, serving as chairman of his department 1936–45. He then returned to Norway. A Knight of the Order of St Olav, Ore wrote many books on mathematical subjects.

During the 1920s and 1930s Ore's primary research interest was abstract algebra. Among other topics, he investigated linear equations in noncommutative fields; most of his work on this subject was summarized in a book he published in 1936 on abstract algebra. He then turned to an examination of number theory, and in particular of algebraic numbers. His investigations in this subject were contained in a text on number theory and its origins which he published in 1948.

Much of Ore's later research dealt with the theory of graphs. He took a special interest in the four-colour problem, the theory that maps require no more than four colours for each region of the map to be coloured but with no zone sharing a common border with another zone of the same colour. Ore wrote a book detailing his investigations into the problem; it appeared in 1967.

Another of Ore's interests was the history of mathematics. He wrote biographies of the 16th-century Italian Gerolamo Cardano and of his fellow Norwegian, the ill-starred Niels ◊Abel; they were published in 1953 and 1957 respectively.

Osborn, Henry Fairfield (1857–1935) US palaeontologist who did much to promote the acceptance of evolutionism in the USA.

The son of a wealthy businessman, Osborn studied at Princeton, developed an interest in natural history, and began a long career of palaeontological exploration in 1877 with an expedition to Colorado and Wyoming. From 1881 he occupied a post at Princeton, moving in 1891 to Columbia University.

Osborn's main work was in vertebrate palaeontology. He eagerly accepted evolutionary theory and was concerned to fill out its main trends and details. He continued Edward Drinker Cope's work on the evolution of mammalian molar teeth and wrote an influential textbook, *The Age of Mammals* (1910). Osborn's evolutionary studies focused on the problem of the adaptive diversification of life. He was particularly concerned with the parallel but independent evolution of related lines of descent, and with the explanation of the gradual appearance of new structural units of adaptive value. He placed great emphasis on the fact that evolution was the resultant of pressures from four major directions: external environment, internal environment, heredity, and selection. A convinced Christian, the interpretation of evolution in religious and moral terms concerned him greatly.

Ostwald, (Friedrich) Wilhelm (1853–1932) Latvian-born German physical chemist famous for his contributions to solution chemistry and to colour science. He was awarded the 1909 Nobel Prize for Chemistry for his work on catalysis, chemical equilibria, and reaction velocities.

Ostwald was born of German parents in Riga, Latvia, on 2 September 1853; his father was a master cooper. He was good at handicrafts when he was a boy, a skill that was later to stand him in good stead when he had to make his own chemical apparatus. He was educated at the Realgymnasium in Riga and in 1872 went to the University of Dorpat (Tartu) in Estonia to study chemistry under Carl Schmidt and Johann Lemberg. He also

studied physics under Arthur von Oettingen, and was awarded his PhD in 1878. While working for his doctorate, he lectured at Dorpat on the theory of chemical affinity and was Oettingen's assistant. He married in 1880; his son Wolfgang (1883–1943) was also to become a notable chemist, and his daughter Grete wrote her father's biography in 1953.

In 1881 Ostwald was appointed professor of chemistry at Riga. Six years later he accepted what was then the only chair in physical chemistry in Germany, at the University of Leipzig, and in 1898 celebrated the official dedication of the new Physico-chemical Institute there, of which he was made director. He retired in 1906, having been appointed the first German exchange professor to Harvard 1905–06. In 1901 he had moved his family and his huge library to 'Landhaus Energie', a house in Grossbothen, and after 1909 devoted an increasing amount of his time to philosophy. He died in Leipzig on 4 April 1932.

As a student Ostwald worked out that the magnitude of a chemical change could be calculated from any measurable change in a physical property that accompanies it. In 1887 he determined the volume changes that take place during the neutralization of acids by bases in dilute solutions, and in 1879 proposed that the rate at which compounds such as zinc sulphide and calcium oxalate are dissolved by various acids be used as a measure of the acids' relative affinities. He read the memoir by Svante ◊Arrhenius on the 'galvanic conductibility of electrolytes' in 1884 and became an enthusiastic supporter of the new theory of ionic dissociation. He was then able to redetermine the affinities of the acids using Arrhenius's electrolytic conductivity method.

In 1885 and 1887 Ostwald published the two volumes of his ambitious textbook *Lehrbuch der allgemeinen Chemie*. Also in 1887, together with Jacobus ◊van't Hoff and Arrhenius, he founded the journal *Zeitschrift für physikalische Chemie*.

In 1888 he proposed the Ostwald dilution law, which relates the degree of dissociation of an electrolyte, α, to its total concentration c expressed in moles per litre (dm^3). It states that:

$$k = \alpha^2 c/(1 - \alpha)$$

The constant, k, neglects the activity coefficient and is therefore not the true thermodynamic constant K. The equation is important historically because it was the form in which the law of mass action was first applied to solutions of weak organic acids and bases. Ostwald then worked on the theory of acid–base indicators.

Ostwald turned his attention to catalysis in 1900. He discovered a method of oxidizing ammonia to convert it to oxides of nitrogen (for making nitric acid) by passing a mixture of air and ammonia over a platinum catalyst. By means of this technique (using ammonia from the Haber process), and by later developments connected with it, Germany became independent of supplies of Chilean nitrates and was able to continue the manufacture of explosives during World War I after the Allies had blockaded its ports. Ostwald patented the Ostwald–Bauer process for the manufacture of nitric acid from ammonia.

From 1909 Ostwald became interested in science methodology and the organizational aspects of science, in a world language, in internationalism, and in pacifism. He enlarged the premises at 'Landhaus Energie' and built a laboratory for colour research. He devised a 'colour wheel' for relating the various colours to their shades and tints. His studies of colour theory and the techniques of painting are noteworthy, and his book *Grosse Männer* on the lives of famous scientists shows great insight into the factors that make for great people.

Otis, Elisha Graves (1811–1861) US engineer who pioneered the development of the lift. Although mechanical lifts and hoists had been known since early in the 19th century, it was the invention by Otis of a safety device that caused them to be generally adopted in commerce and slightly later as passenger-carrying machines. He also invented and patented a number of other important machines.

Otis was born on 3 August 1811 on his father's farm in Halifax, Vermont. His father was a justice of the peace and served four terms in the Vermont state legislature. Elisha's education was received in Halifax. When he was 19 he went to Troy, New York, to work as a builder. Illness and enterprise led him to take up a haulage business. As he accumulated capital he engaged in other businesses with varying degrees of success: first as a miller, and when this failed he converted his mill into a factory to make carriages and wagons. Again ill health caused him to abandon his livelihood. This time he became employed in Albany, New York, as a master mechanic in a factory making beds. Again he acquired capital and opened his own machine shop, which was successful for a time. Misfortune struck again when the Albany authorities diverted the stream that drove the water turbine he had invented to supply the workshop with power. He returned to his old job as a master mechanic, in another factory making beds, this time in New Jersey, where after a time he was put in charge of the preparation of a new factory at Yonkers, New York. During the construction of the building, in 1852, he had to make a hoist and, as many serious accidents had been caused by out-of-control lifting platforms, he sought a way of making this one absolutely safe.

Otis built the frame of his hoist with a ratchet into which could be slotted a horizontal wagon spring attached to the 'cage' of the lift. The rope of the hoist was fixed to the centre of the spring and kept it in tension, so preventing it from engaging with the ratchet. If, however, the rope broke, the spring was released and jammed into the ratchet, immediately immobilizing the lift.

Interest was shown in his lifts, and when the bed factory went out of business he took over its plant to fulfill the initial three orders he received for his invention. Further orders came slowly until Otis exhibited his patented lift at the second season of the Crystal Palace Exposition in New York in 1854. As part of his demonstration he climbed onto his elevator, was hoisted into the air, and then a mechanic cut the hoisting rope. This was a grand advertisement and the orders started to come in. In 1857 the first public passenger lift was opened by the New York china firm of E V Haughwout and Company. Generally the lifts were powered by steam engines and in 1860 Otis patented and improved the double oscillatory machine specially designed for his lifts. Also from the workshops of his company, Otis invented and patented railway trucks and brakes, a steam plough, and a baking oven.

Otis was married twice and had two sons. By the time of his death on 8 April 1861 his business was fairly profitable. Later it was developed to massive proportions with the help of his sons.

Otto, Nikolaus August (1832–1891) German engineer who developed the first commercially successful four-stroke internal-combustion engine – even today, the four-stroke cycle is still sometimes referred to as the Otto Cycle.

Otto was born in Holzhausen, Nassau, the son of a farmer, on 14 June 1832. He left school at the age of 16 to work in a merchant's office, and later moved to Cologne where he became greatly interested in the gas engines developed by Etienne ◊Lenoir. In 1861 he built a small experimental gas engine, and three years later joined forces with Eugen Langen, an industrialist trained at the Karlsruhe Polytechnic, to form a company to market such engines. He received valuable help also from a former fellow student, Franz Reuleaux. At the Paris Exhibition of 1867 the firm's product won a gold medal in competition with 14 other gas engines. Further capital was raised, and a new factory, the Gasmotorenfabrik, was built at Deutz near Cologne in 1869. Otto concentrated on the administrative side of the business, leaving Langen, with his new recruits Gottlieb ◊Daimler and Wilhelm ◊Maybach, to develop the engineering side.

In 1876, Otto described the four-stroke engine for which his name is famous. Unfortunately his patent was invalidated in 1886 when his competitors

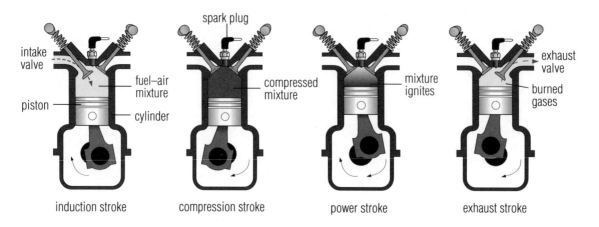

spark plug

intake
valve

piston

fuel–air
mixture

cylinder

compressed
mixture

mixture
ignites

exhaust
valve

burned
gases

induction stroke   compression stroke   power stroke   exhaust stroke

Otto The four-stroke cycle of a modern petrol engine. The cycle is called the Otto cycle after German engineer Nikolaus Otto, who introduced it in 1876. It improved on earlier engine cycles by compressing the fuel mixture before it was ignited.

discovered that Alphonse Beau de Rochas (1815–1893) had described the principle of the four-stroke cycle in an obscure pamphlet. In the period 1860–65 Lenoir sold several hundred of his small double-acting gas engines, but technical weaknesses – especially low compression – limited their potential. Otto's much more efficient and relatively quiet engine, the so-called 'silent Otto' was well received and sold extensively in the first ten years of manufacture. Otto died in Cologne on 26 January 1891.

Otto first designed a successful vertical atmospheric gas engine in 1867. Some ten years later he introduced a horizontal engine, the operation of which was closely similar to the cycle of Rochas. Almost certainly, however, Otto reached his results independently of Rochas and the system has ever since been referred to as 'the Otto cycle'.

In the Otto four-stroke cylinder cycle the explosive mixture, in the first stroke of the piston towards the crankshaft, is drawn into the cylinder (the induction stroke). It is compressed on the return (compression) stroke. Ignition is then effected at or about the top dead-centre position and the burning mixture drives the piston during the third stroke of the cycle. Finally, on the fourth (exhaust) stroke, the burnt gases are driven out of the cylinder. The cycle is then repeated.

The superiority of Otto's new engine over other types was soon apparent. Thousands of them, manufactured by Otto and Langen, were installed throughout the world in a very few years. Other types of engine were still made, such as the low-power vertical Bischop engine, in which expansion of the exploded gases raised the piston, which was then driven downwards by atmospheric pressure during its downward stroke.

Owen, Richard (1804–1892) English anatomist and palaeontologist, one of the leading naturalists of the Victorian era.

Born at Lancaster on 20 July 1804, Owen was apprenticed to a local surgeon before studying medicine at Edinburgh University and completing his medical studies at St Bartholomew's Hospital, London. Showing great proficiency in working with specimens, he was soon appointed curator at Bart's, and later became the first Hunterian Professor at the Royal College of Surgeons. Owen was elected fellow of the Royal Society in 1834 and served as Fullerian Professor of Physiology and Comparative Anatomy at the Royal Institution 1858–62. In 1856 he was made the first superintendent of the Natural History Departments of the British Museum, and was later promoted to director when the collections were moved to South Kensington. On his retirement in 1884 this very eminent and highly public scientist was made a knight. He died in London on 18 December 1892.

Owen's early career was marked by his phenomenal output of high-quality zoological identification, description, and classification in the manner of Georges ◊Cuvier. Owen published more than 360 detailed monographs on recent and fossil invertebrates and vertebrates, the most important being concerned with the pearly nautilus, the moa and other birds of New Zealand, the dodo from Mauritius, and the archaeopteryx – his reconstruction of that extinct primitive bird on comparative anatomical principles being regarded as a classic. His *History of British Fossil Reptiles* (1849–84) was a staggering work of patient erudition; he also produced a popular textbook, *Palaeontology* (1860).

Owen never accepted Darwinian evolution. Among other objections, he contended on taxonomic grounds that the doctrine could not explain human beings; he turned them into the single example of a special sub-class of Mammalia. (In response, T H ◊Huxley demonstrated that the anatomical grounds for Owen's taxonomy were illusory.) Owen also fiercely attacked Charles ◊Darwin's mechanism for evolution, denying natural selection. In so far as Owen was prepared to countenance evolution, it was only in terms of the unfolding of a grand plan of Nature, as suggested by the framework of German *Naturphilosophie.*

Further Reading

Gruber, Jacob W and Thackray, John C, *Richard Owen Commemoration: Three Studies,* Natural History Museum, 1992.

Owen, Richard, *The Hunterian Lectures in Comparative Anatomy, May–June 1837,* University of Chicago Press, 1992.

Rupke, Nicolaas A, *Richard Owen: Victorian Naturalist,* Yale University Press, 1994.

P

Paget, James (1814–1899) English surgeon, one of the founders of pathology. He is best remembered for describing two conditions named after him: Paget's disease of the nipple, a precancerous disorder, and Paget's disease of the bone, or osteodystrophia deformans. From a fairly humble beginning he rose to be one of the greatest and most respected surgeons of his time.

Paget was born in Great Yarmouth on 11 January 1814. He went to school in Yarmouth, but had to leave at the age of 13 when his father's business ran into hard times. At 16 he became apprenticed to the local surgeon apothecary, Charles Costerton, and in 1834 his elder brother George paid for him to go to St Bartholomew's Hospital in London, where despite the poor standard of teaching at the time, he gained his membership of the Royal College of Surgeons in 1836. In his struggle to make up his income, Paget took pupils, worked as a sub-editor on the *Medical Gazette*, reported lectures, reviewed books, and translated works. It was not until he became warden of the students' residential college at St Bartholomew's in 1843 that he was able to give up his journalism. He was one of the original 300 fellows of the Royal College of Surgeons of England in 1843, where he later became professor of anatomy and surgery 1847–52. At the age of 33 he became assistant surgeon at St Bartholomew's Hospital, and four years later in 1851 had his own practice in Cavendish Square. In 1878 he tended the Princess of Wales and his fame spread. He became a rich man, and was appointed surgeon extraordinary to Queen Victoria and became a close friend of the royal family. During a postmortem in 1871, Paget contracted a severe infection through a cut, which left him unable to continue his hospital work, although he did maintain his consulting rooms. He received a baronetcy in 1871 and was a member of the General Medical Council and of the senate of the University of London; in 1874 he was president of the Royal College of Surgeons. He died on 30 December 1899, and his funeral was held at Westminster Abbey.

Paget's original clinical descriptions of the two conditions named after him were so accurate that virtually nothing has needed to be added to them since. Paget's disease of the nipple was described in 1874 and is an eczematous skin eruption that indicates an underlying carcinoma of the breast, although the eruption is not simply an extension of the cancer cells inside the breast. Histologically Paget cells can be identified and are pathognomonic of the condition.

When Paget described the disease of the bone in 1877, he referred to it as osteitis deformans. This implies an inflammation of the bone, which is not accurate and it is now called osteodystrophia deformans. Paget did, however, accurately describe this idiopathic condition, which can affect the bones of the elderly, particularly the femora and tibiae in the legs and the bones of the skull. The bones soften, giving rise to deformity of the limbs, which may also fracture easily. If the skull is affected bony changes cause enlargement of the head, and pressure on the VIIIth cranial nerve can cause deafness.

Further Reading

Hanford, James H, 'Dr Paget's library', *Bull Med Lib Ass*, 1945, v 33, pp 91–99.

Roberts, S, *James Paget: The Rise of Clinical Surgery*, Royal Society of Medicine Press Ltd, 1989.

Turner, G Gray, 'What research owes to the Paget tradition', *Fight Dis*, 1937, v 25, pp 33–41 and 52–58.

Paneth, Friedrich Adolf (1887–1958) Austrian chemist known for his contribution to the development of radiotracer techniques and to organic chemistry.

Paneth was born in Vienna on 31 August 1887, the second of the three sons of the physiologist Joseph Paneth. He was educated in Vienna and attended the universities of Munich and Glasgow before obtaining his PhD from Vienna in 1910. From 1912 to 1918 he worked as assistant to Stefan Meyer at the Vienna Institute for Radium Research – in 1913 he spent a short time with Frederick ◊Soddy in Glasgow and visited Ernest ◊Rutherford's laboratory in Manchester. He spent two years, 1917–19, at the Prague Institute of Technology and three, 1919–22, at the University of Hamburg, before going to the University of Berlin. From 1929 to 1933 he was professor and director of the chemical laboratories at the University of Königsberg (now Kaliningrad in Russia).

Because of the growth of the Nazi movement, Paneth left Germany in 1933 and went to Imperial College, London, as a reader and guest lecturer. Six years later he moved to Durham University as professor of chemistry, where he stayed until 1953. During World War II he was head of the chemical division of the Joint British and Canadian Atomic Energy Team in Montréal, and from 1949–55 served as president of the Joint Commission on Radioactivity, an organization of the International Council of Scientific Unions. In 1953 Paneth returned to Germany to become director of the Max Planck Institute for Chemistry in Mainz. He died in Vienna on 17 September 1958.

One of Paneth's first chemical papers was concerned with the acid-catalysed rearrangement of the two organic compounds quinidine and cinchonidine. But he soon became much more involved with radioactive substances. He unsuccessfully tried to chemically separate radium D and thorium B from lead, and eventually realized that they must both be isotopes of lead. In collaboration with the Hungarian chemist Georg von ◊Hevesy he extended this work into research on using radium D and thorium B as indicators – radioactive tracers – to establish the solubility of the slightly soluble compounds lead sulphide and lead chromate.

A similar experiment to try to separate the radioactive products of thorium decay led to the development and isolation of bismuth hydride, BiH_3, and the discovery that radium E and thorium C are bismuth isotopes. It was only by the use of radioactive isotopes that the minute quantities of bismuth hydride formed could be detected. In order to decompose the hydride and concentrate the metal from the unstable hydrides he studied, such as those of bismuth, lead, tin, and polonium, he used a method known as the mirror deposition technique. The metal formed a metallic mirror on the inside of a heated tube through which the hydride was passed. He then developed a better method involving the electrolysis of the metal sulphate. He prepared several grams of a new tin hydride, SnH_4, and made intensive investigations of its properties.

The work on metal hydrides led, in turn, to that on free radicals. In 1929, while at the University of Berlin, Paneth and Wilhelm Hofeditz announced the preparation and identification of the free methyl radical from lead tetramethyl.

Also in the period up to 1929 he developed sensitive methods for determining trace amounts of helium. Using spectroscopy and, later, mass spectroscopy, he determined the helium content of natural gas from various sources, measured its rate of diffusion through glass, measured the amount of helium in rocks and meteorites, and unsuccessfully tried to measure the helium produced by attempted transmutations from light elements into helium. For the remainder of his life from 1929, meteorites dominated his interests. He calculated that the ages of iron meteorites were in the range 10^8 to 10^9 years, and speculated that they were formed within the Solar System.

In the late 1930s Paneth succeeded in obtaining measurable amounts of helium by the neutron bombardment of boron; he had induced an artificial transmutation. He then began to examine stratospheric trace elements. He determined the helium, ozone, and nitrogen dioxide content of the atmosphere. In the course of establishing the extent of gravitational separation of the components of the atmosphere, he found none below 60 km/37 mi but discovered a measurable change in relative concentration above this altitude. He then went back to studying free radicals and explored the use of radioactive isotopes to combine with them in a mirror removal technique.

Papin, Denis (1647–c. 1712) French physicist and technologist who invented a vessel that was the forerunner of the pressure cooker or autoclave.

Papin was born in Blois, France, on 22 August 1647 and studied medicine at Angers University, where he obtained his MD in 1669. His first job was as an assistant to Christiaan ◊Huygens in Paris, and then in 1675 he went to London to assist Robert ◊Hooke (then responsible for the running of the Royal Society), to write letters for a payment of two shillings (10p) each. Papin was not appointed a fellow of the Royal Society until late in the 1680s. In 1680, he returned to Paris to work with Huygens and in 1681 he went to Venice for three years as director of experiments at Ambrose Sarotti's academy. In 1684 he tried to secure the position of secretary of the Royal Society, but Edmond ◊Halley got it and Papin was appointed 'temporary curator of experiments' with a salary of £30 a year. In November 1687 he was appointed to the chair of mathematics at Marburg University and stayed there until 1696 when he moved to Kassel to take up a place in the court of the Landgrave of Hesse. He returned to London in 1707, but by then his friends had gone and there was no position for him at the Royal Society. He drifted into obscurity and died in about 1712 (certainly not later than 1714).

Papin's first scientific work as Huygens's assistant was to construct an air pump and to carry out a number of experiments. Later, with Robert ◊Boyle, he introduced a number of improvements to the air pump and invented the condensing pump. In 1680 they published *A Continuation of New Experiments*. It was while he was with Boyle that he invented the steam digester – a closed vessel with a tightly fitting lid in which water was heated. This was the prototype of the modern pressure cooker, but it is used more extensively in the chemical industry as the autoclave. In Papin's prototype, the steam was prevented from escaping so that a high pressure was generated, causing the boiling point of the water to rise considerably.

Papin invented a safety valve to guard against excessive rises in pressure. This safety valve was of technical importance in the development of steam power. He showed his invention to the Royal Society in May 1679.

In the early 1680s, when he was employed by the Royal Society, he carried out numerous experiments in hydraulics and pneumatics, which were published in *Philosophical Transactions.*

In 1690 Papin suggested that the condensation of steam should be used to make a vacuum under a piston previously raised by the expansion of the steam. This was the earliest cylinder-and-piston steam engine. His idea of using steam later took shape in the atmospheric engine of Thomas ◊Newcomen. His scheme was unworkable, however, because he proposed to use one vessel as both boiler and cylinder. He proposed the first steam-driven boat in 1690 and in 1707 he built a paddle-boat, but the paddles were turned by human power and not by steam.

Also during this period, he considered the idea of a piston ballistic pump with gunpowder and discussed the project with Huygens. In a letter to Gottfried ◊Leibniz on 6 March 1704, he claimed the idea as his own. In 1705, Leibniz sent him a sketch of Thomas ◊Savery's high-pressure steam pump for raising water. In 1707 Papin devised a modification of this, which was workable but not as productive as the original piston model.

Pappus of Alexandria (lived c. AD 300–350) Greek mathematician, astronomer, and geographer whose chief importance lies in his commentaries on the mathematical work of his predecessors.

Nothing is known of his life and many of his writings survive only in translations from the original Greek. According to the *Suda lexicon,* he lived in the time of the emperor Theodosius I (reigned AD 379–95), but the compiler of the *Suda lexicon* was notoriously unreliable and from other sources it appears that Pappus lived rather earlier. The most important piece of evidence is found in his commentary on ◊Ptolemy, in which he writes of an eclipse of the Sun that took place in AD 320 in language that strongly suggests that he himself witnessed the event as a grown man. It is usual, therefore, to place Pappus in the first half of the 4th century.

Pappus' chief works are the *Synagogue* (more commonly referred to as the *Collection*), the commentary on Ptolemy's *Syntaxis* or *Almagest,* and the commentary on ◊Euclid's *Elements.* He wrote also a commentary on Euclid's *Data* and one on the *Anelemma* of Diodorus; neither of these works, however, survives. Pappus may also have written the section from the fifth book onwards of the commentary on Ptolemy's *Harmonica* which was chiefly the

work of Porphyry. More convincingly established is Pappus' authorship of the *Description of the World,* a geographical treatise that has come down to us only in the form of a book written in Armenian and bearing the name of Moses of Khoren as its author. That the treatise does not exist in Greek is no hindrance to attributing it to Pappus because, of all his works, only the *Collection* and the commentary on the *Almagest* survive in their original form. Some scholars believe that the *Description* should be attributed to Anania Shirakatsi, but the consensus is that the work is either a direct translation or a very close paraphrase of Pappus. It should also be mentioned, in a list of Pappus' work, that a 12th-century Arabic manuscript attributes to Pappus the invention of an instrument to measure the volume of liquids. If Pappus did invent such an instrument – and there seems to be no good reason to doubt it – he may have written a treatise on hydrostatics that has been lost to posterity.

By far the most important of Pappus' works is the *Collection.* Without it, much of the geometrical achievement of his predecessors would have been lost for ever. The *Collection* is written in eight parts, of which the first two have never been found; Pappus may have intended it to extend to twelve parts and may indeed have done so. The *Collection* deals with nearly the whole body of Greek geometry, mostly in the form of commentaries on texts that it is assumed the reader has to hand. It reproduces known solutions to problems in geometry; but it also frequently gives Pappus' own solutions, or improvements and extensions to existing solutions. Thus Pappus handles the problem of inscribing five regular solids in a sphere in a way quite different from Euclid, gives a broader generalization than Euclid to the famous Pythagorean theorem, and provides a demonstration of squaring the circle that is quite different from the method of ◊Archimedes (who used a spiral) or that of Nicomedes (who used the conchoid).

Perhaps the most interesting part of the *Collection,* measured by its influence on modern mathematics, is Book VII, which is concerned with the problems of determining the locus with respect to three, four, five, six, or more than six lines. Pappus' work in this field was called 'Pappus' problem' by René ◊Descartes, who demonstrated that the difficulties that Pappus was unable to overcome could be got round by the use of his new algebraic symbols. Pappus thus came to play an important, if minor, role in the founding of Cartesian analytical geometry. And it is another mark of his originality and skill that he spent much time working on the problem of drawing a circle in such a way that it will touch three given circles, a problem sophisticated enough to engage the interest, centuries later, of both François ◊Viète and Isaac ◊Newton.

For his own originality, even if his chief importance is as the preserver of Greek scientific knowledge, Pappus stands (with ◊Diophantus) as the last of the long and distinguished line of Alexandrian mathematicians.

Further Reading

Berboud, Ali, 'Greek Geometrical Analysis', *Centaurus*, 1994, v 37, pp 52–86.

Jones, A (ed), *Pappus of Alexandria*, Sources in the History of Mathematics and Physical Sciences series, Springer-Verlag, 1985, v 8, 2 parts.

Paracelsus, Philippus Aureolus (1493–1541)

Adopted name of Theophrastus Bombastus von Hohenheim. Swiss physician and chemist whose works did much to overthrow the accepted scientific authorities of his day (such as ◊Galen) and to establish the importance of chemistry in medicine. He adopted the name Paracelsus as a claim to superiority over the Roman physician Celsus, whose works had recently been translated.

Paracelsus was born on or about 10 November 1493 in Einsiedeln, Switzerland, the son of a doctor. On his mother's death, he and his father moved to Villach, Austria, where he attended the Bergschule. This local school specialized in teaching mineralogy to students who would later work in the mines nearby. In 1507 he became, like many of his contemporaries, a wandering scholar. He is said to have obtained a baccalaureate in medicine from the University of Vienna, to have been to the University of Basel, and to have studied at several universities in Italy, and may have received a doctorate from Ferrara. He was a military surgeon in Venice in 1521 and then continued his travels as far as Constantinople (now Istanbul in Turkey). He returned to Villach in 1524 and by 1525 had set himself up in medical practice. He was successful enough to be elected professor of medicine at Basel 1527–28. Here he scandalized other academics by lecturing in the vernacular and by his savage attacks on the accepted medical texts. In 1527 he burned the works of Galen and ◊Avicenna in public and the next year was forced to leave Basel. He spent several years travelling once more and then returned to Villach, when he was appointed physician to Duke Ernst of Bavaria, in 1541. He died in Salzburg on 24 September of that year.

Paracelsus substituted the traditional medical theories with an animistic view of nature, believing that all matter possesses its characteristic spirits or life substances, which he called *entia*. He emphasized the importance of the observation of the properties of all things and it was this principle that led him to discover new remedies and means of treatment for many illnesses, some of which he characterized accurately for the first time.

Chemical therapy had been used in the ancient world, although chiefly externally. Paracelsus, however, realized the therapeutic power of chemicals taken internally, although he imposed strict control on their use, dosage, and purity. Paracelsus was extremely successful as a doctor. His descriptions of miners' diseases first identified silicosis and tuberculosis as occupational hazards. He also recognized goitre as endemic and related to minerals in drinking water, and originated a medical account of chorea, rather than believing this nervous disease to be caused by possession by spirits. Paracelsus was the first to recognize the congenital form of syphilis, and to distinguish it from the infectious form. He showed that it could be successfully treated with carefully controlled doses of a mercury compound.

Paracelsus' study of alchemy helped to develop it into chemistry. His investigations produced new, nontoxic compounds for medicinal use; he discovered new substances arising from the reaction of metals and described various organic compounds, including ether. He was the first to devise such advanced laboratory techniques as the concentration of alcohol by freezing. Paracelsus also devised a specific nomenclature for substances already known but not precisely defined. Paracelsian chemicals were introduced into the *London Pharmacopoeia* of 1618, and his attempt to construct a chemical system, grouping chemicals according to their susceptibility to similar processes, was the first of its kind.

The true use of chemistry is not to make gold but to prepare medicines.
PARACELSUS ATTRIBUTED REMARK

Paracelsus' concept of the human being as a 'microcosm' of the natural world led to his theory of an external agency being the source of disease, overturning contemporary views that regarded illness as an imbalance of the four humours (blood, phlegm, choler, and spleen) within the body. His ideas encouraged new modes of treatment supplanting, for example, blood-letting, and opened the way for new ideas on the source of infection.

Despite Paracelsus' mystical preoccupations such as astrology and the use of magic seals and amulets, his importance to the development of science is substantial. He can be regarded as a founder of modern medicine, as he was the first to demand that a doctor should master all those arts then divided between barbers, field surgeons, apothecaries, alchemists, and local 'wise women'. His revolutionary views and vitriolic nature continually involved him in clashes with authority, and his investigations into 'forbidden fields' led to frequent accusations against him of sorcery and heresy. Nevertheless, within his works lie the stepping stones between ancient and modern science.

Further Reading

Grell, Ole P, *Paracelsus: The Man and His Reputation,* Studies in the History of Christian Thought, Brill, 1998, v 85.

Hartmann, Franz, *The Life and Doctrines of Paracelsus,* Health Research, 1998.

Stillman, John M, *Paracelsus: His Personality and Influence as Physician, Chemist, and Reformer,* Kessinger Publishing Company, 1996.

Telepnef, Basilo, *Paracelsus: A Genius Amidst A Troubled World,* Banton Press, 1991.

Weeks, Andrew, *Paracelsus: Speculative Theory and the Crisis of the Early Reformation,* SUNY Series in Western Esoteric Traditions, State University of New York Press, 1996.

Paré, Ambroise (1509–1590) French surgeon and prolific writer justifiably described as the founder of modern surgery.

Paré was born in Bourg-Hersent, Mayenne, in 1509. His father was a valet and a baker and Ambroise received little in the way of formal education. He started his medical apprenticeship with a barber in Angers, continuing his studies in anatomy and surgery with a barber surgeon in Paris 1532–33. He then found a position at the Hotel-Dieu, the largest Paris hospital. In 1536 he became a military surgeon with the army of Marechal Montejan in the Italian campaign. He remained with the army for most of his life and was also surgeon at the courts of Henri II, Francis II, Charles IX, and Henri III.

Paré published several books on surgery concentrating particularly on battle wounds. He abandoned the brutal practice of cauterizing gunshot wounds with hot irons and boiling oil and used instead an ointment made of egg yolk, oil of roses, and turpentine. He had stumbled on this new treatment by accident when he had run out of boiling oil on a busy battlefield and achieved spectacular results by using the ointment. His book on the subject, *La Méthode de traiter les playes faites par les arquebuses et autres bastons au feu/ Methods of Treating Wounds Inflicted by Arquebuses and Other Firearms* (1545), established his reputation and became a standard military textbook in all European armies. It was also translated into Dutch.

Paré advocated the use of ligatures rather than cauterization to close the blood vessels on an amputated limb, a procedure that has been described as the greatest ever advance in surgery. However, this was a skilled operation that required the cooperation of the patient in a long and painful procedure and was not generally practised until the early 18th century, when the screw tourniquet was invented by Jean Petit. Paré also made innovations in the management of difficult childbirth, the extraction of teeth, and the filling of dental cavities. He devised artificial dentures and made plans for prosthetics – an artificial hand made of iron and an artificial eye.

After the Luxemburg campaign in 1552 he was recommended to Henri II and joined his team of surgeons. Sent by the king to Metz, which was under seige, he was taken prisoner by the Duc de Savoie but retrieved his liberty after he had cured an ulcer on the duc's leg. After the death of Henri II he kept his place as court surgeon through the reigns of Francis I, Charles IX, and Henri III. Paré is believed to have been a Huguenot and it is thought that it was through the intervention of Charles IX that he escaped the St Bartholomew's Day Massacre in 1572.

Paré wrote numerous books. In 1549 he published an anatomical handbook for surgeons, *Brève Collection de l'administration économique, avec la manière de conjoindre les os,* and in 1563 *Dix livres de la chirurgie avec le magasin des intruments necessaires a icelle.* He wrote on the subject of plague and leprosy as well as surgery and childbirth. His *Oeuvres complètes/Complete Works* (1575) was translated into several languages. It had been reprinted three times by the time of his death at the age of 80, on 22 December 1590.

Parsons, Charles Algernon (1854–1931) English mechanical engineer who designed and built the first practical steam turbine and developed its use as the motive power for the generation of electricity in power stations, in centrifugal pumps, and, particularly, as a source of power for steamships. In most areas of its application it replaced the much less efficient reciprocating steam engine. To accompany this invention Parsons developed more efficient screw propellers for ships and suitable gearing to widen the turbine's usefulness, both on land and sea. In his later life he designed searchlights and optical instruments, and developed methods for the production of optical glass.

Parsons, the sixth and youngest son of the Earl of Rose, was born in London on 13 June 1854. He came from a talented family. His grandfather had been vice president of the Royal Society and his father was its president. During his youth in Ireland, Parsons was educated by private tutors. When he was 17 he went to Trinity College, Dublin, where he spent two years. From there he went to St John's College, Cambridge, where he gained high honours in mathematics. He began his training in engineering on leaving Cambridge by becoming an apprentice at William Armstrong and Company near Newcastle upon Tyne. After further experience as an engineer he went to the firm of Clarke,

Chapman and Company at Gateshead as a junior partner in charge of their electrical section. It was there that he succeeded in making a practical steam turbine and applied it to the generation of electricity.

In a steam turbine a cylindrical bladed rotor is enclosed within a casing with static blades, and the steam passes between the two, contacting first one set of turbine blades then being directed on to another set designed to work with the same steam at a slightly lower pressure. At the same time the work done by the expansion of the steam aids the rotation produced. Parsons' first machine was used as a turbogenerator for electricity and can now be seen in the Science Museum, London.

In 1889 he formed his own company near Newcastle upon Tyne. He developed turbogenerators of various kinds and, as time went on, increasing capacities, which formed the basic machinery for national (and much of international) electricity production.

From about 1894 Parsons, with the formation of a new company at Wallsend, applied his turbine to various uses. His first venture, the 48-m/100-ft vessel *Turbinia* (displacement 44 tonnes) achieved initially a speed of 20 knots. Even at this high speed he calculated that the output from the turbine (about 1,500 kW/2,000 hp) was not being used efficiently. He designed a propulsion system that incorporated three shafts, each with three propellers. From this new machinery the *Turbinia,* with Parsons at the controls, created quite a stir when it sailed up and down the assembled rows of British and foreign warships at the naval review celebrating the diamond jubilee of Queen Victoria in 1897. *Turbinia* can still seen in the Museum of Science and Industry at Newcastle upon Tyne.

Prompted by the difficulties of realizing the full power output from the turbine at sea, Parsons investigated the loss of efficiency of screw propellers and the phenomenon of cavitation caused by the water not adhering to the propeller blades at high speeds – and the accompanying damage to the blades. Using steam turbines instead of reciprocating steam engines, high speeds – with less vibration – were to be had by ocean liners, and greater efficiency – with increased fuel economy – was obtained by the slower trading vessels. Parsons turbines fitted to the liners *Lusitania* and *Mauritania* developed some 52,000 kW/70,000 hp.

Parson's work on searchlights and specialist marine and other optical instruments was taken up by the Royal Navy and various maritime trading companies. He also revitalized the British optical glass industry and safeguarded its production for possible military applications at a time when it was about to be eclipsed by German companies. He spent much of his life attempting, without success, to make artificial diamonds by the crystallization of carbon at high pressures and temperatures.

Parsons was a man of considerable courage in so far as he often undertook to produce machines far beyond the current limits of design and expertise. He was, without a doubt, one of the greatest engineers of the late 19th and early 20th centuries and was recognized as such by his election to the Royal Society, the award of a knighthood and various honorary degrees, and in being the first engineer to be admitted to the Order of Merit.

His ingenuity has lasted and benefitted humanity in that now there are turbines in use in a large variety of roles, providing the most convenient, useful, and efficient means of converting power into motion. Parsons died while on a cruise to the West Indies on 11 February 1931, aged 76 years.

Parsons, William (1800–1867) 3rd Earl of Rosse. Irish politician, engineer, and astronomer, whose main interest was in rediscovering the techniques used by William ◊Herschel to build bigger and better telescopes. After considerable expense and dedicated effort he succeeded, and with his new instruments made some important observations, particularly of nebulae.

Parsons was born in York on 17 June 1800, but it was at his ancestral home, Birr Castle in County Offaly, that he received his early education. He then attended Trinity College, Dublin, for a year before going to Magdalen College, Oxford, in 1819, and graduating with a first-class degree in mathematics at the age of 22. A political career commensurate with his family's land ownership and title was virtually obligatory for Parsons, as the eldest son, and even while still an undergraduate he was elected to the House of Commons to represent King's County, a seat he then held at Westminster for 13 years. In 1831 he became Lord Lieutenant of County Offaly, and although he retired from parliamentary life in 1834, seven years later he was back, at the House of Lords, an elected Irish representative peer, having succeeded to the title of Rosse on his father's death. During and after the potato famine of 1846, Parsons worked to alleviate the living conditions of his tenants. It was work that Irish landowners were more or less forced to undertake when the government in London delayed aid; but his tenants were grateful to Parsons, and when he died in Monkstown on 31 October 1867, thousands attended his funeral.

The work of William Herschel was a source of fascination to Parsons. Early on he decided that he too would construct enormous telescopes and make great astronomical discoveries. Accordingly, he learned to grind mirrors, made a few small ones, and then began to seek a material capable of being cast as a large mirror. An alloy using copper and tin was considered but found difficult to cast directly. An attempt at another solution, using sectional mirrors surrounding a central disc soldered on to a brass disc, proved unsatisfactory for instruments with an aperture larger than 46 cm/18 in. Subsequently, Parsons developed a way of casting solid discs, designing a mould ventilator that permitted the even cooling of the metal forming the mirror, in an annealing oven. Thirteen years after his experiments began, Parsons was able to construct a 92-cm/36-in mirror in sections; a solid mirror of the same size was completed a year later. And in 1842 Parsons cast the first 1.8-m/72-in disc, the 'Leviathan of Parsonstown', which weighed nearly 4 tonnes and was incorporated into a telescope with a focal length of 16.2 m/54 ft. It took three years to put together, including setting it up on two masonry piers.

At last Parsons was ready for the observational side of his work. And during the next 13 years, he made a number of important observations. His telescope was, after all, the largest in contemporary use, and with it he researched particularly into nebulae. He was the first to remark that some were shaped in a spiral – in fact he went on to find 15 spiral nebulae – and resolved others into clusters of stars. It was he who named the famous Crab nebula.

In constructing his 'Leviathan', Parsons designed a mechanism (since copied by many others) for grinding and polishing metal mirrors. He also invented a clockwork drive for the large equatorial mounting of an observatory. He was even among the first to take photographs of the Moon.

His other interests included a study of problems in constructing iron-armoured ships.

Pascal, Blaise (1623–1662)

French mathematician, physicist, and religious recluse who was not only a scientist anxious to solve some of the problems of the day but also a gifted writer and a moralist. He is remembered not so much for his original creative work – as are his contemporaries René ◊Descartes and Pierre de ◊Fermat – but for his contributions to projective geometry, the calculus of probability, infinitesimal calculus, fluid statics, and his methodology in science generally. Much of his work has become appreciated only during the last 150 years.

Pascal was born on 19 June 1623 at Clermont-Ferrand, the son of a civil servant in the local administration. His mother died when he was only three, and his father – also a respected mathematician – looked after the family and saw to the education of the children. In 1631 they all moved to Paris, where Pascal's sister Jacqueline showed literary talent and Pascal himself displayed mathematical ability. By

Pascal Engraving of French philosopher and mathematician Blaise Pascal whose main work was in the fields of calculus, hydraulics, and probability. In recognition of his work, the SI unit for pressure is called the pascal. It is equal to one newton per square metre. *Mary Evans Picture Library*

1639, when Pascal was 16, he was already participating in the scientific and philosophical meetings run at the Convent of Place Royale by its director, Father Marin Mersenne (1588–1648); some of these meetings were attended also by Descartes, Fermat, and other celebrated figures. The illness and eventual death of his father led Pascal to commit himself to a more spiritual mode of life, one from which he was at times terrified of lapsing. Converted to the rigorous form of Roman Catholicism known as Jansenism in 1646, he finally experienced a fervently spiritual 'night of fire' on 23 November 1654, and from then on wrote only at the direct request of his spiritual advisers, the order of monks at Port Royal. Five years later his health had become poor enough to prevent him from working at all. After 1661, when his sister died, Pascal became even more solitary and his health deteriorated further. His last project was to design a public transport system for Paris. The system was actually inaugurated in 1662, the year Pascal died. He died from a malignant ulcer of the stomach on 19 August 1662 in Paris, aged only 39.

Pascal's first serious work was actually on someone else's behalf. In 1639 Gérard Desargues (1593–1662) published a work entitled *Brouillon project d'une atteinte aux événements des rencontres du cone avec un plan/Experimental Project Aiming to Describe What*

Happens When the Cone Comes in Contact with a Plane, but its content baffled most of the mathematicians of that time because of its style and vocabulary, and the refusal of Desargues to use Cartesian algebraic symbols. Pascal became Desargues's main disciple, and in the following year published his 'Essai pour les coniques' in explanation of the subject. The paper was an immediate success in the mathematical world; that in itself, coupled with the fact that his own algebraic notational system now had strong competition, left Descartes smarting rather, and he thenceforward regarded Pascal as something of an opponent.

The eternal silence of these infinite spaces terrifies me.

BLAISE PASCAL PENSÉES

Grasping the significance of Desargues's work, Pascal used its basic ideas – the introduction of elements at infinity, the definition of a conic as any plane section of a circular cone, the study of a conic as a perspective of a circle, and the involution determined on any straight line by a conic and the opposite sides of an inscribed quadrilateral – and went on to make his first great discovery, now known as Pascal's mystic hexagram. He stated that the three points of intersection of the pairs of opposite sides of a hexagon inscribed in a conic are collinear. By December 1640 he had deduced from this theorem most of the propositions now known to have been contained in the *Conics* of the ancient Greek mathematician ◊Apollonius of Perga. It was not until 1648, however, that Pascal found a geometric solution to the problem of ◊Pappus of Alexandria (which Descartes had used in connection with demonstrating the strength of his new analytical geometry in 1637). Pascal's solution was important because it showed that projective geometry might prove as effective in this field as the Cartesian analytical methods.

The full treatise that Pascal wrote covering the whole subject was never published; the manuscript was seen later only by Gottfried ◊Leibniz. And in fact, because the work of Desargues was so complicated, it was not until the 19th century, with the researches of Jean-Victor ◊Poncelet, that attention was drawn to the work of Pascal.

In 1642, to help his father in his work, Pascal decided to construct an arithmetical machine that would mechanize the processes of addition and subtraction. He devised a model in 1645, and then organized the manufacture and sale of these first calculating machines. (At least seven of these 'computers' still exist. One was presented to Queen Christina of Sweden in 1652.)

Pascal kept up a long correspondence with Fermat on the subject of the calculus of probabilities. Their main interest was in the study of two specific problems: the first concerned the probability that a player will obtain a certain face of a die in a given number of throws; and the second was to determine the (portion of the) stakes returnable to each player of several if a game is interrupted. Pascal was the first to make a comprehensive study of the arithmetical triangle (called the Pascal triangle) that he then used to derive combinatorial analysis. Together with Fermat, he provided the foundations for the calculus of probability in 1657. In 1658 and the next year, Pascal perfected what he called 'the theory of indivisibles' (which he had first referred to in 1654). This was in fact the forerunner of integral calculus, and enabled him to study problems involving infinitesimals, such as the calculations of areas and volumes.

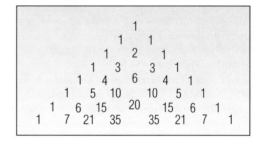

Pascal In Pascal's triangle, each number is the sum of the two numbers immediately above it, left and right – for example, 2 is the sum of 1 and 1, and 4 is the sum of 3 and 1. Furthermore, the sum of each row equals a power of 2 – for example, the sum of the 3rd row is $4 = 2^2$: the sum of the 4th row is $8 = 2^3$.

Pascal's work in hydrostatics was inspired by the experiment of Evangelista ◊Torricelli in 1643, which demonstrated that air pressure supports a column of mercury only about 76 cm/30 in high. In 1647, Pascal succeeded in repeating Torricelli's experiment, but this time using wine and water in tubes 12 m/39 ft high fixed to the masts of ships. He confirmed that a vacuum must exist in the space at the top of the tube, and set out to prove that the column of mercury, wine, or water is held up by the weight of air exerted on the container of liquid at the base of the tube. Pascal suggested that at high altitudes there would be less air above the tube and that the column would be lower. Unable through poor health to undertake the experiment himself, he entrusted it to his brother-in-law who obtained the expected results using a mercury column in the mountains of the Puy de Dôme in 1648.

Pascal's proof that the height of a column of mercury does depend on air pressure led rapidly to investigations of the use of the mercury barometer in weather forecasting. Pascal however turned to a study of pressure in liquids and gases, and found that it is transmitted equally in all directions throughout a fluid and is always exerted perpendicular to any surface in or containing the fluid. This is known as Pascal's principle and it was propounded in the treatise on hydrostatics that Pascal completed in 1654. This principle is fundamental to applications of hydrostatics and governs the operation of hydraulic machines.

Pascal's pioneering work on fluid pressure laid the foundations for both hydraulics and meteorology. In his honour, the SI unit for pressure (equal to one newton per square metre) is called the pascal.

Further Reading

Cole, John Richard, *Pascal: The Man and His Two Loves,* New York University Press, 1995.

Coleman, Francis Xavier Jerome, *Neither Angel Nor Beast: The Life and Work of Blaise Pascal,* Routledge & Kegan Paul, 1986.

Davidson, Hugh M, *Blaise Pascal,* World Authors series, Macmillan Library Reference, 1983.

Nelson, Robert James, *Pascal: Adversary and Advocate,* Harvard University Press, 1981.

Norman, Burford, *Portraits of Thought: Knowledge, Methods, and Styles in Pascal,* Ohio State University Press, 1988.

O'Connell, Marvin R, *Blaise Pascal: Reasons of the Heart,* Library of Religious Biography, Eerdmans Publishing Co, 1997.

Pasteur French chemist and microbiologist Louis Pasteur who developed the germ theory of disease and fermentation. The technique of pasteurization arose from his research into improving the storage properties of wine. *Mary Evans Picture Library*

Pasteur, Louis (1822–1895) French chemist and microbiologist who became world famous for originating the process of pasteurization and for establishing the validity of the germ theory of disease, although he also made many other scientific contributions. Regarded as one of the greatest scientists in history, he received many honours during his lifetime, including the Legion of Honour, France's highest award.

Pasteur was born on 27 December 1822 in Dôle in eastern France, the son of a tanner. While he was still young, his family moved to Arbois, where he attended primary and secondary schools. He was not a particularly good student, but he showed an aptitude for painting and mathematics and his initial ambition was to become a professor of fine arts. He continued his education at the Royal College in Besançon, from which he gained his BA in 1840 and his BSc in 1842. In 1843 Pasteur entered the Ecole Normale Supérieure in Paris, where he began to study chemistry and from which he gained his doctorate in 1847. In the following year he was appointed professor of physics at the Dijon Lycée but shortly afterwards, early in 1849, he accepted the post of professor of chemistry at the University of Strasbourg. In the same

year he married Marie Laurent, the daughter of the university's rector; later they had five children, only two of whom survived beyond childhood. In 1862 Pasteur was elected to the French Academy of Sciences, and in 1863 to a chair at the Ecole Normale Supérieure, a position that was created for him so that he could institute an original teaching programme that related chemistry, physics, and geology to the fine arts. Also in 1863 he became dean of the new science faculty at Lille University, where he initiated the novel concept of evening classes for workers. Meanwhile, in 1857 he had been appointed director of scientific studies at the Ecole Normale Supérieure. Because of the pressure of his research work, Pasteur resigned from the directorship in 1867 but, with financial assistance from Emperor Napoleon III, a laboratory of physiological chemistry was established for him at the Ecole. Pasteur suffered a stroke in 1868 but, although partly paralysed, continued his work. In 1873 he was made a member of the French Academy of Medicine, and in the following year the French parliament granted him a special monetary award to guarantee his financial security while he pursued his research. In 1882 he was elected to the Academic Française. In 1888 the Pasteur Institute was created in Paris for the purpose of continuing Pasteur's pioneering research into rabies; he headed this establishment until his death, in Paris, on 28 September 1895.

Pasteur first gained recognition through his early work on the optical activity of stereoisomers. In 1848 he presented a paper to the Paris Academy of Sciences in which he reported that there are two molecular forms of tartaric acid: one that rotates plane polarized light to the right and another (a mirror image of the first) that rotates it to the left. In addition, he showed that one form can be assimilated by living microorganisms whereas its optical antipode cannot.

Pasteur began his biological investigations – for which he is best known – while at Lille University. After receiving a query from an industrialist about wine- and beermaking, Pasteur started researching the process of fermentation. Using a microscope he found that properly aged wine contains small spherical globules of yeast cells whereas sour wine contains elongated yeast cells. He also proved that fermentation does not require oxygen, but that it nevertheless involves living microorganisms and that to produce the correct type of fermentation (alcohol-producing rather than lactic-acid-producing) it is necessary to use the correct type of yeast. Pasteur also realized that after wine has formed, it should be gently heated to about 50 °C/122 °F to kill the yeast and thereby prevent souring during the ageing process. Pasteurization – as this heating process is called today – is now widely used in the food-processing industry.

In the field of observation, chance only favours those minds which have been prepared.
LOUIS PASTEUR ENCYCLOPAEDIA BRITANNICA 1911, 11TH EDN, VOL 20

Pasteur then turned his attention to spontaneous generation, a problem that had once again become a matter of controversy, despite Lazzaro ◊Spallanzani's disproof of the theory about a century previously. Pasteur showed that dust in the air contains spores of living organisms, which reproduce when introduced into a nutrient broth. Then he boiled the broth in a container with a U-shaped tube that allowed air to reach the broth but trapped dust in the U-bend. He found that the broth remained free of living organisms, thereby again disproving the theory of spontaneous generation.

In the mid-1860s the French silk industry was seriously threatened by a disease that killed silkworms and Pasteur was commissioned by the government to investigate the disease. In 1868 he announced that he had found a minute parasite that infects the silkworms, and recommended that all infected silkworms be destroyed. His advice was followed and the disease eliminated. This stimulated his interest in infectious diseases and, from the results of his previous work on fermentation, spontaneous generation, and the silkworm disease, Pasteur developed the germ theory of disease. This theory was probably the most important single medical discovery of all time, because it provided both a practical method of combating disease by disinfection and a theoretical foundation for further research.

When meditating over a disease, I never think of finding a remedy for it, but, instead, a means of preventing it.
LOUIS PASTEUR ADDRESS AT ECOLE CENTRALE DES ARTS ET MANUFACTURES, PARIS, 15 MAY 1884

Continuing his research into disease, in 1881 Pasteur developed a method for reducing the virulence of certain pathogenic microorganisms. By heating a preparation of anthrax bacilli he attenuated their virulence but found that they still brought about the full immune response when injected into sheep. Using a similar method, Pasteur then inoculated fowl against chicken cholera. He was thus following the work of Edward ◊Jenner, who had first vaccinated against cowpox in 1796. In 1882 Pasteur began what proved to be his most spectacular research: the prevention of rabies. He demonstrated that the causative microorganism (actually a virus, although their existence was not known at that time) infects the nervous system and then, using the dried tissues of infected animals, he eventually succeeded in obtaining an attenuated form of the virus suitable for the inoculation of human beings. The culmination of this work came on 6 July 1885, when Pasteur used his vaccine to save the life of a young boy who had been bitten by a rabid dog. The success of this experiment brought Pasteur even greater acclaim and led to the establishment of the Pasteur Institute in 1888.

Further Reading

Debre, P and Forster, Elborg (transl), *Louis Pasteur*, Johns Hopkins University Press, 1998.

Geison, Gerald L, *The Private Science of Louis Pasteur*, Princeton University Press, 1995.

Parker, Steve, *Louis Pasteur and Germs*, Science Discoveries series, Belitha, 1993.

Yount, Lisa, *Louis Pasteur*, Lucent Books, 1995.

Pauli, Wolfgang (1900–1958) Austrian-born Swiss physicist who made a substantial contribution to

Pauli Austrian-born Swiss physicist Wolfgang Pauli, who won the Nobel Prize for physics in 1945 for his work on atomic structure. He proposed the exclusion principle in 1924, which stated that two electrons could occupy each energy level provided they had different spin. *Mary Evans Picture Library*

USA at the Institute for Advanced Study, Princeton. Pauli became a Swiss citizen on his return and died in Zürich on 15 December 1958.

In the early 1920s, the quantum model of the atom proposed by Bohr in 1913 and elaborated by Sommerfeld in 1916 was in some disarray. Observations of the magnetic anomaly in alkali metals and of the fine spectra of alkaline-earth metals did not accord with the Bohr–Sommerfeld model and it was suggested that the quantum numbers used to describe the energy levels of electrons in atoms in this model would have to be abandoned. Pauli realized that the situation could be explained if a fourth quantum number were added to the three already used (n, l, and m). This number, s, would represent the spin of the electron and would have two possible values. He further proposed that no two electrons in the same atom can have the same values for their four quantum numbers. This is the Pauli exclusion principle, which was announced in 1925.

The exclusion principle means that the energy state of each electron in an atom can be defined by giving a unique set of values to the four quantum numbers. It not only accounted for the unusual properties of the elements that had been observed, but also gave a means of determining the arrangement of electrons into shells around the nucleus that explained the classification of elements into related groups. The successive shells could contain a maximum of 2, 8, 18, 32, and 50 electrons, with most elements containing outer valence electrons and inner complete shells. This discovery was of great importance, for it gave an explanation of the similarities in the properties of elements and revealed the significance of ordering elements by their atomic number.

> *I don't mind you thinking slowly; I mind
> you publishing faster than you think.*
> **WOLFGANG PAULI** ATTRIBUTED (FROM
> H COBLAUS)

quantum theory with the Pauli exclusion principle. For this achievement, Pauli was awarded the 1945 Nobel Prize for Physics. He also postulated the existence of the neutrino.

Pauli was born in Vienna on 25 April 1900. His father was professor of colloid chemistry at the University of Vienna and his godfather was the physicist Ernst ◊Mach. Pauli made rapid progress in science while at school in Vienna and by the time he entered the University of Munich to study under Arnold ◊Sommerfeld, he had already mastered both the special and general theories of relativity proposed by Albert ◊Einstein. Recognizing his ability, Sommerfeld gave Pauli the task of preparing a comprehensive exposition of relativity, as Einstein had not done so. Pauli produced a monograph of extraordinary clarity, an amazing achievement for a student of 19.

Pauli obtained his doctorate in 1922 and then went to Göttingen as an assistant to Max ◊Born. He soon moved to Copenhagen to study with Niels ◊Bohr and then in 1923 went to Hamburg as a *Privatdozent* (unpaid lecturer). In 1928, Pauli was appointed professor of experimental physics at the Eidgenössische Technical University, Zürich. He retained this position until the end of his life, but spent World War II in the

Pauli's other main contribution to physics was made in 1930. The production of beta radiation in a continuous spectrum had puzzled physicists as theory demanded that the spectrum should be discontinuous. It appeared to be caused by a loss of energy when beta particles (electrons) were emitted from atoms, but no explanation could be found for such a loss. It was suggested that the theory of conservation of energy would have to be abandoned, but Pauli proposed that the emission of an electron in beta decay is accompanied by the production of an unknown particle. This particle would have unusual properties, having no charge and zero mass at rest – hence the fact that it had not been observed. Pauli persisted in this opinion, and in 1934 Enrico ◊Fermi confirmed Pauli's view and called the particle the neutrino. It was eventually detected in 1956.

Pauli made substantial advances in our understanding of the nature of the atom by adhering to accepted theories that he felt he could not abandon. He demonstrated exceptional insight, for such an approach usually blinds scientists to progress. Pauli summed up his life in a characteristically succinct fashion when he declared, 'In my youth I believed myself to be a revolutionary; now I see that I was a classicist.'

Further Reading

Lauikainen, K V, *Beyond the Atom: the Philosophical Thought of Wolfgang Pauli*, Springer-Verlag, 1988.

Meyenn, Karl von, *Wolfgang Pauli: Scientific Correspondence with Bohr, Einstein, Heisenberg a o, Part II: 1930–1939*, Sources in the History of Mathematics and Physical Sciences series, Springer-Verlag, 1985, v 6.

Meyenn, Karl von, 'Physics in the making of Pauli's Zurich' in: Sarlemijn, A and Sparnaay, M J (eds), *Physics in the Making: Essays on Developments in 20th Century Physics*, North-Holland, 1989, pp 93–130.

Pauli, Wolfgang; Enz, Charles P; and Meyenn, Karl von (eds); Schlapp, Robert (transl), *Writing on Physics and Philosophy*, Springer-Verlag, 1994.

Weisskopf, Victor F, 'Personal memories of Pauli', *Phys Today*, 1984, v 38 (12), pp 36–41.

Pauling, Linus Carl (1901–1994) US theoretical chemist and biologist whose achievements ranked among the most important of any in 20th-century science. His main contribution was to molecular structure and chemical bonding. He was one of the very few people to have been awarded two Nobel prizes: he received the 1954 Nobel Prize for Chemistry (for his work on intermolecular forces) and the 1962 Peace Prize. Throughout his career his work was noted for the application of intuition and inspiration, assisted by his phenomenal memory; he often carried over principles from one field of science and applied them to another.

Pauling was born in Portland, Oregon, on 28 February 1901, the son of a pharmacist. He began his scientific studies at Oregon State Agricultural College, from which he graduated in chemical engineering in 1922. He then began his research at the California Institute of Technology, Pasadena, gaining his PhD in 1925. From 1925 to 1927 he was a postdoctoral fellow in Europe, where he met the chief scientists of the day who were working on atomic and molecular structure: Arnold ◊Sommerfeld in Munich, Niels ◊Bohr in Copenhagen, Erwin ◊Schrödinger in Zürich, and William Bragg (see William and Lawrence ◊Bragg) in London. He became a full professor at Pasadena in 1931

Pauling US chemist and biologist Linus Pauling who studied the nature of the chemical bond. Pauling held strong pacifist views, and was awarded the Nobel Peace Prize in 1962 for his work in support of a ban on nuclear testing. *Mary Evans Picture Library*

and left there in 1936 to take up the post of director of the Gates and Crellin Laboratories, which he held for the next 22 years. He also held university appointments at the University of California, San Diego, and Stanford University, and during the 1960s spent several years on a study of the problems of war and peace at the Center for the Study of Democratic Institutions at Santa Barbara, California. His last appointment was as director of the Linus Pauling Institute of Science and Medicine at Menlo Park, California.

Pauling's early work reflects his European experiences. In 1931 he published a classic paper, 'The nature of the chemical bond', in which he used quantum mechanics to explain that an electron-pair bond is formed by the interaction of two unpaired electrons, one from each of two atoms, and that once paired these electrons cannot take part in the formation of other bonds. It was followed by the book *Introduction to Quantum Mechanics* (1935), of which he was coauthor. He was a pioneer in the application of quantum mechanical principles to the structures of molecules, relating them to interatomic distances and bond angles by X-ray and electron diffraction, magnetic effects, and thermochemical techniques.

It was Pauling who introduced the concept of hybrid orbitals in molecules to explain the symmetry exhibited by carbon atoms in most of their compounds. The electons in the ground state and in the excited state of the carbon atom can be represented as follows:

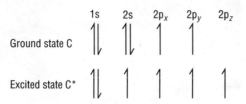

One of the 2p electrons can then form sp hybrid orbitals with the 2s electron, with two 2p atomic orbitals remaining.

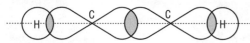

In acetylene (ethyne), for example, the overlap of two sp hybrid orbitals between two carbon atoms results in a linear molecule. A hydrogen atom is bonded to each end by overlap between the carbons' sp orbitals and the s orbitals of the hydrogens. (The remaining carbon p orbitals also overlap to form two π bonds, which, together with the bond just described, account for the traditional triple bond in this molecule.)

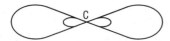

The structures of many other organic molecules can be explained in a similar way.

Pauling also investigated the electronegativity of atoms and polarization (movement of electrons) in chemical bonds. He assigned electronegativities on a scale up to 4.0. A pair of electrons in a bond are pulled preferentially towards an atom with a high electronegativity. In hydrogen chloride, HCl, for example, hydrogen has an electronegativity of 2.1 and chlorine of 3.5. The bonding electrons are pulled towards the chlorine atom, giving it a small excess negative charge (and leaving the hydrogen atom with a small excess positive charge), polarizing the hydrogen–chlorine bond:

$$H - Cl \qquad H \overset{\bullet\bullet}{\underset{\bullet\bullet}{\times}} Cl \qquad H \rightarrow Cl \qquad \overset{\delta+ \quad \delta-}{H - Cl}$$

electron pair pulled towards chlorine atom · · · · · · · · · polarized molecule

Electronegativity values can be used to show why certain substances, such as hydrochloric acid, are acid, whereas others, such as sodium hydroxide, are alkaline.

electronegativities of some elements			
H 2.1			
C 2.5	N 3.0	O 3.5	F 4.0
Si 1.8	P 2.1	S 2.5	Cl 3.0
Ge 1.8	As 2.0	Se 2.4	Br 2.8

For compounds whose molecules cannot be represented unambiguously by a single structure, Pauling introduced the idea of resonance hybridization. An example is carbon dioxide, CO^2:

$$O = C = O \qquad O \leftarrow C \equiv O \qquad O \equiv C \rightarrow O$$

Resonance hybrids (canonical forms) of carbon dioxide.

The true structure is regarded as an intermediate between two or more theoretically possible structures, which are termed canonical forms.

These and Pauling's other ideas on chemical bonding are fundamental to modern theories of molecular structure. Much of this work was consolidated in his book *The Nature of the Chemical Bond* (1939).

In the 1940s Pauling turned his attention to the chemistry of living tissues and systems. He applied his knowledge of molecular structure to the complexity of life, principally to proteins in blood. With Robert Corey, he worked on the structures of amino acids and polypeptides. They proposed that many proteins have structures held together with hydrogen bonds, giving them helical shapes. This concept assisted Francis ◊Crick and James ◊Watson in their search for the structure of DNA, which they eventually resolved as a double helix.

In his researches on blood, Pauling investigated immunology and sickle-cell disease. Later work confirmed his hunch that the disease is genetic and that normal haemoglobin and the haemoglobin in abnormal 'sickle' cells differ in electrical charge. Throughout the 1940s he studied living materials; he also carried out research on anaesthesia. At the end of this period he published two textbooks, *General Chemistry* (1948) and *College Chemistry* (1950), which became academic bestsellers.

Like many of his contemporaries, Pauling became concerned about the proliferation of nuclear weapons and their atmospheric testing during the 1950s. He presented to the United Nations a petition signed by 11,021 scientists from 49 countries urging an end to nuclear-weapons testing, and during the 1960s spent several years on a study of the problems of war and peace at the Center for the Study of Democratic Institutions in Santa Barbara, California. For these efforts he was awarded the Nobel Peace Prize in 1962, the year in which the International Nuclear Test Ban Treaty was signed.

Further Reading

Goertzel, Ted and Goertzel, Ben, *Linus Pauling: A Life in Science and Politics*, Basic Books, 1996.

Hager, Thomas, *Force of Nature: The Life of Linus Pauling*, Simon and Schuster, 1995.

Hager, Thomas, *Linus Pauling and the Chemistry of Life*, Oxford Portraits in Science series, Oxford University Press, 1998.

Maksic, Zvonimir B and Eckert-Maksic, Mirjana, *Molecules in Natural Science and Medicine: An Encomium for Linus Pauling*, Ellis Horwood, 1991.

Newton, David E, *Linus Pauling: Scientist and Advocate*, Makers of Modern Science series, Facts on File, 1994.

Serafini, Anthony, *Linus Pauling: A Man and His Science*, Simon and Schuster, 1989.

Pavlov, Ivan Petrovitch (1849–1936) Russian physiologist, best known for his systematic studies of the conditioning of dogs and other animals. For his observations on the gastrointestinal secretion in animals he received the 1904 Nobel Prize for Physiology or Medicine.

Pavlov Russian physiologist Ivan Petrovich Pavlov who studied conditioned reflexes and the physiology of digestion. Most of his work was carried out in St Petersburg, Russia. *Mary Evans Picture Library*

Pavlov was born in Ryazan on 24 September 1849. He decided to follow in the footsteps of his father, the local priest, and entered a theological college. In 1870, however, he left the seminary to study chemistry and physiology at the University of St Petersburg. There he was taught by the chemists Dmitri ⬧Mendeleyev and Alexander Butlerov (1828–1886). He received his medical degree in 1879 from the Imperial Medical Academy, St Petersburg, and his PhD from the military academy there in 1883. From 1884 to 1886 he studied cardiovascular and gastrointestinal physiology in Germany, under Karl ⬧Ludwig in Leipzig and Rudolf Heidenhain in Breslau (now Wrocław in Poland). He researched at the Botkin laboratory in St Petersburg 1888–90 and in 1890 was appointed professor of physiology at the Imperial Medical Academy, where he remained until he resigned in 1924. He died in St Petersburg (then named Leningrad) on 27 February 1936.

Pavlov's first unaided research was on the physiology of the circulatory system, studying cardiac physiology and the regulation of blood pressure. Using experimental animals, he became a surgeon of some distinction, a typical example of his experiments being the dissection of the cardiac nerves of a living dog to show how the nerves that leave the cardiac plexus control heartbeat strength.

During the years from 1890 to 1900, Pavlov investigated the secretory mechanisms of digestion. He developed an operation to prepare an ancillary miniature stomach or pouch, isolated from salivary and pancreatic secretions but with its vagal-nerve supply intact. In this way he was able to observe the gastrointestinal secretion of a living animal.

Pavlov then went on to develop the idea of the conditional reflex – the discovery for which he is most famous. Pavlov confined a dog in a soundproof room, in order to ensure that there were no distracting influences such as extraneous sounds and smells. The dog was held in a loose harness so that it could not move about too much. Food was delivered to it by an automatic apparatus operated from outside the room, so that the dog was fed at an appropriate moment without direct interference from the person directing the experiment. The flow of saliva from the dog's parotid gland was collected in a small measuring tube attached to the animal's cheek. The experiment was continued until the dog became used to the artificial situation. Pavlov discovered that if a neutral stimulus, such as a bell, was presented simultaneously with a natural stimulus to salivate (such as the sight of food) and the combination repeated often enough, the sound of the bell alone caused salivation.

Pavlov termed salivation the 'unconditioned reflex' and food the 'unconditioned stimulus'. The sound of the bell is the 'conditioned stimulus' and the salivation caused by the bell alone the 'conditioned reflex'. Many inborn reflexes may be conditioned by Pavlov's method, including responses involving the skeletal muscles (knee-jerking and blinking), as well as responses of the smooth muscles and glands.

Experiment alone crowns the efforts of medicine, experiment limited only by the natural range of the powers of the human mind. Observation discloses in the animal organism numerous phenomena existing side by side, and interconnected now profoundly, now indirectly, or accidentally. Confronted with a multitude of different assumptions the mind must guess the real nature of this connection.

IVAN PAVLOV EXPERIMENTAL PSYCHOLOGY
AND OTHER ESSAYS, PT X

A similar approach was developed in Pavlov's work relating to human behaviour and the nervous system, all the time emphasizing the importance of conditioning. He deduced that the inhibitive behaviour of a psychotic person is a means of self-protection. The person shuts out the world and, with it, all damaging stimuli. Following this theory, the treatment of psychiatric patients in Russia involved placing a sick person in completely calm and quiet surroundings.

Pavlov's study of the normal animal in natural conditions enabled him to add greatly to scientific knowledge. He also demonstrated the necessity of providing the right situation for completely objective study and measurement of behaviour, and greatly improved operative and post-operative conditions for animals.

In 1897 Pavlov summarized his findings in his Nobel prizewinning work, *Lectures on the Work of the Principal Digestive Gland.*

Further Reading

Babkin, B P, *Pavlov: A Biography,* Victor Gollancz, 1951.
Frolov, Yuri Petrovich, *Pavlov and His School: The Theory of Conditioned Reflexes,* Kegan, 1937.
Strelau, Jan, *Temperament – Personality – Activity,* Academic Press, 1983.
Wells, Harry Kohlsaat, *Ivan P Pavlov: Toward a Scientific Psychology and Psychiatry,* Pavlov and Freud series, International Publishers, 1956, v 1.

Payne-Gaposchkin, Cecilia Helena (1900–1979)
English-born US astronomer and author whose interest in stellar evolution and galactic structure led to important research in the study of variable, binary, and eclipsing stars.

Payne-Gaposchkin was born Cecilia Helena Payne in Wendover, Buckinghamshire, on 10 May 1900. She attended schools in Wendover and London before entering Newnham College at Cambridge University in 1919. Although her scientific interests were not at first clearly defined, contact with such eminent astronomers as Arthur ◊Eddington quickly induced her to choose astronomy as her main interest and career. After graduation in 1923, she went to the Harvard College Observatory in Cambridge, Massachusetts, to continue her studies under Harlow ◊Shapley. For her research into stellar atmospheres she was awarded her PhD in 1925, and in 1927 was appointed an astronomer at the observatory. In 1938 she was made Phillips Astronomer at Harvard, before being awarded the chair in astronomy there in 1956 (the first woman to receive such an appointment at Harvard).

The author of many scientific papers, Payne-Gaposchkin also wrote a number of successful books on astronomical topics, ranging from introductory texts for the layperson to erudite academic monographs on specialized subjects. Her introductory textbook, first published in 1953, was revised with the help of her daughter in 1970. She died on 7 December 1979.

Stellar astronomy held a prominent place in Payne-Gaposchkin's research from an early stage in her career. One of her earliest significant findings, published in 1925, was the discovery of the relationship between the temperature and spectral class of a star. She continued to employ a variety of spectroscopic techniques in the investigation of stellar properties and composition, and her further investigation of stellar atmospheres during the 1920s led her to encounter some of the first indications of the overwhelming abundance of the lightest elements (hydrogen and helium) in the Galaxy.

During the 1930s Payne-Gaposchkin concentrated increasingly on the study of variable stars; she was particularly concerned to use the information she obtained towards an improvement in the understanding of galactic structure. Much of this work, especially the studies of the Large and Small Magellanic Clouds, was carried out in collaboration with her husband, Sergei Gaposchkin.

Other major areas of her interest included the devising of methods to determine stellar magnitudes, the position of variable stars on the Hertzsprung–Russell diagram, and novae.

Peano, Giuseppe (1858–1932) Italian mathematician who applied the rigorous and axiomatic methods used in mathematics to his study of logic. He is chiefly remembered for his concise logical definitions of natural numbers, devised – not entirely by himself – in order to derive a complete system of notation for logic, and for his discovery in analysis of a curve that fills topological space.

Peano was born on 27 August 1858 in Spinetta, near Cuneo. Living on a farm, he was educated locally until the age of 12 or 13, when he was sent to Turin to receive private lessons. In 1876 he won a scholarship to the Collegio delle Provincie, Turin University. On graduating, he joined the staff of the university and remained there for the rest of his life, first becoming a professor there in 1890. By that time he had already held a professorial appointment for four years, teaching at Turin Military Academy; he retired from this concurrent post in 1901. During his lifetime he received several honours and awards, and participated actively within the Turin Academy of Sciences. He died of a heart attack on 20 April 1932 and, by his request, was buried in Turin General Cemetery; his remains were removed to the family tomb in Spinetta in 1963.

Peano was a pioneer in symbolic logic and a fervent promoter of the axiomatic method – but he himself considered that his work in analysis was more important. It was carried out mainly in the 1880s while Peano was investigating the integrability of functions. In 1886 he was the first to show that the first-order differential equation $dy/dx = f(x,y)$ was solvable using only the one assumption that f is continuous. In 1890 he generalized this result, and in his published study gave the first explicit statement of the axiom of choice.

His first work in logic was published in 1888. It contained his rigorously axiomatically derived postulates for natural numbers which received considerable acclaim, although he studiously acknowledged his debt for some of the work to Richard ◊Dedekind, who had also published during the same year. The postulates are nevertheless now known as the Peano axioms. They formed the basis on which Peano went on to found his system of mathematical notation for logic; *Formulario mathematico* (1895–1908), comprising his work and that of collaborators, contained 4,200 theorems. Later, Bertrand ◊Russell was to say that he reached a turning point in his own life on meeting Peano, and – indeed – part of Peano's work was used in Russell's *Principia Mathematica*.

Peano also applied the axiomatic method to other fields, such as geometry, first in 1889 and again in 1894. A treatise on this work contained the beginnings of geometrical calculus.

His name is in addition particularly associated with the discovery of the 'Peano curves' that fill a space (such as a square), and that are used in topology. He provided new definitions of the length of an arc of a curve and of the area of a surface. He determined an error term in Simpson's formula and became interested in errors in numerical calculations; and he developed a theory of gradual operations that led to new methods for resolving numerical equations.

After 1900, he changed his interests slightly, and created an international language that never really caught on. Between 1914 and 1919 he organized conferences for secondary-school mathematics teachers in Turin. Finally, he became a mathematical historian and recorded many exact origins of mathematical terms and first applications of symbols and theorems.

Pearson, Karl (1857–1936) English mathematician and biometrician who is chiefly remembered for his crucial role in the development of statistics as applied to a wide variety of scientific and social topics.

Pearson was born in London on 27 March 1857. He was tutored at home, except for a period 1866–73 when he attended University College School. He began his university studies at King's College, Cambridge, in 1875, where an indication of Pearson's somewhat uncompromising and unconventional spirit is found in his successful pressuring of the authorities to abolish the mandatory classes in divinity for undergraduates. Pearson graduated with high honours in 1879, and was awarded a fellowship of the college 1880–86 that gave him financial independence without obligation and enabled him to travel and study as he pleased. He visited universities in Germany, took a degree in law in 1881 (although he never practised), and was awarded his master's degree in 1882. In 1884 – still officially a fellow of King's College – Pearson was named Goldsmid Professor of Applied Mathematics and Mechanics at University College, London; he was to hold this post until 1911 although his most productive work during the period was carried out elsewhere. He was also appointed lecturer in geometry at Gresham College, London, in 1891, which required him to give a short series of lectures each year. It was from them on that Pearson became interested in the development of statistical methods for the investigation of evolution and heredity. His efforts in this aim were most fruitful, and were recognized by his election as fellow of the Royal Society in 1896 (which awarded him its Darwin Medal in 1898). He then founded and became editor (until his death) of *Biometrika*, a journal established to publish work on statistics as applied to biological subjects. His work on eugenics led to his appointment as head of the Laboratory of Eugenics at London University upon Francis ◊Galton's retirement in 1906. In 1911 he became the first Galton Professor of Eugenics, a post he retained until 1933, when he retired to become emeritus professor. (His department was then split into two sections, one of which was headed by Pearson's son.) Pearson continued to work in his department until his death in Coldharbour, Surrey, on 27 April 1936.

During the early years of Pearson's career he did little work in mathematics, concentrating instead on law and political issues. His appointment to the Goldsmid Chair required him to focus his attentions on academic duties and on writing. A further marked change overtook his life in the early 1890s with the publication of Francis Galton's book *Natural Inheritance,* and with Pearson's exposure to the ideas of Walter Weldon, the newly appointed professor of zoology at University College.

Weldon was interested in the application of Galton's methods for correlation and regression to the investigation of the validity of Charles ◊Darwin's model of natural selection. Pearson threw himself into this project with great vigour, examining graphical methods for data presentation, studying probability theory and concepts such as standard deviation (a term he himself introduced in 1893, although the idea was by then nearly a century old), and more complex distribution patterns. He submitted many papers on statistical methods to the Royal Society of London, but encountered some stiff opposition to his mathematical approach to biological material. It was this that prompted him to launch his own journal, *Biometrika.*

Early in his investigation he determined a method for finding values for the parameters required to describe a particular distribution. Another major achievement was his classification of the different types of curves produced in the plotting of data into general types. This contributed to putting the Gaussian (or 'normal') distribution into more realistic perspective.

Pearson's discoveries included the Pearson coefficient of correlation (1892), the theory of multiple and partial correlation (1896), the coefficient of variation (1898), work on errors of judgement (1902), and the theory of random walk (1905). The last theory has since been applied to the study of random processes in many fields. In addition, Pearson's *Biometrika* for 1901 is a book of tables of the ordinates, integrals, and other properties of Pearson's curves, and was of great practical use in making statistical methods accessible to a large number of scientists.

Perhaps the most familiar of Pearson's achievements was his discovery in 1900 of the χ^2 (chi-squared) test applied to determine whether a set of observed data deviates significantly from what would have been predicted by a 'null hypothesis' (that is, totally at random). Pearson also demonstrated that it could be applied to examine whether two hereditary characteristics (such as height and hair colour) were inherited independently.

Weldon's death in 1906 dealt a severe blow to Pearson's work in the field of mathematics as applied to biology; Pearson himself lacked the biological background to keep up with the increasingly sophisticated developments in the field of genetics. A great controversy had grown up around the approach of Weldon – who believed in gradual but continuous evolution – as against that of the followers of Gregor ◊Mendel, such as William ◊Bateson – who believed in intermittent variation. Pearson felt that Mendel's results were not incompatible with a statistical approach, although many Mendelians were convinced that they were. But it was the equally celebrated statistician Ronald ◊Fisher who was ultimately able to bring about the beginnings of a reconciliation between the two approaches.

During the rest of Pearson's career he concentrated on the establishment of a thriving department dedicated to the training of postgraduate students so that statistical techniques might be applied to subjects in many areas of academic study. He also worked on eugenics, examining the relative importance of environment and heredity in disorders such as tuberculosis and alcoholism, and in the incidence of infant mortality.

Peierls, Rudolf Ernst (1907–1995) German-born British physicist who made contributions to quantum theory and to nuclear physics.

Peierls was born in Berlin on 5 June 1907. He was educated at the Humboldt School, Oberschöneweide, Berlin, and then at the University of Berlin. He studied with Arnold ◊Sommerfeld in Munich, with Werner ◊Heisenberg in Leipzig, and with Wolfgang ◊Pauli in Zürich. From 1929 to 1932, he worked as Pauli's research assistant at the Federal Institute of Technology in Zürich. He held a Rockefeller Fellowship in Rome and Cambridge 1932–33, and was an honorary research fellow at Manchester University 1933–35. He then became an assistant in research for the Royal Society at the Mond Laboratory in Cambridge in 1935, and in 1937 he was appointed professor of mathematical physics (formerly called applied mathematics) at the University of Birmingham. Peierls worked on the Atomic Project in Birmingham 1940–43 and in the USA 1943–46. He then returned to Birmingham until 1963, when he became Wykeham Professor of Physics at Oxford University. From 1974 to 1977, he was professor of physics at the University of Washington, Seattle. His many honours included a knighthood in 1968 and the award of the Royal Medal from the Royal Society in 1959, the Max Planck Medal of the Association of German Physical Societies in 1963, and the Enrico Fermi Award of the US Department of Energy in 1980.

Peierls began his research in 1928, a very exciting time in the development of quantum theory. The laws of quantum mechanics had been formulated consistently and now was the time to begin to apply them to the many unexplained phenomena in the fields of atomic, molecular, and solid-state physics. His first work was on the theory of solids and concerned a phenomenon called the Hall effect. Then, in 1929, he developed the theory of heat conduction in nonmetallic crystals, concluding that the thermal conductivity of a large perfect crystal should grow exponentially at low temperatures. This was not verified experimentally until 1951. Peierls also proposed a general theory of the diamagnetism of metals.

In nuclear physics, Peierls contributed to the early theory of the neutron–proton system and, in 1938, gave the first complete treatment of resonances in nuclear collisions. During World War II, he was concerned with atomic energy. Uranium fission and the emission of secondary neutrons had been discovered and the possibility of releasing nuclear energy was of wide interest. In 1940, Otto ◊Frisch and Peierls showed that a simple estimate of the energy released in a chain reaction indicated that a fission bomb would make a weapon of fantastic power. They drew the attention of the British government to this in 1940, and Peierls was placed in charge of a small theoretical group concerned with evaluating the chain reaction and its efficiency. In 1943, when the UK decided not to continue its work on nuclear energy, Peierls moved to the USA to help in the work of the Manhattan Project, first in New York and then at Los Alamos.

Pelletier, Pierre-Joseph (1788–1842) French chemist whose extractions of a range of biologically active compounds from plants founded the chemistry of the alkaloids. The most important of his discoveries was quinine, used against malaria.

Pelletier was born in Paris on 22 March 1788, the son of a distinguished chemist and pharmacist. He studied at the Ecole de Pharmacie, qualifying in 1810. He was awarded his doctorate in 1812 and three years later was appointed assistant professor of natural history and drugs at the school. He was promoted to full professor in 1825 and in 1832 made assistant director of the school itself. He was elected to the French Academy in 1840, the same year in which illness forced him to retire from the Ecole de Pharmacie. He died in Paris on 19 July 1842.

Pelletier's early career involved analysing gum resins and plant colourings. In 1813, working with the physiologist François ◊Magendie, he produced reports on opopanax, sagapenum, asafoetida, myrrh, galbanum, and caranna gum. His first major success came in 1817 when he discovered the emetic substance in ipecacuanha root; he called it emetine.

The following four years were particularly productive. Together with Joseph Caventou he investigated the action of nitric acid on the nacreous material of human gall stones and the green pigment in leaves, which they named chlorophyll. In 1818 Pelletier derived crotonic acid from croton oil and carried out an analysis of carmine from cochineal. Pelletier and Caventou then isolated ambrein from ambergris. However, it was their joint discovery of the alkaloids in plants that brought recognition on an international scale: strychnine in 1818, brucine and veratrine in 1819, and – most important of all – quinine in 1820. Quinine is the chief alkaloid in cinchona bark and for the next hundred years was the only effective treatment for malaria, representing the first successful use of a chemical compound in combating an infectious disease.

During the following 20 years Pelletier expanded his alkaloid and phytochemical research. In 1823, with Jean Baptiste ◊Dumas, he proved the presence of nitrogen in alkaloids, something he had failed to confirm in his earlier work with Caventou. He later carried out researches on strychnine and developed procedures for its extraction from nux vomica. He also made chemical examinations of upas, improved the method of manufacturing quinine sulphate, and isolated cahinca acid, the bitter crystalline substance from cahinca root.

In 1832 Pelletier documented his discovery of narceine, a new opium alkaloid; he also claimed to have been the first to isolate thebaine (which he called paramorphine). He went on to study the oily hydrocarbon by-products of the destructive distillation of amber and bitumen. In a similar study 1837–38, focusing on a pine resin by-product used in the production of illuminating gas, he discovered a substance he called retinaphte, later known as toluene (now methylbenzene).

Few people have discovered as many pharmaceutically important natural products as Pelletier did. Their powerful effects and their use in medical practice introduced specific chemical compounds into pharmacology instead of the imprecise plant extracts and mixtures used previously.

Pelton, Lester Allen (1829–1918) US engineer who developed a highly efficient water turbine used to drive mechanical devices and hydroelectric power turbines using large heads of water.

After spending his youth in Vermillion, Ohio, the 20-year-old Pelton, then a carpenter, went to California in search of gold. He failed (like thousands of others) in his quest, but it was while involved in gold-mining that he made a discovery that led him to his invention.

Water wheels were used at the mines to provide power for machinery. The energy to drive these wheels was supplied by powerful jets of water that struck the base of the wheel on flat-faced vanes. In time, these vanes were replaced by hemispherical cups, with the jet striking the centre of the cup. Pelton noticed that one of the water wheels appeared to be rotating faster than usual. It turned out that this was because the wheel had become loose on its axle, and the water jet was striking the inside edge of the cups, rather than the centre.

Pelton went away to reconstruct what he had seen, finding again that the wheel rotated more rapidly and hence developed more power. Working on the construction of stamp mills at Camptonville in California, Pelton found that by using split cups the effect could be enhanced, and by 1879 he had tested a prototype at the University of California. This was so successful that he was awarded a prize. A patent was granted in 1889, and he later sold the rights to the Pelton Water Wheel Company of San Francisco.

By 1890, Pelton wheels developing hundreds of horsepower at efficiencies of more than 80% were in operation. Efficiencies of more than 90% were being achieved using the wheel in hydroelectric schemes of thousands of horsepower by the time of Pelton's death in 1910. The Pelton wheel remains the only hydraulic turbine of the impulse type in common use today.

Pennington, Mary Engle (1872–1952) US chemist known chiefly for her pioneering work in food refrigeration.

Mary Pennington was born in Nashville, Tennessee, on 8 October 1872. She gained an interest in chemistry at an early age and after graduating from high school in 1890 she went to the Towne Scientific School of the University of Pennsylvania where she studied chemistry and biology. She completed the course for a BS in 1892 but was denied a degree on account of her sex and was awarded a certificate of proficiency. She completed her PhD at the University of Pennsylvania in 1895, majoring in chemistry and then worked for two more years at the university as a fellow in botany. After a year at Yale as a fellow in physiological chemistry, Pennington returned to Philadelphia and in 1898 opened her own Philadelphia Clinical Laboratory. She was given a post as a lecturer at the Women's Medical College at Pennsylvania, which she held until 1906. She passed civil-service examinations and in 1907 was appointed as a bacterial chemist in the Bureau of Chemistry of the US Department of Agriculture, being made head the new Food Research Laboratory in 1908. In 1919 she moved to New York City to the American Balsa Company, manufacturers of insulating materials, leaving after three years to be an independent consultant on the storage, handling, and transportation of perishable goods. Pennington never retired and died in New York on 27 December 1952.

Pennington achieved renown for her pioneering work on food preservation. In Philadelphia, from research into the preservation of dairy products, she developed standards of milk inspection that were later used by health boards across the USA. During World War I she conducted experiments into railroad refrigeration cars and recommended standards that were to remain in use into the 1940s. As a consultant, she turned her interest to frozen food, not only carrying out research into food processing but also designing both industrial and household refrigerators. She published widely in technical journals and government reports and coauthored the book *Eggs* (1933). Through her research, Pennington was awarded the Garvan Medal, awarded annually to a US woman chemist, and was the first female member of the American Society of Refrigerating Engineers. She was vice president of the American Institute of Refrigeration.

Pennycuick, Colin James (1933–) English biologist who is best known for his extremely detailed studies of flight.

Pennycuick was born in Virginia Water, Surrey, on 11 June 1933, the son of an army officer. He graduated from Merton College, Oxford, in 1956 and obtained his doctorate from Peterhouse College, Cambridge, in 1962. In 1964 he became a lecturer in zoology at Bristol University, with a break 1971–73 while he was researching at Nairobi University in Kenya. He was reader in zoology at Bristol 1975–83 and then moved to the USA to become Maytag Professor of Ornithology at the University of Miami 1987–92. In 1993 he returned to Bristol University to become research professor in zoology.

Pennycuick's research is unusual in that it interrelates an extremely large number of factors and therefore gives a very detailed account of the various processes involved in flight. In flying vertebrates, for example, he has investigated the mechanics of flapping; the aerodynamic effects of the feet and tail; the physiology of gaseous exchange; heat disposal; the relationship between the size and anatomy of a flying creature and the power it develops; and the frequency of wing beats. In applying the results of his research to bird migration he discovered that many migratory birds have minimal energy reserves and must stop to feed at regular intervals. Therefore the destruction of the intermediate feeding places of these birds could lead to their extinction, even if their summer and winter quarters are conserved. Pennycuick has also hypothesized that migratory birds navigate using the Sun's altitude and its changing position.

Penrose, Roger (1931–) English mathematician who, through his theoretical work, has made important contributions to the understanding of astrophysical phenomena. He has examined especially those anomalies in space–time, the singularities known as black holes, that occur when a sufficiently large mass is contained within a sufficiently small volume so that its gravitational pull prevents the escape of any radiation.

Penrose was born the son of an eminent English human geneticist, Lionel Sharples Penrose (1898–1972), in Colchester, Essex, on 8 August 1931. He grew up amid a family tradition of scholarship and creativity, and completed his education at University College, London. Even as he worked for his doctorate at Cambridge in 1957, Penrose and his father were devising geometrical figures of which the construction is three-dimensionally impossible. (Published the following year in the *British Journal of Psychology,* they became well known when incorporated by the Dutch artist M C Escher into a couple of his lithographs.) A series of lecturing and research posts followed, both in the UK (London and Cambridge) and the USA (Princeton, Syracuse, and Texas). In 1966 Penrose was made professor of applied mathematics at Birkbeck College, London. He was Rouse Ball Professor of Mathematics at Oxford University 1975–83 (emeritus thereafter). Since 1993 he has been Francis and Helen Pentz Distinguished Visiting Professor of Physics and Mathematics at Penn State University, USA. He was elected a fellow of the Royal Society of London in 1972 and a foreign associate of the US National Academy of Sciences in 1998. He was knighted in 1994.

Penrose's early work in mathematics included the formulation of some of the fundamental theorems that describe black holes. The explanation of the occurrence of black holes in terms of gravitational collapse is now usually given in a form that owes a great deal to Penrose's work in stressing the importance of space–time geometry. A model of the behaviour of stars that collapse upon themselves had first been proposed by Oppenheimer and Snyder in 1939 and their results have been proved valid to a remarkable degree by later work. Their model of spherical collapse, together with an interest in gravitational collapse stemming from study of black holes, led to vigorous research on the dynamics and the inevitability of collapse to a singularity. The most important result of such research was a set of theorems formulated by Penrose and Stephen ◊Hawking in 1964, which extend the dynamics of simple spherical collapse to the much more complex situation of gravitational collapse. Singularities in any physical theory might naturally be taken to indicate the breakdown of the theory, but using techniques developed jointly with Hawking and Geroch, Penrose has established that once gravitational collapse has proceeded to a certain degree, assuming the truth of the general theory of relativity that gravitation is always attractive, singularities are inevitable.

These techniques are now famous as the singularity theorems.

The existence of a trapped surface within an 'event horizon' (the interface between the black hole and space–time), from which little or no radiation or information can escape, implies that some events remain hidden to observers outside the black hole. But it remains unknown whether all singularities must be hidden in this way. Penrose has put forward the hypothesis of 'cosmic censorship' – that they are all so hidden – which is now widely accepted.

On moving to Oxford University, Penrose began developing an intuition that first occurred to him in Texas in 1964. This is a model of the universe whose basic building blocks are what he calls 'twistors'. The model arises in response to a dichotomy in physics, in that calculations in the macroscopic world of ordinary objects (including Einstein's theory of gravity and the general theory of relativity) use real numbers, whereas the microscopic world of atoms and quantum theory often requires a system using complex numbers, containing imaginary components that are multiples of the square root of –1. Penrose holds that, as everything is made up of atoms, and as energy exists as discrete quanta bundles, all calculations about both the macroscopic and microscopic worlds should use complex numbers. Logically to maintain such a hypothesis would require reformulation of the major laws of physics and of space–time.

His publications include *The Emperor's New Mind: Concerning Computers, Minds and the Laws of Physics* (1989), which won the 1990 Science Book Prize; *Shadows of the Mind: A Search for the Missing Science of Consciousness* (1994); and *The Nature of Space and Time* (1996), written with Stephen Hawking.

Penzias, Arno Allan (1933–) German-born US radio engineer who shared the 1978 Nobel Prize for Physics with Robert ◊Wilson for their discovery of cosmic microwave background radiation. The existence of this radiation had been predicted on the basis of the Big Bang model of the origin of the universe, and its detection represents some of the strongest evidence in favour of this model.

Penzias was born in Munich, Germany, on 26 April 1933. For political reasons his parents emigrated to the USA, taking their young son with them; all were later naturalized. Studying at the City College of New York (CCNY), Penzias earned his bachelor's degree in physics in 1954. He then continued his studies at Columbia University in New York, where he was awarded his master's degree in 1958 and his doctorate in 1962. In 1961 Penzias joined the Radio Research Laboratory of the Bell Telephone Company. From then to 1972 he was a staff member of the radio research department, and from 1972 to 1974 he was head of the technical research department. He then became head of the radiophysics research department before, in 1976, becoming director of the Radio Research Laboratory. In 1979 he became executive director of research and communication sciences at Bell Telephone Laboratories, and in 1989 vice president of research.

In addition to his posts in the telecommunications industry, Penzias has also concurrently held a series of academic positions. The first of these was as lecturer in the department of astrophysical science of Princeton University 1967–82. He was appointed an associate of the Harvard College Observatory in 1968, a visiting professor at Princeton University in 1972, adjunct professor at the State University of New York (SUNY) at Stony Brook in 1975, and made trustee of Trenton State College in New Jersey in 1976.

Penzias's many important contributions to radio astronomy have brought him widespread acclaim. He received the Henry Draper Medal of the National Academy of Sciences in 1977, the Herschel Medal of the Royal Astronomical Society in 1977, and in 1978, with Robert Wilson and Pyotr ◊Kapitza, the Nobel Prize for Physics.

In 1963 Penzias and Wilson were assigned by the Bell Telephone Company to the tracing of radio 'noise' that was interfering with the development of a communications programme involving satellites. By May 1964 the two had detected a surprisingly high level of radiation at a wavelength of 7.3 cm/2.9 in, which had no apparent source (that is, it was uniform in all directions, or isotropic). They excluded all known terrestrial sources of such radiation and still found that the noise they were detecting was a hundred times more powerful than could be accounted for. They also found that the temperature of this background radiation was 3.5K (–269.7°C/–453.4°F), later revised to 3.1K (–270°C/–454.1°F).

They took this enigmatic result to Robert ◊Dicke, a professor of physics at Princeton University. Dicke was interested in microwave radiation and had predicted that this sort of radiation should be present in the universe as a residual relic of the intense heat associated with the birth of the universe following the Big Bang. His department was then in the process of constructing a radio telescope designed to detect precisely this radiation, at a wavelength of 3.2 cm/1.3 in, when Penzias and Wilson presented their data.

Since then, background radiation has been subjected to intense study. Its spectrum conforms closely to a black-body pattern and its temperature is now known to be just under 3K (– 270°C/–454°F). For cosmologists this constitutes the most convincing evidence in favour of the Big Bang model for the origin of the universe, although it also raises some fundamental questions, such as the possible 'oscillation' of the universe between total contractions and total expansions.

Penzias's later work has been concerned with developments in radio astronomy, satellite communications, atmospheric physics and related matters. It was, however, for his work on the black-body background radiation that he received the Nobel prize.

Peregrinus, Petrus (born c. 1220) Adopted name of Peregrinus de Maricourt. French scientist and scholar about whom little is known except through his seminal work – based largely on experiment – on magnetism.

His real name was Peregrinus de Maricourt and he may have been given the name 'Peter the Pilgrim' because he was a crusader. He was an engineer in the French army under Louis IX and was active in Paris in the middle of the 13th century, where he advised Roger ◊Bacon. He took part in the siege of Lucera in Italy in 1269 and in that year published his findings about magnets in *Epistola de magnete*. In it he described a simple compass (a piece of magnetized iron on a wooden disc floating in water) and outlined the laws of magnetic attraction and repulsion. His ideas were taken up 250 years later by William ◊Gilbert.

Perkin, William Henry (1838–1907) English chemist who achieved international fame for his accidental discovery of mauve, the first aniline dye and the first commercially significant synthetic dyestuff.

Perkin was born in Shadwell, South London, on 12 March 1838, the son of a builder. His father wanted him to become an architect and he was educated at the City of London School, where he became interested in chemistry; encouraged by Thomas Hall, one of his teachers, he carried out experiments at home. At the age of 15 he persuaded his father to let him enter the Royal College of Chemistry, London, and two years later he became an assistant to August ◊Hofmann, who was professor of chemistry there. Perkin's discovery of mauve occurred during the Easter vacation of 1856 when he was still only 18. With the help of his father he set up a factory to manufacture the dye, and so founded the British synthetic dyestuffs industry. He was knighted in 1906 on the 50th anniversary of his famous discovery. He died in Sudbury, Middlesex, on 14 July 1907.

In one of his early home experiments Perkin looked at the reduction products of dinitrobenzene and dinitronaphthalene and obtained a coloured substance initially named nitrosonaphthyline. It was the first example of the group of azo dyes produced from naphthalene.

In 1856 Perkin set himself the ambitious task of trying to synthesize quinine. He used chromic acid to oxidize toluidine (4-methylphenylamine) and obtained only a dirty dark precipitate. He then repeated the experiment using aniline (phenyl amine) and again produced a dark precipitate. But extracted with alcohol it gave an intensely purple solution; this contained the new dye, which Perkin called aniline purple – later named mauve by French textile manufacturers. He sent a sample to the dyestuff company of Pullars in Perth, Scotland, who reported favourably once they had found a satisfactory mordant.

Despite advice to the contrary by Hofmann, Perkin decided to develop the dye himself commercially. His father put up the money and his brother, T D Perkin (1831–1891), helped with the laboratory work. Without any connections in the textile industry and with only a small experimental quantity of the dye, they built a new factory at Greenford Green (now Perivale), to the west of London, which was opened in 1859. Initially they had difficulty getting supplies of benzene (to make aniline, which was at that time a rare substance, found only in a few research laboratories) and nitric acid (to prepare nitrobenzene). Perkin patented the process, after establishing that someone under the age of 21 could do so; it was soon copied but involving more expensive oxidizing agents than the simple acidified potassium dichromate he used.

In the following years Hofmann also patented several commercial dyes based on the methylation and ethylation of magenta (discovered by Verguin in 1859), producing violets and rosanilines. At the company of Roberts and Dale in Manchester, H Caro (1834–1911) discovered a new way of making mauve and with Martins introduced Manchester brown and Martins yellow. Other new dyes included crysaniline, rosolic acid, aniline green, aniline black, and diphenylamine blue. Perkin's chance discovery had resulted in a new dyestuffs industry based on coal tar (the source of benzene and aniline). Commercial demand for mauve died within ten years and it was superseded. Perkin's factory introduced new dyes based on the alkylation of magenta, and in 1868 he established a new route for the synthesis of alizarin (independently of Caro and Karl Graebe, who in the same year patented a process for making alizarin). The natural dye was derived from the madder plant, and within a few years the growing of the crop was no longer a commercial proposition in Europe.

The starting point for alizarin was anthracene, another coal-tar derivative. Eventually one tonne of alizarin was prepared during 1869, and by 1871 Perkin's company was producing one tonne every day. Perkin's business acumen was considerable and he became a wealthy man. He sold the factory and retired from industry in 1874, at the age of 36, to continue his academic research.

Even before this time Perkin had investigated various other organic compounds. In 1860, with B F Duppa (1828–1873), he established that glycine (aminoethanoic acid) can be obtained by heating bromoacetic acid (bromoethanoic acid) with ammonia. They also showed that tartaric acid (2,3-dihydroxybutanoic acid) and fumaric and maleic acid (trans- and cis-ethene-1, 2-dicarboxylic acids) are related and they synthesized racemic acid from dibromosuccinic acid (2,3-dibromobutan-1, 4-dioic acid).

In the late 1860s Perkin prepared unsaturated acids by the action of acetic anhydride on aromatic aldehydes, a method known as the Perkin synthesis. In 1868 he synthesized coumarin, the first preparation of a synthetic perfume. He also investigated the effects of magnetic fields on the chemical structures of substances.

In 1906 on the 50th anniversary of the discovery of mauve a jubilee celebration was held at the Royal Institution in London, attended by major chemists from throughout Europe. Pride of place at the dinner that followed was given to a specimen of benzene first isolated by Michael Faraday in 1825, the parent substance upon which the dyestuffs industry was founded.

Perkin married twice and had three sons and four daughters. The eldest son, also named William Henry (1860–1929), became a professor of chemistry at the University of Manchester, where he established a research team devoted to organic chemistry; he later moved to Oxford University. Another son, Arthur George (1861–1937), was also a skilled organic chemist and was professor of colour chemistry and dyeing at the University of Leeds 1916–37.

Perrin, Jean Baptiste (1870–1942) French physicist who made the first demonstration of the existence of atoms. He did this by the quantitative observation of Brownian motion. In recognition of this achievement, Perrin was awarded the 1926 Nobel Prize for Physics. He also made an important contribution to the discovery that cathode rays are electrons.

Perrin was born in Lille on 30 September 1870. He was educated in Lyon and Paris and in 1891 entered the Ecole Normale Supérieure, gaining his doctorate six years later. He was then appointed to a readership in physical chemistry at the Sorbonne in 1897, and in 1910 he became professor of physical chemistry there. Perrin retained this position until 1940, when his outspoken antifascism caused him to flee the German occupation. He went to New York, where he died on 17 April 1942.

Perrin's first work of significance was done in 1895 on the nature of cathode rays. The cathode rays generated in discharge tubes were allowed to penetrate thin sheets of glass or aluminium and collected in a hollow cylinder. In this way the rays were shown to carry a negative charge, an indication that they consisted of negatively charged particles. The rays could thus be retarded by an electric field, and Perrin carried out further experiments, which included imposing a negative charge on a fluorescent screen onto which various rays were focused. As the negative charge was increased, the intensity of fluorescence fell. He was able in this way to establish crude values for e/m, the charge-to-mass ratio of an electron, which were improved upon by the classic studies of J J ◊Thomson in 1897, which established the existence of the electron.

Perrin's more important contribution to scientific knowledge was in papers published in 1909 on atomic theory. Perrin extended the work of Robert ◊Brown, who in 1827 had reported that pollen grains suspended in water and observed by microscope appeared to be in rapid random motion. It was believed that Brownian motion occurs because the tiny pollen grains are jostled by moving water molecules. Perrin suggested that, this being the case, the principles of the kinetic theory of gases were applicable as the grains and water molecules would both behave like gas molecules even though the pollen grains were much greater in size than water molecules.

The experiments that Perrin performed to measure Brownian motion are classics. One system involved gamboge (gum resin) particles obtained from vegetable sap, and required the isolation of 0.1 g/0.004 oz of particles of the necessary size from a sample weighing 1 kg/2.2 lb; the isolation took several months. In the experiment, the distribution of suspended particles in a container was analysed by depth. It was found that their number decreases exponentially with height and, using principles proposed by Albert ◊Einstein, Perrin was able to deduce a definite value for Avogadro's number that agreed substantially with experimental values obtained in other ways. This showed that Perrin's assumption was correct and that Brownian motion is due to molecular bombardment. Perrin's work on Brownian motion came as close as was possible then to detecting atoms without actually seeing them and it was accepted as a final proof of the existence of atoms.

Perutz, Max Ferdinand (1914–) Austrian-born British molecular biologist who shared the 1962 Nobel Prize for Chemistry for his solution of the structure of the haemoglobin molecule; his co-worker John ◊Kendrew, who had determined the structure of myoglobin, was the other winner of the prize.

Perutz was born in Vienna on 19 May 1914. Both his parents came from families of textile manufacturers and expected their son to study law before entering the family business. But at school at the Theresianum in Vienna he became interested in chemistry and in 1932 entered the University of Vienna to study the subject. A course in organic biochemistry, given by F von Wessely, fired his imagination and after graduation he tried (but failed) to get a place at Cambridge University to study under Frederick Gowland ◊Hopkins.

In 1936 Perutz became a research student at the Cavendish Laboratory, Cambridge, where he worked on X-ray crystallography under John Bernal (1901–1971). After internment in Canada as an enemy alien during World War II, he returned to Cambridge and remained there for the rest of his academic career. In 1939 he received a grant from the Rockefeller Foundation and was appointed research assistant to William Bragg (see William and Lawrence ◊Bragg); he gained his PhD a year later. Perutz continued his researches and in 1947 was appointed head of the newly constituted Molecular Biology Unit of the Medical Research Council. In 1957 he formally proposed to the council the idea of a new laboratory, backed by Nevill ◊Mott, Bragg's successor as Cavendish Professor. Five years later Perutz became chairman of the new Laboratory of Molecular Biology and held this post until his retirement in 1979.

Perutz first applied the methods of X-ray diffraction to proteins at the Cavendish Laboratory. Following a conversation with F Haurowitz in Prague in 1937, he began work on determining the structure of haemoglobin. There were enormous difficulties and it was not until 16 years later, in 1953, that he discovered a suitable method. He found that if he added a single atom of a heavy metal such as gold or mercury to each molecule of protein the diffraction pattern was altered slightly. Kendrew, who had joined Perutz in 1945, used a similar technique for the smaller molecule of myoglobin.

Using high-speed computers, which were just becoming available, they analysed hundreds of X-ray pictures and in 1958 Perutz published his first findings on the structure of haemoglobin. By 1960 they had worked out the precise structures of both proteins. Haemoglobin turned out to have 574 amino-acid units in four folded chains, each similar to the single chain of myoglobin. Their basic helical structure confirmed the prediction made ten years earlier by Linus ◊Pauling that protein strands are twisted.

In his later work on haemoglobin Perutz tried to interpret the mechanism by which the molecule transports oxygen in the blood in terms of its molecular structure. He became especially interested in the effect of the protein globin on the iron-containing haem group, which is related to the effect of protein on the catalytic properties of metals and coenzymes.

The sequences of the 20 different amino-acid residues along the α and ß globin chains are determined genetically; occasionally mutations lead to an alteration in one of the sequences. People who carry some of these mutations may suffer from a lack of red blood cells (anaemia) or have too many red cells, because the stability of the oxygen-carrying mechanism of the haemoglobin molecule is impaired. This was the first time that the symptoms of an inherited disorder had been interpreted in terms of the molecular structure of a biochemical. It holds the hope that a treatment may be found for the most common inherited haemoglobin disorder, sickle-cell disease.

Petit, Alexis-Thérèse (1791–1820) French scientist who worked mainly in physics but whose collaboration with Pierre ◊Dulong resulted in a discovery that was to play an important part in chemistry in the determination of atomic weights (relative atomic masses).

Petit was born in Vesoul, Haute-Saône, on 2 October 1791. He went to school at Besançon and at the age of only 16 entered the Ecole Polytechnique in Paris. He graduated in 1809 – after only two years – and a year later was appointed professor of physics at the Lycée Bonaparte. He was awarded his doctorate in 1811 for a thesis on capillary action. In 1814 he became an assistant professor at the Ecole Polytechnique, succeeding to a full professorship a year later. The last years of his life were darkened by the death in 1817 of his wife (sister of the physicist François ◊Arago) and by illness. He contracted tuberculosis and died, in Paris, on 21 June 1820 in only his 29th year. He was succeeded at the Ecole Polytechnique by his friend and colleague Dulong.

Petit's early research was conducted in collaboration with his brother-in-law Arago. They examined the effect of temperature on the refractive index of gases. Their results led Petit to doubt the validity of the then accepted corpuscular theory of light and to become an early supporter of the wave theory.

In 1815 the offer of a prize in a scientific competition on the measurement of temperature and cooling laws stimulated Petit and Dulong to begin their fruitful, albeit short, collaboration. Their results established the importance of the gas thermometer (they won the competition and were awarded the prize in 1818). They continued working in this area, examining the specific heats (specific heat capacities) of various solids and in 1819 announced the famous Dulong–Petit law of atomic heats. This stated that, for most solid elements, the product of the specific heat and atomic weight is a constant (termed the atomic heat), equal to 5.97. The modern expression of the law is that the product of the specific heat capacity and relative atomic mass is approximately constant and equal to three times the universal gas constant (R), or 25.07 joules per mole per Kelvin ($J \, mol^{-1} \, K^{-1}$).

The law applies at room temperature only, and not to lighter solid elements such as boron and carbon; the constant tends to zero as temperature falls towards absolute zero. Chemists who at that time were having difficulty determining atomic weights (and distinguishing them from equivalent weights) now had a method of estimating the approximate weight merely by measuring the specific heat of a sample of the element concerned.

Pfeffer, Wilhelm Friedrich Philipp (1845–1920) German physiological botanist who is best known for his contributions to the study of osmotic pressures, which is important in both biology and chemistry.

Pfeffer was born in Grebenstein, near Kassel, on 9 March 1845, the son of a pharmacist. He went to Göttingen University to study botany and chemistry, and gained his doctorate in 1865. He then went to Marburg University, where he spent several years studying botany and pharmacy. From 1867 to 1870 he studied botany as a private assistant to Nathanael Pringsheim (1823–1894), a botanist specializing in the study of algae, and then he worked under the plant physiologist Julius von Sachs (1832–1897) at the University of Würzburg 1870–71. In 1871 Pfeffer returned to Marburg as a *Privatdozent* (an official but unpaid lecturer) and in 1873 he became Extraordinarius at Bonn University, a post he held until 1877, when he was appointed to a professorship at Basel University. In the following year Pfeffer accepted a professorship at Tübingen University, then in 1887 became a professor at Leipzig University. He died on 31 January 1920 in Leipzig.

Pfeffer made the first ever quantitative determinations of osmotic pressure in 1877. The apparatus he used consisted of a semipermeable container of sugar solution immersed in a vessel of water. He connected a mercury-filled manometer to the top of the semipermeable container to measure the osmotic pressure after the solute and water had reached equilibrium. Using these pressure measurements he also showed that osmotic pressure varies according to the temperature and concentration of the solute. Other scientists later made independent determinations of osmotic pressure and confirmed Pfeffer's results. In addition, Jacobus ◊van't Hoff established that the osmotic pressure of a solution is analogous to gaseous pressure: a solute (if not dissociated) exerts the same osmotic pressure as the gaseous pressure it would exert if it were a gas occupying the same volume at the same temperature. Pfeffer's work on osmosis led to the modern understanding of osmometry and was of fundamental importance in the study of cell membranes, because semipermeable membranes surround all cells and play a large part in controlling the internal environment of cells.

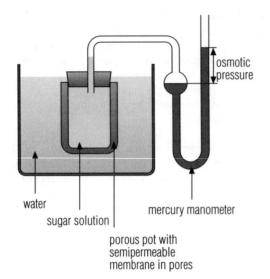

water

sugar solution

mercury manometer

osmotic pressure

porous pot with
semipermeable
membrane in pores

Pfeffer Pfeffer's apparatus for measuring osmotic pressure.

In addition to his work on osmosis, Pfeffer also studied respiration, photosynthesis, protein metabolism, and transport in plants. He published more than a hundred scientific papers and books, and his three-volume *Handbuch der Pflanzenphysiologie* (translated in 1906 as *Physiology of Plants*) was an important text for many years.

Piaget, Jean (1896–1980) Swiss psychologist famous for his pioneering studies of the development of thought processes, particularly in children. He is generally considered to be one of the most important figures in modern developmental psychology and his work has had a great influence on educational theory and child psychology. He received many international honours for his work, including seven scientific prizes and 25 honorary degrees.

Piaget was born on 9 August 1896 in Neuchâtel, Switzerland. He published his first scientific article (about an albino sparrow) when he was only 10 years old, and by the age of 15 he had gained an international reputation for his work on molluscs. Subsequently he studied at the universities of Neuchâtel, Zürich, and Paris, obtaining his doctorate from Neuchâtel in 1918. His interest then turned to psychology and he spent two years at the Sorbonne researching the reasons why children fail intelligence tests. The results of this research gained him the directorship of the Institut J J Rousseau in Geneva in 1921. During his subsequent career Piaget held many academic positions, some of which were concurrent. He was professor of philosophy at Neuchâtel 1926–29; professor of child psychology and history of scientific

thought at Geneva University 1929–39; director of the Institut Universitaire des Sciences de l'Education in Geneva 1933–71; professor of psychology and sociology at Lausanne University 1938–51; professor of sociology 1938–52 and of experimental psychology 1940–71 at Geneva University; professor of genetic psychology at the Sorbonne 1952–63; and director of the International Bureau of Education in Geneva 1929–67. In 1955, with the help of the Rockefeller Foundation and the Swiss National Foundation for Scientific Research, Piaget founded the International Centre of Genetic Epistemology at Geneva University, which he continued to direct after he retired in 1971. He also held several positions with UNESCO at various times during his life. Piaget died in Geneva on 16 September 1980.

Piaget's work on concept formation in children falls into two main phases: an early phase, 1924–37, in which he established the basic differences between thought processes in children and those in adults, and a late phase, after 1937, in which he carried out detailed investigations of thought development and evolved his theories about concept formation in children – his best-known work.

In his early work Piaget showed how radically different are the mental processes of children from those of adults: according to his theory – which resembles Sigmund ◊Freud's ideas about the development of the id, ego, and superego – children's mental processes are dominated by an egocentric attitude, being influenced mainly by the wishes and inner needs of the child, but as the child develops, its thinking becomes increasingly dominated by the influence of the external environment.

After 1937 Piaget carried out much more rigorous investigations into the origin and development of logical and mathematical concepts in children, and attempted to trace the growth of reasoning capacities from birth to maturity. In developing his famous theory of concept development, Piaget invented a new type of logic (called psycho-logic) in an attempt to apply pure logic to experimental psychology, and as a result of this his writings are highly technical. Stated simply, however, Piaget's theory postulates four main stages in the development of mental processes: sensorimeter, pre-operational, concrete operational, and formal operational.

In the sensorimeter stage, which lasts from birth to the age of about two years, infants obtain a basic knowledge of objects by empirical experimentation. Gradually a child forms concepts of objects, and learns that they continue to exist even when out of sight. The pre-operational stage lasts from the age of two years to the age of seven years. In this stage a child learns to imitate and begins to represent concrete objects with words – language starts to develop. From 7 to 12 years old a child is in the concrete operational stage: he or she develops the concept of number, begins to classify objects according to their similarities and differences, and can distinguish between past and present. Finally, from 12 onwards, a child is in the formal operational stage, which is characterized by the development of logical thought and mathematical ability; thinking also becomes more flexible – hypotheses are formed and experimented with, for example.

Although it has been criticized for being based on observations of only a small number of subjects, Piaget's work on the development of mental processes is generally considered to be a major achievement and has greatly influenced educational theory and practice, particularly the teaching of mathematics.

Further Reading

Boden, Margaret A, *Piaget,* Fontana Modern Masters series, Fontana, 1994.

Gruber, Howard E and Vonèche, Jacques, *The Essential Piaget,* Basic Books, 1977.

Inhelder, Bärbel; Cornu-Wells, Angela; and De Caprona, Denys (eds), *Piaget Today,* Erlbaum, 1987.

Silverman, Hugh J, *Piaget, Philosophy, and the Human Sciences,* Humanities Press, 1980.

Smith, Leslie (ed), *Jean Piaget: Critical Assessments,* Critical Assessments of Leading Psychologists series, Routledge, 1992, 4 vols.

Smith, Leslie Allan, *Necessary Knowledge – Piagetian Perspectives on Constructivism: Essays in Developmental Psychology,* Erlbaum, 1993.

Tryphon, Anastasia and Vonèche, Jacques (eds), *Piaget–Vygotsky: The Social Genius of Thought,* Psychology Press, 1996.

Piazzi, Giuseppe (1749–1826) Italian monk, originally trained in theology, philosophy, and mathematics, who nevertheless was put in charge of an observatory, where he carried out astronomical studies of considerable importance. He is, for example, credited with the discovery of the first asteroid, or 'planetoid', as he more logically termed it.

Piazzi was born in Ponte di Valtellina (then part of Italy, now in Switzerland) on 16 July 1746. He studied in various Italian cities and in 1764 entered the Theatine order in Milan, where he lived as a monk for several years. He continued his studies of philosophy and mathematics in Milan and Rome and was awarded a doctorate in both subjects. For ten years after 1769 he worked as a teacher in Genoa and in Malta, before becoming professor of higher mathematics at the Palermo Academy in Sicily. During the latter part of the 1780s the Bourbons, then the rulers of the independent kingdom of Naples, decided to establish observatories in Palermo and Naples. Put in charge of the one at Palermo, Piazzi travelled to observatories in England and France to obtain advice and equipment, and met such great astronomers as William ⚲Herschel, Jesse Ramsden (1735–1800), and Nevil ⚲Maskelyne. He examined their equipment and commissioned from Ramsden a 1.5-m/5-ft vertical circle that he intended to use to determine star positions. The device was installed in Palermo in 1789 and still exists.

The Palermo Observatory opened in 1790 and Piazzi served as its director until his death. He conducted many astronomical studies and became a fellow of the Royal Society in 1804. He also took on additional responsibilities, including the reformation of the Sicilian system of weights and measures in 1812, and finally in 1817 he was put in charge of the other observatory at Naples. For a time Piazzi split his time between the two observatories, but eventually he moved to Naples in 1824 because his health was failing. He died in Naples on 22 July 1826.

Piazzi's first astronomical publication appeared in 1789, but his great project on mapping the positions of the fixed stars did not begin until the 1790s. He was fortunate in working at the southernmost observatory in Europe in a favourable climate. These conditions, together with the quality of his equipment, enabled him to produce new and accurate measurements.

Piazzi was examining the apparent 'gap' in the Solar System between Mars and Jupiter, long a source of speculation for astronomers, when, on 1 January 1801, he detected a faint body that had not previously been noted. He followed it for six weeks, until it could no longer be detected because of its position relative to the Sun. Using Piazzi's data, Karl ⚲Gauss in Germany managed to calculate the orbit of the body, and sent his prediction to Baron von Zach of the Gotha Observatory. The body was rediscovered by Heinrich ⚲Olbers, just where Gauss had predicted it would be found; its dimness, considering its distance from the Earth, indicated that it was very small. (Herschel calculated that it was only 320 km/200 mi in diameter and did not therefore warrant being called a planet. He proposed the name 'asteroid', a term that became popular.) The body that Piazzi discovered was named Ceres, and is now known to have a diameter of 940 km/584 mi. Three more asteroids were discovered before Piazzi's death, and it is now thought that as many as 100,000 may exist.

In 1803 Piazzi published his first catalogue of fixed stars, which located 6,748 stars with unprecedented accuracy. His second catalogue, produced in collaboration with N Cacciatore, appeared in 1813. It described 7,646 stars. Both publications won prizes.

Picard, (Charles) Emile (1856–1941) French mathematician whose work in analysis – and particularly in analytical geometry – brought him deserved fame.

Responsible for the formulation of 'Picard's little theorem' and 'Picard's big theorem', he was also an excellent teacher, interested in applying mathematical principles as much as possible to other branches of science, particularly physics and engineering.

Picard was born on 24 July 1856 in Paris, where his father was the director of a silk factory. He showed talent as a pupil at the Lycée Henry IV, where his excellent memory contributed to his outstanding results. Completing his education, he entered the Ecole Normale Supérieure in 1874. Within three years he had already made some important algebraic discoveries, been consistently placed first among his contemporary fellow students, and had earned his doctorate. He was then retained as an assistant instructor at the Ecole 1877–78. In 1879 he was appointed professor (at the age of 23) in Toulouse. Two years later, however, he returned to Paris as lecturer in physics and experimental mechanics at the Sorbonne and, simultaneously, again at the Ecole Normale Supérieure. Also in 1881 his name was put forward for election to the Paris Academy of Sciences (although his election did not actually occur until 1889). In 1885 he took the chair of differential and integral calculus at the Sorbonne, and served as his own assistant until he reached the prescribed age of 30, at which he was officially able to hold the post. In 1897, at his own request, he exchanged this post for the chair of analysis and higher algebra because he wanted a position in which he could train students for research. He was made a member of the Académie Française in 1924, and received the Grande Croix de la Légion d'Honneur in 1932. He also won the Mittag-Leffler Gold Medal from the Swedish Academy of Sciences, received honorary degrees from five foreign universities, and was a member of 37 academies and learned societies. Highly respected for his administrative capability, and an excellent teacher, Picard died on 11 December 1941 in the Palais de l'Institut in Paris, where he was living as permanent secretary.

Picard's work was mainly in the fields of mathematical analysis and algebraic geometry. In 1878 he studied the integrals of differential equations by making successive substitutions with equations having suitable partial derivatives. A year later, he proved the theorem now known by his name, that an integral function of the complex variable takes every finite value, with one possible exception. He expressed it in this way:

Let $f(z)$ be an entire function. If there exist two values of A for which the equation $f(z) = A$ does not have a finite root, then $f(z)$ is a constant. From this it follows that if $f(z)$ is an entire function that is not a constant, there cannot be more than one value of A for which $f(z) = A$ has no solution.

In the following year he stated a second theorem:

Let $f(z)$ be a function, analytic everywhere except at a where it has an essential isolated singularity; the equation $f(z) = A$ has in general an infinity of roots in any neighbourhood of a. Although the equation can fail for certain exceptional values of the constant A, there cannot be more than two such values.

From these results, generalizations were worked out that are now known as 'Picard's little theorem' and 'Picard's big theorem'.

Picard created a theory of linear differential equations analogous to the Evariste ◊Galois's theory of algebraic equations. (This work was later extended by his pupil, Ernest Vessiot (1865–1952).) His work on the integrals attached to algebraic surfaces, together with the associated topological questions, developed into an area of algebraic geometry that had applications in topology and function theory. Much of Picard's work was recorded in a three-volume book entitled *Traité d'analyse*.

He also applied his method of analysis to the theories of elasticity, heat, and electricity, and produced a solution to the problem of the propagation of electrical impulses along a cable. When he was over 80 he presented a paper to the Academy of Sciences on questions of homogeneity and similarity encountered by physicists and engineers.

Pickering, Edward Charles (1846–1919) US
astronomer, one of the most famous and hard-working of his time, who was a pioneer in three practical areas of astronomical research: visual photometry, stellar spectroscopy, and stellar photography. As director of the Harvard College Observatory for more than 40 years, he was instrumental in educating and inspiring an entire generation of young astronomers; unusually for someone of his generation, he was also keen to encourage women to take up astronomy as a career.

Pickering was born on 19 July 1846 in Boston, Massachusetts. He began his academic career as an assistant instructor of mathematics at the Lawrence Scientific School at Harvard, but after two years he was appointed assistant professor of physics at the newly founded Massachusetts Institute of Technology. During his subsequent ten years in this post the methods used by Pickering were to break new ground in the way the subject was taught. Then, in 1876, he was appointed director of the Harvard College Observatory, a post he was to hold for 42 years. In that time he received honorary doctorates from six US and two European universities; in addition he was awarded the Rumford Gold Medal of the American Academy of Arts and Sciences and was twice a recipient of the Gold Medal of the Royal Astronomical Society. He died in Cambridge, Massachusetts, on 3 February 1919.

As a basis for the photometric work he carried out, Pickering made two critical decisions. First, he adopted the magnitude scale suggested by Norman Pogson (1829–1891) in 1854, on which a change of one magnitude represented a change of a factor of 2.512 in brightness. Second, choosing the Pole Star (Polaris), then thought to be of constant brightness, as the standard magnitude and arbitrarily assigning a value of 2.1 to it, he redesigned the photometer to reflect a number of stars round the meridian at the same time so that comparisons were immediately visible. The photometric work that followed continued for nearly a quarter of a century. (Unfortunately Polaris has since been found to vary in brightness to a small degree.)

The first great catalogue of magnitudes, containing 4,260 stars, was published in 1884. It was known as the *Harvard Photometry*. Pickering's tenacity to carry out the laborious nature of producing this vast work never flagged; in the process he is estimated to have carried out more than 1.5 million photometric readings. Each visible star was measured for its brightness and the process was repeated for the same stars to achieve the most accurate figure possible. Pickering's observations were finally published in 1908 as the *Revised Harvard Photometry*. Printed as Volumes 50 and 54 of the *Annals* of Harvard College Observatory, it tabulates the magnitudes of more than 45,000 stars brighter than the seventh magnitude. It remained the standard reference for many years.

A further production of the Harvard College Observatory was the *Henry Draper Catalogue*, a classification of stellar spectra. Pickering's researches into stellar spectroscopy were made possible by a practical invention of his whereby the spectra of a number of stars could be surveyed simultaneously and by the establishment in 1886 of a fund commemorating the amateur astronomer Henry ◊Draper. Draper's widow supplied the financial backing for Pickering and his assistants to photograph, measure, and catalogue the spectra of stars as a memorial publication to her husband, to appear in the *Annals*. Finally issued in 1918, the complete *Draper Catalogue* contained the spectra of no fewer than 225,000 stars, classified according to the new, improved alphabetical system devised by Pickering's pupil and colleague, Annie Jump ◊Cannon.

Pickering's interest in stellar photography was responsible for the first *Photographic Map of the Entire Sky* (1903). It comprised 55 plates of stars down to the 12th magnitude, taken both at Harvard and at its sister station in the southern hemisphere, at Arequipa in Peru, where Pickering's younger brother, William (1858–1938), was director. In addition, Pickering photographed large areas of the sky on clear nights, building up a 300,000-plate photographic library that has since proved invaluable to astronomers searching for changes in the brightness and position of celestial objects.

One of the most important products of Pickering's researches was the creation of the astronomical colour index: a measure of the apparent colour of a star and thus of its temperature. Cooler stars emit more light at longer wavelengths and so appear redder than hot stars. The colour index is expressed as the difference in a star's brightness when measured on two selected wavelengths. The international colour index, defined by Pickering in about 1890, is the difference between the photographic magnitude (blue light) and the photovisual magnitude (yellow light); it is zero for white stars, positive for red stars, and negative for blue stars. Magnitudes are now seldom measured photographically; instead, colour filters on photoelectric cells measure the colour index between the two wavelengths.

Pippard, (Alfred) Brian (1920–   ) English physicist who has carried out important work in superconductivity.

Pippard was born on 7 September 1920 in London. He was educated at Clifton College, Bristol, and then at Clare College, Cambridge, obtaining his BA in 1941. He then worked as a scientific officer at the Radar Research and Development Establishment at Great Malvern until 1945, when he returned to Cambridge. He gained his PhD in 1949, then became a lecturer in physics in 1950 and a reader in 1959. He was then appointed John Humphrey Plummer Professor of Physics at Cambridge in 1960, and in 1971 he became Cavendish Professor of Physics there (emeritus from 1982). Pippard's honours include a knighthood in 1975, and the award of the Hughes Medal of the Royal Society in 1958.

Pippard is the son of an eminent professor of engineering, and as a boy he was fascinated by low-temperature physics. He was deterred from this, though, thinking his mathematical ability was inadequate. He intended to become a chemist but after graduating in 1941, his work on the design of radar aerials during the war deflected him towards physics. After the war, he became involved in low-temperature work and decided to concentrate his efforts on the task of applying microwaves to the study of superconductors. He worked especially on the way in which electric currents flow without resistance in a thin layer at the surface of the metal. He measured the thickness – about 1,000 Å (10^{-7} m) – of this penetration layer and examined variations with temperature and purity. He found that when he tried to change the properties at one point by applying a disturbance, he influenced the metal over a distance that in pure metals is usually greater than the penetration-layer thickness. Because of this, he said that the electrons of superconductors possess a property that he called 'coherence'.

From this starting point, he worked out an equation relating current to magnetic field. Similar work was being done at the same time in Russia by Lev Landau (1908–1968) and others. In 1957, a definitive theory of superconductivity was derived by John ◊Bardeen, Leon ◊Cooper, and John Schrieffer (1931–) and it was found to provide a consistent explanation for both Pippard's and Landau's work. Soon after this, Pippard's guess that impurities in the metal could shorten the coherence length was confirmed, and 'dirty' superconductors were produced with the important technological property of carrying currents and generating extremely strong magnetic fields without their resistance reappearing.

Pippard also discovered that absorption of microwaves at the surface of a given metal at low temperatures is governed by one particular characteristic of the conduction electrons – the shape of the Fermi surface. This initiated experiments and theoretical work in many laboratories, which transformed understanding of the dynamical laws governing the motion of electrons in metals. It also clarified the understanding of the way in which one metal differs from another in the details of this motion.

Pixii, Hippolyte (1808–1835) French inventor who made the first practical electricity generator.

Following Michael ◊Faraday's announcement to the Royal Society (on 24 November 1831) of his discovery of electromagnetic induction and his suggestions for making a simple dynamo, Pixii (an instrument maker, who had learned the craft from his father) set out to construct a practical electricity generator. Shortly afterwards he made a device that consisted of a permanent horseshoe magnet, rotated by means of a treadle, and a coil of copper wire above each of the magnet's poles. The two coils were linked and the free ends of the wires connected to terminals, from which a small alternating current was obtained when the magnet rotated. This device was first publicly exhibited at the French Academy of Sciences in Paris on 3 September 1832. Later, at the suggestion of André ◊Ampère, a commutator (a simple switching device for reversing the connections to the terminals as the magnet is rotated) was fitted so that Pixii's generator could produce direct-current electricity. This revised generator was taken to England in November 1833 by Count de Predevalli and exhibited in London. Pixii himself died two years later, only 27 years old, in 1835.

Although Pixii's machine generated only a small current, it was nevertheless the first practical electricity generator and the forerunner of all modern generators.

Planck, Max Karl Ernst Ludwig (1858–1947) German physicist who discovered that energy consists

Planck German physicist Max Planck, pioneer of quantum theory, photographed in 1925. Planck was appointed president of the Kaiser Wilhelm Institute in Berlin in 1930, but resigned in 1937 in protest at the Nazis' treatment of Jewish scientists. After the war he was made president of the institute, which was renamed the Max Planck Institute. *Mary Evans Picture Library*

of fundamental indivisible units, which he called quanta. This discovery, made in 1900, marked the foundation of the quantum theory that revolutionized physics in the early 1900s. For this achievement, Planck gained the 1918 Nobel Prize for Physics.

Planck was born in Kiel on 23 April 1858. In 1867, his family moved to Munich, where Planck studied at the Maximilian Gymnasium before entering the University of Munich in 1874. Planck studied mathematics and physics, spending some time 1877–78 with Gustav ◊Kirchhoff and Hermann von ◊Helmholtz at the University of Berlin. Planck gained his PhD at Munich with a dissertation on thermodynamics in 1879 and became a lecturer there in the following year. In 1885, he was appointed extraordinary professor of physics at Kiel and then in 1888 moved to Berlin, where he became assistant professor of physics and director of the newly founded Institute for Theoretical Physics. Planck rose to become professor of physics at Berlin in 1892, a position he retained until 1926. In 1930, he was appointed president of the Kaiser Wilhelm Institute but resigned in 1937 in protest at the Nazis' treatment of Jewish scientists. In 1945, the institute was renamed the Max Planck Institute and moved to Göttingen. Planck was reappointed its president, a position he retained until he died in Göttingen on 4 October 1947.

In 1862, Kirchhoff had introduced the idea of a perfect black body that would absorb and emit radiation at all frequencies, reaching an equilibrium that depended on temperature and not the nature of the surface of the body. A series of investigations were then undertaken into the nature of the thermal radiation emitted by black bodies following the discovery by Josef ◊Stefan in 1879 that the total energy emitted is proportional to the fourth power of the absolute temperature. Measurements of the frequency distribution of black-body radiation by Wilhelm Wien (1864–1928) in 1893 produced the result that the distribution is a function of the frequency and the temperature. A plot of the energy of the radiation against the frequency resulted in a series of curves at different temperatures, the peak value of energy occurring at a higher frequency with greater temperature. This may be observed in the varying colour produced by a glowing object. At low temperatures, it glows red but as the temperature rises the peak energy is emitted at a greater frequency, and the colour become yellow and then white.

We have no right to assume that any physical laws exist, or if they have existed up to now, that they will continue to exist in a similar manner in the future.

MAX PLANCK THE UNIVERSE IN THE LIGHT OF MODERN PHYSICS

Wien found an expression to relate peak frequency and temperature in his displacement law, and then attempted to derive a radiation law that would relate the energy to frequency and temperature. He discovered a radiation law in 1896 that was valid at high frequencies only, while Lord ◊Rayleigh later found a similar equation that held for radiation emitted at low frequencies. Planck was able to combine these two radiation laws to arrive at a formula that represented the observed energy of the radiation at any given frequency and temperature. This entailed making the assumption that the energy consists of the sum of a finite number of discrete units of energy, which he called quanta, and that the energy ϵ of each quantum is given by the equation $\epsilon = h\nu$, where ν is the frequency of the radiation and h is a constant now recognized to be a fundamental constant of nature and called Planck's constant. By thus directly relating the energy of a radiation to its frequency, an explanation was found for the observation that radiation of greater energy has a higher frequency distribution.

Classical physics had been unable to account for the distribution of radiation, for Planck's idea that energy must consist of indivisible particles was revolutionary, totally contravening the accepted belief that radiation consisted of waves. But it found rapid acceptance because an explanation for photoelectricity was provided by Albert ◊Einstein in 1905 using Planck's quantum theory, and in 1913, Niels ◊Bohr applied the quantum theory to the atom and evidence was at last obtained of the behaviour of electrons in the atom. This was later developed into a full system of quantum mechanics in the 1920s, when it also became clear that energy and matter have both a particle and wave nature. Thus the year 1900 marked not only the beginning of a new century but, with the discovery of the quantum theory, the end of the era of classical physics and the founding of modern physics.

Further Reading

Greenberg, Valerie D, *Transgressive Readings: The Texts of Franz Kafka and Max Planck,* University of Michigan Press, 1990.

Heilbron, John L, *The Dilemmas of an Upright Man: Max Planck as a Spokesman for German Science,* University of California Press, 1986.

Planck, Max, *Scientific Autobiography and Other Papers,* Philosophical Library, 1949.

Plaskett, John Stanley (1865–1941) Canadian astronomer and engineer whose work in instrument design and telescope construction led to his becoming director of the Dominion Astrophysical Observatory in Victoria, British Columbia. There, he used the large reflecting telescope that he designed to carry out important research into binary stars and stellar radial velocities.

Plaskett was born in Hickson, near Woodstock, Ontario, on 17 November 1865. After completing his schooling locally, he was employed as a mechanic in various parts of North America. In 1889, however, he became a mechanic in the department of physics at Toronto University, where he decided to take up undergraduate studies; he eventually became a lecturer there. From 1903 Plaskett was in charge of astrophysical work at the new Dominion Observatory in Ottawa and he initiated comprehensive programmes of research into stellar radial velocities using the observatory's 38-cm/15-in reflector. The spectroscope he produced for the reflector so improved the instrument that it was comparable with the best in North America. Having repeatedly urged the Canadian parliament to sanction the construction of a 1.8-m/72-inch reflector, Plaskett was finally appointed to supervise its creation for the Dominion Astrophysical Observatory in Victoria; he was also appointed the observatory's first director in 1917, and remained there until he retired in 1935, at which time he was elected a fellow of the Royal Society and president of the Royal Astronomical Society of Canada. He then supervised the construction of the 205-cm/82-in mirror for the MacDonald Observatory at the University of Texas. He died in Esquimalt, near Victoria, on 17 October 1941.

Using his new telescope at Victoria in conjunction with a spectrograph of high sensitivity, Plaskett discovered many new binary stars, including Plaskett's star, a giant binary-star system previously thought to be a single, massive star. His work on the radial velocities of galactic stars enabled him to confirm the contemporary discovery of the rotation of the Galaxy and to indicate the most probable location of the gravitational centre of the Galaxy. In turn, this led to a study of the motion and distribution of galactic interstellar matter, particularly involving the detection of spatial calcium.

Plato (c. 420–340 BC) Greek mathematician and philosopher who founded an influential school of learning in which the basic precept was not so much one of practical experimentation, as of striving to find mathematical and intellectual harmony. In consequence, most of Plato's astronomical theories involved the most idealistic forms of mathematical wishful thinking, the most fundamental premise being that the Earth, a perfect sphere, was at the centre of a universe in which all other celestial bodies described perfectly circular orbits.

Plato's real name was Aristocles; he was called Plato, 'broad-shouldered', from an early age, however. Born into a patrician Athenian family, he was naturally expected to take up a political career, but as a pupil of Socrates he came to regard politicians with ever-increasing scepticism, and following the trial and death of his mentor in 399 BC, he resolved to become a philosopher and teacher. He travelled for some years, probably to Cyrene, certainly to Sicily, perhaps also to Egypt, before returning at last to Athens in 388 BC where he set up a school that became known as the Academy on part of the premises of a gymnasium. (In one form or another, the Academy continued to exist for about 900 years.) In about 367 BC, Plato returned to Sicily as tutor to King Dionysus II, but after a few years he became disgusted with the sybaritic lifestyle of the court and (it is thought) went back again to Athens; nothing more is known of his life.

The extant works of Plato, believed on good authority to be genuine, consist of philosophical dialogues among which are *Timaeus,* the *Symposium,* the *Republic,* and the *Laws.* In all of them an idealized form of Socrates appears as one of the speakers. Plato divided philosophy into three branches: ethics, physics, and dialectics. The basic tenet behind all his arguments

is the doctrine of ideas. True science, he reasoned, investigates the nature of those purer and more perfect patterns that were the models after which all created things were formed by the great original intelligence.

Accordingly, it was in particular the science of geometry – with its premise of symmetry and the irrefutable logic of its axioms – that had the most appeal to Plato. In several of his works he therefore presents a picture of the world that is purely conceptual in form. Little thought was given to the idea of observing phenomena before putting forward a theory to explain them. According to legend, Plato had been strongly influenced in this by the ideas of ◊Pythagoras, the most famous of the Greek geometricians, some 150 years earlier. For both Pythagoras and Plato, the ideal of mathematical harmony in the attainment of the perfection of the Creator's original intentions simply meant that the universe had to be spherical because the sphere was the perfect volume; for the same reason the movements of the heavenly bodies had to be circular and uniform. Moreover, the Earth, which lay at the exact centre of the cosmos, was a sphere and was surrounded by a band of crystalline spheres that held in place the Sun, the Moon, and the planets.

At one stage, Plato asked one of his pupils, ◊Eudoxus of Cnidus, to make a model showing the circular movements of all celestial bodies. Eudoxus, a skilled mathematician, managed to construct one that demonstrated the movements of Mercury and Venus as epicycles round the Sun, thereby taking the first step towards a heliocentric system.

Despite the high degree of interest shown in such revolutionary concepts, Plato never accepted any concept but that the Earth was at the centre of the universe. This strongly conservative outlook and the unequalled authority that Plato's name gave to it resulted in the acceptance of a geocentric universe until it was invalidated by the findings of Nicolaus ◊Copernicus 19 centuries later.

Further Reading

Cavaliere, Robert, *Plato for Beginners,* Writers & Readers Publishing, 1996.

Hare, Richard M, *Plato,* Past Masters series, Oxford University Press, 1983.

Ophuijsen, J M, Van, *Plato and Platonism,* Studies in Philosophy and the History of Philosophy series, Catholic University of America Press, 1998.

Strathern, Paul, *Plato in 90 Minutes,* Philosophers in 90 Minutes series, Constable & Co, 1996.

Pliny, (Gaius Plinius Secundus) (AD 23–79) Roman military officer, scientific encyclopedist, and historian. Prudently retiring from his commission during the troubled times of the Emperor Nero AD 54–68, Pliny devoted his energy to a massive compilation of all the known sciences of his day. He is usually now called Pliny the Elder to distinguish him from his nephew and biographer, Pliny the Younger.

Born into a wealthy provincial family at Como in the year 23, Pliny completed his studies in Rome and, in his early twenties, took up a military career in Germany, where he became a cavalry commander and friend of Vespasian. He kept out of harm's way while Nero was on the imperial throne, and (it is assumed) spent much of his time writing. But when in 69 his old comrade Vespasian was made emperor, Pliny returned to Rome – where his routine included a daily visit to the emperor to talk of this and that – and took up various public offices. It was in the course of his duties that Pliny's life came to a tragic and untimely end. In the year 79 Pliny was in command of the fleet at Misenum, in the bay of Naples, when the famous eruption of Vesuvius that destroyed the towns of Pompeii and Herculaneum took place. Observing a strange cloud formation, subsequently found to have resulted from the eruption of the volcano, Pliny made for Stabiae where he landed. Here, however, he was fatally overcome by a cloud of poisonous fumes. It is possible that he saw himself as doing his duty, but it is equally possible that he died a martyr to science, his curiosity at this critical moment having been greater than his fears.

Virtually all pursuits, human or scientific, interested Pliny and in his early years he produced a grammar, a history of Rome, a biography of Pomponius Secundus, a report on the Roman military campaign in Germany, and a manual on the use of the lance in warfare. All these texts have long since diappeared, but there remains intact what is by far his most ambitious and large-scale work, the *Historia naturalis/Natural History,* in which he surveys all the known sciences of his day, notably astronomy, meteorology, geography, mineralogy, zoology, and botany. At the commencement of the work he states that he has covered 20,000 subjects of importance drawn from a hundred selected writers to whose observations he has added many of his own.

All the important assumptions of classical astronomy are described in Book 2 of the *Natural History.* It is of special interest in that it presents not only the author's opinions, but also those of ☽Hipparchus and ☽Eratosthenes, major figures in the early history of the science. According to Pliny the Earth lay on the pivot of the heavens and was surrounded by the seven stars: the Sun, the Moon, Mercury, Venus, Mars, Jupiter, and Saturn. Nevertheless, he saw the Sun as the ruler of the heavens, providing the Earth with light and with the changing pattern of the seasons. Ascribing to the Sun a zodiacal orbit round the Earth, divided into 12 equal parts then occupied by the zodiacal constellations,

Pliny goes on to describe in turn the different orbits of the seven stars, correctly adjudging Saturn to be farthest from the Earth and therefore taking 30 years to complete its circuit. Jupiter, being much nearer, is able to finish its journey in only 12 years, and Mars in about two. After the remaining planets have been described, Pliny again discusses the Sun, which, in order that it might concur with a mathematically desirable end, is represented as taking 360 days to complete its circuit, to which a surplus of $5^1/_4$ days has to be added to ensure that this great star is seen to rise at the identical point each successive year. Such were the specifications of the Julian calendar, established by Julius Caesar in 46 BC. (It was to result in the error of overestimating the time of the Sun's journey by 11 minutes, 14 seconds, but in Pliny's time this was too small a miscalculation to have had time to become apparent.) The Moon is the last of the seven stars to be described, its puzzling progress of waning being explained as a result of the slant of the zodiacal sky and highly sinuous nature of its course.

Pliny, having no knowledge of distances in the universe, assumed that the Moon is larger than the Earth, for otherwise he could not see how the entire Sun could be obscured from the Earth during an eclipse by the coming of the Moon between them. The Sun, however, he judged to be of far greater size than the Earth for the reasons, among others, that 'the shadow that it throws of rows of trees along the edges of fields are at equal distances apart for very many miles, just as if over the whole of space the Sun lay in the centre' and that 'during the equinoxes it reaches the vertical simultaneously for all the inhabitants of the southern region'. By his knowledge of the night sky at various latitudes, observed during his military journeys, Pliny even reasoned that the Earth must be a globe. In this connection, he cites the experience of Eratosthenes, who reported that in summer the days are considerably longer the further north the observer travels. He then gives Eratosthenes' famous calculation of the overall circumference of the Earth. As for gravitation, to Pliny the world consisted of four elements – earth, air, fire, and water. Of this number the 'light' substances were prevented from rising by the weight of the 'heavy' ones, while the latter were prevented from falling by the countervailing pressures from the more buoyant elements. Such was the earliest hypothesis on the nature of gravity.

In a discussion of comets, Pliny dismisses the popular belief that their arrival portended dramatic events in the fortunes of the Roman world. He alludes to the great impact the appearance of a comet had on Hipparchus and how in order that the appearance of a new star in the heavens could more surely be assessed he made a catalogue of all the stars visible to the naked eye, in the process systematizing a classification that lasted for more than 17 centuries.

The other books of the *Natural History* are just as detailed. Books 3–6 record the geography and ethnography of the then known world, in which frequent references are made to great cities that have since disappeared. Book 7 is concerned with human physiology, Books 8–9 with that of fishes and other marine animals, Book 10 of birds, and Book 11 of insects. Books 12–19 are concerned with botany, agriculture, and horticulture, the subjects that appear to have awakened Pliny's keenest interest (he is one of our chief sources of information on early Roman gardens and ancient botanical writings). Books 20–27 cover medicine and drugs, Books 28–32 medical zoology, and Books 32–37 minerals, precious stones, and metals, especially those used by Roman jewellers and artisans.

The scientific value of this great undertaking varies. The further the subjects covered are removed from Pliny's own experiences and observations, the more credulous and even silly he becomes, particularly in reporting the existence of strange animals with patently fabulous qualities. His fluency with the Greek language also induced him to translate from it into Latin too freely, often thereby blurring a critical distinction in mathematical or technical passages. The *Natural History* is, however, invaluable in many instances as the only surviving record of people's early reactions to the physical world and the gradual advance of careful observation and systematic classification of natural orders. This great undertaking appears to have been completed in AD 77, only two years before Pliny's death.

Further Reading

Beagon, Mary, *Roman Nature: The Thought of Pliny the Elder*, Oxford Classical Monographs, Clarendon Press, 1992.

Eastwood, Bruce, 'The astronomies of Pliny, Martianus Capella and Isidore of Seville in the Carolingian world' in: Butzer, Paul L and Lohrman, Dietrich (eds), *Science in Western and Eastern Civilization in Carolingian Times*, Birkhauser, 1993, pp 161–180.

French, Roger and Greenaway, Frank (eds), *Science in the Early Roman Empire: Pliny the Elder, his Sources and Influence*, Barnes and Noble, 1986.

Kennedy, Eberhard C, *Pliny: Selections*, Bristol Latin Texts series, Bristol Classical Press, 1984.

White, Horace (ed), *Pliny on Himself*, Blackwell–Bristol Classical Press, 1988.

Plücker, Julius (1801–1868) German mathematician and physicist. He made fundamental contributions to the field of analytical geometry and was a pioneer of the investigations of cathode rays that led eventually to the discovery of the electron.

Plücker was born in Elberfeld on 16 June 1801. He attended the Gymnasium in Düsseldorf, and studied at the universities of Bonn, Heidelberg, Berlin, and Paris. He was awarded his PhD from the University of Warburg in 1824, and he then took up a lectureship at the University of Bonn, where he became a professor of mathematics in 1828. In 1833 he moved to Berlin where he held simultaneous posts as extraordinary professor at the University of Berlin, and as a teacher at the Friedrich Wilhelm Gymnasium. Conflict with one of his colleagues prompted him to move to the University of Halle in 1834, where he held the chair of mathematics for two years. In 1836 Plücker became professor of mathematics at the University of Bonn, a post he held until 1847, when he became professor of physics at the same institution. He held this post until his death.

Plücker was the author of a number of books on advanced mathematics, and he also published many papers on his work in experimental physics. He did not gain much standing at home among other German physicists, but his talents were quickly recognized abroad. He was elected fellow of the Royal Society in 1855, and was awarded the Copley Medal by that body in 1868. He was also made a member of the French Academy of Sciences in 1867. Plücker died in Bonn on 22 May 1868.

The first half of Plücker's career was devoted to the study of mathematics. He found a valuable vehicle for the dissemination of his ideas in a newly founded German mathematical journal. He published books on analytical geometry in 1828, 1831, 1835, and 1839. He resumed the study of geometry shortly before his death, and his latest studies were published in 1868. His mathematics was characterized by elegance and clarity. He was able to correct some errors in work published by Leonhard ◊Euler in 1748. The work he did towards the end of his life was completed by his assistant Felix ◊Klein. During these years Plücker introduced six equations of higher plane curves, which have been named Plücker's coordinates. His work led to the foundation of line geometry.

When Plücker became professor of physics at Bonn in 1847, he turned away from his studies on geometry and plunged into theoretical and experimental physics. He studied optics and gas spectroscopy, recognizing early the potential of the latter technique in analysis. He found the first three hydrogen lines well before Robert ◊Bunsen and Gustav ◊Kirchhoff had begun their experiments in this field.

Plücker was strongly influenced by Michael ◊Faraday, who had experimented with electrical discharge in gases at very low pressures. Plücker took up this work and, unlike Faraday, had the advantage of being able to use high-vacuum tubes, which had been developed by Heinrich Geissler (1814–1879) in 1855. He found in 1858 that the discharge causes a fluorescent glow to form on the glass walls of the tube, and that the glow could be made to shift by applying an electromagnet to the tube. Johann Hittorf (1824–1914), Plücker's student, continued this work and showed in 1869 that the glow was produced by cathode rays formed in the tube; in 1897 J J ◊Thomson demonstrated that these rays consist of electrons.

Poincaré, (Jules) Henri (1854–1912) French mathematician and prolific mathematical writer. His

interests and achievements were wide-ranging, although he is probably best known for his introduction of automorphic functions in pure mathematics, of ergodicity in the theory of probability, and of some of the understanding of the dynamics of the electron later attributed to Albert ◊Einstein in the theory of relativity. He was also renowned for his study of celestial mechanics.

Poincaré was born on 29 April 1854 in Nancy, the son of a doctor. A brilliant student, he won first prize in an open competition between students from throughout France. Completing his education, he entered the Ecole Polytechnique in Paris in 1873, where he graduated. He then studied engineering at the Ecole des Mines, but it was in mathematics that in 1879 his doctoral thesis was successfully composed. Immediately afterwards, Poincaré was appointed to a teaching post at the University of Caen, and only two years later he became professor of mathematics at Paris University. In 1887 he was elected to the Academy of Sciences, and during the remainder of his lifetime he received many other honours and awards. He died in Paris on 17 July 1912.

Poincaré's first great work was in pure mathematics, where he generalized the idea of functional periodicity in his theory of automorphic functions that are invariant under a denumerably infinite group of linear fractional transformations. He showed how these functions could be used to express the coordinates of any point of an algebraic curve as uniform functions of a single parameter, and could also be used to integrate linear differential equations with rational algebraic coefficients. Developing his investigations, he found that one class of automorphic functions – which he called Fuchsian, after the German mathematician Immanuel ◊Fuchs – were associated with transformations arising in non-Euclidean geometry. The originator of the study of algebraic topology, Poincaré has sometimes been compared with Karl ◊Gauss in terms of the innovatory nature of his discoveries and the genuine desire for rigorous and precise presentation of data.

Poincaré contributed to the theory of the figures of equilibrium of rotating fluid masses and discovered the pear-shaped figures used in the researches of George Darwin (Charles ◊Darwin's second son) and others. But perhaps his greatest contribution to mathematical physics was his paper on the dynamics of the electron, published in 1906, in which he obtained many of the results of the theory of relativity later credited to Albert Einstein. Poincaré worked quite independently of Einstein; his treatment was based on the full theory of electromagnetism and limited to electromagnetic phenomena, whereas Einstein developed his theory from elementary considerations involving light signalling. Poincaré's studies of mathematical physics led him inevitably to investigations in the field of celestial mechanics. He made important contributions to the theory of orbits, particularly with the classic three-body problem – the mutual gravitational and other effects of three bodies close together in space – which he generalized to a study of n bodies. In the course of his work he developed powerful new mathematical techniques, including the theories of asymptotic expansions and integral invariants. He made important discoveries about the behaviour of the integral curves of differential equations near singularities, and wrote a massive three-volume treatise on his new mathematical methods in astronomy. From his theory of periodic orbits he developed the entirely new subject of topological dynamics.

Poincaré wrote on the philosophy of science. He believed that some mathematical ideas precede logic, and made an original analysis of the psychology of mathematical discovery and invention in which he stressed the role played by convention in scientific method.

Science is built up with facts, as a house is with stones. But a collection of facts is no more a science than a heap of stones is a house.
HENRI POINCARÉ SCIENCE AND HYPOTHESIS *1905*

He was said, very early in his career, to be a 'mathematical giant'. Certainly Poincaré's output of writings was gigantic – he produced, in all, more than 30 books and 500 papers. But one outstanding quality of his authorship was that it appealed not merely to scientists but to educated people in all walks of life. When he was elected to the Académie Française in 1908, it was to fill the position left vacant following the death of the poet René Sully Prudhomme – a writer, not a scientist.

Further Reading
Folina, Janet, *Poincaré and the Philosophy of Mathematics*, Studies in Contemporary Philosophy series, Macmillan, 1992.

Poincaré, Henri, *Science and Method*, Key Texts series, Thoemmes Antiquarian Books, 1996.

Poincaré, Henri; Goroff, Daniel L (ed and intr), *New Methods of Celestial Mechanics*, History of Modern Physics and Astronomy series, American Institute of Physics, 1993, 13, 3 vols.

Stump, David, 'Henri Poincaré's philosophy of science', *Stud Hist Phil Sci*, 1989, v 20, pp 335–363.

Poiseuille, Jean Louis Marie (1799–1869) French physiologist who made a key contribution to our knowledge of the circulation of blood in the arteries. He also studied the flow of liquids in artificial capillaries.

Poiseuille was born on 22 April 1797 in Paris. Little is known of the positions he held, but he is known to have attended the Ecole Polytechnique in Paris 1815–16 and to have received a doctorate in 1828. In 1842 he was elected to the Académie de Médicine in Paris and the Société Philomathique, both in Paris. He also received the Montyon Medal for his physiological researches in 1829, 1831, 1835, and 1843. Poiseuille is best-known for his studies of the circulation of the blood through arteries. He improved on earlier measurements of blood pressure by using a mercury manometer and filling the connection to the artery with potassium carbonate to prevent coagulation. He used this instrument, known as a hemodynamometer, for his dissertation to show that blood pressure rises during expiration (breathing out) and falls during inspiration. He also discovered that the dilation of an artery falls to less than $1/20$ of its normal value during a heartbeat.

Poiseuille was also interested in the flow of liquids through other small pipes and capillaries. Experiments with distilled water led him to state laws for the volume of liquid discharged per unit time from a capillary to its diameter, length, temperature, and pressure difference between the ends of the pipe. At first this relationship was named after Poiseuille but later it was realized that Hagen had discovered it independently a year earlier. It is now known as the Hagen–Poiseuille law. Poiseuille died in Paris on 26 December 1869.

Poisson, Siméon-Denis (1781–1840) French mathematician and physicist. He is mainly remembered for Poisson's ratio in elasticity, which is the ratio of the lateral contraction of a body to its longitudinal extension. The ratio is constant for a given material. Poisson also made contributions to mathematics, especially in probability theory, and to astronomy, in which he investigated planetary and lunar motion.

Poisson was born on 21 June 1781 in Pithiviers, Loirel, where his father was a civil servant in the local administration. Initially training as a surgeon, but discovering he had neither the manual dexterity for nor

any interest in the profession, he entered the Ecole Centrale in Fontainebleau in 1796 to study mathematics. Two years later he continued his studies in Paris at the Ecole Polytechnique (coming first in the entry examination), where he studied under Pierre ◊Laplace and Joseph ◊Lagrange. After only 12 months there, in 1799 he submitted a paper on the theory of equations that enabled him not only to graduate in 1800 but to begin teaching at the Ecole himself. Two years later he was named deputy professor and, in 1806, became professor. In 1808 he was appointed astronomer at the Bureau des Longitudes, and the following year he was appointed professor of mechanics at the Faculty of Sciences. In 1815 he became an examiner at the Ecole Polytechnique. Nominated Conseil Royal de l'Université in 1820, he became an administrator at the highest level in France's educational system and, as such, played a particularly prominent part in the 'defence' of science against the conservative policies of the government of the day. Seven years later, he was appointed mathematician at the Bureau des Longitudes in succession to Laplace. And in 1837 Poisson became a nobleman on accepting the offer of a baronetcy. He died in Paris on 25 April 1840.

Much of Poisson's work involved applying mathematical principles in theoretical terms to contemporary and prior experiments in physics, particularly with reference to electricity and magnetism but also with special regard to heat and sound. Quite early in his career, Poisson adopted the 'two-fluid' theory of Jean Nollet (1700–1770), according to which the like fluids of electricity repelled and the unlike fluids attracted, and showed that Joseph Lagrange's potential function would be constant over the surface of an insulated conductor. He went on to give an ingenious proof of the formula for the force at the surface of a charged conductor.

Charles ◊Coulomb had already carried out experimental work involving the surface densities of charge for two spherical magnets placed any distance apart. Poisson produced theoretical results that were in agreement with those obtained experimentally by Coulomb and, in 1824, gave a very complete theory of magnetism using Coulomb's model – again incorporating two 'fluids'. Poisson derived a general expression for the magnetic potential at any point: the sum of two integrals due to volume and surface distribution of magnetism respectively.

In his own experiments on the elasticity of materials, Poisson deduced the ratio between the lateral and longitudinal strain in a wire; this is now known as Poisson's ratio. Poisson summed up his work in physics in several books towards the end of his life. They include *Treatise on Mechanics* (1833) and *Mathematical Theory of Heat* (1835). Poisson also published *Researches on the Movement of Projectiles in Air* (1835), which builds on the work of Gaspard ◊Coriolis and was the first account of the effects of the Earth's rotation on motion. It inspired the famous pendulum experiment carried out in 1850 by Léon ◊Foucault that first demonstrated the Earth's rotation.

His significant work in probability theory was considered at first to be a mere popularization of the work of Laplace. Poisson's formula for the great asymmetry between opposite events, such that the prior probability of either event is very small, was not used until the end of the 19th century, when its importance was finally recognized. Poisson was also responsible for a formulation of the 'law of large numbers', which he introduced in his important work on probability theory, *Recherches sur la probabilité des jugements* (1837).

Polanyi, Michael (1891–1976) Hungarian-born British physical chemist, particularly noted for his contributions to reaction kinetics. In later life he diverted his attention to social philosophy, in which he became equally renowned. Throughout his career he voiced his firm belief in the right of the scientist to seek the truth unhampered by external constraints.

Polanyi was born in Budapest on 12 March 1891. He entered the University of Budapest in 1909 to study medicine, but after graduation went to the Technische Hochschule at Karlsruhe as a student of chemistry under Georg ◊Bredig. After service as a medical officer during World War I, he returned briefly to Karlsruhe before joining the Kaiser Wilhelm Institute of Fibre Chemistry in Berlin. In 1923, at the invitation of Fritz ◊Haber, Polanyi moved to the Institute for Physical and Electro-Chemistry. But he became increasingly disturbed by the influence of the Nazi Party, especially its dismissal of Jewish scientists, and in 1933 he accepted the chair of physical chemistry at Manchester, England.

During the 1940s, Polanyi made the decision to concentrate on philosophy and in 1948 he transferred to the newly created chair of social studies at Manchester. On retiring from this position in 1958 he moved to Merton College, Oxford, as senior research fellow. He died in Northampton on 22 February 1976.

Polyani's early researches in chemical physics resulted in several papers on the adsorption of gases by solids. He introduced the idea of the existence of an attractive force between a solid surface and the atoms or molecules of a gas; he also suggested that the adsorbed surface is a multilayer and not subject to simple valency interactions. His other work of about that time extended the theory of Hermann ◊Nernst (which stated that the entropy of a system approaches zero as the temperature decreases towards absolute zero). Polanyi showed that an increase in pressure must have

the same effect, although in practice the highest attainable laboratory pressure is less effective than a very modest temperature increase.

At Berlin Polanyi's interest turned to X-ray analysis, using the newly developed rotating crystal method. He and his co-workers improved the technique and applied it to the determination of the structure of cellulose fibres. He also investigated the physical and mechanical properties of various materials; he grew crystals of metals and devised a special apparatus to measure their shear and rupture strengths.

Even as early as 1920 Polanyi recognized that the current theories of chemical reaction rates were simplifications of the truth. The collision theory postulated that only molecules with a certain critical energy would react. Working first under Haber and then at Manchester Polanyi extended this idea and produced theories of rates of association and dissociation based on the angular momenta of the colliding particles. Then quantum mechanics presented the kineticist with a powerful new tool. Reactions were considered in terms of the variation in potential energy of a system, which could be plotted as a function of the distance between reacting nuclei to produce a diagram somewhat resembling a contour map. The configuration of the components at the 'mountain pass' was defined as the activated complex, and the 'height' of the pass represented the activation energy.

Polanyi and Eyring investigated the reaction between a hydrogen atom and a hydrogen molecule:

$$H + H_2(\text{para}) \rightarrow H + H_2(\text{ortho})$$

and made the first reasonable accurate determination of its energy surface (ortho- and parahydrogen are isomers that differ only in the direction of spin of their nuclei).

Polanyi also played a part in solving a problem that had long been puzzling kineticists. It was known that in the hydrogen–iodine equilibrium:

$$H_2 + I_2 \leftrightarrow 2HI$$

the rate of reaction is given by the equation:

$$\frac{d\,[HI]}{dt} = K[H_2]\,[I_2]$$

where K is a constant. But in the apparently analogous reaction between hydrogen and bromine, experiment showed the reaction rate to be given by:

$$\frac{d\,[HBr]}{dt} = \frac{k[H_2]\,[Br_2]^{1/2}}{m + [HBr]\,/\,[Br_2]}$$

where k and m are constants. This expression implies that the velocity of the reaction is inhibited by the presence of the product HBr. Polanyi and others proposed a chain mechanism for the reaction:

$$
\begin{aligned}
\text{initiation:} && Br_2 &\rightarrow 2Br \\
\text{propagation:} && Br + H_2 &\rightarrow HBr + H \\
&& H + Br_2 &\rightarrow HBr + Br \\
\text{inhibition:} && H + HBr &\rightarrow H_2 + Br_2 \\
\text{termination:} && 2BR &\rightarrow Br_2
\end{aligned}
$$

In his new philosophical role at Manchester, Polanyi was active in the Society for Freedom in Science. He advocated that scientific research need not necessarily have a pre-stated function and expressed the belief that a commitment to the discovery of truth is the prime reason for being a scientist. His principal work was an investigation of the processes by which high-level skills such as craftsmanship and connoisseurship are acquired and the means by which such skills are shared and extended. His move to Oxford in 1958 coincided with the publication of his book *Personal Knowledge,* of which he said 'The principal purpose of this book is to achieve a frame of mind in which I may firmly hold what I believe to be true, even though I know it may conceivably be false'.

Further Reading

Allen, Richard, *Polanyi,* Thinkers of Our Time series, Claridge Press, 1990.

Prosch, Harry, *Michael Polanyi: A Critical Exposition,* SUNY Series in Cultural Perspectives, State University of New York Press, 1986.

Scott, Drusilla, *Michael Polanyi,* Gospel and Culture series, Society for Promoting Christian Knowledge, 1996.

Pólya, George (1887–1985) Hungarian mathematician best known for his work on function theory, probability, and applied mathematics.

Pólya was born in Budapest on 13 December 1887. He studied at the Eotvos Lorand University and was awarded his PhD in mathematics by the University of Budapest in 1912. While there he was a member of a thriving community of mathematicians, but he then chose to devote two years to postgraduate study abroad. He attended courses at the University of Göttingen and in Paris before in 1914 accepting the offer of a position as assistant professor of mathematics at the Swiss Federal Institute of Technology in Zürich. He was promoted to associate professor and in 1928 to full professor of the institute. He served as dean and chairman of the mathematics department from 1938, but in 1940 left to go to the USA. Brown University in Providence, Rhode Island, offered him the post of visiting professor, which he held for two years before moving to Smith College, Northampton, Massachusetts, as professor of mathematics. In 1946 Pólya became professor of mathematics at Stanford University, Palo Alto, California, where he remained until his retirement as professor emeritus in 1953. He frequently made lecture tours to universities throughout North America and Europe after his 'retirement'.

Pólya was a member of numerous scientific and mathematical organizations, including the National Academy of Sciences, the American Academy of Arts and Sciences, and the London Mathematical Society. He was awarded several honorary degrees and wrote numerous books.

One of Pólya's best known achievements was his discovery in 1920 of the theorem since named after him. Pólya's theorem is a solution of a problem in combinatorics theory and method. Much of his other early work was on function theory, and he published studies on analytical functions in 1924 and on algebraic functions in 1927. He also worked on linear homogeneous differential equations in 1924 and transcendental equations in 1930. One of his studies in mathematical physics was an investigation into heat propagation published in 1931. He extended some of the previous results obtained by Andrei ◊Markov on the limit of probability, and probability theory became one of Pólya's major research areas.

Other subjects he examined included the study of complex variables, polynomials, and number theory. His contributions to mathematics can thus be seen to be notable both for their breadth and their depth.

Further Reading

Boas, R P, 'George Pólya, December 1887–September 1985', *Biogr Mem Nat Acad Sci,* 1990, v 59, pp 339–355.

Clements, M A and Ellerton, Nerida, *Pólya, Krutetskii, and the Restaurant Problem,* Deakin University Press, 1991.

Pólya, George; Rota, Gian-Carlo, Boas, Ralph P and Hersch, Joseph (eds), *George Pólya – Collected Papers: Analysis,* Mathematicians of Our Time series, MIT Press, 1984, v 22.

Taylor, Harold D and Taylor, Loretta, *George Pólya: Master of Discovery, 1887–1985,* Seymour, 1993.

Poncelet, Jean-Victor (1788–1867) French military engineer who, to pass the time during two years as a prisoner of war, revised all the mathematics he could remember and went on to make fresh discoveries, particularly in projective geometry. He was among the leaders of those who initiated and developed the concept of duality.

Poncelet was born in Metz on 1 July 1788, the son of Claude Poncelet, a rich landowner and an *advocat* at the parliament of Metz. Born illegitimate and only later acknowledged by his father, Poncelet was sent to live with a family in Saint-Avold, and they were responsible for his educational grounding. At the age of 16 he returned to Metz and attended the school there. In 1807 he went to the Ecole Polytechnique in

Paris, and stayed there for three years. He then fell behind with his studies, however, because of ill health, and in 1810 joined the Corps of Military Engineers. Graduating from the Ecole d'Application in Metz in February 1812, he then assisted in the fortification of the Dutch island of Walcheren. In June of the same year he became lieutenant of engineers and, attached to the staff of the engineer general, took part in the campaign against the Russians. He was captured at the Battle of Krasnoy, and was imprisoned in Saratov, a city on the Volga, until 1814. He then returned to France in September of that year and became captain of the Engineering Corps in Metz. From then until 1824 he was engaged on projects in military engineering there. At the end of that time he was appointed professor of mechanics applied to machines at the Ecole d'Application de l'Artillerie et du Génie in Metz, six years later becoming a member of Metz Municipal Council and secretary of the Conseil-Général of the Moselle. He was elected to the mechanics section of the Académie Française in 1834, and from 1838 to 1848 was professor to the Faculty of Science at Paris. From 1848 to 1850 he was commandant of the Ecole Polytechnique with the rank of general. He died in Paris on 22 December 1867.

Poncelet's first great work was done while he was imprisoned at Saratov. With no textbooks at his disposal, he reconstructed the elements of pure and analytical mathematics (specifically geometry) from memory before undertaking some original research on the systems and properties of conics. It was projective geometry that interested him most, and it was his study of this aspect of conics that established the basis for his later important work, the treatise entitled *Traité des propriétés projectives des figures* (1822). Poncelet had been a pupil of Gaspard ◊Monge, who was the originator of modern synthetic geometry – synthetic geometry's viewing of figures as they exist in space is an alternative mathematical tool to the equation in the analytical method – but was equally conversant with analytical geometry. In fact, Poncelet used both methods and ranks as one of the greatest of those who contributed to the development of the relatively new synthetic (projective) geometry.

Poncelet also discovered the circular points at infinity, although the concept of points at infinity goes back to Gérard Desargues (1591–1661), and many of the individual ideas of projective geometry go back considerably further. But it was Poncelet who first developed them as a distinct branch of the mathematical science. His rather forceful presentation – and his occasionally wild accusations of plagiarism by other geometrists – antagonized the young German mathematician Julius ◊Plücker to such an extent that he turned from using synthetic methods and became

himself one of the greatest of analytical geometrists.

The principle of duality was first recognized and publicized by Poncelet in the *Journal für Mathematik* of 1829, although previously formulated by Joseph Gergonne 1825–27. (It can be illustrated by considering a statement capable of two meanings, both true, one obtained from the other simply by interchanging two words. In projective geometry, in two dimensions, this is achieved by interchanging the words 'point' and 'line'. In three-dimensional geometry, there is a corresponding duality between points and planes; in this case the line is self-dual, in that it is determined by any two distinct points on it or by any two distinct planes through it.) Much of higher geometry is concerned with duality, and every new application practically doubles the extent of existing knowledge.

Poncelet's engineering skills were much used 1814–40, for the first ten years of which he was engaged on projects in topography and the fortification and organization of an engineering arsenal. In 1821 he developed a new model of a variable counterweight drawbridge, which he described and publicized in 1822. His most important technical contributions were concerned with hydraulic engines (such as Poncelet's water wheel), regulations, and dynamometers, as well as in devising various improvements to his own previous fortification techniques. In applied mechanics he worked in three interrelated fields: experimental mechanics, the theory of machines, and industrial mechanics.

Pond, John (1767–1836) English astronomer whose meticulous observations at his private observatory led to his discovering errors in data published by the Royal Observatory in Greenwich. When he himself became Astronomer Royal, he therefore implemented a vigorous programme of renovation and reorganization at Greenwich that restored the observatory to its former standards of excellence.

Pond was born in London in 1767 – no more exact date is known. His scientific talents were apparent from an early age and he entered Trinity College, Cambridge, in 1783 to study chemistry. Forced by poor health to leave the university before he could take his degree, he travelled in warmer climates to recover his strength. He went to several Mediterranean and Middle Eastern countries, making astronomical observations wherever possible. When he returned to England in 1798, he established a small private observatory in Westbury, near Bristol. From there he published observations of considerable astronomical interest, and in 1807 he was elected a fellow of the Royal Society. This prompted him to return to London, and in 1811 he was appointed Astronomer Royal. He immediately set about reorganizing and modernizing the Greenwich Observatory, which until that time had had only one assistant and a collection of equipment that was sadly in need of repair. In 1835, however, he was forced to retire from all professional duties because of ill health. He was awarded the Lalande Prize of the French Academy of Sciences in 1817, and the Copley Medal of the Royal Society in 1823. He died in Blackheath on 7 September 1836.

Pond first demonstrated his skills as an astronomer at the age of 15. He noticed errors in the observations being made at the Greenwich Observatory and made a thorough investigation of the declination of a number of fixed stars. By 1806 he had clearly and publicly demonstrated that the quadrant at Greenwich, designed by Bird, had become deformed with age and needed replacing. It was this in particular that prompted his programme to modernize the whole observatory.

One of the first results of the revitalization programme was his 1813 catalogue of the north polar distances of 84 stars. These data were obtained with the new mural circle designed by Edward Troughton and were highly esteemed by Pond's contemporaries. Pond was able to dispute, in 1817, the validity of J Brinkley's observations on the parallax of a number of fixed stars. Pond held that Brinkley had not, in fact, detected stellar parallax, which was being sought by numerous astronomers as a proof of Copernican cosmology, and he was later proved to be right. The interest that the controversy generated contributed to Friedrich ◊Bessel's later successful efforts in this field.

Another controversy, of an unpleasant kind, surrounded Pond's work a few years later – surprisingly, considering how meticulous (even pedantic) he was known to be. A committee of enquiry, set up by the Royal Society, found that two of Pond's assistants were responsible for work that was less than accurate or conscientious, and reprimanded them; Pond was cleared.

Instituting new methods of observation, Pond went on to produce a catalogue of more than 1,000 stars in 1833. His work continued to be admired by many of his fellow astronomers in the UK and in Europe. Nevertheless, he remains remembered most for his modernization of the Greenwich Observatory.

Pons, Jean-Louis (1761–1831) French astronomer

who, in a career that began at a comparatively late age, nevertheless discovered 37 comets and became director of the Florence Observatory.

Pons was born on Christmas Eve in 1761 at Peyre, near Dauphine. The son of a poor family, he was not well educated and held several labouring jobs until the age of 28, when he became a porter and doorkeeper at the Marseille Observatory. Noting his interest in

astronomy, the directors of the observatory gave him instruction in the subject, paying particular attention to Pons's training in practical observation. Pons learned quickly; knowledge of the sky together with excellent eyesight and considerable patience stood him in good stead. And as a result of his diligence and achievement, Pons was named *astronome adjoint* at the Marseille Observatory in 1813. Five years later he became its assistant director. His achievements were recognized outside the Marseille Observatory when, in 1819, on the recommendation of Baron Frederich von Zach, Pons became director of a newly constructed observatory at Lucca, in northern Italy. Three years later, when the observatory was closed, Pons was invited by Grand Duke Leopold of Tuscany to become director of the Florence Observatory. Before failing eyesight finally forced him to give up much of his observational work, he received many honours and awards (including no fewer than three Lalande prizes). He retired from the observatory a few months before his death on 14 October 1831.

The first Lalande Prize that Pons was awarded by the French Academy of Sciences was for his discovery in 1818 of three small, tailless comets, among which was one that Pons claimed had first been seen in 1805 by Johann ◊Encke of the Berlin Observatory. Alerted to this possibility, Encke carried out further observations and calculations, and finally ascribed to it a period of 1,208 days – which meant that it would return in 1822. Its return was duly observed, in Australia, only the second instance ever of the known return of an identified comet. Encke wanted the comet to be named after Pons, but it continued to be called after its discoverer. Encke received the Gold Medal of the Royal Astronomical Society of London and Pons the Silver.

At Lucca Pons discovered a number of new comets, for one of which he received his second Lalande Prize. His third Lalande Prize followed his discovery of more comets at the Florence Observatory, raising the total number of his discoveries to 37.

Porsche, Ferdinand (1875–1951) German engineer

who designed and built the first mass-produced European people's car and later helped to develop small, high-performance luxury cars destined for series production. He also invented synchronizing gearboxes and torsion-bar suspension.

Porsche was born the son of a tinsmith in Bohemia. From 1923 to 1929 he served as technical director of the German firm of Daimler, which became Daimler–Benz in 1926. During that period his most notable contribution was the Mercedes SSK racing car. He rose from relative obscurity to form a limited liability company on 25 March 1931, registered in Stuttgart in the name of Dr Ing HCF Porsche Ltd.

From 1931 to 1933, Porsche developed his first small-car prototypes for Zündapp and NSU, under contract. In 1932 he devised the first torsion-bar suspension system and in the same year visited Russia to make an extensive study trip through all centres of the Soviet vehicle industry of that period. He was allowed to visit any factory that interested him and was said to have been shown all their designs for vehicles, aircraft, and tractors. At the end of this journey, he was offered the job of Russia's chief national designer, to be accompanied by a wealth of authority and privilege. But Porsche declined; the language barrier, in particular, deterred him.

In 1936 he received a contract from the German government to develop the Volkswagen ('people's car') and plan the factory where it would be built. Just prior to this he had conceived a racing car, without contract. The project was taken over by Auto Union and the car subsequently claimed victories on virtually every race track in Europe 1934–37, as well as many class records.

The first Volkswagen prototypes were on the road by the end of 1935; the years to follow, up to the outbreak of World War II, were years of the utmost concentration on the Volkswagen for Porsche. Some other design jobs, however, had appeared alongside the major Volkswagen contract to cause Porsche to expand his company. During June 1938 the design offices moved from Kronenstrasse 24 in Stuttgart to Spitalwaldstrasse 2 in Suffenhausen, where he led the development of light tractors. Those tractors built to Porsche license and under the firm's supervision after World War II can be traced to these designs. Concepts were also developed by him for aviation engines as well as plans and designs for wind-driven power plants – large windmills with automatic sail adjustment that delivered electric current via generators.

The war cut short further development of the Volkswagen so Porsche designed the Leopard and Tiger tanks used by German Panzer regiments and helped to develop the V-1 flying bomb. During this period he was awarded an honorary professorship.

After internment following the end of the war, Porsche joined his son in Gmünd, Carinthia, Austria, where his company had been moved from Zuffenhausen to help develop the first Type 256 Porsche roadster, later to become the 911 model. He was considerably weakened by his 22-month term of imprisonment, however, and his health caused him to withdraw from engineering by the end of the 1940s. He died in 1951.

The Volkswagen was conceived in 1934 as a utility car of low weight to be 'achieved by new basic measures'. The first prototypes were built in 1935 and 1936, before the contract to build had been signed. A lightweight 'flat-four' cylinder, air-cooled engine of substantial magnesium-alloy construction was rear-mounted in the vehicle. It was united with a similarly constructed gearbox. Independent suspension of all four wheels was by swing axles with torsion-bar springing.

Substantial weight-savings resulted in the absence of axle beams and the combined weight of the rear-mounted engine and gearbox unit was insufficient to cause handling instability. The disposition of major components allowed an aerodynamically efficient saloon-car body of lightweight chassis-less construction to be fitted, giving adequate leg room within the small exterior envelope.

Porsche's first production Volkswagen rolled off the assembly lines in 1945 at the Wolfsburg plant. On 17 February 1972 it became the car with the longest and biggest production run in the history of the motorcar, outpacing the Model T Ford at 15,007,033 units.

Porsche was a brilliant engineer whose genius reached into many disciplines. It has been said that the torsion-bar suspension alone would have sufficed to establish a monument to his name in the automotive industry. He can be considered one of the pioneers of air-cooled engines in the industry. The sports cars bearing his name were developed by his son Ferry and the first, the 356, was based on the incredibly versatile Volkswagen Beetle.

Further Reading

Barker, Richard and Harding, Anthony, *Automobile Design: Twelve Great Designers and Their Work,* Society of Automotive Engineers, 1992.

Peto, James and Ford, Gerard (eds), *Ferdinand Porsche: Design Dynasty 1900–1998,* Design Museum, 1998.

Porter, George (1920–) Baron Porter of Luddenham. English physical chemist who developed the technique of flash photolysis for the direct study of extremely fast chemical reactions, for which achievement he shared the 1967 Nobel Prize for Chemistry with Ronald ◊Norrish and Manfred ◊Eigen. He has also inspired others – particularly young people – by his television appearances and lectures at the Royal Institution in the 1960s.

Porter was born in Stainforth, Yorkshire, on 6 December 1920. He graduated from Leeds University in 1941, during World War II, and spent the next four years as a radar officer in the Royal Navy. He then went to Cambridge University where he carried out research 1945–49 under Ronald Norrish. From 1952 to 1954 he was assistant director of research at Cambridge and assistant director of the British Rayon Research Association for a year in 1955. He then became professor of physical chemistry at Sheffield University and was made head of the chemistry department in 1963.

He was Fullerian Professor of Chemistry at at the Royal Institution 1966–88 (emeritus thereafter) and its director 1966–85. From 1985 to 1990 he was president of the Royal Society. He was knighted in 1972 and created a baron in 1990

In 1947, while working with Norrish, Porter began using quick flashes of light to study transient species in chemical reactions, particularly free radicals and excited states of molecules. He studied very fast reactions having short-lived intermediates. In 1950 he could detect entities that exist for less than a microsecond; by 1967 he had reduced the time limit to a nanosecond, and by 1975 he could detect species that lasted for as little as a picosecond (10^{-12} sec). His early work dealt with reactions involving gases (mainly chain reactions and combustion reactions), but he later extended the technique to solutions. He developed a method of stabilizing free radicals by trapping them in the structure of a supercooled liquid (a glass), a technique called matrix isolation. He enabled flash photolysis to be applied to organic chemistry, biochemistry, and photobiology. Today photochemical methods are used to synthesize hydrocarbons for fuels and chemical feedstocks.

If sunbeams were weapons of war, we would have had solar energy long ago.
GEORGE PORTER OBSERVER *1973*

One of Porter's main interests from the early 1960s was the mechanism of photosynthesis in plants, which proceeds via 'light' and 'dark' stages. He studied the light-harvesting mechanisms of chloroplasts and the primary processes that occur in the first nanosecond of photosynthesis.

Porter, Rodney Robert (1917–1985) English immunologist well known for his contribution to the identification of the structure of antibody molecules. For this work he received the 1972 Nobel Prize for Physiology or Medicine, which he shared with US neuroscientist Gerald Edelman (1929–   ).

Porter was born in Liverpool on 8 October 1917 and was educated at Ashton-in-Makerfield Grammar School, and then at Liverpool University, where he gained a BSc in 1939. From 1940 to 1946, including much of World War II, he was in military service. He then returned to Cambridge (gaining his PhD in 1948) and continued his research, aided by Frederick ◊Sanger. In 1949 he was appointed to the staff of the National Institute for Medical Research, a position he held until 1960 when he became Pfizer Professor of Immunology at St Mary's Hospital Medical School,

London. From 1967 he was Whitley Professor of Biochemistry at Oxford, and honorary director of the Medical Research Council's Immunochemistry Unit.

When Porter started his research after the war, he often referred to Karl ◊Landsteiner's book *The Specificity of Serological Reactions,* and it was from this work that he learnt the technique for preparing certain antibodies. Some aspects of the structural studies of immunoglobulins, or antibody proteins, had been completed, such as those for several human myeloma proteins and some rabbit immunoglobulins. Some work had also been done on the structural basis of the combining specificity of antibodies and in the solution of the genetic origins of antibodies. Porter's major scientific interests have been the structural basis of the biological activities of antibodies – in 1962 he proposed a structure for gamma globulin – and worked on the structure, assembly, and activation mechanisms of the components of a substance known as complement. This is a protein normally present in the blood, but which disappears from the serum during most antigen–antibody reactions. Porter also investigated the way in which immunoglobulins interact with complement components and with cell surfaces.

Powell, Cecil Frank (1903–1969) English physicist who developed photographic techniques for studying subatomic particles and who discovered the pi-meson (pion). For this discovery he was awarded the 1950 Nobel Prize for Physics.

Powell was born in Tonbridge, Kent, on 5 December 1903, the son of a gunsmith. He won a scholarship to Cambridge University in 1921 and graduated four years later. He then went to the Cavendish Laboratory to do research under Ernest ◊Rutherford and Charles ◊Wilson, working on methods of taking improved photographs of particle tracks in a cloud chamber. Powell gained his PhD in 1928 and moved to the Wills Physics Laboratory at Bristol University as research assistant to A M Tyndall (1881–1961). He remained at Bristol, becoming professor of physics in 1948 and director of the laboratory in 1964. He died in Bellano, Italy, on 9 August 1969.

In the early 1930s Tyndall and Powell studied the mobility of ions in gases and the way water droplets condense on ions in a cloud chamber. Then in 1938, instead of photographing the cloud-chamber tracks, Powell made the ionizing particles trace paths in the emulsions of a stack of photographic plates. The technique received a boost with the development of more sensitive emulsions during World War II and in 1947 Powell used it in his discovery of the pi-meson (the existence of which had been predicted by Hideki ◊Yukawa in 1935). Powell collaborated with the Italian physicist Giuseppe Occhislini, and together they published *Nuclear Physics in Photographs* (1947), which became a standard text on the subject.

Powell, John Wesley (1834–1902) US geologist whose enormous and original studies produced lasting insights into erosion by rivers, volcanism, and mountain formation.

The son of intensely pious Methodist immigrants, Powell was intended by his farmer father for the Methodist ministry, but he early developed a love for natural history. In the 1850s he became secretary of the Illinois Society of Natural History, travelling widely and building up his natural history collections and his geological expertise. Fighting in the Civil War, he had his right arm shot off, but continued in the service, rising to the rank of colonel.

After the end of the war, Powell occupied various chairs in geology in Illinois, while continuing with intrepid fieldwork (he was one of the first to steer a way down the Grand Canyon). In 1870 Congress appointed him to lead an official survey of the natural resources of the Utah, Colorado, and Arizona area, the findings of which were published in his *The Exploration of the Colorado River* (1875) and *The Geology of the Eastern Portion of the Uinta Mountains* (1876).

Powell's studies produced lasting insights on fluvial erosion, volcanism, isostasy, and orogeny. His greatness as a geologist and geomorphologist stemmed from his capacity to grasp the interconnections of geological and climatic causes. In 1881 he was appointed director of the US Geological Survey. He encouraged most of the great US geologists of the next generation, including Grove Karl Gilbert, Clarence E Dutton, and W H Holmes.

Powell drew attention to the aridity of the American southwest, and for a couple of decades campaigned for massive funds for irrigation projects and dams, and for the geological surveys necessary to implement adequate water strategies. He also asserted the need in the drylands for changes in land policy and farming techniques. Failing to win political support on such matters, he resigned in 1894 from the Geological Survey.

Poynting, John Henry (1852–1914) English physicist, mathematician, and inventor whose various contributions to science included an equation by which the rate of flow of electromagnetic energy (now called the Poynting vector) can be determined, and the measurement of Isaac ◊Newton's gravitational constant. He received many honours for his work, including the Royal Society's Royal Medal in 1905.

Poynting was born in Monton, Lancashire, on 9 September 1852. He attended his father's school until 1867, when he entered Owens College in Manchester (later Manchester University), where he gained an external BSc from London University in 1872. He then studied at Trinity College, Cambridge, 1872–76. After graduation he served as a physics demonstrator – under Balfour Stewart (1828–1887) – at Owens College until 1878, when he was appointed a research fellow at Trinity College where he researched in the Cavendish Laboratories under James Clerk ◊Maxwell. In 1880 he became professor of physics at Mason College, Birmingham (which became Birmingham University in 1900), a post he held until his death – caused by a diabetic attack – in Birmingham on 30 March 1914.

Poynting's first publications, in the late 1870s, were in the field of mathematics and included such subjects as statistical studies of alcoholism in England. After moving to the Cavendish Laboratories in 1878 he began a long series of experiments to determine Newton's gravitational constant (from which can be calculated the Earth's mean density), which was the subject of a competition at Cambridge. He published his most accurate results in 1891, having obtained them using an ordinary beam balance; his figures differ only slightly from those now generally accepted. His experimental method was refined in 1895 by Charles ◊Boys, who used a quartz-fibre torsion balance. Poynting recognized the value of Boys's apparatus and used it for several later studies of his own, such as the measurement of radiation pressure.

Poynting's best-known work concerned the transmission of energy in electromagnetic fields. In *On the Transfer of Energy in the Electromagnetic Field* (1884) he published an equation (which he worked out using Maxwell's electromagnetic field theory) by which the magnitude and direction of the flow of electromagnetic energy – the Poynting vector – can be determined. This equation is usually expressed as:

$$S = (1/\mu)EB \sin \theta$$

where S is the Poynting vector, μ is the permeability of the medium, E is the strength of the electric field, B is the strength of the magnetic field, and θ is the angle between the vectors representing the electric and magnetic fields.

Poynting, in collaboration with W Barlow, also did important work on radiation. In 1903 he suggested the existence of an effect of the Sun's radiation that causes small particles orbiting the Sun to gradually approach it and eventually plunge in. This idea was later developed by the US physicist Howard Robertson (1903–1961) – who related it to the theory of relativity – and it is now known as the Poynting–Robertson effect. Poynting also devised a method for measuring the radiation pressure from a body; his method can be used to determine the absolute temperature of celestial objects.

Poynting's other work included a theoretical analysis of the solid to liquid phase change, in 1881; a statistical analysis of changes in commodity prices on the stock exchange, in 1884; a study of osmotic pressure; and the construction of a saccharometer and a double-image micrometer.

Prandtl, Ludwig (1875–1953) German physicist who put fluid mechanics on a sound theoretical basis. In particular, he originated the boundary layer theory and did pioneering work in aerodynamics.

Prandtl was born in Freising on 4 February 1875, and entered the Technische Hochschule at Munich in 1894. He specialized in engineering, obtaining his first degree in 1898 and a doctorate in 1900 with a thesis on the lateral instability of beams in bending. In the same year, Prandtl went to work in the Maschinenfabrik Augsburg-Nürnberg, where he became interested in fluid flow. In 1901, he gained a professorship at the Technische Hochschule in Hanover, and then became professor of applied mechanics at Göttingen in 1904. There he constructed the first German wind tunnel in 1909 and built up an important centre for aerodynamics. Prandtl continued to work at Göttingen until his death. A US investigation team arriving there after World War II found that Prandtl, though still active, had not contributed greatly to the German effort. Prandtl died in Göttingen on 15 August 1953.

Prandtl's interest in fluid flow was triggered by his first task in industry, which was to improve a device for the removal of shavings. His studies revealed many weaknesses in the understanding of fluid mechanics. The current theory was unable to explain the observation that in a pipe a fluid would separate from the wall in a sharply divergent section instead of completely filling the pipe. In 1904, Prandtl published a very important paper that proposed that no matter how small the viscosity of a fluid, it is always stationary at the walls of the pipe. This thin static region or boundary layer has a profound influence on the flow of the fluid, and an understanding of the effects of boundary layers was developed to explain the action of lift and drag on aerofoils during the following half century.

In 1906, Prandtl was joined at Göttingen by Theodore von ◊Kármán, who arrived as a student and subsequently became Prandtl's collaborator. In 1907, Prandtl investigated supersonic flow, extending the pioneering work of Ernst ◊Mach to slender bodies. From 1909, Prandtl's aerodynamic studies developed apace as the world became interested in flight. He turned to the problem of drag, which could not be fully explained by the skin friction produced by the boundary layer on a wing. In 1911 and 1912, Kármán and Prandtl discovered how vortices cause drag. Prandtl's major contribution was an explanation of induced drag, which he showed was caused by lift inducing a trailing vortex. Much of this work was published after World War I and resulted in major changes in wing design and the streamlining of aircraft.

The efforts of Prandtl and Kármán in the 1920s led to a greater understanding of turbulent flow. In 1926 Prandtl developed the concept of mixing length – the average distance that a swirling fluid element travels before it dissipates its motion – and was able to produce a plausible theory of turbulence. The concept of mixing length can be thought of as being similar to the mean free path in the kinetic theory of gases. Prandtl's work on turbulence is still the basis of present-day theory.

Modern-day aircraft with their high degree of streamlining and swept-back wings all owe their shapes to the work of Prandtl and Kármán.

Prelog, Vladimir (1906–1998) Bosnian-born Swiss organic chemist famous for his studies of alkaloids and antibiotics, and for his work on stereochemistry. He shared the 1975 Nobel Prize for Chemistry with John ◊Cornforth.

Prelog was born in Sarajevo in Bosnia on 23 July 1906. He spent his early years in Zagreb and went to Hungary to study chemistry at the Institute of Technology in Prague, where he also did postgraduate research. From 1929 to 1934 he worked in Prague as a chemist in a laboratory for the preparation of fine chemicals. Then in 1935 he went to Zagreb in Yugoslavia (now Croatia) to become a lecturer and later associate professor of organic chemistry in the University of Zagreb's Technical Faculty. But in 1941, after the German occupation at the beginning of World War II, Prelog moved to Zürich to lecture at the Swiss Federal Institute of Technology. He became an associate professor in 1947, and ten years later he was made a full professor, succeeding the 1939 Nobel prizewinner Leopold Ruzicka (1887–1976). Prelog retired in 1976. He died on 7 January 1998.

Alkaloids were the subject of Prelog's early research, and one of his first achievements was the determination of the structure of the anti-malarial quinine alkaloids. In 1945 he showed that Robert ◊Robinson's formulae for strychnine alkaloids were incorrect (they were later rectified), and he derived the structures of steroid alkaloids from plants of the genera *Solanum* and *Veratrum* (the latter with Derek ◊Barton). He also investigated many other alkaloids using classical organic chemistry, confirming the findings by X-ray crystallography.

In the 1940s, after his move to Zürich, Prelog studied many lipid extracts from animal organs – working with Ruzicka – and discovered a number of steroids and elucidated their structures. Then, with W Keller-Shlierlein, he investigated metabolic products of microorganisms and with a number of other researchers isolated various new complex natural products that have interesting biological properties. These include antibiotics and bacterial growth factors.

Many of these classes of metabolites have molecules that contain large rings. Prelog became interested in their stereochemistry, and looked at the relationships between the spatial structure and chemistry of many large-membered rings. He researched the steric course of asymmetric syntheses and succeeded in determining the then unknown absolute configurations of the steroids and terpenes. He used asymmetric synthesis as a sensitive tool for studying the details of reaction mechanisms, such as the synthesis of cyanhydrin.

Prelog demonstrated experimentally that some microorganisms have the ability to reduce the carbonyl group of certain alicyclic substrates in a highly stereospecific way. Together with Cahn and Christopher ◊Ingold, he developed a widely used system for defining chirality (or handedness) in organic compounds and of stereoisomerism in general. The comprehensive molecular topology that evolved from this work is gradually replacing classical stereochemistry.

Further Reading

Prelog, Vladimir, *My 132 Semesters of Studies in Chemistry*, Profiles, Pathways and Dreams series, American Chemical Society, 1990.

Prévost, Pierre (1751–1839) Swiss physicist who first showed that all bodies radiate heat, no matter how hot or cold they are.

Prévost was born in Geneva on 3 March 1751. His father, a Calvinist minister, was very keen that his son should have the best possible education and Prévost was sent to study classics, science, and theology, but ultimately he turned to the study of law and gained his degree in 1773. After graduating he became a teacher and held various positions in Holland, Lyon, and Paris. On the death of his father he returned to Geneva and for a time was professor of literature there, but after a year he eventually decided to go back to Paris and work on the translation of a Greek drama.

In 1786 Prévost left Paris once more for Geneva, where he became active in politics. It was at this time that his interest in science re-emerged and he devoted much of his research to the problems of magnetism and then to heat. He was appointed professor of philosophy and general physics at Geneva in 1793 and remained in this post until his retirement in 1823. In his later years, Prévost chose to abandon the earlier research in which he had won such a reputation in favour of studying the human ageing process. He used himself for his observations, noting down in detail every sign of advancement that his mind, body, and

mirror showed. A man of many talents, he used his ability for experimental research to the very end. He died in Geneva on 8 April 1839.

Prévost made his classic analysis of heat radiation in 1791. He conducted experiments to determine the heat properties of different kinds of objects under identical conditions. He found that dark, rough-textured objects give out more radiation than smooth, light-coloured bodies, given that both are at the same temperature. He also found that the reverse is true – that dark, rough objects absorb more heat radiation than light, smooth ones. From these experiments, Prévost conceived of heat as being a fluid composed of particles and that during radiation, the particles streamed out in the form of rays between radiating bodies.

This led to Prévost's theory of heat exchanges. If several objects at different temperatures are placed together, they exchange heat by radiation until all achieve the same temperature. All the objects can then remain at this temperature, however, only if they are receiving as much heat from their surroundings as they radiate away.

Even though Prévost's idea of heat being a fluid, which was the caloric theory current at that time, was erroneous, it did not prevent his basic ideas on heat radiation from being correct. In challenging the notion then prevalent that heat and cold are separate, cold being produced by the entry of cold into an object rather than by an outflow of heat, Prévost made a basic advance in our knowledge of energy. Further consideration of the subject a century later led to the quantum theory of Max ◊Planck and to the idea that heat and other forms of energy are in fact particulate in nature.

Priestley, Joseph (1733–1804) English chemist and theologian. He entered chemistry when it was making the transition from alchemy to a theoretical science. An outstanding practical scientist, he combined experimental flair with quantitative accuracy – skills that led him to discover several new gases, including oxygen. He was less dynamic as a theorist; his conservatism made him a lifelong supporter of Georg ◊Stahl's phlogiston theory of combustion despite mounting evidence – much of it provided by Priestley himself – refuting the principle. Outside his scientific work his life was far from harmonious. He was an outspoken man of radical views, which brought him notoriety and eventually drove him to leave his native country.

Priestley was born in Fieldhead, near Leeds, on 13 March 1733, the son of a cloth-dresser. His mother died when he was only seven years old and he was brought up by an aunt, who introduced him to Calvinism. In 1752 he attended the Dissenting Academy at Daventry, and three years later he entered the ministry as Presbyterian minister at Needham

Market, Suffolk. He moved to Nantwich, Cheshire, in 1758, and in 1761 became tutor in languages at Warrington Academy. A year later he married May Wilkinson, sister of the ironmaster John Wilkinson. On a trip to London in 1766 he met the US scientist Benjamin ◊Franklin, who aroused in Priestley an interest in science; thereafter he combined scientific research with his clerical and social duties.

In 1767 Priestley returned to Leeds as minister of a chapel at Mill Hill. He did his most productive work 1773–80, when he was librarian and literary companion to Lord Shelburne, whom he accompanied on a journey to France in 1774. While in Paris he met Antoine ◊Lavoisier and told him of his experiments with 'dephlogisticated air' (soon to be named oxygen by Lavoisier).

By 1780 Priestley's outspoken criticisms as a Dissenter had become an embarrassment to Lord Shelburne, who retired his companion on a small pension. Priestley moved to Birmingham to become minister of a chapel called the New Meeting. He also joined the Lunar Society, in company with the inventors James ◊Watt and Matthew ◊Boulton, Josiah ◊Wedgwood, Erasmus ◊Darwin (grandfather of Charles ◊Darwin) and a number of less notable inventors and scientists. In Birmingham, Priestley continued to voice loudly his opposition to the established church and his support of the French Revolutionaries. In 1791, on the second anniversary of the storming of the Bastille, the people of Birmingham rioted and vented some of their wrath on Priestley and other Dissenters, whose homes were ransacked. Priestley escaped to London and settled for a while in Hackney, but his unpopularity mounted, exacerbated by an offer of citizenship from France (by the very people who executed Lavoisier in 1794). In that same year Priestley emigrated to the USA, to Northumberland in Pennsylvania. He rejected the offer of a professorship at the University of Pennsylvania, preferring to live a life of comparative solitude in Northumberland, where he died on 6 February 1804.

Influenced by Franklin, Priestley's early work of 1767 onwards was in physics, particularly electricity and optics. He established that electrostatic charge is concentrated on the outer surface of a charged body and that there is no internal force. From this observation he proposed an inverse square law for charges, by analogy with gravitation. Priestley's house in Leeds was near a brewery, and it was his interest in the process of fermentation that turned him to chemistry, particularly gases. He experimented with the gas produced during fermentation – the layer of 'fixed air' (carbon dioxide) over a brewing vat – and showed it to be the same as that reported by Joseph ◊Black in 1756. He dissolved the gas under pressure in water, beginning a European craze for soda water.

At Lord Shelburne's estate at Calne, Wiltshire, Priestley continued experimenting with gases. He used a large magnifying glass to focus the Sun's rays to produce high temperatures. He invented the pneumatic trough for collecting gases over water, and overcame the problem of handling water-soluble gases by collecting them over mercury.

An early discovery, in 1772, was 'nitrous air' (nitric oxide, or nitrogen monoxide, NO). Priestley found that a sample of the gas left in contact with iron filings and sulphur decreased in volume and that the new gas produced supported combustion. He had reduced nitric oxide to nitrous oxide (dinitrogen monoxide, N_2O), Humphry ◊Davy's 'laughing gas'. In the same year he became the first person to isolate gaseous ammonia by collecting it over mercury (previously ammonia was known only in aqueous solution).

It had long been known that burning sulphur gives off a choking gas. In 1774 Priestley made the same gas by heating oil of vitriol (concentrated sulphuric acid) with mercury. He also produced it by heating the acid with copper turnings, a method still used today to make sulphur dioxide (SO_2).

Priestley's most famous discovery was that of oxygen. In 1772 he had shown that a gas necessary to animal life is liberated by plants. Two years later he prepared the same gas by heating red calyx of mercury (mercury(II) oxide, HgO) or minium (red lead, Pb_3O_4). His investigation of the properties of the new gas showed it to be superior to common air. A mouse trapped in a container of it stayed conscious twice as long as in ordinary air, and breathing it had no adverse effects (apart from leaving a peculiar light feeling in the chest). When he mixed the new gas with nitrous air (NO) there was a diminution in volume and yet another, red gas (nitrogen dioxide, NO_2) was formed. From all of these observations Priestley concluded that he had prepared dephlogisticated air – that is, air from which the fiery principle of phlogiston had been removed. The Swedish chemist Karl ◊Scheele independently prepared oxygen in 1772, but his tardiness in publication resulted in Priestley being credited with the discovery.

Further Reading

Anderson, Robert Geoffrey Williams and Lawrence, Christopher (eds), *Science, Medicine, and Dissent: Joseph Priestley (1733–1804)*, Wellcome Trust/Science Museum, 1987.

Clark, John R, *Joseph Priestley: A Comet in the System*, Friends of Joseph Priestley House, 1994.

Graham, Jenny, 'Revolutionary in exile: the emigration of Joseph Priestley to America, 1794–1804', *Transactions of the American Philosophical Society*, American Philosophical Society, 1995, v 85, pt 2.

Hoecher, James J, *Joseph Priestley and the Idea of Progress*, Modern European History series, Garland Publishing, 1987.

McLachlan, John, *Joseph Priestley, Man of Science, 1733–1804: An Iconography of a Great Yorkshireman*, Merlin Books, 1983.

Schofield, Robert E, *The Enlightenment of Joseph Priestley: A Study of His Life and Work from 1733 to 1773*, Pennsylvania State University Press, 1997.

Prigogine, Ilya (1917–) Russian-born Belgian theoretical chemist who was awarded the 1977 Nobel Prize for Chemistry for widening the scope of thermodynamics from the purely physical sciences to ecological and sociological studies.

Prigogine was born in Moscow on 22 January 1917. When he was four years old his parents emigrated to western Europe, and settled in Belgium in 1929. He studied at the University of Brussels, gaining his doctorate in 1941. In 1951 he became professor of the Université Libre de Bruxelles (emeritus from 1987) and in 1959 was appointed director of the Instituts Internationaux de Physique et de Chemie. From 1961 to 1966 he was professor of the department of chemistry at the Enrico Fermi Institute for Nuclear Studies and the Institute for the Study of Metals at the University of Chicago. From 1967 he held the position of director of the Center for Statistical Mechanics and Thermodynamics at the University of Texas in Austin, concurrently with his professorship in Brussels.

Prigogine's work has been concerned with applying thermodynamic principles to new disciplines. Observation of many physical systems has shown that there is a general tendency to assume the state in which they are most disordered. This occurs by means of processes that dissipate energy and which can in principle produce work. But it was not understood how it is possible for a more orderly system, such as a living creature, to arise spontaneously from a less orderly system and yet maintain itself despite the tendency towards disorder. It is now known that order can be created and preserved only by processes that flow 'uphill' in the thermodynamic sense. They are compensated by 'downhill' events. These interrelated occurrences owe their existence to the absorption of energy from the surroundings and are consistent with thermodynamic laws.

During the late 1940s Prigogine developed mathematical models of what he called dissipative systems of this kind, to show how they might have come about. His models demonstrated how matter and energy can interact creatively, forming organisms that can sustain themselves and grow in opposition to the general drift towards universal chaos. Dissipative systems can exist only in harmony with their surroundings.

Prigogine showed that dissipative systems exhibit two types of behaviour: close to equilibrium, their order tends to be destroyed; far from equilibrium, order can be maintained and new structures formed. The probability of order arising out of disorder, by pure chance, is infinitesimal; but the formation of an ordered dissipative system makes it possible to create order out of chaos. These ideas have been applied to examine how life originated on Earth, to the dynamic equilibria in ecosystems, to the preservation of world resources, and even to the prevention of traffic jams.

Pringsheim, Ernst (1859–1917) German physicist whose experimental work on the nature of thermal radiation led directly to the quantum theory.

Pringsheim was born in Breslau, Germany (now Wrocław, Poland) on 11 June 1859. He studied at gymnasia in Breslau and in 1877 entered the University of Heidelberg, moving on to Breslau in 1878 and Berlin in 1879. He gained his PhD at Berlin in 1882 and became a lecturer there in 1886. Pringsheim became professor of physics at Berlin in 1896 and in 1905 moved to Breslau to take up the post of professor of experimental physics. He died in Breslau on 28 June 1917.

In 1881, Pringsheim developed an infrared spectrometer that made the first accurate measurements of wavelengths in the infrared region. He put the instrument to its most important use from 1896 onwards when he began to collaborate with Otto ◊Lummer on a study of black-body radiation. This led to a verification of the Stefan–Boltzmann law that relates the energy radiated by a body to its absolute temperature. Pringsheim and Lummer then proceeded to make careful measurements of the distribution of energy with frequency at various temperatures. They confirmed Wien's displacement law, which relates the peak frequency of maximum energy to the temperature, but in 1899 found anomalies in radiation laws that had been devised to express the energy of the radiation in terms of its frequency and temperature. The results encouraged Max ◊Planck to find a new radiation law that would account for the experimental results and in 1900, Planck arrived at such a law by assuming that the energy of the radiation consists of indivisible units, which he called quanta. This marked the founding of the quantum theory.

Proust, (Joseph) Louis (1754–1826) French chemist who discovered the law of constant composition, sometimes called Proust's law, which states that every true chemical compound has exactly the same composition no matter how it is prepared.

Proust was born in Angers on 26 September 1754, the son of an apothecary. He was brought up to follow his father's profession, studying chemistry under

Guillaume Rouelle at the Jardin du Roi and working as an apothecary chemist in La Salpêtrière Hospital in Paris and lecturing at the Palais Royal. In the 1780s, before the beginning of the French Revolution, he went to Spain and spent the next 20 years in Madrid. He taught at various academies and carried out his own research in a well-equipped laboratory (the Royal Laboratory) provided by his patron, King Charles IV of Spain. In 1808 Napoleon invaded Spain and French soldiers wrecked Proust's laboratory. He returned to France a poor man, was elected to the Academy of Sciences in 1816, and eked out his retirement on a small pension provided to him as an academician by Louis XVIII. He died in Angers on 5 July 1826.

Proust's reputation as a chemist rests on his extraordinary ability as an analyst. He identified grape sugar (glucose) and distinguished between it and sugar from other sources. Before his work on chemical compounds in the early 1800s in Madrid, the prevailing view in chemistry was that of Claude ◊Berthollet who had stated (and in 1803 published in his *Statique chimique*) that the composition of compounds could vary over a wide range, depending on the proportions of reactants used to produce them. In 1799 Proust prepared and analysed copper carbonate produced in various ways and compared the results with those obtained by analysing mineral deposits of the same substance; he found that they all had the same composition. Similar results with other compounds led Proust to propose the law of constant composition (he ascribed the errors in Berthollet's experiments to impurities and inaccurate analyses). Proust's law influenced John ◊Dalton's thinking about atomic theory and in 1808 Dalton proposed the law of definite proportions. The proportions of the elements in a compound result from the linking of definite (usually small) numbers of atoms to form molecules, giving the compound a constant composition. After a long controversy Berthollet finally conceded that Proust was right. Both chemists did agree, however, that the rate of a chemical reaction does depend on the masses of the reactants.

Prout, William (1785–1850) English chemist who pioneered physiological chemistry, but who is best known for formulating Prout's hypothesis, which states that the atomic weights (relative atomic masses) of all elements are exact multiples of the atomic weight of hydrogen. Since at that time (1815) the atomic weight of hydrogen was taken to be 1.0, the hypothesis implied that all atomic weights are whole numbers.

Prout was born in Horton, Gloucestershire, on 15 January 1785 into a prosperous and well-established West Country family. He began by studying medicine at Edinburgh University, qualifying in 1811. He then set up a medical practice in London and established a

private chemical laboratory. From 1813 he wrote about and gave lectures in 'animal chemistry' and began his own researches into the chemistry of physiological processes. He published his atomic-weight hypothesis anonymously in 1815. He continued to experiment, widening his interests to include some physics. He died in London on 9 April 1850.

In his early researches Prout studied various natural secretions and products, including blood, urine, gastric juices, kidney and bladder stones, and even cuttlefish ink. He became convinced that the products of secretion derive from the chemical breakdown of body tissues. In 1818 he isolated urea and uric acid for the first time, and six years later he found hydrochloric acid in digestive juices from the stomach. In 1827 he became the first scientist to classify the components of food into the three major divisions of carbohydrates, fats, and proteins.

His anonymous paper of 1815 was comprehensively entitled 'On the relation between the specific gravities of bodies in their gaseous state and the weight of their atoms'. From the determinations of atomic weights that had been made, Prout observed that many were whole-number multiples of that of hydrogen. The hypothesis implied that all other elements were in some way multiples or compounds of hydrogen, which was therefore the basic building block of matter. In 1920 Ernest ◊Rutherford named the proton (the hydrogen nucleus), which is a constituent of every atomic nucleus and is, therefore, indeed a 'basic building block of matter', after Prout (*proton*).

Prout's hypothesis gave even more stimulus to the making of accurate determinations of atomic weights – work that inevitably proved the hypothesis to be wrong (for example chlorine has an atomic weight of 35.5). The idea was therefore largely abandoned until the work on isotopes by Frederick ◊Soddy and others more than a century later finally accounted correctly for non-integral atomic weights (resulting from a natural mixture of isotopes).

Prout also studied the gases of the atmosphere and in 1832 made accurate measurements of the density of air. He devised a barometer for making precise atmospheric pressure measurements, and the Royal Society adopted its design for a national standard barometer.

Prusiner, Stanley (1942–) US neurologist and biochemist who was awarded the 1997 Nobel Prize for Physiology or Medicine for his pioneering discovery of prions – a new biological principle of infection.

Stanley Prusiner was born in Des Moines, Iowa, on 28 May 1942, the elder of two brothers. His father, an architect, was drafted into the US Navy soon after his birth, and Stanley and his mother lived in Cincinnati, Ohio, until after the war when the family settled back in Des Moines. He was educated at Walnut Hills High School and at the University of Pennsylvania where he majored in chemistry.

In 1963 Prusiner began a research project on hypothermia in the department of surgery with Sidney Wolfson, which led to another project on brown adipose tissue. This excited him and he began to think seriously about a career in biomedical research. While finishing his medical training at the National Institute for Health (NIH) in San Francisco in 1968, he met his wife Sandy, a mathematics teacher.

Prusiner spent three years at the NIH studying glutaminases in the bacterium *Escherichia coli* and learning useful research methods. In 1972 he took up a residency in neurobiology at the University of California in San Francisco. Here it was the death of one of his patients from the dementia resulting from Creutzfeldt–Jakob Disease (CJD), a 'slow virus' infection with unusual properties, that made him determined to make the disease a research project. In 1974 he took up the offer of an assistant professorship at the university and, amid dire warnings from colleagues about the difficulties of the project, set up a laboratory to study scrapie, a disease of sheep thought to be similar to CJD. Scrapie had been documented in Iceland in the 18th century and found in Scotland in the 1940s. He developed a collaboration with William Hadlow and Carl Eklund in Hamilton, Montana. The next few years were fraught with difficulties over funding for a project that seemed to undermine the tenets of molecular biology. Experimental evidence showed that the infectious agent for scrapie, isolated from hamster brains, was a single protein. This did not square with past research, which held that the only way to transmit information from one generation to the next is through nucleic acids. Prusiner and his colleagues' findings were originally seen as heresy and when they were published in *Science* in 1982 they provoked a storm of protest and scepticism amongst virologists by introducing the term 'prion' derived from 'proteinaceous infectious particle' to describe the single protein. A challenge was issued but intensive research failed to find any nucleic acid in scrapie.

Undaunted by attacks in the press, and supported by his wife and two daughters, Prusiner continued his research. In the next decade, a series of experiments by Prusiner and others showed that prions are present in healthy animals but not in the same form as those found in diseased brains. The results have convinced many scientists that the protein is the agent in the transmission of several deadly diseases known to be transmitted through extracts of diseased brains, including bovine spongiform encephalopathy (BSE, or 'mad cow disease'), CJD, scrapie, and kuru, the mysterious disease found among the Fore people in New Guinea and connected with cannibalistic rituals.

Prusiner's discovery added a new infectious agent to the list of well-known agents – bacteria, viruses, fungi, and parasites – and should lead to the development of drugs to treat diseases that still lead to certain death. It may help develop an understanding of other dementia-related diseases such as Alzheimer's. The discovery earned him several scientific awards including the Nobel Prize for Physiology or Medicine in 1997.

Ptolemy, (Claudius Ptolemaeus) (lived 2nd century AD)

Egyptian astronomer, astrologer, geographer, and philosopher, working in a centre of Greek culture technically under Roman domination. His collected works on astronomical themes – known generally as the *Almagest* (although he called it *Syntaxis*) – influenced astronomical and religious conceptions for at least 13 centuries after his death.

Almost nothing is known of Ptolemy's life. His name suggests to some commentators that he was born in the city of Ptolemais Hermii, on the banks of the Nile. Certainly it was in Alexandria that he mostly lived and worked, setting up his observatory on the top floor of a temple in order to view the heavens with greater clarity. Again, the exact date of his death is unknown, although there is some evidence that he may have lived to around the age of 78, and died in either AD 141 or 151.

Ptolemy had often been accused of plagiarizing the theories of ☿Hipparchus, the Greek astronomer and philosopher of two centuries earlier, and of using

Ptolemy Egyptian astronomer and geographer Ptolemy who developed the theory that the Earth is at the centre of the Universe. This stood as the accepted doctrine until Copernicus opposed it in the 16th century. *Mary Evans Picture Library*

☿Plato as his authority for adapting Hipparchus where necessary to maintain his own point of view. It is sometimes forgotten, however, how many sources Ptolemy had at his disposal. Living in Alexandria, whose library was the repository of the greatest store of knowledge in the world, Ptolemy had to hand the entire accumulated wealth of information compiled by Greek and other scholars during the previous four centuries. Some of those scholars, particularly the Greek ones (such as ☿Aristarchos), had proposed a Sun-centred (heliocentric) Solar System. Even Hipparchus favoured a heliocentric universe. Yet Ptolemy managed to put together a cosmology that it would be difficult to make less accurate – and for various reasons (at least as far as western Europe was concerned) the science of astronomy stuck fast at that point.

It was Plato, who loved symmetry and sought mathematical perfection in the workings of nature, who probably inspired Ptolemy as much as Hipparchus did. Ptolemy began with the premise that the Earth was a perfect sphere. Because gravity brought things demonstrably towards the centre of the Earth, all celestial bodies must likewise conform to it. Thus the Earth was at the centre of the cosmos, and the Moon, Mercury, Venus, the Sun, Mars, Jupiter, Saturn, and the stars (in that order), in their various spheres, orbited the Earth. All their orbits were circular, though Mercury and

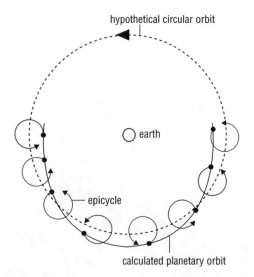

hypothetical circular orbit

earth

epicycle

calculated planetary orbit

Ptolemy The Ptolemaic, Earth-centred model of the universe dominated astronomy for more than 1,400 years, until it was overthrown by Copernicus in the 16th century. Ptolemy believed that the Earth was the centre of the Universe and that the planets and stars follow perfectly circular orbits. In order to reconcile this belief with the observed elliptical orbits of the planets, he proposed a complex theory of epicycles (in essence, that some of the planets orbit a point that is itself orbiting the Earth).

Venus, and possibly Mars (Ptolemy was not sure), had epicyclic orbits (describing small circular orbits about a point that was itself orbiting the Earth). The sphere of the stars comprised a dome with points of light attached or pricked through.

Apart from Ptolemy's interest in astronomy and his desire to find mathematical answers to natural problems, he also studied geography in great detail, producing vivid maps of Asia and large areas of Africa. These, together with his notes on longitude and latitude, were combined into a collection known as his *Geography,* and it was from these maps that Christopher Columbus many centuries later decided that it ought to be possible to reach India by sailing west across the Atlantic.

The work of Ptolemy that is most available today is his thesis on astrology, the *Tetrabiblios,* in which he suggests that some force from the stars may have considerable influence over the lives and events in the human experience.

Ptolemy's legacy to the world was an attempt at a complete understanding of all he could observe. It has not proved accurate, but it was popular and it endured for hundreds of years.

Further Reading

Britton, John Phillips, *Models and Precision: The Quality of Ptolemy's Observations and Parameters,* Sources and Studies in the History and Philosophy of Classical Science, Garland, 1992, v 1.

Ellis, Walter M, *Ptolemy of Egypt,* Routledge, 1994.

Gingerich, Owen, *The Eye of Heaven: Ptolemy, Copernicus, Kepler,* Masters of Modern Physics, American Institute of Physics, 1993.

Grasshoff, Gerd, *The History Ptolemy's Star Catalogues,* Studies in the History of Mathematics and Physical Sciences, Springer-Verlag, 1990.

Swerdlow, N M, 'The enigma of Ptolemy's catalogue of stars', *J Hist Astron,* 1992, v 23, pp 173–183.

Purkinje, Jan Evangelista (1787–1869) Czech histologist and physiologist whose pioneering studies were of great importance to our modern knowledge of vision, the functioning of the brain and heart, pharmacology, embryology, and histology.

Purkinje was born on 17 December 1787 in Libochovice, Bohemia (now in the Czech Republic), and was educated there by piarist monks (members of a religious congregation established in 1597 to educate the poor). Before being ordained a priest, however, he went to Prague University to study philosophy but changed to medicine, in which he graduated in 1819 with his famous thesis on the visual phenomenon now known as the Purkinje effect. After graduating he worked as an assistant in the department of physiology at Prague

University until 1823, when he was appointed professor of physiology and pathology at the University of Breslau (now Wrocław in Poland) – perhaps through the influence of the German poet Wolfgang von Goethe, who had previously befriended Purkinje. (In addition to his scientific work, Purkinje also translated the poetry of Goethe and Friedrich von Schiller.) At Breslau University Purkinje founded the world's first official physiological institute. In 1850 he returned to Prague University as professor of physiology, a post he held until his death, in Prague, on 28 July 1869.

In his famous graduation thesis Purkinje described the visual phenomenon in which, as the light intensity decreases, different coloured objects of equal brightness under high light intensities appear to the eye to be unequally bright – blue objects appear brighter than red objects; this phenomenon is now called the Purkinje effect. In 1832 he was the first to describe what are now known as Purkinje's images: a threefold image of a single object seen by one person reflected in the eye of another person. This effect is caused by the object being reflected by the surface of the cornea and by the anterior and posterior surfaces of the eye lens.

Probably Purkinje's best-known histological work was his discovery in 1837 of large nerve cells with numerous dendrites found in the cortex of the brain's cerebellum; these cells are called Purkinje cells. Two years later he discovered the Purkinje fibres – atypical muscle fibres lying beneath the endocardium that conduct the pacemaker stimulus along the inside walls of the ventricles to every part of the heart. Also in 1839, in describing the contents of animal embryos, Purkinje was the first to use the term 'protoplasm' in the scientific sense.

Purkinje made numerous other important discoveries and observations. In 1823 he recognized that fingerprints can be used as a means of identification. In 1825, while examining birds' eggs, he discovered the germinal vesicle, or nucleus, of unripe ova; this structure is now sometimes called the Purkinje vesicle. He discovered the sweat glands in skin in 1833 and, in 1835, described in detail the structure of the skin. In that year he also described ciliary motion. In 1836 he observed that pancreatic extracts can digest protein, and in 1837 he outlined the principal features of the cell theory – before Theodor ◊Schwann and Matthias ◊Schleiden enunciated this theory in detail. Purkinje also described the effects on the human body of camphor, opium, belladonna, and turpentine. And he did much to improve microscopical techniques, being the first to use the microtome in the preparation of tissue samples; moreover, he was one of the first to teach microscopy as part of his university course.

Pye, John David (1932–) English zoologist who has performed important research in the field of ultrasonic bio-acoustics, particularly in bats.

Pye was born on 14 May 1932 in Mansfield, Nottinghamshire. He was educated at Queen Elizabeth's Grammar School, University College of Wales at Aberystwyth (from which he graduated in 1954), and London University (from which he obtained his doctorate in 1961). From 1958 to 1964 he was a zoology research assistant, after which he became a lecturer at King's College, London. In 1970 he was appointed reader at King's College, then in 1973 he joined the staff of Queen Mary College (now Queen Mary and Westfield College), London, initially as professor of zoology, then from 1977 as head of the zoology department. He became professor emeritus in 1991.

A surprisingly large number of animals use ultrasound (which has a frequency above about 20 kHz and is inaudible to humans) – bats, cetaceaens (whales, porpoises, and dolphins), and many insects, for example. Because of the lack of sufficiently sophisticated detection devices, the phenomenon was not discovered until 1935, although the first indication that bats use a system other than sight for navigation came with Lazzaro ◊Spallanzani's discovery in 1794 that blinded bats still managed to find food. Even today, with sensitive electronic instruments widely available, biological ultrasound is relatively little studied. Pye is one of the few investigators in this field and has examined the use of ultrasound in many different animals, although he is best known for his work on echolocation in bats. In 1971 he calculated the resonant frequencies of the drops of water in fog and found that these frequencies coincided with the spectrum of frequencies used by bats for echolocation. For this reason, fog absorbs the ultrasound emitted by bats and renders useless their echolocation systems; this is probably the reason why bats avoid flying in fog. Pye also found that ultrasound seems to be important in the social behaviour of rodents and insects, which, since a number of these creatures are pests, raises the possibility of developing novel control measures.

Pyman, Frank Lee (1882–1944) English organic chemist, famous for his contributions to pharmaceutics and chemotherapy.

Pyman was born in Malvern on 9 April 1882. He was educated at Dover College, where his interest in chemistry began, and in 1899 entered Owens College in Manchester (later to become Manchester University), at a time when it was the centre of organic chemistry research in the UK. He graduated in 1902 and went to Zürich Polytechnic in Switzerland for two years, but because Zürich University did not at that time recognize polytechnic students he submitted his PhD thesis to Basel University, which granted him the degree in 1904.

On his return to the UK Pyman took a job in the experimental department of the Wellcome Chemical Works at Dartford, Kent, in 1906. During World War I he worked on the preparation of drugs needed to treat British troops overseas. In 1919 he was appointed professor of technological chemistry in Manchester University and head of the department of applied chemistry at the College of Technology. He stayed at Manchester for eight years, then in 1927 took up the appointment of director of research at the Boots Pure Drug Company's laboratories at Nottingham, where he remained until he died, in Nottingham, on 1 January 1944.

Pyman began research at the Wellcome Chemical Works under Jowett and worked with him for nine years, resulting in his lifelong interest in the glyoxalines (glyoxal is ethanedial), cyclic amidines with therapeutic properties. He was particularly interested in the relationship between their chemical constitution and their physiological action. He later tried to relate chemical constitution with the local anaesthetic action of the substituted amino alkyl esters. After 1915 Jowett moved to the Imperial Institute, but he continued to send Pyman samples for examination. From one such (bark of *Calmatambin glabrifolium*) Pyman isolated a glycoside, which led him to study the constitution of the anhydro-bases made from it by the Hofmann degradation – which converts an amide to an amine with one carbon atom less. This work placed him in the forefront of British organic chemistry and revealed the existence of a substance whose molecules contained a ten-membered heterocyclic ring. He also examined alkaloids, and became the first person to isolate a natural substance containing an asymmetric nitrogen atom.

Pyman undertook the preliminary processing work in connection with the preparation of the antibacterial drugs Salvarsan (arsphenamine) and Neosalvarsan, which were needed at the outbreak of World War I to deal with syphilis. He also synthesized an alkaloidal compound used in the treatment of amoebic dysentery among troops during the war. Another alkaloid was used as a uterine haemostat under the name Lodal.

Among compounds synthesized by Pyman were histidine and other simple bases of biological importance, such as guanidine. He continued to work with glyoxalines, synthesizing them and testing their effectiveness as antiseptics, pressor drugs, antimalarials, and hypoglycaemic substances. He also investigated arsenicals, acridines (used as powerful antiseptics), and the organic salts of bismuth. He studied the relationship between chemical constitution and the pungency of amides, and examined the preservative properties of hops.

Pythagoras (c. 572–c. 479 BC) Greek mathematician and philosopher, part of whose mystic beliefs entailed an intense study of whole numbers, the effect of which he sought to find in the workings of nature. He founded a famous school that lived as a cultic community governed by what might now be considered eccentric – if not downright primitive – rules, but which during and after his lifetime discovered an astonishing number of facts and theorems, some immortal.

Pythagoras Greek mathematician and philosopher Pythagoras. Pythagoras was born on the Greek island of Samos and is thought to have had to flee the island's despotic ruler. He went on to found a school and religious brotherhood in Crotona, Italy. *Mary Evans Picture Library*

Very little is known about the life of Pythagoras, other than that he was born on the island of Samos and that, possibly obliged to flee the despotism of its ruler, Polycrates, he probably travelled extensively. His work seems to show the influence of contemporary ideas in Asia Minor; nevertheless, Pythagoras is next authoritatively recorded in southern Italy, in the Dorian colony of Crotona, in about 529 BC. There he became the leader of a religious community that had political pretensions to being an association for the moral reform of society. The Pythagorean brotherhood flourished; as a mathematical and philosophical community it was extending science rapidly, and as a political movement it was extending its influence over several western Greek colonies. More distant colonies put up some physical resistance, however, and it was probably one act of suppression in particular – led by one Cylon –

that saw Pythagoras exiled (yet again) to Metapontum until he died, possibly around 500 BC. The school continued for something like another 50 or 60 years before being finally and totally suppressed.

There is geometry in the humming of the strings. There is music in the spacings of the spheres.

PYTHAGORAS QUOTED IN ARISTOTLE METAPHYSICS

Pythagoras was all but obsessed by numbers. He and his community looked for numerical values in all they saw around them, and strove to create relationships in the values they found. In elementary pure mathematics they studied the properties of the numbers themselves, and their practice of representing numbers as lines, triangles or squares of pebbles has given us our word calculate (from *calculus*, the Greek for 'pebble'). It also led directly to a firm basis for geometrical considerations. In this way, they established that the addition of each successive odd number after 1 to the preceding ones results in a square ($1 + 3 = 2^2$; $1 + 3 + 5 = 3^2$, and so on) and Pythagoras himself is supposed ultimately to have arrived at the theorem to which his name is attached, regarding right-angled triangles. (In fact he is supposed to have proved it from a more general equation he is said also to have formulated:

$$m^2 + \{\tfrac{1}{2}(m^2 - 1)\}^2 = \{\tfrac{1}{2}(m^2 + 1)\}^2$$

And to have noted that if the triangle in question is isosceles, the ratio of the hypotenuse to either side is the irrational number $\sqrt{2}$.)

Using geometrical principles, the Pythagoreans were able to prove that the sum of the angles of any regular-sided triangle is equal to that of two right angles (using the theory of parallels), and to solve any algebraic quadratic equations having real roots. They formulated the theory of proportion (ratio), which enhanced their knowledge of fractions, and used it in their study of harmonics upon their stringed instruments: the harmonic of the octave was made by touching the string at $\tfrac{1}{2}$ its length, of a fifth at $\tfrac{2}{3}$ its length, and so on. Pythagoras himself is said to have made this the basis of a complete system of musical scales and chords.

He is said also to have taken a keen interest in astronomy, seeking numerical consistency among the celestial movements and objects.

Further Reading

Iamblichus; Taylor, Thomas (transl), *Life of Pythagoras*, Kessinger Publishing Company, 1998.

Kaufmann, R, *Pythagoras: The Reality of the New Computer Age*, Heridonius Foundation, 1996.

Lappan, Glenda, et al; Anderson, Cathering, et al (eds), *Looking for Pythagoras: The Pythagorean Theorem*, Connected Mathematics series, Dale Seymour Publications, 1997.

Rutherford, Ward, *Pythagoras: Lover of Wisdom*, Esoteric Themes and Perspective series, Aquarian Press, 1984.

Quetelet, (Lambert) Adolphe (Jacques) (1796–1874) Belgian statistician, astronomer, and social scientist who applied statistical reasoning to social phenomena and was influential to the course of European social science. He organized the first statistics conference in 1833 and his measurement of obesity (the Quetelet index) is still in use today. In his youth he also wrote an opera and published poems and essays.

Born in Ghent on 22 February 1796, Quetelet was the son of a municipal officer. He was educated at the Lycée de Ghent and after graduating spent a year as a teacher in Oudenaarde. At the age of 19 he was appointed professor of mathematics at the College de Ghent and in 1819 became the first to be awarded a doctorate from the New University of Ghent for his dissertation on the theory of conic sections. In the same year he was appointed professor of elementary mathematics at the Athénée in Brussels where he worked on geometry and in 1820 he was elected a member of the Academie Royale des Sciences et Belles-Lettres of Brussels. He founded and co-edited a journal at this time with Professor J C Garnier, *Correspondance mathématique et physique,* in which many of his papers were published.

Quetelet proposed the founding of an observatory in 1820 and in 1823 he was sent to Paris by his government to study astronomy at the Observatory there. There he met several famous scientists, learning astronomy from Dominique ◊Arago and the theory of probability from Joseph ◊Fourier and Pierre ◊Laplace. From 1824 he taught higher mathematics at the Athenée and physics and astronomy at the Musée (later to become the Université Libre). In 1826 he published popular books on astronomy and probability. He travelled to England in 1827 to buy astronomical instruments and to visit observatories and in 1828 he was made astronomer at the Brussels Royal Observatory, which was finally completed in 1833. Quetelet made his home at the observatory from 1832 studying meteorology and geophysics with a strong statistical influence.

After meeting Laplace and Fourier, Quetelet turned some of his attention to statistics and became the first to use the normal curve as other than an error law. He was convinced that probability influenced human affairs more deeply than anyone realized. From 1825 he began preparing a table of births and deaths in Brussels in a project that was extended to cover the whole of Belgium. He also covered the statistics of crime, drawing conclusions using data on sex, age, climate, and education and making improvements in census taking. He wrote a number of papers on social statistics and in 1835 became famous throughout Europe for his controversial essay 'Sur l'homme et le développement de ses facultés, essai d'une physique sociale', in which he presented the concept of the average man (*l'homme moyen*) as the central value around which measurements of a human trait are grouped according to the normal curve. He broke new ground with his idea of *l'homme moyen* in which the normal man was described as both a static and dynamic entity and with his argument for the use of statistics for the discovery of social laws.

Quetelet devoted a great deal of time latterly to organizing international meetings and cooperation in astronomy, meteorology, geophysics, and statistics, although he was forced to slow down by a stroke he suffered in 1855. When Quetelet died in Brussels on 17 February 1874 royalty and many famous scientists gathered at his funeral. A monument was erected in his honour in Brussels in 1880.

R

Rainwater, Leo James US physicist; see ◊Bohr, Mottelson, and Rainwater.

Raman, Chandrasekhara Venkata (1888–1970)
Indian physicist who discovered that light is scattered by the molecules in a gas, liquid, or solid so as to cause a change in its wavelength. This effect is known as Raman scattering and the Raman spectra produced are used to obtain information on the structure of molecules. For its discovery, Raman was awarded the 1930 Nobel Prize for Physics.

Raman was born in Trichinopoly in Madras (now Tiruchchirappalli in Tamil Nadu) on 7 November 1888. He studied at the AVN College in Vizagapatam, where his father was professor of mathematics and physics, and at the Presidency College of the University of Madras where he obtained a BA in 1904 and an MA in 1907. Although aged only 16 and 19 respectively, Raman gained first-class degrees of great distinction. However, he was unable to continue his scientific education as this would have meant leaving India, and because there were no opportunities for a scientific career in India, Raman entered the financial division of the civil service in 1907, working as an accountant in Calcutta for ten years.

During this time, Raman pursued his studies privately, using the facilities at the laboratories of the Indian Association for the Cultivation of Science in Calcutta. He concentrated his efforts on investigations into vibration in sound and the theory of musical instruments, an interest that continued throughout his life. His work on these subjects and on diffraction prompted an offer of the professorship of physics at the University of Calcutta, which Raman took up in 1917.

Raman remained at Calcutta until 1933, and it was during this period of his life that he made the discovery that was his most important contributions to physics. In 1926 he established the *Indian Journal of Physics* and in 1928 was made president of the Indian Science Congress. Further honours came with the award of a knighthood by the British government in 1929 and the Hughes Medal of the Royal Society in 1930, in addition to the Nobel Prize for Physics in the same year.

In 1934, Raman became head of the physics department at the Indian Institute of Science, a post he held until 1948, also serving as president of the Institute 1933–37. The Indian government then built the Raman Research Institute for him at Bangalore and he became its first director in 1948. Raman took his duties as an educator very seriously and trained a great number of young scientists who later rose to positions of responsibility in science. Among his colleagues at the Institute was Homi ◊Bhabha. Raman remained director of his institute until he died in Bangalore on 21 November 1970.

Raman was inspired to work on the scattering of light in 1921, when returning to India by sea from a conference in the UK. He was struck by the intense blue colour of the Mediterranean, which he could not reconcile with the explanation put forward by Lord ◊Rayleigh that attributed the blue colour to the scattering of light by particles suspended in the water. Raman began to investigate this phenomenon upon his arrival in Calcutta. He showed that the blue colour of the sea is produced by the scattering of light by water molecules.

In 1923, Arthur ◊Compton discovered the Compton effect, in which X-rays are scattered on passing through matter and emerge with a longer wavelength. This was explained by assuming that X-ray particles or photons had collided with electrons and lost some energy. In 1925, Werner ◊Heisenberg predicted that this effect should be observed with visible light. Raman had already come to the same conclusion independently and had in fact made a preliminary observation of this light-scattering effect in 1923. He then refined his experiments and in 1928 was able to report the existence of the scattering effect for monochromatic light in dust-free air and pure liquids. The Raman spectra produced show lines displaced to either side of the normal line in a gas and a continuous band in dense liquids. The effect is caused by the internal motion of the molecules encountered, which may impart energy to the light photons or absorb energy in the resulting collisions. Raman scattering therefore gives precise information on the motion and shape of molecules.

Raman's other researches included the effects of sound waves on the scattering of light in 1935 and 1936; he vibration of atoms in crystals in the 1940s; the optics of gemstones, particularly diamonds, and of minerals in the 1950s; and the physiology of human colour vision in the 1960s.

Raman's discovery is important not only because it affords a method for the analysis of molecular structure but also because in demonstrating conclusively that light may behave as particles (photons), it confirms the quantum theory. However Raman is also to be remembered as a pioneer of Indian science.

Ramanujan, Srinavasa Ayengar (1887–1920)

Indian mathematician who, virtually unaided and untaught, made original contributions to function theory and number theory. His work and his evident desire for further study impressed the Cambridge mathematician Godfrey ◊Hardy so much that he was offered a scholarship to Trinity College. Despite the brevity of the remainder of his life, Ramanujan established a worldwide reputation.

Ramanujan was born in Erode, near Kumbakonam in Madras (now Tamil Nadu), on 22 December 1887. His family was poor, although of the high Brahmin caste. At school Ramanujan did himself and his teachers credit until, at the age of 15, he read and became fascinated by G S Carr's textbook *A Synopsis of Elementary Results in Pure and Applied Mathematics* (1880). Obsessed by the section on pure mathematics – which he soon learned by heart – he won a scholarship to the state college at Kumbakonam, but failed at the end of his first year because he had devoted too much of his time and energy to mathematics, to the neglect of other subjects (English in particular). Unemployed, he nevertheless developed his own theorems and hypotheses from the mathematics he knew.

Finances became even worse in 1909 when he got married. In the next three years, however, he was given a small grant by Ramachaudra Rao that enabled him to maintain his mathematical investigations and begin publishing his results, and he found work as a clerk in the offices of the Madras Port Trust. Then began his correspondence with Godfrey Hardy at Cambridge University. Deeply impressed both by the results of Ramanujan's work to date, and by the surprising gaps in his knowledge of certain aspects (later found to be gaps in Carr's textbook), Hardy eventually managed to persuade the somewhat relectant Ramanujan to take up the scholarship offered. Ramanujan arrived in 1914, and published 25 papers in European journals over the next five years. During that time, however, he contracted tuberculosis, and although the pleasure afforded him by his election as fellow of the Royal Society in 1918 temporarily alleviated his condition, he was obliged to return to the more favourable climate of India in the following year.

But although he kept on working, his health deteriorated further, and he died in Chetput on 26 April 1920. His collected papers were edited by Godfrey Hardy and published in 1927.

Carr's textbook, and particularly the section on pure mathematics, was the firm foundation on which Ramanujan based all his original work. In fact, he first scrutinized the book in detail from start to finish, checking its theorems and examples. From the knowledge he gained he was able to proceed beyond the material published and develop his own results in many fields, but particularly in function theory and number theory. When he arrived at Cambridge, Hardy was amazed at the standard he had reached in these areas – although Ramanujan knew nothing of subjects that had not been covered in Carr's book. Hardy was thus obliged to ensure that Ramanujan was given a speedy but thorough grounding in (for example) doubly periodic functions, the techniques of rigorous mathematical proofs, Cauchy's theorem, and other items that were all new ground. Hardy was also astonished to find that Ramanujan did much of his calculation mentally, and had achieved many of his creditable results by working through a large number of examples to check correlation.

It was perhaps in number theory that Ramanujan made his most enduring contribution. With Hardy he published a theory on the methods for partitioning an integer into a sum of smaller integers, called summands. In function theory he found accurate approximations to π, and worked on modular, elliptic, and other functions.

Further Reading

Berndt, Bruce C (ed), *Ramanujan's Notebooks,* Springer-Verlag, 1997.

Berndt, Bruce C and Rankin, Robert A (eds), *Ramanujan: Letters and Commentary,* History of Mathematics series, American Mathematical Society, 1995, v 9.

Kanigel, Robert, *The Man Who Knew Infinity,* Pocket Books, 1992.

Kanigel, Robert, *Apprentice to Genius,* Macmillan Publishing Co, 1986.

Ramón y Cajal, Santiago (1852–1934)

Spanish histologist whose research revealed that the nervous system is based on units of nerve cells (neurons). For his discovery he shared the 1906 Nobel Prize for Physiology or Medicine with the Italian cytologist and histologist Camillo ◊Golgi.

Ramón y Cajal was born on 1 May 1852, in Petilla de Aragón, Spain, the son of a country doctor. At the insistence of his father he studied medicine at the University of Zaragoza, but he took little interest in the course other than in anatomy. He qualified in 1873 and then joined the army medical service, which sent him to Cuba. There he caught malaria and was discharged; he returned to Zaragoza and obtained a doctorate in anatomy in 1877. In 1884 he was appointed professor of descriptive anatomy at the University of Valencia and in 1887 he took up the histology professorship at the University of Barcelona. From 1892 to 1921 he served at the University of Madrid as professor of histology and pathological anatomy, becoming director of the new Instituto Nacional de Higiene in 1900. In 1921 he retired from the university to become director of the Cajal Institute in Madrid, founded in his honour by King Alfonso XIII, and retained this position until he died, in Madrid, on 17 October 1934.

When Ramón y Cajal commenced his research, the path of a nervous impulse was unknown. In his investigations he used potassium dichromate and silver nitrate to stain sections of embryonic tissue, improving on the procedure developed by Golgi.

By this means he demonstrated that the axons of nerve cells end in the grey matter of the central nervous system and never join the endings of other axons or the cell bodies of other nerve cells. He considered that these findings indicate that the nervous system consists entirely of independent units and is not a network as was previously thought. In 1897 Ramón y Cajal investigated the human cerebral cortex using methylene blue (also used by Paul ◊Ehrlich) as well as Golgi's silver nitrate stain. He described several types of nerve cells and demonstrated that there were distinct structural patterns in different parts of the cerebral cortex. His findings indicated that structure might well be related to the localization of a particular function to a specific area. In 1903 he found that silver nitrate stained structures within the cell body, which he identified as neurofibrils, and that the cell body itself was concerned with conduction.

During his years at Madrid University, Ramón y Cajal concerned himself with the generation and degeneration of nerve fibres. He demonstrated that when a nerve fibre regenerates it does so by growing from the stump of the fibre still connected with the cell body. In 1913 he developed a gold sublimate to stain nerve structures, which is now valuable in the study of tumours of the central nervous system.

Modern neurology has its foundations in Ramón y Cajal's meticulous work because his investigations are the basis of modern understanding of the part played by the nerve cell in the nervous function, and of the nervous impulse. He published numerous scientific papers and books, among them the classic *Structure of the Nervous System of Man and Other Vertebrates* (1904) and *The Degeneration and Regeneration of the Nervous System* (1913–14).

Further Reading

Ramón y Cajal, Santiago; Horne Craigie, E and Cano, Juan (transl), *Recollections of My Life,* MIT Press, 1989.

Ramsay, William (1852–1919) Scottish chemist famous for his discovery of the inert gases, for which achievement he was awarded the 1904 Nobel Prize for Chemistry.

Ramsay was born in Glasgow on 2 October 1852, the son of an engineer (whose father, Ramsay's grandfather, founded the Glasgow Chemical Society). Despite this technical and scientific background, Ramsay received a classical education and entered the University of Glasgow in 1866, when he was only 14 years old, to take an arts course. Two years later he went to work in the laboratory of the Glasgow City Analyst, where he soon made up the deficiencies in his science education, and in 1870 he left for Germany to carry out research in organic chemistry under Rudolf Fittig (1835–1910) at Tübingen, gaining his PhD in 1873.

Ramsay then returned to Glasgow as an assistant at Anderson's College (later the Royal Technical College), followed by a post at the university. In 1880 he was appointed professor of chemistry at the newly created University College of Bristol (later Bristol University) and a year later became principal of the college. Then in 1887 he moved to become professor of chemistry at University College, London, as successor to Alexander ◊Williamson, where he remained until he retired in 1912. He was knighted in 1902. After retirement he moved to a house near High Wycombe, Buckinghamshire, where he continued some research in converted stables. At the outbreak of World War I in 1914 he became busy as a member of various committees. But his health deteriorated and he died in High Wycombe on 23 July 1916.

In the early 1870s, in Glasgow, Ramsay initially continued research in organic chemistry, investigating alkaloids and pyridine. During 1876 he met J B Henney, a young chemist who was interested in the chemistry of minerals. Together they studied water loss in salts and later the solubility of gases in solids.

At Bristol 1880–87 Ramsay worked principally on liquid-vapour systems, relying heavily on able assistants such as Sydney Young because much of his time as principal was taken up obtaining financial support for the new college.

At University College, London, his first action was to reorganize the out-of-date laboratory. He and his students investigated diketones, the metallic compounds of ethylene (ethene), and the atomic weight (relative atomic mass) of boron. Ramsay became interested in an article in *Nature* (September 1892) by Lord ◊Rayleigh in which he reported finding a difference in the densities of samples of nitrogen extracted from air and from chemical sources. After corresponding with Rayleigh, Ramsay undertook to study the problem. With the help of his assistant Percy Williams, he passed nitrogen from air over heated magnesium (to form magnesium nitride). After this treatment, about 6% of the gas still remained; further treatments reduced the volume of the residual gas even further, until they were left with an unknown gas of density 20 (oxygen = 16). Despite losing the sample in a laboratory accident, they finally established that it was the new element argon (which had contaminated the nitrogen derived from air).

Early in 1895 Ramsay became interested in helium, a gas known from spectrographic evidence to be present on the Sun but yet to be found on Earth. W F Hillebrand had reported that certain uranium minerals on being heated produced a gas that was chemically inert, and Ramsay repeated these experiments and obtained enough of the gas to send a sample to William ◊Crookes for spectrographic analysis. Crookes confirmed that it was helium. Ramsay and his coworkers soon made the connection between helium and argon and in his book *The Gases of the Atmosphere* (1896) he repeated his earlier suspicion that there was an eighth group of elements at the end of the periodic table. He drew up a table with gaps for the unknown elements.

hydrogen	1.01	?	
fluorine	19.0	?	
chlorine	35.5	?	
bromine	79.0	lithium	7.0
iodine	126.9	sodium	23.0
?	169.0	potassium	39.1
helium	4.2	rubidium	85.5
?		caesium	132.0
argon	39.2	?	170.0

During the next decade Ramsay and Morris ◊Travers sought the remaining inert (also known as rare or noble) gases by the fractional distillation of liquid air. Ramsay often used demonstrations and public lectures to show the existence of these gases, and he announced the discovery of neon in 1894 at a meeting in Toronto, Canada. Krypton and xenon took until 1898 to isolate. The last member of the series, radon, is a product of radioactive decay. It was identified in 1901 from a minute sample prepared by Ramsay and Robert Whytlaw-Gray (1877–1958).

Rankine, William John Macquorn (1820–1872)
Scottish engineer and physicist who was one of the founders of the science of thermodynamics, especially in reference to the theory of steam engines.

Rankine was born in Edinburgh on 5 July 1820, the son of an engineer. He trained as a civil engineer under John Benjamin MacNeil, and was eventually appointed to the chair of civil engineering and mechanics at the University of Glasgow in 1855, a position he continued

to hold until his death on 24 December 1872. In 1853 he became a member (and later a fellow) of the Royal Society, whose official catalogue credits him with 154 papers.

One of Rankine's earliest scientific papers, on metal fatigue in railway axles, led to improved methods of construction in this field. In about 1848 he commenced the series of researches on molecular physics that occupied him at intervals during the rest of his life and which are among his chief claims to distinction in the realm of pure science. In 1849 he delivered two papers on the subject of heat. His first work, 'On an equation between the temperature and the maximum elasticity of steam and other vapours' was published in the *Edinburgh New Philosophical Journal* and at the end of the year he sent to the Royal Society of Edinburgh his paper 'On a formula for calculating the expansion of liquids by heat'.

In 1853, together with James Robert Napier, he projected and patented a new form of air engine, but this patent was afterwards abandoned. It was in 1859 that he produced what is perhaps his most influential work, *A Manual of the Steam Engine and Other Prime Movers,* the 13th attempt at a treatment of the steam engine theory. In it he described a thermodynamic cycle of events (the so-called Rankine cycle) that was used as a standard for the performance of steam-power installations where a considerable vapour provides the working fluid. Rankine here explained how a liquid in the boiler vaporized by the addition of heat converts part of this energy into mechanical energy when the vapour expands in an engine. As the exhaust vapour is condensed by a cooling medium such as water, heat is lost from the cycle. The condensed liquid is pumped back into the boiler. This concept of a power cycle is useful to engineers in developing equipment and designing power plants.

Besides writing in various newspapers, Rankine contributed many papers to scientific journals, the most significant ones being on the subject of thermodynamics. The application of the doctrine that 'heat and work are convertible' to the discovery of new relationships among the properties of bodies was made about the same time by three scientists: William Thomson (afterwards Lord ◊Kelvin), Rankine, and Rudolf ◊Clausius. Lord Kelvin cleared the way with his analysis of Sadi ◊Carnot's work, more than 20 years earlier, on the motive power of heat, which pointed out the error of Carnot's assumption that heat is a substance and therefore indestructible. Rankine in 1849 and Clausius in 1850 showed the further modifications that Carnot's theory required. Lord Kelvin in 1851 put the foundations of the theory in the form they have since retained.

Rankine also made an important contribution to

soil mechanics and his work on earth pressure and the stability of retaining walls was a notable advance. He collaborated with others to produce *The Imperial Dictionary of Universal Biography* and was the corresponding and general editor of *Shipbuilding, Theoretical and Practical* (1866).

Further Reading

Channell, David F, 'W J M Rankine and the Scottish roots of engineering science' in: Garber, Elizabeth, *Beyond History of Science: Essays in Honour of Robert E Schofield*, Lehigh University Press, 1990, pp 194–203.

Channell, David F, *William John MacQuorn Rankine*, Scotland's Cultural Heritage, 1987.

Marsden, Ben, 'Engineering science in Glasgow: economy, efficiency and measurement as prime movers in the differentiation of an academic discipline', *Brit J Hist Sci*, 1992, v 25, pp 319–346.

Ray, John (1627–1705) English naturalist whose plant and animal classifications were the first significant attempts to produce a systematic taxonomy based on a variety of structural characteristics, including internal anatomy. He was also the first to use the term 'species' in the modern sense of the word.

Ray was born on 29 November 1627 in the small Essex village of Black Notley. His father was a blacksmith and his mother an amateur herbalist and medical practitioner. After attending the grammar school in nearby Braintree, Ray spent two years at Catherine's Hall, Cambridge (now St Catherine's College). He transferred to Trinity College, Cambridge in 1646, and graduated in 1648. He was elected a fellow of Trinity College in the following year and remained at that college for the next 13 years, initially teaching Greek, mathematics, and the humanities. In 1650, however, he suffered a serious illness and, while recuperating, spent much time walking through the surrounding countryside; this stimulated his interest in natural history, which thereafter became his main academic pursuit. Ray took holy orders in 1660, but the restoration of King Charles II changed the country's religious climate and Ray was obliged to leave Trinity in 1662 because he refused to sign an agreement to the Act of Uniformity, which required all clergymen to declare their assent to everything contained in the Prayer Book of Queen Elizabeth I and to conform to the liturgy of the Church of England. Thus Ray lost his livelihood and for the rest of his life he depended on financial support from his friends, particularly from Francis Willughby (1635–1672), an affluent younger contemporary at Cambridge who shared Ray's interest in natural history. From 1663 to 1666 Ray and Willughby toured Europe to study the flora and fauna and collect specimens. On their return to England, Ray lived at Willughby's home, where they collaborated on publishing the results of their natural history studies. In 1672 Willughby died unexpectedly, but Ray remained at his family home, supported by an annuity left him by Willughby and by his position as tutor to the Willughby children. In 1673 Ray married a governess in the Willughby household. In 1678, however, Willughby's widow forced Ray and his wife to leave, and they returned to Black Notley, where Ray remained for the rest of his life. He died there on 17 January 1705.

Ray's first publication was *Catalogus plantarum circa Cantabrigiam nascentium/Catalogue of Plants around Cambridge* (1660), compiled from his observations during his walks while convalescing from illness. The work listed 558 species and was the best attempt then available at cataloguing plants. His first attempt at a genuine classification, however, was a table of plants that he contributed to John Wilkin's book *Essay Towards a Real Character* (1668). In 1670 Ray, with Willughby's help, published *Catalogus plantarum Angliae/Catalogue of English Plants*. Ray and Willughby then began producing a definitive catalogue and classification of all known plants and animals, with Ray responsible for the botany and Willughby for the zoology. But Willughby died while this work was in its early stages and Ray assumed the task of completing the entire project, since he was a competent zoologist and was familiar with Willughby's material. This task occupied Ray for the rest of his life.

As a tribute to Willughby, Ray published *F Willughbeii ... ornithologia* (1676; translated in 1678 as *The Ornithology of F Willughby*) and *F Willughbeii ... de historia piscium/History of Fish* (1685) under Willughby's name, although most of the work was Ray's own. Ray continued his botanical studies and, in *Methodus plantarum nova* (1682), developed a clear-cut taxonomic system based on plant physiology, morphology, and anatomy. In his system he laid great emphasis on the division of plants into cryptogams (flowerless plants), monocotyledons, and dicotyledons. Within the dicotyledons Ray defined 36 family groupings, many of which are still used. He also established the species as the fundamental unit of taxonomy, although he mistakenly believed that species are immutable.

The culmination of Ray's work, however, was *Historia generalis plantarum* (1686–1704), a monumental three-volume treatise in which he attempted to produce a complete, natural classification of plants. The book covered about 18,600 species (most of which were European) and, in addition to plant classification, it contained much information on the morphology, distribution, habitats, and pharmacological uses of individual plant species as well as on general aspects of plant life, such as diseases and seed germination. In it he modified his belief in the immutability of species.

Ray also wrote several books on zoology under his own name, notably *Synopsis methodica animalium quadrupedum et serpentini generis/Synopsis of Quadrupeds* (1693), *Historia insectorum/History of Insects* (published posthumously in 1710), and *Synopsis methodica avium et piscium/Synopsis of Birds and Fish* (published posthumously in 1713). In all of these works Ray followed the same format he had used in his *Historia generalis plantarum,* giving details of individual species in addition to classification.

Furthermore, Ray also believed that fossils are the petrified remains of dead animals and plants – a concept that, surprisingly, appeared in his theological writings and did not gain general acceptance until the late 18th century.

Although it was not possible to devise a natural classification system until Charles ◊Darwin and Alfred Russel ◊Wallace had formulated evolutionary theory, Ray's system approached that ideal far more closely than those of any of his contemporaries and remained the best attempt at classification until superseded by Carolus ◊Linnaeus' taxonomic work in 1735.

Rayet, George Antoine Pons (1839–1906) French astronomer who, in collaboration with Charles Wolf (1827–1918), detected a new class of peculiar white or yellowish stars whose spectra contain broad hydrogen and helium emission lines. These stars were subsequently named Wolf–Rayet stars, after their discoverers.

Rayet was born near Bordeaux on 12 December 1839. He did not attend school until the age of 14, when his family moved to Paris. In 1859 he entered the Ecole Normale Supérieure and three years later graduated from there with a degree in physics. He worked as a teacher for a year before becoming a physicist in the new weather forecasting unit set up by Urbain ◊Leverrier at the Paris Observatory. In 1873 Leverrier entrusted the running of the meteorological service to Rayet, but within a year the two men disagreed over the practical forecasting of storms and this led to Rayet's dismissal. Rayet then became a lecturer in physics at the Faculty of Sciences of Marseille and in 1876 he was appointed as professor of astronomy at Bordeaux.

As a result of a government proposal to construct several new observatories in France, Rayet was asked to organize a collective survey of the history and equipment of the world's observatories. Subsequently, he was offered the appointment of director of the new observatory to be built at Floirac, near Bordeaux, and from 1879 he held this post along with his appointment at Bordeaux. During his last years Rayet was troubled by a serious lung complaint; he died in Floirac on 14 June 1906.

At the Paris Observatory, Rayet's collaboration with Charles Wolf came to fruition in 1865 when they successfully photographed the lunar penumbra during an eclipse. A year later they discovered a new phenomenon: on 4 May 1866 a nova appeared and after its brilliance had significantly reduced Rayet and Wolf, on 20 May, discovered bright bands in its spectrum, something that had hitherto not been noticed in stellar spectra. Establishing these as manifestations of the later stages of some novae, Rayet and Wolf went on to investigate the possible presence of this phenomenon in permanently bright stars, and in 1867 three such stars were located in the constellation of Cygnus. These stars, with characteristically broad and intense emission lines, are now known to be relatively rare and are called Wolf–Rayet stars. They are about twice the size of the Sun, very hot, with an expanding outer shell and a disparity between the energy produced in the interior and the radiated energy.

In 1868 Rayet took part in an expedition to the Malay Peninsula to observe a solar eclipse and was given responsibility for the spectroscopic work of the expedition. His valuable recordings of solar prominences together with observations made by others during the same eclipse, notably those of Jules César ◊Janssen, contributed to the establishment of the first precise data on the Sun.

As director, Rayet equipped the new observatory in Floirac with the most modern astrometric equipment and began a programme of accurately measuring the coordinates of stars, the positions of comets and nebulae, and the components of double stars. He was one of the original supporters of the *Carte internationale photographique du ciel,* which was established in order to map the entire sky using identical telescopes around the world, simultaneously. A year before his death in 1906, he had the satisfaction of publishing the first volume of the Bordeaux Observatory's *Catalogue photographique.* Despite his poor state of health, Rayet took part in a 1905 expedition to Spain to study a solar eclipse.

Rayleigh, John William Strutt (1842–1919) 3rd Baron Rayleigh. English physicist who, with William ◊Ramsay, discovered the element argon. For this achievement Rayleigh was awarded the 1904 Nobel Prize for Physics while Ramsay gained the 1904 Nobel Prize for Chemistry. However, Rayleigh possessed a remarkable grasp of all the fundamental areas of classical physics (electromagnetic theory, thermodynamics, and statistical mechanics), producing important contributions in all of these fields.

Rayleigh was born John William Strutt at Langford Grove, Essex, on 12 November 1842. He received private tutoring until 1861 when he entered Trinity College, Cambridge, to study mathematics, graduating in 1865. He was then elected to a fellowship of Trinity College, which he held until his marriage in 1871. After graduating from Cambridge he travelled to the USA until 1868, and then set up a laboratory in the family home at Terling Place. On the death of his father in 1873, Strutt inherited his title and became Lord Rayleigh. He continued his scientific research, which was considered rather eccentric for a person in his privileged position.

The same year marked Rayleigh's election to the fellowship of the Royal Society, which he later served as secretary 1885–96 and president 1905–08, and which awarded him the Rumford and Copley medals. In 1879, he succeeded James Clerk ◊Maxwell as Cavendish Professor of Experimental Physics at the University of Cambridge, a post he held until his return from the Montréal meeting of the British Association for the Advancement of Science in 1884, at which Rayleigh had held the presidency. After 1884, Rayleigh confined most of his research activities to his personal laboratory and study at home. He did serve as professor of natural philosophy at the Royal Institution in London 1887–1905, but his duties there did not require him often to leave home. In 1900, he contributed to the foundation of the National Physical Laboratories in Teddington, Middlesex. In 1908, Rayleigh was appointed chancellor of Cambridge University, a post he held until his death at Terling Place on 30 June 1919.

Rayleigh's early researches at home during the late 1860s and early 1870s were largely concerned with the properties of waves in the fields of optics and acoustics. He did work on resonance, extending the studies of Hermann von ◊Helmholtz, and on vibration. Rayleigh also studied light and colour. In 1871, he explained that the blue colour of the sky arises from the scattering of light by dust particles in the air, and was able to relate the degree of scattering to the wavelength of the light. Rayleigh was also interested in diffraction gratings, and made the first accurate definition of the resolving power of diffraction gratings. This led to improvements in the spectroscope, which in the 1870s was becoming an important tool in the study of solar and chemical spectra. Rayleigh was also responsible for the invention of the optical zone plate.

At Cambridge, Rayleigh's professorial responsibilities enabled him to improve the teaching of experimental physics, causing an explosion in the popularity of the subject that had far-reaching consequences for physics in the UK. In 1884, he completed the project initiated by his predecessor Maxwell that sought the accurate standardization of the three basic electrical units: the ohm, ampere, and volt. His insistence on accuracy led to the designing of more precise electrical instruments.

After leaving Cambridge, Rayleigh continued to do research in a broad range of subjects including light and sound radiation, thermodynamics, electromagnetism, and mechanics. He was very conscientious at keeping up with developments as they appeared in the scientific literature, and having a keen critical eye, he was often able to devise new experiments to rectify weaknesses he found in the work of others.

The work that most caught the public eye began with Rayleigh's careful study of the measurement of the density of different gases. He originally became interested in this problem because of William ◊Prout's hypothesis, more than 60 years earlier, that all the elements are multiples of hydrogen and have atomic weights (relative atomic masses) that are integers. Rayleigh's results did not support this theory, as others had found, but he made the incidental observation that whenever he measured the density of nitrogen in air it was 0.5% greater than the density of nitrogen from any other source. He immediately eliminated all the possible suggestions for the source of the impurity causing the increase, but could not solve the problem. In desperation he published a short note in *Nature* in September 1892, asking for suggestions. Over the next three years, Rayleigh and Ramsay both studied the problem and in the end jointly announced the discovery of a new element: argon. The gas had escaped detection by chemists because of its extreme inertness, which renders it virtually devoid of any chemical properties. Argon might have been discovered a century earlier if Henry ◊Cavendish had followed up his observation of a residual quantity of gas in air that he simply could not oxidize.

The discovery of argon was followed by one of Rayleigh's most important contributions to physics. This was the Rayleigh–Jeans equation, published in 1900, which described the distribution of wavelengths in black-body radiation. This equation could only account for the longer wavelengths, and Wilhelm Wien (1864–1928) later produced an equation to describe the shorter wavelength radiation.

This inconsistency led to the formulation shortly after of the quantum theory by Max ◊Planck, which accounted for the distribution of all wavelengths by assuming that energy exists in indivisible units called quanta. Rayleigh was not enthusiastic about such a revolutionary solution, which overturned classical ideas of radiation. He was likewise unable to agree with the explanation of the hydrogen spectrum produced by Niels ◊Bohr in 1913, which developed from the quantum theory, and he also found the special theory of relativity proposed by Albert ◊Einstein in 1905 distasteful because it dispensed with the ether as a medium for light waves. He had in fact made an attempt to detect the ether in 1901, and his negative result only added to the evidence for relativity.

However, such conservatism should not blind us to Rayleigh's achievements in advancing and consolidating the branches of classical physics that remained valid. And in bringing about the discovery of argon, he initiated the uncovering of a whole family of elements (the inert, or noble, gases) that are of great importance in themselves and to an understanding of chemical bonding.

Reber, Grote (1911–) US radio astronomer – indeed, at one time he was probably the world's only radio astronomer – who may truly be said to have pioneered the new aspect of astronomical science from its inception. His major project was to map all the extraterrestrial sources of radio emission that can be traced.

Reber was born in Wheaton, Illinois, on 22 December 1911. Completing his education at the Illinois Institute of Technology, he became a radio engineer. After Karl ◊Jansky stumbled on the existence of cosmic radio waves, Reber was among the first to explore this new field. Since then his research has taken him all over the world. From Illinois, Reber moved his telescope to Virginia in 1947, where he was appointed chief of the university's Experimental Microwave Radio Section. Four years later he moved to Hawaii, where a new telescope, sensitive to lower frequencies than he had been able to detect previously, was constructed. In 1954 he moved yet again, this time to Australia, where he joined the Commonwealth Scientific and Industrial Research Organization in Tasmania. Although he then went to the National Radio Astronomy Observatory at Green Bank, West Virginia, in 1957 to work with the 43-m/141-ft radio telescope installed there, he returned to Tasmania in 1961 to help complete the mapping project he had helped to begin.

After a first, unsuccessful, attempt, Reber finally completed the construction of a bowl-shaped reflector 9 m/350 in diameter, with an antenna at its focus, in the back garden of his Illinois home in 1957. He immediately began to map radio sources in the sky, noting particularly that many seemed to come from the direction of the Milky Way. He took his first results to the Yerkes Observatory for discussion with the astronomers there. Satisfactory explanations of radio emission and radio sources were to come later, with the

further development of radio astronomy, but at the time, and for a number of years, Reber's was probably the only radio telescope in existence.

Despite the fact that the resolution of his homemade apparatus was no better than 12°, which meant that he could identify only a general direction from which radio waves were coming, he compiled a map of the sky, noting as he did so how many radio sources seemed to have no optically identifiable presence. The most intense radiation he recorded emanated from the direction of Sagittarius, near the centre of the Galaxy.

The radio telescope in Hawaii represented a great improvement in facilities for him, since it was sensitive to lower frequencies. But it was the equipment in Tasmania that really held Reber's attention. The project there was to complete a map of radio sources emitting waves around 144 m/473 ft in length, and it was to this work that he devoted most of the rest of his professional career.

Redman, Roderick Oliver (1905–1975) English astronomer who was chiefly interested in stellar spectroscopy and solar physics. A practical man, he also established a thriving solar observatory in Malta and organized the re-equipping of the Cambridge Observatories after World War II.

Redman was born on 17 July 1905 in Rodborough, Gloucestershire. At the age of 18 he won an exhibition scholarship from Marling School in Stroud to St John's College at Cambridge University, where he studied until 1929. By that time he was working under Arthur ◊Eddington at the university observatory for his PhD in astronomy. The doctorate was awarded in 1930, while Redman was serving as assistant astronomer at the Dominion Astrophysics Observatory in Victoria, British Columbia. The following year, Redman returned to Cambridge to become assistant director under F Stratton at the Solar Physics Observatory. He became chief assistant of the Radcliffe Observatory in 1937 and moved to the new observatory site in Pretoria in 1939. World War II prevented the observatory from being fully equipped so, after being elected fellow of the Royal Society in 1946, Redman returned again to Cambridge in 1947 and was appointed professor of astrophysics and director of the observatory. He retained these positions until 1972, when he was made director of the newly amalgamated observatories and Institute of Theoretical Physics. He retired later that same year, and died not long after, on 6 March 1975.

From the beginning of his career as an astronomer, Redman was interested in spectroscopic analysis. During his years as a research student under Arthur Eddington, Redman contributed to the early analysis of the Hertzsprung–Russell diagram by studying absolute stellar magnitudes. Upon his return to

Cambridge in 1931, Redman concentrated his efforts in stellar spectroscopy, and in the development of spectroscopic techniques.

He applied the method of photographic photometry to the study of elliptical galaxies and later, in South Africa, also to the study of bright stars, for which he developed the 'narrow band technique', which was of great value in stellar photometry.

The Sun was a source of fascination for Redman. He devoted considerable time and energy to studies and analyses of the solar spectrum, and went all over the world in order to observe total eclipses, during which he was able to identify thousands of the emission lines in the chromospheric spectrum and to investigate the question of chromospheric temperature.

Redman's final contribution to astronomy was his initiation of a large stellar photometry programme.

Regnault, Henri Victor (1810–1878) French physical chemist who is best known for his work on the physical properties of gases. In particular he showed that Boyle's law applies only to ideal gases. He also invented an air thermometer and a hygrometer, and he discovered carbon tetrachloride (tetrachloromethane).

Regnault was born in Aachen, Germany, on 21 July 1810. His father, a military officer under Napoleon, was killed in battle during the emperor's 1812 campaign in Russia. Regnault's mother died a few months later. A friend of his father's subsequently took responsibility for his education, and Regnault was found a job in a draper's shop in Paris. In spite of his poverty, Regnault managed to take lessons and in 1830 was admitted to the Ecole Polytechnique in Paris, from where he graduated two years later. He spent two more years at the Ecole des Mines before leaving France to study mining and metallurgical processes in various European locations. He researched briefly under Justus von ◊Liebig at Giessen and Jean-Baptiste Boussingault at Lyon, before returning to the Ecole Polytechnique in 1836 to assist Joseph ◊Gay-Lussac who held the chair in chemistry. After four years Regnault succeeded Guy-Lussac. In the same year Regnault was elected to the chemical section of the Académie des Sciences but by then, in 1840, he was turning his attention to physics and he became professor of physics at the Collège de France in 1841. There, over the next 13 years, he carried out his most significant experimental work.

From 1854 Regnault lived in Sèvres where he was director of the renowned porcelain factory there. In 1870 during the time of the Franco-Prussian War, all his instruments and books were destroyed by Prussian soldiers. Regnault never recovered from this or the further tragedy of the death of his son later in the Franco-Prussian War, and he spent his last years grief stricken and disabled. He died in Auteuil, near Paris, on 19 January 1878.

In his chemical work, nearly all of which dates from between 1835 and 1839, Regnault followed no unified programme of research. His major contributions were to organic chemistry. He studied the action of chlorine on ethers, leading to the discovery of vinyl chloride (monochloroethene), dichloroethylene (dichloroethene), trichloroethylene (trichloroethene), and carbon tetrachloride (tetrachloromethane).

Following Jean Baptiste ◊Dumas's method of investigating atomic composition through the measurement of specific heats, Regnault measured the specific heats of a wide range of substances, during which work, 1839–42, he established the approximate nature of the Dulong–Petit law and endorsed F E Neumann's extension of the law from elements to compounds as a valid progression.

In 1842 he was commissioned by the minister of public works to re-examine the physical constants in the design and operation of steam engines. This was the beginning of the work for which Regnault is now best known, namely the thermal properties of gases. He found that nearly all ordinary gases behave in much the same way and that the nature of this behaviour could generally be described by the perfect gas laws, which can define the volume of a gas in terms of its pressure, temperature, and number of molecules (Boyle's law, Charles's – or Gay-Lussac's – law, and Avogadro's law). He painstakingly measured the coefficients of expansion of various gases and by 1852 had shown how real gases depart from the 'ideal' or 'perfect' behaviour required by Boyle's law – it was left to Johannes ◊van der Waals to formulate a mathematical statement of the variation ten years later. Regnault also calculated that absolute zero is at −273°C/−459°F. He redetermined the composition of air, and performed experiments on respiration in animals.

Remington, Philo (1816–1889) US mechanical engineer largely responsible for perfecting the Remington breech-loading rifle and the Remington typewriter.

Born in Litchfield, New York State, the son of a small-arms manufacturer, Remington entered his father's business, spending 25 years as superintendent of the manufacturing department. It was in this post that he did the work for which he is now remembered.

During the American Civil War, business boomed for the Remingtons but, following the victory of the Union in 1865, the firm looked to diversification to meet the future; in 1873 a perfect answer materialized. After work carried out in the Kleinstuber machine shops in Milwaukee, Wisconsin, the printer and newspaper editor Christopher Sholes (1819–1890) had designed a typewriter capable of being mass-produced. This development attracted the attention of two businessmen, Carlos Glidden and Samuel Soulé, who bought Sholes's patent and then went to Remington with a proposal that the typewriter be manufactured by the company.

The contract was signed in 1873, and what soon became known as the Remington typewriter – based on Sholes's original design – was marketed the following year. This first typewriter had no facility for upper- and lower-case type; only capitals were available. This was soon solved by the simple device of putting both types on each typebar, and providing a mechanism (the shift key) for lifting the key to make contact with the paper. The first typewriter carrying the shift key, the Remington Mark II, appeared in 1878.

To overcome initial market inertia, the Remington machine was loaned to over a hundred firms free of charge. Mark Twain bought one, becoming the first author to provide his publisher with a typewritten manuscript.

Together with his father, Eliphalet (1793–1861), Remington made many improvements to guns and their manufacture. This work went back to 1816, when Remington's father had made a flintlock rifle at his own father's forge in Utica, New York, with an accuracy that soon attracted great attention. That led to the setting up of E Remington and Son at Ilion, beside the Erie Canal. Among the advances made by the father-and-son team was a special lathe for the cutting of gunstocks, a method of producing extremely straight gun barrels, and the making of the first US drilled rifle barrel from cast steel.

Reynolds, Osborne (1842–1912) Irish research engineer, one of the first people to approach engineering as an academic rather than a practical subject. He is particularly remembered for his investigation into turbulent flow in fluids.

Reynolds was born in Belfast on 23 August 1842. His father was a mathematician who became a school-teacher and then rector of the parish of Debach-with-Boulge, Suffolk, (as were his grandfather and great grandfather before). Most of Reynold's early education was at Dedham Grammar School, where his father was a teacher. He left school at the age of 19 and entered an engineering workshop, where he applied his mathematical knowledge to further the understanding of the action and design of machines. He left these practical pursuits to study mathematics at Cambridge University. Like his father he attended Queen's College, from which he graduated in 1867 and was immediately awarded a fellowship. Soon afterwards he went to work in London for John Lawson, a civil engineer.

In 1868 Reynolds was elected to the new chair of engineering at Owens College (now Manchester University). His course of lectures on civil and mechanical engineering included all the mechanical, structural, and thermodynamic principles involved in the subjects and gave rise to a new generation of scientific engineers who were largely to take over from the older, purely practical men.

At the time, academic engineering was not fully divorced from the pure sciences, and much of Reynold's early research into the behaviour of comets, electrical phenomena in the atmosphere, and properties of materials would today be regarded as part of physics. His first real engineering research was concerned with the efficiency of screw propellers for ships, and with their stability. He used scale models, a technique that was to prove of value in his later work.

During the 1880s Reynolds made his famous contribution to hydrodynamics by studying the motion of water at various velocities in parallel channels. Jean Louis ◊Poiseuille and Henri Darcy (1803–1858) had already carried out research in this area but obtained conflicting results. Reynolds showed that for the flow of a liquid to be non-turbulent, it needed a high viscosity, low density, and an open surface. If these and other criteria were not met then the flow was turbulent – a phenomenon he often demonstrated using dyes. The two states, Reynolds found, are separated by a critical velocity, itself dependent on viscous forces (tending to produce stability) and inertial forces (tending to produce instability). The ratio of the two forces, whch gives a measure for any given sytem, is now known as the Reynolds number, Re, and is given by $Re = \rho v l / \eta$, where ρ is the density of the liquid, η its viscocity, v the velocity of flow, and l is a linear dimension, such as the diameter of a tube through which the liquid is flowing.

Reynolds applied much of what he had learned about turbulent flow to the behaviour of the water in river channels and estuaries. For one study he made an accurate model of the mouth of the River Mersey, and pioneered the use of such models in marine and civil engineering projects. His later studies led to discoveries about the forces involved in lubrication with oil and the design of an improved bearing that made use of this knowledge. He also worked on multi-stage steam turbines, but was disappointed by their low efficiency (not realizing that efficiency increases with size and that large efficient turbines are practicable). Using the experimental 75 kW/100 hp steam engine that he had designed for his engineering department, he determined the mechanical equivalent of heat so accurately that it has remained one of the classical determinations of a physical constant.

Reynolds was elected a fellow of the Royal Society in 1877, and during the following decade was honoured with many medals and honourary degrees. He was married twice, his first wife dying a year after the wedding.

Ricardo, Harry Ralph (1885–1974) English engineer who played a leading role in development of the internal-combustion engine. His work was particularly significant during World War I and World War II, enabling the British forces to fight with the advantage of technically superior engines. His work on combustion and detonation led to the octane-rating system for classifying fuels for petrol engines.

Born on 26 January 1885 in London, Ricardo was the eldest son of Halsey Ricardo, an architect, and Catherine Rendel, daughter of Alexander Rendel, a consultant civil engineer. He was educated at Rugby School and designed and built a steam engine, putting it into production when he was 12.

Ricardo went to Cambridge University in 1903, where he designed and built a motor cycle, with its power unit. With it, he won a fuel-economy competition and this success led directly to his concentrating on researching the internal-combustion engine.

In the summer of 1905 he designed and built a two-cylinder, two-stroke engine, called the Dolphin, for automotive applications; but his first production power unit was a four-cylinder version to power his uncle's large car. Ricardo qualified for association membership of the Institution of Civil Engineers and was given charge of a small mechanical engineering department to design site equipment for his grandfather's firm.

During World War I he worked on aircraft engines and designed the engine for the Mk V tank. In July 1917, Ricardo set up his research and consultancy company, which, between the wars, worked on engine development and the categorization of fuels according to their ease of detonation. From 1932 until the outbreak of World War II, it was almost exclusively engaged in the design of light high-speed diesel engines.

When war broke out, Ricardo was living in Tottingon Manor, near Henfield. The house was requisitioned and the company was moved to a less vulnerable site in Oxford. After the war, it moved to Shoreham and Ricardo settled at Wood-side, the family house at Graffham. It was here that he fell and broke his leg, resulting in his death six weeks later on 18 May 1974.

Ricardo was elected a fellow of the Royal Society in 1929 and was president of the Institution of Mechanical Engineers 1944–1945. In 1948 he was knighted and during his life he received 12 medals from various learned bodies.

Ricardo is probably best known for his work on combustion and detonation in spark-ignition engines. In 1912 it was widely believed that the ringing knock in engines with high compression ratios was due to pre-ignition – the firing of the charge in the cylinder before the correct time. Ricardo demonstrated in 1913 that the knock was due to the spontaneous combustion of a part of the charge. One of the factors influencing the tendency for a fuel to ignite spontaneously was its stability, the paraffinic being the worst and the aromatic the best. An early contract won by Ricardo's embryonic company was one from Shell to investigate the behaviour of various fuels. The work led to the evolution of the toluene number system of categorizing fuels, which later became the octane rating.

Ricardo paid great attention to combustion-chamber design and put his ideas into practice during a job to improve the performance of the popular, cheap, side-valve engine. In this he succeeded, so spectacularly, indeed, that his combustion-chamber configuration was produced under licence, or pirated, throughout the world. This led to a patent infringement case, which Ricardo won in 1932. One of the reasons for the success of his valve engine was that the cylinder head, having no valve ports, could be made the best shape for correct combustion. The principle was used for aircraft engines, which were so successful that manufacturers adopted the Ricardo design. This type of engine became the last and best of the British piston engines, powering aircraft of World War II.

During World War I, zeppelin airships bombed the UK from heights of 5,000–6,000 m/16,000–20,000 ft, out of reach of both aircraft and anti-aircraft guns. Ricardo's supercharged engine was re-designed in 1915 and 1916 to power an aircraft to tackle this menace. On its type test, the first engine developed 270 kW/360 hp on supercharged air at ground level and would have been able to intercept the zeppelins with ease. The first engine ran on the test bed in March 1917, exceeding its rated 110 kW/150 hp, developing 125 kW/168 hp at 1,200 rpm and just over 15 kW/200 hp at 1,600 rpm. The first Mk V tank ran in June 1917. When the weight of armour and armaments on tanks was increased, Ricardo designed 168 kW/225 hp and 223.7 kW/ 300 hp units to provide the extra power.

Towards the end of World War II Messerschmitt Me-410s (fast twin-engined fighter bombers) were making hit-and-run raids on British cities and were outdistancing British fighters. Ricardo proposed oxygen enrichment of the Merlin engine and after Mosquitos had been so equipped, the losses of Me-410s increased dramatically and the raids came to an end.

When Ricardo began his work on internal-combustion engine development, the techniques used were more akin to art than to science. He led the revolution in engine design, and his painstaking work laid a firm foundation for the meticulous programmes that have resulted in smaller engines producing more power on less fuel than ever before.

Further Reading

Reynolds, John, *Sir Harry Ricardo: High Priest of the Internal Combustion Engine,* Sutton Publishing, 1999.

Ricardo, Harry, *The Ricardo Story: The Autobiography of Sir Harry Ricardo, Pioneer of Engine Research,* Society of Automotive Engineers, 1992.

Ricci-Curbastro, Gregorio (1853–1925) Italian mathematician who is chiefly remembered for his systematization of absolute differential calculus (also now called the Ricci calculus), which later enabled Albert ◊Einstein to write his gravitational equations, to express the principle of the conservation of energy, and thereby fully to derive the theory of relativity.

Although his complete surname was Ricci-Curbastro, he is often known simply as Ricci. He was born on 12 January 1853 in Lugo, Romagna, where he grew up and was educated at home by private tutors. At the age of 16 he went for a year to Rome University to study mathematics and philosophy, before returning to Lugo. Two years later he enrolled at the University of Bologna. After a year there, in 1872 he enrolled at the Scuola Normale Superiore in Pisa. In 1875 he received his doctorate in the physical and mathematical sciences. After winning a scholarship to travel and study, he spent a year 1877–78 at Munich in Germany, where he met Felix ◊Klein and Enrico ◊Betti. During 1879, Ricci stayed in Pisa and worked as an assistant to the mathematician U Dini.

In December 1880 Ricci was appointed professor of mathematical physics at the University of Padua, and stayed there for the remainder of his life. He published his major work – on absolute calculus – 1888–92, but after being asked in 1891 to teach other aspects of mathematics in addition to those for which he had been appointed, he also published works on higher algebra, infinitesimal analysis, and the theory of real numbers. He received many honours and awards, and was elected to membership of a number of academies. He also made valuable contributions to his local administration: as a magistrate and councillor he was not only concerned with problems of water supply, swamp drainage, and public finance, he was also able to encourage the close collaboration of the government with science and its use in the service of the state. He died in Bologna on 6 August 1925.

Ricci's invention of absolute differential calculus was the result of ten years of research 1884–94. By introducing an invariant element – an element that can also be used in other systems – Ricci was able to modify the existing differential calculus so that the formulae and results remained the same form regardless of the system of variables used. Starting with the idea of co-variant derivation formulated by Elwin ◊Christoffel, the work of Bernhard ◊Riemann on the theory of invariants of algebraic form, and with Rudolf ◊Lipschitz's work on quadratic forms, Ricci realized that the methods used by these mathematicians could be generalized. In 1893 he published his *Di alcune applicazione del calculo differenziale assoluto all teoria delle forme differenzial quadratiche,* in which he gave a specific form to his ideas.

In 1896 he applied absolute calculus to the congruencies of lines on an arbitrary Riemann variety; later, he used the Riemann symbols to find the contract tensor, now known as the Ricci tensor (which plays a fundamental role in the theory of relativity). Ricci also discovered the invariants that occur in the theory of the curvature of varieties.

Later still, he collaborated with a former pupil of his, Tullio ◊Levi-Civita, to produce *Méthodes de calcul différentiel absolu et leurs applications.* This work contains references to the use of intrinsic geometry as an instrument of computation dealing with normal congruencies, geodetic laws, and isothermal families of surfaces. The work also shows the possibilities of the analytical, geometric, mechanical, and physical applications of the new calculus. In application to mechanics, Ricci solved the Lagrange equations with respect to the second derivatives of the coordinates. The application to physics includes equations in electrodynamics, the theory of heat, and the theory of electricity.

Although for some time, however, the new calculus found few applications, when Albert Einstein came to formulate his general theory of relativity Ricci's method proved to be an apt means. Einstein's use of it has since encouraged the intensive study of differential geometry based on Ricci's tensor calculus.

Ricci continued to take an active part in mathematical studies into his very last years. His final major contribution was in 1924, when he presented a paper to the International Congress of Mathematicians held in Toronto, Canada; his subject then was the theory of Riemann varieties.

Richards, Theodore William (1868–1928) US chemist who gained worldwide fame for his extremely accurate determinations of atomic weights (relative atomic masses). For this work he was awarded the 1914 Nobel Prize for Chemistry.

Richards was born in Germantown, Pennsylvania, on 31 January 1868, the son of a painter father and author mother. He received his early education at home, and then in 1882 he went to Haverford College, initially to study astronomy but changing to chemistry because of his poor eyesight. He graduated three years later and went to Harvard, where he gained his chemistry degree in 1886. He remained at Harvard to do research under Josiah Cooke (1827–1894), who set him the task of testing William ◊Prout's hypothesis (that all atomic weights are whole numbers) by determining the ratio by weight of hydrogen to oxygen in water. He was awarded his PhD for this work in 1888. Richards was then granted a travelling fellowship and visited several European universities, where he came into contact with such influential chemists as Viktor ◊Meyer and Lord ◊Rayleigh. He became an instructor in chemistry at Harvard in 1894; he also met Wilhelm ◊Ostwald and Hermann ◊Nernst on a second trip to Europe in 1895. He declined the offer of a professorship at Göttingen University in 1901 in favour of the position of professor of chemistry at Harvard, which he retained for the rest of his career. He died in Cambridge, Massachusetts, on 2 April 1928.

Richards's determinations of atomic weights were based on painstakingly precise quantitative measurements, for which he introduced various new analytical techniques. He devised a method of keeping samples sealed and dry so that they could not absorb moisture before or during weighing. For accurately determining the endpoint in silver nitrate titrations (which usually depend on the first appearance or last disappearance of a precipitate) he invented the nephelometer, a means of comparing the turbidity of two solutions. He made accurate atomic-weight measurements for 25 elements; his co-workers determined 40 more, improving on the 'standard' values obtained by Jean ◊Stas in the 1860s. In 1913 he detected differences in the atomic weights of ordinary lead and samples extracted from uranium minerals (which had arisen by radioactive decay) – one of the first convincing demonstrations of the uranium decay series and confirming Frederick ◊Soddy's prediction of the existence of isotopes. It also revealed a germ of truth in Prout's defunct hypothesis. Richards also investigated the physical properties of the elements, such as atomic volumes and the compressibilities of nonmetallic solid elements.

Richter, Burton (1931–)

US experimental particle physicist. He was a pioneer in colliding beam technology and designed the Stanford Positron Electron Accelerating Ring in the 1960s. He shared the 1976 Nobel Prize for Physics with Samuel Ting (1936–) for their independent discovery of a new subatomic particle. He is Paul Pigott Professor of Physical Sciences at Stanford University.

Richter was born on 22 March 1931 in New York. He studied at the Massachusetts Institute of Technology achieving a BS in 1952 and a PhD in physics in 1956. As a postdoctoral student his interest in the physics of elementary particles took him to Stanford University's high-energy physics laboratory where he was invited to join German-born US physicist Wolfgang Panofsky (1919–) and US physicist G K O'Neill in 1965 in building an electron–electron collider. This led to the building of the first pair of electron-storage rings. Intense beams of particles were made to collide in this machine in order to study the validity of quantum electrodynamic theory.

Richter went on to design the Stanford Positron Electron Accelerating Ring (SPEAR). This was capable of causing collisions of much more energetic particles and in 1974 Richter and his colleagues created a new kind of elementary particle which they called psi. This particle is a hadron with a lifetime of about one thousand times greater than can be expected from its observed mass. Its discovery supported Sheldon ◊Glashow's concept of 'charm' – its properties are consistent with the idea that it is formed from a fourth type of quark. This discovery was announced in a 35-author paper in *Physical Review Letters*.

Meanwhile, Samuel Ting and his colleagues at the Brookhaven Laboratory, Long Island, had simultaneously made the same discovery following a completely different route. Ting's new particle was called J and after Richter and Ting met to discuss their findings the particle became known as J/psi in recognition of its simultaneous origin. This was the first of a 'family' of discoveries and the beginning of new attempts to understand and rationalize the underlying structure of matter. Ting and Richter shared the Nobel Prize for their discovery two years later.

Richter has made over 300 publications in high-energy physics, accelerators and colliding beam systems. He became a professor at Stanford in 1967 and director of the Stanford Linear Accelerator Center in 1984. He is or has been a member of advisory committees to the US Department of Energy, Brookhaven National Laboratory, Fermi National Accelerator Laboratory, MIT Lincoln Laboratory, Argonne National Laboratory, CERN, DESY, the German accelerator laboratory in Hamburg, and the Max Planck Institute in Munich. He is a member of the Director's Council of the Scripp's Institution of Oceanography. He is also interested in the use of science and technology in industry and has had an advisory role with General Motors and with an artificial intelligence company. He is, or has been, a member of the board of directors of several companies including Varian Associates and Litel Instruments and is the chair of the US Liaison Committee for the International Union of Pure and Applied Physics.

In 1979 Richter proposed a scheme to convert the 3-km/1.9-mi long accelerator at Stanford Linear Accelerator Center (SLAC) into an electron–positron accelerator. This later became a useful testing ground for ideas for future accelerators. He was director of SLAC 1984–99.

Ricketts, Howard Taylor (1871–1910) US pathologist who discovered rickettsiae (which are named after
him), a type of microorganism having both viral and
bacterial characteristics. The ten known species in the
Rickettsia genus are all pathogenic in human beings,
causing diseases such as Rocky Mountain spotted fever
and forms of typhus.

Ricketts was born on 9 February 1871 in Findlay,
Ohio. He was educated at the University of Nebraska,
from which he graduated in 1894, and Northwestern
University, Chicago, from which he obtained his medical degree in 1897. He then became a junior resident
doctor at Cook County Hospital, Chicago, before moving to the Rush Medical College (then affiliated with
Chicago University) in 1899 as an instructor in cuta-
neous pathology. In 1901 Ricketts travelled to Europe,
performing laboratory work there. On his return in
1902 he became an instructor and later associate professor in the pathology department of Chicago
University. In 1909 Ricketts went to Mexico City to
investigate typhus; while there he became fatally
infected with the disease and died on 3 May 1910.

Ricketts began studying Rocky Mountain spotted
fever in 1906 and discovered that the disease is transmitted to human beings by the bite of a particular type
of tick that inhabits the skins of animals. In 1908 he
found the causative microorganisms in the blood of
infected animals and in the bodies and eggs of ticks.
This microorganism is now called *Rickettsia rickettsii*,
after its discoverer. In his studies of typhus in Mexico
Ricketts demonstrated that this disease is also caused
by a type of rickettsia and that the microorganisms are
transmitted to humans by the body louse. Before he
died from the disease, Ricketts also showed that typhus
can be transmitted to monkeys, and that, after recovery, they are immune to further attacks.

**Riemann, (Georg Friedrich) Bernhard (1826–
1866)** German mathematician whose work in geometry – both in combining the results of others and in his
own crucial and innovative research – developed that
branch of mathematics to a large degree. His concepts
in non-Euclidean and topological space led to
advances in complex algebraic function theory and in
physics; later Albert ◊Einstein was to make use of his
work in his own theory of relativity. Riemann's study
of analysis was also fundamental to further development. Despite the brevity of his life, he knew most of
the other great mathematicians of his time, and was
himself a famed and respected teacher.

Riemann was born on 17 September 1826 in
Breselenz (in Hannover), one of the six children of a
Lutheran pastor. From a very early age he showed considerable talent in mathematics. Nevertheless, when he
leaft the Lyceum in Hanover in 1846 to enter Göttingen

University, it was to study theology at the behest of his
father. However, he soon obtained his father's permission to devote himself to mathematics and did so, being
taught by the great Karl ◊Gauss. Riemann moved to
Berlin in 1847 and there came into contact with the
equally prestigious teachers Lejeune ◊Dirichlet and
Karl ◊Jacobi; he was particularly influenced by
Dirichlet. Two years later he returned to Göttingen and
submitted a thesis on complex function theory, for
which he was awarded his doctorate in 1851.

During the next two years Riemann qualified as an
unsalaried lecturer, preparing original work on Fourier
series, and working as an assistant to the renowned
physicist Wilhelm ◊Weber. At Gauss's suggestion,
Riemann also wrote a paper on the fundamental postulates of Euclidean geometry, a paper that was to open
up the whole field of non-Euclidean geometry and
become a classic in the history of mathematics.
(Although Riemann first read this paper to the university on 10 June 1854, neither it nor the work on Fourier
series was published until 1867 – a year after
Riemann's death.) Riemann's first course of lectures
concerned partial differential equations as applied to
physics. The course was so admired by physicists that it
was reprinted as long afterwards as in 1938 – 80 years
later. He published a paper on hypergeometric series
and in 1855–56 lectured on his (by now famous) theory of Abelian functions, one of his fundamental
developments in mathematics, which he published in
1857. When Karl Gauss died in 1855, Dirichlet was
appointed in his place, and Riemann was appointed
assistant professor in 1857. On Dirichlet's untimely
death in 1859 Riemann became professor. Three years
later, Riemann married; but in the same year he fell
seriously ill with tuberculosis and he spent much of the
following four years trying to recover his health in
Italy. But he died there, in Selasca, on 16 June 1866 at
the age of 39.

Riemann's first work (his thesis, published when he
was already 25) was a milestone in the theory of complex functions. Augustin ◊Cauchy, who had struggled
with general function theory for 35 years, had discovered most of the fundamental principles, and had
made many daring advances – but some points of
understanding were still lacking. Unlike Cauchy,
Riemann based his theory on theoretical physics
(potential theory) and geometry (conformal representation), and could thus develop the so-called 'Riemann
surfaces' which were able to represent the branching
behaviour of a complex algebraic function.

He developed these ideas further in a paper of 1857
that continued the exploration of Riemann surfaces as
investigative tools to study complex function behaviour, these surfaces being given such properties that
complex functions could map conformally onto them.

In the theory of Abelian functions there is an integer p associated with the number of 'double points' – a double point may be represented on a graph as where a curve intersects itself. Riemann formed, by extension, a multiconnected many-sheeted surface that could be dissected by cross-cuts into a singly connected surface. By means of these surfaces he introduced topological considerations into the theory of functions of a complex variable, and into general analysis. He showed, for example, that all curves of the same class have the same Riemann surface. Extensions of this work become highly abstract – the genus p was in fact discovered by Niels ◊Abel in a purely algebraic context; it is not simply the number of double points. Not until much more work had followed, by Henri ◊Poincaré in particular, did Riemann's ideas in this field reach general understanding. However, his work considerably advanced the whole field of algebraic geometry.

Often his lectures and papers were highly philosophical, containing few formulae, but dealing in concepts. He took into account the possible interaction between space and the bodies placed in it; hitherto space had been treated as an entity in itself, and this new point of view – seized on by the theoretical physicist Hermann von ◊Helmholtz among others – was to become a central concept of 20th-century physics.

Riemann's most profound paper on the foundation of geometry (presented in 1854), also had consequences for physics, for in it he developed the mathematical tools that later enabled Albert Einstein to develop his theory of relativity. The three creators of 'hyperbolic geometry' – Karl Gauss, Nikolai ◊Lobachevsky, and János Bolyai (see Wolfgang and János ◊Bolyai) – all died in the 1850s with their work unacknowledged, and it was Riemann's paper that initiated the revolution in geometry. In 1799 Gauss had claimed to have devised a geometry based on the rejection of Euclid's fifth postulate, which states that parallel lines meet at infinity. Another way of expressing this is to consider a parallelogram in which two opposite corners are right-angled – but in which the other two angles are less than 90°; this is 'hyperbolic' geometry.

One possible case for the two angles to be less than 90° would come about according to two-dimensional geometry on the surface of a sphere. Straight lines are in those circumstances sections of great circles, and a 'rectangle' drawn on the surface of the sphere may have angles of less than 90°. In this way, Riemann invented 'spherical' geometry, which had previously been overlooked (and which can be more disconcerting than hyperbolic geometry). In 1868 Eugenio ◊Beltrami developed this, considering 'pseudo-spheres' – surfaces of constant negative curvature that can realize the conditions for a non-Euclidean geometry on them.

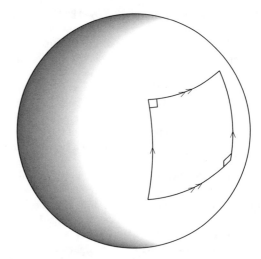

Riemann Georg Riemann showed that in spherical geometry (a form of non-Euclidean geometry), although a parallelogram may have two opposite angles of 90°, it does not necessarily follow that the other two angles are also 90°.

Many other ideas were contained in Riemann's paper. He took up the discussion – and returned again to it later in life – of the properties of topological variabilities (manifolds) with an arbitrary number n of dimensions, and presented a formula for its metric, the means of measuring length within it. He took an element of length, ds, along a curve, and defined it as:

$$\mathrm{d}s^2 = \Sigma g_{ij}{}^2 \, \mathrm{d}x^i \mathrm{d}x^j$$

where $i, j = 1, 2, \dots n$. The structure obtained by this rule is called a Riemann space. It is in fact exactly this sort of concept that Einstein used to deal with time as a 'fourth dimension', and to talk about the 'curvature of space'. Euclidean geometry requires the 'curvature' to be zero. The definition of the curvature of a directed space curve at a point was introduced in this same paper, and implicitly introduces the concept of a tensor. From generalization of this work, and despite opposition at the time, n-dimensional geometries began to be used, especially to examine the properties of differential forms with more than three variables.

Riemann's career was short, and not prolific, but he had a profound and almost immediate effect on the development of mathematics. Everything he published was of the highest quality, and he made a breakthrough in conceptual understanding within several areas of mathematics: the theory of functions, vector analysis, projective and differential geometry, non-Euclidean geometry, and topology. Twentieth-century mathematics bears witness to the extreme fruitfulness of Riemann's ideas.

Ritter, Johann Wilhelm (1776–1810) German physicist who carried out early work on electrolytic cells and who discovered ultraviolet radiation.

Ritter was born in Samnitz, Silesia (now in Poland), on 16 December 1776. He worked first as a pharmacist's apprentice and then after four years, in 1795, went to Jena in Germany to study medicine. Until 1804 he also taught at the University of Jena and at Gotha, before moving to Munich as a member of the Bavarian Academy of Science. He died in Munich six years later on 23 January 1810.

In 1800 Ritter electrolysed water to produce hydrogen and oxygen and two years later developed a dry battery, both of which convinced him that electrical forces were involved in chemical bonding. He also compiled an electrochemical series. At about the same time he was studying the effect of light on chemical reactions, and from the darkening of silver chloride in light he discovered ultraviolet radiation.

Roberts, Richard (1789–1864) Welsh engineer who became one of the greatest mechanical inventors of the 19th century. His inventions included a screw-cutting lathe and a planing machine.

Roberts was born on 22 April 1789 at Carreghofa, Montgomeryshire (now part of Powys), the son of a shoemaker. He had very little formal education and at an early age went to work on the newly opened Ellesmere Canal. From there he obtained work as a labourer in a limestone quarry. At 20 years of age he went to seek work in Liverpool and, later, Manchester – where he became a toolmaker.

To evade military service, Roberts moved to London, where he worked as an apprentice to Henry ◊Maudslay, one of the foremost engineers of the day. Roberts returned to Manchester, which was then the centre of the cotton industry, and in 1814 he set up in business for himself. In 1817 he designed a machine for planing metal – one of the first in his long series of inventions. In 1824, at the request of some manufacturers, he built a self-acting spinning mule that was a vast improvement on that devised by Samuel ◊Crompton in 1779. He took only four months to complete the task.

In 1828 Roberts went into partnership with Thomas Sharpe to found the firm of Sharpe, Thomas and Company. The firm manufactured machines to his design which he continued to improve. For example, in 1832 he improved his mule by adding a radial arm for winding the yarn. When the Liverpool and Manchester Railway opened in 1830 the firm ventured into the business of building locomotives. Their products were bought by railway companies in the UK and elsewhere in Europe. In 1834 they produced a steam carriage with a differential drive to the back wheels. Thomas also designed a steam brake and a system of standard gauges to which all his work was constructed.

The partnership ended when Sharpe died in 1842. The firm split up – the Sharpe family continued to control the manufacture of locomotives, while Roberts retained the remaining part of the company known as the Globe Works. In 1845 he invented an electromagnet – of which examples were placed in the Manchester museum at Peel Park and one was kept by the Scottish Society of Arts. In 1848 Roberts invented a machine for punching holes in steel plates. Incorporating the Jacquard method, he devised a machine for punching holes of any pitch or pattern in bridge plates and boiler plates. He later invented a machine for simultaneously shearing iron and punching both webs of angle iron to any pitch. As with his improvement to the self-acting mule a quarter of a century before, Roberts built his hole-punching machine in response to requests by company owners, who this time found themselves faced with labour difficulties as a result of the strike during the building of Thomas ◊Telford's Conway suspension bridge.

At the Great Exhibition of 1851 Roberts received a medal for a turret clock he had made. Recognition of his contribution to engineering took other forms. He was elected member of the Institution of Civil Engineers in 1838 and was a founder member of the Mechanics Institute in 1824. But, despite his genius as an inventor, Roberts's financial position deteriorated almost to poverty and just before he died on 16 March 1864 a public subscription was being raised to support him.

Robertson, Robert (1869–1949) Scottish chemist whose main work was concerned with improvements to explosives for military use.

Robertson was born in Cupar, Fife, on 17 April 1869. He was educated at the Madras Academy and St Andrews University, where he took extra lessons in chemistry in order to gain a BSc degree as well as his MA. After a short period as assistant to the Glasgow city analyst he obtained a post at the Royal Gunpowder Factory at Waltham Abbey, Essex (at a time when the military were changing from black powder to smokeless nitro compounds as propellant explosives for cartridges). The results of his work on nitrocellulose were incorporated into his doctoral thesis of 1897. He was put in charge of the main laboratory in 1900 and seven years later was appointed superintending chemist in the research department at Woolwich Arsenal. The work of the department increased tremendously during World War I, and in 1918 Robertson was knighted for his services. On the retirement of James Dobbie in 1921 Robertson became the government chemist, a position he held until he left government service in 1936 and went to work at the Davy Faraday Laboratory at the Royal Institution. At the outbreak of World War II in 1939 his offer to return to the explosives research department at Woolwich was gladly accepted; he went back to the Royal Institution in 1945. He died in London on 28 April 1949.

From 1900, at Waltham Abbey, Robertson studied the Will test for measuring the rate of decomposition of nitrocellulose and in 1906 introduced an improved method of purifying nitrocellulose. As a result of his work the propellant in British ammunition was changed from Mark I cordite to the more stable MD cordite. His appointment to Woolwich in 1907 coincided with the analysis of defects in British ammunition that had been revealed during the South African War. The new explosive tetryl (trinitrophenylmethylnitramine) was developed, as were detonators for lyddite (picric aid, 2,4,6-trinitrophenol); work began on the use of TNT (trinitrotoluene, 2,4,6-trinitromethylbenzene) as a high explosive for military purposes. Robertson continued his investigations into the stability of cordite, showing that the presence of impurities can be a critical factor (and leading to improved methods of manufacture and storage).

At the beginning of World War I the British government became concerned about supplies of TNT, which were limited by the availability of toluene (methylbenzene), manufactured from coal tar or extracted from Borneo petroleum, which is rich in aromatic hydrocarbons. Robertson's researchers solved the considerable problems of 'diluting' TNT with ammonium nitrate to produce a new high explosive, amatol.

After Robertson became government chemist in 1921 he welcomed the opportunity to carry out research unfettered by the secrecy that had inevitably surrounded his previous work. Many of his investigations were carried out to assist state departments. These included the carriage of dangerous goods by sea, the determination of sulphur dioxide and nitrous gases in the atmosphere, the elimination of sulphur dioxide from the gaseous products of combustion at power stations, the possible effects on health of tetraethyl lead additives to petrol, the determination of iodine in biological substances, and the preservation of photographic reproductions of valuable documents. He was also concerned with the determination of carbon monoxide and nitrous oxide (dinitrogen oxide) and in an investigation of the extraction of minerals (such as potassium chloride and bromine) from the waters of the Dead Sea.

Later work on infrared absorption spectroscopy in collaboration with J J Fox and E S Hiscocks greatly stimulated research in this field. Robertson's improvements in spectrographic equipment also permitted his study of diamonds from various natural sources.

Robinson, Robert (1886–1975) English organic chemist who, during a long and distinguished career, made many contributions to the science. Among the many and wide-ranging topics he researched were alkaloids, steroids, and aromatic compounds. For his work on alkaloids and other biologically significant substances derived from plants he was awarded the 1947 Nobel Prize for Chemistry.

Robinson was born in Bufford, near Chesterfield, on 13 September 1886, the son of a local manufacturer. It was intended that he should enter his father's business but after graduating in chemistry from Manchester University in 1905, he embarked on an academic career. He obtained his doctorate in 1912 and then held the chair in organic chemistry successively at Sydney University 1912–15, Liverpool 1915–20, St Andrews 1920–22, Manchester 1922–29, and Oxford 1929–55. He was knighted in 1939. In 1957 he founded the influential journal *Tetrahedron*. He died in Great Missenden on 8 February 1975.

Robinson's lifelong interest in plant materials began with his study of the colourless material brazilin and its red oxidation product brazilein, which occur in brazilwood. This work led on to an investigation of anthocyanins (red and blue plant pigments) and anthoxanthins (yellow and brown pigments). He studied their composition and synthesis, and related their structure to their colour. His first synthesis in this area, that of callistephin chloride, was carried out in 1928.

In his research on alkaloids he worked out the structure of morphine in 1925 and by 1946 he had devised methods of synthesizing strychnine and brucine – using only 'classical' techniques of organic chemistry – and so influenced all structural studies of natural compounds that contain nitrogen. He also suggested biosynthetic pathways for the production of such substances in nature. While not always correct, these proposals confirmed his relentless and convincing assertion that, since nature involves chemical substances, it must obey laws recognized by chemists.

He began research on steroids at Oxford and his studies of the sex hormones, bile acids, and sterols were fundamental to the general methods now used to investigate compounds of this type. His discovery that certain synthetic steroids could produce the same biological effects as do the natural oestrogenic sex hormones led to the preparation of stilboestrol, hexoestrol, and dienoestrol, paving the way for pharmaceutical applications such as the contraceptive pill and treatments for infertility in women.

In 1942, spurred on by the needs of World War II, Robinson investigated the properties of the antibiotic penicillin and elucidated its structure. His methods were later applied to structural investigations of other antibiotics.

Throughout his career Robinson was also concerned with the theoretical aspects of organic chemistry. He began by studying the polarization (electron displacement) in the carbon–chlorine covalent bond and progressed to investigating conjugate systems, which involve alternate single and double carbon–carbon bonds. He showed that if the original double bonds are sufficiently weak, pairs of electrons can transfer from them to intervening single bonds along the chain. He introduced the method of representing such electron transfer by means of 'curly arrows' on a structural formula. This theory is particularly relevant to aromatic compounds, in which the presence of a substituent in the benzene ring influences further substitution and how fast such substitution takes place. Robinson worked out the theory that governs this important type of reaction and how it is affected by the nature of the reagent concerned: electrophilic reagents attack preferentially positions in which there are an excess of electrons; nucleophilic reagents attack electron-deficient positions.

In his later years Robinson became interested in the composition of petroleum and how it originated on Earth, and he suggested routes by which petroleum products may have originated from amino acids and other chemicals present before life as we know it began.

He was professor of organic chemistry at St Andrews in the early 1920s at the same time as his predecessor, Norman ◊Haworth, was at Durham University. Between them they led contemporary work on an extremely wide range of natural products (Haworth's main area of study was carbohydrates) and many of today's structural and synthetic methods are based on their pioneering work.

Further Reading

Birch, Arthur J, 'Investigating a scientific legend: The tropinione synthesis of Sir Robert Robinson, FRS', *Notes Rec Roy Soc Lond*, 1993, v 47, pp 227–296.

Saltzman, Martin D, 'Sir Robert Robinson: A centennial tribute', *Chem Brit*, 1986, v 22, pp 543–548.

Synge, R L M, 'How the Robinsons nearly invented partition chromatography in 1934', *Notes Rec Roy Soc Lond*, 1992, v 46, pp 309–312.

Williams, Trevor, *Sir Robert Robinson: Chemist Extraordinary*, Oxford University Press, 1990.

Roe, (Edwin) Alliot Verdon (1877–1958) English aircraft designer, the first Briton to construct and fly an aeroplane and the designer of the Avro series of aircraft.

Roe was born on 26 April 1877 at Patricroft, near Manchester. He was educated at St Paul's School, London, but at the age of 14 he went to British Columbia. Returning from Canada a year later, he served a five-year apprenticeship at the Lancashire and Yorkshire Railway Company's locomotive sheds. He then spent two years at sea, after which he entered the motor industry. He became interested in aircraft design and, in 1908, flew a distance of 23 m/75 ft in a biplane of his own design. This feat was accomplished nearly a year before the first officially recognized flight in England by John Moore-Brabazon (1884–1964).

In 1910, with his brother Humphrey, Roe founded the firm of AV Roé and Company. It became one of the world's major aircraft companies and the builder of one of the most famous aircraft of its time – the Avro 504. In 1928, Roe severed all ties with the company and turned his attention to the design of flying boats. He became associated with the firm of S E Saunders and founded the Saunders–Roe Company at Cowes, Isle of Wight, and became its president. Roe was knighted in 1929, and changed his surname to Verdon-Roe. He died at his home near London on 4 January 1958.

The first aircraft from the Manchester works was the Avro 500, of historic importance because it was one of the first machines to be ordered for use by the British army. The order – for three two-seater biplanes fitted with 37 kW/50 hp Gnome engines – was placed by the government in 1912. Before the Gnome engines appeared, Roe had completed a two-seater biplane powered by a 45 kW/60 hp ENV engine, and it was this aircraft that provided the basis for a succession of very successful planes.

The Avro 500 was an equal-span, two-bay biplane of wooden construction. The undercarriage was of an original design, with wheels mounted on a transverse leaf-spring that attached to a central skid (there was no tail-skid). The machine rested its rear end on the base of a suitably reinforced rudder; a modified rudder, still acting as a tailskid, was fitted later.

The first of the 500s went into service on 12 May 1912, and two were used to form the strength of the Central Flying School of the Royal Flying Corps (RFC), which opened at Upavon on 7 August that year. (Several of these aircraft were later used by the naval and military wings of the RFC.) The original order was increased to 12 and this contract enabled the firm of AV Roe to became solidly established. In 1913 the company produced its first seaplane type, a large biplane originally known as the Avro 503.

The construction of the Avro 504, which followed the 503, began in April 1913. It made its debut in September of that year. The design, construction, and performance were all considerably in advance of its contempories, and it was this aircraft that helped lay the foundations for decades of safe flying instruction. Adapted to a float-plane version in 1914, it is regarded as one of the first production machines. Although not basically a military aircraft, it was used extensively in World War I and took part in some famous actions – the attack on the zeppelin airship sheds at Freidrichshaven being one. Further modification led to a long succession of successful aircraft, from the 504A through to the 504H, which was the first aircraft to be successfully launched by catapult.

Romer, Alfred Sherwood (1894–1973)

US palaeontologist and comparative anatomist who is best known for his influential studies of vertebrate evolution and as the author of several books on the anatomy and evolution of the vertebrates.

Romer was born on 28 December 1894 in White Plains, New York, the son of a journalist. His family moved frequently during his early years, but in 1909 Romer returned to White Plains to live with his grandmother and a more settled phase began. He left high school in 1912 and, because his family was poor, spent a year doing odd jobs to earn money for a college education. In 1913 he entered Amherst College to study history and German literature but his interest soon turned to palaeontology, and he took a course in evolution. He graduated in 1917 after the start of World War I and joined the American Field Service in France; later that year he enlisted in the US Army, and remained in Europe until 1919. On returning to the USA, he did postgraduate work at Columbia University, from which he gained his doctorate in 1921 with a thesis on comparative muscle structure that is still a classic in its field. He then taught anatomy at the Bellevue Hospital Medical College, New York, until 1923, when he was appointed an associate professor in the department of geology and palaeontology at the University of Chicago. He held this post for 11 years, during which period he married Ruth Hibbard; they had three children. In 1934 Romer was appointed professor of biology at Harvard University; he also became director of its biological laboratories in 1945 and of the Museum of Comparative Zoology in the following year. He held these three posts until 1965, when he officially retired, although he continued to work and lecture for the rest of his life. Romer died on 5 November 1973 in Cambridge, Massachusetts.

Romer spent almost all of his career investigating vertebrate evolution. Using evidence from palaeontology, comparative anatomy, and embryology, he traced the basic structural and functional changes that took place during the evolution of fishes to primitive terrestrial vertebrates and from these to modern vertebrates. In these studies he emphasized the evolutionary significance of the relationship between the form and function of animals and the environment.

One of the most important figures in palaeontology since the 1930s, Romer wrote several well-known books on vertebrates, including *Man and the Vertebrates* (1933), *Vertebrate Palaeontology* (1933), which was widely influential in its field for several decades, and *The Vertebrate Body* (1949), a comprehensive study of comparative vertebrate anatomy that is still a standard textbook today. He also collected an extensive range of fossils from his field trips to South Africa, Argentina, and Texas.

Römer, Ole (or Olaus) Christensen (1644–1710)

Danish astronomer and civil servant who, through the precision of both his observations and his calculations, first derived a rate for the speed of light. This was all the more remarkable in that most scientists of his time considered light to be instantaneous in propagation. A practical man, Römer was also talented at designing scientific instruments.

He was born in Århus, in Jutland, on 25 September 1644. Educated in Copenhagen, he attended the university there, where he studied under the Bartholin brothers – Thomas (1616–1680), who professor of mathematics and anatomy, and Erasmus (1625–1698), a physicist and astronomer. First as a student of mathematics and astronomy, then as personal assistant, Römer lived at the house of Erasmus Bartholin, whose daughter he eventually married. In 1671 he collaborated with Jean Picard (1620–1682), who had been sent by the French Academy to verify the exact position of Tycho ◊Brahe's observatory. Evidently impressed by Römer's work, Picard invited him to come back to Paris with him once the investigations were over; Römer gladly accepted. At the academy in Paris, Römer worked initially as an assistant, but within a year was made a member in his own right. He was also appointed tutor to the crown prince. There followed several years in which he conducted observations, designed and improved instruments, and submitted various papers to the academy, all culminating, in 1679, in the exposition of his calculation of the speed of light. With his new-found fame, Römer then visited Britain and met some of the greatest astronomers of his age – Isaac ◊Newton, Edmond ◊Halley, and the Astronomer Royal, John ◊Flamsteed. He returned to Denmark in 1681 to take up the dual post of Astronomer Royal to King Christian V and director of the Royal Observatory in Copenhagen. He also accepted a number of civic duties. He died in Copenhagen on 23 September 1710.

It was while he was in Paris that Römer carried out his famous research that not only demonstrated that light travels at a finite speed but also put a rate to it. His observations of the satellites around Jupiter, especially of the innermost one, Io, led him to notice that the length of time between eclipses of Io by Jupiter was not constant. He found that when the distance between the

Earth and Jupiter was least, the interval between eclipses was also smallest. He therefore measured the inter-eclipse period when the two planets were closest and then announced in September 1679 that the eclipse of Io by Jupiter predicted for 9 November would occur 10 minutes later than expected on the basis of all previous calculations.

Römer's prediction was borne out; his interpretation of the delay provoked a sensation. He said that the delay was caused by the time it took for the light to traverse the extra distance across the Earth's orbit when the positions of Jupiter and the Earth were such that they were not as close to each other as they sometimes were. This meant that light did not traverse space instantaneously, but travelled at a finite speed. Römer estimated that speed to be 225,000 km/140,000 mi per second – which is remarkably close (considering that it was the first estimate ever) to the modern value of 299,792 km/186,291 mi per second. Römer's interpretation of his observations was not accepted by all of his contemporary astronomers, particularly not in France, but was confirmed 60 years later – after Römer's death – by James ◊Bradley (who was also able to improve upon Römer's estimate, obtaining a value of 308,300 km/191,578 mi per second).

Römer's later work was on optics, instrument design, and the systematization of weights and measures. Unsatisfied by the Copenhagen Observatory, he established his own private observatory, which he named the Tuscalaneum and which possessed the first telescope attached to a transit circle, a device of his own invention.

Röntgen, Wilhelm Konrad (1845–1923) German physicist who discovered X-rays. For this achievement, he was awarded the first Nobel Prize for Physics in 1901.

Röntgen was born in Lennep, Prussia, on 27 March 1845. He received his early education in Holland and then went to Zürich Polytechnic, Switzerland, in 1866 to study mechanical engineering. Röntgen received a diploma in this subject in 1868 and a PhD in 1869. He then became an assistant to August ◊Kundt, who was professor of physics at Zürich, and changed direction towards pure science. Under Kundt's guidance, Röntgen made rapid progress in physics. In 1871, he moved to Würzburg and then in 1872 to Strasbourg both times in order to remain with Kundt. He then obtained the position of professor of physics and mathematics at the Agricultural Academy of Hohenheim in 1875, but returned to Strasbourg the following year to teach physics. He was then professor of physics at Giessen 1879–88, when he was appointed to the same position at Würzburg, also becoming director of the Physical Institute there. Finally in 1900,

Röntgen German physicist Wilhelm Konrad Röntgen who discovered X-rays in 1895. He was awarded the Nobel Prize for physics in 1901. Today, the unit of radiation exposure is called the **roentgen**, or röntgen. *Mary Evans Picture Library*

Röntgen became professor of physics and director of the Physical Institute at Munich. He retired in 1920, and died in poverty on 10 February 1923 in Munich, following runaway inflation in Germany.

During his career, Röntgen's worked on such diverse topics as elasticity, heat conduction in crystals, specific heat capacities of gases, and the rotation of plane-polarized light. In 1888, Röntgen made an important contribution to electricity when he confirmed that magnetic effects are produced by the motion of electrostatic charges, following a demonstration of the effect made by Henry ◊Rowland in 1875.

It was during his period in Würzburg that Röntgen made his most momentous discovery. In November 1895 he was investigating the properties of cathode rays emitted by a high-vacuum discharge tube, particularly the luminescence produced when such rays impinged on certain chemicals. One of the substances with which he was experimenting was barium platinocyanide. Surprisingly, he found that it glowed even when the tube was encased in black cardboard. He then removed the chemical to an adjacent room; as before it glowed whenever the tube was activated. Such high penetrating power led Röntgen to the conclusion that the radiation was entirely different from cathode rays. Unable to establish the nature of the radiation, which in fact came from the glass walls of the tube when struck by the cathode rays, he coined the term

'X-rays'. Röntgen was in no doubt that his discovery was unique and therefore decided to look more closely at the nature of his X-rays before publicly announcing their existence. He established that they pass unchanged through cardboard and thin plates of metal, travel in straight lines, and are not deflected by electric or magnetic fields.

By January 1896, Röntgen was ready to reveal his work to the general public. As X-rays are absorbed by bone, he illustrated one lecture with an X-ray photograph of a man's hand. The impact was tremendous. Soon the use of X-ray equipment and photography in medical work developed both in Europe and the USA. The discovery also served as an impetus to other scientists. In France it led Henri ◊Becquerel to the discovery of radioactivity the same year, which in turn caused a revolution in ideas of the atom, while the demonstration of X-ray diffraction in 1912 by Max von ◊Laue brought about methods of investigating atomic and molecular structure.

It is likely that X-rays had been produced by others before Röntgen, because experiments with cathode rays had been going on ever since Julius ◊Plücker first produced them in 1858. William ◊Crookes had noticed that photographic plates kept near cathode-ray tubes became fogged, an effect almost certainly due to X-rays. However it was Röntgen who first realized the existence of X-rays and first investigated their properties. It was only right that he was acclaimed by the world for a discovery that has brought immense benefits both in medicine and science. It is perhaps fitting that it was made by a man of total integrity who refused to make any financial gain out of his good fortune, believing that the products of scientific research should be made freely available to all.

Further Reading

Glasser, Otto, *Wilhelm Conrad Röntgen and the Early History of the Roentgen Rays,* Norman Publishing, 1993.

Röntgen, Wilhelm Konrad, *Röntgen Centennial: X-Rays Today in Natural and Life Sciences,* World Scientific Publishing Company, 1997.

Ross, Ronald (1857–1932) British physician who proved that malaria is transmitted to human beings by the bite of the *Anopheles* mosquito. He also devoted much of his time to public health programmes concerned with the prevention of the disease. For his significant contribution to the battle against malaria, which has plagued people for centuries, he received the 1902 Nobel Prize for Physiology or Medicine.

Ross was born in Almora, India, on 13 May 1857, the son of a British army officer serving there. He was educated in the UK and received his medical training at St Bartholomew's Hospital, London, graduating in 1879. He was unenthusiastic about medicine, his interests at that time being in the arts and mathematics. When he joined the Indian Medical Service in 1881, however, he gradually became absorbed with medical problems. During his first leave in England, 1888–89, he obtained a diploma in public health and took a course in bacteriology. On retiring from the Indian Medical Service in 1899, he returned to the UK and lectured at the new School for Tropical Medicine in Liverpool, later holding the chair in tropical medicine there. He was knighted in 1911 and a year later moved to London, where he established a consulting practice at King's College Hospital. During World War I he was consultant on malaria to the War Office and when the Ross Institute of Tropical Diseases was opened in his honour, in 1926, he became its first director. He died in London on 16 September 1932.

While on leave in England in 1894, Ross became acquainted with the Scottish physician Patrick ◊Manson, who demonstrated that the blood of malarial patients contained pigmented bodies and parasites. (The discovery that malaria was caused by a protozoan in the bloodstream had been made by Charles ◊Laveran in Algeria in 1883.) Manson's suggestion was that malaria was spread by mosquitoes and Ross returned to India determined to investigate this hypothesis and to identify the mosquito responsible. The shortage in India of literature on the subject delayed the identification of species of mosquitoes and parasites, and Ross was also cut off from

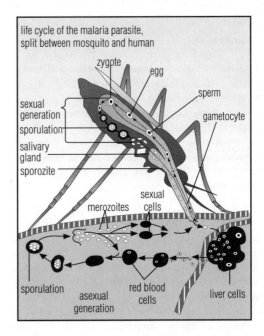

Ross The reproductive life cycle of a malaria parasite is split between *Anopheles* mosquito and human hosts.

the work of others. He missed, for example, Albert King's suggestion that malaria might be transmitted via mosquito bites.

Ross refused to believe the popular idea that malaria was caused by bad air (*mal aria*) or contaminated water, and he continued to collect mosquitoes, identifying the various species and dissecting their internal organs. In the stomachs of some insects he found 'motile filaments', which, although Ross was unaware of it, were gametes. He thought that the filaments might develop to further stages, and dissected a few mosquitoes that had fed on malarial patients. In August 1897 he discovered in an *Anopheles* mosquito a cyst containing the parasites that had been found by Laveran in the blood of malarial patients. These sporozoites of the malarial parasite remain in the human blood for only an hour after a bite, before invading liver cells, and their subsequent developmental stages are distinct from those in the mosquito. The biting mosquito may suck up various stages of the parasite with the blood, but all are digested except those that produce gametes. After fertilization the zygote bores through the stomach wall of the mosquito and forms an external cyst. Sporozoites are formed in the cyst, which migrate to the mosquito's salivary glands, ready for injection into a victim. Later, using caged birds with bird malaria, Ross was able to show that the 'motile filaments' do develop to further stages. The life history of the parasite inside a mosquito was thus revealed and the mode of transmission to the victim was identified as taking place through a mosquito bite.

Further Reading

Bynum, William F and Overy, Caroline, *The Beast in the Mosquito: The Correspondence of Ronald Ross and Patrick Manson,* Wellcome Institute Series in the History of Medicine; Clio Medica, Rodopi, 1998, v 51.

Mégroz, Rodolphe Louis, *Ronald Ross, Discoverer and Creator,* G Allen and Unwin Ltd, 1931.

Nye, E R and Gibson, Mary, *Ronald Ross, Malariologist and Polymath: A Biography,* Macmillan Press Ltd, 1996.

Ross, Ronald, *The Great Malaria Problem and Its Solution,* Keynes, 1988.

Roux, Wilhelm (1850–1924) German anatomist and zoologist who is famous for his work on developmental mechanics in embryology. He founded the first-ever journal of experimental embryology and also helped to produce a dictionary of experimental morphology.

Roux was born on 9 June 1850 in Jena. He attended the Oberrealschule in Meiningen then studied at the universities of Jena – where he was a student of Ernst ◊Haeckel – Berlin, and Strasbourg. In 1873 he matriculated from the medical faculty, and passed his state medical examinations in 1877. After spending several years as an assistant at Franz Hofmann's Institute of Hygiene in Leipzig, Roux moved to the University of Breslau (now Wrocław in Poland), where he eventually became director of his own Institute of Embryology. He was professor of anatomy at the University of Innsbruck 1889–95, when he became director of the Anatomical Institute at the University of Halle, where he remained until his retirement in 1921. Roux died in Halle on 15 September 1924.

Roux's embryological investigations were performed mainly on frogs' eggs. He performed a series of experiments in which he punctured the eggs at the two-cell stage of development (a technique Roux pioneered) and found that they grew into half-embryos; this finding led him to conclude that the fate of the parts had already been determined at the two-cell stage. In the field of embryology Roux also researched into the earliest structures in amphibian development. In 1894 he founded the first journal of experimental embryology; it is still published today and is now called *Roux Archiv für Entwicklungsmechanik.*

Roux also investigated the mechanisms of functional adaptations, examining the physical stresses that cause bones, cartilage, and tendons to adapt to malformations and diseases. In addition, he collaborated with two botanists and an anatomist to produce a dictionary of experimental morphology, which provided a valuable compendium of definitions and historical notes in this discipline.

Roux was not the only scientist who performed embryological experiments at that time, but he nevertheless made substantial contributions to the knowledge of embryological development. However, he grossly overestimated the importance of his work, claiming, for example, that he alone was the first to progress from causal manipulation to a causal analysis of development – an absurd contention because, at the very least, it ignored the work of his contemporaries Oskar Hertwig (1849–1922) and Eduard Pfluger (1829–1910).

Rowland, Henry Augustus (1848–1901) US physicist who is best known for the development of the concave diffraction grating, which heralded a new era in the analysis of spectra.

Rowland was born in Honesdale, Pennsylvania, on 27 November 1848. As a child he displayed a clear interest in science, and entered the Rensselaer Polytechnic Institute in Troy, New York, in 1865, graduating with a degree in civil engineering in 1870. Rowland spent the next year working on surveys as a railway engineer. In 1871, he became a teacher of natural science at Wooster College in Ohio, but returned to the Rensselaer Polytechnic in 1872 to serve first as an instructor, and from 1874 as assistant professor.

The newly established Johns Hopkins University in Baltimore, Maryland, offered Rowland the chair of physics in 1876. He accepted, and spent the next year travelling in Europe meeting scientists such as James Clerk ◊Maxwell and Hermann von ◊Helmholtz, conducting some research and purchasing equipment to make the physics laboratories at Johns Hopkins among the best equipped in the world. Rowland remained as professor of physics there until his death at Baltimore on 16 April 1901. He was also the founder and first president of the American Physical Society.

Rowland felt that he did not comfortably fit into the category of either experimental or theoretical physicist. He designed his experiments so that their results might shed light on questions of theoretical interest, but he was also extremely talented at the practical design of experimental apparatus.

His earliest research, 1873–74, concerned the measurement of the magnetic permeability of nickel, iron, and steel, and the demonstration of its variation with the strength of the magnetizing force. This led to one of his most noteworthy experiments, which was conducted while on a brief visit to Helmholtz's laboratory in Berlin in 1875. The question of whether a moving electrically charged body would demonstrate certain properties of an electric current, such as the ability to create a magnetic field, had arisen from the work of Michael ◊Faraday and Maxwell. If it did, then an electric current could be regarded as a sequence of electric charges in motion. Rowland was able to provide the first demonstration that this is in fact so by showing that a rapidly rotating charged body was able to deflect a magnet. Such was the delicacy of this experiment that it was not confirmed until Wilhelm ◊Röntgen succeeded in repeating it in 1888.

Upon his return to the USA, Rowland began a series of studies aimed at the accurate determination of certain physical constants. He first investigated the value for the ohm, the unit of electrical resistance. The value that he published in 1878 is very close to that accepted today. He then repeated James ◊Joule's determination of the mechanical equivalent of heat in 1879, and was able to improve the accuracy of the result.

The development of the concave diffraction grating in 1882 stands as Rowland's major contribution to physics. The science of spectroscopy was well advanced from the days when prisms had been relied upon for the production of spectra, due particularly to the introduction by Joseph von ◊Fraunhofer of ruled gratings in place of prisms. The quality of the results obtainable depended on the accuracy and density of the scratched rulings on the diffraction gratings. Rowland saw that a critical limiting factor in the ability to produce these lines was the availability of a perfect screw for the ruling machine. He tackled the

problem using his engineering expertise, and was eventually able to produce lines at a density of more than 16,000 per cm/40,000 per in of grating. This gave a much greater revolving power, but Rowland went on to improve spectroscopy even further by the introduction of a concave metal or glass grating. This had the advantage of being self-focusing and thus eliminated the need for lenses, which absorbed some wavelengths of the spectrum.

Rowland's concave diffraction gratings were a sensational success. He sold over a hundred of the devices, which enabled scientists to accomplish in a few hours what had previously taken days to achieve. Rowland then put his invention to use in the years 1886–95 by remapping the solar spectrum, publishing the wavelengths for 14,000 lines with an accuracy ten times better than his predecessors had managed.

Royce, (Frederick) Henry (1863–1933) English engineer who, in cooperation with Charles Rolls (1877–1910), produced the famous Rolls-Royce series of high-performance motorcars.

Royce was born on 27 March 1863 at Alwalton, Huntingdonshire (now Cambridgeshire). On leaving school he became an apprentice engineer with the Great Northern Railway. He later, 1882–83, worked on the pioneer scheme to light London's streets with electricity, and as chief electrical engineer on the project to light the streets of Liverpool. In 1884 he founded the firm of F H Royce and Company Ltd, Mechanical Engineers of Manchester, and manufactured electric cranes and dynamos. In 1904 he built his first car and in 1907, with Rolls, he founded the firm of Rolls-Royce Ltd, motorcar and aeroengine builders, of Trafford Park, Manchester (and later of Derby and London). Royce became the company's director and chief engineer.

By 1914, the firm had established a reputation for building 'the best cars in the world'. In 1920 a US factory was opened at Springfield, Massachusetts, and the Rolls-Royce Ghost was made there until 1926. The Ghost was followed by the Phantom, manufactured 1927–31. In that year the company bought Bentley Motors and two years later the Bentley luxury-model car, based on a Rolls-Royce three-litre engine, made its appearance. It maintained its reputation as a first-class luxury limousine until 1950.

Royce was made a baronet in 1930. He was also awarded the OBE and was a member of the Institute of Mechanical Engineers, the Institute of Aeronautical Engineers, and the Institute of Electrical Engineers. He died in Sussex on 22 April 1933.

Like all other industrialists at the turn of the century, Rolls at first knew nothing about motorcars and could only copy and improve on the good designs of others. In 1903 France led the world in automobile design. Taking a French car, the 7.5 kW/10 hp Decauville as his model, Royce used imported parts and set about improving the design. Because he was a craftsman-mechanic and possessed special skills, the cars he built were just that much better than the others being made at that time.

The first Royce-built car appeared in 1904. It had mechanically operated overhead inlet valves – a great improvement on the Decauville's automatic inlets. Because it was so well made, the Royce car was also very much quieter and smoother-running. Three of these first models were built and, by chance, one of them was bought by a man called Edmunds who was a director of a car-importing firm. Also working for the firm was Charles Rolls. Although he worked as a salesman, Rolls was rich, aristrocratic, and well-known as a pioneer motoring and aviation enthusiast.

Rolls drove and tested the car and was so impressed by its performance that he undertook to sell Royce's entire output. The two men became friends, pooled their talents, and started the world-famous partnership. The Rolls-Royce range was expanded to include three-litre, three-cylinder 'light' and 'heavy' versions of the four-cylinder Twenty and Six to sell at £900.

In 1906 a light Twenty, driven by Rolls, won the Tourist Trophy and also broke the Monte Carlo-to-London record. In that year, also, the partnership embarked upon its one-model policy based on a 30–37 kW/40–50 hp six-cylinder car that was later to win immortality as the Silver Ghost. The car's reputation was assured after a successful 24,000-km/15,000-mi RAC-observed trial in 1907, and it was in that year that the Rolls-Royce firm of car-makers officially came into existence. Over 6,000 of these cars were made at Manchester and later at the Derby works.

Rolls was killed in a flying accident in 1912, but the firm continued to prosper. An armoured version of the Ghost saw service both during and after World War I. Later, the firm was to win a reputation for its production of aeroengines.

Ruffini, Paolo (1765–1822) Italian mathematician, philosopher, and doctor who made valuable contributions in all three disciplines. In his mathematical work he is remembered chiefly for what is now known as the Abel–Ruffini theorem.

Ruffini was born on 22 September 1765 at Valentano, Viterbo. While he was very young his family moved to Modena, and it was there that he grew up and remained for the rest of his life. Studying medicine, philosophy, mathematics, and literature at the University of Modena, Ruffini was an exceptional student. During his own final year of instruction, he also taught one of the courses in mathematics. In 1788 he obtained degrees in philosophy, medicine, and mathe-

matics, and was appointed professor of the foundations of analysis. Three years later he became professor of the elements of mathematics.

Napoleon entered Modena in 1796, and Ruffini found himself obliged to take up an appointment as an official of the republic, until permitted to return to his teaching two years later. Then, however, he refused to swear the oath of allegiance to the republic and was immediately barred from teaching or holding any public office. He busied himself with his medical work and other research, and was soon recalled to the university. After the fall of Napoleon, Ruffini held the chair of applied mathematics as well as the chair of clinical medicine, and in 1814 he was also appointed rector. Three years later he contracted typhus during an epidemic in the city, but with true scientific detachment he observed the progress of the disease and afterwards wrote a paper on the symptoms and treatment of typhus. He died, in Modena, on 9 May 1822.

In the year of his return to the university after being barred, Ruffini published a theorem – later to become known as the Abel–Ruffini theorem – which stated that it was impossible to give a general solution to equations of greater than the fourth degree using only radicals (such as square roots, cube roots, and so on). To try to clarify this, he published a demonstration of the theorem in a paper entitled 'The general theory of equations'; it was not well received. In 1813 he published it in revised form, again to little avail. His methods of proof were regarded as lacking in scientific rigour. In 1824 the Norwegian mathematician Niels ◊Abel demonstrated more convincingly the same theorem, having come independently to the identical conclusion.

Ruffini also made a substantial contribution to the theory of equations, developing the so-called theory of substitutions that was the forerunner of modern group theory. His work became incorporated into the general theory of the solubility of algebraic equations developed by the ill-starred Evariste ◊Galois.

In addition, Ruffini brought his mathematical insight to bear on philosophical and biological matters, publishing a number of papers 1806–21. He considered the possibility that living organisms had come into existence as the result of chance, thus anticipating more modern work on probability.

Rühmkorff, Heinrich Daniel (1803–1877) German-born French instrument-maker, who invented the Rühmkorff induction coil, a type of transformer for direct durrent that outputs a high voltage from a low-voltage input.

Rühmkorff was born in Hannover on 15 January 1803, but virtually nothing is known of his life before he went to Paris in 1819 and became a porter in the laboratory of the French physicist Charles Chevalier (1804–1850). There Rühmkorff became interested in electrical equipment and soon began to manufacture scientific instruments. He opened his own workshop in 1840, but although he eventually became famous throughout Europe for his scientific apparatus, his factory remained small (after his death it was auctioned off for just £42).

Rühmkorff's first notable invention was a thermoelectric battery in 1844. He then turned his attention to developing an induction coil, the principles of which had been worked out by Michael ◊Faraday in 1831. After a long series of experiments, Rühmkorff eventually produced his induction coil in 1851. It consisted of a central cylinder of soft iron on which were wound two insulated coils – an inner primary coil comprising only a few turns of relatively thick copper wire, and an outer secondary coil with a large number of turns of thinner copper wire; an interrupter automatically makes and breaks the current in the primary coil, thereby inducing an intermittent high voltage in the secondary coil.

Rühmkorff demonstrated his invention at the 1855 Paris Exhibition, where it won him a decoration and a medal, and at the 1858 French Exhibition of Electrical Apparatus, where he was awarded the first prize of 50,000 francs. Later, however, the originality of his invention was contested by C G Page (1812–1868) who claimed to have invented a similar device some 20 years earlier in the USA.

The Rühmkorff induction coil played an important part in many later advances, including the development of discharge tubes and, indirectly, the discovery of cathode rays and X-rays. Today, coils working on the same principle are still used to provide the ignition spark in internal-combustion engines.

Widely respected and a great philanthropist, Rühmkorff was made an honorary member of the French Physical Society – despite his lack of early education. He died in Paris on 19 December 1877.

Rumford, Benjamin Thompson, Count Rumford (1753–1814) American-born British physicist who first demonstrated conclusively that heat is not a fluid but a form of motion.

Thompson was born into a farming family at Woburn, Massachusetts, on 26 March 1753. At the age of 19 he became a school teacher as a result of much self instruction and some help from local clergy. He moved to Rumford (now Concord, New Hampshire) and almost immediately married a wealthy widow many years his senior. Thompson's first activities seem to have been political. When the American Revolution broke out he remained loyal to the crown and acted as some sort of secret agent. Obliged to flee to London in 1776 (having separated from his wife the year before), he was rewarded with government work and the appointment as lieutenant colonel of a regiment in New York. After the war, he retired from the army and lived permanently in exile in Europe. Thompson moved to Bavaria and spent the next few years with the civil administration there, becoming war and police minister as well as grand chamberlain to the elector.

In 1781 Thompson was made a fellow of the Royal Society on the basis of a paper on gunpowder and cannon vents. He had studied the relationship between various gunpowders and the apparent force with which the cannon balls were shot forth. This was a topic, part of a basic interest in guns and other weapons, to which he frequently returned, and in 1797 he produced a gunpowder standard.

In 1791 Thompson was made a count of the Holy Roman Empire in recognition of all his work in Bavaria. He took the title from Rumford in his homeland, and it is by this name that we know him today.

Rumford was greatly concerned with the promotion of science and in 1796 established the Rumford medals in the Royal Society and in the Academy of Arts and Science, Boston. These were the best endowed prizes of the time, and they still exist today.

In 1799, Rumford returned to England and with Joseph ◊Banks founded the Royal Institution, choosing Humphry ◊Davy as lecturer. Its aim was the popularization of science and technology, a tradition that still continues there.

Two years later Rumford resumed his travels. He settled in Paris and married the widow of Antoine ◊Lavoisier, who had produced the caloric theory of heat that Rumford overthrew. However, this was a second unsuccessful match and after separating from his wife, Rumford lived at Auteuil near Paris until his death on 21 August 1814. In his will he endowed the Rumford chair at Harvard, still occupied by a succession of distinguished scientists.

Rumford's early work in Bavaria shows him at his most versatile and innovative. He combined social experiments with his lifelong interests concerning heat in all its aspects. When he employed beggars from the streets to manufacture military uniforms, he was faced with a feeding problem. A study of nutrition led to the recognition of the importance of water and vegetables and Rumford decided that soups would fit the requirements. He devised many recipes and developed cheap food emphasizing the potato. Meanwhile soldiers were being employed in gardening to produce the vegetables, Rumford's interest in gardens and landscape giving Munich its huge Englischer Garten, which he planned and which remains an important feature of the city today. The uniform enterprise led to a study of insulation and to the conclusion that heat was lost mainly through convection; thus clothing should be designed to inhibit this.

No application of heat technology was too humble for Rumford's scrutiny. He devised the domestic range – the 'fire in a box' – and special utensils to go with it. In the interests of fuel efficiency, he devised a calorimeter to compare the heats of combustion of various fuels. Smoky fireplaces also drew his attention, and after a study of the various air movements, he produced designs incorporating all the features now considered essential in open fires and chimneys, such as the smoke shelf and damper.

His search for an alternative to alcoholic drinks led to the promotion of coffee and the design of the first percolator.

The work for which Rumford is best remembered took place in 1798. As military commander for the elector of Bavaria, he was concerned with the manufacture of cannon. These were bored from blocks of iron with drills, and it was believed that the cannons became hot because as the drills cut into the cannon, heat was escaping in the form of a fluid called caloric. However, Rumford noticed that heat production increased as the drills became blunter and cut less into the metal. If a very blunt drill was used, no metal was removed yet the heat output appeared to be limitless. Clearly heat could not be a fluid in the metal, but must be related to the work done in turning the drill. Rumford also studied the expansion of liquids of different densities and different specific heats and showed by careful weighings that the expansion was not due to caloric taking up the extra space.

Although the majority of Rumford's scientific work related to heat and its applications, he had an important subsidiary interest in light. He invented the Rumford shadow photometer and established the standard candle, which was the international unit of luminous intensity right up to the 1900s. Transmission of light and shadows cast by coloured sources interested him, and he also looked into concepts of complementary colours. Photosynthesis drew his passing glance and he was probably one of the first to try to relate heat and light in their effects on chemical reaction – the beginnings of the science of photochemistry.

Rumford's contribution to science in demolishing the caloric theory of heat was very important because it paved the way for the realization of the fact that heat is a form of energy and that all forms of energy are interconvertible. However it took several decades to establish the view that caloric does not exist, as the caloric theory readily explained the important conclusions on heat radiation made by Pierre ◊Prévost in 1791 and on the motive power of heat made by Sadi ◊Carnot in 1824.

Further Reading

Rumford, Benjamin T; Brown, Sanborn C (ed), *Light and Armament*, Harvard University Press, 1970.

Rumford, Benjamin T; Brown, Sanborn C (ed), *Public Institutions*, Harvard University Press, 1970.

Schagrin, Morton L, *More Heat than Light: Rumford's Experiments on the Materiality of Light*, Synthese, 1994, v 99, pp 111–121.

Russell, Bertrand Arthur William (1872–1970)

3rd Earl Russell. British philosopher and mathematician who, during a long and active life, made many contributions to mathematics and wrote about morals and politics, but is best remembered as one of the founders of modern logic. He was a prolific writer and was awarded the 1950 Nobel Prize for Literature.

Russell British philosopher and mathematician Bertrand Russell photographed in 1952. Russell wrote many scholarly and popular books about mathematics, logic, and philosophy. Russell was awarded the Nobel Prize for Literature in 1950. Except for during World War II, Russell was a life-long pacifist who campaigned for disarmament and peace. *Mary Evans Picture Library*

Russell was born in Trelleck, Monmouthshire (now Gwent), on 18 May 1872 into a family that had long been prominent in British social and political life. His grandfather was Lord John Russell, who introduced the 1832 Reform Bill in Parliament and went on to serve twice as prime minister. Russell's parents died when he was a child and it was his grandfather who, disapproving of arrangements made by his parents, undertook to bring up Russell and his brother Frank. Instead of being educated by the Nonconformist thinkers his parents had nominated, he was educated at home until he was 18 by governesses and tutors.

In 1890 Russell entered Trinity College, Cambridge, to study mathematics and philosophy. Two years later he was elected to the Apostles – a small informal group that regarded itself as being made up of the best minds in the university. Another member, Alfred North ◊Whitehead, was then a lecturer in mathematics. Russell was elected to a prize fellowship at Trinity in 1895, and in 1910 to a lectureship in logic and the philosophy of mathematics.

Mathematics may be defined as the subject in which we never know what we are talking about, nor whether what we are saying is true.

<small>BERTRAND RUSSELL MYSTICISM AND LOGIC 1917</small>

Russell was a pacifist at the outbreak of World War I in 1914, a stand that was bitterly resented by many people of his class. A leaflet published in 1916, in which he protested at the harsh treatment of a conscientious objector, led to his prosecution and dismissal from the Trinity lectureship. Two years later Russell was imprisoned for six months when his article in *The Tribunal*, a pacifist weekly, was judged to be seditious. While serving the sentence in Brixton Prison, he wrote *Introduction to the Philosophy of Mathematics*.

In 1922, after World War I, Russell stood as a Labour Party candidate in the general election, but was defeated (two other attempts at entering Parliament were also unsuccessful). Soon afterwards he wrote two books that reflected contemporary developments in science: *The ABC of Atoms* (1923) and *The ABC of Relativity* (1925). In 1931 he succeeded his brother and became the 3rd Earl Russell. He was appointed to the staff of City College, New York, in 1940, but was dismissed by a State Supreme Court order following a wave of protest against the liberal views on sex expressed in his book *Marriage and Morals*. He did, however, lecture in philosophy at other US universities.

During the Cold War that followed World War II Russell even more vehemently expressed his views on pacifism, and in 1958 he was the president of the Campaign for Nuclear Disarmament. He was briefly imprisoned once more in 1961, when he was aged 89.

Russell received many honorary degrees, was elected a fellow of the Royal Society in 1908, and made a member of the Order of Merit in 1949. He married four times, three of his marriages ending in divorce. He died in Plas Penrhyn, Merionethshire (now part of Gwynedd), on 2 February 1970.

Russell published the first volume of *Principles of Mathematics* in 1903, expounding his belief that the basic principles of mathematics can be founded on fundamental logical concepts so that all the propositions of pure mathematics can be deduced from this basis using only a few of the most important logical principles. This work was indebted to a symbolic calculus developed by George ◊Boole.

But Russell's most significant publication concerning mathematical logic, derived from his collaboration with Whitehead, was the three-volume *Principia Mathematica* (1910, 1912, and 1913), whose title reflected that of Isaac Newton's fundamental work. The arguments proposed in the *Principia* were explained, without the use of technical logical symbolism, in *Introduction to the Philosophy of Mathematics*. The book is a model of clarity and of the lucid expression of complex and abstract ideas. It was followed by a second edition of the *Principia*, which incorporated an introduction that set out how the system must be modified as a result of the work of other mathematicians such as Leon Chwistek (1884–1944) and Ludwig ◊Wittgenstein.

Further Reading

Blackwell, Kenneth (ed), *A Bibliography of Bertrand Russell*, Collected Papers of Bertrand Russell series, Routledge, 1994, 3 vols.

Hylton, Peter, *Russell, Idealism, and the Emergence of Analytic Philosophy*, Clarendon Press, 1990.

Irvine, Andrew D (ed), *Bertrand Russell: Critical Assessments*, Critical Assessments of Leading Philosophers series, Routledge, 1998, 4 vols.

Monk, Ray, *Bertrand Russell: The Spirit of Solitude*, Vintage, 1997.

Monk, Ray, *Russell: Mathematics, Dreams and Nightmares*, The Great Philosophers series, Phoenix, 1997.

Moorehead, Caroline, *Bertrand Russell*, Viking Penguin, 1999.

Pampapathy, Rao A, *Understanding Principia and Tractatus: Russell and Wittgenstein Revisited*, International Scholars Publications, 1998.

Russell, Bertrand, *My Philosophical Development*, Routledge, 1995.

Russell, Bertrand, *Autobiography*, Routledge, 1998.

Slater, John G, *Bertrand Russell*, Bristol Introductions series, Thoemmes, 1994.

Russell, Frederick Stratten (1897–1984) English marine biologist best known for his studies of the life histories and distribution of plankton. He received many honours for his work, including a fellowship of the Royal Society of London in 1938, the Gold Medal from the Linnean Society in 1961, and a knighthood in 1965.

Russell was born on 3 November 1897 in Bridport, Dorset, and was educated at Oundle School and then at Gonville and Caius College, Cambridge. His studies were interrupted by World War I, during which he served with distinction in the Royal Naval Air Service. He graduated in 1922 and then worked for two years for the Egyptian government as assistant director of fisheries research, after which he returned to the UK and joined the scientific staff of the Marine Biological Association at Plymouth. He remained there for the rest of his working life (although he went on an expedition to the Great Barrier Reef in Australia 1928–29, and served in Air Staff Intelligence during World War II), becoming its director in 1945. From 1950 until he retired in 1965 Russell was also a member of the National Oceanographic Council, and from 1962 to 1975 he was chair of the advisory panel on biological research to the Central Electricity Generating Board. He was knighted in 1965.

While working for the Egyptian government, Russell studied the vertical distribution in the sea of the eggs and larvae of marine fish and their migratory movements. Continuing this line of research at the Marine Biological Association, he investigated the different types of behaviour of individual species of fish at various times of the year. He went on to investigate the distribution of *Calanus* (a crustacean copepod) and *Sagitta* (a chaetognath worm). By combining the results of his research, Russell established the value of certain types of plankton as indicators of different types of water in the English Channel and the North Sea. He also offered a partial explanation for the difference in abundance of herring in different areas. In addition, Russell discovered a means of distinguishing between different species of fish shortly after they have hatched, when they are almost identical in appearance. Russell's studies of plankton and of water movements were extremely valuable in providing information on which to base fishing quotas, the accuracy of which is essential to prevent overfishing and the depletion of fish stocks.

Russell also elucidated the life histories of several species of medusa by rearing the hydroids from parent medusae, and he published the two-volume *The Medusae of the British Isles* (1953, 1970).

Russell, Henry Norris (1877–1957) US astronomer who was chiefly interested in the nature of binary stars, but who is best remembered for his publication in 1913 of a diagram charting the absolute magnitude of stars plotted against their spectral type. Ejnar ◊Hertzsprung had in fact published similar results previously in a photographic journal that was seen by few astronomers (and noted by none), but Russell was the first to put in graphic form what became known as the Hertzsprung–Russell diagram. Its impact on the scientific world was enormous and the diagram remains of great importance for research into stellar evolution,

although some of Russell's initial extrapolations have since been superseded.

Born in Oyster Bay, New York, on 25 October 1877, Russell was five years old when his parents pointed out to him the transit of Venus that inspired him to become an astronomer. He received his early education at home, and then went on to Princeton University, from which he graduated, with distinction, in 1897. He remained at the university, working in the astronomy department, until he received his PhD in 1899 for devising a new way of determining the orbits of binary stars. Russell then travelled to the UK, and joined Arthur Hinks at the Cambridge University Observatories. He worked with Hinks on stellar photography and evolved a technique for the measurement of stellar parallax. Further research into binary stars followed before, in 1905, Russell returned to Princeton, where he was made professor and director of the university observatory. In 1921 he was appointed research associate of the Mount Wilson Observatory, and in 1927 he received the appointment of the C A Young Research Professorship. Russell was awarded many honours from academies and universities. Described as the dean of American astronomers by a contemporary, he died in Princeton in 1957.

Like Hertzsprung, Russell concluded from his early works on stellar distances that stars could be grouped in two main classes, one much brighter than the other. By plotting the luminosities against the spectra of hundreds of stars in a diagram, Russell managed to show a definite relationship between true brightness and type of spectrum. (He used Annie Jump ◊Cannon's system of spectral classification, which also indicated surface temperature.) Most of the stars were grouped together in what became known as the 'main sequence' that appeared to run from the top left of the diagram to the bottom right. But there was a group of very bright stars plotted above the main sequence – indicating that stars of similar spectral type could have very different magnitudes. This was a significant discovery, yet the fact that there was a 'main sequence' at all was profoundly stimulating to Russell, who immediately founded a theory of stellar evolution upon it. He proposed that all stars progress at one time or another either up or down the 'main sequence', depending on whether they are contracting (and therefore becoming hotter) or expanding (thus cooling), and he tried to derive a logical progression. The progression he finally proposed, however, was discredited within a decade – although it provoked considerable scientific research. Stellar evolution is now known to be far more complex than a simple progression.

Russell's lifelong study of binary stars resulted in a method for calculating the mass of each star from a

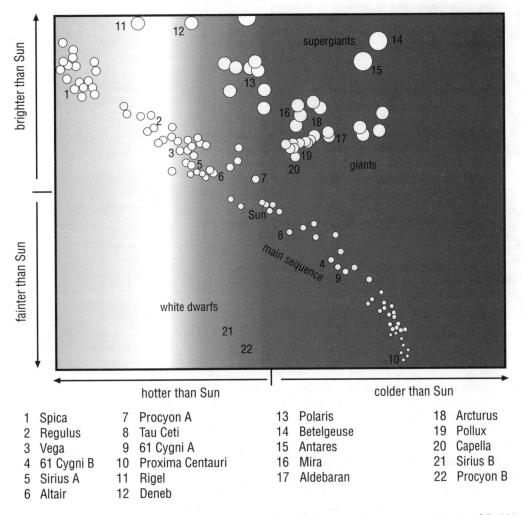

1	Spica	7	Procyon A	13	Polaris	18	Arcturus
2	Regulus	8	Tau Ceti	14	Betelgeuse	19	Pollux
3	Vega	9	61 Cygni A	15	Antares	20	Capella
4	61 Cygni B	10	Proxima Centauri	16	Mira	21	Sirius B
5	Sirius A	11	Rigel	17	Aldebaran	22	Procyon B
6	Altair	12	Deneb				

Russell The Hertzsprung–Russell diagram relates the brightness (or luminosity) of a star to its temperature. Most stars fall within a narrow diagonal band called the main sequence. A star moves off the main sequence when it grows old. The Hertzsprung–Russell diagram is one of the most important diagrams in astrophysics.

study of its orbital behaviour. He pioneered a system using both orbits and masses in order to compute distance from Earth, and his research into eclipsing binary stars (one of which moves in front of the other, from the viewpoint of Earth) led to the amassing of valuable data on variations in light emission.

Finally, his investigation of the solar spectrum and his analysis of the composition of the solar atmosphere led him to a general speculation on the composition of stars. For the first time he suggested that there was a considerable abundance of hydrogen present, and hesitantly put forward a fairly high percentage figure. The 'Russell mixture' turned out in fact to have *under*estimated the abundance of hydrogen (more than 80% of the Sun's volume).

Rutherford, Ernest (1871–1937) 1st Baron Rutherford of Nelson. New Zealand-born British physicist who first explained that radioactivity is produced by the disintegration of atoms and discovered that alpha particles consist of helium nuclei. For these achievements, Rutherford was awarded the 1908 Nobel Prize for Chemistry. Rutherford went on to make two more discoveries of fundamental importance to nuclear physics: he was the first to determine the basic structure of the atom and show that it consists of a central nucleus surrounded by electrons, and he also produced the first artificial transformation, thereby changing one element into another.

Rutherford was born near Nelson on South Island on 30 August 1871. His father was a wheelwright and

Rutherford New Zealand-born British physicist Ernest Rutherford who won the Nobel Prize for Chemistry in 1908 for his work in atomic science. Rutherford came from a family of 12 children who lived near Nelson, New Zealand. In 1895, at the age of 24, he won a scholarship to Cambridge University, England. Three years later he was made professor of physics at McGill University, Canada. *Mary Evans Picture Library*

equipped laboratory in the world. He was attracted back to the UK in 1907, when he succeeded Arthur Schuster (1851–1934) at Manchester, Schuster declaring that he would resign his chair only for Rutherford. Rutherford built up a renowned laboratory at Manchester, and it was there that he made his momentous discoveries of the nuclear atom and artificial transformation.

> *All science is either physics or stamp collecting.*
> **ERNEST RUTHERFORD** QUOTED IN J B BIRKS
> RUTHERFORD AT MANCHESTER

During World War I, Rutherford worked for the Admiralty on methods of locating submarines and then in 1919 moved to Cambridge to become professor of physics and director of the Cavendish Laboratory in succession to Thomson. He retained this position for the rest of his life, and was also professor of natural philosophy at the Royal Institution from 1921. Many honours were accorded to Rutherford in addition to the 1908 Nobel Prize for Chemistry. They included the Royal Society's Copley Medal in 1922, the presidency of the Royal Society 1925–30, a knighthood in 1914, the Order of Merit in 1925, and a peerage in 1921, Rutherford taking the title Baron Rutherford of Nelson. In his last years, Rutherford was active in helping refugee scientists who had escaped from Nazi Germany. Rutherford died in Cambridge on 19 October 1937 and is buried in Westminster Abbey, London.

When Rutherford first came to the Cavendish Laboratory, Thomson put him to work to study the effect that X-rays have on the discharge of electricity in gases. This was early in 1896, only a few weeks after Wilhelm ◊Röntgen had discovered X-rays. Rutherford found that positive and negative ions are formed, and measured the mobility of the ions produced. In 1897 he went on to make a similar study of the effects of ultraviolet light and the radioactivity produced by uranium minerals, which had been discovered by Henri ◊Becquerel the year before. Rutherford then became fascinated by radioactivity and began a series of investigations to explore its nature. In 1899, he found that there are two kinds of radioactivity with different penetrating power. The less penetrating he called alpha rays and the more penetrating beta rays. In 1900, Rutherford discovered a third type of radioactivity with great penetrating power, which he called gamma rays. (Alpha and beta rays were later found to consist of streams of particles and so are now known as alpha particles and beta particles. Gamma rays were found to be

farmer who, like his mother, had emigrated from the UK to New Zealand when a child. Rutherford did not show any great aptitude for science as a child and when he entered Nelson College in 1887, he exhibited an all-round ability. He went on to Canterbury College, Christchurch, in 1889, receiving a BA degree in 1892. He then embarked on a study of mathematics and physics, gaining his MA in 1893 and then a BSc in 1894. Rutherford investigated the magnetic properties of iron by high-frequency electric discharges for his science degree, and constructed a very sensitive detector of radio waves as a result of his research. This was only six years after Heinrich ◊Hertz had discovered radio waves, and the same year that Guglielmo ◊Marconi began his radio experiments.

In 1895, Rutherford went to the UK to study at the Cavendish Laboratory, Cambridge. There he became the first research student to work under J J ◊Thomson. Armed with his radio detector, Rutherford made a big impact on Cambridge, but under Thomson's guidance, he soon turned to the work in atomic physics that was to become his career. In 1898, helped by Thomson, Rutherford obtained his first academic position with a professorship in physics at McGill University, Montréal, Canada, which then boasted the best-

electromagnetic waves of very high frequency and so are still called gamma rays or gamma radiation.)

When Rutherford moved to Montréal in 1898, he began to use thorium as a source of radioactivity instead of uranium. He found that thorium produces an intensely radioactive gas, which he called emanation. This was a decay product of thorium and Rutherford discovered several more, including thorium X. To identify these products, Rutherford enlisted the aid of Frederick ◊Soddy, who was later to discover isotopes. Analysis of the decay products enabled Rutherford and Soddy in 1903 to explain that radioactivity is an atomic phenomenon, caused by the breakdown of the atoms in the radioactive element to produce a new element. Rutherford found that the intensity of the radioactivity produced decreases at a rate governed by the element's half-life. The idea that atoms could change their identity was revolutionary, yet so compelling was Rutherford's explanation of radioactivity that it was accepted immediately with very little opposition.

Rutherford was now concerned to identify alpha rays, which he was sure consisted of positively charged particles and specifically either hydrogen or helium ions. Deflection of the rays in electric and magnetic fields proved in 1903 that they are positive particles, but Rutherford was unable to determine the amount of charge because his apparatus was not sensitive enough.

In 1904, with Bertram Boltwood (1870–1927), Rutherford worked out the series of transformations that radioactive elements undergo and showed that they end as lead. They were able to estimate the rates of change involved and in 1907 Boltwood calculated the ages of mineral samples, arriving at figures of more than a thousand million years. This was the first proof of the age of rocks, and the method of radioactive dating has since been developed into a precise way of finding the age of rocks, fossils, and ancient artefacts.

On returning to the UK in 1907, Rutherford continued to explore alpha particles. In conjunction with Hans ◊Geiger, he developed ionization chambers and scintillation screens to count the particles produced by a source of radioactivity, and by dividing the total charge produced by the number of particles counted, arrived at the conclusion that each particle has two positive charges. The final proof that alpha particles are helium ions came in the same year, when Rutherford and Thomas Royds succeeded in trapping alpha particles in a glass tube and by sparking the gas produced showed from its spectrum that it was helium.

Rutherford's next major discovery came only a year later in 1909. He suggested to Geiger and a gifted student named Ernest Marsden that they investigate the scattering of alpha particles by gold foil. They used a scintillation counter that could be moved around the

foil, which was struck by a beam of alpha particles from a radon source. Geiger and Marsden found that a few particles were deflected through angles of more than 90° by the foil. Rutherford was convinced that the explanation lay in the nature of the gold atoms in the foil, believing that each contained a positively charged nucleus surrounded by electrons. Only such nuclei could repulse the positively charged alpha particles that happened to strike them to produce such enormous deflections. But Rutherford needed proof of this theory. He worked out that the nucleus must have a diameter of about 10^{-13} cm/10^{-14} in – 100,000 times smaller than the atom – and calculated the numbers of particles that would be scattered at different angles. These predictions were confirmed experimentally by Geiger and Marsden, and Rutherford announced the nuclear structure of the atom in 1911.

Few were convinced that the atom could be almost entirely empty space as Rutherford contended. However, among those who agreed with Rutherford was Niels ◊Bohr. He went to Manchester to work in 1912, and in 1913 produced his quantum model of the atom, which assumed a central positive nucleus surrounded by electrons orbiting at various energy levels. Also in 1913, another of Rutherford's co-workers, Henry ◊Moseley, announced his discovery of the atomic number, which identifies elements, and showed that it could only be given by the number of positive charges on the nucleus, and thus the number of electrons around it. Rutherford's view of the nuclear atom was thereby vindicated, and universally accepted.

Several more important discoveries were made at Manchester. In 1914, Rutherford found that positive rays consist of hydrogen nuclei. Also in 1914, Rutherford and Edward Andrade showed that gamma rays are electromagnetic waves by diffracting them with a crystal. They measured the wavelengths of the rays and found that they lie beyond X-rays in the electromagnetic spectrum. Becquerel in 1900 had identified beta rays with cathode rays, which were shown to be electrons, and so the nature of radioactivity was now revealed in full.

Rutherford's work was now interrupted by war and he did not return to physics until 1917, when he made his last great discovery. He made it unaided, unlike most of his earlier discoveries, because all his colleagues and students were still engaged in war work. Rutherford followed up earlier work by Marsden in which scintillations were noticed in hydrogen bombarded by alpha particles well beyond their range in the gas. These were due to hydrogen nuclei knocked on by the alpha particles, which was not unexpected. However Rutherford now carried out the same experiment using nitrogen instead of hydrogen, and he found that hydrogen nuclei were still produced and not nitrogen nuclei. Rutherford announced his interpretation of this result in 1919, stating that the alpha particles had caused the nitrogen nuclei to disintegrate, forming hydrogen and oxygen nuclei. This was the first artificial transformation of one element into another. Rutherford found similar results with other elements and announced that the nucleus of any atom must be composed of hydrogen nuclei. At Rutherford's suggestion, the name proton was given to the hydrogen nucleus in 1920. He also speculated in the same year that uncharged particles, which were later called neutrons, must also exist in the nucleus.

Rutherford continued work on artificial transformation in the 1920s. Under his direction, Patrick ◊Blackett in 1925 used a Wilson cloud chamber to record the tracks of disintegrated nuclei, showing that the bombarding alpha particles combines with the nucleus before disintegration and does not break the nucleus apart like a bullet. Bombardment with alpha particles had its limits as large nuclei repelled them without disintegrating, and Rutherford directed the construction of an accelerator to produce particles of the required energy. The first one was built by John ◊Cockcroft and Ernest ◊Walton, and went into operation at the Cavendish Laboratory in 1932. In the same year, another of Rutherford's colleagues, James ◊Chadwick, discovered the neutron at the Cavendish Laboratory.

Rutherford was to make one final discovery of great significance. In 1934, using some of the heavy water recently discovered in the USA, Rutherford, Marcus Oliphant, and Paul Harteck bombarded deuterium with deuterons and produced tritium. This may be considered the first nuclear fusion reaction.

Rutherford may be considered the founder of nuclear physics, both for the fundamental discoveries that he made and for the encouragement and direction he gave to so many important physicists involved in the development of this science.

Further Reading

Allibone, T E, *Rutherford: The Father of Nuclear Energy,* The
    Rutherford Lectures series, Manchester University Press,
    1973, v 4.
Bunge, Mario Augusto and Shea, William R (eds),
    Rutherford and Physics at the Turn of the Century, Dawson,
    1979.
Moon, Philip Burton, *Ernest Rutherford and the Atom,*
    Pioneers of Science and Discovery, Priory Press, 1974.
Oliphant, Mark, *Rutherford: Recollections of the Cambridge
    Days,* Elsevier, 1972.

Rutherfurd, Lewis Morris (1816–1892) US spectroscopist and celestial photographer.

Rutherfurd was born in Morrisania, New York, on 25 November 1816, into a well-established family of Scottish descent. He showed an early interest in science, and during his student days at Williams College, Massachusetts, he was made an assistant to the professor of physics and chemistry. After graduating, however, he went on to study law. His independent means was augmented by his marriage to Margaret Stuyvesant Chanler, which freed him from the need to practice law and allowed him to travel abroad for seven years. When he returned to the USA in 1856, he had his own observatory built and spent the rest of his life working on astronomical photography and spectroscopy. He died in Tranquility, New Jersey, on 30 May 1892.

From 1858 Rutherfurd produced many photographs that were widely admired of the Moon, Jupiter, Saturn, the Sun, and stars down to the fifth magnitude, using a 29-cm/11.5-in achromatic refracting telescope built by Henry Fitz. He went on to map the heavens by photographing star clusters and, to enable him to analyse the information in his stellar photographs, he devised a new micrometer that could measure the distances between stars more accurately. After 1861 he became more and more interested in the spectroscopic work of Robert ◊Bunsen and Gustav ◊Kirchhoff and from 1862 he began to make spectroscopic studies of the Sun, Moon, Jupiter, Mars, and 16 fixed stars. From his stellar studies, he independently produced a classification scheme of stars based on their spectra that turned out to be remarkably similar to Pietro ◊Secchi's star classification. Apparently, at the January 1864 meeting of the National Adademy of Sciences, he displayed an unpublished photograph of the solar spectrum that had three times the number of lines that had been noted by Kirchhoff and Bunsen. To help his spectroscopic work he began devising more sophisticated diffraction gratings and his innovative skill in producing these became generally well known to other contemporary astronomers, providing them with diffraction gratings with up to 6,700 lines per cm/17,000 lines per in.

Rutherfurd made his last observations in 1878. In 1883 he donated his equipment and large collection of photographic plates to the Observatory of the University of Columbia.

Rydberg, Johannes Robert (1854–1919) Swedish physicist who discovered a mathematical expression that gives the frequencies of spectral lines for elements. It includes a constant named the Rydberg constant after him.

Rydberg was born in Halmstad on 8 November 1854. He was educated at the Gymnasium in Halmstad and in 1873 entered the University of Lund, graduating in mathematics in 1875 and gaining a doctorate in this subject in 1879. He remained at Lund for the rest of his life, beginning work as a lecturer in mathematics in

1880. He became a lecturer in physics in 1882 and was appointed professor of physics provisionally in 1897 and permanently in 1901. He retained this position until a month before his death on 28 December 1919.

Rydberg worked in the field of spectroscopy. He did not do a great amount of experimental investigation, but was concerned to organize the mass of observations of spectral lines into some kind of order. Rydberg began by classifying the lines into three types: principal (strong, persistent lines), sharp (weaker but well-defined lines), and diffuse (broader lines). Each spectrum of an element consists of several series of these lines superimposed over each other. He then sought to find a mathematical relationship that would relate the frequencies of the lines in a particular series. In 1890, he achieved this by using a quantity called the wave number, which is the reciprocal of the wavelength. The formula expresses the wave number in terms of a constant common to all series (the Rydberg constant), two constants that are characteristic of the particular series, and an integer. The lines are then given by changing the value of the integer.

Rydberg then found that Johann ◊Balmer had already developed a formula for a series of lines of the hydrogen spectrum in 1885. However, it turned out to be a special case of his own more general formula. Rydberg then went on to produce another formula that he believed would express the frequency of every line in every series of an element. This formula is:

$$N = R[1/(n + a)^2 - 1/(m + b)^2]$$

where N is the wave number, R is the Rydberg constant, n and m are integers, m being greater than n, and a and b are constants for a particular series.

Rydberg's intuition proved to be correct and five more series of hydrogen lines were subsequently discovered that fitted the formula. Although it was an empirical discovery and Rydberg was unable to explain why his formula expressed the spectral lines, Niels ◊Bohr was able to show that it gave the energy states required for the theory of atomic structure that he presented in 1913.

In 1897 Rydberg put forward the idea of atomic number and the importance of this in revising the periodic table. His views were vindicated in the brilliant research conducted into X-ray spectra by Henry ◊Moseley in 1913. The Rydberg formula also proved to be of use in determining the electronic shell structure of elements, which provided a proper basis for the classification of the elements.

Ryle, Martin (1918–1984) English astronomer who developed the technique of sky-mapping using 'aperture synthesis', combining smaller dish aerials to give the characteristics of one large one. For this work he received the 1974 Nobel Prize for Physics (jointly with his friend and colleague Antony ◊Hewish, the discoverer of pulsars).

Ryle was born in Brighton, Sussex, on 27 September 1918. He studied at Oxford University, graduating in 1939. His interest in radio was already pronounced, and on the outbreak of war he joined the Telecommunications Research Establishment in Malvern, where he was involved in the development of radar and other systems. After the war he was invited by John Ratcliffe (1902–1987), a former colleague at Malvern, to join him at the Cavendish Laboratory in Cambridge, working on the study of solar radio-frequency emissions. As a result of his research, Ryle was appointed to a lectureship in physics in 1948 and, the following year, to a fellowship at Trinity College. Election to a fellowship at the Royal Society came in 1952. He was the first director of the Mullard Radio Astronomy Observatory, serving from 1957 to 1982, and in 1959 he was appointed Cambridge's first professor of radio astronomy (emeritus from 1982). A knighthood was conferred in 1966 and he was Astronomer Royal 1972–82. He died on 12 October 1984.

At the Cavendish Laboratory, Ryle's first task was to study solar emission at 1-m/3.3-ft wavelengths. This necessitated the building of a suitable instrument. His choice lay between a steerable parabolic dish (like the one in use at Jodrell Bank) and an interferometer-type instrument (which consists, in essence, of two separated aerials, each receiving the same signal from the same source, coupled to a receiver). Ryle chose the interferometer variety that the Cambridge observatory is now famous for. This type of telescope was first constructed merely to distinguish and measure sources of different angular size, identifying 'compact' emitters and distinguishing them from diffuse sources, but it was then seen also to allow positions to be measured with much greater accuracy than was possible with a single parabolic reflector. The earliest instruments, built at Grange Road on the outskirts of the city, used a spacing of about 0.75 km/0.5 mi between the two parabolic dishes used as aerials.

One of the interferometers was built specifically to study the compact source of radio emission in the constellation Cygnus noted by James ◊Hey during the war. On the first night of its operation. Cassiopeia-A, the most intense compact source in the sky, was also found – a great discovery. Optical astronomers at Mount Palomar were able to identify both these sources only because of the extreme accuracy (to within one minute of arc) of the later radio measurements: Cygnus as a very distant galaxy and Cassiopeia as a supernova within our own Galaxy.

In 1949 the use of this type of aerial led to a breakthrough in radio telescope design. By making observations from a number of different spacings to construct a radio map of the Sun, the forerunner of the 'synthesis' aerials was produced. This work was extended in 1954 to provide the first radio map of the sky. In the earlier Sun-mapping a certain symmetry of the source had been assumed so as to simplify the complex mathematical treatment of the signal data. Now, with an arbitrary distribution of sources, the accurate Fourier inversion required involved a precise locating of the sites of the aerial components and enough computer capacity – which was just becoming available – to interpret the signal information. In 1956 the group (generously assisted by Mullard Ltd) extended their activities to the Lord's Bridge site as more and larger instruments demanded increasing ground space and freedom from electrical interference with the weak signals.

With such equipment it was now possible to begin the First Cambridge Catalogue Survey (1C): a map of the most powerful known radio sources in the northern sky. By increasing yet further the collecting area of the detectors, the resolution and sensitivity of the instrument are also increased – as are also, unfortunately, the problems of alignment and scale of construction. So for the Second Survey, 2C – the first really comprehensive radio mapping of the sky, completed in 1955 – a collecting area of 0.4 ha/1 acre was used. The definitive 3C survey, published in 1959 and now used as reference by all radio astronomers, was made with a similar arrangement of parabolic reflectors, but working at a shorter wavelength (1.7 m/5.6 ft) which gave better resolution.

As this work went on, the first large-aperture synthesis aerial was being built, and it was that which was used to complete the 4C survey. This survey catalogued no fewer than 5,000 sources.

It was in turn superseded by an extension in concept to 'supersynthesis', in which a fixed aerial maps a band of the sky using solely the rotation of the Earth, and another aerial maps successive rings out from it concentrically. The 'One Mile' telescope was built in 1963 on this principle, and was designed both for the 5C survey – a programme to scan only part of the sky, but in considerable depth and detail – and for the compilation of radio maps of individual sources.

A 5-km/3-mi instrument was completed in 1971, incorporating further advances in design. It can provide a resolution of up to one third of a second of arc – 0.001 of a degree – to give very detailed maps of known sources. The variety of programmes for which it is now in use includes, most importantly, the mapping of extragalactic sources – radio galaxies and quasars – and the study of supernovae and newly born stars. It can provide as sharp a picture as the best groundbased optical telescopes.

Ryle was personally responsible for most of these developments. The site at Cambridge has gained its renown in large measure through his efforts and the results that his team obtained.

S

Sabatier, Paul (1854–1941) French organic chemist who investigated the actions of catalysts in gaseous reactions. He is particularly remembered for his work, with his assistant Jean-Baptiste Senderens (1856–1936), on catalytic hydrogenation of gaseous hydrocarbons. For this research he shared the 1912 Nobel Prize for Chemistry with Victor ◊Grignard.

Sabatier was born in Carcassone, Aude, on 5 November 1854, and was educated locally and in Toulouse. In 1887 he entered the Ecole Normale Supérieure in Paris, graduating three years later. He spent the next year as a teacher at the Lycée in Nîmes and then became assistant to Pierre ◊Berthelot at the Collège de France. He was awarded his doctorate in 1880 for a thesis on metallic sulphides. After a year of further research in Bordeaux he went in 1882 to Toulouse, where he was appointed assistant professor of physics, later transferring to a similar position in chemistry. When in 1884 he reached the age of 30, the minimum for a full professorial appointment, he was duly installed as professor of chemistry. He retained the position for the rest of his long life, declining the offers of the chairs at the Sorbonne and the Collège de France in 1907. He died in Toulouse on 14 August 1941.

Sabatier's early researches were concerned with physical and inorganic chemistry. Among many investigations he correlated the colours of chromates and dichromates with their acidity, and was the first chemist to prepare pure hydrogen sulphide. In 1895 he became interested in the role of metal catalysts through the work on nickel carbonyl by Ludwig ◊Mond. In the following year he produced somewhat similar compounds by the action of the oxides of nitrogen on finely divided metals.

In his next series of experiments, begun in 1897, he studied the reaction of ethylene (ethene) and hydrogen on a heated oxide of nickel. He found that the reduced nickel formed catalysed the hydrogenated acetylene (ethyne) in a similar way, and converted benzene vapour into cyclohexane. With his assistant Sanderens he extended the method to the hydrogenation of other unsaturated and aromatic compounds. He also synthesized methane by the hydrogenation of carbon monoxide using a catalyst of finely divided nickel. He later showed that at higher temperatures the same catalysts can be used for dehydrogenation, enabling him to prepare aldehydes from primary alcohols and ketones from secondary alcohols.

Sabatier later explored the use of oxide catalysts, such as manganese oxide, silica, and alumina. Different catalysts often gave different products from the same starting material. Alumina, for example, produced olefins (alkenes) with primary alcohols, which yielded aldehydes with a copper catalyst.

He explained the action of catalysts in terms of 'chemisorption', the formation of unstable compounds on the surface of a catalyst. He cited an improvement in catalytic action with decreasing particle size and the poisoning effect of impurities as evidence for this theory. He also postulated that the suitability of a catalyst for a particular reaction depends on its chemical nature as well as its physical properties (because different catalysts give different products from the same reaction).

Later catalytic hydrogenation was applied to liquid hydrocarbons by Vladimir ◊Ipatieff, leading to applications such as the hardening of natural oils by hydrogenation and the development of the margarine and modified fats industry.

Sabin, Albert Bruce (1906–1993) Russian-born US virologist who devoted his long and distinguished career to the development of protective vaccines. He is particularly associated with the oral poliomyelitis vaccine.

Sabin was born on 26 August 1906 in Bialystok, Russia (now in Poland). In 1921 he and his family emigrated to the USA where he attended New York University 1926–31, graduating with a medical degree. He then served as house physician to the Bellevue Hospital in New York 1932–33. Between 1935 and 1937 he was an assistant at the Rockefeller Institute and an associate from 1937. Two years later he was made associate professor of research in paediatrics at the University of Cincinnati College of Medicine and, after serving as a medical officer in the army during World War II, he became research professor of paediatrics there 1946–60. He held the position of distinguished service professor 1960–70 and was president of the Weizmann Institute of Science, Israel, 1970–72. On his return to the USA he joined the staff of the Medical College of South Carolina, and between 1973 and 1974 he was an expert consultant to the National Cancer Institute.

Sabin became interested in polio research while working at the Rockefeller Institute. In 1936 he and Peter Olitsky were able to make polio viruses from monkeys grow in tissue cultures from the brain cells of a human embryo that had miscarried. At the same time they were unsuccessful in their attempts to cultivate the virus in other human tissues, which gave weight to the existing theory that the virus attacked nerve cells only. (This theory was disproved in 1949 by John ◊Enders, Thomas Weller, and Frederick Robbins.)

Jonas ◊Salk had become engaged in producing an inactive polio vaccine, but Sabin was not convinced that the Salk technique of using dead virus was adequate. He concentrated on developing a live-virus oral vaccine because he felt that the inactive vaccine could be nothing more than a temporary measure for protection and would require the patient to be re-vaccinated at fairly frequent intervals. Sabin believed that only a living virus could be counted on to produce the necessary antibodies over a long period. Also, the living virus could be taken orally because it would multiply and invade the body of its own accord and would not, like the Salk vaccine, have to be injected. Sabin succeeded in finding virus strains of all three types of polio, each of which is too feeble to produce the disease itself. Sabin's vaccine is known as the live-attenuated vaccine and exerts its effect by inducing a harmless infection of the intestinal tract, thus simulating natural infection without causing any disease. It operates by multiplying in the tissues, giving rise to a mild and invisible infection with subsequent antibody formation and immunity. The vaccine has the advantage of inducing immunity rapidly, a property that is particularly valuable in the face of an epidemic. When given to a significant proportion of a population, the vaccine induces community protection by rendering the alimentary tract of those vaccinated resistant to re-infection by the polio virus.

It took Sabin many years of patient research but by 1957 he had enough confidence after trying the vaccine out on himself, his family, and numerous volunteers, to offer it for field trials to the medical community. He was unable to test his new vaccine in the USA because, at an earlier stage of the Salk vaccine's development in 1954, a faulty batch had caused paralytic polio in some children. However, Sabin managed to interest the Russians in his vaccine, and subsequently was able to report in 1959 that 4.5 million vaccinations had been successfully carried out. The vaccine was commercially available by 1961.

Today, the 'sugar lump' vaccine (as it is now known) has become an accepted and easy method of vaccination against polio. Its success can be measured only by the marked decline of the once prevalent disease, which killed so many young people or crippled them for life.

Sabin, Florence Rena (1871–1953) US anatomist, teacher, and public health reformer. She achieved a number of firsts for women: she was the first woman faculty member and first woman professor at Johns Hopkins medical school; the first woman president of the American Association of Anatomists; the first woman elected to the National Academy of Sciences; the first woman staff member of the Rockefeller Institute; and the first woman to receive the Jane Addams Medal for distinguished service. Among her many awards were 15 honorary degrees.

Sabin was born in 1871 in Central City, Colorado, where her father had unsuccessfully joined the Gold Rush. The family moved to Denver when she was four. Her mother died in childbirth in 1878 and Sabin was brought up by relatives. She was educated at the Vermont Academy at Saxtons River, Vermont, and at Smith College, the first US women's college to grant degrees. Graduating with honours in 1893, she was determined to study medicine in spite of family opposition.

Sabin worked as a teacher to raise money to enter the newly opened Johns Hopkins Medical School in 1897. The school was financed by the daughters of the trustees of Johns Hopkins University, who had insisted that women be admitted on an equal footing with men and that the highest admission standards be required. Sabin was one of 15 women in a class of 42. For one of her research projects she produced a three-dimensional model of the mid and lower brain that came to be used worldwide in the teaching of anatomy. She published *An Atlas of the Medulla and Midbrain* (1901), which became a standard medical textbook for the next 30 years.

Sabin maintained her connection with Johns Hopkins for the next 25 years, becoming assistant professor of anatomy in 1902 and full professor of histology in 1917. She was a dynamic and highly respected teacher. Her study of the lymphatics, small blood vessels, and the development of blood cells in pig embryos led to the discovery that lymphatics were closed at their collecting ends and was a significant contribution to scientific research. It earned her a prize of $1000 and in 1916 she gave the Harvey Memorial Lecture on the subject. Around this time she travelled to Leipzig in Germany to study a new technique that allowed researchers to work on living tissue and identify cells by staining them. She integrated this 'living stain' technique into her own research on monocytes, white blood cells that are involved in tissue reactions to infections.

In 1925 Sabin set up the department of cellular studies at the Rockefeller Institute, one of the leading research centres focusing on infectious diseases. There she continued her research into the relation of monocytes and other white blood cells in the defence of the body against tuberculosis. She joined the research committee of the National Tuberculosis Association in 1926, which was an ambitious cooperative venture coordinating universities, pharmaceutical conpanies, research institutes, and their resources to find the cause of tuberculosis. In 1929 she was received at the White House by President J Edgar Hoover.

Retiring to Denver, Colorado, in 1938 to live with her sister, Sabin continued her research and lecturing and in 1944, at the age of 73, was asked by the governor of Colorado to chair a subcommittee on health. She campaigned for and got passed the Sabin Health Bills, which gave Colorado one of the best public health programmes in the USA. She also set up a tuberculosis X-ray survey that halved the city's death rate from TB in two years, and she achieved a 90% drop in the incidence of syphilis. Within four months, as manager of Denver's department of health and welfare, she improved sewage disposal, rid the city of a rat infestation, and ensured that no unpasteurized milk would enter the city.

Sabin had also taken a lifelong interest in social issues and women's rights: she was involved with the Just Government League in Maryland, working for women's rights; helped on the Maryland *Suffrage News;* and organized letter-writing campaigns and attended suffragist meetings and rallies. Her own achievements in opening doors for women in the fields of medicine and research were remarkable and she always did what she could to help other women reach their full potential.

Sabine, Edward (1788–1883) Irish geophysicist who made important studies of terrestrial magnetism.

Sabine was born in Dublin on 14 October 1788. He received a military education at the Royal Military Academy in Woolwich, London, and never attended any university courses in science. In 1803 Sabine was commissioned in the Royal Artillery, with which he served his military career, rising to the rank of major general in 1859. In 1818, he was elected to the Royal Society, serving in a variety of positions and ultimately becoming its president 1861–71.

In 1818 Sabine accompanied the expedition headed by John Ross (1777–1856) to explore the Northwest Passage as official astronomer. The following year he went with William Parry (1790–1855) to the Arctic. While on this voyage he planned a trip in the southern hemisphere, which he undertook at the behest of the Royal Society 1821–22. Sabine then collaborated with the mathematician Charles ◊Babbage in 1826 on a survey of magnetism in the UK, a project that was not completed until the 1830s and that was repeated by Sabine himself in the late 1850s. Sabine was also active

in the British Association, serving as secretary to the organization 1838–59, with the exception of the year 1852, when he was its president. From 1849 to 1871, he was deeply involved with the administration of the King's Observatory at Kew. Sabine was awarded several honours, including the Copley Medal of the Royal Society, and was knighted in 1869. He died in Richmond, Surrey, on 26 June 1883.

During the 1820s, one of Sabine's major concerns was the use of the pendulum apparatus designed by Henry Kater (1777–1835) to determine the shape of the Earth. It was for these studies, which involved analysing data from 17 field stations around the globe, that Sabine was awarded the Copley Medal. His conclusions have since been somewhat modified because he failed to consider the fact that the density of the crust is not uniform and so obtained an erroneous result for the shape of the Earth.

Sabine's greatest scientific interest was the study of terrestrial magnetism, and he used his considerable influence to instigate a British 'magnetic crusade': an expedition to establish observatories in the southern hemisphere was sent out in 1839 and Sabine managed to extend its duration for two three-year periods beyond its original duration, and thereby accumulated an enormous bulk of data. With this, Sabine in 1851 discovered a 10–11-year periodic fluctuation in the number of magnetic storms. He then brilliantly correlated this magnetic cycle with data Samuel ◊Schwabe had collected on a similar variation in solar activity. Sabine was thereby able to link the incidence of magnetic storms with the sunspot cycle. This work was also done independently by Johann von Lamont (1805–1879) about the same time. Other results also grew out of Sabine's huge mass of data, and in 1851 he was able to demonstrate that the daily variation in magnetic activity comprised two different components.

Sabine's enthusiasm for the subject of terrestrial magnetism yielded important new findings in that field, but it is considered that he caused too great a proportion of the available funding for research to be diverted to fields relevant to that subject and may have compromised other more important fields of research.

Sagan, Carl Edward (1934–1996) US astronomer and popularizer of astronomy whose main research was on planetary atmospheres, including that of the primordial Earth. His most remarkable achievement was to provide valuable insights into the origin of life on our planet.

Sagan was born on 19 November 1934 in New York City. Completing his education at the University of Chicago, he obtained his bachelor's degree in 1955 and his doctorate in 1960. Then, for two years, he was a research fellow at the University of California in

Berkeley, before he transferred to the Smithsonian Astrophysical Observatory in Cambridge, Massachusetts, lecturing also at Harvard, where he became assistant professor. Finally, in 1968 Sagan moved to Cornell University, in Ithaca, New York, and took up a position as director of the Laboratory for Planetary Studies; in 1970 he became professor of astronomy and space science there. He died on 20 December 1996.

The editor of the astronomical journal *Icarus,* Sagan wrote a number of popular books including *Broca's Brain: Reflections on the Romance of Science* (1979); *Cosmos* (1980), based on his television series of that name; and the science-fiction novel *Contact.*

In the early 1960s Sagan's first major research was into the surface and atmosphere of Venus. At the time, although intense emission of radiation had shown that the dark-side temperature of Venus was nearly 600K (327°C/621°F), it was thought that the surface itself remained relatively cool – leaving open the possibility that there was some form of life on the planet. Various hypotheses were put forward to account for the strong emission actually observed: perhaps it was due to interactions between charged particles in Venus' dense upper atmosphere; perhaps it was glow discharge between positive and negative charges in the atmosphere; or perhaps emission was due to a particular radiation from charged particles trapped in the Venusian equivalent of a Van Allen belt. Sagan showed that each of these hypotheses was incompatible with other observed characteristics or with implications of these characteristics. The positive part of Sagan's proposal was to show that all the observed characteristics were compatible with the straightforward hypothesis that the surface of Venus was very hot. On the basis of radar and optical observations the distance between surface and clouds was calculated to be between 44 km/27 mi and 65 km/40 mi; given the cloud-top temperature and Sagan's expectation of a 'greenhouse effect' in the atmosphere, surface temperature on Venus was computed to be between 500K (227°C/440°F) and 800K (527°C/980°F) – the range that would also be expected on the basis of emission rate.

Sagan then turned his attention to the early planetary atmosphere of the Earth, with regard to the origins of life. One way of understanding how life began is to try to form the compounds essential to life in conditions analogous to those of the primeval atmosphere. Before Sagan, Stanley ◊Miller and Harold ◊Urey had used a mixture of methane, ammonia, water vapour, and hydrogen, sparked by a corona discharge that simulated the effect of lightning, to produce amino and hydroxy acids of the sort found in life forms. Later experiments used ultraviolet light or heat as sources of energy, and even these had less energy than would have been available in Earth's primordial state. Sagan followed a similar method and, by irradiating a mixture of methane, ammonia, water, and hydrogen sulphide, was able to produce amino acids – and, in addition, glucose, fructose, and nucleic acids. Sugars can be made from formaldehyde (methanal) under alkaline conditions and in the presence of inorganic catalysts. These sugars include five-carbon sugars, which are essential to the formation of nucleic acids, and the six-carbon sugars glucose and fructose – all common metabolites found as constituents of present-day life forms. Sagan's simulated primordial atmosphere not only showed the presence of those metabolites, it also contained traces of adenosine triphosphate (ATP) – the foremost agent used by living cells to store energy.

In 1966, in work done jointly with Pollack and Goldstein, Sagan was able to provide evidence supporting a hypothesis about Mars put forward by Wells, who observed that in regions on Mars where there were both dark and light areas, the clouds formed over the lighter areas aligned with boundaries of adjacent dark areas. Wells suggested that they were lee clouds formed by the Martian wind as it crossed dark areas. The implication, that dark areas mark the presence of ridges, was given support by Sagan's finding that dark areas had a high radar reflectivity that was slightly displaced in longitude. Sagan concluded that these dark areas were elevated areas with ridges of about 10 km/6 mi and low slopes extending over long distances.

Saha, Meghnad (1893–1956) Indian theoretical physicist and astrophysicist. He contributed to the study of high-temperature ionization and the discovery of the Saha ionization formula.

Born in Scortali, a village near Dacca in India (now Bangladesh) on 6 October 1893, Meghnad Saha was the youngest of the five children of a small shopkeeper. Through the generosity of a local doctor he was able to receive his elementary schooling in a neighbouring town and in 1905 he won a scholarship to study at a government high school in Dacca. In the same year, however, he participated in a boycott of the visit of the British governor of Bengal and was expelled from school, losing his scholarship. He then struggled through private school enrolling in the Calcutta Presidency College in 1911. In 1915 he received an MA in applied mathematics.

He was invited in 1916 to take up a lectureship in mathematics at the new University College of Science in Calcutta by its founder, Asutosh Mukherjee. Not getting along with his head of department, he soon transferred to the physics department where his fascination with astrophysics took root and he began a study of 25 years of the monthly notices of the Royal

Astronomical Society. He was inspired by the work of Danish physicist Niels ◊Bohr and German physicists Arnold ◊Sommerfeld, Max ◊Planck, and Hermann ◊Nernst. He and his colleague Satyendra Bose (1894–1974) translated several of Albert ◊Einstein's papers from German into English. Meanwhile he was also teaching thermodynamics to graduate students and he became interested in the connection between thermodynamics and astrophysics. Inspired by the work of J Eggert in Germany he began work on thermal ionization.

Saha applied thermodynamics and quantum theory to stellar matter and drew an analogy between chemical dissociation and atomic ionization. The resulting formula expressed the degree of ionization in a very hot gas in terms of its temperature and electron pressure. His results were published in papers in the *Philosophical Magazine* in 1920 and the *Proceedings of the Royal Society* in 1921 and are considered to be the starting point of modern astrophysics, on which most of the subsequent research is based. His theory provided the key to understanding for the first time the absence of rubidium and caesium in the solar spectrum. Important knowledge of stellar atmospheres could be found using Saha's theory to analyse their spectra.

In 1919 Saha won the Premchand Roychand Scholarship which allowed him to spend two years in Europe. He visited A Fowler's laboratory at Imperial College, London and also worked with English astrophysicist Edward Milne, who made important extensions to Saha's work. In Berlin he visited Nernst and met Einstein, Planck, ◊Laue, and Sommerfeld. He set up experiments there that confirmed his theory and he published an explanatory article in *Zeitschrift für Physik* in 1921.

Saha was appointed as Khaira Professor of Physics at the University of Calcutta in 1921 but was disappointed by the lack of enthusiasm and lack of funding for his work. In 1923 he became professor and head of the department of physics at Allahabad University, where he taught until 1938. His fame spread and he was the recipient of many honours including the presidency of the physics section of the Indian Science Congress Association in 1925 and membership of the Royal Society from 1927. He moved back to the University of Calcutta in 1938 to take up the Palit chair and in 1950 he created the Institute of Nuclear Physics, now renamed the Saha Institute of Nuclear Physics.

Saha took an interest in the social implications of science but had not become involved in political campaigns after his original foray at the age of 11. He was not a supporter of Gandhi and his khadi campaigns, believing industrialization to be the way forward. In 1935 he founded *Science and Culture*, a socioscientific

journal that became influential. He was sympathetic to the struggle for independence in India but remained on the sidelines until after independence, when he ran as an independent candidate and was elected to parliament. He died on a visit to New Delhi on 16 February 1956.

Saint-Claire Deville, Henri Etienne (1818–1881)

French inorganic chemist who worked on high-temperature reactions and is best known for being the first to extract metallic aluminium in any quantity.

Saint-Claire Deville was born on 11 March 1818 on the island of St Thomas in the Virgin Islands (then Danish territory), the son of the French consul there. He was educated in France and studied science and medicine, learning chemistry under Louis Thénard (1777–1857). He gained his medical degree in 1844 and a year later he became dean and professor of chemistry at the newly established University of Besançon. In 1851 he followed Antoine Balard (an ex-assistant of Thénard) as professor of chemistry at the Ecole Normale in Paris and took over from Jean Baptiste ◊Dumas at the Sorbonne in 1859. He died in Boulogne-sur-Seine on 1 July 1881.

In 1827 Friedrich ◊Wöhler had isolated small quantities of impure aluminium from its compounds by the drastic method of heating them with metallic potassium. Saint-Claire Deville substituted the safer sodium. He first had to prepare sufficient sodium metal but by 1855 he had obtained enough aluminium to cast a block weighing 7 kg/15 lb. The process was put into commercial production and within four years the price of aluminium had fallen to one-hundredth of its former level. (It was to decrease even further 27 years later when Charles Hall in the USA and Paul Héroult in France (see ◊Hall and Héroult) independently discovered the method for electrolytically extracting aluminium.)

Saint-Claire Deville also investigated the chemistry and metallurgy of magnesium and platinum, made the first preparation of a monobasic acid 'anhydride' when he made nitrogen pentoxide (dinitrogen pentoxide, N_2O_5), and studied the high-temperature decomposition of gases into atomic species. In organic chemistry he made one of the first extractions of toluene (methylbenzene), in 1841, while experimenting with tolu balsam and turpentine oil.

Sakharov, Andrei Dmitrievich (1921–1989)

Russian physicist who was closely involved with the development of Soviet thermonuclear weapons. He later repudiated this work and became an active campaigner for nuclear disarmament and human rights. This resulted in the award of the 1975 Nobel Peace Prize and in his banishment in 1980.

Sakharov was born in Moscow on 21 May 1921 and followed in his father's footsteps to become a physicist.

Sakharov Russian physicist and dissident Andrei Sakharov who was awarded the Nobel Peace Prize in 1975. Sakharov was born and educated in Moscow. He was mainly responsible for the development of the Soviet hydrogen bomb, but in the early 1960s campaigned for a nuclear test-ban treaty and human rights, which brought him into conflict with the Soviet authorities. *Mary Evans Picture Library*

He showed exceptional scientific ability early on in his education and studied at Moscow State University, graduating in 1942. In 1945, Sakharov joined the staff of the P N Lebedev Institute of Physics in Moscow as a physicist and spent his research life there. In 1953, at the age of 32, he became the youngest ever to be made a full member of the Soviet Academy of Sciences. Sakharov's other Soviet honours include the Hero of Socialist Labour, the Order of Lenin, and Laureate of the USSR. In addition to the 1975 Nobel Peace Prize, his foreign honours include membership of the American Academy of Arts and Sciences in 1969 and the National Academy of Sciences in 1972, the Eleanor Roosevelt Peace Award in 1973, and the Cino del Duca Prize and the Reinhold Niebuhr Prize from Chicago University in 1974.

In 1980, Sakharov was stripped of his Soviet honours and banished to Gorky (now Nizhniy-Novgorod) for criticizing Soviet action in Afghanistan. He continued to be given honours abroad, receiving the Fritt Ord Prize in 1980 and becoming a foreign associate of the French Academy of Science in 1981.

At the P N Lebedev Institute of Physics, Sakharov worked with Igor Tamm (1895–1971), who was to win the 1958 Nobel Prize for Physics with Pavel Cherenkov (1904–1990) and Ilia Frank (1908–1990) for their work on Cherenkov radiation. In 1948, Sakharov and Tamm published a paper in which they outlined a principle for the magnetic isolation of high-temperature plasma, and in so doing significantly altered the course of Soviet research into thermonuclear reactions. From 1948 to 1956, their work was solely on research connected with nuclear weapons and was top secret. It led directly to the explosion of the first Soviet hydrogen bomb in 1953, but by 1950 Sakharov and Tamm had also formulated the theoretical basis for controlled thermonuclear fusion – the means by which thermonuclear power could be used for the generation of electricity and other peaceful ends.

By the end of the 1950s, Sakharov was becoming interested in wider issues and in 1958, with Yakov B Zeldovich, he published an article in *Pravda* advocating educational reforms that contradicted official pronouncements. Sakharov pointed out that mathematicians and physicists are most creative early on in their careers and proposed early entry into university. Many of Sakharov's ideas were incorporated. In the early 1960s, he joined the controversy between the genetics of Gregor ◊Mendel and that of Trofim ◊Lysenko and was instrumental in breaking Lysenko's hold over Soviet science and in giving science some political immunity. His scientific papers in the 1960s concerned the structure of the universe. In 1965 he wrote on the initial stages of an expanding universe and the appearance of nonuniformity in the distribution of matter, and in the following year on quarks, the basic components of protons.

After the mid-1960s, Sakharov's activities showed a shift of interest. In 1968, he published a famous essay entitled 'Progress, peaceful coexistence and intellectual freedom', which argued for a reduction of nuclear arms by all nuclear powers, an increase in international cooperation, and the establishment of civil liberties in Russia. This was followed in 1970 by the founding of a Committee for Human Rights by Sakharov and other Soviet physicists to promote the principles expressed in the Universal Declaration of Human Rights. Sakharov's subsequent publications on this theme included *Sakharov Speaks* (1974), *My Country and the World* (1975), and *Alarm and Hope* (1979) and made him an international figure. But his fame also brought increasing harassment from the Soviet authorities, and Sakharov was not allowed to go to Norway to collect his Nobel prize. In 1980, he was removed from Moscow and banished to Gorky, but was allowed to return to Moscow at the end of 1986 and resume his place in the Soviet Academy of Sciences. He was elected to the Congress of the USSR People's Deputies (CUPD) in 1989, where he emerged as leader of its radical reform grouping prior to his death later the same year.

Sakharov's fundamental work on controlled thermonuclear fusion may one day result in the production of cheap energy. His bravery in resisting oppression and calling for the peaceful use of science demonstrated a rare strength of character.

Further Reading

Bailey, George, *The Making of Andrei Sakharov,* Allen Lane, 1989.

Bailey, George, *Galileo's Children: Science, Sakharov and the Power of State,* Arcade Publishing, 1999.

Kelley, Donald R, *The Solzhenitsyn–Sakharov Dialogue: Politics, Society, and the Future,* Contributions in Political Science series, Greenwood Press, 1982, v 74.

Sakharov, Andrei D, *Memoirs,* Hutchinson, 1990.

Sakharov, Andrei D, *Collected Scientific Works,* Marcel Dekker Inc, 1982.

Sakharov, Andrei D; Salisbury, Harrison Evans (ed), *Sakharov Speaks,* Collins–Harvill Press, 1974.

Salam, Abdus (1926–1996) Pakistani theoretical physicist who shared the 1979 Nobel Prize for Physics for jointly developing a unified theory of weak and electromagnetic interactions. He also set up the International Centre for Theoretical Physics in Trieste, Italy.

Salam was born on 29 January 1926 in Jhang Maghiana, Pakistan, then part of India. He attended Government College in Lahore before going to Cambridge University in the UK where he graduated in mathematics and physics. Salam then started experimental research at the Cavendish Laboratory – working on tritium–deuterium scattering – but, according to his Nobel lecture, 'soon I knew the craft of experimental physics was beyond me'. Instead he switched to theory and he started to work on quantum field theory with Nicholas Kemmer in Paul ◊Dirac's department. Salam returned to Government College as a mathematics professor in 1951, received his PhD from Cambridge in 1952, and became a lecturer in mathematics at Cambridge in 1954. He was appointed professor of theoretical physics at Imperial College, London, in 1957.

Salam was instrumental in setting up, in 1964, the International Centre for Theoretical Physics in Trieste, Italy, and was its director 1964–93. The ICTP, which is administered by the International Atomic Energy Agency (part of the United Nations), aims to stimulate science and technology in developing countries. Salam was also chief scientific advisor to the president of Pakistan 1961–74. He died in Oxford on 21 November 1996.

> *The whole history of particle physics, or of physics, is one of getting down the number of concepts to as few as possible.*
> **ABDUS SALAM** L WOLPERT AND A RICHARDS
> A PASSION FOR SCIENCE *1988*

Salam shared the Nobel prize with Sheldon Glashow (1932–) and Steven Weinberg (1933–) for unifying the theories of electromagnetism and the weak force, the force responsible for a neutron transforming into a proton, electron, and neutrino (during radioactive decay). It was known that the electromagnetic force was caused by the exchange of photons (particles of light with no mass or charge) while the weak force was transmitted by massive charged particles known as the W^+ and W^- bosons. Glashow had shown that a satisfactory 'electroweak' theory required a fourth neutral particle and, independently in 1967, Salam and Weinberg calculated how the masses of the W^+, W^-, and this new particle (the Z^0) were related. The theory actually involves two new particles (the W^0 and B^0) that combine in different ways to form either the photon or the Z^0. One prediction of the theory was that the exchange of Z^0 particles in certain reactions, such as electron–neutrino scattering, would cause a weak neutral current (similar to the well-known weak charged current caused by the W particles). This neutral current was successfully measured at CERN, the European particles physics laboratory near Geneva, in 1973. Weinberg and Salam also predicted that the electroweak interaction should violate left–right symmetry and this was confirmed by experiments at Stanford University in California. The W and Z particles themselves were not detected until 1983, four years after he received his prizes.

Further Reading

Dalafi, H and Hassan, M H, *Renaissance of Sciences in Islamic Countries: Muhammad Abdus Salam,* World Scientific Publishing Co, 1994.

Isham, C J and Kibble, T (eds), *Selected Papers of Abdus Salam,* Series on Twentieth-Century Physics, World Scientific Publishing Co, 1994.

Lai, C H and Ladwai, Z, *Ideals and Realities: Selected Essays of Abdus Salam,* World Scientific Publishing Co. 1989.

Salk, Jonas Edward (1914–1995) US microbiologist who produced the first successful vaccine against the paralytic disease poliomyelitis.

Salk was born in New York, the son of Polish–Jewish Immigrants on 28 October 1914. He graduated in surgery from the College of the City of New York in 1934, and then became a research fellow at the New York

University College of Medicine, where he studied the chemistry of proteins. In 1939 he was awarded a doctorate in medicine and during the next three years worked at the Mount Sinai Hospital in New York, before joining the research staff of the Virus Research Unit in the University of Michigan, where he worked on influenza vaccines until 1944. The next two years were spent in consultation regarding the protection of the armed forces from epidemics. In 1946 he became an assistant professor in epidemiology at Michigan and the following year he was invited by the University of Pittsburgh to join a special medical research unit there to carry out a three-year programme on the causes and treatment of viral diseases. The development of the Salk vaccine against poliomyelitis was announced in 1955. He was appointed director of the Salk Institute for Biological Studies, San Diego, in 1962. He died on 23 June 1995.

The major obstacle to research on the preparation of vaccines in the 1940s was the difficulty of obtaining sufficient virus. Unlike bacteria, which may be grown in culture, viruses need living cells on which to grow. A breakthrough came when it was found that viruses could be grown in live chick embryos. John ◊Enders improved on this technique with the use of mashed embryonic tissue, supplied with nutrients, and with the addition of penicillin to keep down the growth of bacteria.

Once the method of preparing sufficient quantities of virus was available, Salk set about finding a way of treating the polio virus so that it was unable to cause the disease but was still able to produce an antibody reaction in the human body. He collected samples of spinal cord from many polio victims and grew the virus in the new live-cell culture medium. He studied the reaction of the virus to various chemicals and found that there were three distinct types of virus that cause the disease. Salk experimented with formaldehyde (methanal) to render the virus inactive. By 1952 he had produced a vaccine effective against the three common strains of polio virus in the USA; he tested it on monkeys, which are also susceptible to polio, and found that it worked. Next he tried the vaccine on children who had recovered from polio and were immune to the disease, and he found an increase in the antibody content of their blood. Afterwards, he tried it on his family and children who had not had polio, and again antibodies were formed in the blood.

Salk needed a large-scale clinical trial, however, because a large number of people would need to receive the preventive vaccine if any useful results were to be obtained. The vaccine had to be prepared on a commercial scale and licences were issued to five companies, who were instructed in the technique of vaccine production and were responsible for their own

quality control, because Salk's laboratory could not cope with the volume of work that testing would involve. In 1955, in a big publicity campaign, some vaccine was prepared without adequate precautions and about 200 cases of polio, with 11 deaths, resulted from the clinical trials. Salk recommended that the vaccine should be tested by the public health service in future and more stringent control prevented further disasters.

Salk was the first to make use of Enders's method of growing viruses to prepare a vaccine against poliomyelitis. It saved many people from the crippling and often fatal effects of the disease and prompted Albert ◊Sabin to prepare a polio vaccine that can be administered orally rather than by injection.

Further Reading

Bredeson, Carmen, *Jonas Salk: Discoverer of the Polio Vaccine,* People to Know series, Enslow Publishers, 1993.

Curson, Marjorie and Gallin, Richard (ed), *Jonas Salk,* Pioneers in Change series, Silver Burdett Press, 1990.

Sherrow, Victoria, *Jonas Salk,* Makers of Modern Science series, Facts on File, 1993.

Sanger, Frederick (1918–) English biochemist who worked out the sequence of amino acids in various protein molecules. For his work on insulin he was awarded the 1958 Nobel Prize for Chemistry. For determining the sequence in the DNA molecule, he became one of the very few scientists to receive two Nobel prizes when, in 1980, he shared the Chemistry Prize with the US molecular biologists Paul ◊Berg and Walter ◊Gilbert.

Sanger was born in Rendcomb, Gloucestershire, on 13 August 1918, the son of a doctor. He was educated at Bryanston School and at St John's College, Cambridge, from which he graduated in 1939. He then began research in biochemistry, gaining his PhD in 1943 and working as a research fellow until 1951. In that year he joined the staff of the Medical Research Council and in 1961 became head of the Protein and Nucleic Acid Chemistry Division of the council's Molecular Biology Laboratory at Cambridge. He retired in 1983.

Beginning in 1943 Sanger and his co-workers determined the sequence of 51 amino acids in the insulin molecule, using samples of the hormone obtained from cattle pancreases. By 1945 he had discovered a compound, Sanger's reagent (2, 4-dinitrofluorobenzene), which attaches itself to amino acids and so he was able to break the protein chain into smaller pieces and analyse them using paper chromatography. By 1953 he had determined the sequence for insulin, and even shown that there are small but precise differences between the structures of insulins from different animals. He also worked out the structures of other proteins, including various enzymes.

In the late 1950s Sanger turned his attention to the sequence of the nucleotides that link to form the protein strands in the nucleic acids RNA and DNA. The double-helical structure of DNA had been determined by Francis ◊Crick and James ◊Watson in 1953, and within the next few years other workers had identified enzymes that can join nucleotides to form chains and others that can cut existing chains into shorter pieces. Sanger used the chain-cutting type of enzyme to identify nucleotides and their order along the chain, and in 1977 he and his co-workers announced that they had established the sequence of the more than 5,000 nucleotides along a strand of RNA from the bacterial virus called R17. They later worked out the order for mitochondrial DNA, which has approximately 17,000 nucleotides.

Savery, Thomas (c. 1650–1715) English inventor and engineer who is generally credited with producing the world's first practical steam-driven water pump. It had only limited success and was not adopted widely, probably due to faulty materials and workmanship.

Much of Savery's life is unrecorded. He came from a Devon family and may have been born in Shilston near Modbury. It is possible that he was a captain in the military engineers but it is more likely that he was 'captain' of a mine – a title sometimes used in mining circles. The first definite record comes with the grant of a patent in 1696 for a machine for cutting, grinding, and polishing mirror glass. His patent for a fire engine for raising water from mines, for which he is best known, was granted in July 1698. In 1705 he was appointed Treasurer for Sick and Wounded Seamen, a post he held until 1714. In 1706 he was elected fellow of the Royal Society, and the same year he applied for a patent for a bellows for foundry work.

It is probable that he made a trip to Hannover in Germany in connection with his engine and on his return he applied, in 1710, for a patent for an improved oven. He also invented a mechanism for measuring the distance sailed by a ship. In 1714 Savery was appointed surveyor of the waterworks at Hampton Court and he designed a pumping system, driven by a water wheel, for supplying the fountains.

Obituaries place Savery's death in May 1715 and his will, dated 15 May, was proved on 19 May by his widow, Martha – his executrix and sole legatee. It is not known where he was buried.

For many years up to the first decades of the 18th century, pumping out British mines had been a major problem. Various suggestions had been made for using steam power, but the Miners' Friend, as Savery's invention was called, showed most promise of significant advance.

His invention consisted of a boiler heated by an open fire, so it was technically an 'atmospheric engine' and not a 'steam engine' as we know it today. The engine was connected via a regulator and steam pipe to the top of a receiver, the bottom of which was mounted on a hollow box or 'engine tree'. Also connected to the engine tree was the suction pipe, which extended into the mine, and a force (delivery) pipe. There were one-way valves (opening upwards) in the suction and force pipes.

To work the Miners' Friend, the operator opened the regulator, letting steam into the receiver, and driving air up the force pipe through the one-way valve. When the receiver was full of steam, the regulator was closed then doused with cold water to condense the steam it contained. Atmospheric pressure forced water up the suction pipe through the one-way valve into the receiver. The operator then opened the regulator, and the steam pressure forced the water up the force pipe. The steam in the receiver was again condensed, and the cycle repeated.

A contemporary writer described a basic engine built in 1711 or 1712 at Campden House, Kensington, which had a boiler holding 182 l/40 gall (48 US gall), a receiver of 59 l/13 gall (16 US gall), and 76-mm/3-in wooden suction and delivery pipes, the former 5 m/ 16 ft long and the latter 13 m/42 ft. It could pump 14,180 l/3,120 gall (3,747 US gall) per hour and cost £50.

A model exhibited to the Royal Society had two receivers working alternately to deliver water continuously and it was on this concept that Savery based his description of the Miners' Friend. He reckoned it could lift water 6–8 m/20–26 ft and then force it to a height of 18–24 m/60–80 ft. In deep mines two or more engines, one above the other, were to be used. Savery

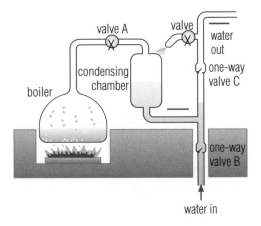

Savery Thomas Savery's steam pump, the 'Miners' Friend', has been described as the precursor of the steam engine. However, it achieved only limited success and was not adopted widely, probably because of faulty materials and poor workmanship.

claimed that the draught to the furnace would help mine ventilation and that the water delivered above ground could be used to turn a water wheel.

There are no records, however, of any engines being installed in mines. A two-receiver engine built at York Buildings waterworks had continuous problems with blowing steam joints. Savery acquired facilities for producing his engines but it appears that poor workmanship and materials made them unworkable.

There is little doubt that Savery produced the world's first, practical, working steam engine. It was probably never used for the purpose for which it was intended and another Devonian, Thomas ◊Newcomen, solved the problem in a different way. Savery's engine did work, however, and for this he deserves to take his place in history.

Scheele, Karl Wilhelm (1742–1786) Swedish chemist, arguably the greatest of the 18th century. He anticipated or independently duplicated much of the pioneering research that was taking place at that time in France and England, and isolated many elements and compounds for the first time. Among his many discoveries were the elements oxygen and chlorine, although delays in publishing his findings often resulted in other chemists being credited with priority. He never took a university appointment, doing all his research privately while practising as an apothecary.

Scheele was born on 9 December 1742 in Stralsund, Pomerania, at a time when it belonged to Sweden (it was more often, as now, German territory), the seventh of 11 children of a poor family. He received little education until 1756 when at the age of 14 he became an apothecary's apprentice at Göteborg (Gothenburg) and learned basic chemistry through reading, observation and experiment. He progressed from position to position, moving to Malmö in 1765, Stockholm in 1768, and finally Uppsala in 1770, still practising as an apothecary. In Uppsala he met Johann Gahn (1745–1818) who introduced him to the Swedish chemist Torbern Bergman (1735–1784), who in turn recognized Scheele's talents and publicized his work. In 1775 Scheele moved to run a pharmacy in the small town of Köping on Lake Malären in Västmanland, where he remained for the rest of his life despite opportunities to take academic posts in Germany and England, and an offer from the Prussian Frederick II to serve as court chemist. Also in 1775 he was elected to the Swedish Royal Academy of Sciences, a unique honour for a mere apothecary's assistant. As Scheele approached middle age his health – never good – began to fail and he suffered from rheumatic pain and possibly the toxic effects of some of the chemicals he experimented with; long hours of intense work also took their toll. He married on his deathbed and died,

in Köping, aged only 43 on 21 May 1786.

Scheele's research did not appear to follow a particular plan, and he seems to have experimented in an indiscriminate way with the various substances he came across in his work. But even if his approach lacked system, he nevertheless made a huge contribution to chemistry. His original discoveries alone make a formidable list, and the major ones are worth itemizing; ignoring chronology and combining inorganic discoveries with those in organic chemistry, they include the following:

arsenic acid, arsine, barium oxide (baryta), benzoic acid, calcium tungstate (scheelite), chlorine, citric acid, copper arsenite (Scheele's green), gallic acid, glycerol, hydrogen cyanide and hydrocyanic acid, hydrogen fluoride, hydrogen sulphide, lactic acid, malic acid, manganese and manganates, molybdic acid, nitrogen, oxalic acid, oxygen, permanganates, silicon tetrafluoride, tartaric acid, tungstic acid, and uric acid

Undoubtedly the most significant of these are chlorine and oxygen. Scheele also discovered that the action of light modifies certain silver salts (50 years before they were first used in photographic emulsions). He isolated phosphorus from calcined bones and obtained uric acid from bladder stones. He studied molybdenum disulphide (molybdenite, MoS_2) and showed how it differs from graphite – both substances have similar physical properties and both are still used as solid lubricants. He demonstrated the different oxidation states of copper, iron, and mercury.

Scheele's discovery of oxygen began – as did Antoine ◊Lavoisier's – with a study of air. He first showed that air consists of two main gases, one of which ('fire air') supports combustion and one of which ('vitiated air' or 'foul air') does not. In various experiments on air he consumed the 'fire air' component to leave the 'vitiated air' – Scheele was a staunch believer in the phlogiston theory of combustion. Then in a series of preparations 1771–72 he produced 'fire air' (oxygen) in various ways chemically: by the action of heat on saltpetre (potassium nitrate) or manganese dioxide; by heating heavy metal nitrates (and absorbing the nitrogen dioxide also formed in lime water), and by heating mercuric (mercury (II)) oxide (Joseph ◊Priestley's method of 1774). He showed that oxygen is involved in the respiration of plants and fish. Scheele described these experiments in his only major publication, *A Chemical Treatise on Air and Fire,* written in about 1773 in German, the language that Scheele normally used in speech and writing. The introduction to the book was written by

Bergman, who took so long to provide his text that publication did not actually take place until 1777. This was three years after Priestley had prepared oxygen and published his findings, and credit is now usually given to him. (The name oxygen – meaning 'acid producer' – was coined by Lavoisier, who mistakenly thought that all acids contain oxygen.)

Following on from this work Scheele isolated chlorine in 1774 by heating manganese dioxide with hydrochloric acid, but he thought that it was a compound of oxygen – 'dephlogisticated muriatic [hydrochloric] acid' – and did not recognize it as an element. This distinction was made a generation later by Humphry ◊Davy, who through his work on hydrochloric acid also discredited Lavoisier's theory that all acids contain oxygen.

Scheiner, Christoph (1573–1650)

German astronomer who carried out one of the earliest and most meticulous studies of sunspots and who made significant improvements to the helioscope and the telescope.

Scheiner was born in Wald, near Mindelheim, on 25 July 1573. He attended the Jesuit Latin School at Augsburg and then the Jesuit College at Landsberg, In 1600 he was sent to Ingolstadt, where he studied philosophy and mathematics. During the years 1603–05 he taught humanities in Dillingen and also invented the pantograph, which enabled the copying of plans and drawings to a different scale. Returning to Ingolstadt, he studied theology until his graduation in 1610 and his subsequent appointment as professor of mathematics and Hebrew at Ingolstadt University. It was there that he began to make his astronomical observations and, as well as carrying out his own research, he also organized public debates on current issues in astronomy. In 1616 Scheiner accepted an invitation to take up residence at the court in Innsbruck and the following year he was ordained to the priesthood. From 1633 to 1639 he lived in Vienna and from then until his death on 18 June 1650 he lived in Neisse (now Nysa in Poland).

Scheiner built his first telescope in 1611 and began making astronomical observations of the Sun. He was among the earliest observers of the Sun and, using one of the first properly mounted telescopes, he was sensible enough to project the image of the Sun onto a white screen so that it would not damage his eyes. Within a matter of weeks of observation, he reported dark spots around the Sun. His superiors in the Jesuit order, fearing discredit to the order if the discovery were proved to be false, prohibited the publication of Scheiner's observations using his own name. He therefore disclosed the nature of his discovery to a friend in Augsburg, Marc Wesler, who had Scheiner's letters printed under a pseudonym and sent copies to ◊Galileo and Johannes ◊Kepler. Scheiner believed that the spots were small planets circling the Sun and in a second series of letters, published in the same year under the same false name, Scheiner described the individual behaviour of the sunspots and the existence of brighter patches, or 'faculae', on the solar surface. Observing the lower conjunction of Venus with the Sun, he ascertained that these bodies revolved around the Sun. But because of his religious beliefs he upheld the traditional view that the Earth is at rest at the centre of the universe.

Although Scheiner had tried to conceal his identity, Galileo identified him and claimed priority for the discovery of sunspots, hinting that Scheiner was guilty of plagiarism. It would seem that this accusation was unjust, however, since the existence of the spots had been reported independently by others apart from Galileo (in Florence) and Scheiner, including Thomas Harriot in Oxford and Johann Fabricius in Wittenberg.

In his *Solellipticus* (1615) and *Refractiones caelestes* (1617), Scheiner drew attention to his observations of the elliptical form of the Sun near the horizon, which he explained as being due to the effects of refraction. In his major work, *Rosa ursina sive sol* (1626–30), Scheiner described the inclination of the axis of rotation of the sunspots to the plane of the ecliptic, which he accurately determined as having a value of 7°30′, the modern value being 7°15′.

Unfortunately, Scheiner lived in an age when observational astronomy posed grave confrontations to his theological principles and this not only affected Scheiner's scientific career, but also hindered the progress of science as a whole.

Schiaparelli, Giovanni Virginio (1835–1910)

Italian astronomer whose long experience of rather ancient equipment led to considerable caution in making his discoveries known, but who nevertheless carried out significant research into the nature of comets and the inner planets of the Solar System. He is best known – and most misunderstood – for allegedly discovering 'canals' on Mars.

Schiaparelli was born in Savigliano, Piedmont, on 14 March 1835. After leaving school, he first trained as a civil engineer. Only after he had graduated from the University of Turin and was teaching mathematics at the university did Schiaparelli begin a study of modern languages and astronomy. Support from the Piedmont government permitted him to engage in advanced studies at the observatories of Berlin and Pulkovo. On his return in 1860, Schiaparelli was appointed astronomer at the Brera Observatory in Milan; he remained there until his retirement in 1900. His first observations, using only the primitive instruments then available to him, resulted in the discovery of the asteroid Hesperia. For most of the next 15 years, Schiaparelli's major interest was in comets. In later years, when more sophisticated instruments became available at Milan, Schiaparelli turned his attention to the planets. Towards the end of his working life, he made use of his linguistic skills by assisting in the translation from the Arabic of a historic work on astronomy; it was published after his death, which occurred on 4 July 1910 in Milan.

Schiaparelli's study of comets began with theoretical research into the nature of a comet's tail. Two years later his work on the tail was extended to a consideration of other features of a comet, including the histories of comets recorded in years previously. From these, and from his own notes on the bright comet of 1862, Schiaparelli was led to conjecture that all meteor showers are the result of the disintegration of comets. Such a hypothesis had been put forward before, but Schiaparelli could point to his compilation of extensive observational evidence to show that all meteors moved in elliptical or parabolic orbits around the Sun, orbits that (as would have to be the case for Schiaparelli's hypothesis to be true) were identical with or similar to those of comets. Schiaparelli also argued that meteors became visible as luminous showers falling from a determinable position in the celestial sphere. Pietro ◊Secchi's observations of the 1862 comet were to confirm this hypothesis; and, in the years following, observations by other astronomers served to confirm Schiaparelli's theory.

In 1877, using new equipment far superior to the instruments he had used before, Schiaparelli began detailed observation of Mars, preparatory to drawing a map of the fundamental features of its surface. In noting what Secchi had previously called 'channels' (*canali*), and while introducing further nomenclature involving 'seas' and 'continents', Schiaparelli made it quite clear, in publishing his results, that such terms were for convenience only and did not represent terrestrial actuality. Nevertheless, possibly through mistranslation – and certainly through wishful thinking – fanciful stories of advanced life on Mars proliferated, especially in France, the USA, and the UK, for the next 40 years or more.

Schiaparelli's observations of Mars continued through the next few years, being more frequent during the seven oppositions between 1879 and 1890. All manner of variations – of inclination to axis, of the apparent diameter, of geometric declination, of observational conditions, and so on – allowed Schiaparelli to build up a complex picture of Mars. During the 1877 opposition Schiaparelli noted that when Mars moved away from the Earth, its diameter appeared to decrease. He also observed that certain canals seemed to be splitting into two parts and he suggested that this

'gemination' had serious implications for the understanding of the physical constitution of Mars. His observations of 1888 occurred under such good atmospheric conditions that Schiaparelli found it impossible to represent all the features of Mars in adequate detail or colour. New geminations, absent from the last observation, led him to propose that they were the effect of a periodic phenomenon related to the solar year on Mars. Schiaparelli also observed that split canals were visible for a few days or weeks before becoming single canals or disappearing entirely. He continued his observations until 1890, and their detail and accuracy far surpassed observations made by others using similar instruments.

Schiaparelli also observed Mercury, studying the dark spots that form shadowy bands on the surface of the planet. He concluded that Mercury revolved around the Sun in such a way as always to present the same side to the Sun. He came to exactly the same conclusion about the rotation of Venus. Other observations included a study of binary stars in order to deduce their orbital systems.

Schiaparelli's role in the history of astronomy extends beyond the part he played through his observations. He also made a noteworthy contribution in helping Nallino to translate the only existing Arabic text of al-Battani's *Opus astronomicum* into Latin and in writing explanatory notes to many chapters. The translation is a major landmark in understanding the development of astronomy in the Arabic world. Schiaparelli intended to compile a major work on the history of ancient astronomy and he published a number of monographs on the subject.

Further Reading

Baudot, François, *Schiaparelli,* Saint Martin's Press, 1997.

Ordway, F I, 'The legacy of Schiaparelli and Lowell', *J Brit Interplanet Soc*, 1986, v 39, pp 19–27.

Turchetta, Massimo and Gavazzi, Giuseppe, 'Nineteenth-century Italian contributions to galactic theory', *J Hist Astron*, 1987, v 18, pp 196–208.

Schleiden, Matthias Jakob (1804–1881) German botanist who, with Theodor ◊Schwann, is best known for the establishment of the cell theory.

Schleiden was born on 5 April 1804 in Hamburg and studied law at Heidelberg University 1824–27. After graduating, he practised as a barrister in Hamburg but soon returned to university, taking courses in botany and medicine at the universities of Göttingen, Berlin, and Jena. After graduating in 1831 he was appointed professor of botany at Jena, where he remained until he became professor of botany at the University of Dorpat, Estonia, in 1862. He returned to Germany after a short time, however, and from 1864 began teaching privately in Frankfurt. Schleiden died in Frankfurt on 23 June 1881.

Although the existence of cells had been known since the 17th century (Robert ⟳Hooke is generally credited with their discovery in 1665), Schleiden was the first to recognize their importance as the fundamental units of living organisms when, in 1838, he announced that the various parts of plants consist of cells or derivatives of cells. In the following year Schwann published a paper in which he confirmed for animals Schleiden's idea of the basic importance of cells in the organization of organisms. Thus Schleiden and Schwann established the cell theory, a concept that is common knowledge today and which is as fundamental to biology as atomic theory is to the physical sciences.

Schleiden also researched into other aspects of cells. He recognized the importance of the nucleus (which he called the cytoblast) in cell division, although he incorrectly believed that new cells budded off from the nuclear surface. In addition, he noted the active movement of intracellular material in plant tissues, calling this movement protoplasmic streaming. The phenomenon is well known today, although the intracellular material is now called cytoplasm.

Schmidt, Bernhard Voldemar (1879–1935)

Estonian lens- and mirror-maker who devised a special sort of lens to work in conjunction with a spherical mirror in a reflecting telescope. The effect of this was to nullify 'coma', the optical distortion of focus away from the centre of the image inherent in such telescopes, and thus to bring the entire image into a single focus, useful for general surveys of the night sky or for photography.

Schmidt was born on the island of Naissaar, Estonia, on 30 March 1879, the child of poor parents. Inclined to scientific pursuits, one of his earliest successes was to make a convex lens by grinding the bottom of a bottle using fine sand. Another experiment had disastrous consequences, however: he made some gunpowder, packed it tightly into a metal tube and ignited it. The explosion caused him to lose most of his right arm. At the age of 21 he began to study engineering at the Institute of Technology at Göteborg (Gothenburg). After one year he went on to the institute at Mittweida in Germany. After graduating in 1904 he stayed in Mittweida making lenses and mirrors for astronomers. One of his early accomplishments, in 1905, was a 40-cm/27-in mirror for the Potsdam Astrophysical Observatory. Schmidt worked independently, producing optical equipment of very high quality until 1926, when Schorr, the director of the Hamburg Observatory, asked him to move into the observatory and work there. Schmidt accepted the invitation. He worked on the mountings and drives of the telescopes,

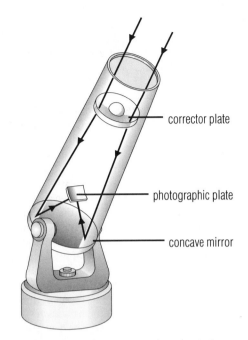

Schmidt The Schmidt Telescope uses a corrective lens (corrector plate) to achieve a wide field of view. It is one of the most widely used tools of astronomy.

as well as on their optics. It was in Hamburg that he perfected his lens and built it into the observatory telescope, specifically for use in photography. He suffered from alcoholism and died in Hamburg, in an asylum, on 1 December 1935.

It is usual for reflecting telescopes to have parabolic mirrors, rather than spherical ones; spherical ones are subject to an optical distortion known as spherical aberration. Parabolic mirrors too, however, suffer from their own optically distortive effect, 'coma'; but they provide an image that is at least centrally clear and focused. What Schmidt devised was a means of correcting the image formed by a spherical mirror – a disc-shaped lens thicker at the centre and edges than at half-radius. By replacing the parabolic mirror of a telescope with a spherical one plus his lens – his 'corrector plate', as he called it – he could produce an image that was sharply focused at every point (generally on a curved photographic plate, although on later models Schmidt used a second lens to compensate for the use of a flat photographic plate).

Later astronomers, opticians, and engineers improved on Schmidt's basic designs to produce such instruments as the super-Schmidt meteor camera, which has been used to great effect at Las Cruces, New Mexico, and the large 120-cm/48-in Schmidt on the same site as the 500-cm/200-in Mount Palomar reflecting telescope, and used in the Palomar Sky Survey.

Further Reading

Schmidt, E, *Optical Illusions: The Life Story of Bernhard Schmidt, the Great Stellar Optician of the 20th Century*, Estonian Academy Publishers Teaduste Akadeemia Kirjastus, 1995.

Schoenheimer, Rudolf (1898–1941) German-born US biochemist who first used isotopes as tracers to study biochemical processes.

Schoenheimer was born in Berlin on 10 May 1898. After graduating in medicine from the University of Berlin in 1923, he spent the next ten years in various teaching posts in Germany. In 1933 he emigrated to the USA, where he became a member of the College of Physicians and Surgeons at the University of Columbia. He committed suicide in New York City on 11 September 1941, while still at the peak of his career.

Schoenheimer introduced the use of isotopic tracers into biochemical research in 1935. Deuterium (heavy hydrogen) had become fairly easily available for the first time, thanks mainly to the work of Harold ◊Urey, who was also at Columbia. Schoenheimer used deuterium to replace some of the hydrogen atoms in molecules of fat, which he then fed to laboratory animals. It had previously been thought that fat stored in body tissues remained immobile, just lying there until starvation demanded its use. On analysing the body fat of rats four days after feeding them deuterated fat, he found that about half of the labelled fat was being stored – that is, ingested fat was being stored by the animal and stored fat was being used. There was a rapid turnover and the body constituents, far from being static, were changing constantly and dynamically.

Urey prepared the isotope nitrogen-15 at about this time, and Schoenheimer soon used it to label amino acids, the basic building blocks of proteins. In a series of experiments, in which he fed a single labelled amino acid to an animal, he traced the fate of that acid in the animal's proteins. He again found that there is constant action, even though the overall movement may be small, with the protein molecules constantly changing and shifting. He had thus established that many component molecules of the body are continually being broken down and built up. He summarized his findings in his book *The Dynamical State of Bodily Constituents*.

After World War II researchers such as Melvin ◊Calvin went on to use radioactive isotopes, such as those of carbon and phosphorus, to investigate biochemical pathways in living animals. These techniques were developed from the pioneering work of Rudolf Schoenheimer.

Schramm, David (1945–1997) US theoretical astrophysicist, an authority on the Big Bang theory of the formation of the universe. His most important work was in cosmology and he was instrumental in merging the fields of particle physics, nuclear physics, and astrophysics in the study of the early universe.

Schramm was born in St Louis, Missouri, on 25 October 1945 and received his MA and BS in physics from the Massachusetts Institute of Technology (MIT) in 1967, going on to study with William Fowler and Gerald Wasserberg at the California Institute of Technology (Caltech), receiving his PhD in 1971.

Schramm joined the faculty at the University of Chicago in 1974, becoming chairman of astronomy and physics 1977–82. He was instrumental in building the cosmology laboratory at Chicago into one of the world's best. He was given the title of Louis Block Distinguished Service Professor of Physical Sciences in 1982. As well as being an extraordinary scientist he was a brilliant teacher from the most elementary to the most advanced levels, and he achieved the faculty award for excellence in graduate teaching in 1994. From 1995 he was also a very effective vice president for research, with his ability to generate enthusiasm for scientific research in the public and the government. Schramm was piloting a twin engine plane on a flight to his second home in Aspen when he was killed at the age of 52 in a crash outside Denver, Colorado, on 19 December 1997.

One of Schramm's great contributions to cosmology was to calculate the number of families of elementary particles in the universe. At a time when two families were known and it was widely assumed that there were many more, he and his colleagues predicted that only one more family was waiting to be discovered. Physicists in Geneva and Stanford confirmed this in 1989. It was the first time astronomy had been crucial to a discovery in physics.

Schramm's work on light elements was fundamental to the Big Bang theory of the birth of the universe. He showed how elements such as lithium, helium, and hydrogen were produced in the Big Bang – work that instigated the new 'hot Big Bang theory'. He also calculated that ordinary matter comprised only a small fraction of the universe, predicting that it was largely made up of 'exotic dark matter'.

Schramm received numerous awards, among which were the Helen B Warner Prize from the American Astronomical Society in 1978 and the Julius Edgar Lilienfield Prize from the American Physical Society in 1993. He wrote and co-wrote over 300 papers and 15 books.

Schrödinger, Erwin (1887–1961) Austrian physicist who founded wave mechanics with the formulation of the Schrödinger wave equation to describe the behaviour of electrons in atoms. For this achievement, he was awarded the 1933 Nobel Peace Prize with Paul ◊Dirac and Werner ◊Heisenberg, who also made important advances in the theory of atomic structure.

Schrödinger was born in Vienna on 12 August 1887. His father was an oilcloth manufacturer who had studied chemistry and his mother was the daughter of a chemistry professor. Apart from a few weeks when he attended an elementary school in Innsbruck, Schrödinger received his early education from a private tutor. In 1898 he entered the Gymnasium in Vienna where he enjoyed mathematics, physics, and ancient languages. He then attended the University of Vienna, specializing in physics. Schrödinger obtained his doctorate in 1910 and a year later he became an assistant in the university's Second Physics Institute. His early research ranged over many topics in experimental and theoretical physics.

During World War I, Schrödinger served as an artillery officer and then returned to his previous post at Vienna. Conditions were difficult in Austria after the war and Schrödinger decided to go to Germany in 1920. After a series of short-lived posts at Jena, Stuttgart, and Breslau, he became professor of physics at Zürich in 1921.

Schrödinger's most productive work was done at Zürich and it resulted in his succeeding Max ◊Planck as professor of theoretical physics at Berlin in 1927. He remained there until the rise of the Nazis in 1933, when Schrödinger went to Oxford, England, where he became a fellow of Magdalen College. Homesick, he returned to Austria in 1936 to take up a post at Graz, but the Nazi takeover of Austria in 1938 placed Schrödinger in danger. The intervention of the prime minister of Ireland, Éamon de Valera (1882–1975), led to his appointment in 1939 to a post at the Institute for Advanced Studies in Dublin. Schrödinger continued work in theoretical physics there until 1956, when he returned to Austria to a chair at the University of Vienna. In the following year Schrödinger suffered a severe illness from which he never fully recovered. He died in Vienna on 4 January 1961.

The origin of Schrödinger's great discovery of wave mechanics began with the work of Louis ◊de Broglie, who, in 1924, using ideas from Albert ◊Einstein's special theory of relativity, showed that an electron or any other particle has a wave associated with it. The fundamental result was that:

$$\lambda = h/p$$

where λ is the wavelength of the associated wave, h is Planck's constant, and p is the momentum of the particle. An immediate deduction from this discovery was that if particles, and particularly electrons, have waves then – like sound and other kinds of waves – their behaviour should be capable of description by a particular type of partial differential equation known as a wave equation. These ideas were taken up by both de Broglie and Schrödinger and in 1926 each published

the same wave equation which, when written in relativistic terms, is:

$$\frac{1}{c^2}\frac{\delta^2\psi}{\delta t^2} = \frac{\delta^2\psi}{\delta x^2} + \frac{\delta^2\psi}{\delta y^2} + \frac{\delta^2\psi}{\delta z^2} - \frac{4\pi m^2 c^2}{h^2}\psi$$

where ψ is the wave function, t is the time, m is the mass of the electron, c is the velocity of light, h is Planck's constant, and x, y, and z represent the position of the electron in Cartesian coordinates. Unfortunately, while the equation is true, it was of very little help in developing further facts and explanations.

Later the same year, however, Schrödinger used a new approach. After spending some time studying the mathematics of partial differential equations and using the Hamiltonian function, a powerful idea in mechanics due to William Rowan ◊Hamilton, he formulated an equation in terms of the energies of the electron and the field in which it was situated. His new equation was:

$$\frac{\delta^2\psi}{\delta x^2} + \frac{\delta^2\psi}{\delta y^2} + \frac{\delta^2\psi}{\delta z^2} + \frac{8\pi^2 m}{h^2}(E - V)\psi = 0$$

where E is the total energy of the electron and V is the potential of the field in which the electron is moving. This equation neglects the small effects of special relativity. Partial differential equations have many solutions and very stringent conditions had to be fulfilled by the individual solutions of this equation in order for it to be useful in describing the electron. Among other things, they had to be finite and possess only one value. These solutions were associated with special values of E, known as proper values or eigenvalues. Schrödinger solved the equation for the hydrogen atom, where:

$$V = -e^2/r$$

e being the electron's charge and r is its distance from the nucleus, and found that the values of E corresponded with those of the energy levels given in the older theory of Niels ◊Bohr. Also, to each value of E there corresponded a finite number of particular solutions for the wave function ψ, and these could be associated with lines in the spectrum of atomic hydrogen. In the hydrogen atom the wave function describes where we can expect to find the electron, and it turns out that while it is most likely to be where Bohr predicted it to be, it does not follow a circular orbit but is described by the more complicated notion of an orbital, a region in space where the electron can be found with varying degrees of probability.

Atoms other than hydrogen and also molecules and ions can be described by Schrödinger's wave equation but such cases are very difficult to solve. In certain cases approximations have been used, usually with the numerical work being carried out on a computer.

Schrödinger's mathematical description of electron waves found immediate acceptance because these waves could be visualized as standing waves around the nucleus. In 1925, a year before Schrödinger published his results, a mathematical system called matrix mechanics, developed by Max ◊Born and Werner Heisenberg had also succeeded in describing the structure of the atom but it was totally theoretical and gave no picture of the atom. Schrödinger's vindication of de Broglie's picture of electron waves immediately overturned matrix mechanics, though it was later shown that wave mechanics is equivalent to matrix mechanics.

The task is ... to think what nobody has yet thought, about that which everybody sees.

ERWIN SCHRÖDINGER L BERTALANFFY PROBLEMS OF LIFE 1952

During his later years, Schrödinger became increasingly worried by the way quantum mechanics, of which wave mechanics is a part, was interpreted, in particular with the probabilistic nature of the wave function. Schrödinger believed he had given a great description to the atom in the same way that Isaac ◊Newton's laws described mechanics and James Clerk ◊Maxwell's equations described electrodynamics, only to find that the structure of the atom became increasingly more difficult to describe explicitly with each new discovery. Much of his later work was concerned with philosophy, particularly as applied to physics and the atom.

Schrödinger made a fundamental contribution to physics in finally producing a solid mathematical explanation of the quantum theory first advanced by Planck in 1900, and the subsequent structures of the atom formulated by Bohr and de Broglie.

Further Reading

Bitbol, Michel, *Schrödinger's Philosophy of Quantum Mechanics,* Boston Studies in the Philosophy of Science series, Kluwer Academic Publishers, 1996, v 188.

Gotschl, Johann (ed), *Erwin Schrödinger's World View: The Dynamics of Knowledge and Reality,* Kluwer Academic Publishers, 1992.

Kilmister, C W, *Schrödinger: Centenary Celebration of a Polymath,* Cambridge University Press, 1987.

Moore, Walter J A, *Erwin Schrödinger: A Life,* Cambridge University Press, 1994.

Schwabe, Samuel Heinrich (1789–1875)

German chemist and astronomer who was the first person to measure the periodicity of the sunspot cycle.

Schwabe was born in Dessau on 25 October 1789; his father was a doctor and his mother ran a pharmacy.

Educated in Berlin, he entered his mother's business as a pharmacist at the age of 17. Three years later he returned to Berlin and took up pharmaceutical studies at the university there, under Martin ◊Klaproth. It was at the university that he became absorbed in both astronomy and botany. His two years' course over, Schwabe went back to the pharmacy in 1812. Seventeen years later his amateur astronomical research – particularly his study of sunspots – became engrossing. He sold his pharmacy business and became an astronomer. As a result of his work he was presented with the Royal Astronomical Society's Gold Medal in 1857 and was elected to the Royal Society in 1868. During his lifetime he published no fewer than 109 scientific papers, and after his death – which occurred on 11 April 1875 – 31 volumes of his astronomical data were presented to the Royal Astronomical Society. They are stored in its archives.

Wanting to commence his astronomical research while still a pharmacist, Schwabe looked for some branch of astronomy that would occupy him during the daytime. His first thought was that he might find a new planet close to the Sun – inside the orbit of Mercury – spotting it as it passed in front of the Sun's disc. He began to watch the Sun in 1825 with a small 5-cm/2-in telescope and could not help but notice sunspots. After a while he forgot his hopes of discovering an intramercurial planet and concentrated on the sunspots, making daily counts of them for most of the rest of his life. Day after day, year after year, he tabulated his results under four headings: the year, the number of sunspots, the number of days free from sunspots, and the number of days when observations were made. Schwabe realized that with his modest apparatus, in a private observatory, numerical determinations were problematical. He acknowledged that on days when there were large numbers of sunspots, it was more than probable that he underestimated the total. Nevertheless, after carefully collating his results, his patience was rewarded when, in 1843, he was able to announce a periodicity. He declared that the sunspots waxed and waned in number according to a ten-year cycle.

His discovery was ignored at the time, but in 1851 it was republished by the explorer and naturalist Alexander von ◊Humboldt in his book *Kosmos* and given the recognition it deserved. Immediately afterwards, Rudolf Wolf of Berne collated all existing support data in other astronomical records, recalculated the value of the periodicity more accurately, and fixed it at 11.1 years.

Schwabe's revelation of the periodicity – which may be considered as marking the precise beginning of solar physics – was all the more remarkable because Joseph ◊Lalande and Jean-Baptiste Delambre

(1749–1822) had previously considered such an investigation and decided it would not be profitable. In 1851, the year the more accurate value for the periodicity was set, the period was first linked with the occurrence of magnetic storms. It was not long before Johann von Lamont (1805–1879) showed that the sunspot cycle had further effects upon the Earth in terms of magnetic disturbances, weather conditions, and plant and animal growth rates. Nor was it long before astronomers began using the photo-heliograph in order to keep daily counts of sunspots.

Although Schwabe was preoccupied with his sunspot counts on every sunny day, he nevertheless found the time for other astronomical research. In December 1827 he rediscovered the eccentricity of Saturn's rings. Four years later he drew a picture of the planet Jupiter on which the Great Red Spot was shown for the first time. And he also found time to write scientific papers on the phenomena of frost patterns, haze, and rock sources.

Schwann, Theodor (1810–1882)

Schwann, Theodor (1810–1882) German physiologist who, with Matthias ◊Schleiden, is credited with formulating the cell theory, one of the most fundamental of all concepts in biology. Schwann also did important work on digestion, fermentation, and histology.

Schwann was born on 7 December 1810 in Neuss. He was educated at the Jesuit college in Cologne then studied medicine at the universities of Bonn, Würzburg, and Berlin, graduating from the last in 1834. He spent the next four years – the most scientifically productive period in his life – working as an assistant to the German physiologist Johannes ◊Müller at the Museum of Anatomy in Berlin. In 1839, however, Schwann's work on fermentation attracted so much adverse criticism that he left Germany for Belgium, where he was professor of anatomy at the Roman Catholic University in Louvain 1839–48, then held the same post at the University of Liège until his death in Cologne on 11 January 1882.

In 1834 Schwann began to investigate digestive processes and two years later isolated from the lining of the stomach a chemical responsible for protein digestion, which he called pepsin. This was the first enzyme to be isolated from animal tissue, although Anselme Payan, a French chemist, had isolated an enzyme from malt in 1833. Schwann then studied fermentation and between 1836 and 1837 showed that the fermentation of sugar is a result of the life processes of living yeast cells (he later coined the term 'metabolism' to denote the chemical changes that occur in living tissue). This work on fermentation was later criticized heavily, especially by the German chemists Friedrich ◊Wöhler and Justus von ◊Liebig, and this led to Schwann leaving

Germany. It was not until Louis ◊Pasteur's work on fermentation in the 1850s that Schwann was proved correct. Meanwhile, however, Schwann investigated putrefaction in an attempt to disprove the theory of spontaneous generation (which had once again become a matter of debate) repeating, with improved techniques, Lazzaro ◊Spallanzani's earlier experiments. Like Spallanzani, Schwann found no evidence to support the theory, despite which it was still believed by some scientists.

In 1839 Schwann published *Mikroskopische Untersuchungen über die Überreinstimmung in der Struktur und dem Wachstum der Tiere und Pflanzen* (translated in 1847 as *Microscopical Researches on the Similarity in the Structure and Growth of Animals and Plants*) in which he formulated the cell theory. In the previous year Matthias Schleiden – whom Schwann knew well – had stated the theory in connection with plants, but it was Schwann who extended the theory to animals and enunciated it in its clearest form.

Schwann and Schleiden are therefore generally credited as co-formulators of the cell theory. Giving numerous examples from many different types of animal tissues, Schwann in his *Microscopical Researches* concluded that all organisms (both animals and plants) consist entirely of cells or of products of cells and that the life of each individual cell is subordinated to that of the whole organism. The cell theory soon became widely accepted and is today recognized as being one of the most important concepts in biology.

Schwann also discovered the cells (now called Schwann cells) that make up the myelin sheath surrounding peripheral nerve axons, and the striated muscle in the upper region of the oesophagus. In addition, he noted that an egg is a single cell that eventually develops into a complex organism – a basic principle in embryology.

Schwarzschild, Karl (1873–1916)

Schwarzschild, Karl (1873–1916) German astronomer and theoretician who achieved great things despite a short life span. In addition to the conceptual work he carried out, he was a practical man who designed and constructed some of his own instruments and devised considerable improvements in the use of photography for astronomical purposes.

Schwarzschild was born in Frankfurt on 9 October 1873, the eldest of a family of five sons and one daughter. His father was a prosperous member of the Jewish business community in Frankfurt, and Schwarzschild spent a happy childhood surrounded by relatives who were talented in art and music. The first in his family to be scientific, he was educated at the local municipal school; in 1891 he went to Strasbourg Univeristy and spent two years there. He then continued his studies at Munich University. After graduating, he became an assistant at the Kuffner Observatory in Ottakring, Vienna, and in 1901 he was appointed associate professor at the University of Göttingen, where the observatory had been equipped by Karl ◊Gauss 80 years previously. In the following year he was appointed full professor at the age of only 28, and he was also made director of the observatory. He left Göttingen in 1909 to succeed Hermann ◊Vogel as director of the Astrophysical Observatory at Potsdam. At the outbreak of World War I he volunteered for service and was sent to Belgium to work at a weather station. He was then transferred to France to calculate trajectories for long-range shells, and to the Eastern Front, in Russia, where he contracted pemphigus, a metabolic disease of the skin that was then incurable. He died in Potsdam, Germany, on 11 May 1916. By his own request he was buried in Göttingen. For his war work he was awarded a posthumous Iron Cross, and in 1960 the Berlin Academy honoured him as the greatest German astronomer of the preceding century.

At secondary school, Schwarzschild bought himself some lenses in order to make a telescope. Aware of the boy's interest, his father introduced him to J Epstein, a mathematician and owner of a private observatory. Under the guidance of Epstein's son – later to become professor of mathematics at the University of Strasbourg – Schwarzschild gained his knowledge of the telescope, at the same time studying advanced mathematics and celestial mechanics. His first published work was a paper on celestial orbits, written at the age of 16. The subject of his PhD thesis was Henri ◊Poincaré's theory of stable configurations in rotating bodies and its application to particular astronomical problems. He investigated the tidal deformation in satellites and the validity of Pierre ◊Laplace's theory on the origin of the Solar System. Even before he graduated, he had devised a multi-slit interferometer enabling him to measure the distance between close double stars. Between 1896 and 1899 he gave lectures that conveyed an infectious natural enthusiasm to non-astronomers and were to become famous.

In observational astronomy Schwarzschild was the first to apply precise methods using photographic photometry, substituting a photographic plate at the telescope in place of the eye and measuring densities with a photometer. He photographed an aggregate of 367 stars and presented the results to the University of Munich as credentials to entitle him to teach there.

In 1900, he suggested that the geometry of space was possibly not in conformity with Euclidean principles. (This was 16 years before the publication of Albert ◊Einstein's general theory of relativity.)

He introduced the concept of radiative equilibrium in astrophysics and was probably the first to see how radiative processes were important in conveying heat in stellar atmospheres. 1906 saw the publication of his work on the transfer of energy at and close to the solar surface. He observed the total solar eclipse on 30 August 1905, and obtained spectrograms, using a camera fitted with an objective prism, which gave information on the chemical composition of regions at various heights on the Sun. He also developed methods and techniques later to become standard in the preparation of stellar statistics.

In 1910 Schwarzschild made measurements from the photographs of Halley's comet taken by the Potsdam expedition to Tenerife, and suggested that fluorescent radiation occurs in the tails of comets. In spectroscopy, he devised a spectrographic system that provided an efficient and accurate way to determine the radial velocities of stars. He then made further important contributions to geometric optics and to the theory behind the design of optical instruments.

Although primarily an astronomer, he was also a theoretical physicist and was one of the great promoters of Niels ◊Bohr's theory of atomic spectra. As he lay dying, he completed a famous paper, in which he developed the 'rules of quantization'. (Work carried out independently by Arnold ◊Sommerfeld gave the theory of the Stark effect and the quantum theory of molecular structure.) These last papers also dealt with the gravitational field of a point mass in empty space and gave the first exact solution of Einstein's field equations.

Schwarzschild, Martin (1912–1997) German-born US astronomer whose most important work was in the field of stellar structure and evolution.

Schwarzschild was born in Potsdam on 31 May 1912, the son of the astronomer and mathematician Karl ◊Schwarzschild. Schwarzschild the younger was educated at the University of Göttingen, where he obtained a PhD in astronomy in 1935. He then emigrated to the USA, eventually becoming a naturalized US citizen. He was Nansen Fellow at the University of Oslo 1936–37 and a Littauer Fellow at Harvard University 1937–40. In 1940 he was made a lecturer in astronomy at Columbia University, later becoming assistant professor in 1944 and professor in 1947. From 1951 Schwarzschild held the position of Eugene Higgins Professor of Astronomy at Princeton University. He was a member of the National Academy of Sciences and the American Astronomical Society, of which he was president 1970–72.

Schwarzschild's research was primarily concerned with the theory of stellar structure and evolution. He wrote numerous articles on the internal constitution of stars and has made astronomical observations with telescopes carried by balloons into the stratosphere. In 1959 he obtained structural details of the surface of the

Sun and photographs of sunspot penumbrae by using a balloon-supported solar telescope at 24,385 m/ 80,032 ft.

Arthur ◊Eddington was interested in the fact that whereas stars differ greatly in brightness, density, and in some physical properties, they differ relatively little in mass. By 1926 the range of known stellar masses lay from 1/6 to 100 times that of the Sun. Since then the upper limit has been reduced and much of the work on assessing these limits was done by Schwarzschild. It is now thought that the upper limit may be only 65 solar masses. The smallest stellar masses known are about 1/100 that of the Sun or about 10 times the mass of Jupiter.

Schwarzschild also worked out a quantity (Z_{He}) for the total mass density of the elements heavier than helium, using the density of hydrogen as one unit. The values of Z_{He} are smallest for old stars (0.003) and largest for young stars (0.04), implying that the most recently formed stellar objects were formed out of a medium of interstellar gas and dust that was already enriched with heavy elements. These elements were probably produced in stellar interiors and expelled by the oldest stars.

Schwarzschild was also involved with what is known as pulsation theory. In 1879, even before variations in radial velocities were known, Arthur Ritter had considered the periodic expansions and contractions of a star, termed radial pulsations. In 1938 Schwarzschild suggested that the star's deepest interior pulsates, but that in the outermost regions the elements of gas do not all vibrate in unison, causing a lag in the light curve by the observed amount.

Throughout his distinguished career, Schwarzschild made an enormous contribution to our understanding of the dynamics and structure of stellar objects.

Scott, Peter Markham (1909–1989) English ornithologist and artist best known for his bird paintings, book illustrations, and wildlife conservation work, including the foundation of the Wildfowl Trust at Slimbridge, Gloucestershire. He received numerous honours from many different countries, including several honorary degrees and, in 1973, a knighthood.

Scott was born on 14 September 1909, the son of Captain Robert Falcon Scott (1868–1912), the Antarctic explorer. He was educated at Oundle School, from which he went to Trinity College, Cambridge, then to the Munich State Academy and finally to the Royal Academy School, London. In 1936 he represented the UK in the Olympic Games, gaining a bronze medal for the single-handed sailing event. During World War II he served with the Royal Navy, and after the war, in 1946, founded the Wildfowl Trust. In 1949 he led his first expedition, which was to explore the uncharted Perry River area in the Canadian Arctic, and in 1951 and 1953 he led expeditions to Iceland to mark geese. In addition, Scott also led ornithological expeditions to Australasia, the Galápagos Islands, the Seychelles, and the Antarctic. From 1961 to 1967 he was the first president of the World Wildlife Fund. In 1963 he became chair of the Survival Service Commission of the International Union for the Conservation of Nature and Natural Resources, and in 1969 he was made president of the Wildlife Youth Service. He became chancellor of Birmingham University in 1974.

Scott did much to promote wildlife conservation, particularly of birds. The Wildfowl Trust contains hundreds of species of birds and attracts thousands of visitors each year. In addition to his conservation work, he made numerous television appearances and wrote several books – including *Key to the Wild Fowl of the World* (1949), *Wild Geese and Eskimos* (1951), and *The Eye of the Wind* (1961) – and illustrated many others, most notably *The Snow Goose,* a novel by Paul Gallico, and *The Swans* (in collaboration with the Wildfowl Trust).

Further Reading
Huxley, Elspeth, *Peter Scott: Painter and Naturalist,* Faber and Faber, 1993.
Scott, Peter Markham; Weston-Smith, Miranda (ed), *Travel Diaries of a Naturalist,* Collins, 1983–85, 2 vols.
Scott, Peter Markham; Scott, Philippa (ed), *The Art of Peter Scott: Images from a Lifetime,* 1992.

Seaborg, Glenn Theodore (1912–1999) US physical chemist who was best known for his researches on the synthetic transuranic elements. For this work he shared the 1951 Nobel Prize for Chemistry with his co-worker Edwin McMillan (1907–1991).

Seaborg was born in Ishpeming, Michigan, on 19 April 1912 into a Swedish immigrant family; his father was a machinist. When he was ten years old the family moved to Los Angeles, where he graduated from high school in 1929. He went to study literature at the University of California but changed to science and graduated in 1934. He then went to study at Berkeley under Gilbert ◊Lewis, gaining his PhD in 1937 and spending a further two years as one of Lewis's research associates; he became an instructor in 1939. During part of World War II Seaborg was a section chief at the metallurgical laboratory at Chicago University, where much of the early work on the atomic bomb was carried out. After the war, in 1945, he was appointed professor of chemistry and director of nuclear chemical research at the Lawrence Radiation Laboratory at Berkeley, becoming associate director of the laboratory 1954–61 and chancellor of the campus 1958–61. In 1961 he was made chair of the US Atomic Energy Commission and held the appointment for ten years. He returned to the Lawrence Radiation Laboratory in 1971 to resume his post as associate director (until 1975) and to become university professor of chemistry. He died on 18 February 1999.

The transuranic elements are all those that lie beyond uranium in the periodic table, that is, all elements of atomic number higher than 92. They constitute the majority of the actinides (elements 89 to 103), so-called by analogy with the lanthanides or rare earths. They are all radioactive and none occurs to any appreciable extent in nature; they are synthesized by transmutation reactions. In the early 1970s, Seaborg was involved in the identification of ten new transuranic elements: plutonium (atomic number 94), americium (95), curium (96), berkelium (97), californium (98), einsteinium (99), fermium (100), mendelevium (101), nobelium (102), and unnilhexium (106). In 1997, unnilhexium was officially named seaborgium (symbol Sg) in his honour.

Seaborg and his collaborators discovered plutonium in 1940 by bombarding uranium with deuterons in the Berkeley 152-cm/60-in cyclotron. The first isotope found had a mass of 238, and the more important (because it is fissionable) plutonium-239 was discovered in 1941 (by neutron bombardment of U-238). In 1944 helium bombardment of Pu-239 yielded Cm-242, the first isotope of curium. Americium, as Am-241, was identified by Seaborg and others at the Metallurgical Laboratory 1944–45. Helium bombardment of Am-241 at Berkeley produced berkelium (as Bk-249) at the end of 1949, and three months later the minute amount of Cm-242 available was also bombarded with helium to form the californium isotope Cf-245. Einsteinium was identified in the debris from the 'Mike' nuclear explosion staged by the Los Alamos Scientific Laboratory in November 1952, where it arose from the radioactive decay of heavy uranium isotopes. Another decay product, fermium-255, was discovered in January 1953. Helium bombardment was again used in early 1955 to create mendelevium-256 out of Es-253. Nobelium, element 102, was discovered in spring 1957 at the Nobel Institute of Physics in Stockholm. In 1974 he was involved in the discovery of the transactinide element seaborgium, element 106, which was created by a Berkeley team led by Albert Ghiorso by bombarding californium-249 with oxygen nuclei.

As chair of the Atomic Energy Commission, Seaborg encouraged the rapid growth of the US nuclear power industry. Many of the isotopes he discovered have also found other uses in industry and in medicine.

Further Reading

Kauffmann, George R, 'Transuranium pioneer: Glenn T Seaborg', *Today's Chemist*, 1991, v 4 (3), pp 18–20, 23, 24, 32.

Seaborg, Glenn T, *A Chemist in the White House: From the Manhattan Project to the End of the Cold War*, American Chemical Society, 1997.

Seaborg, Glenn T, *A Scientist Speaks Out: A Personal Perspective on Science, Society and Change*, World Scientific Publishing Co, 1996.

Seaborg, Glenn T; Kathren, Ronald L, Gough, Jerry B, and Benfield, Gary T (eds), *The Plutonium Story: The Journals of Professor Glenn T Seaborg, 1939–1946*, Battelle Press, 1994.

Secchi, (Angelo) Pietro (1818–1878) Italian astronomer and physicist famous for his work on solar phenomena, stellar spectroscopy, and spectral classification.

Secchi was born on 18 June 1818 in Reggio. At the age of 25 he joined the Jesuit order (Society of Jesus) and trained to become a Jesuit priest before becoming a lecturer in physics and mathematics at the Collegio Romano in 1839. In 1848 he was driven into exile for being a Jesuit and went first to Stonyhurst College, England, then to Georgetown University in Washington, DC, where he continued his mathematical and scientific work. In 1849 he was appointed director of the Gregonia University Observatory at the Collegio Romano and professor of astronomy there. He was made a member of the Royal Society in 1856. He died on 26 February 1878 in Rome.

While the Collegio Romano was in papal hands there was no lack of funds for the observatory. There were plenty of assistants and good equipment. Secchi's memoirs testify to the variety of fields in which he researched, and his position gave him the facilities for gaining the widest publicity for his work. He wrote many papers in astronomy, magnetism, and meteorology.

Secchi's interest in solar physics was aroused in the USA, where he assisted in the first experiments on the heat radiated at different locations on the Sun's disc. His interest in spectroscopy dates from a visit of Jules César ◊Janssen to Rome.

When Secchi returned to Rome in 1849 he equipped his new observatory with a Merz refractor and with this he carried out research into stellar spectroscopy, terrestrial magnetism, and meteorology. With William ◊Huggins, Secchi was the first person to adapt spectroscopy to astronomy in a systematic manner and he made the first spectroscopic survey of the heavens. He pointed out that stellar spectra differ from one another and that stars differ in other respects than brightness, position, and colour. He proposed that the differences in stellar spectra reflected differences in the stars' chemical composition.

In 1867 Secchi suggested the establishment of spectral classes of stars and he divided the spectra he had studied into four groups. Data accumulated since Secchi's day have necessitated a considerably more complex division, but his classification led to schemes of stellar evolution. His groups were based on stars like Sirus, with strong hydrogen lines; stars similar to the Sun, with numerous fine spectral lines; stars of the Herculis type, with nebulous bands towards the red end of the spectrum; and carbon stars with bands in the violet end of the spectrum. The modern system of spectral classification is based on these four groups.

Secchi's other work included photographing the solar eclipse of 1860 in Spain and observing one in Sicily in 1870. In 1867 he demonstrated his universal meteorograph in the Paris Exhibition and gave lectures, some of which eventually formed the basis of his book on the Sun. He also proved that prominences are appendages of the Sun and he determined many features of their behaviour. He was an active observer of double stars and, with Warren ◊de la Rue and William Cranch ◊Bond, was among the first to use the new technique of photography for astronomical purposes. By 1859 he had a complete set of photographs of the Moon. Towards the end of his life, Secchi founded the Società degli Spettroscopisti Italiani, a society formed for the recording of daily spectroscopic observations of the Sun, mainly from various observatories in Italy.

Secchi achieved a great deal during his lifetime. Before outlining his stellar classification he examined 4,000 stars. He observed comets, meteors, and planets – in particular Jupiter, Saturn, and Mars. He published his findings in many volumes and he belonged to most scientific societies of the day. Much of our modern knowledge of astronomy has its roots in Secchi's findings.

Sedgwick, Adam (1785–1873) English geologist who contributed greatly to the understanding of the stratigraphy of the British Isles.

The son of the curate of Dent in northwest Yorkshire, Sedgwick attended Trinity College, Cambridge, where he studied mathematics. He became a fellow of the college in 1810, and was ordained priest in 1818. Though supposedly knowing no geology, he was appointed Woodwardian professor in 1818, holding the chair until his death, 55 years later. He soon made himself, however, one of the most eminent British geologists. An energetic champion of fieldwork, Sedgwick explored such diverse districts as the Isle of Wight, Devon and Cornwall, the Lake District, and northeast England. In the 1830s, he unravelled the stratigraphic sequence of fossil-bearing rocks in north Wales, describing the oldest of them as belonging to the Cambrian period (now dated at 570–510 million

years ago). In south Wales, his companion Roderick ◊Murchison had concurrently developed the Silurian system. The question of where the boundary lay between the older Cambrian and the younger Silurian sparked a celebrated dispute that rumbled on for almost 40 years and was resolved only after their deaths, when in 1879 Charles Lapworth coined the term 'Ordovician' for the middle ground. With Murchison, Sedgwick also identified the Devonian system in southwest England.

Sedgwick commended a highly empirical approach to geological investigation, seeing facts founded on fieldwork as the bedrock of the science. He combined this with passionate Christian convictions. He deplored James ◊Hutton's and Charles ◊Lyell's uniformitarianism; he was suspicious of glacial theory; and completely rejected all theories of evolution, not least those of his former pupil and friend Charles ◊Darwin. Despite these blindspots, Sedgwick shone in two spheres. He was a supreme student of palaeontology, especially of Palaeozoic fossils; and he contributed greatly to our understanding of stratigraphy and geological time, using fossils as an index of relative time, and assuming relatively distinct fauna and flora for each period.

Further Reading

Clark, John Willis and Hughes, Thomas McKenny, *The Life and Letters of the Reverend Adam Sedgwick,* Cambridge University Press, 1890.

Speakman, Colin, *Adam Sedgwick – Geologist and Dalesman, 1785–1873: A Biography in Twelve Themes,* Broad Oak Press, 1982.

Segrè, Emilio Gino (1905–1989) Italian physicist who shared the 1959 Nobel prize for discovering the antiproton (the antiparticle of the proton). He also discovered many new radioactive elements and pioneered the use of thermalized neutrons in experiments.

Segrè was born on 1 February 1905 in Tivoli near Rome. He went to the University of Rome to study engineering but switched to physics in his fourth year, having met Enrico ◊Fermi, who had just arrived in Rome as professor of theoretical physics. He obtained his PhD in 1928 for research into the spectroscopy of lithium. At this time the Rome group were building up expertise in atomic and molecular physics – Segrè had visited Pieter ◊Zeeman's laboratory in Amsterdam and Otto ◊Stern's laboratory in Hamburg – but Fermi reckoned the most interesting physics would be found in the nucleus. In 1934 Irè and Frédéric ◊Joliot-Curie proved him right with their discovery of artificial radioactivity using alpha-particle bombardment. Fermi predicted neutron bombardment would be even better and, as Segrè said, 'we made a discovery practically every week'. Segrè was appointed professor at the University of Palermo in 1936 and quickly he discovered a new element in some old parts from an accelerator at Berkeley that had been heavily radiated by deuterons. The parts were made from molybdenum (atomic number 42) and Segrè called the new element, which had the atomic number 43, technetium (from the Greek for 'artificial'). However, in 1938, during a visit to Berkeley, Mussolini's anti-Semitic laws forced Segrè, a Jew, to remain in the USA. With the exception of wartime research at Los Alamos, Segrè remained at Berkeley for the rest of his career, and was appointed a professor in the physics department in 1947. In 1944 he became a US citizen.

Working with Dale Corson and Kenneth Mackenzie in 1940, Segrè discovered another new element, now called astatine (atomic number 85). In December he again met up with Fermi, now at Columbia University in New York, to discuss using plutonium-239 instead of uranium-235 in atomic bombs. Segrè began working on the production of plutonium at Berkeley and then moved to Los Alamos to study the spontaneous fission of uranium and plutonium isotopes. In 1947 Segrè started work on proton–proton and proton–neutron interaction at the new 467-cm/184-in cyclotron accelerator at Berkeley, switching to the more energetic Bevatron machine in the early 1950s. The Bevatron accelerated protons to 6 billion electron-volts and when this proton beam struck a metal target inside the accelerator, it produced a negative beam composed mostly of pions, muons, and electrons. Using time-of-flight techniques Segrè, Owen Chamberlain (1920–   ), Clyde Wiegand (1915–1996), and others were able to detect the antiproton among these other particles. Antiparticles were a prediction of Paul ◊Dirac's combination of special relativity and quantum mechanics. Although antielectrons (or positrons) had been observed a mere four years after their prediction by Dirac in 1928 – Carl ◊Anderson detected them in cosmic rays in 1932 – physicists had been waiting more than 20 years for the antiproton. Segrè and Chamberlain's discovery, for which they shared the 1959 Nobel prize, confirmed that Dirac's relativistic quantum theory was correct.

Segrè was also well-known for his editing and writing, including a biography of Fermi. He died in Berkeley on 22 April 1989.

Seguin, Marc (1786–1875) French engineer who, in 1825, built the first successful suspension bridge in Europe using cables of iron wire. He also invented the tubular boiler.

Seguin was born in Annonay, Ardèche, on 20 April 1786. He obtained his early education at a small boarding school in Paris, but was self-taught in engineering science. He had arrived in Paris at the age of 13 where his interest in engineering was stimulated by his close contact with his great-uncle Joseph Montgolfier (see Joseph and Jacques ◊Montgolfier). Shortly after Montgolfier's death in 1810, Seguin returned to Annonay.

In 1825, in association with Henri Dufour (1786–1875), using wire cables, Seguin erected the first suspension bridge of its kind in Europe. This bridge was built at Geneva and, over the next 20 years, Seguin and his brothers erected other cable suspension bridges in France – beginning with the one over the River Rhône at Tournon in 1827.

Seguin, again with his brothers, tried to establish a steamboat service on the Rhône, and later turned his attention to railways. He was successful in establishing France's first modern railway between Lyon and Saint-Etienne, completed in 1832. He discovered that the Stephenson steam engine then available was not capable of generating enough power for the high-speed operation he desired, so he invented a new type of boiler – the multi-tabular or fire-tube boiler.

By the time Seguin retired from active work in engineering in 1838, he had produced engineering projects that provided some of the earliest examples of large-scale civil engineering in France. In recognition of his services he was elected corresponding member of the Académie des Sciences in 1845.

Besides practical engineering, Seguin showed a great interest in problems involving heat and light. He published his first statements on the subject, made in 1824 and 1825, in a Scottish journal. He argued that matter consists of small, dense molecules constantly on the move in miniature solar systems and he maintained that magnetic, electrical, and thermal phenomena were the result of their particular velocities and particular orbits. He identified heat as molecular velocity and explained the conversion to a mechanical effect by stating that this occurs when the molecules transmit their velocities to external objects. In 1839 he published his *De l'Influence des chemins de fer* in which he rejected the calorific theory then dominant in France because it implied perpetual motion due to the supposed existence of heat as a fluid conserved in all processes. Seguin assumed that a certain amount of heat disappeared in the very act of the production of mechanical power and that the converse was equally true. He tried to determine the numerical relationship between heat and mechanical power and, in a table of results, he showed that the heat loss as measured by a thermometer was not a true indication of the heat lost by the steam producing the power. However, he was unable to specify a relationship between temperature loss and loss of heat content. He could not, therefore, define a unit of heat or state its mechanical equivalent.

When James ◊Joule succeeded in determining the mechanical equivalent of heat in 1847, Seguin supported his conclusions. Later Seguin attempted to claim priority over Joule, but it was decided that only in retrospect could the suggestions that Seguin made in 1839 be interpreted as a mechanical equivalent of heat. In 1853, Seguin published a weekly scientific magazine called *Cosmos,* and this became an important vehicle for the popularization of science in France. It also served as a forum for Seguin's theories including his particle theories for heat, light, electricity, and magnetism.

Seki Kowa (c.1642–1708) Also called Seki Takakazu. Japanese mathematician who did much to change the role of mathematics in his society; from being an art form indulged in by intellectuals at leisure, he made it a science. To do this he not only created a basic social paradigm embodying scientific curiosity, he even found himself obliged to create a new mathematical notation system. Using his new techniques, Seki discovered many of the theorems and theories that were being – or were shortly to be – discovered in the West. It is likely, for example, that he derived the determinant (part of a method to solve linear equations) before Gottfried ◊Leibniz did in 1693. In his own country Seki is sometimes referred to as 'the sacred mathematician'.

Seki was born probably in Fujioka in Gunma prefecture in about the year 1642 – the exact date is unknown, and even his birthplace is the subject of some doubt. His father's name was Nagaakira Utiyama, but he was adopted by the Seki family and was known either as Seki Kowa or Seki Takakazu. Nothing is known about his life, other than his efforts to popularize mathematics, except that the date of his death has been definitely established as 24 October 1708; he died in what is now called Tokyo.

Much of Seki's reputation stems from the social reform he introduced in order to develop the study of mathematics in Japan. By the time of his death, anyone could take an interest in the subject, and could teach others – although the books available for instruction were still couched in the formal (and possibly condescending) terms of the literati of society. Seki himself was much influenced by the book of Chu Shih-Chieh, which dealt with the solution of problems by transforming them into a one-variable algebraic equation. The challenge of the book was that it contained problems that the author declared to be unsolvable; Seki solved many of these using methods of his own devising. He introduced Chinese ideograms to represent unknowns and variables in equations, and although he was obliged to confine his work to equations up to the fifth degree – his algebraic alphabet (*endan-jutsu*) was not suitable for general equations of the nth degree –

he was able to create equations with literal coefficients of any degree and with several variables, and to solve simultaneous equations.

In this way he was able to derive the equivalent of $f(x)$, and thereby to arrive at the notion of a discriminant – a special function of the root of an equation expressible in terms of the coefficients.

Another of Seki's important contributions was the mathematically rigorous definition (rectification) of the circumference of a circle; he obtained a value for π that was correct to the 18th decimal place. Further work included the rectification of a circular arc and the curvature of a sphere. He established a theorem relating to the solid that results from the revolving of a segment of a circle about a straight line that is in the same plane as the segment. (This theorem was substantially the same as the well known theorem of ◊Pappus of Alexandria.)

Seki is also credited with major discoveries in calculus. He developed a method of finding the approximate value of the root of a numerical equation and also evolved a method of determining the coefficients of an expression in the form:

$$y = a_1x + a_2x^2 + ... + a_nx^n$$

which was similar to the method of finite difference.

Semenov, Nikolai Nikolaevich (1896–1986) Russian physical chemist who studied chemical chain reactions, particularly branched-chain reactions that can accelerate with explosive velocity. For his work in this area he shared the 1956 Nobel Prize for Chemistry (the first Soviet Nobel prizewinner) with the English physical chemist Cyril ◊Hinshelwood.

Semenov was born on 3 April 1896 in Saratov. In 1913 he went to the University of Petrograd (now St Petersburg) and despite the turmoil of World War I and the Russian Revolution he graduated in 1917. During the next 25 years he held appointments at various research establishments in Leningrad (as Petrograd had become). From 1920 to 1931 he worked at the AFI or Physical-Technical Institute, becoming a professor in 1928. From 1931 he directed the Institute of Chemical Physics at the Soviet Academy of Sciences before moving to the Moscow State University in 1944, where he became head of the department of chemical kinetics.

In 1913 Max Bodenstein introduced the idea of a chain reaction to account for various gas reactions. Semenov developed this theory in the 1920s and showed how certain violently explosive reactions – particularly those involving combustion – can be explained in terms of branching chains: each branch in the reaction pathway starts more than one new reaction, thus rapidly accelerating the overall effect. He summarized his results in 1934 in his influential book *Chemical Kinetics and Chain Reactions* (English translation, 1935).

Semenov also played an important part in resisting narrow interpretations of Marxist-Leninism in its application to chemistry. In this way he helped to keep Soviet chemistry progressing and avoiding unprofitable detours such as that caused by Lysenkoism (see Trofim ◊Lysenko) in biology.

Seyfert, Carl Keenan (1911–1960) US astronomer and astrophysicist whose interests in photometry, the spectra of stars and galaxies, and the structure of the Milky Way resulted in the identification and study of the type of galaxy that now bears his name.

Seyfert was born on 11 February 1911 in Cleveland, Ohio. He graduated from Harvard with a BSc in 1933, gaining an MA two years later. His PhD in astronomy was awarded in 1936 while he was Parker Fellow at Harvard. Before joining the Mount Wilson Observatory as national research fellow in 1940, Seyfert worked at the McDonald Observatory in Chicago for four years, carrying out research on the spectra of stars in the Milky Way. He was director of Barnard Observatory 1946–51 and then he was appointed professor of astronomy at Vanderbilt University, where he became director of the Arthur S Dyer Observatory.

Apart from his research work in astronomy, Seyfert held a number of administrative posts, the most important of which was as civilian member of the National Defence Research Committee. He was a member of the International Astronomical Union and the American Astronomical Society and was a fellow of the Royal Astronomical Society. He died on 13 June 1960 in Cleveland.

In 1943 Seyfert was studying a series of 12 active spiral galaxies that possess barely perceivable arms and exceptionally bright nuclei. His investigations showed that these galaxies contain small, unusually bright nuclei, often bluish in colour, and have distinctive spectral lines denoting the emission of radio waves and infrared energy. The highly excited spectra of these galaxies showed that they contain hydrogen as well as ionized oxygen, nitrogen, and neon. Sulphur, iron, and argon were also common to such galaxies. On the basis of their spectra, Seyfert divided the galaxies into two types, I and II.

Radiation from the nuclei of the galaxies is due to the very hot gases that they contain at their centres. The gases are subject to explosions that cause them to move violently, with speeds of many thousands of kilometres per second relative to the centre of the galaxy in the case of Type I, and of several hundreds of kilometres per second in the case of Type II galaxies. Seyfert

galaxies also emit a fairly large quantity of X-rays and differ from other active galaxies in that they exhibit substantial amounts of non-thermal emission.

Only a small percentage of galaxies show these and related phenomena. Seyfert's original list has been extended and these galaxies are still the subject of research. The most intensively studied are NGC 1068, 1275, and 4151. Their spectra are so rich, however, that it is not possible to construct any single model that will satisfactorily account for all their known characteristics.

In 1951 Seyfert began a study of the objects now known as Seyfert's Sextet – a group of diverse extragalactic objects, of which five are spiral nebulae and one an irregular cloud. One member of the group is moving away from the others at a velocity nearly five times that at which the others are receding from each other. Seyfert's original proposal, however, that the six were grouped together because of a chance meeting between objects at different distances is not now the accepted explanation.

Shannon, Claude Elwood (1916–) US mathematical engineer whose work on technical and engineering problems within the communications industry led him to fundamental considerations on the nature of information and its meaningful transmission. His mathematical theory to describe this process was sufficiently general for its applications to other areas of communication to be immediately appreciated. He is therefore regarded as one of the founders of information theory.

Shannon was born in Gaylord, Michigan, on 30 April 1916. He earned his bachelor's degree at the University of Michigan in 1936, and then continued his studies at the Massachusetts Institute of Technology (MIT). There he became a Bowles Fellow in 1939, and a year later was awarded both his master's degree and his doctorate in mathematics. Shannon then worked for a year as a national research fellow at Princeton University before becoming in 1941 a staff member at the Bell Telephone Laboratories. The work that he carried out during the 1940s led him to postulate a theory for communication, which was published in book form as *The Mathematical Theory of Communication* (1949). This theory brought him considerable acclaim, and he was presented with several notable awards and honours. In 1956 Shannon – still technically working for Bell – became visiting professor of electronic communications at MIT; a year later he became professor of communications science and mathematics there; and in 1958 he finally and officially left Bell to become Donner Professor of Science (emeritus from 1978).

As early as 1938 Shannon was examining the question of a mathematical approach to language. At the

Bell laboratories he was given the task of determining which of the many methods of transmitting information was the most efficient, in order to enable the development of still more efficient methods. For this Shannon produced a model in which he reduced a communications system to its most simple form, so that it included only the most essential components. He also reduced the notion of information to a binary system of a series of yes/no choices, which could be presented by a 1/0 binary code. Each 1/0 choice, or piece of information, he called a 'bit'. In this way complex information could be organized according to strict mathematical principles.

An important feature of Shannon's theory was the prominence given to the concept of entropy, which he demonstrated to be equivalent to a shortage in the information content (a degree of uncertainty) in a message. One consequence of this work was the demonstration of the redundancy in most messages constructed using ordinary language; it became evident that many sentences could be significantly shortened without losing their meaning. His methods, although devised in the context of engineering and technology, were soon seen to have applications not only to computer design but to virtually every subject in which language was important, such as linguistics, psychology, cryptography, and phonetics; further applications were possible in any area where the transmission of information in any form was important.

Shapley, Harlow (1885–1972) US astronomer who made what Otto von ◊Struve called 'the most significant single contribution toward our understanding of the physical characteristics of the very close double stars'.

Shapley was born on 2 November 1885 in Missouri, the son of a farmer. By the age of 16 he was working as a reporter on a newspaper in Kansas, having received a limited education. He then attended Carthage Presbyterian Collegiate Institute, graduating after two years with the intention of enrolling in the University of Missouri's School of Journalism. The school did not open for another year and Shapley, not wanting to waste time, took up astronomy. After graduating from a three-year course at Laws Observatory, he became a teaching assistant there and gained an MA a year later.

In 1911 Shapley moved to Princeton where he worked with Henry ◊Russell on eclipsing binary stars. Using a new method of computing and a polarizing photometer with a 58-cm/23-in refractor, Shapley obtained nearly 10,000 measurements of the sizes of stars in order to analyse some 90 eclipsing binaries. He also showed that Cepheid variable stars were pulsating single stars not double stars.

In 1914, having completed his PhD thesis, Shapley moved to Mount Wilson Observatory. In 1921 he was appointed director of the Hale Observatory at Harvard. Under Shapley the observatory became an important centre for astronomical research. He introduced a graduate programme whose alumni included Carl ◊Seyfert, Jesse ◊Greenstein, and Leo ◊Goldberg.

Shapley continued as director until 1952. He was active in retirement, being involved in the grants committee of the American Philosophical Association and undertaking a number of lecture tours. He was subpoenaed and interrogated by the House Un-American Activities Committee, having been named by Senator Joseph McCarthy in 1950 as one of five alleged communists associated with the State Department. Shapley was exonerated, however, by the Senate Foreign Relations Committee.

Shapley received a number of honours during his career, including the Draper Medal, the Rumford Medal of the American Academy of Art and Science, the Gold Medal of the Royal Astronomical Society, and the Pope Pius XI Prize. He played a part in the setting up of UNESCO and was one of the US representatives who participated in drafting its charter. He died on 20 October 1972 in Boulder, Colorado.

While he was at the Mount Wilson Observatory, Shapley began observations of light changes from the variable stars in globular clusters. His studies required a great deal of detailed work, gaining and collating information from these very remote stellar systems. The systems were spherical, containing a concentration of tens of thousands of stars. Shapley discovered many previously unknown Cepheid variables and he devised a method, based on the fact that brighter stars have longer cycles of light variation, to measure distances across space. For this relationship between cycle, period, and luminosity to be useful, it was first necessary to determine the luminosity of one Cepheid. The great distances involved prevented Cepheids from being measured by direct trigonometric methods. Shapley devised a statistical procedure to establish the distance and luminosity of a Cepheid variable.

Shapley's research served to overthrow previous conceptions about the shape and size of the Milky Way. Jacobus ◊Kapteyn had argued that the Sun was at the centre of a flat stellar assemblage in which a high proportion of stars were within a boundary some 10,000 light years in diameter. Shapley proposed that Kapteyn's stellar assemblage was only a small part of a much larger galactic system, extending far beyond the visible stars to which Kapteyn had limited it. The centre of Shapley's system was a congregation of globular clusters some 60,000 light years away in the direction of the constellation of Sagittarius, and the whole system was said to have an equatorial diameter of about 300,000 light years.

Next, Shapley turned his attention to the debate about whether spiral nebulae were satellites of our Galaxy or independent stellar systems, similar to the Milky Way, but located well outside our galactic system. The luminosity of novae discovered in spiral nebulae could be used to measure their distances. The distance of 1,000,000 light years that Shapley proposed for the Andromeda galaxy is close to the figure now accepted, although Shapley withdrew his results soon after publishing them.

In 1919, on Edward ◊Pickering's death, Shapley was offered, but declined, the position of director of the Hale Observatory at Harvard; he did, however, take up the position two years later. He encouraged completion of the Draper Catalogue, preferring its extension by Annie Jump ◊Cannon to the new, more sophisticated spectral catalogue constructed by Antonia ◊Maury. Shapley's study of the Magellanic Clouds was also begun at Harvard. The observatory had maintained a southern station in Peru, keeping photographic records that went back many years. Shapley was able to use these to revise his estimate of the distance of the Clouds to 100,000 light years. He also conducted a study of the giant emission nebula 30 Doraches and published the first photographs of the obscured cluster.

Shapley increasingly turned his attention to galaxies, carrying out surveys that recorded the presence of tens of thousands of them in both hemispheres. The surveys showed the irregular distribution of galaxies, a point Shapley used to refute the homogeneity necessary in Edwin ◊Hubble's cosmological model. As a result of these surveys, Shapley also identified two dwarf systems in the constellations of Sculptor and Fornax.

Shapley's contributions to early 20th-century astronomy are indisputable, especially with regard to galaxies and the structure of the universe. He can be considered one of the founders of modern cosmology.

Sharpey-Schafer, Edward Albert (1850–1935)

English physiologist and endocrinologist who discovered the effects of the hormone adrenaline (although the actual hormone was not isolated until five years after his discovery). He received the Royal Medal of the Royal Society in 1902 and its Copley Medal in 1924.

He was born Edward Albert Schäfer in London on 2 June 1850, the son of a merchant. He went to University College, London, in 1871 and graduated in medicine three years later. His professor of general anatomy and physiology was William Sharpey, who deeply impressed him by his skills. Schäfer became assistant professor when Sharpey retired in 1874, and eventually became Jodrell Professor at University College in 1883. In 1876 Schäfer was one of the founder members of the Physiological Society (he

wrote a history of the society in 1927). In 1899 he left University College to take the post of professor of physiology at Edinburgh University, which he held until his retirement in 1933. In 1913 he was knighted. He had named one of his sons after his mentor, Sharpey, but after both sons were killed in World War I he affixed Sharpey's name to his own and was thereafter known as Sharpey-Schafer. He died in North Berwick, Scotland, on 29 March 1935.

Sharpey-Schafer's most significant contribution to medical research occurred in 1894, when he and his co-worker George Oliver (1841–1915) discovered that an extract from the central part of an adrenal gland injected into the bloodstream of an animal caused a rise in blood pressure by vasoconstriction. They also noted that the smooth muscles of the animal's bronchi relaxed. These effects were caused by the action of the hormone adrenaline (also known as epinephrine), which is produced by the medulla of the adrenal gland; it was later isolated in 1901 by the Japanese-US chemist Jokichi Takamine (1854–1922).

Sharpey-Schafer also suspected that another hormone was produced by the islets of Langerhans in the pancreas. He adopted for it the name 'insulin' (from the Latin for 'island'), a name that persisted, although the scientists who isolated it in 1922 at first called it 'isletin'.

In 1903 Sharpey-Schafer devised the classic position for artificial respiration, the supine position, which was adopted as standard by the Royal Life Saving Society. He was also an ardent fighter for equal opportunities for women in the world of medicine.

Shaw, (William) Napier (1854–1945)

English meteorologist who, in the late 1800s and early 1900s, did much to establish the then young science of meteorology. He is probably best known, however, for introducing in 1909 the millibar as the meteorological unit of atmospheric pressure (not used internationally until 1929) and for inventing the tephigram, a thermodynamic diagram widely used in meteorology, in about 1915. He received numerous honours for his work, including the 1910 Symons Gold Medal (the Royal Meteorological Society's highest award) and a knighthood in 1915.

Shaw was born in Birmingham on 4 March 1854, the third son of a manufacturing goldsmith and jeweller. He was educated at King Edward VI School, Birmingham, then won a scholarship to Emmanuel College, Cambridge, from which he graduated in 1876. In the following year he was elected a fellow of the college and was also appointed a lecturer in experimental physics at the Cavendish Laboratory (part of Cambridge University); he became assistant director of the Cavendish Laboratory in 1898. In 1900 he was appointed secretary of the Meteorological Council, which, because of the large workload involved, necessitated his resigning from the Cavendish Laboratory; he retained his fellowship until 1906, however. In 1905 he was made director of the Meteorological Office, a post he held until his official retirement in 1920; under his directorship the Meteorological Office was transferred to the Air Ministry. From 1907 until 1920 he was also reader in meteorology then, on retiring in 1920, was appointed the first professor of meteorology at the Royal College of Science of the Imperial College of Science and Technology (part of London University), where he remained until 1924. In 1923 he married Sarah Dugdale, a lecturer at Newnham College, Cambridge. Even after retiring (for the second time), Shaw continued his meteorological writings. He died in London on 23 March 1945.

In addition to his introduction of the millibar and invention of the tephigram – both of which are still used in meteorology – Shaw made several other important contributions to the science. While at the Meteorological Office he pioneered the study of the upper atmosphere by using instruments carried by kites and high-altitude balloons. In 1906, working with R Lempfert, he measured the rate of descent of air in two anticyclones (arriving at figures of 350 m/1,150 ft and 450 m/1,480 ft per day) and, in the case of one particular depression, calculated that 2 million million tonnes of air must have moved to account for the pressure drop. From these studies – described in *Life History of Surface Air Currents* (1906) – Shaw came near to proposing the polar-front theory of cyclones later put forward by Jacob Bjerknes (1897–1975).

Again in collaboration with Lempfert, Shaw wrote *Weather Forecasting* (1911) and *The Air and its Ways* (1923), in which they described their work in determining the paths of air (by means of synoptic charts) in and around the north Atlantic pressure system. This work on pressure fronts formed the basis of a great deal of later work in the field. As a successor to *Forecasting Weather,* Shaw wrote the four-volume *Manual of Meteorology* (1926–31), his most important book and still a valuable standard reference work.

Shaw also studied hygrometry, evaporation, and ventilation, and (with J S Owens), wrote *The Smoke Problem of Great Cities* (1925), an early work on atmospheric pollution.

Sherrington, Charles Scott (1857–1952)

English neurologist who is renowned for his research on the physiology of the nervous system; his laboratories came to be regarded as the best in the world for teaching and research in neurophysiology. For his innovative work on the function of the nerve cell he was awarded the 1932 Nobel Prize for Physiology or Medicine, which he shared with Edgar ◊Adrian.

Sherrington was born on 27 November 1857 in Islington, London. His father died when he was young, and his mother remarried. Sherrington's stepfather was Dr Caleb Rose, a classical scholar and archaeologist who influenced the young boy and interested him in medicine. He went to Ipswich Grammar School and then entered St Thomas's Hospital, London, in 1876. He interrupted his studies in 1880 to go to Cambridge as a non-collegiate student, where he became a demonstrator in the physiology department and a member of Gonville and Caius College. There he studied under the British physiologist Michael Foster (1836–1907).

In 1881 the International Medical Congress was held in London, and it was there that Sherrington was introduced to and became interested in experimental neurophysiology. He also met Santiago ◊Ramón y Cajal whose interests were similar. The following year Sherrington went to Spain as a member of a research team to study a cholera outbreak. He gained his medical degree at Cambridge in 1885 and the next year qualified as a doctor and published his first paper, on the nervous system. In the same year he travelled to Italy to study cholera and then went to Berlin where he visited the pathologist Rudolf Virchow (1821–1902) and Robert ◊Koch. He returned to St Thomas's as a lecturer in physiology and in 1891 was appointed professor-superintendent of the Brown Institute, London University's veterinary hospital. He took up the physiology professorship at Liverpool University in 1895, where he developed many of his original ideas on practical teaching. In 1913 he became professor of physiology at Oxford, a position he retained, although with interruptions, until 1935. During World War I he was heavily involved in government committees on the study of industrial fatigue and for three months he worked incognito as a labourer in a munitions factory. The observations he made there did much to improve safety for factory workers. He was elected president of the Royal Society in 1920 and was knighted two years later. Sherrington was also a poet and philosopher, and published his writings. He was made president of the British Association in 1922. He died in Eastbourne on 4 March 1952.

One of Sherrington's important findings, published in 1894, was that the nerve supply to muscles contains 25–50% sensory fibres, as well as motor fibres concerned with stimulating muscle contraction. The sensory fibres carry sensation to the brain so that it can determine, for example, the degree of tension in the muscles. His discovery helped to explain some of the disorders of the nervous system in which there is a deterioration in muscular coordination.

Sherrington then went on to study reflex actions and formulated theories of the way in which antagonistic muscles coordinate behaviour. He showed that reflex actions do not occur independently, as a result of reflex arcs, but in a movement integrated with the movement of other muscles (that is, when one set of muscles is activated, the opposing set is inhibited). This theory of reciprocal innervation is known as Sherrington's law.

Sherrington divided the sense organs into three groups: interoceptive, characterized by taste receptors; exteroceptive, such as receptors that detect sound, smell, light, and touch; and proprioceptive, which involve the function of the synapse (Sherrington's word) and which respond to events inside the body. In 1906 he investigated the scratch reflex of a dog using an 'electric flea' and found that the reflex stimulated 19 muscles to beat rhythmically five times a second, and brought into action a further 17 muscles that kept the dog upright. The exteroceptive sensors initiated the order to scratch, and the proprioceptors initiated the muscles to keep the animal upright. Sherrington then removed the cerebrum of the dog and cut the epidermal tactile receptors and found that the proprioceptors still worked, against gravity, and activated the muscles to keep the dog upright.

Sherrington also plotted the motor areas of the cerebral cortex of the brain and identified the regions that govern movement and sensation in particular parts of the body. He experimented on the brain of a live gorilla, which caused an observer to comment that he did not know whether to admire most the skill or the courage of the experimenter.

In 1893, while Sherrington was in charge of the Brown Institute, he investigated diphtheria antitoxins. While experimenting for the first time on a horse (used to produce the antitoxin), an urgent message reached him that a young relative was desperately ill with diphtheria. He bled the horse, prepared the antitoxin, and on reaching the boy found that he had only a few hours to live. He injected the child with the antitoxin, and the boy recovered. It was the first use of diphtheria antitoxin in the UK.

Sherrington carried out significant work in the development of antitoxins, particularly those for cholera and diphtheria. In addition his observations of the nervous function in animals, described in *The Integrative Action of the Nervous System* (1906), greatly influenced modern neurophysiology, particularly brain surgery and the treatment of nervous disorders.

Further Reading

Cohen, Henry, *Sherrington: Physiologist, Philosopher and Poet,* Sherrington Lectures series, Liverpool University Press, 1958, v 4.

Eccles, John Carew and Gibson, William Carleton (eds), *Sherrington: His Life and Thought,* Springer International, 1979.

Granit, Ragnar, *Charles Scott Sherrington: An Appraisal,* Doubleday, 1966.

Liddell, Edward George Tandy, *The Discovery of Reflexes,* Clarendon Press, 1960.

Sherrington, Charles Scott; Denny-Brown, Derek (ed), *Selected Writings of Sir Charles Sherrington: A Testimonial Presented by the Neurologists Forming the Guarantors of the Journal Brain,* Oxford University Press, 1979.

Shrapnel, Henry (1761–1842) English artillery officer who invented the artillery shell that bears his name. He also invented the brass tangent slide and some types of fuses, compiled range tables, and improved the construction of mortars and howitzers.

Shrapnel was born in Bradford-on-Avon, Wiltshire, on 3 June 1761. He received a commission in the Royal Artillery in 1779, and in the following year he went to Newfoundland. In 1781 he was promoted to first lieutenant, and on returning to England two years later he commenced his investigations into the problems connected with hollow spherical projectiles filled with bullets and bursting charges and with their discharge from light and heavy ordnance. He was promoted captain and served in the Duke of York's unsuccessful campaign against the French in 1793, being wounded in the seige of Dunkirk.

Promotions followed fairly regularly and by 1804 he was regimental lieutenant-colonel. In that year also, he was appointed inspector of artillery at the Royal Arsenal at Woolwich and, while he was there, succeeded in perfecting many of his inventions connected with ordnance. Further promotion followed and in 1814 he became regimental colonel. By this time, Shrapnel had spent more than 30 years and several thousand pounds of his own money in perfecting his inventions. The treasury granted him a pension of £1,200 a year for life, but he was disappointed not to receive a baronetcy. In 1819 he was promoted major-general and, in 1837, lieutenant-general. Shrapnel died at his home in Southampton on 13 March 1842.

When Shrapnel invented his new shell, he introduced a new name into artillery nomenclature. Although shells had been used for more than 400 years, Shrapnel's shell was different. It was fused and filled with musket balls – plus a small charge of black powder that was just sufficient to explode the container after a pre-determined period of time. When the fuse acted, the container – or shell-case – was blown open and the musket balls it had contained scattered in all directions, causing great damage to anyone or anything with which they came into contact. The Duke of Wellington reported the success of Shrapnel's case-shot and wrote telling him of the performance of his invention against the enemy at Vimiera in 1808. Other generals, in other actions, also acclaimed the new weapon.

Although the first shells used as containers for the musket balls (or shrapnel as they came to be known) were round, later they were of an elongated form with added velocity. Shrapnel's shells continued to be used right up to World War I. They proved to be especially effective against large infantry units on open ground. They were less effective, however, against dispersed or protected personnel.

After World War I there came a period of rapid development and improvement in the design of artillery ammunition. Technological advances in metallurgy, chemistry, and electronics led to the Shrapnel shell being replaced by more powerful projectiles containing bursting charges of TNT, amatol, and cyclonite (RDX). As a result it was no longer necessary to pack the shell with steel fragments – the disintegration of the shell case itself provided the same effect. Because the final effect was still achieved in the way Shrapnel had envisaged – by the blast of the explosion and the spraying of steel fragments – the term 'shrapnel' continued to be used, although erroneously, so perpetuating the association with Shrapnel's name.

Sidgwick, Nevil Vincent (1873–1952) English theoretical chemist best known for his contributions to the theory of valency and chemical bonding.

Sidgwick was born in Oxford on 8 May 1873 into a talented family. His father and two of his uncles were faculty members at the universities of Oxford and Cambridge, and another uncle was archbishop of Canterbury. He was educated at home until he was 12 years old, when he went to Rugby School to study classics and science. His application for a classical scholarship to Oxford in 1891 was unsuccessful, but the following year he was offered a scholarship in natural sciences to Christ Church College. His tutor, the physical chemist Vernon Harcourt, was one of the first people to study reaction kinetics in physical chemistry. Sidgwick graduated in natural sciences in 1895 and went on to perform the extraordinary feat of graduating also in classics two years later. After a year as a laboratory demonstrator, he went to Germany in 1899 to study under Georg ◊Bredig in Wilhelm ◊Ostwald's department at Leipzig. He returned to the UK for a while to recover from an illness, then went back to Germany for two years to work in Tübingen. He was awarded his doctorate in 1901 and became a fellow at Lincoln College, Oxford. He remained at Oxford for the rest of his life, becoming a reader in 1924 and a supernumerary professor of chemistry in 1935, although he did travel abroad frequently in the 1920s and 1930s. He died in Oxford on 15 March 1952.

Sidgwick did little significant work before 1920, spending much of his time teaching and writing his successful and readable book *The Organic Chemistry of Nitrogen* (1910). On a sea voyage to attend a meeting of the British Association in Australia in 1914 he travelled with Ernest ◊Rutherford, and the two scientists forged a lifelong friendship. Sidgwick became absorbed by the study of atomic structure and its importance in chemical bonding, although this work was interrupted by World War I, during which he acted as an unpaid consultant to the department of explosive supplies.

After the war Sidgwick's productivity increased. He extended Gilbert ◊Lewis's ideas on electron sharing to explain the bonding in coordination compounds (complexes) then being studied by Alfred ◊Werner, with a convincing account of the significance of the dative bond. Together with his students he demonstrated the existence of and wide-ranging importance of the hydrogen bond. He summarized this stage of his work in *The Electronic Theory of Valency* (1927).

In 1931 Sidgwick made his first visit to the USA as Baker Nonresident Lecturer in Chemistry at Cornell University. He assimilated the new advances in theoretical chemistry such as Erwin ◊Schrödinger's wave mechanics and Werner ◊Heisenberg's uncertainty principle. He also took notice of the new techniques for the determination of physical forces between atoms and the structures of molecules. These advances were surveyed in his book *Some Physical Properties of the Covalent Link in Chemistry* (1933).

World War II sharply reduced the extent of Sidgwick's overseas travel and the amount of academic research being carried out throughout the world. This permitted him to catch up on the vast amount of literature that had been published in the 1930s and to produce another monumental, definitive two-volume work *The Chemical Elements and their Compounds*, which was published in 1950. Once more he demonstrated his ability to consider and systematize the diverse work of other people and to provide an insight into a broad subject area for the benefit of scholars and students.

Siemens, Ernst Werner von (1816–1892) German electrical engineer who discovered the dynamo principle and who organized the construction of the Indo-European telegraph system between London and Calcutta via Berlin, Odessa, and Tehran.

Siemens was born on 13 December 1816 at Lenthe, near Hannover. In 1832 he entered the Gymnasium in Lubeck. Three years later he became an officer cadet at the artillery and engineering school in Berlin, and studied mathematics, physics, and chemistry 1835–38.

As a serving officer he continued his studies and, in his spare time, he made many practical scientific inventions. He invented a process for gold- and silverplating and a method for providing the wire in a telegraph system with a seamless insulation using gutta-percha. Other inventions included the ozone tube, an alcohol meter, and an electric standard or resistance based on mercury.

In 1847, Siemens founded with scientific instrumentmaker Johan Halske (1814–1890), the firm of Siemens–Halske to manufacture and construct telegraph systems. The company was responsible for constructing extensive systems in Germany and Russia. In 1870, the firm laid the London–Calcutta telegraph line and later became involved in underwater cable telegraphy. In the UK, Siemens became scientific consultant to the British government and helped to design the first cable-laying ship, the *Faraday*.

Valuing the contribution science was already making to technological advancement, Siemens helped to establish scientific standards of measurement and was mainly responsible for establishing the Physicalische-Technische Reichsastalt in Berlin in 1887. He was also cofounder of the Physical Society. His contributions to science were rewarded with a honorary doctorate from the University of Berlin in 1860. He was elected member of the Berlin Academy of Science in 1873 and was ennobled in 1888. In 1889 Siemens retired from active involvement with his firm. He died on 6 December 1892 in Charlottenberg.

Siemens's genius for invention was developed on a very wide scale through the firm he established in Germany with Halske and also through the firm of Siemens Brothers, which had been established in the UK. In 1846 he succeeded in improving the Wheatstone telegraph, making it self-acting by using 'make-and-break' contacts. He subsequently developed an entire telegraph system that included the seamless insulation of the wire. The firm obtained government contracts to provide extensive telegraph networks in Germany. But because of disagreements, these Prussian contracts were cancelled in 1850, so Siemens went to Russia and established an extensive telegraph network there – one that included the line used during the Crimean War.

His greatest single achievement was the discovery of the dynamo principle. Siemens announced his discovery to the Berlin Academy of Science in 1867. He had already introduced the double-T armature and had succeeded in connecting the armature, the electromagnetic field, and the external load of an electric generator in a single current. This enabled manufacturers to dispense with the very costly permanent magnets previously used. Unlike other workers in the field, including Charles ◊Wheatstone, Siemens foresaw the use of his dynamo in machines involving heavy currents. This enabled his companies to become pioneers in the development of electric traction in such applications as streetcars and mini-locomotives and also of electricity-generating stations.

Again unlike some inventor-engineers of his time, Siemens valued the contribution that science could make to practical engineering advancement. He advocated that technique should be based on scientific theory. He often published analyses of his telegraph and cable-laying technology in reports to the Berlin Academy of Science. He also maintained that a nation, in times of harsh international competition, would never maintain its status in the world if it did not base its technology on continuing research work.

Sikorsky, Igor Ivan (1889–1972) Ukrainian-born US aeronautical engineer, one of the great pioneers of aircraft design. He built the first multi-engined aeroplane, was the designer of a famous series of large passenger flying-boats, and built the first practical helicopter.

Sikorsky was born in Kiev on the 25 May 1889. His father was professor of psychology at Kiev University. He was brought up in a cultured family atmosphere and developed an interest in art and a particular fondness for the life and works of ◊Leonardo da Vinci. During his studies of Leonardo he came across the well-known design for a helicopter. He developed an interest in model aeroplanes, and when he was 12 he built a small rubber-powered helicopter that could actually fly. In 1903, at the age of 14, he entered the Russian Naval Academy for a career as an officer in the navy. Three years later he resigned because he wanted to devote his time to practical mechanical pursuits. He went first to Paris, where he studied briefly, and then entered the Kiev Polytechnic Institute. After only a year he left these studies because he wished to be a practical engineer, and he found the gap between the theoretical studies of physics and practical engineering too wide. His family was rich and he was not short of money, so he equipped his own experimental workshop and attempted to develop his ideas.

In 1908 he spent the summer in France and came into contact with the US aeronautical pioneer Wilbur Wright (see Orville and Wilbur ◊Wright), reviving his interest in aviation. He returned to Kiev, believing that he could build a helicopter with a horizontal rotor that would rise straight up into the air, and show that fixed wings were not necessary for flight. The following January he went to Paris to buy a suitable engine for his new machine, and in May 1909 he began to construct his first helicopter. Structural difficulties and the weight of the engine led him to begin work on a second, improved machine. This helicopter did not fly either, and he abandoned his attempts until materials and engines became available that would make his designs practicable.

He decided to concentrate his efforts on fixed-wing aeroplanes and soon built his first biplane, the S-1, with an 11-kW/15-hp engine. It was underpowered, but with a larger engine his S-2 made a short flight. With these early designs he began the practice of taking the controls on the first flight, which he was to continue throughout his career as a designer and builder of aeroplanes. The same year, 1910, two more designs were built. In 1911 his S-5 aeroplane with a 37-kW/50-hp engine flew for more than an hour and achieved altitudes of 450 m/1,480 ft. His cross-country flights enabled him to obtain an international pilot's licence. By now he had achieved recognition and his next aeroplanes had military applications: the S-6 was offered to the army. His famous aeroplanes *Le Grand* and the even larger *Ilia Mourometz* had four engines, upholstered seats, an enclosed cabin for crew and passengers, and even a toilet. They became the basis for the four-engined bomber that Russia used during World War I.

After the war and the Russian Revolution, Sikorsky emigrated to the USA but found it difficult to gain a foothold in US aviation. After a number of years as a teacher and lecturer he founded the Sikorsky Aero Engineering Corporation on a farm on Long Island, and when this company showed promise it was taken over by the United Aircraft Corporation. This arrangement allowed Sikorsky a lot of freedom and gave him the money to build new aeroplanes. In 1929 he produced the twin-engined S-38 Amphibian, and by 1931 the S-40 American Clipper was in production. This large flying boat allowed Pan American Airways to develop routes in the Carribean and South America. In 1937 the even larger S-42 Clipper III was built. But with the coming of World War II and the demise of the flying boat as the most popular method of passenger transport, Sikorsky again took up the idea of a helicopter.

1939 saw the construction of the VS-300 helicopter. The new materials and expertise made his design practical, and on 14 September 1939 Sikorsky piloted his helicopter a few feet into the air; the machine had a four-cylinder 56-kW/75-hp air-cooled engine, driving a 8.2-m/28-ft three-bladed rotor. In May 1941 an endurance record of more than 90 minutes was set by a Sikorsky helicopter, and in 1943 the R-3, the world's first production helicopter, was flown. There quickly followed a whole series of production designs using one then two piston engines. With their usefulness for rescue and transport work in inaccessible or densely populated places helicopters came into their own and were designed for specific purposes. Later Sikorsky models had distinguished military service in Korea. During the late 1950s piston engines were replaced by the newly developed gas-turbine engines as the source of power, and helicopters were built for even more rugged duties.

In 1957 Sikorsky retired as engineering manager from his company. During his lifetime he had received many honours. He married in 1924 and had been proud to become a US citizen in 1928. After a lifetime devoted to aviation he died at Easton, Connecticut, on the 26 October 1972.

Further Reading

Finne, K N; Bobnow, Carl J (ed) and Von Hardesty (transl), *Igor Sikorsky: The Russian Years*, Smithsonian Institution Press, 1987.

Otfinoski, Steven, *Igor Sikorsky: Father of the Helicopter*, Masters of Invention series, Rourke Enterprises, 1993.

Simon, Franz Eugen (1893–1956) German-born British physicist who developed methods of achieving extremely low temperatures and who also established the validity of the third law of thermodynamics.

Simon was born in Berlin on 2 July 1893. In 1903, he entered the Kaiser Friedrich Reform Gymnasium, Berlin, and received a classical education. However, Simon's interest in science enabled him in 1912 to enter the University of Munich to read physics, chemistry, and mathematics. He spent a year in Munich under Arnold ◊Sommerfeld and then a term at Göttingen before he was called up for military service in 1913. Simon was wounded twice and became one of the first poison-gas casualties, but was awarded the Iron Cross first class. In 1919, he resumed his studies at Berlin, obtaining his DPhil in 1921 under Hermann ◊Nernst. In 1922, Simon became assistant to Nernst at the Physical Chemical Institute of the University of Berlin and remained there for ten years, becoming a *Privatdozent* (unpaid lecturer) in 1924 and associate professor in 1927.

In 1931, Simon took over the chair of physical chemistry at the Technical University in Breslau (now Wroc|aw in Poland). With the rise to power of Hitler in 1933, Simon foresaw trouble because he was Jewish. He resigned his post in that year, and accepted an invitation from Frederick ◊Lindemann (Lord Cherwell) to work at the Clarendon Laboratory, Oxford. In 1936, Simon became a reader in thermodynamics there. He then decided to stay in the UK and became a British citizen in 1938. During World War II, Simon worked on the atomic bomb project, being concerned with the separation of uranium isotopes by gaseous diffusion.

After the war, Simon became professor of thermodynamics at Oxford in 1945 and held this post until 1956, when he was appointed Dr Lee's Professor of Experimental Philosophy at Oxford, succeeding Lindemann. He held this position for only a few weeks, dying in Oxford on 31 October 1956. Among the honours Simon received were the Rumford Medal of the Royal Society in 1948 and a knighthood in 1955.

Simon's first scientific work was his PhD thesis under Nernst on the study of specific heats at low temperatures. While he was at the Physical Chemistry Institute at Berlin University, he built up the low-temperature department. He worked on the solidification of helium and other gases by the use of high pressure, and discovered the specific heat anomaly in solid orthohydrogen. In 1930, he installed a new hydrogen liquefier into his laboratory to his own design and this design was adopted by many other laboratories. In 1932, Simon worked out a method for generating liquid helium by single-stroke adiabatic expansion, and this too came to be used widely for its simplicity and cheapness.

From 1933, when Simon went to the UK, his work was concerned with magnetic cooling and investigations below 1K (−271.5 °C/−456.6 °F), the properties of liquid helium, and specific heats. He made a major contribution to physics by showing that the third law of thermodynamics is obeyed at very low temperatures. This law was proposed by Nernst in 1905 and it states that the entropy of a substance approaches zero as its temperature approaches absolute zero. There were subsequently doubts that this is a universal law applicable in all cases, but Simon's low-temperature work dispelled them and the expression of the third law in this form is largely due to his efforts.

Simon also did a lot of work on helium. Helium is the only substance that, under its vapour pressure, remains liquid down to absolute zero. Liquid helium is unique too in that at low temperatures, its internal energy is smaller than that of the solid in equilibrium with it. Simon succeeded in establishing the helium-vapour-pressure scale below 1.7K (− 271.5°C/−456.6°F) and heat transport in liquid helium below 1K. He worked on the properties of fluids at high pressure and low temperature, and showed that helium could be solidified at a temperature ten times as high as its liquid/gas critical point. He also worked on heat conductivity in connection with radiation damage.

In the magnetic field, Simon is most noted for his lead in using magnetic cooling to open up a new range of very low temperatures for a wide variety of physical experiments. In the UK in the 1930s, he developed adiabatic demagnetization to investigate properties of substances below 1K. He then went on to investigate nuclear cooling, showing that the cooling effect is limited by interaction energies and that if, instead of a paramagnetic salt, a substance is chosen whose paramagnetism is due to nuclear spins, then lower temperatures can be reached as the interaction energies for nuclear magnetic moments are smaller than for electron moments. In this way, Simon finally achieved temperatures nearly one millionth of a degree above absolute zero.

Simpson, George Clark (1878–1965) English meteorologist whose numerous contributions to meteorology included studies of atmospheric electricity and of the effect of radiation on the polar ice, and the standardization of the Beaufort scale of wind speed. Among the many honours he received for his work were the Symons Gold Medal from the Royal Meteorological Society in 1930 and a knighthood in 1935.

Simpson was born in Derby on 2 September 1878, the son of a successful tradesman. In about 1887 he was sent to the Diocesan School, Derby, a small school (with a limited curriculum) for educating the sons of tradesmen and artisans. He left school in 1894 and entered his father's business. After reading popular science books, however, he became interested in optics and began to attend evening classes. On his father's suggestion, he then decided to try to further his education at Owens College, Manchester (later Manchester University) and, after private coaching, passed the entrance examination and began studying at the college in 1897. Because of his lack of higher education, he was initially advised to study for an ordinary degree but, at the instigation of Arthur Schuster (1851–1934), changed to an honours degree course. He gained a first-class honours degree in 1900 and became an unsalaried tutor at Owens College. In 1902 he won a travelling scholarship and went to Göttingen University to study under Emil Wiechert (1861–1928), after which he visited Lapland to investigate atmospheric electricity before returning to the UK. In 1905 Schuster set up a small meteorology department at Manchester University (as Owens College had become) and placed Simpson in charge; this position was the first lectureship in meteorology at a British university. In the same year Simpson also accepted an invitation to assist Napier ◊Shaw, the newly appointed director of the British Meteorological Office. While holding these posts Simpson travelled widely, spending a period from 1906 with the Indian Meteorological Office inspecting meteorological stations throughout India and Burma (now Myanmar); travelling to the Antarctic in 1910 as a meteorologist on Robert Scott's last expedition; and visiting Mesopotamia (now part of Iraq) from 1916 as a meteorological adviser to the British Expeditionary Force. In 1920, when in Egypt as a member of the Egyptian government's Nile Project Commission, he was summoned back to the UK to succeed Shaw as director of the Meteorological Office in London, a post he held until officially retiring in 1938. In the following year, however, with the outbreak of World War II, he returned from retirement to take charge of Kew Observatory, continuing research into the electrical structure of thunderstorms until 1947. Simpson spent his last years in Westbury-on-Trym, near Bristol, and died in Bristol on 1 January 1965.

Simpson's early work – carried out while at Owens College – concerned magnetism and electricity. At

Göttingen University, however, his interest turned to meteorology and he demonstrated that the Earth's permanent negative charge cannot be maintained by the absorption of negative ions from the atmosphere. Continuing this line of research in Lapland, he measured dissipation of atmospheric electricity and ionization and radioactivity in the atmosphere; he described the results of these studies in *Atmospheric Electricity in High Altitudes* (1905). He also investigated ionization, radioactivity, and potential gradients while on the Antarctic expedition.

When Simpson became Shaw's assistant at the Meteorological Office, he began working on the Beaufort scale. This scale, which was devised in 1805 by the British admiral and hydrographer Francis ⓗBeaufort, described and classified wind force at sea but made no reference to actual wind speeds (as originally formulated it was based on the effect of the wind on a fully rigged man-o'-war sailing ship). Simpson devised a revised form of the scale in which the numbers of the original scale were assigned wind speeds measured by a freely exposed anemometer at a height of 11 m/36 ft above ground level. In 1921 he was asked by the International Meteorological Committee to reconcile international differences between sets of Beaufort scale equivalent wind speeds, and in 1926 the committee accepted the scale Simpson himself had devised earlier. In 1939, however, the committee adopted a new scale based on wind-speed measurements from an anemometer at 6 m/20 ft above ground level, although for some time the US and British weather services continued to use Simpson's 11-m/ 36-ft elevation scale.

As director of the Meteorological Office, Simpson investigated the effects of solar radiation on the polar ice caps. He concluded that excessive solar radiation would increase the amount of cloud and that the resultant increase in precipitation would lead to enlargement of the ice caps. He then investigated the possibility that this conclusion might explain the ice ages. In a series of papers on this subject he showed that, in glaciated regions, the initial effect of increased radiation is greater precipitation (in the form of snow), which, in turn, leads to enlargement of the ice sheet, followed by recession of the ice as the radiation increases further. Then, when the radiation decreases, the resultant drop in temperature causes the precipitation to fall as snow again, which leads to a second advance of the ice.

Simpson, George Gaylord (1902–1984) US palaeontologist who studied the evolution of mammals and applied population genetics to the subject and to the migrations of animals between continents.

Simpson was born on 16 June 1902 in Chicago,

Illinois, the son of a lawyer. He attended the University of Colorado and after graduation went to Yale University, where he gained his PhD in 1926 with a thesis on Mesozoic mammals. A year later he took a post in New York City at the American Museum of Natural History, where he remained for 32 years, continuing his palaeontological research and becoming curator in 1942. He took a professorial appointment at Columbia University in 1945, and from 1959 to 1970 he was Alexander Agassiz Professor of Vertebrate Palaeontology at the Museum of Comparative Zoology, Harvard. He went to Tucson in 1967 to take up an appointment as professor of geosciences at the University of Arizona. He died there on 6 October 1984.

Simpson's chief work in the 1930s concerned early mammals of the Mesozoic, Palaeocene, and Eocene, which entailed many extensive field trips throughout the Americas and to Asia to study fossil remains. This led him to consider the taxonomy of mammals, and in the 1940s he began applying genetics to mammalian evolution and classification. Much of his work was summarized in a series of textbooks, including *Tempo and Mode in Evolution* (1944), *The Meaning of Evolution* (1949), *The Major Features of Evolution* (1953), and *The Principles of Animal Taxonomy* (1961), which were influential in establishing the neo-Darwinian theory of evolution.

Simpson, James Young (1811–1870) Scottish obstetrician and one of the founders of gynaecology, who pioneered the use of chloroform as an anaesthetic.

Simpson was born in Bathgate near Linlithgow on 7 June 1811, the son of a village baker. He was a brilliant pupil at school and at the age of only 14 he went to Edinburgh University to study medicine, and graduated in 1832 to become assistant to one of the university professors on the merit of his exceptional thesis. He became professor of midwifery in 1840 at the age of 29, and seven years later his skill as an obstetrician was acknowledged when he was requested to attend Queen Victoria during her stays in Scotland. By this time he had a thriving private practice and was making pioneering advances in modern gynaecology; he was eventually appointed physician to Queen Victoria. He was made a baronet in 1866, and died in London on 6 May 1870.

Although Simpson made great advances in gynaecology, his most famous work was in the field of anaesthesia. In 1846 the US dentist William ⓗMorton had successfully extracted a tooth painlessly by using ether as an anaesthetic. Simpson was impressed and began experimenting himself, but he was not particularly successful with ether, although he did use it on a patient in childbirth in early 1847. He then heard of the work of the French physiologist Jean Flourens

(1794–1867), who was experimenting with chloroform on animals, and of the successful use of chloroform in surgery by Robert Liston at University College Hospital, London. In November 1847 Simpson introduced the use of chloroform in his practice, particularly to relieve the pain of childbirth. He described his cases in *Account of a New Anaesthetic Agent* (1847). This caused a storm of opposition from some Calvinists, who regarded labour pains as God-given and heretic to relieve. It was not until royal intervention in 1853 that the controversies died down. Queen Victoria, who never pretended that pregnancy and childbirth were anything but loathsome, accepted the use of chloroform during the birth of Prince Leopold, her seventh child. She described the new drug as 'miraculous' and her praise of Simpson knew no bounds. Thus criticism of his techniques abated, and they were soon universally adopted.

Further Reading

Atkinson, Richard Stuart, *James Simpson and Chloroform,* Pioneers of Science and Discovery series, Priory Press, 1973.

Russell, Kenneth and Forster, Frank, *A List of the Works of Sir James Young Simpson 1811–1870: A Centenary Tribute,* Medical History Unit, University of Melbourne, 1971.

Shepherd, John A, *Simpson and Syme of Edinburgh,* Livingstone, 1969.

Simpson, Eve (Evelyne) Blantyre, *Sir James Y Simpson,* Famous Scots series, Oliphant, Anderson & Ferrier, 1896.

Simpson, Myrtle, *Simpson, the Obstetrician: A Biography,* Gollancz, 1972.

Simpson, Thomas (1710–1761) English mathematician and writer who, after a somewhat erratic start in life, contributed greatly to the development of mathematics in the 18th century. He is particularly remembered for Simpson's rule, which simplifies the calculation of areas under graphic curves.

Born at Market Bosworth, Leicestershire, on 20 August 1710, Simpson was the son of a weaver. Uninterested in his studies, he left home and lodged at the house of a widow in Nuneaton, whom he married in 1730. A few years later, following an eclipse of the Sun, Simpson became obsessed by astrology and gained a reputation in the locality for divination. But after he had apparently frightened a girl into having fits by 'raising a devil' from her, he was obliged to flee with his wife to Derby. In 1735 or 1736 he moved to London and worked as a weaver at Spitalfields, teaching mathematics in his spare time. It was there that he published his first mathematical works, which created a better sort of reputation and even won some acclaim. Soon after 1740 he was elected to the Royal Academy of Stockholm, and in 1743 he was appointed professor of mathematics at the Royal Academy at Woolwich, largely through the interest of William Jones (1675–1749). Finally, on 5 December 1745 he was elected a fellow of the Royal Society. From then on he was a constant contributor to *The Ladies' Diary,* acting as its editor 1754–60. He died in Market Bosworth on 14 May 1761, and was buried at Sutton Cheynell, Leicestershire. (Mrs Simpson survived him and received a pension from the crown after her husband's death, until she herself died in 1782 – at the age of 102.)

Simpson's first mathematical work, in 1737, was to study Edmund Stone's translation of Guillaume L'Hôpital's *Analyse des infiniements petits,* and from it to write a new treatise on 'fluxions' (calculus). This was an important contribution to the subject – although it also showed up the defects in the mathematical training that Simpson had received. In 1740 he wrote *The Nature and Laws of Chance,* and some essays on several subjects in speculative and general mathematics. In 1742 *The Doctrine of Annuities and Reversions* appeared; in 1743, *Mathematical Dissertation on a Variety of Physical and Analytical Subjects. A Treatise of Algebra* followed in 1745, and in its appendix contained some extremely ingenious solutions to algebraic problems. Ingenuity also distinguished his *Elements of Geometry* (1747). His next works were *Trigonometry, Plane and Spherical* (1748) and *Select Exercises in Mathematics* (1752). In a paper he produced in 1755, Simpson proved that the arithmetic mean of n repeated measurements (which was already in limited use) was preferable to a single measurement in a precisely specifiable case. His final major publication was *Miscellaneous Tracts on Some Curious Subjects in Mechanics, Physical Astronomy and Special Mathematics* (1757). He also contributed several papers to the *Transactions* of the Faraday Society, most of which have been republished.

Simpson is most famous for having devised a method for determining approximately the area under a curve, known as Simpson's rule. The method is to join the extremities of the ordinates by parabolic segments. In a general parabola whose axis is parallel to the y-axis between two coordinates (for example) $x = -h$ and $x = h$ each side of zero, and whose equation is (for example):

$$y = ax^2 + bx + c$$

Simpson found that the approximate area under the curve between those ordinates is:

$$\int_{-h}^{h} (ax^2 + bx + c)\, dx = [\tfrac{1}{3}ax^3 + \tfrac{1}{2}bx^2 + cx]_{h-1}^{h}$$

which he then reduced to:

$$\tfrac{1}{3}h\,[y_3 + 4y_2]$$

This result gives the area under a quadratic curve exactly, and gives an approximation to the area under a curve that is not parabolic. Greater accuracy can be obtained by dividing the range of integration into a larger number of intervals and successively applying the rule for three ordinates.

On another occasion, Simpson worked out a way to calculate the volume of a prismoid, a solid bounded by any number of planes, two of which are parallel and contain all the vertices. The two parallel faces are called the bases. He said that the volume:

$$V = \tfrac{1}{6}h(B + B' + 4M)$$

where M is a section made by a plane parallel to the bases B and B' and midway between them, and h is the distance between the bases. This formula can be used to find the volume of any solid bounded by a ruled surface and two parallel planes.

Singer, Isaac Merrit (1811–1875) US inventor. His name will always be associated with the domestic sewing machine, which became such a feature of 'every good home' in the late 1800s.

Singer was born in Pittstown, New York, on 27 October 1811. He began his career simply enough as an apprentice machinist, and during his early working life patented a rock-drilling machine and, later, a metal- and wood-carving machine. It was while he was employed in a machine shop in Boston that his main chance arrived. One day he was asked to carry out some repairs to a Lerow and Blodgett sewing machine. Singer not only did that, but at the same time decided he could add many improvements to the design. Eleven days later he produced a new model which he patented under his own name.

Litigation against his patent followed from Elias ◊Howe, another maker, who claimed Singer had used his patented stitch method. Although Howe eventually won the case, Singer was already in production with his machine, having formed the I M Singer Company in 1851 and, as a measure of his machine's success, his business went from strength to strength. Singer had formed a partnership with an Edward Clark in the June of 1851, and by 1860 the company was the largest sewing-machine manufacturer in the world. In 1863 Singer and Clark formed the Singer Manufacturing Company and Singer retired to England where he settled in Torquay, Devon. He died there on 23 July 1875.

Sewing as a means of constructing clothes dates back to prehistoric times when bone needles were used to stitch skins together. From that, people progressed to using an awl with which first to make a hole, followed by a type of crochet needle for the stitch. The use of a steel sewing needle appears to have originated in the 16th century and hand sewing continued as the only method of stitching up to the end of the 18th century, when inventive minds turned their attention to this domestic chore.

Barthélemy Thimonnier of France is credited with devising the first practical sewing machine as a means of speeding up the production of army uniforms in 1841. By 1845, Howe in the USA had designed his answer, the first lockstitch machine, using a threaded needle and shuttle (bobbin). When Singer patented his improved machine in 1851, he used the best of Howe's design and altered some of the other features. The basic mechanism was the same, however: as the handle turned, the needle paused at a certain point in its stroke so that the shuttle could pass through the loop formed in the cotton. When the needle continued the threads were tightened, forming a secure stitch.

Singer's machines were very popular (and still are) and his marketing, aimed at the ordinary family – he introduced the first instalment-plan payment system – was such a success that by 1869 more than 110,000 sewing machines had been produced for the US market alone.

Skinner, B(urrhus) F(rederic) (1904–1990) US psychologist famous for his staunch advocacy of behaviourism, which attempts to explain human behaviour solely in terms of observable responses to external stimuli. He is also well known for his controversial ideas about the relationship between individuals and society, for inventing the Skinner box and the teaching machine, and for developing programmed learning.

Skinner was born on 20 March 1904 in Susquehanna, Pennsylvania, and was educated at Harvard University. After obtaining his doctorate in 1931 he remained at the university as an instructor until 1936, when he moved to the University of Minnesota, Minneapolis – initially as an instructor, then as assistant professor 1937–39. During World War II he was an associate professor in a research programme for the US Office of Scientific Research and Development. In 1945, after the war, he was appointed professor of psychology at Indiana University, Bloomington, then in 1948 he returned to Harvard as professor of psychology, becoming Edgar Pierce Professor of Psychology there in 1958.

Skinner's best-known research work concerns operant conditioning, which, in general, involves influencing voluntary behaviour patterns by means of rewards or punishments or a combination of both. In his research, Skinner took a firm behaviouristic standpoint, believing that behaviour can be studied properly only by objective experimentation and observation of reactions to definable stimuli, and that all subjective phenomena should be discounted. Although many psychologists consider Skinner's ideas to be rather extreme, he succeeded in bringing a considerable degree of methodological rigidity to psychological experimentation.

In the field of operant conditioning, Skinner conducted many highly original experiments, mainly using pigeons. For example, during World War II he trained pigeons to pilot bombs and torpedoes, although the pigeons were never actually used as missile guides; and later, at Harvard, he taught pigeons to play table tennis. In the course of his work on training animals he developed the Skinner box, which, in its basic form, comprises a box with a lever-operated food-delivery device inside; when the experimental animal presses the lever, a pellet of food is delivered. More sophisticated versions of the Skinner box have since been developed and have proved extremely useful in studying the behaviour of a wide variety of animals.

The step-by-step training of experimental animals led Skinner to develop teaching machines and the associated concept of programmed learning. Similar in many respects to the Skinner box, a teaching machine presents information to a student at a pace determined by the student himself, and then tests the student on the material previously presented; correct answers are 'rewarded', thereby reinforcing learning.

Skinner first gained public attention, however, with his invention in the mid-1940s of the air crib, a large, air-conditioned, soundproof box intended to serve as a mechanical baby minder and designed to provide the optimum environment for child growth during the first two years of life. (His own daughter was partially reared in such a box until the age of two.) But Skinner aroused the greatest controversy with *Walden Two* (1948), a fictional description of a modern utopia, and *Beyond Freedom and Dignity* (1971), a nonfiction work in which, using the results of modern psychological research to support his case, Skinner presents his ideas for the improvement of society. The central theme in both of these books is essentially the same: an ideal society can be attained and maintained only if human behaviour is modified – by means of such techniques as conditioning – to fit society instead of society adapting to the needs of individuals.

Further Reading

Bjork, Daniel W, *B F Skinner: A Life*, APA Books, 1997.

Dilman, Ilham, *Mind, Brain, and Behaviour: Discussions of B F Skinner and J R Searle*, Routledge, 1988.

Nye, Robert D, *Three Psychologies: Perspectives from Freud, Skinner, and Rogers*, Brooks/Cole Pub Co, 1986.

Nye, Robert D, *The Legacy of B F Skinner: Concepts and Perspectives, Controversies and Misunderstandings*, Brooks/Cole Pub Co, 1992.

Richelle, Marc N, *B F Skinner: A Reappraisal*, Erlbaum, 1993.

Smith, Laurence D and Woodward, William R, *B F Skinner and Behaviorism in American Culture*, Lehigh University Press, 1996.

Wiener, Daniel N, *B F Skinner: Benign Anarchist*, Allyn & Bacon Inc, 1995.

Skolem, Thoralf Albert (1887–1963) Norwegian mathematician who did important work on Diophantine equations and who helped to provide the axiomatic foundations for set theory in logic.

Skolem was born in Sandsvaer on 23 May 1887 and was educated at the University of Oslo, where he studied mathematics, physics, and life sciences. He graduated with the highest distinction in 1913, having written a dissertation on the algebra of logic. By that time he had for four years been working as an assistant to Otto Birkeland, with whom he published his first papers, on the subject of the 'northern lights'. In 1918 he was made an assistant professor of mathematics at Oslo, eight years before he finally submitted, in 1926, at the age of 40, a doctoral thesis. From 1930 to 1938 Skolem was able to conduct his research, without teaching duties, as a fellow of the Christian Michaelson Institute in Bergen. In 1938 he was appointed professor of mathematics at Oslo, where he lectured on algebra and number theory to the virtual exclusion of mathematical logic, his area of specialization. He retired in 1957, but continued to do research until his death at Oslo, just before a projected lecture tour of the USA, on 23 March 1963.

Skolem was a retiring man, devoted almost entirely to mathematical research. He wrote 182 scientific papers and, unusually for a mathematician, most of them were written after he had reached the age of 40. It was not, indeed, until he was 33 that he published his first papers in mathematical logic, but those papers of 1920 elevated him at once to a leading place in the field. To the chagrin of his foreign colleagues Skolem published chiefly in Norwegian journals (a number of which he edited) and so were inaccessible; lectures given on his frequent visits to the USA went some way to break down this barrier.

Skolem's early work was in the highly abstruse field of formal mathematical logic. From papers published in the 1920s emerged what is now known as the Löwenheim–Skolem theorem, one consequence of which is Skolem's paradox. It takes the following form. If an axiomatic system (such as Ernst ◊Zermelo's axiomatic set theory, which intends to generate arithmetic, including the natural numbers, as part of set theory) is consistent (that is, satisfiable), then it must be satisfiable within a countable domain; but Georg ◊Cantor had shown the existence of a never-ending sequence of transfinite powers in mathematics (that is, uncountability). How to resolve this paradox? Skolem's answer was that there *is* no complete axiomatization of mathematics. Certain concepts must be interpreted only relatively; they can have no 'absolute' meaning.

In this work Skolem was ahead of his time, so much so that in the 1930s he had to take pains to summarize his work of a decade earlier in order to bring it to the attention of mathematicians. As his papers remained largely unread (admittedly partly because they were written in Norwegian), he became somewhat dispirited and turned away from mathematical logic to more conventional topics in algebra and number theory. In particular, he began to work on Diophantine equations, publishing what was for many years the definitive text on the subject.

Nevertheless, his main field remained the logical foundations of mathematics. Before such subjects as model theory, recursive function theory, and axiomatic set theory had become separate branches of mathematics, he introduced a number of the fundamental notions that gave rise to them.

Slipher, Vesto Melvin (1875–1969) US astronomer whose important work in spectroscopy increased our knowledge of the universe and paved the way for some of the most important results obtained in more recent astrophysics.

Slipher was born on 11 November 1875 in Mulberry, Indiana. He attended Indiana University and then in 1902, shortly after graduating, joined the Lowell Observatory in Arizona at the request of Percival ◊Lowell. There he began the spectroscopic analyses that led to important conclusions about planetary and nebular rotation, planetary and stellar atmospheres, and diffuse and spiral nebulae.

Slipher's academic and administrative positions show the range of his achievements. He received an MA in 1903 and a PhD in 1909 from the University of Indiana, and he was awarded honorary degrees from a number of universities. He became acting director of Lowell Observatory in 1916 and was director from 1926 until his retirement in 1952. He instigated the search that resulted in the discovery of the planet Pluto by Clyde ◊Tombaugh in 1930. Slipher was active in the International Astronomical Union and the American Association for the Advancement of Science, and he was a member of a number of other astronomical and scientific societies. He died in Flagstaff, Arizona, on 8 November 1969.

Slipher studied Venus, Mars, and Jupiter. The lack of surface detail on Venus made calculation of the rotation period difficult. Slipher's method was to measure changes in the inclination of the spectral lines while keeping a spectrograph perpendicular to the terminator. The 26 photographs that he took gave a result that

was close to the figure now generally accepted on the basis of more modern methods of computation. In the years following, Slipher also published measurements of the period of rotation for Mars, Jupiter, Saturn, and Uranus, and in 1933 he was awarded the Royal Astronomical Society's Gold Medal for his work on planetary spectroscopy.

Slipher was responsible for a number of planetary discoveries. His work on Jupiter first showed the existence of bands in the planet's spectrum, and he and his colleagues were able to identify the bands as belonging to metallic elements, including iron and copper. He also showed that the diffuse nebula of the Pleiades had a spectrum similar to that of the stars surrounding it and concluded that the nebula's brightness was the result of light reflected from the stars.

Another of Slipher's discoveries was instrumental to work done by Edwin ◊Hubble, Ejnar ◊Hertzsprung, and others on emission and absorption nebulae. This work depended on Slipher's recognition of the existence of particles of matter in interstellar space. His discovery of a non-oscillating calcium line in the spectra of various celestial objects showed that there was gas between the stars and the Earth.

Slipher's most significant contribution to astronomy concerned spiral nebulae. His investigations paved the way for an understanding of the motion of galaxies and for cosmological theories that explained the expansion of the universe. While Hubble must be given the credit for formulating the relationship between velocity and distance in interstellar space, his work used results gained by Slipher in his research into spiral nebulae. In 1912 Slipher gained a set of spectrographs that showed that the Andromeda spiral nebula was approaching the Sun at a velocity of 300 km/985 mi per second. He continued his observations of this and other nebulae, looking at the Doppler shifts for 14 spirals. By 1925 Slipher's catalogue included measurements of the radial velocities of nearly all the 44 known spirals. His results suggested that spirals were external to our Galaxy as their radial velocities could not be contained within the Milky Way system. His work influenced not only Heber ◊Curtis and Hubble, who each put forward an account of the nature of the phenomenon, but also other astronomers who were interested in discovering the relationship between velocity and distance in interstellar space. Slipher's contribution to this field of study was outstanding and fundamental.

Smalley, Richard Errett (1943–) US chemist who, with his colleagues US chemist Robert ◊Curl (1933–) and English chemist Harold ◊Kroto, discovered buckminsterfullerene (carbon 60) in 1985. Smalley also pioneered the technique that they used to discover this molecule – supersonic jet laser beam spectroscopy. He shared the 1996 Nobel Prize for Chemistry with Curl and Kroto.

Born on 6 June 1943 in Akron, Ohio, Smalley was educated at Michigan University (obtaining a BS in 1965) and at Princeton (where he gained an MA in 1971 and a PhD in 1973). He worked at the James Franck Institute in Chicago 1973–76 before moving to Rice University in Houston, where he was made professor in 1981.

In 1981 Smalley devised a procedure to produce microclusters of a hundred or so atoms using a technique involving laser bombardment. The released atoms are cooled by a jet of helium and they condense into clusters of various sizes. Harold Kroto, who was interested in the carbon chains identified by radio astronomers in space, heard of this in 1984 and had a suspicion that Smalley's clusters might produce the chains of carbon atoms he was looking for. He visited Houston in 1985 to work with Smalley and Robert Curl and he persuaded a reluctant Smalley to direct his laser beam at a graphite target. This produced the small chains that Kroto was looking for but more interestingly they also found a mass-spectrum signal for a molecule of exactly 60 carbon atoms, in a sphere in which 12 pentagons and 20 hexagons are arranged like the panels on a soccer ball. This structure also resembles the framework of US architect Buckminster Fuller's geodesic dome, hence the name buckminsterfullerene (later shortened to fullerene, the molecules being informally known as buckyballs). Their discovery added another allotrope to well-known diamond and graphite forms of carbon.

Since Smalley, Kroto, and Curl's discovery, other fullerenes have been identified with 28, 32, 50, 70, and 76 carbon atoms. New molecules have been made based on the buckyball enclosing a metal atom, and buckytubes have been made consisting of cylinders of carbon atoms arranged in hexagons. In 1998 these were proved, in laboratories in Israel and the USA, to be 200 times tougher than any other known fibre. Possible uses for these new molecules are as lubricants, superconductors, semiconductors, and as a starting point for new drugs.

Smalley's research laboratory is best known for the discovery of C_{60} and the other fullerenes but in the 1990s it moved away from the study of clusters levitated in the gas phase to develop nanoscale structures and the probes for these structures. An example of this new direction is the nanowire, a metallic structure only a few nanometres in diameter but hundreds of micrometres in length. The aim is to produce these wires by polymerizing carbon and producing a single fullerene molecule in the shape of a continuous graphene tube. These fullerene nanospheres are expected to have very high electrical conductivity and a tensile strength about a hundred times higher than steel. The nanowires will make excellent probes and will make a connection between macroscopic and nanoscopic worlds. Smalley and his colleagues have published several articles on the progress of this research including one in *Nature* (1997) and two in *Science* (1997 and 1998).

Smalley is an Alfred P Sloan Fellow, a fellow of the National Academy of Sciences and the American Academy of Arts and Sciences. He has received the Robert A Welch Award in Chemistry, the 1993 Europhysics Prize, the 1996 Franklin Medal, the 1997 Distinguished Civilian Public Service Award, as well as the Nobel prize.

Smeaton, John (1724–1792) British civil engineer who rebuilt the Eddystone lighthouse in 1759 and was also greatly influential in directing the scientific research that was being carried out in the mid-18th century. It was he who first adopted the term 'civil engineer' in contradistinction to the fast-growing number of military engineers graduating from the military colleges.

Smeaton was born of Scottish ancestry in Austhorpe, near Leeds on 8 June 1724. He was encouraged to practise law, and after a good elementary education he served in his father's firm of solicitors. Later he went to London for further training, but his natural inclination for mechanical science led him to leave law and become a maker of scientific instruments.

He soon introduced many technical innovations – one of which was a novel instrument with which he was able to measure and study the expansion characteristics of various materials. From 1756 to 1759 he was engaged in the rebuilding of the Eddystone lighthouse in the English Channel. He was also a consultant in the field of structural engineering, and from 1757 onwards he was responsible for many engineering projects including bridges, power stations operated by water or wind, steam engines, and river and harbour facilities.

He was a charter member of the first professional engineering society, the Society of Civil Engineers (founded in 1771), which, after his death, became known as the Smeatonian Society. He was a fellow of the Royal Society and, in 1759, received its Copley Medal. He died on 28 October 1792, at Austhorpe.

Although Smeaton's best known achievement was the rebuilding of Eddystone, his main contribution to engineering was his innovative ability to combine engineering with applied science. His work on water wheels and windmills served to underline the importance of scientific research to practical engineering problems. It was his own research work that led him to question the relative efficiency of the then firmly established undershot water wheel (which operates through the action of the flow of water against blades in the wheel) and the overshot wheel (which is operated by water moving the wheel by the force of its weight).

Experimenting with models, Smeaton showed that overshot wheels were twice as efficient as undershot ones. He went further and speculated on the cause of this difference in efficiency. From his experiments, he concluded that the loss of 'mechanic power' in the undershot wheel was caused by turbulence, which he described as the loss of power by water and other non-elastic bodies in changing their 'figure' in consequence of their 'stroke'. Thus, only part of their original power is communicated when acting by impulse or collision.

In 1759 Smeaton presented his important paper to the Royal Society, 'An experimental enquiry concerning the natural power of water and wind to turn mills and other machines depending on a circular motion'. This paper was followed by two others, one on the necessary mechanical power to be employed in giving different degrees of velocity to heavy bodies from a state of rest, and the other on some 'fundamental experiments upon the collision of bodies'.

Smeaton's work, with its emphasis on scientific investigation into practical engineering problems, provided one of the first examples of the interdependence of engineering and applied science. This led to other designers adopting his approach. (One early result of this was that the undershot water wheel was abandoned as uneconomical.) It also lent a sense of urgency to the recurrent controversy raging at the time over the measure of force, in the discussions of which Smeaton's own research findings played a prominent role.

Later on in life Smeaton performed extensive tests on the experimental steam engine of Thomas ◊Newcomen, which led to significant improvements in its design and efficiency.

Further Reading

Anonymous, *Smeaton and Lighthouses: A Popular Biography with an Historical Introduction and Sequel,* John W Parker, 1844.

Holmes, John, *A Short Narrative of the Genius Life and Works of the Late Mr J Smeaton, Civil Engineer,* privately published, 1793.

Smiles, Samuel, *Life of John Smeaton, in: Lives of the Engineers,* John Murray, 1861, v II:6, pp 1–90.

Smith, Francis Graham (1923–) English astronomer, one of the leaders in radio astronomy since its earliest postwar days.

Smith was born in Roehampton, Surrey, on 25 April 1923. He studied at Epsom College before entering Downing College, Cambridge, in 1941 to read natural sciences. His undergraduate studies were interrupted in 1943, when he was assigned to the Telecommunications Research Establishment at Malvern as a scientific officer. In 1946 Smith returned to Cambridge to complete his degree, and he then became a research student in the radio research department at the Cavendish Laboratories. He was awarded the 1851 Exhibition Scholarship in 1951 and received a PhD the following year.

In 1952 Smith went to the Carnegie Institute in Washington, DC, where he spent a year as a research fellow before returning to Cambridge. He was appointed professor of astronomy at the University of Manchester in 1964 and then moved to Jodrell Bank, where he worked under Bernard ◊Lovell for the next ten years. He was director of the Royal Greenwich Observatory 1976–81, then, in 1981, he moved back to Jodrell Bank to become director of the Nuffield Radio Astronomy Laboratories – remaining in that post until 1988. In 1987 he was appointed Langworthy Professor of Physics at Manchester (emeritus from 1990). From 1982 to 1990 Smith was Astronomer Royal. He was knighted in 1986.

As director of the Royal Greenwich Observatory, Smith's interests were divided between the running of the observatory itself and the supervision of the early stages of the Northern Hemisphere Observatory (an international venture dedicated to both optical and radio research). He was active in the choice of site (Las Palmas in the Canary Islands), the specificiations of the new observatory, and in setting up the team to run it. He also organized the equipping of the site with new telescopes.

In addition to his many academic papers, Smith wrote successful books on radio astronomy. He is a fellow of the Royal Society and a fellow of the Royal Astronomical Society. He served the latter body as secretary 1964–70 and as president 1975–77.

The disruptive effect on Smith's education of his assignment to the Telecommunications Research Establishment in 1943 was more than compensated for by the valuable opportunity it afforded him of learning the sophisticated techniques used in radar research. These methods were to be most useful in his later work in radio astronomy. His earliest experiments at the Cavendish Laboratories were conducted with a small group of scientists that included Martin ◊Ryle. Their initial interest lay in studying radio waves emanating from the Sun, using the radio interferometer that had been designed by Ryle. Methods that evolved during this and other projects were soon applied to the study of other celestial sources of radio waves.

Other early radio astronomers – most notably Karl ◊Jansky, Grote ◊Reber, and James ◊Hey – had established that there were powerful localized sources of radio waves in the sky. In 1948 Smith and Ryle set out to investigate the source that had been found in the constellation of Cygnus. They set up a radio interferometer and recorded oscillations in receiver output that indicated that they had found two sources of radio waves. One of these was the Cygnus source. Smith analysed the timing and duration of the second signal in order to work out its position. This source lay in the constellation Cassiopeia.

The interferometer that Smith and Ryle used to obtain this important result had not been aligned with great accuracy; so Smith set himself the task of determining the precise location of both sources. He used interferometers that were more correctly aligned and devised methods of calibrating the interferometers more accurately. It was not until 1951 that he began to seek the assistance of an experienced optical astronomer. He approached D Dewhirst at the Cambridge Observatory and asked him to attempt to correlate the radio location with an observable optical feature. Dewhirst gave, as a tentative identification, a faint nebulous structure in Cassiopeia. He was not able to provide any details about the nebula.

Smith then wrote to Jan ◊Oort, who put him in touch with Walter ◊Baade, and Rudolph ◊Minkowski at Mount Palomar in the USA. These two astronomers had at their disposal the most powerful optical instrument in the world, the Hale telescope, and they were able to pinpoint optical counterparts. Cassiopeia A, as the source is now known, was shown to derive from a Type II supernova explosion within our Galaxy; and the Cygnus A is a double radio galaxy.

These discoveries provided a powerful impetus to the development of radio astronomy. They presented a valuable new method for observing strong signals from sources that would otherwise have been invisible and inaccessible to study. In essence, this opened up a whole new dimension to the universe.

During the 1950s Smith participated in a systematic search for radio sources, which culminated in 1959 in the publication of the 3C catalogue. This still provides the standard system of nomenclature for the field. Smith and Ryle were the first to publish (in 1957) a paper on the possibility of devising an accurate navigational system that depended on the use of radio signals from an orbiting satellite. This was proposed in the wake of the first Sputnik satellite.

During the early 1960s Smith was active in early scientific experiments that used artificial satellites. In 1962 he installed a radio receiver in *Aeriel II,* one of a series of joint US–UK satellites. It was able to make the first investigation of radio noise above the ionosphere.

At Jodrell Bank 1964–74 Smith studied radio waves from our Galaxy and from pulsars. His most important discoveries were the strongly polarized nature of radiation from pulsars (1968), an estimate of the strength of the magnetic field in interstellar space, and a theory of the mechanism of radiation in pulsars (1970). This theory is known as the theory of 'relativistic beaming'. Current opinion in the field of pulsar research is divided between supporting this theory and the 'polar cap' theory.

Smith's contributions to radio astronomy have been to the experimental, theoretical, and administrative aspects of the field. He has seen the subject grow from a hardly recognized discipline to an integral part of modern astronomy.

Smith, Hamilton Othanel US microbiologist; see ◊Nathans and Smith.

Smith, William (1769–1839) 'Strata Smith'. English geologist who was one of the founders of stratigraphical geology.

Born at Churchill, Oxfordshire, to a farming family, on 23 March 1769, Smith received little formal education and became a drainage expert, a canal surveyor, and a mining prospector – occupations affording him abundant opportunity to examine the varying landforms and outcrops of much of England and Wales. In 1791 he moved to the coal-mining district of Somerset, and became an expert in the construction of canals. In 1794 he undertook a six weeks' tour by post-chaise to the north of England that permitted him to see the rocks over wide stretches of terrain. During the 1790s his geological ideas matured, and by 1799 he was able to set out a detailed list of the secondary strata of England. This led him to the construction of geological maps, beginning with the Bath area. Smith was not the first geologist to recognize the principles of stratigraphy, or the usefulness of type fossils. The real measure of his achievement was less theoretical than practical, for it was he who actually determined in greater particularity than previously the succession of English strata, across the whole country, from the Carboniferous up to the Cretaceous. He also established their fossil specimens. Beyond this, his primary accomplishment lay in mapping. Smith ingeniously viewed the map as the perfect medium for presenting stratigraphical knowledge. In developing a map type showing outcrops in block, he set the essential pattern for geological cartography throughout the 19th century.

Always slow to publish, in 1815 he brought out, after much delay, *A Delineation of the Strata of England and Wales,* a geological map using a scale of five miles to the inch. Between 1816 and 1824 he published *Strata Identified by Organized Fossils,* which displayed the fossils characteristic of each formation, and his *Stratigraphical System of Organized Fossils* a descriptive catalogue. He also issued various charts and sections, and geological maps of 21 counties.

Smith's relations with the elite British geological community remained ambiguous and often tense. Ever in financial difficulties, Smith felt scorned and snubbed. In 1831, however, his work was belatedly recognized when the Geological Society of London awarded him the first Wollaston Medal. He died in Northampton on 28 August 1839.

Snell, Willebrord van Roijen (1580–1626)

Dutch physicist who discovered the law of refraction. He also founded the method of determining distances by triangulation.

Snell was born in Leiden in 1580. His father was professor of mathematics at the University of Leiden, and Snell studied law there. From 1600 to 1604 he travelled throughout Europe, working with and meeting such scientists as Tycho ◊Brahe and Johannes ◊Kepler. In 1613, Snell succeeded to his father's position at the University of Leiden and there taught mathematics, physics, and optics. He died in Leiden on 30 October 1626.

Snell developed the method of triangulation in 1615, starting with his house and the spires of nearby churches as reference points. He used a large quadrant over 2 m/7 ft long to determine angles, and by building up a network of triangles, was able to obtain a value for the distance between two towns on the same meridian. From this, Snell made an accurate determination of the radius of the Earth.

Snell is best known for Snell's law of refraction in optics, which states that the ratio of the sines of the angles of the incident and refracted rays to the normal is a constant. This constant is now called the refractive index of the two media involved. Snell discovered this law after much experimental work in 1621, and he formulated it in terms of the lengths of the paths traversed by the rays rather than the sines of the angles. Snell did not publish his law, and it first appeared in *Dioptrique* (1637) by René ◊Descartes. There Descartes expressed the law using the sines of the angles, which could easily be derived from Snell's original formulation. Whether Descartes knew of Snell's work or discovered the law independently is not known.

Snyder, Solomon Halbert (1938–)

US pharmacologist and neuroscientist who has studied the chemistry of the brain, and co-discovered the receptor mechanism for the body's own opiates, the encephalins.

Snyder was born in Washington, DC, on 26 December 1938 and graduated in medicine from Georgetown University in 1962. He joined the National Institutes of Health in Bethesda as a research associate, and in 1965 moved to the Johns Hopkins Medical School, becoming professor of psychiatry and pharmacology in 1970, and distinguished service professor in 1977.

His doctoral research under the supervision of the Nobel laureate Julius Axelrod (1912–   ) was the study of neurotransmitters, naturally occurring chemicals that are involved in the working of the nervous system, and the effects of drugs on them. In the early 1970s, in collaboration with his research student Candace Pert (1946–   ), Snyder realized that the very specific effects of synthetic opiates given in small doses suggested that they must bind to highly selective target receptor sites. Using radioactively labelled compounds they located such receptors in specialized areas of the mammalian brain and from this finding arose the suggestion that there might therefore be natural opiate-like substances in the brain that used these sites. These chemicals, the encephalins, were discovered by Hans Kosterlitz (1903–1996) and John Hughes (1942–   ) shortly afterwards. In 1978 Snyder, Hughes, and Kosterlitz were awarded the Lasker award for this work.

Snyder continues to examine the relationships of chemicals to neural functioning and has made a particular study of the naturally occurring receptor sites for the benzodiazepine drugs that are widely used in psychiatry.

Soddy, Frederick (1877–1956)

English chemist who was responsible for major advances in the early developments of radiochemistry, being mainly concerned with radioactive decay and the study of isotopes. For this work he was awarded the 1921 Nobel Prize for Chemistry. He was also a controversial character, holding firm views – with which very few people agreed – about the relationship between science and society.

Soddy was born in Eastbourne, Sussex, on 2 September 1877, the youngest of seven children. He attended Eastbourne College and became much influenced by his chemistry teacher R E Hughes, with whom he published his first scientific paper in 1894 (at the age of only 17). He went to the University College of Wales at Aberystwyth for a year after leaving school, winning an open scholarship to Merton College, Oxford, in 1895. He graduated with top honours three years later; William ◊Ramsay was his external examiner. He spent two years doing research at Oxford, but achieved little of note.

Then in 1900, at the age of 23, he applied for but was refused the professorship of chemistry at the University of Toronto in Canada. He followed this up with a personal visit, which did little to promote his case, and visited Montréal on his way back to the UK. There he was offered a junior demonstrator's post at McGill University, in Ernest ◊Rutherford's department. Soddy accepted and formed a fruitful partnership with Rutherford.

Soddy returned to London in 1902 and worked with Ramsay at University College. In 1904 he went on a brief tour of Australia as an extension lecturer for London University and on his return took up an appointment as a lecturer in physical chemistry at the University of Aberdeen, where he developed the theory of isotopes. In 1914 he was promoted to the chair in chemistry, finally achieving the professorship he had striven for since 1900. During World War I he was involved in research aimed at contributing to the war effort.

Then in 1919 he was appointed Dr Lee's Professor of Chemistry at Oxford, in the hope that he would build up an active research group in the field of radiochemistry. Soddy was instrumental in modernizing the laboratories and active in teaching, but he did little further original research. His interests turned increasingly to political and economic theory and, although he wrote prolifically on these subjects, he was unable to raise the interest or enthusiasm of others, particularly the university authorities. He retired early, in 1936, soon after the death of his wife, which affected him deeply. He travelled in Asia for a while, visiting thorium mines. During and after World War II he became increasingly concerned with how atomic energy was being put to use (as early as 1906 he had realized the tremendous potential in the energy locked up in uranium), and tried to arouse a more active sense of social responsibility among his fellow scientists to halt what he saw as a dangerous trend in the development of human society. He died in Brighton on 22 September 1956.

Soddy's first major scientific contribution, the disintegration law, was the result of his work with Rutherford in Montréal. They postulated that radioactive decay is an atomic or subatomic process, a theory that was immediately accepted. They proposed that there are two radioactive decay series beginning with uranium and thorium and both ending in lead, in which a parent radioactive element breaks down into a daughter element by emitting either an alpha particle or a beta particle. Soon a third series, beginning with actinium, was also demonstrated; it too ends in lead. (A fourth series beginning with neptunium and ending with bismuth was not discovered until after World War II.)

Soddy and Rutherford also predicted that helium should be a decay product of radium, a fact that Soddy and Ramsay proved spectrographically in 1903. In 1911 Soddy published his alpha-ray rule, which states that the emission of an alpha particle from an element results in a reduction of two in the atomic number (Russel's beta-ray rule holds that the emission of a beta particle causes an increase of one in atomic number). The displacement law, introduced by Soddy in 1913, combines these rules and explains the changes in atomic mass and atomic number for all the radioactive intermediates in the decay processes.

Also in 1913 Soddy and Theodore ◊Richards in the USA independently demonstrated the occurrence of different forms of lead in minerals from different sources. These could be added to the plethora of chemically inseparable 'elements' that displayed different radioactive properties – there were far more new elements than there were available places in the periodic table. Then Soddy brought order to chaos by proposing that the inseparable elements are in fact identical substances (in the chemical sense), differing only in atomic weight (relative atomic mass) but having the same atomic number. He named the multiple forms isotopes, meaning *same place* because they occupied the same place in the periodic table. It is now known that all the elements above bismuth (atomic number 83) have at least one radioactive isotope, as do many lighter elements (such as phosphorus). The existence of isotopes also explained anomalies in atomic-weight determinations, which were often found to be caused by the existence of isotopes in elements that were neither radioactive nor formed by radioactive decay.

Soddy was a scientist of great foresight; he predicted the use of isotopes in geological dating and the possibility of harnessing the energy of radioactive nuclei. He was capable of thorough experimentation and dramatic interpretation of the results, having the courage to propose unifying hypotheses. The change in interest that overtook him in middle life was a consequence of what he regarded as the disturbing events that were taking place in the world around him.

Further Reading

Howorth, Muriel, *Pioneer Research on the Atom – Rutherford and Soddy in a Glorious Chapter of Science: The Life Story of Frederick Soddy, MA, LLD, FRS, Nobel Laureate,* New World Publications, 1958.

Kauffman, George B (ed), *Frederick Soddy, 1877–1956: Early Pioneer in Radiochemistry,* Kluwer Academic Press, 1985.

Merricks, Linda, *The World Made New: Frederick Soddy, Science, Politics and Environment,* Oxford University Press, 1996.

Trenn, Thaddeus J, *The Self-Splitting Atom: The History of the Rutherford–Soddy Collaboration,* Taylor and Francis, 1977.

Wise, Leonard, *Frederick Soddy,* Great Money Reformers series, Holborn, 1946, v 3.

Solvay, Ernest (1838–1922) Belgian industrial chemist who invented the ammonia–soda process, also known as the Solvay process, for making the alkali sodium carbonate (soda).

Solvay was born in Rebecq-Rognon, near Brussels, on 16 April 1838, the son of a salt refiner. He was not a healthy child and had little formal education; by his late teens he was working as a bookkeeper for his father. In his spare time he carried out chemical experiments in a small home laboratory. In 1860 he went to Schaarbeek to work for an uncle who directed a gasworks, and there learned about the industrial handling of ammonia both as a gas and as an aqueous solution. Within a year he had discovered and patented the reactions that are the basis of the Solvay process. Trial production at a small plant in Schaarbeek failed; for two years Solvay knew he had the chemistry right, but could not solve the considerable problems of chemical engineering (problems that had nearly bankrupted several other industrial chemists earlier in the century). With the help of his brother Alfred he raised the necessary capital to build a full-scale works at Couillet, which was opened in 1863. By the summer of 1866 the process was well established, and a second factory was opened at Dombasle in 1873.

Solvay was as much an entrepreneur as a chemist and he soon realized that there was more money to be made from granting licences to other manufacturers than there was in making soda. (One of the licensees was the Brunner Mond Company in Cheshire, England, whose alkali division was later to become part of Imperial Chemical Industries.) Throughout the world, the Solvay process replaced the old Leblanc process (see Nicolas ◊Leblanc), which required more energy (heat) and produced obnoxious waste materials, releasing huge quantities of hydrogen chloride into the atmosphere. Towards the end of the 19th century the price of soda fell dramatically. Solvay became a very rich man and entered politics, becoming a member of the Belgian senate and a minister of state. He endowed many educational institutions throughout Belgium. During World War I he helped to organize food distribution. He lived to be 84 years old and died in Brussels on 26 May 1922.

The Solvay process uses as raw materials sodium chloride (common salt), calcium carbonate (limestone), and heat energy; ammonia is also used as a carrier of carbon dioxide, but is theoretically not consumed by the process. First the limestone is heated to yield calcium oxide (lime) and carbon dioxide:

$$CaCO_3 \rightarrow CaO + CO_2$$

The ammonia is dissolved in a solution of sodium chloride (brine), and the ammoniacal brine allowed to trickle down a tower against an upflow of carbon dioxide. The products of the resulting reaction are ammonium chloride (which stays in solution) and sodium bicarbonate (sodium hydrogen carbonate), which forms a precipitate:

$$NH_3(aq) + CO_2(g) + NaCl(aq) + H_2O \rightarrow NaHCO_3(s) + NH_4Cl(aq)$$

Finally the sodium bicarbonate is filtered off and heated to yield sodium carbonate:

$$2NaHCO_3 \rightarrow Na_2CO_3 + CO_2 + H_2O$$

Ammonia is recovered from the filtrate by reacting it with the calcium oxide from the heated limestone, producing calcium chloride as the only waste product. The key technical development is the use of countercurrent carbonating towers, which are usually employed in series to get maximum yield.

Somerville, Mary Greig (1780–1872) Born Fairfax. Scottish astronomer and mathematician who popularized astronomy and wrote several textbooks. Somerville College, Oxford, was named after her in 1879.

Born in Jedburgh, Scotland on 26 December 1780, Mary Fairfax, whose father was a naval officer, received only a year's formal education and ran wild as a child. At 15 she became interested in algebra and studied ◊Euclid and classics with her younger brother's tutor. This was disapproved of by her immediate family, who thought education was a waste of time for girls. Her uncle, however, supported her in her classical pursuits.

When she was 24, she married a cousin, Samuel Greig, who also disapproved of intellectual women. She had two children with him, one of whom died. Greig's death three years after their marriage left her free to study mathematics. She won a prize in a mathematical journal for solving a problem on Diophantine equations and bought herself a small library of mathematical books. In 1832, she married another cousin, the surgeon William Somerville, and lived with him in London. He encouraged her in her studies and introduced her to intellectual society.

Despite having no formal education, Somerville produced several textbooks that became widely used. In 1826 she presented a paper to the Royal Society entitled 'The magnetic properties of the violet rays of the solar spectrum' and she was commissioned by Lord Brougham to write an English version of Pierre ◊Laplace's treatise on celestial mechanics. Her 1831 translation *Mechanism of the Heavens* met with widespread approval and she was elected an honorary member of the Royal Astronomical Society. Her bust was placed in the Great Hall at the Royal Society and she was given a government pension of £200.

Several books and papers followed, including *On the Connection of the Physical Sciences* (1834), 'Physical geography' (1848), and *On Molecular and Microscopic Science* (1869). She also published a treatise on *Finite Differences* and books of 'popular science'.

Somerville was a suffragist and was first to sign John Stewart Mill's petition to the government for women's suffrage. She spent most of the latter part of her life in Italy and she died in Naples on 29 November 1872.

Further Reading

Patterson, Elizabeth Chambers, *Mary Somerville, 1780–1872,* Somerville College, 1979.

Patterson, Elizabeth Chambers,'A Scotswoman abroad: Mary Somerville's 1817 visit to France' in: North, J D and Roche, J J (eds), *The Light of Nature: Essays Presented to A C Crombie,* Nijhoff, 1985, pp 321–362.

Weitzenhoffer, Kenneth, 'The education of Mary Somerville', *Sky Telesc,* 1987, v 73, pp 138–139.

Sommerfeld, Arnold Johannes Wilhelm (1868–1951) German physicist who made an important contribution to the development of the quantum theory of atomic structure. He was also a gifted teacher of science.

Sommerfeld was born in Königsberg in Prussia (now Kaliningrad in Russia) on 5 December 1868. After attending the local Gymnasium, he entered Königsberg University in 1886 and opted for mathematics. He received his PhD in 1891 and then obtained an assistantship at the Mineralogical Institute in Göttingen 1893–94. In 1895, he became a *Privatdozent* (unpaid lecturer) in mathematics at Göttingen University and in 1897, was appointed professor of mathematics at the Mining Academy in Clausthal. In 1900, Sommerfeld became professor of technical mechanics at the Technical Institute in Aachen and in 1906 moved to Munich University as director of the Institute of Theoretical Physics, which was established there for him. Sommerfeld built his institute into a leading centre of physics and attracted many gifted scientists as students, notably Peter ◊Debye, Wolfgang ◊Pauli, Werner ◊Heisenberg, and Hans ◊Bethe. It was also under Sommerfeld's direction that Max von ◊Laue and his colleagues made the famous discovery of X-ray diffraction in 1912. Sommerfeld also helped to spread and advance physics by publishing several important books that summed up current knowledge in several fields. The most influential of these were *Atombau und Spektrallinien/Atomic Structure and Spectral Lines* (1919) and *Wellenmechanischer Ergänzungsband/Wave Mechanics* (1929).

Sommerfeld remained at Munich until 1940, when he retired. He courageously defended Albert ◊Einstein and other Jewish scientists in the Weimar and Nazi periods when anti-Semitism was prevalent in Germany. Sommerfeld returned to his post at the Institute of Theoretical Physics in Munich after World War II. He died in Munich on 26 April 1951 after being struck by a car.

Sommerfeld was active as a theoretician in several fields both in physics and engineering, and he produced a four-volume work on the theory of gyroscopes 1897–1910 in association with Felix ◊Klein. However, his principal contribution to science was in the development of quantum theory. Sommerfeld promoted the theory as a fundamental law of nature, and inspired Niels ◊Bohr to apply the theory to the structure of the atom. Sommerfeld took the quantum model of the atom that Bohr proposed in 1913 and worked out in 1915 that electrons must move in elliptical and not circular orbits around the nucleus. This led him in 1916 to predict a series of spectral lines based on the relativistic effects that would occur with elliptical orbits. Friedrich Paschen (1865–1945) immediately undertook the spectroscopic work required and confirmed Sommerfeld's predictions. This evidence for Bohr's ideas led to a rapid acceptance of the quantum theory of the atom.

Sommerville, Duncan MacLaren Young (1879–1934) Scottish mathematician who made significant contributions to the study of non-Euclidean geometry.

Sommerville was born on 24 November 1879 at Beawar, Rajasthan, India, the son of Scottish parents. He was educated in Scotland, first at Perth Academy and then at the University of St Andrews. From 1902 to 1904 he was a lecturer in the mathematics department there. In 1911 he became president of the Edinburgh Mathematical Society, which he had helped to found.

In 1915 Sommerville went to New Zealand as professor of pure and applied mathematics at Victoria University College, Wellington. He also became the first executive secretary of the Royal Astronomical Society of New Zealand, of which he was a founder member. He presided over the mathematical section of the Australasia Association for the Advancement of Science in 1924 and four years later was awarded the Hector Medal of the Royal Society of New Zealand. He retained his post of professor of mathematics in Wellington until he died there on 31 January 1924.

Sommerville wrote numerous papers, nearly all of them on geometrical topics. The first appeared in 1905 under the title 'Networks of the plane in absolute geometry', which was followed by 'Semi-regular networks of the plane in absolute geometry' (1906). He also wrote two other papers in that year which gave a pure mathematical treatment to the questions of a statistical nature that arose from the biometric researches of Karl ◊Pearson.

Sommerville was an accomplished teacher and taught in both Scotland and New Zealand. His contribution to this area was enhanced by the publication of four textbooks on non-Euclidean geometry. Two of these indicated his major research specialties: *Elements of Non-Euclidean Geometry* and *An Introduction to the Geometry of n Dimensions,* which included concepts that Sommerville himself had originated. He explained how non-Euclidean geometries arise from the use of alternatives to ◊Euclid's postulate of parallels, and showed that both Euclidean and non-Euclidean geometries – such as hyperbolic and elliptic geometries – can be considered as sub-geometries of projective geometry. He stated that projective geometry is the invariant theory associated with the group of linear fractional transformations. He studied the tesselations of Euclidean and non-Euclidean space and showed that, although there are only three regular tesselations in the Euclidean plane, there are five congruent regular polygons of the same kind in the elliptical plane and an infinite number of such patterns in the hyperbolic plane. The variety is even greater if 'semi-regular' networks of regular polygons of different kinds are allowed (because the regular patterns are topologically equivalent to the non-regular designs). In his later work on n-dimensional geometry, Sommerville generalized his earlier analysis to include 'honeycombs' of polyhedra in three-dimensional spaces and of polytopes in spaces of 4, 5, ... n dimensions – including both Euclidean and non-Euclidean geometries.

Sommerville also studied astronomy, anatomy, and chemistry. His interest in crystallography played a significant part in motivating him to investigate repetitive space-filling geometric patterns. He was also a skilful artist, as was exhibited in the models he constructed to illustrate his abstract conceptions.

Sorby, Henry Clifton (1826–1908)

Sorby, Henry Clifton (1826–1908) English geologist who made huge advances in the field of petrology.

The only son of a wealthy Sheffield tool manufacturer, Sorby was Born on 10 May 1826 and was privately Educated, soon displaying a single-minded enthusiasm for science. After a brief interest in agricultural chemistry he turned to geology. His father's death allowed the 21-year-old Sorby the leisure to spend his life as an independent scientific researcher (he never married). He became fascinated with the microscopic study of rocks. David ◊Brewster had earlier explored the molecular structure of minerals by investigating the passing of light through them, but he had been limited to investigating well-crystallized specimens. Operating from his own laboratory, Sorby overcame this problem by drawing upon the art of thin-slicing hard minerals, analysing the specimens obtained under the microscope. Microscopic examination of thin sections of rocks had the virtue of enabling the constituent minerals to be scrutinized in transmitted light. Sorby also recognized the value of the Nicol prism for distinguishing the different component minerals in terms of the effect they produced on polarized light. His interest in studying meteorites led him in 1863 to discover the crystalline nature of steel, thus instituting the study of metallography. Though his early papers met with hostility, Sorby's work became credited with opening up a new science – though it

proved to be more energetically cultivated in Germany than in the UK.

Sorby's interests were wide. He employed his microscopic techniques to investigate the structures of iron and steel under stress. He attempted to utilize quantitative techniques for geological phenomena, extrapolating from laboratory models and small-scale natural processes in the expectation of explaining vast events in geological history. In 1857 he was elected fellow of the Royal Society, and he was to play a large role in the foundation of Firth College (later the University of Sheffield), where he endowed a chair of geology and a research fellowship. He died in Sheffield on 10 March 1908.

South, James (1785–1867)

South, James (1785–1867) English astronomer noted for the observatory that he founded and his observations of double stars.

South was born in London in October 1785. He first studied medicine and surgery and became a member of the Royal College of Surgeons before renouncing medicine at the age of 31 in order to devote himself to astronomy. His marriage in 1816 made him wealthy enough to establish observatories in London and in Paris and to equip them with the best telescopes then available.

South became a member of the Royal Society of London in 1821 and he held a variety of positions in the Astronomical Society of London. When the latter body gained a royal charter in 1831, a technicality barred South from serving as its first president and he resigned from the society. He was knighted in that year and two years later was awarded an honorary LLD by Cambridge University. He was also a member of a number of scientific organizations in Scotland, Ireland, France, Belgium, and Italy. He died on 19 October 1867 in London.

South's contribution to astronomy and the development of scientific work in the UK has been obscured by his argumentative temperament. His public criticism of the Royal Society for participating in the decline of the sciences in the UK offended other members. He published criticisms of other works, including the *Nautical Almanac,* finding it inferior to continental work. None of this endeared him to his peers. South's quarrel with Troughton about the quality of the latter's workmanship was consistent with South's apprehension about declining standards, but it led to a law suit which South lost. He then publicly destroyed the equipment that Troughton had made for him.

Despite such quarrels, South continued to work until his retirement. He is perhaps best remembered for his work with John ◊Herschel in observing double stars. They charted and catalogued changes in the positions of some 380 such stars. Their work was presented to the Royal Society in 1824 and rewarded with the Gold Medal of the Astronomical Society and the first prize of the Institut de France. In 1826 South completed another catalogue of double stars and for this he was awarded the Copley Medal of the Royal Society.

Spallanzani, Lazzaro (1729–1799) Italian physiologist who is famous for disproving the theory of spontaneous generation. In his later years Spallanzani became widely renowned for his biological investigations and received many academic honours, including a fellowship of the Royal Society of London in 1768.

Spallanzani was born on 12 January 1729, the son of a distinguished lawyer. He attended the local school until he was 15, when he went to the Jesuit college at Reggio. He was invited to join the Jesuit order, but declined. He then studied law at the University of Bologna where, under the influence of his cousin Laura ◊Bassi, who was professor of physics and mathematics there, Spallanzani became interested in science and broadened his education to include mathematics, chemistry, natural history, and French. In 1754, after obtaining his doctorate, he was appointed professor of logic, metaphysics, and Greek at Reggio College. Three years later he was ordained a priest, but performed his priestly duties irregularly and devoted himself almost entirely to his scientific studies – which were greatly facilitated by the moral protection and financial assistance provided by the church. Spallanzani was professor of physics at Modena University 1760–69, when he became professor of natural history at the University of Pavia, a position he held for the rest of his life. In his later years Spallanzani travelled widely in order to further his scientific investigations. He died in Pavia on 11 February 1799.

Spallanzani is best known for finally disproving the theory of spontaneous generation. The experiments of Francesco Redi (1626–1697) on fly maggots in 1668 proved that complex animals do not arise spontaneously, but until Spallanzani's investigations, it was still generally believed that simple life forms were generated spontaneously from rotting food. After performing hundreds of experiments in which he boiled infusions of vegetable matter in hermetically sealed flasks and found that no microorganisms had grown in the broth, Spallanzani was able to report in 1765 that this was not the case.

Spallanzani also investigated many other biological problems, such as the physiology of blood circulation. In 1771, while examining the vascular network in a chick embryo, he discovered the existence of vascular connections between arteries and veins – the first time this connection had been observed in a warm-blooded animal. He also studied the effects of growth on the circulation in chick embryos and tadpoles; the influ-ence of gravity and the effects of wounds on various parts of the vascular system; and changes that occur in the circulation of dying animals. In addition, Spallanzani showed that the arterial pulse is caused by sideways pressure on the expansile artery walls from heartbeats transmitted by the bloodstream.

Spallanzani also studied digestion and, after administering food samples in perforated containers to a wide variety of animals and then recovering the containers and examining them, concluded that the fundamental factor in digestion is the solvent property of gastric juice – a term first used by him. In his investigations of reproduction, he showed that the clasp reflex in amphibians persists after the male has been severely mutilated or even decapitated. (The clasp reflex is an automatic action on the part of the male in which he tightly holds the female during mating.) And in 1765 he performed an artificial insemination of a dog. Spallanzani's other biological investigations included the resuscitation of rotifers; the regeneration of decapitated snails' heads; the migration of swallows and eels; the flight of bats; and the electric discharge of torpedo fish (electric rays). In his later years Spallanzani studied respiration, proving that tissues use oxygen and give off carbon dioxide.

In addition to his biological work, Spallanzani also studied various problems in physics, chemistry, geology, and meteorology, as well as pioneering the science of vulcanology.

Spemann, Hans (1869–1941) German embryologist who discovered the phenomenon now called embryonic induction – the influence exerted by various regions of an embryo that controls the subsequent development of cells into specific organs and tissues. For this outstanding achievement he was awarded the 1935 Nobel Prize for Physiology or Medicine. In carrying out his embryological research, Spemann also pioneered techniques of microsurgery.

Spemann was born on 27 June 1869 in Stuttgart, the eldest of the four children of a bookseller. He attended school at the Eberhard-Ludwigs-Gymnasium, after which he was obliged to do a year of military service with the Kassel Hussars. When his military service ended, Spemann went to Heidelberg University to study medicine, but soon abandoned it in order to study zoology. On his graduation in 1894 he went to Würzburg University to study for his doctorate. and in 1898 was appointed lecturer in zoology there. Spemann remained at Würzburg until 1908, when he was appointed to the chair of zoology at Rostock University. From 1914 to 1919 he was director of the Kaiser Wilhelm Institute of Biology in Berlin-Dahlem, after which he became professor of zoology at the University of Freiburg im Breisgau, a position he held until his retirement in 1935. Spemann died in Freiburg on 12 September 1941.

Spemann's Nobel prizewinning research was carried out on newt embryos. Previous workers had already shown that, as a newt embryo develops, an outgrowth of its brain comes into contact with the ectoderm (the outer germ layer in the very early embryo) and that this outgrowth develops into the retina of the eye while the area of ectoderm it has come into contact with develops into the lens. By carefully destroying the outgrowths at an early stage in their development, Spemann found that neither the retina nor the lens subsequently develop. This finding led him to the conclusion that the stimulus causing ectoderm to develop into lens tissue comes from the brain outgrowth. In his next series of experiments, Spemann – using delicate microsurgical techniques that he himself had developed – removed the piece of ectoderm that would normally become the lens and replaced it with a piece of ectoderm from elsewhere in the embryo. He found that, regardless of its site of origin, the transplanted ectoderm develops into a lens if it is in contact with the developing retina.

Spemann continued his line of research by investigating the effect of ligaturing embryos into halves. Embryos at an early stage of development either died or developed into a whole embryo: there were no half embryos formed. Similar results were obtained using embryos in the blastula stage (when the embryo is a hollow ball of cells), but when performed after gastrulation and invagination, ligaturing resulted in half embryos. It seemed, therefore, that as the embryo developed, the fates of different parts became determined. Spemann next began to search for the cause of specific aspects of embryonic development. Working with Otto Mangold, he transplanted various embryonic parts to other areas of the embryo and to different embryos. They discovered that any part of the ectoderm that comes into contact with the mesoderm (middle germ layer) during gastrulation eventually develops into the central nervous system. By transplanting mesoderm from the dorsal lip region of one embryo into an intact second embryo, Spemann managed to induce the development of a second central nervous system. Thus Spemann and Mangold demonstrated that one area of embryonic tissue influences the development of neighbouring tissues. Spemann named these influential regions organizers.

To investigate whether or not there was any predetermination within embryos, Spemann next conducted a series of experiments in which he exchanged tissue between newt and frog embryos. He found that embryonic tissue from newts always gives rise to newt organs, even when transplanted into a frog embryo, and that frog tissue always develops into frog organs in a newt embryo. Thus Spemann demonstrated that embryonic tissue responds to induction from foreign tissue but has the potential to develop only into the organs of the species from which it originated and is therefore predetermined to some extent.

Further Reading

Allen, Garland E, 'Inducers and 'organizers': Hans Spemann and experimental embryology', *Hist Phil Life Sci*, 1993, v 15, pp 229–236.

Hamburger, Viktor, *The Heritage of Experimental Embryology: Hans Spemann and the Organizer*, Monographs on the History and Philosophy of Biology, Oxford University Press, 1988.

Saha, Margaret, 'Spemann seen through a lens' in: Gilbert, Scott F (ed), *A Conceptual History of Modern Embryology*, Plenum Press, 1991, pp 91–108.

Sperry, Elmer Ambrose (1860–1930) US inventor and engineer who exploited the technology of the gyroscope to develop the first commercially successful gyrostabilizer for ships, and the gyrocompass and gyro-controlled autopilot for aircraft and ships. In doing this work he laid the foundations for modern control theory, cybernetics, and automation.

Sperry was born on 21 October 1860, the son of Stephen Sperry, a farmer of Cortland County, New York, and Mary Burst from nearby Cincinnatus who died soon after his birth. He attended the Cortland Normal School until January 1880 and then made informal arrangements to sit in on lectures at nearby Cornell and at the same time to develop his first invention (a generator with characteristics suited to arc lighting).

Sperry married Zula Goodman on 28 June 1887 and the following year set up his own research and development enterprise. He formed a mining machinery company and, moving to Cleveland, Ohio in 1893, developed and manufactured streetcars. He produced a superior storage battery, teaching himself chemistry in the process. He perfected a process for the production of caustic soda (sodium hydroxide) and was closely involved in a complicated process for the detinning of scrap from tin-can manufacture.

The family moved to Brooklyn in 1907 and in the same year his interest in the gyroscope began to show itself, leading to the work for which he is best known. Sperry's gyroscope company, from a research and development concern, gradually evolved into a manufacturing organization and World War I brought a dramatic upsurge in foreign sales.

Sperry was also active in researching internal-combustion engines. He spent $1 million on a compounded diesel but the idea never came to fruition. He developed a track-recorder car for detecting substandard railway track and went on to invent a device for revealing defective rails that were undetectable visually.

Sperry resigned as president of the Sperry Gyroscope Company in 1926 to become chairman of the board. During his lifetime he and his company filed about 360 patent applications that finally matured as patents. His wife died on 11 March 1930 and Sperry died in Brooklyn on 16 June the same year.

A gyroscope's major active component is a rapidly spinning wheel. This follows the natural laws of motion and inertia so that if its spindle is moved in one direction it will respond by forcing the spindle to move at right angles to the original direction of motion. This behaviour is called precession.

A considerable amount of work had already been done in Europe and the USA on gyrostabilization and in 1908 Sperry filed a massive patent application for a ship's gyroscope. It encapsulated the principle of an active system rather than the passive systems already used by the German naval engineer Ernst Otto Schlick.

Sperry's scheme mounted the gyro with its axis vertical in the hold of the ship. The axis was free to move in a fore and aft direction, but not from side to side. He used an electric motor to precess the gyro (tilt its rotor) artificially just as the ship began to roll. The gyro responded by exerting a force to one side or the other. Since it was fixed rigidly to the ship in the plane, the ship's roll was largely counteracted.

In 1912 a full-sized prototype with two gyro wheels, each weighing 1,800 kg/4,000 lb, was installed in the USS *Worden,* a 433-ton torpedo-boat destroyer. The installation cut a total roll of 3° to about 6°.

A gyrocompass feels the force of gravity and precesses until the axis of rotation of the spinning wheel is parallel to the axis of rotation of the Earth. On a ship, however, the pendulous gyro will also sense the ship's motion so it precesses away from the meridian. Sperry solved this problem by incorporating a servomechanism and a mechanical analogue computer that together compensated for the unwanted inputs.

Dr Hermann Anschutz-Kaempfe (1872–1931) installed a system in the German fleet's flagship, *Deutschland,* in 1908. The prototype Sperry unit was fitted to the Dominion Line ship *Princess Anne* early in 1911 and the first production unit went into the USS *Utah* in November the same year.

The Sperry aircraft stabilizer had two components – one providing roll control and the other pitch control. Each unit opened compressed air valves, admitting air to slave cylinders. The pistons acted on the aircraft's controls to correct the error.

The roll component of the equipment was first flown in a Curtiss aircraft on Thanksgiving Day 1912, with the founder of the company, Glenn Curtiss

(1878–1930), himself at the controls. In the winter of 1913–14 Sperry and his son designed and built an improved unit in which its four gyros were mounted together on a single stable platform. This arrangement has since become an essential component of guidance systems for missiles, aircraft, and submarines.

The problems of blind-flying instruments proved to be extrememly tough and by the end of World War I virtually the only workable gyro instrument was for indicating rate of turn. The all-important gryocompass and artificial horizon eluded Sperry himself and his research teams due to the rapid accelerations of aircraft in bumpy air.

At the instigation of the US forces, Sperry designed the control equipment for a specially built Curtiss pilotless aircraft that was to deliver a 450-kg/1,000-lb load of explosives to a target 80–160 km/50–100 mi away. This was officially called the 'flying bomb', thus anticipating the German V1s of World War II and the cruise missiles of the early 1980s.

After the war Sperry turned his attention to marine autopilots and a trial installation on an oil tanker performed well. Sales of the equipment increased until 1,000 merchant ships were so equipped by 1932.

Sperry introduced many of the concepts that are common in modern control theory. He did not use present-day jargon to describe his innovations but nevertheless he was one of the first in the fields of cybernetics and automation.

Further Reading

Hughes, Thomas Parke, 'Model builders and instrument makers', *Sci Context,* 1988, v 2, pp 59–75.

Hughes, Thomas Parke, *Elmer Sperry: Inventor and Engineer,* Johns Hopkins University Press, 1971.

Hunsaker, Jerome Clarke, *Biographical Memoir of Elmer Ambrose Sperry, 1860–1930,* National Academy of Sciences, 1955.

Spitzer, Lyman (1914–1997) US astrophysicist who made important contributions to cosmogony (the study of the origin and evolution of stars and planetary systems).

Spitzer was born on 26 June 1914 in Toledo, Ohio. He graduated from Yale in 1935 and then went to Cambridge University in the UK to work with the astronomer Arthur ◊Eddington. In 1936 he returned to Yale, where he gained a PhD two years later. Spitzer stayed at Yale until 1947, when he moved to Princeton as professor, head of the astrophysical department, and director of the Princeton Observatory, holding these posts until 1979. In 1951 he founded the Princeton Plasma Physics Laboratory and was its director until 1961. From 1982 he was senior research astronomer at Princeton. He died on 31 March 1997.

Spitzer's initial interest was in star formation. One hypothesis proposed that stars were formed when gases and dust in interstellar space fused together under the influence of weak magnetic forces. A satisfactory understanding of this hypothesis required an appreciation of the fusion power of gases at temperatures as high as 100 million degrees, by which point hydrogen gas fuses to form helium. Spitzer proposed that only a magnetic field could contain gases at these temperatures, and he devised a figure-of-eight design to describe this field. His model remained important to later attempts to bring about the controlled fusion of hydrogen.

Spitzer's interest in the origin of planetary systems led him to criticize the tidal theory, proposed by James ◊Jeans amongst others. This was the idea that our planetary system is the result of an encounter between the Sun and a passing star: the star's closeness set up a tidal effect on the Sun, causing it to give off gaseous filaments that subsequently broke off from the main body to become planetary fragments. Spitzer showed that such a theory overlooked the fact that a gas would be dispersed into interstellar space long before it had cooled sufficiently to condense into planets. This objection also applied to Fred ◊Hoyle's hypothesis that the Sun was a binary star whose companion long ago exploded as a supernova, leaving a gas cloud that condensed into planets.

Stahl, Franklin William US molecular biologist; see ◊Meselson and Stahl.

Stahl, Georg Ernst (1660–1734) German chemist and physician who founded the phlogiston theory of combustion. This theory was one of the great dead-ends of chemistry, which was to dominate – and mislead – the science for nearly a century. Nevertheless it was instrumental in stimulating much thought and experiment, and helped to bring about the change from alchemy to chemistry.

Stahl was born in Ansbach, Franconia, on 21 October 1660, the son of a Protestant clergyman. He studied medicine under Georg Wedel (1645–1721) at the University of Jena, where a fellow student was Friedrich Hoffmann (1660–1742); Stahl occupied a teaching post at Jena a year before he gained his medical degree in 1684. He became a physician to the duke of Sachsen Weimar in 1687 and seven years later, on the recommendation of Hoffmann, he moved to the new University of Halle as its first professor of medicine, where his course included lectures in chemistry. In 1716 he moved again to Berlin to become personal physician to King Frederick I of Prussia, a position he retained until his death. He died in Berlin on 14 May 1734.

The phlogiston theory had its beginnings in 1667 in the ideas of Jochim Becher (1635–1681), who thought that combustible substances contain an active principle, which he termed *terra pinguis* (fatty earth). Jan van ◊Helmont called the combustible element 'phlogiston', but it was Stahl who formulated the theory. The phlogiston theory is simple: when a substance is burned or heated it loses phlogiston; reduction of the products of combustion (with, say, charcoal) reverses the process and phlogiston is restored. For example, when metallic lead is heated it forms a powdery calx (so the metal must have been a combination of calx and phlogiston). Then when the calx is heated with charcoal, it absorbs phlogiston from the charcoal and becomes metallic lead again. When charcoal is heated on its own, it leaves hardly any ash (calx) and so must be particularly rich in phlogiston.

The theory was the first attempt at a rational explanation for combustion (and what we would term oxidation), and had obvious appeal to the chemists of the time who were familiar with the reduction processes – often using charcoal – associated with the smelting of metals. The first doubts about the phlogiston theory came when chemists began weighing the reactants and products of such reactions. When metals are calcined (oxidized by heating in air) they get heavier – and yet they should *lose* phlogiston and become lighter. Also a calx demonstrably becomes lighter when it is reduced back to metal, instead of getting heavier as it once more takes up phlogiston. Stahl himself made such quantitative determinations, but accounted for the observations by stating that phlogiston is weightless or can even have negative weight; it might be as insubstantial as 'caloric' (heat) and flow from one substance to another. The falsity of these assumptions and of the whole phlogiston theory was finally proved by Antoine ◊Lavoisier in the 1770s with his experiments on combustion (and by the discovery of oxygen in 1774 by Karl ◊Scheele and Joseph ◊Priestley).

Stark, Johannes (1874–1957) German physicist who is known for his discovery of the phenomenon (now called the Stark effect) of the division of spectral lines in an electric field, and for his discovery of the Doppler effect in canal rays (high-velocity rays of positively charged ions). For this work he received the 1919 Nobel Prize for Physics.

Stark was born in Schickenhof, Bavaria, on 15 April 1874. He studied chemistry, physics, mathematics, and crystallography at the University of Munich, from which he graduated in 1898 and where he spent the following two years working at the Physical Institute. In 1900 he became a lecturer at the University of Göttingen, then in 1906 was appointed extraordinary professor at the Technische Hochschule in Hannover. In 1909 he moved to the Technische Hochschule in

Aachen, where he held a professorship until 1917. From 1917 to 1922 he was professor of physics at the University of Greifswald, lecturing also at the University of Würzburg 1920–22. He then attempted to set up a porcelain factory in northern Germany but this scheme failed, largely because of the depressed state of the German economy, and so he tried – unsuccessfully – to return to academic life. A vehement anti-Semite, Stark was attracted to the rising Nazi movement and joined the Nazi party in 1930. Three years later he became president of the Reich Physical-Technical Institute and also president of the German Research Association. But his attempts to become an important influence in German physics brought him into conflict with the authorities and he was forced to resign in 1939. Nor did his decline end there: because of his Nazi background, in 1947 he was sentenced to four years' internment in a labour camp by a German denazification court. Stark died on 21 June 1957 in Traunstein (then in West Germany).

In 1902 Stark predicted that the high-velocity canal rays produced in a cathode-ray tube should exhibit the Doppler effect (the change in the observed frequency of a wave resulting from movement of the wave's source or the observer or both). Three years later he proved his prediction correct by demonstrating the frequency shift in hydrogen canal rays.

His next major work was his discovery (announced in 1913) of the spectral phenomenon now called the Stark effect. Following Pieter ◊Zeeman's demonstration in 1896 of the division of spectral lines caused by the influence of a magnetic field, Stark succeeded in showing (by photographing the spectrum emitted by canal rays – consisting of hydrogen and helium atoms – as they passed through a strong electric field) that an electric field produces a similar splitting effect on the spectral lines. The Stark effect is produced because the electric field causes the radiating atom's electron cloud to alter its position with respect to the nucleus, which distorts the electron orbitals. Light is emitted when an excited electron moves from a high to a lower energy orbital, so distortion of the orbitals also distorts the emitted light, this effect being manifested as splitting of the spectral lines.

Stark is also known for his modification (in 1913) of the photo-equivalence law proposed by Albert Einstein in 1906. Now called the Stark–Einstein law, it states that each molecule involved in a photochemical reaction absorbs only one quantum of the radiation that causes the reaction.

Starling, Ernest Henry (1866–1927) English physiologist, remembered for his work on the heart, on body functions, and on hormones (which he named).

Starling was born in London on 17 April 1866; his father was a barrister who worked in India, and whom he rarely saw. He was educated at King's College, London, 1880–82, and then at Guy's Hospital. He gained his medical degree there in 1889, having spent a summer in Heidelberg in Germany in 1885 working in the laboratories of the physiologist Willy Kühne (1837–1900), and was a demonstrator at Guy's in 1887. In 1889 he was appointed a lecturer in physiology at Guy's and retained the position until 1899. During that period he was a part-time researcher at University College, London, in 1890, where he got to know William ◊Bayliss, with whom he was to work a few years later. In 1892 he went to Breslau in Germany (now Wrocław in Poland) where he spent some time in the laboratories of Rudolf Heidenhain. From 1899 to 1923 he was professor of physiology at University College. World War I interrupted this appointment and in 1914 he became director of research at the Royal Army Medical Corps College, where he investigated antidotes to poisonous gases. From 1917 to 1919 he served as chairman of the Royal Society's food committee and as scientific adviser to the Ministry of Food. He retired from University College in 1922 and became a research professor of the Royal Society. He died while on a Caribbean cruise, in Kingston, Jamaica, on 2 May 1927.

Starling spent several years studying the conditions that cause fluids to leave blood vessels and enter the tissues. In 1896 he demonstrated the Starling equilibrium – the balance between hydrostatic pressure, causing fluids to flow out of the capillary membrane, and osmotic pressure, causing the fluids to be absorbed from the tissues into the capillary. The most important plasma protein in this fluid exchange, which helps to generate intravascular pressure, was found to be albumin.

When he started working at University College with Bayliss, Starling researched the nervous mechanisms that control the activities of the organs of the chest and abdomen, and together they discovered the peristaltic wave in the intestine. Their most important discovery, however, was in 1902, when they found the hormone secretin. This substance is found in the epithelial cells of the duodenum and excites the pancreas to secrete its digestive juices when acid chyme passes from the stomach into the duodenum – hence the name 'secretin'. It was the first time that a specific chemical substance had been seen to act as a stimulus for an organ at a distance from its site of origin. Starling and Bayliss coined the word 'hormone' in 1905 to characterize secretin and other similar substances produced internally and carried in the bloodstream to other parts of the body where they affect the function of organs.

Starling is probably best known for his work on the heart and on circulation. In 1918 he devised a heart–lung preparation by which the heart was isolated from all the other organs except the lungs, and attached only by the pulmonary blood vessels. The blood circulation in the heart was recorded by manometers. In this experiment Starling demonstrated the mechanism by which the heart is able to increase automatically the energy of each contraction in proportion to the mechanical demand made upon it and how it can adapt its work to the needs of the body independently of the nervous system. This mechanism, which Starling called the law of the heart, states that the more the heart is filled during diastole (relaxation), the greater is the following systole (contraction) – that is, that the one is directly proportional to the other. This mechanism enables the heart to adjust the strength of its beat to variations in bloodflow without changing its rate. If a heart is impaired, it has to dilate more to achieve the same amount of work as it did when undamaged. Constant dilation of the heart is therefore used as a primary indication that it is damaged. This physiological phenomenon is not a feature exclusive to cardiac muscle but occurs in all contractile tissues, although in the heart the function is more immediately vital.

In 1924 Starling succeeded in maintaining the mammalian kidney in isolation from the body, and found that substances lost in the excretory filtrate, such as carbonates, glucose, and chlorides, are reabsorbed in the lower parts of the glomeruli.

Stas, Jean Servais (1813–1891) Belgian analytical chemist who is remembered for making the first accurate determinations of atomic weights (relative atomic masses).

Stas was born in Louvain on 21 August 1813. He initially studied medicine, and although he qualified as a doctor he never practised. After graduation he went to Paris as an assistant to Jean Baptiste ◊Dumas, working mainly in organic chemistry. In 1840 he was appointed professor of chemistry at the Ecole Royale Militaire in Brussels, and he advised the Belgian government on military topics related to chemistry. In middle age he developed a disorder of the throat, which made it difficult for him to give lectures. He left the military school in 1869 and three years later he became commissioner of the Mint, but his liberalist views did not coincide with the monetary policy of the government and he left the post in 1872. He spent the rest of his life in retirement, although he still voiced his anti-clerical opinions and was openly critical of the part played by the church in education. He died in Brussels in 13 December 1891.

While he was working with Dumas in Paris, Stas helped to re-determine the atomic weights of oxygen and carbon, showing them both to be almost exactly whole numbers (and that of carbon to be 12, not 6 as had previously been assumed). These results gave new support to William ◊Prout's hypothesis of 1815 (that all atomic weights are whole numbers). Beginning in the mid-1850s, Stas spent more than ten years measuring accurately the atomic weights of many elements, using oxygen = 16 as a standard. He gradually found more and more elements with non-integral atomic weights, and finally he discredited completely Prout's hypothesis. His results provided the foundation for the work of Dmitri ◊Mendeleyev and others on the periodic table, and remained the standards of accuracy until they were superseded 50 years later by the determinations of the US chemist Theodore ◊Richards.

Staudinger, Hermann (1881–1965) German organic chemist who pioneered polymer chemistry. His contribution was finally recognized when he was 72 years old with the award of the 1953 Nobel Prize for Chemistry.

Staudinger was born in Worms, Hesse, on 23 March 1881, the son of a physician. His university education included studies at Halle (where he obtained his PhD in 1903), Munich, and Darmstadt. He taught in Strasbourg, at the Technische Hochschule in Karlsruhe 1908–12 as professor of organic chemistry in association with Fritz ◊Haber, and as professor of general chemistry at Zürich 1912–26, where he succeeded Richard ◊Willstätter. In 1926 he was appointed professor of chemistry at the University of Freiburg im Breisgau, where he remained until he retired in 1951. In 1940 he was made director of the Chemical Laboratory and Research Institute for Macromolecular Chemistry. After 1951 his department at Freiburg became the State Research Institute for Macromolecular Chemistry and he was made an emeritus professor. He died in Freiburg on 8 September 1965.

Staudinger's first research, at Halle, concerned the malonic esters of unsaturated compounds. Then in 1907 under Johannes Thiele (1865–1918) at Strasbourg he made the unexpected discovery of the highly reactive ketenes, the substances that give the aroma to coffee.

It was in Karlsruhe that Staudinger began the work for which he was to become famous, the study of the nature of polymers. He devised a new and simple synthesis of isoprene (the monomer for the production of the synthetic rubber polyisoprene) and with C L Lautenschläger prepared polyoxymethylenes. All this work was done at a time when most chemists thought that polymers were disorderly conglomerates of small molecules. From 1926 Staudinger put forward the view – not immediately accepted – that polymers are giant molecules held together with ordinary chemical bonds. To give credence to the theory he made chemical changes to polymers that left their molecular weights almost unchanged; for example, he hydrogenated rubber to produce a saturated hydrocarbon polymer.

To measure the high molecular weights of polymers he devised a relationship, now known as Staudinger's law, between the viscosity of polymer solutions and their molecular weight. Viscometry is still widely used for this purpose in the plastics industry and in polymer research. Eventually X-ray crystallography was to confirm some of his predictions about the structures of polymers, particularly the long-chain molecular strands common to many of them.

Although Staudinger had no conception of how information is stored in nucleic acids or how such information is transferred to proteins, in 1936 he made a remarkably accurate prediction: 'Every gene macromolecule possesses a quite different structural plan which determines its function in life.' In his book *Macromolekulare Chemie und Biologie* (1947) he anticipated the molecular biology of the future.

Stebbins, Joel (1878–1966) US astronomer, the first to develop the technique of electric photometry in the study of stars.

Stebbins was born on 30 July 1878 in Omaha, Nebraska. He was interested in astronomy from an early age, and pursued his studies in the subject at the universities of Nebraska, where he received a BA in 1899, Wisconsin, and California. He worked at the Lick Observatory 1901–03, where he earned a PhD. He was then appointed instructor in astronomy at the University of Illinois and was made assistant professor in 1904. After a sabbatical year at the University of Munich 1912–13, he became professor of astronomy at the University of Illinois and was made director of the university observatory. In 1922 Stebbins became director of the Washburn Observatory and professor of astronomy at the University of Wisconsin. He retired as professor emeritus in 1948, but continued active research at the Lick Observatory until 1958. Stebbins was a member of the National Academy of Sciences, the American Association for the Advancement of Science, and other prominent scientific organizations. He was the recipient of the Draper Medal of the National Academy of Sciences in 1915, the Gold Medal of the Royal Astronomical Society in 1950, and other honours. He died in Palo Alto on 16 March 1966.

Stebbins's earliest astronomical research was in spectroscopy and photometry. In 1906 he began attempting to use electronic methods in photometry. The results were encouraging, although at first only the brightest objects in the sky (such as the Moon) could be studied in this manner. From 1909 to 1925 he devoted much of his time to improving the photoelectric cell and using it to study the light curves of eclipsing binary stars. As the sensitivity of the device

was increased, it could be used to measure the light of the solar corona during total eclipses. Stebbins discovered that although there was no detectable variations in the light output of the Sun, he could observe variations in the light of cooler stars.

During the 1930s Stebbins applied photoelectric research to the problem of the nature and distribution of interstellar dust and its effects on the transmission of stellar light. He analysed the degree of reddening of the light of hot stars and of globular clusters. His discoveries contributed to an understanding of the structure and size of our Galaxy. He investigated whether interstellar material absorbed light of all wavelengths equally, and found that over a range from the infrared as far as the ultraviolet absorption was constant, but that absorption of ultraviolet light itself was less strong.

Stebbins's other work included studies using photoelectric equipment of the magnitudes and colours of other galaxies. He demonstrated that his method was more accurate than those that relied on the eye or photography, and the advent of the photomultiplier extended the usefulness of his technique even further.

Steele, Edward John (1948–) Australian immunologist whose research into the inheritance of immunity has lent a certain amount of support to the Lamarckian theory of the inheritance of acquired characteristics, thus challenging modern theories of heredity and evolution.

Steele was born in Darwin, Northern Territory, on 27 October 1948 and educated at the University of Adelaide, from which he graduated in molecular biology in 1971 and gained his doctorate in 1975. In 1976 he began his postdoctoral work at the John Curtin School of Medical Research, Canberra, studying naturally occurring autoimmune disease. He moved to Canada in 1977 and continued his research at the Ontario Cancer Institute. In 1978 he became interested in evolutionary theory, and early in 1980 he moved to the UK to the Clinical Research Centre of the Medical Research Council in Harrow, London.

The modern neo-Darwinistic theory of evolution is a synthesis of Darwin's idea of survival of the fittest by means of natural selection, and Mendelian genetics: according to neo-Darwinism, chance, in the form of genetic mutations, plays an important role in evolution; and competition for limited resources – natural selection – eventually kills off the 'bad' mutations. These ideas are in direct opposition to Jean Baptiste ◊Lamarck's theory of the inheritance of acquired characteristics, according to which various parts of the body develop or disappear as necessitated by changes in habits resulting from environmental changes. Lamarck, however, believed that these acquired changes could be passed on to subsequent generations and that, if continued for a long time, a new species would eventually develop. Steele, working with Reginald Gorczynski, found that mice that have been made immune to certain antigens can pass on this acquired immunity to first and second generations of their offspring. This finding suggests that although Lamarck's original ideas are too unsophisticated to be correct, in a subtler, more refined form they may make a valuable contribution towards a better understanding of evolutionary processes.

Further Reading

Hutchings, Alice, *Edward Steele: The Journal of a Victorian,* James (Charlotte) Publishers, 1983.

Stefan, Josef (1835–1893) Austrian physicist who first determined the relation between the amount of energy radiated by a body and its temperature. This expression is usually known as the Stefan–Boltzmann radiation law because Ludwig ◊Boltzmann gave a theoretical explanation of it.

Stefan was born in Klagenfurt on 24 March 1835. He entered the University of Vienna in 1853 and, after completing his studies, became a lecturer there in 1858, rising to be professor of higher mathematics and physics in 1863. He retained this position for the rest of his life, and was also director of the Institute for Experimental Physics at Vienna from 1866. From 1885 to his death, Stefan served as vice president of the Imperial Academy of Sciences. He died in Vienna on 7 January 1893.

Stefan's discovery of his radiation law was made in 1879. For a long time, it had been known that Isaac ◊Newton's law of cooling, which held that the rate of cooling of a hot body is proportional to the difference in temperature between the body and its surroundings, is incorrect for large temperature differences. Many people had found that the amount of heat given out by a very hot body is far greater than expected by Newton's law.

Stefan followed up experimental work by the Irish physicist John ◊Tyndall, who had measured the amount of radiant heat produced by a platinum wire heated to varying degrees of incandescence by an electric current. He found that over the greatest range, from about 525°C/977°F up to about 1,200°C/2,192°F, the intensity of radiation increased by 11.7 times. Stefan realized that this increase in intensity was equal to the ratio of the absolute temperatures raised to the fourth power, and from this deduced his radiation law. This states that the total energy E radiated in a given time by a given area of a body is given by:

$$E = \sigma T^4$$

where T is the absolute temperature and σ is a constant known as the Stefan constant. Stefan confirmed the validity of his law over wide temperature ranges.

In 1884, Boltzmann, a former student of Stefan, gave a theoretical explanation of Stefan's law based on thermodynamic principles and the kinetic theory developed by James Clerk ◊Maxwell in the 1860s. Boltzmann pointed out that it held only for perfect black bodies, and Stefan had in fact been able to derive the law because platinum approximates to a black body. However, from his law, Stefan was able to make the first accurate determination of the surface temperature of the Sun, obtaining a value of approximately 6,000°C/11,000°F.

Stefan also made several other contributions to physics. He was an able experimental physicist, and produced accurate measurements of the conductivities of gases that helped to confirm Maxwell's kinetic theory. He also investigated diffusion in gases, making theoretical derivations that confirmed experimental results.

Steiner, Jakob (1796–1863) Swiss mathematician, the pre-eminent geometrician of the 19th century and the founder of modern synthetic, or projective, geometry.

Steiner was born in Utzenstorf, near Bern, on 18 March 1796. Because he had to help out in the family business his early education was neglected and colleagues in later years were astonished to discover that he had not learnt to read and write until the age of 14. When he was 18 he left home to enrol at the Pestalozzi school in Yverdon; it was run on the monitorial system and in a very short time Steiner was employed as an instructor in mathematics. For a while he maintained himself by teaching and in 1821 received a teacher's certificate in Berlin. He had also attended some mathematical lectures at Heidelberg and acquired sufficient skill and knowledge to be given a place as a student at the University of Berlin in 1822. By 1825 he was teaching at the university and in 1834 a chair of geometry was created for him; he held the chair for the rest of his life. His health began to deteriorate in the 1850s and he died in Bern on 1 April 1863.

When Steiner began to publish his epoch-making geometrical discoveries in the 1820s, mathematics was in that exciting transitional stage that has produced the modern explosion in mathematics. Steiner played an important role in the transition. His first published paper, which appeared in *Crelle's Journal* in 1826, contained his discovery of the geometrical transformation known as inversion geometry. His most important work, the *Systematische Entwicklung der Abhängigkeit geometrischer Gestalten von Einander* appeared in 1832. The work was notable for its full discussion and examination of the principle of duality and for the wealth of fundamental concepts and results in projective geometry that it contained. In it are to be found the two discoveries to which he had lent his name, the Steiner surface (also called the Roman surface), which has a double infinity of conic sections on it, and the Steiner theorem. The theorem states that two pencils (collections of geometric objects) by which a conic is projected from two of its points are projectively related. The book also included a supplement listing problems to be solved, and it remained a rich quarry for geometers for the next hundred years.

Steiner's other principal result was the theorem now known as the Steiner–Poncelet theorem, an extension of work done by Jean-Victor ◊Poncelet in 1822. Steiner proved that any Euclidean figure could be generated using only a straight rule if the plane of construction had drawn on it already a circle with its centre marked. (In 1904 it was shown by Francesco Severi (1879–1961) that only the centre of the circle and a small arc of its circumference were necessary.)

Steiner's consistent aim was to discover fundamental principles from which the rest of geometry could be derived in an orderly and coherent manner. His work, in general, was marked by his disdain of using analysis and algebra; he preferred to rely on entirely synthetic methods. It is for that reason that whether he was, as some believe, the finest geometer since ◊Apollonius of Perga, he is universally recognized as the founder of projective geometry.

Steno, Nicolaus (1638–1686) (Latinized form of Niels Stensen) Danish naturalist widely regarded as one of the founders of stratigraphy.

Born a Protestant in Copenhagen on 10 January 1638, Steno converted to Catholicism and settled in Florence, Italy. Having studied medicine in Leiden in the Netherlands, in 1666 he was appointed personal physician to Ferdinand, Grand Duke of Tuscany, before becoming royal anatomist at Copenhagen in 1672. He was ordained a priest in 1675, and gave up science on being appointed vicar-apostolic to north Germany and Scandinavia. He died on 6 December 1686, and is buried in the Medici crypt in Florence.

As a physician he discovered Steno's duct of the parotid gland, and investigated the workings of the ovaries. A passionate anatomist, Steno showed that a pineal gland resembling the human one is found in other creatures, using this finding to challenge René ◊Descartes's claim that the gland was the seat of the uniquely human soul. Steno's examination of quartz crystals disclosed that, despite differences in the shapes, the angle formed by corresponding faces is invariable for a particular mineral. This constancy (Steno's law), follows from internal molecular ordering.

Steno is perhaps best remembered for his contribu-

tions to geology and palaeontology. Having found fossil teeth (glossopetrae) far inland closely resembling those of a shark he had dissected, in his *Sample of the Elements of Mylogy* (1667) he championed the organic origin of fossils against those who postulated they were 'sports of nature' or similar concretions. On the basis of his palaeontological views, he also set out a view of geological history, contending that sedimentary strata had been deposited in former seas. He assumed six successive periods of Earth history: first, an age of deposition of non-fossiliferous strata from an ocean; then several periods of undermining and collapse; then another epoch of the deposition of strata, this time fossiliferous; followed by further undermining and collapse. This explained why the deepest strata contained no fossils but were overlain by fossiliferous strata, and also why certain strata were found horizontal while others were tilted to the horizon. To accompany his ideas, Steno sketched what are generally regarded as the earliest geological sections.

Making significant advances in anatomy, geology, crystallography, palaeontology, and mineralogy, Steno was one of the great all-rounders of 17th-century science.

Stephenson, George (1781–1848) English engineer who pioneered the building of the first railways in the UK and of steam locomotives to run on them.

Stephenson English railway engineer George Stephenson whose work resulted in great improvements in railways and steam locomotives. In 1821 he was appointed engineer for the construction of the Stockton and Darlington railway. *Mary Evans Picture Library*

Stephenson was born on 9 June 1781 in Wylam, a village near Newcastle upon Tyne, the son of a fireman. He received no formal education and was employed when a boy to look after cattle. When he was 14 years old he became an assistant fireman to his father at Darley Colliery. He was illiterate until the age of 17 when, frustrated by his inability to follow the daily newspaper reports of the Napoleonic Wars, he attended evening classes and learned to read and write.

In 1808, at a time when his prospects seemed so bleak that he seriously thought of emigrating, Stephenson took a contract to work the engine of the Killingworth pit. While there he regularly took the steam pumping engine to pieces in order to understand its construction. The reward came with his success in modifying a Newcomen engine (see Thomas ◊Newcomen) that was performing its pumping function inefficiently, when in 1812 he was appointed engine-wright to the colliery at £100 a year.

Stephenson's first invention was a safety lamp for miners. This device avoided the dangers of combustion by allowing the air to enter along narrow tubes. He demonstrated the success of his discovery by entering gas-filled tunnels at the Killingworth pit with perfect safety. The simultaneous development of a safety lamp by Humphry ◊Davy produced fierce and sometimes acrimonius controversy as to who was the real inventor, before it was accepted that both had reached the same goal independently and by different approaches.

In 1811 John Blenkinsop (1783–1831) constructed a steam locomotive for hauling coal wagons in a Yorkshire colliery but the machine, which used toothed wheels on a racked track, was ponderous and unwieldy. At Wylam colliery they were now anxious to introduce steam power on the horse tramways, and Stephenson produced a smooth-wheeled locomotive called the *Blucher,* which, in 1814, successfully drew 30 tonnes of coal in eight wagons up an incline of 1 in 150 at 7 kph/4 mph. Not satisfied, Stephenson introduced the 'steam blast' by which exhaust steam was redirected into the locomotive's chimney through a blast pipe, bringing in air with it and increasing the draught through the fire. This further development made the locomotive truly practical.

Subsequently Stephenson started to make experiments with various gradients. He found that a slope of 1 in 200, common enough on roads, reduced the haulage power of a locomotive by 50% (on a completely even surface, a tractive force of less than 5 kg/ 10 lb would move a tonne). Furthermore he discovered that friction was virtually independent of speed. The obvious conclusion from such findings was that railway gradients should always be as low as possible. Cuttings, tunnels, and embankments were therefore necessary. In 1819 the proprietors of Hetton Colliery, under Stephenson's direction, laid down a railway

11 km/8 mi long. It was opened in 1822, with traction provided partly by stationary engines and partly by locomotives.

In 1821 Stephenson succeeded in persuading Edward Pease, chief promotor of the scheme, that Stockton and Darlington could be better connected by steam locomotion than by the proposed horse traction. He was appointed engineer to the project and advocated the use of malleable iron rails instead of the cast iron used hitherto. The gauge for the new railway was assessed by Stephenson at 1.4 m/4 ft 8 in, a historic decision, since this has remained the 'standard gauge' for railways throughout the world.

Stephenson then induced Pease and Michael Longridge to support him and his son Robert ◊Stephenson in establishing locomotive works at Newcastle, where the engines were to be made for the Stockton and Darlington Railway. On 27 September 1825 the world's first public railway came into operation with the opening of the line. Stephenson's engine *Locomotion* took a party of passengers from Darlington at a top speed of 24 kph/15 mph.

Before the Stockton and Darlington Railway was opened, Stephenson had been engaged to design a railway from Manchester to Liverpool, the trade between the towns having already grown too great to be accommodated on the existing canals. Surveyors for the projected railway met fierce opposition from the farmers and landowners through whose estates the railway was to run. A bill to implement the scheme was thrown out by its opponents in Parliament, but a second bill, introduced in 1826 (and showing an improved overall plan), was accepted. The greatest physical obstacle to Stephenson's plans was a large area of marshy ground known as Chat Moss. By distributing the load over a considerable surface of the bog Stephenson was able to take his line over the treacherous ground.

Having eventually convinced the railway directors that locomotives and not fixed engines should operate on the line, Stephenson took part in an open competition to discover the most efficient locomotive for the railway, the prize being £500. A mean speed of 16 kph/10 mph was to be attained and steam pressure was not to exceed 345,000 pascals/50 psi.

Stephenson saw that if he was to succeed he had to find some means of increasing the heating surface of the boilers of his locomotives. He therefore adopted tubes passing through the cylindrical barrel and connecting the firebox with the smokebox. The engine Stephenson produced for the great trial, the *Rocket,* was built at the Newcastle works under the direct supervision of his son Robert, and after many failures the problem of securing the tubes to the tube plates was overcome. The locomotive had a weight of 4.2 tonnes, half the weight of *Locomotion.*

Three other engines were entered for the competition but basic inadequacy or ill-luck overtook them. On the testing day, the *Rocket,* the only engine ready on time, ran 19 km/12 mi in 53 minutes, and was duly awarded the prize. On 15 September 1830 the line was opened with great ceremony. If the Stockton and Darlington Railway announced the arrival of the steam locomotive, the Manchester and Liverpool Railway, providing the first regular passenger service, showed that it had come to stay. An unwelcome event on the opening day was the first railway accident in which William Huskisson, president of the Board of Trade, was killed. Ironically he had been Stephenson's most influential supporter in Parliament.

For the remainder of his life Stephenson worked as a consultant engineer to several newly emerging railway companies, all in the north of England or the Midlands. There was hardly a railway scheme in which he was not consulted or an important line constructed without his help and advice. The last great issue with which Stephenson was concerned arose in 1845, in the battle between the supporters of the locomotive and those who advocated the atmospheric railway system developed by Stephenson's great contemporary Isambard Kingdom ◊Brunel. The dispute arose in connection with the extension of the railway from Newcastle to Berwick. Although Brunel had many influential friends in the Board of Trade, Stephenson's supporters in Parliament were the more numerous and carried the day. This ended the last attempt to challenge the advent of the steam locomotive. Stevenson died on 12 August 1848 in Chesterfield.

Further Reading

Beckett, Derrick, *Stephensons' Britain,* David & Charles, 1984.

Donnelly, Peter, *An Introduction to Railways and George Stephenson,* John Sinclair Railway Collection, 1992.

Dorman, C C, *The Stephensons and Steam Railways,* Pioneers of Science and Discovery series, Priory Press, 1975.

Rolt, L T C, *George and Robert Stephenson: The Railway Revolution,* Penguin, 1984.

Rowland, John, *Railway Pioneer: The Story of George Stephenson,* Lutterworth Press, 1971.

Skeat, William Oswald, *George Stephenson: The Engineer and His Letters,* Institution of Mechanical Engineers, 1973.

Smiles, Samuel, *The Lives of George and Robert Stephenson,* The Folio Society, 1975.

Stephenson, Robert (1803–1859) English civil engineer. He constructed railway bridges such as the high-level bridge at Newcastle upon Tyne, England, and the Menai and Conway tubular bridges in Wales. He was the only son of engineer George ◊Stephenson.

Born at Willington Quay, near to Newcastle upon Tyne, on 16 October, Stephenson began his working life assisting his father in the survey of the Stockton and Darlington Railway in 1821. The following year he spent six months at Edinburgh University studying mathematics. He then returned to Newcastle to manage the locomotive factory that his father had established there. His health began to decline seriously, however, and seeking a warmer climate he accepted an offer to superintend some gold and silver mines in Colombia in South America. He was away three years, but difficulties in the management of the Newcastle locomotive factory led to a request for his return. He returned to England in 1827, when the controversy over the most suitable form of traction for the Manchester and Liverpool Railway was at its height. The successful *Rocket* steam locomotive was eventually built under his personal direction, as were subsequent improvements to it.

In 1833 a scheme to construct a railway from Birmingham to London was introduced, and Stephenson became engineer for the line. The project was very important, being the first railway to be taken into the capital. Stephenson overcame with outstanding engineering skill many of the obstacles encountered, notably with the Blisworth cutting and the Kilsby tunnel. The railway was completed in 1838, and from then on he was engaged on railway work for the rest of his life. He died in London on 12 October 1859.

Probably the most important and certainly the most conspicuous of Stephenson's achievements were the various railway bridges which he built in the UK and elsewhere. The High Level Bridge over the River Tyne in Newcastle and the Victoria Bridge over the River Tweed at Berwick are among his earliest and most striking achievements. The former, spanning the river between Gateshead and Newcastle, comprises six iron arches; James ◊Nasmyth's newly invented steam hammer was used to drive in its foundations. In 1844 construction began, under Stephenson's supervision, of a railway line from Chester to Holyhead. He gave long and detailed thought to the best type of bridges for crossing the River Conway and the Menai Straits. For the Menai Straits he designed a bridge in which the railway tracks were completely enclosed in parallel iron tubes. This proved so successful when put into service that the same plan was adopted for other bridges. One such, the Victoria Bridge over the St Lawrence at Montréal, was constructed by Stephenson 1854–59, and was for many years the longest bridge in the world.

Further Reading

Beckett, Derrick, *Stephensons' Britain,* David & Charles, 1984.

Dorman, C C, *The Stephensons and Steam Railways,*
Pioneers of Science and Discovery series, Priory Press,
1975.

Rolt, L T C, *George and Robert Stephenson: The Railway
Revolution,* Penguin, 1984.

Smiles, Samuel, *The Lives of George and Robert Stephenson,*
The Folio Society, 1975.

Smith, Donald John, *Robert Stephenson: An Illustrated Life,*
Lifelines series, Shire Publications, 1989, v 8.

Steptoe, Patrick Christopher English obstetric surgeon; see ◊Edwards and Steptoe.

Stern, Otto (1888–1969) German-born US physicist
who showed that beams of atoms and molecules have
wave properties. He also determined the magnetic
moment of the proton. For these achievements, Stern
gained the 1943 Nobel Prize for Physics.

Stern was born in Sohrau, Upper Silesia (now Zory
in Poland), on 17 February 1888. His family moved to
Breslau (now Wrocław in Poland) in 1892. Following
the custom of the time, Stern attended a number of
German universities. He went to Freiburg im Breisgau,
Munich, and Breslau, giving him the opportunity to
attend lectures by such prominent scientists as Arnold
◊Sommerfeld, Otto ◊Lummer, and Ernst ◊Pringsheim.
Stern received his PhD from Breslau in 1912 for a dissertation on the kinetic theory of osmotic pressure in
concentrated solutions with special reference to solutions of carbon dioxide.

Although Stern's thesis work had been in the field of
physical chemistry, he was fascinated by theoretical
physics. He arranged to join Albert ◊Einstein in Prague
as a postdoctoral associate. When Einstein moved to
Zürich in 1913, Stern followed him and took up a post
as *Privatdozent* (unpaid lecturer) in physical chemistry
at the technical high school in Zürich.

Stern served in the army in World War I and was
assigned to meteorological work on the Russian front.
He was able to work on theoretical physics in his spare
time, and was then transferred to more congenial laboratory work in Berlin towards the end of the war. In
1918, he took up the position of *Privatdozent* in the
department of theoretical physics at the University of
Frankfurt. Stern obtained his first professional position in 1921, when he was made associate professor of
theoretical physics at the University of Rostock, but he
soon moved to the University of Hamburg where, in
1923, he became professor of physical chemistry and
director of the Institute of Physical Chemistry.

The next ten years marked the peak of Stern's career.
He made important contributions to the understanding of quantum theory, and built up a thriving research
group. Many of his associates were Jewish as indeed
was Stern himself, and life became increasingly diffi-

cult during the early 1930s as the Nazis rose to power.
The sacking of Stern's longtime associate Immanuel
Estermann and an order to remove a portrait of
Einstein from the laboratory were the last straws. Stern
resigned his post in 1933 and went to the Carnegie
Technical Institute in Pittsburg in the USA, where he
was given the post of research professor and set up a
new department for the study of molecular beams.

Stern was granted US citizenship in 1939 and
worked as a consultant to the US War Department
during World War II. After the war he retired and
moved to Berkeley, California, where he maintained
contact with the scientific community on a private
basis only. He died in Berkeley of a heart attack on 17
August 1969.

The first phase of Stern's scientific career covers the
period 1912–18. During these years he was absorbed in
purely theoretical work and in learning how to choose
the really central issues for study in an experimental
context. His theoretical work was partly in the field of
statistical thermodynamics, in which he proposed an
elegant derivation of the entropy constant.

After World War I, Stern began to concentrate on
the molecular beam method, which had been discovered by Louis Dunoyer (1880–1963) in 1911. This
method consisted of opening a tiny hole in a heated
container held inside a region of high vacuum. The
vapour molecules inside the heated container flowed
out to form a straight beam of moving particles suffering virtually no collisions in the vacuum. The beam
could be narrowed still further by the use of slits, and
a system of rotating slits could be used to select only
those particles travelling at particular velocities. This
was a powerful tool in the study of the magnetic and
other properties of particles, atoms, and molecules.

Stern's first experiments with this device were completed in 1919. They dealt with the measurement of
molecular velocities and confirmed the Maxwellian
distribution of velocities. He then began an experiment with Walther Gerlach (1899–1979) that was
intended to measure the magnetic moment of metal
atoms and also to investigate the question of spatial
quantization.

Developing the quantum model of the atom proposed by Niels ◊Bohr in 1913, Sommerfeld had derived
a formula for the magnetic moment of the silver atom
and predicted that silver atoms in a magnetic field
could orient in only two directions with respect to that
field. This latter idea was not compatible with classical
theory. The Stern–Gerlach experiment would determine which of these theories was correct. The
experiment consisted of passing a narrow beam of silver atoms through a strong magnetic field. Classical
theory predicted that this field would cause the beam
to broaden, but spatial quantization predicted that the

beam would split into two distinct separate beams. The result, showing a split beam, was the first clear evidence for space quantization. Stern and Gerlach also obtained a measurement of the magnetic moment of the silver atom.

Stern then went on to improve this molecular beam technique and in 1931 was able to detect the wave nature of particles in the beams. This was an important confirmation of wave–particle duality, which had been proposed in 1924 by Louis ◊de Broglie for the electron and extended to all particles.

In 1933 Stern measured the magnetic moment of the proton and the deuteron. The magnetic moment of the proton had been predicted by Paul ◊Dirac to be one nuclear magneton. Stern's group, despite much advice not to attempt the difficult experiment whose result was in any case already 'known', caused much astonishment when they demonstrated that the proton's magnetic moment was 2.5 times greater than expected. The explanation for this discrepancy lies partly in parallel proton movements.

Stern's experiments with molecular beams came at a critical time in the development of quantum theory and nuclear physics as they provided the firm experimental evidence that was needed for theories in quantum mechanics that were hitherto highly controversial. Stern's great talent lay in his experimental foresight, which was based on a solid theoretical grounding, coupled with an almost fanatical obsession with experimental and technical detail.

Stevens, Nettie Maria (1861–1912) US biologist whose researches concentrated on the role of chromosomes and their relationship to heredity.

Stevens was born in Cavendish, Vermont, on 7 July 1861, the daughter of a carpenter. After local schooling she became a librarian at the Free Public Library of Chelmsford, Massachusetts, until 1892. In that year, aged 31, she returned to education by attending classes at a high school, and in 1896 moved to Stanford University as an undergraduate, receiving a bachelor's degree in physiology in 1899 and a master's degree the following year. She was already interested in marine biology and registered at Bryn Mawr College for her PhD, which she was awarded in 1903 for a dissertation on ciliate protozoa. She spent research periods at marine laboratories in Europe and also visited the Zoological Institute at Würzburg where she met Theodor ◊Boveri. Whilst serving as a research fellow at Bryn Mawr, she was awarded a fellowship to work at the Stazione Zoologica, Naples, in 1905. She became an associate professor in the same year, and apart from a further year in Würzburg in 1908, remained at Bryn Mawr until her early death from carcinoma on 4 May 1912.

Her early work on the morphology of ciliate protozoa developed her interests in cytology in general and she studied regenerative processes in lower invertebrates. From there she moved on to working on the development of the roundworm (nematode), examining its regenerative properties after exposure to ultraviolet radiation, and showed that even in very early embryonic life cells were restricted in their regenerative capabilities. Her most significant work was in examining the relationship between chromosomes and the units of heredity postulated by the work of Gregor ◊Mendel in the 19th century. Stevens's experiments with a species of beetle showed that sex was determined by a specific chromosome, a conclusion that the biologist Edmund Wilson (1856–1939) arrived at independently. This was the first direct evidence that Mendel's factors were associated with chromosomes.

Stevinus, Simon (c. 1548–1620) Flemish scientist who, in physics, developed statics and hydrodynamics and who introduced decimal notation into mathematics.

Stevinus was born in Bruges (now in Belgium) in about 1548. He began work in Antwerp as a clerk and then entered Dutch government service, using his engineering skills to become quartermaster general to the army. (For Prince Maurice of Nassau he designed sluices that could be used to flood parts of Holland to defend it from attack.) He married very late in life and died in The Hague in the early part of 1620.

Stevinus's interests were wide-ranging. In statics he made use of the parallelogram of forces and in dynamics he made a scientific study of pulley systems. In hydrostatics Stevinus noted that the pressure exerted by a liquid depends only on its height and is independent of the shape of the vessel containing it. He is supposed to have anticipated ◊Galileo in an experiment in which he dropped two unequal weights from a tall building to demonstrate that they fell at the same rate.

Stevinus wrote in the vernacular (a principle he advocated for all scientists). Even so his book on mechanics *De Beghinselen der Weeghcoust* (1586), written in Flemish, was 20 years later translated into Latin (as *Hypomnemata mathematica*) by Willebrord ◊Snell.

Stieltjes, Thomas Jan (1856–1894) Dutch-born French mathematician who contributed greatly to the theory of series and is often called the founder of analytical theory.

Stieltjes was born in Zwolle on 29 December 1856, the son of a distinguished civil engineer. Almost all his scientific and mathematical training was received at the Ecole Polytechnique in Delft. He graduated from the school in 1877 and was appointed to a post at the Leiden Observatory. He remained there until 1883, and though little is known of his mathematical doings in those years, it seems probable that he continued to do research, since in 1884 he was appointed to the chair of mathematics at the University of Groningen. In that year also he was awarded an honorary doctorate by the University of Leiden. Two years later he was elected to the Dutch Academy of Science. In 1886 he went to France, became a naturalized French citizen, and for the rest of his short life taught mathematics at the University of Toulouse. Although he was never elected to the French Academy (despite being nominated in 1892), he won the academy's Ormoy Prize in 1893 for his work on continued fractions. He died in Toulouse on 31 December 1894.

In a short working life Stieltjes studied almost all the problems in analysis then known – the theory of ordinary and partial differential equations, Leonhard ◊Euler's gamma functions, elliptic functions, interpolation theory, and asymptotic series. But his lasting reputation rests on his investigations into continued fractions. The fruit of those researches is contained in his last memoir, *Recherches sur les fractions continués*, completed just before he died. The memoir was a milestone in mathematical history. Before its appearance only special cases of continued fractions had been considered. Stieltjes was the first mathematician to give a general treatment of continued fractions as part of complex analytical function theory. He did so, moreover, in a book of exemplary clarity and beauty.

A continued fraction is derived from a sequence of ordinary fractions:

$$\frac{a_1}{b_1}, \frac{a_2}{b_2}, \frac{a_3}{b_3}$$

which are called partial quotients, by adding each fraction to the denominator of the preceding fraction. In such series, a_1, a_2, a_3, and so on are called partial numerators; b_1, b_2, b_3 and so on are called partial denominators. They may be real or complex numbers. To this day one of the most important continued fractions in analytic theory remains the Stieltjes-fraction, or S-fraction.

In this fraction the values of k are constants other than zero and z is a complex variable. Taking the values of k as real and positive, Stieltjes was able to solve what is known as the Stieltjes moment problem – that is, the problem of determining a distribution of mass which has pre-assigned moments. His solution has been very fruitful, as has the very problem itself, extended as it has been into many fields.

Stieltjes's researches also raised the mathematical status of discontinuous functions and divergent series. He advanced the theory of Riemann's function (see Bernhard ◊Riemann), especially by the appearance, in his last great paper, of the integral:

$$\int_a^b f(u)\, \delta g(u)$$

which is a generalized form of the Riemann integral and is now known as the Stieltjes integral. Stieltjes came upon it in his search for a way to express the limit of a certain sequence of analytic functions. What he did was to replace lengths of intervals (in the approximating sums for Riemann integration) by masses spread on them. He introduced this distribution of masses by means of a non-decreasing function, g, which gives the increment $g(b) - g(a)$ of the function g to every interval $[a, b]$. From this he was able to obtain his integral.

Stieltjes's analysis of continued fractions has had immense influence in the development of mathematics. His ideas greatly helped David ◊Hilbert in his working out of the theory of quadratic forms in infinitely numerous variables. They were also used by Felix ◊Hausdorff in his work on divergent series. Indeed, so varied are the fields that have profited from Stieltjes's creative imagination – number theory, the theory of equations, the theory of integration, infinite matrices, the theory of functions, and, in the physical sciences, dynamics and the construction of electrical networks – that he well deserves to be known as the chief pioneer of modern analysis.

Stirling, Robert (1790–1878) Scottish inventor who is credited with the invention of the first practicable hot-air engine. The principle has a large number of inherent advantages that could make it as important as the internal-combustion engine, so intensive research has been being carried out on the Stirling engine.

Stirling was born in Cloag, Perthshire, on 25 October 1790. He attended Glasgow and Edinburgh universities, studying advanced Latin and Greek, logic and mathematics, metaphysics, and rhetoric. He was licensed to preach by the presbytery of Dunbarton in 1815 and was ordained to the ministry in 1816. In the same year he took out his patent on the air engine and heat regenerator. The patent was also signed by his younger brother, James, who was in fact a mechanical engineer. It seems probable, therefore, that Robert had the idea for the engine and that James developed it. Robert also designed and made scientific instruments and various other patents relating to air engines in the names of R and J Stirling were granted over the years, the last being in 1840. In 1819 Robert Stirling married Jane, eldest daughter of William Rankine, a wine merchant at Galston, and five years later became minister of the church there. He remained at Galston for the rest of his life, retiring in 1876 and dying two years later on 6 June 1878.

There were several patents for air engines before Stirling's first patent of 1816 but it is doubtful if any of them would have worked, with the probable exception of that of George ◊Cayley.

The Stirling cycle engine differs from the internal-combustion engine in that the working fluid (in Stirling's case, air) remains in the working chambers. The heat is applied from an external source, so virtually any fuel, from wood to nuclear fuel, can be used. It also means that combustion can be made to take place under the best conditions, making the control of emissions (pollution) considerably easier. The burning of the fuel is continuous, not intermittent as in an internal-combustion engine, so there is less noise and vibration. Another advantage is the high theoretical thermal efficiency; in practice the thermal efficiencies of Stirling engines of different designs are better than those of conventional diesel engines.

There are many arrangements for Stirling engines but the essential factor is that they use what is effectively two pistons to push the working fluid between two working spaces. One space is kept at a high temperature by the heat source and the other at a low temperature. Between these two spaces is a regenerator that alternately receives and gives up heat to the working fluid. The pistons are connected to a mechanism that keeps them out of phase (usually by 90°). It is this differential motion that moves the working fluid from one space to the other. On its way to the hot space the fluid passes through the regenerator, gaining heat. In the hot space it gains more heat and expands, giving power. After the power stroke the fluid is pushed back through the regenerator, where it gives up its residual heat into the cold space and is ready to start the cycle again.

Stirling's first engine appeared in 1818. It had a vertical cylinder about 60 cm/2 ft in diameter. It produced about 1.5 kW/2 hp, pumping water from a quarry and ran for two years before the hot sections of the cylinder burnt out. This burning out is a problem that has plagued virtually every engine of the type ever since.

In 1824 the Stirling brothers started work on improved engines and in 1843 converted a steam engine at a Dundee factory to operate as a Stirling engine. It is said to have produced 28 kW/37 hp and to have used less coal per unit of power than the steam design it replaced. In any event, the hot parts burned out regularly after a few months, and after several replacements it was re-converted to steam.

The type lived on, however, until well into the next century and was used extensively for powering small pumps and similar domestic applications. Improved Otto cycle engines and the standardization and spread of electricity supplies helped to establish the small electric motor and led to the Stirling engine's eventual demise.

The renaissance of the Stirling engine began in 1938 in the Philips laboratories in the Netherlands. In the early 1980s most effort was directed towards developing the principle for automotive applications. A joint Ford–Philips programme resulted in a Stirling-engined vehicle that was cleaner and had a fuel economy 9–35% better than the conventionally engined car.

The Stirling engine has yet to live up to its promise. Possibly the greatest hurdle is the huge investment already made in conventional internal-combustion engines. For them to be deposed, the Stirling principle will have to show substantial advantages in most respects.

Further Reading

Sier, Robert, *Reverend Robert Stirling, D D: A Biography of the Inventor of the Heat Economiser and Stirling Cycle Engine*, L A Mair, 1995.

Stock, Alfred (1876–1946) German inorganic chemist best known for his preparations of the hydrides of boron (called boranes) and for his campaign for better safety measures in the use of mercury in chemistry and industry.

Stock was born in Danzig (now Gdansk, Poland) on 16 July 1876. He studied chemistry at the University of Berlin under Emil ◊Fischer, and after receiving his doctorate became Fischer's assistant. In 1909 he moved to Breslau (now Wrocław, Poland), to join the staff of the Inorganic Chemistry Institute. After a period at the Kaiser Wilhelm (later Max Planck) Institute in Berlin, he became director of the chemistry department at the Technische Hochschule in Karlsruhe in 1926, where he remained until he retired ten years later. He died in Karlsruhe on 12 August 1946.

Stock began studying the boron hydrides – general formula B_xH_y – in 1909 at Breslau. By treating magnesium boride (Mg_3B_2) with an acid he produced B_4H_{10}. He went on to prepare several other hydrides and in 1912 devised a high-vacuum method for separating mixtures of them. Many contain more hydrogen atoms in their molecules than ordinary valency rules will allow, at least if normal covalent bonds are involved. Their structures were finally worked out by Linus ◊Pauling, Hugh ◊Longuet-Higgins, William ◊Lipscomb, and others. In the 1960s boron hydrides found their first practical use as additives to rocket fuels.

In 1921 Stock prepared beryllium (scarcely known before in the metallic state) by electrolysing a fused mixture of sodium and beryllium fluorides. This successful extraction method made beryllium available for industrial use, as in special alloys and glasses and for making windows in X-ray tubes. By 1923 Stock was suffering from chronic mercury poisoning caused by prolonged exposure to the liquid metal and its vapour – a fate previously shared by many other chemists. He introduced sensitive tests for mercury and devised improved laboratory techniques for dealing with the metal to minimize the risk of accidental poisoning.

Stokes, George Gabriel (1819–1903)

Irish physicist who is mainly remembered for Stokes's law, which relates the force moving a body through a fluid to the velocity and size of the body and the viscosity of the fluid. He also made important contributions in optics, particularly in the field of fluorescence, a term that he coined.

Stokes was born in Skreen, Sligo, in Ireland on 13 August 1819 and went to school in Dublin and to college in Bristol, England, before entering Cambridge University in 1837. He graduated in mathematics in 1841, and became a fellow of Pembroke College. In 1849, Stokes was appointed Lucasian Professor of Mathematics at Cambridge, a position he retained until his death. Among the honours accorded to him were the presidency of the Royal Society 1885–90, a knighthood in 1889, and the Royal Society's Copley Medal in 1893. He died in Cambridge on 1 February 1903.

Much of Stokes's extensive reputation was gained through the work he carried out on the theory of viscous fluids 1845–50. He derived the equation later known as Stokes's law, which determines the movement of a small sphere through viscous fluids of various density. The equation can be stated as $F = 6\pi\eta rv$, where F is the force acting on the sphere, η the coefficient of viscosity, r the radius of the sphere, and v its velocity. Stokes's law enables the resistance of fluids to motion to be assessed and the terminal velocity of a body to be calculated. It was to be of enormous importance to science as the basis of the famous oil-drop experiments to determine the charge on the electron performed by Robert ◊Millikan 1909–13.

Stokes's investigation into fluid dynamics led him to consider the problem of the ether, the hypothetical medium that was believed to exist for the propagation of light waves. In 1848, Stokes showed that the laws of optics held if the Earth pulled the ether with it in its motion through space and from this assumed the ether to be an elastic substance that flowed with the Earth. The classic Michelson–Morley experiments of 1881 and 1887 did not totally negate this contention; it was shown to be untrue by Oliver ◊Lodge in 1893 and the existence of the ether was finally disproved.

Stokes made another important contribution with the first explanation of fluorescence in 1852. He had examined the blue light that is emitted in certain circumstances by a solution of quinine sulphate that is normally colourless. Stokes showed that ultraviolet light was being absorbed by the solution and then re-emitted as visible light. He was then able to use fluorescence as a method to study ultraviolet spectra. Stokes went on in 1854 to realize that the Sun's spectrum is made up of the spectra of the elements it contains and concluded that the dark Fraunhofer lines are the spectral lines of elements absorbing light in the Sun's outer layers. He did not, however, develop this important idea. It was left to Robert ◊Bunsen and Gustav ◊Kirchhoff to propose the method of spectrum analysis in 1860.

Another field in which Stokes made his mark was geodesy and in 1849 he published an important study of the variation of gravity at the surface of the Earth. Stokes was also a gifted mathematician and helped to develop Fourier series.

Further Reading

Buchwald, Jed Z, 'Why Stokes never wrote a treatise on optics', in: Harman, P M, Shapiro, Alan E (eds), *The Investigation of Difficult Things: Essays on Newton and the History of the Exact Sciences in Honour of D T Whiteside*, Cambridge University Press, 1992, pp 451–476.

Wilson, David B (ed), *The Correspondence Between Sir George Gabriel Stokes and Sir William Thomson, Baron Kelvin of Largs*, Cambridge University Press, 1990, 2 vols.

Wright, Thomas, 'Scale Models, Similitude and Dimensions: Aspects of mid-19th Century Engineering Science', *Ann Sci*, 1992, v 49, pp 233–254.

Stokes, William

Irish physician; see ◊Cheyne and Stokes.

Stopes, Marie Charlotte Carmichael (1880–1958)

Scottish advocate of birth control who, in 1921, founded the first instructional clinic for contraception in the UK.

Marie Stopes was born on 15 October 1880 in Edinburgh. Her mother was a feminist and one of the first woman members of Edinburgh University; her father was an English brewing engineer from Essex. She read botany at University College, London, graduating in 1902, then went to the University of Munich in Germany, from which she gained her doctorate in 1904. She was awarded her DSc from London University in 1905, when only 25 years old, and then taught at the University of Manchester – the first woman to be appointed to the science staff there. For several years she continued her palaeobotanical research into fossil plants and primitive cycads and became one of the foremost investigators in her field. In 1911 she married Reginald Ruggles Gates, a Canadian botanist, and left Manchester University. But the marriage was not consummated and was annulled in 1916.

The breakdown of her marriage stimulated Marie Stopes's interest in the subject of sexual intercourse, personal relationships, and marriage, and in 1918 she published *Married Love*, the underlying theme of which is that women should be able to enjoy sexual intercourse on the basis of equality with men; in the book she also referred briefly to contraceptive methods. This topic was extremely controversial in the UK at that time and she had great difficulty in finding a publisher. Even after it was published, *Married Love* met with considerable opposition: for example, C P Blacker (later to help in the creation of the International Planned Parenthood Foundation) said that the book was 'responsible for printing instructions to girls of initially dubious virtues as to how to adopt the profession of more or less open prostitution'. Nevertheless, Marie Stopes received many requests for more information and advice about contraception from women who had read her book, so later in the same year she wrote and published *Wise Parenthood*, in which she attempted to answer the queries she had received.

Also in 1918 Marie Stopes married for the second time; her husband was Humphrey Verdon Roe, the co-founder (with Alliot Verdon ◊Roe) of the A V Roe aircraft company. Roe supported Marie Stopes's ideas and sponsored her birth control clinic, the first one in the UK, which opened in 1921 in Marlborough Road, Holloway, London. This event re-aroused vehement opposition, especially from the Roman Catholic Church, and Marie Stopes spent the next few years both promoting and defending the idea of contraception. In 1934 she published another book *Birth Control Today*, in which she voiced her disapproval of abortion as a means of population control, describing women who sought abortions as 'a danger to the human race'. She continued to champion the cause of birth control in her later years, travelling to many different countries to do so. She died on 2 October 1958 near Dorking, Surrey, having brought about a considerable change in general attitudes towards a more widespread acceptance of contraception, a trend that continued after her death – although even today the subject still arouses controversy and opposition, particularly from certain religious groups.

Further Reading

Coldrick, Jack, *Dr Marie Stopes and Press Censorship of Birth-Control*, Athol Books, 1992.

Hall, Ruth, *Marie Stopes: A Biography*, Quality Book Club, 1978.

Peetl, Robert (ed), *Marie Stopes, Eugenics, and the English Birth Control Movement*, The Galton Institute, 1997.

Rose, June, *Marie Stopes and the Sexual Revolution*, Faber and Faber, 1993.

Stopes-Roe, Harry Verdon, *Marie Stopes and Birth Control*, Pioneers of Science and Discovery series, Priory Press, 1974.

Strömgren, Bengt Georg Daniel (1908–1987)

Swedish astronomer best known for his hypothesis about the so-called 'Strömgren spheres' – zones of ionized hydrogen gas surrounding hot stars embedded in interstellar gas clouds.

Strömgren was born on 21 January 1908 in Göteborg, the son of Elis Strömgren, who was also an astronomer of distinction. In 1927 he received an MA from the University of Copenhagen and he was awarded a PhD from the same university in 1929. He was appointed a lecturer there, but in 1936 he moved to the University of Chicago as an assistant (and later associate) professor. In 1938 he became professor of astronomy at the University of Copenhagen and in 1940 he succeeded his father as director of the observatory there.

In 1946 Strömgren served as visiting professor to the University of Chicago. He was appointed a special lecturer in astronomy at the University of London in 1949 and was visiting professor to both the California Institute of Technology and to Princeton University in 1950. From 1951 to 1957 he was professor at the University of Chicago and director of both the Yerkes and McDonald observatories. From 1957 to 1967 he was a member of the Institute of Advanced Study at Princeton. He was a member of many scientific associations in Europe and the USA and was awarded the Bruce Medal of the Astronomical Society of the Pacific in 1959. Strömgren retired in 1967.

Some gaseous nebulae that can be observed within our Galaxy are luminous. In 1940 Strömgren proposed that this light was caused by hot stars embedded within obscuring layers of gas in the nebulae. He suggested that extremely hot stars ionize hydrogen gas and that the dimensions of the ionized zone (the H II zone) depend on both the density of the surrounding gas and the temperature of the star.

Strömgren's calculations of the sizes of these H II zones or 'Strömgren spheres' have been shown by observations to be largely correct. This concept was fundamental to our understanding of the structure of interstellar material. Strömgren's other work included an analysis of the spectral classification of stars by means of photoelectric photometry, and research into the internal make-up of stars, all these areas being fundamental to the development of modern astronomy.

Strutt, John William

English physicist; see Lord ◊Rayleigh.

Struve, (Gustav Wilhelm) Ludwig (Ottovich) von (1858–1920)

Russian astronomer, the younger brother of Hermann von ◊Struve and son of Otto Wilhelm von ◊Struve, who was an expert on the occultation of stars and stellar motion.

Struve was born on 1 November 1858 at Pulkovo, near St Petersburg. He attended school at Vyborg and followed the family tradition by studying astronomy at the University of Dorpat (now Tartu, Estonia). After his graduation in 1880 he began research at the Pulkovo Observatory. From 1883 to 1886 Struve travelled through Europe, visiting observatories in many countries.

When he returned to Pulkovo in 1886 Struve continued his work at the observatory. He wrote a thesis on the constant of precession and was awarded his doctorate in 1887. In 1894 he moved to the University of Kharkov in the Ukraine, where he was made extraordinary professor of astronomy. In 1897 he became a full professor and director of the university observatory. In 1919 he left Kharkov for Simferopol, where he was appointed professor at the Tauris University. He died in Simferopol on 4 November 1920.

Struve's father had done excellent work on determining the constant of precession. Struve was also interested in this subject and he investigated the whole question of motion within the Solar System. This led him on to work on the positions and motions of stars, and to an estimation of the rate of rotation of the Galaxy.

Struve was best known for his expert knowledge about the occultation of stars during a total lunar eclipse. Much of his early work on this subject was done in the 1880s, but his interest in it continued until the end of his career.

Struve, (Karl) Hermann (Ottovich) von (1854–1920)

Russian astronomer, third in the line of famous astronomers, who was an expert on Saturn. His other work was largely concerned with features of the Solar System, although he also shared the family interest in stellar astronomy.

Struve was born on 30 October 1854 at Pulkovo. He studied at Karlsruhe in Germany, Vyborg in Karelia, and Reval (Tallinn) in Estonia, before enrolling at the University of Dorpat (Tartu) in Estonia in 1872. On completing his undergraduate studies in 1877, Struve travelled in Europe and visited major centres of astronomical research. He was awarded his PhD from Dorpat in 1882.

A year later Struve was appointed astronomer at Pulkovo and he became director there in 1890. In 1895 he left to become professor of astronomy at the University of Königsberg in Germany (now Kaliningrad in Russia). He was appointed director of the Observatory of Berlin-Babalsberg in 1904, and in 1913 he became the founder director of the Neubabalsberg Observatory. He was a member of numerous scientific societies and the recipient of the 1903 Gold Medal of the Royal Astronomical Society. He died in Herrenalb, Germany, on 12 August 1920.

Among the many features of the Solar System studied by Struve were the transit of Venus, the orbits of Mars and Saturn, the satellites (especially Iapetus and Titan) of Saturn, and Jupiter and Neptune. Struve's best work was his 1898 paper on the ring system of Saturn. Data in this publication formed the basis of much of his later research.

Struve, F(riedrich) G(eorg) W(ilhelm) von (1793–1864)

German-born Russian astronomer who was an expert on double stars and one of the first astronomers to measure stellar parallax. He was also the founder of a dynasty of famous astronomers that spanned four generations.

Struve was born in Altona, Schleswig-Holstein, on 15 April 1793. To avoid conscription into the German army, he fled to Dorpat (now Tartu) in Estonia in 1808. He entered the University of Dorpat and graduated in 1810. His interest in astronomy led to his appointment as an observer at the Dorpat Observatory in 1813. In the same year he was awarded his PhD and became extraordinary professor of mathematics and astronomy at the University of Dorpat.

From 1817 onwards Struve served as director of the Dorpat Observatory, but after 1834 he was primarily concerned with the construction and equipping of an observatory at Pulkovo near St Petersburg in Russia, which was opened in 1839. He retired in 1862 and was succeeded as director of the Pulkovo Observatory by his son Otto Wilhelm von ◊Struve. Struve died in Pulkovo on 23 November 1864. At the time of his death he was a member of virtually every European scientific academy.

Struve's earliest research dealt with questions of geodesy and stellar motion. His primary interest, however, was in the discovery and measurement of double stars. In 1822 he published a catalogue of about 800 known double stars, and he instigated an extensive observational programme. The number of such stars known had increased to more than 3,000 by 1827. Struve published a paper in 1843 in which he described more than 500 multiple stars in addition to his earlier work on double stars.

Struve was one of the first astronomers to detect stellar parallax successfully. His interest in that subject dated from 1822, and in 1830 he measured the parallax of Alpha Lyrae. Other work of particular note included his observations, published in 1846, of the absorption of stellar light in the galactic plane, which he correctly deduced to be caused by the presence of interstellar material. He also investigated the distribution of stars in space. In addition to his work in astronomy, Struve made significant contributions to geodesy with his survey of Livonia on the Baltic coast 1816–19 and his measurements of the arc of meridian 1822–27.

Struve, Otto von (1897–1963) Russian-born US astronomer, the last of four generations of a family of eminent astronomers. He contributed to many areas of stellar astronomy, but was best known for his work on interstellar matter and stellar and nebular spectroscopy.

Struve was born on 12 August 1897 at Kharkov in Russia. He studied at the Gymnasium at Kharkov before entering a school for artillery training in Petrograd (now St Petersburg) in 1915. He served in the Imperial Russian Army on the Turkish front during World War I. After the war he studied at the University of Kharkov, where he was awarded a degree with top honours in 1919. He was conscripted into the counter-revolutionary White Army during the Civil War in 1919, but he fled to Turkey in 1920.

With the aid of E B Frost, director of the Yerkes Observatory, Struve went to the USA in 1921. He became an assistant at the observatory and studied for his doctorate, which was awarded in 1923. He then rose to the ranks of instructor (1924), assistant (1927) and associate (1930) professor, and assistant director of the observatory (1931). He became professor of astrophysics at the University of Chicago in 1932. When Frost retired in 1932, Struve was made director of the Yerkes Observatory. He was also the founder director of the McDonald Observatory in Texas.

Struve taught at the University of Chicago until 1950, when he became professor of astrophysics and director of the Leuschner Observatory at the University of California at Berkeley. He left in 1959 to become director of the newly established National Radioastronomy Observatory at Green Bank, West Virginia. He retired because of ill-health in 1962, but was appointed joint professor of the Institute of Advanced Studies and California Institute of Technology.

Struve was a member of the National Academy of Sciences, the Royal Society, and the Royal Astronomical Society. He was the recipient of numerous honours including the Gold Medal of the Royal Astronomical Society in 1944 and the Draper Medal of the National Academy of Sciences in 1950. He died on 6 April 1963 in Berkeley.

Struve's early work was on stellar spectroscopy and the positions of comets and asteroids. Spectroscopic analysis of interstellar space had fascinated him from early in his career, as had double stars. He did early work on stellar rotation and demonstrated the rotation of blue-giant stars and the relationship between stellar temperature (and hence spectral type) and speed of rotation. In 1931 he found, as he had anticipated, that stars that spun at a high rate deposited gaseous material around their equators.

In 1936, together with C T Elvey, Struve developed a nebular spectrograph that was used to study interstellar gas clouds. In 1938 they were able to demonstrate for the first time that ionized hydrogen is present in interstellar matter. They also determined that interstellar hydrogen is concentrated in the galactic plane. These observations had important implications for later work on the structure of our Galaxy and for radio astronomy.

Struve was also interested in theories of the evolution of stars, planetary systems, and the universe as a whole. He believed that the establishment of a planetary system should be thought of as the normal course of events in stellar evolution and not a freak occurrence. Struve's contributions to astronomy were of fundamental importance to the fast-growing science of the present century, just as his forefathers' work had been in their time.

Struve, Otto Wilhelm von (1819–1905) Russian astronomer, an active collaborator with his father, F G W von ◊Struve, in many astronomical and geodetic investigations. He is best known for his accurate determination of the constant of precession.

Struve was born in Dorpat (now Tartu), Estonia, on 7 May 1819. He took his degree at the University of Dorpat in 1839, although he had begun work as an astronomer two years earlier. From 1839 to 1848 he worked at the Pulkovo Observatory, near St Petersburg in Russia, becoming its deputy director in 1848, and its director in 1862. From 1847 to 1862 he held a concurrent post as a military adviser in St Petersburg. In 1889 he retired from the Pulkovo Observatory and moved to Karlsruhe, Germany. He was a member of numerous scientific academies and received the Gold Medal of the Royal Astronomical Society. He died in Karlsruhe on 16 April 1905.

One of the most ambitious observational programmes initiated at the Pulkovo Observatory in its early days was a systematic survey of the northern skies for the purpose of discovering and observing double stars. Struve was one of the most active participants in this programme and has been credited with the discovery of about 500 double stars. He also made detailed measurements of binary systems.

Struve was interested in the Solar System and he made a careful study of Saturn's rings. He discovered a satellite of Uranus and calculated the mass of Neptune. He also concerned himself with the measurement of stellar parallax, the movement of the Sun through space, and the structure of the universe, although he was among those astronomers who erroneously believed our Galaxy to be the extent of the whole universe. His determination of the constant of precession, which served as the best estimate for nearly half a century, served to seal his reputation as an astronomer of distinction.

Sturgeon, William (1783–1850) English physicist and inventor who made the first electromagnets.

Sturgeon was born on 22 May 1783, at Whittington, Lancashire, the son of a shoemaker. Sturgeon was himself apprenticed to a shoemaker in 1796, but in 1802 went into the army, enlisting in the Royal Artillery two years later. He studied natural sciences in the evenings, but in 1820 (at the age of 37) he went back to shoemaking and set up a business in Woolwich. He became a member of the Woolwich Literary Society and in 1824 became a lecturer in science and philosophy at the East India Royal Military College of Addiscombe. In 1832 he was appointed to the lecturing staff of the Adelaide Gallery of Practical Science, and in 1840 he was appointed as superintendent of the Royal Victoria Gallery of Practical Science. At this time, as an itinerant lecturer he was able to support his family from an income. As a member of the Manchester Literary and Philosophical Society, he was supported by the president of the society in acquiring a grant of £200 from Lord Russell. In 1849 he was granted an annuity of £50 to promote his work on electromagnetism, but died in the following year on 4 December in Prestwick, Manchester.

Sturgeon was the founder of electromagnetism, and the first English-language journal to be devoted wholly to electricity was started by him. His scientific work only began in earnest when he returned to civilian life at the age of 37, although he had carried out occasional electrical experiments in Woolwich where he had developed various mechanical skills that were useful for making scientific apparatus, and was often in demand to lecture to schools and other groups.

In 1828 he put into practice the idea of a solenoid, first proposed by André ◊Ampère, by wrapping about 18 turns of wire round an iron core so that they became magnetic when a current was passed through them. He found that each coil reinforced the next, since they effectively formed a set of parallel wires with the current moving in the same direction through all of them. He also noticed that the magnetic field seemed to be concentrated in the iron core and that it disappeared as soon as the current was switched off. He varnished the core to insulate it and keep it from short-circuiting the wires, and also tried using a core that was bent into a horseshoe shape. (Joseph ◊Henry in the USA was later to insulate the wires themselves.) His device was capable of lifting 20 times its own weight.

He later invented an important new galvanometer. Sturgeon was one of a small group of lecturers and instrument-makers who worked at demonstrating electrical science in new ways. Between 1836 and 1843 he published a monthly periodical *Annals of Electricity*. He then founded *Annals of Philosophical Discovery* and *Monthly Report of Progress of Science and Art*, which terminated at the end of 1843. They were nevertheless landmarks, being the first electrical journals ever to be published in English.

Sturtevant, Alfred Henry (1891–1970) US geneticist who was the first to map the position of genes on a chromosome. He worked with US biologist Thomas Hunt ◊Morgan.

Born in Jacksonville, Illinois, on 21 November 1891, Sturtevant was the youngest of six children. His grandfather was a founder and president of Illinois College and his father was a mathematics teacher turned farmer. The family moved to a farm in southern Alabama, when Alfred was seven and he was educated in a one-room country school there and for three years in a public school in Mobile. In 1908 Sturtevant entered Columbia University, lodging with his oldest brother, Edgar, a classics teacher who encouraged him in his studies. His interest in genetics had begun as a boy when he became curious about the cause of the different coat colours of his father's horses on the farm and drew up their pedigrees and also those of his family. At Columbia, he pursued this hobby and was encouraged by his brother to learn more about it. He was inspired by a book on Mendelism by geneticist R C Punnett and wrote an account of the genetic relationships that explained the patterns of inheritance of coat colours in horses, which he gave to Morgan, who was professor of experimental zoology at Columbia. Morgan had worked out the principles of sex linkage in mutant fruit flies (*Drosophila*) only months before and was impressed by Sturtevant's work, helping him to get it published in *Biological Bulletin* (1910). He also gave him a place in his research laboratory, which was later to become famous as the 'fly room'. A small room with as many as eight people at a time in it conducting research, the fly room had an exhilarating and collaborative atmosphere. Sturtevant completed his doctorate with Morgan in 1914 and remained at Columbia until 1928 while also working as a research investigator for the Carnegie Institution.

In 1928, Sturtevant joined Morgan in Pasadena as professor of genetics in the new division of biology established by Morgan at the California Institute of Technology (Caltech). He maintained an active research programme and kept up the collaborative spirit of the 'fly room', working closely with other members of staff, including George ◊Beadle, Theodosius ◊Dobzhansky, and Jack Schultz. He lectured in biology and taught genetics and entomology, remaining at Caltech until his death, apart from a year spent as a visiting professor in Europe in 1932, and shorter visits to other US universities. In his later years, Sturtevant took an interest in the genetic effects of radiation and in 1954 he issued a public warning on the genetic hazards of the fallout from the atmospheric testing of atomic bombs.

In May 1910, Morgan and Sturtevant discovered a variant of *Drosophila* with a white eye instead of the normal red. Using these variant flies, Sturtevant developed the technique of 'chromosome mapping' – a method for finding the linear arrangement of genes along a chromosome that relies on the frequencies between linked genes. His 1913 paper describing the location of the sex-linked genes is one of the classics of genetics. Sturtevant and Morgan determined the gene order along the chromosome by working out the recombination frequencies between the linked genes. During meiosis in a heterozygous, phenotypically normal female, an X chromosome will rearrange or crossover. Males derived from these females will carry a combination of mutations. Those mutations that are closest together on the chromosome will be seen with the greatest frequency in the phenotypes of the male flies. The discovery of the inheritance of these mutations in flies did not strictly accord with Mendel's rules since female flies had to inherit two mutated X chromosomes to demonstrate the phenotype, whereas males only had to acquire a single mutated X chromosome.

In his last published work on *Drosophila* (1956) Sturtevant gave an account of a mutant gene that had no apparent effect on the fly itself but in combination with another mutant gene that determined a prune-coloured eye, it was lethal to the organism.

Sturtevant wrote many important papers ands books including *An Analysis of the Effects of Selection* (1918), *The North American Species of Drosophila* (1921), and *A History of Genetics* (1965) – his last book, which contained an appendix with detailed pedigrees of a number of his fellow geneticists. With Morgan, he wrote *The Mechanism of Mendelian Heredity* (1915) and, with Morgan, Muller, and Bridges, *An Introduction to Genetics* (1939).

Suess, Eduard (1831–1914) Austrian geologist who helped pave the way for modern theories of the continents.

Suess was born in London on 20 August 1831 of Bohemian ancestry. He was educated in Vienna and at the University of Prague. He moved to Vienna in 1856 and became professor of geology there in 1861. As well as his geological interests, he occupied himself with public affairs, serving as a member of the Reichstag for 25 years. His geological researches took several directions. As a palaeontologist, he investigated graptolites, brachiopods, ammonites, and the fossil mammals of the Danube Basin. He wrote an original text on economic geology. He undertook important research on the structure of the Alps, the tectonic geology of Italy, and seismology. The possibility of a former landbridge

between North Africa and southern Europe caught his attention. Suess died in Marz, Austria, on 26 April 1914.

The outcome of these interests was *The Face of the Earth* (1885–1909), a massive work devoted to analysing the physical agencies contributing to the Earth's geographical evolution. Suess offered an encyclopedic view of crustal movement, of the structure and grouping of mountain chains, of sunken continents, and of the history of the oceans. He also made significant contributions to rewriting the structural geology of each continent.

In many respects, Suess cleared the path for the new views associated with the theory of continental drift in the 20th century. In view of geological similarities between parts of the southern continents, Suess suggested that there had once been a great supercontinent, made up of the present southern continents; this he named Gondwanaland, after a region of India. Alfred ◊Wegener's work was later to establish the soundness and penetration of such speculations.

Sutherland, Earl Wilbur Jr (1915–1974) US biochemist who was awarded the 1971 Nobel Prize for Physiology or Medicine for his work with cyclic adenosine monophosphate (cyclic AMP), the chemical substance that moderates the action of hormones.

Sutherland was born in Burlingame, Kansas, on 19 November 1915. He graduated from Washburn College, Topeka, in 1937 and received his MD from Washington University Medical School, St Louis, in 1942. After serving as an army officer during World War II he took an appointment at Washington University to do research on hormones under Carl and Gerty ◊Cori. In 1953 he became director of the department of medicine at Western Reserve (now Case Western Reserve) University in Cleveland. Ten years later he was appointed professor of physiology at Vanderbilt University, Nashville, and from 1973 until his death he was a member of the faculty of the University of Miami Medical School. He died in Miami on 9 March 1974.

Sutherland began working with hormones at Washington under the Coris and then spent the 1950s doing research on his own – other workers took little interest in his studies. At that time it was thought that hormones, carried in the bloodstream, activated their target organs directly. Sutherland showed that the key to the process – the activating agent of the organ concerned – is cyclic adenosine 3-,5-monophosphate (cyclic AMP). The arrival of a hormone increases the organ's cellular level of cyclic AMP, which in turn triggers or inhibits the cellular activity.

Cyclic AMP is present in every animal cell and therefore affects 'everything from memory to toes', as Sutherland himself said, so the implications of his discovery were enormous. The 1971 Nobel prize committee commented that it is rare for such a discovery to be credited to only one person. By the end of the 1960s Sutherland was no longer alone in his research; hundreds of scientists throughout the world were keen to do research on the newly discovered substance.

Sutherland, Gordon Brims Black McIvor (1907–1980)

Scottish physicist who is best known for his work in infrared spectroscopy, particularly the use of this technique for studying molecular structure. He received many honours for his work, including a knighthood in 1960.

Sutherland was born in Caithness on 8 April 1907. He was educated at the Morgan Academy, Dundee, and graduated from St Andrew's University, then did postdoctoral work at Trinity College, Cambridge, where he joined one of Eric Rideal's research groups working on infrared spectroscopy. From 1931 to 1933 he was in the USA as a Commonwealth Fund Fellow at the University of Michigan, Ann Arbor (one of the leading centres for spectroscopy studies), working with D Dennison. After returning to the UK he was elected to the Stokes Studentship at Pembroke College, Cambridge, in 1934 and was made a fellow of the college in the following year. During his fellowship – which he held until 1949 – he spent a year as an assistant to the director of production of the Ministry of Supply, was a proctor of the university 1943–44, and served on the council of the university senate 1946–49; he was also appointed university reader in spectroscopy in 1947. While at Cambridge he established a successful research group, first in the department of physical chemistry and later in the newly founded department of colloid science. In 1949 he left Cambridge to take up the position of professor of physics at the University of Michigan, a post he held until 1956, when he returned to the UK to become director of the National Physical Laboratory at Teddington. In 1962 he visited China with one of the first postwar delegations from the Royal Society. From 1964 until his retirement in 1977 Sutherland was master of Emmanuel College, Cambridge. He died in Cambridge on 27 June 1980.

Sutherland spent most of his career using infrared spectroscopy to elucidate molecular structure. Working with William Penney (1909–1991), he showed that the four atoms of hydrogen peroxide (H_2O_2) do not lie in the same plane but that the molecule's structure resembles a partly opened book, with the oxygen atoms aligned along the spine and the O–H bonds lying across each cover. Later, during World War II, Sutherland and his research group at Cambridge analysed fuel from crashed German aircraft in order to discover their sources of oil. At Michigan University he was one of the first to use spectroscopy to study biophysical problems; he also continued his investigations into simpler molecules and crystals.

As director of the National Physical Laboratory, Sutherland reorganized the institution along similar lines to that of the US National Bureau of Standards and established departments of pure physics, applied physics, and standards. The scientific reputation of the laboratory was greatly enhanced under Sutherland's management and, while there, he also researched into the structure of a wide range of substances from proteins to the different forms of diamonds. After his appointment as master of Emmanuel College, he became less active in fundamental research and turned his attention to educational issues.

Sutherland, Ivan Edward (1938–)

US electronics engineer who pioneered the development of computer graphics, the method by which computers display pictorial (as opposed to alphanumeric) information on a visual display unit (VDU).

Sutherland was born in Hastings, Nebraska, on 16 May 1938. His university education began at the Carnegie Institute of Technology, where he obtained a bachelor's degree in 1959, and continued at the Massachusetts Institute of Technology (MIT), where he obtained a master's degree in 1960 and a PhD in electrical engineering in 1963. He was then called into the US Army Signals Corps. In 1964 he became director of information-processing techniques at the Advanced Research Projects Center of the Department of Defense. He stayed in this position until 1966 when he was appointed associate professor of electrical engineering at Harvard University. Two years later he moved to Salt Lake City, to a position as associate professor at the University of Utah, and there founded the Evans and Sutherland Computer Corporation. He became a full professor at Utah in 1972, but left in 1976 to become Fletcher Jones Professor of Computer Science and head of department at the California Institute of Technology. He is currently Sun Fellow and vice president of Sun Microsystems.

From 1960 to 1963 he worked in the Lincoln Laboratory at MIT on the 'Sketchpad' project. This was the first system of computer graphics that could be altered by the operator in the course of its use for calculation and design. Sketchpad used complex arrangements of the data fed into the computer to produce representations of the objects in space as well as fine geometrical detail. Programs could be altered using light pens that touch the surface of the VDU.

While at Utah, Sutherland was engaged in the design of a colour-graphics system able to represent fine distinctions of colour as well as accurate perspective. The image could be moved, rotated, expanded, or made smaller to give a realistic image of the object, rendering the computer suitable for use in engineering and architectural design.

Sutton-Pringle, John William (1912–1982) British zoologist best known for his substantial contribution to our knowledge of insect flight.

Sutton-Pringle was born on 22 July 1912 and was educated at Winchester College and King's College, Cambridge. After graduation he was appointed demonstrator in zoology at Cambridge in 1937, a post he held for two years. From 1938 to 1945 he was a fellow of King's College, Cambridge. In 1945 he was appointed to a lectureship at Cambridge, and became a fellow of Peterhouse College in the same year. He was a reader in experimental cytology 1959–61, when he became emeritus fellow at Peterhouse. In 1977 he was elected president of the Society for Experimental Biology.

Sutton-Pringle helped to establish much of our present knowledge of the anatomical mechanisms involved in insect flight. Most insects have two hindwings and two forewings, and in many species each hindwing is linked to its anterior forewing, thus enabling each pair of wings to act in unison. Not all species use both pairs of wings for flight, however; in the housefly, for example, the hindwings are reduced in size and serve as balancing organs during flight.

Insect flight is achieved by simple up-and-down movements of the wings. In aphids, for example, these wing movements are brought about by the contractions of two separate sets of muscles: contraction of the longitudinal muscles results in depression of the wings; contraction of the dorso-ventral muscles causes elevation of the wings. When moving through the air, the anterior edge of the wings remains rigid while the posterior edge bends. On the downward stroke, the posterior edge is displaced upwards, and on the upward stroke the posterior edge is displaced downwards. This, in turn, causes the development of a localized region of high pressure air behind the insect, which propels the insect forwards. The faster the rate of wing-beats, the greater the displacement of the posterior wing edges, the greater the pressure exerted on the insect from behind, and therefore the faster the insect flies.

Svedberg, Theodor (1884–1971) Swedish physical chemist who invented the ultracentrifuge to facilitate his work on colloids. For his contributions to colloid chemistry he was awarded the 1926 Nobel Prize for Chemistry.

Svedberg was born in Fleräng, near Gävle, on 30 August 1884. As a secondary-school student he became interested in natural sciences (particularly botany), and resolved to study chemistry in the belief that chemical phenomena could explain several of the hitherto unsolved problems of biology. He entered Uppsala University in 1904 and remained associated with it for the rest of his life. He obtained a BSc in 1905 and a PhD two years later, with a thesis on his studies of colloidal solutions. In 1912 he was appointed to the first chair in physical chemistry in Sweden. When he retired from this post in 1949, he became head of the new

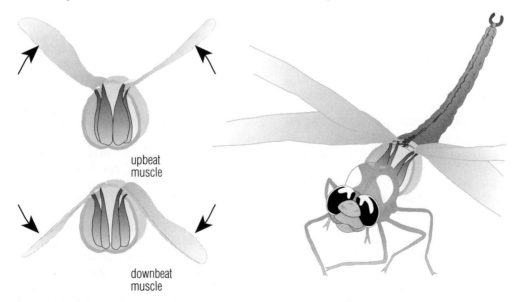

upbeat muscle

downbeat muscle

Sutton-Pringle Sutton-Pringle showed that the rapid wing-beats necessary for flight in insects are achieved by alternate sets of muscles.

Gustav Werner Institute of Nuclear Chemistry. He resigned in 1967 and died in Örebro on 25 February 1971.

Colloid chemistry was Svedberg's interest for 20 years. By 1903 he was already influenced by the work of Hermann ◊Nernst, Richard ◊Zsigmondy, and, particularly, Georg ◊Bredig. Bredig had devised a method of preparing metal sols by passing an electric arc between metal electrodes submerged in a liquid. Svedberg used alternating current with an induction coil having its spark gap in a liquid. In this way he prepared a number of new organosols from more than 30 metals, which were purer in form and had a finer dispersion than Bredig's. Also,the method was able to be reproduced, so that such sols could be used for quantitative analyses in physicochemical studies. Using an ultramicroscope, he studied the Brownian motion of particles in these sols and correlated the observations with the effects of temperature, viscosity, and the nature of the original solvent. These experiments confirmed Albert ◊Einstein's theories about Brownian motion.

Svedberg also had a continuing interest in radioactive processes and, with D Stronholm, experimented with isomorphic co-precipitation of various radioactive substances. He discovered that thorium-X crystallizes with lead and barium salts (but not with others), anticipating Frederick ◊Soddy's demonstration of the existence of isotopes. By about 1923 Svedberg had also investigated a totally different subject, the chemistry involved in the formation of latent images in photographic emulsions.

In 1924 Svedberg constructed the first ultracentrifuge, a development that made a timely and significant contribution to the study of large molecules. Its ability to sort particles by weight can reveal the presence of contaminants in a sample of a new protein, or distinguish between various long-chain polymers in substances such as cellulose and other natural polymers. His other researches in the 1930s confirmed his view that these substances consist of well-defined uniform molecules.

During World War II the Swedish government asked Svedberg to investigate methods of producing synthetic rubber (at that time, polychloroprene). This research led to the establishment of a small manufacturing plant in the north of Sweden. He also studied other synthetic polymers, introducing electron microscopy to study natural and regenerated cellulose, X-ray diffraction techniques to investigate cellulose fibres, and electron diffraction to analyse colloidal micelles and crystallites.

In the late 1930s Svedberg's interest in radiochemistry prompted a need to increase the capacity for making radioactive isotopes. Finance from the Swedish industrialist Gustaf Werner was used to build a large cyclotron, founding the Gustaf Werner Institute of Nuclear Chemistry.

After his official retirement in 1949, Svedberg became the head of the institute and recruited the staff. One group worked on the biological and medical applications of the cyclotron, while another group investigated the effects of radiation on macromolecules, together with problems in radiochemistry and radiation physics.

Swammerdam, Jan (1637–1680) Dutch naturalist who investigated many aspects of biology but who is probably best known for his outstanding microscope observations, his detailed and accurate anatomical descriptions, and his studies of insects. He is considered by many to be a founder of both comparative anatomy and entomology.

Swammerdam was born in Amsterdam on 12 February 1637. He was the son of an apothecary whose hobby was a museum of curiosities, a hobby that stimulated the younger Swammerdam's interest in natural history, particularly in insects. He graduated with a medical degree from Leiden University in 1667 but never practised as a physician, preferring to pursue his interest in natural history. Subsequently his father, who wanted his son to become a priest, withdrew his financial support – despite which the younger Swammerdam continued his biological studies, although he suffered severe privations and became chronically ill, both physically and mentally. In 1673 Swammerdam came under the influence of the religious zealot Antoinette Bourignon and became increasingly embroiled in religious controversy until he died, only 43 years old, in Amsterdam on 15 February 1680.

Swammerdam made many important contributions to biological knowledge but most of his studies were of insects. He accurately described and illustrated the life cycles and anatomies of many species, including bees, mayflies, and dragonflies. In mayflies and dragonflies the change from the last nymph stage to the winged adult is outwardly the most striking, but Swammerdam showed that rudimentary wings occur in the aquatic nymphs some time before the final moult. He also showed that caterpillars develop wings and adult-type legs shortly before pupating. From his observations of their metamorphic development Swammerdam classified insects into four major groups, three of which are still used in a modified form in modern insect classification. In addition, he disproved many false beliefs about insects – for example, that their bodies are structureless, fluid-filled cavities without fully formed internal organs.

Swammerdam also studied vertebrates, about which he provided a substantial body of new knowledge, most of which was correct. He showed that the lungs of newly born mammals sink in water when the lungs are taken from the animals before breathing has started but that lungs taken from young animals whose respiration has been established float. He also erroneously believed, however, that the movements of the chest in mammals are unrelated to inhalation and exhalation but are associated with transferring air from the lungs to the heart. Swammerdam demonstrated that muscles removed from a frog could be stimulated to contract and that when muscle (including heart muscle) contracts it does not increase in volume. Furthermore, he anticipated the discovery of the role of oxygen in respiration by postulating that air contained a volatile element that could pass from the lungs to the heart (contributing to the respiration operation of the heart) and then to the muscles, providing the energy for muscle contraction. Investigating the anatomy of the frog, he observed that the frog's egg passes through a stage when it consists of four joined globules (now known to be the second cleavage of the fertilized egg). He was also probably the first to discover red blood corpuscles when he observed oval particles in frog's blood in 1658.

In his work on human and mammalian anatomy, Swammerdam discovered valves in the lymphatic system; these valves are now called Swammerdam valves. He also investigated the human reproductive system and was one of the first to show that female mammals produce eggs, analogous to birds' eggs. In addition he perfected a technique for injecting dyes into dissected cadavers in order to display anatomical details.

Swammerdam's work – particularly his insect studies – had a profound impact on scientific thinking, although his manuscripts were not published in full until 1737, when Hermann ◊Boerhaave published *Biblia naturae/Bible of Nature,* a two-volume Latin translation of Swammerdam's Dutch text that included illustrations engraved from Swammerdam's own drawings. The work is one of the finest collections of biological observations ever published and, even today, many of Swammerdam's illustrations remain unsurpassed.

Swan, Joseph Wilson (1828–1914) English inventor and electrical engineer – trained originally as a chemist – who invented an incandescent electric lamp. He also made major contributions to photographic processing, and lesser ones to electroplating methods, electrolytic cells, and the production of artificial fibres.

Swan was born on 31 October 1828 in Sunderland. For a time during his childhood his parents allowed him to roam about Sunderland, where he became fascinated with the busy industries, towns, and ports. Eventually he was sent to a dame school run by three elderly women, and from there he went to a large school under the direction of Dr Wood, a Scottish minister. When he left school he became apprenticed to a Sunderland firm of retail chemists. Before his apprenticeship was finished both partners in the business died. Joseph then went to join his brother-in-law, John Mawson, in his chemical firm at Newcastle upon Tyne. During these times he was fascinated by scientific and engineering inventions, and he attended lectures and read books and journals that described them. It was then that he learned of the early interest in the electric lamp of J W Starr and W E Staite.

Swan quickly proved his worth and soon the firm was producing photographic chemicals. He developed a deep interest in the photographic process, making an experimental study of the various methods. One particular wet process for producing photographic prints, using a gelatine film impregnated with carbon or other pigment granules and photosensitized using potassium dichromate, was patented by Swan in 1864. This was known as the carbon or autotype process. A few years later, in 1879, he invented and patented a bromide printing paper, now a standard photographic medium.

Swan's interest in electric lighting is said to stem from a lecture given by Staite in Sunderland in 1845. From about 1848 he began making filaments by cutting strips of cardboard or paper and baking them at high temperatures to produce a carbon fibre. The recipes he used were often exotic, sometimes entailing cooking with syrup of tar. These filaments were made into coils or circles. In making the first lamps he connected the ends of a filament to wire (itself a difficult task), placed the filament in a glass bottle, and attempted to evacuate the air and seal the bottle with a cork. Usually the filament burned away very quickly in the remaining air, blackening the glass at the same time.

In 1865 the German chemist Hermann Sprengel (1834–1906) invented a mercury vacuum pump, which was used to evacuate the air from radiometer tubes produced by William ◊Crookes in the UK. Swan read of Crookes's work and saw the pump as a means of producing an improved vacuum for his lamps. He came across Charles Stearn, who had become familiar with the technique of producing a vacuum using Sprengel's pump, when he read a newspaper advertisement. Swan them produced filaments for Stearn to use to make lamps using the Sprengel pump. Although their first experiments were not very successful they found that if, after first producing the best possible vacuum, a strong current was passed to make the filament burn brightly, and if the bulb was further evacuated (thus drawing out the products of the combustion of the carbon with the remnants of the air), then a fairly durable incandescent lamp was produced. Swan demonstrated his electric light and exhibited it throughout the northeast of England in 1878 and 1879, at the same time producing a new type of filament from cotton thread partly dissolved by sulphuric acid.

From the summer of 1880 onwards, Swan's electric lamps were manufactured. First they were made in a factory in Benwell, Newcastle upon Tyne, but soon a larger London company was formed. Thomas ◊Edison, famous for his electrical inventions (including the phonograph), developed an electric light in the USA on a similar principle to Swan's. Edison was quick to take out patents while Swan hesitated. In 1882 he initiated litigation for patent infringement against Swan, but this was dismissed and the joint company Edison and Swan United Electric Light Company came into being in 1883.

In the 1880s electrical supply was in its infancy. There were few electric companies, and those that did exist distributed over very small areas; usually electricity users had their own generators. But the availability of the electric lamp had a great stimulus on the electricity industry, first in public buildings and the private residences of a few notables and then, within a few years, in shops, factories, offices, and ships of the Merchant and Royal Navy. Also its potential for advertising was soon recognized.

Swan did not rest to merely reap the financial rewards of his invention. He made a miner's electric safety lamp that, although far too costly to be adopted at the time, was the ancestor of the modern miner's lamp. In the course of this invention he devised a new lead cell (battery) that would not spill acid. He had a lifelong interest in electrical cells and attempted to make an early type of fuel cell.

In the course of developing a method of producing uniform carbon filaments, Swan devised a process in which nitrocellulose (made by nitrating cotton) was dissolved in acetic acid and extruded through a fine die. This process had obvious advantages in producing lighting filaments, but it was also seen by Swan to be capable of producing an artificial silk. His wife and daughter crocheted some of the material and it was exhibited as 'artifical silk' at an exhibition in 1885, but Swan never considered commercial production.

Throughout his life Swan was an ardent and determined experimenter, with interests ranging from photography to electroplating. He carried out a very extensive study of the best conditions for the electrodeposition of copper and a number of other metals. Many of his discoveries were of practical use, and he took out more than 70 patents. He was elected a fellow of the Royal Society in 1894, and ten years later he was knighted. He held high offices in a number of professional socities and was in receipt of medals from both the Royal Society and the Royal Photographic Society.

He died at home in Warlingham, Surrey, on 27 May 1914, aged 85.

Swinburne, James (1858–1958) Scottish engineer, a pioneer in electrical engineering and plastics.

Swinburne was born in Inverness on 28 February 1858. He was the third of six sons of a naval captain and spent most of his childhood on the lonely island of Eileen Shona, in Loch Mordart, where the common spoken language was Gaelic. Eventually he was sent to study at Clifton College, where the accent was on science subjects, a bias Swinburne's talents were quick to appreciate.

Swinburne began his career in engineering with an apprenticeship to a locomotive works in Manchester, after which he travelled to Tyneside and found employment with an engineering firm. It was during this time that his lifelong interest in electrical engineering developed, and in 1881 Joseph ◊Swan engaged him to take responsibility for setting up a new factory in Paris for the manufacture of Swan's electric lamps. Swinburne carried out the task so successfully that in the following year Swan sent him to the USA to set up a factory there. From 1885 Swinburne was employed as technical assistant to the engineer Rookes ◊Crompton, at his Chelmsford factory. He worked on many aspects of electrical engineering and was particularly involved in the development of dynamos and the well-known 'hedgehog' transformer.

In 1894, Swinburne decided to set up his own laboratory and made himself available as a consultant. Some of the research carried out in his laboratory focused on the reaction between phenol and formaldehyde (methanal) and its commercial potential. Unfortunately when Swinburne came to patent the product in 1907 he was beaten to the idea by the Belgium chemist Leo ◊Baekeland (with his invention of Bakelite). Swinburne was able to obtain a patent on the production of a laquer, however, and set up his own manufacturing concern, Damard Laquer Company, in Birmingham. Baekeland bought him out in the early 1920s and formed Bakelite Limited, Great Britain, of which Swinburne became the first chairman, a position he maintained until 1948. From then until his retirement in 1951 he remained on its board of directors. He died in Bournemouth on 30 March 1958.

Swinburne lived to be 100 years old and was greatly respected by the scientific and industrial world, being affectionately known as the 'father of British Plastics'.

It was in the 1880s that the great march of electrical progress began to gather momentum. Swan and his filament lamp inspired the idea of using electricity for domestic purposes, and other great engineers concentrated on the development of heavier equipment such as dynamos and transformers. When Swinburne joined Crompton's team the impetus was reaching its peak, with many of the problems in electrical engineering being solved and with modifications being made to existing ideas.

Swinburne's own contributions were wide-ranging and included the invention of the watt-hour meter and the 'hedgehog' transformer for stepping up medium-voltage alternating current to high voltages for long-distance power transmission. He was also responsible for numerous smaller inventions and for work on the theory of dynamos. The words 'motor' and 'stator', thought to have been coined by him, are now in common use in electrical engineering.

Swings, Pol(idore) F F (1906–1983) Belgian astrophysicist with a particular interest in cometary spectroscopy.

Swings was born in Ransart, near Charleroi, on 24 September 1906. He studied mathematics and physics at the University of Liège, where he earned his doctorate in mathematics in 1927. He served as an assistant at the university 1927–32, although he spent much of his time abroad conducting his postdoctoral research. In 1930 he was awarded a special DSc in physics. From 1932 to 1975 he was professor of astrophysics at the University of Liège.

During the 1930s and 1940s, Swings spent several years in the USA as visiting professor at a number of universities, including Chicago and California. He was a member of numerous professional bodies including the International Astronomical Union, which he served both as vice president and president, the National Academy of Sciences in the USA, the Royal Astronomical Society in London, and the Royal Belgian Academy of Sciences. He received the Francqui Prize in 1947 and the Decennial Prize in 1958, the highest Belgian honours. Swings was coauthor of an atlas of cometary spectra, published in 1956, and the recipient of several honorary degrees.

Swings's early astronomical studies concentrated on celestial mechanics, but he soon displayed an interest in the more modern discipline of spectroscopy. At first he approached the subject in an experimental laboratory fashion, but later he applied his expertise in spectral analysis to an investigation of the constitution of a number of types of celestial bodies. His most influential work dealt with the study of cometary atmospheres, and he is credited with the discovery of the Swings bands and the Swings effect. Swings bands are emission lines resulting from the presence of certain atoms of carbon; the Swings effect was discovered with the aid of a slit spectrograph and is attributed to fluorescence resulting partly from solar radiation.

Swings also made spectroscopic studies of inter-stellar space and investigated stellar rotation, as well as nebulae, novae, and variable stars.

Sylow, Ludwig Mejdell (1832–1918) Norwegian mathematician who is remembered for his fundamental theorem on groups and for the special type of subgroups that are named after him.

Sylow was born in Christiania (now Oslo) on 12 May 1832 and attended the cathedral school there until 1850, when he entered the University of Christiania to study mathematics. After graduating, he trained to become a teacher and received his certificate in 1856. For the next 40 years he taught in a school at Halden, although he travelled around Europe on a scholarship in 1861 and lectured at the University of Christiania in 1862. From 1873 to 1877 he was given a leave of absence from his teaching duties to collaborate with Sophus ◊Lie on producing an edition of the works of Niels ◊Abel. A year earlier Sylow had published his theorem, the first major advance in group theory since Augustin ◊Cauchy's work of the 1840s, and still regarded as essential for work on finite groups. At the same time he introduced the concept of subgroups, now known by his name. The edition of Abel's work prepared by Sylow and Lie was published in 1881; it was followed by Sylow's edition of Abel's letters in 1901. Through Lie's influence, Sylow was rewarded with a chair of mathematics at the University of Christiania in 1898, where he remained until his death on 7 September 1918.

Sylvester, James Joseph (1814–1897) English mathematician, one of the pre-eminent algebraists of the 19th century and the discoverer, with Arthur ◊Cayley, of the theory of algebraic invariants.

Sylvester was born in London on 3 September 1814, the sixth of nine children in the family of Abraham Sylvester. He was educated at a school for Jewish boys in north London and in 1828 entered the new University of London, founded especially for Dissenters and others outside the Anglican church who were still unable to take degrees at the ancient universities and dedicated to establishing the sciences on a finer basis in the university curriculum. After only five months there he was expelled for attempting to wound a fellow student with a table knife. In 1829 he enrolled at the Royal Institution school in Liverpool, where he won a prize of £250 for a paper on arrangements before running away to Dublin, apparently to escape from anti-Semitic persecution. He was sent back to England by a cousin of his mother and in 1831 entered St John's College, Cambridge. In the final honours examination of 1837 he emerged with the second highest results, but, unable to subscribe to the Thirty-Nine Articles (articles of faith) of the Church of England, he was ineligible to compete for the Smith's Prize or to take his degree. He therefore went to Trinity College, Dublin, where he gained his BA in 1841.

In the meantime he had been appointed to the chair of natural philosophy at University College, London, in 1837 and elected to the Royal Society in 1839. In 1841 he went to the USA to become professor of mathematics at the University of Virginia, but after some sort of personal squabble (the truth has never been established) resigned the chair and returned to England in 1845. For the next ten years he abandoned academic life, although he took in private pupils, including Florence Nightingale. He worked for the Equity and Law Life Assurance Company 1845–55, entered the Inner Temple in 1846, and was called to the bar in 1850. At about this time he also founded the Law Reversionary Interest Society.

In 1855 he returned to academic life, becoming professor of mathematics at the Royal Military Academy at Woolwich and editor of the *Quarterly Journal of Pure and Applied Mathematics* from its first edition in 1855 to 1877. He remained at Woolwich until 1877, when he again went to the USA to become professor of mathematics at the newly founded Johns Hopkins University at Baltimore. During his tenure there he founded, in 1883, the US *Journal of Mathematics*. In that year he took up his last academic post as Savilian Professor of Geometry at Oxford University, where he was elected a fellow of New College. He died at London, three years after his retirement, on 15 March 1897.

Sylvester was a prolific writer of mathematical papers, but he was unmethodical, and his brilliant inventiveness was somewhat dulled by his failure to provide rigorous proofs for the ideas that, born of his creative intuition, he was confident in asserting. He is remembered chiefly for his algebra, especially for laying the foundations with Arthur Cayley (with whom he did not collaborate) of modern invariant algebra. He also wrote two long memoirs (1853 and 1864) on the nature of roots in quintic equations and did brilliant work on the theory of numbers, especially in partitions and Diophantine analysis. He introduced the concept of a denumerant and he coined the term 'matrix' in 1850 to describe a rectangular array of numbers out of which determinants can be formed. His high achievements were acknowledged by the Royal Society, which awarded him the Royal Medal in 1861 and the Copley Medal in 1880.

Further Reading

Feuer, Lewis S, 'Sylvester in Virginia', *Math Intellig*, 1987, v 9 (2), pp 13–19.

Hogan, Edward, 'A proper spirit is abroad: Peirce, Sylvester, Ward and American mathematics, 1829–1843', *Hist Math*, 1991, v 18, pp 158–172.

Parshall, Karen Hunger, *James Joseph Sylvester: Life and Work in Letters*, Oxford University Press, 1998.

Parshall, Karen Hunger, 'America's first school of mathematical research: James Joseph Sylvester at the John Hopkins University', 1876–1883, *Arch Hist Exact Sci*, 1988, v 38, pp 153–196.

Parshall, Karen Hunger and Rowe, David E, *The Emergence of the American Mathematical Research Community, 1876–1900: J J Sylvester, Felix Klein, and E H Moore*, History of Mathematics series, American Mathematical Society, 1994, v 8.

Synge, Richard Laurence Millington (1914–1994)

English biochemist who carried out research into methods of isolating and analysing proteins and related substances. He is best known for the work on paper chromatography he did with Archer ◊Martin, for which they shared the 1952 Nobel Prize for Chemistry.

Synge was born in Liverpool on 28 October 1914, the son of a stockbroker. He attended Winchester School 1928–33 and then went to Trinity College, Cambridge, graduating in 1936; he gained his PhD five years later. He went to work as a biochemist at the Wool Industries Research Association in Leeds, and then in 1943 moved to the Lister Institute of Preventive Medicine in London. In 1948 he was put in charge of protein chemistry at the Rowett Research Institute in Aberdeen. He spent the year 1958–59 with the New Zealand Department of Agriculture at its Ruakura Animal Research Station. From 1967 until his retirement in 1974 he worked as a biochemist at the Food Research Institute of the Agricultural Research Council in Norwich. He was also honorary professor of biology at the University of East Anglia. He died on 18 August 1994.

In the early 1940s there were crude chromatographic techniques for separating proteins in a reasonably large sample, but no sufficiently refined method existed for the separation of individual amino acids. Martin and Synge, who worked together both at Cambridge and Leeds, evolved the technique of using porous filter paper in chromatography. A spot of mixed amino-acid solution is placed at the end of a strip of filter paper and allowed to dry. The paper is then dipped in a solvent that either creeps up it by capillary action (ascending chromatography) or down the paper if it hung below the level of the solvent. As the solvent passes the mixture the various amino acids move with it, but at different rates. The filter paper is then dried, and sprayed with a 'developer' such as ninhydrin solution. On heating the paper the positions of the amino acids are revealed as dark spots and can be identified by comparing them with the spots produced by known amino acids. Several mixtures can be analysed at once by applying several spots to a wide piece of paper.

The technique described is one-dimensional paper (or partition) chromatography, because the solvent spreads the amino acids in only one direction. If the chromatogram is dried but, before being treated with ninhydrin, is rotated through 90° and dipped in solvent again (either the same or a different one), the amino acids can be resolved even more clearly. This version is known as two-dimensional chromatography.

Martin and Synge announced their method in 1944 and it became an immediate success, being applied widely and adapted to many experimental problems. It was soon demonstrated that not only the type but the concentration of each amino acid can be determined. Synge was able to work out the exact structure of Gramicidin-S, a simple antibiotic peptide, which led in 1953 to Frederick ◊Sanger's elucidation of the complete sequence of insulin. Other chromatographic techniques since developed include gas, thin-layer, ion-exchange, gel-filtration, and, most recently, high-pressure liquid chromatography.

Szent-Györgyi, Albert von Nagyrapolt (1893–1986)

Hungarian-born US biochemist who studied the physiology of muscle contraction and carried out research into cancer. He was best known, however, for his work on vitamin C, for which he was awarded the 1937 Nobel Prize for Physiology or Medicine.

Szent-Györgyi was born in Budapest on 16 September 1893, into a family of scientists. He completed his early education in Budapest and entered the medical school at the university there in 1911. During his first year he began research in his uncle's laboratory, and three years later he had published a series of papers on the structure of the vitreous body in the eye. During World War I he served in the Austro-Hungarian army on the Russian and Italian fronts, and was decorated for bravery. But he soon left the army with a (self-inflicted) wound and returned to his studies in Budapest, gaining his medical degree in 1917. During the 1920s he studied at various universities in Germany, the Netherlands, Belgium, the USA, and the UK. He obtained his PhD from Cambridge University in 1927 and returned to Hungary in 1937 to the University of Szeged. Szent-Györgyi was active in the anti-Nazi underground movement during World War II; after the war he became professor of biochemistry at the University of Budapest. Unhappy with the Soviet regime, in 1947 he emigrated to the USA where he joined the staff of the Marine Biological Laboratories at Woods Hole, Massachusetts. He became a US citizen in 1955. For 32 years he was director of the National Institute of Muscle Research and was scientific director of the National Foundation for Cancer Research from 1975. He died at Woods Hole on 22 October 1986.

Szent-Györgyi published his first significant piece of research in 1928 while he was at Cambridge working under Frederick Gowland ◊Hopkins. He isolated a substance from the adrenal glands and called it hexuronic acid because the molecule appeared to contain six carbon atoms. He isolated the same substance from cabbages and oranges. Back in Hungary in the early 1930s he discovered that paprika – a major crop in the locality around Szeged – is an extremely rich source of the acid, which he prepared as pure white crystals and in 1932 proved to be the same as the substance (first discovered in 1907) that prevents scurvy in human beings; his announcement was anticipated by only two weeks by Charles King. Szent-Györgyi suggested that the acid be called antiscorbutic acid, although it finally became known as ascorbic acid (vitamin C). His work made it possible for Norman ◊Haworth and Paul ◊Karrer to synthesize ascorbic acid, for which they were awarded the 1937 Nobel Prize for Chemistry, the same year in which Szent-Györgyi received the Physiology Prize.

Discovery consists of seeing what everybody has seen, thinking what nobody has thought.
ALBERT SZENT-GYÖRGYI QUOTED IN I G GOOD (ED) THE SCIENTIST SPECULATES *1962*

Szent-Györgyi also studied the uptake of oxygen by minced muscle tissue. Left undisturbed, the tissue gradually absorbed less and less oxygen as some substance in it was used up. In 1935 he found that activity was restored by adding any one of four closely related four-carbon compounds: fumaric acid, malic acid, succinic acid, or oxaloacetic acid. This discovery was later used by Hans ◊Krebs in working out the Krebs (tricarboxylic acid) cycle.

In 1940 Szent-Györgyi isolated two kinds of muscle protein from myosin, which, until then, had been thought to be the single basic component of muscle tissue. One was composed of rod-shaped particles and the other was in the form of minute globular beads. The former retained the name myosin and the latter was called actin; he re-named the combined compound actomyosin. When adenosine triphosphate (ATP) is added to it, a change takes place in the relationship of the two components that results in the contraction of the muscle itself.

During the late 1940s Szent-Györgyi made further investigations into the chemistry of the citrus fruits and extracted the so-called vitamin P from lemon peel. It is a complex compound of three flavonoids whose function is to reduce the fragility of capillary blood vessels. The breakdown of capillaries is a common result of prolonged radiation therapy in cancer patients, and can be countered by administering 'vitamin P'.

In the 1960s Szent-Györgyi began studying the thymus gland, which had been shown to play a part in the setting up of the body's immunological system. He isolated several compounds from the thymus that seem to be involved in the control of growth. At the National Foundation for Cancer Research he carried out research on the processes of cell division. In 1976, in his 84th year he published a book entitled *Electronic Biology and Cancer*.

Szilard, Leo (1898–1964) Hungarian physicist and one of the 20th century's most original minds. He made major contributions to statistical mechanics, nuclear physics, nuclear engineering, molecular biology, political science, and genetics but was best known for his work on nuclear chain reaction. He was a central figure in the Manhattan Project and after the war became a strong proponent of the peaceful uses of atomic energy.

Leo Szilard was born in Budapest, the oldest of three children of a Jewish architect and engineer. A sickly child, he was mostly taught at home by his mother. He started studying electrical engineering in Budapest but his studies were interrupted when he was drafted into the Austro-Hungarian army in World War I. In 1920 he continued his studies in Berlin at the Technische Hochschule but transferred to read physics at the university, receiving a doctorate in 1922. His PhD thesis was on thermodynamics and the continuation of this work led to the publication of a famous 1929 paper establishing the connection between entropy and information. This was a forerunner to the theory of cybernetics.

In Berlin he was a research worker at the Kaiser Wilhelm Institute and a *Privatdozent* (unpaid lecturer) at the university. He worked on X-ray crystallography with Herman Marks and began work on patenting some of his pioneering inventions which included a prototype of the modern nuclear particle accelerator.

With Albert ◊Einstein he patented an electromagnetic pump for liquid refrigerants, which is still used in nuclear reactors today.

In 1933, Szilard fled Hitler's Germany for the UK, working in the field of nuclear chain reactions at St Bartholomew's Hospital in London and the Clarendon Laboratory, Oxford. This work led to the establishment of the Szilard–Chambers reaction and the discovery of the emission of neutrons from beryllium. When Szilard emigrated to the USA in 1938, he learned that Otto ◊Hahn and Lise ◊Meitner had discovered fission in Germany. Recognizing the significance of this he persuaded Einstein (who commanded world respect) to write to President Roosevelt, warning him of the possibility of atomic bombs and encouraging him to develop them before the Germans did. This was the start of the Manhattan Project and initiated a programme that was to culminate in the dropping of a nuclear bomb on Hiroshima in Japan in 1945.

Szilard started work immediately at Columbia University to demonstrate the fission process and measure the number of neutrons released. In 1942 he joined Enrico ◊Fermi at Chicago University, where they worked on the first controlled chain reaction on 2 December 1942. Fermi and Szilard were awarded the patent for the nuclear fission reactor in 1945. In the last months of the war, Szilard and others made a futile attempt to dissuade President Truman from dropping the bomb on Hiroshima, predicting the nuclear stalemate that would follow.

After the war Szilard moved into molecular biology, becoming professor of biophysics at Chicago in 1946. He was also prominent in the campaign for nuclear-arms control and in 1962 he founded the Council for a Livable World, a Washington lobby on arms control. He joined the Salk Institute of Biological Sciences at La Jolla in California in 1956, where he worked on genetics and immunology until his death on 30 May 1964.

Szilard was a fellow of the American Physical Society and the American Academy of Arts and Sciences and he received the Einstein Award in 1958 and the Atoms for Peace Award in 1959.

T

Tabor, David (1913–) English physicist who has worked mainly in tribology, the study of the effects between solid surfaces.

Tabor was born in London on 23 October 1913. He was educated at Regent Street Polytechnic, London, 1925–31, and then read physics at the Royal College of Science, London, obtaining his BSc in 1934. From 1934 to 1936, he researched under George ◊Thomson and then from 1936 to 1939 under Frank ◊Bowden at Cambridge. He gained his PhD in 1939, and then went to Australia in 1940 to work in tribophysics at a division of the Commonwealth Scientific Research Organization in Melbourne. In 1946 he returned to Cambridge, and worked in the section of the Cavendish Laboratory concerned with the physics and chemistry of solids. He was assistant director of research there until 1961, when he was made a lecturer in physics. He subsequently became a reader in physics in 1964 and professor of physics in 1973, a position he held until 1981 (emeritus thereafter). Among his many awards is the Guthrie Medal of the Institute of Physics in 1974.

Tabor's research interests have been very wide. Early investigations were into the friction and lubrication of metals, low-energy and high-energy electron-diffraction techniques and high-vacuum methods for studying clean surfaces, the adsorption of vapours, and the first stages of conversion of a chemisorbed film to a chemically formed film. Bowden had introduced the idea of using mica to study the contact between two surfaces since the cleavage faces are molecularly smooth. Tabor extended this to a study of forces between two curved mica surfaces and showed that normal van der Waals forces operate for separations less than 100 Å (10^{-8} m), and retarded van der Waals forces for separations larger than 500 Å (5×10^{-8} m). As a byproduct of an investigation of the action of windscreen wiper blades, Tabor was able to study directly the repulsive forces between electrically charged double-layers. These and the attractive van der Waals forces are of basic importance in colloid stability.

Tabor also looked at the friction and transfer of polymers. This work includes the effect of speed and temperature and he attempted to correlate the behaviour with viscoelastic properties. He showed that the low friction of Teflon (polytetrafluoroethene, PTFE) is not due to poor adhesion but to its molecular structure, and worked on the self-lubrication of polymers by incorporating surface materials into the polymer itself. A study of the friction of rubber led to the introduction of high-hysteresis rubber into automobile tyres as means of increasing their skid-resistance. Tabor also examined the effect of hydrostatic pressure on the viscoelastic properties of polymers and showed that by decreasing the free volume, hydrostatic pressure increases the glass transition temperature.

Tabor researched into the shear properties of molecular films of long-chain organic molecules as an extension of earlier work on the mechanism of boundary lubrication, and showed that the shear strength of these materials rises sharply when they are subjected to high pressure. This sheds light on the mechanism of thin-film lubrication.

Tabor's work on the hardness of solids includes an explanation of the indentation hardness of metals in terms of their basic yield properties and the first account of plastic indentation and elastic recovery that explains rebound in terms of plastic and elastic properties (rebound hardness). He has also examined the effect of temperature and loading time on indentation hardness, and made the first correlation of the hardness behaviour with the creep properties of the material (hot-hardness), and offered a physical explanation of the Mohs scale used in the testing of minerals.

He has also carried out a broad study of the creep of polycrystalline ice over a wide range of temperatures and strain rates, and has explained this behaviour in terms of various dislocation and grain-boundary properties. These results have a bearing on the flow of glaciers.

Tabor has looked at diffusion in polymers, studying the diffusion of suitably tagged organic molecules through a polymer matrix. By increasing the length of the diffusant, he has provided experimental evidence for the first time for the process of reptation, whereby the diffusant worms its way through the free volume of the polymer. He has also examined the effect of hydrostatic pressure on diffusion since this shows how the polymer matrix restricts the movement of the diffusant.

Talbot, William Henry Fox (1800–1877) English classical scholar, mathematician, and scientist who invented the calotype (or talbotype) photographic process. This was a negative-to-positive process on paper that laid the foundation for modern photography.

Talbot was born on 11 February 1800 in Melbury, Dorset, the son of William Davenport Talbot, an officer in the Dragoons, and Lady Elizabeth Fox Strangeways, daughter of the second Earl of Ilchester. He was educated at Harrow and Trinity College, Cambridge, and was elected Liberal member of Parliament for Chippenham, taking his seat in 1833. During a trip to Italy he resolved to try to capture the images obtained in a camera obscura and by 1835 had succeeded in fixing outlines of objects laid on sensitized paper. Images of his home, Lacock Abbey, followed and Talbot then appeared to give up his experiments until the announcement of Louis Daguerre's (1789–1851) success on 7 January 1839.

Talbot rushed into publication in case Daguerre's process was the same as his own (there were similarities). He exhibited his work at the Royal Institution and again at the Royal Society on 31 January where he presented a hastily prepared paper. Some of the exhibits were positives and were probably taken between 1835 and 1839.

To publicize his process, Talbot set up a laboratory for printing calotypes in Reading. This produced *The Pencil of Nature*, the first book in the world to be illustrated by photographs. It came out irregularly in six parts, beginning 29 June 1844, each part containing from three to seven photographs. Other books followed.

Talbot patented an enlarger in June 1843 and took the first successful photograph by electric light. This was also the first successful motion-freezing photograph taken by flash and it was demonstrated at the Royal Institution in 1851. He applied the principle of dichromate and gelatine to photoglyphic engraving and tried to lay claim to the collodion process. Squabbling over this claim culminated in a court case in which on 20 December 1854 it was found that collodion photography did not infringe calotype patents.

In parallel with his photographic work, Talbot was giving papers at Royal Society meetings, many of them on mathematical and scientific subjects. He published papers on archaeology and, with Henry Rawlinson and Edward Hincks, was one of the first to decipher the cuneiform inscriptions of Nineveh. He was also the author of *English Etymologies*. He died at Lacock Abbey on 17 September 1877.

Talbot's calotype process was patented on 8 February 1841. Good-quality writing paper was coated successively with solutions of silver nitrate and potassium iodide, forming silver iodide. The iodized paper was made more sensitive by brushing with solutions of gallic acid and silver nitrate, and then it was exposed (either moist or dry). The latent image was developed with an application of gallo-silver nitrate solution, and when the image became visible the paper was warmed for one to two minutes. It was fixed with a solution of potassium bromide (later replaced by sodium hyposulphite). Calotypes did not have the sharp definition of daguerreotypes and were generally considered inferior.

In the decade to 1851, Talbot took out four patents, many of which contained previously published claims. He stirred up considerable resentment by his activities, which are considered to have hindered the development of photography in the UK. However on 30 July 1852 he announced that he wished only to retain licensing on professional portraiture. This cleared the way for amateurs to use processes developed in other countries.

Further Reading

Arnold, Harry John Philip, *William Henry Fox Talbot: Pioneer of Photography and Man of Science*, Hutchinson Benham, 1977.

Buckland, Gail, *Fox Talbot and the Invention of Photography*, Scolar Press, 1980.

Hannavy, John, *Fox Talbot: An Illustrated Life*, Lifelines series, Shire Publications, 1976, v 38.

Hawkyard, Alasdair, *William Henry Fox Talbot: Scientist, Inventor, Classicist*, A Hawkyard, 1989.

Schaaf, Larry John (ed), *Correspondence of William Henry Fox Talbot: A Draft Calendar*, Glasgow University Library Studies series, Department of Accounting and Finance, University of Glasgow, 1995.

Schaaf, Larry John, *Out of the Shadows: Herschel, Talbot, and the Invention of Photography*, Yale University Press, 1992.

Talbot, William Henry Fox; Weaver, Mike (ed), *Talbot, William Henry Fox, 1800–1877*, World Photographers Reference Series, Clio, 1992, v 3.

Tansley, Arthur George (1871–1955) English botanist who was a pioneer in the science of plant ecology. He helped to promote the subject through his teaching and by writing and editing textbooks and journals (including contributing to and editing the first major book on the vegetation of the British Isles). He was also instrumental in the formation of organizations devoted to the study of ecology and the protection of wildlife.

Tansley was born in London on 15 August 1871. He was educated at Highgate School 1886–89 (and later commented on the inadequacy of the science teaching of that time), after which he attended science classes at University College, London, where he received his first instruction in botany from Francis Oliver. In 1890 he went to Trinity College, Cambridge, graduating in 1894. He combined his last year of study with a teaching post at University College and, after graduation, returned there as an assistant to Oliver and as a demonstrator in botany, a position he held until 1906.

Between 1900 and 1901 Tansley visited Ceylon (now Sri Lanka), the Malay peninsula, and Egypt to study their flora. On his return, he found that there was no suitable journal in which to publish his findings, so he founded *The New Phytologist* in 1902, remaining its editor for 30 years. In 1907 he was appointed university lecturer in Botany at Cambridge University.

After World War I, however, his interest turned temporarily towards psychology, and in 1923 he resigned his lectureship in order to study under Sigmund ◊Freud in Austria. Tansley returned to the UK the following year, and in 1927 was appointed Sherardian Professor of Botany at Oxford University, a position that carried with it a fellowship of Magdalen College. He remained at Oxford until his retirement in 1939. Tansley continued to be active after retiring. He was chairman of the Nature Conservancy Council (now divided into English Nature, Scottish Natural Heritage, and the Countryside Council for Wales) 1949–53 and president of the Council for the Promotion of Field Studies (now called the Field Studies Council) 1947–53, having played a large part in the establishment of these organizations. He died in Grantchester on 25 November 1955.

Most of Tansley's work concerned British plants and plant communities. He coordinated a large project 1903–07 to map the vegetation of the British Isles; the surveys that were completed are still models of vegetation-mapping technique. The scientists involved in this project published their findings in *Types of British Vegetation* (1911), of which Tansley was the editor and major contributor. Although this book was a masterly summary of British flora, Tansley and the other scientists felt that a wider approach to plant ecology was needed, so on 12 April 1913 the group founded the British Ecological Society, with Tansley as its president. The society founded the *Journal of Ecology*, which Tansley edited 1916–38.

While professor of botany at Oxford, Tansley enlarged and rewrote *Types of British Vegetation.* The new work, *The British Islands and Their Vegetation* (1939), was Tansley's greatest single achievement. In it he showed how vegetation is affected by soil, climate, the presence of wild and domesticated animals, previous land management, and contemporary human activities. He also reviewed all known accounts of British flora and then linked the two themes, thereby demonstrating which factors are important in influencing the various types of vegetation. In 1949 he published *Britain's Green Mantle,* a shorter and more popular version.

Tansley also helped to promote the study of plant ecology through his teaching; by writing several practical guides, such as *Practical Plant Ecology* (1923); and by campaigning for the establishment of ecological

organizations. His contributions to botany were recognized by the award of several honours, including a fellowship of the Royal Society of London in 1915, the Gold Medal of the Linnaean Society in 1941, and a knighthood in 1950.

Tartaglia (c. 1499–1557) Adopted name of Niccolò Fontana. Italian mathematician, mathematical physicist, and writer who, despite an unpromising youth, worked hard eventually to find fame for his work in mathematics, topography, and mechanical physics.

Tartaglia was born in Brescia, Lombardy, in either 1499 or 1500. His father was a postman and his family was very poor. When he was 12, the French marched in and sacked Brescia, and Fontana was seriously injured. Only the careful nursing by his mother of the savage sword-thrust wound in his mouth saved his life, but thereafter he was called Tartaglia – 'stammerer' – because of speech defects caused by the wound. Virtually self-educated, Tartaglia developed a true scientific curiosity and absorbed knowledge from every source he could find, particularly in mathematics and physics. In 1516 he moved to Verona and became a teacher of the abacus. Later he took charge of a school there 1529–33. After that he went on to Venice, where he was to remain for the rest of his life. Although he gained a position of professor of mathematics, and published many papers on his work during the later stages of his life, he never made much money from his skills and died alone and poor in humble dwellings near the Rialto Bridge on 15 December 1557.

With the coming of the 16th century, a revival took place in most branches of science, and Tartaglia was perhaps one of the more important contributors to it. Mathematics, in particular, had made little progress since the Greek scholars set down the basic rules; succeeding generations had evidently been content with simple counting and the ability to undertake elementary explanations to problems. Capable of applying his mind to most things, Tartaglia read all he could and then chose – among other enquiries – to explore the complexities of third-degree (cubic) equations. (Solutions had by then already been found for the linear and quadratic equations.) He was only one among many concerned with the task, however, most of the others also being Italian. There was keen rivalry, and Tartaglia more than once entered into a public contest of skills with another mathematician. In one particular confrontation with a certain Antonio Fior, Tartaglia emerged the victor by applying his methods and solving all the problems set for him by Fior, whereas Fior could not solve those set by Tartaglia.

He next turned his attention to solving the problem of calculating the volume of a tetrahedron from the length of its sides. Successful in that endeavour, he attempted Malfatti's problem – to inscribe within a triangle three circles tangent to one another, and managed to do that too.

Although Tartaglia spent much of his time teaching mathematics, he was also responsible for translating ◊Euclid's *Elements* into Italian in 1543 – the first translation of Euclid into a contemporary European language.

His greatest love, however, appears to have been in using his mathematical (and other relevant) skills to solve military problems. He delighted in planning the disposition of artillery, surveying the topography in relation to the best means of defence, and in designing fortifications. He also attempted a study of the motion of projectiles, and formulated what is now generally known as Tartaglia's theorem: the trajectory of a projectile is a curved line everywhere, and the maximum range at any speed of its projection is obtained with a firing elevation of 45°.

A practical man and a colourful character, Tartaglia fired the imagination of many in an age when imagination and scientific curiosity were beginning once more to bloom.

Telford, Thomas (1757–1834) Scottish civil engineer, famous for building roads and bridges. He was also the first president the Institute of Civil Engineers.

Telford was born in Westerkirk, Dumfries, on 9 August 1757, the son of a shepherd. He began his career as a stonemason, but he had strong ambitions and educated himself in architecture in his spare time. In search of work he travelled to London and found employment building the additions to Somerset House in the Strand under the supervision of William Chambers. Recognizing his talents, the rich and famous were soon consulting him about their own buildings and consequently he was launched upon a career that was to make him into one of the outstanding civil engineers of that time.

In 1786 Telford was appointed official surveyor to the county of Shropshire. This proved to be the start of 30 years' intense construction work for different organizations, dealing with anything and everything requiring his particular skills. He was responsible for reconstructing roads; building canals, aqueducts, and harbours; erecting suspension bridges; and surveying railway lines. Above all, he will be remembered for the Menai Bridge in north Wales, which must remain his most famous achievement.

The state of the roads in Britain during the 18th century depended very much on the individual turnpike trust and whether it chose to pay for repairs. Telford and his contemporary, John ◊McAdam, set about rebuilding the existing Roman routes, digging down to the foundations of these roads and levelling them to meet the need for faster travel. It was recorded that after such work had been carried out on a road, a mail coach travelling on it could attain speeds of up to 19 kph/12 mph and could average at least 13 kph/8 mph.

In 1793 Telford was appointed engineer to the Ellesmere Canal Company, where he was responsible for the building of aqueducts over the Ceirog and Dee valleys in Wales, using a new method of construction consisting of troughs made from cast-iron plates and fixed in masonry. Ten years later he was asked to take charge of the Caledonian Canal project, an enormous conglomeration of plans that included not only the canal but harbour works at Aberdeen and Dundee and more than 1,450 km/900 mi of link roads with several bridges.

Throughout his entire career, bridges had formed an important part of his construction work. In his early days in Shropshire he had built three over the River Severn (at Montford, Buildwas, and Dewdley) and later he tackled a complicated structure over the River Conway, but by far the most impressive was the Menai Bridge. Built as a suspension bridge over the Menai Straits to join Anglesey to the Welsh mainland, it took from 1819 to 1826 to erect and had a finished span of 176 m/580 ft with huge wrought-iron links supporting it. Telford died in Westminster on 2 September 1834.

Although Telford was well aware of the need for faster communications and improvements to the transport system, he chose almost to disregard the railways that were just beginning to be accepted as a means of transport, and concentrated entirely on roads and canals. Nevertheless, his contribution to the advancement of civil engineering was considerable during the latter half of the 18th century and in the early part of the 19th, and it was only just that the Institute of Civil Engineers should reward him with the presidency.

Teller, Edward (1908–) Hungarian-born US physicist widely known as the 'father of the hydrogen bomb'. He is also known for his vigorous promotion of nuclear weapons, opposition to communism, and for testifying against J Robert ◊Oppenheimer at the security hearings of 1954.

Teller was born on 15 January 1908 in Budapest, where he attended the Institute of Technology. He also attended a series of universities in Germany, including Leipzig where he obtained his PhD in 1930. He left Germany in 1933 when Hitler came to power and after periods in Copenhagen and London, was appointed professor of physics at George Washington University, Washington, DC, in 1935. There he developed the Gamow–Teller selection rule for beta decay. In 1941 he became a US citizen and joined the staff of Columbia University, New York, and then the University of

Chicago in 1942 to work with Enrico ◊Fermi on atomic fission.

Between 1942 and 1946, Teller was a member of the Manhattan Project, Los Alamos, New Mexico, which developed the first atomic bombs. He worked initially on the fission bomb, but later convinced the Los Alamos director, J Robert Oppenheimer, to let him work on the fusion, or hydrogen (H-) bomb. By the end of World War II, Teller had designed a H-bomb (then also known as the 'Super') but it required a refrigeration plant to make it work and in 1949 the General Advisory Committee (GAC), chaired by Oppenheimer, advised the Atomic Energy Commission not to pursue the project. The situation changed on 29 August 1949, however, when the Soviet Union exploded its first fission bomb. Teller, now a professor at the University of Chicago, and Ernest ◊Lawrence of the Radiation Laboratory in Berkeley, lobbied President Truman and on 31 January 1951, Truman announced a crash programme to build the H-bomb, with Teller appointed assistant director of weapons development at Los Alamos with responsibility for the bomb. The Super was successfully tested on Eniwetok Atoll in the Pacific Ocean in November 1952.

Teller's exact role in the development of the H-bomb has, however, been surrounded with controversy, for he has been repeatedly accused of down-playing, or ignoring, the contribution of Polish-born mathematician Stanislaw Ulam (1909–1985) to the bomb's design. The original idea of using a fission explosion to ignite a thermonuclear (fusion) explosion in deuterium (heavy hydrogen) came from Enrico Fermi. Ulam and others had proved Teller's original ideas to be unworkable. Ulam then suggested a configuration in which shock waves from the fission explosion would compress and heat the deuterium, causing it to explode. Teller later modified this idea to use X-rays from the first explosion, rather than shock waves. (Teller and Ulam's report on the design remains classified.)

After the war, Teller successfully championed the establishment of a second nuclear weapons research facility, which opened in 1952 as the Lawrence Livermore Laboratory near Berkeley, California. Teller was Livermore's associate director from 1954 until his retirement in 1975, and has been director emeritus ever since. He has also been a professor at the University of California since 1953, becoming university professor in 1970 and university professor emeritus in 1975.

Oppenheimer (and the GAC) had opposed setting up a second weapons laboratory just as he had opposed the H-bomb, but in 1954 his security clearance was revoked. It was the height of the McCarthy era and Oppenheimer was suspected of being a communist and Soviet spy. Teller was called to give evidence at his security hearing and, although he testified that he did not believe Oppenheimer to be disloyal, concluded: 'I would feel personally more secure if public matters would rest in other hands.' Oppenheimer lost his security clearance and many physicists never forgave Teller.

In the 1980s Teller returned to the public eye when he convinced President Reagan of the feasibility of placing fission-bomb-powered X-ray lasers in space to destroy incoming Soviet nuclear missiles. Billions of dollars were spent on the Strategic Defense Initiative ('Star Wars') before technical problems, and the disintegration of the former Soviet Union, rendered it obsolete. However Teller remains in favour of nuclear technology and defence, having suggested 'brilliant pebbles' – thousands of intelligent missile-interceptors based in space – and the use of nuclear explosions to prevent asteroids hitting the Earth.

Further Reading

Blumberg, Stanley A and Owens, Gwinn, *Energy and Conflict: The Life and Times of Edward Teller,* G P Putnams, 1976.
Blumberg, Stanley A and Panos, Louis G, *Edward Teller: Giant of the Golden Age of Physics,* Charles Scribner, 1990.

Temin, Howard Martin (1934–1994) US virologist concerned with cancer research. For his work on the genetic inheritance of viral elements he received the 1975 Nobel Prize for Physiology or Medicine, which he shared with David Baltimore (1938–) and Renato Dulbecco (1914–).

Temin was born in Philadelphia on 10 December 1934 and educated at Swarthmore College, Pennsylvania, where he gained a BA in 1955. He then obtained his PhD at the California Institute of Technology, Pasadena, in 1959 for a thesis on animal virology. During the following year he was a postdoctoral fellow there. Between 1960 and 1964 he became assistant professor of oncology at the University of Wisconsin, and then associate professor 1964–69. He was appointed professor of oncology at Wisconsin in 1969 and professor of cancer research in 1971. In 1974 he became professor of viral oncology and cell biology at Wisconsin.

In the early attempts at organ transplants in the human body, the patient did not live long after the operation because the transplanted organ was rejected by the recipient's body as foreign tissue. Peter ◊Medawar in the UK experimented with mice and found that if the intended recipient was injected at the embryo stage with cells from the future donor, its body did not reject the transplant, but accepted the foreign cells as its own. He also found that this acquired immunological tolerance can be handed down to a second generation. Following on Medawar's experiments, Macfarlane ◊Burnet in Australia found that the ability of the human body to produce antibodies is not learnt through a process of evolution but he suggested that the genes of the antibody-producing cells contain a region that is continually mutating, with each mutation leading to the production of a new antibody variant.

Temin's prizewinning research was on a virus that has a mechanism that incorporates its material into mammalian genes. He discovered that beneficial mutations outside the germ line are naturally selected and that the mechanism adds genetic information from outside into the germ line.

It has been suggested since that this inheritance might operate in the blood cells, the gut lining, and perhaps in the nervous system, from where it enters the germ line. Experimental evidence suggests that acquired characteristics can be passed on through genes, in agreement with Jean Baptiste ◊Lamarck. For instance, the incidence of chemically induced brain tumours has been found to be very high in the offspring of affected parents.

Further Reading

Cooper, Geoffrey M; Temin, Rayla G; and Sudgen, Bill, *The DNA Provirus: Howard Temin's Scientific Legacy*, American Society for Microbiology, 1995.

Tesla, Nikola (1856–1943) Croatian-born US physicist and electrical engineer who was one of the great pioneers of the use of alternating-current electricity. In particular, he invented the alternating-current induction motor and the high-frequency coil that bears his name.

Tesla was born at midnight between 9 and 10 July 1856 in Smiljan, Croatia (then part of Austria–Hungary). His father was a priest of the Serbian Orthodox Church. Tesla was very clever as a child and grew up with a liking for writing poetry and experimentation. It was intended that he should follow his father and become a priest, but Tesla developed an interest in scientific pursuits while he was at the Real Gymnasium in Karlovac. On leaving school he studied engineering at the Technical University at Graz, Austria. In 1880 he went to the University of Prague to continue his studies but the death of his father caused him to leave without graduating.

In 1881, Tesla went to Budapest as an engineer for a telephone company and a year later took up a similar position in Paris. He went to the USA in 1884, and worked for Thomas ◊Edison for a year before setting up on his own. From 1888, Tesla was associated with

Tesla Croation-born US physicist and engineer Nikola Tesla who made several inventions, including the alternating current induction motor. Tesla emigrated to the USA in 1884, and became a naturalized citizen. *Mary Evans Picture Library*

the industrialist George ◊Westinghouse, who bought and successfully exploited Tesla's patents, leading to the introduction of alternating current for power transmission. Tesla became a US citizen in 1889, and after 1892, when his mother died, became increasingly withdrawn and eccentric. In 1912 both he and Edison were proposed for the Nobel Prize for Physics but Tesla refused to be associated with Edison, who had conducted an unscrupulous campaign for the adoption of direct current. In the event, neither received the prize. Tesla neglected to patent many of his discoveries and made little profit from them. He lived his last years as a recluse and died in New York on 7 January 1943.

In 1878, during his student days at Graz, Tesla saw a direct-current electric dynamo and motor demonstrated and felt that the machine could be improved by eliminating the commutator and sparking brushes, which were sources of wear. His idea for the induction motor came to him in Budapest four years later. He had the notion of an iron rotor spinning between stationary coils that were electrified by two out-of-phase alternating currents producing a rotating magnetic field. Like many of his other ideas, Tesla mentally developed his motor for all kinds of practical applications before ever a model was built.

Tesla built his first working induction motor while he was on assignment in Strasbourg in 1883. However, he found that he could raise little interest in his inventions in Europe so he set off for New York, where he eventually set up his own laboratory and workshop in 1887 to develop his motor in a practical way. Only months later he applied for and was granted a complicated set of patents covering the generation, transmission, and use of alternating-current electricity. At about the same time he lectured to the American Institute of Electrical Engineers on polyphase alternating current. After learning about the talk, Westinghouse quickly bought Tesla's patents.

Westinghouse was able to back Tesla's ideas and as a demonstration, employed his system for lighting at the 1893 World Columbian Exposition in Chicago. Months later Westinghouse won the contract to generate electricity at Niagara Falls, using Tesla's system to supply local industries and deliver polyphase alternating current to the town of Buffalo 35 km/22 mi distant.

After 1888 Tesla's interests turned to alternating currents at very high frequencies, which he felt might be useful for lighting and for communication. After first using high-frequency alternators for these purposes, he designed what has come to be known as the Tesla coil. This is an air-core transformer with the primary and secondary windings tuned in resonance to produce high-frequency, high-voltage electricity. Using this device, Tesla produced an electric spark 40 m/135 ft long in 1899. He also lit more than 200 lamps over a distance of 40 km/25 mi without the use of intervening wires. Gas-filled tubes are readily energized by high-frequency currents and so lights of this type were easily operated within the field of a large Tesla coil. Characteristic of his way of working, Tesla soon developed all manner of coils that have since found numerous applications in electrical and electronic devices.

Tesla was very interested in the possibility of radio communication and as early as 1897 he demonstrated the remote control of two model boats on the lake in Madison Square Gardens in New York. He extended this to guided weapons, in particular a remote-control torpedo. In 1900 he began to construct a broadcasting station on Long Island in the hope of developing 'World Wireless'; this eventually proved too expensive for his backers and was abandoned. However, many of his ideas have come to fruition at the hands of others. Tesla also outlined a scheme for detecting ships at sea, which was later developed as radar. One of his most ambitious ideas was to transmit alternating-current electricity to anywhere in the world without wires by using the Earth itself as an enormous oscillator. There were many other inventions, including electrical clocks and turbines, but often they remained in his head, there being no money to put them into practice.

Tesla gave the world one of the most practical devices of all time, the alternating-current induction motor. This, coupled with the distinct advantage that alternating current can be transmitted over much greater distances than direct current, has given the motive power for most of our present-day machines.

Further Reading

Anderson, Leland I; Peterson, Gary L; and Hull, Richard L, *Nikola Tesla: Guided Weapons and Computer Technology,* Tesla Presents series, Twenty-First Century Books, 1998.

Beckhard, Arthur J, *Nikola Tesla: Electrical Genius,* Dennis Dobson, 1961.

Martin, Thomas C, *The Inventions, Researches, and Writings of Nikola Tesla,* Health Research, 1997.

O'Neill, John Joseph, *Prodigal Genius: The Life of Nikola Tesla,* Brotherhood of Life, 1998.

Peat, Francis David, *In Search of Nikola Tesla,* Ashgrove Press, 1997.

Seifer, Marc J, *Wizard: The Life and Times of Nikola Tesla,* Citadel Press, 1998.

Tesla, Nikola and Childress, David Hatcher, *The Fantastic Inventions of Nikola Tesla,* The Lost Science series, Adventures Unlimited, 1993.

Thales of Miletus (c. 624–c. 547 BC) Greek philosopher who was among the first early Greek philosophers to reject mythopoetic forms of thought for a basically scientific approach to the world.

Thales was born in Miletus, the son of Examyas and Cleobuline, both of whom were members of distinguished Miletan families. Thales' precise date of birth is unknown, but his peak of activity is traditionally dated as 585 BC, the year in which he predicted an eclipse of the Sun. It is his prediction of this eclipse that is the basis of his reputation as a scientist.

Claims are made also for his ingenuity and practicality as an astronomer, mathematician, politician, and businessman. ◊Aristotle, writing more than 200 years later, records that, when Thales was reproached for being impractical, he, having predicted that weather conditions the next year would be conducive to a large olive harvest, bought up all the olive presses in Miletus and exploited his monopoly to make a large profit. Herodotus gives another example of Thales' belief in the control of physical nature when he recounts that Thales diverted the River Halys to enable Croesus' army to cross. Such engineering required that any divine connotations attaching to the flow of rivers be ignored and objects and events in the world treated much as they are in present-day scientific research.

Thales sought unifying and general hypotheses that relied on the relationships between natural phenomena to explain natural events. The order he believed to be inherent in the world was not to be explained by reference to divine or mystical forces, but was to be discovered and articulated in terms of natural causes.

In astronomy Thales is credited with defining the constellation of Ursa Minor (Little Bear) and with writing a work on navigation in which the Little Bear is commended for its usefulness in this regard. But his reputation as an astronomer rests on a number of doubtful sources that, for example, ascribe to him the introduction of Egyptian mathematics to Greece and the use of a 'Babylonian saros' (a cycle of 223 lunar months) to calculate the solar eclipse. It has been argued that the Babylonian saros was the invention of the English astronomer Edmond ◊Halley more than 2,200 years later and could not have been the basis of Thales' calculation.

Cosmological views attributed to Thales are known almost entirely from the writings of Aristotle. Thales is said to have proposed that water was the material constituent of all things and that the Earth floats on water. He explained the occurrence of earthquakes by reference to this idea of a floating Earth. Thales' explanation of events is couched in terms of natural phenomena and objects, not in the usual terms of activity by the god Poseidon. His cosmology may be

reminiscent of Near Eastern mythology, but the Greek thinkers who followed the path he established by seeking explanations of natural events in terms of natural agencies were the precursors of modern scientists and astronomers.

Thales' greatest achievement (again, it should remembered, a matter for doubt) was his geometry. If Proclus' account is right, Thales was an important innovator in geometry, particularly for introducing the notion of proof by the deductive method, whereas his Babylonian and Egyptian predecessors had not progressed beyond making generalizations from experience on a rough-and-ready inductive principle. In five fundamental propositions Thales laid down the foundations on which classical geometry was raised.

(1) A circle is bisected by its diameter. (2) In an isosceles triangle the two angles opposite the equal sides are themselves equal to each other. (3) When two straight lines intersect, four angles are produced, the opposite ones being equal. (4) The angle in a semicircle is a right angle. (5) Two triangles are congruent if they have two

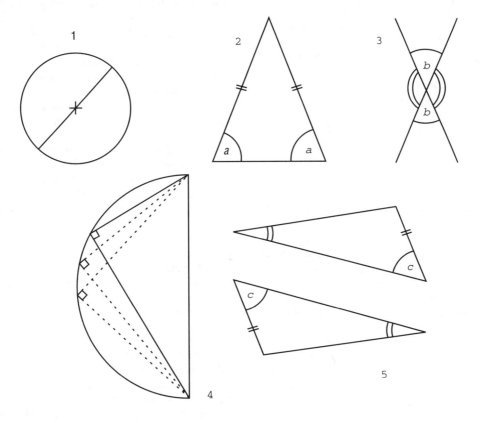

Thales of Miletus Some of the basic rules of geometry were laid down by ancient Greek philosopher Thales: (1) a circle is bisected by its diameter; (2) in an isosceles triangle, the two angles opposite the equal sides are themselves equal; (3) when straight lines cross, the opposite angles created are equal; (4) the angle in a semicircle is a right-angle: and (5) two triangles are congruent (the same shape and size) if they have two angles and one side identical.

angles and one side that are respectively equal to each other.

Thales' proofs were not always very rigorous. But they had the nub of logical unassailability in them. Consider the proof of the proposition that the angle in a semicircle is a right angle. It is obvious that the diagonals of a rectangle are of equal length and that they bisect one another. It is obvious, also, that any quadrilateral possessing these properties is a rectangle. If we draw two diameters, AOC and BOD, of a circle with centre O, we therefore get a rectangle. Omit the dotted lines in the figure and we are left with the proposition that, if A is any point on the are of a semicircle with the diameter BD, then the angle BAD is necessarily a right angle. Without this method of reasoning – so like ◊Euclid's – the original proposition would not appear obvious. It is abstract reasoning of this kind that makes Thales such an important figure in the history of European thought. It is entirely in the proper spirit that Thales, on making his discovery of his fourth proposition, sacrificed a bull to the gods in thanks.

Further Reading

Anglin, W S and Lambek, J, *The Heritage of Thales,* Undergraduate Texts in Mathematics series, Springer-Verlag, 1995.

Clodd, Edward, *Pioneers of Evolution from Thales to Huxley,* Lessinger Publishing Co, 1997.

Guthrie, William, *Greek Philosophers: From Thales to Aristotle,* Routledge, 1990.

Lesser, Harry, *Ancient Philosophy: Thales to Aristotle,* Fundamentals of Philosophy series, UCL Press, 1998.

Said, Dibinga, *The African Origins of Thales' Cosmology,* The African Origins of Greek Philosophy series, Omenana, 1995.

Theiler, Max (1899–1972) South African-born US microbiologist who developed an effective vaccine against yellow fever, an achievement that gained him the 1951 Nobel Prize for Physiology or Medicine. He also researched into various other diseases, including Weil's disease and poliomyelitis.

Theiler was born on 30 January 1899 in Pretoria, the son of a Swiss-born veterinary surgeon. After doing his preliminary medical training at Rhodes University College and the University of Cape Town, Theiler went to the UK and completed his training at St Thomas's Hospital and the London School of Hygiene and Tropical Medicine, from which he received his medical degree in 1922. After graduating, Theiler went to the USA and joined the department of tropical medicine at Harvard University Medical School. In 1930 he moved to the Rockefeller Institute for Medical Research (now Rockefeller University), New York City, becoming director of the Virus Laboratory there in

1950. In the same year he was also made a director of the Division of Medicine and Public Health. Theiler was appointed professor of epidemiology and microbiology at Yale University in 1964 and held this post until he retired in 1967. He died on 11 August 1972 in New Haven, Connecticut.

By the time Theiler began his research into yellow fever, Walter Reed (1851–1902), a US army doctor, had proved in 1900 that the disease is carried by the *Aêdes aegypti* mosquito, and Stokes, Bauer, and Hudson had discovered that the causative agent is a virus. Furthermore it had been established that certain mammals can act as reservoirs of infection and that *A. aegypti* is not the only species of mosquito that can transmit yellow fever.

Theiler's early work on the disease – carried out at Harvard – demonstrated that common albino mice are susceptible to yellow fever, and that when they are infected, the virus undergoes certain changes. Continuing his research at the Rockefeller Institute, he found that when the mice are given intracerebral injections of yellow fever virus they develop encephalomyelitis but, unlike monkeys and human beings, do not develop heart, liver, or kidney disorders. He passed the virus through the brains of several mice in order to produce a fully mouse-adapted strain of the virus, which he then injected subcutaneously into monkeys and human volunteers. Theiler found that this mouse-adapted strain produced full, active immunity in monkeys but still affected the kidneys in humans. But when he combined the mouse-adapted viral strain with serum from the blood of people who had recovered from yellow fever and injected the mixture into humans, he found that it produced immunity without affecting the kidneys; he had succeeded in producing a safe vaccine against yellow fever.

This method of making the vaccine is not suitable for large-scale production, however, because human serum containing antibodies against yellow fever is difficult to obtain. Theiler therefore began working on a method of producing yellow fever vaccine that did not require human serum, and in 1937 he developed vaccine 17-D, still the main form of protection against yellow fever. In 1931 E W Goodpasture developed a method of culturing viruses by injecting them into chick embryos. Theiler made vaccine 17-D by combining Goodpasture's technique with his own method of making mouse-adapted viral strain. He passed yellow fever virus successively through 200 mice then cultured the virus in 100 chick embryos; this yielded a mutant form of the virus that caused only mild symptoms when injected into humans yet gave complete immunity against yellow fever.

In addition to his work on yellow fever, Theiler also investigated Weil's disease, amoebic dysentery, and poliomyelitis (polio). He hypothesized that the polio virus is widespread in the intestines, where it is harmless, and that symptoms are produced only in the rare instances where the virus enters the central nervous system.

Theon of Smyrna (lived c. AD 130) Greek mathematician and astronomer who is remembered chiefly for his *Expositio rerum mathematicarum ad legendum Platoneum utilium,* much of the text of which is in two manuscripts, one on mathematics and one on astronomy and astrology.

Little is known of Theon's birth or life. The latest thinkers he names in the *Expositio* are Thrasyllus and Adrastus. Assuming that Theon tried to take account of the most modern contemporary writers, and as Thrasyllus was active when Tiberius was emperor of Rome and Adrastus died in the late 100s, Theon is generally taken to have been active in the early 2nd century AD. He is also referred to by other writers: ◊Ptolemy's work includes Theon's observations of Venus and Mercury between 127 and 132.

Theon's *Expositio* is useful as a source of quotations from other writers. Its main task, in keeping with the suppositions of Platonic philosophy (see ◊Plato), is to articulate the interrelationships between arithmetic, geometry, music, and astronomy. The section on mathematics deals with prime, geometrical, and other numbers in the Pythagorean pantheon (see ◊Pythagoras), while the section on music considers instrumental music, mathematical relations between musical intervals, and the harmony of the universe. Neither the mathematical nor the musical sections exhibit any great originality. Theon was concerned to collate and organize discoveries made by his predecessors. His own contribution seems at times to consist of a mysticism about numbers and mathematical calculations.

The astronomical section is by far the most important. Music is included: the planets, Sun, Moon, and the sphere of fixed stars are all set at intervals congruent with an octave. The Earth is a sphere standing at the centre of the universe, surrounded by several circles of the heavens. The text sets out the different explanations of the order of heavenly bodies and of deviations in latitude of the Sun, Moon, and planets. Theon also shows how different writers, including ◊Aristotle, Callipus (*c.* 370–*c.* 330 BC), and ◊Eudoxus of Cnidus, accounted for the workings of the system of rotating spheres, and he puts forward what was then known about conjunctions, eclipses, occultations, and transits. Other subjects covered include descriptions of eccentic and epicyclic orbits, and estimates of the greatest arcs of Mercury and Venus from the Sun.

No other works of Theon have survived, although he is known to have written a commentary on Plato's *Republic.*

Theophrastus (*c.* 372–*c.* 287 BC) Greek thinker who wrote on a wide range of subjects – science, philosophy, law, literature, music, and poetry, for example – but who is best known as the founder of botany.

Theophrastus was born in Eresus on the Greek island of Lesvos. He studied under ◊Plato at the Academy in Athens, where ◊Aristotle was also working, and then under Aristotle after he had left the Academy in 348 BC. When Aristotle returned to Athens and founded the Lyceum in 335 BC, Theophrastus became his chief assistant, eventually succeeding him as head of the Lyceum in 323 BC, when Aristotle again left Athens. Enrolment at the Lyceum reached its peak under Theophrastus, and he employed the pupils, many of whom came from distant parts of Greece, to make botanical observations near their homes. He remained head of the Lyceum until his death in *c.* 287 BC.

Theophrastus was a prolific writer: more than 200 books are attributed to him but most are known only by their titles. The most important of his surviving works are those on botany. In these books he covered most aspects of the subject – descriptions of plants, their classification, distribution, propagation, germination, and cultivation. He described and discussed more than 500 species and varieties of plants from lands bordering the Atlantic and Mediterranean and from India, referring in his descriptions to information from people who had been on Alexander the Great's campaigns and so had first-hand knowledge of foreign flora. On the basis of his collection of information about a wide range of flora, Theophrastus classified plants into trees, shrubs, undershrubs, and herbs. In his detailed study of flowers, he noted that some flowers bear petals whereas others do not, and observed the different relative positions of the petals and ovary. He also distinguished between two major groups of flowering plants – dicotyledons and monocotyledons in modern terms – and between flowering plants and cone-bearing trees – angiosperms and gymnosperms. In his work on propagation and germination, Theophrastus described the various ways in which specific plants and trees can grow – from seeds, from roots, from pieces torn off, from a branch or twig, or from a small piece of cleft wood. He also accurately described the germination of seeds.

Theophrastus provided an excellent foundation for the science of botany – his writings are comprehensive and are generally very accurate, even by modern standards, although he was not infallible – for example, like all pre-17th-century scientists Theophrastus believed in spontaneous generation. But he usually substantiated statements with observed facts, thus helping to establish a sound method of scientific investigation.

Further Reading

Fortenbaugh, William Wale (ed), *Theophrastus of Eresus: Sources for His Life, Writings, Thought, and Influence*, Philosophia Antiqua series, Brill, 1991, v 54, 2 vols.

Fortenbaugh, William Wale; Huby, Pamela M; and Long, Anthony A (eds), *Theophrastus of Eresus: On His Life and Work*, Rutgers University Studies in Classical Humanities series, Transaction Books, 1985, v 2.

Ophuijsen, J M van and Raalte, Marlein van (eds), *Theophrastus: Reappraising the Sources*, Rutgers University Studies in Classical Humanities series, Transaction Publishers, 1998, v 8.

Thom, René Frédéric (1923–   ) French mathematician who is a leading specialist in the fields of differentiable manifolds and topology and is famous for his model popularly known as 'catastrophe theory'.

Thom was born in Montbéliard on 2 September 1923. He studied in Paris at the Ecole Normale Supérieure, where he received a degree in mathematical sciences, 1943–46, and then spent four years at the Centre National de la Recherche Scientifique. In 1951 he was awarded a doctorate by the University of Paris for his thesis on algebraic topology. From 1954 to 1963 he was a professor in the faculty of science at the University of Strasbourg and in 1963 he became a professor at the Institute of Advanced Scientific Studies at Bures-sur-Yvette. He was awarded the Fields Medal by the International Congress of Mathematicians in 1958, the Brouwer Medal of the Academy of Sciences of the Netherlands in 1970, and the Grand Prix of Science by the city of Paris in 1974.

Since his student days Thom's major interest has been in problems of topology. Much of his early work was done just at the time that the operations of the US mathematician Norman Steenrod had been discovered. In his doctoral thesis he related Steenrod's definition of powers to the action of a cyclic group of permutations. From there he went on, with the help of H Cartan, to formulate a precise series associated with 'space spherical bundles' and to demonstrate that the fundamental class of open spherical bundles showed topological invariance and formed a differential geometry. This led him to his famous theorem, the theorem of signature, which states that in order that a directed form M^{4K} of dimension 4K may become cuspal, it is necessary that the quadratic curve defined by the cusp produced on $H^{2K} (M^{4K}, Q)$ contains as many positive points as negative points (in order to be of zero index). In his work on the the-

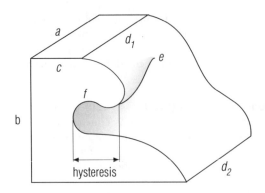

Thom The cusp is one of seven elementary catastrophes in catastrophe theory; *a*, *b* and *c* are axes describing interacting factors in a process: *d* is a folded sheet with an upper zone (d_1) and a lower zone (d_2) describing the behaviour under investigation. At *e* there is a bifurcation, beyond which (d_1) and (d_2) are separate: *f* is the intermediate zone.

ory of forms Thom has shown that there are complete homological classes that cannot be the representation of any differential form. He was able to improve the understanding of this Steenrodian problem (although it is far from being completely understood) by formulating auxiliary spaces. These are now known as 'Thom spaces'.

In 1956 Thom developed the theory of transversality, and contributed to the examination of singularities of smooth maps. This work laid the ground for his later statement of the 'catastrophe theory', which he first published in 1968. The theory is, in fact, a model (not yet an explanation) for the description of processes that proceed by sudden changes, so that their action is not continuous, but discontinuous. They are thus not able to be described by means of mathematical tools derived from calculus. Catastrophe theory seeks to describe sudden changes from one equilibrium state to another and to do so Thom proposed seven 'elementary catastrophes', which he hoped would be sufficient to describe processes within human experience of space–time dimensions. The seven elementary catastrophes are the fold, cusp, swallow-tail, butterfly, hyperbolic, elliptic, and parabolic. Of these the cusp is both the simplest and the most likely to provide immediate applied use.

The important features of the cusp are the following:

a, *b*, and *c*: axes that describe interacting factors in a process;

d: a folded sheet, divided into an upper zone, d_1, and a lower zone, d_2, which describes the behaviour of a substance, person, or group under investigation;

e: the bifurcation point, a singularity, beyond which d_1 and d_2 separate;

f: the intermediate zone between d_1 and d_2.

The region of overlap between d_1 and d_2 is called the hysteresis. It is the existence of this overlap that makes possible sudden and dramatic changes from the equilibrium state d_1 and the equilibrium state d_2.

Thom is perhaps best known for his book published in 1972, *Structural Stability and Morphogenesis*. It is there that he introduced the notion of the 'universal unfolding' of a singularity. The book itself is not so much a mathematical treatise as a discussion of how the concept of structural stability may be applied to the appearance and evolution of natural forms in physics and the life sciences. In particular, the book attempts to use the model of catastrophe theory to analyse embryogenesis. The model has been used also to study nerve transmission and the heartbeat, to analyse change of phase in physics (for example, from liquid to gas), and even, by sociologists, to study human events such as the outbreak of riot or war. Whether the catastrophe theory will ultimately prove of great moment in the history of mathematics (it is, after all, fundamentally simply an argument by analogy) may be doubtful, but Thom's work has been of central importance to research in topology since 1945.

Thomas, Sidney Gilchrist (1850–1885) English metallurgist and inventor who, with his cousin Percy ◊Gilchrist, developed a process for removing phosphorus impurities from the iron melted during steel manufacture.

Thomas was born in Canonbury, London on 16 April 1850. His father died before he was 17, and the need for Thomas to earn a living became imperative. He spent a few months teaching and then in that same year, 1867, he obtained a post as a clerk at Marlborough Street Police Court. In the summer of 1868 he was transferred to a similar position at the Thames Court, Arbour Square, Stepney, where, at a very modest salary, he remained until 1879.

His deep interest was in industrial chemistry, and he made his discoveries in his spare time. From about 1870 onwards one crucial problem in this field monopolized his attention – namely, the need to dephosphorize pig iron when it was loaded into a Bessemer converter. Both the Bessemer and the Siemens–Martin processes (the most popular methods for converting pig iron into steel) suffered from the serious drawback that in neither were phosphorus impurities removed. The steel produced from such phosphoric ores was brittle and of little use. Because only non-phosphoric ores could be used, the great mass of British, French, German, and Belgian iron ore was unusable for converting into steel. From 1860 onwards Henry ◊Bessemer and a great host of experimentalists looked unsuccessfully for the solution.

Thomas devoted the whole of his spare time to this question, experimenting systematically at home and attending the laboratories of various chemistry teachers. Towards the end of 1875 he arrived at a theoretic and provisional solution to the problem. The key was the chemical nature of the lining of the converter or furnace, which varied in composition but always contained silica. The phosphorus in the pig iron was rapidly oxidized during the process to form phosphoric acid, which, because of the silicous character of the slag was reduced back to phosphorus and re-entered the metal. The answer lay in providing a substance that would combine with the phosphoric acid and incorporate it into the slag. A long series of experiments had led Thomas to the conclusion that the material that could best withstand the intense heat of the furnace as well as providing the durability that would make it economical to use was lime, or the chemically similar magnesia or magnesian limestone. Thomas foresaw that by using such a lining he was removing phosphorus from the pig iron and also that phosphorus 'deposited' in the basic slag would itself prove to be of immense commercial use (as a fertilizer).

In establishing this theory, his cousing Percy Gilchrist, a chemist at a large ironworks in Blaenavon, south Wales, proved to be of the greatest assistance to Thomas. In March 1878, at a meeting of the Iron and Steel Institute of Great Britain, Thomas announced that he had successfully dephosphorized iron in a Bessemer converter. This announcement was disregarded, but the complete specification of his patent was filed in May 1878, to be followed by successive patents over the next few years.

Two notable developments followed. One was that the high-phosphorus iron ore of Lorraine and other areas in Europe could now be used for steel-making. The other was that by lining furnaces with a lime or other alkaline material, the basic slag that was formed could be an important by-product, with application in the developing artificial fertilizer industry.

Thomas did not long enjoy the fruits of his discovery. Not until 1879 did he give up his clerkship, but he was already suffering from a lung infection. Following a cruise round the world he died in Paris on 1 February 1885. After providing for his next of kin (he was unmarried), he left all his considerable fortune to charitable institutions.

Thompson, Benjamin American-born British physicist; see Count ◊Rumford.

Thompson, D'Arcy Wentworth (1860–1948) Scottish biologist and classical scholar who is best known for his book *On Growth and Form*, first published in 1917. He also studied fisheries and oceanography and published several works on classical science.

Thompson was born on 2 May 1860 in Edinburgh; his father was an authority on ancient Greece. He was educated at the Edinburgh Academy, Edinburgh University, and Trinity College, Cambridge. In the late 1870s, while studying medicine at Edinburgh University, he came under the influence of Charles Thomson (1830–1882) – the university's professor of natural history, who had recently returned from the *Challenger* Expedition for the exploration of the ocean depths – and became interested in biology and oceanography. In 1884 Thompson was appointed professor of biology at University College, Dundee, then became senior professor of natural history at St Andrews University in 1917 – a post he held for the remainder of his career. Concerned about conservation, in 1896 and 1897 Thompson went on expeditions to the Pribilof Islands as a member of the British–US commission on fur-seal hunting in the Bering Sea. He was also one of the British representatives on the International Council for the Exploration of the Sea and a member of the Fishery Board of Scotland. Thompson died on 21 June 1948 in St Andrews.

Thompson's principal contribution to biology was his highly influential *On Growth and Form* (1917), in which he interpreted the structure and growth of organisms in terms of the physical forces to which every individual is subjected throughout its life. He also hypothesized that the evolution of one species into another results mainly from major transformations involving the entire organism – a view contrary to the traditional Darwinistic theory of species arising as a result of numerous minor alterations in the body parts over several generations. In the 1942 revised edition of his book, however, Thompson admitted that his evolutionary theory did not adequately account for the cumulative effect of successive small modifications.

In addition to his theoretical work on growth, form, and evolution, Thompson wrote many papers on fisheries and oceanography. He also published works on classical natural history, notably *A Glossary of Greek Birds* (1895) and an edition of Aristotle's *Historia animalium* (1910).

Thomson, George Paget (1892–1975) English physicist who in 1927 first demonstrated electron diffraction, a confirmation of the wave nature of the electron. Clinton ◊Davisson also made the same discovery independently using a different method and in recognition of their achievement, Thomson and Davisson shared the 1937 Nobel Prize for Physics.

Thomson was born in Cambridge on 3 May 1892, the only son of the physicist J J ◊Thomson. He was educated at Perse School, Cambridge, and then at Trinity College, Cambridge, where he took a first-class

honours degree in mathematics and in physics in 1913. For a year he joined his father's research team but on the outbreak of World War I joined the infantry and saw active service in France. Thomson then transferred to the Royal Air Force and spent the rest of the war investigating the stability of aeroplanes. In 1919, he returned to Cambridge to become a fellow and lecturer at Corpus Christi College. Then in 1922 he became professor of natural philosophy at the University of Aberdeen, holding the post until 1930, when he moved to Imperial College, London, as professor of physics.

During World War II, Thomson headed many government committees, including the British Committee on Atomic Energy, which investigated the possibility of atomic weapons. For part of 1942 he was scientific liaison officer at Ottawa, Canada, where he built up close contact with the US atomic bomb project, and later in the war he became scientific adviser to the Air Ministry. Thomson returned to Imperial College after the war, interesting himself in thermonuclear fusion and undertaking vital research in this field. He retained his professorship there until 1952, when he became master of Corpus Christi College, Cambridge. Among the many honours he received were a knighthood in 1943 and presidency of the Institute of Physics 1958–60 and of the British Association for the Advancement of Science in 1960. Thomson retired in 1962 and died in Cambridge on 10 September 1975.

During the mid-1920s, Thomson carried out a series of experiments hoping to verify a hypothesis initially presented in 1924 by Louis ◊de Broglie that electrons possess a duality, acting both as particles and as waves. The basis of the experiment involved the bombardment of very thin metal (aluminium, gold, and platinum) and celluloid foils with a narrow beam of electrons. The beam was scattered into a series of rings in a similar manner to the rings associated with X-ray diffraction in metals. Applying mathematical formulae to measurements of the rings together with a knowledge of the crystal lattice, Thomson showed in 1927 that all the readings were in complete agreement with de Broglie's theory. Electrons were therefore shown to possess wave–particle duality. Several modifications to the initial experiments proved that the scattering effects were not the result of X-rays produced by the impact of electrons on the metal foil.

George Thomson's achievements parallel those of his father to an extraordinary degree. Both made fundamental discoveries concerning the electron, J J Thomson proving the existence of the electron as a particle in 1897 and his son demonstrating its wave nature 30 years later. Both men also became professors by the age of 30, both gained knighthoods, and both were awarded the Nobel prize.

Thomson, J(oseph) J(ohn) (1856–1940) English physicist who is famous for discovering the electron and for his research into the conduction of electricity through gases, for which he was awarded the 1906 Nobel Prize for Physics. He also received several other honours, including a knighthood in 1908 and the Order of Merit in 1912.

Thomson was born in Cheetham Hill, near Manchester, on 18 December 1856, the son of an antiquarian bookseller. At the age of 14 he went to Owens College, Manchester (later Manchester University), to study engineering. When his father died two years later, however, his family could not afford the premium for engineering training and so, with the help of a scholarship, Thomson studied physics, chemistry, and mathematics. In 1876 he won a scholarship to Trinity College, Cambridge, where he remained – except for visiting lectureships to Princeton University in 1896 and to Yale University in 1904, both in the USA – for the rest of his life.

After graduating in mathematics in 1880, he worked at the Cavendish Laboratory under Lord ◊Rayleigh, succeeding him as Cavendish Professor of Experimental Physics in 1884. In 1919 he resigned the Cavendish professorship (being succeeded in turn by his student Ernest ◊Rutherford), having been elected master of Trinity College the previous year. He held this post until his death (in Cambridge) on 30 August 1940.

Thomson's first important research concerned vortex rings, which won him the Adam's Prize in 1883. It was then thought that atoms might exist in the form of vortex rings in the 'ether', an idea that although untrue, led Thomson to begin his investigations into cathode rays and these, in turn, led to his famous discovery of the electron in 1897. At the end of the 19th century there was considerable debate as to whether cathode rays were charged particles or whether they were some undefined process in the ether. The German physicist Heinrich ◊Hertz had apparently shown that cathode rays were not deflected by an electric field (a finding that indicated that they were not particulate) but Thomson proved this to be incorrect in 1897, and demonstrated that Hertz's failure to obtain a deflection was caused by his use of an insufficiently evacuated cathode-ray tube. Having proved the particulate nature of cathode rays, Thomson went on to determine their charge-to-mass ratio, finding it to be constant – irrespective of the gas in the cathode ray tube – and with a value nearly 1,000 times smaller than that obtained for hydrogen ions in liquid electrolysis. He also measured the charge of the cathode-ray particles and found it to be the same in the gaseous discharge as in electrolysis. Thus he demonstrated that cathode rays are fundamental, negatively charged particles with a mass much less than the lightest atom known. He announced these findings during a lecture at the Royal Institution on 30 April 1897, calling the cathode-ray particles 'corpuscles'. The Dutch physicist Hendrik ◊Lorentz later named them 'electrons' (a term first used – with a slightly different meaning – by the Irish physicist George Stoney), which became generally accepted.

The assumption of a state of matter more finely subdivided than the atom of an element is a somewhat startling one.
J J THOMSON ROYAL INSTITUTION LECTURE 1897

Thomson then spent several years investigating the nature and properties of electrons, after which he began researching into 'canal rays', streams of positively charged ions, which Thomson named positive rays. Using magnetic and electric fields to deflect these rays, he found (in 1912) that ions of neon gas are deflected by different amounts, indicating that they consist of a mixture of ions with different charge-to-mass ratios. The English chemist Frederick ◊Soddy had earlier proposed the existence of isotopes and Thomson proved this idea correct when he identified – also in 1912 – the isotope neon-22. This work was later continued by Francis ◊Aston (one of Thomson's students and, later, the developer of the mass spectrograph), A J Dempster, and other scientists and led to the discovery of many other isotopes.

In addition to his pioneering research, Thomson wrote several notable works that were widely used in British universities, including *Notes on Recent Researches in Electricity and Magnetism* (1893), *Elements of the Mathematical Theory of Electricity and Magnetism* (1895), and, with John Poynting, the four-volume *Textbook of Physics*. Equally important, Thomson developed the Cavendish Laboratory into the world's leading centre for subatomic physics in the early 20th century. Furthermore, he trained a generation of scientists who subsequently made fundamental contributions to physics: seven of his research assistants – including his only son, George ◊Thomson – later won Nobel prizes.

Further Reading

Dahl, Per F, *Flash of the Cathode Rays: A History of J J Thomson's Electron,* Institute of Physics Publishing, 1997.

Morgan, Bryan, *Men and Discoveries in Electricity,* J Murray, 1952.

Thomson, George Piaget, *J J Thomson and the Cavendish Laboratory in His Day,* British Men of Science series, Nelson, 1964.

Thomson, James (1822–1892) Irish physicist and engineer who discovered that the melting point of ice decreases with pressure. He was also an authority on hydrodynamics and invented the vortex water wheel.

Thomson was born on 16 February 1822 in Belfast into a family of scientists. His father was professor of mathematics at Belfast and his younger brother was William Thomson, later Lord ◊Kelvin. Thomson received his early education from his father and then at the age of only ten began to attend Glasgow University, obtaining an MA in 1839. He subsequently held a succession of engineering posts, and then settled in Belfast in 1851 as a civil engineer. In 1857, Thomson became professor of civil engineering at Belfast and in 1873 moved to Glasgow to take up the same position there. He resigned his chair in 1889 and died in Glasgow on 8 May 1892.

As a young man Thomson was most interested in engineering projects, especially those involving paddles and water wheels, and while still a student he invented a device for feathering paddles. In 1850, Thomson invented the vortex water wheel, which was a smaller and more efficient turbine than those in use at the time, and it came into wide use. On moving to Belfast, Thomson continued his investigations into whirling fluids, making improvements to pumps, fans, and turbines.

Thomson's most important discovery was made in 1849, when he determined the lowering of melting point caused by pressure on ice. This led him to reach an understanding of the way in which glaciers flow. Thomson also carried out painstaking studies of the phase relationships of solids, liquids, and gases, and was involved in both geology and meteorology, producing scientific papers on currents and winds.

Tinbergen, Niko(laas) (1907–1988) Dutch-born British ethologist who studied many animals in their natural environments but is best known for his investigations into the courtship behaviour of sticklebacks and the social behaviour of gulls. He did much to revitalize the science of ethology, for which, among many other honours, he shared the 1973 Nobel Prize for Physiology or Medicine with Konrad ◊Lorenz (with whom he worked on several research projects) and Karl von ◊Frisch.

Tinbergen was born on 15 April 1907 in The Hague and was educated at Leiden University, from which he gained his doctorate in 1932. During 1931 and 1932 he went with a scientific expedition to the Arctic and on his return became a lecturer at Leiden University. Except for a period of military service during World War II, Tinbergen remained at Leiden – becoming professor of experimental zoology in 1947 – until 1949, when he was appointed professor of zoology at Oxford University in the UK. He established a school of animal behaviour studies at Oxford and remained at the university until he retired in 1974. He died in Oxford on 21 December 1988.

One of Tinbergen's best-known studies was of the three-spined stickleback, described in *The Study of Instinct* (1951). During the spring mating season the male stickleback marks out its individual territory and attacks any other male stickleback that enters its domain. If a female stickleback enters his territory, however, the male does not attack but courts her instead. Tinbergen showed that the aggressive behaviour of the male is stimulated by the red coloration on the underside of other males (this red patch develops on the underbelly of males during the mating season but does not appear on females). Tinbergen also demonstrated that the courtship dance of the male is stimulated by the sight of the swollen belly of a female that is ready to lay eggs. If the female responds to the male's zig-zag courtship dance, she follows him to the nest that he has already prepared. The female enters the nest first and is followed by the male who pokes her under the tail with his snout, causing her to release eggs and to emit a chemical that stimulates the male to ejaculate sperm into the water.

In *The Herring Gull's World* (1953) Tinbergen described the social behaviour of gulls, again emphasizing the importance of stimulus-response processes in territorial behaviour. Defence of territory is particularly important for birds such as herring gulls, which nest in large, densely populated colonies. Although these gulls possess a large vocabulary of warning calls, Tinbergen's findings suggest that gestures are equally, if not more important in warning off other gulls. For example, he found that when two male herring gulls meet at territorial boundaries, one or both of the gulls tugs at the grass with his beak, rather than immediately fighting. Another similar behaviour pattern – the choking gesture – is performed by male and female gulls to warn off invaders: again, rather than fight, the gulls lower their heads, open their mouths and appear to choke. Tinbergen hypothesized that these gestures are normal behaviour patterns (grass-pulling, for example, occurs during nest-building) that have become adapted to denote aggression – and are recognized as aggressive by other birds – in order to prevent fighting and the possible injury or death that could result.

Tinbergen investigated other aspects of animal behaviour, such as the importance of learning in the feeding behaviour of oystercatchers, and also studied human behaviour, particularly aggression, which he believed to be an inherited instinct that developed when humans changed from being predominantly herbivorous to being hunting carnivores.

Tiselius, Arne Wilhelm Kaurin (1902–1971)

Swedish physical biochemist who discovered the complex nature of proteins in blood serum and developed electrophoresis as a technique for studying proteins. For this work he was awarded the 1948 Nobel Prize for Chemistry.

Tiselius was born in Stockholm on 10 August 1902 into an academic family. His father died when he was only four years old, and the remaining family moved to Göteborg. At school he became interested in chemistry and biology and in 1921 he went to Uppsala University to study under Theodor ◊Svedberg, the leading Swedish physical chemist at that time. In 1924 he gained an MA in chemistry, physics, and mathematics and later the same year submitted his doctoral thesis on electrophoresis (the migration of charged colloidal particles in an electric field). He became an assistant to Svedberg and remained associated with the university for the rest of his career. He joined the faculty in 1930 and eight years later he was made director of the new Institute of Biochemistry. From 1934 to 1935 he worked in the USA at the Frick Chemical Laboratory at Princeton University. He retired in 1968 and died in Stockholm on 29 October 1971.

Tiselius began his research in Svedberg's laboratory in 1925. At that time Svedberg was developing the ultracentrifuge and Tiselius used the new machine to study the sizes and shapes of protein molecules. He observed that many substances that appeared to be homogeneous in the ultracentrifuge could be separated by electrophoresis. This was especially the case with serum proteins, but he changed the direction of his research and did not return to this problem for a number of years.

He then investigated zeolite minerals, which are unique in their ability to substitute their water of crystallization with different substances, while the crystal structure remains intact despite the removal of the water under vacuum. Tiselius studied the optical changes that occur when the dried crystals are rehydrated. He did this work at Princeton, and while he was there his discussions with such scientists as Karl ◊Landsteiner and Leonor Michaelis (1875–1949) made him reopen his research into more effective separation methods for biochemistry.

On his return to Uppsala he reconstructed his electrophoresis apparatus and used it to separate the proteins in horse serum. He obtained four bands of protein with varying mobilities. The band with the fastest movement coincided with the serum albumin boundary and the next three revealed, uniquely, the existence of three electrophoretically varying components which he named α-, ß-, and γ-globulin. He observed the bands optically by measuring changes in their refractive indices.

He also became interested in adsorption methods of separation and devised a new quantitative optical technique for observing the eluate (previously adsorbed material washed out of the chromatography column in solution). In 1943, he showed that 'tailing' during elution can be prevented by introducing to the eluting solution a substance whose adsorption affinity was higher than the rest of the components making up the mixture. He called this method 'displacement analysis'. In 1954, he used calcium phosphate in the form of hydroxyl-apatite for the purpose of adsorbing protein, with phosphate buffers as the agents for elution.

Tiselius made a decisive contribution to chromatography. His characteristic method of working was to take well-recognized, qualitative experimental phenomena and establish their theoretical basis. As a result he was able to introduce improvements to existing techniques and to devise new ones. During the last ten years of his life he became very concerned about the possible threat to humanity by the advance of science. He believed that the Nobel Foundation was in a unique position to be able to bring pressure to bear on the most pertinent problems facing humanity, and he founded the Nobel Symposia, which take place every year in each of the five prize fields to discuss the social, ethical, and other implications of the award-winning work.

Todd, Alexander Robertus (1907–1997)

Baron Todd. Scottish chemist who made outstanding contributions to the study of natural substances. For his work on nucleotides and coenzymes he was awarded the 1957 Nobel Prize for Chemistry.

Todd was born in Glasgow on 2 October 1907. He was educated at Allan Glen School and at Glasgow University, graduating in 1929. He went to the University of Frankfurt in Germany for two years, gaining his doctorate in 1931. From 1931 to 1934 he studied at Oxford University under the organic chemist Robert ◊Robinson. After leaving Oxford he spent two years at the University of Edinburgh as assistant in medical chemistry, and from there he went to the Lister Institute of Preventive Medicine in London. In 1937 he became reader in biochemistry at the University of London and a year later was appointed the Sir Samuel Hall Professor of Chemistry and director of the chemical laboratories at Manchester University. He took up the professorship of organic chemistry at Cambridge University in 1944, where he remained until he retired in 1971. He was knighted in 1954 and in 1962 was created Baron Todd of Trumpington; he became Master of Christ's College, Cambridge, in 1963.

Todd began his research in 1931 with Robinson, investigating the synthesis of the water-soluble plant pigments called anthocyanins. In 1936 he began his work on vitamins with the synthesis of the water-soluble vitamin B_1 (thiamine), deficiency of which causes the disease beriberi. It is essential for the correct metabolism of carbohydrates; its diphosphate forms the coenzyme of carboxylase. He went on to study pantothenic acid, the so-called 'filtrate factor' of B vitamins, which has been of therapeutic value in treating certain anaemias. Todd later worked on the structure of the fat-soluble vitamin E (tocopherol), deficiency of which affects fertility or muscular activity. In 1955 Todd and his co-workers, with Dorothy ◊Hodgkin, established the structure of vitamin B_{12} (cyanocobalamin), deficiency of which causes pernicious anaemia.

In the late 1940s and early 1950s Todd also worked on nucleotides – compounds of a base (such as purine), a pentose sugar, and phosphoric (V) acid. The term is applied to certain coenzymes, such as nicotinamide adenine dinucleotide (NAD); to compounds formed by partial hydrolysis of nucleic acids; and to nucleic acids themselves, which can be regarded as polynucleotides. He synthesized adenosine triphosphate (ATP) and adenosine diphosphate (ADP), the key substances in the energy-generating biochemical processes in the body. He developed new methods for the synthesis of all the major nucleotides and their related coenzymes, and established in detail the chemical structures of the nucleic acids, such as the hereditary material DNA (deoxyribonucleic acid). During the course of this work, which provided the essential basis for further developments in the fields of genetics and of protein synthesis in living cells, Todd also devised an approach to the synthesis of the nucleic acids themselves.

Tolansky, Samuel (1907–1973) English physicist who made important contributions to the fields of spectroscopy and interferometry.

Tolansky was born in Newcastle upon Tyne on 17 November 1907. He attended Snow Street School and Rutherford College and then in 1925 went to Armstrong College, part of Durham University, where he was awarded his BSc in 1928. He undertook scientific research at Armstrong College 1929–31, when he spent a year at the Physikalische Technische Reichsanstalt in Berlin, Germany, under Friedrich Paschen (1865–1947).

On his return to England, Tolansky went to London to spend two years doing research at Imperial College and received his PhD in 1934. He then moved to the physics department of Manchester University, where he served as an assistant lecturer under Lawrence Bragg (see William and Lawrence ◊Bragg). In 1936 Tolansky was awarded a DSc by Manchester University,

and he subsequently became a lecturer in 1937 and senior lecturer in 1945, and in 1946 was given the post of reader in physics. In the following year, Tolansky moved to Royal Holloway College, part of London University, to take up the chair of physics. He retained this position until he died in London on 4 March 1973.

Tolansky's early research centred on the study of line and band spectra and at Paschen's department in Berlin he was exposed to studies in virtually all areas of spectroscopy. His main interest until his move to London in 1947 was the analysis of hyperfine structures in atomic spectra. He made a particular study of the spectrum of mercury, but the occurrence of multiple isotopes in his samples complicated the analysis. He also studied the hyperfine structure of the spectra of halogen gases such as chlorine and bromine, and of arsenic, iron, copper, and platinum. He used the analysis of spectra to investigate nuclear spin, and magnetic and quadruple moments.

During World War II, Tolansky was requested by Tube Alloys (a euphemistic name for the body that was coordinating British research into the possibilities of constructing an atomic bomb) to obtain information on the spin of uranium-235, which is the isotope capable of fission in a nuclear chain reaction. Tolansky was unable to obtain any material in which the proportion of uranium-235 was enriched, so he had to use samples in which the proportion was only 0.7%. He was nevertheless able to demonstrate that the spin is in excess of 1/2, and suggested that it was most likely to be 5/2 or 7/2. The latter figure is the value that is currently accepted.

After the war, Tolansky concentrated on the applications of multiple-beam interferometry. He used it to investigate the fine details of surface structure as the method is able to resolve structure as small as 15 Å (15 $\times$ 10^{-9} m) in height. He examined the vibration patterns in oscillating quartz crystals and the microtopography of many different crystals, particularly diamonds. He was especially interested in the growth features of crystals such as growth spirals. A quantitative means of assessing the hardness of materials grew out of Tolansky's work on interferometry as the depths of indentations made by the impact of a standard hardness tester could be accurately assessed by using interferometry. Another application for the technique lay in the measurement of the thickness of thin film.

Tombaugh, Clyde William (1906–1997) US astronomer whose painstaking work led to his discovery of Pluto.

Tombaugh was born on 4 February 1906 in Streator, Illinois. He had a deep fascination for astronomy and constructed a 23-cm/9-in telescope out of parts of old machinery on his father's farm. His family could not afford to send him to college and he joined the Lowell Observatory in 1929 in the hope that he would learn about the subject while working there as an assistant. In 1933, after his discovery of Pluto, Tombaugh won a scholarship to the University of Kansas, from where he obtained an MA in 1936.

Several astronomers had shown that the orbital motions of Uranus and Neptune exhibited gravitational perturbations suggestive of the existence of a planet beyond them. Percival ◊Lowell made the first generally accepted calculation of the new planet's likely position and, as director of the Lowell Observatory, he set up a team to look for the planet. This work continued when Vesto ◊Slipher became director in 1926.

On joining the observatory, Tombaugh worked on Slipher's team. There were various problems. The new planet would be too dim for a telescope to reveal without bringing thousands of dim stars into view also and, because of its distance from the Earth, any visible motion would be very slight. Tombaugh devised a technique by means of which he compared two photographs of the same part of the sky taken on different days. Each photograph could be expected to show anything between 50,000 and 500,000 stars. Tombaugh looked to see if any of the spots of light had moved in a way not expected of stars or the then known planets. Any movement would be noticeable if the different photographic plates were focused at a single point and alternately flashed rapidly on to a screen. A planet moving against the background of stars would appear to move back and forth on the screen.

It was a painstaking process. On 18 February 1930 Tombaugh discovered a moving light in the constellation of Gemini. On 13 March the discovery of the new planet was announced and it was named after the god of the nether darkness, which seemed appropriate for the most distant planet.

There was some doubt that this could be the planet that Lowell had predicted, since it was only one-tenth as bright and too small to account for all the gravitational perturbations, but the doubt was soon dispelled and Tombaugh was recognized for his great contribution to the furthering of our knowledge of the Solar System.

Further Reading

Levy, David H, *Clyde Tombaugh: Discoverer of Planet Pluto*, University of Arizona Press, 1992.

Tombaugh, Clyde W, *The Discovery of Pluto: Unknown Aspects of the Story*, Mercury, 1986, v 15, pp 66–72, 98–102.

Wetterer, Margaret, *Clyde Tombaugh and the Search for Planet X*, The Lerner Publishing Group, 1996.

Tomonaga, Sin-Itiro (1906–1979) Japanese theoretical physicist who was one of the first to develop a

consistent theory of relativistic quantum electrodynamics. He shared the Nobel Prize for Physics in 1965 with US quantum physicist Julian Schwinger (1918–1994) and US physicist Richard ◊Feynman for 'fundamental work in quantum electrodynamics'.

Sin-Itiro Tomonaga was born in Tokyo on 31 March 1906, the son of a professor at Shinsu University. In 1907 the family moved to Kyoto where his father became professor of philosophy. He was a sickly child who often missed school. One of his classmates at school, Hideki ◊Yukawa, was also to become a Nobel laureate in physics.

Tomonaga was inspired to study physics by Albert ◊Einstein's visit to Japan in 1922 and by reading a book on relativity by Jun Ishiwara. He also studied the atomic theory of Danish physicist Nils ◊Bohr at school. Tomonago and Yukawa both entered Kyoto Imperial University in 1926. In his reminiscences *My Teachers, My Friends,* Tomonaga describes his experience as a university student as deeply unsatisfactory, with mediocre and tedious lectures and laboratories that did not live up to his expectations. In their final year at university Tomonaga and other ambitious students studied quantum mechanics on their own, and after their graduation in 1929 he and Yukawa continued their studies as unpaid assistants to Kajuro Tamaki.

In 1932 Tomonaga joined the laboratory of Yoshio Nishina at the Tokyo Institute of Physical and Chemical Research and began a collaboration with Nishina, publishing five papers together on the positron and another on neutron–proton interaction. In 1937 he joined the group of German physicist Werner ◊Heisenberg in Leipzig and in 1940 he developed an intermediate coupling theory for mesons. He remained in Leipzig until just before the outbreak of war, producing three papers in German on nuclear structure and one with Tamaki in 1937, which treated for the first time the collision of a very high energy neutrino with a neutron, emphasizing the rapid rise with increased energy of the probability of neutrino interaction. Tomonaga, and Yukawa who was visiting him, were urgently advised by the Japanese embassy to return home in August 1939. On his return Tomonaga continued his association with Nishima's laboratory.

In 1940 he married Ryoko Sekiguchi, the daughter of the director of the Tokyo Astromomical Observatory who was also a professor at Tokyo Imperial University. They had three children. In 1941 Tomonaga was made professor at Tokyo Bunrika Daigaku (University of Literature and Science) and in 1944 he became a part-time lecturer at Tokyo University, also being obliged to be involved in research for the navy. He undertook war work on microwave circuits and wave guides and on the theory of the magnetron oscillator used to generate short radio waves for radar and was awarded the Japan Academy Prize with Masao Kotani in 1948 for this work.

Tomonaga's family fled to the countryside during the intense bombing of Tokyo in 1944 and he shared his house with several other physicists whose families had also left, while working on radar at the naval research laboratory. Meanwhile he was also teaching at the university and he and his students at this time became co-authors of over 20 papers on cosmic ray phenomena, quantum theory, and renormalization theory. Tomonaga and a number of colleagues had been working on the formulation of quantum electrodynamics in super-many-time theory and the group presented 23 papers at Kyoto University in November 1946.

Postwar communication with the west was difficult but in 1947 Tomonaga read in *Time* and *Newsweek* of exciting developments that partially explained the renormalization method that he himself had been working on. In 1949 Tomonaga joined Yukawa in Princeton, USA, for a year, working on the nature of collective oscillations in a one-dimensional fermion system. He published his book *Quantum Mechanics* in the same year. It was translated into English in 1963 and sales ran to hundreds of thousands.

Tomonaga continued to do his research in the 1950s but also became a member and president of the Science Council of Japan in 1951. He was president of Tokyo University of Education 1956–62, and from 1957 he was an active anti-nuclear campaigner and a member of the Pugwash conference. Other honours awarded to him include the Japanese Cultural Medal in 1952 and the USSR Lomonosov Medal in 1964. He was also a member of the Japan Academy, the American Philosophical Society, the US National Academy of Sciences, and the Royal Swedish Academy of Sciences.

Tomonaga wrote two books on the history of physics: *The Spin is Spinning*, containing stories about quantum theory, and a first volume of *What Would Be Physics*, describing the ideas behind mechanics and thermodynamics. He was working on the second volume of this when he died of cancer in Tokyo on 8 July 1979.

Torricelli, Evangelista (1608–1647) Italian physicist and mathematician who is best known for his invention of the barometer.

Torricelli was born on 15 October 1608 in Faenza and was educated, mainly in mathematics, at the Sapienza College, Rome. He was impressed by the works of ◊Galileo and the respect became mutual when Galileo read Torricelli's *De motu* (1641), which dealt with movement. In that same year Galileo invited him to Florence, and after Galileo's death the following year became professor of mathematics at Florence, where he remained for the rest of his life. He died there on 25 October 1647.

Galileo had been puzzled why a lift pump could not lift a column of water more than about 9 m/30 ft – current explanations were based on Nature's supposed abhorrence of a vacuum. Torricelli realized that the atmosphere must have weight, and the height of the water column is limited by atmospheric pressure. In 1643 he filled a long glass tube, closed at one end, with mercury and inverted it in a dish of mercury. Atmospheric pressure supported a column of mercury about 76 cm/30 in long; the space above the mercury was a vacuum. Mercury is nearly 14 times as dense as water, and the mercury column was only about 1/14 the height of the maximum water column.

Torricelli also noticed that the height of the mercury column varied slightly from day to day and finally came to the conclusion that this was a reflection of variations in atmospheric pressure. Thus by 1644 he had developed the mercury barometer.

Townes, Charles Hard (1915–   ) US physicist who is best known for his investigations into the theory, and subsequent invention in 1953, of the maser. He has received numerous honours for this work, including the 1964 Nobel Prize for Physics, which he shared with Nikolai Basov (1922–   ) and Aleksandr Prokhorov (1916–   ), two Russian scientists who independently invented the maser in 1955.

Townes, the son of a lawyer, was born in Greenville, South Carolina, on 28 July 1915. He was educated at Furman University, Greenville, from which he graduated in 1935, studied for his master's degree at Duke University and then moved to the California Institute of Technology to work for a PhD, which he gained in 1939. From 1939 to 1947 he worked at the Bell Telephone Laboratories designing radar bomb-aiming systems, after which he joined the physics department of the University of Columbia, becoming professor of physics in 1950. Next, he worked at the Massachusetts Institute of Technology 1961–67, when he was appointed professor of physics at the University of California, Berkeley (emeritus from 1986).

In about 1950 Townes became interested in the possibility of constructing a device that could generate high-intensity microwaves, and by 1951 he had concluded that it might be possible to build such a device based on the principle that molecules emit radiation when they move from one energy level to a lower one. Ammonia molecules can occupy only two energy levels and, Townes argued, if a molecule in the high energy level can be made to absorb a photon of a specific frequency, then the molecule should fall to the lower energy level, emitting two photons of the same frequency and producing a coherent beam of single-frequency radiation.

Using ammonia molecules, the radiation emitted would have a wavelength of 1.25 cm/0.5 in and would therefore be in the microwave region of the electromagnetic spectrum. But in constructing a device using this principle Townes had to develop a method (now called population inversion) for separating the relatively scarce high-energy molecules from the more common lower-energy ones. He succeeded by using an electric field that focused the high-energy ammonia molecules into a resonator, and by 1953 he had constructed the first working maser (an acronym for *m*icrowave *a*mplification by *s*timulated *e*mission of *r*adiation).

Masers quickly found numerous applications – in atomic clocks (still the most accurate timepieces available) and radiotelescope receivers, for example. In the late 1950s solid-state masers (in which molecules of a solid were used instead of gaseous ammonia) were made and were used to amplify weak signals reflected from the *Echo I* passive communications satellite and radar reflections from Venus.

In 1958 Townes published a paper that demonstrated the theoretical possibility of producing an optical maser to produce a coherent beam of single-frequency visible light, rather than a microwave beam. But the first working optical maser (or laser, from *l*ight *a*mplification by *s*timulated *e*mission of *r*adiation) was built by Theodore ◊Maiman in 1960.

Townsend, John Sealy Edward (1868–1957) Irish mathematical physicist who was responsible for the development of the study of the kinetics of electrons and ions in gases. He was the first to obtain a value for the charge on the electron and to explain how electric discharges pass through gases.

Townsend was born in Galway on 7 June 1868. He attended Corrig School and in 1885 entered Trinity College, Dublin. There he studied mathematics, physics, and experimental science, graduating in 1890. He spent the next four years teaching and lecturing, especially on mathematics, and in 1895 Townsend went to England, where he remained for the rest of his life. He gained entry to Cambridge University as a research student, and he and Ernest ◊Rutherford became the first such students to work under J J ◊Thomson. Townsend was soon recognized as a scientist of rare quality, and when Oxford University established a new chair of experimental physics in 1900 with the intention of improving the standard of instruction in the fields of electricity and magnetism, Townsend was invited to become the first Wykeham Professor. He accepted, and most of the rest of his professional career was spent in Oxford.

During his early years at Oxford, Townsend was deeply involved with the construction of a permanent electrical laboratory. This was completed in 1910, but Townsend's research was then disrupted by the outbreak of World War I. He spent the war years at Woolwich, researching into radio telegraphy for the Royal Naval Air Service. Townsend resumed his work on gaseous ionization at Oxford after the war and continued there until 1941, when he was knighted and retired from his university duties. He did not, however, cease working. He spent a period teaching at Winchester School, and then returned to Oxford where he wrote a number of monographs. Townsend died in Oxford on 16 February 1957.

Townsend's earliest research at Cambridge was in the field of magnetism, but he soon turned to the subject that would occupy him for the rest of his career, namely the properties of ionized gases. He studied the conductivity of gases ionized by the newly discovered X-rays and in 1897 developed a method for producing ionized gases using electrolysis. This method enabled Townsend to obtain the first estimate for the electron charge in 1898. It was later modified by J J Thomson and Charles ◊Wilson, and formed part of the basis for the famous oil-drop experiments performed by Robert ◊Millikan 1909–13.

In 1898 Townsend began the first study of ionic diffusion in gases. He studied diffusion in gases that had been ionized (or electrified) by means of the so-called Townsend discharge. This involved the passage of a weak current through low-pressure gases. He found that the coefficient of diffusion of an ion was only a quarter of that of a neutral molecule, indicating a smaller mean free path for ions.

Around the time of Townsend's move to Oxford, he began to develop his collision theory of ionization. He based this theory on results he had himself obtained and those of Aleksandr Stoletov (1839–1896), which indicated that the ionization potential of molecules was ten times less than was generally accepted. This meant that collisions by negative ions or electrons could induce the formation of secondary ions, thus carrying an electric charge through a gas.

The study of the multiplication of charges in a gas was Townsend's major preoccupation for the next few years. He determined the coefficient of multiplication, also called Townsend's first ionization coefficient, which describes the number of pairs of ions produced by the movement of one electron through 1 cm/0.4 in in the direction of an electric field.

Townsend also studied the electrical conditions that lead to the production of a spark in a gas, and on the confusing role played in this by the positive ions that are produced simultaneously with the electrons.

During the 1920s, Townsend was involved with the measurement of the average fraction of energy lost by an electron in a single collision. He discovered in 1924 that this fraction was very small when the electrons were passed through a monatomic gas such as helium or argon. Carl Ramsauer (1879–1955) was independently engaged in a similar study and their results, which are called the Ramsauer–Townsend effect, were later found to be analogous to electron diffraction and were important in understanding the wavelike nature of the electron.

Tradescant, John (1570–1638) and John (1608–1662)

English horticulturalists, father and son, who were pioneers in the collection and cultivation of plants. Carolus ◊Linnaeus named the flowering plant genus *Tradescantia* (the spiderworts) after them.

Tradescant senior is generally considered to be the earliest collector of plants and other natural history objects. In 1604 he became gardener to the Earl of Salisbury, who, in 1610, sent him to Belgium to collect plant specimens; the Brussels strawberry was one of the plants that he brought back. The following year he went to France, visiting Rouen and the Apothecary Garden in Paris, and in 1618 went to Russia with an official party sent by King James I. Two years later Tradescant accompanied another official expedition – this time one against the North African Barbary pirates – and brought back to England gutta-percha, mazer wood, and various fruits and seeds. Between 1625 and 1628 he was employed by the Duke of Buckingham and during this period joined an expedition to La Rochelle, France. Later, when he became gardener to King Charles I, Tradescant set up his own garden and museum in Lambeth, London, which he stocked from his private collection of plants and other natural history specimens. In 1624 he published a catalogue of 750 plants grown in his garden; the only known copy of this catalogue is now in the library of Magdalen College, Oxford.

The younger Tradescant, sharing his father's enthusiasm for plants, became a member of the Company of Master Gardeners of London when only 26 years old. Three years later, in 1637, he went to Virginia, America, to collect plants and shells for his father's museum. After his father's death in 1638, the younger Tradescant succeeded him as gardener to Charles I, and went on several plant-collecting expeditions, adding to his father's collection. He published two lists of plants in the collection – in 1634 and 1656, the latter incorporating his father's specimens – most of which were unknown in England before 1600.

The younger Tradescant died on 22 April 1662 in Lambeth. His collection was eventually incorporated with that of Elias Ashmole (1617–1692) who, in turn, gave it to Oxford University in 1683, thereby founding the Ashmolean Museum.

Travers, Morris William (1872–1961)

English chemist famous for his association with William ◊Ramsay on the discovery of the inert, or noble, gases.

Travers was born in Kensington, London, on 24 January 1872, the second of four sons of a London physician. He was educated at Ramsgate 1879–82 and Woking 1882–85, before going to Blundell's School in Tiverton, Devon, because it had a good chemistry laboratory. He went to University College, London, in 1889 and graduated in chemistry in 1893. He was then advised to study organic chemistry, and in 1894 went to France to carry out research at Nancy University with Alban Haller. But after a few months he returned to London to University College and became a demonstrator under William Ramsay. In 1898 he gained his DSc and became an assistant professor, being promoted to professor of chemistry in 1903. He went to Bangalore in 1906 as director of the new Indian Institute of Scientists.

He returned to the UK at the outbreak of World War I in 1914 and directed the manufacture of glass at Duroglass Limited, Walthamstow, becoming president of the Society of Glass Technology. In 1920 he became involved with high-temperature furnaces and fuel technology, including the gasification of coal. He was made honorary professor of chemistry at Bristol University in 1927, and retired in 1937. During World War II he served as an adviser and consultant to the Explosives Section of the Ministry of Supply. He died at his home in Stroud, Gloucestershire, on 25 August 1961.

Travers returned to London to assist Ramsay in 1894, at the time of the discovery of argon, the first of the inert, or noble, gases to be found. Then after the discovery of helium a year later, he helped Ramsay to determine the properties of both new gases. They also heated minerals and meteorites in the search for further gases, but found none. Then in 1898 they obtained a large quantity of liquid air and subjected it to fractional distillation. Spectral analysis of the least volatile fraction revealed the presence of krypton. They examined the argon fraction for a constituent of lower boiling point, and discovered neon. Finally xenon, occurring as an even less volatile companion to krypton, was found and identified spectroscopically.

The physicist James ◊Dewar had succeeded in liquefying hydrogen in 1898, but Travers independently constructed the necessary apparatus. Using liquid hydrogen, Ramsay and Travers were able to condense the neon fraction from air while the helium fraction remained gaseous. In this way they obtained enough neon by mid-1900 to complete their study of the inert gases. Travers continued his researches in cryogenics and made the first accurate temperature measurements of liquid gases. He also helped to build several experimental liquid air plants in Europe.

In his later work at Bristol, Travers studied the thermal decomposition of organic vapours and investigated gas and heterogeneous reactions. In 1956, when he was over 80 years old, he published *Life of Sir William Ramsay*, a biography of his partner of 50 years earlier.

Trésaguet, Pierre-Marie-Jérôme (1716–1796)

French civil engineer best known for his improved methods of road-building.

Trésaguet was born in Nevers into a family that was connected with all aspects of engineering. He grew up absorbing the general principles of the subject, and spent many years working for the Corps des Ponts et Chaussées, where his learning was put to good use in civil-engineering projects. At first he was a sub-inspector in Paris, then chief engineer in Limoges, before he finally became inspector general. He died in Paris on 12 March 1796.

In the 17th and 18th centuries most roads consisted of stretches of old Roman roads and rough tracks, well worn over the years by the passage of horses and farm carts. Pitted, pot-holed, and often completely impassable for several months each winter because of mud, they presented an awesome prospect to anyone wishing to travel a long distance. Turnpike roads, with the levying of tolls to pay for maintenance, effected some improvements, although often the tolls were simply pocketed and the repairs left undone. Even for new roads, the emphasis was on providing a suitable surface. Trésaguet realized that the key to the problem was to provide a solid foundation, one that could withstand winter rains and frost and the effects of traffic. He chose to dig out the road bed to a depth of about 25 cm/10 in and lay first a course of uniform flat stones, laid on edge to permit drainage. Well hammered in, they provided a solid base on top of which he spread a layer of much smaller stones for a smoother surface. His roads were built 5.4 m/18 ft wide, with a crown that rose 15 cm/6 in above the outside edge.

His method was first used for a major road that ran from Paris to the Spanish border, via Toulouse. It proved so successful that many other countries copied the idea, including the UK. The Scottish civil engineer Thomas ◊Telford put the principle into practice when he was surveyor to the county of Shropshire.

Trevithick, Richard (1771–1833)

English engineer who constructed one of the first steam railway locomotives.

Trevithick was born on 13 April 1771, in Illogan, Cornwall, the son of a mine manager. As a boy he was fascinated by the mining machinery and the large stationary steam engines that worked the pumps. In 1797 he made a model of a steam road locomotive, which he ran round a table in his home. He built various full-sized engines in the early 1800s and by 1808 he had built the engine *Catch-me-who-can*, and ran it in London as a novelty for those willing to pay a shilling for a ride. Then in 1816 he left England for Peru. When he returned, after making and losing a fortune, he found that in his absence others had developed steam transport until it was a thriving concern, with the first railway being authorized to carry passengers by an act of Parliament in 1823. Trevithick was never able to resume his earlier position at the forefront of transport invention, and he died a poor man in Dartford, Kent, on 22 April 1833.

The first steam-powered road vehicle was invented by the French army officer Joseph ◊Cugnot in 1769, for hauling cannon. It probably did not carry passengers, and credit for first doing this is usually given to Trevithick's *Puffing Devil* of 1801. It made its famous debut on Christmas Eve, but unfortunately burnt out while Trevithick and his friends were celebrating their success at a nearby inn.

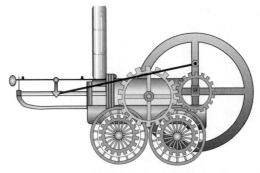

Trevithick The first steam engine to run on rails was invented by Richard Trevithick 1804. The locomotive was first used on rails designed for horse-drawn wagons, hauling up to 10 metric tons and 70 people to and from the Penydarren ironworks, near Merthyr Tydfil, Wales.

By 1804 Trevithick had produced his first railway locomotive, able to haul 10 tonnes and 70 people for 15 km/9.5 mi on rails used by horse-trains at the Penydarren Mines, near Merthyr Tydfil in south Wales. A few years later he hired some land near Euston, London, where he set up his money-making novelty ride. He also applied his inventive genius to many other machines, including steamboats, river dredgers, and threshing machines. But he will always be best remembered for his steam locomotives.

Trumpler, Robert Julius (1886–1956)

Swiss-born US astronomer who is known for his studies and classification of star clusters found in our Galaxy. He also carried out observational tests of the general theory of relativity.

Trumpler was born in Zürich on 2 October 1886, the third son of a family of ten children of the Swiss industrialist Wilhelm Trumpler. He attended the University of Zürich for two years and then transferred to the University of Göttingen, where he gained his PhD in 1910. For the following four years, Trumpler work on the Swiss Geodetic Survey determining longitudes and latitudes, and it was during this time that he developed a personal interest in the annual proper motion of the stars in the Pleiades cluster. The latter interest coincided with that of Frank Schlesinger (1871–1943), director of the Allegheny Observatory, near Pittsburgh, Pennsylvania. A meeting between the two led Trumpler in 1915 to accept an invitation by Schlesinger to work at the Allegheny Observatory on comparative studies of galactic star clusters. In 1919 Trumpler was invited to work with William ◊Campbell at the Lick Observatory, near Chicago, to assist with tests of the general theory of relativity. Trumpler was appointed as professor of astronomy at the University of California in 1930. He was elected to the National Academy of Sciences in 1932 and in the same year he became president of the Astronomical Society of the Pacific, being re-elected to the presidency in 1939. He retired in 1951 and died five years later in Oakland, California, on 10 September 1956.

At the Allegheny Observatory Trumpler showed that galactic star clusters contain different classes of stars, with no observable regularity in the occurrence of blue stars, yellow stars, or red giants, and these observations paved the way for later theories about stellar evolution. In 1930 he showed that interstellar material was responsible for obscuring some light from galaxies, which had led to overestimations of their distances from Earth; this work supported Harlow ◊Shapley's research on the size of our Galaxy.

Three years after joining Campbell at the Lick Observatory, Trumpler took part in a test of the theory of relativity in which stars near the totally eclipsed Sun were photographed from Australia and compared with photographs taken simultaneously from Tahiti. Readings showed that light suffered an outward deflection of 4.4501 cm/1.752 in at the edge of the Sun, compared with Einstein's prediction that the amount of deflection would be 4.4323 cm/1.7463 in.

Trumpler also used the refractor at the Lick Observatory to study the planet Mars, concluding that, while most of Giovanni ◊Schiaparelli's observations were incorrect, there was still a possibility that some of the supposed observations of 'canals' could be volcanic faults. This conclusion exemplifies the accuracy of Trumpler's observational astronomy because his hypothesis was made in 1924 and it only gained real support on the return of the photographs taken by the *Mariner 9* space probe to Mars, more than 50 years later.

Further Reading

Eyles, Joan M and William Smith, 'Richard Trevithick and Samuel Homfray: their correspondence on steam engines, 1804–1806', *J Trevithick Soc*, 1985, v 12, pp 10–35.

Hodge, James, *Richard Trevithick,* Shire Publications, 1989.

Tsiolkovskii, Konstantin (1857–1935) Russian theoretician and one of the pioneers of space rocketry, hailed by his country as the 'father of Soviet cosmonautics'.

Tsiolkovskii was born on 17 September 1857 in the village of Izheskaye, in the Spassk district. His parents were peasants and he had very little formal education. Despite this disadvantage and despite being impeded by deafness, he showed a marked aptitude for scientific invention and from boyhood was particulary intrigued by anything connected with flight.

During the 1880s, Tsiolkovskii earned his living as a schoolteacher, but contined to work in his spare time on theoretical heavier-than-air flying machines and the possibility of flight into outer space. In 1883 he defined the 'principle of rocket motion', which proved that it is feasible for a rocket-propelled craft to travel through the vacuum of space. His brilliant conceptions on rocketry and space flight covered all aspects, including the use of 'high-energy' propellants. He never actually constructed a rocket, but his theories, sketches, and designs were fundamental in helping to establish the reality of space flight as we know it today. He died on 19 September 1935, just at the time when Robert Goddard (1882–1945) in the USA was launching his first liquid-fuelled rocket.

When Tsiolkovskii began his theoretical research, early flight in the form of balloons, airships, and fragile uncrewed aircraft had already determined many things about the Earth's atmosphere and gravitation. He calculated that in order to achieve flight into space, speeds of 11 km/7 mi per second or 40,200 kph/25,000 mph would be needed – the so-called escape velocity for Earth. Known solid fuels were too heavy for such rocket propulsion, so Tsiolkovskii concentrated on potential liquid fuels as propellants. In his notes he recorded, 'In a narrow part of the rocket tube the explosives mix, producing condensed and heated gases. At the other, wide end of the tube, the gases – rarefied and, consequently, cooled – escape through the nozzle with a very high relative velocity'. He also emphasized the value of what he called 'rocket trains' as a means of interplanetary travel. He suggested the 'piggyback' (or step) principle, with one rocket on top of another. When the lower one was expended, it could be jettisoned (reducing the weight) while the next one fired and took over.

Tsiolkovskii was one of three important pioneers working independently on the possibility of space flight. In the 1920s Hermann Oberth (1894–1989) in Germany wrote a book about his ideas and stimulated much interest, while in the USA Goddard carried the work further by designing and actually constructing a liquid-fuelled rocket in 1935. It attained a speed of more than 1,125 kph/700 mph and rose to a height of over 300 m/1,000 ft. How much of today's achievement in space travel can be attributed directly to the self-taught Russian genius is debatable, although Tsiolkovskii's work must at least have had a profound effect on thinking in his own country.

Tswett, Mikhail Semyonovich (1872–1919) Italian-born Russian scientist who made an extensive study of plant pigments and developed the technique of chromatography to separate them.

Tswett was born in Asti on 14 May 1872 of a Russian father and an Italian mother. His father was a civil servant in Russia, where his mother had grown up; they had stopped in Asti en route to Switzerland when he was born. His mother died soon afterwards and his father had to leave the baby with a nurse in Lausanne when he returned to Russia. Tswett spent his childhood and youth in Lausanne and Geneva and in 1891 he entered the department of mathematics and physics at Geneva University. He graduated in physical and natural sciences in 1893 and obtained his doctorate three years later. His first scientific publication, of 1894, was on plant anatomy. In 1897 he went to Russia to do research at the Academy of Sciences and the St Petersburg Biological Laboratory. His foreign degrees were not acceptable in Russia so he took an MSc degree at Kazan University in 1901. For the next six years he worked at Warsaw University in Poland before being offered a teaching appointment at the Warsaw Veterinary Institute. In 1908 he moved to the Warsaw Technical University and obtained a doctorate in botany in 1910. During World War I he organized the work of the botany department of the Warsaw Polytechnic Institute, which was evacuated to Moscow and Gorky (now Nizhniy-Novgorod). In 1917 he was appointed professor of botany and director of the Botanical Gardens at Yuriev University (Estonia), but under threat of German invasion had to move once again to Voronezh. He died there on 26 June 1919.

Tswett opposed the view that green leaves contain only two plant pigments, chlorophyll and xanthophyll. In 1900 he showed that there are two types of chlorophyll, termed chlorophyll *a* and chlorophyll *b,* which differ in colour and absorption spectra. He obtained a pure sample of chlorophyll *a,* but isolating the *b* type proved to be troublesome. By 1906 he had devised an adsorption method of separating the pigments. He ground up leaves in petroleum ether and let the liquid trickle down a glass tube filled with powdered chalk or alumina. As the mixture seeped downwards, each pigment showed a different degree of readiness to attach itself to the absorbent, and in this way the pigments became separated as different coloured layers in the tube. To get samples of single pigments, he pushed the adsorbent out of the tube, cut off the coloured pieces of the column with a knife, and extracted the pigment from each piece separately using a solvent. Tswett called the new technique 'chromatography' from the fact that the result of the analysis was 'written in colour' along the length of the adsorbent column. Eventually he found six different pigments. The new method attracted little attention until it was rediscovered by scientists such as Richard ◊Willstätter and Richard ◊Kuhn. By the late 1940s it had become one of the most versatile methods of chemical analysis, particularly in biochemistry, especially after Archer ◊Martin and Richard ◊Synge had developed paper chromatography.

Tull, Jethro (1674–1741) English lawyer and inventor of agricultural machinery, whose development of the seed drill revolutionized farming methods and helped to initiate the agricultural revolution.

Tull was born in Basildon, Berkshire (baptized 30 March). He attended St John's College, Oxford, and later became a law student at Gray's Inn, London, where he was called to the bar in May 1699. Ill-health, which had dogged him throughout much of his life, eventually forced him to return to the country, where he began to look with new eyes at the long-established methods of farming. He realized much could be done to improve the old system and his first invention, the seed drill of 1701, was an attempt to bring some order and economy into the process. Although local farmers were intrigued by his invention, they were reluctant to alter their ways until the advantages had been thoroughly proven. For the next 30 years, Tull was to struggle to bring his new ideas and inventions to agriculture, trying to change the system by simple reasoning and example. All of this he set down in his classic book on farming *The New Horse Houghing Husbandry* (1733).

When Tull turned to farming at the beginning of the 18th century, the strip system was still generally practised in most parts of the UK. Three common fields in a settlement were cultivated in rotation – two in use, one fallow. The fields were then divided up into approximately half-acre (0.2 hectare) strips, each one separated from the next by a grass balk or pathway; each person had the right to a strip in all three common fields.

Tull's first invention was the seed drill, designed to surmount the problems related to broadcast sowing, which was the traditional method. It was a revolutionary piece of equipment, designed to incorporate three previously separate actions into one: drilling, sowing, and covering the seeds. The drill consisted of a seed box capable of delivering the seed in a regulated amount, a hopper mounted above it for holding the seed, and a plough and harrow for cutting the drill (groove in the soil) and turning over the soil to cover the sown seeds.

Tull then experimented with implements for ploughing, paying particular attention to the different requirements for different types of soil. He devised the 'common two-wheeled plough' (or 'plow', as he called it), which could cut a furrow to a depth of about 17.5 cm/7 in on the lighter lands of the Midlands and southern England. It had a single coulter for making the vertical cut and a share for the horizontal one. This type of plough was not suitable for the heavy clay lands of the eastern region, and for these he developed a more sturdy swing plough with a longer horizontal beam and no wheels.

Although these ploughs proved successful to a certain extent, they did not solve one of the most difficult problems the farmer had to face: removing the top layer of grass and weeds. Often it was necessary to use a breast plough to cut through these before the main ploughing could take place. Tull solved this eventually by making a four-coulter plough, with blades set in such as way that the grass and roots were pulled up and left on the surface to dry. This was the final stage in the development of the plough, and basically the design is much the same today.

Tull was perhaps the initiator of the farming revolution that during the next hundred years was to raise the productivity of the land beyond the requirements of the immediate village. He and such contempories as Charles Townsend (1674–1738), nicknamed 'Turnip Townsend' because he was responsible for the introduction of turnips as a field crop for feeding livestock, enabling farmers to keep them alive through the winter, and Robert Bakewell (1725–1795) of Leicestershire, who did much to improve animal breeding, laid the foundation of the new agriculturalism, by which enough food would be provided to feed the masses in the coming Industrial Revolution.

Further Reading

Bourde, André J, *The Influence of England on the French Agronomes, 1750–1789*, Cambridge Studies in Economic History, Cambridge University Press, 1953.

Hidden, Norman, 'Jethro Tull, I, II, and III', *Agr Hist Rev*, 1989, v 37, pp 26–35.

Turing, Alan Mathison (1912–1954) English mathematician who worked in numerical analysis and played a major part in the early development of British computers.

Turing was born in London on 23 June 1912 into a family distinguished by its diplomats and engineers, three of whom had been elected to the Royal Society. He was educated at Sherborne School 1926–31, when he went to King's College, Cambridge to study mathematics. After receiving his BA in 1935, he was elected a fellow of the college on the strength of his paper 'On the Gaussian error function', which won a Smith's prize in mathematics in 1936. The paper was a characteristic example of the headstrong but brilliant nature of Turing's mathematical method throughout his life. He 'discovered' the central limit theorem in utter ignorance of the fact that it had already been discovered and proved.

In 1936 Turing went to the USA for two years to work at Princeton University with the mathematical logician Alonso ◊Church. There he worked on the theory of computation and in 1937 he presented to the London Mathematical Society the paper 'On computable numbers', which was his most famous contribution to mathematics. It constituted a proof that there exist classes of mathematical problems that are not susceptible of solution by fixed and definite processes, that is to say by automatic machines. He returned to King's College in 1938 and after the outbreak of World War II in 1939 was employed by the government Code and Cipher School at Bletchley Park. For his work in designing machines to break the German Enigma codes he was awarded an OBE in 1946.

After the war Turing joined the mathematics division of the National Physical Laboratory at Teddington, where he began immediately to work on the project to design the general computer known as the Automatic Computing Engine, or ACE. Although he left the project in 1947 to return to Cambridge, Turing played an important part in the theoretical work for the production of the ACE; a pilot version of the machine was in operation by 1950 and the mature version (like most computers of the time quickly rendered obsolete by newer machines) by 1957.

In 1948 Turing was appointed reader in the theory of computation at the University of Manchester and was made assistant director of the Manchester Automatic Digital Machine (MADAM). Two years later he published in *Mind* his trenchant discussion of the arguments against the notion that machines were able to think: 'Computing machinery and intelligence'. His conclusion was that, by his definition of 'thinking', it *was* possible to make intelligent machines.

In his last years at Manchester much of his work was done at home. All his life he had been concerned with mechanistic interpretations of the natural world and he now devoted himself to attempting to erect a mathematical theory of the chemical basis of organic growth. In this he was partly successful, since he was able to formulate and solve complicated differential equations to express certain examples of symmetry in biology and also certain phenomena such as the shapes of brown and black patches on cows. On 7 June 1954 he committed suicide by taking poison following a prosecution for a minor homosexual offence.

We do not need to have an infinity of different machines doing different jobs. A single one will suffice. The engineering problem of producing various machines for various jobs is replaced by the office work of 'programming' the universal machine to do these jobs.

ALAN TURING QUOTED IN A HODGES ALAN TURING: THE ENIGMA OF INTELLIGENCE 1985

Turing's place in the history of mathematics rests on the theory of computation which he worked out in 1936 and 1937. He suggested a basic machine that was not a mechanical device, but an abstract concept representing the operation of a computer. Quite simply, it was a paper tape, divided into squares, with a head for erasing, reading, or writing on each square and a mechanism for moving the tape to either the left or the right. The tape could have instructions already written on it and it was of either limited or unlimited length. So Turing's concept contained, in embryonic form, the now familiar notions of program, input, output, and – by implication – the processing of information. Turing machines were therefore of two types: machines designed to carry out a specific function and process information in a specified way and machines of a universal function capable of carrying out any procedure.

Further Reading

Clark, Andy and Millican, Peter (eds), *Connectionism, Concepts, and Folk Psychology: The Legacy of Alan Turing*, Mind Association Occasional series, Oxford University Press, 1997, v 2.

Gottfried, Ted, *Alan Turing: The Architect of the Computer Age*, Impact Biographies series, Franklin Watts Inc, 1996.

Hodges, Andrew, *Alan Turing: The Enigma of Intelligence*, Vintage, 1992.

Hodges, Andrew, *Turing: A Natural Philosopher*, The Great Philosophers series, Phoenix, 1997, v 3.

Millican, Peter and Clark, Andy (eds), *Machines and Thought: The Legacy of Alan Turing*, Mind Association Occasional series, Oxford University Press, 1997, v 1.

Strathern, Paul, *Turing and the Computer*, Big Idea series, Arrow, 1997.

Turing, Alan, *Enigma*, Springer-Verlag, 1994.

Turner, Charles Henry (1867–1923) US biologist and teacher who was internationally known for his research into insect behaviour patterns.

Turner was born on 3 February 1867 in Cincinnati, Ohio. On graduating from Cincinnati High School he went to study biology at the University of Cincinnati, receiving a BS degree in 1891 and an MS in 1892. He remained at the university for a year as an assistant instructor in the biology laboratory and then moved to Clark College, Atlanta, as professor of biology there until 1895. Turner went on to teach in public schools in Evansville, Indiana, and Cincinnati and in 1906 was principal of College Hill High School, Cleveland. From 1907 to 1908 he was professor of biology at Haines Normal and Industrial Institute, Augusta, Georgia, after which he moved to St Louis, Missouri, and taught biology at Sumner High School until his death in 1923.

Turner was an outstanding teacher but he is chiefly known for his research into insect behaviour. From 1892 until his death he conducted experiments on ants, bees, moths, spiders, and cockroaches and published over 50 papers on neurology, animal behaviour, and invertebrate ecology. In 1907, with his dissertation 'The homing of ants: an experimental study of ant behaviour', he was awarded a PhD by the University of Chicago. Turner was the first to prove that insects can hear and distinguish pitch and that cockroaches learn by trial and error; in French literature the turning movement of the ant towards its nest was given the name 'Turner's circling'. As well as scientific research, Turner also wrote nature stories for children and was active in the civil-rights movements in St Louis. After his death, a school for the physically handicapped was erected in St Louis and named the Charles H Turner School, renamed the Turner Middle School in 1954.

Twort, Frederick William (1877–1950) English bacteriologist, the original discoverer of bacteriophages (often called phages), the relatively large viruses that attack and destroy bacteria. He also researched into Johne's disease, a chronic intestinal infection of cattle. The only major honour that Twort received for his work was his election as a fellow of the Royal Society in 1929.

Twort was born on 22 October 1877 in Camberley, Surrey, the son of a physician. He studied medicine at St Thomas's Hospital, London, obtaining his degree in 1900. He then spent a year as assistant superintendent of the clinical laboratory at St Thomas's before becoming assistant bacteriologist at the London Hospital in 1902. In 1909 Twort was appointed superintendent of the Brown Institute, a pathology research centre. He remained there (except for a period of war service during World War I) until he retired 35 years later, having also been made professor of bacteriology at the

University of London in 1919. He died in Camberley on 20 March 1950.

Twort is probably best known for his discovery in 1915 of what is now called a bacteriophage. While working with cultures of *Staphylococcus aureus* (the bacterium that causes the common boil), he noticed that colonies of these bacteria were being destroyed. Twort isolated the substance that produced this effect and found that it was transmitted indefinitely to subsequent generations of the bacterium. He then suggested that the substance was a virus, a prediction that was later proved correct. He was unable to continue his work, however, and his discovery aroused little interest at the time. Two years later, in 1917, the same discovery was made independently by a Canadian bacteriologist, Félix d'Hérelle, who named the active substance 'bacteriophage'. Again, bacteriophages were virtually ignored and it was not until the 1950s, with the work of Heinz ◊Fraenkel-Conrat and others, that their importance was recognized. Since then bacteriophages have been widely used in microbiology, mainly for studying bacterial genetics and cellular control mechanisms.

Twort was also the first to culture the causative bacillus of Johne's disease, and showed that a specific substance is essential for the growth of this bacillus. In addition, he discovered that vitamin K is needed by growing leprosy bacteria, which opened a new field of research into the nutritional requirements of microorganisms.

Tyndall, John (1820–1893) Irish physicist who is mainly remembered for the Tyndall effect, which is the scattering of light by very small particles suspended in a medium. The discovery of this effect enabled Tyndall to explain the blue colour of the sky.

Tyndall was born in Leighlinbridge, Carlow, on 2 August 1820. He went to school in Carlow and then held a succession of surveying and engineering jobs in Ireland and England. In 1847, he became a teacher of mathematics at Queenswood College, Hampshire, where he was a colleague of the chemist Edward Frankland (1825–1899). Drawn to the study of science by Frankland, Tyndall left with him in 1848 to enter the University of Marburg, Germany. There Tyndall studied physics and mathematics, and also chemistry under Robert ◊Bunsen. Obtaining his doctorate in 1850, he returned to Queenwood in 1851, and in 1853 became professor of natural philosophy at the Royal Institution. From 1859 to 1868, Tyndall was also professor of physics at the Royal School of Mines.

In 1867, Tyndall became superintendent of the Royal Institution, succeeding Michael ◊Faraday. In his position as lecturer at the Royal Institution and as a journalist and writer, he did much to popularize science in the UK and also in the USA, where he toured 1872–73. Tyndall also championed those he believed had been wrongly treated, and was responsible for the recognition of the UK of the pioneering work done on the conservation of energy by Julius ◊Mayer. In 1886, Tyndall became seriously ill and he retired from the Royal Institution in the following year. He died from an accidental overdose of drugs at Hindhead, Surrey, on 4 December 1893.

The discovery of the Tyndall effect was made in 1869 when Tyndall was investigating the passage of light through liquids. He found that light passes unimpeded through a pure solvent or an ordinary solution, but that the beam becomes visible in a colloidal solution. Tyndall realized that the colloidal particles although invisible to the eye were big enough to scatter the light, and reasoned that a similar suspension of dust particles in the atmosphere causes the blue light in the sunlight passing through the atmosphere to be scattered more than the red, producing a blue sky. This explanation was confirmed by Lord ◊Rayleigh in 1871, who showed that the scattering is inversely proportional to the fourth power of the wavelength.

This work led Tyndall to consider the likelihood that the air contains living microorganisms, and he was able to show that pure air devoid of any suspended particles as indicated by the absence of the Tyndall effect did not produce putrefaction in foods. The air must therefore contain bacteria. This result was important in confirming the work of Louis ◊Pasteur that rejected the idea of the spontaneous generation of life, and it also inspired Tyndall to develop methods of sterilizing by heat treatment.

Tyndall also carried out experimental work on the absorption and transmission of heat by gases, especially water vapour and atmospheric gases, which was important in the development of meteorology.

Further Reading

Barton, Ruth, *John Tyndall, Oantheist: A Rereading of the Belfast Address,* Osiris, 1987, v 3, pp 111–134.

Kim, Stephen S, *John Tyndall's Transcendental Materialism and the Conflict Between Religion and Science in Victorian England,* Mellen University Press, 1996.

Sugiyama, Shigeo, 'The significance of the particulate conception of matter in John Tyndall's physical researches', *Hist Scientiarum,* 1992, v 2, pp 119–138.

U

Ulugh Beg (1394–1449) Title of Muhammad Taragay (Turkish 'great prince'). Mongol mathematician and astronomer, ruler of Samarkand from 1409 and of the Mongol Empire from 1447.

Beg was born in Sulaniyya in Central Asia (Persia) on 22 March 1394 and was brought up at the court of his grandfather Timur (Tamerlane). At the age of 15 Ulugh Beg became ruler of the city of Samarkand and the province of Maverannakhr. Although his grandfather was interested in conquest, Ulugh Beg's leanings were towards science and, in particular, astronomy. In 1420 he founded an institution of higher learning, or 'madrasa', in Samarkand. It specialized in astronomy and higher mathematics. Four years later he built a three-storey observatory and a 'Fakhrī' sextant of sufficiently large dimensions to enable very accurate observations to be made. The institution and observatory were advanced for the time and consequently the work of Ulugh Beg and his handpicked team of scientists held good for many centuries. In 1447 he succeeded his father, Shahrukh, to the Timurid throne, but he met a tragic and violent death when he was murdered at the instigation of his own son on 27 October 1449.

The observatory was reduced to ruins by the beginning of the 16th century and its precise location remained unknown until 1908, when the archaeologist V L Vyatkin found its remains. The main instrument proved to be the Fakhrī sextant, the arc of which was placed in a trench about 2 m/16.5 ft wide. The trench itself was dug into a hillside along the line of the meridian. One of the preserved artefacts is a piece of the arc consisting of two walls faced with marble and 51 cm/20 in apart. Other instruments used at the observatory included an armillary sphere, a triquetram, and a 'shamila', an instrument serving as astrolabe and quadrant.

The Fakhrī sextant was used mainly for determining the basic constants of astronomy by observing the Sun and, in particular, the Moon and planets. Since the radius of the arc was 40.4 m/132.6 ft, the divisions of the arc were correspondingly large, allowing for very accurate measurements to be made. By observing the altitude of the Sun at noon every day, Ulugh Beg was able to deduce the Sun's meridianal height, its distance from the zenith, and the inclination of the ecliptic. The value that he obtained for the inclination of the eclip-

tic differs by only 32 seconds from the true value for his time.

The *Zij* of Ulugh Beg and his school is a large work that was originally written in the Tadzhik language. It consists of a theoretical section and the results of observations made at the Samarkand Observatory. Included in the work are tables of calendar calculations, of trigonometry, and of the positions of planets, as well as a star catalogue.

Ulugh Beg and his collaborator Alkashi took great pains to determine accurately the sine of 1° by two independent methods. The tables give the values of sines and tangents for every minute to 45°, and for every 5 minutes between 45° and 90°. Cotangents are given for every degree. The values in the tables differ from the true values by a maximum of only one digit in the ninth decimal place.

The great accuracy to which the school worked is also evident in the values obtained for the movements of the planets Saturn, Jupiter, Mars, Venus, and Mercury. The differences between Beg's data and that of modern times are amazingly small, the discrepancies being within the limits of 2–5 seconds for the first four planets and 10 seconds at the most for Mercury. The somewhat larger discrepancy for the latter is attributable to Mercury's being smaller and having a higher orbital velocity and a greater eccentricity of orbit, which makes it more difficult to observe with the naked eye.

The catalogue of stars in the *Zij* contains 1,012 stars and includes 992 fixed stars whose positions Beg redetermined with unusual precision. This was the first star catalogue to be produced since that of Ḍal-Sufi, nearly five centuries earlier. Its great value lies in the fact that it was original, even though Beg was influenced by Ptolemy in the coordinates he used.

An expedition headed by T N Kari-Niazov discovered the tomb of Ulugh Beg in Samarkand in 1941. It was found that Ulugh Beg had been laid to rest fully clothed – a sign that, according to the Islamic religion, Ulugh Beg had been deemed a martyr, therefore a testament to his great contribution to the advancement of science, particularly astronomy.

Urey, Harold Clayton (1893–1981) US chemist who in 1931 discovered heavy water and deuterium, the isotope of hydrogen of mass 2. For this extremely significant discovery, which was to have a profound effect on future research in chemistry, physics, biology, and medicine, he was awarded the 1934 Nobel Prize for Chemistry.

Urey was born in Walkerton, Indiana, on 29 April 1893 and educated at schools in De Kelb County, Kendallville, and Walkerton. He graduated from high school in 1911 and worked as a schoolteacher for three years in Indiana and Montana. He went to Montana State University, Missoula, in 1917, gaining his BS degree three years later. During 1918 and 1919 he worked as a research chemist at the Barrett Chemical Company in Philadelphia, where he helped to produce war materials. From 1919 to 1921 he was an instructor in chemistry at Montana State University, and then went to the University of California in Berkeley, where he developed his interest in physical and mathematical chemistry. He received his PhD in 1923 and during the following year was a fellow of the American Scandinavian Foundation and attended the Institute of Theoretical Physics at the University of Copenhagen. He studied there under Niels ⟡Bohr, who was engaged on his pioneering work on the theory of atomic structure.

After Urey returned to the USA he worked for five years as an associate in chemistry at Johns Hopkins University in Baltimore, Maryland. Then from 1929 to 1934 he was associate professor of chemistry at Columbia University, New York City, and was Ernest Kempton Adams Fellow there 1933–36. He was appointed full professor of chemistry in 1934, and was the executive officer of the chemistry department 1939–42. During World War II he was director of research of the Substitute Alloy Materials Laboratories at Columbia, which became part of the Manhattan Project for the development of the atomic bomb. In 1945 Urey became professor of chemistry at the Institute of Nuclear Studies at the University of Chicago, and from 1952 to 1958 was Martin A Ryerson Professor of Chemistry there. In 1958 he was named professor-at-large of chemistry at the University of California in La Jolla; he was also a member of the Space Science Board of the Academy of Sciences. He died in La Jolla on 5 January 1981.

Urey discovered deuterium (heavy hydrogen, symbol D) in 1931 with F G Brickwedde and G M Murphy. He predicted that it would be possible to separate hydrogen from HD (whose molecules contain one hydrogen atom and one deuterium atom) by the distillation of liquid hydrogen, taking advantage of the difference in their vapour pressures. In heavy water, D_2O, both hydrogen atoms of normal water (H_2O) are replaced by deuterium atoms. Two years after its discovery by Urey, the US chemist Gilbert Newton obtained nearly pure heavy water by fractional electrolysis of water. Today it is manufactured by a process that involves isotopic chemical exchange between hydrogen sulphide and water. Its chief use is as a moderator to slow down fast neutrons in a nuclear reactor.

Urey was one of the first to calculate thermodynamic properties from spectroscopic data, particularly the equilibrium constants for exchange reactions between isotopes. He went on to isolate heavy isotopes of carbon, nitrogen, oxygen, and sulphur. Urey's group provided the basic information for the separation of the fissionable isotope uranium-235 from the much more common uranium-238 by gaseous diffusion of their fluorides. After World War II he worked on tritium for use in the hydrogen bomb.

The evolution of the Earth was another topic that exercised Urey's mind. It was traditionally believed a molten Earth had formed by processes similar to those that occur in oil-smelting furnaces. Today there is evidence to suggest that the Earth and other planets were formed by condensation and accumulation from a dust cloud at low temperatures. Urey theorized that the final accumulation of the Earth had occurred at 0°C/32°F from small planetary particles containing metallic iron, carbon, iron carbide, titanium nitride, and some ferrous (iron(II)) sulphide. He considered that most gases had been lost during the previous high-temperature phase, leaving a primitive atmosphere consisting of hydrogen, ammonia, methane, water vapour, nitrogen, and hydrogen sulphide. In 1952 he suggested that some of these molecules could have united spontaneously to form the basic 'building blocks' of life. The iron core of the Earth would have accumulated slowly through geological history from a mixture of metallic iron and silicates, meaning that the Earth was not molten at the time when its materials had accumulated. Urey also contributed to theories about the origin of the Moon, subscribing to the view that it had not formed from the Earth but had a separate origin.

Van Allen, James Alfred (1914–) US physicist who was closely involved with the early development of the US space programme and discovered the magnetosphere, the zone of high levels of radiation around the Earth caused by the presence of trapped charged particles. This region is popularly known as the Van Allen belt.

Van Allen was born in Mount Pleasant, Iowa, on 7 September 1914. He grew up there and then went to the Iowa Wesleyan College, where he received his BS degree in 1935. He then went to the University of Iowa, where he earned his MS in 1936 and his PhD in 1939. From 1939 to 1942, Van Allen worked as a research fellow at the Carnegie Institute in Washington, DC, in the department of terrestrial magnetism. During World War II, Van Allen served as an ordnance and gunnery officer with the US Navy. He participated in the development of the proximity fuse, which was a device attached to a missile such as an anti-aircraft shell so that it detonated when it neared the target and the radio waves it emitted were reflected back to it with sufficient intensity from the target. This meant that detonation could occur even when the missile had not been aimed sufficiently accurately for a direct hit, and this greatly increased the effectiveness of anti-aircraft weapons.

Van Allen's wartime work gave him experience with the miniaturization of sophisticated equipment, and it was put to good use in his next post 1946–50 as supervisor of the High Altitude Research Group and Proximity Fuse Unit in the applied physics department at Johns Hopkins University. During the period 1949–57, Van Allen organized and led scientific expeditions to Peru, the Gulf of Alaska, Greenland, and Antarctica to study cosmic radiation.

From 1951 to 1985, Van Allen was professor of physics and head of the physics department at the University of Iowa. From 1953 to 1954 he participated in Project Matterhorn (later the Princeton Plasma Physics Laboratory), which was concerned with the study of controlled thermonuclear reactions, and he also served as a research associate at Princeton University. Van Allen was then closely involved with the organization of International Geophysical Year, which took place from July 1957 to December 1958. From 1985 he was Carver Professor of Physics at Iowa, becoming Regent Distinguished Professor in 1990.

Van Allen's work immediately after the end of World War II involved utilization of the unused German stock of V2 rockets and of Aerobee rockets for research purposes. Devices for the measurement of the levels of cosmic radiation were sent to the outer regions of the atmosphere in these rockets, and the data were radioed back to Earth. In 1949 Van Allen conceived of rocket balloons (rockoons), which began to be used in 1952. They consisted of a small rocket that was lifted by means of a balloon into the stratosphere and then fired off, thus being able to reach heights attainable otherwise only by a much larger rocket. Van Allen's experience in the miniaturization of electronic equipment enabled him to include a maximum amount of instrumentation in the limited payload of these rockets, and this was to be crucial to the early stages of the US space programme.

The possibility of sending a rocket into orbit around the Earth, thereby creating an artificial satellite, was finally given serious consideration by the US government in the mid-1950s. President Eisenhower announced the Vanguard Program in 1955, which promised to put an artificial satellite into orbit within two years to coincide with the scheduled International Geophysical Year, which was itself timed to coincide with a peak in solar activity. Van Allen was given the responsibility for the instrumentation of the proposed satellites.

Van Allen was on a scientific expedition to the Antarctic when the news of the world's first artificial satellite, the Russian *Sputnik 1,* broke on 4 October 1957. This precipitated great activity in the US camp, and the first US satellite, *Explorer 1,* was launched on 31 January 1958. Part of *Explorer*'s payload was a Geiger counter that Van Allen had intended to use to measure the levels of cosmic radiation, but at a height of about 800 km/500 mi the counters registered a radiation level of zero. This was an absurd reading, and instrument failure was suspected. When the same result was recorded by *Explorer 3,* which was launched on 26 March 1958, Van Allen realized that the zero reading could have resulted from the counters being swamped with very high counts of radiation. The counter that was sent up with *Explorer 4* on 26 July 1958 was shielded with lead in order to allow less radiation to penetrate, and this showed clearly that parts of space contained much higher levels of radiation than had previously been suspected.

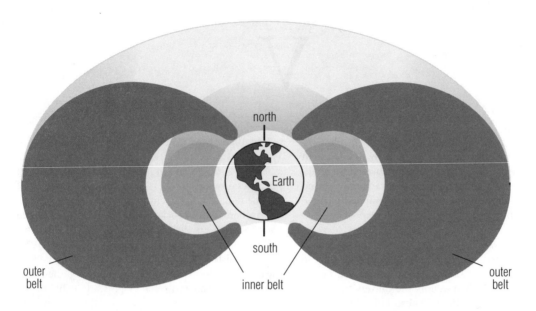

Van Allen The Van Allen belts of trapped charged particles are a hazard to spacecraft, affecting on-board electronics and computer systems. Similar belts have been discovered around the planets Mercury, Jupiter, Saturn, Uranus, and Neptune.

Van Allen studied the size and distribution of the high radiation zones. He found that it consists of two toroidal belts around the Earth, which arise by the trapping of charged particles in the Earth's magnetic field. They were named the Van Allen belts, but are now more usually known as the magnetosphere.

van de Graaff, Robert Jemison (1901–1967) US physicist who designed and built the electrostatic high-voltage generator named after him.

Van de Graaff was born in Tuscaloosa, Alabama, on 20 December 1901. He studied to be an engineer, obtaining a BS degree from the University of Alabama in 1922 and an MS a year later. He worked for a short while for the Alabama Power Company, but left in 1924 to attend the Sorbonne in Paris for further study. There van de Graaff was deeply impressed by lectures given by Marie Curie (see Marie and Pierre ◊Curie), which focused his attentions on the exciting developments in atomic physics. In 1925, he went to the UK to study at Oxford under John ◊Townsend, receiving a BSc in 1926 and a PhD in 1928. Van de Graaff conceived the idea of his generator at this time and returned to the USA in 1929 to develop it. He built a working model at Princeton University, where he served as a national research fellow 1929–31. He then undertook further development at the Massachusetts Institute of Technology (MIT), where he was appointed research associate in 1931. Van de Graaff then became associate professor of physics at MIT in 1934, and retained his position until 1960, when he

resigned to devote all his time to the High Voltage Engineering Corporation (HVEC), a company he had set up in 1946 with John Trump. Van de Graaff died in Boston on 16 January 1967.

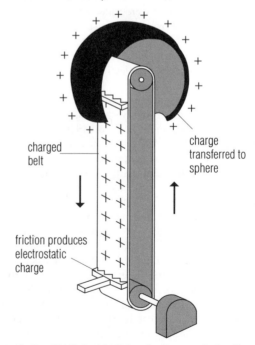

van de Graaff US physicist Robert Jemison van de Graaff developed this high-powered generator that can produce more than a million volts. Experiments involving charged particles make use of van de Graaff generators as particle accelerators.

Van de Graaff's main work at Oxford concerned the mobility of ions in the gaseous state, but he saw the need for beams of high-energy subatomic particles in the study of the properties of atoms. He realized that a high potential could be built up by storing electrostatic charge within a hollow sphere and that this could be achieved by depositing charges on to a moving belt that carries the charges into the sphere, where a collector transfers them to the sphere's outer surface. Van de Graaff's first working model, constructed in 1929, operated at 80,000 volts and he soon upgraded this to 2 million volts, and eventually to 5 million volts. At MIT, the generator was developed so that it could be used to accelerate subatomic particles to very high velocities, and this technology was then immediately applied to nuclear investigations and also to clinical research. Trump and van de Graaff collaborated to modify the generator so that it could be used in the generation of hard X-rays for use in radiotherapy in treating internal tumours and the first machine, a 1-MeV (1 million electronvolts) X-ray generator, was installed in a Boston hospital in 1937.

During World War II, the US Navy commissioned the production of five generators with 2-MeV capacity for use in the X-ray examination of munitions. The experience gained during these years enabled van de Graaff to set up HVEC for the commercial production of generators. The company developed the van de Graaff generator for the wide variety of scientific, medical, and industrial research purposes in which it is employed today. The tandem principle of particle acceleration and a new insulating core transformer invented by van de Graaff contributed to these advances.

Further Reading

Rowlands, J J, 'Van de Graaff electrostatic generator', *Technol Rev*, 1961, v 63 (3), pp 33–36.

Vandermonde, Alexandre-Théophile (1735–1796)

French musician and musical theorist who wrote original and influential papers on algebraic equations and determinants.

Vandermonde was born in Paris on 28 February 1735. Being a somewhat sickly child he was educated privately – at first chiefly in music, the sphere in which he was expected to make his career. But the tuition of the French geometrician Alexis Fontaine des Bertins (1705–1771), awakened his mathematical interest, and although he later wrote some skilful papers on musical composition, the early years of his maturity were devoted to mathematics. Fontaine introduced him to leading members of the French Academy of Sciences and in 1771, before he had written a single scientific paper or made any very

remarkable discovery, he was elected to the academy. In the next two years he presented to the academy the only four mathematical papers he ever wrote. He played a part in the founding of the Conservatoire des Arts et des Métiers and served as its director from 1782. In the 1780s he also collaborated with his close friend Gaspard ◊Monge and with the chemist Claude ◊Berthollet in an analysis of the difference between pig iron and steel, which was published in 1786. He died in Paris on 1 January 1796.

Of Vandermonde's four mathematical papers, the most celebrated are the first and the fourth. The first, regarded by some mathematicians as his best, considered the solvability of algebraic equations. Vandermonde found formulae for solving general quadratic equations, cubic equations, and quartic equations. Joseph ◊Lagrange published similar results at about the same time, but Vandermonde's two methods of solution for solving lower order equations – called substitution and combination – were independently worked out by him. In addition he found the solution to the equation:

$$x^{11} - 1 = 0$$

and stated, without giving a proof, that

$$x^n - 1 = 0$$

must have a solution where n is a prime number.

The fourth paper occupies a controversial place in the history of mathematics. Some mathematicians regard it as a decisive moment in the establishment of the theory of determinants; others consider that, although it might be the first coherent statement of the theory, its content had mostly already been published in other forms. Whatever the truth of the matter, the paper did include the Vandermonde determinant, his best-known contribution to mathematics.

The second paper may have influenced Karl ◊Gauss in his work on electrical potentials; the third was a relatively unimportant work on factorials. It is really on the strength of two papers, written within a year of each other, that Vandermonde (who subsequently contributed nothing at all to mathematics) earned a permanent place in the subject's history.

van der Waals, Johannes Diderik (1837–1923)

Dutch scientist whose theoretical work on gases made an important contribution to chemistry and physics, a fact recognized by the award to him of the 1910 Nobel Prize for Physics. His theories about interatomic forces also added to knowledge about molecular structure and chemical bonding.

Van der Waals was born in Leiden on 23 November 1837, the son of a carpenter. He began his career as a primary school teacher, then entered Leiden University in 1862 to study physics, while at the same time working as a secondary school physics teacher, becoming headmaster of a school at The Hague in 1866. Following on from the work of Rudolf ◊Clausius and other molecular theorists, van der Waals laid the foundation for most of his future studies in his doctoral thesis of 1873, 'Over de continuiteit van den gasen vloeistoftoestand/On the continuity of the gaseous and liquid states'. It received immediate recognition and was soon translated into other European languages. In 1887 he became professor of physics at the new University of Amsterdam (formerly the Amsterdam Athenaeum), and remained there until he retired in 1907; he was succeeded by his son. He died in Amsterdam, after a long illness, on 8 March 1923.

Using fairly simple mathematics, van der Waals's 1873 thesis explained in molecular terms various phenomena of vapours and liquids that had been observed experimentally by Thomas ◊Andrews and others, especially the existence of critical temperature (above which a gas or vapour cannot be liquefied by pressure alone, no matter how great). The law of corresponding states that van der Waals developed some years later gave a somewhat better 'fit' between the theory and the experimental data and became a useful guide in work on the liquefaction of the so-called permanent gases.

The van der Waals equation of state attempts to explain the behaviour of real gases, as opposed to the 'ideal' or 'perfect' gas laws of Robert ◊Boyle, Jacques ◊Charles, and Joseph ◊Gay-Lussac, which combined to give the equation:

$$PV = RT$$

it still links pressure P, volume V, and absolute temperature T, but introduces two other constants a and b (R remains the universal gas constant):

$$(P + a/V^2)(V - b) = RT$$

The term a/V^2 accounts for intermolecular attraction, determined by integrating over an 'attraction sphere' that extends round each molecule. The constant b accounts for the non-overlapping of molecules and their finite size. Both constants, a and b, are different for different gases. Van der Waals was also able to work out equations for isotherms (how the volume of a gas or liquid changes with pressure at a particular temperature) and calculate the parameters of the critical point.

By extension, van der Waals's results were also applied to other thermodynamic quantities and phenomena, such as the Joule–Thomson effect, saturated vapour pressures, supercooling, and so on.

The cohesive attraction between molecules in a liquid became known as van der Waals forces. The same forces are postulated for molecular crystals such as those of graphite and naphthalene. In graphite, for

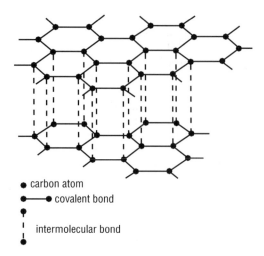

● carbon atom
●——● covalent bond
●
¦ intermolecular bond
¦
●

van der Waals van der Waals's forces in graphite.

example, normal covalent bonds hold together hexagonal arrays of carbon atoms in planes, which are themselves bonded in parallel 'layers' by van der Waals forces. A shearing force can fairly readily overcome these weak forces, allowing the planes to slip or slide over each other, which accounts for the existence of well-defined cleavage planes in solid graphite and its effectiveness as a lubricant.

Further Reading

Kipnis, A; Yavelov, B E; and Rowlinson, J S, *Van Der Waals and Molecular Science*, Oxford University Press, 1996.

Langbein, D, *Theory of Van Der Waals Attraction*, Tracts in Modern Physics series, Springer-Verlag, 1974, v 72.

Rowlinson, J S (ed), *J D Van Der Waals: On the Continuity of the Gaseous and Liquid States*, Studies in Statistical Mechanics series, Elsevier Science, 1988, v 14.

van't Hoff, Jacobus Henricus (1852–1911) Dutch theoretical chemist who made major contributions to stereochemistry, reaction kinetics, thermodynamics, and the theory of solutions. In 1901 he was awarded the first Nobel Prize for Chemistry.

Van't Hoff was born in Rotterdam on 30 August 1852, the son of a doctor. At school he showed great ability at mathematics, but decided to study chemistry at the polytechnic at Delft. In 1871 he attended the University of Leiden, and a year later went to Bonn to study under Friedrich ◊Kekulé, who was unimpressed by his Dutch student, so van't Hoff moved to Paris and worked with Charles Adolphe ◊Wurtz at the Ecole de Médecine. He returned to the Netherlands and obtained his doctorate at Utrecht in 1874, taking up a lectureship in physics at the veterinary college there two years later. In 1878 he became professor of chemistry, mineralogy, and geology at the University of Amsterdam and stayed there until 1896. In that year he moved to Berlin to become a professor to the Prussian Academy of Sciences, with an honorary professorship at Berlin University as well. He remained there until he died, in Berlin, on 1 March 1911.

Van't Hoff had made his first major contribution to chemistry even before he was awarded his doctorate. In 1874 he announced the results of his research into conformational analysis of organic compounds, which hinged on what we would now call the stereochemistry of the carbon atom. He postulated that the four valencies of a carbon atom are directed towards the corners of a regular tetrahedron. This allows it to be asymmetric (connected to four different atoms or groups) in certain compounds, and it is these compounds that exhibit optical activity. Van't Hoff ascribed the ability to rotate the plane of polarized light to the asymmetric carbon atom in the molecule, and showed that optical isomers are left- and right-handed forms (mirror images) of the same molecule. A similar idea was put forward independently in Paris two months later by Joseph le Bel, who had studied under Wurtz at the same time as had van't Hoff.

Van't Hoff's first ideas about chemical thermodynamics and affinity were published in 1877, and consolidated in his *Etudes de dynamique chimique* (1884), translated into English in 1886. He applied thermodynamics to chemical equilibria, developing the principles of chemical kinetics and describing a new method of determining the order of a reaction. He deduced the connection between the equilibrium constant and temperature in the form of an equation known as the van't Hoff isochore. He generalized it in the form of what he called the principle of mobile equilibrium, which is a special case of Le Châtelier's principle, which he had independently formulated in the same year. It may be stated thus:

If a change occurs in one of the factors (such as temperature or pressure) under which a system is in equilibrium, the system will adjust itself so as to annul, as far as possible, the effect of that change.

In the field of reaction kinetics, van't Hoff announced his findings at the same time as, but independently of, Cato Guldberg, and Peter Waage in 1867. They all developed the fundamental law of reaction kinetics that assumes that, at constant temperature, the rate of any simple chemical reaction is proportional to the product of the concentrations of the various reacting substances – a statement of the law of mass action.

Van't Hoff also introduced the modern concept of chemical affinity as the maximum work obtainable as the result of a reaction, and he showed how it can be calculated from measurements of osmotic pressure, gas pressure, and the electromotive force of reversible galvanic cells. In 1886 he published the results of his study of dilute solutions and showed the analogy between them and gases, because they both obey equations of the type $PV = RT$.

In the 1880s he became a friend of Svante ◊Arrhenius. The theories of van't Hoff on osmotic pressure and those of Wilhelm ◊Ostwald on the affinity of acids accorded well with Arrhenius's views on electrolytes and the three scientists worked together to get their new theories accepted. In 1887 they started the important journal *Zeitschrift für physikalische Chemie*, whose first volume contained the famous paper by Arrhenius on electrolytic dissociation and the fundamental paper of van't Hoff. He was the first to apply thermodynamies systematically to solutions, although the treatment could have been more generally applicable had he used the thermodynamic system derived by Willard ◊Gibbs 1875–79.

Further Reading

Ramsay, Ogden B (ed), *Van't Hoff – LeBel Centennial: A Symposium*, ACS Symposium Series, American Chemical Society, 1974, v 12.

Holleman, A F, 'My reminiscences of Van't Hoff', *J Chem Educ*, 1952, v 29, pp 379–382.

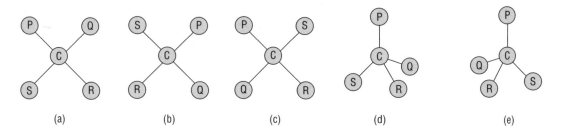

(a)   (b)   (c)   (d)   (e)

van't Hoff van't Hoff introduced the idea of a tetrahedral carbon atom. The three square structures (a), (b), and (c) are all equivalent (rotating (b) 90° anticlockwise gives (a): rotating (c) 180° along the axis P–R also gives (a)). The tetrahedral structures (d) and (e) are mirror images of each other, but one cannot be rotated in any way to make it the same as the other: they represent a pair of (optical) stereoisomers.

Van Vleck, John Hasbrouck (1899–1980) US physicist who made important contributions to our knowledge of magnetism, as a result of which he is widely considered to be one of the founders of modern magnetic theory. He received many honours for his work, including the 1977 Nobel Prize for Physics, which he was awarded jointly with Philip ◊Anderson and Nevill ◊Mott.

Van Vleck was born in Middletown, Connecticut, on 13 March 1899, the son of a mathematics professor. He was educated at the University of Wisconsin, from which he graduated in 1920, and at Harvard University, from which he gained his master's degree in 1921 and his doctorate in 1922. He then stayed at Harvard as an instructor in physics until 1923, when he went to the University of Minnesota as an assistant professor. In 1927 he married Abigail Pearson, and was promoted to full professor of physics at Minnesota. He was professor of physics at Wisconsin University 1928–34 – during which period he was a Guggenheim Foundation Fellow 1930 – then returned to Harvard. He remained at Harvard until formally retiring in 1969, having been Hollis Professor of Mathematics and Natural Philosophy since 1951; on retiring he was made an emeritus professor. While at Harvard he held various other positions in addition to the Hollis professorship: dean of engineering and applied physics 1951–57, Lorentz Professor at Leiden University, the Netherlands, in 1960; and Eastman Professor at Oxford University 1962–63. Van Vleck died in Cambridge, Massachusetts, on 27 October 1980.

Van Vleck devoted most of his career to studying magnetism, particularly its relationship to atomic structure. With the coming of quantum wave mechanics in the early 1930s he began investigating its implications for magnetism and devised a theory – using wave mechanics – that gives an accurate explanation of the magnetic properties of individual atoms in a series of chemical elements. He also introduced the idea of temperature-independent susceptibility in paramagnetic materials – a phenomenon now called Van Vleck paramagnetism – and drew attention to the importance of electron correlation (the interaction between the movements of electrons) in the appearance of localized magnetic moments in metals. His most important work, however, was probably his formulation of the ligand field theory, which is still one of the most useful tools for interpreting the patterns of chemical bonds in complex compounds. This theory explains the magnetic, electrical, and optical properties of many elements and compounds by considering the influences exerted on the electrons in particular atoms by other atoms nearby.

Van Vleck also worked on radar during World War II. He found that water molecules in the atmosphere absorb radar waves with a wavelength of about 1.25 cm/0.5 in, and that oxygen molecules have a similar effect on radar waves with a wavelength of 0.5 cm/0.2 in. This finding was important for the development of effective radar systems and, later, in microwave communications and radio astronomy.

Vauquelin, Louis Nicolas (1763–1829) French chemist who worked mainly in the inorganic field analysing minerals and is best known for his discoveries of chromium and beryllium. He rose from humble origins to be one of the most influential scientists of his time.

Vauquelin was born in Saint-André d'Héberôt, Calvados, on 16 May 1763, the son of a Normandy farm labourer. He too worked on the land as a boy until 1777 when he became apprenticed to an apothecary in Rouen. Two years later he moved to Paris and eventually became a laboratory assistant at the Jardin du Roi under Antoine Fourcroy (1755–1809), who recognized Vauquelin's ability, befriended him, and began a nine-year collaboration. In 1791 he was made a member of the Academy of Sciences and from that time he helped to edit the journal *Annales de chimie*, although two years later he left the country for a while during the height of the French Revolution. On his return in 1794 he became professor of chemistry at the Ecole des Mines in Paris. He described various analytical techniques in his *Manuel de l'essayeur* (1799), which led in 1802 to his being appointed to the position of assayer to the Mint. On Fourcroy's death in 1809 he succeeded him as professor of chemistry at the University of Paris (and gave a home to Fourcroy's two elderly sisters). He was elected to the Chamber of Deputies in 1828 and died a year later, in his birthplace, on 14 November 1829.

Vauquelin did most of his important work in inorganic chemistry in the late 1790s while he was at the Ecole des Mines. He analysed various minerals, often using specimens supplied by the mineralogist René ◊Haüy. In a Siberian lead mineral called crocolite he discovered chromium in 1797, naming the element from the Greek *chroma* ('colour') because so many of its compounds are brightly coloured. (Martin ◊Klaproth made the same discovery a few months later.) Vauquelin also examined emeralds and the mineral beryl and recognized that they contained another new element that was eventually called beryllium, although at first he called it glucinium because of the sweet taste of some of its salts. The element itself was not isolated until 1828 by Friedrich ◊Wöhler.

In organic chemistry, Vauquelin also made some significant discoveries. In 1806, working with asparagus, he isolated the amino acid aspargine, the first one to be discovered. He also discovered pectin and malic acid in apples, and isolated camphoric acid and quinic acid.

Vening Meinesz, Felix Andries (1887–1966)

Dutch geophysicist who originated the method of making very precise gravity measurements in the stable environment of a submarine. The results he obtained were important in the fields of geophysics and geodesy.

Vening Meinesz was born in The Hague on 30 July 1887, and took a degree in civil engineering at the Technical University of Delft in 1910. He was first employed by the government to take part in a gravimetric survey of Holland. Over the next decade he took measurements at over 50 sites, and was particularly concerned with overcoming the problem of inaccuracies caused by unstable support for his apparatus. His PhD thesis, submitted to the Technical University of Delft in 1915, dealt with this problem. Vening Meinesz developed a device that required the measurement of the mean periods of two pendulums swinging from the same apparatus. The mean of the two periods is not affected by disturbances in the horizontal plane, and so can be used to determine the local gravitational force accurately.

From 1923 to 1939, Vening Meinesz undertook 11 scientific expeditions at sea in submarines. He was fortunate in receiving the cooperation of the Royal Netherlands Navy. The outbreak of World War II put a temporary stop to such peaceful uses of submarines, but expeditions were resumed in the late 1940s. By then it was Vening Meinesz's younger associates who actually put out to sea, but his pendulum apparatus was the only one suited to marine gravimetric measurement until the end of the 1950s. Spring gravimetric devices have since been developed that can be mounted on stable platforms in surface vessels, but Vening Meinesz's method has been applied in thousands of measurements around the world.

Vening Meinesz became professor of cartography at the University of Utrecht in 1927, and in 1935 was also made professor of geophysics at the same university. He held both these posts until 1957, and from 1938 to 1957 he also held the simultaneous post of professor of physical geodesy at the University of Delft. Vening Meinesz died in Amersfort on 10 August 1966.

During the course of his early research, Vening Meinesz realized that measurements of the Earth's gravitational field could yield important indications of the nature of the internal features of the Earth itself. A prerequisite of such study would be the ability to make accurate measurements of the Earth's gravitational field in as many different places as possible. Values could be obtained on land with relative ease, although they might be subject to large distortions by the presence of local features such as mountains. Measurement at sea was made impossible by turbulence caused by waves and wind, but was most desirable because so much of the Earth's surface is covered by ocean and because there are fewer problems with local geographic features as the sea bed is the nearest source of distortion.

It was suggested to Vening Meinesz that gravimetric experiments could be conducted below the sea's surface in submarines because disruption from waves decreases exponentially with the depth of the submarine. On his first voyage, Vening Meinesz found that once he had modified the design of his apparatus to compensate for the craft's rolling, he was indeed able to make very accurate measurements.

One of the earliest important findings to arise from these studies was the discovery of low-gravity belts in the Indonesian Archipelago running from Sumatra to the Mindanao Deep. Vening Meinesz proposed this to have arisen as a result of a downward buckling of the crust causing light sediments to fill the resulting depressions. This is the origin of the concept of the geosyncline. Vening Meinesz later returned to the question of crustal deformation and suggested it to be a consequence of convection currents arising from the cooling of the Earth at its surface. He elaborated this into a short-lived hypothesis that denied the existence of continental drift, but abundant evidence was soon amassed to support the view that continental drift does occur and is driven by convection currents in the mantle.

The results Vening Meinesz obtained on his expeditions at sea were also applied in the field of geodesy, which is concerned with the analysis of the Earth's shape. He showed that the equilibrium shape of a rotating ellipsoid is disrupted by irregularly distributed masses, but that the height of these anomalous masses does not exceed 40 km/25 mi. He was able to discount the model of the Earth's shape that proposed a flattening at the equator.

Venn, John (1834–1923)

English logician whose diagram, known as the Venn diagram, is much used in the teaching of elementary mathematics.

Venn was born in Drypool, Hull, on 4 August 1834 into a prominent Anglican family. When he was a young boy his father moved to London to take up an appointment as honorary secretary to the Church Missionary Society and he was educated first at Sir Roger Cholmley's School (now Highgate School). In 1853 he matriculated at Gonville and Caius College, Cambridge. He was elected a mathematical scholar in 1854 and gained his BA in 1857. In the same year he was elected a fellow of the college; he remained a fellow all his life.

Given his family background it was no surprise that Venn was ordained as a deacon at Ely in 1858 and as a priest in 1859. He then held curacies at Cheshunt, Hertfordshire, and Mortlake, Surrey, before returning to Cambridge in 1862 as a college lecturer in moral sciences. For the next 30 years his chief interest was in logic, a subject to which he contributed a trilogy of standard texts: *The Logic of Chance* (1866), *Symbolic Logic* (1881), and *The Principles of Empirical Logic* (1889). While he was pursuing his logical research, Venn became infected by the crisis of belief prevalent in high Victorian, post-Darwinian England and, although he never lost his faith, he found himself unable any longer to subscribe to the Thirty-Nine Articles of the Church of England and abjured his clerical orders in 1883. In the same year he was elected to the Royal Society and awarded a ScD by the University of Cambridge. After publishing his third volume of logic, he turned increasingly to the history of the uni-

versity and the three-volume biographical history of Gonville and Caius (1897) was almost entirely his work. He died in Cambridge on 4 April 1923.

Venn is remembered chiefly for his logical diagrams. The use of geometrical representations to illustrate syllogistic logic was not new (they had been used consistently by Gottfried ◊Leibniz), and Venn came to be highly critical of the various diagrammatic methods prevalent in the 19th century, in particular those of George ◊Boole and Augustus ◊De Morgan. Neither Boole's algebraic logic nor De Morgan's formal logic satisfied him and it was largely in order to interpret and correct Boole's work that he wrote his *Symbolic Logic*. In it appeared the diagrams that have since become universally known as Venn diagrams.

Before publishing *Symbolic Logic*, Venn had adopted the method of illustrating propositions by means of exclusive and inclusive circles; in the new book he added the new device of shading the segments of the circles to represent the possibilities that were excluded by the propositions at issue. It was these diagrams, more than his attempt to clarify what he considered to be inconsistencies and ambiguities in Boole's logic, which constituted the real merit of the book. His diagrams were based on his belief that those that merely represented the relations between two classes or two propositions were not sufficiently general; later, he extended his method by proposing a series of circles dividing the plane into compartments, so that each successive circle should intersect all the compartments already existing. It was this idea, taken up and refined by Charles ◊Dodgson (Lewis Carroll), which led to the use of the closed compartment enclosing the whole diagram to define the universe of discourse – or what is now known as the universal set.

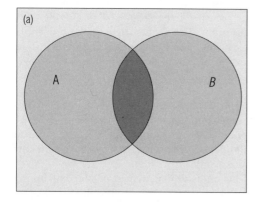

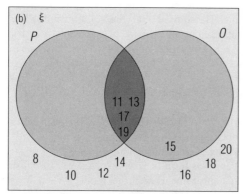

ξ = set of whole numbers from 1 to 20
O = set of odd numbers
P = set of prime numbers

Venn Sets and their relationships are often represented by Venn diagrams. The sets are drawn as circles – the area of overlap between the circles shows elements that are common to each set, and thus represent a third set. Here (a) is a Venn diagram of two intersecting sets and (b) a Venn diagram showing the set of whole numbers from 1 to 20 and the subsets P and O of prime and odd numbers, respectively. The intersection of P and O contains all the prime numbers that are also odd.

Vernier, Pierre (1584–1638) French engineer and instrument-maker who devised the precision measuring scale now named after him.

Vernier inherited an interest in scientific measuring instruments from his father, who was keeper of the château of Ornans, a lawyer by training, and probably also an engineer. Vernier worked as an engineer for the military under the Spanish Habsburgs, who at the time ruled the Franche-Comté, and he realized the need for a more accurate way of reading angles on the surveying instruments he used in mapmaking. He was aware of the work of the Portuguese mathematician and astronomer Filde Nunez Salaciense, who, working on the same problem in about 1540, arrived at the idea of engraving on the face of an astrolabe a series of fixed scales laid out in concentric circles. On any one circle the scale was determined by dividing its circumference into an equal number of parts, one fewer than those dividing the next circle out but one more than those on the next circle in. Thus a line of sight (to, say, a star) would inevitably fall very close to a whole division on one of the scales. By calculation or by using tables it was possible accurately to determine the angle in degrees, minutes, and seconds. But in practice it was extremely difficult to engrave with precision a different scale on each of the circles. As Tycho ◊Brahe remarked, Nunez's method failed to live up to its promise.

Fifty years later Clavius (a former student of Nunez) found a way of engraving the scales and his associate Jacobus Curtins further simplified the system so that angles could be read off directly (although 60 separate scales were required). The system was described in Clavius's *Geometrica practica* of 1604, which Vernier probably studied.

Vernier's solution to the problem was to use a single moveable scale, rather than a series of fixed ones, thus avoiding the difficulties of multiple engraving. The mobile scale was graduated with nine divisions equalling the space occupied by ten graduations on the main scale. In this way the accuracy of the reading was increased by a factor of ten. By this time, 1630, his reputation as an outstanding engineer was established and Vernier was appointed Conseiller et Général des Monnaies to the Count of Burgundy. He made a special journey to Brussels to present his invention to Isabelle-Clair-Eugénie, the Infanta of Spain and ruler of Franche-Comté, who told him to publish a description of it. After doing so in 1631 Vernier returned to Dôle where he designed and directed the building of fortifications. His other engineering projects included the design of a building for the harquebusiers of Dôle, but in 1636 ill health forced him to give up engineering and he returned to Ornans, where he died a few years later on 16 September 1638.

Vesalius, Andreas (1514–1564) Belgian physician who was a founder of modern anatomy.

Vesalius was born in Brussels on 13 December 1514, to a family of physicians from Wesel (the derivation of Vesalius) in Germany. His father was the royal pharmacist to Charles V of Germany, and from an early age Vesalius showed an inclination to follow in the family tradition, by dissecting dead birds and mice. He was educated at the University of Louvain and then studied medicine in Paris. After a period as a military surgeon, he moved to Padua, Italy, where he gained his medical degree in 1537, and was then appointed lecturer in surgery and anatomy. At Padua he published his famous book *De humani corporis fabrica/On the Structure of the Human Body* (1543), which met with vigorous opposition and led to bitter controversy. In a fit of despondency, he gave up anatomy and resigned his chair at Padua. He became court physician to Charles V and later to his son Philip II of Spain. On his way back from

Vesalius Belgian medical scientist Andreas Vesalius, the founder of modern anatomy. He introduced the practice of hands-on dissection and anatomical drawing, techniques which allowed him to make accurate observations. *Mary Evans Picture Library*

a pilgrimage to Jerusalem, on 15 October 1564, he died in a shipwreck off the Greek island of Zante (Zákynthos).

Vesalius was taught anatomy in the Galenist tradition. ◊Galen had never dissected a human body – all his accounts of the human anatomy were based on his research of the Barbary ape – although he was regarded as infallible and was venerated until the Renaissance; Vesalius was therefore taught principles of anatomy that had not been questioned for 1,300 years.

The artists of Vesalius's time encouraged the study of anatomy because they wanted accurate representations of the human body. The greatest of these were ◊Leonardo da Vinci, Albrecht Dürer (1471–1528), and Michelangelo (1475–1564). Leonardo, who made more than 750 anatomical drawings, paved the way for Vesalius. Vesalius became dissatisfied with the instruction he had received and resolved to make his own observations, which disagreed with Galen's. For instance, he disproved that men had one rib fewer than women – a belief that had been widely held until then. He also believed, contrary to ◊Aristotle's theory of the heart being the centre of the mind and emotion, that the brain and the nervous system are the centre.

Between 1539 and 1542 Vesalius prepared his masterpiece, a book that employed talented artists to provide the illustrations. The finished work, published in 1543 in Basel, is one of the great books of the 16th century. The quality of anatomical depiction introduced a new standard into all illustrated works and especially into medical books. The text, divided into seven sections, is of great importance in expressing the need to introduce scientific method into the study of anatomy. The *De humani corporis fabrica* did for anatomy what ◊Copernicus's book did for astronomy (they were both published in the same year). Vesalius upset the authority of Galen and his book, the first real textbook of anatomy, marks the beginning of biology as a science.

Further Reading

Fulton, John Farquhar, *Vesalius Four Centuries Later: Medicine in the Eighteenth Century,* Logan Clendening Lectures on the History and Philosophy of Medicine, First Series, University of Kansas Press, 1950.

Heseler, Baldasar; Erikkson, Ruben (ed), *Andreas Vesalius' First Public Anatomy at Bologna, 1540: An Eyewitness Report,* Lychnos-Bibliotek, Almqvist & Wiksells, 1959, v 18.

O'Malley, Charles Donald, *Andreas Vesalius of Brussels, 1514–1564,* University of California Press, 1964.

Viète, François (1540–1603) French mathematician, the first extensively to use letters of the alphabet to represent numerical quantities and the foremost algebraist of the 16th century.

Viète was born in Fontenay-le-Comte, in the Poitou region, in 1540. He was educated locally until 1556, when he entered the University of Poitiers to study law. He graduated in 1560 and for the next four years or so practised law at Fontenay, studying cryptography and mathematics in his spare time. From about 1566 to 1570 he was tutor to Catherine of Oarthenay at La Rochelle. In 1570 he moved to Paris and entered the service of Charles IX. He remained in the royal employment until 1584, when persecution of the Huguenots forced him to flee to Beauvoir-sur-Mer. The years at Beauvoir provided him with the opportunity to devote himself to serious mathematical work and it was in these years that his most fruitful algebraic research was carried out. On the accession of Henry IV in 1589, Viète returned to the royal service, and in the succeeding years of the continued war against Spain he gave valuable service to the French crown by deciphering letters of Phillip II of Spain. He was dismissed from the court in 1602 and died in Paris on 13 December 1603.

Although his stock of astronomical knowledge was slight, Viète's mathematical achievements were the result of his interest in cosmology. One of his first major results was a table giving the values of six trigonometri-cal lines based on a method originally used by ◊Ptolemy. The table, which worked out the values of trigonometric lines from degree to degree and the length of the arc expressed in parts of the radius, appeared in his *Canon mathematicus seu ad triangula* (1579), almost certainly the first book to treat systematically of plane and spherical triangle solution methods by means of all six trigonometric functions. Viète was the first person to use the cosine law for plane triangles and he also published the law of tangents. He was, above all, eager to establish trigonometry as something more than a poor relation of astronomy and his work went a good way towards doing so.

Viète is most celebrated for introducing the first uniformly symbolic algebra. His *In artem analytica isogoge* (1591) used letters for both known and unknown quantities, an innovation that paved the way for the development of 17th-century algebra. More specifically, his use of vowels for unknown quantities and consonants for known ones was a pointer to the later development of the concepts of variables and parameters.

In 1593 Viète gave the first explicit explanation of the notion of 'contact'. He asserted that 'the circle may be regarded as a plane figure with an infinite number of sides and angles, but a straight line touching a straight line, however short it may be, will coincide with that straight line and will not form an angle'. His last important work, *De aequationum recognitione et emandatione,* appeared in 1615, more than a decade after his death. In it Viète gave solutions to the lower-order equations and established connections between the positive roots of an equation and the coefficients and the different powers of the unknown quantities. He is credited with introducing the term 'coefficient' into algebra to denote either of the two rational factors of a monomial.

Mathematics to Viète was little more than a hobby, yet by providing the first systematic notation and, as a general tendency, substituting algebraic for geometric proofs in mathematics, he gave algebra a symbolic and analytical framework.

Vine, Frederick John (1939–1988) English geophysicist whose work was an important contribution to the development of the theory of plate tectonics.

Vine was born in Brentford, Essex, on 17 June 1939, and was educated at Latymer Upper School, London and at St John's College, Cambridge. From 1967 to 1970 he worked as assistant professor in the department of geological and geophysical sciences at Princeton University, before returning to the UK in 1970 to become reader and then, from 1974, professor in the school of environmental sciences at the University of East Anglia.

In Cambridge in 1963, Vine collaborated with his supervisor Drummond Hoyle Matthews (1931–), and wrote a paper, 'Magnetic anomalies over ocean ridges', which provided additional evidence for Harry ◊Hess's seafloor-spreading hypothesis of 1962. Alfred ◊Wegener's original 1912 theory of continental drift (Wegener's hypothesis) had been met with hostility at the time because he could not explain why the continents had drifted apart, but Hess had continued his work developing the theory of seafloor spreading to explain the fact that as the oceans grew wider, the continents drifted apart.

Following the work of Brunhes and Matonori Matuyama in the 1920s on magnetic reversals, Vine and Matthews predicted that new rock emerging from the oceanic ridges would intermittently produce material of opposing magnetic polarity to the old rock. They applied palaeomagnetic studies to the ocean ridges in the North Atlantic and were able to argue that parallel belts of different magnetic polarities existed on either side of the ridge crests. This evidence was vital proof of Hess's hypothesis. Studies on ridges in other oceans also showed the existence of these magnetic anomalies.

Vine and Matthews's hypothesis was widely accepted in 1966 and was confirmation of Hess's earlier work. Their work was crucial to the development of the theory of plate tectonics and revolutionized the earth sciences.

Vogel, Hermann Carl (1841–1907) German astronomer who became the first director of the Potsdam Astrophysical Observatory. He is renowned for his work on the spectral analysis of stars and his discovery of spectroscopic binary stars.

Vogel was born in Leipzig on 3 April 1841, the sixth child of Carl Christoph Vogel, the principal of a Leipzig grammar school. Vogel attended his father's school up to the age of 18 and then continued his education at the Polytechnical School in Dresden. In 1863 he returned to Leipzig to study natural science at the university and, shortly after beginning his course, he became second assistant at the university observatory. He showed remarkable dexterity at manipulating instruments and as a result the director of the observatory, Karl Brühns, asked him to take part in the Astronomische Gesellschaft's 'zone project'. This was part of a much larger programme that aimed to scan the northern skies and to ascertain the coordinates of all stars down to the ninth magnitude. Vogel's contribution was to observe all nebulae within a specific zone and this work formed the basis of his inaugural dissertation. In 1870, at the joint recommendation of Brühns and Johann Karl Friedrich Zöllner, the professor of Leipzig Observatory, Vogel was appointed director of an observatory at Bothkamp, near Kiel, that belonged to the amateur astronomer F G von Bülow. Vogel's work on the spectra of planets, undertaken while he was at the Bothkamp Observatory, won him a prize from the Royal Danish Academy of Sciences. In 1874 he was asked to become an observer at the proposed astrophysical observatory at Potsdam, near Berlin. The Potsdam Observatory was officially opened in 1879, and in 1882 he was appointed its first director, a position he held until his death on 13 August 1907.

During his time at the Bothkamp Observatory, Vogel was given complete scientific freedom, sole discretion in determining the observatory's research programme, and excellent equipment. He worked intensively on the spectroscopic properties of stars, planets, nebulae, the northern lights, comet III 1871, and the Sun. With the aid of a reversible spectroscope, he attempted to ascertain the rotational period of the Sun and, following attempts made by William ◊Huggins in England in 1868, he also attempted spectroscopically to determine the radial velocity of fixed stars.

Having been appointed as an observer to the future Potsdam Observatory in 1874, Vogel became increasingly interested in spectrophotometry. He used this technique to study Nova Cygni in 1876 and his results provided the first evidence that changes occur in the spectrum of a nova during its fading phase. He also began an extensive study of the solar spectrum, but the results of his painstaking measurements were soon superseded by more precise tables compiled by using diffraction gratings. At this point in his career Vogel decided to specialize in spectroscopy, and in response to a proposal made by the Italian astronomer Pietro ◊Secchi he examined the spectra of some 4,000 stars. His original intention was to classify the stars according to their spectra, a procedure he believed would reflect their stage of development. However, he became dissatisfied with his findings and abandoned this work to pursue a problem that had intrigued him since his days at Bothkamp Observatory – measuring the Doppler shift in the spectral lines of stars to ascertain their velocity.

Vogel's use of photography to record stellar spectra led to his most sensational discovery – spectroscopic binary stars. His success was based on a study of the periodic displacements of the spectral lines of the stars Algol and Spica, eclipsing binary stars whose components could not, at the time, be detected as separate entities by optical means. From his spectrographs, Vogel derived the dimensions of this double-star system, the diameter of both components, the orbital velocity of Algol, the total mass of the system, and, in 1889, he derived the distance between the two component stars from each other.

Vogel's work ended the controversy over the value of Christian ◊Doppler's theory for investigating motion in the universe. His discovery of spectroscopic binary stars not only led to the realization that such systems are a relatively common feature of the universe; it also played an important role in the discovery of interstellar calcium absorption lines.

Volhard, Jacob (1834–1910) German chemist who is best remembered for various significant methods of organic synthesis. He also made contributions to inorganic and analytical chemistry.

Volhard was born in Darmstadt on 4 June 1834. He completed his undergraduate studies and worked under Justus von ◊Liebig at the University of Giessen. He then held professorial appointments at three German universities: Munich 1864–79, Erlangen 1879–82, and Halle 1882–1910. He remained at Halle until his death on 16 June 1910.

Volhard is best known for his development of a method of quantitatively analysing for an element via silver chloride. A chloride solution of the element to be determined is titrated with an excess of standard silver nitrate solution, and the residual silver nitrate analysed against standard ammonium (or potassium) thiocyanate solution. Bromides can also be determined using this technique. The end-point is usually detected by using a ferric (iron(III)) indicator, such as iron alum.

During the 1860s Volhard developed methods for the syntheses of the amino acids sarcosine (N-methylaminoethanoic acid) and creatine, and the heterocyclic compound thiophen; he also did research on guanidine and cyanimide. His method of preparing halogenated organic acids has become known as the Hell–Volhard–Zelinsky reaction, in which the acid is treated with chlorine or bromine in the presence of phosphorus (iodine is not sufficiently reactive to take part in the reaction). It is specific for α-hydrogen atoms (generating the α-chloro- or α-bromo-acid) and can therefore be used to detect their presence. The α-hydrogens are replaced selectively, and the reaction can be stopped at the mono- or di-halogen stage by using the correct amount of halogen; with excess halogen, all the α-hydrogens are substituted. The reaction is also useful for syntheses because the substituted halogen atom(s) can easily be replaced by a cyanide group (by treatment with potassium cyanide), which in the presence of an aqueous acid and ethyl alcohol (ethanol) yields the corresponding malonic ester (diethylpropandioate), from which barbiturate drugs can be synthesized.

Volta, Alessandro Giuseppe Antonio Anastasio (1745–1827) Count Volta. Italian physicist who discovered how to produce electric current and built the first electric battery. He also invented the electrophorus as a ready means of producing charges of static electricity.

Volta Italian physicist Alessandro Volta who invented the first battery, or voltaic cell. This was constructed from a pile of alternating zinc and silver discs, with absorbent material soaked in salt water between them. It gave other scientists access to a reliable source of electric currents, to study the effects of electricity. *Mary Evans Picture Library*

Volta was born in Como on 18 February 1745. He received his early education at various religious institutions but showed a flair for science, particularly the study of electricity, which had been brought to the forefront of attention by the experiments and theories of Benjamin ◊Franklin. Volta began to experiment with static electricity in 1765 and soon gained a reputation as a scientist, leading to his appointment as principal of the Gymnasium at Como in 1774 and, a year later, as professor of experimental physics there. In 1778, Volta took up the same position at Pavia and remained there until 1819. In 1799, the conflict between Austria and France over the region caused him to lose his post but he was reinstated following the French victory in 1800. Volta then travelled to Paris in 1801 to demonstrate his discoveries in electricity to Napoleon, who made him a count and awarded him a pension. Volta retained his academic post when Austria returned to power in 1814, but retired in 1819. He died in Como on 5 March 1827.

Volta's first major contribution to physics was the invention of the electrophorus in 1775. He had researched thoroughly into the nature and quantity of electrostatic charge generated by various materials, and he used this knowledge to develop a simple practical device for the production of charges. His electrophorus consisted of a disc made of turpentine, resin, and wax, which was rubbed to give it a negative charge. A plate covered in tinfoil was lowered by an insulated handle on to the disc, which induced a positive charge on the lower side of the foil. The negative charge that was likewise induced on the upper surface was removed by touching it to ground the charge, leaving a positive charge on the foil. This process could then be repeated to build up a greater and greater charge. Volta went on to realize from his electrostatic experiments that the quantity of charge produced is proportional to the product of its tension and the capacity of the conductor. He developed a simple electrometer similar to the gold-leaf electroscope but using straws so that it was much cheaper to make. This instrument was very sensitive and Volta was able to use it to measure tension, proposing a unit that was equivalent to about 13,500 volts.

Volta's next important work did not concern electricity but the air and gases. In 1776, he discovered methane by isolating and examining the properties of marsh gas found in Lake Maggiore. He then made the first accurate estimate of the proportion of oxygen in the air by exploding air with hydrogen to remove the oxygen. Later, in about 1795–96, Volta recognized that the vapour pressure of a liquid is independent of the pressure of the atmosphere and depends only on temperature. This anticipated the law of partial pressures put forward by John ◊Dalton in 1801.

Volta's greatest contribution to science began with the discovery by Luigi ◊Galvani in 1791 that the muscles in dead frogs contract when two dissimilar metals (brass and iron) are brought into contact with the muscle and each other. Volta successfully repeated Galvani's experiments using different metals and different animals, and he also found that placing the two metals on his tongue produced an unpleasant sensation. The effects were due to electricity and in 1792, Volta concluded that the source of the electricity was in the junction of the metals and not, as Galvani thought, in the animals. Volta even succeeded in producing a list of metals in order of their electricity production based on the strength of the sensation they made on his tongue, thereby deriving the electromotive series.

Volta's tongue and Galvani's frogs proved to be highly sensitive detectors of electricity – much more so than Volta's electrometer. In 1796, Volta set out to measure the electricity produced by different metals, but to register any deflection in the electrometer he had to increase the tension by multiplying that given by a single junction. He soon hit upon the idea of piling discs of metals on top of each other and found that they had to be separated by a moist conductor to produce a current. The political upheavals of this period prevented Volta from proceeding immediately

to construct a battery but he had undoubtedly achieved the 'voltaic pile', as it came to be called, by 1800. In that year, he wrote to the president of the Royal Society, Joseph ◊Banks, and described two arrangements of conductors that produced an electric current. One was a pile of silver and zinc discs separated by cardboard moistened with brine, and the other a series of glasses of salty or alkaline water in which bimetallic curved electrodes were dipped.

Volta's discovery was a sensation, for it enabled high electric currents to be produced for the first time. It was quickly applied to produce electrolysis, resulting in the discovery of several new chemical elements, and then led throughout the 1800s to the great discoveries in electromagnetism and electronics that culminated in the invention of the electrical machines and electronic devices that we use today. Volta's genius lay in an ability to construct simple devices and in his tenacity to follow through his convictions. He was not a great theoretician and did not attempt to explain his discovery. However, he did see the need for establishing proper measurement of electricity, and it is fitting that the unit of electric potential, tension, or electromotive force is named the volt in his honour.

Further Reading

Pancaldi, Giuliano, 'Electricity and life: Volta's path to the battery', *Hist Stud Phys Biol Sci*, 1990, v 21, pp 123–160.

Pera, Marcello, 'Radical theory change and empirical equivalence: the Galvani–Volta controversy' in: Shea, William R (ed), *Revolutions in Science: Their Meaning and Relevance*, Science History, 1988, pp 133–156.

Volterra, Vito (1860–1940) Italian mathematician whose chief work was in the fields of function theory and differential equations.

Volterra was born in Ancona on 3 May 1860, but after his father's death, when he was two, he lived at Florence with his mother and her brother. He attended the Scuola Tecnica Dante Alighieri and the Istituto Tecnico Galileo Galilei. As a young boy he gave signs of a distinct flair for mathematics and physics and by the time he had reached his early teens he had studied a number of sophisticated mathematical texts, including Adrien ◊Legendre's *Eléments de géométrie*. Not only was he able to solve difficult problems, he set himself interesting new ones. So, at the age of 13, after reading Jules Verne's *From the Earth to the Moon* (published eight years before), he became interested in projectile problems and came up with a plausible determination for the trajectory of a spacecraft that had been fired from a gun. His solution was based on the device of breaking time down into small intervals during which it could be assumed that the force was constant. The trajectory could thus be viewed as a series of small parabolic arcs. This was the essence of the argument that he developed in detail 40 years later in a series of lectures at the Sorbonne.

When Volterra was still at school, his mother wished him to abandon his academic studies and become a bank clerk in order to supplement the small family income. His teacher Antonio Roiti averted this by finding him a job as an assistant at the physics laboratory of the University of Florence. He was thus able to continue at the institute and in 1878 he entered the University of Florence to study natural sciences. Two years later he entered the Scuola Normale Superiore at Pisa, and there he began to work with Enrico ◊Betti, who was to have a profound influence on his career. It was Betti who turned him in the direction of function theory (while still a student, Volterra published papers offering solutions to functions previously believed to be nonderivable), and then on to mechanics and mathematical physics.

In 1882 Volterra was awarded a doctorate and in the following year he was appointed professor of mechanics at the University of Pisa. He remained there until 1892, when he moved to the University of Turin. In 1900 he succeeded Eugenio ◊Beltrami in the chair of mathematical physics at the University of Rome. During World War I he established the Italian Office of War Inventions, where he played an important part in designing armaments for airships. He also proposed that helium be used in place of hydrogen dirigible airships. After the war he became increasingly involved in politics, speaking in the Senate and openly voicing his opposition to the Fascist regime. For his views he was eventually dismissed from his chair at Rome in 1931 and banned from taking part in any Italian scientific meeting, although he was elected to the Pontifical Academy of Sciences in 1936 on the nomination of Pope Pius XI. From 1931 onwards, although deprived of an official post, he continued to write papers and to lecture abroad, principally at the Sorbonne. He died in Rome on 11 October 1940.

Volterra's achievements were numerous, but most of them involved function theory and differential equations. He contributed especially to the foundation of the theory of functionals, the solution of integral equations with variable limits, and the integration of hyperbolic partial differential equations. His chief method, hit upon as a young boy, was based on dividing a problem into a small interval of time and assuming one of the variables to be constant during each time period. Thus his papers on partial differential equations of the early 1890s included the solution of equations for cylindrical waves:

$$\frac{d^2u}{dt^2} = \frac{d^2u}{dx^2} + \frac{d^2u}{dy^2}$$

He also brought his knowledge of mathematics to bear on biological matters. One example of this is his construction of a model for population change, in which the prey, x, and the predator, y, interact in a continuous manner expressed in these differential equations:

$$\frac{dx}{dt} = x(g - ky)$$

and

$$\frac{dy}{dt} = y(-d + kx)$$

Volterra's mathematics was given its broadest statement in his two most important publications, *The Theory of Permutable Functions* (1915) and *The Theory of Functionals and of Integral and Integro-differential Equations* (1930).

von Baeyer, Johann Friedrich Wilhelm Adolf

German organic chemist; see Johann von ◊Baeyer.

von Braun, Wernher Magnus Maximilian (1912–1977)

German-born US rocket engineer who was instrumental in the design and development of German rocket weapons during World War II and who, after the war, was a prime mover in the early days of space rocketry in the USA.

Von Braun was born on 23 March 1912 in Wirsitz, Germany (now in Poland), the son of a baron. He was educated in Zürich and at Berlin University where he was awarded his PhD in 1934. In 1930 he had joined a group of scientists who were experimenting with rockets, and within four years they had developed a solid-fuelled rocket that reached an altitude of about 2.5 km/1.5 mi. In 1938 von Braun became technical director of a military rocket establishment at Peenemünde on the Baltic coast. In that year a rocket was produced that had a range of 17.5 km/11 mi. In 1940 he joined the Nazi party, and two years later the first true missile – a liquid-fuelled rocket with an explosive warhead – was fired from Peenemünde. The next developments were the V1 (a flying bomb powered by a pulse-jet engine) and the V2 (a supersonic liquid-fuelled rocket), both of which were launched against the UK from sites on the western coast of the European mainland. Some 4,300 V2s were fired, 1,230 of which hit London. The rocket weapons came too late, however, to affect the outcome of the war.

In the last days of the war in 1945 von Braun and his staff, not wishing to be captured in the Russian-occupied part of Germany, travelled to west to surrender to US forces. They went to the USA and soon afterwards von Braun began work at the US Army Ordinance Corps testing grounds at White Sands, New Mexico. In 1952 he moved to Huntsville, Alabama, as technical director of the US Army's ballistic missile programme.

In October 1957 the Soviet Union launched the first artificial satellite, *Sputnik 1*, and US anxiety was not eased for several months until 31 January of the following year, when von Braun and his team sent up the first US satellite *Explorer 1*. Von Braun became a deputy associate administrator of the National Aeronautical and Space Administration (NASA) in March 1970, but two years later left the organization to become an executive in a private business. He died on 16 June 1977 in Alexandria, Virginia..

Further Reading

Piszkiewicz, Dennis, *Wernher von Braun: The Man Who Sold the Moon,* Praeger Publishers, 1998.

Spangenburg, Ray and Moser, Diane K, *Wernher von Braun: Space Visionary and Rocket Engineer,* Makers of Modern Science series, Facts on File, 1995.

Stuhlinger, Ernst and Ordway, Frederick I, *Wernher von Braun: Crusader for Space,* Krieger Publishing Company, 1996.

Bergaust, Erik, *Wernher von Braun,* National Space Institute, 1976.

David, Heather M, *Von Braun, Wernher,* Putnam, 1967.

von Liebig, Justus German organic chemist; see Justus von ◊Liebig.

Von Neumann, John (originally Johann) (1903–1957) Hungarian-born US physicist and mathematician who originated games theory and developed the fundamental concepts involved in programming computers. He also made a valuable contribution to quantum mechanics.

Von Neumann was born in Budapest on 28 December 1903. He received private instruction until 1914, when he entered the Gymnasium, and even then continued to be tutored outside school in mathematics because of the exceptional ability that he displayed in the subject. Von Neumann left Hungary in 1919 in the wake of the disruptions arising as a result of the defeat suffered by Austria-Hungary in World War I. He attended several universities, studying in Berlin 1921–23 and then in Zürich until 1925. He received a degree in chemical engineering from the Zürich Institute in 1925, and was awarded a PhD in mathematics from the University of Budapest a year later. He then studied in Göttingen, where he worked with J Robert ◊Oppenheimer, and held the post of *Privatdozent* (unpaid lecturer) in mathematics at the University of Berlin 1927–29.

After a year as lecturer at the University of Hamburg, Von Neumann travelled to the USA in 1930. Holding first the position of visiting professor, he became full professor of mathematics at the University of Princeton in 1931. He held this position until 1933, when he was invited to become the youngest member of the newly established Institute of Advanced Studies at Princeton University. Von Neumann was a member of this institute for the rest of his career, although he also held a number of important advisory posts with the US government 1940–54.

During World War II, Von Neumann served as a consultant for various committees within the navy, army, the Atomic Energy Commission, and the Office for Scientific Research and Development. He was associated with research projects at Los Alamos 1943–55, working under Oppenheimer on the A-bomb project and also under Edward ◊Teller on the H-bomb project. The importance of Von Neumann's scientific contributions brought him widespread recognition, including the award of the Medal of Freedom, the Albert Einstein Award, and the Enrico Fermi Award – all in 1956. His health had begun to fail in 1955, and he died of cancer in Washington, DC, on 8 February 1957.

Pure mathematics was Von Neumann's primary scientific interest during the first years of his career. He made important contributions to the subjects of mathematical logic, set theory, and operator theory and his theory of rings of operators is highly regarded.

In mathematics you don't understand things. You just get used to them.
JOHN VON NEUMANN ATTRIBUTED REMARK

In 1928 Von Neumann read a paper on games theory to a scientific meeting in Göttingen. This was an entirely new subject originated by Von Neumann himself. It consisted of proving that a quantitative mathematical model could be constructed for determining the best strategy, that is, the one that, in the long term, would produce the optimal result with minimal losses for any game, even one of chance or one with more than two players. The sort of games for which this theory found immediate use were business, warfare, and the social sciences – games in which strategies must be worked out for defeating an adversary. Games theory has also found application in the behavioural sciences. Von Neumann began work on this subject in the late 1920s, but did not devote himself exclusively to it by any means.

Applied mathematics in the field of theoretical physics held a strong fascination for Von Neumann. He began to work on the axiomization of quantum mechanics in 1927, and in 1932 published a book entitled *The Mathematical Foundations of Quantum Mechanics.* This defended mathematically the uncertainty principle of Werner ◊Heisenberg. In 1944, Von Neumann made another very important contribution to quantum mechanics when he showed that the systems of matrix mechanics developed by Heisenberg and Max ◊Born and of wave mechanics developed by Erwin ◊Schrödinger were equivalent. Von Neumann also published papers with Subrahmanyan ◊Chandrasekhar on gravitational fields. Work on pure mathematics also continued and in particular he collaborated with Francis Murray in an investigation of noncommutative algebras during the latter part of the 1940s.

Work on the atom bomb project brought a variety of new problems, many of them completely different from those Von Neumann had previously encountered. The necessity for quickly producing approximate models for complex physical problems encouraged Von Neumann to examine and develop improvements for the available computing machines. During the war he contributed to work on hydrodynamics and on shock waves, and afterwards he spent a great deal of effort designing and then supervising the construction of the first computer able to use a flexible stored program (named MANIAC-1) at the Institute of Advanced Study in 1952. This work laid the foundations for the design of all subsequent programmable computers.

Von Neumann also developed his games theory, and in 1944 published *Theory of Games and Economic Behavior* with Oskar Morgenstern, his major work on the subject. Games theory was also used during the H-bomb project in the early 1950s, in which Von Neumann played an active role. The possibility of developing automata to the point where they might be self-producing, and the similarities between the nervous system and computers were areas that absorbed much of Von Neumann's interest during his last years.

Von Neumann was a mathematician with an exceptional talent for absorbing the essential features of all the important branches of both mathematics and theoretical physics, and he was also adept at the applications of his theoretical work. He demonstrated great originality and imagination in his pioneering efforts in the areas of computer design and especially in games theory.

Further Reading

Aspray, William, *John Von Neumann and the Origins of Modern Computing*, History of Computing series, MIT Press, 1990.

Dore, Mohammed; Chakravarty, Sukhamoy; and Goodwin, Richard M (eds), *John Von Neumann and Modern Economics*, Oxford University Press, 1989.

Glimm, James, *The Legacy of John Von Neumann*, Proceedings of Symposia in Pure Mathematics series, American Mathematical Society, 1990, v 50.

Vonneumann, Nicholas, *John Von Neumann as Seen By His Brother*, Nicholas A Vonneuman, 1992.

von Stradonitz, Friedrich August Kekulé German organic chemist; see Friedrich August ◊Kekulé von Stradonitz.

Vorontsov-Vel'iaminov, Boris Aleksandrovich (1904–) Russian astronomer and astrophysicist. Besides being the author of several successful textbooks on astronomy, he compiled astronomical catalogues and published several advanced specialized tests. In 1962 he was honoured by being awarded the Bredikhin Prize.

Vorontsov-Vel'iaminov was born on 14 February 1904 and became a professor at the University of Moscow in 1934. In 1930, independently of Robert ◊Trumpler, he demonstrated the occurrence of the absorption of stellar light by interstellar dust. This fact had not been taken into consideration in 1922 by Jacobus ◊Kapteyn in his model of the universe, one of the most serious flaws in his calculations. The significance of Vorontsov-Vel'iaminov's discovery was that it became possible to determine astronomical distances and, in turn, the size of the universe more accurately.

Vorontsov-Vel'iaminov devoted considerable energy to the study of gaseous nebulae, the observations of novae, and analysis of the Hertzsprung–Russell diagram, with reference to the evolution of stars. He made particularly important contributions to the study of the blue–white star sequence, which was the subject of a book he published in 1947.

In 1959 Vorontsov-Vel'iaminov compiled a list and recorded the positions of 350 interacting galaxies that are clustered so closely that they seem to perturb each other slightly in structure. Besides this catalogue, he compiled a more extensive catalogue of galaxies in 1962, in which he listed and described more than 30,000 examples.

Wald, George (1906–1997) US biochemist who investigated the biochemical processes of vision that take place in the retina of the eye. For this work he shared the 1967 Nobel Prize for Physiology or Medicine with the Swedish physiologist Ragnar Granit (1900–1991) and the US physiologist Haldan Hartline (1903–1983).

Wald was born in New York City on 18 November 1906 and educated at the university there, graduating in 1927. He gained his PhD from Columbia University five years later. From 1932 to 1934 he studied in Europe as a National Research Council fellow, first in Berlin under Otto ◊Warburg and then in Zürich with Paul ◊Karrer, who did the pioneering work on vitamin A. When Wald returned to the USA he joined the staff at Harvard University and remained there for the rest of his career; he was appointed professor of biology in 1948. In the 1970s Wald rose to fame outside the area of science for his outspoken comments against US involvement in the Vietnam War.

Wald began his work on the chemistry of vision in the early 1930s. The key to the process is the pigment called visual purple, or rhodopsin, which occurs in the rods (dim-light receptors) of the retina. In 1933 he discovered that this substance consists of the colourless protein opsin in combination with retinal, a yellow carotenoid compound that is the aldehyde of vitamin A. Rhodopsin molecules are split into these two compounds when they are struck by light, and the enzyme alcohol dehydrogenase then further reduces the retinal to form vitamin A. In the dark the process is reversed and the compounds recombine to restore the rhodopsin to the retinal rods. The process does not work with 100% efficiency and over a period of time some of the retinal is lost. This deficiency has to be made up from the body's stores of vitamin A (which is supplied through the diet), but if the stores are inadequate the visual process in dim light is affected and night blindness results.

Wald and his co-workers went on to investigate how these biochemical changes trigger the electrical activity in the retina's nerves and the optic nerve. In the 1950s they found the retinal pigments that detect red and yellow–green light, and a few years later identified the pigment for blue light. All of these – the three primary colour pigments – are related to vitamin A, and in the 1960s Wald demonstrated that the

absence of one or more of them results in colour blindness.

Wallace, Alfred Russel (1823–1913) Welsh naturalist who is best known for proposing a theory of evolution by natural selection independently of Charles ◊Darwin.

Wallace was born in Usk, Monmouthshire, on 8 January 1823. After a rudimentary education (he left school when he was 14 years old), he joined an elder brother in a surveying business. In 1844, however, he became a teacher at the Collegiate School, Leicester, where he met H W ◊Bates, who interested him in entomology. Together they planned a collecting trip to the Amazon, and arrived in South America in 1848; Bates remained there for 11 years but Wallace returned to England in 1852. Unfortunately, the ship sank on the return voyage and although Wallace survived, all his specimens were lost, the only remaining ones being those previously sent to England. In 1853 he published an account of his experiences in South America in *A Narrative of Travels on the Amazon and Rio Negro.*

From 1842 to 1862 Wallace explored the Malay Peninsula and the East Indies, from which he collected more than 125,000 specimens. During this expedition he observed the marked differences that exist between the Australian and Asian faunas and later, when writing about this phenomenon, drew a hypothetical line that separates the areas in which each of these two distinct faunas exist. This line, now called the Wallace line, follows a deep-water channel that runs between the larger islands of Borneo and Celebes and the smaller ones of Bali and Lombok. In 1855, while in Borneo, he wrote *On the Law Which Has Regulated the Introduction of New Species,* in which he put forward the idea that every species had come into existence coincidentally, both in time and place, with a pre-existing, closely allied species. He also believed that the Australian fauna was less highly developed than the Asian fauna, the survival of the Australian fauna being due to the separation of Australia and its nearby islands from the Asian continent before the more advanced Asian fauna had developed. These ideas then led Wallace to the same conclusion that Charles Darwin had reached (but had not published at that time) – the idea that species evolve by natural selection. Then, while suffering from malaria, in 1858,

Wallace wrote an essay outlining his ideas on evolution and sent it to Darwin, who was surprised to find that Wallace's ideas were the same as his own. The findings of the two men were combined in a paper read before the Linnean Society on 1 July 1858. Wallace's section, entitled 'On the tendency of varieties to depart indefinitely from the original type', described how animals fight to survive, the rate of their reproduction, and their dependence on supplies of suitable food. In the conclusion to his section Wallace wrote 'those that prolong their existence can only be the most perfect in health and vigour; ... the weakest and least perfectly organised must always succumb'. He described his work more fully in *The Malay Archipelago,* published in 1869; Darwin's *On the Origin of Species* had appeared in 1859.

Wallace continued to gather evidence to support the theory of evolution and in 1870, while on an expedition to Borneo and the Molucca (Maluku) islands, published *Contributions to the Theory of Natural Selection.* In this work he diverged from Darwin's views: both thought that the human race had evolved to its present physical form by natural selection but, in keeping with his spiritualistic beliefs, Wallace was of the opinion that humans' higher mental capabilities had arisen from some 'metabiological' agency. Wallace also differed from Darwin about the origins of the brightly coloured plumage of male birds and the relative drabness of female birds; Wallace believed that it was merely natural selection that had led to the development of dull, protectively coloured plumage in females, rather than subscribing to Darwin's idea that females are attracted by brightly coloured plumage in males.

Wallace also studied mimicry in the swallowtail butterfly and wrote a pioneering work on zoogeography, *Geographical Distribution of Animals* (1876). In addition he spent much time promoting socialism by, for example, campaigning for women's suffrage and land nationalization.

Public recognition of Wallace's important work on evolution came late in his life; he was elected a fellow of the Royal Society in 1893 and received the Order of Merit in 1910. He died in Broadstone, Dorset, on 7 November 1913.

Further Reading

Brooks, John Langdon, *Just Before the Origin: Alfred Russel Wallace's Theory of Evolution,* Columbia University Press, 1984.

George, Wilma, *Biologist Philosopher: A Study on the Life and Writings of Alfred Russel Wallace,* Life of Science Library, Abelard-Schuman, 1964, v 43.

Green, Len, *Alfred Russel Wallace: His Life and Work,* Hertford and Ware History Society, Occasional Paper, Hertford and Ware Local History Society, 1995, v 4.

Green, Len, *Alfred Russel Wallace: His Life and Work,*

Occasional Papers of the Hertford and Ware Local History Society series, Hertford and Ware Local History Society, 1995, v 4.

Smith, Charles H, *Alfred Russel Wallace on Spiritualism, Man, and Evolution: An Analytical Essay,* C H Smith, 1992.

Wallace, Alfred Russel, *My Life: A Record of Events and Opinions,* AMS Press – Chapman & Hall, 1995, 2 vols.

Wallis, Barnes Neville (1887–1979)

Wallis, Barnes Neville (1887–1979) English aircraft designer who gained fame during World War II for his association with the development of a 'bouncing' bomb. used by the Allies to attack dams in Germany.

Wallis, later known as Barnes Wallis, was born in Derbyshire on 26 September 1887. He was educated at Christ's Hospital School and trained as a marine engineer at J S White and Company, shipbuilders of Cowes, Isle of Wight. In early 1911 he joined the Vickers Company, and from 1913 to 1915 he worked in the design department of Vickers Aviation. During World War I he served briefly as a private in the Artist's Rifles, then returned to Vickers as chief designer in the airship department of their works at Barrow-in-Furness.

From 1916 to 1922 he was chief designer for the Airship Guarantee Company, a subsidiary of Vickers. From 1923 onwards he was chief designer of structures at Vickers's Weybridge works where he stayed as a designer until the end of World War II. In 1945 he became chief of aeronautical research and development at the British Aircraft Corporation Division at Weybridge – a post he held until his retirement in 1971.

Wallis was widely honoured by his fellow engineers and by a grateful government. He received the CBE in 1943 and was made a fellow of the Royal Society in 1945; he held honorary degrees from London, Bristol, Oxford, and Cambridge universities. In 1965 he was made an honorary fellow of Churchill College, Cambridge, and in 1968 he was knighted. He died on 31 October 1979.

Towards the end of 1911 Wallis left shipbuilding to join H B Pratt as an apprentice designer. (Pratt had been commissioned by Vickers to design a new rigid airship after the *Mayfly* debacle of 1911.) A series of successful designs followed, and in 1913 the British government initiated the famous R series of airships — starting with the R-26. Wallis himself designed the R-80; and the performance of this machine was a significant advance on that of all the others.

In 1924 Wallis began designing the R-100, and it was during this work that he got the initial ideas which he later incorporated in his geodetic structures for aircraft. Despite the success of the R-100 and its proven structural strength, the disaster that befell its government-built (and differently designed) sister ship, the R-101, brought an end to rigid airship building in the UK.

Following the cessation of work on rigid airships, Wallis was transferred to the Vickers Weybridge works as chief structures designer, and one of his first tasks was to design a lighter wing structure for the Vickers-built Viastra 2, which was being used commercially in Australia. The experience Wallis gained in this job – together with that gained in other structural research, particularly the design of the A1-30 torpedo-carrier and the 'wandering web' of the Vivid and Valiant – later enabled him to evolve the now-famous geodesic system for fixed-wing aircraft.

The breakaway from established structural-design practice in airframes was made when a Wallis-designed fuselage was incorporated in the G4-31 biplane in 1932. In this design, Wallis sought to dispense with the primary and secondary members by substituting a latticework system of main members only – an idea he had originally derived from the wire netting used to contain the gas bags on the airship R-100. An exploratory structure of this type had been used on the ill-fated M1-30 torpedo-carrier. The G4-31 structure represented a halfway stage between that and the full geodetic structure employed in the monoplane that was later to achieve worldwide fame as the Wellesley bomber.

A geodetic line is, by definition, the shortest distance between two points on the Earth – that is, on a sphere. Applied to airframes, the theory had many advantages, one being that the load transfer from member to member was by the shortest possible route. In the Wallis lattice pattern, if one series of members was in tension, the opposite members were in compression – thus the system was stress-balanced in all directions. The Wellesley was responsible for the great technical advance in design that took place in the mid-1930s and which eventually produced the Wellington bomber of World War II.

Critics of the geodetic form of construction condemned it on the grounds that, for quality production, it was impractical. Wallis and his team at Weybridge rebutted this criticism by devising the necessary tools and methods: a complete Wellington airframe could be assembled in 24 hours. But the real proof of the essential simplicity of the Wellington structure came when nearly 9,000 airframes were produced for the war effort at Blackpool and Chester using only a minimum of skilled personnel – much of the workforce was made up of semi-skilled workers new to aircraft production.

In all, 11,461 Wellington bombers were produced – the largest number of any British bomber. The Wellington served throughout World War II in almost every role possible for a twin-engined aircraft and in conditions as widely different as those in Iceland and the Middle East. Without it, the war might well have taken a different course.

By applying his considerable knowledge of aerodynamic streamlining to ballistic problems, Wallis also devised new means of attacking the enemy by devising novel, but very effective, bombs. Among others, he designed the 544-kg/1,200-lb Tallboy and the 10-tonne Grandslam. But his most notable invention in this field was the famous Wallis 'bouncing bomb'. The bomb itself was used to destroy vital and hitherto practically impregnable targets – the huge Möhne and Eder dams, which were of paramount military importance to Germany because they fed the waterways essential for the production of war material.

To smash the dams, Wallis designed a cylindrical bomb to be hung crosswise in the bomb-bay of the aircraft. Each one, 1.5 m/5 ft in length and almost the same in diameter, was designed so that if it was dropped at the correct height and speed, it would skim across the water enabling it to reach the target presented by the wall of the dam. To achieve this, ten minutes before being dropped, the bomb was given a back-spin of 500 revolutions per minute by an auxillary motor. Upon impact with the water, the backward spin caused the bomb to skim across the surface, bouncing along, in shorter and shorter leaps, until it hit the wall of the dam. Then instead of rebounding away from the wall, the back-spin caused a downwards 'crawl' to a depth of 9 m/30 ft, where a hydrostatic fuse caused it to explode. The raids on the dams were successfully carried out in 1943 by Lancaster aircraft of RAF 617 squadron.

Further Reading

Heap, Christine, *The Papers of Sir Barnes Wallis in the Science Museum Library: A Handlist*, Science Museum, 1987.
Morpurgo, J E, *Barnes Wallis: A Biography*, I Allan, 1981.

Wallis, John (1616–1703) English mathematician who made important contributions to the development of algebra and analytical geometry and who was one of the founders of the Royal Society.

Wallis was born in Ashford, Kent, on 23 October 1616. He began his education at Ashford, but was sent to boarding school at Ley Green, near Tenterden, on the outbreak of plague at Ashford in 1625. In the years 1630–31 he attended the Martin Holbeach School in Felsted, Essex. There he learned Greek, Latin, and Hebrew and was introduced to the elements of logic. It was his brother who, in the Christmas vacation of 1631, instructed him in the fundamentals of arithmetic. In 1632 he went to Emmanuel College, Cambridge, to study physics, medicine, and moral philosophy. He received his BA in 1637. In 1640 he was ordained in the Church of England and for the next four years earned his living as a private chaplain in

Yorkshire and later in Essex. On his mother's death in 1643 he came into a large inheritance that left him financially independent.

In 1644 Wallis was elected a fellow of Queen's College, Cambridge, but was compelled to relinquish the fellowship a year later when he married. He moved to London and assisted the parliamentary side by deciphering captured coded letters during the Civil War. In gratitude for that work Oliver Cromwell overlooked Wallis's signature on the 1648 remonstrance against the execution of Charles I and, in 1649, appointed him Savilian Professor of Geometry at Oxford University. It was then that Wallis began to study mathematics in earnest. In 1655 he published his most famous work, the *Arithmetica infinitorum,* which immediately raised him to international scientific eminence. In 1658 he was appointed keeper of the university archives. In 1660 Charles II chose him as his royal chaplain. In the meantime Wallis had, ever since 1649, been meeting regularly with other lovers of science, notably Robert ◊Boyle, at the discussions that led to the founding of the Royal Society in 1660.

In the second half of his life Wallis's chief publications were his *Mechanica* (1669–71), which was the fullest treatment of the subject then existing, and his *Algebra* (1685). He also became involved in a long and acrimonious dispute with the political philosopher Thomas Hobbes over what he considered to be the anti-Christian tendencies of Hobbes's philosophy – a quarrel that lasted for 25 years and ended only with Hobbes's death in 1679. He also conducted experiments in speech and attempted to teach, with some success, deaf mutes to speak. His method was described in his *Gramatica linguae Anglicanae* (1652). After the revolution of 1688–89 that drove James II from the throne, he was employed by William III as a decipherer. He held the Savilian Chair until his death, in Oxford, on 28 October 1703.

Wallis's two great works established him as one of the foremost mathematicians of the 17th century. The *Arithmetica* was the most substantial single work on mathematics yet to appear in England. In it he applied Cartesian analysis to Evangelista ◊Torricelli's method of indivisibles and (in an appendix) applied analysis for the first time to conic sections as curves of the second degree. The treatise also introduced the symbol ∞ to represent infinity, the germ of differential calculus, and, by an impressive use of interpolation (the word was Wallis's invention), the famous value for π (pi) and the celebrated formula:

$$\frac{4}{\pi} = \frac{3 \times 3 \times 5 \times 5 \times 7 \times 7}{2 \times 4 \times 4 \times 6 \times 6 \times 8} \cdots$$

The *Algebra* was the first treatise ever to attempt to combine a full exposition of the subject with its history and was important for introducing the principles of analogy and continuity into mathematics.

Walton, Ernest Thomas Sinton (1903–1995) Irish physicist best known for his work with John ◊Cockcroft on the development of the first particle accelerator, which produced the first artificial transmutation in 1932. In recognition of this achievement, Walton and Cockcroft were awarded the 1951 Nobel Prize for Physics.

Walton was born in Dungarvan, County Waterford, on 6 October 1903. He attended the Methodist College in Belfast and went on to Trinity College, Dublin, where he earned his bachelor's degree in 1926. He was later awarded an MSc in 1928 and an MA in 1934 from the same institution. In 1927, Walton continued his studies at the Cavendish Laboratories at Cambridge University, remaining there until 1934. He obtained his PhD in 1931, and in 1934 returned to Ireland to become a fellow of Trinity College, Dublin. In 1947 Walton also became professor of natural and experimental philosophy at Trinity College. After his retirement in 1974, Walton held the post of emeritus fellow of Trinity College. He received many honours in recognition of his scientific achievements. In particular Walton was the joint recipient with Cockcroft of the Hughes Medal of the Royal Society in 1938 as well as the Nobel Prize for Physics in 1951.

Before Walton and Cockcroft began their investigation of artificial transmutation, the only means of changing one element into another was by bombarding it with alpha particles from a natural source – that is, a radioactive substance. This placed a variety of constraints on the possible procedures in such work. Walton investigated several approaches for the production of fast particles. Two of the methods he attempted in 1928 failed because of difficulties in focusing the particles, and these methods were developed later by others to build the first successful betatron and the early linear accelerators.

In 1929 Walton and Cockcroft were joined at the Cavendish Laboratory by George ◊Gamow. Gamow made calculations on the feasibility of producing transmutations by bombardment with proton beams. Protons were preferable to alpha particles because their smaller charge makes them less susceptible to repulsive interactions with the target nuclei. Furthermore, hydrogen gas is more readily ionized than helium, so protons are produced more easily than are alpha particles.

The device that Cockcroft and Walton constructed, the first successful particle accelerator, used an arrangement of condensers to build up very high potentials and was completed in 1932. It could produce a beam of protons accelerated at over 500,000 electronvolts. In 1932 Walton and Cockcroft used the proton beam to bombard lithium. They observed the production of large quantities of alpha particles, showing that the lithium nuclei had captured the protons and formed unstable beryllium nuclei that instantaneously decayed into two alpha particles travelling in opposite directions. Walton and Cockcroft detected these alpha particles with a fluorescent screen. They later investigated the transmutation of other light elements using proton beams, and also deuterons (nuclei of deuterium) derived from heavy water.

These experiments were a pioneering venture, representing the first investigations of artificial transmutation. The type of generator built by Cockcroft and Walton suffers electric breakdown at very high voltages, and has a limit of 1.5 MeV (1.5 million electronvolts). Other generators, particularly that designed by Robert ◊van de Graaff and the cyclotron developed by Ernest ◊Lawrence soon superseded it. The particle accelerator thereby became a vital research tool at an extremely turbulent time in the development of nuclear physics, and has been developed to a far more advanced state in recent years.

Wankel, Felix (1902–1988) German engineer known for his research into the development of the rotary engine that bears his name.

Wankel was born in Luhran on 13 August 1902. He attended Vohlschule and Gymnasium before becoming employed by Druckerie-Verlay in Heidelberg in 1921. In 1927 he became a partner in an engineering works before opening his own research establishment, where he carried out work for Bayerisch Motorenwerke (BMW) in 1934. Later he carried out work for the German Air Ministry. At the end of World War II in 1945 he began to work for a number of German motor manufacturers at the Technische Entwicklungstelle in Lindow. In 1960 he was made director of this institute. He died in Lindau on 9 October 1988.

During the 1930s Wankel carried out a systematic

investigation of internal-combustion engines. He became particularly interested in rotary engines and gradually began to make mechanical sense of the number of possible arrangements and engine cycles. Although many of his early ideas turned out to be only marginally successful, the German motor firm NSU sponsored the development of his engine with a view to its possible use in motorcycles. Eventually, after the war, he rearranged his early designs and produced a successful prototype of a practical engine in 1956.

The Wankel engine consists of one chamber of epitrochoidal shape (the path described by a point on a circle rolling round another circle), which looks like an elongated circle with two dents in it. Inside this chamber is a rotor in the shape of an equilateral triangle with rounded sides. In one revolution the rotor successively isolates various parts of the chamber, allowing for the intake of fuel and air, compression, ignition, expansion, and exhaust to take place. While this driving cycle is taking place relative to one face of the rotor, two more are taking place relative to the other two faces; as a result the crankshaft rotates three times for every turn of the rotor. Thus the Wankel engine produces more power for its weight than the more conventional Otto and Diesel engines. There are no separate valves, because the induction and exhaust of vapours is controlled by the movement of the rotor. The great problem with the Wankel engine has been the effective and efficient sealing of the chamber into three parts by the rotor.

Wankel engines are easily connected together in pairs. There are very few moving parts compared with an ordinary motorcar engine; there are no piston rods or camshafts. The saving in engine weight means that slightly less power is required from engines of this type when they are used in cars.

Over the years a number of motor companies have produced cars with this engine, including NSU in Germany and Toyo Kogyo of Japan. Other companies

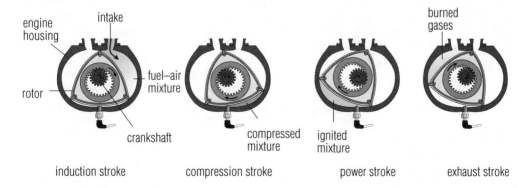

Wankel The rotary Wankel engine uses the same four stages as the four-stroke Otto cycle; induction, compression, combustion, and exhaust.

throughout the world have bought the rights to manufacture and use the Wankel engine. As yet it has not displaced the conventional engine, but this is mainly because of the difficulty of efficiently sealing the chambers for a long duration, and because of the now very stringent tests for pollution which any new engine has to undergo in many countries.

Warburg, Otto Heinrich (1883–1970) German biochemist who made several important discoveries about metabolic processes, particularly intracellular respiration and photosynthesis, and pioneered the use of physicochemical methods for investigating the biochemistry of cells. Probably his most important contribution was his outstanding work on respiratory enzymes, for which he was awarded the 1931 Nobel Prize for Physiology or Medicine.

Warburg was born on 8 October 1883 in Freiburg im Breisgau, the son of a physics professor at the University of Berlin. He studied chemistry under Emil ◊Fischer at the University of Berlin, obtaining his doctorate in 1906, and then read medicine at the University of Heidelberg, gaining his medical degree in 1911. In 1913 he went to the Kaiser Wilhelm (later Max Planck) Institute for Cell Physiology in Berlin-Dahlem, becoming a professor there in 1918 and its director in 1931 (having served in the Prussian Horse Guards during World War I). In 1941 Warburg, being part-Jewish, was removed from his post by the Nazi regime, but such was his international prestige and so important was his research that he was soon reinstated and he remained the director of the institute for the rest of his life. In 1944 he was nominated for a second Nobel prize but was not allowed to accept the award because Germans were forbidden to do so. Warburg died in West Berlin on 1 August 1970.

One of Warburg's chief interests was intracellular respiration, and in the early 1920s he devised a method for determining the uptake of oxygen by living tissue using a manometer. Continuing this general line of research, he began to investigate oxidation–reduction reactions involved in intracellular respiration. Warburg and the German chemist Heinrich ◊Wieland held opposite views about the mechanism of the reaction:

$$AH_2 \;+\; B \;\xrightarrow{\text{catalyst}}\; A \;+\; BH_2$$

$$\begin{array}{cccc} \text{(hydrogen} & \text{(hydrogen} & \text{(oxidized)} & \text{(reduced)} \\ \text{donor)} & \text{acceptor)} & & \end{array}$$

Warburg believed that the hydrogen acceptor had to be activated and made capable for accepting hydrogen, whereas Wieland thought that the hydrogen donor was activated and made to yield its hydrogen to a hydrogen

carrier. Warburg demonstrated that his proposed mechanism was possible and postulated that, in living cells, an iron-containing enzyme activated oxygen (the hydrogen acceptor) and rendered it capable of accepting the hydrogen. He noted that animal charcoal, produced by heating blood, catalyses the oxidation of many organic compounds – oxygen being consumed in the process – whereas vegetable charcoal produced by heating sucrose does not behave in this way. From this finding Warburg concluded that the difference in the behaviour of the two types of charcoal was due to the presence of iron in the blood. He discovered that charcoal systems and living cells behave in similar ways in some respects: in each case, the uptake of oxygen is inhibited by the presence of cyanide or hydrogen sulphide, both of which combine with heavy metals and inhibit respiration. He also showed that, in the dark, carbon monoxide inhibits the respiration of yeast but does not do so in the light. He was aware that heavy metals form complexes with carbon monoxide and that the iron complex is dissociated by light, which provided further evidence for the existence of an iron-containing respiratory enzyme. Warburg then investigated the efficiency of light in overcoming the carbon monoxide inhibition of respiration, finding that the light's efficiency depended on its wavelength. And by plotting the wavelength against the light's efficiency, he determined the photochemical absorption spectrum of the respiratory enzyme, which proved to be a haemoprotein (a protein with an iron-containing group) similar to haemoglobin; he called it iron oxygenase. It was for this work that Warburg was awarded a Nobel prize in 1931.

Meanwhile, the British biologist David Keilin (1887–1963) had discovered cytochromes (the hydrogen carriers in intracellular respiration whose existence had been postulated by Wieland) and cytochrome oxidase, believed to be identical to Warburg's iron oxygenase. Therefore both Wieland and Warburg had been correct in their views about the mechanisms involved in intracellular respiration; they had merely been investigating different stages in this extremely complex pathway.

Warburg also studied coenzymes and he and his collaborators isolated NADP (nicotinamide adenine dinucleotide phosphate) in 1935 and FAD (flavine adenine dinucleotide) in 1938, both of which are important in respiration.

Working on photosynthesis Warburg showed that, given suitable conditions, it can take place with almost total thermodynamic efficiency – that is, virtually 100% of the light energy can be converted to chemical energy. Later he discovered the mechanism for the conversion of light energy to chemical energy that occurs in photosynthesis. In addition, he studied cancer and was the first to discover that malignant cells require less oxygen than do normal cells. This finding was unique at the time, and even today remains one of the relatively few facts that applies to all types of cancer.

Warming, Johannes Eugenius Bülow (1841–1924) Danish botanist whose pioneering studies of the relationships between plants and their natural environments established plant ecology as a new discipline within botany.

Warming was born on 3 November 1841 on the island of Mando. He studied at the University of Copenhagen but, while still a student, spent the years 1863–66 at Lagoa Santa, Brazil, assisting the Danish zoologist P W Lund in a project involving the excavation of fossils. During this expedition, Warming undertook a thorough study of tropical vegetation, the results of which took 25 years to publish fully, although a summary, *Lagoa Santa: A Contribution to Biological Phytogeography*, appeared in 1892. After his return from Brazil, Warming studied for a year at Munich University under Karl von Nägeli (1817–1891) and then spent another year at Bonn University under J L von Hanstein. In 1871 Warming gained his doctorate from the University of Copenhagen and he taught botany there 1873–82, when he became professor of botany at the Royal Institute of Technology in Stockholm, Sweden. He went on an expedition to Greenland in 1884 and to Norway in 1885, after which he returned to Copenhagen to become professor of botany at the university and director of the Botanical Gardens, positions he held until his retirement in 1911. His last major expedition, 1890–92, was to the West Indies and Venezuela. Warming died in Copenhagen on 2 April 1924.

Warming's most important contribution to botany was in the area of plant ecology. Ernst ◊Haeckel had coined the term 'ecology' in 1866 and it was introduced into botany by Reiter in 1885, but it was Warming who provided the foundation for the study of plant ecology. He investigated the relationships between plants and various environmental conditions, such as light, temperature, and rainfall, and attempted to classify types of plant communities (he defined a plant community as a group of several species that is subject to the same environmental conditions, which he called ecological factors). Warming set out the results of his work in *Plantesamfund* (1895), in which he not only provided a theoretical basis for the study of plant ecology but also formulated a programme for future research into the subject, including the investigation of factors responsible for the congregation of plants into communities, and of the evolutionary and environmental pressures that lead to the development of particular habits and habitats in each plant species. *Plantesamfund* was translated into several languages, including English (as *Oecology of Plants* in 1909), and had a tremendous impact in stimulating research into plant ecology.

Warming also investigated a wide range of other areas in botany – including tropical, temperate, and arctic flora (about which he provided a vast amount of data), flower ovules, and the classification of flowering plants.

Waterston, John James (1811–1883) Scottish physicist who first formulated the essential features of the kinetic theory of gases. Unfortunately, his work was not recognized during his lifetime and Waterston was considered to be an eccentric scientist of no outstanding merit, best known for his work on solar heat. This assessment of his abilities was considerably revised after his death when his contribution to kinetic theory came to light, but by that time the theory had been independently developed by others.

Waterston was born in Edinburgh in 1811. He attended Edinburgh High School and then joined a civil engineering firm. His employers permitted him to attend courses at Edinburgh University, where he studied a broad range of scientific and medical subjects. He showed particular aptitude in mathematics and physics, and began publishing scientific papers as early as 1830.

The expanding British railway system attracted many young engineers to its service, and Waterston moved to London in 1833 to do surveying and draughtsmanship work for it. He wrote papers on matters arising from his work and also continued to do experiments and research into pure science in his own time. He became affiliated with the Institute of Civil Engineers, and took a less time-consuming job in the hydrographers' department of the Admiralty in order to spend more time on science.

A complete change in Waterston's life came in 1839 when he went to India to take up a post as teacher of the East India Company's cadets in Bombay. He spent his spare time in the library of the Grant College in Bombay, and continued to write scientific papers, which he sent back to the UK – including the ill-fated submission on kinetic theory.

Waterston spent nearly 20 years in Bombay, but when he had saved enough money he retired and in 1857 he returned to Edinburgh to devote all his efforts to research. He wrote papers on a variety of topics covering a broad scientific spectrum, but had difficulty in getting them published. He became increasingly bitter over this and towards the end of his life withdrew completely from all contacts with the rest of the scientific community. On 18 June 1883 he disappeared from his home and was never heard of again.

Waterston's first scientific paper, published when he was only 19 years old, concerned a model that he proposed might explain gravitational force without the necessity for postulating an effect that operated at great distances. This was a topic of lively debate at the time, and although he did not carry his work along these lines any further, the paper did contain some formative ideas that were developed in his kinetic theory of gases 15 years later.

In 1843, Waterston wrote a book on the nervous system in which he attempted to apply molecular theory to physiology. It included several fundamental features of the kinetic theory of gases, among them the idea that temperature and pressure are related to the motion of molecules. However, Waterston's ideas on neurophysiology and psychology were ahead of their time and, perhaps for this very reason, the book aroused little interest.

The work of James ◊Joule on heat stimulated Waterston to consider more fully its application to the properties of gases. He produced a paper that contained the first formulation of the equipartition theory and was thus an early application of statistical mechanics, and submitted it to the Royal Society in 1845. The society, following its standard practice, had the paper read by two scientists, who both commented unfavourably on the efforts of this obscure scientist writing from the other side of the globe, and the paper was firmly rejected. An abstract of the paper did appear in the *Transactions* of the Royal Society in 1846, and a short note was published on it by the British Association in 1851.

Waterston was unable to retrieve the paper from the society, and as he had not kept a copy for himself, he was unable to publish his theory elsewhere. A longer abstract of the paper was the best he could provide, and that purely for private circulation. Hermann von ◊Helmholtz published an abstract of his theory in a German journal, which may conceivably have stimulated interest in kinetic theory in Germany. But it was Rudolf ◊Clausius, James Clerk ◊Maxwell, and Ludwig ◊Boltzmann who received the credit for the development of the kinetic theory from 1857 onwards. The rejection of Waterston's work had delayed progress to the kinetic theory by about 15 years. Waterston's priority was finally established by Lord ◊Rayleigh, who discovered his 1845 paper on the kinetic theory in the Royal Society's vaults in 1891 and published it in the following year with an introduction warning young scientists of the resistance to new ideas often displayed by scientific societies.

Waterston did gain some recognition for a paper he presented to the British Association in 1853 on the basis for the generation of solar heat. He proposed that meteoric material falling into the Sun would produce heat. In 1857 he published an estimate of the solar temperature at 13 million degrees, which is not far from the present value accepted for the Sun's interior. Waterston wrote other papers on sound, capillarity, latent heat, and various aspects of astronomy. The rejection of two of his papers by the Royal Astronomical Society in 1878 may well have been related to his resignation from that society shortly thereafter, after having been a member for over a quarter of a century, and his subsequent progressive withdrawal from science.

Waterston must therefore be regarded rather as a tragic figure, a scientist whose originality and talent were frustrated to the detriment not only of himself but also of science as a whole.

Watson, James Dewey (1928–) US geneticist who, with ◊Crick and ◊Wilkins discovered the molecular structure of DNA, for which they shared the Nobel Prize for Physiology or Medicine in 1962. Their discovery of the double helix is considered to be the most important biological advance of the 20th century.

Watson was born on 6 April 1928 in Chicago, Illinois, the son of a businessman. He attended the Horace Mann Grammar School and the South Shore

Watson US geneticist James Dewey Watson who won the Nobel Prize for Physiology or Medicine in 1962, together with Francis Crick and Maurice Wilkins, for his work on determining the structure of DNA. *Mary Evans Picture Library*

High School in Chicago and at the age of 15 he entered the University of Chicago on a tuition scholarship to study zoology. In 1947 he received a BSc in zoology and was awarded a fellowship for graduate study at the Indiana University in Bloomington. In 1950 he achieved his PhD in zoology.

At Indiana he was influenced by geneticists H J ◊Muller and T M Sonneborn (1905–1981) who were both in the bacteriology department. His PhD thesis, supervised by Italian biologist S E Luria (1912–1991), was on the effect of hard X-rays on bacteriophage multiplication. From 1950 to 1951 he continued his work on viruses as a Merck Fellow of the National Research Council. While he was there he studied bacteria viruses and the DNA of infecting viruses. It was in the spring of 1951, on a visit to the Zoological Station in Naples, that he met Maurice Wilkins, who showed him the X-ray diffraction pattern of crystalline DNA that he had discovered. This inspired his interest in molecular biology and later that year he moved to the Cavendish Laboratory at the University of Cambridge where he met Francis Crick. They found that they shared an interest in elucidating the detailed structure of DNA, and started to work together.

By incorporating the results of Rosalind ◊Franklin's and Maurice Wilkins's X-ray diffraction studies, Edwin ◊Chargaff's discovery that nucleic acids contain only four different organic bases and Alexander ◊Todd's demonstration that nucleic acids contain sugar and phosphate groups, Crick and Watson postulated that DNA consists of a double helix consisting of two parallel chains of alternate sugar and phosphate groups linked by pairs of organic bases. They then built a series of accurate molecular models, eventually making one that incorporated all known features of DNA and which gave the same diffraction pattern as that found by Wilkins. They envisaged replication occurring by a parting of the two strands of the double helix, each organic base thus exposed linking with a nucleotide (from the free nucleotides within a cell) bearing the complementary base. Thus two complete DNA molecules would eventually be formed by this step-by-step linking of nucleotides, with each of the new DNA molecules comprising one strand from the original DNA and one new strand. Their model also explained how genetic information could be coded – in a sequence of organic bases. Crick and Watson published their work on the proposed structure of DNA in 1953 and their hypothetical model has been confirmed by many other researchers and accepted as correct.

In 1953 Watson returned to the US becoming senior research fellow in biology (at the age of 25) at the California Institute of Technology and studying RNA with X-ray diffraction with Alexander Rich. He returned to the Cavendish in 1955 to 1956 to work with Crick again and they published papers together on the principles of virus construction. Watson became a member of Harvard Biology Department faculty in 1956 as assistant professor, was promoted to associate professor in 1958 and to professor in 1961. At Harvard he researched the role of RNA in protein synthesis. From 1968 to 1993 he was director of the Cold Spring Harbour Laboratory of Quantitative Biology, and has been president from 1994.

As well as receiving the Nobel Prize for Physiology or Medicine in 1962 with Crick and Wilkins, Watson has received several other awards and honours including the John Collins Warren Prize of the Massachusetts General Hospital with Crick in 1959, the Eli Lilly Award for Biochemistry in 1959, the Lasker Award with Crick and Wilkins in 1960, the Research Corporation Prize with Crick in 1962. He also has membership of the Danish Academy of Arts and Sciences, is consultant to the President's Scientific Advisory Committee. He wrote *The Double Helix* (1968) the story of their discovery of the double helix, and from 1989 to 1992 he was head of the US government's Human Genome Project.

Watson-Watt, Robert Alexander (1892–1973)

Scottish physicist and engineer who was largely responsible for the early development of radar. He patented his first 'radiolocator' in 1919, and perfected his equipment and techniques from 1935 through the years of World War II. His radar was employed in the deployment of British fighter aircraft during the Battle of Britain.

Watson-Watt was born in Brechin, Angus, and educated at the University of St Andrews where he also taught 1912–21. His interest in the reflection of radio waves was first aroused during his time at the university and this subject became his life's work.

The first patent for a radar-like system had been granted in several countries to a German engineer Christian Hulsmeyer in 1904. Evolving from the search for a means of detecting radio waves from ships, his system worked, was demonstrated to the German Navy, but was never accepted. The principles used in Hulsmeyer's system had been discovered much earlier through the experimental work of the English physicist Michael ◊Faraday and the mathematical investigations of the Scottish physicist James Clerk ◊Maxwell, who predicted the existence of radio waves and formulated the electromagnetic theory of light. The German physicist Heinrich ◊Hertz tested Maxwell's theories experimentally, and in 1886 proved the existence of radio waves.

When Watson-Watt started his work it was known that radio waves can be reflected, for it was their reflection from ionized layers in the upper atmosphere that made long-distance broadcasting possible. The reflection was sharper as wavelength decreased. The device that Watson-Watt patented in 1919 was concerned with radio-location by means of short-wave radio waves. It was based on quite simple principles. Radio waves travel at an accurately known velocity (the velocity of light), which for purposes of approximation may be taken as 300,000 km/186,000 mi per second. When radio waves are radiated from a transmitting antenna and are interrupted by any object – such as a ship, plane, or even a mountain – part of the energy is reflected back toward the receiver. The direction from which the echo is obtained is the direction of the obstacle.

Watson-Watt continued his experiments and by 1935 had patented improvements that made it possible to follow an aeroplane by the radio-wave reflections it sent back. The system was called 'rádio detection and ranging' and from this comes the present abbreviation 'radar'. Research and development was being conducted during the 1930s in the UK, France, Germany, and the USA, although as the decade wore on only the British researched with any great energy. Watson-Watt's work was heavily subsidized by the British government, and was carried out in great secrecy. By 1938, when it was apparent that war was inevitable, radar stations were in operation, and during the Battle of Britain in 1940 radar made it possible for the British to detect incoming German aircraft as easily by night as by day, and in all weathers including fog. Early in 1943 microwave aircraft-interceptor radars were operational, ending night-bombing raids on Britain.

The first radar sets specifically designed for airborne surface-vessel detection had been flown early in 1943. Wartime pressures and the enthusiastic hard work of Watson-Watt had given the UK a clear lead in the field of radar, and before the USA joined the war Watson-Watt visited the USA to advise on the setting up of radar systems. In 1942 he was knighted.

Radar as a navigational aid and for collision avoidance has become a standard accessory on ships and aircraft. Harbour surveillance sets now guide ships when visibility is poor. Radar on planes detects storms and helps pilots to avoid bad weather and a phenomenon known as clear-air turbulence. A familiar police application is the use of radar to determine the speed of a car by the Doppler shift in frequency of the reflected signal. In weather forecasting the tracking of distant clouds and their development is accomplished by the use of radar, while in the military field it is used in the steering of guided missiles and in warning of their approach. The great radio telescope at Jodrell Bank, Cheshire, which has a bowl-shaped reflector 76 m/250 ft across that can be pointed to any part of the sky, can be used as a radar set, the reflector being used to

direct the pulses of microwaves in a narrow beam towards a chosen object. In this way echoes have been obtained from the Moon and the paths of satellites and spacecraft have been tracked.

Much research and development of computer-controlled and computer-linked radar continues. Development of higher power sources also continues and it is probable that further improvements in radar performance will be achieved by advances in receiving techniques. Here again, the computer will play an important role, storing information, separating signals from noise, and generally increasing the sensitivity of the receiver. But however sophisticated, all uses of radar owe a debt to Watson-Watt's original invention.

Watt, James (1736–1819) Scottish mechanical engineer who is popularly credited with inventing the steam engine. In fact he modified the engine of Thomas ◊Newcomen to the extent that it became a practical, efficient machine capable of application to a variety of industrial tasks. In particular he devised the separate condenser and eventually made a double-acting machine that supplied power with both directions of the piston; this was a great help in developing rotary motion. He also invented devices associated with the steam engine, artistic instruments, and a copying process, and devised the horsepower as a description of

Watt Scottish engineer James Watt, who developed the steam engine. The first working engine was produced in 1776 in partnership with manufacturer Matthew Boulton, but it was not until the 1780s that the firm began to show a profit. *Mary Evans Picture Library*

an engine's rate of working. The modern unit of power, the watt, is named after him.

Watt was born in Greenock on 19 January 1736, the son of a chandler and joiner. Throughout his life he suffered from serious attacks of migraine, and at school both his peers and his teachers took a poor view of this 'weakness'. His great delight was to work in his father's workshop, where a corner had been set aside for him with his own forge and workbench. Soon he developed great skill, and he wished to become an instrument-maker. In his attempt to find an apprenticeship in this trade, he went first to Glasgow, where he worked with an optician and odd-job man for a year. Then, on advice from a friend, he went to London. Eventually, he secured a position with very unfavourable conditions. He did, however, learn the skills of instrument-making before illness forced him to return home to Greenock. After recovering, he set up in business as an instrument-maker in Glasgow and in 1757 obtained work from Glasgow University that allowed him to work in a room within its precincts, and he proudly described himself as 'Instrument Maker to Glasgow University'.

During this period he was asked to repair a small working model of Newcomen's steam engine. The machine proved to be temperamental and difficult to operate without air entering the cylinder and destroying the vacuum. He set about investigating the properties of steam and making measurements of boilers and pistons in the hope of improving Newcomen's machine, which was, at best, slow, temperamental, inefficient, and extremely costly to run in terms of the coal required to keep a sufficient head of steam in a practical engine. During a short period of inspiration, in the course of a Sunday afternoon walk, he had the idea of a separate condenser (separate from the piston). In Newcomen's engine, the steam in the cylinder was condensed by a jet of water, thus creating a vacuum that, in turn, was filled during the power stroke by the atmosphere pressing the piston to the bottom of the cylinder. On each stroke the cylinder was heated by the steam and cooled by the injected water, thus absorbing a tremendous amount of heat. With his separate cylinder, Watt could keep the cylinder hot, and the condenser fairly cold by lagging, thus improving the thermal efficiency of the machine and the economics of its operation. Watt's original engine of 1765 is now in the Science Museum, London. It was only a working model, and reveals the haste in which it was built.

As far as practical engines were concerned, Watt had a great deal of trouble in efficiently lagging the cylinder so that heat was retained and at the same time allowing the piston to move freely. He was helped with facilities and labour by John Roebuck of Kinneil, who eventually employed Watt's engine to pump water from his mines. In 1767 Watt again travelled to England, this time to patent his engine (patent granted in 1769). On his way back to Scotland he visited some friends of Roebuck in Birmingham and met Matthew ◊Boulton. Boulton was a major manufacturer in Birmingham and had the finance to exploit Watt's engine. Because of the patent arrangements between Watt and Roebuck it was not until the latter got into severe financial difficulties that Boulton could buy him out and begin manufacturing the engine. In fact, between 1767 and 1774, Watt made his living as a canal surveyor. Although he was successful at this, his health was not up to an outside job in harsh weather and he suffered accordingly.

From 1775, financial difficulties being solved, Boulton and Watt went into partnership and manufactured Watt's engines at the famous Soho Foundry, near Birmingham. In 1782 Watt improved his machine by making it double-acting. By means of a mechanical linkage known as 'parallel motion' and an extra set of valves, the engine was made to drive on both the forward and backward strokes of the piston, and a 'sun-and-planet' gear (also devised by Watt) allowed rotary motion to be produced. This new and highly

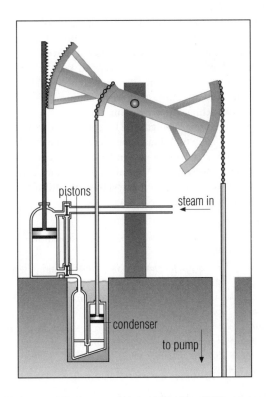

Watt James Watt's steam engines, dating from 1769, were an improvement on that of Thomas Newcomen in that they had a separate condenser and permitted steam to be admitted alternately on either side of the piston.

adaptable engine was quickly adopted by cotton and woollen mills. A universally practical means of producing power for the evolving British industry was therefore at hand, with the consequent rapid rise in the adoption of larger machines.

During this same period, 1775–90, Watt invented an automatic centrifugal governor, which cut off the steam when the engine began to work too quickly and turned it on again when it had slowed sufficiently. He also devised a steam engine indicator, which showed steam pressure and the degree of vacuum within the cylinder. Because of the secretarial duties connected with the business, Watt invented a way of copying letters and drawings; this was a chemical process and was displaced only with the advent of the typewriter and photocopier. Although his steam engines were usually built for specific purposes and individually priced, it was important to have a rational method upon which charges could be made. For this he considered the rate at which horses worked and, after many experiments, concluded that a 'horsepower' was 15,000 kg/33,000 lb raised through 0.3 m/1 ft each minute. He rated his engines in horsepower and in the English-speaking world this method of describing the capability of an engine continued until recent years.

In 1785 Watt was elected a fellow of the Royal Society. During the last decade of the 18th century the active management of the Soho Works was taken over increasingly by Boulton and Watt's sons and in 1800, when the patent rights to the engine expired, Watt retired. He then kept an attic workshop and busied himself designing and constructing copying machines.

Watt died on 25 August 1819, aged 83, leaving the legacy of highly useful machine power for the development and proliferation of industry. His name has become immortalized as the unit of power; a watt is one joule per second, and one horsepower is equivalent to about 746 watts.

Further Reading

Davenport, A N, *James Watt and the Patent System*, British Library, 1989.

Murihead, James P, *Life of James Watt*, Industrial Antiquities series, Archival Facsimiles Ltd, 1989.

Smiles, Samuel, *Lives of the Engineers Boulton and Watt: The Steam-Engine*, Murray, 1904.

Smiles, Samuel, *Lives of Boulton and Watt*, Collected Works of Samuel Smiles series, Routledge/Thoemmes Press, 1996.

Unwin, Richard James, *James Watt: Pioneer of the Machine Age*, Artisan, 1991.

Weber, Heinrich (1842–1913) German mathematician whose chief work was in the fields of algebra and number theory.

Weber was born in Heidelberg on 5 May 1842. He entered the university there to study mathematics and physics and, after a year's interval at the University of Leipzig, received his doctorate in 1863. He then went to Königsberg (now Kaliningrad in Russia), where for three years he worked with Franz Neumann (1798–1895) and Friedrich Richelot (1808–1875). He began to teach at the University of Heidelberg in 1866 and was made an extraordinary professor in 1869. Thereafter he taught at a number of institutions – the Zürich Polytechnic, the University of Königsberg, the Technical High School at Charlottenburg, and the universities of Marburg and Göttingen – before taking up his last post at Strasbourg in 1895. He died in Strasbourg on 17 May 1913.

The three years that Weber spent at Königsberg as a young man had a decisive influence on his mathematical career. The influence of Karl ◊Jacobi was then very powerful there and much of Weber's work shows his solid grounding in Jacobian methods. His early work was based on the theory of differential equations, and he was encouraged by Neumann to apply his knowledge to problems in physics. Yet it was not until late in his career that Weber's work in such subjects as heat, electricity, and electrolytic dissociation was published. Most of it was contained in his *Die partiellen Differentialgleichungen der mathematischen Physik* (1900–01), which was essentially a reworking of, and a commentary upon, a book of the same title, based on lectures given by Bernhard ◊Riemann and written by Karl Hattendorff.

In the decades before that book appeared Weber produced most of his important work, especially his most outstanding contribution to mathematics, his demonstration of Niels ◊Abel's theorem in its most general form. Another brilliant result was his proof of Leopold ◊Kronecker's theorem that the absolute Abelian fields are cyclotomic – that is, that they are derived from the rational numbers by the adjunction of roots of unity. This work on Abel's mathematics reflected the influence of Richelot, under whose guidance Weber became an expert in the manipulation of algebraic functions.

In the 1890s Weber produced several important results, chief among them his demonstration of the critical importance of linking analysis and number theory in investigating problems involving complex multiplication. In 1896 there appeared his culminating work in algebra, the two-volume *Lehrbuch der Algebra*, which for a generation was the standard algebra text. That book, and his editorship of the three-volume *Enzylopädie Elementär-Mathematik* (1903–07), commended Weber not just to higher mathematicians but also to the host of teachers and students who came after him.

Weber, Wilhelm Eduard (1804–1891) German physicist who made important advances in the measurement of electricity and magnetism by devising sensitive instruments and defining electric and magnetic units. In recognition of his achievements, the SI unit of magnetic flux density is called the weber. Weber was also the first to reach the conclusion that electricity consists of charged particles.

Weber was born in Wittenberg on 24 October 1804. The family was highly gifted, for Weber's father was professor of theology at the University of Wittenberg and his older brother Ernst Weber (1795–1878) became a pioneer in the physiology of perception. In 1814, the family moved to Halle, where Weber entered the university in 1822. He obtained his doctorate in 1826, and then became a lecturer at Halle, rising to an assistant professorship in 1828.

In 1831, Weber moved to Göttingen to become professor of physics and there began a close collaboration with Karl ◊Gauss. He lost this post in 1837 following a protest at the suspension of the constitution by the new ruler of Hannover. However Weber managed to continue working at Göttingen and then in 1843 he obtained the position of professor of physics at Leipzig. In 1849, Weber returned to his former post at Göttingen. He remained in this position until he retired in the 1870s, and died in Göttingen on 23 June 1891.

Weber's work in magnetism dates from the time when he joined Gauss at Göttingen. They conceived absolute units of magnetism that were defined by expressions involving only length, mass, and time, and Weber went on to construct highly sensitive magnetometers. He also built a 3-km/2-mi telegraph to connect the physics laboratory with the astronomical observatory where Gauss worked, and this was the first practical telegraph to operate anywhere in the world. It was not subsequently developed as a commercial invention, though, from 1836–41, Gauss and Weber organized a network of observation stations to correlate measurements of terrestrial magnetism made around the world.

In 1840, Weber extended his work on magnetism into the realm of electricity. He defined an electromagnetic unit for electric current that was applied to measurements of current made by the deflection of the magnetic needle of a galvanometer. In 1846, he developed the electrodynamometer, in which a current causes a coil suspended within another coil to turn when a current is passed through both. This instrument could be used to measure alternating currents. Current could also be measured by the Coulomb torsion balance in electrostatic units, and in an experiment carried out with Rudolph Kohlrausch in 1855, Weber found that the ratio of the electro-

magnetic unit to the electrostatic unit is a constant equal to the velocity of light. They did this by discharging a condenser through a torsion balance and a ballistic galvanometer. Weber and Kohlrausch attached no great importance to their strange result, but it later proved to be vital to James Clerk ◊Maxwell in his development of the electromagnetic theory of light.

In 1852, Weber defined the absolute unit of electrical resistance and also began to conceive of electricity in terms of moving charged particles of positive and negative electricity, resistance being produced by a combining of the two particles. In 1846, he had produced a general law of electricity that attempted to express electrical effects mathematically and although it was not successful, it did help Weber to develop his ideas on the nature of electricity. In a remarkable piece of foresight, he put forward in 1871 the view that atoms contain positive charges that are surrounded by rotating negative particles and that the application of an electric potential to a conductor causes the negative particles to migrate from one atom to another. It was not until 1913, with the proposal of the Rutherford–Bohr model of the atom, that Weber's ideas were seen to be essentially correct. Weber also provided similar explanations of thermal conduction and thermoelectricity that were later fully developed by others.

Weber also did important work in acoustics with his brother Ernst Weber. In 1825, they made the first experimental study of interference in sound. Their findings were important in enabling Hermann von ◊Helmholtz to achieve explanations of the perception of sound and mechanism of hearing.

Weber's insistence on precise experimental work to produce correct definitions of electrical and magnetic units was very important to the development of these sciences and to electromagnetism. His far-reaching views on the nature of electricity were influential in creating a climate for the acceptance of such ideas when evidence for them was later found.

Wedderburn, Joseph Henry Maclagan (1882–1948) Scottish mathematician who opened new lines of thought in the subject of mathematical fields and who had a deep influence on the development of modern algebra.

Wedderburn was born in Forfar on 26 February 1882 and was educated at the University of Edinburgh, which he entered in 1898. He received a degree in mathematics in 1903 and in the following year was awarded a Carnegie Fellowship to study at the University of Chicago. In 1905 he returned to Scotland, where he was appointed a lecturer in mathematics at the University of Edinburgh and editor of the *Proceedings of the Edinburgh Mathematical Society*. In

1908 he was awarded a doctorate and in 1909 he went back to the USA to teach at Princeton University. During World War I he saw active duty in France as a soldier in the British army. He then returned to Princeton, where he remained until his retirement in 1945. For the last 20 years of his life he was in poor health and he stopped publishing in 1938. He died in Princeton on 9 October 1948.

The first paper that Wedderburn published, 'Theorem on finite algebra' (1905), was a milestone in algebraic history. Before it appeared little was known about hyper-complex numbers and their roles in algebra. The classification of semi-simple algebras had been investigated only for fields composed of real or complex numbers. Wedderburn was able to show, by introducing new methods, that it was possible to arrive at a complete understanding of the structure of these algebras over any field.

From that foundation he went on to derive the two theorems to which his name has become attached. The first was contained in his paper 'On hyper-complex numbers' (1907), in which he demonstrated that a simple algebra consists of matrices of a given degree with elements taken from a division of algebra. This paper marked the beginning of a new approach to this type of algebra. The first Wedderburn theorem states that 'if the algebra is a finite division algebra (that is, that it has only a finite number of elements and always permits division by a non-zero element), then the multiplication law must be commutative, so that the algebra is actually a finite field'.

Wedderburn's second theorem states that a central-simple algebra is isomorphic to the algebra of all $n \times n$ algebras. He arrived at it by an investigation of skew fields with a finite number of elements. When he started, all commutative fields with a given number of elements had been classified; but it was assumed that no noncommutative field existed, because none had ever been found. Wedderburn's discovery that every field with a finite number of elements is commutative under multiplication thus led to a complete classification of all semi-simple algebras with a finite number of elements.

The modern study of mathematical fields owes an enormous debt to Wedderburn, who may rightly be regarded as one of the creative geniuses of his age.

Wedgwood, Josiah (1730–1795) English pottery manufacturer, one of the most celebrated and influential of all time.

Wedgwood was born in about June 1730 in Burslam, Staffordshire, the youngest son of Thomas Wedgwood, who was also a renowned potter. After his father's death in 1739 the young Josiah worked in the family business at Churchyard Works, Burslam, and in 1744

was apprenticed to his brother Thomas. At about this time he contracted smallpox, and had to have his right leg amputated. During the period of forced inactivity he studied books about pottery and did much experimental work. He was refused a partnership with his brother in 1749, but shared one with John Harrison of Stoke-on-Trent, which lasted until 1753. A year later he joined Thomas Wheildon of Fenton Low, Staffordshire, who was also a leading potter of his day.

The partnership flourished, which enabled Wedgwood to become a master of the art and to continue with what he termed his *Experimental Book,* which proved to be an invaluable source of information on the production of Staffordshire pottery. He also invented and produced his improved 'green glaze', which has remained popular until the present day.

Wedgwood then set up in business on his own at the Ivy House Factory in Burslem, and there he perfected cream-colonial earthenware, which became known as queen's ware because of the interest and patronage of Queen Charlotte in 1765. In 1768 he went into partnership with the Liverpool business-man Thomas Bentley and they expanded the company into the Brick House Bell Works Factory. They produce unglazed stoneware in various colours, formed and decorated in the popular Neo-Classical style. Wedgwood also continued with his black basalts, which, with added red acaustic painting, allowed him to imitate Greek red-figure vases and fine-grained jasper ware. He then built the Etruria Factory, using his engineering skills in the design of its machinery and high-temperature beehive-shaped kilns, which were more than 4 m/12 ft wide. He named the factory after Etruria in northern Italy where coincidentally he died on 3 January 1795.

Further Reading
Burton, Anthony, *Josiah Wedgwood: A Biography,* Deutsch, 1976.

Reilly, Robin, *Josiah Wedgwood, 1730–1795,* Macmillan, 1992.

Smiles, Samuel, *Josiah Wedgwood: His Personal History,* Collected Works of Samuel Smiles series, Routledge/Thoemmes, 1997.

Tames, Richard, *Josiah Wedgwood, 1730–1795: An Illustrated Life,* Lifelines series, Shire Publications, 1972, v 4.

Young, Hilary (ed), *The Genius of Wedgwood,* Victoria and Albert Museum, 1995.

Wegener, Alfred Lothar (1880–1930) German meteorologist and geologist who perhaps did most to revolutionize scientific study of the Earth in the 20th century.

Born in Berlin in 1880, Wegener studied at Heidelberg, Innsbruck, and Berlin, obtaining his

Wegener German meteorogist and geologist Alfred Lothar Wegener whose theory of continental drift was accepted after initial rejection. Most of his observation and exploration was carried out in Greenland, where he died in 1930 while attempting to cross from the central ice-cap to the base at Kamarujuk on the west coast. *Mary Evans Picture Library*

doctorate in astronomy in 1905. Before World War I he taught at Marburg, specializing in meteorology. From 1924 he held a specially created chair in meteorology and geophysics at Graz, Austria.

If it turns out that sense and meaning are now becoming evident in the whole history of the Earth's development, why should we hesitate to toss the old views overboard?

ALFRED WEGENER IN MARTIN SCHWARZBACH
ALFRED WEGENER, THE FATHER OF CONTINENTAL
DRIFT

From 1910 Wegener began developing a theory of continental drift. Empirical evidence for such displacement lay, he thought, in the close jigsaw-fit between coastlines on either side of the Atlantic, and notably in palaeontological similarities between Brazil and Africa. Wegener was also convinced that geophysical and geodetic factors would corroborate the conjecture of a

flight from the poles and of wandering continents – though he himself was rather confused about the causes of such displacement, believing partly in tidal forces.

Wegener supposed that a united supercontinent, Pangaea, had existed in the Mesozoic. This had developed numerous fractures and had drifted apart, some 200 million years ago. During the Cretaceous, South America and Africa had largely been split, but not until the end of the Quaternary had North America and Europe finally separated; the same was true of the break between South America and Antarctica. Australia had been severed from Antarctica during the Eocene. Wegener's hypothesis met with widespread hostility. Only with the development of a satisfactory mechanism for displacement, that is, with the rise of plate tectonics since World War II, has the modified hypothesis won support.

An intrepid polar explorer, Wegener died while crossing the Greenland ice sheet on his fourth expedition on 21 November 1930. Wegener may well be remembered as the most influential geologist of the 20th century. Though not the first theorist of continental drift, his accounts of the theory, especially his

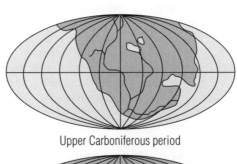

Upper Carboniferous period

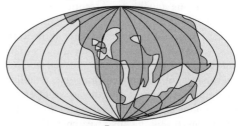

Eocene

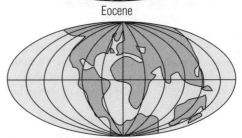

Lower Quaternary

Wegener Continental drift.

Origin of Continents and Oceans (1929), gave the premise scientific plausibility.

Further Reading

Georgi, Johannes, *Mid-Ice: The Story of the Wegener Expedition to Greenland,* K Paul, Trench, Trubner & Co, 1934.

Macrakis, Kirstie, 'Alfred Wegener: self-proclaimed scientific revolutionary', *Arch Int Hist Sci,* 1984, v 34, pp 163–176.

Schwarzbach, Martin, *Alfred Wegener, the Father of Continental Drift,* Scientific Revolutionaries: A Biographical Series, Science Tech Publishers – Springer-Verlag, 1986.

Weierstrass, Karl Theodor Wilhelm (1815–1897)

German mathematician who is remembered especially for deepening and broadening the understanding of functions.

Weierstrass was born in Ostenfelde, Westphalia, on 31 October 1815. Because of his family's frequent change of residence he attended many schools as a young boy and it was not until he entered the Roman Catholic school at Paderborn in 1829 that he began to reveal his mathematical ability. In deference to his father's wish that he should pursue a 'respectable career', he entered the University of Bonn in 1834 to study law, administration, and finance. By 1837 he was certain that mathematics alone interested him and in that year he left Bonn, without taking a degree, to enter the Theological and Philosophical Academy at Münster, with the dual intention of gaining a teacher's certificate and devoting himself to the study of advanced mathematics.

He received his teaching certificate in 1841. From 1842 to 1848 he taught at a secondary school in Deutsch-Krone, West Prussia, then moved to Braunsberg, where he became a lecturer at the Roman Catholic school. In his spare time he did his mathematical research and in 1854 he published in *Crelle's Journal* a paper on Abelian integrals that established his reputation and earned him the award of an honorary doctorate from the University of Königsberg. The strain of combining his research with a heavy teaching load (physics, botany, and history in addition to mathematics) told on his health. From 1850 he suffered from debilitating attacks of vertigo and for the rest of his life he was rarely in good health. He was therefore happy to be given leave of absence in 1855 to complete his work on function theory, begun in the 1854 paper.

That paper marked a turning point in his academic life. Until the age of 40 Weierstrass had worked in isolation. Then, in 1856, he was appointed professor of mathematics at the Royal Polytechnic School in Berlin and, jointly with it, associate professor at the University of Berlin, although he did not begin actually to lecture at the university until 1864. In 1861 he suffered a complete physical breakdown, and although a year of convalescence brought an end to the attacks of vertigo, he thereafter suffered from bronchitis and phlebitis. By 1894 he was confined to a wheelchair; he died of pneumonia in Berlin on 19 February 1897.

Weierstrass's most important work was in function theory, the subject that he first treated seriously in the examination paper for his teacher's certificate in 1841. This was followed up by the 1854 paper, which solved the inversion of hyperelliptic integrals, and a second paper of 1856. His greatest achievement was the demonstration, published in 1871, that there exist continuous functions in an interval that have derivatives nowhere in the interval. In fact he published very little. Much of his reputation rested on his lectures at Berlin, which ranged over the whole of mathematics and which became famous for their 'Weierstrassian rigour'. In particular, Weierstrass did much (again more in lectures than in publications) to clarify the meaning of basic concepts such as 'function', 'derivative', and 'maximum'. His development of the modern theory of functions was described in his *Abhandlungen aus der Funktionlehre* (1886), a text derived chiefly from his students' lecture notes. In the 1890s Weierstrass planned the publication of his life's work, again to be compiled from lecture notes. Two volumes were published before his death and five more appeared during the next three decades. Three volumes of the projected ten-volume set remain unpublished, but even the incomplete work remains a rich quarry for the present-day mathematician.

Weil, André (1906–1998)

French mathematician whose main fields of activity were number theory, group theory, and algebraic geometry.

Weil was born on 6 May 1906 in Paris, where he grew up, was educated, and attended the university, receiving his doctorate in 1928. In 1930 he went to India for two years as professor of mathematics at Aligarh Muslim University. Returning to France, he took up a similar post at Strasbourg University and remained there until 1940. Then, after a year's lecturing in the USA, he moved to Brazil where in 1945 he became professor of mathematics at the University of São Paolo. From 1947 to 1958 he was professor of mathematics at the University of Chicago, and then transferred to a similar post at the school of mathematics at the Institute of Advanced Studies of the University of Princeton. He died on 6 August 1998.

One of Weil's earliest contributions to number theory came in 1929, when he extended some earlier work by Henri ◊Poincaré. This resulted in the postulation of what is now called the Mordell–Weil theorem, a theorem that is closely connected to the theory of Diophantine equations.

Weil worked on quadratic forms with algebraic coefficients and extended Emil ◊Artin's work on the theory of quadratic number fields. He also contributed to the generalization of algebraic geometry.

In addition, Weil was a founder member of a secretive and esoteric club that published mathematical papers under the pseudonym Nicolas Bourbaki. (Although there was no limit to the number of members in the Bourbaki group, its membership was always changing because retirement was compulsory on reaching the age of 50.)

Weil's own major work, *Foundations of Algebraic Geometry*, was published in 1946.

Weinberg, Steven (1933–)

US theoretical physicist best known for developing the unified electroweak theory. In 1957 he demonstrated with Pakistani theoretical physicist Abdus ◊Salam that the weak nuclear force and the electromagnetic force (two of the fundamental forces of nature) are variations of a single underlying force that is now called the electroweak force. Weinberg, Salam, and US physicist Sheldon ◊Glashow shared a Nobel Prize for Physics for this work in 1979.

Born in New York on 3 May 1933, the son of a court stenographer, Steven Weinberg was educated at the Bronx High School of Science in the same class as Glashow. With Glashow he entered Cornell in 1950, graduating in 1954 and then moving on to Princeton where he gained a PhD in 1957. He held positions at Columbia for two years, at Berkeley 1959–69, and at the Massachusetts Institute of Technology 1969–73. He was Higgins Professor of Physics at Harvard 1973–86 before becoming professor of physics and astronomy at the University of Texas at Austin.

At Berkeley in 1967, working with Glashow's early explanation, Weinberg produced a gauge theory that correctly predicted electromagnetic and weak nuclear forces. This was later to become known as the electroweak theory. In his paper, 'A model of leptons', he showed that although electromagnetism is much stronger than the weak force of everyday energies, the only way to devise a theory of the weak force is to include the electromagnetic force. Weinberg showed how what was seemingly impossible could be achieved and the forces could be unified through the interchange of particles in spite of the difference in their strengths. Abdus Salam had independently reached the same conclusions and what became known as the Weinberg–Salam model was a major advance on earlier models that had originally applied to leptons. The model's most striking prediction was

that of the presence of neutral-current weak interactions (which had previously been believed to be absent). It also predicted the cross sections and other properties of a large number of neutral-current processes in terms of a single parameter, and together with the Glashow– Iliopoulis–Maiani charm scheme is the basis for an understanding of particle physics. The fundamental constituents of the model are six quarks and six leptons . The quarks interact through the strong and the electroweak interactions, but the leptons have only electroweak interactions. The strong interactions are mediated by a neutral boson, the gluon, and the theory that describes these interactions is called quantum chromodynamics, while the weak force is mediated by the W+ and W– boson. In 1979 Weinberg shared the Nobel Prize for Physics for this work with Salam and his old school friend Sheldon Glashow, who had extended the work that Weinberg and Salam had independently developed.

Weinberg also took an interest in cosmology and published *Gravitation and Cosmology* (1972). While he was at Harvard in 1979 he published *The First Three Minutes*, which described the early universe and was immensely popular with a general audience. In *Dreams of a Final Theory* (1993) he put the case that contemporary theories contained glimpses of an outline of a final theory. In the book he suggests that if the US government were to go ahead with the planned construction of the Superconducting Super Collider in Texas, it would be powerful enough to reveal the boson described by English physicist Peter Higgs (1929–) in 1964 and used by Weinberg to support his model.

Weismann, August Friedrich Leopold (1834–1914)

German zoologist who is best known for his 'germ plasm' theory of heredity and for his opposition to Jean Baptiste ◊Lamarck's doctrine of the inheritance of acquired characteristics. Weismann was one of the founders of the science of genetics, and many of the ideas he put forward on the subject are essentially correct. For his outstanding contribution towards elucidating the mechanism of inheritance, Weismann received many honours, including a medal awarded by the Linnaean Society of London at the Darwin–Wallace celebration in 1908 and the Darwin Medal, which was awarded at the anniversary meeting of the Royal Society of London.

Weismann was born on 17 January 1834 in Frankfurt am Main, the son of a classics professor at the Gymnasium there. In 1852 he went to the University of Göttingen to study medicine and graduated in 1856, after which he briefly held several positions, including those of a doctor in the Baden army (Baden was then an autonomous grand duchy) and private physician to Archduke Stephen of Austria. In 1860 Weismann visited Freiburg im Breisgau, which impressed him so much that he felt he would like to live there. In the following year a brief period studying under Karl Leuckart (1822–1898) in Giessen reawakened Weismann's childhood interest in natural history, and in 1863 he joined the University of Freiburg's medical faculty as a teacher of zoology and comparative anatomy. He persuaded the university to build a zoological institute and museum, and he became its first director. Weismann remained at the University of Freiburg until his retirement in 1912. During his later years he travelled extensively and became famous for his lectures on heredity and evolution. He was extremely patriotic and renounced all the British honours awarded him when World War I broke out. He died in Freiburg on 5 November 1914.

In his early years at Freiburg, Weismann studied insect metamorphosis and the sex cells of hydrozoa. In the mid-1860s, however, his eyesight began to deteriorate and he was unable to perform the microscope work necessary for this research. After a rest his eyesight improved and he resumed his earlier work, but the improvement was only temporary and by the mid-1880s he was forced to abandon the observational part of his work and to concentrate on theory.

Although an admirer of Charles ◊Darwin, Weismann began by questioning pangenesis (Darwin's theory that every cell of the body contributes minute particles – gemmules – to the germ cells and therefore participates in the transmission of inherited characteristics) and then proceeded to attack the Lamarckian theory of the inheritance of acquired characteristics. Weismann's early work on hydrozoan sex cells led him to postulate that every living organism contains a special hereditary substance, the germ plasm, that controls the development of every part of the organism and is transmitted from one generation to the next in an unbroken line of descent. Furthermore, he realized that repeated mixing of the germ plasm at fertilization would lead to a progressive increase in the amount of hereditary material, and therefore predicted that there must be a type of nuclear division at which each daughter cell receives only half of the original germ plasm. This prediction was proved correct by the cytological work of Oskar Hertwig (1849–1922) and others, which then led Weismann to propose that the germ plasm was situated in what were later called the chromosomes of the egg nucleus.

Weismann's germ-plasm theory is still basically true today, although we now use the terms chromosomes, genes, and DNA to refer to the hereditary material Weismann called germ plasm. In one important respect, however, Weismann was not completely correct: he believed that the germ plasm cannot be altered by the action of the environment and that variations among individuals arise from different combinations and permutations of the germ plasm. Although different combinations of the hereditary material do give rise to individual variations, the genetic material can be modified by environmental influences – as was later demonstrated by Hugo ◊de Vries and Hermann ◊Muller.

Weizsäcker, Carl Friedrich von (1912–)

German theoretical physicist who has made fundamental contributions to astronomy by investigating the way in which energy is generated in the cores of stars. He is also known for his theory on the origin of the Solar System.

Weizsäcker was born in Kiel on 28 June 1912. He earned his PhD at the University of Leipzig in 1933, and was an assistant at the Institute of Theoretical Physics there 1934–36. He worked at the Kaiser Wilhelm Institute of Physics in Berlin-Dahlem and lectured at the University of Berlin 1936–42, when he was appointed to a chair at the University of Strasbourg. Weizsäcker returned to the Kaiser Wilhelm Institute in 1944. During World War II, he was a member of the German research team investigating the feasibility of constructing nuclear weapons and harnessing nuclear energy. One of his overriding concerns in this work was that his team should not develop a nuclear weapon that might be placed at the disposal of the Nazi government.

In 1946 Weizsäcker became director of a department in the Max Planck Institute of Physics in Göttingen, holding an honorary professorship at the University of Göttingen. He became professor of philosophy at the University of Hamburg in 1957 and retired in 1969 with an appointment to an honorary chair at the University of Munich. From 1970 to 1980 he was director of the Max Planck Institute in Starnberg.

In 1938, Weizsäcker and Hans ◊Bethe independently proposed the same theory of stellar evolution, one that accounted both for the incredibly high temperatures in stellar cores and for the production of ionizing and particulate radiation by stars. They proposed that hydrogen atoms fused to form helium via a proton–proton chain. Bethe and his collaborators went on to outline the complex of reactions that might follow to produce the energy created by a star. Weizsäcker turned to a study of the atomic reactions that take place in the fission of uranium and the problems of constructing an atomic pile.

In 1944 Weizsäcker revived an old cosmogenic theory, the so-called 'nebular hypothesis' of Immanuel ◊Kant and Pierre ◊Laplace, which had carried much weight during the 19th century, but which by the end of the century had given way to the 'collision' theory.

The collision theory proposed that planets were produced after another star approached our Sun so closely that a proportion of the solar mass became detached in the form of a wisp of hot gas and dust and then coalesced to form the planets. The chief difficulty with this theory was that, since stellar interactions of that nature must be exceedingly rare, planetary systems must be exceedingly uncommon in the universe. Furthermore, the stability of the solar material disturbed in such a manner was unlikely to be sufficient to permit the formation of planets.

Weizsäcker suggested that multiple centres, or vortices, formed in the spinning gaseous discoid mass that preceded our Solar System, and that from them the planets condensed. This model indicated that planetary systems were formed as a natural by-product of stellar evolution, and that they were therefore not likely to be as rare as would have been predicted by the collision theory.

Wells, Horace (1815–1848)

US dentist who discovered nitrous oxide anaesthesia and, in 1844, was the first to use the gas in dentistry – although ether anaesthesia had previously been used in other surgical operations.

Wells was born in Hartford, Vermont, on 21 January 1815. He was educated at private institutions in Massachusetts and New Hampshire, then, at the age of 19, began to study dentistry in Boston. He subsequently set up a dental practice in Hartford, Connecticut, initially in partnership with William ◊Morton – who later pioneered the use of ether as an anaesthetic – and with John Riggs (1810–1885) as one of his students. In late 1844, while watching an exhibition of the effects of laughing gas (nitrous oxide) staged by a travelling show, Wells observed that the gas induced anaesthesia – an effect also noticed previously by Crawford Long (1815–1878), another pioneer of anaesthesia. Wells then arranged to have one of his wisdom teeth extracted by Riggs while the showman administered nitrous oxide. Having felt no pain during this operation, he subsequently used nitrous oxide anaesthesia to perform painless extractions on his patients.

In January 1845 Wells went to Boston where, with the help of Morton (then no longer his partner), the chemist Charles Jackson (1805–1880), and the surgeon John Warren (1778–1856), he arranged to demonstrate a painless tooth extraction using nitrous oxide anaesthesia to students at the Massachusetts General Hospital. During the demonstration, however, the patient cried out and, although the patient later claimed to have felt no pain, the audience believed that the demonstration had failed. After this debacle Wells gave up his dental practice and became a travelling salesman, selling canaries and then showerbaths in Connecticut. In 1846 Morton gave a successful demonstration of ether anaesthesia in the same operating theatre that Wells had used, and in the following year Wells went to Paris to try to establish his priority in using anaesthesia. At about this time he also began experimenting on himself with nitrous oxide, ether, and various other intoxicating chemicals; as a result he became addicted to chloroform and mentally unstable. In 1848, having returned to the USA, he was imprisoned in New York City for throwing acid in the face of a prostitute and, while in his prison cell, committed suicide on 24 January of that year. Ironically, during his imprisonment the Paris Medical Society accepted Wells's claim to priority in the discovery of anaesthesia.

Welsbach, Carl Auer, Baron von Welsbach (1858–1929)

Austrian chemist and engineer who discovered two rare-earth elements and invented the incandescent gas mantle.

Welsbach was born Carl Auer on 1 September 1858 in Vienna. He was the son of the director of the Imperial Printing Press. He went to Heidelberg for his university training and studied under the German chemist Robert ◊Bunsen, developing a strong interest in spectroscopy and lighting. He showed that didymium, previously thought to be an element, actually consisted of the two very similar but different elements: praseodymium and neodymium. He also found that another rare-earth element, cerium, added as its nitrate salt to a cylindrical fabric impregnated with thorium nitrate, produced a fragile mantle that glowed with white incandescence when heated in a gas flame. The 'Welsbach mantle' was patented in 1885.

The major development in artificial lighting in the 19th century was the introduction of methods of generating and distributing coal gas in urban communities. The first successful experiments in this field are usually credited to Witham ◊Murdock, a Scottish engineer working in Cornwall who lit his own home by gas before being commissioned to install gas lighting in London. For several decades the source of light was from the yellow gas flame itself, produced by a simple 'bat's-wing' burner. During the 1820s a new type of burner was introduced, in which a controlled amount of air was admitted to the gas current (as in a laboratory Bunsen burner) producing a high-temperature but non-luminous flame that heated a refractive material. At very high temperatures this material became the light source. But the method proved to be expensive and unreliable until the invention of the Welsbach mantle, which, in its final form of a woven net (usually spherical or cylindrical) impregnated with the salts of thorium and cerium, could be made sufficiently strong and durable to be transported. (When a mantle was first used, the cotton burned away to leave a mesh of metal oxides that was fragile but continued to function as long as it was not roughly handled.)

Thomas ◊Edison's electric lamp eventually replaced gas lamps for nearly all applications, although mantles are still used for kerosene lamps and for portable lamps powered by 'bottled' gas. More often than not, such lamps are lit using a cigarette lighter or automatic gas lighter that makes use of a 'flint', another of Welsbach's discoveries. Most lighter flints consist of what he called Mitschmetal, a pyrophoric mixture containing about 50% cerium, 25% lanthanum, 15% neodymium, and 10% other rare metals and iron. When it is struck or scraped it produces hot metal sparks. Mitschmetal is also used as a deoxidizer in vacuum tubes and as an alloying agent for magnesium.

When the emperor of Austria conferred upon him the title Freiherr, Welsbach chose as his baronial motto 'more light'. This has proven to be a prophetic choice, for both Welsbach's discoveries are still used in the production of light.

Wenner-Gren, Axel Leonard (1881–1961) Swedish industrialist who developed a monorail system of transport.

Wenner-Gren was born on 5 June 1881 in Uddevalla. He was educated in Germany and began his working career as a salesman for the Swedish Electric Lamp Company. Over a period of years he gradually gained promotion and eventually became a majority shareholder. In 1921 he founded the Electrolux Company to manufacture vacuum cleaners and, later, refrigerators. With the success of his first company well established, he widened his interests to include many aspects of Swedish industry, including the ownership of one of the country's largest wood-pulp mills and of the Bofors munition works. From the profits, he donated a large sum of money for the foundation of an institute for the development of scientific research in Sweden, which became known as the Wenner-Gren Foundation for Nordic Cooperation and Research.

Engineers have been experimenting with monorails for more than 150 years but almost always their construction has proved to be more complicated than expected. The first monorail patent was taken out in 1821 by Henry Robinson Palmer, an engineer to the London Dock Company, who built a line that ran between the Royal Dock Victualling Yard and the River Thames. It consisted of an elevated rail made from wooden planks set on edge and capped by an iron bar to take the wear and tear of the horse-drawn 'car' wheels. The 'cars' were in two parts that hung down on each side of the rail like saddle bags. Similar later designs were built by Lartigue in France and, in 1869, by J L Hadden who built a steam-operated monorail in

Syria. An electric version of the Lartigue line was operated in France in the late 1890s. Later systems used gyroscopes to stabilize the train.

Wenner-Gren's monorail, the Alweg line, consisted of a concrete beam carried on concrete supports. The cars straddled the beam on rubber-tyred wheels, and there were also horizontal wheels in two rows on each side of the beam. The system proved to be commercially successful, and it was used for the 13-km/8-mi line in Japan from Tokyo to Haneda Airport.

Werner, Abraham Gottlob (1749–1817) German geologist who developed the first influential paradigms of Earth structure and history.

Born in Silesia into a family involved for generations in mines engineering, Werner studied between 1769 and 1771 at the Mining School at Freiberg, Saxony, before proceeding to the University of Leipzig. An early product of his studies was *On the External Characteristics of Fossils* (1774), an examination of minerals in the light of their surface features. In 1775 he was appointed to the Freiberg Academy, where he continued to teach for the rest of his long life. He proved easily the most influential instructor in the history of geology, most of the leading students of the next generation learning their science under him.

Though now judged largely erroneous, Werner's geology was of cardinal significance in its day for establishing a physically based stratigraphy, grounded on precise mineralogical knowledge. Werner proposed a general succession of the creation of rocks, beginning with Primary rocks (precipitated from the water of a universal ocean), then passing through Transition, Flötz (sedimentary), and finally Recent and Volcanic. The oldest rocks had been chemically deposited; they were crystalline and without fossils. Later rocks had been mechanically deposited. Formed out of the denuded debris of the first creations, they were fossiliferous and superincumbent.

Werner's approach was particularly important for linking the order of the strata to the history of the Earth, and relating studies of mineralogy and strata. Its 'neptunism' (that is, belief in water as the chief strataforming agent) was attacked by the Huttonian 'plutonists' who saw heat or fire as playing that role. 19th-century geology drew on the work of both Werner and James ◊Hutton to develop a balanced view of the significant geomorphological forces.

Werner, Alfred (1866–1919) French-born Swiss chemist who founded the modern theory of coordination bonding in molecules (formerly inorganic coordination compounds were known by the generic term 'complexes'). For this achievement he was awarded the 1913 Nobel Prize for Chemistry.

Werner was born on 12 December 1866 in Mulhouse, Alsace, when it was part of France (four years later at the end of the Franco-Prussian War it became German territory). He was the son of a foundry worker and, despite his parents' French sympathies, received a German education. He began studying chemistry and experimenting when he was 18 years old, and in 1885, while doing military service with the German army, attended lectures at the Karlsruhe Technische Hochschule. A year later he entered the Zürich Polytechnic, graduating with a diploma in chemistry in 1889. He spent 1890 with Pierre ◊Berthelot in Paris, but returned to Zürich the following year, becoming a full professor in 1895. He ceased work in 1915 because of severe arteriosclerosis, and he died in Zürich on 15 November 1919.

Although Werner is recognized mainly for his discoveries in inorganic chemistry, his first major success was in organic chemistry in 1890. With his teacher Arthur Hantzsch (1857–1935) he described the structure and stereochemistry of oximes (organic compounds containing the =N–OH group, prepared by adding hydroxylamine, NH_2OH, to aldehydes or ketones). He showed that these compounds could exhibit geometrical isomerism in the same way as a compound containing a carbon–carbon double bond, and explained their structures by suggesting that the nitrogen bonds are directed in space tetrahedrally (extending the theories of Jacobus ◊van't Hoff and Joseph le Bel about the carbon atom).

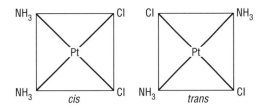

syn (*trans*)   anti (*cis*)

Werner The two stereoisomers of benzaldoxime.

Werner developed his theory about bonding in coordination compounds as part of his thesis for obtaining a university teaching position. In addition to ionic and covalent bonds, Werner proposed the existence of a set of coordination bonds resulting from an attractive force from the centre of an atom acting uniformly in all directions. The number of groups or 'ligands' that can thus be bonded to the central atom depends on its coordination number and determines the structure (geometry) of the resulting molecules. Common coordination numbers are 4, 6, and 8. Neutral ligands (such as ammonia and water) leave the central atom's ionic charge unchanged; ionic ligands (such as chloride or cyanide ions) alter the central charge accordingly.

A typical Werner-type coordination compound is hexamminocobalt(III) chloride, $[Co(NH_3)_6]Cl_3$, in which the cobalt has a coordination number of 6 – there are six coordinate bonds from it to the six ammonia molecules. The cobalt's valence (oxidation state) of +3 is balanced by the three negatively-charged chloride ions. The six ammonias are located at the corners of a regular octahedron. Werner was able to demonstrate the theory experimentally by preparing geometrical isomers of compounds of the type diamminoplatinum chloride, which is square planar in shape.

Werner Stereoisomers of diamminoplatinum chloride, $Pt(NH_4)_2CL_2$, each with a coordination number of 4.

More complicated molecules, particularly those having as a ligand ethylene diamine (1,2-diaminoethene, abbreviated to 'en'), exhibit optical isomerism through a pair of mirror-imaged stereoisomers.

Ethylene diamine is bi-functional and acts as a bridge between a pair of coordinate bonds. Some ligands of this type, such as ethylene diamine tetra-acetic acid (EDTA) and its salts, are used to 'mop up' metal

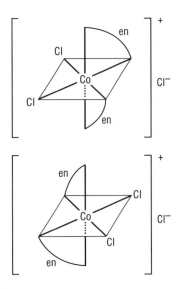

Werner A pair of optically isomeric coordination compounds; mirror images of cis- $[Co(en)_2Cl_2]^+Cl^-$, each with a coordination number of 6.

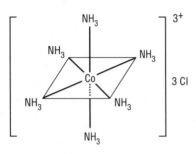

Werner Hexamminocobalt chloride, $[Co(NH_3)_6]\,Cl_3$, with a coordination number of 6.

ions – for example, as antidotes for poisoning by heavy metals such as copper and lead.

Westinghouse, George (1846–1914) US engineer and industrialist at a time of rapid commercial expansion in the USA. His early fame came from his invention of a safe and speedy braking system for railway trains, but later his ideas and influence spread to gas and electricity distribution systems, and to the electrical industry generally.

Westinghouse was born on 6 October 1846 at Central Bridge, New York. He was the eighth of ten children, and his father was a manufacturer of agricultural implements. When he was 15 he ran away from school to fight for the Union in the American Civil War. His parents soon brought him home again, but 18 months later allowed him to join the Union army. In 1864 he joined the navy, but left the following year, having achieved the rank of acting third-assistant engineer. Westinghouse then spent a period of three months as a student at Union College, Schenectady, New York, after which he decided his place was in his father's workshop. In October of the same year (1865), he took out a patent for a railway steam locomotive – the first of his more than 400 patents. During the next four years he concentrated on inventing railway devices, the most important of which was his famous air brake system, patented in 1869.

Up to this time railway trains were slowed only by brakes on the locomotive, and then by manually applied brakes on each individual truck or carriage if necessary. Westinghouse's invention allowed the driver of the locomotive to apply the brakes on all the cars simultaneously – a so-called continuous braking system. This allowed the train to brake smoothly and rapidly, and consequently it became safer for trains to travel at much higher speeds. In the same year Westinghouse formed the Westinghouse Air Brake Company.

The increased efficiency of the railways was quickly realized. Westinghouse further helped both himself and the nation with his pioneer efforts to standardize railway components and systems, including the development of a completely new signalling system. This needed electricity and electrical components, and he went on to invent and manufacture devices in this area. As his business grew he formed more home and foreign companies to manufacture his inventions.

Gas was then a source of power to industry and required efficient distribution; Westinghouse developed a system of gas mains whereby the gas was fed into the network at high pressure but was at the required pressure when it was received by the consumer. His initial high-pressure mains were narrow-diameter pipes that fed into wider pipes (with a consequent drop in pressure), which in turn fed into even wider pipes until the gas was at the correct pressure in the right place.

During the 1880s electricity as well as gas was important, and Westinghouse built a single-phase alternating-current distribution system in Pittsburg with French transformers and generators. He quickly realized its potential, and got his own engineers to design equipment suitable for a new high-tension (voltage) system. Westinghouse saw that high-tension distribution avoided much of the loss through electrical resistance, which limited moderate voltage systems to a small distribution area, and enabled the building of large electrical networks. Alternating current (AC) allowed step-down transformers to be used to bring the voltage to a suitable level for use.

At about this time he secured the services of the Croatian-born electrical engineer Nikola ◊Tesla. He also bought the patents for the AC polyphase induction motor that made his AC system even more useful, because up to that time AC motors had to be started by rotating them at their running speed before the current was switched on. In 1893 the Westinghouse Electric Company lit the world's first Columbia Exposition in Chicago. Two years later the same company harnessed the Niagara Falls to generate electricity for the lights and trams of the town of Buffalo, 35 km/22 mi away.

Many of the Westinghouse industries were based in Pittsburgh and nearby in Turtle Creek Valley, where in 1889 Westinghouse built a model town for his workers. During the period 1907–08 a series of financial crises and takeovers caused him to lose control of the Westinghouse industries. He returned to active experimentation, designing a new steam turbine and reduction gear system and an air spring for use in motorcars. He also spent time reorganizing a large insurance society. From 1913 he suffered increasing ill health from heart disease, and he died in New York on 12 March 1914.

Further Reading

Ravage, Barbara, *George Westinghouse: A Genius for Invention,* Innovative Minds series, Raintree Steck-Vaughn Publishers, 1997.

Usselman, Steven W, From novelty to utility: 'George Westinghouse and the business of innovation during the age of Edison', *Bus Hist Rev,* 1992, v 66, pp 251–304.

Weyl, Hermann (1885–1955) German mathematician and mathematical physicist whose range of research and interests was remarkably wide, and found expression also in published works on philosophy, logic, and the history of mathematics. A one-time pupil of the renowned David ◊Hilbert and a colleague of Albert ◊Einstein, it was probably inevitable that Weyl is remembered chiefly for his studies on topological space and Riemannian geometry.

Weyl was born in Elmshorn, near Hamburg, on 9 November 1885. Attending the high school in Altona, he evinced a strong interest in mathematics and in philosophy. At the age of 18 he entered Göttingen University where, four years later, he received his doctorate for a dissertation on singular integral equations. Until 1913 he then became an unsalaried lecturer at the university, but at that time turned down a professorship in order to take up the chair of mathematics at the Technische Hochschule in Zürich. He held the post until 1930 – despite temporary conscription into the German army during World War I and a year as visiting professor at Princeton University in the USA in 1928. He then succeeded David Hilbert to the chair of mathematics at the University of Göttingen, but the unfavourable political climate of Nazi Germany prompted him to move to the Institute of Advanced Studies back at Princeton, where he then held a permanent post as professor of mathematics. After his retirement in 1951, Weyl divided his time between Princeton and Zürich in Switzerland. During his lifetime Weyl's mathematical talents and contributions were recognized by the award of many honorary degrees and his election to the membership of prestigious scientific societies such as the National Academy of Sciences and the Royal Society. In addition to his many articles published in various journals, Weyl also wrote 15 books that were published both in the USA and Europe. He died in Zürich on 8 December 1955.

Weyl's early university days were strongly influenced by two great mathematicians in his department at Göttingen: David Hilbert and Herman ◊Minkowski. Weyl was to develop interests in fields that included and went beyond those of these two important men.

The whole of Weyl's mathematical career is permeated by his abilities in analysis, but it was during his earliest years, from 1908 to around 1915, that these interests were dominant. He first examined the problems of singular eigenvalues for differential equations, and then turned his attention to oscillations in structures such as membranes and elastic bodies.

As a colleague of Einstein during 1913, he became interested in the developing the general theory of relativity and differential geometry. He lectured on both topics, and consolidated these lectures into a book he published in 1918, entitled *Raum–Zeit–Materie/ Space–Time–Matter,* which in five years ran to five editions. Weyl's interest in relativity theory took him to the point where he believed (erroneously) that he had found a way to a grand unification of gravitation and electromagnetism – something towards which Einstein was to strive for the rest of his life (and which is still being sought). Also in theoretical physics, Weyl was able to anticipate the non-conservation of parity, which has now been found to be characteristic of weak interactions between leptons (a class of subatomic particles that obeys Fermi–Dirac statistics).

Weyl's lectures on Riemann surfaces (see Bernhard ◊Riemann) prompted him to write a book on the subject, which was first published in 1913 (and then republished in 1955). His most important work in this field was the definition of the complex manifold of the first dimension, which has been important in all later work on the theory of both complex and of differential manifolds. This work demanded skills in topology, geometry, and other areas quite different from those he had previously applied in his work in analysis.

The number of papers Weyl produced on the subject of number theory was small – but their impact was great. In 1916 he published one of his best papers, on the definition of the uniform distribution modulo 1, which was to be of great significance in the later work of Godfrey ◊Hardy and John Littlewood (1885–1977) on number theory. Other productive research areas during Weyl's fruitful tenure at the Technische Hochschule in Zürich included calculus, continuous groups, and Lie groups. He applied his work on group theory to the analysis of the atom in a book on quantum mechanics he published in 1928.

During the rest of Weyl's career he returned to these subjects and explored them further. He published books on classic groups in 1939 and on number theory in 1940. His interest in the philosophy of mathematics led him to write a book on this theme as well, in 1949. A mathematician of profound and diverse talents, Weyl made significant contributions to several fields of both mathematics and mathematical physics.

Further Reading

Chandrasekharan, K (ed), *Hermann Weyl, 1885–1985,* Springer-Verlag, 1986.

Chandrasekharan, K (ed), *Hermann Weyl 1885–1985:*

Centenary Lectures Delivered by C N Yang, R Penrose, A Borel at the ETH Zurich, Springer-Verlag, 1986.
Scholz, Erhard, 'Hermann Weyl's contribution to geometry, 1917–1923', in: Chikara, Sasaki, et al (eds), *The Intersection of History and Mathematics*, Birkhauser, 1994, pp 203–230.

Wheatstone, Charles (1802–1875)

English physicist who is known principally for the Wheatstone bridge, a method of making accurate determinations of electrical resistance. However, Wheatstone did not invent this method but popularized it. He in fact made several important but lesser-known original contributions to science, including the invention of the stereoscope and the rheostat, and the first determination of the velocity of electricity along a wire. He was also a pioneer of the telegraph and he invented the concertina.

Wheatstone was born in Gloucester on 6 February 1802. His family were involved in the manufacture of musical instruments and he received no formal education in science. Wheatstone entered the music business as an apprentice to an uncle in 1816. He became an instrument-maker, inventing the concertina in 1829, and also investigated the acoustic properties of instruments. Wheatstone's work in acoustics led to his appointment as professor of experimental physics at King's College, London, in 1834, a position he retained for the rest of his life. His interests then extended to electricity and optics and, in 1837, he formed a partnership with William Cooke (1806–1879) to develop a commercial telegraph. This too continued for life and led to Wheatstone being knighted in 1868, Cooke receiving the same honour the following year. Wheatstone died on a visit to Paris on 19 October 1875.

Wheatstone's early interest in acoustics was stimulated by his family's business, which was principally concerned with the manufacture of flutes. In 1827, he invented an ingenious device called the kaleidophone which visually demonstrated the vibration of sounding surfaces by causing an illuminated spot to vibrate and produce curves by the persistence of vision. Wheatstone went on to investigate the transmission of sound in instruments and subsequently discovered modes of vibration in air columns in 1832 and vibrating plates in 1833.

Wheatstone's contributions to light and optics are also important. In 1860, he demonstrated how the visual combination of two similar pictures in a stereoscope gives an illusion of three dimensions. However, work of greater significance came much earlier with a paper presented at the British Association meeting in Dublin in 1835 entitled 'Prismatic analysis of electric light'. There, Wheatstone showed that different spectra are produced by spark discharges from metal electrodes, analysis of the spectra proving that different lines and colours are formed by different electrodes. He showed the sensitivity of the method and predicted correctly that with development, it would become a technique for the analysis of elements. Wheatstone said, 'We have a mode of discriminating metallic bodies more readily than by chemical examination and which may hereafter be employed for useful purposes'. Many years were to pass before the classic development of spectroscopy by Robert ◊Bunsen and Gustav ◊Kirchhoff in 1860.

In 1848 Wheatstone described a polar clock, which was an instrument for telling the time based on the change in plane of polarization of sunlight in the direction of the Pole. With this clock, it was possible to tell the hour of the day by the light from the sky even if the Sun was be obscured.

In 1834 Wheatstone began a series of important experiments with Cooke on the transmission of electricity along wires. The early work involved the pursuit of pure scientific knowledge, such as the determination of the velocity of electricity related below, but later work was directed towards the public transmission of messages – that is, commercial telegraphy. A series of successes was achieved, the first being a patent in 1837 for the five-needle telegraph. This was an instrument in which five magnetic needles on a panel were deflected by electric signals to various positions that indicated letters of the alphabet, thus transmitting written messages. This device was developed by Wheatstone and Cooke, culminating in a portable two-needle telegraph in 1845 and a single-needle telegraph the following year. These instruments were direct ancestors of the teleprinter.

In the field of electricity, Wheatstone made several important contributions. In 1834, he made the first determination of the velocity of electricity through a wire by using a rotating mirror to determine the delay that occurred between sparks as a current produced several spark gaps in a long loop of wire. The result was very high – 30% greater than the speed of light – possibly because the wire was not straight, but the method was taken up and used by Armand ◊Fizeau in 1849 to make the first accurate determination of the velocity of light.

Wheatstone also improved on early versions of the dynamo invented by Michael ◊Faraday by combining several armatures on one shaft so that current was generated continuously; previously only intermittent generation was possible. He also recognized the theoretical and practical importance of Ohm's law (see Georg ◊Ohm), developing the rheostat (variable resistance) and Wheatstone bridge method for the accurate determination of resistance. This important method was published in the *Transactions of the Royal Society* in 1843, but it had been invented ten years earlier by

Samuel Christie (1784–1865). It involves placing an unknown resistance in a simple circuit with three known resistances and varying one of them until no current flows through a galvanometer connected like a bridge to all four resistances. The unknown resistance can then be determined from the values of the other three resistances.

It is ironic that Wheatstone is mainly remembered for a device that he himself did not invent, and this must not blind us to the extraordinary range of his talents and great value of his original work in telegraphy, electricity, optics, and acoustics.

Further Reading

Bowers, Brian, *Sir Charles Wheatstone FRS, 1802–1875*, HMSO, 1975.

Dawes, Howard A L, 'Wheatstone's wave machine: a physical model of light' in: Anderson, R G W, et al (eds), *Making Instruments Count: Essays Presented to Gerard L'Estrange Turner*, Variorum, 1993, pp 127–138.

Hubbard, Geoffreay, *Cooke and Wheatstone and the Invention of the Electric Telegraph*, Routledge and K Paul, 1965.

Whipple, Fred Lawrence (1906–   ) US astronomer known for his discoveries of comets and his contribution to the understanding of meteorites.

Whipple was born in Red Oak, Iowa, on 5 November 1906. He was educated in California and received his bachelor's degree from the University of California at Los Angeles in 1927; he went on to become a teaching fellow at the University of California at Berkeley. He spent some time at the Lick Observatory and received his PhD in 1931. In the same year he was appointed to the staff of the Harvard College Observatory and a year later he became an instructor at Harvard. He was gradually promoted to posts of increasing responsibility until, in 1950, he was made professor, a post he held until 1977. During World War II, Whipple carried out radar research at the Office of Scientific Research and Development, and in 1948 he was awarded the Presidential Certificate of Merit for his work there. He also held a number of advisory posts on scientific bodies such as the Rocket and Satellite Research Panel. In 1955 he became director of the Smithsonian Institution Astrophysics Observatory, a post he retained until 1973, when he became the senior scientist at the observatory. He was awarded the Donahue Medal six times and in 1971 he received the Kepler Medal of the American Association for the Advancement of Science.

In addition to discovering six new comets, Whipple contributed to the understanding of the constitution and behaviour of comets. In 1949 he produced the 'icy comet' or 'dirty snowball' model, proposing that the nucleus of a comet consists of a frozen mass of water, ammonia, methane, and other hydrogen compounds and that embedded within it is a quantity of silicates, dust, and other materials. As the comet's orbit brings it nearer to the Sun, solar radiation causes the frozen material to evaporate, thus producing a large amount of silicate dust that forms the comet's tail. This explanation has found general acceptance among astronomers, and was confirmed in 1986 by spaceprobe studies of Halley's comet.

Whipple has also worked on ascertaining cometary orbits and defining the relationship between comets and meteors. His other interests include the evolution of the Solar System, stellar evolution, and planetary nebulae. He actively participated in the organization of the International Geophysical Year 1957–58 and in the 1950s became active in the programme to devise effective means of tracking artificial satellites.

Whipple, George Hoyt (1878–1976) US pathologist, physician, and physiologist whose work on the formation of haemoglobin led to a cure for pernicious anaemia. He also discovered the cause of thalassaemia. He shared the Nobel Prize for Physiology or Medicine with US physicians George Minot (1885–1950) and William Murphy (1892–1987) in 1934.

Whipple was born at Ashland, New Hampshire, on 28 August 1878 into a medical family. He took an undergraduate degree at Yale University before entering Johns Hopkins University Medical School in 1901. He was inspired to take up medical research by his teachers there who included J J Abel and W H Welch and he remained in Welch's department of pathology after his graduation in 1905 for training and research. At this time he recognized the rare condition that became known as Whipple's disease – a condition which he described as being characterized by the deposition of fat in the intestinal and mesenteric lymphatic tissues. In 1907 he took a year out in the Canal Zone (Panama) to study tropical diseases including amoebic dysentery, filariasis, and blackwater fever.

On his return to Johns Hopkins in 1908 he concentrated his research on the liver, blood coagulation, and jaundice, and in 1914 he became director of the Hooper Foundation for Medical Research and a professor at the University of California at San Francisco. In California he began researching into bile pigments, going on to study the formation of haemoglobin (of which bile pigments are the breakdown products). Working with Frieda Robbins, his experiments involved bleeding dogs until their haemoglobin levels had been reduced to a third of normal, and then measuring the rate of haemoglobin regeneration when the dogs were given various diets. They found a variation in the rate according to the diet of the individual dogs and reported that raw liver, kidney, and meat (in that order) in their diet produced marked increases in haemoglobin production in the blood cells. Whipple published over 200 papers on the topic of haemoglobin production and experimental anaemia.

Following Whipple's reports, Harvard physicians George Minot and William Murphy investigated the use of liver and other foods in the treatment of pernicious anaemia in humans and the three shared the 1934 Nobel Prize for Physiology or Medicine. Other scientists later made the connection between vitamin B_{12} deficiency and pernicious anaemia.

Whipple became dean of the new medical school at Rochester, New York, in 1922, and he was active in the development of the school and in his own researches, remaining there for the rest of his career. As well as his research into blood pigments he worked on blood proteins and blood clot formation and was the discoverer of what he named thalassaemia, a genetic disorder in which there is an abnormality in the protein portion of the haemoglobin molecule, leading to severe anaemia in some people of Mediterranean extraction.

Whipple married Katherine Waring in 1914 and they had a daughter and a son. Among his many other responsibilities Whipple was a trustee of the Rockefeller Foundation 1927–43 and a member of the board of trustees of the Rockefeller Institute 1939–60. He died in Rochester on 1 February 1976.

White, Gilbert (1720–1793) English naturalist and cleric who is remembered chiefly for his book *The Natural History and Antiquities of Selborne* (1789), a classic work in which White vividly records his acute observations of the flora and fauna in the area of Selborne (now in Hampshire).

White was born on 18 July 1720 in Selborne and, after attending schools in Farnham and Basingstoke, went to Oriel College, Oxford, in 1740. He graduated in 1743, was elected a fellow of his college in 1744, and obtained a master's degree in 1746. Although many of his associates believed him capable of a successful academic career, White chose to become a cleric and took deacon's orders in 1747, subsequently becoming a curate in his uncle's parish of Swarraton, near Selborne. White was ordained a priest in 1750 and, after refusing several positions, eventually accepted a post at Moreton Pinkney, Northamptonshire, where his living was paid by Oriel College. But he was strongly attracted to the countryside of his birthplace, so he left the care of the Moreton Pinkney parish to a curate and returned to the family home in Selborne. White subsequently held curacies in several parishes in the neighbourhood but continued to live in Selborne itself until his death on 26 June 1793.

After his return to Selborne, White spent much of his time studying the wildlife in the area. He kept a diary of his observations and also wrote of his findings to two naturalist friends Thomas Pennant and Daines Barrington. These letters, which cover a period of about 20 years, form the basis of *The Natural History of Selborne*. Elegantly written, it is characterized by acute observations of a wide variety of natural history subjects, as well as descriptions of rural life in 18th-century England. The book is more than merely a record, however, it also contains White's theories and speculations and several important discoveries, such as the migration of swallows, the recognition of three distinct species of British leaf warblers, and the identification of the harvest mouse and the noctule bat as British species. On its publication in 1789, *The Natural History of Selborne* was widely praised by leading naturalists; it also has great popular appeal and has been reprinted many times.

White also wrote *Calendar of Flora and the Garden* (1765), an account of observations he made in his garden in 1751, and *Naturalist's Journal* (begun in 1768), a similar but more sophisticated work.

Further Reading
Campbell, Colin (ed), *Gilbert White*, Silent Books Ltd, 1993.
Mabey, Richard, *Gilbert White: A Biography of the Author of the Natural History of Selbourne*, Century, 1986.
White, Gilbert; Francesca Greenoak (ed), *The Journals of Gilbert White*, Century, 1988–89, 3 vols.

Whitehead, Alfred North (1861–1947) English mathematician and philosopher whose research in mathematics involved a highly original attempt – incorporating the principles of logic – to create an extension of ordinary algebra to universal algebra, a meticulous re-examination of the relativity theory of Albert ◊Einstein, and, in work carried out together with his friend and collaborator Bertrand ◊Russell, the production of what is probably one of the most famous mathematics books of the century, *Principia Mathematica*. This book endeavoured to show that logic could be regarded as the basis of mathematics.

Whitehead was born in Ramsgate, Kent, on 15 February 1861, the son of a headteacher who, when Whitehead was aged six, became the vicar of a large parish near Ramsgate. From 1875 to 1880 the boy went to Sherborne School; he then went to Trinity College, Cambridge. Receiving his doctorate in 1884, he was elected to a fellowship of the college and was appointed lecturer. One of his pupils there was Bertrand Russell; the two struck up a friendship and together attended the 1900 International Congress of Philosophy in Paris. The result of this excursion was the publication of their joint work, *Principia Mathematica* (1910). In that year, however, Whitehead left Cambridge and held a number of positions at University College, London, before being appointed professor of applied mathematics at Imperial College, London, in 1914. There he produced his book on relativity theory. It gave a thorough, but obscure, analysis and projected further development of the subject. But his interests were already turning more and more to actual philosophy, and the book is a complicated mixture of mathematics, physics, and philosophy. In 1924 – at the age of 63 – he was invited to become professor of philosophy at Harvard University. During his subsequent years in the USA he produced many fine contributions to philosophy but very little in the way of mathematics. At Harvard he still considered himself an Englishman, and his services to his home country were recognized in the presentation to him of the country's highest award, the Order of Merit, in 1945. A fellow of the Royal Society from 1903, Whitehead died at Harvard on 30 December 1947.

A science which hesitates to forget its founders is lost.

ALFRED NORTH WHITHEAD ATTRIBUTED REMARK

Even in his mathematical studies, Whitehead preferred to think of the philosophical aspects; he was convinced that to regard the various branches of mathematics in a theoretical way, as manifestations of the human intellect, was far preferable to considering them as real, concrete structures, as was the prevailing fashion at the turn of the century. It was from this viewpoint that he produced his first major work *A Treatise of Universal Algebra* (1898), an attempt at a total expansion of algebraic principles that also demonstrated his growing interest in philosophy itself.

At the International Congress of Philosophy in 1900, Whitehead and Russell heard Giuseppe ◊Peano describe the rigorously axiomatic method by which he had arrived at the axioms concerning the natural numbers – for which, despite the acknowledged prior work by Richard ◊Dedekind, Peano is now famous. He was using logical methods to derive mathematical instruments. It occurred, apparently first to Bertrand Russell, that similar methods to those of Peano could be used to deduce mathematics from logic in a general and fundamental way. The collaboration of Russell and Whitehead on the project lasted ten years, and culminated in the publication of the very complicated three-volume treatise *Principia Mathematica*. The book did not quite accomplish its objectives – in fact, in some ways, some of it was nullified by events of its own instigation – but it did have a momentous influence on mathematical thought about the foundations

of the subject. It had a considerable effect on many individual branches, from the development of Boolean algebra to Kurt ◊Gödel's work in which he demonstrated – devastatingly – that arithmetic, and hence mathematics, can never be proved to be consistent.

There was to have been a fourth volume, by Whitehead alone, devoted entirely to geometry, but it was never completed.

Further Reading
Ford, Lewis S, *The Emergence of Whitehead's Metaphysics, 1925–1929,* SUNY Series in Philosophy, State University of New York Press, 1985.

Ford, Lewis S and Kline, George L, *Explorations in Whitehead's Philosophy,* Fordham University Press, 1983.

Kline, George L, *Alfred North Whitehead: Essays on His Philosophy,* University Press of America, 1989.

Lowe, Victor, *Alfred North Whitehead: The Man and His Work,* Johns Hopkins University Press, 1990, v 2.

McHenry, Leemon B, *Whitehead and Bradley: A Comparative Analysis,* SUNY Series in Philosophy series, State University of New York Press, 1991.

Nobo, Jorge L, *Whitehead's Metaphysics of Extension and Solidarity,* State University of New York Press, 1986.

Whitehead, John Henry Constantine (1904–1960) English mathematician who achieved eminence in the more abstract areas of diffential geometry, and of algebraic and geometrical topology.

Whitehead was born on 11 November 1904 in Madras, India, where his father was the Anglican bishop; he was the nephew of the mathematician and philosopher Alfred North ◊Whitehead. Educated first in Oxford then at Eton, he entered Balliol College, Oxford, and gained a BA in mathematics. After graduating he joined a firm of stockbrokers but left after 18 months to return to Oxford. For his mathematical researches he was, in 1929, awarded a scholarship to the University of Princeton, New Jersey, where he met and worked with Oswald Veblen (1880–1960). Four years later he returned again to Oxford and was elected fellow of Balliol College; he took up the Wayneflete Chair of Pure Mathematics there in 1947. On a visit to Princeton in 1960, he suffered a heart attack and died in May of that year.

Whitehead's early research was on differential geometry and the application of differential calculus and differential equations to the study of geometrical figures. It was the results of his years of study in these fields that he took with him to Princeton to meet Veblen, a man he had already known by reputation for some considerable time. Yet Veblen's primary interest at the time was in topology – the study of shapes and figures that retain their essential properties despite being 'stretched' or 'squeezed'. Nevertheless, each mathematician influenced the other. Veblen learned so much about differential geometry that he and Whitehead wrote a textbook together on the subject: *Foundations of Differential Geometry* (1932).

Whitehead, in turn, learned a great deal about topology. Combining his interests thereafter, much of his mathematics became very complex and advanced. Some of his most significant work, however, was in the study of knots. In geometry a knot is a two-dimensional representation of a three-dimensional curve that because of its dimensional reduction (by topological distortion) appears to have nodes (to loop onto itself).

Whitehead, Robert (1823–1905) English engineer, best known for his invention of the self-propelled torpedo.

Whitehead was born on 3 January 1823 in Bolton, Lancashire, one of the eight children of the owner of a cotton-bleaching business. He was educated at the local grammar school and at the age of 14 was apprenticed to a Manchester engineering company: Richard Ormond and Son. His uncle, William Smith, was the manager of the works, and Whitehead received a thorough grounding in practical engineering. He also trained in draughtsmanship by studying at evening classes at the Mechanics Institute in Manchester. His uncle became manager of the works of Philip Taylor and Sons in Marseilles, and in 1844 Whitehead joined him there. Three years later he set up in business on his own in Milan (then part of the Austrian Empire), designing machinery.

Whitehead took out various patents under the Austrian government, but these were annulled by the revolutionary Milanese government of 1848. He moved to Trieste and worked for the Austrian Lloyd Company for two years. From 1850 to 1856 he was manager there of the Studholt works, and then, at the neighbouring naval port of Fiume, he began working at the Stabilimento Tecnico Fiumano. It was there that in 1866 he invented the torpedo.

In 1872, with his son-in-law George Hoyos, Whitehead bought the Fiume establishment, devoting the works to the construction of torpedoes and accessory equipment. His son John became the third partner. In 1890 a branch was founded at Portland Harbour, England, under Captain Payne-Gallway and in 1898 the original works at Fiume were rebuilt on a larger scale.

Whitehead was presented with a diamond ring by the Austrian Empire for having designed and built the engines of the ironclad warship *Ferdinand Max*, which rammed the Italian *Re d'Italia* at the Battle of Lissa in 1866. In May 1868 he was decorated with the Austrian Order of Francis Joseph in recognition of the excellence of his engineering exhibits at the Paris Exhibition

of 1867. He also received honours and awards from many other European countries. In his later years he formed a large estate at Worth, Sussex. He died on 14 November 1905 near Shriveham, Berkshire, and was buried in Worth.

While in business in Milan (1847) Whitehead designed pumps for draining part of the Lombardy marshes and made improvements to silkweaving looms. From 1856, in Fiume, he built naval marine engines (for Austria) and in 1864 he was invited to cooperate in perfecting a 'fireship' or floating torpedo designed by Captain Lupins of the Australian Navy. But in secret, with his son John and a mechanic, he carried out a series of experiments that led in 1866 to the invention of the Whitehead torpedo. It travelled at 7 knots for up to 630 m/2,070 ft but had difficulty in maintaining a uniform depth. Within two years he had remedied this defect by an ingenious but simple device called a balance chamber, which for many years was guarded as the torpedo's 'secret'. A typical torpedo of this time was about 4 m/13 ft long, weighed 150 kg/330 lb (including a 9-kg/20-lb dynamite warhead) and was powered by a compressed-air motor driving a simple propellor.

Nonexclusive manufacturing rights were bought by the Austrian government in 1870, by the British in 1871, the French in 1872, and by Germany and Italy in 1873; by 1900 the right to build the torpedoes had been purchased by almost every country in Europe, the USA, China, Japan, and some of the South American republics.

In 1876 Whitehead developed a servomotor, which controlled the steering gear and gave the torpedo a truer path through the water. Speed and range were gradually improved, so that by 1889 the weapons could maintain 29 knots for 900m/3,000ft. He devised methods of accurately firing torpedoes either above or below water from the fastest ships no matter what the speed or bearing of the target. The weapon was finally perfected in 1896 by the addition of a gyroscope, invented by an Austrian naval engineer, which was coupled to the servo and steering mechanism. Any doubts about the torpedo's usefulness were dispelled when, on 9 February 1904, outside Port Arthur, a few Japanese destroyers armed with torpedoes reduced the Russian battlefleet to impotence.

Whitney, Eli (1765–1825) US lawyer who invented the cotton gin, a machine for plucking cotton fibres off the seeds on which they grow.

Whitney was born on 8 December 1765 at Westborough, Massachusetts, the son of a farmer. His exceptional mechanical ability was evident at an early age, and when he was 15 he began manufacturing nails in a small metalworking shop on the family farm. Then in 1789 he went to Yale University to study law. After graduating three years later he moved to Savannah, Georgia, intending to become a tutor, but he continued to make various mechanical contrivances for domestic use. He became acquainted with Mrs Nathanael Green, the widow of the Revolutionary general, who pointed out to Whitney the local need for a machine for picking cotton. He devised such a machine, the cotton gin ('gin' being short for 'engine'), and in May 1793 formed a partnership with Phineas Millar to manufacture the invention. The cotton gin was patented in March the following year. It was widely copied and, although the courts vindicated his patent rights in 1807, five years later Congress refused to extend the patent. Meanwhile, in January 1798, Whitney had secured a government order to make 10,000 guns. It took him eight years to complete the two-year contract, but even so he received a second order in 1812 and his manufacturing methods were later adopted by both the Federal armouries. Whitney died in New Haven, Connecticut, on 8 January 1825.

Even at Yale, Whitney earned pocket money by making and mending mechanical bits and pieces. In Georgia, Mrs Green introduced him to cotton growers, who realized that a mechanical picker could expand the cotton industry and bring wealth to the Southern States. Whitney's machine had metal 'fingers' that separated the cotton from the seeds. It consisted of a wooden cylinder bearing rows of slender spikes set 1.3 cm/0.5 in apart, which extended between the bars of a grid set so closely together that only the cotton lint (and not the seeds) could pass through. A revolving brush cleaned the cotton off the spikes and the seeds fell into another compartment. The machine was hand-cranked, and one gin could produce about 50 lb/23 kg of cleaned cotton per day – a fifty-fold increase in a worker's output.

The introduction of a machine to clean cotton led to the expansion of the plantations and the demand for more labour, which in turn led to the increasing use of slaves – indeed the cotton gin has been cited as a contributory factor to the American Civil War. Courts in South Carolina awarded Whitney and Millar a $50,000 grant, with which they built a factory at New Haven, Connecticut. But the gin was so easy to copy and simple to manufacture that blacksmiths constructed their own machines. Whitney spent so much of his money in legislation to defend his patent, that he eventually gave up the struggle and in 1798 turned to the manufacture of firearms.

In his arms factory, also in New Haven, Whitney used skilled workers and machine tools to make arms with fully interchangeable parts. It is said that he once took a batch of unassembled rifles and threw then at a government official's feet, inviting him to pick out parts at random and build up a working firearm. This time Whitney made a fortune and kept it.

In 1818 he made a small milling machine, with a power-driven table that moved horizontally beneath and at right angles to a rotating cutter. This device is all that remains today of the machinery with which he launched what became known in Europe as the American system of manufacture. He also introduced division of labour in his musket factory, the beginnings of a production line and mass production.

Further Reading

Green, Constance M, *Eli Whitney and the Birth of American Technology*, Library of American Biography, Addison-Wesley Educational Publishers, 1965.

Latham, Jean L, *Eli Whitney: Great Inventor*, Chelsea House Publishers, 1991.

Whittle, Frank (1907–1996) English engineer and inventor of the jet engine. The developments from his original designs were first used in the Gloster Meteor fighter at the end of World War II. Direct descendants of these engines are now the sources of power for all kinds of military and civil aircraft.

Whittle was born in Coventry on 1 June 1907. When he was ten the family moved to Leamington Spa where he attended secondary school. His aptitude and interest in engineering and invention was encouraged and often demanded by his father, who was himself a designer and craftsman of sufficient skill to run his own workshop. The workshop stimulated Whittle's interests further than his father's ideas. He became interested in aeronautics from a practical as well as a scientific point of view, and at about the same time he developed a preoccupation with the idea of finding a source of power superior to that of the piston engine. On leaving school he joined the Royal Air Force (RAF) as an apprentice. His ability was such that he later entered the RAF College, Cranwell as a cadet, and trained as a fighter pilot. During the training, which included all aspects of the theory of flight and motive power for aircraft, he was able to further his ideas for an improved aero-engine and impress his instructors with the high standard of his flying.

In about 1928 the idea of using a jet of hot gas to cause motion (in accordance with Newton's third law: every action produces an equal and opposite reaction) seemed promising. Whittle realized that a gas turbine could be incorporated to drive a compressor to compress the air entering an engine and the air would rapidly expand when fuel was ignited in it, causing a thrust of exhaust gases and hot air to push the aeroplane through the sky. The faster the turbine turned, the more the air was compressed and the greater the expansion and combustion, and thus increased thrust was obtained.

This idea was beautiful and simple; perhaps too simple since it took Whittle a long time and considerable frustration to convince the Air Ministry that the jet was a source of power with greater potential than piston engines, which were still being developed to new heights of performance. After initially being turned down, Whittle's idea sank into oblivion until about 1935 when, with some support, encouragement and financial backing, he formed the Power Jets Company. The RAF now gave him support and a partial release from his duties. In 1936 he began experiments with his engine at British Thomson-Houston, Rugby. His first engine looked like something between an ancient gramophone and an old vacuum cleaner, but soon his designs took a form that would be recognizable today as a jet engine. His intention was to create a power plant that would propel a small aeroplane at about 800 kph/500 mph. These early assemblies vibrated alarmingly and emitted a terrifying noise.

The prospect of war in 1939 finally prompted the Air Ministry to encourage Whittle's invention by giving Power Jets a contract to power an air frame designed and constructed by Gloster Aircraft. These developments culminated in the maiden flight of the experimental Gloster E-28/39 in May 1941. By the end of 1944 the twin-engined Gloster Meteor, the production model developed from the E-28/39, was coming into service. Although it was the first Allied jet aeroplane, the Germans had produced the Messerschmitt Me-262 slightly earlier.

In the years following the end of the war, the jet engine made possible the new generation of supersonic fighters and eventually the high-speed civil air travel that is now commonplace. The power and thrust of jets have increased by very large factors since Whittle's original designs, but his ideas, developments, and innovations have influenced the invention's whole development to a degree that is very rare for original and early ideas.

For his inventions, Whittle received considerable financial compensation and a knighthood, but eventually Power Jets was removed from his grasp. In 1918 he retired from the RAF with the relatively senior rank of air commodore. He went to the USA, where he took up a university appointment. The famous prototype jet aeroplane, the Gloster E-28/39, can still be seen hanging from the ceiling of the Science Museum, London.

Further Reading

Golley, John, *Whittle: The True Story,* Airlife, 1987.
Golley, John, *Genesis of the Jet: Frank Whittle and the Invention of the Jet Engine,* Airlife Publishing Ltd, 1998.
Golley, John and Gunston, Bill, *Whittle: The True Story: In Association with Sir Frank Whittle,* Smithsonian Institution Press, 1987.

Whitworth, Joseph (1803–1887) English engineer who established new standards of accuracy in the production of machine tools and precision measuring instruments. He devised standard gauges and screw threads, and introduced new methods of making gun barrels.

Whitworth was born in Stockport, Cheshire on 20 December 1803, the son of a schoolteacher. He was educated first at his father's school and then, after the age of 12, at Idle, near Leeds. When he was 14 he went to work in his uncle's cotton mill in Derbyshire. He was so fascinated by the mill machinery that, without permission, he left his uncle's employment and took a job as a mechanic with a firm that made machinery. When he was 22 (and newly married) he went to work for the engineer and toolmaker Henry ◊Maudslay in his London workshops. In 1833 Whitworth moved to Manchester and set up in business as a toolmaker in a rented room that had access to power from a stationary steam engine. From this small beginning the large Whitworth works developed.

At that time it was the usual practice to build every machine and each machine part separately. Parts were not interchangeable and screw threads were often used by only one firm or workshop. Whitworth, recognizing the advantages, brought standardization to his company and the engineering industry as a whole by developing means of measuring to tolerances never before possible so that shafts, bearings, and gears could be interchanged. The well-known Whitworth standard for screw threads was part of this process of modernization.

The Whitworth company produced many machines to work to his new standards and to cope with the new methods of production. There were machines for cutting, shaping, and gear-cutting, but of particular importance for the rapid production of high-quality goods was the planning machinery, which substantially reduced the time spent by skilled workmen on routine tasks. Whitworth also designed a knitting machine and a horse-drawn mechanical road-sweeper.

During the later part of the 19th century steel became available on a large scale from the Bessemer and Siemens open-hearth processes. At the Whitworth works, steel ingots of hexagonal cross-section were used to make gun barrels, axles, propellor shafts, and the like. Whitworth cast these under pressure applied by a hydraulic press so that imperfections caused by bubbles of air or variable cooling rates were minimized. Guns of all sizes were produced, and Whitworth supervised many experiments to investigate the forces acting on the breech and barrel of a gun and the amount of barrel wear (which affected the accuracy of the weapon). He also made advances in the design of rifling for the barrels of small-calibre weapons.

Whitworth was also concerned with the training,

lives, and leisure time of his workers. He created 30 Whitworth scholarships for university engineering students and donated large sums of money to the various Manchester colleges (now Manchester University) and other educational organizations. He received many honours, including a knighthood, fellowship of the Royal Society, and admission to the Légion d'Honneur. Whitworth died after a long illness on 22 January 1887 while on holiday in Monte Carlo in Monaco.

Further Reading

Atkinson, Norman, *Sir Joseph Whitworth: The World's Best Mechanician,* Sutton Publishing, 1997.

Atkinson, Norman, *Sir Joseph Whitworth,* Sutton Publishers, 1996.

Wieland, Heinrich Otto (1877–1957) German organic chemist, particularly noted for his work in determining the structures of steroids and related compounds. He also studied other natural compounds, such as alkaloids and pterins, and contributed to the investigation of biological oxidation. For his work on steroids, he was awarded the 1927 Nobel Prize for Chemistry.

Wieland was born in Pforzheim in the Black Forest on 4 June 1877, the son of a chemist, and was educated at the local school. From 1896 he attended several universities: at Munich, Berlin, Stuttgart, and finally Munich again under the chemist Johannes Thiele (1865–1918). He obtained his PhD in 1901 and spent most of his career in the chemistry faculty of the University of Munich. He became a lecturer there in 1904 and senior lecturer in organic chemistry in 1913. During World War I, in 1917, he moved to the Technische Hochschule (also in Munich) and almost immediately took a year's leave of absence to work on chemical warfare research under Fritz ◊Haber at the Kaiser Wilhelm Institute of Chemistry at Berlin-Dahlem. After the war Wieland returned to his post as professor at the Technische Hochschule, moving to the University of Freiburg in 1921. He finally returned to Munich in 1925 as professor of chemistry and director of the Baeyer Laboratory as successor to Richard ◊Willstätter. He remained there until he retired in 1950, when he was made emeritus professor. He died in Munich on 5 August 1957.

Most of Wieland's early work was concerned with organic nitrogen compounds. He investigated the addition of nitrogen oxides to double bonds in compounds such as terpenes (proposing the existence of nitrogen–nitrogen bonds in dimeric nitrogen oxides). In 1909 he published a method for, and described the mechanism whereby, fulminic acid (cyanic acid) could be prepared from ethyl alcohol (ethanol), nitric acid, and mercury. Two years later he gave the first demon-stration of the existence of nitrogen free radicals by oxidizing diphenylamine to form tetra-arylhydrazine, and decomposing it by heating it in toluene.

After World War I Wieland's interest turned to the chemistry of biologically important compounds. He had begun studying the bile acids as early as 1912, showing that the three newly discovered acids have similar structures related to that of cholesterol – at that time being investigated by Adolf Windaus (1876–1959) at Göttingen. The importance of steroids became even more apparent with the realization that vitamin D and the gonadotrophic hormones also belong to this class of compound. Using classical chemical methods Wieland later worked out what he thought was the basic skeleton of a steroid molecule (for which he was awarded the Nobel prize), but it was found to be incorrect. In 1932 he collaborated with O Rosenheim (who used X-ray analysis) and H King to produce the somewhat modified structure that is still accepted today.

Wieland did other work with the bile acids, demonstrating their role in converting fats into water-soluble cholic acids (a key process in digestion). He was the first to prepare the carcinogen methylcholanthrene, and went on to study the poisons produced in the skins of some species of toads, which are chemically similar to the bile salts. He also determined the structures of and synthesized many toadstool poisons, such as phalloidine from the deadly *Amanita* fungus. This led him to an investigation of alkaloids from both plant and animal sources. He isolated and determined the structures of the *Lobelia* alkaloids, and made incomplete studies of the structures of strychnine and curare. At the suggestion of one of his students he began research into the composition and synthesis of pterins, the pigments that give the colour to butterflies' wings (and one of which is the precursor of the essential human dietary factor folic acid).

Also after World War I Wieland began work on biological oxidation – the process within living tissues by which food substances such as glucose are converted to carbon dioxide and water with the liberation of energy for metabolism. He held the view that the oxidation was in fact a catalytic dehydrogenation. Using palladium as a catalyst in the absence of oxygen he was able to prove experimentally that this was the case; he also experimented with anaerobic microbial systems. This proposal was in direct opposition to the findings of Otto ◊Warburg, who had shown that biological oxidation was an addition of oxygen moderated by iron-containing enzymes. The controversy sparked a long and lively debate, and stimulated a great deal of research. In the end both workers were shown to be correct; both catalytic dehydrogenation and oxidation steps do occur in the complex biochemical pathway of energy production in tissues.

Wiener, Norbert (1894–1964) US statistician whose main interest lay in devising the means to describe continuously changing conditions and phenomena. His work in a number of fields involving such random processes led him to develop, and later to popularize, the theory of cybernetics and to contribute fundamentally towards an understanding of the concept of decision-making.

Wiener was born in Columbia, Missouri, on 26 November 1894. A child prodigy, he was put under pressure by his father to excel academically. He was reading fluently at the age of three, entered high school when only nine, and completed the four-year high-school course in two years. He went on to take his bachelor's degree at Tuft's College at the age of 14. The following year, Wiener began postgraduate studies at Harvard University, intending to concentrate on zoology; he transferred to Cornell University in 1910 but returned to Harvard in 1911, having finally chosen to specialize in the philosophy of mathematics. He earned his master's degree in 1912, and his PhD a year later. A travelling fellowship then enabled Wiener in 1913 to visit the UK and go to Cambridge University, where he studied logic under Bertrand ◊Russell, and afterwards to go to the University of Göttingen, Germany, to work with David ◊Hilbert.

On his return to the USA, Wiener took up successive teaching posts at Columbia, Harvard, and Maine universities; worked for a year as a staff writer for the *Encyclopedia Americana* in Albany, New York; spent another year working as a journalist for the *Boston Herald*; and then took up his first appointment at the Massachusetts Institute of Technology (MIT). He worked first as an instructor in the mathematics department 1919–24, then as an assistant professor 1924–28, as associate professor 1928–32, and finally as full professor from 1932 until his retirement in 1960 as emeritus professor.

Many professional awards were bestowed on Wiener in recognition of the value of his contribution to mathematics; a member of prestigious international mathematical and scientific organizations, he was also the author of both academic and popular texts. He died in Stockholm, Sweden, on 18 March 1964.

Wiener's commitment to pure mathematics developed somewhat slowly, and it was only in 1918 (at the age of 24) that he began to take a serious interest in integral and differential equations. From the beginning, he worked in areas that had some application to physical processes. His results on the Lebesgue integral are important in the study of wave mechanics. He produced a mathematical theory for Brownian motion in 1920, and the enthusiasm of the engineering department at MIT spurred him then to examine problems in harmonic analysis. This led him to make certain deductions about information flow along a wave.

Newtonian analytical methods are not amenable to the investigation of continuously changing processes, so Wiener devoted much of his efforts to methodology, developing mathematical approaches that could usefully be applied to such phenomena. During the 1930s he carried out some work in collaboration with others on Fourier transformations, on Tauberian theorems, on radiation equilibrium, and on the application of mathematics to the study of physiology.

During World War II, Wiener worked on the control of anti-aircraft guns (which required him to consider factors such as the machinery itself, the gunner, and unpredictable evasive action on the part of the target's pilot), on filtering 'noise' from useful information for radar, and on coding and decoding. His investigations stimulated his interest in information transfer and processes such as information feedback. He related the occurrence of these processes in, for instance, the firing of anti-aircraft weapons and in mental processes.

The statistically random (stochastic) components of this process made it familiar material for Wiener. He published a book in 1948 about his ideas on the communication of information and its control. He thereby established and named a new branch of science: cybernetics, the theory of which involves a mathematical description of the flow of information. It is applied to many areas outside mathematics, including neurophysiology, computer design, and biochemical regulation. Wiener's book had an immediate impact; the common usage of such terms as 'input', 'feedback', and 'output' in everyday speech is, to a large measure, due to him.

A revised edition of the book, *Cybernetics*, was published in 1961. But soon after it was first produced, Wiener stopped doing research and decided to devote the rest of his life to awakening world leaders to the inevitable prospect of automation in many spheres of ordinary life.

Further Reading

Jerison, David; Singer, I M; and Stroock, Daniel W (eds), *The Legacy of Norbert Wiener: A Special Symposium in Honor of the 100th Anniversary of Norbert Wiener's Birth*, Proceedings of Symposia in Pure Mathematics Series, American Mathematical Society, 1997, v 60.

Mandrekar, V R and Asani, Pesi R (eds), *Proceedings of the Norbert Wiener Centenary Congress, 1994*, Proceedings of Symposia in Applied Mathematics Series, American Mathematical Society, 1996, v 52.

Masani, Pesi R, *Norbert Wiener, 1894–1964*, Vita Mathematica Series, Birkhauser, 1989.

Wiener, Norbert, *Invention: The Care and Feeding of Ideas*, MIT Press, 1993.

Wigglesworth, Vincent Brian (1899–1994)
English entomologist whose research covered many areas of insect physiology but who is best known for his investigations into the role of hormones in growth and metamorphosis. He received many honours for his contributions towards an understanding of insect physiology, including the Royal Medal of the Royal Society in 1955 and a knighthood in 1964.

Wigglesworth was born on 17 April 1899 in Kirkham, Lancashire, the son of a doctor. He was educated at Repton then won a scholarship to Gonville and Caius College, Cambridge. During World War I, he served in France in the Royal Field Artillery before resuming his university education and graduating in physiology and biochemistry. He did two years' research under Frederick Gowland ◊Hopkins, during part of which time he worked with J B S ◊Haldane, and then qualified in medicine at St Thomas's Hospital, London. In 1926 he was appointed lecturer in medical entomology at the London School of Hygiene and Tropical Medicine, and then reader in entomology at London University 1936–44. Wigglesworth became director of the Agricultural Research Council Unit of Insect Physiology at Cambridge in 1943 and remained there until he retired in 1967. During his directorship, he also held the post of Quick Professor of Biology at Cambridge 1952–66.

Wigglesworth's work on insect metamorphosis was carried out mainly on the bloodsucking insect *Rhodnius prolixus* (the kissing bug), which was brought from South America by E Brumpt (1877–1951) and proved suitable for experimentation. In 1917 it had been demonstrated that the hormone responsible for growth and moulting is secreted only when the insect's brain is present; decapitated insects live but do not moult. By transplanting various parts of the brain into decapitated *Rhodnius* specimens, Wigglesworth proved that this hormone (which he called moulting hormone) is produced in the region of the brain containing the neurosecretory cells. In addition, he showed that another hormone – one that prevents the development of adult characteristics until the insect larva is fully grown – is also produced in the head. He then demonstrated that this second hormone (which he called juvenile hormone) is secreted by the corpus allatum, an endocrine gland near the brain. Wigglesworth investigated the effects of the two hormones and found that insect larvae exposed to juvenile hormone grow but remain in the larval form; that adult insects exposed to moulting hormone moult again and, when also exposed to juvenile hormone, some of their organs partly regress to the larval forms. He also found that juvenile hormone is necessary for normal reproduction in many insects.

Although best known for his work on insect growth and metamorphosis, Wigglesworth also investigated many other aspects of insect anatomy and physiology, including the mechanisms involved in hatching, the mode of action of adhesive organs in walking, the role of the outer waxy layer on insects' bodies in preventing water loss, the respiration of insect eggs, insect sense organs and their use in orientation, and the functions of insect blood cells. His book *The Principles of Insect Physiology* (1939) has been reprinted in several editions as the standard general text on insect physiology.

Wilcox, Stephen (1830–1893) US inventor who, with George ◊Babcock, designed a steam-tube boiler that was developed into one of the most efficient sources of high-pressure steam, remaining so from the latter part of the 19th century until the demise of steam engines in the 20th century.

Wilcox was born on 12 February 1830 in Westerley, Rhode Island, the son of a prosperous banker and anti-slavery campaigner. He went to a local school and developed an interest in mechanisms in his spare time. After leaving school he went to work on improving old machines and inventing new ones – such as a hot-air engine for operating fog signals.

In about 1856, with his first partner D M Stillman, Wilcox patented a steam boiler in which slightly bent water tubes were set an an angle in the firebox. It was not entirely successful, largely because of difficulties in making joints that were water- and steam-tight at the high pressures involved. Ten years later, with a new partner and boyhood friend George Babcock, he designed an improved safety water-tube boiler.

The new boiler had straight tubes, although they were still inclined to the horizontal. Banks of tubes were connected together at their ends, through which the hot water gradually rose by convention. The firebox surrounded the tubes to give rapid heating and there was a reservoir of hot water above the firebox and tubes, with steam above the water. A patent was granted in 1867 and Babcock and Wilcox formed a company to manufacture the boiler. Their steam engines were used in the first US electricity generating stations and played an important part in the subsequent development of electric lighting.

Wilcox continued research into steam engines and boilers for the rest of his life. During his later years he worked on a marine version of the boiler with his assistant and nephew William Hoxie. Much of this work was carried out using his yacht *Reverie* for sea trials. Wilcox died in Brooklyn, New York, on 27 November 1893.

Throughout his inventing career Wilcox acquired nearly 50 patents and accrued a considerable fortune. He endowed a public library at Westerley and, after his death, his widow used the money to aid the building of parks and schools.

Wilkes, Maurice Vincent (1913–) English mathematician who led the team at Cambridge University that built the EDSAC (electronic delay storage automatic calculator), one of the earliest of the British electronic computers.

Wilkes was born on 26 June 1913. He attended King Edward's School, Stourbridge, and then went on to St John's College, Cambridge. He graduated in mathematics and then carried out research in physics at the Cavendish Laboratories. After a short period as a university demonstrator, he became involved with war work in the development of radar and operational research. At the end of World War II he became head of the Computer Laboratory of the University of Cambridge, moving to the USA in 1980 to join the Digital Equipment Corporation in Maynard, Massachusetts. In 1986 he returned to the UK to become a founding member of the Olivetti and Oracle Research Laboratory in Cambridge.

In the late 1940s Wilkes and his team began to build the EDSAC. At the time electronic computer developments were in their infancy, with only John ◊Mauchly and Presper ◊Eckert's ENIAC (electronic numerical integrator and calculator) in the USA having come into operation. There were many rival ideas concerning the principles on which a computer should be designed and how data should be stored. Of the rival serial and parallel systems, Wilkes chose the serial mode, in which the information in the computer is processed in sequence (and not several parts at once, as in the parallel type). This choice of design involved the incorporation of mercury delay lines as the elements of the memory.

A means of delaying the passage of information was developed at the Radiation Laboratory at the Massachusetts Institute of Technology from an original idea of William Shockley of Bell Telephones, who was later to share a Nobel prize as one of the inventors of the transistor. It was originally intended that the device would be used in radar equipment. The delay lines were made up from tubes about 1.5 m/5 ft long and filled with mercury. At each end of each tube was a suitably cut quartz crystal. By the piezoelectric effect, when alternating electric current met one of the crystals it altered its shape slightly; this sent a small ripple through the mercury, which in turn struck the other crystal and in disturbing it produced the current again. The time taken for the ripple to travel through the mercury was sufficient to store the signal, and the process could be repeated indefinitely provided suitable auxilliary amplification equipment was used.

At the time that EDSAC was being built there was considerable interest in this type of memory device, and a number of US computers were being built that incorporated them. It was by no means certain that

either the delay line or the computer would work satisfactorily, but on 6 May 1949 it ran its first program and became the first delay-line computer in the world to come into operation. From early 1950 it offered a regular computing facility to the members of Cambridge University, the first service of its kind involving a general-purpose computer. Much time was spent by the research group on the development of programming and in the compilation of a library of programs. The EDSAC was in operation until July 1958, although it had been modified during its period of operation. The expertise that Wilkes and his colleagues had gained was passed on to T R Thompson and JMM Pinkerton who, with the Lyons Catering Company, developed the LEO (Lyons Electric Office) as a commercial computer.

In the mid-1950s EDSAC II was built, and it came into service in 1957. This, however, was a parallel machine and the delay line was abandoned in favour of the superior magnetic storage methods.

Maurice Wilkes played a leading part in subsequent computer developments and has written many books and papers on the subject, including *Memoirs of a Computer Pioneer* (1985) and *Computing Perspectives* (1995). In 1950 he was elected a fellow of St John's College, Cambridge; he was elected a fellow of the Royal Society in 1956, and in 1957 he became the first president of the British Computer Society.

Wilkins, Maurice Hugh Frederick (1916–) New Zealand-born British biophysicist who contributed to the discovery of the structure of DNA. He shared the Nobel Prize for Physiology or Medicine with Francis ◊Crick and James ◊Watson in 1962.

Born on 15 December 1916 at Pongaroa, New Zealand, Wilkins was sent to King Edward's School, Birmingham, England at the age of six. He then studied physics at St John's College, Cambridge, graduating in 1938. He was taken on as a research assistant at Birmingham University and gained a PhD from there in 1940. His thesis was on the study of the thermal stability of trapped electrons in phosphors. During the war he joined the Ministry of Home Security and Aircraft Production where he worked to improve cathode ray tube screens for radar and studied the separation of uranium isotopes in bombs under the Australian nuclear physicist M L E Oliphant (1901–). He moved with the rest of the research group to the site of the Manhattan Project in Berkeley, California.

Becoming disillusioned with nuclear physics, Wilkins followed up his interest in biophysics and took up a position on a project in St Andrews, Scotland, in 1945. In 1946 his research moved him to King's College, London, and the same year he became a member of the Medical Research Council of the Biophysics Research Unit there, becoming assistant director in

1950, deputy director in 1955, and director 1970–72. His work led to the development of reflecting microscopes for ultraviolet microspectrophotometric study of nucleic acid. He also studied the position and groupings of pyramidines and purines in nucleic acids and the tobacco mosaic virus. With the use of a visible light polarizing microscope he could see the position of the virus particles in crystallized tobacco mosaic virus. Following the discovery in 1946 that genes consist of DNA, Wilkins began to investigate the structure of the DNA molecule. Studying the X-ray diffraction pattern of DNA, he discovered that the molecule has a double helical structure and his colleague, Rosalind ◊Franklin also showed that DNA's phosphate groups are situated on the outside of the helix. Wilkins passed on these findings to Francis Crick and James Watson at Cambridge who were trying to elucidate the detailed structure of DNA and they incorporated his and Franklin's information into their models. He was later able to prove their double helix hypothesis by X-ray studies and he went on to apply his X-ray diffraction technique to RNA.

Wilkins married Ann Chidgey in 1959 and they had two children. He was awarded the 1960 Albert Lasker Award with Crick and Watson, and in 1961 he was made honorary lecturer of the department of biophysics at King's College, Cambridge. He was awarded a CBE in 1962, the same year as he shared the Nobel prize with Crick and Watson. He was appointed professor of biophysics and head of department at King's College in 1970 and retired in 1981, becoming emeritus professor.

Wilkinson, Geoffrey (1921–1996) English inorganic chemist who shared the Nobel Prize for Chemistry in 1973 for his pioneering work on the organometallic compounds of the transition metals with Ernst ◊Fischer. He was knighted in 1976.

Born in Todmorden, Yorkshire, on 14 July 1921, Wilkinson was educated at the local grammar school, obtaining a scholarship to Imperial College, London, in 1939 from where he graduated with a BSc in 1941 and a PhD in 1946. From 1943 to 1946 he worked as a junior scientific officer at the Atomic Energy Division of the National Research Council of Canada on a secret uranium project. He then moved to the USA taking up various appointments: at the Radiation Laboratory at Berkeley, California, 1946–50, where he practised nuclear chemistry with Glenn ◊Seaborg, and in the chemistry department of the Massachusetts Institute of Technology 1950–51. In 1951 he joined the theoretical and experimental research school of US organic chemist Robert ◊Woodward at Harvard becoming assistant professor 1951–56 and professor 1956–78. From 1978 until his retirement in 1988 he was the Sir

Edward Frankland Professor of Inorganic Chemistry at the University of London, working at Imperial College.

Wilkinson wrote several books and papers, among which is *Advanced Inorganic Chemistry* (1962), which was co-authored with F A Cotton, one of his US ex-students. It has reached several editions. He was also the general editor of the multi-volumed *Advanced Coordination Chemistry*. He was the recipient of many awards and fellowships. He was made John Simon Guggenheim Fellow in 1954, he received the American Chemical Society's inorganic chemistry award in 1966, the Lavoisier Medal of the French Chemical Society in 1987, and the Hiroshima University Medal in 1978. He was made an honorary fellow of the Institute of Technology at Manchester in 1989 and was also fellow of the Royal Society and an honorary fellow of Imperial College. He died on 26 September 1996.

It was while he was working with Woodward at Harvard in 1951 that Wilkinson read an article in *Nature* about a synthetic compound called ferrocene, which was presenting a puzzle to scientists. Working on this, he concluded that each molecule of ferrocene consisted of a single atom sandwiched between two flat five-sided carbon rings, resulting in a 'sandwich compound' and in 1952 he published a paper with Woodward and others on this remarkable compound – $(C_2H_5)_2Fe$. Thousands of sandwich-type molecules have since been made, containing other chemicals and other sizes of rings – the metallocenes. Meanwhile, German chemist Ernst Fischer had read the same *Nature* article and also had been independently working along the same lines as Wilkinson. They jointly received the Nobel Prize for Chemistry in 1973 for their work on sandwich compounds.

In 1954 Wilkinson synthesized a rhodium triphenylphosphine complex that became known as 'Wilkinson's catalyst'. The compound, $RhCl(P(C_6H_5)_3P)$ was the first such complex to be used as a homogeneous catalyst for adding hydrogen to the double bonds of alkalenes. It has been widely used in industry in the hydrogenation of ethene and propene to form aldehydes. This type of compound can also be used as a catalyst for the reaction of hydrogen and carbon monoxide with alkalenes (hydroformylation).

Wilks, Samuel Stanley (1906–1964) US statistician whose work in data analysis enabled him to formulate methods of deriving valid information from small samples. He also concentrated on the developments and applications of techniques for the analysis of variance.

Wilks was born on 17 June 1906 in Little Elm, Texas. Educated locally, he studied architecture at the North Texas State College, obtaining his bachelor's degree there in 1926, and his master's two years later at the University of Texas. A two-year scholarship then took him to Iowa University, where he studied statistics and received his doctorate in 1931. Three further scholarships enabled him to continue studying, in New York, London, and Cambridge, England, before he finally joined the staff of Princeton University. Initially an instructor, he became assistant professor in 1936, associate professor in 1938, and professor of mathematical statistics in 1944. Active as a government advisory panellist, he received a number of awards and honours; he was also the author of several textbooks on statistics. He died in Princeton on 7 March 1964.

Much of Wilks's early work concerned problems associated with the statistical analysis of data obtained from small samples, such as those derived from experiments in psychology. His investigations of the analysis of variance were devoted especially to multivariate analysis. Two of his most original contributions were the Wilks criterion and his multiple correlation coefficient.

The US College Entrance Examination Board, which carries out extensive educational tests, found his assistance invaluable in analysing their results. Seeking also to apply these methods to industrial problems, Wilks did fundamental work in the establishment of the theory of statistical tolerance.

Williams, Frederic Calland (1911–1977) English electrical and electronics engineer with many accomplishments and inventions to his credit. He is particularly remembered for his pioneering work on electronic computers at the University of Manchester.

Williams was born on 26 June 1911 in Romiley, near Stockport, Cheshire. After attending a private primary school near his home he went on to Stockport Grammar School, and in 1929 he was awarded an entrance scholarship to the University of Manchester. He studied engineering and graduated in 1932. The following year he carried out research and was awarded an MSc. After working for a short time with Metropolitan Vickers Electrical Company, he was awarded the Ferranti Scholarship of the Institution of Electical Engineers, which he took up at Oxford University by doing research on 'noise' in electronic circuits and valves. For this work he was awarded a doctorate in 1936. Also in that year he returned to Manchester as an assistant lecturer, where he stayed until the outbreak of World War II in 1939.

During the war Williams was involved in many applications of circuit design. He played a major part in the development of radar and allied devices and in the design of the feedback systems known as servomechanisms, which had applications in aircraft controls and gunnery. In 1945, at the end of the war, he visited the Radiation Laboratory at the Massachusetts Institute of Technology (MIT) where he worked on circuitry and also learned of attempts to use cathode-ray tubes to store information. On his return to the UK after his second visit to MIT in 1946 he began to develop cathode-ray tube storage devices, in which information was coded and stored as dots on the screen. The phosphor in the tubes allowed an image to persist for only a fraction of a second, and so the system needed considerable development. At first he transferred information to and from two tubes, but later he designed the appropriate circuitry to repeat the dots in one tube so that they would persist indefinitely.

In December 1946 Williams was appointed to the chair of Electrotechnics at Manchester University and began to work with MHA Newman, who had a grant from the Royal Society for the development of computers. Their first machine began operation on 21 June 1948, becoming the first stored-program computer. The cathode-ray storage tubes allowed for immediate access to data. After modification, the machine went into production with Ferranti Limited, the first of several such computers. William's tubes, as they came to be known, were in great demand during the early 1950s because of their simplicity and cheapness. They were adopted in many computers in the UK and the USA; in particular they were a feature of the early 700 series of IBM computers.

Williams turned from computers when, because of their circuitry, they ceased to be a challenge to him and in the 1950s he began work on electrical machines, principally induction motors and induction-excited alternators. During his later years he worked on an automatic transmission for motor vehicles. He also played an increasingly large part in the administration of the University of Manchester. He received many awards, including the fellowship of the Royal Society in 1950 and a knighthood in 1976. He died on 11 August 1977.

Williamson, Alexander William (1824–1904) British organic chemist who made significant discoveries concerning alcohols and ethers, catalysis, and reversible reactions.

Williamson was born in London on 1 May 1824, of Scottish parents; his father was a clerk in the East India Company. A boyhood accident cost him an arm and the sight of one eye; when he was 16 years old his father retired and the family moved abroad. Williamson went to Heidelberg University in Germany to study medicine, but was persuaded by Leopold Gmelin (1788–1853) to change to chemistry. He then studied under Thomas ◊Graham at University College, London, and Justus von ◊Liebig at Giessen University, from which he gained his PhD in 1846. After a period in Paris studying methematics, he became professor of chemistry at University College, London, in 1849, where he remained until he retired in 1887. He died in Haslemere, Surrey, on 6 May 1904.

From 1850 Williamson studied alcohols and ethers and showed that they are both of the same type – the theory of types was fast gaining ground in organic chemistry. For example, amines are regarded as belonging to the 'ammonia type' (NH_3), with one or more of ammonia's hydrogen atoms replaced by organic (alkyl) radicals. Williamson ascribed alcohols and ethers to the 'water type'. In an alcohol, one of the hydrogen atoms of water (H_2O or HOH) is replaced by an alkyl radical (R) to give a compound R·OH, such as ethyl alcohol (ethanol) C_2H_5OH. In an ether, both of water's hydrogens are replaced, either by the same alkyl radical (R) or by two different ones (R and R') to give compounds of the form R·O·R – such as diethyl ether (ethoxyethane), $(C_2H_5)_2O$ – or of the form R·O·R' – such as methyl ethyl ether (methoxyethane), $CH_3OC_2H_5$. Williamson was the first to make 'mixed' ethers, with two different alkyl groups, and his method is still known as the Williamson synthesis. It involves treating an alkoxide with an alkyl halide (haloalkane). For example:

$$CH_3I + C_2H_5ONa \rightarrow CH_3OC_2H_5 + NaI$$

The original way of making diethyl ether (ethoxyethane) is by treating ethyl alcohol (ethanol) with sulphuric acid. In 1854 Williamson suggested that the reation takes place in two stages. First the substances react to form ethyl sulphate:

$$2C_2H_5OH + H_2SO_4 \rightarrow (C_2H_5)_2SO_4 + 2H_2O$$

Then the ethyl sulphate reacts with further alcohol to form diethyl ether and liberate sulphuric acid:

$$(C_2H_5)_2SO_4 + 2C_2H_5OH \rightarrow 2(C_2H_5)_2O + H_2SO_4$$

The sulphuric acid turns up unchanged at the end of the reactions but has been essential to them: it has acted as a catalyst. This was the first time that anyone had explained the action of a catalyst in terms of the the formation of an intermediate compound.

The theory of types has now outlived its usefulness. But it was important in the mid-19th century because through the work of Williamson and others it established some sort of order among the confusion that then prevailed in organic chemistry.

Some of the reactions of alcohols and ethers are reversible (that is, the products of a reaction may recombine to form the reactants), a phenomenon first noted and described by Williamson in the early 1850s. Using modern notation, if P and Q are the reactants and R and S are the products, the reversible reaction is written:

$$P + Q \leftrightarrow R + S$$

An example is the esterification reaction between ethyl alcohol (ethanol) and acetic acid (ethanoic acid) to form ethyl acetate (ethyl ethanoate):

$$C_2H_5OH + CH_3COOH \leftrightarrow CH_3COOC_2H_5 + H_2O$$

If the rate of the forward reaction is the same as that of the reverse reaction, all four compounds (P, Q, R, and S) coexist and the system is said to be in dynamic equilibrium (a term also introduced by Williamson).

Willstätter, Richard (1872–1942) German organic chemist best known for his investigations of alkaloids and plant pigments, such as chlorophyll, for which he was awarded the 1915 Nobel Prize for Chemistry.

Willstätter was born in Karlsruhe on 13 August 1872, the son of a textile merchant. He studied chemistry at the Munich Technische Hochschule under Johann von ◊Baeyer, and after graduation worked under A Einhorn (1857–1917) and was awarded his doctorate in 1894 for a thesis on the structure of cocaine. He worked as Baeyer's assistant for several years, and then in 1905 became a professor at the Technische Hochschule in Zürich, Switzerland. From 1912 to 1916 he was director of the chemistry section of the Kaiser Wilhelm Institute at Berlin-Dahlem, but his work was interrupted by World War I and at the request of Fritz ◊Haber he turned his attention to the design of an effective gas mask. In 1916 he succeeded Baeyer as a full professor at Munich, but resigned in 1925 because of mounting anti-Semitism. He continued working privately – supervising over the telephone some research at the university. At the start of World War II in 1939 he finally left Germany and went to live in exile in Switzerland. He died in Locarno on 3 August 1942.

Willstätter's first research work was on alkaloids. Following his doctoral study of cocaine in 1894, he went on to investigate tropine and atropine, and by 1898 had determined their structures and syntheses. From the pomegranate alkaloid pseudopelletierine he prepared cyclo-octatetraene, an eight-carbon ring compound with alternate single and double bonds, analagous to benzene.

He also worked on quinones, and by following William ◊Perkin's method of oxidizing aniline (phenylamine) with chromic acid determined the structure of the dyestuff aniline black.

Willstätter then began his research into blood pigments and plant pigments. He showed that chlorophyll is not a single homogeneous substance but is made up of four components: two green ones, chlorophyll a ($C_{55}H_{72}O_5N_4Mg$) and chlorophyll b ($C_{55}H_{70}O_6N_4Mg$), and two yellow ones, carotene ($C_{40}H_{56}$) and xanthophyll ($C_{40}H_{56}O_2$). He found that the blue–green chlorophyll a and the yellow–green chlorophyll b exist in the ratio of 3:1, and that the ratio of xanthophyll to carotene is 2:1.

In order to separate the complex substances he re-developed the technique of chromatography, first used in studies of chlorophyll by Mikhail ◊Tswett in Russia in 1906, at about the same time as Willstätter was doing his work in Switzerland. It came as a surprise that the chlorophylls contain magnesium, later shown to be linked to four pyrrole rings like the iron atom in the haem group of the red blood pigment haemoglobin.

Soon after his return to Germany Willstätter had to abandon his research into plant pigments because during World War I the large quantities of solvents needed for chromatography became unobtainable. After the war he took up the study of enzymes and of catalytic hydrogenation, particularly in the presence of oxygen. He worked on the degradation of cellulose, investigated fermentation, and pioneered the use of hydrogels for absorption. He tried to prove, incorrectly, that enzymes are not proteins.

Wilson, Charles Thomson Rees (1869–1959)

Scottish physicist who invented the Wilson cloud chamber, the first instrument to detect the tracks of atomic particles. For this achievement, Wilson shared the 1927 Nobel Prize for Physics with Arthur ◊Compton, who gained his award for the discovery of the Compton effect.

Wilson was born on 14 February 1869 at a farmhouse near Glencorse, just outside Edinburgh. His father, a successful farmer, died when Wilson was four and the family moved to Manchester. After studies at Owens College (now the University of Manchester), he gained a BSc in 1887 and then attended Sidney Sussex College, Cambridge, obtaining a BA in natural sciences in 1892. After four years' teaching at Bradford Grammar School, Wilson returned to Cambridge where he was the Clerk Maxwell Student 1896–99. In 1900 he became a lecturer at Sidney Sussex College and in 1925 was appointed Jacksonian Professor of Natural Philosophy at Cambridge. Wilson held this post until 1934 and retired from Cambridge two years later. He continued to be active in research, producing his last paper (on thundercloud electricity) at the age of 87, by which time he was the oldest fellow of the Royal Society. Wilson gained many honours, including the society's Hughes Medal in 1911, the Royal Medal in 1922, and the Copley Medal in 1935. He died in Carlops, near Edinburgh, on 15 November 1959.

Wilson's great discovery of the cloud chamber was brought about by a thorough study of atmospheric cloud formation, an interest that began with observations of clouds on Ben Nevis (Britain's highest mountain) while on holiday in 1894. The wonderful optical effects fascinated Wilson, and on his return to Cambridge he tried to simulate them in his laboratory. In 1895 he began to construct a device to reproduce

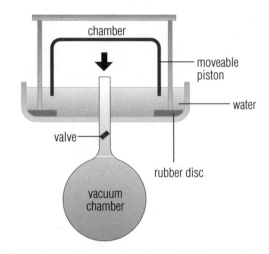

Wilson The cloud chamber devised by C T R Wilson was the first instrument to detect the tracks of atomic particles. It consisted originally of a cylindrical glass chamber fitted with a hollow piston, which was connected, via a valve, to a large evacuated flask. The piston falls rapidly when the valve is opened, and water vapour condenses along the tracks of any particles in the chamber.

cloud formation and was successful in the production of an artificial cloud by causing the adiabatic expansion of moist air. From 1895 to 1899, Wilson carried out many experiments and established that the nucleation of droplets is able to take place in the absence of dust particles. Until this experiment, it was considered essential for each water droplet to form on a nucleus of dust. Wilson demonstrated that once supersaturated with water vapour, nucleation can occur and that furthermore it is greatly improved by exposure to X-rays. This showed that ions are the nucleation sites on which water droplets form in the absence of dust.

Another unforgettable experience on Ben Nevis in 1895 had inspired a lifelong interest in atmospheric electricity. In Wilson's own words, 'Mist hid the top of Ben Nevis; there was a faint muttering of distant thunder. Suddenly I felt my hair stand up; I did not await any further developments but started to run ... the storm broke overhead with a bright flash and loud thunder just after I had left the summit. ...' During the years 1900–10, Wilson's attentions were devoted to the study of electrical conduction in dust-free air. He devised a gold-leaf electroscope in which surface leakage from the leaf to the case was impossible. With this instrument, he was able to show that some electrical leakage always occurs in air, and that the conductivity of the air inside the electroscope is the same in daylight as in the dark, and is independent of the sign of the charge for leaf potential. Wilson hoped to establish some link with an outside source of ions, and he even undertook some experiments underground to collect data. Later work by others was to show cosmic radiation to be the probable explanation.

Wilson returned to the cloud chamber in 1910, having realized that it could possibly show the track of a charged particle moving through it because water droplets could condense along the particle's path. Applying a magnetic field to the chamber would cause the track to curve, giving a measure of the charge and mass of the particle. In 1911, after many attempts, Wilson succeeded in producing a working model of his cloud chamber. The chamber was constructed in the form of a short cylinder in which supersaturation was achieved and controlled by the movement of a piston through a determined distance. The condensation effects were monitored through the other end. The Wilson cloud chamber immediately became vital to the study of radioactivity. It was used to confirm the classic alpha-particle scattering and transmutation experiments first performed by Ernest ◊Rutherford, and Rutherford is reputed to have said it was 'the most original apparatus in the whole history of physics'.

The Wilson cloud chamber and its successors proved to be indispensable tools in the investigation of the structure of the nucleus. Wilson himself was a lone researcher and did not contribute greatly to the development of his discovery. Modifications by Patrick ◊Blackett and Carl ◊Anderson brought about the discovery of the positron in 1932 and meson in 1936. The development of the cloud chamber into the bubble chamber by Donald ◊Glaser in 1952 produced a highly sensitive detector that has revealed whole families of new particles.

Wilson, Edward Osborne (1929–) US biologist and a leading authority on ants. He is a pioneer of biodiversity and sociobiology, the study of the social behaviour of all animals including humans. Through his books he has become a great popularizer of science and he has won several awards including two Pulitzer prizes.

Wilson was born in Birmingham, Alabama, on 10 June 1929 and graduated in biology from the University of Alabama in 1949, obtaining a PhD from Harvard in 1955. In the same year he completed a taxonomic analysis of the ant genus *Lasius*. He was appointed to the Harvard faculty in 1956, after which he made as number of important discoveries about ants, including the fact that they communicate through chemical substances called pheromones. He developed the concept of the taxon cycle in which he links speciation and species dispersal with the habitats encountered by organisms in the process of expanding their populations.

With Canadian ecologist Robert ◊MacArthur, Wilson developed a theory of the equilibrium of island populations, which they published in *Theory of Island Biogeography* (1967). He subsequently conducted experiments with Daniel Simberloff in mangrove clumps in the Florida Keys to confirm their hypothesis that a 'dynamic equilibrium number of species exists in any island'. To do this, they enumerated the species of insect in each island population, then eliminated all of them by fumigation, finding in the succeeding months that the same number of species returned to recolonize the islands.

Wilson's book *The Insect Societies* (1971) was a comprehensive survey of his entomological work and revealed in detail the complicated relationships and behaviour patterns of ants and other social insects in their own environments. His second book, *Sociobiology: The New Synthesis* (1975), caused controversy among certain groups of scientists who saw one chapter in particular as politically inflammatory. In this chapter he elucidated his theory on the biological basis of human society. He proposed that human social behaviour followed the same basic biological principles as the behaviour of groups of animals, attributing 90% of human behaviour to environment and only 10% to genetic factors. In 1979 with his exploration of the implications of sociobiology for human aggression, morality, and sexuality, *On Human Nature*, Wilson won a Pulitzer prize. In another controversial theory, he showed how apparently altruistic behaviour in insects, birds, and mammals is actually genetically and biologically programmed and may have evolved through natural selection. In this theory the individual can be sacrificed to preserve the genes of closely related individuals.

Among his other books, *The Ants* (1990) is a summary of all that is known about ants, *In Search of Nature* is an introduction to all Wilson's ideas, and *Consilience The Unity of Knowledge* (1998) draws on the physical sciences, biology, anthropology, psychology, religion, and philosophy to show how human intellectual mastery of the truths of the universe has its roots in the ancient Greek philosophy of the intrinsic orderliness governing the cosmos – an idea that flourished in the Enlightenment. He explains why the original goals of the Enlightenment are reappearing in science and the humanities. *Consilience* was a candidate for the first Samuel Johnson Prize for Non-fiction in 1999.

Wilson was professor of zoology at Harvard from 1964, becoming F B Baird Professor of Science in 1976, and has been curator of entomology at the Museum of Comparative Zoology at Harvard since 1972.

Wilson, John Tuzo (1908–1993) Canadian geologist and geophysicist. He was the first to use the term 'plate' to describe the rigid portions into which the Earth's crust is divided. He was a major contributor, along with US geophysicist Robert Dietz (1914–), US geologist Harry ◊Hess, and English geophysicists Drummond Matthews (1931–) and Frederick ◊Vine, to the development of plate tectonics theory in the 1960s and 1970s.

Born in Ottawa on 24 October 1908, Wilson was the first student to study geophysics in Canada (at the University of Toronto). After graduating he studied further at Cambridge and Princeton achieving his PhD in geology in 1936. From 1936 to 1939 he worked for the Canadian Geological Survey before joining the army for the duration of World War II. He was appointed professor of geophysics at the University of Toronto in 1946, a position he held until his retirement in 1974.

Wilson was interested in the mobile Earth hypothesis of German geologist Alfred ◊Wegener and had been inspired by the lectures of Hess at Princeton. In 1963 he provided some of the first proof of Hess's 1962 hypothesis of seafloor spreading by showing that islands became progressively older the further they were from mid-ocean ridges. Wilson introduced the idea of 'hot spots' in the mantle that remain stationary under the moving plates and produce plumes of mantle material that form volcanic chains of islands such as Hawaii and Japan. At the time his hotspot manuscript was considered too radical for publication by all the major international scientific journals but it was eventually published in the *Canadian Journal of Physics*. Numerous studies subsequently supported his hypothesis.

Wilson developed a new concept in plate tectonics theory in his 1965 paper 'A new class of faults and their bearing on continental drift', in which he introduced the idea of a transform fault. He hypothesized a third type of plate boundary to connect oceanic ridges and trenches. They could end abruptly and transform into major faults that slip horizontally, an example of which is the San Andreas Fault. He replied to critics of his plate tectonics theory with a persuasive account in *A Revolution in Earth Science* (1965).

An inspiring teacher, Wilson could explain complex concepts such as the movement of continents, the formation of island chains, and the spreading of ocean floors using simple diagrams and models. He was also a pioneer of hands-on interactive museum exhibits. He was an active outdoor man and led expeditions in the remote northern regions of Canada. He also made the first ascent of Mount Hague in Montana, USA, in 1935. The Wilson Range in Antarctica is named after him.

Wilson held the prestigious position of president of the International Union of Geodesy and Geophysics in 1957 and was the first non-US president of the American Geophysical Union, which changed its rules to allow his election. After his retirement he became director of the Ontario Science Center and later became chancellor at York University, Toronto, from which he retired in 1987. He was a tireless traveller and lecturer until his death at Los Gatos, California, on 15 April 1993.

Wilson, Robert Woodrow (1936–) US radio astronomer who, with Arno ◊Penzias, detected the cosmic microwave background radiation, which is thought to represent a residue of the primordial 'Big Bang' with which the universe is believed to have begun. For this they were awarded the 1978 Nobel Prize for Physics.

Wilson was born in Houston, Texas, on 10 January 1936. He studied at Rice University and earned his bachelor's degree in 1957. He began postgraduate research at the California Institute of Technology and was awarded his PhD in 1962. In 1963 he joined the technical staff of the Bell Telephone Laboratories in Holmdel, New Jersey, becoming head of the radiophysics department 1976–94. Wilson detected the 'three-degree background radiation' in 1965, only two years after he began working at Bell, and the sensational news of this discovery rapidly earned him international acclaim. He was awarded the Henry Draper Award of the National Academy of Sciences in 1977 and the Herschel Award of the Royal Astronomical Society in the same year. In 1994 he became senior scientist at the Harvard–Smithsonian Center for Astrophysics.

Some of the earliest quantitative work on the 'Big Bang' hypothesis, the theory of the origin of the universe, was proposed and carried out by Ralph ◊Alpher, Hans ◊Bethe, and George ◊Gamow in 1948. They predicted the existence of isotropic cosmic background radiation, at a temperature of 25K (−248°C/−414°F). But this estimate, which turned out to be too high, could not be confirmed at the time, because the radio wavelengths in the shorter range of the radio spectrum would have been swamped by other sources and radio astronomy had not been developed sufficiently to be applied to this problem. The theory required a number of modifications and so its prediction of microwave radiation was soon forgotten as other issues assumed greater importance in astronomy.

In 1964, Wilson and Penzias tested a radio telescope and receiver system for the Bell Telephone Laboratories with the intention of tracking down all possible sources of static that were causing interference in satellite communications. They found a high level of isotropic background radiation at a wavelength of 7.3 cm/2.9 in, with a temperature of 3.1K (−276°C/−529°F) – their initial result had been a temperature of 3.5K (−277°C/−500°F). This radiation was a hundred times more powerful than any that could be accounted for on the basis of any known sources.

As they could not explain this residual signal, Wilson and Penzias contacted Robert ◊Dicke, at Princeton University, who was also interested in microwave radiation. Independently of Gamow, Dicke had followed a somewhat different line of reasoning to predict that microwave radiation, which was the remnant of the tremendous heat generated by the primordial fireball, was theoretically detectable. At the time his research team was constructing a radio telescope designed specifically to pick up radiation at a wavelength of 3.2 cm/1.3 in. When he heard of Wilson's and Penzias' observations, he immediately realized that their findings confirmed his predictions. The discovery of microwave radiation by Wilson and Penzias was almost a repeat of Karl ◊Jansky's discovery, also at the Bell Telephone Laboratories, of radio astronomy itself in the 1930s.

Microwave radiation has since become the subject of intense investigation. Its spectrum appears to conform closely with that of black-body radiation and its temperature is only three degrees above absolute zero (−273°C/−459°F). It is thought to be the direct consequence of an explosively expanding universe; the temperature theoretically decreases as the universe continues to expand. Radio astronomers continue to scrutinize this radiation for any evidence of anisotropy, which may indicate an unsuspected pattern of distribution of matter in the universe.

Winsor, Frederick Albert (1763–1830) German inventor, one of the pioneers of gas lighting.

Winsor was born in Brunswick and educated in Hamburg, where he learned English. He travelled to England before 1799 and became interested in the technology and economics of fuels. In 1802 he went to Paris to investigate the 'thermo-lamp', which Philippe ◊Lebon had patented in 1799. He returned to England at the end of 1803 and began a series of lectures at the Lyceum Theatre, London. A retired coachmaker named Kenzie lent him premises near Hyde Park to use as a gasworks. In 1804 Winsor was granted a patent for 'an improved oven, stove or apparatus for extracting inflammable air, oil, pitch, tar and acid and reducing into coke and charcoal all kinds of fuel' (there was no specific mention of coal, although that was the 'fuel' mainly used). In 1806 he moved to Pall Mall, where, during the following year, he lit one side of the street with gas lamps. In that year he was also granted a second patent for a new gas furnace and purifier, followed in 1808 and 1809 by others for refining gas to reduce its smell. Another 1809 patent was for a 'fixed and moveable telegraph lighthouse for signals of intelligence in rain, storm and darkness'. 1809 also saw an application to Parliament for a charter for the Light and Heat Company. The bill was thrown out but the Westminster Gas-Light and Coke Company was finally incorporated, with the blessing of Parliament, in June 1810, although this time Winsor was not involved. He went to Paris in 1815 and tried to form a similar company there. He made a point of mentioning that he had been one of the first to credit Lebon with the original invention of the gas oven (on his 1802 visit). In 1817 he lit Passage des Panoramas with gas, but his company made little progress and was liquidated in 1819. Winsor died in Paris on 11 May 1830 and was buried in the cemetery of Pére Lachaise. A cenotaph was erected to his memory in Kensal Green Cemetery, London, with the inscription 'At evening time it shall be light'. He had a son, F A Winsor Jr (1797–1874), who obtained a patent for the production of light as late as 1843.

In 1802, Winsor published *Description of the Thermo-lamp invented by Lebon of Paris* with remarks by himself. It was published in English, French, and German and re-issued in English in 1804 as *An account of the most Ingenious and Important Discovery of some Ages*. There was also *Analogy between Animal and Vegetable Life, Demonstrating the Beneficial Application of the Patent light Stoves to all Green and Hot Houses* (1807), and others.

Winsor started his career as a company-promoting expert. At the time of his visit to Paris in 1802, the Scottish engineer William ◊Murdock had been working in the UK on lines similar to Winsor's and his experiments had first yielded gas as a practical illuminant between 1792 and 1798, when he built gasworks at the Soho factory of Matthew ◊Boulton and James ◊Watt near Birmingham. There had been similar projects by Archibald Cochrane between 1782 and 1783, but apart from those of Murdock and Lebon experiments in gas-lighting had not progressed further than 'philosphical fireworks'. These were exhibited by a German named Diller (died 1789) in London and Paris. Similar fireworks were shown by the inventor Edmund ◊Cartwright at the London Lyceum in May 1800, and the population was sceptical when Winsor advertised 'The superiority of the New Patent Coke over the use of coals in Family Concerns, displayed every evening at the Large Theatre, Lyceum, Strand, by the New Imperial Patent Light Stove Company'. He kept secret how he obtained and purified the gas, but he demonstrated how he carried it to the different rooms of a house. He showed a chandelier, in the form of a long flexible tube hanging from the ceiling, connected to a burner in the shape of a cupid grasping a torch with one hand and holding the tube with the other. He explained how the flame could be modified and showed how it did not go out in wind and rain, produced no smoke and did not scatter dangerous sparks. Winsor was a man with plenty of perseverance (but with less chemical knowledge and mechanical skill) and was undeterred by the fact that his gas was sneered at as offensive, dangerous, expensive, and unmanageable.

The distilling retort Winsor used consisted of an iron pot with a fitted lid. The lid had a pipe in the centre leading to the conical condensing vessel, which was compartmented inside with perforated divisions to spread the gas to purify it of hydrogen sulphide and ammonia. The device was not very successful, and the gas being burnt was impure and emitted a pungent smell. He also tried lime as a purifier, with a little success.

When Winsor applied to Parliament for a charter he was opposed by Murdock and Watt, and the writer Walter Scott wrote that he was a madman to propose to light London with smoke. The Corporation of the Westminster Gas-Light and Coke Company were from then on advised by Samuel Clegg, an old disciple of Murdock's, and not by Winsor.

Withering, William (1741–1799) English physician, botanist, and mineralogist, best known for his work on the drug digitalis (from the foxglove plant), which he initially used as a diuretic to treat dropsy (oedema).

Withering was born on 17 March 1741 in Wellington, Shropshire, where his father was an apothecary. He went to the Edinburgh Medical School and graduated in 1766, taking the post of physician at Stafford Infirmary for the next nine years. In 1775 Erasmus ◊Darwin suggested that Withering should take over a practice in Birmingham that had belonged to William Small (1734–1775), founder of the Lunar Society, who had just died. Withering did so, and also became a member of the Lunar Society, where he met Matthew ◊Boulton, Joseph ◊Priestley, and other contemporary scientists. His practice in Birmingham did well and he became a physician at Birmingham General Hospital. He contracted tuberculosis and retired in 1783; he was elected a fellow of the Royal Society a year later. He publicly expressed his sympathies with the French Revolution, and in 1791 his house was attacked by a mob (as was Priestley's). He visited Portugal for a year 1792–93 and died in Birmingham on 6 October 1799.

In 1785 Withering published *Account of the Foxglove*, which detailed the controlled use of the drug digitalis for the treatment of dropsy. The drug was made from the leaves of the native British foxglove *Digitalis purpurea*. He had begun studying digitalis in 1775, after noting its use in traditional herbal remedies. He worked out precise dosages of dried foxglove leaves. He also suggested the possible use of the drug in the treatment of heart disease, and in this he was correct because digitalis increases the heart's output without increasing the heart rate, thus clearing the interstitial fluid that is responsible for dropsy. Digitalis, in the form of digoxin, is still one of the most widely used drugs for treating heart failure.

Withering also made a name for himself in the field of botany after the publication of his *Botanical Arrangement* (1776), which was based on the work of Carolus ◊Linnaeus and became a standard work, and his activities in geology are remembered through the mineral ore witherite (barium carbonate), which was named after him.

Further Reading

Aronson, J K, *An Account of the Foxglove and its Medical Uses, 1785–1985*, Oxford University Press, 1985.

Mann, R D; Townsend, Helen; and Townsend, Josephine, *William Withering and the Foxglove*, MTP, 1986.

Withering, William, *Withering and the Discovery of the Foxglove: An Autobiographical Extract by William Withering (1741–1799)*, Roseneath Classics series, Roseneath Scientific Publications, 1992.

Wittgenstein, Ludwig Josef Johann (1889–1951) Austrian mathematician and philosopher who is best known for his philosophical theories of language.

Wittgenstein was born in Vienna on 26 April 1889, the youngest boy of eight children. His father was prominent in the iron and steel industry, and his mother was the daughter of a banker. He was educated at home until he was 14, and in 1903 went to school in Linz to study mathematics and the physical sciences, going on to the Technische Hochschule at Charlottenburg in Berlin to study engineering. He went to the UK in 1908 and registered as a research student in aeronautical engineering at the University of Manchester.

On the advice of Friedrich ◊Frege, Wittgenstein moved to Trinity College, Cambridge, in 1912 to study philosophy under Bertrand ◊Russell. In late 1913 he went to live on a farm in Skjolden, Norway, to have seclusion in which to develop his ideas on logic. On the outbreak of World War I in 1914 Wittgenstein volunteered for the Austrian Army and saw service on the eastern front and in southern Tyrol. He continued his philosophical work, however, and when he was captured in 1918 he had with him the completed manuscript of *Tractatus Logico-Philosophicus*. Through a mutual friend, the economist John Keynes (1883–1946), the manuscript was delivered to Russell in Cambridge and eventually published in 1921.

After the war Wittgenstein abandoned philosophy – saying his mind was 'no longer flexible' – and he became a schoolteacher in various Austrian villages. Then in January 1929 he returned to Cambridge, his interest in philosophy having apparently been rekindled by a lecture given in Vienna by Luitzen ◊Brouwer on the foundations of mathematics. From 1930 to

1936 Wittgenstein gave lectures in Cambridge, and then spent a year in Norway, returning to the UK in 1937. Two years later he succeeded G E Moore as professor of philosophy.

During World War II Wittgenstein worked first as a hospital porter in Guy's Hospital, London, and then as a laboratory assistant at the Royal Victoria Infirmary in Newcastle upon Tyne. He went back to Cambridge in 1944 and following his retirement in 1947 moved to Ireland to live. Two years later he was found to have cancer and during his last days he returned to Cambridge, to his doctor's house, where he died on 24 April 1951.

Wittgenstein's *Tractatus* is concerned with the presuppositions and conditions of ordinary everyday language. He argued that a sentence literally represents the world in such a way that any significant proposition in language can be 'logically analysed' into simple 'elementary propositions' which are a nexus of names that stand for definite objects. The structuring of the parts of a proposition depicts a possible real combination of elements. Logical and mathematical propositions are exceptions – lacking reference to real or possible states of affairs and yet not being nonsensical.

Wittgenstein began work on his *Philosophical Investigations* in 1936, although it was not published until 1953, after his death. It took a more subtle and complex view than the *Tractatus*, retaining an interest in the problem of meaning but arguing that the meanings of words depends on their role within particular 'language games'. He postulated that no single feature may be supposed to be present in all forms of language, just as no single definitive feature is common to all of the practices we call games. The unity of language games is like a family resemblance, and to understand the workings of a language we must understand the complex of usages present in language games: words are used to do things rather than merely stand for objects, and the meaning of a concept depends on how it is used in a particular language game. So that in mathematics, the force of a proof – the necessity of mathematical proof – is based on convention or agreement about what is to count as following a rule in the language game of mathematics. But we do not agree *because* the proof follows a rule; rather, agreement with a mathematical calculation fixes its meaning as a proof or a rule, and human practice determines what the rules shall be.

Further Reading

Hintikka, Jaakko, *Ludwig Wittgenstein*, Kluwer Academic Publishers, 1996.

McGuinness, Brian, *Wittgenstein and His Times*, Wittgenstein Studies series, Thoemmes Antiquarian Books, 1998.

Rhees, Rush, *Discussions on Wittgenstein*, Wittgenstein Studies series, Thoemmes Antiquarian Books, 1996.

Shanker, S G, *Wittgenstein and the Turning Point in the Philosophy of Mathematics*, State University of New York Press, 1987.

Shanker, S G (ed), *Ludwig Wittgenstein: Critical Assessment*, Critical Assessments of Leading Philosophers series, Routledge, 1996.

Sluga, Hans and Stern, David G (eds), *The Cambridge Companion to Wittgenstein*, Cambridge Companions to Philosophy series, Cambridge University Press, 1996.

Strathern, Paul, *Wittgenstein in 90 Minutes*, Philosophers in 90 Minutes series, Constable and Co, 1996.

Wittig, Georg (1897–1987) German chemist, best known for his method of synthesizing olefins (alkenes) from carbonyl compounds, a reaction often termed the Wittig synthesis. For this achievement he shared the 1979 Nobel Prize for Chemistry with the US chemist Herbert Brown (1912–).

Wittig was born in Berlin on 16 June 1897. He was educated at the Wilhelms-Gymnasium and then at Kassel and Marburg universities. He was a lecturer at Marburg 1926–32, and then head of department at the Technische Hochschule in Brunswick 1932–37. He became a special professor at the University of Freiburg in 1937, and then from 1944 until 1956 was professor and institute director at Tübingen. He became a professor at Heidelberg in 1956, and remained there until 1967, when he became emeritus professor. Wittig died in Heidelburg on 26 August 1987.

In the Wittig reaction, which he first demonstrated in 1954, a carbonyl compound (aldehyde or ketone) reacts with an organic phosphorus compound, an alkylidenetriphenylphosphorane, $(C_6H_5)_3P=CR_2$, where R is a hydrogen atom or an organic radical. The alkylidene group ($=CR_2$) of the reagent reacts with the oxygen atom of the carbonyl group to form a hydrocarbon with a double bond, an olefin (alkene). In general,

$$(C_6H_5)_3P=CR_2 + R_2'CO \rightarrow (C_6H_5)_3PO + R_2C=CR_2'$$

The reaction is widely used in organic synthesis, for example to make squalene (the synthetic precursor of cholesterol) and vitamin D_3 (cholecalciferol).

Wöhler, Friedrich (1800–1882) German chemist who is generally credited with having carried out the first laboratory synthesis of an organic compound, although his main interest was inorganic chemistry.

Wöhler was born in Eschershein, near Frankfurt am Main, on 31 July 1800, the son of a veterinary surgeon in the service of the crown prince of Hesse-Kassel. He entered Marburg University in 1820 to study medicine, and after a year transferred to Heidelberg, where he studied in the laboratory of Leopold Gmelin (1788–1853). He gained his medical degree in 1823, but Gmelin had persuaded Wöhler to study chemistry and so he spent the following year in Stockholm with Jöns ◊Berzelius, beginning a lifelong association between the two chemists. From 1825 to 1831 he occupied a teaching position in a technical school in Berlin, and from 1831 to 1836 he held a similar post at Kassel. In 1836 he became professor of chemistry in the medical faculty of Göttingen University, as successor to Friedrich Strohmeyer (1776–1835), and remained there for the rest of his career, making it one of the most prestigious teaching laboratories in Europe. He died in Göttingen on 23 September 1882.

Organic chemistry just now is enough to drive one mad. It gives one the impression of a primeval, tropical forest full of the most remarkable things, a monstrous and boundless thicket, with no way of escape, into which one may well dread to enter.

FRIEDRICH WÖHLER LETTER TO BERZELIUS
28 JAN 1835

In Wöhler's first research in 1827 he isolated metallic aluminium by heating its chloride with potassium; he then prepared many different aluminium salts. In 1828 he used the same procedure to isolate beryllium. Also in 1828 he carried out the reaction for which he is best known. He heated ammonium thiocyanate – a crystalline, inorganic substance – and converted it to urea (carbamide), an organic substance previously obtained only from natural sources. Until that time there had been a basic misconception in scientific thinking that the chemical changes undergone by substances in living organisms were not governed by the same laws as were inanimate substances; it was thought that these 'vital' phenomena could not be described in ordinary chemical or physical terms. This theory gave rise to the original division between inorganic (non-vital) and organic (vital) chemistry, and its supporters were known as vitalists, who maintained that natural products formed by living organisms could never be synthesized by ordinary chemical means. Wöhler's synthesis of urea was a bitter blow to the vitalists and did much to overthrow their doctrine. It involved an isomerization reaction:

$$NH_4OCN \xrightarrow{\text{heat}} O = C \begin{array}{c} NH_2 \\ \\ NH_2 \end{array}$$

ammonium cyanate

urea (carbamide)

Wöhler worked with Justus von ◊Liebig on a number of important investigations. In 1830 they proved the polymerism of cyanates and fulminates, and two years later announced a series of studies of benzaldehyde (benzenecarbaldehyde) and the benzoyl (benzenecarboxyl) radical. In 1837 they investigated uric acid and its derivatives. Wöhler also discovered quinone (cyclohexadiene-1,4-dione), hydroquinone or quinol (benzene-1,4-diol), and quinhydrone (a molecular complex composed of equimolar amounts of quinone and hydroquinone).

In the inorganic field Wöhler isolated boron and silicon and prepared silicon nitride and hydride. He prepared phosphorus by the modern method, and discovered calcium carbide and showed that it can be reacted with water to produce acetylene (ethyne):

$$CaC_2 + 2H_2O \rightarrow Ca(OH)_2 + C_2H_2$$

He demonstrated the analogy between the compounds of carbon and silicon, and just missed being the first to discover vanadium and niobium. He also obtained pure titanium and showed the similarity between this element and carbon and silicon. He published little work after 1845, but concentrated on teaching.

Wolf, Maximilian Franz Joseph Cornelius (1863–1932) German astronomer particularly noted for his application of photographic methods to observational astronomy.

Wolf was born in Heidelberg on 21 June 1863. He was fascinated by astronomy from an early age and his father, who was fairly wealthy, built a small observatory for him in 1885 which he used for most of his research until 1896. He studied at the University of Heidelberg and was awarded his PhD in 1888 for a thesis on celestial mechanics. He then spent a year in Stockholm, before returning to Heidelberg to join the staff of the university there as a lecturer. In 1893 he travelled to the USA and was then appointed extraordinary professor of astrophysics at Heidelberg. With the assistance of wealthy benefactors, Wolf supervised the construction of a new observatory at Königstuhl, near Heidelberg. He was appointed director of that observatory in 1896 and made professor of astronomy in 1901. Wolf held both these posts until his death, on 3 October 1932, in Heidelberg.

Wolf made his first important astronomical discovery in 1883, when he observed a comet that has an orbital period of 7.7 years. In Wolf's honour it now bears his name. He devoted much of his time to developing new photographic methods for application to astronomy. One of his most successful innovations was a technique for discovering large numbers of asteroids. Until this time, asteroids had always been discovered visually, the first, Ceres, being noticed by Giuseppe

◊Piazzi in 1801; more and more of these bodies had gradually been discovered over subsequent years. Wolf arranged for time-lapse photographs to be taken, using a camera mounted on a telescope whose clock mechanism followed as exactly as possible the proper motions of the 'fixed stars'. On the developed plate, the stars would appear as discrete spots – the size being a function of the star's magnitude – whereas any asteroids present would appear as short streaks in the foreground.

The first asteroid Wolf discovered using this technique was number 323, afterwards named Brucia. He subsequently discovered more than 200 other asteroids using the same method. In September 1903, he discovered a special asteroid, number 588, later named Achilles. Its particular significance was that it was the first of the so-called 'Trojan satellites' whose orbits are in precise synchrony with that of Jupiter's; they form a gravitationally stable configuration between Jupiter and the Sun. The possibility of the existence of this kind of triangular three-bodied system was first analysed and predicted theoretically by Joseph Lagrange in the 1770s and Wolf's discovery of the 'Trojan satellites' provided the observational evidence to substantiate Lagrange's theory.

Wolf also detected several new nebulae, both within the Milky Way and outside our Galaxy. Independently of Edward ◊Barnard, he discovered that the dark 'voids' in the Milky Way are in fact nebulae that are obscured by vast quantities of dust, and he studied their spectral characteristics and distribution. Among the nebulae that Wolf himself discovered is the North America Nebula (NCG 7000), which resembles that continent in shape and is found in the constellation of Cygnus.

Wolf, with Carl Pulfrich (1858–1929), invented the stereocomparator, which was used for various kinds of observational astronomy. He also carried out research on the sunspot cycle and was the first to observe Halley's Comet when it approached the Earth in 1909. Besides being a keen observational astronomer and a dedicated and inspiring teacher, Wolf is best remembered for his innovative photographic techniques that led to the discovery of many new asteroids.

Wolff, Heinz Siegfried (1928–) German-born British biomedical engineer who has worked on high-technology instruments and the application of technology to medicine.

Wolff was born in Berlin on 29 April 1928. He worked in the physiological laboratory at Oxford University 1946–50 and then for a year in the Medical Research Unit in Glamorgan. He then went to University College, London, to study physiology and after graduating in 1954 he was employed in the Division of Human Physiology at the Medical Research Council's National Institute for Medical Research, where he specialized in the development of instrumentation suitable for field work. In 1965 he was appointed head of the institute's Division of Biomedical Engineering. He then became director of the Biomedical Division of the MRC's Clinical Research Centre in Harrow, London, 1983–95.

Wolff's interests range from the invention of new high-technology instruments to the widespread and sensible application of technology to the problems of the elderly and the disabled. He believes that small, specialized pieces of equipment that can be worked by doctors and nurses might be preferable to large centralized units to which patients have to go for tests or treatment. Machines should be simple to use and should show when they are not working properly and be capable of repair on the spot by the operator. The researcher should collaborate more with the manufacturer, and manufacturers should spend some resources on creating a market for the next generation of equipment as well as fulfilling existing market requirements. Technology should also be used to make the chronically ill more comfortable and to allow the disabled to remain in their own homes.

Wolff, Kaspar Friedrich (1733–1794) German surgeon and physiologist who has become regarded as the founder of embryology, although his findings were largely ignored for more than 50 years.

Wolff was born in Berlin on 18 January 1733 and studied at Halle and the Berlin Medical School, from which he graduated in 1759. He was an army surgeon during the Seven Years' War (1756–63), and then lectured in pathology in Berlin. Despite the success of his lectures he was not offered a professorship, and so in 1766 he accepted an invitation from Catherine II of Russia to take the post of academician for anatomy and physiology in St Petersburg. He remained there until his death on 22 February 1794.

Wolff produced his revolutionary work *Theoria generationis* in 1759. Until that time it was generally believed that each living organism develops from an exact miniature of the adult within the seed or sperm – the so-called preformation, or homunculus, theory. Wolff introduced the idea that cells that are initially unspecialized later differentiate to produce the separate organs and systems of the plant or animal body with their distinct types of tissues. In fact Wolff's view that plants and animals are composed of cells was still a subject of controversy. His name is also associated with, among other parts of the anatomy, the Wolffian body, a structure in an animal embryo that eventually develops into the kidney.

Wollaston, William Hyde (1766–1828)

English chemist and physicist who developed the technique of powder metallurgy and discovered rhodium and palladium, two elements similar to platinum.

Wollaston was born in East Dereham, Norfolk, on 6 August 1766, one of 17 children of an academic family. His father Francis Wollaston was a cleric and amateur astronomer, and his elder brother Francis John Hyde Wollaston became a professor of chemistry at Cambridge University. Wollaston was educated at Charterhouse School and at Gonville and Caius College, Cambridge, from which he graduated in medicine in 1793. He practised as a doctor for seven years and then in 1800 moved to London and devoted the rest of his life to scientific research. He died of a brain tumour on 22 December 1828.

Wollaston initiated the technique of powder metallurgy when working with platinum and trying to get it into a workable, malleable form. Using aqua regia (a mixture of concentrated nitric and hydrochloric acids) he dissolved the platinum from crude platina, a mixed platinum–iridium ore. He then prepared ammonium platinichloride, which he decomposed by heating to yield fine grains of platinum metal. The grains were worked using heat, pressure, and hammering to form sheets, which he sold to industrial chemists for making corrosion-resistant vessels; manufacturers of sulphuric acid were willing to pay high prices for such a useful metal. Wollaston kept his method secret, and made £30,000 from selling platinum, much of which he donated to various scientific societies to help finance their researches.

In 1803, while investigating platinum ores, Wollaston discovered the element palladium. Within a year he also found rhodium, another metal with similar properties to platinum.

He was a great supporter of John ◊Dalton's atomic theory and published several papers based on the law of multiple proportions. In 1808 he suggested that a knowledge of the arrangements of atoms in three dimensions would be a great leap forward (although a century was to pass before this became possible). He advocated the use of 'equivalents' in quantitative chemical calculations, from which the concept of normality (now superseded by molarity) was developed.

Wollaston also worked in various areas of physics. In optics he suggested the total reflection method for measuring refractivity (later developed by Carl Pulfrich and Ernst ◊Abbe) and drew attention to the dark lines (later called Fraunhofer lines) in the solar spectrum. In 1807 he developed the camera lucida, which was to inspire William Fox ◊Talbot to his discoveries in photography. He also invented a reflecting goniometer for accurately measuring the angles of crystals in minerals.

In 1801 Wollaston established the important physical principle that 'galvanic' and 'frictional' electricity are the same. He also stated that the action in the common voltaic cell is due to the oxidation of the zinc electrode. In early 1821 he reported that there is 'a power ... acting circumferentially round the axis of a wire carrying a current' and tried in Humphry ◊Davy's laboratory at the Royal Institution to make a current-carrying wire revolve on its axis. These experiments were unsuccessful and the final demonstration of the effect is now attributed to Michael ◊Faraday. In 1824 the British Weights and Measures Act incorporated the imperial gallon, equivalent to 10 lb weight of water as suggested by Wollaston in 1814. (But as a member of a Royal Commission in 1819 Wollaston was instrumental in the rejection of the decimal system of weights and measures.)

Woodger, Joseph Henry (1894–1981)

English biologist known principally for his theoretical work on the underlying philosophical basis of scientific methodology in biology, especially for his attempt to provide biology with a strict and logical foundation on which observations, theories, and methods could be based.

Woodger was born on 2 May 1894 in Great Yarmouth, Norfolk, and was educated at Felsted School then University College, London (where he studied under J P Hill, one of the leading British zoologists of the time). Woodger enrolled in the army in 1915 and after World War I spent a brief period in Baghdad (then part of the Ottoman Empire). He returned to London in 1919 and began investigating newly discovered cell organelles, including Golgi bodies and mitochondria. In 1924 he was appointed reader in biology at the Middlesex Hospital Medical School in London, and became a professor there in 1947. He retired in 1959.

Woodger's transition from practical work to the theoretical and philosophical aspects of biology dated from his appointment to the readership in biology. Confronted for the first time with having to teach, he found no textbooks that gave an adequate grounding in the fundamental scientific principles involved in biology and medicine, so he wrote one – *Elementary Morphology and Physiology* (1924). He became increasingly concerned with the problems of methodology and interpretation in biological experimentation and with the need for 'a critical sorting of fundamental concepts to promote a strictness of thought equal to the strictness of investigation required in the new biology'.

There was at that time no generally accepted (biological) theory of the organism, only a host of facts and conflicting ideas ranging from total mechanism to vitalism. The new biology required a causal description for each vital process and a means of understanding how such processes as nutrition, development, and behaviour are related to the life of a particular organism or species.

Woodger began by teaching himself philosophy, with particular reference to Alfred North ♢Whitehead and Bertrand ♢Russell's *Principia Mathematica*. He developed the idea that one of the characteristics of a living system is the organization of its substance, and that this order is of a hierarchical nature. Thus the components of an organism can be classified on a scale of increasing size and complexity: molecular, macromolecular, cell components, cells, tissues, organs, and organisms. Each class exhibits specifically new modes of behaviour, which cannot be interpreted as being merely additive phenomena from the previous class.

Woodger's major work, *Biological Principles: A Critical Study* (1929), examines the fundamental requirements of theories in biology. He was able to show how to resolve many of the apparent antitheses in biology (such as those between structure and function, preformation and development, and mechanism and vitalism). He also made the first attempt to put embryological ideas on a logistic basis by analysing at length, and in strict logical form, the process of cell division. He demonstrated that living matter shows not only spatial hierarchical order but also divisional hierarchies (each cell or group of cells has a parent cell), and that many difficulties in biological theory arose originally through the abstraction from time – that is, viewing an organism as a series of spatially ordered components only. He summarized many of these ideas in his book *The Technique of Theory Construction* (1939).

Woodward, Robert Burns (1917–1979) US organic chemist famous for his syntheses of complex biochemicals. For his outstanding contribution to this area of science he was awarded the 1965 Nobel Prize for Chemistry.

Woodward was born in Boston on 10 April 1917. He went to the Massachusetts Institute of Technology in 1933, while he was still only 16 years old, gaining his BS degree three years later and his PhD a year after that. He went to Harvard in 1938, at the age of 21, and remained there for the rest of his academic career. He held various appointments, including assistant professor 1944–46, associate professor 1946–50, full professor 1950–53, Morris Loeb Professor 1953–60, and Donner Professor of Science from 1960. From 1973 to 1974 he was also Todd Professor of Chemistry and a fellow of Christ's College, Cambridge. He died in Cambridge, Massachusetts, on 8 July 1979.

Woodward's first important research was in collaboration with William Doering when in 1944 they achieved a total synthesis of quinine (from simple starting materials). In 1947 he worked out the structure of penicillin and two years later that of strychnine. In the early 1950s he began to synthesize steroids, such as cholesterol and cortisone in 1951 and lanosterol in 1954. In that same year he synthesized the poisonous alkaloid strychnine and lysergic acid, the basis of the hallucinogenic drug LSD. In 1956 he made reserpine, the first of the tranquillizing drugs, and four years later he prepared chlorophyll. Turning his attention again to antibiotics, he and his co-workers produced a tetracycline in 1962 and cephalosporin C in 1965. In 1971 came the culmination of ten years' work, involving collaboration with Swiss chemists – the synthesis of vitamin B_{12} (cyanocobalamin). Many of these syntheses were among the most complicated ever attempted in organic chemistry, involving many stages that had to be carefully selected for stereospecificity and maximum yield. Yet so well worked out were they that many have become the basis of commercial manufacture of drugs and other useful biochemicals.

Wooley, Richard van der Riet (1906–1986) English astronomer, best known for his work on the dynamics of the Galaxy, observational and theoretical astrophysics, and stellar dynamics.

Wooley was born in Weymouth, Dorset, on 24 April 1906; his father was Rear Admiral Charles Wooley. He was educated at Allhallows School, Honiton, and at the universities of Cape Town in South Africa and Cambridge. He was a Commonwealth Fund Fellow at Mount Wilson Observatory 1929–31 and an Isaac Newton Student at Cambridge 1931–33, when he was appointed chief assistant at the Royal Observatory, Greenwich. He remained at Greenwich for four years, until he was appointed first assistant observer – John Couch Adams Astronomer – at the University Observatory in Cambridge. In 1939 he became the director of the Commonwealth Observatory at Mount Stromlo, Canberra, Australia. Finally, in 1955, Wooley was appointed as the 11th Astronomer Royal, succeeding Harold Spencer Jones (1890–1960) at the Royal Observatory; he retained this position until his retirement in 1970. Even after his retirement, he held the post of first director of the South African Astronomical Observatory until he reached the age of 70. He received a knighthood in 1963 and was president of the Royal Astronomical Society 1963–65, receiving its Gold Medal in 1971. He died in Cape Town on 24 December 1986.

While Wooley was chief assistant at the Royal Observatory, he became well acquainted with the more traditional aspects of astronomy. His duties included meridian astronomy with the Airy transit circle, time service control with small reversible transits and pendulum clocks, double star observations, solar spectroscopy, and spectrohelioscope observations. The observatory at Mount Stromlo was devoted mainly to solar physics and so while he was director there he devoted much of his time to the study of photospheric convection, emission spectra of the chromosphere, and the solar corona. Besides these investigations, he pioneered the observation of monochromatic magnitudes and constructed colour magnitude arrays for globular clusters. Under Wooley's control, the Commonwealth Observatory grew in stature and its equipment was updated to include a 188-cm/74-in reflecting telescope.

When Wooley was appointed Astronomer Royal, the Royal Observatory had recently been moved from Greenwich to Herstmonceux in Sussex. At the time of his appointment the establishment seemed to lack purpose and direction; observations were being amassed using obsolete equipment and methods that had been devised by George ◊Airy in the 19th century. Wooley's first priorities were to press for an agreement on the design of the new Isaac Newton Telescope and to redistribute resources for astrophysical research projects. During the 15 years that he spent as Astronomer Royal he was noted for the balance that he maintained between theoretical studies and observational astronomy. His personal interests during this period were globular clusters, the evolution of galactic orbits, improvements of radial velocities, and a re-evaluation of RR Lyrae luminosities. He appointed several physicists to the staff whose studies involved galactic cluster fields, elemental abundance, and the evolution of galaxies.

Wright, Almroth Edward (1861–1947) English bacteriologist who did pioneering work in the field of immunology, notably in the development of a vaccine against typhoid fever. He received numerous honours for his work, including a knighthood in 1906.

Wright was born on 10 August 1861 in Middleton Tyas, a small village near Richmond in Yorkshire. His father was an Irish Presbyterian cleric who, between 1863 and 1885, held ministries in Dresden, Boulogne, and Belfast, and Wright received his early education from his parents and private tutors. While his family was in Belfast, however, he attended the Royal Academic Institution and then in 1878 entered Trinity College, Dublin, from which he graduated in modern literature in 1882 and in medicine in the following year. Subsequently he studied – on a travelling scholarship – pathological anatomy at the universities of Leipzig and Marburg and physiological chemistry at Strasbourg. He then went to Australia, where he was a demonstrator of physiology at Sydney University 1889–91. After his return to England, Wright worked for a short time in the laboratories of the College of Physicians and Surgeons in London until, in 1892, he was appointed professor of pathology at the Army

Medical School in Netley, Hampshire. It was while he held this post that he developed a vaccine against typhoid, but he disagreed with the army authorities over the use of his vaccine and he resigned his professorship in 1902. In the same year he became professor of pathology at St Mary's Hospital in London and held this post until he retired in 1946; in 1908 he also became responsible for the department of therapeutic inoculation (later called the Institute of Pathological Research) at St Mary's. In 1911 Wright went to South Africa, where he introduced prophylactic inoculation against pneumonia for workers in the Rand gold mines. On returning to England, he was appointed director of the department of bacteriology of the newly founded Medical Research Committee (later the Medical Research Council) at the Hampstead Laboratory, London. During World War I he served in France as a temporary colonel in the Army Medical Service, afterwards returning full-time to his professorship at St Mary's Hospital. Wright died at his home in Farnham Common on 30 April 1947.

Wright first began bacteriological research while he was professor at the Army Medical School, and by 1896 he had succeeded in developing an effective antityphoid vaccine, which he prepared from killed typhoid bacilli. Preliminary trials of the vaccine on troops of the Indian Army proved its effectiveness and the vaccine was subsequently used successfully among the British soldiers in the Boer War. In addition to this important development, Wright established a new discipline within medicine, that of therapeutic immunization by vaccination, which was aimed at treating microbial diseases rather than preventing them. He proved that the human bloodstream contains bacteriatrophins (opsonins) in the serum and that these substances can destroy bacteria by phagocytosis. He researched into wound infections, his work in this area leading to the use of salt solution as an osmotic agent to draw lymph into wounds, thereby accelerating their closure. He also originated vaccines against enteric tuberculosis and pneumonia.

Wright, Louis Tompkins (1891–1952) US physician, surgeon, and civil-rights leader, known for his work on fractures (especially head injuries), venereal disease, and cancer.

Born on 23 July 1891 in LaGrange, Georgia, Wright was educated at Clark University, Atlanta, from which he received a BA, graduating as valedictorian in 1911, and at Harvard Medical School, receiving his MD *cum laude* in 1915. After his internship at Freedmen's Hospital, Washington, DC, and having taken medical examinations for licensing in Maryland, Georgia, and New York, in 1917 he joined the US Army as first lieutenant in the Medical Corps. Returning to New York after World War I, he combined private practice and serving on the staff of the Harlem Hospital – in 1919 as a clinical assistant visiting surgeon, rising to director of surgery 23 years later and director of the medical board of Harlem Hospitals in 1948. He was the first black doctor to be appointed to a municipal hospital position in New York City. In 1929, after passing the civil-service examinations, Wright was also appointed as the first black police surgeon in the history of the city. Wright remained in New York until his death on 8 October 1952; he had married in 1918 and had two daughters.

Wright is best known for his work as a physician and surgeon. His criticism of the Schick test for diphtheria carried out at the Freedmen's Hospital is said to be the first original work to be published from the hospital. While in the army he originated the intradermal method of vaccination against smallpox, published in the *Journal of the American Medical Association* (1918). Wright specialized in head injuries and fractures; he devised a brace for neck fractures, a blade for the treatment of fractures of the knee joint, and a plate made out of tantalum for the repair of recurrent hernias. As an authority on the subject he wrote the chapter on head injuries in C Scudder's *Treatment of Fractures* (11th edition, 1938) and published many articles in medical journals. Wright also became an authority on the venereal disease lymphogranuloma venereum and was the first physician to experiment with the new antibiotics Aureomycin (the 'wonder drug') and Terramycin, publishing 30 and 8 papers respectively on the two drugs 1948–52. In 1948 Wright moved into the field of cancer research and founded the Harlem Hospital Cancer Research Foundation, where he dealt with the effectiveness of chemotherapeutic drugs.

As well as his professional activities, Wright was involved with civil-rights activities, promoting better health assurance and expanding equal opportunities for black people. He was active on the local branch of the National Association for the Advancement of Colored People (NAACP) and was chair of its national board of directors for 17 years. His work led to many honours and awards including the Purple Heart in World War I, a DSc from Clarke University in 1938, and the Spingarn Medal in 1940. He was made a fellow of the New York Surgical Society in 1949 and a fellow of the International College of Surgeons in 1950, and was also a fellow of the American Medical Association and the National Medical Association. In 1952 the Louis T Wright Library of Harlem Hospital was named after him as was a public school in Harlem in 1976.

Wright, Orville (1871–1948) and Wilbur (1867–1912) US aeronautical engineers famous for their achievement of the first controlled, powered flight in a

Wright brothers US engineers Orville (left) and Wilbur Wright who pioneered piloted flight. They were the first to make a successful powered flight, near Kitty Hawk, North Carolina.
Mary Evans Picture Library

heavier-than-air machine (an aeroplane) and for their design of the aircraft's control system.

Wilbur, the elder of the two brothers, was born in Millville, Indiana, on 16 April 1867 and Orville was born in Dayton, Ohio, on 19 August 1871. Their father was a bishop of the United Brethren Church. He brought up his sons to think for themselves, to have initiative, and to have the enterprise to use their abilities and express themselves fully. They both went to the local high school in Dayton. During and after their schooldays they developed an interest in mechanical things. They taught themselves mathematics and read as much as they could about current developments in engineering. After some attempts at editing and printing small local newspapers, the two brothers formed the Wright Cycle Company in 1892. For the next ten years they designed, built, and sold bicycles.

Like any other serious innovative engineers, the Wright brothers must have considered the possibility of powered flight and how to achieve it, but the exploits of Otto ◊Lilienthal, the German pioneer of gliders who was killed in 1896, brought home to them that much might be achieved in this direction with perseverance and daring.

Lilienthal's death convinced Wilbur that in order to avoid dangerous accidents it was important that they not only build successful aeroplanes but that they also learn to fly them correctly. Control of direction and stability were problems that occupied them for the next few years; in August 1899 they flew a kite with a wingspan of about 1.5 m/5 ft with controls for warping the wings to achieve control of direction and stability. Their wing-warping method was the forerunner of the later idea of ailerons. They discovered that the kite would fly with the horizontal tailplane either forward or aft of the wings.

The following year, 1900, the Wrights built a larger kite of 5-m/17-ft wingspan to carry a pilot. After taking advice as to where to find steady winds together with suitable sandy banks, they decided on Kitty Hawk, North Carolina. The kite flew well and Wilbur achieved a few seconds of piloted flight. They also flew a glider with the tailplane in front of the wings. The following July they returned to Kitty Hawk and built a wooden sled at Kill Devil Hills, where there were large sand dunes. Their new machine was longer and had a different wing camber to the previous model; it also had a hand-operated elevator attached to the tail plane. Again they achieved encouraging results, particularly after further alterations to the wing camber. There were still however problems with stability and control.

During the following winter the Wrights built a small wind tunnel and tested various wing designs and cambers. In the course of these tests they compiled the first accurate tables of lift and drag, the important parameters that govern flight and stability. The new glider had a 9.6-m/32-ft wingspan and had, at first, a double vertical fin mounted behind the wings. Turning was still difficult, however, and so this was converted to a single moveable rudder operated by the wing-warping controls. This configuration proved so successful that they decided to attempt powered flight the following summer. During the winter of 1902 they searched in vain for a suitable engine for their craft and for knowledge of propeller design. They eventually constructed their own 9-kW/12-hp motor and made their own very efficient propeller. After some initial trouble with the propeller shafts, the Wright biplane took to the air and made a successful flight on 17 December 1903 at Kill Devil Hills near Kitty Hawk. The aeroplane had a wingspan of 12 m/40 ft and weighed 340 kg/750 lb with the pilot. The two brothers took it in turns to fly. Wilbur, in the last of the flights, stayed in the air for 59 seconds and travelled 255 m/852 ft at a little under 16 kph/10 mph relative to the ground.

The following year the Wrights incorporated a 12-kW/16-hp engine and separated the wing-warping and rudder controls. They flew their new model at their home town of Dayton, learning to make longer flights and tighter turns.

In 1905 the Wrights were sufficiently confident of their design to offer it to the US War Department. The following year they patented their control system of elevator, rudder, and wing-warping. Although they spent time patenting and finding markets for their machines during the next few years, they did not feel sufficiently confident to exhibit them publicly until 1908. That year Wilbur flew in France and Orville in the USA. In 1909 Wilbur flew in Rome and Orville in Berlin. Their aeroplanes were now sufficiently well controlled and stable to allow Wilbur to make a flight of 32 km/20 mi in the USA.

During the next few years they and their Wright Company built aeroplanes, but by 1918 their competitors had gained ground and their patents were under pressure. During the ensuing litigation Wilbur caught typhoid fever and died at Dayton, Ohio, on the 30 May 1912.

Orville sold his interest in the Wright Company in 1915 and later pursued aviation research. He eventually became a member of the National Advisory Committee on Aeronautics. He died in Dayton on 30 January 1948 having received during his lifetime many awards and honours as tokens of the momentous achievement of the Wright brothers.

Further Reading

Gibbs-Smith, Charles Harvard, *The Wright Brothers: A Brief Account of Their Work, 1899–1911,* HMSO, 1963.

Howard, Fred, *Wilbur and Orville: A Biography of the Wright Brothers,* Dover Publications, 1998.

Hudson, Margaret, *The Wright Brothers,* Lives and Times series, Heinemann, 1998.

Jakab, Peter L, *Visions of a Flying Machine: The Wright Brothers and the Process of Invention,* Smithsonian History of Aviation Series, Airlife, 1990.

Kelly, Fred C, *The Wright Brothers: A Biography,* 1989.

Sabin, Louis, *Wilbur and Orville Wright: The Flight to Adventure,* Troll Communications, 1997.

Woods, Andrew, *Young Orville and Wilbur Wright: First to Fly,* Troll Communications, 1997.

Wright, Thomas (1711–1786) English astronomer and teacher who carried out theoretical work in astronomy that anticipated modern discoveries.

Wright was born in Byer's Green, near Durham, on 22 September 1711. He left school at the age of 13 to take up an apprenticeship, which he did not complete, with a clockmaker. Although he was interested in instrument-making, he held a number of jobs outside this field. His most successful work was as a private mathematics teacher and lecturer on popular scientific subjects. In 1742 he was offered the chair of mathematics at the Academy of Sciences at St Petersburg. He refused this position, however, on the grounds that the salary offered was inadequate. He spent the rest of his days in Byer's Green as a writer and teacher. He died on 25 February 1786.

The main drive behind most of Wright's scientific work was his desire to reconcile his religious beliefs with his telescopic observations and with the knowledge he obtained through his extensive reading. In his early works Wright described the universe as a series of concentric spheres – hardly an original concept – in which the centre was occupied by some divine power. Then in 1750 he wrote his most influential work, 'An original theory or new hypothesis of the universe'. It did not, however, express his final thoughts on the subject. He wrote another manuscript on the subject, but it was never published. His first essay was, however, a classic work and it created sufficient interest to warrant a new edition to be published in the USA, in Philadelphia, in 1937. In it, Wright describes the Milky Way as a flattened disc, in which the Sun does not occupy a central position. Furthermore, he stated that nebulae lay outside the Milky Way. These views were more than 150 years ahead of their time and did not become accepted by the scientific community until they were substantiated by observational evidence in the 1920s.

However, Wright's model does not completely conform with modern views because he persisted in his belief that the centre of the system was occupied by a divine presence. Wright's other work included thoughts on the particulate nature of the rings of Saturn, anticipating the writings of James Clerk ◊Maxwell by nearly a century, and thoughts on such diverse fields as architecture and reincarnation.

Wu Chien-Shiung (1912–1997)

Chinese-born US physicist, teacher, and researcher in nuclear physics. Her work changed the accepted view of the structure of the universe. She was the first woman to receive an honorary doctorate of science from Princeton University, New Jersey, the first woman elected president of the American Physical Society, and the first woman awarded the Wolf Prize from the state of Israel. She was also the first living scientist to have an asteroid named after her.

Born in Liu-ho, Kiangsu Province, on 31 May 1912, Wu received a BSc from the National Central University in 1934. She moved to the USA in 1936 to work under US physicist Ernest O ◊Lawrence at the University of California at Berkeley, gaining a PhD in 1940. She spent a short time teaching at Smith College, Northampton, Massachusetts, and then took up a post at Princeton University. In 1944 she worked on radiation detection in the division of war research at Columbia University, becoming a staff member in 1946. She spent the rest of her career there, becoming professor of physics in 1957. In 1972 she became the Pupin Professor of Physics at Columbia.

In the 1950s Wu's research focused on the mechanism of beta disintegration in radioactive decay. She demonstrated in 1956 that the direction of the emission of beta rays is strongly correlated with the direction of spin of the emitting nucleus. Her experiment, performed by cooling cobalt-60 in a magnetic field so that the their spins were aligned, confirmed the hypotheses of Chinese physicists Yang Chen Ning and Lee Tsung Dao (see ◊Yang and Lee) that the 'law of symmetry' was violated in 'weak' nuclear interactions. Yang and Lee received the Nobel Prize in 1957 for their theory, which overturned many of the central tenets of physics. In 1958 Wu experimentally confirmed US physicists Richard ◊Feynman and Murray ◊Gell-Mann's theory of conservation of vector current in beta decay.

Wu made many contributions to elementary particle physics including demonstrating that the electromagnetic radiation from the annihilation of positrons and electron is polarized, proving that electrons and positrons have opposite parity, as predicted by Paul ◊Dirac's theory of the electron. In recognition of her contributions to atomic research and the understanding of beta decay and weak interactions, she was awarded the Research Corporation Award and the Comstock Prize from the National Academy of Sciences. Wu also undertook studies of the X-ray spectra of muonic atoms and in her later years became interested in the structure of haemoglobin. She retired from Columbia in 1981.

Wurtz, Charles Adolphe (1817–1884)

French organic chemist, best known for his synthetic reactions and for discovering ethylamine and ethylene glycol (1,2-ethanediol). His major contribution, however, was the elevation of the standard of organic chemistry research in mid-19th-century France to a level that challenged the excellence of the German universities.

Wurtz was born in Wolfisheim, near Strasbourg, on 26 November 1817, the son of a clergyman. Given the choice of studying theology or medicine, he chose the latter as being nearer his real interest, chemistry. He attended the University of Strasbourg and graduated with a medical degree in 1843. He spent a year at Giessen, where he met and studied with Justus von ◊Liebig and August ◊Hofmann. In 1844 he moved to Paris and became an assistant to Jean Baptiste ◊Dumas at the Faculty of Medicine. He later succeeded him as lecturer in organic chemistry (1849), professor of organic chemistry (1853), and dean of the faculty. In 1874 he accepted the professorship of organic chemistry at the Sorbonne and was able to relinquish the heavy administrative duties of dean and concentrate on teaching and writing. He also held public office as mayor of the Seventh Arrondissement of Paris and as a senator. He died in Paris on 12 May 1884.

Wurtz initially worked on the oxides and oxyacids of phosphorus; in 1846 he discovered phosphorus oxychloride ($POCl_3$). He later turned to organic chemistry, at first studying aliphatic amines. In 1849 he made his famous discovery of ethylamine, the first organic derivative of ammonia (whose existence had been predicted by Liebig), and went on to prepare various amines and diamines.

In 1855 Wurtz discovered a method of producing paraffin hydrocarbons (alkanes) using alkyl halides (halogenoalkanes) and sodium in ether. The method was named the Wurtz reaction (sometimes also known as the Wurtz–Fittig reaction) and has subsequently been used to synthesize hydrocarbons as high up the homologous series as $C_{60}H_{122}$.

Wurtz discovered ethylene glycol (1,2-ethanediol) in 1856, which led to methods of preparing glycolic acid (hydroxyethanoic acid), choline, and other substances. He discovered aldol (3-hydroxybutanal) while investigating the polymerization of acetaldehyde (ethanal), devised a method of making esters from alkyl halides, and in 1867, with Friedrich ◊Kekulé, synthesized phenol from benzene.

Throughout his work in organic chemistry, Wurtz enthusiastically applied the theory of types as propounded by Charles Gerhardt (1816–1856). He was active at a time when chemistry was undergoing great upheavals, and took clear stands on the many issues under debate.

Yalow, Rosalyn Sussman (1921–) US medical physicist who shared the 1977 Nobel Prize for Physiology or Medicine, with Roger ◊Guillemin and Andrew Schally (1926–), for her work in developing the radioimmunoassay (RIA) technique. The Nobel citation called Yalow's work 'a spectacular combination of immunology, isotope research, mathematics, and physics.' Although Yalow's research concentrated on the human endocrine system – the glands and the hormones they secrete into the blood to control the organs – the RIA technique has been applied throughout medicine.

Rosalyn Sussman was born on 19 July 1921 in New York City. She graduated in physics from Hunter College, New York, in 1941 and obtained a PhD in experimental nuclear physics from the University of Illinois in 1945. There she met Aaron Yalow whom she married in 1943. Rosalyn then returned to Hunter College to teach; she also started working part-time in the Radioisotope Unit of the Veterans Administration (VA) Hospital in the Bronx. In 1950 Yalow began working full-time at the VA. For the first 22 years, Yalow worked with a medical doctor called Sol Berson. Recalling their partnership, she said: 'He wanted to be a physicist and I wanted to be a doctor'. When Berson died in 1972, their laboratory was renamed the Solomon A Berson Research Laboratory and Yalow was appointed its director. She retired from the post in 1992.

In the Radioisotope Unit at the VA, radioactive isotopes were used in diagnosis, therapy, and research. Yalow and Berson started studying the thyroid gland with radioactive iodine and developed methods to measure the amount of blood in circulation and the rate of removal of proteins from the blood. Next they studied the behaviour of insulin (a small protein or peptide hormone) in the blood. They injected diabetic and non-diabetic volunteers with radioactive-labelled insulin and discovered that the insulin disappeared more slowly from the blood of the diabetics. This was surprising because diabetes was thought to result from the absence of insulin. However the diabetics had a history of taking insulin and this 'foreign' insulin was triggering the production of antibodies in the blood. The insulin was binding to the antibodies. In developing methods to measure the antibody concentration, Yalow and Berson invented RIA.

To measure the concentration of a natural hormone, a solution containing a known amount of the radioisotope-labelled form of the hormone and its antibody is prepared. When a solution containing the natural hormone is added to the first solution, some of the labelled hormone is displaced from the hormone–antibody complex. The fraction of labelled hormone displaced is proportional to the amount of the natural hormone (which is unknown). The hormone–antibody complex can then be removed from the solution and the amount of labelled hormone in each sample determined from measurements of radioactivity. This in turn enables the amount of natural hormone to be calculated. This technique is known as radioimmunoassay.

Further Reading

Straus, Eugene W, *Rosalyn Yalow, Nobel Laureate: Her Life and Work in Medicine, A Biographical Memoir,* Plenum Publishing Co, 1998.

Strauss, Eugene W (ed), *Festschrift for Rosalyn Yalow: Hormones, Metabolism and Society,* Mount Sinai Hospital Committee on Medical Education and Publications, 1992.

Yang and Lee, Yang Chen Ning (1922–) and Lee Tsung Dao (1926–) Chinese particle physicists best known for their joint discovery of parity volition for which they shared the Nobel Prize for Physics in 1957.

Yang was born in Hofei, Anwhei, on 22 September 1922, the son of a mathematics professor. He gained a BSc in physics in 1942 at the Southwest Associated University at Kunming, Yunnan. Attracted by the reputation of Enrico ◊Fermi he moved to the University of Chicago in 1945, from where he received his PhD in 1948. He moved to the Institute of Advanced Studies in Princeton in 1949, where he remained until 1965, becoming a professor in 1955. Yang made his first major contribution to the theory of elementary particles with US physicist Robert G Mills (1924–) in 1954, when they devised a theory for the conservation of the property isospin, which was important for the development of the standard model of particles and their interactions. What became known as the Yang–Mills theory was a non-Abelian theory in which a mathematical principle is used to describe fundamental interactions for elementary particles and fields.

Lee was born in Shanghai on 24 November 1926 and was educated at the National Checkiang University in Guizhou province, southern China, where his studies were interrupted by the Japanese invasion during World War II. Fleeing to Kunming, he too studied at the National Southwest Associated University. In 1946 he was awarded a Chinese government scholarship to study under Fermi at the University of Chicago, and with Hungarian-born US physicist Edward ◊Teller. He completed his PhD on white dwarf stars in 1950. In Chicago he also began his long collaboration with Yang. Lee then worked as a research associate in astronomy at the Yerkes Astronomical Observatory in Wisconsin and taught physics at the University of California at Berkeley. He worked at Princeton University, New Jersey, 1951–53 and then at Columbia University, where he became the youngest professor in the faculty in 1956 and was made the Enrico Fermi Professor of Physics in 1963.

After Lee left Princeton for Columbia in 1953, he and Yang kept in touch with weekly visits to each others' faculties, working on the problems of elementary particle physics. In their best known contribution to physics they challenged one of the central concepts of the time – the conservation of parity – which assumed that the laws of nature are unchanged in mirror-image transformations. Yang and Lee realized that this had never been sufficiently put to the test and with the help of a colleague at Columbia, Chien Shiung Wu (1912–1997), who tested their hypotheses, they showed that the law of parity is indeed violated in weak nuclear interactions. They published their findings in 1956 in a controversial paper, and were jointly awarded the Nobel Prize for Physics in 1957.

Lee and Yang argued in 1960 that the neutrino – a very light nuclear particle – produced in an electron emission was different from the one associated with muon emission. This was also verified by experiment in 1961. In their paper on the subject they also predicted the existence of the W-boson as the heavy particle carrying the weak nuclear force. They later indicated the existence of the neutral weak currents observed in 1973.

Yang became a US citizen in 1964 and in 1965 he moved to the State University of New York at Stoney Brook, to become Einstein Professor and Director of Theoretical Physics. He has continued to work on the principles of symmetry and in statistical mechanics. Lee went on to consider some of the implications of their discoveries, particularly the effect on ideas about the neutrino. He has continued to make contributions to a number of fields including nuclear physics, turbulence, and statistical mechanics and has remained in the physics department at Columbia since 1953 (with a break at Princeton 1960–63).

Yersin, Alexandre Emile John (1863–1943) Swiss bacteriologist. He worked at the Institut Pasteur in Paris on the diphtheria bacterium, discovered the bacterium responsible for plague and made the first anti-plague serum. He made and enormous contribution to disease control in Indochina and helped found a medical school in Hanoi.

Born in Aubonne, near Lausanne, Switzerland on 23 September 1863, Yersin went to school in Lausanne before studying medicine at the University of Marburg and the Paris Faculty of Medicine. His life was saved by French bacteriologist Emile Roux (1853–1933) who administered a new serum when he cut himself while performing a post mortem on a patient who had died of rabies. This brought the two close and Yersin became Roux's assistant in 1888 at the Pasteur Institute in Paris. They collaborated on research into rabies and he began his own research into the toxins produced by the diphtheria bacillus. He also briefly worked with German bacteriologist Robert ◊Koch on the tubercle bacillus before suddenly deciding to take a job as ship's doctor for the Messageries Maritimes in 1889 on a steamer bound for Indochina. He subsequently made three expeditions into the interior of Indochina, founding a small colonial village on a plateau at Langbiang, which became a holiday centre for Europeans, and developed into the city of Dalat.

Yersin became a medical officer in the French colonial service in 1894, the same year that a disastrous bubonic plague epidemic raged through China and Hong Kong. Working in a primitive straw hut that he built himself, he examined samples from the corpses and discovered the plague bacterium *Pasteurella pestis* (now known as *Yersinia pestis)* simultaneously with Japanese bacteriologist, Shibasaburo ◊Kitasato, who had also worked with Koch in Germany and had been sent by his government to investigate the plague. The two teams had been working independently because of the language difficulties involved in collaborating. Yersin returned to Paris to develop the anti-plague serum with Roux and Amédée Borrel. He persuaded Roux to set up a laboratory for him in Nha Trang (now Vietnam) where he studied human diseases and local epizootics (outbreaks of diseases in animals). In 1904, he was recalled to Paris and continued his research at the Insitut Pasteur, now with Roux as director and, working with Borrel and French bacteriologist Albert Calmette (1863–1933), he observed that injections of dead plague bacteria led to immunization against the plague in certain animals. Returning to Nha Trang he perfected his anti-plague serum, which reduced the death rate from plague from 90% to around 7%. Yersin's work in Indochina substantially reduced and controlled epidemics in the area.

Yersin helped to found a new medical school in Hanoi and was its director for many years, supervising study and research. He became interested in tropical agronomy and was fascinated by the flora and fauna of the area. He started a number of ecological studies and was also a champion of the poor and sick. He was made honorary director of the Institut Pasteur, in recognition of his contributions to medicine, in 1905 his laboratory was officially named the Institut Pasteur de Nha Trang, and in 1935 the Lycée Yersin was established at Dalat. He died in Nha Trang on 1 March 1943.

Young, Charles Augustus (1834–1908) US astronomer who made some of the first spectroscopic investigations of the Sun.

Young was born in Hanover, New Hampshire, on 15 December 1834. From the age of 14 he was educated at Dartmouth College in Hanover, and he graduated in 1852. Initially his ambitions lay elsewhere and it may only have been family tradition that eventually drew Young towards a career in astronomy. His maternal grandfather, Ebenezer Adams, had held the chair in mathematics and philosophy at Dartmouth College and had been succeeded to the chair by his son-in-law, Ira Young, in 1833, the year before Charles was born, Young's first appointment was at the Phillips Academy, Massachusetts, teaching classics. In 1855 he enrolled, part-time, at the Andover Theological Seminary to train as a missionary. He abandoned this idea a year later, however, when he became professor of mathematics and natural philosophy at the Western Reserve College in Hudson, Ohio. Apart from a brief interlude during the American Civil War, Young stayed at the Western Reserve College until 1866, when he accepted the chair at Dartmouth College that had previously been held by his father and grandfather. Eleven years later Young moved from Hanover to the College of New Jersey, which has since become Princeton University. Three years after retiring from his post at Princeton he died, at Hanover, on 3 January 1908.

Most of Young's serious researches in astronomy were carried out during his years at Dartmouth College. The facilities and modern equipment provided by the college inspired Young's interest in the recently developed field of spectroscopy. He was particularly interested in the Sun and many of his investigations were carried out during solar eclipses. He was the first person to observe the spectrum of the solar corona and he also discovered the reversing layer in the solar atmosphere in which the dark hues of the Sun's spectrum are momentarily reversed but only at the moment of a total solar eclipse. Young published a series of papers relating his spectroscopic observations of the solar chromosphere, solar prominences, and sunspots. He also compiled a catalogue of bright spectral lines in the Sun and used these to measure its rotational velocity.

Besides his solar research, Young wrote several excellent textbooks that introduced astronomy to succeeding generations of astronomers. His first book, *General Astronomy,* was published in 1888 and a more basic text for younger students, *Lessons in Astronomy,* was published in 1891. By 1910, 90,000 copies of these two books had been sold, making them best-sellers of their day. Young's most famous work was his *Manual Astronomy* (1902), which was aimed at a more intermediate level. It was so popular that it underwent numerous reprints and in 1926 was republished in an edition revised by Henry ♭Russell.

Young, J(ohn) Z(achary) (1907–1997) English zoologist whose discovery of and subsequent work on the giant nerve fibres in squids contributed greatly to knowledge of nerve structure and function. He also carried out research on the central nervous system of octopuses, demonstrating that memory stores are located in the brain. Young is probably most widely known, however, for his zoological textbooks *The Life of Vertebrates* (1950) and *The Life of Mammals* (1957). As a result of his work, he received many honorary university degrees, and in 1967 was awarded the Royal Medal of the Royal Society of London.

Young was born on 18 March 1907 in Bristol and was educated at Wells House, Malvern Wells, and at Marlborough College, Wiltshire. He graduated from Magdalen College, Oxford, in 1928 then went to Naples as a biological scholar. After his return to England, Young was elected a fellow of Magdalen College in 1931 and remained there until 1945, when he became professor of anatomy at University College, London – the first non-medical scientist in the UK to hold a professorship in anatomy. In the same year he was also made a fellow of the Royal Society. He remained at University College until he retired in 1974. He died in Oxford on 4 July 1997.

Young began his work on the nerves in squids before World War II. He discovered that certain of their nerve fibres are exceptionally thick – up to 1 mm/0.04 in in diameter (about 100 times the diameter of mammalian nerve cells) – and are covered with a relatively thin myelin sheath (unlike mammalian nerve fibres, which have thick sheaths), properties that make them easy to experiment on. For example, almost all the intracellular contents can be extracted without destroying the fibre's ability to conduct nerve impulses, and electrodes can easily be inserted into the fibres because of their large diameter. Moreover, extracting the contents of the giant fibres is still the only way of obtaining intracellular nerve material uncontaminated by the myelin sheath or other cells. Young's work on the giant nerve fibres in squids has been invaluable, not only because of his own findings, but also because these fibres are extremely useful for experimentation and have been used by many other researchers in their investigations of nerves.

During the war, Young set up a unit at Oxford to study nerve regeneration in mammals and, with Peter ◊Medawar and others, devised a method of rejoining small severed nerves by using intracellular plasma as a 'glue'. Young also researched into the rates of neuron (nerve cell) growth and the factors that determine neuron size.

After the war Young turned his attention to the central nervous system, using octopuses as research animals. Working with Brian Boycott, he showed that octopuses can learn to discriminate between different orientations of the same object – when presented with horizontal and vertical rectangles, for example, the octopuses attacked one but avoided the other. He also demonstrated (this time working with M J Wells) that octopuses can learn to recognize objects by touch. In addition, Young proved that the memory stores are located in the brain and proposed a model to explain the processes involved in memory.

Young, Thomas (1773–1829) English physicist and physician who discovered the principle of interference of light, showing it to be caused by light waves. He also made important discoveries in the physiology of vision and is also remembered for Young's modulus, the ratio of stress to strain in elasticity. In addition, Young was also an Egyptologist and was instrumental in the deciphering of hieroglyphics.

Young was born in Milverton, Somerset, on 13 June 1773. He was an infant prodigy, learning to read by the age of two, whereupon he read the whole Bible twice through. Young was largely self-taught, although he did attend school. He developed great ability at languages, taking particular interest in the ancient languages of the Middle East, and mastered mathematics, physics, and chemistry while still a youth. He also showed great mechanical dexterity and for a short time made optical instruments.

In 1792, under the guidance of his great-uncle Richard Brocklesby (1722–1797), a distinguished London physician, Young commenced studying for the medical profession at St. Bartholomew's Hospital. At the early age of 21 he became a member of the Royal Society. He moved to Edinburgh to continue his medical studies in 1794 and then to Göttingen in Germany in 1795, where he was awarded his MD in 1796. He travelled throughout Germany for several months, visiting museums before settling in Cambridge in 1797 for two years. He resided as a fellow-commoner at Emmanuel College, where he became known as 'Phenomenon Young'. At Cambridge, Young used his time to pursue original scientific studies and made his

early investigations into interference.

Brocklesby left Young his London house and a fortune, and in 1800 Young returned to London and opened a medical practice there. In 1801, he was appointed professor of natural philosophy at the Royal Institution and although he delivered many lectures, he was a disappointing lecturer to popular audiences. He resigned this post in July 1803 to concentrate on his practice as a physician. He was awarded an MB in 1803 from Cambridge University and an MD five years later. In 1811, Young became a physician at St. George's Hospital, London, and held this post until his death. He also held several other appointments, including secretary of the Commission on Weights and Measures, secretary of the Board of Longitude, and foreign secretary of the Royal Society. Young died in London on 10 May 1829.

Young's early work was concerned with the physiology of vision. In 1793 he recognized that the mechanism of accommodation of the eye in focusing the eye on near or distant objects is due to a change of shape in the lens of the eye, the lens being composed of muscle fibres. Young confirmed this view in 1801 after obtaining experimental proof of it. He also showed that astigmatism, from which he himself suffered, is due to irregular curvature of the cornea. In 1801, Young was also the first to recognize that colour sensation is due to the presence in the retina of structures that respond to the three colours red, green, and violet, showing that colour blindness is due to the inability of one or more of these structures to respond to light. Young's work in this field was elaborated into a proper theory of vision by Hermann von ◊Helmholtz and James Clerk ◊Maxwell.

Young also made a thorough study of optics at the same time. There was great controversy as to the nature of light – whether it consisted of streams of particles or of waves. In the UK, the particulate theory was strongly favoured because it had been advanced by Isaac ◊Newton a century before. In 1800, Young reopened the debate by suggesting that the wave theory of Christiaan ◊Huygens gave a more convincing explanation for the phenomena of reflection, refraction, and diffraction. He assumed that light waves are propagated in a similar way to sound waves and are longitudinal vibrations but with a different medium and frequency. He also proposed that different colours consist of different frequencies.

In the following year, Young announced his discovery of the principle of interference. He explained that the bright bands of fringes in effects such as Newton's rings result from light waves interfering so that they reinforce each other. This was a hypothetical deduction and over the next two years, Young obtained experimental proof for the principle of interference by

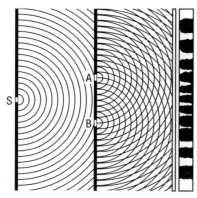

Young Young demonstrated the interference of light by passing monochromatic light through a narrow slit S (he originally used a small hole) and then letting it pass through a pair of closely-spaced slits (A and B). Reinforcement and cancellation of the wave trains as they reached the screen produced characteristic interference fringes of alternate light and dark bands.

passing light through extremely narrow openings and observing the interference patterns produced.

Young's discovery of interference was convincing proof that light consists of waves, but it did not confirm that the waves are longitudinal. The discovery of the polarization of light by Etienne ◊Malus in 1808 led Young to suggest in 1817 that light waves may contain a transverse component. In 1821, Augustin ◊Fresnel proved that light waves are entirely transverse, and the wave nature of light was finally established.

In mechanics, Young established many important concepts in a course of lectures published in 1807. He was the first to use the terms 'energy' for the product of the mass of a body with the square of its velocity and the expression 'labour expended' (that is, work done) for the product of the force exerted on a body 'with the distance through which it moved'. He also stated that these two products are proportional to each other. He introduced absolute measurements in elasticity by defining the modulus as the weight that would double the length of a rod of unit cross-section. Today it is usually referred to as Young's modulus, and equals stress divided by strain in the elastic region of the loading of a material. Young also published in 1805 a theory of capillary action and accounted for the angle of contact in surface-tension effects for liquids.

From 1815 onwards, Young published papers on Egyptology, mostly concerning the reading of tablets involving hieroglyphics. He was one of the first to interpret the writings on the Rosetta Stone, which was found at the mouth of the Nile in 1799. The hieroglyphic vocabulary that he established of approximately 200 signs has stood the test of time remarkably well.

Thomas Young was a scientist who possessed an extraordinary range of talents and a rare degree of insight, and he was able to initiate important paths of investigation that others were to take up and complete. His discoveries in vision are fundamental to an understanding of visual problems and to colour reproduction, and his discovery of interference was a vital step to a full explanation of the nature of light.

Further Reading

Kahlow, Andreas, 'Knowledge transfer in the 19th century: Young, Navier, Ruebling, and the Brooklyn Bridge' in: Woodward, William R and Cohen, Robert S (eds), *World Views and Scientific Discipline Formation*, Kluwer, 1991, pp 377–386.

Kipnis, Nahum, *History of the Principle of Interference of Light*, Science Networks Historical Studies series, Birkhauser, 1991.

Kline, Daniel L, *Thomas Young: Forgotten Genius*, Vidan Press, 1993.

Yukawa, Hideki (1907–1981) Japanese physicist famous for his important theoretical work on elementary particles and nuclear forces, particularly for predicting the existence of the pi-meson (or pion) and the short-range strong nuclear force associated with this particle. He received numerous honours for his work, including the 1949 Nobel Prize for Physics, being the first Japanese to receive a Nobel prize.

Yukawa Japanese physicist Hideki Yukawa who developed the theory of nuclear forces. He was awarded the Nobel Prize for Physics in 1949. *Mary Evans Picture Library*

Yukawa was born in Kyoto on 23 January 1907 and was educated at Kyoto University (where his father was professor of geology), graduating in 1929. He then moved to Osaka University, where he both taught and studied for his doctorate, which he gained in 1938. In the following year he returned to Kyoto University and, except for various visiting professorships, remained there for the rest of his career – as professor of theoretical physics 1939–50, emeritus professor 1950–53, and director of the university's newly created Research Institute for Fundamental Physics from 1953. His visiting professorships included one to the Institute for Advanced Study, Princeton University (at the invitation of J Robert ◊Oppenheimer) 1948–49, and one to Columbia University 1949–53.

Yukawa proposed his new theory of nuclear forces in 1935 at a time when there was much controversy over what holds the nucleus together. In 1932 James ◊Chadwick had discovered the neutron but, Yukawa pointed out, this meant that because the nucleus contains only positively charged protons and neutral neutrons, the protons should repel each other and disrupt the integrity of the nucleus. He therefore postulated the existence of a nuclear 'exchange force' that counteracted the mutual repulsion of the protons and therefore held the nucleus together. He predicted that this exchange force would involve the transfer of a particle (the existence of which was then unknown),

that the force would be of very short range (effective over a distance of only about 10^{-8} m), and that it would be strong enough to overcome the repulsive forces between the protons yet decrease in intensity with sufficient rapidity so as to have a negligible effect on the innermost electrons. He also calculated, using quantum theory, that his predicted exchange particle would have a mass of about 200 times that of an electron (but would have the same charge as an electron) – about one-ninth the mass of a proton or neutron – and that the particle would be radioactive, with an extremely short half-life. At the time no particle having these characteristics had been found. In the following year (1936) Carl ◊Anderson discovered the muon (or mumeson), which possesses several of the properties of Yukawa's predicted particle but not all of them. In 1947, however, Cecil ◊Powell discovered the pion (or pi-meson), a particle similar to Anderson's muon but which fulfilled all of the requirements of Yukawa's exchange particle.

Meanwhile, in 1936 Yukawa predicted that a nucleus could absorb one of the innermost orbiting electrons and that this would be equivalent to emitting a positron. These innermost electrons belong to the 1K electron shell, and this process of electron absorption by the nucleus is known as K capture. In 1947 Yukawa began working on a more detailed theory of elementary particles.

Zassenhaus, Hans Julius (1912–1991) German mathematician whose main area of study lay in the fields of group therapy and number theory.

Born in Koblenz on 28 May 1912, Zassenhaus completed his education by entering the University of Hamburg, from which he received his doctorate in 1934, qualifying as a lecturer there in the same year. For 15 years he worked there and at Rostock University; then he spent ten years as Redpath Professor of Mathematics in Montréal, Canada. Transferring to the USA, he finally became professor of mathematics at Ohio State University in 1964, holding that position until he retired. He died in Columbus, Ohio, on 21 November 1991.

Zassenhaus's research work concentrated on group theory – the study of systems in which the product of any two members of a system results in another member of the same system (for example, even numbers) – and on number theory. His most significant results were obtained in his investigations into finite groups, a class of which has been named Zassenhaus groups and forms part of the basis for the contemporary development of finite group theory. The work of Zassenhaus and Issai Schur (1875–1941) on group extensions led to the postulation of what has become known as the Schur–Zassenhaus theory.

Zassenhaus also made contributions to the study of Lie algebra, the geometry of numbers, and applied mathematics.

Zeeman, (Erik) Christopher (1925–) English mathematician noted for his work in topology and for his research into models of social behaviour that accord with the relatively recent formulation of catastrophe theory.

Born on 4 February 1925, Zeeman was educated at Christ's Hospital, Sussex. At the age of 18, during World War II, he joined the Royal Air Force and became a flying officer. After the war he took up a scholarship to Christ's College, Cambridge, receiving his bachelor's degree in 1948, his master's degree in 1950, and a doctorate in 1954. From then for ten years he was a fellow of Gonville and Caius College, Cambridge, and a lecturer there. Thereafter, he became professor of mathematics at the University of Warwick, where he founded – and became director of – the Mathematics Research Centre. He remained there until 1988, while holding, at various times, visiting professorships in Europe, the USA, and Brazil. From 1988 to 1995 he was master of Hertford College, Oxford. Elected a fellow of the Royal Society in 1975, the following year he was made senior fellow of the Science Research Council.

Between 1951 and 1958 Zeeman researched into algebraic topology; between 1958 and 1967 he studied geometric topology and brain modelling; and his interests since then have been concerned with catastrophe theory and its applications to the physical, biological, and behavioural sciences, and with dynamical systems.

Probably Zeeman's most significant work has been on the recently formulated catastrophe theory. Mathematical analysis cannot easily be used for things that change suddenly, or that have intermittent fits and starts. Where the change is smooth and continuous, it can be described in terms of differential equations. (Isaac ◊Newton's laws of motion and gravitation and James Clerk ◊Maxwell's theory of electromagnetism can all be described in terms of differential equations. Even Albert ◊Einstein's general theory of relativity culminates in a set of differential equations.) A mathematical method for dealing with discontinuous and divergent phenomena was developed only in 1968, and derived from topology – the branch of geometry concerned with the properties of shapes and figures that remain unchanged even when the shape or figure is deformed. This method, the catastrophe theory, has great potential; it can describe the evolution of forms in all aspects of nature and so has great generality. It can be applied to situations where gradually changing forces lead to abrupt changes in behaviour. Many events in physics have now been identified as examples of catastrophe theory, but ultimately its most important applications may be in the 'inexact' sciences – biology and social science.

The theory was first devised by René ◊Thom, who saw it as a development of topology in that the underlying forces in nature can be described as the smooth surfaces of equilibrium, and when equilibrium breaks down, catastrophe occurs. The problem for catastrophe theory then is to describe shapes of all the possible equilibrium surfaces. Thom showed that for processes controlled by not more than four factors, there are two elementary catastrophes. His proofs are very complicated, but the results are easier to understand and can be applied to scientific problems without reference to the proof.

If the two elementary catastrophes (two conflicting behavioural drives, for example) are plotted as axes on the horizontal plane – called the control surface – and the complementary result (the resulting behaviour, to carry the example further) is plotted on a third axis perpendicular to the first two, from most likely result to next most likely, and so on, resultant points can be plotted for the entire control surface, and when connected form a surface of their own. Concerning behavioural results, the application in which Zeeman was particularly interested, this surface is known as the behaviour surface. Catastrophe theory reveals that in the middle of the surface is a pleat, without creases, which becomes narrower towards the back of the surface, and it is this pleat that gives the model its most interesting characteristics. For Zeeman, all the points on the behaviour surface represent the most probable behaviour, with the exception of those on the pleated middle part, which represent the least likely behaviour. At the edge of the pleat, the sheet on which the behaviour points have been travelling folds under and is wiped out. The behaviour state falls to the bottom sheet of the graph and there is a sudden change in behaviour. In an argument, for instance, an aggressive protagonist may waver in his opinion, abandon his position and apologize; the timid opponent may make repeated concessions, then lose his temper and become aggressive.

Zeeman, with J Hevesi, a psychotherapist, has in particular worked on the problems of anorexia nervosa, an illness especially common in adolescent girls, which involves sudden changes from dieting to obsessive fasting. Catastrophe theory has been able to predict behaviour patterns in this disorder and help towards treating the sufferers.

The theory is still a young offshoot of science. But it has already been applied to the propagation of shock waves, the minimum areas of surfaces, non-linear oscillations, scattering, and elasticity. Zeeman has constructed catastrophe models of heartbeat, the propagation of nerve impulses, and the formation of the gastrula and of somites in an embryo. Considerable research on the subject still remains to be done.

Zeeman, Pieter (1865–1943) Dutch physicist who discovered the Zeeman effect, which is the splitting of spectral lines in an intense magnetic field. This achievement was important in determining the structure of the atom and Zeeman shared the 1902 Nobel Prize for Physics with Hendrik ◊Lorentz, who had predicted the Zeeman effect.

Zeeman was born in Zonnemaire, Zeeland, on 25 May 1865. He was educated at local schools and at the Gymnasium in Delft before entering the University of Leiden in 1885. There Zeeman studied under Heike ◊Kamerlingh Onnes and Lorentz, gaining his PhD with a dissertation on the Kerr effect in 1893. He then remained at Leiden as a tutor and in 1897 moved to the University of Amsterdam to take up a lectureship. Zeeman became professor of physics at Amsterdam in 1900. He retained this position until he retired in 1935, and in 1923 became director of a new laboratory that was named the Zeeman Laboratory. In addition to the Nobel prize, among his many honours was the award of the Royal Society's Rumford Medal in 1922. Zeeman died in Amsterdam on 9 October 1943.

While Zeeman was at Leiden, Lorentz proposed that light is caused by the vibration of electrons and suggested that imposing a magnetic field on light would result in a splitting of spectral lines by varying the wavelengths of the lines. Zeeman undertook the first experimental work in search of this in 1896. Using a sodium flare between the poles of a powerful electromagnet and producing spectra with a large concave diffraction grating, Zeeman was able to detect a broadening of the spectral lines when the current was activated. A similar effect was achieved with the sodium absorption spectra, so the changed shape of the flame was not responsible. In 1897, Zeeman refined the experiment and was successful in resolving the broadening of the narrow blue–green spectral line of cadmium produced in a vacuum discharge into a triplet of three component lines. Later work led Zeeman to evaluate the ratio e/m for the oscillating particles involved, which was in agreement with the value obtained for the electron by J J ◊Thomson. This confirmed that the magnetic field was affecting the forces that control the electrons within the atom. However, Zeeman's subsequent experimental work suffered as a consequence of his promotion to the University of Amsterdam, where the facilities were much poorer than in Leiden. By the time he was able to acquire a purpose-built laboratory in 1923, many other workers had overtaken Zeeman's team in expertise and experience.

Study of the Zeeman effect led to important theoretical advances in physics. Zeeman's observations confirmed Lorentz's electromagnetic theory and later investigators were able to show that the spectral effects are caused by electron spin. As a result, the quantum theory was expanded to include these findings. Spectral observations of the Sun carried out by George ◊Hale in 1908 led him to believe that light emitted by sunspots is affected in a similar fashion to Zeeman's laboratory observations. The conclusion reached was that sunspots must be associated with intense magnetic fields within the Sun.

In later years, Zeeman's attention turned to the velocity of light in moving media and his experiments involved glass and quartz. Many difficulties were successfully overcome and Zeeman was able to show that the results were in agreement with the theory of relativity. He also studied isotopes, particularly those of argon, in which he identified a new isotope with a mass number of 38.

Zel'dovich, Yakov Borisovich (1914–1987)
Soviet astrophysicist who was originally a specialist in nuclear physics, but who became interested in particle physics and cosmology during the 1950s.

Zel'dovich was born in Minsk (now in Belarus) on 18 March 1914. He studied at the University of Leningrad (now St Petersburg) in Russia and when he graduated in 1931 he began his work at the Soviet Academy of Sciences in the Institute of Chemical Physics. He was made a corresponding member of the Academy of Sciences in 1946 and became a full academician in 1958. During World War II he contributed research towards the war effort and was awarded the Stalin Prize in 1943. He later worked at the Institute of Cosmic Research at the Space Research Institute of the Soviet Academy of Sciences in Moscow.

During the 1930s Zel'dovich participated in a research programme that was aimed at discovering the mechanism of oxidation of nitrogen during an explosion, and he and his colleagues reported the results of this work in a book published in 1947. During the 1940s he also maintained an interest in, and wrote about, the chemical reactions of explosions, the subsequent generation of shock waves, and the related subjects of gas dynamics and flame propagation. Zel'dovich, together with Y B Khariton, participated in the early work on the mechanism of fission during the radioactive decay of uranium, one of the most significant discoveries of the late 1930s. Their calculations on the chain reaction in uranium fission were published in 1939 and 1940. Besides this, Zel'dovich was also interested in the role played by slow neutrons in the fission process.

It was not until the 1950s that he began to develop an interest in cosmology and Zel'dovich's later writings dealt with such diverse subjects as quark annihilation, neutrino detection, and the applicability of relativistic versus Newtonian theories to the study of the expanding and evolving universe and the earliest stages of the universe – the quantum, hadron, and lepton eras. In 1967, together with C W Misher, A G Doroshkevich, and I D Novikov, he proposed that in its initial stages the universe was highly isotropic, but that as it has expanded, this isotropy has diminished.

Zel'dovich was a prolific writer and carried out extensive research in the fields of physics and astronomy. His later cosmological theories led to more accurate determinations of the abundance of helium in older stars.

Further Reading
Barenblatt, G I; Zeldovich, Y B; Librovich, V B; and Makhviladze, G M, *The Mathematical Theory of Combustion and Explosions,* Plenum Publishing Corporation, 1985.

Gershtein, S S, 'From Reminiscences about Ya B Zeldovich', *Sov Phys Usp,* 1991, v 34, p 444.

Ostriker, Jeremiah P (ed), *Selected Works of Yakov Borisovich Zeldovich,* Princeton University Press, 1993, 2 vols.

Zeppelin, Ferdinand Adolf August Heinrich (1838–1917)
Count von Zeppelin. German soldier and builder of airships.

Zeppelin Airship pioneer Ferdinand von Zeppelin. During World War I his company built 88 airships, many of which were used for air raids to Britain. After the war the Goodyear-Zeppelin company was formed to manufacture airships in the USA. *Mary Evans Picture Library*

Zeppelin was born in Constance, Baden, on 8 July 1838. He was educated in Stuttgart and trained to enter the army, which he did as an infantry officer in 1858. In the early 1860s he was appointed to the Union Army of the Potamac in the American Civil War. This enabled him to join an expedition to explore the sources of the River Mississippi, and in 1870 at Fort Snelling, Minnesota, he made his first ascent in a (military) balloon. After returning home Zeppelin rose to the rank of brigadier general. He finally retired from the army in 1891 and turned his energies to the design and construction of an airship.

After many setbacks, and helped by royal patronage and public subscriptions, he launched his first craft in July 1900. Eight years later he made a 12-hour flight to Lucerne, Switzerland. His exploits aroused the enthusiasm of the German people, who raised a national fund of more than 6 million marks with which he founded the Zeppelin Institution. Many airships – now called zeppelins – were built in the period leading up to World War I, which offered a chance to test their military potential. But enthusiasm for the machine rapidly waned in 1914, the first year of the war, when 13 zeppelins were destroyed in action and many lives lost. Their chief targets – they were used as bombers – were in Belgium and the UK. Their vulnerability to anti-aircraft guns and the rapid development of faster and more manouevrable aeroplanes sealed the fate of the airship as an effective weapon of war. Zeppelin died before the end of the war, on 8 March 1917, at Charlottenburg near Berlin.

The early airships – the LZ5, for example – had chain-driven propellors and, in the stern, multiple rudders and elevators. The main principle of Zeppelin's invention was streamlining the all-over envelope, inside which separate hydrogen-filled gas-bags were raised inside a steel skeleton structure. In some craft, as in the design of the LZ1, a balancing rod ran the whole length of the ship below the envelope, and could be used for horizontal trimming. On the LZ18, German naval engineers incorporated several improvements by providing a covered-in passageway and fully enclosed cars directly beneath the hull. The disastrous end to the *Hindenburg*, which burst into flames over Lakehurst in 1937 on its momentous flight via New York, effectively put an end to any airship being inflated with hydrogen. Since then the non-inflammable helium has almost always been used.

Further Reading

Eckener, Hugo and Farnell, H Leigh, *Count Zeppelin: The Man and His Work,* Massie Publishing Co, 1938.

Goldsmith, Margaret Leland, *Count Zeppelin: A Biography,* Jonathan Cape, 1931.

Guttery, Thomas Ewart, *Zeppelin: An Illustrated Life,* Lifelines series, Shire Publications, 1973, v 23.

Zermelo, Ernst Friedrich Ferdinand (1871–1953)

German mathematician who made many important contributions to the development of set theory, particularly in developing the axiomatic set theory that now bears his name.

Zermelo was born on 27 July 1871 in Berlin, the son of a university professor. Educated locally, he passed his final examinations in 1889 and went to study mathematics, physics, and philosophy first at Halle University, then at Freiburg University. Among his teachers were Georg ◊Frobenius, Immanuel ◊Fuchs, and Max ◊Planck. Zermelo received his doctorate at Berlin in 1894 and went to Göttingen where, five years later, he was appointed as an unsalaried lecturer. In 1904 he supplied a proof of the well-ordering theorem, and in the following year he was appointed professor. A few years later he moved to Zürich after accepting a professorship there; poor health forced him to resign this post in 1916. A gift of 5,000 marks from the Wolfskehl Fund enabled him to live quietly in the Black Forest for the next ten years, restoring himself once more to full health. In 1926 he was appointed honorary professor at the University of Freiburg im Breisgau. He stayed there for nine years, but in 1935 resigned his post once more, this time in protest against the Nazi regime. He was reinstated in 1946 at his own request, and remained in Freiburg until he died, on 21 May 1953.

Zermelo's first research was on the applications of the theorem formulated by Henri ◊Poincaré. He detected some apparent anomalies in kinetic theory, following Poincaré's research, notably that the recurrence theorem arising from Poincaré's work in mechanics seems to make any mechanical model such as the kinetic theory incompatible with the second law of thermodynamics.

It was in 1900 that Zermelo turned his attention to set theory. He provided an ingenious proof to the well-ordering theorem, which states that every set can be well ordered (that is, can be arranged in a series in which each subclass – not being null – has a first term).

He said that a relation $a < b$ (a comes before b) can be introduced such that for any two statements a and b, either $a = b$, or $a < b$, or $b < a$. If there are three elements a, b, and c, then if $a < b$ and $b < c$, then $a < c$. This gave rise to the Zermelo axiom that every class can be well ordered.

Zermelo subsequently pointed out that for any infinite system of sets, there are always relations under which every set corresponds to one of its elements. Because of a storm of criticism from other mathematicians, however, he felt obliged to produce a second proof.

In 1904 Zermelo defined the axiom of choice, the use of which had previously been unrecognized in mathematical reasoning. The first formulations of axioms for set theory – an axiom system for Georg ◊Cantor's theory of sets – were made by Zermelo in

1908. This system has since proved of great value in the development of mathematics. There are seven axioms (which found written formulation rather later), in which only two terms are used: the set, and the element of the set. Every set except the null set is an object of B for which there is another object b of B such that $a \in b$. The axioms state:

(1) that $m = n$ if, and only if, $a \in m$ is equivalent to $a \in n$;

(2) that there is a null set;

(3) that if a property E is definite for the elements of a set m, then there is a subset mE of m consisting of exactly those elements of m for which E holds;

(4) that for any set m there is a set $P(m)$ that has the subsets of m for its elements;

(5) that for any set m there is a set $\cup\, m$ (the union of m) consisting of the elements of m;

(6) that if m is a set of disjoint non-void sets, then $\cup\, m$ contains a subset n that contains exactly one element from every set of m;

(7) and that there is a set A that has the null set as an element and has the property that, if x is an element of A, then $\{x\}$ is also an element of A.

However, Zermelo's axioms involved an unexplained notion of a 'definite property'. This difficulty was overcome later by Abraham ◊Fraenkel. Fraenkel had criticized Zermelo's conclusions, particularly axiom 7, because of weakness. Zermelo afterwards improved on them by describing the set of definite properties as the smallest set containing the basic relations of the domain B and satisfying certain close conditions. A logical formulation of Zermelo's axioms was later achieved by Thoralf ◊Skolem in 1923.

Ziegler, Karl (1898–1973)

Ziegler, Karl (1898–1973) German organic chemist famous for his studies of polymers, for which he shared the 1963 Nobel Prize for Chemistry with Giulio ◊Natta.

Ziegler was born in Helsa, near Kassel, on 26 November 1898, the son of a cleric. He gained his doctorate from Marburg University in 1923 and then held teaching appointments at Frankfurt am Main, Heidelberg, and Halle. In 1943 he became director of the Kaiser Wilhelm (later Max Planck) Institute for Coal Research at Mülheim, where he remained for the rest of his career. He died in Mülheim on 12 August 1973.

In 1933 Ziegler discovered a method of making compounds that contain large rings of carbon atoms, later used to synthesize musks for making perfumes, and in 1942 he developed the use of N-bromosuccinimide for brominating olefins (alkenes). In 1945, after World War II, he began research on the organic compounds of aluminium. He found a method of synthesizing aluminium tri-alkyls from aluminium metal, hydrogen, and olefins, and demonstrated that it is possible to add ethylene (ethene) stepwise to the aluminium–carbon bond of aluminium tri-alkyls to make higher aluminium tri-alkyls. These higher compounds can be converted into alcohols for use in the manufacture of detergents. He also discovered that nickel will catalyse the exchange of groups attached to aluminium by ethylene and liberate higher olefins. Using electrochemical techniques, he prepared various other metal alkyls from the aluminium ones, the most important of which is tetraethyl lead, which is used as an anti-knock additive to petrol.

His most important discovery came in 1953 when he and a student (E Holzkamp) were repeating a preparation of higher aluminium tri-alkyls by heating ethylene with aluminium tri-alkyl. To their surprise the ethylene monomer ($CH_2{=}CH_2$) was completely converted to the dimer butylene (but-1,2-ene, $CH_3CH_2CH{=}CH_2$). They found the explanation to be that the autoclave used for the experiment contained traces of colloidal nickel left from a previous catalytic hydrogenation experiment. This led them to the discovery that organometallic compounds mixed with certain heavy metals polymerize ethylene at atmospheric pressure to produce a linear polymer of high molecular weight (relative molecular mass) and with valuable properties, such as high melting point. All previous processes have the disadvantage of needing high pressures and produced low-melting, partly branched polymers.

Also in 1953 Ziegler and Natta discovered a family of stereospecific catalysts that are capable of introducing an exact and regular structure to various polymers. They found that they could use the Ziegler-type catalyst tri-ethyl aluminium conbined with titanium tetrachloride (titanium(IV) chloride) to polymerize isoprene so that each molecule in the long-chain polymer formed is in a regular position and almost identical to the structure of natural rubber. This discovery formed the basis of nearly all later developments in synthetic plastics, fibres, rubbers, and films derived from such olefins as ethylene and butadiene (but-1,2:3,4-diene).

Zsigmondy, Richard Adolf (1865–1929)

Zsigmondy, Richard Adolf (1865–1929) Austrian-born German colloid chemist who invented the ultramicroscope. For this achievement, and his other work with colloids, he was awarded the 1925 Nobel Prize for Chemistry.

Zsigmondy was born in Vienna on 1 April 1865, the son of a dentist. His early education and first year at university were at Vienna, then he went to Munich and obtained his PhD in organic chemistry in 1889. He became a research assistant in Berlin and then a lecturer in chemical technology at the Technische Hochschule in Graz. In 1897 he joined the Glass Manufacturing Company in Jena, but left in 1900 to carry out his own private research. From 1908 he was professor of inorganic chemistry at Göttingen University. He retired a few months before his death, in Göttingen, on about 23 September 1929.

In Berlin, Zsigmondy worked with the physicist August ◊Kundt on inorganic inclusions in glass. At Jena he became concerned with coloured and turbid glasses and he invented the famous Jena milk glass. This was the work that aroused his interest in colloids, because it is colloidal inclusions that give glass its colour or opacity. He recognized that the red fluids first prepared by Michael ◊Faraday by the reduction of gold salts are largely colloidal analogues of ruby glass and worked out a technique for preparing them reproducibly. His belief that the suspended particles in such gold sols are kept apart by electric charges was generally accepted, and the sols became model systems for much of his later work on colloids.

In 1903, working with HFW Siedentopf, he constructed the first ultramicroscope, with which it is possible to view individual particles in a colloidal solution. Unlike a conventional microscope, in which the illumination is parallel with the instrument's axis, the ultramicroscope uses perpendicular illumination. With such dark-field illumination, individual particles become visible by scattering light (the Tyndall effect), much as moving dust particles are illuminated by a sunbeam. Furthermore the technique makes it possible to detect particles much smaller than the resolving power of the microscope. Ernst Abba, director of the Jena Glass Company, put all the company's facilities at Zsigmondy's disposal to develop the apparatus, even though at that time he had no formal links with the firm and no professional attachments at all. It was for this work that Zsigmondy was made a professor at Göttingen.

Using the ultramicroscope Zsigmondy was able to count the number of particles in a given volume and indirectly estimate their sizes; he could detect particles down to a diameter of 3 nm (3×10^{-9} m). Much of his research continued to centre on gold sols ('purple of Cassius'). Several notable chemists had already studied such sols, but it was not known whether they contained a mixture or a compound. In 1898 he showed that they are a mixture of very small gold and stannic acid particles. He also showed that colour changes in sols reflect changes in particle size caused by coagulation when salts are added, and that the addition of agents such as gelatin stabilizes the colloid by inhibiting coagulation. At Göttingen he investigated ultrafiltration and its use for colloids; he also studied such systems as silica gels and soap gels.

Zsigmondy's work began a study of importance to the understanding of all sols, smokes, fogs, foams, and films. His conclusions clarified problems in biochemistry, bacteriology, and soil physics. The ultramicroscope has remained of great importance in colloid research, although somewhat superseded by the electron microscope.

Zwicky, Fritz (1898–1974) Swiss astronomer and astrophysicist who was distinguished for his discoveries of supernovae, dwarf galaxies, and clusters of galaxies, and also for his theory on the formation of neutron stars.

Zwicky was born in Varna, Bulgaria, but his parents were Swiss and he retained his Swiss nationality throughout his life. He was educated in Switzerland, gaining his BA and his PhD by 1922 from the Federal Institute of Technology at Zürich. He was awarded a fellowship from the International Education Board in 1925 and left Switzerland for the USA to join the California Institute of Technology (Caltech). He was appointed assistant professor at Caltech in 1927 and continued to work there until his retirement in 1968, by which time he had been promoted to the position of professor of astronomy. After his retirement, Zwicky continued to live in the USA. He received the Royal Astronomical Society's Gold Medal in 1973. He died on 8 February 1974.

Zwicky began his research by scouring our neighbouring galaxies for the appearance of a supernova explosion, hoping to discover one that was bright enough for its spectrum to be studied. But since the late 15th and early 16th centuries when Johannes ◊Kepler and Tycho ◊Brahe were fortunate enough to observe such events, no other supernovae have been seen to appear in our Galaxy. Zwicky therefore calculated that only one supernova appears every 300–400 years in any galaxy. He was among the first to suggest that there is a relationship between supernovae and neutron stars. He suggested that the outer layers of a star that explodes as a supernova leave a core that collapses upon itself as a result of gravitational forces. He put forward this theoretical model in the early 1930s, when there seemed to be no hope of actually observing such a phenomenon.

In 1936 Zwicky began a study of galaxy clusters. He used the 46-cm/18-in Schmidt telescope at Mount Palomar Observatory to photograph large areas of the sky. This telescope was specially designed to provide a relatively wide field of view, so that a large portion of the sky could be viewed at one glance without sacrificing a high resolution of separate images. Zwicky observed that most galaxies occur in clusters, each of which contains several thousand galaxies. The nearest is the Virgo cluster, which is also the most conspicuous of large clusters. It contains a number of spiral galaxies and Zwicky's spectroscopic studies of the Virgo and the Coma Berenices clusters showed that there is no evidence of any systematic expansion or rotation of clusters. Zwicky also calculated that the distribution of galaxies in the Coma Berenices cluster was similar, at least statistically, to the distribution of molecules in a gas when its temperature is at equilibrium. He compiled a six-volume catalogue of galaxies and galaxy clusters in which he listed 10,000 clusters located north of declination $-30°$. He completed the catalogue shortly before his death and it is still generally regarded as the classic work in this field.

Zwicky's research interests were not limited to astronomy, but extended to the study of crystal structure, superconductivity, rocket fuels, propulsive systems, and the philosophy of science. But his work on galaxies, galaxy clusters, interstellar matter, and supernova stars outweighs these other interests in importance and has made a vital contribution to the field of astronomy.

Zworykin, Vladimir Kosma (1889–1982) Russian-born US electronics engineer and inventor whose major inventions – the iconoscope television camera tube and the electron microscope – have had ramifications far outside the immediate field of electronics. Electronic television has become the major entertainments medium, and the electron microscope has proved to be a key tool in the development of molecular biology and microbiological research.

Zworykin was born in Murom on 30 July 1889, and received his higher education at the St Petersburg Institute of Technology, from which he graduated with a degree in electrical engineering in 1912. He then went to Paris to do X-ray research at the College of France, but at the outbreak of World War I in 1914 he returned to Russia, where he remained for the next four years working as a radio officer. When the war ended in 1918 he travelled widely throughout the world, before deciding to settle in the USA.

Having learnt to speak English, Zworykin joined the Westinghouse corporation in Pittsburgh, Pennsylvania, and in 1923 took out a patent for the iconoscope, followed a year later by the kinescope (a television receiver tube). In 1929 he demonstrated an improved electronic television system and was then offered the position of director of electronic research for the Radio Corporation of America (RCA) at Camden, New Jersey.

He subsequently moved to the nearby Princeton University to continue the development of television. He obtained his PhD degree from the University of Princeton in 1926.

In 1967 Zworykin was awarded the National Medal of Science by the National Academy of Sciences for his contributions to science, medicine, and engineering and for the application of electronic engineering to medicine. He died on 18 August 1982.

Among the first of Zworykin's developments was an early form of an electric eye. Somewhat later, he invented an electronic image tube sensitive to infrared light, which was the basis for World War II inventions for seeing in the dark.

In 1957 Zworykin patented a device that uses ultraviolet light and television, thereby permitting a colour picture of living cells to be thrown upon a screen, which opened up new prospects for biological investigation. It is, however, the electron microscope, to the development of which Zworykin also contributed, that represents the greatest boon that physics has given to biology.

Vastly extending the range of detail covered by an optical microscope, the electron microscope uses a beam of electrons to form a magnified image of a specimen. Useful magnifications of one million times can be obtained on the viewing screen of a powerful electron microscope, producing an amplification sufficiently large to disclose a disarranged cluster of atoms in the lattice of a crystal. (Optical microscopes have a useful magnification range of only several thousand times.)

The high degree of magnification of an electron microscope comes from its extremely low resolution. If, for example, a microscope has a resolution of a thousandth of a millimetre, it can reveal objects larger than that size. Smaller objects however appear blurred or distorted. The electron microscope image has a resolution several thousand times better than that achieved by the best optical microscope because the resolving power of the latter is limited by the wavelength of light, whereas the effective wavelength of an electron beam is several thousand times shorter.

Electron microscopes may be classified as either transmission or scanning instruments. With the former the image is usually produced by an electron beam that has passed through the specimen. In scanning instruments a finely focused electron beam sweeps through the specimen, and the image is formed by a process similar to that used in television.

Appendices

Scientific Discoveries

Discovery	Date	Discoverer	Nationality
Absolute zero, concept	1848	William Thomson, 1st Baron Kelvin	Irish
Adrenalin, isolation	1901	Jokichi Takamine	Japanese
Alizarin, synthesized	1869	William Perkin	English
Allotropy (in carbon)	1841	Jöns Jakob Berzelius	Swedish
Alpha particles	1899	Ernest Rutherford	New Zealand-born British
Alternation of generations (ferns and mosses)	1851	Wilhelm Hofmeister	German
Aluminium, extraction by electrolysis of aluminium oxide	1886	Charles Hall, Paul Héroult	US, French
Aluminium, improved isolation	1827	Friedrich Wöhler	German
Anthrax vaccine	1881	Louis Pasteur	French
Antibacterial agent, first specific (Salvarsan for treatment of syphilis)	1910	Paul Ehrlich	German
Antiseptic surgery (using phenol)	1865	Joseph Lister	English
Argon	1894	William Ramsay	Scottish
Asteroid, first (Ceres)	1801	Giuseppe Piazzi	Italian
Atomic theory	1803	John Dalton	English
Australopithecus	1924	Raymond Dart	Australian-born South African
Avogadro's hypothesis	1811	Amedeo Avogadro	Italian
Bacteria, first observation	1683	Anton van Leeuwenhoek	Dutch
Bee dance	1919	Karl von Frisch	Austrian
Benzene, isolation	1825	Michael Faraday	English
Benzene, ring structure	1865	Friedrich Kekulé	German
Beta rays	1899	Ernest Rutherford	New Zealand-born British
Big Bang theory	1948	Ralph Alpher, George Gamow	US
Binary arithmetic	1679	Gottfried Leibniz	German
Binary stars	1802	William Herschel	German-born English
Binomial theorem	1665	Isaac Newton	English
Blood, circulation	1619	William Harvey	English
Blood groups, ABO system	1900	Karl Landsteiner	Austrian-born US
Bode's law	1772	Johann Bode, Johann Titius	German
Bohr atomic model	1913	Niels Bohr	Danish
Boolean algebra	1854	George Boole	English
Boyle's law	1662	Robert Boyle	Irish
Brewster's law	1815	David Brewster	Scottish
Brownian motion	1827	Robert Brown	Scottish
Cadmium	1817	Friedrich Strohmeyer	German
Caesium	c. 1860	Robert Bunsen	German
Carbon dioxide	1755	Joseph Black	Scottish
Charles' law	1787	Jacques Charles	French
Chlorine	1774	Karl Scheele	Swedish
Conditioning	1902	Ivan Pavlov	Russian
Continental drift	1912	Alfred Wegener	German
Coriolis effect	1835	Gustave-Gaspard Coriolis	French
Cosmic radiation	1911	Victor Hess	Austrian
Diphtheria bacillus, isolation	1883	Edwin Krebs	US
DNA, double-helix structure	1953	Francis Crick, James Watson	English, US
Doppler effect	1842	Christian Doppler	Austrian
Earth's magnetic pole	1546	Gerardus Mercator	Flemish
Earth's molten core	1916	Albert Michelson	German-born US
Earth's rotation, demonstration	1851	Léon Foucault	French
Eclipse, prediction	585 BC	Thales of Miletus	Greek
Electrolysis, laws	1833	Michael Faraday	English
Electromagnetic induction	1831	Michael Faraday	English

Discovery	Date	Discoverer	Nationality
Electromagnetism	1820	Hans Christian Oersted	Danish
Electron	1897	J J Thomson	English
Electroweak unification theory	1967	Sheldon Lee Glashow, Abdus Salam, Steven Weinberg	US, Pakistani, US
Enzyme, first animal (pepsin)	1836	Theodor Schwann	German
Enzymes, 'lock and key' hypothesis	1899	Emil Fischer	German
Evolution by natural selection	1858	Charles Darwin	English
Exclusion principle	1925	Wolfgang Pauli	Austrian-born Swiss
Fullerenes	1985	Harold Kroto, David Walton	English
Gay-Lussac's law	1808	Joseph-Louis Gay-Lussac	French
Geometry, Euclidean	300 BC	Euclid	Greek
Germ theory	1861	Louis Pasteur	French
Global temperature and link with atmospheric carbon dioxide	1896	Svante Arrhenius	Swedish
Gravity, laws	1687	Isaac Newton	English
Groups, theory	1829	Evariste Galois	French
Helium, production	1896	William Ramsay	Scottish
Homo erectus	1894	Marie Dubois	Dutch
Homo habilis	1960	Louis Leakey, Mary Leakey	Kenyan, English
Hormone, first	1902	William Bayliss, Ernest Starling	English
Hubble's law	1929	Edwin Hubble	US
Hydraulics, principles	1647	Blaise Pascal	French
Hydrogen	1766	Henry Cavendish	English
Iapetus	1671	Giovanni Cassini	Italian-born French
Infrared solar rays	1800	William Herschel	German-born English
Insulin, isolation	1921	Frederick Banting, Charles Best	Canadian
Insulin, structure	1969	Dorothy Hodgkin	English
Interference of light	1801	Thomas Young	English
Jupiter's satellites	1610	Galileo	Italian
Kinetic theory of gases	1850	Rudolf Clausius	German
Krypton	1898	William Ramsay, Morris Travers	Scottish, English
Lenses, how they work	1039	Ibn al-Haytham Alhazen	Arabic
Light, finite velocity	1676	Ole Römer	Danish
Light, polarization	1678	Christiaan Huygens	Dutch
Linnaean classification system	1735	Linnaeus	Swedish
Malarial parasite in *Anopheles* mosquito	1897	Ronald Ross	British
Malarial parasite observed	1880	Alphonse Laveran	French
Mars, moons	1877	Asaph Hall	US
Mendelian laws of inheritance	1866	Gregor Mendel	Austrian
Messenger RNA	1960	Sydney Brenner, François Jacob	South African, French
Microorganisms as cause of fermentation	1856	Louis Pasteur	French
Monoclonal antibodies	1975	César Milstein, Georges Köhler	Argentine-born British, German
Motion, laws	1687	Isaac Newton	English
Natural selection	1859	Charles Darwin	English
Neon	1898	William Ramsay, Morris Travers	Scottish, English
Neptune	1846	Johann Galle	German
Nerve impulses, electric nature	1780	Luigi Galvani	Italian
Neutron	1932	James Chadwick	English
Normal distribution curve	1733	Abraham de Moivre	French
Nuclear atom, concept	1911	Ernest Rutherford	New Zealand-born British
Nuclear fission	1938	Otto Hahn, Fritz Strassman	German
Nucleus, plant cell	1831	Robert Brown	Scottish

Discovery	Date	Discoverer	Nationality
Ohm's law	1827	Georg Ohm	German
Organic substance, first synthesis (urea)	1828	Friedrich Wöhler	German
Oxygen	1774	Joseph Priestley	English
Oxygen, liquefaction	1894	James Dewar	Scottish
Ozone layer	1913	Charles Fabry	French
Palladium	1803	William Hyde Wollaston	English
Pallas (asteroid)	1802	Heinrich Olbers	German
Pendulum, principle	1583	Galileo	Italian
Penicillin	1928	Alexander Fleming	Scottish
Penicillin, widespread preparation	1940	Ernst Chain, Howard Florey	German, Australian
Pepsin	1834	Theodor Schwann	German
Periodic law for elements	1869	Dmitri Mendeleyev	Russian
Piezoelectric effect	1880	Pierre Curie	French
Pi meson (particle)	1947	Cecil Powell, Giuseppe Occhialini	English, Italian
Planetary nebulae	1790	William Herschel	German-born English
Planets, orbiting Sun	1513	Copernicus	Polish
Pluto	1930	Clyde Tombaugh	US
Polarization of light by reflection	1808	Etienne Malus	French
Polio vaccine	1952	Jonas Salk	US
Polonium	1898	Marie and Pierre Curie	French
Positron	1932	Carl Anderson	US
Potassium	1807	Humphry Davy	English
Probability theory	1654	Blaise Pascal, Pierre de Fermat	French
Probability theory, expansion	1812	Pierre Laplace	French
Proton	1914	Ernest Rutherford	New Zealand-born British
Pulsar	1967	Jocelyn Bell Burnell	Irish
Pythagoras' theorem	c. 550 BC	Pythagoras	Greek
Quantum chromodynamics	1972	Murray Gell-Mann	US
Quantum electrodynamics	1948	Richard Feynman, Julian Schwinger, Shin'chiro Tomonaga	US, US, Japanese
Quark, first suggested existence	1964	Murray Gell-Mann, George Zweig	US
Rabies vaccine	1885	Louis Pasteur	French
Radioactivity	1896	Henri Becquerel	French
Radio emissions, from Milky Way	1932	Karl Jansky	US
Radio waves, production	1887	Heinrich Hertz	German
Radium	1898	Marie and Pierre Curie	French
Refraction, laws	1621	Willebrord Snell	Dutch
Relativity, general theory	1915	Albert Einstein	German-born US
Relativity, special theory	1905	Albert Einstein	German-born US
Rhesus factor	1940	Karl Landsteiner, Alexander Wiener	Austrian, US
Rubidium	c. 1860	Robert Bunsen	German
Sap flow in plants	1733	Stephen Hales	English
Saturn's satellites	1655	Christiaan Huygens	Dutch
Smallpox inoculation	1796	Edward Jenner	English
Sodium	1807	Humphry Davy	English
Stars, luminosity sequence	1905	Ejnar Hertzsprung	Danish
Stereochemistry, foundation	1848	Louis Pasteur	French
Sunspots	1611	Galileo, Christoph Scheiner	Italian, German
Superconductivity	1911	Heike Kamerlingh Onnes	Dutch
Superconductivity, theory	1957	John Bardeen, Leon Cooper, John Schrieffer	US
Thermodynamics, third law	1906	Hermann Nernst	German
Thermoelectricity	1821	Thomas Seebeck	German

Discovery	Date	Discoverer	Nationality
Thorium-X	1902	Ernest Rutherford, Frederick Soddy	New Zealand-born British, English
Titius–Bode law	1772	Johan Bode, Johann Titius	German
Tranquillizer, first (reserpine)	1956	Robert Woodward	US
Transformer	1831	Michael Faraday	English
Tuberculosis bacillus, isolation	1882	Robert Koch	German
Uranus	1781	William Herschel	German-born English
Urea cycle	1932	Hans Krebs	German
Urea, synthesis	1828	Friedrich Wöhler	German
Valves, in veins	1603	Geronimo Fabricius	Italian
Van Allen radiation belts	1958	James Van Allen	US
Virus, first identified (tobacco mosaic disease, in tobacco plants)	1898	Martinus Beijerinck	Dutch
Vitamin A, isolation	1913	Elmer McCollum	US
Vitamin A, structure	1931	Paul Karrer	Russian-born Swiss
Vitamin B, composition	1957	Dorothy Hodgkin	English
Vitamin C	1928	Charles Glen King, Albert Szent-Györgi	US, Hungarian-born US
Wave mechanics	1926	Erwin Schrödinger	Austrian
Xenon	1898	William Ramsay, Morris Travers	Scottish, English
X-ray crystallography	1912	Max von Laue	German
X-rays	1895	Wilhelm Röntgen	German

Nobel Prize for Chemistry

Year	Winner(s)[1]	Awarded for
1901	Jacobus van't Hoff (Netherlands)	laws of chemical dynamics and osmotic pressure
1902	Emil Fischer (Germany)	sugar and purine syntheses
1903	Svante Arrhenius (Sweden)	theory of electrolytic dissociation
1904	William Ramsay (UK)	discovery of inert gases in air and their locations in the periodic table
1905	Adolf von Baeyer (Germany)	work in organic dyes and hydroaromatic compounds
1906	Henri Moissan (France)	isolation of fluorine and adoption of electric furnace
1907	Eduard Buchner (Germany)	biochemical research and discovery of cell-free fermentation
1908	Ernest Rutherford (UK)	work in atomic disintegration, and the chemistry of radioactive substances
1909	Wilhelm Ostwald (Germany)	work in catalysis, and principles of equilibria and rates of reaction
1910	Otto Wallach (Germany)	work in alicyclic compounds
1911	Marie Curie (France)	discovery of radium and polonium, and the isolation and study of radium
1912	Victor Grignard (France)	discovery of Grignard reagent
	Paul Sabatier (France)	finding method of catalytic hydrogenation of organic compounds
1913	Alfred Werner (Switzerland)	work in bonding of atoms within molecules
1914	Theodore Richards (USA)	accurate determination of the atomic masses of many elements
1915	Richard Willstäter (Germany)	research into plant pigments, especially chlorophyll
1916	no award	
1917	no award	
1918	Fritz Haber (Germany)	synthesis of ammonia from its elements
1919	no award	
1920	Walther Nernst (Germany)	work in thermochemistry
1921	Frederick Soddy (UK)	work in radioactive substances, especially isotopes
1922	Francis Aston (UK)	work in mass spectrometry of isotopes of radioactive elements, and enunciation of the whole-number rule
1923	Fritz Pregl (Austria)	method of microanalysis of organic substances
1924	no award	
1925	Richard Zsigmondy (Austria)	elucidation of heterogeneity of colloids
1926	Theodor Svedberg (Sweden)	investigation of dispersed systems
1927	Heinrich Wieland (Germany)	research on constitution of bile acids and related substances
1928	Adolf Windaus (Germany)	research on constitution of sterols and related vitamins
1929	Arthur Harden (UK) and Hans von Euler-Chelpin (Sweden)	work on fermentation of sugar, and fermentative enzymes
1930	Hans Fischer (Germany)	analysis of haem (the iron-bearing group in haemoglobin) and chlorophyll, and the synthesis of haemin (a compound of haem)
1931	Carl Bosch (Germany) and Friedrich Bergius (Germany)	invention and development of chemical high-pressure methods
1932	Irving Langmuir (USA)	discoveries and investigations in surface chemistry
1933	no award	
1934	Harold Urey (USA)	discovery of deuterium (heavy hydrogen)
1935	Irène and Frédéric Joliot-Curie (France)	synthesis of new radioactive elements
1936	Peter Debye (Netherlands)	work in molecular structures by investigation of dipole moments and the diffraction of X-rays and electrons in gases
1937	Norman Haworth (UK)	work in carbohydrates and ascorbic acid (vitamin C)
	Paul Karrer (Switzerland)	work in carotenoids, flavins, retinol (vitamin A) and riboflavin (vitamin B_2)
1938	Richard Kuhn (Germany) (declined)	carotenoids and vitamins research
1939	Adolf Butenandt (Germany) (declined)	work in sex hormones
	Leopold Ruzicka (Switzerland)	polymethylenes and higher terpenes
1940	no award	
1941	no award	
1942	no award	
1943	Georg von Hevesy (Hungary)	use of isotopes as tracers in chemical processes
1944	Otto Hahn (Germany)	discovery of nuclear fission
1945	Artturi Virtanen (Finland)	work in agriculture and nutrition, especially fodder preservation
1946	James Sumner (USA)	discovery of crystallization of enzymes
	John Northrop (USA) and Wendell Stanley (USA)	preparation of pure enzymes and virus proteins

Year	Winner(s)[1]	Awarded for
1947	Robert Robinson (UK)	investigation of biologically important plant products, especially alkaloids
1948	Arne Tiselius (Sweden)	researches in electrophoresis and adsorption analysis, and discoveries concerning serum proteins
1949	William Giauque (USA)	work in chemical thermodynamics, especially at very low temperatures
1950	Otto Diels (West Germany) and Kurt Alder (West Germany)	discovery and development of diene synthesis
1951	Edwin McMillan (USA) and Glenn Seaborg (USA)	discovery and work in chemistry of transuranic elements
1952	Archer Martin (UK) and Richard Synge (UK)	development of partition chromatography
1953	Hermann Staudinger (West Germany)	discoveries in macromolecular chemistry
1954	Linus Pauling (USA)	study of nature of chemical bonds, especially in complex substances
1955	Vincent du Vigneaud (USA)	investigations into biochemically important sulphur compounds, and the first synthesis of a polypeptide hormone
1956	Cyril Hinshelwood (UK) and Nikolay Semenov (USSR)	work in mechanism of chemical reactions
1957	Alexander Todd (UK)	work in nucleotides and nucleotide coenzymes
1958	Frederick Sanger (UK)	determination of the structure of proteins, especially insulin
1959	Jaroslav Heyrovský (Czechoslovakia)	discovery and development of polarographic methods of chemical analysis
1960	Willard Libby (USA)	development of radiocarbon dating in archaeology, geology, and geography
1961	Melvin Calvin (USA)	study of assimilation of carbon dioxide by plants
1962	Max Perutz (UK) and John Kendrew (UK)	determination of structures of globular proteins
1963	Karl Ziegler (West Germany) and Giulio Natta (Italy)	chemistry and technology of high polymers
1964	Dorothy Crowfoot Hodgkin (UK)	crystallographic determination of the structures of biochemical compounds, notably penicillin and cyanocobalamin (vitamin B_{12})
1965	Robert Woodward (USA)	organic synthesis
1966	Robert Mulliken (USA)	molecular orbital theory of chemical bonds and structures
1967	Manfred Eigen (West Germany), Ronald Norrish (UK), and George Porter (UK)	investigation of rapid chemical reactions by means of very short pulses of energy
1968	Lars Onsager (USA)	discovery of reciprocal relations, fundamental for the thermodynamics of irreversible processes
1969	Derek Barton (UK) and Odd Hassel (Norway)	concept and applications of conformation
1970	Luis Federico Leloir (Argentina)	discovery of sugar nucleotides and their role in carbohydrate biosynthesis
1971	Gerhard Herzberg (Canada)	research on electronic structure and geometry of molecules, particularly free radicals
1972	Christian Anfinsen (USA), Stanford Moore (USA), and William Stein (USA)	work in amino-acid structure and biological activity of the enzyme ribonuclease
1973	Ernst Fischer (West Germany) and Geoffrey Wilkinson (UK)	work in chemistry of organometallic sandwich compounds
1974	Paul Flory (USA)	studies of physical chemistry of macromolecules
1975	John Cornforth (UK)	work in stereochemistry of enzyme-catalysed reactions
	Vladimir Prelog (Switzerland)	work in stereochemistry of organic molecules and their reactions
1976	William Lipscomb (USA)	study of structure and chemical bonding of boranes (compounds of boron and hydrogen)
1977	Ilya Prigogine (Belgium)	work in thermodynamics of irreversible and dissipative processes
1978	Peter Mitchell (UK)	formulation of a theory of biological energy transfer and chemiosmotic theory
1979	Herbert Brown (USA) and Georg Wittig (West Germany)	use of boron and phosphorus compounds, respectively, in organic syntheses
1980	Paul Berg (USA)	biochemistry of nucleic acids, especially recombinant DNA
	Walter Gilbert (USA) and Frederick Sanger (UK)	base sequences in nucleic acids
1981	Kenichi Fukui (Japan) and Roald Hoffmann (USA)	theories concerning chemical reactions

Year	Winner(s)[1]	Awarded for
1982	Aaron Klug (UK)	determination of crystallographic electron microscopy: structure of biologically important nucleic-acid–protein complexes
1983	Henry Taube (USA)	study of electron-transfer reactions in inorganic chemical reactions
1984	Bruce Merrifield (USA)	development of chemical syntheses on a solid matrix
1985	Herbert Hauptman (USA) and Jerome Karle (USA)	development of methods of determining crystal structures
1986	Dudley Herschbach (USA), Yuan Lee (USA), and John Polanyi (Canada)	development of dynamics of chemical elementary processes
1987	Donald Cram (USA), Jean-Marie Lehn (France), and Charles Pedersen (USA)	development of molecules with highly selective structure-specific interactions
1988	Johann Deisenhofer (West Germany), Robert Huber (West Germany), and Hartmut Michel (West Germany)	discovery of three-dimensional structure of the reaction centre of photosynthesis
1989	Sidney Altman (USA) and Thomas Cech (USA)	discovery of catalytic function of RNA
1990	Elias James Corey (USA)	new methods of synthesizing chemical compounds
1991	Richard Ernst (Switzerland)	improvements in the technology of nuclear magnetic resonance (NMR) imaging
1992	Rudolph Marcus (USA)	theoretical discoveries relating to reduction and oxidation reactions
1993	Kary Mullis (USA)	invention of the polymerase chain reaction technique for amplifying DNA
	Michael Smith (Canada)	invention of techniques for splicing foreign genetic segments into an organism's DNA in order to modify the proteins produced
1994	George Olah (USA)	development of technique for examining hydrocarbon molecules
1995	F Sherwood Rowland (USA), Mario Molina (USA), and Paul Crutzen (Netherlands)	explaining the chemical process of the ozone layer
1996	Robert Curl Jr (USA), Harold Kroto (UK), and Richard Smalley (USA)	discovery of fullerenes
1997	John Walker (UK), Paul Boyer (USA), and Jens Skou (Denmark)	study of the enzymes involved in the production of adenosine triphospate (ATP), which acts as a store of energy in bodies called mitochondria inside cells
1998	Walter Kohn (USA), John Pople (USA)	research into quantum chemistry
1999	Ahmed Zewail (USA)	devising a technique to photograph molecules as they react

[1] Nationality given is the citizenship of recipient at the time award was made.

Nobel Prize for Physics

Year	Winner(s)[1]	Awarded for
1901	Wilhelm Röntgen (Germany)	discovery of X-rays
1902	Hendrik Lorentz (Netherlands) and Pieter Zeeman (Netherlands)	influence of magnetism on radiation phenomena
1903	Henri Becquerel (France)	discovery of spontaneous radioactivity
	Pierre Curie (France) and Marie Curie (France)	research on radiation phenomena
1904	John Strutt (Lord Rayleigh, UK)	densities of gases and discovery of argon
1905	Philipp von Lenard (Germany)	work on cathode rays
1906	Joseph J Thomson (UK)	theoretical and experimental work on the conduction of electricity by gases
1907	Albert Michelson (USA)	measurement of the speed of light through the design and application of precise optical instruments such as the interferometer
1908	Gabriel Lippmann (France)	photographic reproduction of colours by interference
1909	Guglielmo Marconi (Italy) and Karl Ferdinand Braun (Germany)	development of wireless telegraphy
1910	Johannes van der Waals (Netherlands)	equation describing the physical behaviour of gases and liquids
1911	Wilhelm Wien (Germany)	laws governing radiation of heat
1912	Nils Dalén (Sweden)	invention of light-controlled valves, which allow lighthouses and buoys to operate automatically
1913	Heike Kamerlingh Onnes (Netherlands)	studies of properties of matter at low temperatures
1914	Max von Laue (Germany)	discovery of diffraction of X-rays by crystals
1915	William Bragg (UK) and Lawrence Bragg (UK)	X-ray analysis of crystal structures
1916	no award	
1917	Charles Barkla (UK)	discovery of characteristic X-ray emission of the elements
1918	Max Planck (Germany)	formulation of quantum theory
1919	Johannes Stark (Germany)	discovery of Doppler effect in rays of positive ions, and splitting of spectral lines in electric fields
1920	Charles Guillaume (Switzerland)	discovery of anomalies in nickel-steel alloys
1921	Albert Einstein (Switzerland)	theoretical physics, especially law of photoelectric effect
1922	Niels Bohr (Denmark)	discovery of the structure of atoms and radiation emanating from them
1923	Robert Millikan (USA)	discovery of the electric charge of an electron, and study of the photoelectric effect
1924	Karl Siegbahn (Sweden)	X-ray spectroscopy
1925	James Franck (Germany) and Gustav Hertz (Germany)	discovery of laws governing the impact of an electron upon an atom
1926	Jean Perrin (France)	confirmation of the discontinuous structure of matter
1927	Arthur Compton (USA)	transfer of energy from electromagnetic radiation to a particle
	Charles Wilson (UK)	invention of the Wilson cloud chamber, by which the movement of electrically charged particles may be tracked
1928	Owen Richardson (UK)	work on thermionic phenomena and associated law
1929	Louis Victor de Broglie (France)	discovery of the wavelike nature of electrons
1930	Chandrasekhara Raman (India)	discovery of the scattering of single-wavelength light when it is passed through a transparent substance
1931	no award	
1932	Werner Heisenberg (Germany)	creation of quantum mechanics
1933	Erwin Schrödinger (Austria) and Paul Dirac (UK)	development of quantum mechanics
1934	no award	
1935	James Chadwick (UK)	discovery of the neutron
1936	Victor Hess (Austria)	discovery of cosmic radiation
	Carl Anderson (USA)	discovery of the positron
1937	Clinton Davisson (USA) and George Thomson (UK)	diffraction of electrons by crystals
1938	Enrico Fermi (Italy)	use of neutron irradiation to produce new elements, and discovery of nuclear reactions induced by slow neutrons
1939	Ernest Lawrence (USA)	invention and development of the cyclotron, and production of artificial radioactive elements

Year	Winner(s)[1]	Awarded for
1940	no award	
1941	no award	
1942	no award	
1943	Otto Stern (USA)	molecular-ray method of investigating elementary particles, and discovery of magnetic moment of proton
1944	Isidor Isaac Rabi (USA)	resonance method of recording the magnetic properties of atomic nuclei
1945	Wolfgang Pauli (Austria)	discovery of the exclusion principle
1946	Percy Bridgman (USA)	development of high-pressure physics
1947	Edward Appleton (UK)	physics of the upper atmosphere
1948	Patrick Blackett (UK)	application of the Wilson cloud chamber to nuclear physics and cosmic radiation
1949	Hideki Yukawa (Japan)	theoretical work predicting existence of mesons
1950	Cecil Powell (UK)	use of photographic emulsion to study nuclear processes, and discovery of pions (pi mesons)
1951	John Cockcroft (UK) and Ernest Walton (Ireland)	transmutation of atomic nuclei by means of accelerated subatomic particles
1952	Felix Bloch (USA) and Edward Purcell (USA)	precise nuclear magnetic measurements
1953	Frits Zernike (Netherlands)	invention of phase-contrast microscope
1954	Max Born (UK)	statistical interpretation of wave function in quantum mechanics
	Walther Bothe (West Germany)	coincidence method of detecting the emission of electrons
1955	Willis Lamb (USA)	structure of hydrogen spectrum
	Polykarp Kusch (USA)	determination of magnetic moment of the electron
1956	William Shockley (USA), John Bardeen (USA), and Walter Houser Brattain (USA)	study of semiconductors, and discovery of the transistor effect
1957	Tsung-Dao Lee (China) and Chen Ning Yang (China)	investigations of weak interactions between elementary particles
1958	Pavel Cherenkov (USSR), Ilya Frank (USSR), and Igor Tamm (USSR)	discovery and interpretation of Cherenkov radiation
1959	Emilio Segrè (USA) and Owen Chamberlain (USA)	discovery of the antiproton
1960	Donald Glaser (USA)	invention of the bubble chamber
1961	Robert Hofstadter (USA)	scattering of electrons in atomic nuclei, and structure of protons and neutrons
	Rudolf Mössbauer (West Germany)	resonance absorption of gamma radiation
1962	Lev Landau (USSR)	theories of condensed matter, especially liquid helium
1963	Eugene Wigner (USA)	discovery and application of symmetry principles in atomic physics
	Maria Goeppert-Mayer (USA) and Hans Jensen (Germany)	discovery of the shell-like structure of atomic nuclei
1964	Charles Townes (USA), Nikolai Basov (USSR), and Aleksandr Prokhorov (USSR)	work on quantum electronics leading to construction of oscillators and amplifiers based on maser–laser principle
1965	Shin'ichiro Tomonaga (Japan), Julian Schwinger (USA), and Richard Feynman (USA)	basic principles of quantum electrodynamics
1966	Alfred Kastler (France)	development of optical pumping, whereby atoms are raised to higher energy levels by illumination
1967	Hans Bethe (USA)	theory of nuclear reactions, and discoveries concerning production of energy in stars
1968	Luis Alvarez (USA)	elementary-particle physics, and discovery of resonance states, using hydrogen bubble chamber and data analysis
1969	Murray Gell-Mann (USA)	classification of elementary particles, and study of their interactions
1970	Hannes Alfvén (Sweden)	work in magnetohydrodynamics and its applications in plasma physics
	Louis Néel (France)	work in antiferromagnetism and ferromagnetism in solid-state physics
1971	Dennis Gabor (UK)	invention and development of holography
1972	John Bardeen (USA), Leon Cooper (USA), and John Robert Schrieffer (USA)	theory of superconductivity
1973	Leo Esaki (Japan) and Ivar Giaever (USA)	tunnelling phenomena in semiconductors and superconductors
	Brian Josephson (UK)	theoretical predictions of the properties of a supercurrent through a tunnel barrier

Year	Winner(s)[1]	Awarded for
1974	Martin Ryle (UK) and Antony Hewish (UK)	development of radioastronomy, particularly the aperture- synthesis technique, and the discovery of pulsars
1975	Aage Bohr (Denmark), Ben Mottelson (Denmark), and James Rainwater (USA)	discovery of connection between collective motion and particle motion in atomic nuclei, and development of theory of nuclear structure
1976	Burton Richter (USA) and Samuel Ting (USA)	discovery of the psi meson
1977	Philip Anderson (USA), Nevill Mott (UK), and John Van Vleck (USA)	contributions to understanding electronic structure of magnetic and disordered systems
1978	Pyotr Kapitsa (USSR)	invention and application of low-temperature physics
	Arno Penzias (USA) and Robert Wilson (USA)	discovery of cosmic background radiation
1979	Sheldon Glashow (USA), Abdus Salam (Pakistan), and Steven Weinberg (USA)	unified theory of weak and electromagnetic fundamental forces, and prediction of the existence of the weak neutral current
1980	James W Cronin (USA) and Val Fitch (USA)	violations of fundamental symmetry principles in the decay of neutral kaon mesons
1981	Nicolaas Bloembergen (USA) and Arthur Schawlow (USA)	development of laser spectroscopy
	Kai Siegbahn (Sweden)	high-resolution electron spectroscopy
1982	Kenneth Wilson (USA)	theory for critical phenomena in connection with phase transitions
1983	Subrahmanyan Chandrasekhar (USA)	theoretical studies of physical processes in connection with structure and evolution of stars
	William Fowler (USA)	nuclear reactions involved in the formation of chemical elements in the universe
1984	Carlo Rubbia (Italy) and Simon van der Meer (Netherlands)	contributions to the discovery of the W and Z (weakons)
1985	Klaus von Klitzing (West Germany)	discovery of the quantized Hall effect
1986	Erns Ruska (West Germany)	electron optics, and design of the first electron microscope
	Gerd Binnig (West Germany) and Heinrich Rohrer (Switzerland)	design of scanning tunnelling microscope
1987	Georg Bednorz (West Germany) and Alex Müller (Switzerland)	superconductivity in ceramic materials
1988	Leon M Lederman (USA), Melvin Schwartz (USA), and Jack Steinberger (USA)	neutrino-beam method, and demonstration of the doublet structure of leptons through discovery of muon neutrino
1989	Norman Ramsey (USA)	measurement techniques leading to discovery of caesium atomic clock
	Hans Dehmelt (USA) and Wolfgang Paul (Germany)	ion-trap method for isolating single atoms
1990	Jerome Friedman (USA), Henry Kendall (USA), and Richard Taylor (Canada)	experiments demonstrating that protons and neutrons are made up of quarks
1991	Pierre-Gilles de Gennes (France)	work on disordered systems including polymers and liquid crystals; development of mathematical methods for studying the behaviour of molecules in a liquid on the verge of solidifying
1992	Georges Charpak (France)	invention and development of detectors used in high-energy physics
1993	Joseph Taylor (USA) and Russell Hulse (USA)	discovery of first binary pulsar (confirming the existence of gravitational waves)
1994	Clifford Shull (USA) and Bertram Brockhouse (Canada)	development of technique known as 'neutron scattering' which led to advances in semiconductor technology
1995	Frederick Reines (USA)	discovery of the neutrino
	Martin Perl (USA)	discovery of the tau lepton
1996	David Lee (USA), Douglas Osheroff (USA), and Robert Richardson (USA)	discovery of superfluidity in helium-3
1997	Claude Cohen-Tannoudji (France), William Phillips (USA), and Steven Chu (USA)	discovery of a way to slow down individual atoms using lasers for study in a near-vacuum
1998	Robert B Laughlin (USA), Horst L Störmer (USA), and Daniel C Tsui (USA)	discovery of a new form of quantum fluid with fractionally charged excitations
1999	Gerardus 't Hooft (Netherlands) and Martinus Veltman (Netherlands)	work in quantum mechanics that elucidated the quantum structure of electroweak interactions

[1] Nationality given is the citizenship of recipient at the time award was made.

Nobel Prize for Physiology or Medicine

Year	Winner(s)[1]	Awarded for
1901	Emil von Behring (Germany)	discovery that the body produces antitoxins, and development of serum therapy for diseases such as diphtheria
1902	Ronald Ross (UK)	work on the role of the *Anopheles* mosquito in transmitting malaria
1903	Niels Finsen (Denmark)	discovery of the use of ultraviolet light to treat skin diseases
1904	Ivan Pavlov (Russia)	discovery of the physiology of digestion
1905	Robert Koch (Germany)	investigations and discoveries in relation to tuberculosis
1906	Camillo Golgi (Italy) and Santiago Ramón y Cajal (Spain)	discovery of the fine structure of the nervous system
1907	Charles Laveran (France)	discovery that certain protozoa can cause disease
1908	Ilya Mechnikov (Russia) and Paul Ehrlich (Germany)	work on immunity
1909	Emil Kocher (Switzerland)	work on the physiology, pathology, and surgery of the thyroid gland
1910	Albrecht Kossel (Germany)	study of cell proteins and nucleic acids
1911	Allvar Gullstrand (Sweden)	work on the refraction of light through the different components of the eye
1912	Alexis Carrel (France)	work on the techniques for connecting severed blood vessels and transplanting organs
1913	Charles Richet (France)	work on allergic responses
1914	Robert Bárány (Austria-Hungary)	work on the physiology and pathology of the equilibrium organs of the inner ear
1915	no award	
1916	no award	
1917	no award	
1918	no award	
1919	Jules Bordet (Belgium)	work on immunity
1920	August Krogh (Denmark)	discovery of the mechanism regulating the dilation and constriction of blood capillaries
1921	no award	
1922	Archibald Hill (UK)	work in the production of heat in contracting muscle
	Otto Meyerhof (Germany)	work in the relationship between oxygen consumption and metabolism of lactic acid in muscle
1923	Frederick Banting (Canada) and John Macleod (UK)	discovery and isolation of the hormone insulin
1924	Willem Einthoven (Netherlands)	invention of the electrocardiograph
1925	no award	
1926	Johannes Fibiger (Denmark)	discovery of a parasite *Spiroptera carcinoma* that causes cancer
1927	Julius Wagner-Jauregg (Austria)	use of induced malarial fever to treat paralysis caused by mental deterioration
1928	Charles Nicolle (France)	work on the role of the body louse in transmitting typhus
1929	Christiaan Eijkman (Netherlands)	discovery of a cure for beriberi, a vitamin-deficiency disease
	Frederick Hopkins (UK)	discovery of trace substances, now known as vitamins, that stimulate growth
1930	Karl Landsteiner (USA)	discovery of human blood groups
1931	Otto Warburg (Germany)	discovery of respiratory enzymes that enable cells to process oxygen
1932	Charles Sherrington (UK) and Edgar Adrian (UK)	discovery of function of neurons (nerve cells)
1933	Thomas Morgan (USA)	work on the role of chromosomes in heredity
1934	George Whipple (USA), George Minot (USA), and William Murphy (USA)	work on treatment of pernicious anaemia by increasing the amount of liver in the diet
1935	Hans Spemann (Germany)	organizer effect in embryonic development
1936	Henry Dale (UK) and Otto Loewi (Germany)	chemical transmission of nerve impulses
1937	Albert Szent-Györgyi (Hungary)	investigation of biological oxidation processes and of the action of ascorbic acid (vitamin C)
1938	Corneille Heymans (Belgium)	mechanisms regulating respiration
1939	Gerhard Domagk (Germany)	discovery of the first antibacterial sulphonamide drug

Year	Winner(s)[1]	Awarded for
1940	no award	
1941	no award	
1942	no award	
1943	Henrik Dam (Denmark)	discovery of vitamin K
	Edward Doisy (USA)	chemical nature of vitamin K
1944	Joseph Erlanger (USA) and Herbert Gasser (USA)	transmission of impulses by nerve fibres
1945	Alexander Fleming (UK)	discovery of the bactericidal effect of penicillin
	Ernst Chain (UK) and Howard Florey (Australia)	isolation of penicillin and its development as an antibiotic drug
1946	Hermann Muller (USA)	discovery that X-ray irradiation can cause mutation
1947	Carl Cori (USA) and Gerty Cori (USA)	production and breakdown of glycogen (animal starch)
	Bernardo Houssay (Argentina)	function of the pituitary gland in sugar metabolism
1948	Paul Müller (Switzerland)	discovery of the first synthetic contact insecticide DDT
1949	Walter Hess (Switzerland)	mapping areas of the midbrain that control the activities of certain body organs
	Antonio Egas Moniz (Portugal)	therapeutic value of prefrontal leucotomy in certain psychoses
1950	Edward Kendall (USA), Tadeus Reichstein (Switzerland), and Philip Hench (USA)	structure and biological effects of hormones of the adrenal cortex
1951	Max Theiler (South Africa)	discovery of a vaccine against yellow fever
1952	Selman Waksman (USA)	discovery of streptomycin, the first antibiotic effective against tuberculosis
1953	Hans Krebs (UK)	discovery of the Krebs cycle
	Fritz Lipmann (USA)	discovery of coenzyme A, a nonprotein compound that acts in conjunction with enzymes to catalyse metabolic reactions leading up to the Krebs cycle
1954	John Enders (USA), Thomas Weller (USA), and Frederick Robbins (USA)	cultivation of the polio virus in the laboratory
1955	Hugo Theorell (Sweden)	work on the nature and action of oxidation enzymes
1956	André Cournand (USA), Werner Forssmann (West Germany), and Dickinson Richards (USA)	work on the technique for passing a catheter into the heart for diagnostic purposes
1957	Daniel Bovet (Italy)	discovery of synthetic drugs used as muscle relaxants in anaesthesia
1958	George Beadle (USA) and Edward Tatum (USA)	discovery that genes regulate precise chemical effects
	Joshua Lederberg (USA)	work on genetic recombination and the organization of bacterial genetic material
1959	Severo Ochoa (USA) and Arthur Kornberg (USA)	discovery of enzymes that catalyse the formation of RNA (ribonucleic acid) and DNA (deoxyribonucleic acid)
1960	Macfarlane Burnet (Australia) and Peter Medawar (UK)	acquired immunological tolerance of transplanted tissues
1961	Georg von Békésy (USA)	investigations into the mechanism of hearing within the cochlea of the inner ear
1962	Francis Crick (UK), James Watson (USA), and Maurice Wilkins (UK)	discovery of the double-helical structure of DNA and of the significance of this structure in the replication and transfer of genetic information
1963	John Eccles (Australia), Alan Hodgkin (UK), and Andrew Huxley (UK)	ionic mechanisms involved in the communication or inhibition of impulses across neuron (nerve cell) membranes
1964	Konrad Bloch (USA) and Feodor Lynen (West Germany)	work on the cholesterol and fatty-acid metabolism
1965	François Jacob (France), André Lwoff (France), and Jacques Monod (France)	genetic control of enzyme and virus synthesis
1966	Peyton Rous (USA)	discovery of tumour-inducing viruses
	Charles Huggins (USA)	hormonal treatment of prostatic cancer
1967	Ragnar Granit (Sweden), Haldan Hartline (USA), and George Wald (USA)	physiology and chemistry of vision
1968	Robert Holley (USA), Har Gobind Khorana (USA), and Marshall Nirenberg (USA)	interpretation of genetic code and its function in protein synthesis
1969	Max Delbrück (USA), Alfred Hershey (USA), and Salvador Luria (USA)	replication mechanism and genetic structure of viruses

Year	Winner(s)[1]	Awarded for
1970	Bernard Katz (UK), Ulf von Euler (Sweden), and Julius Axelrod (USA)	work on the storage, release, and inactivation of neurotransmitters
1971	Earl Sutherland (USA)	discovery of cyclic AMP, a chemical messenger that plays a role in the action of many hormones
1972	Gerald Edelman (USA) and Rodney Porter (UK)	work on the chemical structure of antibodies
1973	Karl von Frisch (Austria), Konrad Lorenz (Austria), and Nikolaas Tinbergen (UK)	work in animal behaviour patterns
1974	Albert Claude (USA), Christian de Duve (Belgium), and George Palade (USA)	work in structural and functional organization of the cell
1975	David Baltimore (USA), Renato Dulbecco (USA), and Howard Temin (USA)	work on interactions between tumour-inducing viruses and the genetic material of the cell
1976	Baruch Blumberg (USA) and Carleton Gajdusek (USA)	new mechanisms for the origin and transmission of infectious diseases
1977	Roger Guillemin (USA) and Andrew Schally (USA)	discovery of hormones produced by the hypothalamus region of the brain
	Rosalyn Yalow (USA)	radioimmunoassay techniques by which minute quantities of hormone may be detected
1978	Werner Arber (Switzerland), Daniel Nathans (USA), and Hamilton Smith (USA)	discovery of restriction enzymes and their application to molecular genetics
1979	Allan Cormack (USA) and Godfrey Hounsfield (UK)	development of the computed axial tomography (CAT) scan
1980	Baruj Benacerraf (USA), Jean Dausset (France), and George Snell (USA)	work on genetically determined structures on the cell surface that regulate immunological reactions
1981	Roger Sperry (USA)	functional specialization of the brain's cerebral hemispheres work on
	David Hubel (USA) and Torsten Wiesel (Sweden)	visual perception
1982	Sune Bergström (Sweden), Bengt Samuelsson (Sweden), and John Vane (UK)	discovery of prostaglandins and related biologically active substances
1983	Barbara McClintock (USA)	discovery of mobile genetic elements
1984	Niels Jerne (Denmark-UK), Georges Köhler (West Germany), and César Milstein (Argentina)	work on immunity and discovery of a technique for producing highly specific, monoclonal antibodies
1985	Michael Brown (USA) and Joseph L Goldstein (USA)	work on the regulation of cholesterol metabolism
1986	Stanley Cohen (USA) and Rita Levi-Montalcini (USA-Italy)	discovery of factors that promote the growth of nerve and epidermal cells
1987	Susumu Tonegawa (Japan)	work on the process by which genes alter to produce a range of different antibodies
1988	James Black (UK), Gertrude Elion (USA), and George Hitchings (USA)	work on the principles governing the design of new drug treatment
1989	Michael Bishop (USA) and Harold Varmus (USA)	discovery of oncogenes, genes carried by viruses that can trigger cancerous growth in normal cells
1990	Joseph Murray (USA) and Donnall Thomas (USA)	pioneering work in organ and cell transplants
1991	Erwin Neher (Germany) and Bert Sakmann (Germany)	discovery of how gatelike structures (ion channels) regulate the flow of ions into and out of cells
1992	Edmond Fisher (USA) and Edwin Krebs (USA)	isolating and describing the action of the enzyme responsible for reversible protein phosphorylation, a major biological control mechanism
1993	Phillip Sharp (USA) and Richard Roberts (UK)	discovery of split genes (genes interrupted by nonsense segments of DNA)

Year	Winner(s)[1]	Awarded for
1994	Alfred Gilman (USA) and Martin Rodbell (USA)	discovery of a family of proteins (G-proteins) that translate messages – in the form of hormones or other chemical signals – into action inside cells
1995	Edward Lewis (USA), Eric Wieschaus (USA), and Christiane Nüsslein-Volhard (Germany)	discovery of genes which control the early stages of the body's development
1996	Peter Doherty (Australia) and Rolf Zinkernagel (Switzerland)	discovery of how the immune system recognizes virus- infected cells
1997	Stanley Prusiner (USA)	discoveries, including the 'prion' theory, that could lead to new treatments of dementia-related diseases, including Alzheimer's and Parkinson's diseases
1998	Robert Furchgott (USA), Ferid Murad (USA), and Louis Ignarro (USA)	discovery that nitric oxide (NO) acts as a key chemical messenger between cells
1999	Günter Blobel (Germany)	discovery that newly synthesized proteins get to their correct destination by being guided by specific peptide tags

[1] Nationality given is the citizenship of recipient at the time award was made.

Fields Medal

This international prize for achievement in the field of mathematics is awarded every four years by the International Mathematical Union.

Year	Winner(s)
1936	Lars Ahlfors (Finland); Jesse Douglas (USA)
1950*	Atle Selberg (USA); Laurent Schwartz (France)
1954	Kunihiko Kodaira (USA); Jean-Pierre Serre (France)
1958	Klaus Roth (UK); René Thom (France)
1962	Lars Hörmander (Sweden); John Milnor (USA)
1966	Michael Atiyah (UK); Paul J Cohen (USA); Alexander Grothendieck (France); Stephen Smale (USA)
1970	Alan Baker (UK); Heisuke Hironaka (USA); Sergei Novikov (USSR); John G Thompson (USA)
1974	Enrico Bombieri (Italy); David Mumford (USA)
1978	Pierre Deligne (Belgium); Charles Fefferman (USA); G A Margulis (USSR); Daniel Quillen (USA)
1982	Alain Connes (France); William Thurston (USA); S T Yau (USA)
1986	Simon Donaldson (UK); Gerd Faltings (West Germany); Michael Freedman (USA)
1990	Vladimir Drinfeld (USSR); Vaughan F R Jones (USA); Shigefumi Mori (Japan); Edward Witten (USA)
1994	L J Bourgain (USA/France); P-L Lions (France); J-C Yoccoz (France); E I Zelmanov (USA)
1998	Richard E Borcherds (UK); W Timothy Gowers (UK); Maxim Kontsevich (Russia); Curtis T McMullen (USA)

* The Fields Medal was not awarded during and shortly after World War II.

Chronology: Astronomy

c. 3500 BC The Grand Menhir of Locmariaquer is erected in Brittany, France. Set among other menhirs (standing stones) it is the largest in the world (20 m/66 ft high; 380 tonnes), and is probably used for astronomical observations.

c. 2800 BC The first (pre-megalithic) Stonehenge is built in England near Salisbury, Wiltshire. It is a Neolithic monument comprising a circular earthwork 97.5 m/320 ft in diameter with 56 small pits around the circumference (later known as the Aubrey holes). It is probably an astronomical observatory with religious functions; the motions of the Sun and Moon are followed with the aid of carefully aligned rocks.

c. 2700 BC A lunar calendar is developed in Mesopotamia in which new months begin at each new Moon. A year is 354 days long and the calendar is used primarily for administrative purposes.

2296 BC The Chinese record the earliest sighting of a comet.

1361 BC Chinese astronomers make the first recording of an eclipse of the Moon.

c. 1300 BC The Shang dynasty in China establishes the solar year at $365\frac{1}{4}$ days. The calendar consists of 12 months of 30 days each, with intercalary months added to adjust the lunar year to the solar.

1217 BC Chinese astronomers make the first recording of an eclipse of the Sun.

15 June 763 BC Assyrian archivists record an eclipse of the Sun. The same event is recorded in the Bible (Amos 8:9).

28 May 585 BC The Greek philosopher Thales of Miletus, pioneer of Greek rational thinking, correctly predicts the eclipse of the Sun.

c. 366 BC Greek mathematician and astronomer Eudoxus of Cnidus builds an observatory and constructs a model of 27 nested spheres to give the first systematic explanation of the motion of the Sun, Moon, and planets around the Earth.

352 BC Chinese astronomers make the earliest known record of a supernova.

c. 350 BC Aristotle defends the doctrine that the Earth is a sphere, in *De caelo/Concerning the Heavens,* and estimates its circumference to be about 400,000 stadia (one stadium varied from 154 m/505 ft to 215 m/705 ft). It is the first scientific attempt to estimate the circumference of the Earth.

240 BC Chinese astronomers make the first recorded sighting of Halley's Comet.

c. 200 BC The Greeks invent the astrolabe – the first scientific instrument. It is used for observing the positions and altitudes of stars.

c. 165 BC Chinese astronomers first observe and record sunspots. Continuous records of sunspots are kept by Imperial astronomers from 28 BC to AD 1638.

129 BC Greek scientist Hipparchus of Bithynia creates the first known star catalogue. It gives the latitude and longitude and brightness of nearly 850 stars and is later used by Ptolemy.

150 Egyptian astronomer Claudius Ptolemy publishes the work known as the *Almagest,* a highly influential astronomical textbook that outlines a theory of a geocentric (Earth-centred) universe based on years of observations.

516 The Indian astronomer and mathematician Aryabhata I produces his *Aryabhatiya,* a treatise on quadratic equations, the value of π, and other scientific problems, in which he adds tilted epicycles to the orbits of the planets to explain their movement.

772 Muslim astronomer Al-Fazārī translates the Indian astronomical compendium *Mahāsiddhānta/Treatise on Astronomy,* and begins the establishment of a uniquely Arabic astronomy.

800 The Peruvian city of Machu Picchu, built at this time, contains an astronomical altar, 'the hitching post of the Sun', which can be used to measure solar and lunar movements with great accuracy.

987 Toltec conquerors of the Central American Mayan city of Chichén Itzá construct monuments with ritual astronomical alignments to the rising and setting of the Sun and the sacred planet Venus.

1050 The astrolabe, a new device for making astronomical measurements and calculations, arrives in Europe from the East, where Muslim scientists developed it two centuries ago.

4 July 1054 A bright new star, visible in daylight, appears in the constellation Taurus. The supernova (which forms the Crab Nebula) is observed in China and Korea, and is recorded in rock paintings in southwestern America.

1066 The comet later known as Halley's Comet appears in the sky, and is taken as an omen by both the Norman and English sides before the Battle of Hastings. The victorious Normans record its appearance in the Bayeux Tapestry.

1091 The French-born Prior Walcher of Malvern Abbey, England, records his observations in Italy of an eclipse of the Moon. This is one of the earliest accurate western European observations of the phenomenon.

1424 Mongolian ruler and astronomer Ulugh Beg, Prince of Samarkand, builds a great observatory, including a 40 m/132 ft sextant, which enables extremely accurate measurements to be made, cataloguing over 1,000 stars.

1519 The conquistador Hernán Cortés sends the Mayan 'Dresden Codex' to Charles V of Spain – it demonstrates the elaborate Mayan calendar based on the movements of the planet Venus.

1543 Polish astronomer and priest Nicolaus Copernicus publishes *De revolutionibus orbium coelestium/On the Revolutions of the Celestial Sphere,* detailing his theory that the Earth and other planets orbit the Sun on circular paths. A copy of the book is brought to him on his deathbed.

1588 Giovanni Paolo Gallucci's *Theatrum mundi/Theatre of the World* features the first star chart marked with a celestial coordinate system.

1602 Danish astronomer Tycho Brahe's *Astronomia instauratae progymnasmata/Introducing Exercises toward a Restored Astronomy* is published posthumously, giving accurate positions for 777 fixed stars and a description of the 1572 supernova in Cassiopeia.

1603 German astronomer Johann Bayer publishes his *Uranometria* star atlas, the most detailed yet, including the 12 new southern constellations, and introducing the practice of giving the stars Greek identifiers.

1609 German astronomer Johannes Kepler publishes *Astronomia nova/New Astronomy,* which describes the orbit of Mars accurately. His first two laws of planetary motion state that all planets move in elliptical orbits around the Sun, and that they sweep out equal areas in equal times. Italian astronomer Galileo Galilei, having obtained a Dutch telescope, makes his own instruments, including one which magnifies objects 32 times. They are the first telescopes that can be used for astronomical observation.

1610 Italian astronomer Galileo Galilei publishes *Sidereus nuncius/The Starry Messenger,* revealing his telescopic discoveries, including the moons of Jupiter, the phases of Venus, sunspots, and the curious shape of Saturn.

1611 German astronomer Simon Marius is the first to observe the Andromeda Nebula. He has also discovered the four moons of Jupiter independently of Galileo, and names them Io, Europa, Ganymede, and Callisto.

1613 Convinced by his telescopic observations of the Solar System, Italian astronomer Galileo Galilei promotes the heliocentric system devised by Polish astronomer Copernicus.

1647 German astronomer Johannes Hevelius first charts the lunar surface accurately in his *Selenographia/Moon Map.* The work also describes his discovery of the Moon's libration in longitude, and detailed observations of the Sun.

1651 British scientist William Gilbert's book *A New Philosophy of Our Sublunar World* is published posthumously, proposing theories that the fixed stars are not all at the same distance from Earth, and that magnetism holds the planets in orbit around the Sun.

1676 Danish astronomer Ole Römer calculates the speed of light from the delay in the expected eclipses of Jupiter's satellites when the planet is farthest from Earth. He estimates the Sun's rays reach the Earth in 11 minutes.

1705 English astronomer Edmund Halley conjectures that a comet seen in 1682 was identical with comets observed in 1607, 1531, and earlier; he correctly predicts its return in 1758.

1728 English astronomer James Bradley discovers the aberration of starlight – the difference in the angle at which starlight arrives, depending on whether the Earth is moving away from or towards it.

1750 French astronomer Nicolas de Lacaille leads a French expedition to the Cape of Good Hope. Over four years, he records 10,000 southern stars, identifies new constellations, and draws up the first list of 'nebular stars'.

1755 In his *Allgemeine Naturgeschichte und Theorie des Himmels/Universal Natural History and Theory of the Heavens,* German philosopher Immanuel Kant proposes a theory for the formation of the Solar System from a primordial nebula, predicts the existence of Uranus, and proposes that our galaxy is just one of many in the universe.

1772 German astronomer Johan Elert Bode publicizes the Titius–Bode law (proposed in 1766 by Johann Titius) which states that the distances to the planets are proportional to the terms of the series 0, 3, 6, 12, 24, ...

13 March 1781 German-born English astronomer William Herschel discovers the planet Uranus.

1785 Herschel argues in his work *On the Construction of the Heavens* that the Milky Way galaxy is composed of individual stars and is not some luminous fluid.

1786 Herschel's *Catalogue of Nebulae* is published. It is a catalogue of nearly 2,500 nebulae.

1796 French astronomer Pierre-Simon Laplace, in *Exposition du système du monde/ Account of the System of the World,* enunciates the 'nebular hypothesis', that the Solar System formed from a cloud of gas; it forms the basis of modern theory.

1798 Laplace predicts the existence of black holes.

1800 Herschel discovers the existence of infrared solar rays.

1 January 1801 The Italian astronomer Giuseppe Piazzi discovers the first asteroid, Ceres.

1802 Herschel discovers that some stars revolve around others, forming binary pairs. He catalogues 848 of them.

11 October 1838 Using the method of parallax, German astronomer Friedrich Bessel calculates the star 61 Cygni to be 10.3 light years away from Earth. It is the first determination of the distance of a star other than the Sun.

1842 Bessel accurately explains that the wavy course of Sirius is due to the existence of a companion star – the first binary star to be discovered.

1842–1845 Irish astronomer William Parsons Rosse builds the 180-cm/72-in reflecting telescope Leviathan. Used to observe nebulae, its size is not exceeded until the 250-cm/100-in Mount Wilson Observatory telescope is built in 1917.

23 September 1846 German astronomer Johann Gottfried Galle discovers the planet Neptune on the basis of French astronomer Urbain Le Verrier's calculations of its position.

1862 US astronomer Alvan Clark observes the companion star of Sirius – the first white dwarf to be discovered.

1864 By examining their spectra, English astronomer William Huggins demonstrates that the Orion Nebula (and hence all nebulae) consists of gases, while the Andromeda Nebula is composed of stars and is therefore a galaxy.

1872 US astronomer Henry Draper develops astronomical spectral photography and takes the first photograph of the spectrum of a star – that of Vega.

1881 German-born US physicist Albert Michelson develops an interferometer to measure distances between stars. He later uses it to measure the speed of the Earth through the 'ether'.

1885–1890 British astronomer David Gill photographs over 450,000 stars of 11th magnitude or brighter in the southern hemisphere, in South Africa. The plates are catalogued by Dutch astronomer Jacobus Cornelius Kapteyn to produce the Cape Photographic Durchmusterung star catalogue in 1900.

1890 The first version of the Henry Draper Star Catalogue is published. Produced by astronomers at Harvard College Observatory, it lists the position, magnitude, and type of over 10,000 stars, and begins the alphabetical system of naming stars according to temperature. Subsequent editions increase the listing to 400,000 stars.

1905 US astronomer Percival Lowell, after a study of the gravitation of Uranus, predicts the existence of the planet Pluto.

1905–1907 Danish astronomer Ejnar Hertzsprung discovers that there is a relationship between the colour and absolute brightness of stars and classifies them according to this relationship. The relationship is used to determine the distances of stars and forms the basis of theories of stellar evolution.

1920 US physicist Albert Michelson, using a stellar interferometer, measures the diameter of the star Betelgeuse to be 386,160,000 km/241,350,000 mi, which is about 300 times the diameter of the Sun. It is the first time an accurate measurement of the size of a star other than the Sun has been made.

1924 US astronomer Edwin Hubble demonstrates that certain Cepheid variable stars are several hundred thousand light years away and thus outside the Milky Way galaxy. The nebulae they are found in are the first galaxies to be discovered that are proved to be independent of the Milky Way.

1925 English astrophysicist Arthur Eddington publishes *Internal Constitution of the Stars,* in which he shows that the luminosity of a star is a function of its mass.

1927 Belgian astronomer Georges Lemaître proposes that the universe was created by an explosion of energy and matter from a 'primaeval atom' – the beginning of the Big Bang theory. Hubble shows that galaxies are receding and that the further away they are, the faster they are receding.

1929 English philosopher Alfred North Whitehead publishes *Process and Reality: An Essay in Cosmology.* Hubble publishes Hubble's Law, which states that the ratio of the speed of a galaxy to its distance from Earth is a constant (now known as Hubble's constant).

18 February 1930 US astronomer Clyde Tombaugh, at the Lowell Observatory, Arizona, discovers the ninth planet, Pluto.

1931 US engineer Karl Jansky discovers that the interference in telephone communications is caused by radio emissions from the Milky Way. He thus begins the development of radio astronomy.

1932 US scientist Carl David Anderson, while analysing cosmic rays, discovers positive electrons ('positrons'), the first form of antimatter to be discovered.

1933 Eddington publishes *The Expanding Universe,* in which he lays out his theory that the universe is constantly increasing in size.

1942 US astronomer Grote Reber makes the first radio maps of the sky, locating individual radio sources.

1950 Dutch astronomer Jan Hendrik Oort proposes that comets originate in a vast cloud of bodies (the 'Oort cloud') that orbits the Sun at a distance of about one light year.

1951 US astronomer Gerard Kuiper proposes the existence of a ring of small, icy bodies orbiting the Sun beyond Pluto, thought to be the source of comets. They are discovered in the 1990s and it is named the Kuiper belt.

1963 Dutch-born US astronomer Maarten Schmidt discovers the first quasar (3C 273), an extraordinarily distant object brighter than the largest known galaxy yet with a star-like image.

1965 US astronomers Arno Penzias and Robert Wilson detect microwave background radiation in the universe and suggest that it is the residual radiation from the Big Bang.

7 July 1967 Irish astronomer Jocelyn Bell and English astronomer Anthony Hewish discover the first pulsar (announced in 1968). A new class of stars, they are later shown to be collapsed neutron stars emitting bursts of radio energy. The Crab Nebula supernova remnant is discovered to be a pulsar the following year.

1974 English physicist Stephen Hawking suggests that black holes emit subatomic particles until their energy is diminished to the point where they explode.

23 February 1987 Astronomers around the world observe a spectacular supernova in the Large Magellanic Cloud, the galaxy closest to ours, when a star (SN1987A) suddenly becomes a thousand times brighter than our own Sun. It is the first supernova visible to the naked eye since 1604.

1993 US astronomers identify part of the dark matter in the universe as stray planets and brown dwarfs. Known as MACHOs (massive astrophysical compact halo objects), they may constitute approximately half of the dark matter in the Milky Way's halo.

July 1995 US astronomers Alan Hale and Thomas Bopp discover the Hale-Bopp comet. The brightest periodic comet, its icy core is estimated to be 40 km/25 mi wide.

24 March 1996 Comet Hyakutake makes its closest approach, passing within 15.4 million km/9.5 million mi of Earth. It is the brightest comet for decades, with a tail extending over 12 degrees of the sky.

23 March 1997 The comet Hale–Bopp comes to within 196 million km/122 million mi of Earth, the closest since 2000 BC. NASA launches rockets to study the comet. Its icy nucleus is estimated to be 40 km/25 mi wide, making it at least ten times larger than that of Comet Hyakutake and twice the size of Comet Halley.

27 January 1998 Al Schultz of the Space Science Institute in Baltimore, Maryland, using the Hubble Space Telescope, announces the discovery of a giant planet, larger than the Sun, orbiting Proxima Centauri, the closest star to Earth. It is the first planet outside the Solar System to be directly observed.

4 July 1998 Astronomers from the University of Hawaii discover the first asteroid entirely within the Earth's orbit; it is 40 m/130 ft in diameter.

Chronology: Biology

c. 2650 BC Chinese emperor Huang Di begins the canon of internal medicine, with the text *Nei Jing/Inner Canon of Medicine,* which balances ideas of yin and yang. Most subsequent Chinese medical literature is founded on it. There is some evidence, however, suggesting that the *Nei Jing* may actually date from only the 3rd century BC.

c. 2650 BC The Egyptian physician and architect Imhotep is the first to attempt to find nonreligious causes of disease.

c. 2600 BC The Egyptians begin the art of mummification; internal organs are removed and preserved in jars containing a salt solution. The body is prepared with bitumen, which is thought to have medicinal properties.

c. 2500 BC The practice of acupuncture is developed in China.

c. 1600 BC The Edwin Smith papyrus is written. The first medical book, it contains clinical descriptions of the examination, diagnosis, and treatment of injuries, and reveals an accurate understanding of the workings of the heart, stomach, bowels, and larger blood vessels. The papyrus is named after US scientist Edwin Smith, a pioneer in the study of Egyptian science who acquired it in Luxor, Egypt, in 1862.

c. 1122 BC Smallpox is first described, in China. Pharaoh Ramses V, who dies in 1157 BC, is considered the first known victim of the disease.

c. 500 BC Greek physiologist Alcmaeon is the first person to dissect the human body for research purposes. He discovers the optic nerve, describes the difference between arteries and veins, and recognizes that the brain, which he describes in detail, is the source of intelligence. He also possibly practises vivisection.

c. 320 BC Greek philosopher Theophrastus begins the science of botany with his books *De causis plantarum/The Causes of Plants* and *De historia plantarum/The History of Plants.* In them he classifies 500 plants, develops a scientific terminology for describing biological structures, distinguishes between the internal organs and external tissues of plants, and gives the first clear account of plant sexual reproduction, including how to pollinate the date palm by hand.

c. 285 BC Herophilus, an anatomist working at Alexandria, dissects human bodies and compares them with large mammals. He distinguishes the cerebrum and cerebellum, establishes the brain as the seat of thought, writes treatises on the human eye and on general anatomy, and writes a handbook for midwives.

c. 255 BC The doctrine of the pulse, which emphasizes feeling the pulse as the most important aspect of diagnosis, and that a healthy life is achieved by a balance of yin and yang, is introduced in China. It will be compiled into the *Mo Jing* in about 300 AD by Wang Shu-he.

c. 90 BC The Roman scholar Marcus Terentius Varro writes that disease is caused by the entry of imperceptible particles into the body – the first enunciation of germ theory.

77 Pliny the Elder's *Historia Naturalis/Natural History* is completed. Divided into 37 books, it covers such topics as cosmology, astronomy, zoology, botany, agricultural techniques, medicine, drugs, minerals, and metals. The book brings together the scattered material of earlier writers and also makes original contributions, combining keen observation with absurd hearsay.

c. 400 The Graeco-Roman physician Caelius Aurelianus is practising. His *De morbis acutis et chronicis/ Concerning Acute and Chronic Illness,* a guide to acute and chronic diseases, becomes a highly respected text in the Middle Ages.

c. 501 The Indian medical manual *Susruta* is compiled. It becomes a standard text for Indian physicians.

800 Muslim scholar Al-Batrīq produces Arabic translations of major works by the Greek physicians Galen and Hippocrates; they will have a lasting effect on Arab medicine.

1127 Stephen of Pisa writes *Liber regius/Royal Book,* which translates the work of the 10th-century Persian physician 'Ali ibn al-'Abbas' (Haly Abbas), and introduces Arab and Greek medicine into the West.

1160 The Muslim scholar ibn-Rushd (Averroês) writes his great medical encyclopedia *Kitāb al-Kullīyāt fī-al-Tibb/Generalities of Medicine.*

1193 The Italian physician and scholar Burgundo of Pisa translates Galen's medical works from Greek into Latin, thus reintroducing much of Galen's thinking into western Europe.

1195 The physician Roger of Salerno, a teacher at the medical school there, writes *Practica chirurgiae/ Surgical Practice.* This is the earliest European textbook on surgery.

1248 Spanish-born Muslim Al-Baytār, 'chief of botanists' in Cairo, Egypt, writes *Kitāb al-jāmi/ Collection of Simple Drugs,* which lists 1,400 different remedies and is the largest and most popular Arab pharmacopoeia.

1257 The Italian physician Aldobrandon of Siena writes his treatise *Le régime du corps/The Bodily Regimen* on the need for good hygiene and diet, which is a new concept in western medicine.

1316 The Italian physician Mondino de Liuzzi conducts the first properly recorded dissection of a human corpse at Bologna University, Italy. His book *Anatomia* will become the standard work on anatomy for two centuries.

1472 Italian physician Giovanni Matteo Ferrari, writes his *Useful Repertory of the Precepts of Avicenna,* a commentary on the work of the great 11th century Arab physician Avicenna.

1478 The *De medicina/On Medicine* of classical physician Galen is produced in print for the first time, giving new currency to his theories.

1500 Swiss doctor and sow gelder Jacob Nufer performs the first recorded Caesarean operation on a living woman, helping his wife to give birth safely.

1530 A manual of dentistry is published at Leipzig, Germany – the first methodical approach to the subject.

1536 The Swiss physician Paracelsus (Theophrastus von Hohenheim) produces *Die grosse Wundartzney/Great Surgery Book,* a landmark break with Galenic medicine.

1540 Flemish anatomist Andreas Vesalius performs dissections on human cadavers at the University of Bologna. His discoveries contradict the writings of the ancient Greek physician Galen, until now the highest authority.

1542 Vesalius writes *De humani corporis fabrica/On the Fabric of the Human Body,* a highly illustrated, clearly written study of the human body, and effectively the beginning of the science of anatomy.

1546 Italian physician Girolamo Fracastoro publishes *De contagione et contagiosis morbis et curatione/On Contagion and the Cure of Contagious Disease,* in which he describes typhus for the first time, and also proposes that diseases are spread through microscopic bodies.

1563 Italian physician and anatomist Gabriele Falloppio invents the condom, made of pig intestine, as a means to prevent the spread of syphilis. He describes his design in *De morbo Gallico/On the French Disease.*

1599 The Italian naturalist Ulisse Aldrovandi publishes the first three volumes of his *Natural History,* methodically listing and describing bird species in the first serious zoological study.

1604 Italian surgeon Hieronymus Fabricius of Acquapendente publishes *De formata foetu/On the Formation of the Fetus,* the first important study of embryology, in which the placenta is identified for the first time.

1628 English anatomist William Harvey publishes his theory on the circulation of the blood in *Exercitatio anatomica de motu cordis et sanguinis/Anatomical Treatise on the Motion of the Heart and the Blood.*

1658 Dutch microscopist Jan Swammerdam records oval particles in the blood of frogs – the first observation of red blood cells.

1664 English physician Thomas Willis, professor of natural philosophy at Oxford, England, publishes *Anatome cerebri nervorumque descriptio et usus/Use and Description of the Anatomy of the Brain and Nerves,* the most complete description of the brain yet written. It identifies the arteries which supply blood to the base of the brain.

1665 English scientist Robert Hooke publishes *Micrographia,* the first serious scientific work on microscopy, describing the function of the microscope, and coining the name 'cells' to describe cavities he has found in the structure of cork.

1669 Dutch microscopist Jan Swammerdam writes a *History of Insects,* which lists the reproductive parts of insects and correctly describes metamorphosis. Italian anatomist Marcello Malpighi publishes a treatise on the anatomy and development of the silkworm, the first description of the anatomy of an invertebrate.

1674 Dutch microscopist Anton van Leeuwenhoek develops the single-lens microscope, and begins a series of important discoveries by observing protozoa.

March 1676 English physician Thomas Sydenham publishes *Observationes medicae/Medical Observations,* which will be a standard medical text for two centuries. In it, he analyses fevers and suggests cooling treatment for smallpox.

1682 English botanist Nehemiah Grew's *Anatomy of Plants,* identifies the stamens and pistils as male and female sex organs for the first time. English naturalist John Ray's *Methodus plantarum nova/New Method for Plants* is published, in which he makes a fundamental distinction between monocotyledons and dicotyledons.

1683 Dutch microscopist Anton van Leeuwenhoek is the first to observe bacteria.

1684 Van Leeuwenhoek first describes red blood cells accurately.

1704 Ray completes publication of his three-volume *Historia generalis plantarum/General Study of Plants,* a classification of over 18,000 different plant species.

1717 Lady Mary Wortley Montagu writes *Inoculation Against Smallpox,* reporting the method of immunization known in the East for centuries and introducing the practice of inoculation for smallpox into England; the inoculation of the Princess of Wales makes it fashionable.

1727 English botanist Stephen Hales's book *Vegetable Staticks* gives the first accurate scientific explanation of the nutrition of plants, and describes numerous experiments in plant physiology.

1734 French scientist René-Antoine Ferchault de Réaumur publishes *History of Insects,* a founding work of entomology.

1735 In his *Systema Naturae/System of Nature,* Swedish botanist Carolus Linnaeus introduces a system for classifying plants by genus and species – a taxonomy that will survive the upheavals of evolutionism and remains in use today.

1762 Swedish writer Nils von Rosenstein establishes the science of paediatrics with the publication of *The Diseases of Children and Their Remedies.*

1763 English clergyman Edmund Stone describes the effective treatment of fever using willow bark, from which the active ingredient of aspirin is later derived. French surgeon Claudius Aymand performs the first successful appendectomy, in Paris, France.

1766 Swiss biologist Albrecht von Haller shows that nerves stimulate muscles to contract, and that all nerves lead to the spinal column and brain. His work lays the foundation of modern neurology.

1767 Italian biologist Lazzaro Spallanzani disproves Georges Buffon's theories of spontaneous generation by preserving organic material in vials sealed by fusing the glass.

1791 Italian physiologist Luigi Galvani announces his observations on the muscular contraction of dead frogs, which he argues are caused electrically.

1796 English physician Edward Jenner performs the first vaccination against smallpox.

1797 French anatomist Georges Cuvier establishes the science of comparative anatomy with the publication of *Tableau élémentaire de l'histoire naturelle des animaux/An Elementary Natural History of Animals.*

1809 French biologist Jean-Baptiste de Lamarck publishes *Philosophie zoologique/Zoological Philosophy* in which he theorizes that organs improve with use and degenerate with disuse and that these environmentally adapted traits are inheritable.

1823 Italian botanist Giovanni Battista Amici proves the existence of sexual processes in flowering plants, by observing pollen approaching the plant ovary.

1827–1838 US ornithologist John James Audubon publishes the first volume of his multi-volume work *Birds of America.*

1828 Estonian embryologist Karl von Baer describes the notochord, the development of the neural folds into the nervous system, and the main brain vesicles in *Über die Entwicklungsgeschichte der Thiere/On the Development of Animals.* In doing so he establishes the science of comparative embryology. French physiologist Henri Dutrochet discovers osmosis – the passage of a solvent through a semipermeable membrane.

1831 Scottish botanist Robert Brown discovers the nucleus in plant cells.

27 December 1831–2 October 1836 The English naturalist Charles Darwin undertakes a five-year voyage, to South America and the Pacific, as naturalist on the *Beagle.* The voyage convinces him that species have evolved gradually but he waits over 20 years to publish his findings.

1833 US army surgeon William Beaumont publishes *Experiments and Observations on the Gastric Juice and the Physiology of Digestion* – the first detailed book on human digestion.

1836 German physiologist Theodor Schwann discovers pepsin, the first known animal enzyme to be isolated.

1837 French physiologist Henri Dutrochet establishes chlorophyll's essential role in photosynthesis.

1838 German botanist Matthias Jakob Schleiden publishes the article 'Contributions to phytogenesis', in which he recognizes that cells are the fundamental units of all plant life. He is thus the first to formulate cell theory.

1839 Schwann publishes *Microscopic Investigations on the Accordance in the Structure and Growth of Plants and Animals,* in which he argues that all animals and plants are composed of cells. Along with Matthias Schleiden, he thus founds modern cell theory.

1843 US physician and author Oliver Wendell Holmes maintains that puerperal fever (a disease common to women at childbirth) is contagious and recommends that attending doctors wash their hands and wear clean clothes.

1844 US dentist Horace Wells uses nitrous oxide as an anaesthetic to perform painless dental operations. In January 1845 he gives a demonstration in which the patient proves unresponsive.

1846 English palaeontologist Richard Owen publishes *Lectures on Comparative Anatomy and Physiology of the Vertebrate Animals,* one of the first textbooks on comparative vertebrate anatomy. 30 September: US dentist William Thomas Morton gives the first successful demonstration of ether as an anaesthetic during a dental operation to extract a tooth. He uses it in Boston, Massachusetts, on 16 October, to anaesthetize a patient while removing a tumour from his neck.

1847 Scottish physician James Simpson, in *Account of a New Anaesthetic Agent 1847,* first describes the use of chloroform as an anaesthetic. He uses it to assist women during childbirth.

1855 French physiologist Claude Bernard discovers that ductless glands produce hormones, which he calls 'internal secretions'. German biologist Rudolf Virchow discovers that 'every cell is derived from a cell' – the principle of cell division.

1856 French chemist and microbiologist Louis Pasteur establishes that microorganisms are responsible for fermentation, thus establishing the discipline of microbiology.

1858 British physician Henry Gray publishes *Anatomy of the Human Body, Descriptive and Surgical (Gray's Anatomy).* It remains the standard text in anatomy for over 100 years. Virchow publishes *Die Cellularpathologie in ihrer Begründung auf physiologische und pathologische Gewebenlehre/Cellular Pathology as Based upon Physiological and Pathological Histology.* In it he expands his ideas on the cell as the basis of life and disease, establishing cellular pathology as essential in understanding disease.

24 November 1859 Darwin publishes *On the Origin of Species by Natural Selection,* which expounds his theory of evolution by natural selection, and by implication denies the truth of biblical creation and God's hand in Nature. It sells out immediately and revolutionizes biology.

1861 Pasteur develops the germ theory of disease.

1863 French parasitologist Casimir-Joseph Davaine shows that anthrax is due to the presence of rodlike microorganisms in the blood. It is the first disease of animals and humans to be shown to be caused by a specific microorganism.

1865 Austrian monk and botanist Gregor Mendel publishes a paper in the *Proceedings* of the Natural Science Society of Brünn that outlines the fundamental laws of heredity. French physiologist Claude Bernard develops the concept of homeostasis when he notes that 'all the vital mechanisms, varied as they are, have only one object: that of preserving constant the conditions of life'.

1866 German embryologist Ernst Haeckel proposes a third category of living beings intermediate between plants and animals. Called Protista, it consists mostly of microscopic organisms such as protozoans, algae, and fungi.

1874 Austrian surgeon Theodor Billroth develops the study of the bacterial causes of fever associated with

wounds with the publication of *Untersuchungen über die Vegetationsformen von Coccobacteria septica/Investigations of the Vegetal Forms of Coccobacteria septica.*

26 October 1877 English surgeon Joseph Lister performs the first operation to repair a fractured kneecap. Conducted under antiseptic conditions, its success convinces other surgeons of the value of antisepsis.

1881 Billroth initiates modern abdominal surgery by removing the cancerous lower part of a patient's stomach. Cuban physician Carlos Juan Finlay discovers that the mosquito *Aêdes aegypti* is the carrier of yellow fever. His results are published in 1886 but his experiments are ignored until 1900. 5 May: Pasteur vaccinates sheep against anthrax. It is the first infectious disease to be treated effectively with an antibacterial vaccine, and his success lays the foundations of immunology.

1882 German chemist Emil Hermann Fischer shows that proteins are polymers, or large molecules, comprised of amino acids.

1883 German physiologist Paul Ehrlich publishes 'The requirement of the organism for oxygen', in which he shows that different tissues consume oxygen at different rates and that the rate of consumption can be used to measure biological activity.

6 July 1885 Pasteur develops a vaccine against rabies and uses it to save the life of a young boy, Joseph Meister, who has been bitten by a rabid dog.

1889 German physiologists Oskar Minkowski and Joseph von Mering remove the pancreas from a dog, which then develops diabetic symptoms. It leads them to conclude that the pancreas secretes an antidiabetic substance, which is now known as insulin.

1890 German bacteriologist Emil von Behring, along with Japanese bacteriologist Shibasaburo Kitazato, develop tetanus and diphtheria antitoxins, in Berlin, Germany. They inject minute amounts of the toxins into animals, which then produce the antitoxin.

1891 Ehrlich treats malaria with methylene blue. Its use marks the beginning of chemotherapy.

1897 British bacteriologist Ronald Ross discovers the malaria parasite in the gastrointestinal tract of the *Anopheles* mosquito, and realizes that the insect is responsible for the transmission of the disease. Dutch physician Christian Eijkman, working in the Dutch East Indies (now Indonesia), shows that a beriberi-like disease is produced in chickens fed on a diet of polished rice. Although he believes it is caused by a toxin produced by microorganisms, his work eventually leads to the discovery of vitamins.

1898 Martinus Willem Beijerinck identifies the first virus; it is the cause of tobacco mosaic disease.

1900 Dutch geneticist Hugo Marie de Vries, German botanist Carl Erich Correns, and Austrian botanist Erich Tschermak von Seysenegg, simultaneously and independently, rediscover Mendel's 1865 work on heredity. US army pathologist Walter Reed establishes that yellow fever is caused by the bite of an *Aêdes aegypti* mosquito infected with the yellow fever parasite. His discovery leads to the creation of a vaccine and makes possible the completion of the Panama Canal.

1901 Austrian immunologist Karl Landsteiner discovers the ABO blood group. Dutch physician Gerrit Grijns demonstrates that beriberi is caused by a nutritional deficiency of vitamin B_1. English biochemist Frederick Gowland Hopkins isolates the amino acid tryptophan.

1902 British physiologists William Bayliss and Ernest Starling discover that a substance, which they call secretin, is released into the bloodstream by cells in the duodenum. It stimulates the secretion of digestive juices by the pancreas and is the first hormone to be discovered.

1903 Dutch physiologist Willem Einthoven invents the string galvanometer (electrocardiograph), which measures and records the tiny electrical impulses produced by contractions of the heart muscle. He uses it to diagnose different types of heart disease.

1904 Spanish physiologist Santiago Ramón y Cajal demonstrates that the neuron is the basis of the nervous system.

1906 Russian botanist Mikhail Semyonovich Tsvet develops chromatography for separating plant pigments.

1910 US geneticist Thomas Hunt Morgan discovers that certain inherited characteristics of the fruit fly *Drosophila melanogaster* are sex linked. He later argues that because all sex-related characteristics are inherited together they are linearly arranged on the X-chromosome.

1912 Gowland Hopkins publishes the results of his experiments that prove that 'accessory substances' (vitamins) are essential for health and growth and that their absence may lead to diseases such as scurvy or beriberi. In the same year, Polish-born US biochemist Casimir Funk discovers that pigeons fed on rice polishings can be cured of beriberi, and suggests that the absence of a vital nitrogen-containing substance known as an amone causes such diseases. He calls these substances 'vitamines'.

1914 German biochemist Fritz Albert Lepmann explains the role of adenosine triphosphate (ATP) as the carrier of chemical energy from the oxidation of food to the energy consumption processes in the cells.

1919 Austrian zoologist Karl von Frisch discovers that bees communicate the location of nectar through wagging body movements and rhythmic dances.

1921 Canadian physiologists Frederick Banting, Charles Best, and John James MacLeod isolate insulin. A diabetic patient in Toronto, Canada, receives the first insulin injection.

1928 Scottish bacteriologist Alexander Fleming discovers penicillin when he notices that the mould *Penicillium notatum,* which has invaded a culture of staphylococci, inhibits the bacteria's growth.

1930 English geneticist Ronald Fisher publishes *The Genetical Theory of Natural Selection* in which he synthesizes Mendelian genetics and Darwinian evolution.

1935 Austrian zoologist Konrad Lorenz founds the discipline of ethology by describing the learning behaviour of young ducklings; visual and auditory stimuli from the parent object cause them to 'imprint' on the parent. German chemist Gerhard Domagk uses Prontosil to cure a streptococcal infection in his youngest daughter; this is the first use of a sulfa drug on a human.

1937 French microbiologist Max Theiler develops a vaccine against yellow fever; it is the first antiviral vaccine.

24 August 1940 Australian pathologist Howard Florey and German-born British biochemist Ernst Chain develop penicillin, in Oxford, England, for general clinical use as an antibiotic, announcing their results in *The Lancet.*

1943 US biologist Selman A Waksman discovers the antibiotic streptomycin, which is used as a treatment for tuberculosis; he coins the term 'antibiotic'.

1947 The poliomyelitis virus is isolated by US physician Jonas E Salk.

1948 US biologist Alfred Mirsky discovers ribonucleic acid (RNA) in chromosomes.

1952 British doctor Douglas Bevis develops amniocentesis, a diagnostic test on the fetus. English biophysicist Rosalind Franklin uses X-ray diffraction to study the structure of DNA. She suggests that its sugar-phosphate backbone is on the outside – an important clue that leads to the elucidation of the structure of DNA the following year.

25 April 1953 English molecular biologist Francis Crick and US biologist James Watson announce the discovery of the double helix structure of DNA, the basic material of heredity. They also theorize that if the strands are separated then each can form the template for the synthesis of an identical DNA molecule. It is perhaps the most important discovery in biology.

1955 Spanish-born US molecular biologist Severo Ochoa discovers polynucleotide phosphorylase, the enzyme responsible for the synthesis of RNA (ribonucleic acid), which allows him to synthesize RNA.

1955 US geneticists Joshua Lederberg and Norton Zinder discover that some viruses carry part of the chromosome of one bacterium to another; called transduction it becomes an important tool in genetics research.

1956 US biochemist Arthur Kornberg, using radioactively-tagged nucleotides, discovers that the bacteria *Escherichia coli* uses an enzyme, now known as DNA polymerase, to replicate DNA (deoxyribonucleic acid). It allows him to synthesize DNA in the test tube. US biologists Maklon Hoagland and Paul Zamecnik discover transfer RNA (ribonucleic acid) which transfers amino acids, the building blocks of proteins, to the correct site on the messenger RNA.

1957 Interferon, a natural protein that fights viruses, is discovered by Scottish virologist Alick Isaacs and Swiss virologist Jean Lindemann.

1959 French researcher Jérôme Lejeune discovers that Down's syndrome is due to an extra chromosome 21. It is the first chromosomal disorder discovered.

1961 English molecular biologist Francis Crick and South African chemist Sydney Brenner discover that each base triplet on the DNA strand codes for a specific amino acid in a protein molecule. French biochemists François Jacob and Jacques Monod discover messenger ribonucleic acid (mRNA), which transfers genetic information to the ribosomes, where proteins are synthesized.

3 December 1967 South African surgeon Christiaan Barnard performs the first heart transplant operation. The patient, Louis Washkansky, survives for 18 days.

1969 US geneticist Jonathan Beckwith and associates at the Harvard Medical School isolate a single gene for the first time.

1970 US biochemists Howard Temin and David Baltimore separately discover the enzyme reverse transcriptase, which allows some cancer viruses to transfer their RNA to the DNA of their hosts turning them cancerous – a reversal of the common pattern in which genetic information always passes from DNA to RNA. Indian-born US biochemist Har Gobind Khorana assembles an artificial yeast gene from its chemical components.

1972 English engineer Godfrey Hounsfield performs the first successful CAT (computerized axial tomography) scan, which provides cross-sectional X-rays of the human body. US microbiologist Daniel Nathans uses a restriction enzyme that splits DNA (deoxyribonucleic acid) molecules to produce a genetic map of the monkey virus (SV40), the simplest virus known to produce cancer; it is the first application of these enzymes to an understanding of the molecular basis of cancer.

1973 US biochemists Stanley Cohen and Herbert Boyer develop the technique of recombinant DNA (deoxyribonucleic acid). Strands of DNA are cut by restriction enzymes from one species and then inserted into the DNA of another; this marks the beginning of genetic engineering. US chemist and medical information scientist Paul Lauterbur obtains the first NMR (nuclear magnetic resonance) image, in Britain. Radio waves are beamed through a patient's body while subjected to a powerful magnetic field; an image is generated because different atoms absorb radio waves at different frequencies under the influence of a magnetic field.

1975 Argentine immunologist César Milstein and German immunologist Georges Köhler develop the first monoclonal antibodies – lymphocyte and myeloma tumour cell hybrids that are cloned to secrete unlimited amounts of specific antibodies – in Cambridge, England. British scientist Derek Brownhall produces the first clone of a rabbit, in Oxford, England. The gel-transfer hybridization technique for the detection of specific DNA (deoxyribonucleic acid) sequences is developed; it is a key development in genetic engineering.

1977 English biochemist Frederick Sanger describes the full sequence of 5,386 bases in the DNA (deoxyribonucleic acid) of virus *phi* X174 in Cambridge, England; the first sequencing of an entire genome. In-vitro fertilization (IVF) is developed by the British gynaecologists Patrick Steptoe and Robert Edwards. The first IVF baby is born in 1978.

1981 US geneticists J W Gordon and F H Ruddle of the University of Ohio inject genes from one animal into the fertilized egg of a mouse that develop into mice with the foreign gene in many of the cells; the gene is then passed on to their offspring creating permanently altered (transgenic) animals; it is the first transfer of a gene from one animal species to another.

1982 US researcher Stanley Prusiner discovers prions (proteinaceous infectious particles); they are responsible for several neurological diseases including 'mad cow disease' (first identified in 1986).

1983 US medical researcher Robert Gallo at the US National Cancer Institute, Maryland, and French medical researcher Luc Montagnier at the Pasteur Institute in Paris, France, isolate the virus thought to cause AIDS; it becomes known as the HIV virus (human immunodeficiency virus).

1988 Several US and European firms develop microcapsule reservoirs only 250 nanometres in diameter and made of a biodegradable polymer. They contain insulin which is delivered when the microcapsule dissolves; it constitutes a fundamentally new method of treating diabetes.

1990 A four-year-old girl in the USA has the gene for adenosine deaminase inserted into her DNA (deoxyribonucleic acid); she is the first human to receive gene therapy.

1992 US biologist Philip Leder receives a patent for the first genetically engineered animal, the oncomouse, which is sensitive to carcinogens.

1996 Two US dentists discover a new muscle running from the jaw to just behind the eye socket. About 3 cm/1 in long, it helps to support and raise the jaw.

1997 27 February: Scottish researcher Ian Wilmut of the Roslin Institute in Edinburgh, Scotland, announces that British geneticists have cloned an adult sheep. A cell was taken from the udder of the mother sheep and its DNA (deoxyribonucleic acid) combined with an unfertilized egg that had had its DNA removed. The fused cells were grown in the laboratory and then implanted into the uterus of a surrogate mother sheep. The resulting lamb, Dolly, came from an animal that was six years old. This is the first time cloning has been achieved using cells other than reproductive cells. The news is met with international calls to prevent the cloning of humans. August: US geneticist Craig Venter and colleagues publish the genome of the bacterium *Helicobacter pylori,* a bacterium that infects half the world's population and which is the leading cause of stomach ulcers. It is the sixth bacterium to have its genome published, but is clinically the most important. It has 1,603 putative genes, encoded in a single circular chromosome that is 1,667,867 nucleotide base-pairs of DNA long. Complete genomes are increasingly being published as gene-sequencing techniques improve. 18 September: US geneticist Bert Vogelstein and colleagues demonstrate that the p53 gene, which is activated by the presence of carcinogens, induces cells to commit suicide by stimulating them to produce large quantities of poisonous chemicals, called 'reactive oxygen species' (ROS). The cells literally poison themselves. It is perhaps the human body's most effective way of combating cancer. Many cancers consist of cells with a malfunctioning p53 gene. 2 October: UK scientists Moira Bruce and, independently, John Collinge and their colleagues show that the new variant form of the brain-wasting Creutzfeldt-Jakob disease (CJD) is the same disease as bovine spongiform encephalopathy (BSE or 'mad cow disease') in cows.

1998 22 April: Scientists at the Public Health Laboratory Service in London, England, report the discovery of a bacterium *Pseudonas aeruginosa* that is resistant to all known antibiotics. It causes a wide range of infections in people with impaired immune systems. 28 April: UK researchers at Guy's Hospital in London, England, announce the development of a vaccine against *Streptococcus mutans* the bacterium that causes tooth decay. They hope it will be incorporated into toothpaste to eradicate decay. 10 December: In a joint effort by scientists around the world, the first genetic blueprint for a whole multicellular animal is completed. The 97 million-letter code, which is published on the Internet, is for a tiny worm called *C elegans.* The study began 15 years ago and cost £30 million.

1999 Canadian researchers engineer an artificial chromosome that can be inserted into mammal cells and then transmitted from one generation to the next. The development has important implications for germ-line therapy where a defect is corrected in the gametes and the change passed to future generations.

Chronology: Chemistry

c. 100 BC The Romans produce mercury by heating the sulphide mineral cinnabar and condensing the vapours.

c. 100 Mary the Jewess, an alchemist, succeeds in her laboratory inventions with metals and lays the foundation for later work in chemistry. She creates the world's first distillation device, a double boiler, a way to capture vapours of metals, and a metal alloy called Mary's Black.

297 The tomb of a Chinese military commander of this date contains metal belt ornaments made of aluminium, not isolated by Western scientists until 1827.

c. 725 The Arab alchemist Abu Masa Dshaffar is working. According to some sources, he discovers methods for the manufacture of mineral acids and silver nitrate.

742 The most famous alchemist of the period, Jābir ibn-Hayyān of Kufa (Geber in Iraq) practises as a physician at Kufa, Persia. He becomes court physician to the caliph Harun ar-Rashid. He is said to have been the first person to manufacture mineral acids (nitric acid, etc.)

c. 1313 The German Grey Friar Berthold der Schwarze is traditionally credited with the independent invention of gunpowder. He is also said to have cast the first bronze cannon.

1509 German chemist Erasmus Eberner of Nuremberg discovers zinc (atomic number 30) at Rammelsburg, Germany, and identifies it as a new metal. Swiss alchemist Paracelsus names it 'zinken' in 1541.

1610 French chemist Jean Beguin publishes *Tyrocinium chymicum/An introduction to chemistry,* the first textbook on chemistry rather than alchemy.

1646 German chemist Johann Glauber publishes *Furni novi philosophici/New Philosophy of Furnaces,* outlining principles for industrial-scale manufacture of chemicals.

1665 Using vacuum pumps, Anglo-Irish chemist and physicist Robert Boyle proves that air is necessary for candles to burn and for animals to live.

1666 German chemist Otto Tachenius publishes his *Hippocrates chimicus/Chemistry of Hippocrates,* proposing that all salts arise from the combination of an acid with a base.

1669 The element phosphorus (atomic number 15) is isolated from urine by German alchemist Hennig Brand. He names it 'light-bearer' because it glows in the dark.

1670 Boyle discovers hydrogen (atomic number 1), produced when certain metals react with acid, although he does not identify it as an element.

1697 German chemist Georg Stahl theorizes that all combustible substances contain a material called phlogiston, which escapes during burning. The theory will be widely accepted for several decades.

1742 Swedish scientist Anders Celsius proposes an international fixed temperature scale to the Swedish Academy of Sciences, with 0° set as the boiling point of water, and 100° set as the freezing point.

1754 Scottish chemist Joseph Black discovers carbonic acid gas by heating limestone – the first time a gas other than common air has been positively identified.

1755 Black discovers carbon dioxide, which he calls 'fixed air'.

1766 English natural philosopher Henry Cavendish discovers the element hydrogen (atomic number 1) and delivers papers to the Royal Society, London, England, on the chemistry of gases.

1 November 1772 French chemist Antoine-Laurent Lavoisier demonstrates that when sulphur or phosphorus burns, the gain in weight is due to its combination with air.

1774 Lavoisier demonstrates the conservation of mass in chemical reactions. 1 August: English clergyman, chemist, and natural philosopher Joseph Priestley discovers the element oxygen (atomic number 8), which he calls 'dephlogisticated air'.

1777 Lavoisier shows that air is made up of a mixture of gases, and that one of them (oxygen) is the substance necessary for combustion and rusting to take place. He also assigns the name 'oxygen' to Priestley's dephlogisticated air. Swedish chemist Karl Wilhelm Scheele discovers that silver nitrate, when exposed to light, results in a blackening effect, an important discovery for the development of photography.

1784 Cavendish discovers that water is a compound of hydrogen and oxygen.

1785 English chemist Henry Cavendish discovers the composition of nitric acid. French chemist Claude-Louis Berthollet discovers the composition of ammonia and introduces chlorine ('eau de Javel') as a bleaching agent. Previously, the only bleaching agents were sunlight and urine.

1787 Lavoisier, with collaborators, publishes *Méthode de nomenclature chimie/Method of Chemical Nomenclature,* a system for naming chemicals based on scientific principles. It is the first modern chemical textbook.

1790 French chemist Nicolas Leblanc develops an inexpensive process for making sodium carbonate from sodium chloride (common salt). Sodium carbonate is used in making paper, soap, glass, and porcelain.

1799 French chemist Joseph-Louis Proust discovers that the elements in a compound are combined in definite proportions.

1801 English chemist and physicist John Dalton formulates the law of partial pressure in gases – Dalton's Law – that states that each component of a gas mixture produces the same pressure as if it occupied the container alone.

1802 French chemist and physicist Joseph-Louis Gay-Lussac demonstrates that all gases expand by the same fraction of their volume when subjected to the same temperature increase; it permits the establishment of a new temperature scale.

1803 Dalton formulates his atomic theory of matter: that all elements are made of minute indestructible particles, called atoms, that are all identical.

1808 English chemist Humphry Davy isolates the alkaline-earth metals magnesium (element no 12), calcium (element no 20), strontium (element no 38), and barium (element no 56). 31 December: Gay-Lussac, in *The Combination of Gases,* announces that gases combine chemically in simple proportions of volumes, and that the contraction in volume observed when they combine is a simple relation to the original volume of the gases – Gay-Lussac's Law.

1811 Swedish chemist Jöns Jakob Berzelius introduces the modern system of chemical symbols.

1828 German chemist Friedrich Wöhler synthesizes urea from ammonium cyanate. It is the first synthesis of an organic substance from an inorganic compound and signals the beginning of organic chemistry.

1837 German chemist Karl Friedrich Mohr enunciates the theory of conservation of energy.

1845 German chemist Hermann Kolbe synthesizes acetic acid from carbon disulphide – the first organic compound to be synthesized from inorganic materials.

1854 French scientist Henri-Etienne St Claire Deville develops a new process for making aluminium. Through the action of metallic sodium on aluminium chloride he produces marble-sized lumps of the metal and at the Paris Exposition in 1855 he exhibits a 7-kg/15-lb ingot. His process becomes the foundation of the aluminium industry.

1856 English chemist William Henry Perkin synthesizes the first artificial aniline dye ('mauve'). His commercial production of it the following year leads to the development of other dyes and lays the foundation of the synthetic organic chemical industry.

1858 German chemist Friedrich Kekulé publishes *Uber die Konstitution und die Metamorphosen der chemischen Verbindungen und über die chemische Natur des Kohlenstoffs/On the Constitution and Changes of Chemical Compounds and on the Chemical Nature of Carbon,* in which he shows that carbon atoms can link together to form long chains – the basis of organic molecules.

1860 German chemists Robert Wilhelm von Bunsen and Gustav Kirchhoff discover that each element emits a characteristic wavelength of light. It initiates spectrum analysis, a valuable tool for both chemist and astronomer. English chemists W H Perkin and B F Duppa synthesize glycine, the first amino acid to be manufactured.

1861 Belgian chemist Ernest Solvay patents a method for the economic production of sodium carbonate (washing soda) from sodium chloride, ammonia, and carbon dioxide. Used to make paper, glass, and bleach, and to treat water and refine petroleum, it is a key development in the Industrial Revolution. The first production plant is established in 1863.

1863 English chemist John Newlands devises the first periodic table.

1865 Kekulé suggests that the benzene molecule has a six-carbon ring structure. His theory refines current knowledge of organic chemistry.

1867 Swedish chemist Alfred Nobel patents dynamite. It consists of 75% nitroglycerin and 25% of an absorbent material known as ghur which makes the explosive safe and easy to handle.

1869 Based on the fact that the elements exhibit recurring patterns of properties when placed in order of increasing atomic weight, Russian chemist Dmitry Ivanovich Mendeleyev develops the periodic classification of the elements. He leaves gaps for elements yet to be discovered. US scientist John Wesley Hyatt, in an effort to find a substitute for the ivory in billiard balls invents (independently of Alexander Parkes) celluloid. The first artificial plastic, it can be produced cheaply in a variety of colours, is resistant to water, oil, and weak acids, and quickly finds use in making such things as combs, toys, and false teeth.

1874 Dutch chemist Jacobus Henricus van't Hoff and French chemist Joseph-Achile Le Bel, independently and simultaneously, develop stereochemistry by proposing a three-dimensional structure for organic molecules including a tetrahedron-shaped molecule for carbon.

1886 Swedish chemist Svante August Arrhenius introduces the idea that acids are substances that disassociate in water to yield hydrogen ions (H+) and that bases are substances that disassociate to yield hydroxide ions (OH–), thus explaining the properties of acids and bases through their ability to yield ions. US chemist Charles Martin Hall and French chemist Paul–Louis–Toussaint Héroult, working independently, each develop a method for the production of aluminium by the electrolysis of aluminium oxide. The process reduces the price of the metal dramatically and brings it into widespread use.

1894 Scottish chemist William Ramsay discovers argon (atomic no 18), the first inert gas.

1898 Ramsay and English chemist Morris William Travers discover the noble gases neon (element no 10), krypton (element no 36), and xenon (element no 54). French chemists Pierre and Marie Curie discover the radioactive elements radium (element no 88) and polonium (element no 84). Radium is discovered in pitchblende and is the first element to be discovered radiochemically.

1899 German chemist Emil Fischer postulates the 'lock and key' hypothesis to explain the specificity of enzyme action.

1905 US chemist Bertram Boltwood suggests that lead is the final decay product of uranium.

1906 British biochemists Arthur Harden and William Young discover catalysis among enzymes.

1909 Danish biochemist Søren Sørensen devises the pH scale for measuring acidity and alkalinity.

1913 English physicist Henry Moseley equates the atomic number of an atom with the positive charge on its nucleus, and shows that the characteristics of an element depend on its atomic number not its atomic weight. He draws up the periodic table, based on atomic numbers, that is in use today.

1914 Polish-born US biochemist Casimir Funk isolates vitamin B, a vital discovery in the treatment of beriberi.

1923 Danish chemist Johannes Brønsted and British chemist Thomas Martin Lowry simultaneously and independently introduce the idea that an acid tends to lose a proton and a base tends to gain a proton.

1925 Austrian physicist Wolfgang Pauli discovers the exclusion principle, which accounts for the chemical properties of the elements.

1926 German chemist Hermann Staudinger shows that plastics consist of small molecules (monomers) that form long chainlike structures (polymers) and that they do so through chemical interaction and not by simple aggregation.

1930 Swedish biochemist Arne Tiselius invents electrophoresis, a method of separating proteins in suspension based on their electrical charge.

1932 German-born British biochemist Hans Krebs discovers the urea cycle, in which ammonia is turned into urea in mammals.

1934 French physicists Frédéric and Irène Joliot-Curie bombard boron, aluminium, and magnesium with alpha particles and obtain radioactive isotopes of nitrogen, phosphorus, and aluminium – elements that are not normally radioactive. They are the first radioactive elements to be prepared artificially.

1937 German-born British biochemist Hans Krebs describes the citric acid cycle in cells, which converts sugars, fats, and proteins into carbon dioxide, water, and energy – the 'Krebs cycle'.

1944 British chemists Archer J P Martin and Richard L M Synge separate amino acids by using a solvent in a column of silica gel. The beginnings of partition chromatography, the technique leads to further advances in chemical, medical, and biological research. The role of deoxyribonucleic acid (DNA) in genetic inheritance is first demonstrated by US bacteriologist Oswald Avery, US biologist Colin MacLeod, and US biologist Maclyn McCarthy; it opens the door to the elucidation of the genetic code.

1946 US physicists Edward Mills Purcell and Felix Bloch independently discover nuclear magnetic resonance, which is used to study the structure of pure metals and composites.

1948 British biochemist Dorothy Hodgkin analyses the complex structure of vitamin B_{12} and makes the first X-ray photographs of it.

1951 US chemists Linus Pauling and Robert Corey establish the helical or spiral structure of proteins.

1954 Einsteinium and fermium are synthesized.

1955 Ilya Prigogine describes the thermodynamics of irreversible processes (the transformations of energy that take place in, for example, many reactions within living cells).

1962 Neil Bartlett prepares the first compound of an inert gas, xenon hexafluoroplatinate; it was previously believed that inert gases could not take part in a chemical reaction.

1965 Robert B Woodward synthesizes complex organic compounds.

1981 Quantum mechanics is applied to predict the course of chemical reactions by US chemist Roald Hoffmann and Kenichi Fukui of Japan.

1982 Element 109, unnilennium, is synthesized.

1983 US biochemist Kary Mullis invents the polymerase chain reaction (PCR); a method of multiplying genes or known sections of the DNA molecule a million times without the need for the living cell.

1985 Harold Kroto and David Walton at the University of Sussex, England, discover a new unusually stable elemental form of solid carbon made up of closed cages of 60 carbon atoms shaped liked soccer balls; they call them buckminsterfullerines or 'buckyballs'.

1988 Researchers at IBM's Almaden Research Center in San José, California, using a scanning tunnelling microscope, produce the first image of the ring structure of benzene, the simplest aromatic hydrocarbon. The image confirms the structure of the molecule envisioned by Frederick Kekulé in 1865.

1999 Russian scientists create element 114 by colliding isotopes calcium 48 and plutonium 44. Shortly afterwards US physicists create element 118, which decays into another new element, 116, by bombarding lead with krypton.

Chronology: Earth Science

c. 780 BC Chinese scholars make the first record of an earthquake.

c. 530 BC Pythagoras of Samos proposes the notion of a spherical Earth.

500 BC Greek traveller and geographer Hecataeus of Miletus, writes *Ges periodos/Tour Around the World,* a description of the geography and ethnography of Europe, northern Africa, and Asia – the first book on geography.

c. 295 BC Greek philosopher Theophrastus writes *De lapidibus/On Stones,* a classification of 70 different minerals. It is the oldest known work on rocks and minerals and is the best treatise on the subject for nearly 2,000 years.

c. 20 The Greek geographer Strabo's *Geography* is finished. A multi-volume geography of the world, it is the only extant work covering the history and geography of peoples and countries known to the Greeks and Romans.

114 A Chinese sculpture of this date shows an early form of compass – a polished magnetite spoon that spins to align with the Earth's magnetic field when placed on a smooth surface.

132 Chinese engineer Zhang Heng develops the first seismograph for determining the position of an earthquake's epicentre. It uses a series of balls suspended in the mouths of eight carved dragons. The balls that are dislodged indicate the direction of the earthquake centre.

1154 Al-Idrisi, geographer to Roger II of Sicily, produces a planisphere and writes *al-Kitāb al-Rujarī/Roger's Book,* the most thorough description of the world in medieval times.

1356 The influential geography text *The Travels of Sir John Mandeville* appears for the first time. Although wildly inaccurate, it will be a standard work for several centuries.

1492 German navigator Martin Behaim, with painter Georg Glockendon, constructs a terrestrial globe at Nuremberg, the earliest still in existence.

1537 Flemish cartographers Gemma Frisius and Gerardus Mercator collaborate to produce a celestial globe, complementary to their terrestrial globe of the previous year.

1544 German mineralogist Agricola (Georg Bauer) writes *De ortu et causis subterraneis/On Subterranean Origin and Causes,* a founding work in geology, identifying the erosive power of water, and the origin of mineral veins as depositions from solution.

1546 Mercator states that the Earth must have a magnetic pole separate from its 'true' pole, in order to explain the deviation of a compass needle from true North.

1568 Mercator devises the cylindrical map projection named after him, for use on sea charts. It enables navigators to plot straight-line courses without having to continually adjust their compass readings.

1576 English scientist Robert Norman discovers the magnetic 'dip' or inclination in a compass needle that is caused by the Earth's magnetic field not running exactly parallel to the surface.

1579 English cartographer Christopher Saxton publishes his *County Atlas of England and Wales,* the first detailed regional atlas anywhere.

1660 German scientist Otto von Guericke discovers the sudden drop in air pressure preceding a violent storm – a discovery that will revolutionize weather forecasting. He also suggests comets might return periodically, pre-empting Edmond Halley's work on this subject by 45 years.

1686 English scientist Edmond Halley publishes a map of the world showing the directions of prevailing winds in different regions – the first meteorological chart.

1749 French naturalist Georges-Louis de Buffon publishes the first book of of his 36-volume *Histoire naturelle, genérale et particulière/Natural History, General and Particular,* the first attempt to bring together the various fields of natural history.

June 1752 North American scientist and statesman Benjamin Franklin performs his most famous experiment, flying a kite during a thunderstorm and charging a Leyden jar to which it is connected. He thereby demonstrates the electrical nature of lightning.

1754 French mathematician Jean d'Alembert explains the precession of the equinoxes, and perturbations in the Earth's orbit, using the mathematics of calculus.

1774 French naturalist Nicolas Desmarest's essays on extinct volcanoes demonstrate the volcanic origin of basalt, disproving the theory that all rocks are formed by sedimentation from primeval seas.

1778 In *Epoques de la nature/Epochs of Nature,* French scientist George-Louis Leclerc, comte de Buffon, reconstructs geological history as a series of stages – the first to recognize such stages. It contradicts the doctrine that the Earth is only 6,000 years old.

1788 Scottish geologist James Hutton's paper *Theory of the Earth* expounds his uniformitarian theory of continual change in the Earth's geological features and marks a turning point in geology.

1801 French mineralogist René-Just Haüy publishes *Traité de minéralogie/Treatise on Mineralogy,* a theory of the crystal structure of minerals that establishes him as one of the founders of crystallography.

1806 British navy commander Francis Beaufort devises the Beaufort wind force scale.

1830–1833 Scottish geologist Charles Lyell publishes his three-volume work *Principles of Geology* in which he argues that geological formations are the result of presently observable processes acting over millions of years. It creates a new time frame for other sciences such as biology and palaeontology.

1842 British palaeontologist Richard Owen coins the term 'dinosaur' to describe the great reptiles that inhabited the Earth until 65 million years ago.

1845–1858 German naturalist and explorer Alexander von Humboldt lays the basis of modern geography with the publication of *Kosmos/Cosmos,* in which he arranges geographic knowledge in a systematic fashion.

1851 French scientist Jean-Bernard-Léon Foucault proves that the Earth rotates by using a pendulum 67 m/220 ft long (Foucault's pendulum), in Paris, France. The pendulum always swings in the same plane and the Earth rotates underneath it.

1854 English astronomer George Biddell Airy calculates the mass of the Earth by swinging a pendulum at the top and bottom of a deep coal mine and measuring the different gravitational effects on it.

28 August 1859 US engineer Edwin Drake drills the world's first oil well, at Titusville, Pennsylvania. Drilled to a depth of 21 m/69 ft, it produces 1,818 l/400 gal per day. His success, coinciding with a growing demand for oil products, especially kerosene, leads to further drilling.

7 December 1872–26 May 1876 The British ship *Challenger* undertakes the world's first major oceanographic survey. Under the command of the Scottish naturalist Wyville Thomson, it discovers hundreds of new marine animals, and finds that at 2,000 fathoms the temperature of the ocean is a constant 2.5°C/36.5°F.

1897 Norwegian meteorologist Vilhelm Bjerknes develops mathematical theorems applicable to the motions of large-scale air masses, which are essential to weather forecasting.

1904 In a lecture at St Louis, Missouri, French mathematician Jules-Henri Poincaré proposes a theory of relativity to explain Michelson and Morley's failed experiment to determine the velocity of the Earth.

1906 Irish geologist Richard Oldham proves that the Earth has a molten core, by studying seismic waves.

1907 US chemist Bertram Boltwood uses the ratio of lead and uranium in some rocks to determine their age. He estimates his samples to be 410 million to 2.2 billion years old.

1909 Croatian physicist Andrija Mohorovičić discovers the Mohorovičić discontinuity in the Earth's crust. Located about 30 km/18 mi below the surface, it forms the boundary between the crust and the mantle.

1912 German meteorologist Alfred Wegener suggests the idea of continental drift and proposes the existence of a supercontinent (Pangaea) in the distant past.

1913 French physicist Charles Fabry discovers the ozone layer in the upper atmosphere.

1914 German-born US geologist Beno Gutenberg discovers the discontinuity that marks the boundary between the Earth's lower mantle and outer core, about 2,800 km/1,750 mi below the surface.

1935 US seismologist Charles Richter introduces the Richter scale for measuring the magnitude of earthquakes at their epicentre.

1956 US geologists Bruce Heezen and William Ewing discover a global network of oceanic ridges and rifts 60,000 km/37,000 mi long that divide the Earth's surface into 'plates'.

May 1958 Using data from the *Explorer* rockets, US physicist James Van Allen discovers a belt of radiation around the Earth. Now known as the Van Allen belts (additional belts were discovered later), they consist of charged particles from the Sun trapped by the Earth's magnetic field.

1960 US geophysicist Harry Hess develops the theory of sea-floor spreading, in which molten material wells up along the mid-oceanic ridges forcing the sea floor to spread out from the ridges. The flow is thought to be the cause of continental drift.

1963 British geophysicists Fred Vine and Drummond Matthews analyse the magnetism of rocks in the Atlantic Ocean floor, which assume a magnetization aligned with the Earth's magnetic field at the time of their creation. It provides concrete evidence of sea-floor spreading.

1965 Canadian geologist John Tuzo Wilson publishes *A New Class of Faults and Their Bearing on Continental Drift,* in which he formulates the theory of plate tectonics to explain continental drift and seafloor spreading.

1969 The Joint Oceanographic Institutions Deep Earth Sampling (JOIDES) project begins. It makes boreholes in the ocean floor and confirms the theory of seafloor spreading and that the oceanic crust everywhere is less than 200 million years old.

1985 A British expedition in the Antarctic discovers a hole in the ozone layer above the South Pole.

1987 At a conference in Montréal, Canada, an international agreement, the Montréal Protocol, is reached to limit the use of ozone-depleting chlorofluorocarbons (CFCs) by 50% by the end of the century; the agreement is later condemned by environmentalists as 'too little, too late'.

1991 A borehole in the Kola Peninsula in Arctic Russia, begun in the 1970s, reaches a depth of 12,261 m/ 40,240 ft (where the temperature is found to be 210°C/410°F).

1996 US geophysicists discover that the Earth's core spins slightly faster than the rest of the planet.

1999 A NASA report revealed that the Arctic is losing 2.8% of its ice per decade. This accounts to 34,000 km/21,000 mi per year.

Chronology: Engineering and Technology

c. 3000 BC The abacus, which uses rods and beads for making calculations, is developed in the Middle East and adopted throughout the Mediterranean. A form of the abacus is also used in China at this time.

c. 230 BC Copper-lined pottery jars, with asphalt plugs, containing metal rods – the first electric battery – are used in Baghdad to coat objects with thin layers of gold or silver – the first example of electroplating.

83 The first compass is described in a Chinese book, the *Louen Heng/Discourses Weighed in the Balance*. It consists of a spoon-shaped piece of magnetite which spins on a bronze plate, the handle of the spoon pointing north. It is derived from a divining board – where objects are scattered on a platter and the direction of their pointing is found significant – and is not likely to have been used for navigation.

100 Indian metallurgists invent cast steel. The proportion of carbon within the steel is tightly controlled at less than 1.7% of the total.

c. 270 The Chinese invent gunpowder, a mixture of saltpetre, sulphur, and charcoal. At first, it appears to have been used only for fireworks.

1440 German craftsman Johann Gutenberg of Mainz, Germany, is the first European to develop a method of printing by movable metal type, improving on the current Chinese and Korean methods.

1454 Gutenberg produces the first printed calendar, in Mainz, Germany.

1502 Spanish printer Juan Pablos sets up a printing press in Mexico and produces the first printed book in the Americas, *Christian Doctrine in the Mexican and Castilian Language*.

1640 The Marquis of Worcester uses the expansion of bursts of steam to turn a bladed wheel – the first working 'steam engine' of the modern world.

1674 Dutch scientist and instrumentmaker Christiaan Huygens makes a watch using a balance wheel controlled by the oscillations of a spring to keep time.

1712 The first recorded practical steam-engine to use a piston and cylinder, constructed by English inventor Thomas Newcomen, is installed at Dudley Castle, near Wolverhampton, England, where it is used for pumping out underground mineworkings.

26 May 1733 English inventor John Kay patents his flying shuttle, a loom shuttle which can be automatically shot across the weave and retrieved by an attached thread. The invention cuts the workpower needed for a loom by one third.

1740 English clockmaker Benjamin Huntsman rediscovers the principle of producing steel in a crucible. Huntsman's Sheffield steel is far superior to any other being made.

1758 English engineer John Wilkinson installs the first blast furnace at his works in Bilston, Staffordshire, England.

1764 English inventor James Hargreaves invents the spinning jenny, which allows one individual to spin several threads simultaneously.

1769 English inventor Richard Arkwright patents a spinning machine (or 'water frame' because it operates by water) that produces cotton yarn suitable for warp; it is one of the key inventions of Britain's Industrial Revolution.

1781 Scottish engineer James Watt discovers how to convert the up-and-down motion of his steam engine into rotary motion which can then turn a shaft.

1782 Watt patents the double-acting steam engine, which provides power on both the upstroke and the downstroke of the piston.

1783 English inventor Henry Cort develops a rolling mill which makes the production of iron cheaper and easier by making hammering unnecessary.

1784 American scientist and statesman Benjamin Franklin invents glasses with bifocal lenses. English iron manufacturer Henry Cort discovers the 'puddling process' of converting pig iron into wrought iron by stirring to burn off impurities. It revolutionizes the manufacture of iron, production of which quadruples over the next 20 years. Swiss inventor Aimé Argand invents an oil-burner consisting of a cylindrical wick, two concentric metal tubes to provide air, and a glass chimney to increase the draught. It gives a light ten times brighter than previous lamps and the principle is later used in gas-burners. US engineer Oliver Evans invents an automated process for grinding grain and sifting flour; it marks the beginning of automation in America.

1795 English inventor Joseph Bramah invents a hydraulic press capable of exerting a force of several thousand tonnes.

1807 German promoter Frederick Albert Winsor's National Light and Heat Company lights one side of Pall Mall, London, England, with gas lamps – the first street-lighting in the world.

1816 Scottish clergyman Robert Stirling patents the Stirling hot-air engine. It is powered by the expansion and displacement of air inside an externally heated cylinder. It is forgotten until the Dutch company Philips becomes interested in it in the 1970s.

1834 English mathematician William George Horner develops the zoetrope, a motion picture device that is an improvement over the phenakistoscope. It consists of two discs with images on one side observed through slits on the other.

1836 Swedish engineer John Ericsson patents a screw propeller. Other screw propellers are patented about this time by British engineer Francis Pettit Smith (1836), Austrian engineer Joseph Ressel (1832), Scottish engineer Robert Wilson (1832), and US engineer John Stevens (1826).

1837 French engineer Benoît Fourneyron builds a water turbine which rotates at 2,300 revolutions per minute and generates 60 horsepower. Weighing only 18 kg/40 lb, and with a wheel only 0.3 m/1.0 ft in diameter it is far more productive than the waterwheel and is used to power factories, especially the textile industry, in Europe and the USA.

1841 English mechanical engineer Joseph Whitworth standardizes the size of threads on screws, which becomes internationally accepted. German chemist Robert Wilhelm von Bunsen invents the carbon–zinc battery.

10 September 1846 US inventor Elias Howe patents a practical sewing machine; it revolutionizes garment manufacture in both the factory and home.

1852 US inventor and machine-shop owner Elisha Otis installs, in a factory in Albany, New York, a freight lift equipped with an automatic safety device that prevents it from falling if the lifting chain or rope breaks. This leads to the passenger elevator, making the building of skyscrapers more practical. The first permanent Otis and Son elevator is installed in the Haughwort Department Store in New York, in 1857.

1856 English inventor Henry Bessemer obtains a patent for the Bessemer converter which converts cast iron into steel by injecting air into molten iron to remove carbon and increase the temperature of the molten mass. It allows iron to be poured and thus shaped and brings down prices.

16 August 1858 Queen Victoria of Britain and US president James Buchanan are the first to exchange messages on the first successful Atlantic telegraph cable laid between Valentia, Ireland, and Newfoundland, Canada. The cable lasts for only 27 days.

1859 Belgian inventor Etienne Lenoir builds the first internal combustion engine in Paris, France. Operating on coal gas it has only a 4% efficiency.

1861 German engineer Nikolaus August Otto constructs an internal combustion engine that runs on gasoline.

1865 Swedish inventor Alfred Nobel invents the blasting cap. Used to detonate nitroglycerine safely and dependably, it expands the use of explosives in industry.

10 March 1876 Scottish-born US scientist Alexander Graham Bell becomes the first person ever to transmit speech from one point to another by electrical means.

21 October 1879 US inventor Thomas Edison demonstrates his carbon-filament incandescent lamp light. He lights his Menlo Park power station with 30 lamps that burn for two days; later filaments burn for several hundred hours. Each light can be turned on or off separately in the first demonstration of parallel circuit.

1884 German-born US inventor Ottmar Mergenthaler patents the first Linotype typesetting machine. Characters are cast as metal type in complete lines rather than as individual letters as in a monotype machine.

1888 Serbian-born US inventor Nikola Tesla invents the first alternating current (AC) electric motor, which serves as the model for most modern electric motors. He sells the patent to George Westinghouse, who manufactures the motors in competition with Edison's direct current (DC) electric generators.

1890 US inventor and statistician Herman Hollerith uses punched cards to automate counting the US census. The holes, which represent numerical data, are sorted and tabulated by an electric machine, the forerunner of modern computers. In 1896 Hollerith forms the Tabulating Machine Company, which later changes its name to International Business Machines (IBM).

1892 German engineer Rudolf Diesel patents the diesel engine, a new type of internal combustion engine which runs on a fuel cheaper than petrol and which, because ignition of the fuel is achieved by compression rather than electric spark, is simpler in construction.

1897 German physicist Karl Ferdinand Braun improves the cathode-ray tube. By varying the voltage, he can control the narrow beam of electrons. His 'Braun tube' is the forerunner of television tubes, radar screens, and oscilloscopes.

1917 The US inventor Edwin Armstrong invents the superheterodyne radio circuit. It allows easy tuning of weak radio waves, which it also amplifies. Its design becomes the basis of radar, television, and all amplitude modulation (AM) radios.

1921 US physicist Albert Hull invents the magnetron, an oscillator that generates microwaves.

1922 Italian physicist Guglielmo Marconi suggests that radio waves may be used to detect moving objects. The US Naval Research Laboratory tests the idea and detects a ship moving between the receiver and transmitter. It is the first example of a sophisticated radar system.

1923 The Russian-born US engineer Vladimir Zworykin develops the iconoscope in the USA, an image-scanner that can produce electronic signals for reconstitution on the screen of a cathode-ray tube – the basis of television.

1924 Zworykin patents the kinescope television receiver. It develops into the modern television picture tube. Scottish engineer John Logie Baird produces televised images in outline.

1930 US electrical engineer Vannevar Bush builds the differential analyser. The first analogue computer, it is used to solve differential equations. It is the forerunner of modern computers.

1933 German engineer Ernst August Friedrich Ruska builds the first electron microscope; it has a magnification power of 12,000.

12 April 1937 English engineer Frank Whittle tests the first prototype jet engine. A similar engine is developed in Germany at the same time.

1938 A scanning electron microscope is demonstrated by German physicist Manfred von Ardenne. German inventor Konrad Zuse constructs the first binary calculator using a binary code (Boolean algebra); it is the first working computer.

1943 French oceanographer Jacques Cousteau invents the aqualung (or self-contained underwater breathing apparatus, 'scuba'), the first fully automatic compressed-air breathing apparatus. It allows him to dive to a depth of 64 m/210 ft.

1944 US mathematician Howard Aitken builds the Harvard University Mark I, or Automatic Sequence Controlled Calculator. The first programme-controlled computer, it is 15 m/50 ft long and 2.4 m/8 ft high, and its operations are controlled by a sequence of instruction codes on punched paper that operate electromechanical switches. Simple multiplication takes 4 sec and division 11 sec.

1946 ENIAC (acronym for 'Electronic Numerical Integrator, Analyser, and Calculator'), the first general purpose, fully electronic digital computer, is completed at the University of Pennsylvania for use in military research. It uses 18,000 vacuum tubes instead of mechanical relays, and can make 4,500 calculations a second. It is 24 m/80 ft long and is built by electrical engineers John Presper Eckert and John Mauchly, with input from John Atanasoff.

1947 US-Hungarian mathematician John Von Neumann introduces the idea of a stored-program computer, in which both instruction codes and data are stored.

1948 US physicists John Bardeen, William Bradley Shockley and Walter Brattain develop the transistor in research at Bell Telephone Laboratories in the USA. A solid-state mechanism for generating, amplifying, and controlling electrical impulses, it revolutionizes the electronics industry by enabling the miniaturization of computers, radios and televisions, as well as the development of guided missiles.

1949 BINAC (acronym for binary automatic computer) is built by US scientists John W Mauchly and John Presper Eckert. It is the first electronic stored-program computer to store data on magnetic tape.

1955 English radio astronomer Martin Ryle builds the first radio interferometer. Consisting of three antennae spaced 1.6 km/1 mi apart, it increases the resolution of radio telescopes, permitting the diameter of a radio source to be determined, or two closely spaced sources to be separated.

1973 German physicists Hans Dehmelt, Philip Ekstron, and David Wineland invent the Penning trap; an electron-capturing device that can hold a single electron in place for months at a time.

1986 German physicist Johannes Bednorz and Swiss physicist Karl Alex Müller announce the discovery of a superconducting ceramic material in which superconductivity occurs at a much higher temperature (30 K) than hitherto known, increasing the potential for use of superconductivity for more energy-efficient motors and computers. They receive the Nobel Prize for Physics – in record time – for their discovery.

14 July 1989 The LEP (Large Electron Positron Collider) is inaugurated at the CERN research centre in Switzerland; the new accelerator has a circumference of 27 km/16.8 mi and is the largest scientific apparatus in the world.

1990 The British company Imperial Chemical Industries (ICI) develops the first practical biodegradable plastic, Biopal.

1991 The US General Instrument Corporation develops the first digital high-definition television (HDTV) prototype.

1995 The US company Ultralife introduces the first rechargeable battery made from lightweight solid materials.

1999 US scientists succeed in transforming a diamond into metal, using a very powerful laser to compress it. The WHO announces that it is organizing a large study to compare the mobile phone use of 3,000 mobile phone users with brain tumours with the usage by a cancer-free control group. The $6 million study will be partly financed by mobile phone companies.

Chronology: Mathematics

c. 30000 BC Palaeolithic peoples record tallies on bone in central Europe and France; one wolf bone has 55 cuts arranged in groups of five – the earliest counting system.

c. 3400 BC The first symbols for numbers, simple straight lines, are used in Egypt.

c. 3000 BC The Sumerians of Babylon develop a sexagesimal (based on 60) numbering system. Used for recording financial transactions, the order of the numbers determines their relative, or unit value (place-value), although no zero value is used. It continues to be used for mathematics and astronomy until the 17th century AD, and is still used for measuring angles and time.

876 BC The Hindus in India invent a symbol for zero – one of the greatest inventions in mathematics.

530 BC Pythagoras of Samos, scientist and philosopher, moves to Croton and starts researching and teaching theories of mathematics, geometry, music, and reincarnation. A mystic as well as a mathematician, he argues that the key to the universe lies in numbers, while preaching immortality and the transmigration of souls. He founds a brotherhood in Croton which is to remain influential for several generations. His work leads to a number of important results, including Pythagoras' theorem of right-angled triangles and the discovery of irrational numbers (those that cannot be represented by fractions).

c. 360 BC Greek mathematician and astronomer Eudoxus of Cnidus develops the theory of proportion (dealing with irrational numbers), and the method of exhaustion (for calculating the area bounded by a curve) in mathematics.

c. 300 BC Alexandrian mathematician Euclid sets out the laws of geometry in his *Stoicheion/Elements;* it remains a standard text for 2,000 years. He also sets out the laws of reflection in *Catoptrics.*

c. 250 BC Greek mathematician and inventor Archimedes, in his *On the Sphere and the Cylinder,* provides the formulae for finding the volume of a sphere and a cylinder; in *Measurement of the Circle* he arrives at an approximation of the value of pi; in *The Sand Reckoner* he creates a place-value system of notation for Greek mathematics.

c. 230 BC Alexandrian mathematician Apollonius of Perga, writes *Conics,* a systematic treatise on the principles of conics in which he introduces the terms, parabola, ellipse, and hyperbola. Greek scholar Eratosthenes of Cyrene develops a method of finding all prime numbers. Known as the sieve of Eratosthenes it

involves striking out the number 1 and every *n*th number following the number *n*. Only prime numbers then remain.

c. 190 BC Chinese mathematicians use powers of 10 to express magnitudes.

200 Greek astronomer and mathematician Claudius Ptolemy produces many important geometrical results with applications in astronomy.

1175 Arabic numerals are introduced into Europe with Gerard of Cremona's translation of the Egyptian astronomer Ptolemy's astronomical work the *Almagest.*

1202 Italian mathematician Fibonacci writes *Liber abaci/The Book of the Abacus,* which introduces the famous sequence of numbers now called the Fibonacci sequence.

1225 Fibonacci writes *Liber quadratorum/The Book of the Square,* the first major Western advance in arithmetic since the work of Diophantus a thousand years earlier.

1335 The English abbot of St Albans Richard of Wallingford writes *Quadripartitum de sinibus demonstratis,* the first original Latin treatise on trigonometry.

1591 The French mathematician François Viète writes *In artem analyticam isagoge/Introduction to the Analytical Arts,* in which he uses letters of the alphabet (x and y are now standard) to represent unknown quantities. Before this, equations had been written out in long descriptive sentences.

1614 Scottish mathematician John Napier invents logarithms, a method for doing difficult calculations quickly. His results are published in *Mirifici logarithmorum canonis descriptio/Description of the Marvellous Rule of Logarithms.*

1617 Napier devises a system of numbered sticks, called Napier's bones, to aid complex calculations. He explains their function in his last work *Rabdologiae/Study of Divining Rods.*

1622 English mathematician William Oughtred invents an early form of circular slide rule, adapting the principle behind Napier's 'bones'.

1642 French mathematician Blaise Pascal, aged only 19, builds an adding machine to help his father, the Intendant of Rouen, with tax calculations.

1653 Pascal publishes his 'triangle' of numbers. This has many applications in arithmetic, algebra, and combinatorics (the study of counting combinations).

1657 French mathematician Pierre de Fermat claims to have proved a certain theorem, but leaves no details of his proof. Known as Fermat's last theorem, it is finally proved by US mathematician Andrew Wiles in 1994.

1666 In order to calculate the Moon's orbit accurately, English physicist Isaac Newton develops a new type of mathematics, calculus or 'fluxions', to add infinitesimally small elements of the orbit together.

1669 English mathematician John Wallis publishes his *Mechanica/Mechanics*, a detailed mathematical study of mechanics.

1673 German mathematician Gottfried von Leibniz presents a calculating machine to the Royal Society. It is the most advanced yet, capable of multiplication, division, and extracting roots.

1679 Leibniz introduces binary arithmetic, in which only two symbols are used to represent all numbers. It will eventually pave the way for computers.

1684 Leibniz invents the differential calculus, a fundamental tool in studying rates of change.

1687 English mathematician Isaac Newton publishes *Philosophiae naturalis principia mathematica/The Mathematical Principles of Natural Philosophy,* his most important work. It presents his theories of motion, gravity, and mechanics, which form the basis of much of modern physics.

1707 French mathematician Abraham de Moivre uses trigonometric functions to understand complex numbers for the first time.

1713 Swiss mathematician Jacques Bernoulli's book *Ars conjectandi/The Art of Conjecture* is the first to deal with probability.

1715 English mathematician Brook Taylor publishes *Methodus incrementorum directa et inversa/Direct and Indirect Methods of Incrementation,* an important contribution to Isaac Newton's calculus.

1718 Bernoulli's work on the calculus of variations (the study of functions that are close to their maximum and minimum values) is published posthumously.

1722 De Moivre proposes an equation that is fundamental to the development of complex numbers.

1733 De Moivre describes the normal distribution curve.

1746 D'Alembert develops the theory of complex numbers.

1748 Swiss mathematician Leonhard Euler introduces a formula linking the value of pi to the square root of –1.

c. 1750 French mathematician Jean d'Alembert works with other mathematicians, including Euler, Lagrange, and Laplace, on the 'three body problem', applying calculus to problems of celestial mechanics.

1763 The Reverend Thomas Bayes, the English mathematician and theologian, publishes 'An Essay Towards Solving a Problem in the Doctrine of Chances'. This includes Bayes' Theorem, which is an important theorem in statistics.

1797 The French mathematician Joseph-Louis Lagrange publishes *Théorie des fonctions analytiques/Theory of Analytical Functions,* which introduces the modern notation for derivatives.

1799 The German mathematician Karl Friedrich Gauss proves the fundamental theorem of algebra: that every algebraic equation has as many solutions as the exponent of the highest term.

1799–1825 French mathematician and physicist Pierre-Simon Laplace publishes the five-volume *Traité de mécanique céleste/Celestial Mechanics,* which extends and corrects Isaac Newton's theories of the Solar System.

1801 Gauss publishes *Disquisitiones Arithmeticae/Discourses on Arithmetic,* which deals with relationships and properties of integers and leads to the modern theory of algebraic equations.

c. 1820 Gauss introduces the normal distribution curve ('Gaussian distribution') – a basic statistical tool.

1822 French mathematician Augustin-Louis Cauchy formulates the basic mathematical theory of elasticity; he defines stress as the load per unit area of the cross-section of a material. French mathematician Jean-Baptiste-Joseph Fourier publishes *Théorie analytique de la chaleur/Analytical theory of heat,* introducing a technique now known as Fourier analysis, which has widespread applications in mathematics, physics, and engineering.

1823 English mathematician Charles Babbage begins construction of the 'difference' engine, a machine for calculating logarithms and trigonometric functions.

1824 Norwegian mathematician Niels Henrik Abel proves that equations involving powers of x greater than four cannot be solved using a standard formula like that used for quadratic equations.

1827 French physicist André Ampère publishes *Mémoirs sur la théorie mathématique des phénomènes electrodynamiques uniquement déducte de l'expérience,* in which he formulates the mathematical laws governing electric currents and magnetic fields. It lays the foundation for electromagnetic theory. Gauss introduces the subject of differential geometry that describes features of surfaces by analysing curves that lie on it – the intrinsic-surface theory.

1829 French mathematician Evariste Galois introduces the theory of groups – collections whose members obey simple rules of addition and multiplication but which are necessary for solving higher algebraic equations. Russian mathematician Nikolay Ivanovich Lobachevsky develops hyperbolic geometry, in which a plane is regarded as part of a hyperbolic surface shaped like a saddle. It is the beginning of non-Euclidean geometry.

1835 Belgian statistician Adolphe Quetelet publishes *Sur l'homme et le développement de ses facultés/A treatise on Man and the Development of his Faculties,* in which he presents the idea of the 'average man' in whom measurements of various traits are normally distributed around a central value.

1836 French mathematician Jean-Victor Poncelet publishes *Cours de mécanique appliquée aux machines/A Course in Mechanics Applied to Machines;* it introduces the use of mathematics to machine design.

1837 French mathematician Siméon-Denis Poisson publishes *Recherches sur la probabilité des judgements/Researches on the Probabilities of Opinions,* in which he establishes the rules of probability and describes the Poisson distribution.

1843 Irish mathematician William Rowan Hamilton invents quaternions, which make possible the application of arithmetic to three-dimensional objects.

1845 English mathematician Arthur Cayley publishes *Theory of Linear Transformations,* which lays the foundation of the school of pure mathematics. French mathematician Baron Augustine-Louis Cauchy proves the fundamental theorem of group theory, subsequently known as Cauchy's theorem.

1847 The English mathematician George Boole publishes *The Mathematical Analysis of Logic,* in which he shows that the rules of logic can be treated mathematically. Boole's work lays the foundation of computer logic.

1872 German mathematician (Julius Wilhelm) Richard Dedekind demonstrates how irrational numbers (those that cannot be written as a fraction) may be defined formally.

1874 German mathematician Georg Cantor is the first person rigorously to describe the notion of infinity.

1881 English mathematician John Venn introduces the idea of using pictures of circles to represents sets, subsequently known as Venn diagrams.

1882 German mathematician Ferdinand Lindemann proves π is a transcendental number.

1888 German mathematician Richard Dedekind publishes *Was sind und was sollen die Zahlen?/The Nature and Meaning of Numbers.* He gives a rigorous foundation for arithmetic, later known as the Peano axioms.

1895 Jules-Henri Poincaré publishes the first paper on topology, often referred to as 'rubber sheet geometry'.

1899 German mathematician David Hilbert publishes *Grundlagen der Geometrie/Foundations of Geometry,* which provides a rigorous basis for geometry.

1906 Russian mathematician Andrey Andreyevich Markov studies random processes that are subsequently known as Markov chains.

1908 English mathematician Godfrey Hardy and German physician Wilhelm Weinberg establish the mathematical basis for population genetics.

1913 English mathematician and philosopher Bertrand Russell publishes the final volume of *Principia Mathematica/Principles of Mathematics* in collaboration with another English mathematician and philosopher, Alfred North Whitehead. They attempt to derive the whole of mathematics from a logical foundation.

1931 Austrian mathematician Kurt Gödel publishes 'Gödel's proof' (*On Formally Undecidable Propositions of Principia Mathematica and Related Systems*). His proof questions the possibility of establishing dependable axioms in mathematics, showing that any formula strong enough to include the laws of arithmetic is either incomplete or inconsistent.

1936 British mathematician Alan Turing supplies the theoretical basis for digital computers by describing a machine, now known as the Turing machine, capable of universal rather than special-purpose problem solving.

1944 Hungarian-born US mathematician John von Neumann and the German-born US economist Oskar Morgenstern publish *Theory of Games and Economic Behavior.* Games theory is important in the study of economics, biology, and sociology.

1961 US meteorologist Edward Lorenz discovers a mathematical system with chaotic behaviour, leading to a new branch of mathematics known as chaos theory.

1972 French mathematician René Frédéric Thom formulates catastrophe theory, an attempt to describe biological processes mathematically.

1976 US mathematicians Kenneth Appel and Wolfgang Haken use a computer to prove the four-colour problem – that the minimum number of colours needed to colour a map such that no two adjacent sections have the same colour is four. The proof takes 1,000 hours of computer time and hundreds of pages.

1980 Mathematicians worldwide complete the classification of all finite and simple groups, a task that has taken over 100 mathematicians more than 35 years to complete. The results take up more than 14,000 pages in mathematical journals. Polish-born French mathematician Benoit Mandelbrot discovers fractals. The Mandelbrot set is a spectacular shape with a fractal boundary (a boundary of infinite length enclosing a finite area).

1993 English mathematician Andrew Wiles submits a proof for Fermat's last theorem, a problem that had remained unsolved since 1657. The proof is finally accepted in 1996 after some revision.

1999 The 38th Mersenne prime is discovered as part of the Great Internet Prime Search. It is 2 million digits long.

Chronology: Physics

c. 435 BC Greek philosopher Leucippus is the first to propose the atomic theory. It is developed later by his pupil Democritus.

c. 420 BC Greek philosopher Democritus of Abdera develops Leucippus' atomic theory and states that space is a vacuum and that all things consist of eternal, invisible and indivisible *atomon* (atoms). He also posits necessary laws by which they interact.

c. 250 BC Greek mathematician and inventor Archimedes discovers the principle that bears his name – that submerged bodies are acted upon by an upward or buoyant force equal to the weight of the fluid displaced.

1260 The English friar and scholar Roger Bacon investigates the laws governing optical phenomena such as refraction and reflection.

1537 Italian mathematician Niccolò Tartaglia lays the foundations of ballistics in his *Nova scientia/New Science,* attempting for the first time to establish the laws governing falling bodies.

1583 Italian scientist Galileo Galilei discovers that the period of a pendulum is dependent only on its length, not on the arc of its swing, traditionally after watching a swinging lamp in the cathedral at Pisa.

1600 The English physician William Gilbert writes *De magnete/On Magnetism,* a pioneering study of electricity and magnetism, which distinguishes between electrostatic and magnetic effects.

1604 Italian scientist Galileo Galilei discovers his law of falling bodies, proving that gravity acts with the same strength on all objects, independent of their mass. Traditionally, he is believed to have demonstrated this by dropping balls of the same size but different masses from the top of the Leaning Tower at Pisa.

1621 Dutch physicist Willebrord Snell discovers his law of refraction, relating the angle by which light is refracted at a boundary to the properties of the media it passes between.

1641 Italian scientist Evangelista Torricelli publishes *De Motu/On Motion,* a study of the physics of motion, which leads him to study with the aged Galileo Galilei at Florence, Italy.

1648 French mathematician Blaise Pascal proves, with his brother-in-law, that the pressure of air decreases with increasing height, by measuring the column of height of a mercury barometer carried up a mountain.

1662 Anglo-Irish chemist and physicist Robert Boyle describes the law that will bear his name, stating that, for a fixed mass of gas in a container, the volume occupied by the gas is inversely proportional to the pressure it exerts.

1664 English physicist Robert Hooke suggests that planetary orbits may be maintained by the constant attractive force of gravity between two bodies.

1678 Hooke discovers the law now named after him – that the extension of an elastic material such as a spring is in proportion to the force exerted on it. Dutch physicist and astronomer Christiaan Huygens records his discovery of the polarization of light, responsible for phenomena such as double refraction, in his *Traité de la lumière/Treatise on Light* (published 1690).

1680 English physicist Isaac Newton calculates that an inverse-square law of gravitational attraction between the Sun and planets would explain the elliptical orbits discovered by Kepler. He also puts forward a theory that the air resistance encountered by a body increases in proportion to the square of its speed.

1686 English mathematician and physicist Isaac Newton presents his great work, the *Philosophiae naturalis principia mathematica/Mathematical Principles and Natural Philosophy,* to the Royal Society, but they are short of funds, and unable to finance its publication. They recommend he approach his friend the English astronomer Edmond Halley. The work is published in 1687.

1704 English physicist Isaac Newton publishes *Optics,* the result of decades of research, delayed until after the death of English physicist Robert Hooke to avoid a priority argument. In the book, Newton strongly defends the corpuscular theory of light as a particle rather than a wave.

1709 Polish-born Dutch physicist Gabriel Fahrenheit creates a thermometer using the expansion of alcohol with temperature. He devises a temperature scale with the freezing point of water at 32°, and boiling point at 212°.

1745 German scientist Ewald Georg von Kleist invents the Leyden jar, a simple capacitor that accumulates and preserves electricity. The following year Dutch scientist Pieter von Musschenbroek makes the same discovery independently.

1750 English physicist John Michell describes magnetic induction and the inverse-square law for magnetic attraction in *A Treatise on Artificial Magnets.* Scandinavian physicist Martin Stromer modifies the temperature scale devised by his mentor, Swedish astronomer Anders Celsius. He inverts it, setting freezing point as 0°C and boiling point as 100°C, creating the Celsius scale still used today.

1752 North American scientist and statesman Benjamin Franklin performs his most famous experiment, flying a kite during a thunderstorm and charging a Leyden jar to which it is connected. He thereby demonstrates the electrical nature of lightning.

1757 Croatian-born Italian astronomer and mathematician Roger Boscovich, in *Theoris philosophiae naturalis redacta ad unicam legem virium in natura existentium/Theory of Natural Philosophy Reduced to A Single Law of the Strength Existing in Nature,* propounds an atomic theory of matter for the first time in modern Europe.

1777 French scientist Charles Augustin Coulomb invents the torsion balance in which weights are measured by the amount of twist induced in a metal wire.

1785 Coulomb publishes *Recherches théoriques et expérimentales sur la force de torsion et sur l'élasticité des fils de métal/Theoretical and Experimental Research on the Force of Torsion and on the Elasticity of Iron Threads,* in which he makes the first precise measurements of the electric forces of attraction and repulsion between charged bodies.

1787 French physicist Jacques-Alexandre Charles demonstrates that different gases expand by the same amount for the same temperature rise. It later becomes known as Charles's law.

1800 Italian physicist Alessandro Volta invents the voltaic pile made of discs of silver and zinc – the first battery.

1801 English physician and physicist Thomas Young discovers the interference of light when he observes that light passing through two closely spaced pinholes produces alternating bands of light and dark in the area of overlap. He thereby establishes the wave theory of light.

1810 German physicist Thomas Johann Seebeck discovers that silver chloride takes on the colour of the incident light it is exposed to.

1811 Italian physicist Amedeo Avogadro proposes Avogadro's law which states that equal volumes of different gases under the same temperature and pressure conditions will contain the same number of molecules.

25 July 1814 German physicist Joseph von Fraunhofer plots more than 500 absorption lines (Fraunhofer lines) and discovers that the relative positions of the lines is constant for each element. His work forms the basis of modern spectroscopy.

c. 1820 French physicist André Ampère develops an instrument that uses a needle to measure the flow of electricity. It is the first measurement of electricity.

1821 English physicist Michael Faraday builds an apparatus that transforms electrical energy into

mechanical energy – the principle of the electric motor. German physicist Thomas Seebeck discovers thermoelectricity – the conversion of heat into electricity – when he generates a current by heating one end of a metal strip comprising two metals joined together.

1827 German physicist Georg Ohm formulates Ohm's Law, which states that the current flowing through an electric circuit is directly proportional to the voltage, and indirectly proportional to the resistance.

1828 Scottish botanist Robert Brown observes the continuous motion of tiny particles in a liquid solution, now known as Brownian motion.

29 August 1831 Faraday discovers electromagnetic induction – the production of an electric current by change in magnetic intensity (and also the principle of the electric generator). US scientist Joseph Henry makes the same discovery independently of Faraday, and shortly before him, but does not publish his work.

1832 English physicist William Sturgeon constructs an electric motor. French inventor Hippolyte Pixii builds the first magneto or magneto-electric generator. A magnet rotates in front of two coils to produce an alternating current, making it the first induction electric generator, and the first machine to convert mechanical energy into electrical energy.

1833 Faraday announces the basic laws of electrolysis: that the amount of a substance deposited on an electrode is proportional to the amount of electric current passed through the cell, and that the amounts of different elements are proportional to their atomic weights.

1834 French physicist Benoît-Pierre Clapeyron develops the second law of thermodynamics: entropy always increases in a closed system.

1836 French physicist Edmund Becquerel discovers the photovoltaic effect when he observes the creation of a voltage between two electrodes, one of which is exposed to light.

1842 Austrian physicist Christian Doppler publishes *Über das farbige Licht der Doppelsterne/On the Coloured Light of Double Stars,* in which he describes how the frequency of sound and light waves changes with the motion of their source relative to the observer – the 'Doppler effect'. He also theorizes that the wavelength of light from a star will vary according to the star's velocity relative to Earth.

1843 English physicist James Joule determines the value for the mechanical equivalent of heat (now known as the joule), that is the amount of work required to produce a unit of heat.

1847 Joule discovers the law of conservation of energy – the first law of thermodynamics. German physicist Franz Neumann states the mathematical laws of electrical induction – the process of converting mechanical energy into electrical.

1848 Scottish physicist William Thomson (Lord Kelvin), devises the absolute temperature scale. He defines absolute zero as –273°C/–459.67°F, where the molecular energy of molecules is zero. He also defines the quantities currently used to describe magnetic forces: magnitude of magnetic flux, beta, and H the magnetizing force.

c. **1850** British physicist William Grove demonstrates that steam in contact with a hot platinum wire decomposes into hydrogen and oxygen, thus proving the thermal dissociation of atoms within a molecule.

1857 German mathematical physicist Rudolf Clausius develops the mathematics of the kinetic theory of heat and demonstrates that evaporation occurs when more molecules leave the surface of a liquid than return to it, and that the higher the temperature, the greater the number of molecules that will leave.

1864 Scottish physicist James Clerk Maxwell introduces mathematical equations that describe the electromagnetic field, and predict the existence of radio waves.

1868 Swedish physicist Anders Ångström expresses the wavelengths of Fraunhofer lines in units of 10^{-10} m, a unit now known as the angstrom.

1873 German physicist Ernst Abbe discovers that to distinguish two separate objects under the microscope the distance between them must be more than half the wavelength of the light that illuminates them. The discovery becomes important in the later development of electron and X-ray microscopes. Scottish physicist James Clerk Maxwell publishes *A Treatise on Electricity and Magnetism,* in which he provides a mathematical model of electromagnetic waves and identifies light as being one such wave.

1882 Scottish physicist Balfour Stewart postulates the existence of an electrically conducting layer of the outer atmosphere (now known as the ionosphere) to account for the daily variation in the Earth's magnetic field. US physicist Henry Augustus Rowland invents the concave diffraction grating, in which 20,000 lines to the inch are engraved on spherical concave mirrored surfaces. The grating revolutionizes spectrometry by dispersing light and permitting spectral lines to be focused.

1883 Irish physicist George Francis FitzGerald suggests that electromagnetic waves (radio waves) can be created by oscillating an electric current. A later demonstration of such waves by the German physicist Heinrich Hertz leads to the development of wireless telegraphy. US inventor Thomas Edison observes the flow of current between a hot electrode

and a cold electrode in one of his vacuum bulbs. Known as the 'Edison effect', it results from the thermionic emission of electrons from the hot electrode, and is the principle behind the working of the electron tube, which is to form the basis of the electronics industry.

1885 Croatian-born US physicist and electrical engineer Nikola Tesla sells his polyphase system of alternating current (AC) dynamos, transformers, and motors to US industrialist George Westinghouse, who begins a power struggle to establish alternating current (AC) technology over US inventor Thomas Edison's direct current (DC) systems.

1887 German physicist Heinrich Hertz discovers the photoelectric effect, in which a material gives off charged particles when it absorbs radiant energy, when he observes that ultraviolet light affects the voltage at which sparking between two metal plates takes place. Later work on this phenomenon leads to the conclusion that light is composed of particles called photons. US physicist Albert Michelson and US chemist Edward Williams Morley fail in an attempt to measure the velocity of the Earth through the 'ether' by measuring the speed of light in two directions. Their failure discredits the idea of the ether and leads to the conclusion that the speed of light is a universal constant, a fundamental premise of Einstein's theory of relativity.

1892 German-born US electrical engineer Charles Proteus Steinmetz discovers the law of hysteresis, which, by explaining why all electrical devices lose power when magnetic action is converted to heat, allows engineers to improve the efficiency of electric motors, generators, and transformers through design, rather than trial and error.

1893 Steinmetz develops a mathematical method for making calculations about alternating current (AC) circuits. By allowing the performance and efficiency of electrical equipment to be predicted, it leads to the rapid development of devices using alternating current (AC).

1895 Scottish physicist Charles Thomson Rees Wilson develops the first cloud chamber. He builds it to duplicate the effects of clouds on mountain tops, but later realizes its potential in nuclear physics. 8 November: German physicist Wilhelm Röntgen discovers X-rays. Named because of their unknown origin, they revolutionize medicine and usher in the age of modern physics.

1897 English physicist J J Thomson demonstrates the existence of the electron, the first known subatomic particle. It revolutionizes knowledge of atomic structure by indicating that the atom can be subdivided.

1898 German physicist Wilhelm Wien discovers the proton. He also discovers that a magnetic field can deflect a beam of charged particles. His discovery lays the foundations of mass spectroscopy.

1899 New Zealand-born British physicist Ernest Rutherford discovers alpha and beta rays, produced by the radioactivity of uranium.

1900 French physiologist Paul Ulrich Villard discovers gamma rays. German physicist Max Planck suggests that black bodies (perfect absorbers) radiate energy in packets or quanta, rather than continuously. He thus begins the science of quantum physics, which revolutionizes the understanding of atomic and subatomic processes.

1902 British physicist Oliver Heaviside and US electrical engineer Arthur Kennelly independently predict the existence of a conducting layer in the atmosphere that reflects radio waves. Canadian-born US physicist Reginald Fessenden discovers the heterodyne principle whereby high-frequency radio signals are converted to lower frequency signals that are easier to control and amplify. It leads to the superheterodyne principle essential in modern radio and television.

1903 Rutherford discovers that a beam of alpha particles is deflected by electric and magnetic fields. From the direction of deflection he is able to prove that they have a positive charge and from their velocity he determines the ratio of their charge to their mass. He also names the high-frequency electromagnetic radiation escaping from the nuclei of atoms as gamma rays. English physicist Charles Glover Barkla demonstrates that each element can be made to emit X-rays of a characteristic frequency.

1904 English physicist John Fleming patents the diode valve, which allows electricity to flow in only one direction. It is an essential development in the evolution of television. Japanese physicist Hantaro Nagaoka proposes a model of the atom in which the electrons are located in an outer ring and orbit the positive charge which is located in a central nucleus. The model is ignored because it is thought the electrons would fall into the nucleus.

1905 German physicist Albert Einstein develops his special theory of relativity in a series of four papers in Switzerland. In 'On the motion – required by the molecular kinetic theory of heat – of small particles suspended in a stationary liquid' he explains Brownian motion. In 'On a heuristic viewpoint concerning the production and transformation of light' he explains the photoelectric effect by proposing that light consists of photons and also exhibits wavelike properties. In 'On the electrodynamics of moving bodies' he proposes that space and time are one and that time and motion are relative to the observer. In 'Does the inertia of a body depend on its energy content?' he argues that mass and energy are equivalent, which can be expressed by the formula $E=mc^2$.

1906 German physicist Walther Herman Nernst formulates the third law of thermodynamics, which states that matter tends towards random motion and that energy tends to dissipate at a temperature above absolute zero (–273.12°C/ –350 ° F).

1907 US physicist Lee De Forest invents the 'audion tube', a triode vacuum tube with a third electrode, shaped like a grid, between the cathode and anode that controls the flow of electrons and permits the amplification of sound. It is an essential element in the development of radio, radar, television, and computers.

1908 German physicist Hans Geiger and Rutherford develop the Geiger counter, which counts individual alpha particles emitted by radioactive substances. US physicist Percy Williams Bridgman invents equipment that can create atmospheric pressures of 100,000 atmospheres (later 400,000) creating a new field of investigation.

1909 Einstein introduces his idea that light exhibits both wave and particle characteristics.

1911 Dutch physicist Heike Kamerlingh-Onnes discovers superconductivity, the characteristic of a substance to display zero electrical resistance when cooled to just above absolute zero. Rutherford proposes the concept of the nuclear atom, in which the mass of the atom is concentrated in a nucleus occupying 1/10,000 of the space of the atom and which has a positive charge balanced by surrounding electrons.

1912 Scottish physicist Charles Thomson Rees Wilson perfects the cloud chamber, which detects ion trails since water molecules condense on ions. It is used to study radioactivity, X-rays, cosmic rays, and other nuclear phenomena.

1913 US physicist Robert Millikan measures the electric charge on a single electron in his oil-drop experiment, in which the upward force of the electric charge on an oil droplet precisely counters the known downward gravitational force acting on it. English physicists William and Lawrence Bragg develop X-ray crystallography by establishing that the orderly arrangement of atoms in crystals display interference and diffraction patterns. They also demonstrate the wave nature of X-rays.

1916 Einstein publishes *The Foundation of the General Theory of Relativity,* in which he postulates that space is a curved field modified locally by the existence of mass and that this can be demonstrated by observing the deflection of starlight around the Sun during a total eclipse. This replaces previous Newtonian ideas which invoke a force of gravity. Einstein also derives the basic equations for the exchange of energy between matter and radiation.

1917 Rutherford splits the atom by bombarding a nitrogen nucleus with alpha particles, discovering that it ejects hydrogen nuclei (protons). It is the first artificial disintegration of an element and inaugurates the development of nuclear energy.

29 May 1919 English astrophysicist Arthur Eddington and others observe the total eclipse of the Sun on Príncipe Island (West Africa), and discover that the Sun's gravity bends the light from the stars beyond the edge of the eclipsed sun, thus confirming Albert Einstein's theory of relativity.

1921 German physicist Max Born develops a mathematical description of the first law of thermodynamics.

1926 Austrian physicist Erwin Schrödinger develops wave mechanics. German-born US physicist Albert Michelson determines the speed of light to be 299,853 kps/186,329 mps.

1927 German physicist Werner Heisenberg propounds the 'uncertainty principle' in quantum physics, which states that it is impossible to simultaneously determine the position and momentum of an atom. It explains why Newtonian mechanics is inapplicable at the atomic level.

1928 Russian physicist George Gamow shows that the atom can be split using low-energy ions. It stimulates the development of particle accelerators.

1929 Irish physicist Ernest Walton and English physicist Douglas Cockcroft develop the first particle accelerator.

1935 Japanese physicist Hideki Yukawa proposes the existence of a new particle, the meson, to explain nuclear forces.

1939 French physicists Frédéric Joliot and Irène Curie-Joliot demonstrate the possibility of a chain reaction when they split uranium nuclei. German physicists Hans Bethe and Carl von Weizsäcker propose that nuclear fusion of hydrogen is the source of a star's energy.

1940 US physicists Edwin McMillan and Philip Abelson synthesize the first transuranic element, neptunium (element 93), by bombarding uranium with neutrons at the cyclotron at Berkeley, California.

1947 US physicist Willard Libby develops carbon-14 dating.

1948 Hungarian-born British physicist Dennis Gabor invents holography, the production of three-dimensional images. US physicists George Gamow and Ralph Alpher develop the 'Big Bang' theory of the origins of the universe, which says that a primeval thermonuclear explosion led to the universe expanding rapidly from a highly compressed original state.

1951 US physicist Edward Purcell discovers line radiation (radiation emitted at only one specific wavelength) at 21 cm/8 in emitted by hydrogen in space. It allows the distribution of hydrogen clouds in galaxies and the speed of the Milky Way's rotation to be determined.

1952 US nuclear physicist Donald Glaser develops the bubble chamber to observe the behaviour of subatomic particles. It uses a superheated liquid instead of a vapour to track particles.

1956 US physicists Clyde Cowan and Fred Reines detect the existence of the neutrino, a particle with no electric charge and no mass, at the Los Alamos Laboratory.

29 December 1959 US theoretical physicist Richard Feynman delivers a paper entitled 'There's plenty of room at the bottom' to the American Physical Society, in which he describes the manufacture of transistors and other electronic components one atom at a time. It marks the beginning of nanotechnology.

1961 US physicist Murray Gell-Mann and Israeli physicist Yuval Ne'eman independently propose a classification scheme for subatomic particles that comes to be known as the eightfold way.

1964 Gell-Mann and US physicist George Zweig independently suggest the existence of the quark, a subatomic particle and the building block of hadrons, that experiences the strong nuclear force.

1986 Scientists use 10 laser beams, which deliver a total energy of 100 trillion watts during one-billionth of a second, to convert a small part of the hydrogen nuclei contained in a glass sphere to helium at the Lawrence Livermore National Laboratory in California; it is the first fusion reaction induced by a laser.

1995 US physicists announce the discovery of a new form of matter, called a Bose–Einstein condensate (because its existence had been predicted by Albert Einstein and Indian physicist Satyendra Bose), created by cooling rubidium atoms to just above absolute zero.

4 January 1996 A team of European physicists at the CERN research centre in Switzerland create the first atoms of antimatter: nine atoms of antihydrogen survive for 40 nanoseconds.

11 July 1998 Researchers at the Fermi National Accelerator laboratory in Batavia, Illinois, announce the discovery of the tau neutrino.

1999 Scientists succeed in slowing down the speed of light from its normal speed of 299,792 km/186,282 mi per second to 61 km/38 min per hour.

Glossary

A

Abelian functions in mathematics, functions of the form $\int f(x,y)\,dx$, where y is an algebraic function of x, and $f(x,y)$ is an algebraic function of x and y.

aberration in biology, an abnormal structure or deviation from the type.

aberration of starlight apparent displacement of a star from its true position, due to the combined effects of the speed of light and the speed of the Earth in orbit around the Sun (about 30 km per second/18.5 mi per second).

aberration, optical any of a number of defects that impair the image in an optical instrument. Aberration occurs because of minute variations in lenses and mirrors, and because different parts of the light ◊spectrum are reflected or refracted by varying amounts.

abiotic factor nonorganic variable within the ecosystem, affecting the life of organisms. Examples include temperature, light, and soil structure. Abiotic factors can be harmful to the environment, as when sulphur dioxide emissions from power stations produce acid rain.

ablation in earth science, the loss of snow and ice from a glacier by melting and evaporation. It is the opposite of accumulation. Ablation is most significant near the snout, or foot, of a glacier, since temperatures tend to be higher at lower altitudes. The rate of ablation also varies according to the time of year, being greatest during the summer. If total ablation exceeds total accumulation for a particular glacier, then the glacier will retreat, and vice versa.

ablation in astronomy, progressive burning away of the outer layers (for example, of a meteor) by friction with the atmosphere.

abscissa in coordinate geometry, the x-coordinate of a point – that is, the horizontal distance of that point from the vertical or y-axis. For example, a point with the coordinates (4, 3) has an abscissa of 4. The y-coordinate of a point is known as the ordinate.

absolute magnitude in astronomy, a measure of the intrinsic brightness of a celestial body in contrast to its apparent brightness or ◊magnitude as seen from Earth.

absolute value or *modulus* in mathematics, the value, or magnitude, of a number irrespective of its sign. The absolute value of a number n is written $|n|$ (or sometimes as mod n), and is defined as the positive square root of n^2. For example, the numbers –5 and 5 have the same absolute value:

$$|5| = |{-5}| = 5$$

absolute weight the weight of a body considered apart from all modifying influences such as the atmosphere. To determine its absolute weight, the body must, therefore, be weighed in a vacuum or allowance must be made for buoyancy.

absolute zero lowest temperature theoretically possible according to kinetic theory, zero kelvin (0 K), equivalent to –273.15°C/–459.67°F, at which molecules are in their lowest energy state. Although the third law of ◊thermodynamics indicates the impossibility of reaching absolute zero in practice, a temperature of 2.8×10^{-10} K (0.28 billionths of a degree above absolute zero) has been produced in 1993 at the Low Temperature Laboratory in Helsinki, Finland, using a technique called nuclear demagnetization. Near absolute zero, the physical properties of some materials change substantially; for example, some metals lose their electrical resistance and become superconducting.

absorption the taking up of one substance by another, such as a liquid by a solid (ink by blotting paper) or a gas by a liquid (ammonia by water). In physics, absorption is the phenomenon by which a substance retains radiation of particular wavelengths; for example, a piece of blue glass absorbs all visible light except the wavelengths in the blue part of the spectrum; it also refers to the partial loss of energy resulting from light and other electromagnetic waves passing through a medium. In nuclear physics, absorption is the capture by elements, such as boron, of neutrons produced by fission in a reactor.

absorption spectroscopy or *absorptiometry* in analytical chemistry, a technique for determining the identity or amount present of a chemical substance by measuring the amount of electromagnetic radiation the substance absorbs at specific wavelengths; see ◊spectroscopy.

absorption trough in astronomy, range of ◊wavelengths (around 21 cm/8 in) at which atomic hydrogen absorbs (or emits) radiation; this is a concept used in the attempt to detect ◊intergalactic matter.

abstract algebra in mathematics, generalization of ◊algebra; the word 'abstract' merely draws attention to the level of generality.

abstract group in mathematics, generalization of a group; the word 'abstract' merely indicates that a group is to be considered with reference not to a specific example but to its more general properties (which are shared therefore by other examples).

abundance of helium see ◊helium abundance.

abundant number in mathematics, natural number that is less than the sum of its divisors (factors).

acceleration rate of change of the velocity of a moving body. It is usually measured in metres per second per second (m s^{-2}) or feet per second per second (ft s^{-2}). Because velocity is a vector quantity (possessing both magnitude and direction) a body travelling at constant speed may be said to be accelerating if its direction of motion changes. According to Newton's second law of motion, a body will accelerate only if it is acted upon by an unbalanced, or resultant, ◊force.

Acceleration due to gravity is the acceleration of a body falling freely under the influence of the Earth's gravitational field; it varies slightly at different latitudes and altitudes. The value adopted internationally for gravitational acceleration is 9.806 m s^{-2}/32.174 ft s^{-2}.

acceleration, secular in astronomy, the continuous and nonperiodic change in orbital velocity of one body around another, or the axial rotation period of a body.

acceleration, uniform in physics, acceleration in which the velocity of a body changes by equal amounts in successive time intervals. Uniform acceleration is represented by a straight line on a speed–time graph.

accelerator in physics, a device to bring charged particles (such as protons and electrons) up to high speeds and energies, at which they can be of use in industry, medicine, and pure physics. At low energies, accelerated particles can be used to produce the image on a television screen and generate X-rays (by means of a cathode-ray tube), destroy tumour cells, or kill bacteria. When high-energy particles collide with other particles, the fragments formed reveal the nature of the fundamental forces.

accelerator nerve in biology, nerve that conducts impulses to the heart. On stimulation of the cardiac sympathetic nerves, the rate and strength of the heartbeat increases.

accretion in astrophysics, a process by which an object gathers up surrounding material by gravitational attraction, so simultaneously increasing in mass and releasing gravitational energy. Accretion on to compact objects such as ◊white dwarfs, ◊neutron stars and ◊black holes can release large amounts of gravitational energy, and is believed to be the power source for active galaxies. Accreted material falling towards a star may form a swirling disc of material known as an ◊accretion disc that can be a source of X-rays.

accretion disc in astronomy, a flattened ring of gas and dust orbiting an object in space, such as a star or ◊black hole. The orbiting material is accreted (gathered in) from a neighbouring object such as another star. Giant accretion discs are thought to exist at the centres of some galaxies and ◊quasars.

accumulator in electricity, a storage ◊battery – that is, a group of rechargeable secondary cells. A familiar example is the lead–acid car battery.

ACE inhibitor or *angiotensin-converting enzyme inhibitor* any of a group of drugs used to treat raised blood pressure (hypertension). They limit production of angiotensin, a protein involved in the constriction of blood vessels. Side effects include a precipitate drop in blood pressure and a dry, persistent cough. ACE inhibitors are also used to treat chronic heart failure.

acetylcholine (ACh) chemical that serves as a ◊neurotransmitter, communicating nerve impulses between the cells of the nervous system. It is largely associated with the transmission of impulses across the ◊synapse (junction) between nerve and muscle cells, causing the muscles to contract.

acetyl coenzyme A compound active in processes of metabolism. It is a heat-stable coenzyme with an acetyl group ($-COCH_3$) attached by sulphur linkage. This linkage is a high-energy bond and the acetyl group can easily be donated to other compounds. Acetyl groups donated in this way play an important part in glucose breakdown as well as in fatty acid and steroid synthesis.

acetylene common name for ◊ethyne.

achondrite type of ◊meteorite. They comprise about 15% of all meteorites and lack the *chondrules* (silicate spheres) found in chondrites.

achromatic lens in optics, lens (or combination of lenses) that brings different ◊wavelengths within a ray of light to a single focus, thus overcoming chromatic ◊aberration.

acid in chemistry, compound that releases hydrogen ions (H^+ or protons) in the presence of an ionizing solvent (usually water). Acids react with ◊bases to form salts, and they act as solvents. Strong acids are corrosive; dilute acids have a sour or sharp taste, although in some organic acids this may be partially masked by other flavour characteristics. The strength of an acid is measured by its hydrogen-ion concentration, indicated by the ◊pH value. All acids have a pH below 7.0.

acid amide any organic compound that may be regarded as being derived from ammonia by the substitution of acid or acyl groups for atoms of hydrogen. They are described as primary, secondary, tertiary, and so on, according to the number of atoms of hydrogen displaced. Thus the general formula for a primary amide is $RCONH_2$. The main acid amides are ethanamide and methanamide.

acid rain acidic precipitation thought to be caused principally by the release into the atmosphere of sulphur dioxide (SO_2) and oxides of nitrogen, which dissolve in pure rainwater making it acidic. Sulphur dioxide is formed by the burning of fossil fuels, such as coal, that contain high quantities of sulphur; nitrogen oxides are contributed from various industrial activities and from car exhaust fumes.

aconitine extremely poisonous alkaloid found in the plants aconite and larkspur. It has no smell but is very bitter and produces a tingling sensation when applied externally. If it is eaten or enters the body through a mucous membrane or a wound, it causes death by respiratory or heart failure.

acoustics in general, the experimental and theoretical science of sound and its transmission; in particular, that branch of the science that has to do with the phenomena of sound in a particular space such as a room or theatre.

acquired character feature of the body that develops during the lifetime of an individual, usually as a result of repeated use or disuse, such as the enlarged muscles of a weightlifter.

acquired immune deficiency syndrome full name for the disease AIDS.

actin in zoology, protein that occurs in muscles. See ◊myosin.

actinium (Greek *aktis* 'ray') white, radioactive, metallic element, the first of the actinide series, symbol Ac, atomic number 89, relative atomic mass 227; it is a weak emitter of high-energy alpha particles.

Actinium occurs with uranium and radium in pitchblende and other ores, and can be synthesized by bombarding radium with neutrons. The longest-lived isotope, Ac-227, has a half-life of 21.8 years (all the other isotopes have very short half-lives). Chemically, it is exclusively trivalent, resembling in its reactions the lanthanides and the other actinides. Actinium was discovered 1899 by the French chemist André Debierne (1874–1949).

action potential in biology, a change in the ◊potential difference (voltage) across the membrane of a nerve cell when an impulse passes along it. A change in potential (from about –60 to +45 millivolts) accompanies the passage of sodium and potassium ions across the membrane.

activation analysis in analytical chemistry, a technique used to reveal the presence and amount of minute impurities in a substance or element. A sample of a material that may contain traces of a certain element is irradiated with ◊neutrons, as in a reactor. Gamma rays emitted by the material's radioisotope have unique energies and relative intensities, similar to the spectral lines from a luminous gas. Measurements and interpretation of the gamma-ray spectrum, using data from standard samples for comparison, provide information on the amount of impurities present.

activation energy in chemistry, the energy required in order to start a chemical reaction. Some elements and compounds will react together merely by bringing them into contact (spontaneous reaction). For others it is necessary to supply energy in order to start the reaction, even if there is ultimately a net output of energy. This initial energy is the activation energy.

addition reaction chemical reaction in which the atoms of an element or compound react with a double bond or triple bond in an organic compound by opening up one of the bonds and becoming attached to it, for example

$$CH_2=CH_2 + HCl \rightarrow CH_3CH_2Cl$$

An example is the addition of hydrogen atoms to unsaturated compounds in vegetable oils to produce margarine. Addition reactions are used to make useful polymers from ◊alkenes.

adenosine triphosphate compound present in cells. See ◊ATP.

adiabatic change in biology, process that takes place without any heat entering or leaving the system.

adipocere waxlike substance produced by the exposure of fleshy tissue to moisture with the exclusion of air, as in the earth or under water. Human bodies in moist burial places often undergo this change.

adipose tissue type of connective tissue of vertebrates that serves as an energy reserve, and also pads some organs. It is commonly called fat tissue, and consists of large spherical cells filled with fat. In mammals, major layers are in the inner layer of skin and around the kidneys and heart.

Fatty acids are transported to and from it via the blood system. An excessive amount of adipose tissue is developed in the course of some diseases, especially obesity.

ADP abbreviation for adenosine diphosphate, the chemical product formed in cells when ◊ATP breaks down to release energy.

adsorption taking up of a gas or liquid at the surface of another substance, most commonly a solid (for example, activated charcoal adsorbs gases). It involves molecular attraction at the surface, and should be distinguished from ◊absorption (in which a uniform solution results from a gas or liquid being incorporated into the bulk structure of a liquid or solid).

aeolian deposits in geology, carried, formed, eroded, or deposited by the wind.

Such sediments include desert sands and dunes as well as deposits of windblown silt, called loess, carried long distances from deserts and from stream sediments derived from the melting of glaciers.

aeon or *eon* in astronomical terms, 1,000 million years.

aerial oxidation in chemistry, a reaction in which air is used to oxidize another substance, as in the contact process for the manufacture of sulphuric acid:

$$2SO_2 + O_2 \rightleftharpoons 2SO_3$$

and in the souring of wine.

aerobic in biology, term used to describe those organisms that require oxygen (usually dissolved in water) for the efficient release of energy contained in food molecules, such as glucose. They include almost all organisms (plants as well as animals) with the exception of certain bacteria, yeasts, and internal parasites.

aerodynamics branch of fluid physics that studies the forces exerted by air or other gases in motion. Examples include the airflow around bodies moving at speed through the atmosphere (such as land vehicles, bullets, rockets, and aircraft), the behaviour of gas in engines and furnaces, air conditioning of buildings, the deposition of snow, the operation of air-cushion vehicles (hovercraft), wind loads on buildings and bridges, bird and insect flight, musical wind instruments, and meteorology. For maximum efficiency, the aim is usually to design the shape of an object to produce a streamlined flow, with a minimum of turbulence in the moving air. The behaviour of aerosols or the pollution of the atmosphere by foreign particles are other aspects of aerodynamics.

aestivation in zoology, a state of inactivity and reduced metabolic activity, similar to hibernation, that occurs during the dry season in species such as lungfish and snails. In botany, the term is used to describe the way in which flower petals and sepals are folded in the buds. It is an important feature in plant classification.

aether alternative form of ◊ether, the hypothetical medium once believed to permeate all of space.

aetiology in medicine, the systematic investigation into the causes of disease.

afferent nerve in biology, nerve that carries impulses towards the central nervous system (that is, the spinal cord or brain).

affine geometry geometry that preserves parallelism and the ratios between intervals on any line segment.

affinity in chemistry, the force of attraction (see ◊bond) between atoms that helps to keep them in combination in a molecule. The term is also applied to attraction between molecules, such as those of biochemical significance (for example, between ◊enzymes and substrate molecules). This is the basis for affinity ◊chromatography, by which biologically important compounds are separated.

agglutination in biology, the clumping together of ◊antigens, such as red blood cells or bacteria, to form larger, visible clumps, under the influence of ◊antibodies. As each antigen clumps only in response to its particular antibody, agglutination provides a way of determining blood groups and the identity of unknown bacteria.

aggression in biology, behaviour used to intimidate or injure another organism (of the same or of a different species), usually for the purposes of gaining territory, a mate, or food. Aggression often involves an escalating series of threats aimed at intimidating an opponent without having to engage in potentially dangerous physical contact. Aggressive signals include roaring by red deer, snarling by dogs, the fluffing-up of feathers by birds, and the raising of fins by some species of fish.

agonist in biology, a muscle that contracts and causes a movement. Contraction of an agonist is complemented by relaxation of its ◊antagonist. For example, the biceps (in the front of the upper arm) bends the elbow whilst the triceps (lying behind the biceps) straightens the arm.

agonist in medicine, a drug or other substance that has a similar effect to normal chemical messengers in the body through its actions at receptor sites of cells. Examples are sympathomimetic drugs that mimic the actions of adrenaline and are used in the treatment of certain heart disorders.

agranulocytosis virtual absence from the blood of the white cells known as neutrophils that destroy bacteria. It is a life-threatening condition that results from toxic damage to the bone marrow by some drugs. It is treated with antibiotics and sometimes transfusion of white blood cells.

air the mixture of gases making up the Earth's ◊atmosphere.

airglow faint and variable light in the Earth's atmosphere produced by chemical reactions (the recombination of ionized particles) in the ionosphere.

air mass large body of air with particular characteristics of temperature and humidity. An air mass forms when air rests over an area long enough to pick up the conditions of that area. When an air mass moves to another area it affects the weather of that area, but its own characteristics become modified in the process. For example, an air mass formed over the Sahara will be hot and dry, becoming cooler as it moves northwards. Air masses that meet form *fronts*.

air pump device used to pump air from one vessel to another, or to evacuate a vessel altogether to produce a ◊vacuum.

albedo fraction of the incoming light reflected by a body such as a planet. A body with a high albedo, near 1, is very bright, while a body with a low albedo, near 0, is dark. The Moon has an average albedo of 0.12, Venus 0.76, Earth 0.37.

albinism rare hereditary condition in which the body has no tyrosinase, one of the enzymes that form the pigment ◊melanin, normally found in the skin, hair, and eyes. As a result, the hair is white and the skin and eyes are pink. The skin and eyes are abnormally sensitive to light, and vision is often impaired. The condition occurs among all human and animal groups.

alcohol any member of a group of organic chemical compounds characterized by the presence of one or more aliphatic OH (hydroxyl) groups in the molecule, and which form ◊esters with acids. The main uses of alcohols are as solvents for gums, resins, lacquers, and varnishes; in the making of dyes; for essential oils in perfumery; and for medical substances in pharmacy. The alcohol produced naturally in the ◊fermentation process and consumed as part of alcoholic beverages is called ethanol.

alcoholic solution solution produced when a solute is dissolved in ethanol.

aldehyde any of a group of organic chemical compounds prepared by oxidation of primary alcohols, so that the OH (hydroxyl) group loses its hydrogen to give an oxygen joined by a double bond to a carbon atom (the aldehyde group, with the formula CHO).

algebra branch of mathematics in which the general properties of numbers are studied by using symbols, usually letters, to represent variables and unknown quantities. For example, the algebraic statement $(x + y)^2 = x^2 + 2xy + y^2$ is true for all values of x and y. If $x = 7$ and $y = 3$, for instance:

$$(7 + 3)^2 = 7^2 + 2(7 \times 3) + 3^2 = 100$$

An algebraic expression that has one or more variables (denoted by letters) is a polynomial equation. Algebra is used in many areas of mathematics – for example, matrix algebra and Boolean algebra (the latter is used in working out the logic for computers).

algebraic curve geometrical curve that can be precisely described by an (algebraic) equation.

algebraic fraction in mathematics, fraction in which letters are used to represent numbers – for example, $\frac{a}{b}$, $\frac{xy2}{z}$, and $\frac{1}{(x+y)}$. Like numerical fractions, algebraic fractions may be simplified or factorized. Two equivalent algebraic fractions can be cross-multiplied; for example, if $\frac{a}{b} = \frac{c}{d}$ then $ad = bc$. (In the same way, the two equivalent numerical fractions $\frac{2}{3}$ and $\frac{4}{6}$ can be cross-multiplied to give cross-products that are both 12.)

algebraic numbers in mathematics, numbers that satisfy a polynomial equation with rational coefficients: for example, $\sqrt{2}$ solves $x^2 - 2 = 0$. ◊Real numbers that are not algebraic are called ◊trancendental numbers. Although there is an infinity of

algebraic numbers, there is in fact a 'larger' infinity of transcendental numbers.

algebraic topology in mathematics, study of surfaces and similar but more general objects in higher dimensions, using algebraic techniques. It is based upon ◊homology.

alginate in chemistry, salt of alginic acid, $(C_6H_8O_6)_n$, obtained from brown seaweeds and used in textiles, paper, food products, and pharmaceuticals.

algorithm procedure or series of steps that can be used to solve a problem.

In computer science, it describes the logical sequence of operations to be performed by a program. A flow chart is a visual representation of an algorithm.

aliphatic compound any organic chemical compound in which the carbon atoms are joined in straight chains, as in hexane (C_6H_{14}), or in branched chains, as in 2-methylpentane ($CH_3CH(CH_3)CH_2CH_2CH_3$).

alizarin or *1,2-dihydroxy-anthraquinone* $C_6H_4(CO)_2C_6H_2(OH)_2$, a derivative from anthraquinone. It is now prepared synthetically from anthracene. Alizarin crystallizes in dark red prisms and sublimes in orange-coloured needles, melting at 290°C/554°F. It is almost insoluble in water, but dissolves in alcohol.

alk resin obtained from the turpentine tree *Pistacia terebinthus*, which grows chiefly in the Mediterranean region. A yellow to green liquid, Chian or Chio turpentine, is distilled from it.

alkali in chemistry, a ◊base that is soluble in water. Alkalis neutralize acids and are soapy to the touch. The strength of an alkali is measured by its hydrogen-ion concentration, indicated by the ◊pH value. They may be divided into strong and weak alkalis: a strong alkali (for example, potassium hydroxide, KOH) ionizes completely when disssolved in water, whereas a weak alkali (for example, ammonium hydroxide, NH_4OH) exists in a partially ionized state in solution. All alkalis have a pH above 7.0.

The hydroxides of metals are alkalis. Those of sodium and potassium are chemically powerful; both were historically derived from the ashes of plants.

alkali metal any of a group of six metallic elements with similar chemical properties: lithium, sodium, potassium, rubidium, caesium, and francium. They form a linked group (Group One) in the ◊periodic table of the elements. They are univalent (have a valency of one) and of very low density (lithium, sodium, and potassium float on water); in general they are reactive, soft, low-melting-point metals. Because of their reactivity they are only found as compounds in nature.

alkaline-earth metal any of a group of six metallic elements with similar bonding properties: beryllium, magnesium, calcium, strontium, barium, and radium. They form a linked group in the ◊periodic table of the elements. They are strongly basic, bivalent (have a valency of two), and occur in nature only in compounds.

alkaloid any of a number of physiologically active and frequently poisonous substances contained in some plants. They are usually organic bases and contain nitrogen. They form salts with acids and, when soluble, give alkaline solutions.

alkane member of a group of ◊hydrocarbons having the general formula CnH_{2n+2}, commonly known as *paraffins*. As they contain only single ◊covalent bonds, alkanes are said to be saturated. Lighter alkanes, such as methane, ethane, propane, and butane, are colourless gases; heavier ones are liquids or solids. In nature they are found in natural gas and petroleum.

alkene member of the group of ◊hydrocarbons having the general formula C_nH_{2n}, formerly known as *olefins*. Alkenes are unsaturated compounds, characterized by one or more double bonds between adjacent carbon atoms. Lighter alkenes, such as ethene and propene, are gases, obtained from the cracking of oil fractions. Alkenes react by addition, and many useful compounds, such as poly(ethene) and bromoethane, are made from them.

alkyl any radical of the formula C_nH_{2n+1}; the chief members are methyl, ethyl, propyl, butyl, and amyl. These radicals are not stable in the free state but are found combined in a large number of types of organic compounds such as alcohols, esters, aldehydes, ketones, and halides.

alkyl any of a series of hydrocarbon ◊radicals derived from the ◊alkanes and having the general formula C_nH_{2n+1}. Examples include the methyl radical ($-CH_3$) and the ethyl radical ($-C_2H_5$).

alkyne member of the group of ◊hydrocarbons with the general formula C_nH_{2n-2}, formerly known as the *acetylenes*. They are unsaturated compounds, characterized by one or more triple bonds between adjacent carbon atoms. Lighter alkynes, such as ethyne, are gases; heavier ones are liquids or solids.

allantois bladder in the embryo of reptiles, birds and mammals, that grows outside the embryo into the wall of the yolk sac of reptiles and birds and under the ◊chorion of mammals. In mammals, blood vessels in the allantois carry blood to the ◊placenta; in reptiles and birds the blood vessels permit respiration. As they develop, the vessels become the umbilical vein and arteries.

allele one of two or more alternative forms of a ◊gene at a given position (locus) on a chromosome, caused by a difference in the ◊DNA. Blue and brown eyes in humans are determined by different alleles of the gene for eye colour.

allene any of a class of dienes with adjacent double bonds. The simplest example is CH_2-C-CH_2, allene itself. Because of the stereochemistry of the double bonds, the terminal hydrogen atoms lie in planes mutually at right angles. Allenes behave mainly as typical unsaturated compounds, but are less stable than dienes with nonadjacent double bonds.

allosteric effect regulatory effect on an enzyme which takes place at a site distinct from that enzyme's catalytic site. For example, in a chain of enzymes the end product may act on an enzyme in the chain to regulate its own production.

allotropy property whereby an element can exist in two or more forms (allotropes), each possessing different physical properties but the same state of matter (gas, liquid, or solid). The allotropes of carbon are diamond, fullerenes, and graphite. Sulphur has several allotropes (flowers of sulphur, plastic, rhombic, and monoclinic). These solids have different crystal structures, as do the white and grey forms of tin and the black, red, and white forms of phosphorus.

alloy metal blended with some other metallic or nonmetallic substance to give it special qualities, such as resistance to corrosion, greater hardness, or tensile strength. Useful alloys include bronze, brass, cupronickel, duralumin, German silver, gunmetal, pewter, solder, steel, and stainless steel.

allyl in chemistry, an unsaturated organic radical corresponding to the formula $CH_2:CHCH_2-$.

allyl-metal complex coordination compound of a metal and the organic allyl ($CH_2:CHCH_2-$) group. Allyl-metal complexes are very reactive to oxygen, inflaming in air. The allyl groups are easily replaced by other ligands such as the carbonyl group, CO.

Almagest *(Arabic al 'the' and a corruption of the Greek megiste 'greatest')* book compiled by the Greek astronomer Ptolemy during the 2nd century AD, which included the idea of an Earth-centred universe; it was translated into Arabic in the 9th century. Some medieval books on astronomy, astrology, and alchemy were given the same title.

Alpha Centauri or ***Rigil Kent*** brightest star in the constellation Centaurus and the third-brightest star in the night sky. It is actually a triple star (see ◊binary star); the two brighter stars orbit each other every 80 years, and the third, Proxima Centauri, is the closest star to the Sun, 4.2 light years away, 0.1 light years closer than the other two.

alpha chain particular secondary structure of the polypeptide chain (of a protein) brought about by hydrogen bonding between adjacent ◊peptide units. Alpha chains occur, for example, in the ◊haemoglobin molecule.

alpha decay disintegration of the nucleus of an atom to produce an ◊alpha particle. See also ◊radioactivity.

alpha particle positively charged, high-energy particle emitted from the nucleus of a radioactive atom. It is one of the products of the spontaneous disintegration of radioactive elements (see ◊radioactivity) such as radium and thorium, and is identical with the nucleus of a helium atom – that is, it consists of two protons and two neutrons. The process of emission, *alpha decay*, transforms one element into another, decreasing the atomic (or proton) number by two and the atomic mass (or nucleon number) by four.

Altair or ***Alpha Aquilae*** brightest star in the constellation Aquila and the 13th-brightest star in the night sky. It is a white star 16 light years away from the Sun and forms the Summer Triangle with the stars Deneb (in the constellation Cygnus) and Vega (in Lyra).

altazimuth astronomical instrument designed for observing the altitude and azimuth of a celestial object. It is essentially a large precision theodolite.

alternating current (AC) electric current that flows for an interval of time in one direction and then in the opposite direction, that is, a current that flows in alternately reversed directions through or around a circuit. Electric energy is usually generated as alternating current in a power station, and alternating currents may be used for both power and lighting.

altitude measurement of height, usually given in metres above sea level.

alum any double sulphate of a monovalent metal or radical (such as sodium, potassium, or ammonium) and a trivalent metal (such as aluminium, chromium, or iron). The commonest alum is the double sulphate of potassium and aluminium, $K_2Al_2(SO_4)_4.24H_2O$, a white crystalline powder that is readily soluble in water. It is used in curing animal skins. Other alums are used in papermaking and to fix dye in the textile industry.

alumina or ***corundum*** Al_2O_3 oxide of aluminium, widely distributed in clays, slates, and shales. It is formed by the decomposition of the feldspars in granite and used as an abrasive. Typically it is a white powder, soluble in most strong acids or caustic alkalis but not in water. Impure alumina is called 'emery'. Rubies, sapphires, and topaz are corundum gemstones.

aluminium lightweight, silver-white, ductile and malleable, metallic element, symbol Al, atomic number 13, relative atomic mass 26.9815, melting point 658°C. It is the third most abundant element (and the most abundant metal) in the Earth's crust, of which it makes up about 8.1% by mass. It is non-magnetic, an excellent conductor of electricity, and oxidizes easily, the layer of oxide on its surface making it highly resistant to tarnish. In the USA the original name suggested by the scientist Humphry Davy, 'aluminum', is retained.

aluminium chloride $AlCl_3$ white solid made by direct combination of aluminium and chlorine.

$$2Al + 3Cl_2 \rightarrow 2AlCl_3$$

The anhydrous form is a typical covalent compound.

aluminium hydroxide or *alumina cream* $Al(OH)_3$ gelatinous precipitate formed when a small amount of alkali solution is added to a solution of an aluminium salt.

$$Al_{(aq)} + 3OH_{(aq)} \rightarrow Al(OH)_{3(s)}$$

It is an ◊amphoteric compound as it readily reacts with both acids and alkalis.

amalgam any alloy of mercury with other metals. Most metals will form amalgams, except iron and platinum. Amalgam is used in dentistry for filling teeth, and usually contains copper, silver, and zinc as the main alloying ingredients. This amalgam is pliable when first mixed and then sets hard, but the mercury leaches out and may cause a type of heavy-metal poisoning.

amatol explosive consisting of ammonium nitrate and TNT (trinitrotoluene) in almost any proportions.

amaurosis (Greek *amauros* 'dark') partial or total blindness where the outward appearance of the eye is unaffected. It is usually caused by disease of the brain or blood vessels supplying the retina.

amide any organic chemical derived from a fatty acid by the replacement of the hydroxyl group (–OH) by an amino group (–NH_2). One of the simplest amides is acetamide ($CH_3\text{CONH}_2$), which has a strong mousy odour.

amine any of a class of organic chemical compounds in which one or more of the hydrogen atoms of ammonia (NH_3) have been replaced by other groups of atoms.

amino acid water-soluble organic ◊molecule, mainly composed of carbon, oxygen, hydrogen, and nitrogen, containing both a basic amino group (NH_2) and an acidic carboxyl (COOH) group. They are small molecules able to pass through membranes. When two or more amino acids are joined together, they are known as ◊peptides; ◊proteins are made up of peptide chains folded or twisted in characteristic shapes.

aminoglycoside any of a group of antibiotics, including gentamicin, neomycin, and streptomycin, that are effective against a wide range of bacteria. As they are not absorbed from the intestine, they are usually given by injection. Drugs in this group are quite toxic, with side effects including damage to the ears and kidneys. For this reason they are only used for infections that do not respond to other antibiotics.

ammeter instrument that measures electric current (flow of charge per unit time), usually in ◊amperes, through a conductor. It should not to be confused with a voltmeter, which measures potential difference between two points in a circuit. The ammeter is placed in series with the component through which current is to be measured, and is constructed with a low internal resistance in order to prevent the reduction of that current as it flows through the instrument itself. A common type is the moving-coil meter, which measures direct current (DC), but can, in the presence of a rectifier, measure alternating current (AC) also. Hot-wire, moving-iron, and dynamometer ammeters can be used for both DC and AC.

ammonia NH_3 colourless pungent-smelling gas, lighter than air and very soluble in water. It is made on an industrial scale by the ◊Haber (or Haber–Bosch) process, and used mainly to produce nitrogenous fertilizers, nitric acid, and some explosives.

ammoniacal solution in chemistry, a solution produced by dissolving a solute in aqueous ammonia.

ammonium carbonate $(NH_4)_2CO_3$ white, crystalline solid that readily sublimes at room temperature into its constituent gases: ammonia, carbon dioxide, and water. It was formerly used in smelling salts.

ammonium chloride or *sal ammoniac* NH_4Cl a volatile salt that forms white crystals around volcanic craters. It is prepared synthetically for use in 'dry-cell' batteries, fertilizers, and dyes.

ammonium nitrate NH_4NO_3 colourless, crystalline solid, prepared by neutralization of nitric acid with ammonia; the salt is crystallized from the solution. It sublimes on heating.

amnion innermost of three membranes that enclose the embryo within the egg (reptiles and birds) or within the uterus (mammals). It contains the amniotic fluid that helps to cushion the embryo.

ampere SI unit (symbol A) of electrical current. Electrical current is measured in a similar way to water current, in terms of an amount per unit time; one ampere represents a flow of about 6.28×10^{18} ◊electrons per second, or a rate of flow of charge of one coulomb per second.

Ampère's rule rule developed by French physicist André Ampère connecting the direction of an electric current and its associated magnetic currents. It states that if a person were travelling along a current-carrying wire in the direction of conventional current flow (from the positive to the negative terminal), and carrying a magnetic compass, then the north pole of the compass needle would be deflected to the left-hand side.

amphoteric term used to describe the ability of some chemical compounds to behave either as an ◊acid or as a ◊base depending on their environment. For example, the metals aluminium and zinc, and their oxides and hydroxides, act as bases in acidic solutions and as acids in alkaline solutions.

amplifier electronic device that magnifies the strength of a signal, such as a radio signal. The ratio of output signal strength to input signal strength is called the *gain* of the amplifier. As well as achieving high gain, an amplifier should be free from distortion and able to operate over a range of frequencies. Practical amplifiers are usually complex circuits, although simple amplifiers can be built from single transistors or valves.

amplitude or *argument* in mathematics, the angle in an ◊Argand diagram between the line that represents the complex number and the real (positive horizontal) axis. If the complex number is written in the form $r (\cos \theta + i \sin \theta)$, where r is radius and $i = \sqrt{-1}$, the amplitude is the angle θ (theta). The amplitude is also the peak value of an oscillation.

amplitude modulation (AM) method by which radio waves are altered for the transmission of broadcasting signals. AM waves are constant in frequency, but the amplitude of the transmitting wave varies in accordance with the signal being broadcast.

amylase one of a group of ◊enzymes that break down starches into their component molecules (sugars) for use in the body. It occurs widely in both plants and animals. In humans, it is found in saliva and in pancreatic juices.

anaerobic (of living organisms) not requiring oxygen for the release of energy from food molecules such as glucose. Anaerobic organisms include many bacteria, yeasts, and internal parasites.

anaesthetic drug that produces loss of sensation or consciousness; the resulting state is *anaesthesia,* in which the patient is insensitive to stimuli. Anaesthesia may also happen as a result of nerve disorder.

Ever since the first successful operation in 1846 on a patient rendered unconscious by ether, advances have been aimed at increasing safety and control. Sedatives may be given before the anaesthetic to make the process easier. The level and duration of unconsciousness are managed precisely. Where general anaesthesia may be inappropriate (for example, in childbirth, for a small procedure, or in the elderly), many other techniques are available. A topical substance may be applied to the skin or tissue surface; a local agent may be injected into the tissues under the skin in the area to be treated; or a regional block of sensation may be achieved by injection into a nerve. Spinal anaesthetic, such as epidural, is injected into the tissues surrounding the spinal cord, producing loss of feeling in the lower part of the body.

analgesic agent for relieving pain. Opiates alter the perception or appreciation of pain and are effective in controlling 'deep' visceral (internal) pain. Non opiates, such as aspirin, paracetamol, and NSAIDs (nonsteroidal anti-inflammatory drugs), relieve musculoskeletal pain and reduce inflammation in soft tissues.

analogous in biology, term describing a structure that has a similar function to a structure in another organism, but not a similar evolutionary path. For example, the wings of bees and of birds have the same purpose – to give powered flight – but have different origins.

Compare ◊homologous.

analogue signal in electronics, current or voltage that conveys or stores information, and varies continuously in the same way as the information it represents (compare digital signal). Analogue signals are prone to interference and distortion.

analogue-to-digital converter (ADC) electronic circuit that converts an analogue signal into a digital one. Such a circuit is needed to convert the signal from an analogue device into a digital signal for input into a computer. For example, many sensors designed to measure physical quantities, such as temperature and pressure, produce an analogue signal in the form of voltage and this must be passed through an ADC before computer input and processing. A digital-to-analogue converter performs the opposite process.

analysis in chemistry, the determination of the composition of substances; see ◊analytical chemistry.

analysis branch of mathematics concerned with limiting processes on axiomatic number systems; ◊calculus of variations and infinitesimal calculus is now called analysis.

analytical chemistry branch of chemistry that deals with the determination of the chemical composition of substances. *Qualitative analysis* determines the identities of the substances in a given sample; *quantitative analysis* determines how much of a particular substance is present.

AND gate in electronics, a type of logic gate.

Andromeda major constellation of the northern hemisphere, visible in autumn. Its main feature is the Andromeda galaxy. The star Alpha Andromedae forms one corner of the Square of Pegasus. It is named after the princess of Greek mythology.

Andromeda galaxy galaxy 2.2 million light years away from Earth in the constellation Andromeda, and the most distant object visible to the naked eye. It is the largest member of the ◊Local Group of galaxies.

Like the Milky Way, it is a spiral orbited by several companion galaxies but contains about twice as many stars. It is about 200,000 light years across.

AND rule rule used for finding the combined probability of two or more independent events both occurring. If two events E_1 and E_2 are independent (have no effect on each other) and the probabilities of their taking place are p_1 and p_2, respectively, then the combined probability p that both E_1 and E_2 will happen is given by:

$$p = p_1 \times p_2$$

anechoic chamber room designed to be of high sound absorbency. All surfaces inside the chamber are covered by sound-absorbent materials such as rubber. The walls are often covered with inward-facing pyramids of rubber, to minimize reflections. It is used for experiments in ◊acoustics and for testing audio equipment.

anemometer device for measuring wind speed and liquid flow. The most basic form, the *cup-type anemometer,* consists of cups at the ends of arms, which rotate when the wind blows. The speed of rotation indicates the wind speed.

anemophily type of pollination in which the pollen is carried on the wind. Anemophilous flowers are usually unscented, have either very reduced petals and sepals or lack them altogether, and do not produce nectar. In some species they are borne in catkins. Male and female reproductive structures are commonly found in separate flowers. The male flowers have numerous exposed stamens, often on long filaments; the female flowers have long, often branched, feathery stigmas.

angiography technique for X-raying major blood vessels. A radiopaque dye is injected into the bloodstream so that the suspect vessel is clearly silhouetted on the X-ray film.

angioplasty surgical repair of damaged or diseased blood vessels. A thin wire with a balloon at its tip is inserted into the blocked artery. The balloon is inflated to push the artery walls apart.

angiosperm flowering plant in which the seeds are enclosed within an ovary, which ripens into a fruit. Angiosperms are divided into ◊monocotyledons (single seed leaf in the embryo) and ◊dicotyledons (two seed leaves in the embryo). They include the majority of flowers, herbs, grasses, and trees except conifers.

angle of incidence angle between a ray of light striking a mirror (incident ray) and the normal to that mirror. It is equal to the ◊angle of reflection.

angle of parallelism in non-Euclidean geometry involving the application of classical geometrical principles to nonflat surfaces, the angle at which a line perpendicular to one of two parallel lines meets the other – which may also be 90°, or may be less.

angle of reflection angle between a ray of light reflected from a mirror and the normal to that mirror. It is equal to the ◊angle of incidence.

angle of refraction angle between a refracted ray of light and the normal to the surface at which ◊refraction occurred. When a ray passes from air into a denser medium such as glass, it is bent towards the normal so that the angle of refraction is less than the ◊angle of incidence.

angular momentum in physics, a type of ◊momentum.

anhydride chemical compound obtained by the removal of water from another compound; usually a dehydrated acid. For example, sulphur(VI) oxide (sulphur trioxide, SO_3) is the anhydride of sulphuric acid (H_2SO_4).

anhydrite naturally occurring anhydrous calcium sulphate ($CaSO_4$).

It is used commercially for the manufacture of plaster of Paris and builders' plaster.

anhydrous of a chemical compound, containing no water. If the water of crystallization is removed from blue crystals of copper(II) sulphate, a white powder (anhydrous copper sulphate) results. Liquids from which all traces of water have been removed are also described as being anhydrous.

aniline (Portuguese *anil* 'indigo') $C_6H_5NH_2$ or phenylamine one of the simplest aromatic chemicals (a substance related to benzene, with its carbon atoms joined in a ring). When pure, it is a colourless oily liquid; it has a characteristic odour, and turns brown on contact with air. It occurs in coal tar, and is used in the rubber industry and to make drugs and dyes.

It is highly poisonous.

anion ion carrying a negative charge. During electrolysis, anions in the electrolyte move towards the anode (positive electrode).

anisotropic or *aelotropic* describing a substance that has different physical properties in different directions. Some crystals, for example, have different refractive indices in different directions.

annelid any segmented worm of the phylum Annelida. Annelids include earthworms, leeches, and marine worms such as lugworms.

annular eclipse solar ◊eclipse in which the Moon does not completely obscure the Sun and a thin ring of sunlight remains visible. Annular eclipses occur when the Moon is at its furthest point from the Earth.

anode in chemistry, the positive electrode of an electrolytic ◊cell, towards which negative particles (anions), usually in solution, are attracted. See ◊electrolysis.

anode in electronics, the positive electrode of a thermionic valve, cathode ray tube, or similar device, towards which electrons are drawn after being emitted from the ◊cathode.

antagonist in biology, a muscle that relaxes in response to the contraction of its agonist muscle. The biceps, in the front of the upper arm, bends the elbow whilst the triceps, lying behind the biceps, straightens the arm.

antagonist in medicine, a drug or body chemical with the reverse effect of another drug or chemical. The drug naloxone is an antagonist of morphine.

Antares or *Alpha Scorpii* brightest star in the constellation Scorpius and the 15th-brightest star in the night sky. It is a red supergiant several hundred times larger than the Sun and perhaps 10,000 times as luminous. It lies about 300 light years away from the Sun, and varies in brightness.

antheridium organ producing the male gametes, ◊antherozoids, in algae, bryophytes (mosses and liverworts), and pteridophytes (ferns, club mosses, and horsetails). It may be either single-celled, as in most algae, or multicellular, as in bryophytes and pteridophytes.

antherozoid motile (or independently moving) male gamete produced by algae, bryophytes (mosses and liverworts), pteridophytes (ferns, club mosses, and horsetails), and some gymnosperms (notably the cycads). Antherozoids are formed in an antheridium and, after being released, swim by means of one or more flagella, to the female gametes. Higher plants have nonmotile male gametes contained within pollen grains.

anthracene white, glistening, crystalline, tricyclic, aromatic hydrocarbon with a faint blue fluorescence when pure. Its melting point is about 216°C/421°F and its boiling point 351°C/664°F. It occurs in the high-boiling-point fractions of coal tar, where it was discovered in 1832 by the French chemists Auguste Laurent (1808–1853) and Jean Dumas (1800–1884).

anthropic principle in science, the idea that 'the universe is the way it is because if it were different we would not be here to observe it'. The principle arises from the observation that if the laws of science were even slightly different, it would have been impossible for intelligent life to evolve. For example, if the electric charge on the electron were only slightly different, stars would have been unable to burn hydrogen and produce the chemical elements that make up our bodies. Scientists are undecided whether the principle is an insight into the nature of the universe or a piece of circular reasoning.

anthropometry science dealing with the measurement of the human body, particularly stature, body weight, cranial capacity, and length of limbs, in samples of living populations, as well as the remains of buried and fossilized humans.

antibiotic drug that kills or inhibits the growth of bacteria and fungi. It is derived from living organisms such as fungi or bacteria, which distinguishes it from synthetic antimicrobials.

antibody protein molecule produced in the blood by lymphocytes in response to the presence of foreign or invading substances (◊antigens); such substances include the proteins carried on the surface of infecting microorganisms. Antibody production is only one aspect of ◊immunity in vertebrates.

anticholinergic any drug that blocks the passage of certain nerve impulses in the central nervous system by inhibiting the production of acetylcholine, a neurotransmitter.

anticline in geology, rock layers or beds folded to form a convex arch (seldom preserved intact) in which older rocks comprise the core. Where relative ages of the rock layers, or stratigraphic ages, are not known, convex upward folded rocks are referred to as *antiforms*.

anticoagulant substance that inhibits the formation of blood clots. Common anticoagulants are heparin, produced by the liver and some white blood cells, and derivatives of coumarin. Anticoagulants are used medically in the prevention and treatment of thrombosis and heart attacks. Anticoagulant substances are also produced by blood-feeding animals, such as mosquitoes, leeches, and vampire bats, to keep the victim's blood flowing.

anticonvulsant any drug used to prevent epileptic seizures (convulsions or fits) or reduce their severity.

antiferromagnetic material material with a very low magnetic susceptibility that increases with temperature up to a certain temperature, called the Néel temperature. Above the Néel temperature, the material is only weakly attracted to a strong magnet.

antigen any substance that causes the production of ◊antibodies by the body's immune system. Common antigens include the proteins carried on the surface of bacteria, viruses, and pollen grains. The proteins of incompatible blood groups or tissues also act as antigens, which has to be taken into account in medical procedures such as blood transfusions and organ transplants.

antihistamine any substance that counteracts the effects of histamine. Antihistamines may occur naturally or they may be synthesized.

antihypertensive therapy any treatment that controls hypertension. The first step is usually exercise and a change in diet to reduce salt and, if necessary, caloric intake. If further measures are required, drugs regimen may be prescribed.

anti-inflammatory any substance that reduces swelling in soft tissues. Antihistamines relieve allergic reactions; aspirin and NSAIDs are effective in joint and musculoskeletal conditions; and rubefacients (counterirritant liniments) ease painful joints, tendons, and muscles.

antilogarithm or *antilog* the inverse of ◊logarithm, or the number whose logarithm to a given base is a given number. If $y = \log a\ x$, then $x = $ antilog$a\ y$.

antimatter in physics, a form of matter in which most of the attributes (such as electrical charge, magnetic moment, and spin) of ◊elementary particles are reversed. Such particles (◊antiparticles) can be created in particle accelerators, such as those at CERN in Geneva, Switzerland, and at Fermilab in the USA. In 1996 physicists at CERN created the first atoms of antimatter: nine atoms of antihydrogen survived for 40 nanoseconds.

antiparticle in nuclear physics, a particle corresponding in mass and properties to a given ◊elementary particle but with the opposite electrical charge, magnetic properties, or coupling to other fundamental forces. For example, an electron carries a negative charge whereas its antiparticle, the positron, carries a positive one. When a particle and its antiparticle collide, they destroy each other, in the process called 'annihilation', their total energy being converted to lighter particles and/or photons. A substance consisting entirely of antiparticles is known as ◊antimatter.

antipruritic any skin preparation or drug administered to relieve itching.

antipyretic any drug, such as aspirin, used to reduce fever.

antiseptic any substance that kills or inhibits the growth of microorganisms. The use of antiseptics was pioneered by Joseph Lister. He used carbolic acid (◊phenol), which is a weak antiseptic; antiseptics such as TCP are derived from this.

antiserum substance used to treat or give temporary protection against a particular disease. It contains antibodies against the ◊antigens associated with the disease.

The term is used in connection with preparations made from animal plasma; protective antibodies acquired from human plasma are called ◊immunoglobulins. See ◊immunization.

antitoxin antibody produced by the immune system to counteract a ◊toxin.

antitussive any substance administered to suppress a cough. Coughing, however, is an important reflex in clearing secretions from the airways; its suppression is usually unnecessary and possibly harmful, unless damage is being done to tissue during excessive coughing spasms.

antiviral any drug that acts against viruses, usually preventing them from multiplying. Most viral infections are not susceptible to antibiotics. Antivirals have been difficult drugs to develop, and do not necessarily cure viral diseases.

aperture size of the opening admitting light into an optical instrument such as a telescope or camera.

aperture synthesis in astronomy, a technique used in radio astronomy in which several small radio dishes are linked together to simulate the performance of one very large radio telescope, which can be many kilometres in diameter.

aphelion point at which an object, travelling in an elliptical orbit around the Sun, is at its furthest from the Sun. The Earth is at its aphelion on 5 July.

Apollonius' problem problem set by Apollonius of Perga, to describe a circle touching three other given circles.

Apollo project US space project to land a person on the Moon, achieved 20 July 1969, when Neil Armstrong was the first to set foot there. He was accompanied on the Moon's surface by 'Buzz' Aldrin; Michael Collins remained in the orbiting command module.

aposematic coloration in biology, the technical name for *warning coloration* markings that make a dangerous, poisonous, or foul-tasting animal particularly conspicuous and recognizable to a predator. Examples include the yellow and black stripes of bees and wasps, and the bright red or yellow colours of many poisonous frogs. See also ◊mimicry.

apparent in astronomy, term synonymous with 'observed'. It is used, for example, in *apparent magnitude* and *apparent star place* – the observed position which will only yield the mean position given in star catalogues when it has been corrected for the effects of aberration, precession, and nutation.

apparent depth depth that a transparent material such as water or glass appears to have when viewed from above. This is less than its real depth because of the ◊refraction that takes place when light passes into a less dense medium. The ratio of the real depth to the apparent depth of a transparent material is equal to its ◊refractive index.

Appleton layer or *F layer* band containing ionized gases in the Earth's upper atmosphere, at a height of 150–1,000 km/94–625 mi, above the E layer (formerly the Kennelly– Heaviside layer). It acts as a dependable reflector of radio signals as it is not affected by atmospheric conditions, although its ionic composition varies with the sunspot cycle.

application in mathematics, a curved line that connects a series of points (or 'nodes') in the smoothest possible way. The shape of the curve is governed by a series of complex mathematical formulae. Applications are used in computer graphics and ◊CAD.

approximation rough estimate of a given value. For example, for pi (which has a value of 3.1415926 correct to seven decimal places), 3 is an approximation to the nearest whole number.

aqualung or *scuba* underwater breathing apparatus worn by divers, developed in the early 1940s by French diver Jacques Cousteau. Compressed-air cylinders strapped to the diver's back are regulated by a valve system and by a mouth tube to provide air to the diver at the same pressure as that of the surrounding water (which increases with the depth).

aqueduct any artificial channel or conduit for water, originally applied to water supply tunnels, but later used to refer to elevated structures of stone, wood, or ironcarrying navigable canals across valleys.One of the first great aqueducts was built in 691 BC, carrying water for 80 km/50 mi to Ninevah, capital of the ancient Assyrian Empire. Many Roman aqueducts are still standing, for example the one carried by the Pont du Gard at Nîmes in southern France, built about 8 BC (48 m/160 ft high).

aqueous humour watery fluid found in the chamber between the cornea and lens of the vertebrate eye. Similar to blood serum in composition, it is constantly renewed.

arc in geometry, a section of a curved line or circle. A circle has three types of arc: a *semicircle,* which is exactly half of the circle; *minor arcs,* which are less than the semicircle; and *major arcs,* which are greater than the semicircle.

Archaean or *Archaeozoic* widely used term for the earliest era of geological time; the first part of the Precambrian *Eon,* spanning the interval from the formation of Earth to about 2,500 million years ago.

Archimedes' principle in physics, the principle that the weight of the liquid displaced by a floating body is equal to the weight of the body. The principle is often stated in the form: 'an object totally or partially submerged in a fluid displaces a volume of fluid that weighs the same as the apparent loss in weight of the object (which, in turn, equals the upwards force, or upthrust, experienced by that object).' It was discovered by the Greek mathematician Archimedes.

arc minute, arc second units for measuring small angles, used in geometry, surveying, map-making, and astronomy. An arc minute (symbol ′) is one-sixtieth of a degree, and an arc second (symbol ′) is one-sixtieth of an arc minute. Small distances in the sky, as between two close stars or the apparent width of a planet's disc, are expressed in minutes and seconds of arc.

Arcturus or *Alpha Boötis* brightest star in the constellation Boötes and the fourth-brightest star in the night sky. Arcturus is a red giant about 28 times larger than the Sun and 70 times more luminous, 36 light years away from the Sun.

Argand diagram in mathematics, a method for representing complex numbers by Cartesian coordinates (x, y). Along the x-axis (horizontal axis) are plotted the real numbers, and along the y-axis (vertical axis) the nonreal, or ◊imaginary, numbers.

Aries zodiacal constellation in the northern hemisphere between Pisces and Taurus, near Auriga, represented as the legendary ram whose golden fleece was sought by Jason and the Argonauts.

Its most distinctive feature is a curve of three stars of decreasing brightness. The brightest of these is Hamal or Alpha Arietis, 65 light years from Earth.

armature rotating coils of wire in an electric motor or dynamo, or any electrically powered device where a voltage is induced by a ◊magnetic field.

armillary sphere earliest known astronomical device, in use from the 3rd century BC. It showed the Earth at the centre of the universe, surrounded by a number of movable metal rings representing the Sun, Moon, and planets. The armillary sphere was originally used to observe the heavens and later for teaching navigators about the arrangements and movements of the heavenly bodies.

aromatic compound organic chemical compound in which some of the bonding electrons are delocalized (shared among several atoms within the molecule and not localized in the vicinity of the atoms involved in bonding). The commonest aromatic compounds have ring structures, the atoms comprising the ring being either all carbon or containing one or more different atoms (usually nitrogen, sulphur, or oxygen). Typical examples are benzene (C_6H_6) and pyridine (C_5H_5N).

artillery large-◊calibre guns used in warfare.

aryl any organic ◊radical derived from an ◊aromatic compound; for example, the phenyl radical ($-C_6H_5$) is derived from benzene (C_6H_6).

associative operation in mathematics, an operation in which the outcome is independent of the grouping of the numbers or symbols concerned. For example, multiplication is associative, as $4 \times (3 \times 2) = (4 \times 3) \times 2 = 24$; however, division is not, as $12 \div (4 \div 2) = 6$, but $(12 \div 4) \div 2 = 1.5$. Compare ◊commutative operation and distributive operation.

asteroid or *minor planet* any of many thousands of small bodies, composed of rock and iron, that orbit the Sun. Most lie in a belt between the orbits of Mars and Jupiter, and are thought to be fragments left over from the formation of the ◊Solar System. About 100,000 may exist, but their total mass is only a few hundredths the mass of the Moon.

astigmatism aberration occurring in the lens of the eye. It results when the curvature of the lens differs in two perpendicular planes, so that rays in one plane may be in focus while rays in the other are not. With astigmatic eyesight, the vertical and horizontal cannot be in focus at the same time; correction is by the use of a cylindrical lens that reduces the overall focal length of one plane so that both planes are seen in sharp focus.

astrolabe ancient navigational instrument, forerunner of the sextant. Astrolabes usually consisted of a flat disc with a sighting rod that could be pivoted to point at the Sun or bright stars.

From the altitude of the Sun or star above the horizon, the local time could be estimated.

astronomical colour index difference in a star's brightness when measured on two selected ◊wavelengths, in order to determine the star's temperature. Cooler stars emit more light at longer wavelengths (and so appear redder than hot stars). Modern methods involve ◊photoelectric filtering and the UBV photometry system.

astronomical unit unit (symbol AU) equal to the mean distance of the Earth from the Sun: 149,597,870 km/ 92,955,800 mi. It is used to describe planetary distances. Light travels this distance in approximately 8.3 minutes.

astrophysics study of the physical nature of stars, galaxies, and the universe. It began with the development of spectroscopy in the 19th century, which allowed astronomers to analyse the composition of stars from their light. Astrophysicists view the universe as a vast natural laboratory in which they can study matter under conditions of temperature, pressure, and density that are unattainable on Earth.

asymptote in coordinate geometry, a straight line that a curve approaches progressively more closely but never reaches. The x and y axes are asymptotes to the graph of $xy =$ constant (a rectangular ◊hyperbola).

asystole failure of the heart to beat. It is seen in cardiac arrest.

atmosphere mixture of gases surrounding a planet. Planetary atmospheres are prevented from escaping by the pull of gravity. On Earth, atmospheric pressure decreases with altitude. In its lowest layer, the atmosphere consists of nitrogen (78%) and oxygen (21%), both in molecular form (two atoms bonded together) and 1% argon. Small quantities of other gases are important to the chemistry and physics of the Earth's atmosphere, including water and carbon dioxide. The atmosphere plays a major part in the various cycles of nature (the water cycle, the carbon cycle, and the nitrogen cycle). It is the principal industrial source of nitrogen, oxygen, and argon, which are obtained by fractional distillation of liquid air.

atmosphere or *standard atmosphere* in physics, a unit (symbol atm) of pressure equal to 760 torr, 1013.25 millibars, or 1.01325×10^5 newtons per square metre. The actual pressure exerted by the atmosphere fluctuates around this value, which is assumed to be standard at sea level and 0°C/32°F, and is used when dealing with very high pressures.

atmospheric pressure pressure at any point on the Earth's surface that is due to the weight of the column of air above it; it therefore decreases as altitude increases. At sea level the average pressure is 101 kilopascals (1,013 millibars, 760 mmHg, or 14.7 lb per sq in).

Changes in atmospheric pressure, measured with a barometer, are used in weather forecasting. Areas of relatively high pressure are called anticyclones; areas of low pressure are called depressions.

atom (Greek *atomos* 'undivided') smallest unit of matter that can take part in a chemical reaction, and which cannot be broken down chemically into anything simpler. An atom is made up of protons and neutrons in a central nucleus surrounded by electrons (see ◊atomic structure). The atoms of the various elements differ in atomic number, relative atomic mass, and chemical behaviour.

atom, electronic structure of the arrangement of electrons around the nucleus of an atom, in distinct energy levels, also called orbitals or shells (see ◊orbital, atomic). These shells can be regarded as a series of concentric spheres, each of which can contain a certain maximum number of electrons; the noble gases have an arrangement in which every shell contains this number. The energy levels are usually numbered beginning with the shell nearest to the nucleus. The outermost shell is known as the ◊valency shell as it contains the valence electrons.

atomic force microscope (AFM) microscope that produces a magnified image using a diamond probe, with a tip so fine that it may consist of a single atom, dragged over the surface of a specimen to 'feel' the contours of the surface. In effect, the tip acts like the stylus of a record player, reading the surface. The tiny up-and-down movements of the probe are converted to an image of the surface by computer and displayed on a screen. The AFM is useful for examination of biological specimens since, unlike the scanning tunnelling microscope, the specimen does not have to be electrically conducting.

atomic heat product of relative atomic mass and specific heat capacity. It is approximately constant for many solid elements and equal to 6 calories per gram atom per degree (25.2 joules per mole per Kelvin).

atomicity number of atoms of an ◊element that combine together to form a molecule. A molecule of oxygen (O_2) has atomicity 2; sulphur (S_8) has atomicity 8.

atomic mass see ◊relative atomic mass.

atomic mass unit or *dalton unit* (symbol amu or u) unit of mass that is used to measure the relative mass of atoms and molecules. It is equal to one-twelfth of the mass of a carbon-12 atom, which is equivalent to the mass of a proton or 1.66×10^{-27} kg. The ◊relative atomic mass of an atom has no units; thus oxygen-16 has an atomic mass of 16 daltons but a relative atomic mass of 16.

atomic number or *proton number* the number (symbol Z) of protons in the nucleus of an atom. It is equal to the positive charge on the nucleus.

In a neutral atom, it is also equal to the number of electrons surrounding the nucleus. The chemical elements are arranged in the ◊periodic table of the elements according to their atomic number.

atomic orbital region in space occupied by an electron associated with the nucleus of an atom. Atomic orbitals have various shapes, depending on the energy level of the electron and the degree of hybridization. Atomic orbitals overlap to form molecular orbitals, or chemical bonds between atoms.

atomic radiation energy given out by disintegrating atoms during ◊radioactive decay, whether natural or synthesized. The energy may be in the form of fast-moving particles, known as ◊alpha particles and ◊beta particles, or in the form of high-energy electromagnetic waves known as ◊gamma radiation. Overlong exposure to atomic radiation can lead to radiation sickness.

Radiation biology studies the effect of radiation on living organisms. Exposure to atomic radiation is linked to chromosomal damage, cancer, and, in laboratory animals at least, hereditary disease.

atomic radius effective radius of an atom. Atomic radii vary periodically with atomic number, being largest for the alkali metals and smallest for the rare gases.

atomic size or *atomic radius* size of an atom expressed as the radius in angstroms or other units of length.

The sodium atom has an atomic radius of 1.57 angstroms (1.57×10^{-8} cm). For metals, the size of the atom is always greater than the size of its ion. For non-metals the reverse is true.

atomic structure internal structure of an ◊atom.

the nucleus The core of the atom is the *nucleus,* a dense body only one ten-thousandth the diameter of the atom itself. The simplest nucleus, that of hydrogen, comprises a single stable positively charged particle, the *proton*. Nuclei of other elements contain more protons and additional particles, called *neutrons,* of about the same mass as the proton but with no electrical charge. Each element has its own characteristic nucleus with a unique number of protons, the atomic number. The number of neutrons may vary. Where atoms of a single element have different numbers of neutrons, they are called ◊isotopes. Although some isotopes tend to be unstable and exhibit ◊radioactivity, they all have identical chemical properties.

electrons The nucleus is surrounded by a number of moving *electrons,* each of which has a negative charge equal to the positive charge on a proton, but which weighs only $\frac{1}{1,839}$ times as much. In a neutral atom, the nucleus is surrounded by the same number of electrons as it contains protons. According to quantum theory, the position of an electron is uncertain; it may be found at any point. However, it is more likely to be found in some places than others. The region of space in which an electron is most likely to be found is called an orbital (see ◊orbital, atomic). The chemical properties of an element are determined by the ease with which its atoms can gain or lose electrons from its outer orbitals.

atomic volume volume of one gram-atom of an element.

atomic weight another name for ◊relative atomic mass.

ATP abbreviation for a nucleotide molecule found in all cells. It can yield large amounts of energy, and is used to drive the thousands of biological processes needed to sustain life, growth, movement, and reproduction. Green plants use light energy to manufacture ATP as part of the process of ◊photosynthesis. In animals, ATP is formed by the breakdown of glucose molecules, usually obtained from the carbohydrate component of a diet, in a series of reactions termed ◊respiration. It is the driving force behind muscle contraction and the synthesis of complex molecules needed by individual cells.

attenuation in biology and medicine, the reduction in the virulence of a pathogenic microorganism by culturing it in unfavourable conditions, by drying or heating it, or by subjecting it to chemical treatment. Attenuated viruses, for example, are used in vaccines.

audiometer electrical apparatus used to test hearing.

aurora spectacular array of light in the night sky, caused by charged particles from the Sun hitting the Earth's upper atmosphere. The *aurora borealis* is seen in the north of the northern hemisphere; the *aurora australis* in the south of the southern.

autoclave reactor vessel constructed to allow chemical reactions to take place at high temperature and pressure. Such vessels are used, for example, in the manufacture of chemicals and materials for the construction industry.

autogyro V/STOL aircraft able to take off and land without the use of a runway. It uses horizontal rotor to achieve take-off and sustain height, and forward propeller to provide forward motion through the air.

automorphic function function that in relation to a group of ◊transformations has a value on the transformed point identical with the value on the original point.

autophagy process in which a cell synthesizes substances and then metabolizes and absorbs them for its own sustenance.

autumnal equinox see ◊equinox.

Avogadro's hypothesis in chemistry, the law stating that equal volumes of all gases, when at the same temperature and pressure, have the same numbers of molecules. It was first propounded by Italian scientist Amedeo Avogadro.

Avogadro's number or *Avogadro's constant* the number of carbon atoms in 12 g of the carbon-12 isotope (6.022045×10^{23}). The relative atomic mass of any element, expressed in grams, contains this number of atoms. It is named after Italian scientist Amedeo Avogadro.

axiom in mathematics, a statement that is assumed to be true and upon which theorems are proved by using logical deduction; for example, two straight lines cannot enclose a space. The Greek mathematician Euclid used a series of axioms that he considered could not be demonstrated in terms of simpler concepts to prove his geometrical theorems.

axis *plural axes* in geometry, one of the reference lines by which a point on a graph may be located. The horizontal axis is usually referred to as the x-axis, and the vertical axis as the y-axis. The term is also used to refer to the imaginary line about which an object may be said to be symmetrical (*axis of symmetry*) – for example, the diagonal of a square – or the line about which an object may revolve (*axis of rotation*).

axon long threadlike extension of a nerve cell that conducts electrochemical impulses away from the cell body towards other nerve cells, or towards an effector organ such as a muscle. Axons terminate in ◊synapses, junctions with other nerve cells, muscles, or glands.

axoplasm in a nerve fibre, the ◊cytoplasm of an ◊axon, containing the ◊neurofibrils.

azimuth in astronomy, the angular distance of an object eastwards along the horizon, measured from due north, between the astronomical ◊meridian (the vertical circle passing through the centre of the sky and the north and south points on the horizon) and the vertical circle containing the celestial body whose position is to be measured.

azo dye synthetic dye containing the azo group of two nitrogen atoms (N=N) connecting aromatic ring compounds. Azo dyes are usually red, brown, or yellow, and make up about half the dyes produced. They are manufactured from aromatic ◊amines.

B

background radiation radiation that is always present in the environment. By far the greater proportion (87%) of it is emitted from natural sources. Alpha and beta particles, and gamma radiation are radiated by the traces of radioactive minerals that occur naturally in the environment and even in the human body, and by radioactive gases such as radon and thoron, which are found in soil and may seep upwards into buildings. Radiation from space (◊cosmic radiation) also contributes to the background level.

bacteria singular *bacterium* microscopic single-celled organisms lacking a nucleus. Bacteria are widespread, present in soil, air, and water, and as parasites on and in other living things. Some parasitic bacteria cause disease by producing toxins, but others are harmless and may even benefit their hosts. Bacteria usually reproduce by binary fission (dividing into two equal parts), and this may occur approximately every 20 minutes. Only 4,000 species of bacteria are known; bacteriologists believe that around 3 million species may actually exist.

bacteriology the study of ◊bacteria.

bacteriophage virus that attacks ◊bacteria. Such viruses are now of use in genetic engineering.

bacteriotropin or *opsonin* substance in blood serum that helps to make bacteria more vulnerable to ◊leucocytes (white blood cells), which can then engulf and destroy them.

Baily's beads bright spots of sunlight seen around the edge of the Moon for a few seconds immediately before and after a total ◊eclipse of the Sun, caused by sunlight shining between mountains at the Moon's edge. Sometimes one bead is much brighter than the others, producing the so-called *diamond ring* effect. The effect was described in 1836 by the English astronomer Francis Baily (1774–1844), a wealthy stockbroker who retired in 1825 to devote himself to astronomy.

Bakelite first synthetic ◊plastic, created by Leo Baekeland in 1909. Bakelite is hard, tough, and heatproof, and is used as an electrical insulator. It is made by the reaction of phenol with formaldehyde, producing a powdery resin that sets solid when heated. Objects are made by subjecting the resin to compression moulding (simultaneous heat and pressure in a mould).

balance of nature in ecology, the idea that there is an inherent equilibrium in most ecosystems, with plants and animals interacting so as to produce a stable, continuing system of life on Earth. The activities of human beings can, and frequently do, disrupt the balance of nature.

ballistics study of the motion and impact of projectiles such as bullets, bombs, and missiles. For projectiles from a gun, relevant exterior factors include temperature, barometric pressure, and wind strength; and for nuclear missiles these extend to such factors as the speed at which the Earth turns.

Balmer series visible ◊spectrum of hydrogen, consisting of a series of distinct ◊spectral lines with wavelengths in the visible region.

bandwidth range of ◊frequencies over which the capability of a receiver or other electric device does not differ from its peak by a given amount.

Bardeen–Cooper–Schrieffer theory or *BCS theory* theory that accounts for the zero electrical resistance of some superconducting metals by invoking an attractive interaction between electrons binding them into 'Cooper pairs'.

barium (Greek *barytes* 'heavy') soft, silver-white, metallic element, symbol Ba, atomic number 56, relative atomic mass 137.33. It is one of the alkaline-earth metals, found in nature as barium carbonate and barium sulphate. As the sulphate it is used in medicine: taken as a suspension (a 'barium meal'), its movement along the gut is followed using X-rays. The barium sulphate, which is opaque to X-rays, shows the shape of the gut, revealing any abnormalities of the alimentary canal. Barium is also used in alloys, pigments, and safety matches and, with strontium, forms the emissive surface in cathode-ray tubes. It was first discovered in barytes or heavy spar.

Barnard's star second-closest star to the Sun, six light years away in the constellation Ophiuchus. It is a faint red dwarf of 10th magnitude, visible only through a telescope. It is named after the US astronomer Edward E Barnard (1857–1923), who discovered in 1916 that it has the fastest proper motion of any star, crossing 1 degree of sky every 350 years.

barometer instrument that measures atmospheric pressure as an indication of weather. Most often used are the *mercury barometer* and the *aneroid barometer*.

barycentric calculus coordinate geometry calculations using a coordinate system devised by August Möbius in which numerical coefficients are assigned to points on a plane, giving the position of a general point by reference to four or more non-coplanar points. Described in this way, the general point thus represents a centre of gravity for a distribution of mass at the four (or more) points proportional to the assigned numbers.

base in chemistry, a substance that accepts protons. Bases can contain negative ions such as the hydroxide ion (OH^-), which is the strongest base, or be molecules such as ammonia (NH_3). Ammonia is a weak base, as only some of its molecules accept protons.

$$OH^- + H^+_{(aq)} \rightarrow H_2O_{(l)} \quad NH_3 + H_2O \leftrightarrow NH_4^+ + OH^-$$

Bases that dissolve in water are called alkalis.

Inorganic bases are usually oxides or hydroxides of metals, which react with dilute acids to form a salt and water. Many carbonates also react with dilute acids, additionally giving off carbon dioxide.

base pair in biochemistry, the linkage of two base (purine or pyrimidine) molecules in ◊DNA. They are found in nucleotides, and form the basis of the genetic code.

battery any energy-storage device allowing release of electricity on demand. It is made up of one or more electrical ◊cells. Primary-cell batteries are disposable; secondary-cell batteries, or ◊accumulators, are rechargeable. Primary-cell batteries are an extremely uneconomical form of energy, since they produce only 2% of the power used in their manufacture. It is dangerous to try to recharge a primary-cell battery.

behaviourism school of psychology originating in the USA, of which the leading exponent was John B Watson.

Behaviourists maintain that all human activity can ultimately be explained in terms of conditioned reactions or reflexes and habits formed in consequence. Leading behaviourists include Ivan Pavlov and B F Skinner.

Bernoulli numbers or *B numbers* sequence of ◊rational numbers that may be represented by the symbolic form $B_n = (B + 1)^n$, corresponding to the sequence:

$B_0 = 1$ $B_1 = -\frac{1}{2}$ $B_2 = \frac{1}{6}$
$B_3 = 0$ $B_4 = -\frac{1}{30}$ $B_5 = 0$
$B_6 = -\frac{1}{42}$ $B_7 = 0$ $B_8 = -\frac{1}{30}$

and so on. *B* numbers of odd order (except B_1) are zero; *B* numbers of even order alternate to sign. They are named after Swiss mathematician Jean Bernoulli and were first discussed in his work on probability *Ars Conjectandi*.

Bernoulli's theorem sum of the ◊pressure, potential ◊energy, and ◊kinetic energy of a fluid flowing along a tube is constant, provided the flow is steady, incompressible and nonviscous.

Bessemer process first cheap method of making ◊steel, invented by Henry Bessemer in England 1856. It has since been superseded by more efficient steel-making processes, such as the basic–oxygen process. In the Bessemer process compressed air is blown into the bottom of a converter, a furnace shaped like a cement mixer, containing molten pig iron. The excess carbon in the iron burns out, other impurities form a slag, and the furnace is emptied by tilting.

beta decay disintegration of the nucleus of an atom to produce a beta particle, or high-speed electron, and an electron antineutrino. During beta decay, a neutron in the nucleus changes into a proton, thereby increasing the atomic number by one while the mass number stays the same. The mass lost in the change is converted into kinetic (movement) energy of the beta particle.

Beta decay is caused by the weak nuclear force, one of the fundamental forces of nature operating inside the nucleus.

beta particle electron ejected with great velocity from a radioactive atom that is undergoing spontaneous disintegration. Beta particles do not exist in the nucleus but are created on disintegration, beta decay, when a neutron converts to a proton to emit an electron.

Betelgeuse or *Alpha Orionis* red supergiant star in the constellation of Orion. It is the tenth-brightest star in the night sky, although its brightness varies. It is 1,100 million km/700 million mi across, about 800 times larger than the Sun, roughly the same size as the orbit of Mars. It is over 10,000 times as luminous as the Sun, and lies 650 light years from the Sun. Light takes 60 minutes to travel across the giant star.

Bethe–Weizsäcker cycle see ◊proton–proton cycle.

Betti numbers numbers characterizing the connectivity of a ◊variety. They are named after Italian mathematician Enrico Betti.

Bhabha scattering scattering process involving ◊electrons and ◊positrons, first determined by Indian physicist Homi Bhabha in 1935.

Big Bang in astronomy, the hypothetical 'explosive' event that marked the origin of the universe as we know it. At the time of the Big Bang, the entire universe was squeezed into a hot, superdense state. The Big Bang explosion threw this compact material outwards, producing the expanding universe (see ◊red shift). The cause of the Big Bang is unknown; observations of the current rate of expansion of the universe suggest that it took place about 10–20 billion years ago. The Big Bang theory began modern ◊cosmology.

bile brownish alkaline fluid produced by the liver. Bile is stored in the gall bladder and is intermittently released into the duodenum (small intestine) to aid digestion. Bile consists of bile salts, bile pigments, cholesterol, and lecithin. *Bile salts* assist in the breakdown and absorption of fats; *bile pigments* are the breakdown products of old red blood cells that are passed into the gut to be eliminated with the faeces.

bimetallic strip strip made from two metals each having a different coefficient of thermal expansion; it therefore bends when subjected to a change in temperature. Such strips are used widely for temperature measurement and control, for instance in the domestic thermostat.

binary star pair of stars moving in orbit around their common centre of mass. Observations show that most stars are binary, or even multiple – for example, the nearest star system to the Sun, ◊Alpha Centauri.

biochemistry science concerned with the chemistry of living organisms: the structure and reactions of proteins (such as enzymes), nucleic acids, carbohydrates, and lipids.

bioluminescence production of light by living organisms. It is a feature of many deep-sea fishes, crustaceans, and other marine animals. On land, bioluminescence is seen in some nocturnal insects such as glow-worms and fireflies, and in certain bacteria and fungi. Light is usually produced by the oxidation of luciferin, a reaction catalysed by the ◊enzyme luciferase. This reaction is unique, being the only known biological oxidation that does not produce heat. Animal luminescence is involved in communication, camouflage, or the luring of prey, but its function in other organisms is unclear.

biosynthesis synthesis of organic chemicals from simple inorganic ones by living cells – for example, the conversion of carbon dioxide and water to glucose by plants during ◊photosynthesis.

Other biosynthetic reactions produce cell constituents including proteins and fats.

biplane aircraft with two parallel wings, set one above the other.

biquaternions type of ◊quaternions devised by English mathematician William Clifford to use specifically in association with linear algebra to represent motions in three-dimensional non-Euclidean space.

birefringence another name for ◊double refraction.

black body in physics, a hypothetical object that completely absorbs all electromagnetic radiation striking it. It is also a perfect emitter of thermal radiation.

black-body radiation radiation of a thermal nature emitted by a theoretically perfect emitter of radiation at a certain temperature.

black hole object in space whose gravity is so great that nothing can escape from it, not even light. Thought to form when massive stars shrink at the end of their lives, a black hole sucks in more matter, including other stars, from the space around it. Matter that falls into a black hole is squeezed to infinite density at the centre of the hole. Black holes can be detected because gas falling towards them becomes so hot that it emits X-rays.

blast furnace smelting furnace used to extract metals from their ores, chiefly pig iron from iron ore. The temperature is raised by the injection of an air blast.

blastocyst in mammals, the hollow ball of cells which is an early stage in the development of the embryo, roughly equivalent to the ◊blastula of other animal groups.

blastoderm sheet of cells that grows on the surface of a fertilized ovum. In mammals it forms a disc of cells that eventually develops into the embryo between the amniotic cavity and the yolk sac. The ◊endoderm, ◊mesoderm, and ◊ectoderm also develop from the blastoderm.

blastula early stage in the development of a fertilized egg, when the egg changes from a solid mass of cells (the morula) to a hollow ball of cells (the blastula), containing a fluid-filled cavity (the blastocoel).

blood group any of the types into which blood is classified according to the presence or otherwise of certain ◊antigens on the surface of its red cells. Red blood cells of one individual may carry molecules on their surface that act as antigens in another individual whose red blood cells lack these molecules. The two main antigens are designated A and B. These give rise to four blood groups: having A only (A), having B only (B), having both (AB), and having neither (O). Each of these groups may or may not contain the ◊rhesus factor. Correct typing of blood groups is vital in transfusion, since incompatible types of donor and recipient blood will result in coagulation, with possible death of the recipient.

blue dwarf, blue giant high-temperature stars (as opposed to red stars). Blue giants are generally on or near the main sequence of the ◊Hertzsprung–Russell diagram; blue dwarfs represent the very dense, but very small, near-final form of what was once a ◊red giant.

***B* number** abbreviation for ◊Bernoulli number.

bobbin in weaving, the spool onto which yarn is wound.

Bode's law or ***Titius-Bode law*** numerical sequence that gives the approximate distances, in astronomical units (distance between Earth and Sun = one astronomical unit), of the planets from the Sun by adding 4 to each term of the series 0, 3, 6, 12, 24, ... and then dividing by 10. Bode's law predicted the existence of a planet between Mars and Jupiter, which led to the discovery of the asteroids. It was popularized by German astronomer Johann Bode.

Bohr model model of the atom conceived by Danish physicist Neils Bohr in 1913. It assumes that the following rules govern the behaviour of electrons: (1) electrons revolve in orbits of specific radius around the nucleus without emitting radiation; (2) within each orbit, each electron has a fixed amount of energy; electrons in orbits farther away from the nucleus have greater energies; (3) an electron may 'jump' from one orbit of high energy to another of lower energy causing the energy difference to be emitted as a ◊photon of electromagnetic radiation such as light. The Bohr model has been superseded by wave mechanics (see ◊quantum theory).

boiling point for any given liquid, the temperature at which the application of heat raises the temperature of the liquid no further, but converts it into vapour.

Bok's globule small, circular dark spot in a ◊nebula, with a mass comparable to that of the Sun. Bok's globules are possibly gas clouds in the process of condensing into stars. They were first discovered by Dutch astrophysicist Bart Bok.

bond in chemistry, the result of the forces of attraction that hold together atoms of an element or elements to form a molecule. The principal types of bonding are ◊ionic, ◊covalent, metallic, and intermolecular (such as hydrogen bonding).

Boolean algebra set of algebraic rules, named after English mathematician George Boole, in which TRUE and FALSE are equated to 0 and 1. Boolean algebra includes a series of operators (AND, OR, NOT, NAND (NOT AND), NOR, and XOR (exclusive OR)), which can be used to manipulate TRUE and FALSE values. It is the basis of computer logic because the truth values can be directly associated with bits.

Bose-Einstein statistics treatment of particles which have integral ◊spin in statistical mechanics, enabling properties of systems made up of such particles to be calculated.

boson in physics, an elementary particle whose spin can only take values that are whole numbers or zero. Bosons may be classified as gauge bosons (carriers of the four fundamental forces) or ◊mesons. All elementary particles are either bosons or ◊fermions.

boundary value in applied mathematics, a natural phenomenon in a given region may be described by functions that satisfy certain differential equations in the interior of the region and take specific values on the boundary of the region. The latter are referred to as boundary values.

Bourdon gauge instrument for measuring pressure, patented by French watchmaker Eugène Bourdon in 1849. The gauge contains a C-shaped tube, closed at one end. When the pressure inside the tube increases, the tube uncurls slightly causing a small movement at its closed end. A system of levers and gears magnifies this movement and turns a pointer, which indicates the pressure on a circular scale. Bourdon gauges are often fitted to cylinders of compressed gas used in industry and hospitals.

box girder girder made from four lengths of metal sheet formed into a box cross section.

Boyle's law law stating that the volume of a given mass of gas at a constant temperature is inversely proportional to its pressure. For example, if the pressure of a gas doubles, its volume will be reduced by a half, and vice versa. The law was discovered in 1662 by Irish physicist and chemist Robert Boyle.

brachiopod or ***lamp shell*** any member of the phylum Brachiopoda, marine invertebrates with two shells, resembling but totally unrelated to bivalves.

There are about 300 living species; they were much more numerous in past geological ages. They are suspension feeders, ingesting minute food particles from water. A single internal organ, the lophophore, handles feeding, aspiration, and excretion.

Bragg's law in physics, law that states that the maximum intensity of X-rays diffracted (see ◊X-ray diffraction) through crystal occurs when the sine of the complement of the angle of incidence of the X-rays onto the crystal satisfies the relation:

$$n\lambda = 2d \sin \theta$$

where λ is the wavelength of the radiation; d is the lattice spacing; and n is an integer. The equation was determined by Australian-born British physicist Lawrence Bragg.

braid theory part of the study of nodes in three-dimensional space, first devised by Austrian mathematician Emil Artin.

Bremsstrahlung ◊electromagnetic radiation produced by the rapid deceleration of charged particles such as electrons, as occurs in the collison between electrons and nuclei.

Brewster's law in physics, law that states that the ◊refractive index of a medium is given by the tangent of the angle at which maximum polarization occurs. It was determined by Scottish physicist David Brewster.

British Standard Whitworth thread see ◊Whitworth standard.

broad gauge rail track introduced by Isambard Kingdom Brunel, where the inside edges of the steel rails were separated by a distance of 7 ft/2.2m.

Brownian movement the continuous random motion of particles in a fluid medium (gas or liquid) as they are subjected to impact from the molecules of the medium. The phenomenon was explained by German physicist Albert Einstein in 1905 but was observed as long ago as 1827 by the Scottish botanist Robert Brown. Brown was looking at pollen grains in water under a microscope when he noticed the pollen grains were in constant, haphazard motion. The motion of these particles was due to the impact of moving water molecules. It provides evidence for the ◊kinetic theory of matter.

bubble chamber in physics, a device for observing the nature and movement of atomic particles, and their interaction with radiation. It is a vessel filled with a superheated liquid through which ionizing particles move and collide. The paths of these particles are shown by strings of bubbles, which can be photographed and studied. By using a pressurized liquid medium instead of a gas, it overcomes drawbacks inherent in the earlier ◊cloud chamber. It was invented by US physicist Donald Glaser in 1952.

Bunsen burner gas burner used in laboratories, consisting of a vertical metal tube through which a fine jet of fuel gas is directed. Air is drawn in through airholes near the base of the tube and the mixture is ignited and burns at the tube's upper opening.

Burali–Forte's paradox paradox stating that to every collection of ordinal numbers there corresponds an ordinal number greater than any element of the collection. In particular it would follow that the collection of all ordinal numbers is itself an ordinal number. This contradiction demonstrated the need for a rigorous exposition of set theory in which not all collections may be accepted as valid subjects of discourse. There is thus no such thing as a 'set of all sets', nor a 'set of all ordinals' (indicating that the ◊foundations of mathematics cannot be expressed in purely logical terms). One therefore distinguishes between sets, which may be manipulated, and ◊classes, which may not (except in the simplest of circumstances).

C

CAD acronym for *computer-aided design* use of computers in creating and editing design drawings. CAD also allows such things as automatic testing of designs and multiple or animated three-dimensional views of designs. CAD systems are widely used in architecture, electronics, and engineering, for example in the motor-vehicle industry, where cars designed with the assistance of computers are now commonplace. With a CAD system, picture components are accurately positioned using grid lines. Pictures can be resized, rotated, or mirrored without loss of quality or proportion.

A related development is CAM (computer-assisted manufacturing).

calculus (Latin '*pebble*') branch of mathematics which uses the concept of a derivative (see ◊differentiation) to analyse the way in which the values of a ◊function vary. Calculus is probably the most widely used part of mathematics. Many real-life problems are analysed by expressing one quantity as a function of another – position of a moving object as a function of time, temperature of an object as a function of distance from a heat source, force on an object as a function of distance from the source of the force, and so on – and calculus is concerned with such functions.

calculus of variations method of calculation for solving problems in which one of the unknowns cannot be expressed as a number or a finite set of numbers, but is representable as a curve, a function or a system of functions. (A classic problem in the subject is to show that a circle, among all curves of fixed length, encloses the maximum area.)

calibre internal diameter or a bore or pipe.

Callisto second-largest moon of Jupiter, 4,800 km/3,000 mi in diameter, orbiting every 16.7 days at a distance of 1.9 million km/1.2 million mi from the planet. Its surface is covered with large craters.

caloric theory theory that ◊heat consists of a fluid called 'caloric' that flows from hotter to colder bodies. It was abandoned by the mid-eighteenth century.

calorimeter instrument used in physics to measure various thermal properties, such as heat capacity or the heat produced by fuel. A simple calorimeter consists of a heavy copper vessel that is polished (to reduce heat losses by radiation) and covered with insulating material (to reduce losses by convection and conduction).

calorimeter instrument used in the determination of quantities of heat change.

calorimetry measurement of the heat-related constants of material, for example, thermal capacity, ◊latent heat of vaporization.

calotype paper-based photograph using a wax paper negative, the first example of the negative/positive process invented by the English photographer Fox Talbot around 1834.

camber curved surface of an aerofoil, road, and so on.

Cambrian period of geological time 570–510 million years ago; the first period of the Palaeozoic era. All invertebrate animal life appeared, and marine algae were widespread. The *Cambrian Explosion* 530–520 million years ago saw the first appearance in the fossil record of all modern animal phyla; the earliest fossils with hard shells, such as trilobites, date from this period.

Cambridge Catalogues results of five intensive radio-astronomical surveys (1C, 2C, 3C, 4C, and 5C) under the direction of English astronomers Martin Ryle and Antony Hewish, during the 1950s, 1960s, and 1970s, at Cambridge.

camera obscura darkened box with a tiny hole for projecting the inverted image of the scene outside on to a screen inside.

canal rays streams of positively charged ◊ions produced from an ◊anode in a discharge tube, in which gas is subjected to an electric discharge.

cantilever beam or structure that is fixed at one end only, though it may be supported at some point along its length; for example, a diving board. The cantilever principle, widely used in construction engineering, eliminates the need for a second main support at the free end of the beam, allowing for more elegant structures and reducing the amount of materials required. Many large-span bridges have been built on the cantilever principle.

capacitance, electrical property of a capacitor that determines how much charge can be stored in it for a given potential difference between its terminals. It is equal to the ratio of the electrical charge stored to the potential difference. It is measured in farads.

carbohydrate chemical compound composed of carbon, hydrogen, and oxygen, with the basic formula $C_m(H_2O)_n$, and related compounds with the same basic structure but modified functional groups. As sugar and starch, carbohydrates are an important part of a balanced human diet, providing energy for life processes including growth and movement. Excess carbohydrate intake can be converted into fat and stored in the body.

Carboniferous period of geological time 362.5–290 million years ago, the fifth period of the Palaeozoic era. In the USA it is divided into two periods: the Mississippian (lower) and the Pennsylvanian (upper).

Typical of the lower-Carboniferous rocks are shallow-water limestones, while upper-Carboniferous rocks have delta deposits with coal (hence the name). Amphibians were abundant, and reptiles evolved during this period.

carbon–nitrogen cycle use of carbon and nitrogen as intermediates in the ◊nuclear fusion process of the Sun. Cooler stars undergo the ◊proton–proton cycle.

carboxylic acid organic acid containing the carboxyl group (-COOH) attached to another group (R), which can be hydrogen (giving methanoic acid, HCOOH) or a larger molecule (up to 24 carbon atoms). When R is a straight-chain alkyl group (such as CH_3 or CH_3CH_2), the acid is known as a ◊fatty acid.

carburation mixing of a gas, such as air, with a volatile hydrocarbon fuel, such as petrol, kerosene, or fuel oil, in order to form an explosive mixture. The process, which ensures that the maximum amount of heat energy is released during combustion, is used in internal-combustion engines. In most petrol engines the liquid fuel is atomized and mixed with air by means of a device called a *carburettor*.

carburettor device in an ◊internal-combustion engine that mixes air with a jet of petrol to produce a combustible mixture, which, when ignited, produces driving power via pistons and crankshaft.

carcinogenesis in medicine, the means by which the changes responsible for the development of cancer are brought about.

Carnot cycle series of changes in the physical condition of a gas in a reversible heat engine, necessarily in the following order: (1) isothermal expansion (without change of temperature), (2) adiabatic expansion (without change of heat content), (3) isothermal compression, and (4) adiabatic compression.

Carnot's theorem theorem in ◊thermodynamics stating that the efficiency of any (reversible) heat engine depends only on the temperature range through which the machine operates. It was determined by French physicist Sadi Carnot.

carrier wave wave of ◊electromagnetic radiation of constant frequency and amplitude used in radio communication. Modulation of the wave allows information to be carried by it.

Cassegrain telescope or *Cassegrain reflector* type of reflecting telescope in which light collected by a concave primary mirror is reflected on to a convex secondary mirror, which in turn directs it back through a hole in the primary mirror to a focus behind it. As a result, the telescope tube can be kept short, allowing equipment for analyzing and recording starlight to be mounted behind the main mirror. All modern large astronomical telescopes are of the Cassegrain type.

Cassini Division gap between Saturn's Rings A and B. It was named after Italian astronomer Giovanni Cassini who was the first to realize that Saturn had more than one ring.

cast iron cheap but invaluable constructional material, most commonly used for car engine blocks. Cast iron is partly refined pig (crude) ◊iron, which is very fluid when molten and highly suitable for shaping by casting; it contains too many impurities (for example, carbon) to be readily shaped in any other way. Solid cast iron is heavy and can absorb great shock but is very brittle.

catalyst substance that alters the speed of, or makes possible, a chemical or biochemical reaction but remains unchanged at the end of the reaction. ◊Enzymes are natural biochemical catalysts. In practice most catalysts are used to speed up reactions.

catastrophism theory that regards the variations in fossils from different geological strata as having resulted from a series of natural catastrophes that gave rise to new species.

catenary curve taken up by a flexible cable suspended between two points, under gravity; for example, the curve of overhead suspension cables that hold the conductor wire of an electric railway or tramway.

cathode in chemistry, the negative electrode of an electrolytic ◊cell, towards which positive particles (cations), usually in solution, are attracted. See ◊electrolysis.

cathode in electronics, the part of an electronic device in which electrons are generated. In a thermionic valve, electrons are produced by the heating effect of an applied current; in a photocell, they are produced by the interaction of light and a semiconducting material. The cathode is kept at a negative potential relative to the device's other electrodes (anodes) in order to ensure that the liberated electrons stream away from the cathode and towards the anodes.

cathode ray stream of fast-moving electrons that travel from a cathode (negative electrode) towards an anode (positive electrode) in a vacuum tube. They carry a negative charge and can be deflected by electric and magnetic fields. Cathode rays focused into fine beams of fast electrons are used in cathode-ray tubes, the electrons' ◊kinetic energy being converted into light energy as they collide with the tube's fluorescent screen.

cation ◊ion carrying a positive charge. During electrolysis, cations in the electrolyte move to the cathode (negative electrode).

caustic curve curve formed by the points of intersection of rays of light reflected or refracted from a curved surface.

cavitation formation of partial vacuums (or cavities) in fluids at high velocities, produced by propellers or other machine parts in hydraulic engines, in accordance with Bernoulli's principle. When these vacuums collapse, pitting, vibration, and noise can occur in the metal parts in contact with the fluids.

celestial mechanics branch of astronomy that deals with the calculation of the orbits of celestial bodies, their gravitational attractions (such as those that produce the Earth's tides), and also the orbits of artificial satellites and space probes. It is based on the laws of motion and gravity laid down by Isaac Newton.

celestial sphere imaginary sphere surrounding the Earth, on which the celestial bodies seem to lie. The positions of bodies such as stars, planets, and galaxies are specified by their coordinates on the celestial sphere. The equivalents of latitude and longitude on the celestial sphere are called ◊declination and ◊right ascension (which is measured in hours from 0 to 24). The *celestial poles* lie directly above the Earth's poles, and the *celestial equator* lies over the Earth's Equator. The celestial sphere appears to rotate once around the Earth each day, actually a result of the rotation of the Earth on its axis.

cell in biology, the basic structural unit of life. It is the smallest unit capable of independent existence which can reproduce itself exactly. All living organisms – with the exception of ◊viruses – are composed of one or more cells. Single cell organisms such as bacteria, protozoa, and other microorganisms are termed **unicellular,** while plants and animals which contain many cells are termed **multicellular** organisms. Highly complex organisms such as human beings consist of billions of cells, all of which are adapted to carry out specific functions – for instance, groups of these specialized cells are organized into tissues and organs. Although these cells may differ widely in size, appearance, and function, their essential features are similar.

Cells divide by ◊mitosis, or by ◊meiosis when ◊gametes are being formed.

cell, electrical or *voltaic cell* or *galvanic cell* device in which chemical energy is converted into electrical energy; the popular name is ◊'battery', but this actually refers to a collection of cells in one unit. The reactive chemicals of a *primary cell* cannot be replenished, whereas *secondary cells* – such as storage batteries – are rechargeable: their chemical reactions can be reversed and the original condition restored by applying an electric current. It is dangerous to attempt to recharge a primary cell.

cell, electrolytic device to which electrical energy is applied in order to bring about a chemical reaction; see ◊electrolysis.

cell theory theory that regards all living things as being composed of cells and that their replication and growth result from cell division. The theory was proposed by German botanist Matthias Schleiden and German physiologist Theodor Schwann in 1838–39.

celluloid transparent or translucent, highly flammable, plastic material (a ◊thermoplastic) made from cellulose nitrate and camphor. It was once used for toilet articles, novelties, and photographic film, but has now been replaced by the nonflammable substance cellulose acetate.

Cenozoic or *Caenozoic* era of geological time that began 65 million years ago and continues to the present day. It is divided into the Tertiary and Quaternary periods. The Cenozoic marks the emergence of mammals as a dominant group, including humans, and the formation of the mountain chains of the Himalayas and the Alps.

centre of gravity the point in an object about which its weight is evenly balanced. In a uniform gravitational field, this is the same as the ◊centre of mass.

centre of mass point in or near an object at which the whole mass of the object may be considered to be concentrated. A symmetrical homogeneous object such as a sphere or cube has its centre of mass at its geometrical centre; a hollow object (such as a cup) may have its centre of mass in space inside the hollow.

centrifugal force useful concept in physics, based on an apparent (but not real) force. It may be regarded as a force that acts radially outward from a spinning or orbiting object, thus balancing the ◊centripetal force (which is real). For an object of mass m moving with a velocity v in a circle of radius r, the centrifugal force F equals mv^2/r (outward). Compare with ◊centripetal force.

centrifugal governor governor that controls the behaviour of an engine by means of a feedback process involving ◊centrifugal forces. As the engine speed increases, the arms of the governor are lifted by the centrifugal force, the power supply to the engine is thereby reduced, cutting the speed.

centrifuge apparatus that rotates containers at high speeds, creating centrifugal forces. One use is for separating mixtures of substances of different densities.

centripetal force force that acts radially inward on an object moving in a curved path. For example, with a weight whirled in a circle at the end of a length of string, the centripetal force is the tension in the string. For an object of mass m moving with a velocity v in a circle of radius r, the centripetal force F equals mv^2/r (inward). The reaction to this force is the ◊centrifugal force.

centrosome cell body that contains the centrioles. During cell division the centrosomes organize the microtubules to form the spindle that divides the chromosomes into daughter cells. Centrosomes were first described in 1887, independently by German biologist Theodor Boveri (1862–1915) and Belgian biologist Edouard van Beneden.

Cepheid variable yellow supergiant star that varies regularly in brightness every few days or weeks as a result of pulsations. The time that a Cepheid variable takes to pulsate is directly related to its average brightness; the longer the pulsation period, the brighter the star.

chain reaction in chemistry, a succession of reactions, usually involving free radicals, where the products of one stage are the reactants of the next. A chain reaction is characterized by the continual generation of reactive substances.

chain reaction in nuclear physics, a fission reaction that is maintained because neutrons released by the splitting of some atomic nuclei themselves go on to split others, releasing even more neutrons. Such a reaction can be controlled (as in a nuclear reactor) by using moderators to absorb excess neutrons. Uncontrolled, a chain reaction produces a nuclear explosion (as in an atom bomb).

Chandrasekhar limit or *Chandrasekhar mass* in astrophysics, the maximum possible mass of a ◊white dwarf star. The limit depends slightly on the composition of the star but is equivalent to 1.4 times the mass of the Sun. A white dwarf heavier than the Chandrasekhar limit would collapse under its own weight to form a ◊neutron star or a ◊black hole. The limit is named after the Indian-US astrophysicist Subrahmanyan Chandrasekhar who developed the theory of white dwarfs in the 1930s.

charge see ◊electric charge.

charge conservation feature of ◊quantum mechanics, in which reactions between ◊elementary particles occur in such a way that there is no change in the total charge of the system after the event has occurred.

Charles's law law stating that the volume of a given mass of gas at constant pressure is directly proportional to its absolute temperature (temperature in kelvin). It was discovered by French physicist Jacques Charles 1787, and independently by French chemist Joseph Gay-Lussac in 1802.

chemotherapy any medical treatment with chemicals. It usually refers to treatment of cancer with cytotoxic and other drugs. The term was coined by the German bacteriologist Paul Ehrlich for the use of synthetic chemicals against infectious diseases.

Cherenkov detector apparatus through which it is possible to observe the existence and velocity of high-speed particles, important in experimental nuclear physics and in the study of ◊cosmic radiation. It was originally built to investigate the Cherenkov radiation effect, in which charged particles travel through a medium at a speed greater than that of light in that medium.

chi-squared function (X^2 function) function that in ◊probability theory provides a test for deviation from a ◊null hypothesis. It is usually represented as being made up of:

$$\frac{(\text{observed frequency of result} - \text{expected frequency of result})^2}{\text{expected frequency of result}}$$

in which the top line indicates the (squared) deviation from the expected.

Chladni figures visual manifestations of sound waves resulting from the behaviour of small particles on plates vibrated in sympathy to a particular sound. They were first recognized by German physicist Ernst Chladni.

chlorophyll green pigment present in most plants; it is responsible for the absorption of light energy during ◊photosynthesis.

The pigment absorbs the red and blue-violet parts of sunlight but reflects the green, thus giving plants their characteristic colour.

chloroplast structure (◊organelle) within a plant cell containing the green pigment chlorophyll. Chloroplasts occur in most cells of the green plant that are exposed to light, often in large numbers. Typically, they are flattened and disclike, with a double membrane enclosing the stroma, a gel-like matrix. Within the stroma are stacks of fluid-containing cavities, or vesicles, where ◊photosynthesis occurs.

choke valve in the ◊carburettor of an ◊internal combustion engine that can reduce the amount of air being mixed into the petrol jet.

chondrite type of meteorite characterized by *chondrules,* small spheres, about 1 mm in diameter, made up of the silicate minerals olivine and orthopyroxene.

chordate animal belonging to the phylum Chordata, which includes vertebrates, sea squirts, amphioxi, and others. All these animals, at some stage of their lives, have a supporting rod of tissue (notochord or backbone) running down their bodies.

chorion outermost of the three membranes enclosing the embryo of reptiles, birds, and mammals; the ◊amnion is the innermost membrane.

chromatic aberration an optical effect commonly found in simple lens instruments in which coloured fringes are seen around an image as a result of the ◊wavelength-dependence of the ◊refractive index for glass.

chromatin nucleoprotein found in ◊chromosomes and thought to be the molecular substance of heredity. It is readily stained by basic dyes and is therefore easily identified and studied under the microscope.

chromatography (Greek *chromos* 'colour') technique for separating or analysing a mixture of gases, liquids, or dissolved substances. This is brought about by means of two immiscible substances, one of which (*the mobile phase)* transports the sample mixture through the other (*the stationary phase)*. The mobile phase may be a gas or a liquid; the stationary phase may be a liquid or a solid, and may be in a column, on paper, or in a thin layer on a glass or plastic support. The components of the mixture are absorbed or impeded by the stationary phase to different extents and therefore become separated. The technique is used for both qualitative and quantitive analyses in biology and chemistry.

chromosome structure in a cell nucleus that carries the ◊genes. Each chromosome consists of one very long strand of DNA, coiled and folded to produce a compact body. The point on a chromosome where a particular gene occurs is known as its locus. Most higher organisms have two copies of each chromosome, together known as a *homologous pair* (they are diploid) but some have only one (they are haploid). There are 46 chromosomes in a normal human cell. See also ◊mitosis and ◊meiosis.

chromosome map description of the position of ◊genes along a ◊chromosome.

chromosphere (Greek 'colour' and 'sphere') layer of mostly hydrogen gas about 10,000 km/6,000 mi deep above the visible surface of the Sun (the photosphere). It appears pinkish red during ◊eclipses of the Sun.

circuit in physics or electrical engineering, an arrangement of electrical components through which a current can flow. There are two basic circuits, series and parallel. In a series circuit, the components are connected end to end so that the current flows through all components one after the other. In a parallel circuit, components are connected side by side so that part of the current passes through each component. A circuit diagram shows in graphical form how components are connected together, using standard symbols for the components.

cis- prefix used in ◊stereochemistry to distinguish an ◊isomer that has two substituents or groupings on the same side of the main axis or plane of the molecule. The isomer with the two on opposite sides is denoted by the prefix *trans-*.

class in mathematics another name for a ◊set.

class field theory theory involving the mathematical structure known as a ◊field, dealing specifically with those that extend a given field in a special kind of way.

Clausius–Clapeyron equation relationship between the pressure, temperature and latent heat in a change of state, for example, liquid to gas. It was determined by German physicist Rudolf Clausius and French mathematician Emile Clapeyron (1799–1864).

clone an exact replica. In genetics, any one of a group of genetically identical cells or organisms. An identical twin is a clone; so, too, are bacteria living in the same colony. The term 'clone' has also been adopted by computer technology to describe a (nonexistent) device that mimics an actual one to enable certain software programs to run correctly.

closed curve curve of which the end point coincides with the initial point, for example, a circle or an ellipse.

cloud chamber apparatus for tracking ionized particles. It consists of a vessel fitted with a piston and filled with air or other gas, saturated with water vapour. When the volume of the vessel is suddenly expanded by moving the piston outwards, the vapour cools and a cloud of tiny droplets forms on any nuclei, dust, or ions present. As fast-moving ionizing particles collide with the air or gas molecules, they show as visible tracks.

cluster group of stars or of ◊galaxies, usually with some recognizably systematic configuration. It appears that both types of cluster are a structural feature of the universe, which form over the passage of time.

coacervate collection of particles in an emulsion that can be reversed into droplets of liquid before they flocculate.

coal gas fuel gas comprising mostly hydrogen and methane and carbon monoxide produced by processing coal.

coccyx lowermost component of the spine. It consists of four vestigial vertebrae fused to form a single triangular bone.

coefficient of expansion quantity that describes the amount of expansion undergone by a material for a degree rise in temperature. It is expressed as the increase in length per unit length, per degree centigrade. For example, the metal with the lowest coefficient of expansion is Invar, at 2.3×10^{-6} m of expansion for every metre in length, per degree centigrade rise in temperature.

coenzyme small nonprotein compound that attaches to an ◊enzyme and is necessary for its correct functioning. Tightly bound coenzymes are known as prosthetic groups; more loosely bound ones are called cofactors. The coenzyme itself is not usually changed during a reaction. If it is, it is usually converted rapidly back to its original form.

coherence in physics, property of two or more waves of a beam of light or other electromagnetic radiation having the same frequency and the same ◊phase, or a constant phase difference.

cohomology or *cohomology theory* algebraic study, using group theory, of geometric objects with specific reference to the operation of finding a boundary. Cohomology theory represents a modification of ◊homology in which it is possible both to add and to multiply ◊classes.

coil, electric length of conducting wire that has been formed into a long series of loops. Used to form, for example, transformers, and electromagnets.

coke solid, porous material produced from the carbonization of coal, all the volatile material having been driven off. It is used in the production of steel.

collinear in mathematics, lying on the same straight line.

collodion process in photography, technique that uses iodized cellulose tetranitrate to coat a plate after being sensitized to light using silver nitrate solution.

colloid substance composed of extremely small particles of one material (the dispersed phase) evenly and stably distributed in another material (the continuous phase). The size of the dispersed particles (1–1,000 nanometres across) is less than that of particles in suspension but greater than that of molecules in true solution. Colloids involving gases include *aerosols* (dispersions of liquid or solid particles in a gas, as in fog or smoke) and *foams* (dispersions of gases in liquids).

Those involving liquids include *emulsions* (in which both the dispersed and the continuous phases are liquids) and *sols* (solid particles dispersed in a liquid). Sols in which both phases contribute to a molecular three-dimensional network have a jellylike form and are known as *gels*; gelatin, starch 'solution', and silica gel are common examples.

colour index in astronomy, a measure of the colour of a star made by comparing its brightness through different coloured filters. It is defined as the difference between the ◊magnitude of the star measured through two standard photometric filters. Colour index is directly related to the surface temperature of a star and its spectral classification.

coma in astronomy, the hazy cloud of gas and dust that surrounds the nucleus of a ◊comet.

combustion burning, defined in chemical terms as the rapid combination of a substance with oxygen, accompanied by the evolution of heat and usually light. A slow-burning candle flame and the explosion of a mixture of petrol vapour and air are extreme examples of combustion. Combustion is an exothermic reaction (exothermic reaction) as heat energy is given out.

comet small, icy body orbiting the Sun, usually on a highly elliptical path. A comet consists of a central nucleus a few kilometres across, and has been likened to a dirty snowball because it consists mostly of ice mixed with dust. As a comet approaches the Sun its nucleus heats up, releasing gas and dust which form a tenuous coma, up to 100,000 km/60,000 mi wide, around the nucleus. Gas and dust stream away from the coma to form one or more tails, which may extend for millions of kilometres.

commutative operation in mathematics, an operation that is independent of the order of the numbers or symbols concerned. For example, addition is commutative: the result of adding 4 + 2 is the same as that of adding 2 + 4; subtraction is not as 4 − 2 = 2, but 2 − 4 = −2. Compare ◊associative operation and distributive operation.

compact spaces *and bicompact spaces* special kinds of topological space exhibiting the property that, internally, every family of open sets whose union is the whole space necessarily contains a finite subfamily whose union is already the whole space. An alternative definition, first formulated with regard to a special class of such spaces, requires every sequence of points to have a converging subsequence. Russian mathematicians initially used the word *bicompact* (not now used in the West) to distinguish between the specialized and the general definitions.

companion star either one of a ◊binary star system (although usually the less massive), sometimes only detectable by ◊spectroscopy.

competitive exclusion principle in evolution, principle of natural selection whereby similar species are forced to specialize ever more minutely so as not to overlap with each other in a particular niche; if they do not specialize adequately, they die and become extinct.

complement protein substance in blood serum which reacts with almost all antibody–antigen systems, lysing (breaking down) the antigen from the antibody and disappearing in the process.

complement in mathematics, the set of the elements within the universal set that are not contained in the designated set. For example, if the universal set is the set of all positive whole numbers and the designated set *S* is the set of all even numbers, then the complement of *S* (denoted *S'*) is the set of all odd numbers.

complex in chemistry, any of a class of substances with a characteristic structure in which a central metal atom (often a transition element) is surrounded by – and bonded to – several nonmetallic atoms or groups of atoms (◊ligands). Complexes are also called ◊coordination compounds.

complex in psychoanalysis, an association of mental factors in the unconscious that relate to an emotional experience involving something unacceptable to the individual, often affecting the individual's behaviour.

complex number in mathematics, a number written in the form $a + ib$, where a and b are ◊real numbers and i is the square root of -1 (that is, $i^2 = -1$); i used to be known as the 'imaginary' part of the complex number. Some equations in algebra, such as those of the form $x^2 + 5 = 0$ cannot be solved without recourse to complex numbers, because the real numbers do not include square roots of negative numbers.

complex number astrophysics basis of ◊twistor theory.

complex variable ◊variable representing a complex number.

compound chemical substance made up of two or more ◊elements bonded together, so that they cannot be separated by physical means. Compounds are held together by ionic or covalent bonds.

Compton effect in physics, the increase in wavelength (loss of energy) of a photon by its collision with a free electron (*Compton scattering*). The Compton effect was first demonstrated with X-rays and provided early evidence that electromagnetic waves consisted of particles – photons – which carried both energy and momentum. It is named after US physicist Arthur Compton.

computer-aided design use of computers to create and modify design drawings; see ◊CAD.

computerized axial tomography medical technique, usually known as CAT scan, for noninvasive investigation of disease or injury.

concave of a surface, curving inwards, or away from the eye. For example, a bowl appears concave when viewed from above. In geometry, a concave polygon is one that has an interior angle greater than 180°. Concave is the opposite of ◊convex.

concentric circles two or more circles that share the same centre.

conchoid curve an ◊algebraic curve represented by an equation of the general form:

$$x^2y^2 = (x - a)^2 (c^2 - x^2)$$

conditioned stimulus in psycholgy, an originally neutral stimulus applied in conditioning experiments that evokes a trained or conditioned response. In Pavlov's classical experiments with dogs, the neutral stimulus (the sound of a bell) originally evoked no salivation reflex; but after being presented for a time with an ◊unconditioned stimulus (food), it became the conditioned stimulus which evoked the conditioned response.

conduction, electrical flow of charged particles through a material giving rise to electric current. Conduction in metals involves the flow of negatively charged free ◊electrons. Conduction in gases and some liquids involves the flow of ◊ions that carry positive charges in one direction and negative charges in the other. Conduction in a ◊semiconductor such as silicon involves the flow of electrons and positive holes.

conduction, heat flow of heat energy through a material without the movement of any part of the material itself (compare ◊conduction, electrical). Heat energy is present in all materials in the form of the kinetic energy of their vibrating molecules, and may be conducted from one molecule to the next in the form of this mechanical vibration. In the case of metals, which are particularly good conductors of heat, the free electrons within the material carry heat around very quickly.

conductivity, thermal (unit W m^{-1} K^{-1}) measure of how well a material conducts heat. A good conductor, such as a metal, has a high conductivity; a poor conductor, called an insulator, has a low conductivity.

conductor any material that conducts heat or electricity (as opposed to an insulator, or nonconductor). A good conductor has a high electrical or heat conductivity, and is generally a substance rich in free electrons such as a metal. A poor conductor (such as the nonmetals, glass and porcelain) has few free electrons. Carbon is exceptional in being nonmetallic and yet (in some of its forms) a relatively good conductor of heat and electricity. Substances such as ◊silicon and germanium, with intermediate conductivities that are improved by heat, light, or impurities, are known as ◊semiconductors.

congruence in geometry, two sets are congruent if either can be transformed by translations and rotations into the other.

conics study initiated by Apollonius of Perga of how a cone can be 'cut' so as to produce circles, ellipses, parabolas, and hyperbolas; he stated 'a conic section is the locus of a point that moves so that the ratio of its distance f from a fixed point, to its distance d from a straight line, is constant'. Whether the constant c is greater than, equal to, or less than one determines the type of a curve the section represents.

conic section curve obtained when a conical surface is intersected by a plane. If the intersecting plane cuts both extensions of the cone, it yields a ◊hyperbola; if it is parallel to the side of the cone, it produces a ◊parabola. Other intersecting planes produce circles or ◊ellipses.

conjugation in organic chemistry, the alternation of double (or triple) and single carbon–carbon bonds in a molecule – for example, in penta-1,3-diene, $H_2C=CH–CH=CH–CH_3$. Conjugation imparts additional stability as the double bonds are less reactive than isolated double bonds.

conservation of energy in chemistry, the principle that states that in a chemical reaction, the total amount of energy in the system remains unchanged.

conservation of mass in chemistry, the principle that states that in a chemical reaction the sum of all the masses of the substances involved in the reaction (reactants) is equal to the sum of all of the masses of the substances produced by the reaction (products) – that is, no matter is gained or lost.

constant of precession see ◊precession of the equinoxes.

continental drift in geology, the theory that, about 250–200 million years ago, the Earth consisted of a single large continent (◊Pangaea), which subsequently broke apart to form the continents known today. The theory was proposed 1912 by German meteorologist Alfred Wegener, but such vast continental movements could not be satisfactorily explained until the study of ◊plate tectonics in the 1960s.

contingency table table listing information classified as variable according to two or more independent attributes. Such tables are used commonly in commerce, notably by insurance companies.

continued fraction development of any ◊real number in the form of a sequence of integers from which approximations to the number may be calculated successively; for example:

$$k_1 + \cfrac{1}{k_1 + \cfrac{1}{k_2 + \cfrac{1}{k_3 + \cfrac{1}{k_4}}}}$$

and so on. The sequence can be finite or infinite. The development will be finite in the case of a rational number, and the calculation will then terminate on reaching the rational number. In the case of an irrational number, a termination will be reached only as the ◊limit of the sequence of values calculated.

continuous function or *continuity* in mathematics, representation of continuous motion, uniform variation of ◊transformations. More precisely, a function f is said to be continuous at an argument value x if the function value for arguments close to x can be held down to a value as near to $f(x)$ is required by keeping the argument close enough to x.

convection heat energy transfer that involves the movement of a fluid (gas or liquid). Fluid in contact with the source of heat expands and tends to rise within the bulk of the fluid. Cooler fluid sinks to take its place, setting up a convection current. This is the principle of natural convection in many domestic hot-water systems and space heaters.

convection process in the Sun (and possibly other stars) perhaps caused by ◊solar rotation, that produces the immensely powerful electrical and magnetic fields associated with ◊sunspots.

convergence in mathematics, the property of a series of numbers in which the difference between consecutive terms gradually decreases. The sum of a converging series approaches a limit as the number of terms tends to ◊infinity.

convex of a surface, curving outwards, or towards the eye. For example, the outer surface of a ball appears convex. In geometry, the term is used to describe any polygon possessing no interior angle greater than 180°. Convex is the opposite of ◊concave.

Cooper pairs see ◊Bardeen–Cooper–Schrieffer theory.

coordination compound any of a diverse group of complex compounds characterized by a structure in which several ◊ligands surround – and are covalently bonded to – a central metal atom. Such compounds may be electrically neutral, or positive or negative ions. Similarly the central metal atom may be neutral, anionic or, rarely, cationic, but it is always one that is able to accept an electron pair(s) to form a coordinate bond(s). The total number of bonds between the central atom and the ligands is the coordination number, which, in general, ranges from two to twelve; four and six are the most common.

coordination number see ◊coordination compound.

Copernican model of the universe model of the universe with the Sun at its centre (◊heliocentric) that replaced the Earth centred (geocentric) ◊Ptolemaic model, and was thus a considerable improvement. The model, however, still involved ◊epicycles and the spheres.

cordite explosive consisting of nitroglycerine and cellulose nitrate.

Coriolis effect effect of the Earth's rotation on the atmosphere and on all objects on the Earth's surface. In the northern hemisphere it causes moving objects and currents to be deflected to the right; in the southern hemisphere it causes deflection to the left. The effect is named after its discoverer, French mathematician Gaspard de Coriolis (1792–1843).

corona faint halo of hot (about 2,000,000°C/3,600,000°F) and tenuous gas around the Sun, which boils from the surface. It is visible at solar ◊eclipses or through a *coronagraph,* an instrument that blocks light from the Sun's brilliant disc. Gas flows away from the corona to form the ◊solar wind.

coronagraph device for studying the solar ◊corona at any time of the day. It was first invented by French astronomer Bernard Lyot.

corpuscle in biology, a small body. The cellular components of blood are sometimes referred to as corpuscles.

cortex in biology, the outer part of a structure such as the brain, kidney, or adrenal gland. In botany the cortex includes nonspecialized cells lying just beneath the surface cells of the root and stem.

corticosteroid any of several steroid hormones secreted by the cortex of the adrenal glands; also synthetic forms with similar properties. Corticosteroids have anti-inflammatory and ◊immunosuppressive effects and may be used to treat a number of conditions, including rheumatoid arthritis, severe allergies, asthma, some skin diseases, and some cancers. Side effects can be serious, and therapy must be withdrawn very gradually.

cosecant in trigonometry, a ◊function of an angle in a right-angled triangle found by dividing the length of the hypotenuse (the longest side) by the length of the side opposite the angle. Thus the cosecant of an angle A, usually shortened to cosec A, is always greater than (or equal to) 1. It is the reciprocal of the sine of the angle, that is, cosec A = 1/sin A.

cosine in trigonometry, a ◊function of an angle in a right-angled triangle found by dividing the length of the side adjacent to the angle by the length of the hypotenuse (the longest side). It is usually shortened to *cos*.

cosmic censorship theory that the hidden interior within all ◊event horizons is the same and is always, necessarily, hidden.

cosmic radiation streams of high-energy particles from outer space, consisting of protons, alpha particles, and light nuclei, which collide with atomic nuclei in the Earth's atmosphere, and produce secondary nuclear particles (chiefly ◊mesons, such as pions and muons) that shower the Earth.

cosmic year time the Sun takes to 'orbit' in ◊galactic rotation: about 225 million years.

cosmological principle in astronomy, a hypothesis that any observer anywhere in the universe has the same view that we have; that is, that the universe is not expanding from any centre but all galaxies are moving away from one another.

cosmology branch of astronomy that deals with the structure and evolution of the universe as an ordered whole. Its method is to construct 'model universes' mathematically and compare their large-scale properties with those of the observed universe.

coulomb SI unit (symbol C) of electrical charge. One coulomb is the quantity of electricity conveyed by a current of one ◊ampere in one second.

Coulomb field field of force surrounding an electric charge. Its intensity can be deduced from ◊Coulomb's law.

Coulomb's law in physics, law that states that the ◊force between two charged bodies varies directly as the product of the two charges, and inversely as the square of the distance between them. It was determined by French physicist Charles Coulomb.

covalent bond chemical ◊bond produced when two atoms share one or more pairs of electrons (usually each atom contributes an electron). The bond is often represented by a single line drawn between the two atoms. Covalently bonded substances include hydrogen (H_2), water (H_2O), and most organic substances.

CP violation breaking of a fundamental ◊quantum theory conservation rule by some unstable particles undergoing decay into other particles. C represents charge conjugation that relates particles to ◊antiparticles and P stands for parity.

Cramer's paradox in mathematics, paradox that although two different cubic curves intersect at nine points, part of the definition of a single cubic curve is that it is itself determined by nine points. It was observed by Swiss mathematician Gabriel Cramer.

Cramer's rule method of solving a simultaneous system of linear equation by using ◊determinants. It is named after Swiss mathematician Gabriel Cramer.

Crêpe Ring rather transparent inner ring (Ring C) of the Saturn ring system. Its diameter measures about 149,300 km/92,800 mi.

cresol or *hydroxytoluene* an important constituent of explosives, plastics, and dyestuff intermediates.

Cretaceous (Latin *creta* 'chalk') period of geological time approximately 144.2–65 million years ago. It is the last period of the Mesozoic era, during which angiosperm (seed-bearing) plants evolved, and dinosaurs reached a peak before their extinction at the end of the period. The north European chalk, which forms the white cliffs of Dover, was deposited during the latter half of the Cretaceous.

critical temperature temperature above which a particular gas cannot be converted into a liquid by pressure alone. It is also the temperature at which a magnetic material loses its magnetism (the Curie temperature or point).

critical velocity velocity above which the flow of a liquid ceases to be smooth following ◊streamlines, and becomes ◊turbulent.

Crookes's radiometer instrument consisting of an evacuated glass dome in which sits a freely rotating system of vanes, whose opposite sides are white and black respectively. The rotation of the vanes when put near a source of heat is a demonstration of the ◊kinetic theory of gases. It was devised by English physicist William Crookes.

crossing over in biology, a process that occurs during ◊meiosis. While the chromosomes are lying alongside each other in pairs, each partner may twist around the other and exchange corresponding chromosomal segments. It is a form of genetic recombination, which increases variation and thus provides the raw material of evolution.

cross ratio in projective geometry, a ratio expressing a relationship between two other ratios determined by four points on a given line, namely the ratio:

$$\frac{CA}{CB} : \frac{DA}{DB}$$

For the purposes of projection, the 'point at infinity' may be any one of A, B, C, or D; if the given line is then projected onto another, the cross ratio of the projected points will remain the same – hence the importance of the cross ratio.

crust the outermost part of the structure of Earth, consisting of two distinct parts, the oceanic crust and the continental crust. The *oceanic* crust is on average about 10 km/6.2 mi thick and consists mostly of basaltic types of rock. By contrast, the *continental* crust is largely made of granite and is more complex in its structure. Because of the movements of ◊plate tectonics, the oceanic crust is in no place older than about 200 million years. However, parts of the continental crust are over 3 billion years old.

cryogenics science of very low temperatures (approaching ◊absolute zero), including the production of very low temperatures and the exploitation of special properties associated with them, such as the disappearance of electrical resistance (◊superconductivity).

crystal lattice regular system of points in space (for example, the corners of a cube) about which atoms, molecules, or ions in solids vibrate.

crystalloid substance that, when dissolved in a solvent, can pass through a ◊semipermeable membrane (as opposed to a ◊colloid, which cannot).

cubic curve geometrical curve in three-dimensional space. It may be parametrized after a change of variables as $(x, y, z) = (at^3, bt^2, ct)$ and may thus be said to be determined by nine points. See also ◊Cramer's paradox.

cupola furnace brick-lined furnace used in the conversion of pig iron (cast iron) into iron castings. Air is driven in underneath a charge of heated material; raising the temperature sufficiently to bring about the transformation.

current, alternating see ◊alternating current.

current, direct see ◊direct current.

cybernetics study of communication and control mechanisms in machines (including humans).

cyclotron circular type of particle ◊accelerator.

Cygnus-A source in the constellation Cygnus of strong radio emission, possibly caused by the collisions of interstellar dust within two colliding galaxies. It was identified optically in 1952 as a tiny area of magnitude 17.9.

cyst hollow cavity in an animal or plant, lined with ◊epithelium and usually filled with fluid. Cysts may be normal, for example the urinary bladder, or pathological, for example an ovarian cyst.

cytochrome protein responsible for part of the process of ◊respiration by which food molecules are broken down in ◊aerobic organisms. Cytochromes are part of the electron transport chain, which uses energized electrons to reduce molecular oxygen (O_2) to oxygen ions (O^{2-}). These combine with hydrogen ions (H^+) to form water (H_2O), the end product of aerobic respiration. As electrons are passed from one cytochrome to another, energy is released and used to make ◊ATP.

cytoplasm the part of the cell outside the ◊nucleus. Strictly speaking, this includes all the ◊organelles (mitochondria, chloroplasts, and so on), but often cytoplasm refers to the jellylike matter in which the organelles are embedded (correctly termed the cytosol). The cytoplasm is the site of protein synthesis.

D

daguerreotype in photography, a single-image process using mercury vapour and an iodine-sensitized silvered plate; it was invented by Louis Daguerre 1838.

Daniell cell primary cell that uses a ◊cathode of zinc, immersed in sulphuric acid contained in a porous pot that itself stands in a container of copper sulphate, in which the copper ◊anode stands. An ◊electromotive force of about 1.1 volts is produced by this cell.

dark reaction series of reactions in ◊photosynthesis that do not require light. During the dark reaction, carbon dioxide is incorporated into three-carbon sugar phosphate molecules; this reaction is dependant on the ◊light reaction which does require light.

deamination removal of the amino group (-NH$_2$) from an unwanted ◊amino acid. This is the nitrogen-containing part, and it is converted into ammonia, uric acid, or urea (depending on the type of animal) to be excreted in the urine.

In vertebrates, deamination occurs in the liver.

de Broglie hypothesis cornerstone of quantum physics which relates the wave nature of systems to their particlelike characteristics. For a particle with velocity v and mass m, one can associate a de Broglie wave of wavelength λ given by the de Broglie equation:

$$\lambda = h/mv$$

where h is Planck's constant. It was determined by French physicist Louis de Broglie.

declination in astronomy, the coordinate on the ◊celestial sphere (imaginary sphere surrounding the Earth) that corresponds to latitude on the Earth's surface. Declination runs from 0° at the celestial equator to 90° at the north and south celestial poles.

decomposition process whereby a chemical compound is reduced to its component substances. In biology, it is the destruction of dead organisms either by chemical reduction or by the action of decomposers, such as bacteria and fungi.

Dedekind's cuts mathematical device by which ◊irrational numbers can be referred to by means of sets of fractions (rational numbers). It was defined by German mathematician Julius Dedekind.

deflection of light gravitational effect that bends a ray of light. Such an effect was predicted within the general theory of ◊relativity, although previously considered impossible.

degradation breaking down of compounds into simpler molecules; for example, the action of enzymes brings about the degradation of proteins to amino acids.

delta δ symbol used by German mathematician Leopold Kronecker's in the evaluations of ◊determinants (in matrix the-

ory), to the effect that $\delta(i, j) = 1$ if $i = j$, otherwise it equals zero. (It thus measures whether i and j are different.) The δ used by Gottfried Leibniz in his notation for differential calculus, as in dy/dx, was based on an intended association with the delta.

Delta Δ term meaning 'difference'; Δx represents the difference between consecutive x values according to context.

de Moivre's equation statement that for integers n ($\cos z + \text{i} \sin z)n = \cos nz + \text{i} \sin z$ where $\text{i} = \sqrt{-1}$. The equation was determined by French mathematician Abraham de Moivre.

dendrite part of a nerve cell or neuron. The dendrites are slender filaments projecting from the cell body. They receive incoming messages from many other nerve cells and pass them on to the cell body.

If the combined effect of these messages is strong enough, the cell body will send an electrical impulse along the axon (the threadlike extension of a nerve cell). The tip of the axon passes its message to the dendrites of other nerve cells.

denominator in mathematics, the bottom number of a fraction, so called because it names the family of the fraction. The top number, or numerator, specifies how many unit fractions are to be taken.

density measure of the compactness of a substance; it is equal to its mass per unit volume and is measured in kg per cubic metre/lb per cubic foot. Density is a ◊scalar quantity. The average density D of a mass m occupying a volume V is given by the formula:

$$D = \frac{m}{V}$$

Relative density is the ratio of the density of a substance to that of water at 4°C/32.2°F.

depressor nerve nerve that, when stimulated induces reflex vasodilation and thus slows the heartbeat (resulting in a fall in blood pressure).

derivative or *differential coefficient* in mathematics, the limit of the gradient of a chord linking two points on a curve as the distance between the points tends to zero; for a function of a single variable, $y = f(x)$, it is denoted by $f'(x)$, D$f(x)$, or dy/dx, and is equal to the gradient of the curve.

derivative ◊function derived from another by the application of differentiation or partial differentiation. A derivative of a derivative is called a derivative of the second order.

descriptive geometry branch of mathematics in which three-dimensional objects are represented as two-dimensional (plane) figures, using any of many types of projection.

determinant in mathematics, an array of elements written as a square, and denoted by two vertical lines enclosing the array. For a 2×2 matrix, the determinant is given by the difference between the products of the diagonal terms. Determinants are used to solve sets of simultaneous equations by matrix methods.

determinates 'known' values, as opposed to indeterminates, 'unknown', values.

deuterium naturally occurring heavy isotope of hydrogen, mass number 2 (one proton and one neutron), discovered by US chemist Harold Urey in 1932. It is sometimes given the symbol D. In nature, about one in every 6,500 hydrogen atoms is deuterium. Combined with oxygen, it produces 'heavy water' (D$_2$O), used in the nuclear industry.

Devonian period of geological time 408–360 million years ago, the fourth period of the Palaeozoic era. Many desert sandstones from North America and Europe date from this time. The first land plants flourished in the Devonian period, corals were abundant in the seas, amphibians evolved from air-breathing fish, and insects developed on land.

diacaustic ◊caustic curve formed by refraction.

diamagnetism form of magnetism induced in one substance by the magnetic field of another. Its basic cause lies in the shift of the orbital motion of the ◊electrons of a substance resulting from the external magnetic field of the other substance. It occurs in all materials.

dialysis technique for removing waste products from the blood suffering chronic or acute kidney failure. There are two main methods, haemodialysis and peritoneal dialysis.

diaphragm in telecommunications, thin membrane found in telephone receivers and microphones onto which ◊sound waves impinge, being converted into electrical impulses by a device that takes its input from the diaphragm movements.

diaphragm in zoology, thin membrane found in the mammalian ear onto which ◊sound waves impinge, being converted into electrical impulses through movement of fluid in the cochlea, which is connected to the auditory nerve.

diastole in biology, the relaxation of a hollow organ. In particular, the term is used to indicate the resting period between beats of the heart when blood is flowing into it.

dicotyledon major subdivision of the ◊angiosperms, containing the great majority of flowering plants. Dicotyledons are characterized by the presence of two seed leaves, or cotyledons, in the embryo, which is usually surrounded by the endosperm. They generally have broad leaves with netlike veins.

dielectric an insulator or nonconductor of electricity, such as rubber, glass, and paraffin wax. An electric field in a dielectric material gives rise to no net flow of electricity. However, the applied field causes electrons within the material to be displaced, creating an electric charge on the surface of the material. This reduces the field strength within the material by a factor known as the dielectric constant (or relative permittivity) of the material. Dielectrics are used in capacitors, to reduce dangerously strong electric fields, and have optical applications.

dielectric constant or *relative permittivity* or *specific inductive capacity* capacitance of a capacitor (condenser) with a certain dielectric divided by the capacitance of the same capacitor with a vacuum (or, in practice, air) as a dielectric.

diesel engine ◊internal combustion engine that uses heavy (diesel) oil as the fuel in the ignition and compression power cycle that produces motive power.

difference equation equation that relates the value of a function at time t to its values at a specified number of past times, from among $t-1$, $t-2$, $t-3$, ...

differential calculus branch of ◊calculus involving applications such as the determination of maximum and minimum points and rates of change.

differential equations equations involving ◊derivatives. In a linear differential equation, the unknown function and its derivatives never appear in a power other than one. Partial differential equations involve unknown functions of several variables, and partial derivatives do therefore appear.

differential gear gear that allows two shafts to rotate at different rates. Such a system is used in cars to allow the wheels on the outside edge of a corner to rotate relative to those on the inside edge.

differential geometry investigation of geometrical surfaces using differential calculus.

differential rotation of a stellar cluster or galaxy, the different rates of 'orbiting' of stars. Those nearer the centre move faster than those at the edge. It is also used to describe the axial rotation of equatorial latitudes faster than polar latitudes of a single body (such as the Sun or a gaseous planet).

differentiation in embryology, the process by which cells become increasingly different and specialized, giving rise to more complex structures that have particular functions in the adult organism. For instance, embryonic cells may develop into nerve, muscle, or bone cells.

differentiation in mathematics, a procedure for determining the ◊derivative or gradient of the tangent to a curve f(*x*) at any point *x*.

diffraction the spreading out of waves when they pass through a small gap or around a small object, resulting in some change in the direction of the waves. In order for this effect to be observed the size of the object or gap must be comparable to or smaller than the ◊wavelength of the waves. Diffraction occurs with all forms of progressive waves – electromagnetic, sound, and water waves – and explains such phenomena as why long-wave radio waves can bend round hills better than short-wave radio waves.

diffraction grating polished metallic surface (usually a metallic mirror on a block of glass or quartz) on which has been ruled a great number (in thousands) of parallel lines, used to split light to produce a ◊spectrum.

diffusion spontaneous and random movement of molecules or particles in a fluid (gas or liquid) from a region in which they are at a high concentration to a region of lower concentration, until a uniform concentration is achieved throughout. The difference in concentration between two such regions is called the *concentration gradient*. No mechanical mixing or stirring is involved. For instance, if a drop of ink is added to water, its molecules will diffuse until their colour becomes evenly distributed throughout. Diffusion occurs more rapidly across a higher concentration gradient and at higher temperature.

dimorphism property of a chemical substance that allows it to crystallize in two different forms.

diode combination of a cold anode and a heated cathode, or the semiconductor equivalent, which incorporates a *p–n* junction. Either device allows the passage of direct current in one direction only, and so is commonly used in a ◊rectifier to convert alternating current (AC) to direct current (DC).

Diophantine equations algebraic equations involving one or more unknowns (indeterminates) with ◊integers (whole numbers) as coefficients, to which one or more solutions are sought, also in integers. The classic form is:

$$ax + by = c$$

Part of the significance of this is that even if not enough information is given to derive a single solution, enough is given to reduce the answer to a definite type. Diophantus, who lived in the third century AD, thus began the investigations into ◊number theory that still continue.

diphosphate chemical compound containing two phosphate groups, as in adenosine diphosphate (ADP).

dipole the uneven distribution of magnetic or electrical characteristics within a molecule or substance so that it behaves as though it possesses two equal but opposite poles or charges, a finite distance apart.

direct current (DC) electric current that flows in one direction, and does not reverse its flow as ◊alternating current does. The electricity produced by a battery is direct current.

discharge, electric release of a stored ◊electric charge.

discharge tube device containing (usually two) electrodes and a vacuum or gas at low pressure; a (high) voltage applied to the electrodes causes an electric discharge to take place between them. A gas-filled tube (such as a neon tube) may emit visible light and other forms of radiation.

discriminants special functions of the coefficients of an equation, used to find roots of a polynomial equation.

disproportionation or *dismutation* the splitting of a molecule into two or more simpler molecules.

dissociation in chemistry, the process whereby a single compound splits into two or more smaller products, which may be capable of recombining to form the reactant.

distributive law law expressing the principle operative in the equation:

$$a\,(b + c) = ab + ac$$

divergent in mathematics, of a sequence or series, when the fact that there is no ◊limit for it to approach; it is the opposite of convergent.

DNA *abbreviation* for *deoxyribonucleic acid* complex giant molecule that contains, in chemically coded form, the information needed for a cell to make proteins. DNA is a ladderlike double-stranded ◊nucleic acid which forms the basis of genetic inheritance in all organisms, except for a few viruses that have only ◊RNA. DNA is organized into ◊chromosomes and, in organisms other than bacteria, it is found only in the cell nucleus.

domain set of objects within a mathematical structure on which operations are to be performed. In a simpler context it is the set of arguments (inputs) for which a function is defined.

dominance in genetics, the masking of one allele (an alternative form of a gene) by another allele. For example, if a ◊heterozygous person has one allele for blue eyes and one for brown eyes, his or her eye colour will be brown. The allele for blue eyes is described as recessive and the allele for brown eyes as dominant.

Doppler effect change in the observed frequency (or wavelength) of waves due to relative motion between the wave source and the observer. The Doppler effect is responsible for the perceived change in pitch of a siren as it approaches and then recedes, and for the ◊red shift of light from distant galaxies. It is named after the Austrian physicist Christian Doppler.

double refraction or *birefringence* in a crystal, when an unpolarized ray of light entering the crystal is split into two polarized rays, one of which does obey Snell's law of refraction, and the other does not. Calcite is such a crystal.

double star 'system' of two stars that appear – because of coincidental alignment when viewed from Earth – to be close together; it is, however, an optical effect only, and therefore not the same as a ◊binary star system. Before the twentieth century there were few means of distinguishing double and binary stars.

double theta functions ◊elliptic functions in the form of ◊theta functions of higher degree.

doubling the cube ancient Greek problem in geometrical construction, to derive a cube of exactly twice the volume of another cube of given measurement, using ruler and compass only.

dry cell source of ◊electromotive force which does not contain a liquid. Usually taken to imply the Leclanché type of metal and paste cell.

duality principle that a law or theorem remains valid if one particular element within that law is exchanged for another equally pertinent element. In projective geometry, a statement of two-dimensional proposition remains valid if the word 'point' is exchanged for 'line' (and vice versa); a three-dimensional proposition likewise if 'point' is exchanged for 'plane'.

ductile material material that can sustain large deformations beyond its elastic limit (see ◊elasticity) without fracture. Metals are very ductile, and may be pulled out into wires, or hammered or rolled into thin sheets without breaking.

dynamics or *kinetics* in mechanics, the mathematical and physical study of the behaviour of bodies under the action of forces that produce changes of motion in them.

dynamometer instrument for measuring the power generated by a device.

dynamo theory theory of the origin of the magnetic fields of the Earth and other plants having magnetic fields in which the rotation of the planet as a whole sets up currents within the planet capable of producing a weak magnetic field.

E

e symbol for ◊Euler's number.

earth pressure in civil engineering ◊pressure exerted horizontally by earth behind a retaining wall.

earthquake abrupt motion that propagates through the Earth and along its surfaces. Earthquakes are caused by the sudden release in rocks of strain accumulated over time as a result of tectonics. The study of earthquakes is called seismology. Most earthquakes occur along faults (fractures or breaks) and Benioff zones. Plate tectonic movements generate the major proportion: as two plates move past each other they can become jammed. When sufficient strain has accumulated, the rock breaks, releasing a series of elastic waves (seismic waves) as the plates spring free. The force of earthquakes (magnitude) is measured on the Richter scale, and their effect (intensity) on the Mercalli scale. The point at which an earthquake originates is the *seismic focus* or *hypocentre*; the point on the Earth's surface directly above this is the *epicentre*.

eccentricity in astronomy, the extent to which an elliptical orbit departs from a circular one. It is usually expressed as a decimal fraction, regarding a circle as having an eccentricity of 0.

echolocation or *biosonar* method used by certain animals, notably bats, whales, and dolphins, to detect the positions of objects by using sound. The animal emits a stream of high-pitched sounds, generally at ultrasonic frequencies (beyond the range of human hearing), and listens for the returning echoes reflected off objects to determine their exact location.

eclipse passage of an astronomical body through the shadow of another. The term is usually used for solar and lunar eclipses, which may be either partial or total, but may also refer to other bodies, for example, to an eclipse of one of Jupiter's satellites by Jupiter itself. An eclipse of a star by a body in the Solar System is also called an occultation.

eclipsing binary binary (double) star in which the two stars periodically pass in front of each other as seen from Earth.

ecliptic path, against the background of stars, that the Sun appears to follow each year as it is orbited by the Earth. It can be thought of as the plane of the Earth's orbit projected on to the ◊celestial sphere (imaginary sphere around the Earth).

ectoderm outer layer of cells in an embryo and all the tissues that it gives rise to.

Edison effect electrical ◊conduction between a negatively charged filament, and a positively charged ◊electrode kept together, though separated, in a vacuum chamber.

efferent nerve nerve that conducts impulses away from the central nervous system (brain and spinal cord). Most efferent nerves are motor nerves and run to effector organs.

efficiency in physics, a general term indicating the degree to which a process or device can convert energy from one form to another without loss. It is normally expressed as a fraction or percentage, where 100% indicates conversion with no loss. The efficiency of a machine, for example, is the ratio of the work done by the machine to the energy put into the machine; in practice it is always less than 100% because of frictional heat losses. Certain electrical machines with no moving parts, such as transformers, can approach 100% efficiency.

efflux in aerodynamics, the combination of combustion products and air forming the propulsive medium of a jet or rocket engine.

ego (Latin 'I') in psychology, the processes concerned with the self and a person's conception of himself or herself, encompassing values and attitudes. In Freudian psychology, the term refers specifically to the element of the human mind that represents the conscious processes concerned with reality, in conflict with the ◊id (the instinctual element) and the ◊superego (the ethically aware element).

eigenvalue for a matrix A, the number λ is said to be an eigenvalue of the matrix if there is a nonzero vector x such that $Ax = \lambda x$. Eigenvalues are used to derive a change of base to simplify the matrix to one that has entries only on its diagonal. More generally, the number λ is an eigenvalue of a linear transformation T if there is a nonzero vector x so that $T(x) = \lambda x$.

eightfold-way in quantum mechanics, scheme for the classification of ◊elementary particles into families, grouped according to common properties as expressed by various ◊quantum numbers.

elasticity in physics, the ability of a solid to recover its shape once deforming forces (stresses modifying its dimensions or shape) are removed. An elastic material obeys ◊Hooke's law, which states that its deformation is proportional to the applied stress up to a certain point, called the *elastic limit,* beyond which additional stress will deform it permanently. Elastic materials include metals and rubber; however, all materials have some degree of elasticity.

electrical conduction see ◊conduction, electrical.

electrical energy form of energy carried by an electric current. It may be converted into other forms of energy such as heat, light, and motion.

The electrical energy W watts converted in a circuit component through which a current I amperes passes and across which there is a potential difference of V volts is given by the formula:

$$W = IV$$

electric cell device in which chemical energy is converted into electrical energy; see ◊cell, electric.

electric charge property of some bodies that causes them to exert forces on each other. Two bodies both with positive or both with negative charges repel, each other, whereas bodies with opposite or 'unlike' charges attract each other, since each is in the electric field of the other. In atoms, ◊electrons possess a negative charge, and ◊protons an equal positive charge. The ◊SI unit of electric charge is the coulomb (symbol C).

electricity all phenomena caused by ◊electric charge, whether static or in motion. Electric charge is caused by an excess or deficit of electrons in the charged substance, and an electric current is the movement of charge through a material. Substances may be electrical conductors, such as metals, that allow the passage of electricity through them readily, or insulators, such as rubber, that are extremely poor conductors. Substances with relatively poor conductivities that can be improved by the addition of heat or light are known as ◊semiconductors.

electric motor a machine that converts electrical energy into mechanical energy. There are various types, including direct-current and induction motors, most of which produce rotary motion. A linear induction motor produces linear (in a straight line) rather than rotary motion.

electrochemical series or *electromotive series* list of chemical elements arranged in descending order of the ease with which they can lose electrons to form cations (positive ions). An element can be displaced (displacement reaction) from a compound by any element above it in the series.

electrochemistry the branch of science that studies chemical reactions involving electricity. The use of electricity to produce chemical effects, ◊electrolysis, is employed in many industrial processes, such as the manufacture of chlorine and the extraction of aluminium. The use of chemical reactions to produce electricity is the basis of electrical ◊cells, such as the dry cell and the Leclanché cell.

electrode any terminal by which an electric current passes in or out of a conducting substance; for example, the ◊anode or ◊cathode in a battery or the carbons in an arc lamp. The terminals that emit and collect the flow of electrons in thermionic valves (electron tubes) are also called electrodes: for example, cathodes, plates, and grids.

electrode potential electric potential between an element and its ions in solution.

electrodynamics the branch of physics dealing with electric charges, electric currents and associated forces. ◊Quantum electrodynamics (QED) studies the interaction between charged particles and their emission and absorption of electromagnetic radiation. This field combines quantum theory and relativity theory, making accurate predictions about subatomic processes involving charged particles such as electrons and protons.

electroencephalogram (EEG) graphic record of the electrical discharges of the brain, as detected by electrodes placed on the scalp. The pattern of electrical activity revealed by electroencephalography is helpful in the diagnosis of some brain disorders, in particular epilepsy.

electrolysis in chemistry, the production of chemical changes by passing an electric current through a solution or molten salt (the electrolyte), resulting in the migration of ions to the electrodes: positive ions (cations) to the negative electrode (cathode) and negative ions (anions) to the positive electrode (anode).

electrolyte solution or molten substance in which an electric current is made to flow by the movement and discharge of ions in accordance with Faraday's laws of ◊electrolysis.

electrolytic cell device in which an externally applied voltage brings about a chemical reaction; see ◊electrolysis.

electromagnet coil of wire wound around a soft iron core that acts as a magnet when an electric current flows through the wire. Electromagnets have many uses: in switches, electric bells, solenoids, and metal-lifting cranes.

electromagnetic force one of the four fundamental forces of nature, the other three being gravity, the strong nuclear force, and the weak nuclear force. The ◊elementary particle that is the carrier for the electromagnetic force is the photon.

electromagnetic induction in electronics, the production of an ◊electromotive force (emf) in a circuit by a change of magnetic flux through the circuit or by relative motion of the circuit and the magnetic flux. In a closed circuit an induced current will be produced. All dynamos and generators make use of this effect. When magnetic tape is driven past the playback head (a small coil) of a tape-recorder, the moving magnetic field induces an emf in the head, which is then amplified to reproduce the recorded sounds.

electromagnetic induction, Faraday's law of in physics, law stating that the induced ◊electromotive force is equal to the rate of decrease of ◊magnetic flux. The law was determined by English physicist Michael Faraday.

electromagnetic interaction interaction between two charged particles (for example an ◊electron and a ◊proton) which appears as a ◊force (attractive if the two charges are different in sign). In ◊quantum theory, the electromagnetic interaction is carried between particles by ◊photons.

electromagnetic radiation transfer of energy in the form of ◊electromagnetic waves.

electromagnetic spectrum the complete range, over all wavelengths and frequencies, of ◊electromagnetic waves. These include radio and television waves, infrared radiation, visible light, ultraviolet light, X-rays, and gamma radiation.

electromagnetic waves oscillating electric and magnetic fields travelling together through space at a speed of nearly 300,000 km/186,000 mi per second. The (limitless) range of possible wavelengths and ◊frequencies of electromagnetic waves, which can be thought of as making up the *electromagnetic spectrum,* includes radio waves, infrared radiation, visible light, ultraviolet radiation, X-rays, and gamma rays.

electromotive force (emf) loosely, the voltage produced by an electric battery or generator in an electrical circuit or, more precisely, the energy supplied by a source of electric power in driving a unit charge around the circuit. The unit is the ◊volt.

electron stable, negatively charged ◊elementary particle; it is a constituent of all atoms, and a member of the class of particles known as leptons. The electrons in each atom surround the nucleus in groupings called shells; in a neutral atom the number of electrons is equal to the number of protons in the nucleus. This electron structure is responsible for the chemical properties of the atom (see ◊atomic structure).

electron acceptor in chemistry, compound that can accept an electron and is reduced in doing so; it can therefore take part in oxidation–reduction reactions.

electronegativity the ease with which an atom can attract electrons to itself. Electronegative elements attract electrons, so forming negative ions.

electronics branch of science that deals with the emission of ◊electrons from conductors and ◊semiconductors, with the subsequent manipulation of these electrons, and with the construction of electronic devices. The first electronic device was the thermionic valve, or vacuum tube, in which electrons moved in a vacuum, and led to such inventions as radio, television, ◊radar, and the digital computer. Replacement of valves with the comparatively tiny and reliable ◊transistor from 1948 revolutionized electronic development. Modern electronic devices are based on minute integrated circuits (silicon chips), wafer-thin crystal slices holding tens of thousands of electronic components.

electron microscope means of achieving very high magnification of objects. It uses high-energy electrons, whose characteristic wavelength is much shorter than that of visible light used in ordinary microscopes. Its ◊resolving power is thus far higher.

electrophilic describing a reagent that readily accepts electrons during a chemical reaction. Such reagents, therefore, typically react at centres of high electron density.

electrophoresis movement of electrically charged solute particles in a ◊colloid towards the oppositely charged electrode when a pair of electrodes is immersed in the colloidal solution and connected to an external source of direct-current electricity. It is used as an analytical technique similar to ◊chromatography.

electrophorus means of inducing a charge in one body into another. Usually consists of a metal plate with an insulating handle, the plate being capable of carrying ◊electrostatic charges.

electroplating deposition of metals upon metallic surfaces by electrolysis for decorative and/or protective purposes. It is used in the preparation of printers' blocks, 'master' audio discs, and in many other processes.

electropositivity in chemistry, a measure of the ability of elements (mainly metals) to donate electrons to form positive ions. The greater the metallic character, the more electropositive the element.

electrostatics the study of stationary electric charges and their fields (not currents).

electrovalent bond another name for an ◊ionic bond, a chemical bond in which the combining atoms lose or gain electrons to form ions.

element substance that cannot be split chemically into simpler substances. The atoms of a particular element all have the same number of protons in their nuclei (their ◊atomic number). Elements are classified in the ◊periodic table of the elements. Of the known elements, 92 are known to occur in nature (those with atomic numbers 1–92). Those elements with atomic numbers above 96 do not occur in nature and are synthesized only, produced in particle accelerators. Of the elements, 81 are stable; all the others, which include atomic numbers 43, 61, and from 84 up, are radioactive.

element in mathematics, a member of a ◊set.

elementary particle in physics, a subatomic particle that is not made up of smaller particles, and so can be considered one of the fundamental units of matter. There are three groups of elementary particles: quarks, leptons, and gauge bosons.

Elements title of the major mathematical work by Euclid. Various other mathematical authors have since also used the title.

elevator in aircraft, moveable part of a horizontal aerodynamic surface that changes the aircraft's ◊pitch.

ellipse curve joining all points (loci) around two fixed points (foci) such that the sum of the distances from those points is always constant. The diameter passing through the foci is the major axis, and the diameter bisecting this at right angles is the minor axis. An ellipse is one of a series of curves known as ◊conic sections. A slice across a cone that is not made parallel to, and does not pass through, the base will produce an ellipse.

elliptic function integral of the general form $f\,(x,\sqrt{R})dx$, where f is any rational function of x and R is a quartic polynomial corresponding to: $a_0x^4 + a_1x^3 + a_2x^2 + a_3x + a_4$ with no multiple roots. French mathematician Adrien Legendre proved that any elliptic integral can be reduced to the sum of an elementary function and of scalar multiples of three special functions. ◊Abelian functions and ◊theta functions are both extensions. Elliptic functions are used in the integration of the square root of a cubic or a ◊quartic, and are thus important to many mathematical operations.

elliptic geometry system of ◊non-Euclidean geometry developed as the initial form of ◊Riemann geometry, and regarding all geometrical operations as carried out in 'curved' space, for example, as though on the surface of an ellipsoid or sphere. A 'straight line' is thus defined (then) as the shortest curve (geodesic) on the curved surface joining two points.

ellipticity of the shape of a planet or ◊galaxy, the amount of distortion by which it departs from a perfect sphere. The overall ellipticity of the Earth is given as $\frac{1}{299}$. One class of galaxy is defined in terms of ellipticity, subdivided E0 to E7, according to degree.

elliptic modular functions functions defined in the upper half of an Argand plane that are automorphic relative to a group of modular transformations, that is, transformations T such as:

$$T\,(z) = \frac{az + b}{cz + d}$$

elution in chemistry, washing of an adsorbed substance from the adsorbing material; it is used, for example, in the separation processes of chromatography and electrophoresis.

empirical formula chemical formula of a substance in which only the relative proportions of each of its constituent elements are given. The empirical formula does not necessarily reflect a substance's ◊molecular formula nor its structure. The empirical formula of benzene, for example, is CH, whereas its molecular formula is C_6H_6.

emulsion stable dispersion of a liquid in another liquid – for example, oil and water in some cosmetic lotions.

enantiomorph or *antimer*, *optical antipode*, or *enantiomer* compound that has two asymmetric structures, each a mirror image of the other. Enantiomorphs, such as the optically active forms of lactic acid, have identical chemical and physical properties, except in reactions with other enantiomorphs or in interactions with polarized light. See ◊optical isomerism.

Encke's Division gap within Saturn's Ring A. It is named after German astronomer Johann Encke.

endocytosis ingestion of material by a cell, including ◊phagocytosis and ◊pinocytosis. *Phagocytosis* is the engulfment and ingestion by a white blood cell of bacteria or other foreign particles; *pinocytosis* involves the absorption and ingestion by a cell of surrounding fluid by the folding-in of the cell membrane to form a vesicle which (eventually) releases some of its contents into the cell's ◊cytoplasm.

endoderm innermost of the three germ layers of an embryo.

endoplasmic reticulum (ER) a membranous system of tubes, channels, and flattened sacs that form compartments within eukaryotic cells. It stores and transports proteins within cells and also carries various enzymes needed for the synthesis of ◊fats. The ◊ribosomes, or the organelles that carry out protein synthesis, are attached to parts of the ER.

endoscope in medicine, tubular instrument inserted into a cavity in the body to investigate and treat diseases during a process known as endoscopy.

endplate mass of motor nerve endings that penetrate a muscle fibre.

end-point point during a ◊titration when the two reagents involved are at exact equivalence, that is, when all of each of the reagents has reacted and there is no excess of either.

energy, electrical see ◊electrical energy.

energy, kinetic see ◊kinetic energy.

energy, law of conservation of fundamental principle of physics stating that energy can neither be created nor destroyed, but only changed from one form to another in a closed system.

energy levels, electronic series of specific, discrete energy states that electrons orbiting a nucleus can occupy. In certain processes an electron may absorb external energy and move to a higher energy level (in which case the electron is said to be excited) or it may release energy (usually in the form of light) and move to a lower energy level. Because the energy levels are discrete, these movements of electrons to different energy levels involve specific amounts (quanta) of energy.

energy, magnetic see ◊magnetic energy.

energy, potential see ◊potential energy.

engineering the application of science to the design, construction, and maintenance of works, machinery, roads, railways, bridges, harbour installations, engines, ships, aircraft and airports, spacecraft and space stations, and the generation, transmission, and use of electrical power. The main divisions of engineering are aerospace, chemical, civil, computer, electrical, electronic, gas, marine, materials, mechanical, mining, production, radio, and structural.

enteric in medicine, relating to the intestine, an old term used to qualify infective fevers such as typhoid fever.

enthalpy in chemistry, alternative term for energy of reaction, the heat energy associated with a chemical change.

entropy in ◊thermodynamics, a parameter representing the state of disorder of a system at the atomic, ionic, or molecular level; the greater the disorder, the higher the entropy. Thus the fast-moving disordered molecules of water vapour have higher entropy than those of more ordered liquid water, which in turn have more entropy than the molecules in solid crystalline ice.

enzyme biological ◊catalyst produced in cells, and capable of speeding up the chemical reactions necessary for life. They are large, complex ◊proteins, and are highly specific, each chemical reaction requiring its own particular enzyme. The enzyme's specificity arises from its *active site,* an area with a shape corresponding to part of the molecule with which it reacts (the substrate). The enzyme and the substrate slot together forming an enzyme–substrate complex that allows the reaction to take place, after which the enzyme falls away unaltered.

enzyme induction stimulation of enzyme formation by the presence of its ◊substrate or a derivative of the substrate.

epicycle circular orbit of a body round a point that is itself in a circular orbit round a parent body. Such a system was formulated to explain some planetary orbits in the Solar System before they were known to be elliptical.

epithelium in animals, tissue of closely packed cells that forms a surface or lines a cavity or tube. Epithelium may be protective (as in the skin) or secretory (as in the cells lining the wall of the gut).

epitrochoid or *hypotrochoid* ◊locus of a point on a rolling circle moving round the circumference of another circle, that is not on the circumference of the rolling circle. The locus is of importance in the Wankel engine.

equilibrium in physics, an unchanging condition in which an undisturbed system can remain indefinitely in a state of balance. In a *static equilibrium,* such as an object resting on the floor, there is no motion. In a *dynamic equilibrium,* in contrast, a steady state is maintained by constant, though opposing, changes. For example, in a sealed bottle half-full of water, the constancy of the water level is a result of molecules evaporating from the surface and condensing on to it at the same rate.

equilibrium constant numerical value that expresses the position of a chemical equilibrium at a given temperature and pressure. It is given by the product of the concentrations of the reactants divided by the product of the concentrations of the products.

equinox points in spring and autumn at which the Sun's path, the ◊ecliptic, crosses the celestial equator, so that the day and night are of approximately equal length. The *vernal equinox* occurs about 21 March and the *autumnal equinox,* 23 September.

equivalent weight mass of a substance that exactly reacts with, or replaces, an arbitrarily fixed mass of another substance in a particular reaction. The combining proportions (by mass) of substances are in the ratio of their equivalent masses (or a multiple of that ratio) and a common standard has been adopted: for elements, the equivalent weight is the quantity that reacts with, or replaces, 1.00797 g/0.035279 oz of hydrogen or 7.9997 g/0.28215 oz of oxygen, or the mass of an element liberated during ◊electrolysis by the passage of 1 faraday (96,487 coulombs per mole) of electricity. The equivalent weight of an element is given by its gram ◊atomic mass divided by its ◊valency. For oxidizing and reducing agents, the equivalent weight is the gram molecular mass divided by the number of electrons gained or lost by each molecule. Some substances have several equivalent weights, depending on the specific reaction in which they are involved.

ergodics in dynamics, study of the mathematical principles involved in the kinetic theory of gases.

Erlangen programme expression used by German mathematician Felix Klein to denote his unification and classification of geometries Euclidean and non-Euclidean as 'members' of one 'family', corresponding to the transformations found in each.

erosion wearing away of the Earth's surface, caused by the breakdown and transportation of particles of rock or soil (by contrast, weathering does not involve transportation). Agents of erosion include the sea, rivers, glaciers, and wind.

Water, consisting of sea waves and currents, rivers, and rain; ice, in the form of glaciers; and wind, hurling sand fragments against exposed rocks and moving dunes along, are the most potent forces of erosion.

People also contribute to erosion by bad farming practices and the cutting down of forests, which can lead to the formation of dust bowls.

error theory or *theory of errors* in statistics and probability theory, method of evaluating the effects and the significance of errors, for example when obtaining a mean value from a small sample.

escape velocity in physics, minimum velocity with which an object must be projected for it to escape from the gravitational pull of a planetary body. In the case of the Earth, the escape velocity is 11.2 kps/6.9 mps; the Moon, 2.4 kps/1.5 mps; Mars, 5 kps/3.1 mps; and Jupiter, 59.6 kps/37 mps.

ester organic compound formed by the reaction between an alcohol and an acid, with the elimination of water. Unlike ◊salts, esters are covalent compounds.

etalon instrument that uses ◊interference phenomena to make possible very high resolution observations of ◊spectral lines.

ether in chemistry, any of a series of organic chemical compounds having an oxygen atom linking the carbon atoms of two hydrocarbon radical groups (general formula R-O-R'); also the common name for ethoxyethane $C_2H_5OC_2H_5$ (also called diethyl ether).

This is used as an anaesthetic and as an external cleansing agent before surgical operations. It is also used as a solvent, and in the extraction of oils, fats, waxes, resins, and alkaloids.

ether or **aether** in the history of science, a hypothetical medium permeating all of space. The concept originated with the Greeks, and has been revived on several occasions to explain the properties and propagation of light. It was supposed that light and other electromagnetic radiation – even in outer space – needed a medium, the ether, in which to travel. The idea was abandoned with the acceptance of ◊relativity.

ethology comparative study of animal behaviour in its natural setting. Ethology is concerned with the causal mechanisms (both the stimuli that elicit behaviour and the physiological mechanisms controlling it), as well as the development of behaviour, its function, and its evolutionary history.

ethyne common name **acetylene** CHCH colourless inflammable gas produced by mixing calcium carbide and water. It is the simplest member of the alkyne series of hydrocarbons. It is used in the manufacture of the synthetic rubber neoprene, and in oxyacetylene welding and cutting.

Euclid's fifth postulate states that parallel lines meet only at infinity.

eugenics (Greek *eugenes* 'well-born') study of ways in which the physical and mental characteristics of the human race may be improved. The eugenic principle was abused by the Nazi Party in Germany during the 1930s and early 1940s to justify the attempted extermination of entire social and ethnic groups and the establishment of selective breeding programmes. Modern eugenics is concerned mainly with the elimination of genetic disease.

Euler's number (e) the limit of the sequence: $an = 1 + 1/1! + 1/2! + 1/3! + ... + 1/n!$ An irrational number introduced originally by Swiss mathematician Leonhard Euler, e may be represented to the sixth decimal place as 2.718282; it has useful theoretical properties in differential calculus and serves as a natural base for logarithms (known as 'natural logarithms').

event horizon 'edge' of a black hole; the interface between four-dimensional space and a ◊singularity.

excitation in physiology, the stimulation of a sense receptor or nerve.

excited state, electronic condition of an electron that has absorbed external energy and, as a result, moved from its normal, ◊ground state energy level to a higher energy level. The excitation energy is the difference in energy between the ground state and the excited state.

excluded middle, law of the law in logic, that a statement is either true or false, leaving no room for any further alternatives. There are nonclassical systems of logic that distinguish between true = proven true and false = proven false, and so allow intermediate values (such as 'possibly true'). Boolean-valued logic systems attach probability values to statements that may therefore also have intermediate values other than merely true or false the values form a ◊Boolean algebra.

exclusion principle in physics, a principle of atomic structure originated by Austrian–US physicist Wolfgang Pauli. It states that no two electrons in a single atom may have the same set of quantum numbers. Hence, it is impossible to pack together certain elementary particles, such as electrons, beyond a certain critical density, otherwise they would share the same location and quantum number. A white dwarf star, which consists of electrons and other elementary particles, is thus prevented from contracting further by the exclusion principle and never collapses.

exocytosis ejection from a cell of undigested remnants of material.

exothermic describing a process or reaction that involves the release of energy (usually in the form of heat). Combustion, for example, is an exothermic reaction.

Explorer series of US scientific satellites. *Explorer 1,* launched January 1958, was the first US satellite in orbit and discovered the Van Allen radiation belts around the Earth.

exponent or **index** in mathematics, a superscript number that indicates the number of times a term is multiplied by itself; for example $x^2 = x \times x$, $4^3 = 4 \times 4 \times 4$.

exteroceptive describing receptors that receive stimuli from outside the body, such as those of the ear and the eye.

F

factorial of a positive number, the product of all the whole numbers (integers) inclusive between 1 and the number itself. A factorial is indicated by the symbol '!'. Thus $6! = 1 \times 2 \times 3 \times 4 \times 5 \times 6 = 720$. Factorial zero, $0!$, is defined as 1.

factorization reduction into constituent factors (which when multiplied together produce the original number or expression).

faculae bright areas on the face of the Sun, commonly in the vicinity of ◊sunspots. Named by German astronomer Johannes Hevelius, they are thought to be caused by luminous hydrogen clouds close to the ◊photosphere. They last on average about 15 Earth-days.

Faraday effect in physics, rotation of the plane of polarization of polarized light by passing it through a transparent medium subjected to a transverse magnetic field. It is named after English physicist Michael Faraday.

fat in the broadest sense, a mixture of ◊lipids – chiefly triglycerides (lipids containing three ◊fatty acid molecules linked to a molecule of glycerol). More specifically, the term refers to a lipid mixture that is solid at room temperature (20°C); lipid mixtures that are liquid at room temperature are called *oils*. The higher the proportion of saturated fatty acids in a mixture, the harder the fat.

fatigue in metallurgy, failure of metals under cyclic applications of a stress.

fatty acid or *carboxylic acid* organic compound consisting of a hydrocarbon chain, up to 24 carbon atoms long, with a carboxyl group (–COOH) at one end. The covalent bonds between the carbon atoms may be single or double; where a double bond occurs the carbon atoms concerned carry one instead of two hydrogen atoms. Chains with only single bonds have all the hydrogen they can carry, so they are said to be *saturated* with hydrogen. Chains with one or more double bonds are said to be *unsaturated*. Fatty acids are produced in the small intestine when fat is digested.

Saturated fatty acids include palmitic and stearic acids; unsaturated fatty acids include oleic (one double bond), linoleic (two double bonds), and linolenic (three double bonds). Linoleic acid accounts for more than one third of some margarines. Supermarket brands that say they are high in polyunsaturates may contain as much as 39%. Fatty acids are generally found combined with glycerol in ◊lipids such as triglycerides.

Fermat's last theorem in mathematics, theorum that states that the equation: $xn + yn = zn$ is not solvable in the integers if n is greater than 2. Fermat's own proof has never been found and the theorem remained unproved until 1994, when English mathematician Andrew Wiles verified it.

fermentation breakdown of sugars by bacteria and yeasts using a method of respiration without oxygen (◊anaerobic).

Fermentation processes have long been utilized in baking bread, making beer and wine, and producing cheese, yoghurt, soy sauce, and many other foodstuffs.

Fermi–Dirac statistics mathematical treatment of particles with half-integer ◊spin in statistical mechanics, enabling properties of systems made up by such particles to be calculated. They are named after Italian-born US physicist Enrico Fermi and English physicist David Dirac.

fermion in physics, a subatomic particle whose spin can only take values that are half-integers, such as $\frac{1}{2}$ or $\frac{3}{2}$. Fermions may be classified as leptons, such as the electron, and baryons, such as the proton and neutron. All elementary particles are either fermions or ◊bosons.

ferromagnetism form of ◊magnetism that can be acquired in an external magnetic field and usually retained in its absence, so that ferromagnetic materials are used to make permanent magnets. A ferromagnetic material may therefore be said to have a high magnetic ◊permeability and susceptibility (which depends upon temperature). Examples are iron, cobalt, nickel, and their alloys.

Ultimately, ferromagnetism is caused by spinning electrons in the atoms of the material, which act as tiny weak magnets. They align parallel to each other within small regions of the material to form domains, or areas of stronger magnetism. In an unmagnetized material, the domains are aligned at random so there is no overall magnetic effect. If a magnetic field is applied to that material, the domains align to point in the same direction, producing a strong overall magnetic effect. Permanent magnetism arises if the domains remain aligned after the external field is removed. Ferromagnetic materials exhibit hysteresis (time lag between the application or removal of a force or field and its effect).

Fibonacci series sequence in which each term after the first two is the sum of the two terms immediately preceding it; it begins 1, 1, 2, 3, 5, 8, 13, 21, ... and has a variety of important applications (for example, in search algorithms).

field in physics, a region of space in which an object exerts a force on another separate object because of certain properties they both possess. For example, there is a force of attraction between any two objects that have mass when one is in the gravitational field of the other.

field strength see ◊magnetic field strength.

field theory in mathematics, theory involving the mathematical structure known as a field, which displays the operations of addition and multiplication and their inverses (subtraction and division). An elementary example other than the real numbers is constituted by the rational numbers; there are many other types. A ring is much like a field but does not include the inverse operations. A group is a more restricted concept still.

filament thin wire, usually of tungsten, that is capable of acting as a light source when an electric current is passed through it.

filariasis collective term for several diseases, prevalent in tropical areas, caused by certain roundworm (nematode) parasites. About 120 million people worldwide are infected with filarial worms, mostly in India and Africa.

fine structure splitting of individual ◊spectral lines seen when viewed under high resolution. This can be produced by external magnetic fields acting on ◊atoms, for example.

finite having a countable number of elements, the opposite of infinite.

first order in differential equations, involving only the first ◊derivative.

fission in physics, the splitting of a heavy atomic nucleus into two or more major fragments. It is accompanied by the emission of two or three neutrons and the release of large amounts of nuclear energy.

flare star dim red dwarf star that suddenly lights up with great – but brief – luminosity, corresponding to an equally powerful but short-lived burst of radio emission. The cause is thought to be a sudden and intense outburst of radiation on or above the star's surface.

fluid any substance, either liquid or gas, in which the molecules are relatively mobile and can 'flow'.

fluorescence short-lived ◊luminescence (a glow not caused by high temperature). Phosphorescence lasts a little longer.

flux density see ◊magnetic flux density.

fluxions another name for ◊calculus. It is no longer used.

flywheel massive wheel fixed to a shaft, either to store rotational energy for propulsive purposes, or to smooth fluctuations in rotation rates.

food chain in ecology, a sequence showing the feeding relationships between organisms in a particular ecosystem. Each organism depends on the next lowest member of the chain for its food. A pyramid of numbers can be used to show the reduction in food energy at each step up the food chain.

force any influence that tends to change the state of rest or the uniform motion in a straight line of a body. The action of an unbalanced or resultant force results in the acceleration of a body in the direction of action of the force, or it may, if the body is unable to move freely, result in its deformation (see ◊Hooke's law). Force is a vector quantity, possessing both magnitude and direction; its SI unit is the newton.

force, centrifugal see ◊centrifugal force.

force, centripetal see ◊centripetal force.

force, electromagnetic see ◊electromagnetic force.

force, electromotive see ◊electromotive force.

fossil (Latin *fossilis* 'dug up') cast, impression, or the actual remains of an animal or plant preserved in rock. Fossils were created during periods of rock formation, caused by the gradual accumulation of sediment over millions of years at the bottom of the sea bed or an inland lake. Fossils may include footprints, an internal cast, or external impression. A few fossils are preserved intact, as with mammoths fossilized in Siberian ice, or insects trapped in tree resin that is today amber. The study of fossils is called palaeontology. Palaeontologists are able to deduce much of the geological history of a region from fossil remains.

Foucault pendulum pendulum consisting of a long wire to which is attached a heavy weight, which is then free to swing in any plane. Once it starts swinging in one particular plane, the plane slowly rotates, this being the result of the rotation of the Earth beneath the pendulum. This phenomenon was observed by French physicist Léon Foucault in 1851.

foundation part of the structure that ensures stability by providing mechanical fixing with solid earth.

foundations of mathematics or *foundations of arithmetic* subject of attempts to derive the basic precepts of elementary mathematics from a standpoint of pure logic (thence to derive the more complex principles).

Fourier analysis see ◊Fourier theorem.

Fourier series series in which the terms comprise multiples of the cosine and/or sine of multiple angles. Represented by the formula: $\frac{1}{2} a_0 + \Sigma(a_n \cos nx + b_n \sin nx)$ it is used to analyse periodic functions (that is, functions whose graph repeats itself periodically).

Fourier theorem adaptation of the process developed by French mathematician Joseph Fourier as the ◊Fourier series to the investigation of energy propagated in the form of waves (particularly heat, sound, and light). A further developed version of this method is known as harmonic analysis. Use of the theorem in investigating wave forms is known as Fourier analysis.

four-stroke cycle the engine-operating cycle of most petrol and diesel engines. The 'stroke' is an upward or downward movement of a piston in a cylinder. In a petrol engine the cycle begins with the induction of a fuel mixture as the piston goes down on its first stroke. On the second stroke (up) the piston compresses the mixture in the top of the cylinder. An electric spark then ignites the mixture, and the gases produced force the piston down on its third, power, stroke. On the fourth stroke (up) the piston expels the burned gases from the cylinder into the exhaust.

four-stroke engine an ◊internal combustion engine using the Otto cycle.

fraction (from Latin *fractus* 'broken') in mathematics, a number that indicates one or more equal parts of a whole. Usually, the number of equal parts into which the unit is divided (denominator) is written below a horizontal line, and the number of parts comprising the fraction (numerator) is written above; thus $\frac{2}{3}$ or $\frac{3}{4}$. Such fractions are called *vulgar* or *simple* fractions. The denominator can never be zero.

frame of reference set of axes fixed in such a way as to define uniquely the position of an object in space.

Fraunhofer lines dark lines crossing the solar ◊spectrum. They are caused by the absorption of light from hot regions of the Sun's surface by gases in the cooler, outer regions. They were first investigated by German physicist Joseph von Fraunhofer.

free energy sum of ◊enthalpy and ◊entropy, that is, the capacity of a system to perform work. The change in free energy accompanying a chemical reaction is a measure of its completeness.

freezing point for any given liquid, the temperature at which any further removal of heat will convert the liquid into the solid state. The temperature remains at this point until all the liquid has solidified. It is invariable under similar conditions of pressure – for example, the freezing point of water under standard atmospheric pressure is 0°C/32°F.

frequency in physics, the number of periodic oscillations, vibrations, or waves occurring per unit of time. The SI unit of frequency is the hertz (Hz), one hertz being equivalent to one cycle per second. Frequency is related to wavelength and velocity by the relationship

$$f = \frac{v}{\lambda}$$

where f is frequency, v is velocity and λ is wavelength.

Frequency is the reciprocal of the period T:

$$f = \frac{1}{T}$$

frequency modulation (FM) method by which radio waves are altered for the transmission of broadcasting signals. FM varies the frequency of the carrier wave in accordance with the signal being transmitted. Its advantage over AM (◊amplitude modulation) is its better signal-to-noise ratio. It was invented by the US engineer Edwin Armstrong.

friction in physics, the force that opposes the relative motion of two bodies in contact. The ***coefficient of friction*** is the ratio of the force required to achieve this relative motion to the force pressing the two bodies together.

front in meteorology, the boundary between two air masses of different temperature or humidity. A ***cold front*** marks the line of advance of a cold air mass from below, as it displaces a warm air mass; a ***warm front*** marks the advance of a warm air mass as it rises up over a cold one. Frontal systems define the weather of the mid-latitudes, where warm tropical air is constantly meeting cold air from the poles.

Froude brake ◊dynamometer that measures power by determining ◊torques. It was devised by English engineer William Froude.

fuel cell cell converting chemical energy directly to electrical energy.

It works on the same principle as a battery but is continually fed with fuel, usually hydrogen. Fuel cells are silent and reliable (no moving parts) but expensive to produce.

fuel injection system used in high-performance ◊internal combustion engines whereby pure fuel is injected into the cylinder during the intake phase of the cycle. This eliminates the need for a ◊carburettor and gives greater control over the burning mixtures.

fulcrum point of support of a ◊lever, about which the lever can pivot in lifting and lowering loads applied to it.

function in mathematics, a function f is a non-empty set of ordered pairs $(x, f(x))$ of which no two can have the same first element. Hence, if $f(x) = x^2$ two ordered pairs are $(-2,4)$ and $(2,4)$. The set of all first elements in a function's ordered pairs is called the ***domain***; the set of all second elements is the ***range***. In the algebraic expression $y = 4x^3 + 2$ the dependent variable y is a function of the independent variable x, generally written as $f(x)$.

functions analysis see ◊function theory.

functions of real variables, theory of involves ◊functions of which the arguments are ◊real numbers.

function theory or ***theory of functions*** use of ◊functions, primarily in order to denote mathematical relationships, but also in application to other sciences. Functional analysis, for example, considers problems in which an unknown function is to be found; at this stage ◊variables may represent functions as opposed to numerical values.

furnace device in which very high temperatures are produced to bring about chemical reactions.

fuse device that prevents the passage of electric current above a predetermined level in a ◊circuit, by melting through the consequent temperature rise, and thus breaking the circuit.

fusion in physics, the fusing of the nuclei of light elements, such as hydrogen, into those of a heavier element, such as helium. The resultant loss in their combined mass is converted into energy. Stars and thermonuclear weapons are powered by nuclear fusion.

G

gain in electronics, the ratio of the amplitude of the output signal produced by an amplifier to that of the input signal.

In a voltage amplifier the voltage gain is the ratio of the output voltage to the input voltage; in an inverting operational amplifier (op-amp) it is equal to the ratio of the resistance of the feedback resistor to that of the input resistor.

galactic centres phenomena that are now thought to comprise black holes – which would explain why the centre of our Galaxy appears strangely obscure, and emits only ◊infrared radiation.

galactic rotation revolving of a galaxy round its central nucleus even as it continues its ◊proper motion. Such rotation, however, is not uniform but differential. One revolution of the Sun within our own Galaxy takes about 225 million years, or 1 cosmic year.

galaxy congregation of millions or billions of stars, held together by gravity. *Spiral galaxies,* such as the Milky Way, are flattened in shape, with a central bulge of old stars surrounded by a disc of younger stars, arranged in spiral arms like a Catherine wheel.

Barred spirals are spiral galaxies that have a straight bar of stars across their centre, from the ends of which the spiral arms emerge. The arms of spiral galaxies contain gas and dust from which new stars are still forming.

Elliptical galaxies contain old stars and very little gas. They include the most massive galaxies known, containing a trillion stars. At least some elliptical galaxies are thought to be formed by mergers between spiral galaxies. There are also irregular galaxies. Most galaxies occur in clusters, containing anything from a few to thousands of members.

gallic acid or *trihydroxybenzoic acid* yellow crystalline substance used in making inks.

galvanometer instrument for detecting small electric currents by their magnetic effect.

gamete cell that functions in sexual reproduction by merging with another gamete to form a ◊zygote. Examples of gametes include sperm and egg cells. In most organisms, the gametes are haploid (they contain half the number of chromosomes of the parent), owing to reduction division or ◊meiosis.

game theory group of mathematical theories, developed in 1944 by German born US mathematician Oscar Morgenstern (1902–1977) and Hungarian-born US mathematician John Von Neumann, that seeks to abstract from invented game-playing scenarios and their outcome the essence of situations of conflict and/or cooperation in the real political, business, and social world.

gamma globulin one of a group of proteins or ◊immunoglobulins in the blood that act as ◊antibodies to specific infections. Gamma globulins extracted from the blood of a patient who has recovered from an infection may be used as ◊vaccines to stimulate artificial immunity in others.

gamma radiation very high-frequency electromagnetic radiation, similar in nature to X-rays but of shorter wavelength, emitted by the nuclei of radioactive substances during decay or by the interactions of high-energy electrons with matter. Cosmic gamma rays have been identified as coming from pulsars, radio galaxies, and quasars, although they cannot penetrate the Earth's atmosphere.

gas in physics, a form of matter, such as air, in which the molecules move randomly in otherwise empty space, filling any size or shape of container into which the gas is put.

gas mantle illumination device made from impregnating a dome-shaped piece of rayon with compounds of thorium and cerium, which are decomposed by heat.

gastrula stage in embryonic development following the ◊blastula stage in which ◊gastrulation occurs.

gastrulation cell movements during embryonic development (after cleavage) in which cells move to the positions in which they eventually give rise to the organs of the growing embryo.

gas turbine engine that uses internal combustion to convert the chemical energy locked up in a liquid fuel into mechanical energy. They are mostly used in aircraft and trains.

gauge distance between the inside edges of a railway for trains. Also, the diameter or wires, rods, and so on.

gauss cgs unit (symbol Gs) of magnetic induction or magnetic flux density, replaced by the SI unit, the ◊tesla, but still commonly used. It is equal to one line of magnetic flux per square centimetre. The Earth's magnetic field is about 0.5 Gs, and changes to it over time are measured in gammas (one gamma equals 10^{-5} gauss).

Gaussian distribution another name for ◊normal distribution.

gegenschein faint oval patch of light, opposite the Sun, visible from Earth only at certain times of the year. Its nature and cause are still not known. It is sometimes known as 'counter-glow'.

Geiger counter any of a number of devices used for detecting nuclear radiation and/or measuring its intensity by counting the number of ionizing particles produced (see ◊radioactivity). It detects the momentary current that passes between ◊electrodes in a suitable gas when a nuclear particle or a radiation pulse causes the ionization of that gas. The electrodes are connected to electronic devices that enable the number of particles passing to be measured. The increased frequency of measured particles indicates the intensity of radiation. The device is named after the German physicist Hans Geiger.

gelatine soluble protein-based substance with the ability to form a jelly on cooling. It is used in photography and the making of glues.

gemmule in early genetic theory, minute particles thought to consist of miniature copies of all parts of the body carried in the blood to the ◊gametes and from which their larger forms eventually developed. In modern usage, a gemmule is a bud formed on a sponge that may break free and develop into a new animal.

gene unit of inherited material, encoded by a strand of ◊DNA and transcribed by ◊RNA. In higher organisms, genes are located on the ◊chromosomes. A gene consistently affects a particular character in an individual – for example, the gene for eye colour. Also termed a Mendelian gene, after Austrian biologist Gregor Mendel, it occurs at a particular point, or locus, on a particular chromosome and may have several variants, or ◊alleles, each specifying a particular form of that character – for example, the alleles for blue or brown eyes. Some alleles show ◊dominance. These mask the effect of other alleles, known as recessive.

gene pool total sum of ◊alleles (variants of ◊genes) possessed by all the members of a given population or species alive at a particular time.

generator machine that produces electrical energy from mechanical energy, as opposed to an ◊electric motor, which does the opposite. A simple generator (dynamo) consists of a wire-wound coil (armature) that is rotated between the poles of a permanent magnet. The movement of the wire in the magnetic field induces a current in the coil by ◊electromagnetic induction, which can be fed by means of a commutator as a continuous direct current into an external circuit. Slip rings instead of a commutator produce an alternating current, when the generator is called an alternator.

genetic engineering deliberate manipulation of genetic material by biochemical techniques. It is often achieved by the introduction of new ◊DNA, usually by means of a virus or plasmid. This can be for pure research, gene therapy, or to breed functionally specific plants, animals, or bacteria. These organisms with a foreign gene added are said to be transgenic.

genetics branch of biology concerned with the study of heredity and variation; it attempts to explain how characteristics of living organisms are passed on from one generation to the next. The science of genetics is based on the work of Austrian biologist Gregor Mendel whose experiments with the cross-breeding (hybridization) of peas showed that the inheritance of characteristics and traits takes place by means of discrete 'particles' (◊genes). These are present in the cells of all organisms, and are now recognized as being the basic units of heredity. All organisms possess ◊genotypes (sets of variable genes) and ◊phenotypes (characteristics produced by certain genes). Modern geneticists investigate the structure, function, and transmission of genes.

genotype particular set of ◊alleles (variants of genes) possessed by a given organism. The term is usually used in conjunction with ◊phenotype, which is the product of the genotype and all environmental effects.

geocentric having the Earth at the centre.

geodesic shortest route between two points on any surface.

geodesy methods of surveying the Earth for making maps and correlating geological, gravitational, and magnetic measurements. Geodesic surveys, formerly carried out by means of various measuring techniques on the surface, are now commonly made by using radio signals and laser beams from orbiting satellites.

geological time time scale embracing the history of the Earth from its physical origin to the present day. Geological time is traditionally divided into eons (Archaean or Archaeozoic, Proterozoic, and Phanerozoic in ascending chronological order), which in turn are subdivided into eras, periods, epochs, ages, and finally chrons.

geometric curve curve that can be precisely expressed by an equation (unlike a mechanical curve); for example, a circle, parabola, or hyperbola.

germ plasm theory in early genetics, the theory that of the two tissue types in multicellular animals (somatoplasm in body

cells and germ plasm in reproductive cells) only the integrity of germ plasm is necessary for the inheritance of characteristics.

gland specialized organ of the body that manufactures and secretes enzymes, hormones, or other chemicals. In animals, glands vary in size from small (for example, tear glands) to large (for example, the pancreas), but in plants they are always small, and may consist of a single cell. Some glands discharge their products internally, endocrine glands, and others, externally exocrine glands. Lymph nodes are sometimes wrongly called glands.

globular cluster spherical or near-spherical star cluster containing from approximately 10,000 to millions of stars. More than a hundred globular clusters are distributed in a spherical halo around our Galaxy. They consist of old stars, formed early in the Galaxy's history. Globular clusters are also found around other galaxies.

gluon in physics, a gauge boson that carries the ◊strong nuclear force, responsible for binding quarks together to form the strongly interacting subatomic particles known as hadrons. There are eight kinds of gluon.

glycolysis conversion of glucose to ◊lactic acid. It takes place in the ◊cytoplasm of cells as part of the process of cellular respiration.

Golgi apparatus or *Golgi body* stack of flattened membranous sacs found in the cells of eukaryotes. Many molecules travel through the Golgi apparatus on their way to other organelles or to the endoplasmic reticulum. Some are modified or assembled inside the sacs. The Golgi apparatus is named after the Italian physician Camillo Golgi.

gondola personnel-carrying car of an airship or balloon.

Gondwanaland or *Gondwana* southern landmass formed 200 million years ago by the splitting of the single world continent ◊Pangaea. (The northern landmass was Laurasia.) It later fragmented into the continents of South America, Africa, Australia, and Antarctica, which then drifted slowly to their present positions. The baobab tree found in both Africa and Australia is a relic of this ancient land mass.

governor device that regulates the speed of a motor or engine. See ◊centrifugal governor.

graph pictorial representation of numerical data, such as statistical data, or a method of showing the mathematical relationship between two or more variables by drawing a diagram.

gravitational constant fundamental constant (symbol g) of physics that relates the force of ◊gravity produced by a body to the masses involved and the separation. According to some physicists, its present value of 6.67×10^{-11} m^3/(kg s^2) is decreasing at a rate proportional to the age of the universe.

gravity force of attraction that arises between objects by virtue of their masses. On Earth, gravity is the force of attraction between any object in the Earth's gravitational field and the Earth itself. It is regarded as one of the four fundamental forces of nature, the other three being the ◊electromagnetic force, the ◊strong nuclear force, and the ◊weak nuclear force. The gravitational force is the weakest of the four forces, but it acts over great distances. The particle that is postulated as the carrier of the gravitational force is the graviton.

gravity, acceleration due to see ◊acceleration due to gravity.

gravity, centre of see ◊centre of gravity.

Great Red Spot prominent oval feature, 14,000 km/8,500 mi wide and some 30,000 km/20,000 mi long, in the atmosphere of the planet Jupiter, south of the Equator. It was first observed in the 19th century. Space probes show it to be an anticlockwise vortex of cold clouds, coloured possibly by phosphorus.

greenhouse effect phenomenon of the Earth's atmosphere by which solar radiation, trapped by the Earth and re-emitted from the surface as infrared radiation, is prevented from escaping by various gases in the air. Greenhouse gases trap heat because they readily absorb infrared radiation. The result is a rise in the Earth's temperature (global warming). The main greenhouse gases are carbon dioxide, methane, and chlorofluorocarbons (CFCs) as well as water vapour. Fossil-fuel consumption and forest fires are the principal causes of carbon dioxide build-up; methane is a by product of agriculture (rice, cattle, sheep).

Gregorian calendar calendar established with the authority of the Roman Catholic Church by Pope Gregory XIII in 1582. Correcting at a stroke the 10 day accumulated margin of error of the ◊Julian calendar, the main difference was that century years were discounted as leap years unless they were divisible by 400.

Gregorian telescope reflecting telescope devised – but never constructed – by James Gregory, in which an auxiliary concave mirror reflects the magnified image, the right way up, through a hole in the centre of the main objective mirror, that is, through the end of the telescope itself. The ◊Cassegrain telescope is similar but produces an inverted image.

grid an ◊electrode in the form of a mesh that, when placed between the anode and cathode of a thermionic valve, controls the flow of electrons.

ground state (electronic) the state of an electron in its lowest energy level. When all the electrons orbiting a nucleus are in their lowest energy levels, the atom as a whole has its minimum possible energy and is therefore in its most stable state.

group theory investigation and classification of the properties of the mathematical structures known as groups. A group possesses two operations – 'multiplication' and 'inverting of an element' – and a further designated element called 'unity'. An example is provided by the set of nonzero real numbers with ordinary multiplication and reciprocation (that is, being multiplied or becoming reciprocals). Another example is provided by the integers for which the operation of multiplication ($n \times m$), is to be addition ($n + m$), with the inverse of n being $-1/n$, and the 'unity element' is in fact zero. A third example is provided by a collection of ◊transformations of the plane where $S \times T$ effectively means applying transformation T and then S; such a collection is a group if it includes the identity transformation I (the transformation that leaves all points unchanged) and for each transformation T its inverse, T^{-1} (the transformation of which the effect is to return each point to its original position before it was transformed by T).

gunpowder or **black powder** the oldest known explosive, a mixture of 75% potassium nitrate (saltpetre), 15% charcoal, and 10% sulphur. Sulphur ignites at a low temperature, charcoal burns readily, and the potassium nitrate provides oxygen for the explosion. As gunpowder produces lots of smoke and burns quite slowly, it has progressively been replaced since the late 19th century by high explosives, although it is still widely used for quarry blasting, fuses, and fireworks. Gunpowder has high ◊activation energy; a gun based on gunpowder alone requires igniting by a flint or a match.

gymnosperm (Greek 'naked seed') in botany, any plant whose seeds are exposed, as opposed to the structurally more advanced ◊angiosperms, where they are inside an ovary. The group includes conifers and related plants such as cycads and ginkgos, whose seeds develop in cones. Fossil gymnosperms have been found in rocks about 350 million years old.

gyroscope mechanical instrument, used as a stabilizing device and consisting, in its simplest form, of a heavy wheel mounted on an axis fixed in a ring that can be rotated about another axis, which is also fixed in a ring capable of rotation about a third axis. Applications of the gyroscope principle include the gyrocompass, the gyropilot for automatic steering, and gyro-directed torpedoes.

H

Haber process or *Haber–Bosch process* industrial process by which ammonia is manufactured by direct combination of its elements, nitrogen and hydrogen. The reaction is carried out at 400–500°C/752–932°F and at 200 atmospheres pressure. The two gases, in the proportions of 1:3 by volume, are passed over a ◊catalyst of finely divided iron.

Around 10% of the reactants combine, and the unused gases are recycled. The ammonia is separated either by being dissolved in water or by being cooled to liquid form.

haemoglobin protein used by all vertebrates and some invertebrates for oxygen transport because the two substances combine reversibly. In vertebrates it occurs in red blood cells (erythrocytes), giving them their colour.

haemoprotein protein containing an iron porphyrin group. The green plant pigment ◊chlorophyll and the red blood pigment ◊haemoglobin are both haemoproteins.

halide any compound produced by the combination of a ◊halogen, such as chlorine or iodine, with a less electronegative element (see ◊electronegativity). Halides may be formed by ◊ionic bonds or by ◊covalent bonds.

Hall effect production of a voltage across a conductor or semiconductor carrying a current at a right angle to a surrounding magnetic field. It was discovered in 1897 by the US physicist Edwin Hall (1855–1938). It is used in the *Hall probe* for measuring the strengths of magnetic fields and in magnetic switches.

Halley's comet comet that orbits the Sun about every 76 years, named after English astronomer Edmond Halley who calculated its orbit. It is the brightest and most conspicuous of the periodic comets. Recorded sightings go back over 2,000 years. It travels around the Sun in the opposite direction to the planets. Its orbit is inclined at almost 20° to the main plane of the Solar System and ranges between the orbits of Venus and Neptune. It will next reappear in 2061.

halo nebulous quality round a celestial body (particularly round a red giant); the galactic halo, however, describes the spherical collection of stars forming a surrounding 'shell' for our otherwise compact, discoid Galaxy.

halogen any of a group of five nonmetallic elements with similar chemical bonding properties: fluorine, chlorine, bromine, iodine, and astatine. They form a linked group in the ◊periodic table of the elements, descending from fluorine, the most reactive, to astatine, the least reactive. They combine directly with most metals to form salts, such as common salt (NaCl). Each halogen has seven electrons in its valence shell, which accounts for the chemical similarities displayed by the group.

halogenoalkane any of a group of organic compounds (formerly called alkyl halides) formed by the halogenation of (addition of a halogen to) an alkane. In the presence of ultraviolet light, alkanes react with halides by substitution. In the chlorination of methane, for example, one, two, three or all four of the methane's hydrogens may be substituted by chlorine – depending on how far the reaction is allowed to proceed – with the release of hydrogen chloride at each substitution; the resulting halogenoalkanes are chloromethane (methyl chloride, CH_3Cl), dichloromethane (methylene chloride, CH_2Cl_2), trichloromethane (chloroform, $CHCl_3$) and tetrachloromethane (carbon tetrachloride CCl_4).

hang glider an unpowered crewed glider that achieves great manoeuvrability through a basically triangular-shaped expanse of fabric stretched over cross-struts.

harmonic analysis see ◊Fourier theorem.

head of water vertical distance between the top of a water stream and the point at which its energy is to be extracted.

heat form of energy possessed by a substance by virtue of the vibrating movement (kinetic energy) of its molecules or atoms. Heat energy is transferred by conduction, convection, and radiation. It always flows from a region of higher temperature (heat intensity) to one of lower temperature. Its effect on a substance may be simply to raise its temperature, or to cause it to expand, melt (if a solid), vaporize (if a liquid), or increase its pressure (if a confined gas).

heat capacity in physics, the quantity of heat required to raise the temperature of an object by one degree. The *specific heat capacity* of a substance is the heat capacity per unit of mass, measured in joules per kilogram per kelvin ($J\,kg^{-1}\,K^{-1}$).

heat death in cosmology, a possible fate of the universe in which it continues expanding indefinitely while all the stars burn out and no new ones are formed.

helical screw screw whose thread is in the form of a helix.

heliocentric having the Sun at the centre.

heliograph device for recording the positions of ◊sunspots.

heliometer instrument to measure the apparent diameter of the Sun at different seasons, also used to measure angular distances between stars.

helium (Greek *helios* 'Sun') colourless, odourless, gaseous, nonmetallic element, symbol He, atomic number 2, relative atomic mass 4.0026. It is grouped with the inert gases, is nonreactive, and forms no compounds. It is the second-most abundant element (after hydrogen) in the universe, and has the lowest boiling (−268.9°C/−452°F) and melting points (−272.2°C/−458°F) of all the elements. It is present in small quantities in the Earth's atmosphere from gases issuing from radioactive elements (from ◊alpha decay) in the Earth's crust; after hydrogen it is the second lightest element.

helium abundance presence – and dominance – of ◊helium atoms in the universe. The fact that about 8% of *all* atoms are helium can be traced, through the alpha-beta-gamma theory, to the primordial ◊Big Bang.

helix in mathematics, a three-dimensional curve resembling a spring, corkscrew, or screw thread. It is generated by a line that encircles a cylinder or cone at a constant angle.

hematite principal ore of iron, consisting mainly of iron(III) oxide, Fe_2O_3. It occurs as *specular hematite* (dark, metallic lustre), *kidney ore* (reddish radiating fibres terminating in smooth, rounded surfaces), and a red earthy deposit.

hermaphrodite organism that has both male and female sex organs. Hermaphroditism is the norm in such species as earthworms and snails, and is common in flowering plants. Cross-fertilization is the rule among hermaphrodites, with the parents functioning as male and female simultaneously, or as one or the other sex at different stages in their development. Human hermaphrodites are extremely rare.

hertz SI unit (symbol Hz) of frequency (the number of repetitions of a regular occurrence in one second). Radio waves are often measured in megahertz (MHz), millions of hertz, and the clock rate of a computer is usually measured in megahertz. The unit is named after German physicist Heinrich Hertz.

Hertzsprung–Russell diagram in astronomy, a graph on which the surface temperatures of stars are plotted against their luminosities. Most stars, including the Sun, fall into a narrow band called the ◊main sequence. When a star grows old it moves from the main sequence to the upper right part of the graph, into the area of the giants and supergiants. At the end of its life, as the star shrinks to become a white dwarf, it moves again, to the bottom left area. It is named after the Danish astronomer Ejnar Hertzsprung and the US astronomer Henry Norris Russell, who independently devised it in the years 1911–13.

heterodyne effect superimposition of two waves of different ◊frequency in a radio receiver, one of which is being received, the other transmitted within the device itself, producing an intermediate frequency that can be demodulated.

heterozygous in a living organism, having two different ◊alleles for a given trait. In ◊homozygous organisms, by contrast, both chromosomes carry the same allele. In an outbreeding population an individual organism will generally be heterozygous for some genes but homozygous for others.

high-energy particles particles of ◊electromagnetic radiation that contain high energies, measured in terms of electronvolts. The energy in gamma radiation is of the order of 8×10^7 to 8×10^5 electronvolts and in X-rays of 8×10^3 to 8×10^1 electronvolts.

hodometer device that enables the ◊acceleration of an object moving with known velocity over a path to be determined.

hoist an engine used to power a wire-round drum, whose cable is used to lift heavy objects, usually using a ◊jib and pulleys.

holography method of producing three-dimensional (3-D) images, called holograms, by means of ◊laser light. Holography uses a photographic technique (involving the splitting of a laser beam into two beams) to produce a picture, or hologram, that contains 3-D information about the object photographed. Some holograms show meaningless patterns in ordinary light and produce a 3-D image only when laser light is projected through them, but reflection holograms produce images when ordinary light is reflected from them (as found on credit cards).

hominids humans and their humanlike ape predecessors, which together constitute the family Hominidae.

homologous series any of a number of series of organic chemicals with similar chemical properties in which members differ by a constant relative molecular mass.

homology branch of ◊topology involving the study of closed curves, closed surfaces and similar geometric arrangements in two- to n–dimensional space, and investigating the ways in which such spatial structures may be dissected. The formulation of the homological theory of dimensionality led to several basic laws of ◊duality (relating to topological properties of an additional part of space).

homozygous in a living organism, having two identical ◊alleles for a given trait. Individuals homozygous for a trait always breed true; that is, they produce offspring that resemble them in appearance when bred with a genetically similar individual; inbred varieties or species are homozygous for almost all traits.

Recessive alleles are only expressed in the homozygous condition. See also ◊heterozygous.

Hooke's law law stating that the deformation of a body is proportional to the magnitude of the deforming force, provided that the body's elastic limit (see ◊elasticity) is not exceeded. If the elastic limit is not reached, the body will return to its original size once the force is removed. The law was discovered by English physicist Robert Hooke in 1676.

hormone in biology, chemical secretion of the ductless endocrine glands and specialized nerve cells concerned with control of body functions. The major glands are the thyroid, parathyroid, pituitary, adrenal, pancreas, ovary, and testis. There are also hormone-secreting cells in the kidney, liver, gastrointestinal tract, thymus (in the neck), pineal (in the brain), and placenta. Hormones bring about changes in the functions of various organs according to the body's requirements. The hypothalamus, which adjoins the pituitary gland at the base of the brain, is a control centre for overall coordination of hormone secretion; the thyroid hormones determine the rate of general body chemistry; the adrenal hormones prepare the organism during stress for 'fight or flight'; and the sexual hormones such as oestrogen and testosterone govern reproductive functions.

horsepower British unit of power, equivalent to 745.7 ◊watts.

hot big bang later, but fundamental, concept within the ◊Big Bang model, that the primordial explosion occurred in terms of almost unimaginable heat. The concept, formulated by George Gamow, led to considerable study of thermonuclear reactions and the search for ◊background radiation.

Hubble expansion apparent recession of galaxies as seen from any point within the universe, the velocity of recession being proportional to the distance of the galaxy from the observer.

Hubble's law law that relates a galaxy's distance from us to its speed of recession as the universe expands, announced in 1929 by US astronomer Edwin Hubble. He found that galaxies are moving apart at speeds that increase in direct proportion to their distance apart. The rate of expansion is known as Hubble's constant.

hydration special type of solvation in which water molecules are attached – either by electrostatic forces or by coordinate (covalent) bonds – to ions or molecules of a solute. Some salts, called hydrates, retain associated water molecules in the solid state (this water is called the water of crystallization); in solid copper(II) sulphate, for example, the hydrated ion is $[Cu(H_2O)_4]^{2+}$ or $[Cu(H_2O)_6]^{2+}$

hydraulic press device that uses an ◊incompressible fluid, such as water or oil, to transmit a small downward force applied to a piston of small area to a larger area piston, which then produces a proportionately large upward force. Such a press is a demonstration of ◊Pascal's law of pressures.

hydraulics field of study concerned with utilizing the properties of water and other liquids, in particular the way they flow and transmit pressure, and with the application of these properties in engineering. It applies the principles of hydrostatics and hydrodynamics. The oldest type of hydraulic machine is the *hydraulic press,* invented by Joseph Bramah in England in 1795. The hydraulic principle of pressurized liquid increasing a force is commonly used on vehicle braking systems, the forging press, and the hydraulic systems of aircraft and excavators.

hydrocarbon any of a class of chemical compounds containing only hydrogen and carbon (for example, the alkanes and alkenes). Hydrocarbons are obtained industrially principally from petroleum and coal tar.

hydrodynamics branch of physics dealing with fluids (liquids and gases) in motion.

hydroelectric power electricity generated by moving water. In a typical scheme, water stored in a reservoir, often created by damming a river, is piped into water ◊turbines, coupled to electricity generators. In pumped storage plants, water flowing through the turbines is recycled. A tidal power station exploits the rise and fall of the tides. About one-fifth of the world's electricity comes from hydroelectric power.

hydrogen (Greek *hydro* + *gen* 'water generator') colourless, odourless, gaseous, nonmetallic element, symbol H, atomic number 1, relative atomic mass 1.00797. It is the lightest ồf all the elements and occurs on Earth chiefly in combination with oxygen as water. Hydrogen is the most abundant element in the universe, where it accounts for 93% of the total number of atoms and 76% of the total mass. It is a component of most stars, including the Sun, whose heat and light are produced through the nuclear-fusion process that converts hydrogen into helium. When subjected to a pressure 500,000 times greater than that of the Earth's atmosphere, hydrogen becomes a solid with metallic properties, as in one of the inner zones of Jupiter. Hydrogen's common and industrial uses include the hardening of oils and fats by hydrogenation, the creation of high-temperature flames for welding, and as rocket fuel. It has been proposed as a fuel for road vehicles.

hydrogen bomb bomb that works on the principle of nuclear ◊fusion. Large-scale explosion results from the thermonuclear release of energy when hydrogen nuclei are fused to form helium nuclei. The first hydrogen bomb was exploded at Enewetak Atoll in the Pacific Ocean by the USA in 1952.

hydrogen bond weak electrostatic bond that forms between covalently bonded hydrogen atoms and a strongly ◊electronegative atom with a lone electron pair (for example, oxygen, nitrogen, and fluorine). Hydrogen bonds (denoted by a dashed line –) are of great importance in biochemical processes, particularly the N–H– – –H bond, which enables proteins and nucleic acids to form the three-dimensional structures necessary for their biological activity.

hydrogen carrier compound that accepts hydrogen ions in biochemical reactions and is therefore important in oxidation-reduction reactions such as the intracellular use of oxygen.

hydrogen ion concentration number of grams of hydrogen ions per litre of solution; denoted by [H^+]. It is a measure of the acidity of a solution, in which context it is normally expressed in terms of pH values, given by $pH = \log_{10}(1/[H^+])$.

hydrography study and charting of Earth's surface waters in seas, lakes, and rivers.

hydrolysis chemical reaction in which the action of water or its ions breaks down a substance into smaller molecules. Hydrolysis occurs in certain inorganic salts in solution, in nearly all nonmetallic chlorides, in esters, and in other organic substances. It is one of the mechanisms for the breakdown of food by the body, as in the conversion of starch to glucose.

hydrometer in physics, an instrument used to measure the relative density of liquids (the density compared with that of water). A hydrometer consists of a thin glass tube ending in a sphere that leads into a smaller sphere, the latter being weighted so that the hydrometer floats upright, sinking deeper into less dense liquids than into denser liquids. Hydrometers are used in brewing and to test the strength of acid in car batteries.

hydroxyl group an atom of hydrogen and an atom of oxygen bonded together and covalently bonded to an organic molecule. Common compounds containing hydroxyl groups are alcohols and phenols.

hygrometer in physics, any instrument for measuring the humidity, or water vapour content, of a gas (usually air). A wet and dry bulb hygrometer consists of two vertical thermometers, with one of the bulbs covered in absorbent cloth dipped into water. As the water evaporates, the bulb cools, producing a temperature difference between the two thermometers. The amount of evaporation, and hence cooling of the wet bulb, depends on the relative humidity of the air.

hyperbola in geometry, a curve formed by cutting a right circular cone with a plane so that the angle between the plane and the base is greater than the angle between the base and the side of the cone. All hyperbolae are bounded by two asymptotes (straight lines which the hyperbola moves closer and closer to but never reaches).

A hyperbola is a member of the family of curves known as ◊conic sections.

hyperbolic geometry system of non-Euclidean geometry developed by German mathematician Bernhard Riemann, complementary to ◊elliptic geometry and comprising the geometry of ◊geodesics in the neighbourhood of a point on the (curved) surface at which a tangential plane intersects the surface in a hyperbolic curve.

hypercomplex numbers numbers that expand on complex numbers, for example, ◊quaternions.

hyperfine structure very fine splitting of individual lines in a ◊spectrum, which can be the result of the presence of different ◊isotopes of an element in the source.

hyperon in physics, any of a group of highly unstable ◊elementary particles that includes all the baryons with the exception of protons and neutrons. They are all composed of three quarks. The lambda, xi, sigma, and omega particles are hyperons.

hysteria according to the work of Sigmund Freud, the conversion of a psychological conflict or anxiety feeling into a physical symptom, such as paralysis, blindness, recurrent cough, vomiting, and general malaise. The term is little used today in diagnosis, psychosomatic illness being the modern term.

I

ice age any period of glaciation occurring in the Earth's history, but particularly that in the Pleistocene epoch, immediately preceding historic times. On the North American continent, glaciers reached as far south as the Great Lakes, and an ice sheet spread over northern Europe, leaving its remains as far south as Switzerland.

There were several glacial advances separated by interglacial stages during which the ice melted and temperatures were higher than today.

iconoscope type of television camera where a beam of ◊electrons scans a special mosaic, which can store an optical image electrically, and converts the image stored to electrical signals for transmission.

id in Freudian psychology, the mass of motivational and instinctual elements of the human mind, whose activity is largely governed by the arousal of specific needs. It is regarded as the unconscious element of the human psyche, and is said to be in conflict with the ◊ego and the ◊superego.

ideal in projective geometry and algebra, describes a point (one on every line) at infinity in such a way that the point has a coordinate position. In number theory, the term describes a collection of elements in a ring that has specific properties within a universal set, that is, that form a closed system under addition (among themselves) and under scaling by any element from the universal set. For example, the even numbers form an ideal within the universal set of integers in that when added (or multiplied) together, even numbers result.

ideal gas or **perfect gas** gas obeying the gas laws of Boyle, Charles, and Joule exactly. This would imply that the gas consists of perfectly elastic molecules, each of which has zero volume and no attractive or repulsive interaction with its neighbours.

igneous rock rock formed from cooling magma or lava, and solidifying from a molten state. Igneous rocks are largely composed of silica (SiO_2) and they are classified according to their crystal size, texture, method of formation, or chemical composition, for example by the proportions of light and dark minerals.

imaginary number term often used to describe the non-real element of a ◊complex number. For the complex number ($a + ib$), ib is the imaginary number where $i = \sqrt{-1}$, and b any real number.

immunity the protection that organisms have against foreign microorganisms, such as bacteria and viruses, and against cancerous cells. The cells that provide this protection are called white blood cells, or leucocytes, and make up the immune system. They include neutrophils and macrophages, which can engulf invading organisms and other unwanted material, and natural killer cells that destroy cells infected by viruses and cancerous cells..Some of the most important immune cells are the B cells and T cells. Immune cells coordinate their activities by means of chemical messengers or lymphokines, including the antiviral messenger interferon. The lymph nodes play a major role in organizing the immune response.

immunization conferring immunity to infectious disease by artificial methods. The most widely used technique is ◊vaccination.

Immunization is an important public health measure. If most of the population has been immunized against a particular disease, it is impossible for an epidemic to take hold.

immunoglobulin human globulin ◊protein that can be separated from blood and administered to confer immediate immunity on the recipient. It participates in the immune reaction as the antibody for a specific ◊antigen (disease-causing agent).

immunosuppressive any drug that suppresses the body's normal immune responses to infection or foreign tissue. It is used in the treatment of autoimmune disease; as part of chemotherapy for leukaemias, lymphomas, and other cancers; and to help prevent rejection following organ transplantation.

Immunosuppressed patients are at greatly increased risk of infection.

imprinting in ◊ethology, the process whereby a young animal learns to recognize both specific individuals (for example, its mother) and its own species.

impulse in mechanics, the product of a force and the time over which it acts. An impulse applied to a body causes its ◊momentum to change and is equal to that change in momentum. It is measured in newton seconds (N s).

impulse in nerves, the electrical signal that is transmitted along a nerve fibre which has been sufficiently stimulated.

incandescence emission of light from a substance in consequence of its high temperature. The colour of the emitted light from liquids or solids depends on their temperature, and for solids generally the higher the temperature the whiter the light. Gases may become incandescent through ionizing radiation, as in the glowing vacuum discharge tube.

inclination angle between the ◊ecliptic and the plane of the orbit of a planet, asteroid, or comet. In the case of satellites orbiting a planet, it is the angle between the plane of orbit of the satellite and the equator of the planet.

incoherent light light that is not of a single ◊phase. Daylight is an example.

incompressible fluid fluid that resists changes in density – for example, oil.

indeterminate problems problems involving one or more unknown or variable quantities. See also ◊Diophantine equations.

indicator in chemistry, a compound that changes its structure and colour in response to its environment. The commonest chemical indicators detect changes in ◊pH (for example, litmus and universal indicator), or in the oxidation state of a system (redox indicators).

induction in physics, an alteration in the physical properties of a body that is brought about by the influence of a field.

induction motor device that produces rotation by induction. An alternating current is fed to a winding of wires which thus induces electrical currents to flow in a second set of windings in a central rotor. Interaction between the two currents and the magnetic flux involved causes rotation.

industrial melanism dark or highly pigmented colouring in a 'variety' of a species that evolves in a region with high atmospheric pollution.

inertia in physics, the tendency of an object to remain in a state of rest or uniform motion until an external force is applied, as described by Isaac Newton's first law of motion (see ◊Newton's laws of motion).

infinitesimal number that is not zero but is less than any finite number. Infinitesimal numbers clearly do not exist in the conventional system of real numbers, but modern developments in logic allow the use of an extended system of numbers that includes infinitesimal numbers. Calculations with these adhere to certain restrictions and require a good understanding of ◊limits.

infinitesimal calculus original name for 'calculus', that is, differential and ◊integral calculus, and so called because it was thought to rely on 'infinitely small' quantities. (It is now seen to be based upon a precise theory of ◊limits.)

infinity mathematical quantity that is larger than any fixed assignable quantity; symbol ∞. By convention, the result of dividing any number by zero is regarded as infinity.

infrared radiation invisible electromagnetic ◊radiation of wavelength between about 0.75 micrometres and 1 millimetre – that is, between the limit of the red end of the visible spectrum and the shortest microwaves. All bodies above the ◊absolute zero of temperature absorb and radiate infrared radiation. Infrared radiation is used in medical photography and treatment, and in industry, astronomy, and criminology.

ingot mould shape into which metal is poured in a molten state for further processing.

ingot iron iron that has been produced in such a way as to reduce the amount of impurities within it, in the form of carbon, manganese, and silicon.

inoculation injection into the body of dead or weakened disease-carrying organisms or their toxins (◊vaccine) to produce immunity by inducing a mild form of a disease.

insulator any poor ◊conductor of heat, sound, or electricity. Most substances lacking free (mobile) ◊electrons, such as nonmetals, are electrical or thermal insulators. Usually, devices of glass or porcelain, called insulators, are used for insulating and supporting overhead wires.

integer any whole number. Integers may be positive or negative; 0 is an integer, and is often considered positive. Formally, integers are members of the set $Z = \{... -3, -2, -1, 0, 1, 2, 3,... \}$ Fractions, such as $\frac{1}{2}$ and 0.35, are known as non-integral numbers ('not integers').

integral calculus branch of mathematics using the process of ◊integration. It is concerned with finding volumes and areas and summing infinitesimally small quantities.

integral equations equations involving integrals of the unknown function.

integration in mathematics, a method in ◊calculus of determining the solutions of definite or indefinite integrals.

An example of a definite integral can be thought of as finding the area under a curve (as represented by an algebraic expression or function) between particular values of the function's variable. In practice, integral calculus provides scientists with a powerful tool for doing calculations that involve a continually varying quantity (such as determining the position at any given instant of a space rocket that is accelerating away from Earth). Its basic principles were discovered in the late

1660s independently by the German philosopher Leibniz and the British scientist Newton.

intelligence quotient (IQ) an intelligence rating ascertained through answers to a test, which are expressed as a score and placed on an index of scores. Formerly, IQ was defined as (mental age/calendar age) × 100.

intensity interferometry use of two telescopes linked by computer to study the intensity of light received from a star. Analysis of the combined results has enabled measurement of the diameters of stars as apparently small as 2×10^{-4} sec of arc.

interference in physics, the phenomenon of two or more wave motions interacting and combining to produce a resultant wave of larger or smaller amplitude (depending on whether the combining waves are in or out of ◊phase with each other).

intergalactic matter hypothetical material within a cluster of galaxies, whose gravitational effect is to maintain the equilibrium of the cluster. Theoretically comprising 10–30 times the mass of the galaxies themselves (in order to have the observed effect), it has yet to be detected in any form – although the most likely form is as ◊hydrogen.

internal combustion transformation of the chemical energy of a fuel into mechanical energy in controlled combustion in an enclosed cylinder sealed at one end by a piston.

internal-combustion engine heat engine in which fuel is burned inside the engine, contrasting with an external-combustion engine (such as the steam engine) in which fuel is burned in a separate unit. The diesel engine and petrol engine are both internal-combustion engines. Gas ◊turbines and jet and rocket engines are also considered to be internal-combustion engines because they burn their fuel inside their combustion chambers.

interoceptive describing the receptor that receives stimuli that originate within the body.

interstellar hydrogen presence of hydrogen gas between the stars of a galaxy, thus 'filling out' the shape of the galaxy in a way that can be detected by spectral analysis and radio monitoring.

interstellar space space between the stars of a galaxy. It is generally not, however, a void vacuum, and is the subject of considerable spectral research.

intrinsic geometry study of a surface without reference to any point, condition or space outside it. All measurements and operations carried out on the surface are therefore in terms of its own (intrinsic) form.

intuitional mathematics or *intuitionism* an alternative foundational basis for mathematics that adopts a stricter logic in its approach to proofs concerning the infinite. For example, it dismisses the law of the ◊excluded middle, and so disregards 'proofs' derived by double negatives if the relevant positive statement has not actually been demonstrated to be true. Although this may be considered a sort of philosophical puritanism, the outlook leads to a more refined classification of proof material than merely 'true' or 'false'. The fact that such a critical attitude can itself be formalized in a mathematically sound system is an important achievement. Nevertheless, most practising mathematicians remain unconcerned by this logical analysis.

invagination formation of an inner pocket within a layer of cells by part of the layer pushing inwards to form a cavity that remains open to the original surface. See also ◊endocytosis.

Invar an ◊alloy of approximately 64% iron, 36% nickel, and a small amount of carbon, which possesses a very low coefficient of expansion. As a result, it is used in devices such as pendulums whose correct operation depend on maintaining constant length despite temperature changes.

invariant as a general term, describes a property that is preserved through specified mathematical operations.

inverse function ◊function that exactly reverses the transformation produced by a function f; it is usually written as f^{-1}. For example $3x + 2$ and $\frac{(x-2)}{3}$ are mutually inverse functions. Multiplication and division are inverse operations.

in vitro process biological experiment or technique carried out in a laboratory, outside the body of a living organism (literally 'in glass', for example in a test tube). By contrast, an in vivo process takes place within the body of an organism.

in vivo process biological experiment or technique carried out within a living organism; by contrast, an in vitro process takes place outside the organism, in an artificial environment such as a laboratory.

ion atom, or group of atoms, that is either positively charged (◊cation) or negatively charged (◊anion), as a result of the loss or gain of electrons during chemical reactions or exposure to certain forms of radiation. In solution or in the molten state, ionic compounds such as salts, acids, alkalis, and metal oxides conduct electricity. These compounds are known as ◊electrolytes.

ionic bond or *electrovalent bond* bond produced when atoms of one element donate electrons to atoms of another element, forming positively and negatively charged ◊ions respectively. The attraction between the oppositely charged ions constitutes the bond. Sodium chloride (Na^+Cl^-) is a typical ionic compound.

ionic radius effective radius of an ion. In positively charged ◊cations, the ionic radius is less than the ◊atomic radius (because the electrons are more tightly bound); in ◊anions the ionic radius is more than the atomic radius. Some elements, such as the transition metals, can have several different ionization states and their ionic radii vary according to the state involved.

ionization process of ion formation. It can be achieved in two ways. The first way is by the loss or gain of electrons by atoms to form positive or negative ions.

$$Na - e^- \rightarrow Na^+$$

$$\tfrac{1}{2}\,Cl_2 + e^- \rightarrow Cl^-$$

In the second mechanism, ions are formed when a covalent bond breaks, as when hydrogen chloride gas is dissolved in water. One portion of the molecule retains both electrons, forming a negative ion, and the other portion becomes positively charged. This bond-fission process is sometimes called dissociation.

$$HCl_{(g)} + aq \leftrightarrow H^+_{(aq)} + Cl^-_{(aq)}$$

ionosphere ionized layer of Earth's outer ◊atmosphere (60–1,000 km/38–620 mi) that contains sufficient free electrons to modify the way in which radio waves are propagated, for instance by reflecting them back to Earth. The ionosphere is thought to be produced by absorption of the Sun's ultraviolet radiation.

iron hard, malleable and ductile, silver-grey, metallic element, symbol Fe (from Latin *ferrum*), atomic number 26, relative atomic mass 55.847. It is the fourth most abundant element (the second most abundant metal, after aluminium) in the Earth's crust. Iron occurs in concentrated deposits as the ores hematite (Fe_2O_3), spathic ore ($FeCO_3$), and magnetite (Fe_3O_4). It sometimes occurs as a free metal, occasionally as fragments of iron or iron–nickel meteorites.

iron lung negative pressure ventilator used to assist breathing. The patient lies inside the chamber with only the head free. It is associated mainly with the polio epidemics of the 1940s and 1950s, but is still occasionally used for patients with chronic breathing problems.

irrational number in mathematics, number that cannot be expressed as an exact ◊fraction. Irrational numbers include some square roots (for example, $\sqrt{2}$, $\sqrt{3}$, and $\sqrt{5}$ are irrational) and numbers such as π (the ratio of the circumference of a circle to its diameter, which is approximately equal to 3.14159) and e (the base of ◊natural logarithms, approximately 2.71828). If an irrational number is expressed as a decimal it would extend infinitely without repeating. If an irrational number is divided or multiplied by another irrational number, it becomes rational.

isomer chemical compound having the same molecular composition and mass as another, but with different physical or chemical properties owing to the different structural arrangement of its constituent atoms. For example, the organic compounds butane ($CH_3\,(CH_2)_2CH_3$) and methyl propane ($CH_3CH(CH_3)CH_3$) are isomers, each possessing four carbon atoms and ten hydrogen atoms but differing in the way that these are arranged with respect to each other.

isomorphism existence of substances of different chemical composition but with similar crystalline form.

isoperimetry branch of geometry involving the study and measurement of figures with equal perimeters.

isostasy the theoretical balance in buoyancy of all parts of the Earth's ◊crust, as though they were floating on a denser layer beneath. There are two theories of the mechanism of isostasy, the Airy hypothesis and the Pratt hypothesis, both of which have validity. In the *Airy hypothesis* crustal blocks have the same density but different depths: like ice cubes floating in water, higher mountains have deeper roots. In the *Pratt hypothesis*, crustal blocks have different densities allowing the depth of crustal material to be the same.

isotherm line on a map, linking all places having the same temperature at a given time.

isotope one of two or more atoms that have the same atomic number (same number of protons), but which contain a different number of neutrons, thus differing in their atomic mass (see ◊relative atomic mass). They may be stable or radioactive (see ◊radioisotope), naturally occurring, or synthesized. For example, hydrogen has the isotopes ^{2}H (◊deuterium) and ^{3}H (tritium). The term was coined by English chemist Frederick Soddy, pioneer researcher in atomic disintegration.

isotropic having equal and uniform properties at all points and in all directions. In astronomy the term describes microwave ◊background radiation.

J

Jacquard system use of punched cards to direct the operation of a loom in weaving patterns. It was devised by French engineer Joseph Jacquard.

jet engine ⟡gas turbine in which air taken in through the front is compressed, and then used to provide oxygen for the combustion of fuel. The consequent backward flow of heated, expanding gas provides propulsion, and also drives a turbine, which powers the compressor bringing the air into the combustion chamber.

jib boom of a crane, made from a framework of girders in most cases. Half its length approximately defines the range of operation of the crane, the circle in which loads can be lifted and deposited.

Josephson effect in physics, superconducting (see ⟡superconductivity) ring interrupted by a thin layer of insulating material gives rise to an ⟡alternating current (AC) in the barrier when a steady external voltage is applied to it. This AC effect has a direct-current analogue, occurring when a steady magnetic field is applied to the insulating material. The effect is named after Welsh physicist Brian Josephson.

joule SI unit (symbol J) of work and energy, replacing the calorie (one joule equals 4.2 calories).

Joule–Kelvin effect or *Joule–Thomson effect* in physics, the fall in temperature of a gas as it expands adiabatically (without loss or gain of heat to the system) through a narrow jet. It can be felt when, for example, compressed air escapes through the valve of an inflated bicycle tyre. It is the basic principle of most refrigerators.

Joule's electrical law heat H in joules produced by the passing of a current of I amperes through a resistance of R ohms for a time t seconds is given by:

$$H = I^2Rt$$

Joule's thermal law internal energy of a gas at constant temperature is independent of its volume, provided the gas is ⟡ideal.

Julian calendar calendar established by Julius Caesar in 46 BC, which overestimated the duration of the ⟡sidereal year by 11 minutes and 14 seconds. It was replaced, from 1582, by the ⟡Gregorian calendar, by which time it was inaccurate by a total of 10 days.

Jurassic period of geological time 208–146 million years ago; the middle period of the Mesozoic era. Climates worldwide were equable, creating forests of conifers and ferns; dinosaurs were abundant, birds evolved, and limestones and iron ores were deposited.

K

kelvin scale temperature scale used by scientists. It begins at ◊absolute zero (−273.15°C/−459.67°F) and increases by the same degree intervals as the Celsius scale; that is, 0°C is the same as 273.15 K and 100°C is 373.15 K.

Kennelly–Heaviside layer former term for the E layer of the ionosphere.

Kepler's laws in astronomy, three laws of planetary motion formulated in 1609 and 1619 by the German mathematician and astronomer Johannes Kepler: (1) the orbit of each planet is an ellipse with the Sun at one of the foci; (2) the radius vector of each planet sweeps out equal areas in equal times; (3) the squares of the periods of the planets are proportional to the cubes of their mean distances from the Sun.

kerosene thin oil obtained from the distillation of petroleum; a highly refined form is used in jet aircraft fuel. Kerosene is a mixture of hydrocarbons of the ◊paraffin series.

Kerr cell device making use of the ◊Kerr effect. The cell consists of a transparent container of a special liquid in which there are two electrodes, placed between two polarizing materials in the container. Only if the planes of polarization of all the various layers in the cell are aligned will light pass, and so the Kerr cell can be used as a shutter device.

Kerr effect elliptical polarization of light as a result of the beam of light being reflected from a pole of an electromagnet. A similar effect also exists for liquids, if a ◊potential difference is applied to the liquid itself, the angle of polarization depending on the size of the potential difference.

kinematic relativity theory proposed by English astrophysicist Edward Milne as a viable alternative to Einstein's general theory of ◊relativity, and based generally on kinematics (the science of pure motion, without reference to matter or force), from which Milne successfully derived new systems of dynamics and electrodynamics.

kinematics branch of ◊mechanics that relates ◊accelerations to the velocities and changes in distance they produce, without considering the forces that generate the accelerations involved. See also ◊dynamics.

kinetic energy the energy of a body resulting from motion. It is contrasted with ◊potential energy.

kinetic theory theory describing the physical properties of matter in terms of the behaviour – principally movement – of its component atoms or molecules. The temperature of a substance is dependent on the velocity of movement of its constituent particles, increased temperature being accompanied by increased movement. A gas consists of rapidly moving atoms or molecules and, according to kinetic theory, it is their continual impact on the walls of the containing vessel that accounts for the pressure of the gas. The slowing of molecular motion as temperature falls, according to kinetic theory, accounts for the physical properties of liquids and solids, culminating in the concept of no molecular motion at ◊absolute zero (0 K/−273.15°C).

knocking in a spark-ignition petrol engine, a phenomenon that occurs when unburned fuel-air mixture explodes in the combustion chamber before being ignited by the spark. The resulting shock waves produce a metallic knocking sound. Loss of power occurs, which can be prevented by reducing the compression ratio, re-designing the geometry of the combustion chamber, or increasing the octane number of the petrol (usually by the use of tetraethyl lead anti-knock additives, or increasingly by MTBE – methyl tertiary butyl ether in unleaded petrol).

knot in two- and three-dimensional geometry, a closed curve that loops over or through itself; representations of such structures are commonly presented as congruency problems.

Kuiper band one of a number of bands in the spectra of Uranus and Neptune at ◊wavelengths of 7,500 Å; (7.5×10^{-7}m), indicating the presence of ◊methane. They are named after Dutch-born US astronomer Gerard Kuiper.

kymograph recording produced by an instrument that detects variations such as small muscular contractions or slight changes in arterial blood pressure.

L

lactic acid or *2-hydroxypropanoic acid* $CH_3CHOH\ COOH$ organic acid, a colourless, almost odourless liquid, produced by certain bacteria during fermentation and by active muscle cells when they are exercised hard and are experiencing oxygen debt. An accumulation of lactic acid in the muscles may cause cramp. It occurs in yoghurt, buttermilk, sour cream, poor wine, and certain plant extracts, and is used in food preservation and in the preparation of pharmaceuticals.

Lamarckism theory of evolution, now discredited, advocated during the early 19th century by French naturalist Jean Baptiste Lamarck.

Lamarckism is the theory that acquired characteristics were inherited. It differs from the Darwinian theory of evolution.

Landé splitting factor calculational device used in quantum theory that enables the ◊fine and ◊hyperfine structure of a ◊spectral line to be determined by a knowledge of the various ◊spin and orbital angular momenta of the electrons in the atom.

lanthanide any of a series of 15 metallic elements (also known as rare earths) with atomic numbers 57 (lanthanum) to 71 (lutetium).

One of its members, promethium, is radioactive. All occur in nature. Lanthanides are grouped because of their chemical similarities (most are trivalent, but some can be divalent or tetravalent), their properties differing only slightly with atomic number.

laparoscope in medicine, another name for an ◊endoscope.

large-number hypothesis theory in ◊cosmology that tries to understand the basic reason for an apparent coincidence of size in ratios of fundamental quantities in atomic and cosmological theory. If the apparent radius of the universe is divided by the radius of the ◊electron, the resulting large number (about 10^{43}) is remarkably similar to the ratio of the strengths of the ◊electrostatic and gravitational force between the ◊electron and the ◊proton. The reason for this is not clear at present, but if the relationship is to hold true for all time, it can be shown that on a ◊Big Bang model of the universe the ◊gravitational constant g must decrease with time, that is, the strength of gravity must decrease.

large numbers, laws of theorems in probability theory that predict that the observed frequencies of events for a large number of repeated trials are more and more likely to approach their theoretical probability as the number of repetitions increases.

laser acronym for *light amplification by stimulated emission of radiation* device for producing a narrow beam of light, capable of travelling over vast distances without dispersion, and of being focused to give enormous power densities (10^8 watts per cm^2 for high-energy lasers). The laser operates on a principle similar to that of the ◊maser (a high-frequency microwave amplifier or oscillator). The uses of lasers include communications (a laser beam can carry much more information than can radio waves), cutting, drilling, welding, satellite tracking, medical and biological research, and surgery. Sound wave vibrations from the window glass of a room can be picked up by a reflected laser beam. Lasers are also used as entertainment in theatres, concerts, and light shows.

latent heat in physics, the heat absorbed or released by a substance as it changes state (for example, from solid to liquid) at constant temperature and pressure.

lathe tool used to produce objects with cylindrical symmetry, such as bars, screws, barrels.

lattice in chemistry, the arrangement of positions in, for example, a crystal in which the atoms, ions or molecules remain virtually stationary.

law of universal attraction Isaac Newton's formulation of the law of ◊gravity.

least squares, method of method of deriving as exact an average value as possible from a set of approximate or inaccurate values by introducing the errors as unknown variables and requiring the sum of their squares to be minimized. The method was devised by German mathematician Karl Gauss as a precise way of best fitting a straight line through a set of plotted data points that are not collinear.

Legendre functions functions that satisfy the second-order differential equation:

$$(1 - x^2)\ d^2y/dx^2 - 2x\ dy/dx + n\ (n + 1)y = 0$$

lemniscate curve represented by the equation:

$$(x^2 + y^2)^2 = a^2\ (x^2 - y^2)$$

where a is constant and x and y are variables.

Lenz's law in physics, a law stating that the direction of an electromagnetically induced current (generated by moving a magnet near a wire or a wire in a magnetic field) will be such as to oppose the motion producing it. It is named after the German physicist Heinrich Friedrich Lenz (1804–1865), who announced it in 1833.

Leonid meteor shower shower of meteors emanating from an apparent point in Leo every 33 years.

leucocyte another name for a ◊white blood cell.

lever simple machine consisting of a rigid rod pivoted at a fixed point called the fulcrum, used for shifting or raising a heavy load or applying force. Levers are classified into orders according to where the effort is applied, and the load-moving force developed, in relation to the position of the fulcrum.

Leyden jar an early form of condenser consisting of a glass jar with an interior and exterior coating of metal foil, used to store static electricity.

libration in astronomy, a slight, apparent wobble in the rotation of the Moon due to its variable speed of rotation and the tilt of its axis.

Lie groups or *Lie rings* collections of mathematical objects in groups or rings that have further (topological) structure under which the collective operations are ◊continuous, for example, vectors in the plane (where open discs define a topological structure).

ligand in chemistry, a group that bonds symmetrically to a central atom or ion of a metal; the result is called a *coordination complex*. An example of a neutral ligand is ammonia; the nitrosyl ion NO^+ is a charged ligand. An example of a coordination complex is hexaminocobalt chloride, $[Co(NH_3)_6]Cl_3$, in which the central cobalt ion (Co^{3+}) is surrounded by covalent bonds with six ammonia molecules and ionic bonds with three chloride ions.

Ligands are used in medicine as an antidote to heavy metal poisoning, removing the metal ions by attaching themselves to form a harmless compound.

light ◊electromagnetic waves in the visible range, having a wavelength from about 400 nanometres in the extreme violet to about 770 nanometres in the extreme red. Light is considered to exhibit particle and wave properties, and the fundamental particle, or quantum, of light is called the photon. The speed of light (and of all electromagnetic radiation) in a vacuum is approximately 300,000 km/186,000 mi per second, and is a universal constant denoted by c.

light reaction part of the ◊photosynthesis process in green plants that requires sunlight (as opposed to the ◊dark reaction, which does not). During the light reaction light energy is used to generate ATP (by the ◊phosphorylation of ADP), which is necessary for the dark reaction.

light, speed of (symbol c) a fundamental constant of nature, the speed of light is the limiting velocity that any body can travel at. It is equal to 2.997925×10^8 m/186,180 mi per second, and is the same for all observers, no matter how fast they move themselves.

light, theories of the nature of before the advent of modern physics, theories of the basic nature of light fell into two camps: those who viewed light as made up of a stream of particles (corpuscular theory), and those who viewed it as a wave motion (wave theory). Each attempted to explain all phenomena in optics, such as ◊reflection, ◊refraction, and so on, on the basis of these two viewpoints. It is now known that light exists in quanta known as photons that exhibit both corpuscular and wavelike behaviour in certain circumstances.

light year in astronomy, the distance travelled by a beam of light in a vacuum in one year, approximately 9.46 trillion (million million) km/5.88 trillion miles.

limit in mathematics, in an infinite sequence, the final value towards which the sequence is tending. For example, the limit of the sequence $\frac{1}{2}$, $\frac{3}{4}$, $\frac{7}{8}$, $\frac{15}{16}$ ... is 1, although no member of the sequence will ever exactly equal 1 no matter how many terms are added together. The limit of the ratios of a Fibonacci sequence is $(\sqrt{5} + 1)/2$. This number is also the golden section.

linear function or *linear transformation* in its simplest context, a transformation such as $y = mx$ that may be depicted as a line through the origin. More generally, a transformation T defined on a vector space with the property that:

$$T(\alpha x + \beta y) = \alpha T(x) + \beta T(y)$$

for x, y vectors and α, β scalars.

linear motor device that uses ◊induction to produce forward motion along a track.

line spectrum ◊spectrum made up of discrete lines of intensity at certain ◊wavelengths, characterizing an ◊atom in a particular state.

linkage in genetics, the association between two or more genes that tend to be inherited together because they are on the same chromosome.

The closer together they are on the chromosome, the less likely they are to be separated by crossing over (one of the processes of recombination) and they are then described as being 'tightly linked'.

lipid any of a large number of esters of fatty acids, commonly formed by the reaction of a fatty acid with glycerol. They are soluble in alcohol but not in water. Lipids are the chief constituents of plant and animal waxes, fats, and oils.

liquid state of matter between a ◊solid and a ◊gas. A liquid forms a level surface and assumes the shape of its container. Its atoms do not occupy fixed positions as in a crystalline solid, nor do they have freedom of movement as in a gas. Unlike a gas, a liquid is difficult to compress since pressure applied at one point is equally transmitted throughout (Pascal's principle). ◊Hydraulics makes use of this property.

Lissajous figures path followed by a point subjected to two or more simultaneous simple wave motions, for example, at right angles to one another. They were developed by French physicist Jules Lissajous.

lithium (Greek *lithos* 'stone') soft, ductile, silver-white, metallic element, symbol Li, atomic number 3, relative atomic mass 6.941. It is one of the ◊alkali metals, has a very low density (far less than most woods), and floats on water (specific gravity 0.57); it is the lightest of all metals. Lithium is used to harden alloys, and in batteries; its compounds are used in medicine to treat manic depression.

ln symbol for natural logarithm.

load generally, the burden inflicted on a system. Thus, in ◊mechanics, the load is the weight supported by a structure, whereas in electrical engineering it is the output of an electrical device such as a ◊transformer.

Local Group in astronomy, a cluster of about 30 galaxies that includes our own, the Milky Way. Like other groups of galaxies, the Local Group is held together by the gravitational attraction among its members, and does not expand with the expanding universe. Its two largest galaxies are the Milky Way and the Andromeda galaxy; most of the others are small and faint.

locus (Latin 'place') in mathematics, traditionally the path traced out by a moving point, but now defined as the set of all points on a curve satisfying given conditions. For example, the locus of a point that moves so that it is always at the same distance from another fixed point is a circle; the locus of a point that is always at the same distance from two fixed points is a straight line that perpendicularly bisects the line joining them. The locus of points a fixed distance from a line is two parallel lines running either side.

log in mathematics, abbreviation for ◊logarithm.

logarithm or *log* the ◊exponent or index of a number to a specified base – usually 10. For example, the logarithm to the base 10 of 1,000 is 3 because $10^3 = 1,000$; the logarithm of 2 is 0.3010 because $2 = 10^{0.3010}$. The whole-number part of a logarithm is called the *characteristic*; the fractional part is called the *mantissa*.

Before the advent of cheap electronic calculators, multiplication and division could be simplified by being replaced with the addition and subtraction of logarithms.

logic branch of philosophy that studies valid reasoning and argument. It is also the way in which one thing may be said to follow from, or be a consequence of, another (deductive logic). Logic is generally divided into the traditional formal logic of Aristotle and the symbolic logic derived from Friedrich Frege and Bertrand Russell.

logistic curve curve that represents logarithmic functions, from which logarithms of ordinary numbers can be read off.

longitudinal wave wave in which the displacement of the medium's particles is in line with or parallel to the direction of travel of the wave motion.

loom machine for weaving textiles.

Lorentz transformation means of relating measurements of times and lengths made in one frame of reference to those made in another frame of reference moving at some velocity relative to the first. These formulae, which can be derived directly from Einstein's special theory of ◊relativity, predict that at velocities approaching that of light, lengths appear to contract (the Lorentz contraction) and time intervals appear to increase (time dilation), as measured in a stationary frame of reference.

lubricant substance used between moving surfaces to reduce friction. Carbon-based (organic) lubricants, commonly called grease and oil, are recovered from petroleum distillation.

luminescence emission of light from a body when its atoms are excited by means other than raising its temperature. Short-lived luminescence is called fluorescence; longer-lived luminescence is called phosphorescence.

luminosity or *brightness* in astronomy, the amount of light emitted by a star, measured in ◊magnitudes. The apparent brightness of an object decreases in proportion to the square of its distance from the observer. The luminosity of a star or other body can be expressed in relation to that of the Sun.

luteinization development of an ovum in a ruptured Graafian follicle within the ovary, initiated by oestrogen which in turn is activated by luteinizing ◊hormone.

Lyman series series of lines in the ◊spectrum of hydrogen that lie in the ultraviolet region of the spectrum. It is named after US physicist Theodor Lyman.

lysogeny presence of nonvirulent or temperate ◊bacteriophages in a bacterium, that do not lyse it (damage the outer cell membrane). The phage does not replicate after entering the bacterial cell, although its DNA combines with that of the bacterium and is reproduced with it every time the bacterium multiplies. The basic characteristics of the host bacterium remain unchanged.

lysosome membrane-enclosed structure, or organelle, inside a ◊cell, principally found in animal cells. Lysosomes contain enzymes that can break down proteins and other biological substances. They play a part in digestion, and in the white blood cells known as phagocytes the lysosome enzymes attack ingested bacteria.

M

machine device that allows a small force (the effort) to overcome a larger one (the load). There are three basic machines: the inclined plane (ramp), the lever, and the wheel and axle. All other machines are combinations of these three basic types. Simple machines derived from the inclined plane include the wedge, the gear, and the screw; the spanner is derived from the lever; the pulley from the wheel.

Mach number ratio of the speed of a body to the speed of sound in the undisturbed medium through which the body travels. Mach 1 is reached when a body (such as an aircraft) has a velocity greater than that of sound ('passes the sound barrier'), namely 331 m/1,087 ft per second at sea level. It is named after Austrian physicist Ernst Mach (1838–1916).

macromolecule in chemistry, a very large molecule, generally a ◊polymer.

Magellanic Clouds in astronomy, the two galaxies nearest to our own galaxy. They are irregularly shaped, and appear as detached parts of the Milky Way, in the southern constellations Dorado, Tucana, and Mensa.

magic numbers in atomic physics certain numbers of ◊neutrons or ◊protons (2, 8, 20, 28, 50, 82, 126) in the nuclei of elements of outstanding stability, such as lead and helium.

Such stability is the result of neutrons and protons being arranged in completed 'layers' or 'shells'.

magma molten rock material beneath the Earth's (or any of the terrestrial planets) surface from which ◊igneous rocks are formed. Lava is magma that has extruded on to the surface.

magnetic detector device used in early radio systems, in which high-frequency currents were detected through their demagnetizing effect on a magnetized ◊iron core surrounded by the wire-carrying currents.

magnetic energy property of a magnet described by the multiplication of the flux density by the ◊field strength on the demagnetization curve of a permanent magnet.

magnetic field region around a permanent magnet, or around a conductor carrying an electric current, in which a force acts on a moving charge or on a magnet placed in the field. The field can be represented by lines of force, which by convention link north and south poles and are parallel to the directions of a small compass needle placed on them. A magnetic field's magnitude and direction are given by the ◊magnetic flux density, expressed in ◊teslas.

magnetic field strength property measured to define the strength of a ◊magnetic field. The ◊SI unit is the ◊ampere per metre.

magnetic flux measurement of the strength of the magnetic field around electric currents and magnets. Its SI unit is the ◊weber; one weber per square metre is equal to one tesla.

magnetic flux density ◊magnetic flux passing through one square metre of area of a magnetic field in a direction at right angles to the magnetic force. The ◊SI unit is the ◊tesla.

magnetic moment product of the strength and length of a magnet.

magnetic monopole prediction of one quantum theory (proposed by Dirac) that involves the existence of individual magnetic poles, analogous to the individual charges found in ◊electrostatics (that is, ◊electrons). Such an entity has not yet been definitely observed to exist, but is expected to be rare in any case.

magnetic permeability ◊magnetic flux density in a body, divided by the external magnetic field strength producing it. It can be used as a way of classifying materials into different types of magnetism, such as ◊ferromagnetic.

magnetism phenomena associated with ◊magnetic fields. Magnetic fields are produced by moving charged particles: in electromagnets, electrons flow through a coil of wire connected to a battery; in permanent magnets, spinning electrons within the atoms generate the field.

magnetohydrodynamics study of the behaviour of ◊plasmas under the influence of magnetic fields.

magnetosphere volume of space, surrounding a planet, controlled by the planet's magnetic field, and acting as a magnetic 'shell'. The Earth's magnetosphere extends 64,000 km/40,000 mi towards the Sun, but many times this distance on the side away from the Sun.

magnitude in astronomy, measure of the brightness of a star or other celestial object. The larger the number denoting the magnitude, the fainter the object. Zero or first magnitude indicates some of the brightest stars. Still brighter are those of negative magnitude, such as Sirius, whose magnitude is –1.46. *Apparent magnitude* is the brightness of an object as seen from Earth; *absolute magnitude* is the brightness at a standard distance of 10 parsecs (32.6 light years).

main sequence in astronomy, the part of the ◊Hertzsprung–Russell diagram that contains most of the stars, including the Sun. It runs diagonally from the top left of the diagram to the lower right. The most massive (and hence brightest) stars are at the top left, with the least massive (coolest) stars at the bottom right.

make-and-break circuit circuit that contains a device which, when current flows in one part of the circuit, causes the device to break that part of the circuit, and allow current to flow in another part, and vice versa.

Malfatti's problem medieval European problem, to inscribe within a triangle three circles tangent to one another.

Malus's law law giving the intensity of light after having been polarized through a certain angle.

mandrel accurately turned cylinder onto which a boretube can be fitted for further turning and milling.

manifold in two-dimensional space, a regular surface that locally looks like a flat plane slightly distorted. It can be represented by differentiable functions. There are analogues in spaces of more dimensions.

mapping in mathematics, another name for ◊transformation.

marine engineering branch of ◊engineering devoted to the design and production of propulsive devices and other mechanical devices for marine vessels such as ships and submarines.

Mariner spacecraft series of US space probes that explored the planets Mercury, Venus, and Mars 1962–75.

Markov chain in statistics, an ordered sequence of discrete states (random variables) $x_1, x_2, ..., x_i, ..., x_n$ such that the probability of x_i depends only on n and/or the state xi_{-1} which has preceded it. If independent of n, the chain is said to be homogeneous.

mascon contraction of *mass concentration* one of a number of apparent regions on the surface of the Moon where gravity is somehow stronger. The effect is presumed to be due to localized areas of denser rock strata.

maser acronym for *microwave amplification by stimulated emission of radiation* in physics, a high-frequency microwave amplifier or oscillator in which the signal to be amplified is used to stimulate excited atoms into emitting energy at the same frequency. Atoms or molecules are raised to a higher energy level and then allowed to lose this energy by radiation emitted at a precise frequency. The principle has been extended to other parts of the electromagnetic spectrum as, for example, in the ◊laser.

mass in physics, the quantity of matter in a body as measured by its inertia. Mass determines the acceleration produced in a body by a given force acting on it, the acceleration being inversely proportional to the mass of the body. The mass also determines the force exerted on a body by ◊gravity on Earth, although this attraction varies slightly from place to place. In the SI system, the base unit of mass is the kilogram.

mass number or *nucleon number* sum (symbol A) of the numbers of protons and neutrons in the nucleus of an atom. It is used along with the ◊atomic number (the number of protons) in nuclear notation: in symbols that represent nuclear isotopes, such as $^{14}_{6}C$, the lower number is the atomic number, and the upper number is the mass number.

mass spectrograph an instrument for determining the masses of individual atoms by means of positive-ray analysis, which involves deflecting streams of positive ◊ions using electric and magnetic fields. Ions with different masses are deflected by different amounts and can be detected (for example, photographically) to produce a mass spectrum. ◊Isotopes were first discovered in this way.

mass spectrometer in physics, an apparatus for analysing chemical composition. Positive ions (charged particles) of a substance are separated by an electromagnetic system, which permits accurate measurement of the relative concentrations of the various ionic masses present, particularly isotopes.

mass spectrometry means of analysing a substance in order to determine its basic chemical composition which makes use of the way in which the deflection of an ◊ion in a magnetic and electric field depends on its mass to charge ratio. A mass spectrometer measures the relative abundances of particles of each mass rather than their individual masses.

mast cell in medicine, one of the histamine-containing cells involved in the production of inflammatory reactions, in response to an external trigger factor. For example, cells in the airways or in the bronchial epithelium release histamine and other mediators in response to allergic stimuli, such as allergens, infection, stress, and exercise.

mathematical logic view of mathematics and logic that relates the two disciplines, and to do so uses mathematical or similar notation in the expression of axiomatic statements. ◊Boolean algebra was the original form, and led to German philosopher Gottlob Frege's symbolic logic.

mathematical structure collection of objects that display a) one or more relationships, and b) one or more operations of which the properties may be summarized as a list of ◊axioms; for example, a group, vector, space or ring.

matrix in mathematics, a square ($n \times n$) or rectangular ($m \times n$) array of elements (numbers or algebraic variables) used to facilitate the study of problems in which the relation between the elements is important. They are a means of condensing information about mathematical systems and can be used for, among other things, solving simultaneous linear equations.

matrix mechanics mathematical description of subatomic phenomena that views certain characteristics of the particles involved as being matrices, and hence obeying the rules of matrix mathematics that differ in significant ways from the rules obeyed by ordinary arithmetic.

matter, continuous creation of phenomenon invoked in certain cosmological theories, especially the ◊steady-state model of the universe. In that particular theory, matter is considered to be constantly created, either evenly throughout space, or in localized regions of creation, so as to make up for the diluting effect the Hubble expansion of the universe has on the average density of matter. By continually creating matter, it is then possible for the universe to maintain a steady-state appearance.

Maxwell–Boltzmann distribution in physics, a statistical equation describing the distribution of velocities among the molecules of a gas. It is named after Scottish physicist James Maxwell and Austrian physicist Ludwig Boltzmann, who derived the equation, independently of each other, in the 1860s.

Maxwell's equations set of four vector equations showing the interdependence of electricity and magnetism. The concepts of charge conservation are built into them, as are the experimental results of Faraday, Gauss, and Ampère.

mean in mathematics, a measure of the average of a number of terms or quantities. The simple *arithmetic mean* is the average value of the quantities, that is, the sum of the quantities divided by their number. The *weighted mean* takes into account the frequency of the terms that are summed; it is calculated by multiplying each term by the number of times it occurs, summing the results and dividing this total by the total number of occurrences. The *geometric mean* of n quantities is the nth root of their product. In statistics, it is a measure of central tendency of a set of data.

measure theory extension of the notion of length, area or volume (as appropriate) to general sets of points on the line, plane or in space. Used commonly in analysis (especially integration theory), functional analysis, probability theory, and game theory (in the assessment of the size of coalitions), its definitive form was derived by French mathematician Henri Lebesgue.

mechanical advantage (MA) in physics, the number of times the load moved by a machine is greater than the effort applied to that machine. In equation terms: MA = load/effort.

mechanical curve curve that cannot be precisely expressed as an equation (unlike a geometric curve).

mechanical engineering branch of ◊engineering devoted to the study and production of devices, such as tools and vehicles, that are capable of carrying out tasks.

mechanical equivalent of heat in physics, a constant factor relating the calorie (the *c.g.s.* unit of heat) to the joule (the unit of mechanical energy), equal to 4.1868 joules per calorie. It is redundant in the SI system of units, which measures heat and all forms of energy in ◊joules (so that the mechanical equivalent of heat is 1).

mechanics branch of physics dealing with the motions of bodies and the forces causing these motions, and also with the forces acting on bodies in ◊equilibrium. It is usually divided into ◊dynamics and ◊statics.

medium in bacteriology, an environment in which microorganisms can be cultured. Common mediums include agar, broth, and gelatine, often with added salts and trace elements.

meiosis in biology, a process of cell division in which the number of ◊chromosomes in the cell is halved. It only occurs in eukaryotic cells, and is part of a life cycle that involves sexual reproduction because it allows the genes of two parents to be combined without the total number of chromosomes increasing.

melanin brown pigment that gives colour to the eyes, skin, hair, feathers, and scales of many vertebrates. In humans, melanin helps protect the skin against ultraviolet radiation from sunlight. Both genetic and environmental factors determine the amount of melanin in the skin.

melanocyte cell that produces ◊melanin.

membrane potential potential difference that exists across a membrane or cell wall, such as that across the wall of a nerve cell (neuron).

meridian half a great circle drawn on the Earth's surface passing through both poles and thus through all places with the same longitude. Terrestrial longitudes are usually measured from the Greenwich Meridian.

mesoderm central layer of embryonic cells between the ◊ectoderm and the ◊endoderm.

meson in physics, a group of unstable subatomic particles made up of two indivisible elementary particles, a ◊quark and an antiquark. It has a mass intermediate between that of the electron and that of the proton, is found in cosmic radiation, and is emitted by nuclei under bombardment by very high-energy particles. There are believed to be 15 ordinary types. The last of these to be found was identified by physicists at Fermilab, USA in 1998.

Mesozoic era of geological time 245–65 million years ago, consisting of the Triassic, Jurassic, and Cretaceous periods. At the beginning of the era, the continents were joined together as Pangaea; dinosaurs and other giant reptiles dominated the sea and air; and ferns, horsetails, and cycads thrived in a warm climate worldwide. By the end of the Mesozoic era, the continents had begun to assume their present positions, flowering plants were dominant, and many of the large reptiles and marine fauna were becoming extinct.

messenger RNA (*mRNA*) single-stranded nucleic acid (made up of ◊nucleotides) found in ◊ribosomes, ◊mitochondria, and nucleoli of cells that carries coded information for building chains of ◊amino acids into polypeptides.

Messier catalogue in astronomy, a catalogue of 103 ◊galaxies, ◊nebulas, and star clusters (the Messier objects) published in 1784 by French astronomer Charles Messier. Catalogue entries are denoted by the prefix 'M'. Well known examples include M31 (the ◊Andromeda galaxy), M42 (the Orion Nebula), and M45 (the Pleiades star cluster).

metabolism the chemical processes of living organisms enabling them to grow and to function. It involves a constant alternation of building up complex molecules (*anabolism*) and breaking them down (*catabolism*). For example, green plants build up complex organic substances from water, carbon dioxide, and mineral salts (◊photosynthesis); by digestion animals partially break down complex organic substances, ingested as food, and subsequently resynthesize them for use in their own bodies. Within cells, complex molecules are broken down by the process of ◊respiration. The waste products of metabolism are removed by excretion.

metallurgy the science and technology of producing metals, which includes extraction, alloying, and hardening. *Extractive,* or *process, metallurgy* is concerned with the extraction of metals from their ◊ores and refining and adapting them for use. *Physical metallurgy* is concerned with their properties and application. *Metallography* establishes the microscopic structures that contribute to hardness, ductility, and strength.

metamorphic rock rock altered in structure and composition by pressure, heat, or chemically active fluids after original formation. (If heat is sufficient to melt the original rock, technically it becomes an igneous rock upon cooling.) The term was coined in 1833 by Scottish geologist Charles Lyell (1797–1875).

meteor flash of light in the sky, popularly known as a *shooting* or *falling star,* caused by a particle of dust, a *meteoroid,* entering the atmosphere at speeds up to 70 kps/45 mps and burning up by friction at a height of around 100 km/60 mi. On any clear night, several *sporadic meteors* can be seen each hour.

meteorite piece of rock or metal from space that reaches the surface of the Earth, Moon, or other body. Most meteorites are thought to be fragments from asteroids, although some may be pieces from the heads of comets. Most are stony, although some are made of iron and a few have a mixed rock-iron composition.

meteorology scientific observation and study of the ◊atmosphere, so that weather can be accurately forecast.

Data from meteorological stations and weather satellites are collated by computer at central agencies, and forecast and weather maps based on current readings are issued at regular intervals. Modern analysis, employing some of the most powerful computers, can give useful forecasts for up to six days ahead.

methane CH_4 the simplest hydrocarbon of the paraffin series. Colourless, odourless, and lighter than air, it burns with a bluish flame and explodes when mixed with air or oxygen. It is the chief constituent of natural gas and also occurs in the explosive firedamp of coal mines. Methane emitted by rotting vegetation forms marsh gas, which may ignite by spontaneous combustion to produce the pale flame seen over marshland and known as will-o'-the-wisp.

method of lest squares see ◊least squares, method of.

micrometer instrument for measuring minute lengths or angles with great accuracy; different types of micrometer are used in astronomical and engineering work.

microorganism or *microbe* living organism invisible to the naked eye but visible under a microscope. Microorganisms include viruses and single-celled organisms such as bacteria, protozoa, yeasts, and some algae. The term has no taxonomic significance in biology. The study of microorganisms is known as microbiology.

microscope instrument for forming magnified images with high resolution for detail. Optical and electron microscopes are the ones chiefly in use; other types include acoustic, scanning tunnelling, and ◊atomic force microscopes.

microsome minute particle occurring in the cytoplasm of a cell composed of vesicles with attached ◊ribosomes, which are thought to derive from the ◊endoplasmic reticulum. Microsomes are also thought to give rise to ◊mitochondria.

microtome device for cutting extremely thin slices of tissue for microscopic examination. The tissue is embedded in wax or a synthetic resin (or is frozen) for ease of handling.

microwave radiation radiation in the ◊electromagnetic spectrum between ◊infrared and radio waves. This range has ◊wavelengths of between abut 20 cm/8 in and about 1 mm/0.04 in. Radiation of this type was detected as ◊background radiation.

mimicry imitation of one species (or group of species) by another. The most common form is *Batesian mimicry* (named after English naturalist H W Bates), where the mimic resembles a model that is poisonous or unpleasant to eat, and has aposematic, or warning, coloration; the mimic thus benefits from the fact that predators have learned to avoid the model. Hoverflies that resemble bees or wasps are an example. Appearance is usually the basis for mimicry, but calls, songs, scents, and other signals can also be mimicked.

mineral naturally formed inorganic substance with a particular chemical composition and a regularly repeating internal structure. Either in their perfect crystalline form or otherwise, minerals are the constituents of rocks. In more general usage, a mineral is any substance economically valuable for mining (including coal and oil, despite their organic origins).

minor in the theory of ◊determinants, smaller determinant obtained by deleting one of the rows and one of the columns of a ◊matrix.

minor planet another name for an ◊asteroid.

mitochondria singular *mitochondrion* membrane-enclosed organelles within eukaryotic cells, containing enzymes responsible for energy production during ◊aerobic respiration. Mitochondria absorb O_2 and glucose and produce energy in the form of ◊ATP by breaking down the glucose to CO_2 and H_2O. These rodlike or spherical bodies are thought to be derived from free-living bacteria that, at a very early stage in the history of life, invaded larger cells and took up a symbiotic way of life inside. Each still contains its own small loop of DNA called mitochondrial DNA, and new mitochondria arise by division of existing ones.

mitosis in biology, the process of cell division by which identical daughter cells are produced. During mitosis the DNA is duplicated and the chromosome number doubled, so new cells contain the same amount of DNA as the original cell.

The genetic material of eukaryotic cells is carried on a number of ◊chromosomes. To control movements of chromosomes during cell division so that both new cells get the correct number, a system of protein tubules, known as the spindle, organizes the chromosomes into position in the middle of the cell before they replicate. The spindle then controls the movement of chromosomes as the cell goes through the stages of division: *interphase, prophase, metaphase, anaphase,* and *telophase*. See also ◊meiosis.

Mizar ◊double star in Ursa Major.

M number designation used in the ◊Messier catalogue.

modulation in radio transmission, the variation of frequency, or amplitude, of a radio carrier wave, in accordance with the audio characteristics of the speaking voice, music, or other signal being transmitted.

modulo in number theory, two numbers are said to be equivalent modulo a fixed number if their difference is divisible by the fixed number.

molarity in chemistry, concentration of a solution expressed as the number of ◊moles in grams of solute per cubic decimetre of solution.

mole SI unit (symbol mol) of the amount of a substance. It is defined as the amount of a substance that contains as many elementary entities (atoms, molecules, and so on) as there are atoms in 12 g of the ◊isotope carbon-12.

molecular biology study of the molecular basis of life, including the biochemistry of molecules such as DNA, RNA, and proteins, and the molecular structure and function of the various parts of living cells.

molecular formula in chemistry, formula indicating the actual number of atoms of each element present in a single molecule of a chemical compound. This is determined by two pieces of information: the empirical formula and the ◊relative molecular mass, which is determined experimentally.

molecular weight see ◊relative molecular mass.

molecule molecules are the smallest particles of an element or compound that can exist independently. Hydrogen ◊atoms, at room temperature, do not exist independently. They are bonded in pairs to form hydrogen molecules. A molecule of a compound consists of two or more different atoms bonded together. Molecules vary in size and complexity from the hydrogen molecule (H_2) to the large ◊macromolecules of proteins. They may be held together by ionic bonds, in which the atoms gain or lose electrons to form ◊ions, or by covalent bonds, where electrons from each atom are shared in a new molecular orbital.

Each compound is represented by a chemical symbol, indicating the elements into which it can be broken down and the number of each type of atom present. The symbolic representation of a molecule is known as its formula. For example, one molecule of the compound water, having two atoms of hydrogen and one atom of oxygen, is shown as H_2O.

moment in statistics and probability theory, a generalization to a higher power of the mean. The rth moment of a random variable is the expected value of the rth power of the variable less its mean.

moment of inertia in physics, the sum of all the point masses of a rotating object multiplied by the squares of their respective distances from the axis of rotation. It is analogous to the ◊mass of a stationary object or one moving in a straight line.

momentum the product of the mass of a body and its velocity. If the mass of a body is m kilograms and its velocity is v m s^{-1}, then its momentum is given by:

$$momentum = mv$$

Its unit is the kilogram metre-per-second (kg m s^{-1}) or the newton second.

The momentum of a body does not change unless a resultant or unbalanced force acts on that body (see ◊Newton's laws of motion).

monochromatic literally, one colour, this is the property of some sources of radiation to emit waves of the one ◊frequency (or wavelength). ◊Lasers and ◊masers are examples.

monoclonal describing genetically identical cells produced from one ◊clone.

monocotyledon angiosperm (flowering plant) having an embryo with a single cotyledon, or seed leaf (as opposed to ◊dicotyledons, which have two). Monocotyledons usually have narrow leaves with parallel veins and smooth edges, and hollow or soft stems. Their flower parts are arranged in threes. Most are small plants such as orchids, grasses, and lilies, but some are trees such as palms.

monoplane an aircraft (powered or glider) that has only one major aerofoil structure providing lift.

monotonic of a sequence, that its terms are increasing or decreasing along the sequence.

Mordell's equation equation named after US-born British mathematician Louis Mordell (1888–1972) that is represented by $y^2 = x^3 + k$.

morphogenesis development of forms and structures in an organism.

morphology in biology, the study of the physical structure and form of organisms, in particular their soft tissues.

Moseley's law frequency of the characteristic ◊X-ray line spectra for elements is directly proportional to the square of the ◊atomic number, Z.

Mössbauer effect the recoil-free emission of gamma rays from atomic nuclei under certain conditions. The effect was discovered in 1958 by German physicist Rudolf Mössbauer, and used in 1960 to provide the first laboratory test of Einstein's general theory of relativity.

motor nerve in anatomy, any nerve that transmits impulses from the central nervous system to muscles or organs. Motor nerves cause voluntary and involuntary muscle contractions, and stimulate glands to secrete hormones.

mural arc astronomical apparatus, used from the sixteenth to the nineteen century, comprising a carefully oriented wall on which a calibrated device was fixed, by which the altitudes of celestial objects could be measured.

mutant gene, organism, or population that has undergone a change in character because of ◊mutation.

mutation in biology, a change in the genes produced by a change in the ◊DNA that makes up the hereditary material of all living organisms. Mutations, the raw material of evolution, result from mistakes during replication (copying) of DNA molecules. Only a few improve the organism's performance and are therefore favoured by ◊natural selection. Mutation rates are increased by certain chemicals and by radiation.

myelin fatty substance that forms a sheath around the nerve fibres of vertebrates.

myeloma or *multiple myeloma* malignant disease of the bone marrow, usually occurring in older people. The symptoms include fatigue, severe bone pain, and backache. It causes anaemia, vertebral collapse, clotting problems, and damage to the eyes and internal organs. It is treated with ◊chemotherapy and ◊radiotherapy.

myofibril one of many minute fibrils that together make up a fibre of smooth or striped muscle, running along the length of the muscle.

myosin protein made up of a chain of polypeptides that forms filaments in smooth (or striped) muscle fibrils. During muscle contraction it combines with ◊actin (another muscle protein, contained in thinner filaments) to form actomyosin; the actin filaments are pulled into the myosin filaments, which shortens the ◊myofibrils.

N

n in mathematics, variable used to denote an indefinite number.

n! factorial *n* that is, $1 \times 2 \times 3 \times ... n$.

nacelle streamlined housing on the fuselage of an aircraft, containing the engine intakes, radio antenna, and so on.

Napier's bones primitive mechanical calculation device created by Scottish mathematician John Napier and consisting of a set of little bone rods with which to multiply or divide.

national grid the network of cables, carried overhead on pylons or buried under the ground, that connects consumers of electrical power to power stations, and interconnects the power stations. It ensures that power can be made available to all customers at any time, allowing demand to be shared by several power stations, and particular power stations to be shut down for maintenance work from time to time.

natural logarithm in mathematics, the ◊exponent of a number expressed to base e, where e represents the ◊irrational number 2.71828... .

Natural ◊logarithms are also called Napierian logarithms, after their inventor, the Scottish mathematician John Napier.

natural number one of the set of numbers used for counting. Natural numbers comprise all the positive integers, excluding zero.

natural selection the process whereby gene frequencies in a population change through certain individuals producing more descendants than others because they are better able to survive and reproduce in their environment.

The accumulated effect of natural selection is to produce adaptations such as the insulating coat of a polar bear or the spadelike forelimbs of a mole. The process is slow, relying firstly on random variation in the genes of an organism being produced by ◊mutation and secondly on the genetic recombination of sexual reproduction. It was recognized by Charles Darwin and English naturalist Alfred Russel Wallace as the main process driving evolution.

n-dimensional in mathematics, having an unstated but finite number of dimensions. A typical example is the set of all runs of *n*-numbers (that is, $x_1, ..., xn$), which is the basis of a coordinate geometry generalizing three-dimensional coordinates (x_1, x_2, x_3).

nebula cloud of gas and dust in space. Nebulae are the birthplaces of stars, but some nebulae are produced by gas thrown off from dying stars (see ◊planetary nebula; ◊supernova). Nebulae are classified depending on whether they emit, reflect, or absorb light.

nebula variable star or *T Tauri variable* variable star of ◊spectral classification F, G, or K (a giant above the ◊main sequence on the ◊Hertzsprung–Russell diagram that loses an appreciable proportion of its mass in its (irregular) more luminous periods, and is thus surrounded by volumes of gas and dust.

neighbourhood in topology, subsets of points in a topological space defining a 'locality' round a specific point, which includes an open set to which the specific point belongs. Axioms describing neighbourhoods were first formulated by German mathematician Felix Hausdorff.

neural fold one of two longitudinal (ectodermal) ridges along the dorsal surface of a vertebrate embryo. The ridges fuse to form the ◊neural tube.

neural tube embryological structure from which the brain and spinal cord are derived. It forms when two edges of a groove in a plate of primitive nerve tissue fuse. Incomplete fusion results in neural tube defects such as spinal bifida.

neurofibril one of the many fibrils in the cytoplasm of a neuron, which extend into its ◊axon and ◊dendrites.

neuron another name for a nerve cell.

neurosecretory cell nerve cell that secretes a chemical substance, such as a ◊hormone.

neurosis in psychology, a general term referring to emotional disorders, such as anxiety, depression, and phobias. The main disturbance tends to be one of mood; contact with reality is relatively unaffected, in contrast to ◊psychosis.

neurotransmitter chemical that diffuses across a ◊synapse, and thus transmits impulses between nerve cells, or between nerve cells and effector organs (for example, muscles). Common neurotransmitters are noradrenaline (which also acts as a hormone) and acetylcholine, the latter being most frequent at junctions between nerve and muscle. Nearly 50 different neurotransmitters have been identified.

neutrino in physics, any of three uncharged ◊elementary particles (and their antiparticles) of the lepton class, having a mass too close to zero to be measured. The most familiar type, the antiparticle of the electron neutrino, is emitted in the beta decay of a nucleus. The other two are the muon and tau neutrinos.

neutron one of the three main subatomic particles, the others being the ◊proton and the ◊electron. The neutron is a composite particle, being made up of three ◊quarks, and therefore belongs to the baryon group of the hadrons. Neutrons have about the same mass as protons but no electric charge, and occur in the nuclei of all atoms except hydrogen. They contribute to the mass of atoms but do not affect their chemistry.

neutron star very small, 'superdense' star composed mostly of ◊neutrons. They are thought to form when massive stars explode as ◊supernovae, during which the protons and electrons of the star's atoms merge, owing to intense gravitational collapse, to make neutrons. A neutron star may have the mass of up to three Suns, compressed into a globe only 20 km/12 mi in diameter.

newton SI unit (symbol N) of ◊force. One newton is the force needed to accelerate an object with mass of one kilogram by one metre per second per second. The weight of a medium size (100 g/3 oz) apple is one newton.

Newton's law of cooling rate of loss of ◊heat from a body is directly proportional to the instantaneous temperature difference between the body and the surroundings. This leads to an exponential law of temperature decline.

Newton's laws of motion in physics, three laws that form the basis of Newtonian mechanics. (1) Unless acted upon by an unbalanced force, a body at rest stays at rest, and a moving body continues moving at the same speed in the same straight line. (2) An unbalanced force applied to a body gives it an acceleration proportional to the force (and in the direction of the force) and inversely proportional to the mass of the body. (3) When a body A exerts a force on a body B, B exerts an equal and opposite force on A; that is, to every action there is an equal and opposite reaction.

Newton's rings an ◊interference effect occurring in observations made of thin films separated by an air gap, ◊reflections between various surfaces being allowed.

Nicol prism device which uses the optical properties of calcite to produce ◊plane-polarized light by passing rays of light through it. It is named after Scottish physicist William Nicol who invented it in 1828.

node in two- and three-dimensional geometry, where a curve intersects itself.

no hair theorem proposed by John Wheeler, it states that the only properties of matter conserved after entering a black hole are its mass, its angula momentum and its electrical charge; it thus becomes neither matter nor ◊antimatter.

noise unwanted sound. Permanent, incurable loss of hearing can be caused by prolonged exposure to high noise levels (above 85 decibels). Over 55 decibels on a daily outdoor basis is regarded as an unacceptable level.

In scientific and engineering terms, a noise is any random, unpredictable signal.

noncommutative in which the principle of commutation (see ◊commutative operation) does not apply.

non-Euclidean geometry study of figures and shapes in three-or-more-dimensional (or curved) space, in which Euclid's postulates may not apply fully or at all. There are now many forms of non-Euclidean geometry, probably the best known being those propounded by Bernhard Riemann; the first proponents of such systems, however, were Karl Gauss, Nikolai Lobachevsky, and János Bolyai.

normal distribution in statistics, a distribution widely used to model variation in a set of data which is symmetrical about its mean value. It can be expressed in the form:

$$f(x) = \frac{1}{\sigma\sqrt{2\pi}} \exp\left\{-\frac{(x-\mu)^2}{2\sigma^2}\right\}$$

where $f(x)$ is the relative frequency of data value x, σ is the ◊standard deviation, μ is the mean, exp is the exponential function, and π is a mathematical constant. The curve resulting when $f(x)$ is plotted against x is called the **normal distribution curve.**

North Polar sequence or circumpolar stars, comprises those stars which never set, from the viewpoint of an observer on Earth.

notochord the stiff but flexible rod that lies between the gut and the nerve cord of all embryonic and larval chordates, including the vertebrates. It forms the supporting structure of the adult lancelet, but in vertebrates it is replaced by the vertebral column, or spine.

nova plural *novae* faint star that suddenly erupts in brightness by 10,000 times or more, remains bright for a few days, and then fades away and is not seen again for very many years, if at all. Novae are believed to occur in close ◊binary star systems, where gas from one star flows to a companion ◊white dwarf. The gas ignites and is thrown off in an explosion at speeds of 1,500 kps/930 mps or more. Unlike a ◊supernova, the star is not completely disrupted by the outburst. After a few weeks or months it subsides to its previous state; it may erupt many more times.

nuclear fusion process whereby two atomic nuclei are fused, with the release of a large amount of energy. Very high temperatures and pressures are thought to be required in order for the process to happen. Under these conditions the atoms involved are stripped of all their electrons so that the remaining particles, which together make up a *plasma,* can come close together at very high speeds and overcome the mutual repulsion of the positive charges on the atomic nuclei. At very close range the strong nuclear force will come into play, fusing the particles together to form a larger nucleus. As fusion is accompanied by the release of large amounts of energy, the process might one day be harnessed to form the basis of commercial energy production. Methods of achieving controlled fusion are therefore the subject of research around the world.

nuclear isomer atoms of an element of a given mass that differ in their rates of ◊radioactive decay are known as nuclear isomers.

nucleic acid complex organic acid made up of a long chain of ◊nucleotides, present in the nucleus and sometimes the cytoplasm of the living cell. The two types, known as ◊DNA (deoxyribonucleic acid) and ◊RNA (ribonucleic acid), form the basis of heredity. The nucleotides are made up of a sugar (deoxyribose or ribose), a phosphate group, and one of four purine or pyrimidine bases. The order of the bases along the nucleic acid strand contains the genetic code.

nucleophilic describing an atom, molecule or ion that seeks a positive centre (for example, the atomic nucleus) during a chemical reaction. Nucleophiles react at centres of low electron density because they have electron pairs available for bonding. Common nucleophiles include the hydroxide ion (OH^{-1}), ammonia (NH_3), water (H_2O), and halide anions. See also ◊electrophilic.

nucleosynthesis cosmic production of all the species of chemical elements by large-scale nuclear reactions, such as those in progress in the Sun or other stars. One element is changed into another by reactions that change the number of protons or neutrons involved.

nucleotide organic compound consisting of a purine (adenine or guanine) or a pyrimidine (thymine, uracil, or cytosine) base linked to a sugar (deoxyribose or ribose) and a phosphate group. ◊DNA and ◊RNA are made up of long chains of nucleotides.

nucleus in biology, the central, membrane-enclosed part of a eukaryotic cell, containing threads of DNA. During cell division these coil up to form chromosomes. The nucleus controls the function of the cell by determining which proteins are produced within it (see ◊DNA for details of this process). Because proteins are the chief structural molecules of living matter and, as enzymes, regulate all aspects of metabolism, it may be seen that the genetic code within the nucleus is effectively responsible for building and controlling the whole organism.

nucleus in physics, the positively charged central part of an ◊atom, which constitutes almost all its mass. Except for hydrogen nuclei, which have only protons, nuclei are composed of both protons and neutrons. Surrounding the nuclei are electrons, of equal and opposite charge to that of the protons, thus giving the atom a neutral charge.

null hypothesis in probability theory, assumes that events occur on a purely random (chance) basis.

null set conventional ◊set that has no members.

null vector another name for a zero vector.

number theory in mathematics, the abstract study of the structure of number systems and the properties of positive integers (whole numbers). For example, the theories of factors and prime numbers fall within this area, as do the work of mathematicians Giuseppe Peano (1858–1932), Pierre de Fermat, and Karl Gauss.

nutation in astronomy, a slight 'nodding' of the Earth in space, caused by the varying gravitational pulls of the Sun and Moon. Nutation changes the angle of the Earth's axial tilt (average 23.5°) by about 9 seconds of arc to either side of its mean position, a complete cycle taking just over 18.5 years.

O

objective system of lenses in a telescope or microscope nearest to the object being observed.

occlusion obstruction or closing off of a hollow organ or vessel.

occultation in astronomy, the temporary obscuring of a star by a body in the Solar System. Occultations are used to provide information about changes in an orbit, and the structure of objects in space, such as radio sources.

octane rating numerical classification of petroleum fuels indicating their combustion characteristics.

ohm SI unit (symbol Ω) of electrical ◊resistance (the property of a conductor that restricts the flow of electrons through it).

Ohm's law law that states that the current flowing in a metallic conductor maintained at constant temperature is directly proportional to the potential difference (voltage) between its ends. The law was discovered by German physicist Georg Ohm in 1827.

Olbers' paradox question put forward 1826 by Heinrich Olbers, who asked: If the universe is infinite in extent and filled with stars, why is the sky dark at night? The answer is that the stars do not live infinitely long, so there is not enough starlight to fill the universe. A wrong answer, frequently given, is that the expansion of the universe weakens the starlight.

olefin common name for ◊alkene.

ontogeny process of development of a living organism, including the part of development that takes place after hatching or birth. The idea that 'ontogeny recapitulates phylogeny' (the development of an organism goes through the same stages as its evolutionary history), proposed by the German scientist Ernst Heinrich Haeckel, is now discredited.

open-hearth process or *Siemens–Martin process* method of producing steel in which cast iron and steel scrap or iron ore are heated together in measured amounts with ◊producer gas on a hearth in a furnace.

operant conditioning conditioning of an individual's response (to a stimulus) by means of a reward so that the individual eventually behaves so as to be rewarded.

opposition in astronomy, the moment at which a body in the Solar System lies opposite the Sun in the sky as seen from the Earth and crosses the ◊meridian at about midnight.

optical activity in chemistry, the ability of certain crystals, liquids, and solutions to rotate the plane of ◊polarized light as it passes through them. The phenomenon is related to the three-dimensional arrangement of the atoms making up the molecules concerned. Only substances that lack any form of structural symmetry exhibit optical activity.

optical fibre thin thread of glass so constructed that it permits light to be transmitted down its length, even round corners, by ◊total internal reflection.

optical isomer or *enantiomorph* one of a pair of compounds whose chemical composition is similar but whose molecular structures are mirror images of each other. The presence of an asymmetric (usually carbon) atom makes each isomer optically active (that is, its crystals or solutions rotate the plane of polarized light); the direction of rotation is different (left or right, denoted by *d* or *l*) for each isomer.

optical isomerism type of ◊stereoisomerism in which the isomers differ in their ◊optical activity because of the different spatial arrangements of their atoms. ◊Enantiomorphs (isomers with asymmetrical structures, each isomer being a mirror image of the other) are optical isomers.

optic vessel one of two bulges on each side of the anterior expansion of the neural tube in a vertebrate embryo, from which arise the essential nervous structures of the eyes.

orbit path of one body in space around another, such as the orbit of Earth around the Sun, or the Moon around Earth. When the two bodies are similar in mass, as in a ◊binary star, both bodies move around their common centre of mass. The movement of objects in orbit follows Johann Kepler's laws, which apply to artificial satellites as well as to natural bodies.

orbital, atomic region around the nucleus of an atom (or, in a molecule, around several nuclei) in which an ◊electron is likely to be found. According to quantum theory, the position of an electron is uncertain; it may be found at any point. However, it is more likely to be found in some places than in others, and it is these that make up the orbital.

Ordovician period of geological time 510–439 million years ago; the second period of the ◊Palaeozoic era. Animal life was confined to the sea: reef-building algae and the first jawless fish are characteristic.

ore body of rock, a vein within it, or a deposit of sediment, worth mining for the economically valuable mineral it contains. The term is usually applied to sources of metals. Occasionally metals are found uncombined (native metals), but more often they occur as compounds such as carbonates, sulphides, or oxides. The ores often contain unwanted impurities that must be removed when the metal is extracted.

organelle discrete and specialized structure in a living cell; organelles include mitochondria, chloroplasts, lysosomes, ribosomes, and the nucleus.

organizer in embryology, a part of the embryo that causes changes to occur in another part, through induction, thus 'organizing' development and ◊differentiation.

organ of Golgi an elongated structure that occurs at the junction of a muscle and a tendon, which responds to ◊proprioceptive stimuli.

organometallic compound any of a group of substances in which one or more organic ◊radicals are chemically bonded to a metallic atom – excluding the ionic salts of metals and organic acids. A typical organometallic compound is tetraethyl lead, the 'antiknock' substance commonly added to petrol.

orogeny or *orogenesis* the formation of mountains. It is brought about by the movements of the rigid plates making up the Earth's crust and upper-most mantle (described by ◊plate tectonics). Where two plates collide at a destructive margin rocks become folded and lifted to form chains of mountains (such as the Himalayas).

orthogonal in geometry, having a right angle, right-angled or perpendicular.

orthohydrogen ◊molecules of hydrogen in which the ◊spins of the two atoms are parallel as opposed to parahydrogen in which spins are opposed.

osmosis movement of water through a selectively permeable membrane separating solutions of different concentrations. Water passes by ◊diffusion from a *weak solution* (high water concentration) to a *strong solution* (low water concentration) until the two concentrations are equal. The selectively permeable membrane allows the diffusion of water but not of the solute (for example, sugar molecules). Many cell membranes behave in this way, and osmosis is a vital mechanism in the transport of fluids in living organisms – for example, in the transport of water from soil (weak solution) into the roots of plants (stronger solution of cell sap).

osmotic pressure pressure that must be applied to a solution so that it no longer takes up pure solvent (usually water) across a membrane that is permeable to solvent but not to solute (the dissolved substance). See also ◊osmosis.

Otto engine an ◊internal-combustion engine that produces power by four strokes: intake, compression, ignition, and expansion, followed by exhaust and further intake. This involves two revolutions of the crankshaft.

oxidation number Roman numeral often seen in a chemical name, indicating the ◊valency of the element immediately before the number. Examples are lead(II) nitrate, manganese(IV) oxide, and potassium manganate(VII).

oxygenation combination of (gaseous or dissolved) oxygen with a substance, such as with the blood in the lungs during respiration.

P

pair production creation of an ◊electron and antielectron (◊positron) pair by the interaction between a high-energy particle or ◊photon and the electrostatic field around a nucleus. It can also be used to describe the creation out of the vacuum state of particle–antiparticle pairs as allowed by Heisenberg's ◊uncertainty principle.

Palaeozoic era of geological time 570–245 million years ago. It comprises the Cambrian, Ordovician, Silurian, Devonian, Carboniferous, and Permian periods. The Cambrian, Ordovician, and Silurian constitute the Lower or Early Palaeozoic; the Devonian, Carboniferous, and Permian make up the Upper or Late Palaeozoic. The era includes the evolution of hard-shelled multicellular life forms in the sea; the invasion of land by plants and animals; and the evolution of fish, amphibians, and early reptiles. The earliest identifiable fossils date from this era.

panchromatic film photographic film that is reasonably sensitive to all ◊frequencies within the visible ◊light spectrum.

Pangaea or *Pangea* (Greek 'all-land') single land mass, made up of all the present continents, believed to have existed between 300 and 200 million years ago; the rest of the Earth was covered by the Panthalassa ocean. Pangaea split into two land masses – Laurasia in the north and ◊Gondwanaland in the south – which subsequently broke up into several continents. These then drifted slowly to their present positions (see ◊continental drift).

pangenesis an erroneous theory that stated that bodies in ◊gemmules transported by the blood to a parent's reproductive cells represented invisible (but exact) copies of the rest of the organism. After fertilization and combination with the other parent's gemmules these bodies were supposed to develop and grow into the 'adult' forms.

papilla small growth from the surface of a tissue, such as the papillae on the surface of the tongue.

parabola in mathematics, a curve formed by cutting a right circular cone with a plane parallel to the sloping side of the cone. A parabola is one of the family of curves known as ◊conic sections. The graph of $y = x^2$ is a parabola.

paraffin common name for ◊alkane, any member of the series of hydrocarbons with the general formula C_nH_{2n+2}. The lower members are gases, such as methane (marsh or natural gas). The middle ones (mainly liquid) form the basis of petrol, kerosene, and lubricating oils, while the higher ones (paraffin waxes) are used in ointment and cosmetic bases.

parahydrogen ◊molecules of hydrogen in which the ◊spins of the two atoms are opposed, in contrast to orthohydrogen in which spins are parallel.

parallax change in the apparent position of an object against its background when viewed from two different positions. In astronomy, nearby stars show a shift owing to parallax when viewed from different positions on the Earth's orbit around the Sun. A star's parallax is used to deduce its distance from the Earth.

parallelogram of forces in physics and applied mathematics, a method of calculating the resultant (combined effect) of two different forces acting together on an object. Because a force has both magnitude and direction it is a vector quantity and can be represented by a straight line. A second force acting at the same point in a different direction can be represented by another line drawn at an angle to the first. By completing the parallelogram (of which the two lines are sides) a diagonal may be drawn from the original angle to the opposite corner to represent the resultant force vector.

paramagnetism property of most elements and some compounds (but excluding the ferromagnetic substances – iron, cobalt, nickel, and their alloys) whereby they are weakly magnetized by relatively strong magnetic fields. See also ◊ferromagnetism.

parity concept in ◊quantum theory related to the mirror-symmetry of the functions describing mathematically the behaviour of the particles.

parsec in astronomy, a unit (symbol pc) used for distances to stars and galaxies. One parsec is equal to 3.2616 ◊light years, 2.063 x 10^5 ◊astronomical units, and 3.086 x 10^{13} km.

parthenogenesis development of an ovum (egg) without any genetic contribution from a male. Parthenogenesis is the normal means of reproduction in a few plants (for example, dandelions) and animals (for example, certain fish). Some sexually reproducing species, such as aphids, show parthenogenesis at some stage in their life cycle to accelerate reproduction to take advantage of good conditions.

partial differentiation form of differential calculus in which instead of a function $y = f(x)$ – which has one variable – a function of two or more variables is considered; for example, $z = f(x,y)$. Such functions represent a surface in three-dimensional space.

partitioning of an integer in number theory, breaking the integer down into its constituent parts in as many ways as possible; for example, the number 6 can be partitioned in three ways: 5 + 1, 4 + 2, and 3 + 3. Each of these contributory numbers is known as a summand.

pascal SI unit (symbol Pa) of pressure, equal to one newton per square metre. It replaces bars and millibars (10^5 Pa equals one bar). It is named after the French mathematician Blaise Pascal.

Pascal's pressure law ◊pressure applied within a fluid is transmitted equally in all directions, the ◊force per unit area being everywhere the same.

Pascal's principle law of hydrostatics stating that the application of ◊pressure to a fluid results in that pressure being equally transmitted throughout the fluid, in all directions.

pasteurization treatment of food to reduce the number of microorganisms it contains and so protect consumers from disease. Harmful bacteria are killed and the development of others is delayed. For milk, the method involves heating it to

72°C/161°F for 15 seconds followed by rapid cooling to 10°C/50°F or lower. The process also kills beneficial bacteria and reduces the nutritive property of milk.

pathogen (Greek 'disease producing') in medicine, any microorganism that causes disease. Most pathogens are parasites, and the diseases they cause are incidental to their search for food or shelter inside the host. Nonparasitic organisms, such as soil bacteria or those living in the human gut and feeding on waste foodstuffs, can also become pathogenic to a person whose immune system or liver is damaged. The larger parasites that can cause disease, such as nematode worms, are not usually described as pathogens.

Pauli exclusion principle in physics, a principle of atomic structure. See ◊exclusion principle.

Peano axioms axioms that formally introduce the properties of the positive whole numbers (originally devised, despite being named after Italian mathematician Guiseppe Peano, by German mathematician Julius Dedekind).

penumbra the region of partial shade between the totally dark part (umbra) of a shadow and the fully illuminated region outside. It occurs when a source of light is only partially obscured by a shadow-casting object. The darkness of a penumbra varies gradually from total darkness at one edge to full brightness at the other. In astronomy, a penumbra is a region of the Earth from which only a partial ◊eclipse of the Sun or Moon can be seen.

peptide molecule comprising two or more ◊amino acid molecules (not necessarily different) joined by **peptide bonds,** whereby the acid group of one acid is linked to the amino group of the other (–CO.NH). The number of amino acid molecules in the peptide is indicated by referring to it as a di-, tri-, or polypeptide (two, three, or many amino acids).

perfect number number that is equal to the sum of all its factors (except itself); for example, 6 is a perfect number, being equal to 1 + 2 + 3.

perfusion ◊in vitro-induced passage of blood or a nutrient fluid through the blood vessels of an organism to keep it supplied with oxygen and nutrients.

perihelion point at which an object, travelling in an elliptical orbit around the Sun, is at its closest to the Sun. The point at which it is furthest from the Sun is the aphelion.

periodic law generalization that there is a recurring pattern in the properties of elements when they are arranged in order of increasing atomic number. The law is most apparent when the elements are arranged in the ◊periodic table, in which the elements in each vertical column (group) show similar properties.

periodic table of the elements in chemistry, a table in which the elements are arranged in order of their atomic number. The table summarizes the major properties of the elements and enables predictions to be made about their behaviour.

period–luminosity curve graph depicting the variation in ◊luminosity of a ◊Cepheid variable star with time. In general, the longer the period, the greater the luminosity. By measuring the period it is possible thus to derive an ◊absolute magnitude; comparison of this with the star's observed (apparent) ◊magnitude gives an indication of the distance.

peristalsis wavelike contractions, produced by the contraction of smooth muscle, that pass along tubular organs, such as the intestines. The same term describes the wavelike motion of earthworms and other invertebrates, in which part of the body contracts as another part elongates.

permanent magnet magnet that retains its magnetism permanently, and not just when subject to some external energy source (as is the case with an ◊electromagnet).

permeability in physics, the degree to which the presence of a substance alters the magnetic field around it. Most substances have a small constant permeability. When the permeability is less than 1, the material is a diamagnetic material; when it is greater than 1, it is a paramagnetic material. Ferrimagnetic materials have very large permeabilities. See also ◊magnetism.

Permian period of geological time 290–245 million years ago, the last period of the Palaeozoic era. Its end was marked by a significant change in marine life, including the extinction of many corals and trilobites. Deserts were widespread, terrestrial amphibians and mammal-like reptiles flourished, and cone-bearing plants (gymnosperms) came to prominence. In the oceans, 49% of families and 72% of genera vanished in the late Permian. On land, 78% of reptile families and 67% of amphibian families disappeared.

permutation group group consisting of all the transformations (operations) permutating a fixed number of objects among themselves. Such groups were studied first by French mathematician Evariste Galois in connection with permutations of roots (solutions) of a polynominal equation.

perpetual motion the idea that a machine can be designed and constructed in such a way that, once started, it will continue in motion indefinitely without requiring any further input of energy (motive power). Such a device would contradict at least one of the two laws of thermodynamics that state that (1) energy can neither be created nor destroyed (the law of conservation of energy) and (2) heat cannot by itself flow from a cooler to a hotter object. As a result, all practical (real) machines require a continuous supply of energy, and no heat engine is able to convert all the heat into useful work.

persistence of vision brief retention of the sensation of light by the brain, once the initial stimulus has been removed. Essential phenomenon for the success of televisual and cinematographic images.

perturbation apparent irregularity in an orbit, or occasionally in a star's ◊proper motion, caused by the gravitational effects of a nearby celestial body.

pH scale from 0 to 14 for measuring acidity or alkalinity. A pH of 7.0 indicates neutrality, below 7 is acid, while above 7 is alkaline. Strong acids, such as those used in car batteries, have a pH of about 2; strong alkalis such as sodium hydroxide are pH 13.

phagocyte type of white blood cell, or ◊leucocyte, that can engulf a bacterium or other invading microorganism. Phagocytes are found in blood, lymph, and other body tissues, where they also ingest foreign matter and dead tissue. A macrophage differs in size and life span.

phagocytosis process by which ◊phagocytes surround foreign particles (by an amoeboid movement), engulf and digest them. See also ◊endocytosis.

Phanerozoic (Greek *phanero* 'visible') eon in Earth history, consisting of the most recent 570 million years. It comprises the Palaeozoic, Mesozoic, and Cenozoic eras. The vast majority of fossils come from this eon, owing to the evolution of hard shells and internal skeletons. The name means 'interval of well-displayed life'.

phase in astronomy, the apparent shape of the Moon or a planet when all or part of its illuminated hemisphere is facing the Earth.

The Moon undergoes a full cycle of phases from new (when between the Earth and the Sun) through first quarter (when at 90° eastern elongation from the Sun), full (when opposite the Sun), and last quarter (when at 90° western elongation from the Sun).

phase in physics, a stage in an oscillatory motion, such as a wave motion: two waves are in phase when their peaks and their troughs coincide. Otherwise, there is a *phase difference,* which has consequences in ◊interference phenomena and ◊alternating current electricity.

phenol member of a group of aromatic chemical compounds with weakly acidic properties, which are characterized by a hydroxyl (OH) group attached directly to an aromatic ring. The simplest of the phenols, derived from benzene, is also known as phenol and has the formula C_6H_5OH. It is sometimes called *carbolic acid* and can be extracted from coal tar.

phenotype in genetics, visible traits, those actually displayed by an organism. The phenotype is not a direct reflection of the ◊genotype because some alleles are masked by the presence of other, dominant alleles (see ◊dominance). The phenotype is further modified by the effects of the environment (for example, poor nutrition stunts growth).

philosophy of mathematics has three main aspects: the logical (in which mathematics is simply a branch of logic), the formalist (involving the study of the structure of objects and the property of symbols), and the intuitional (grounded on the basic premise of the possibility of constructing an infinite series of numbers).

phloem tissue found in vascular plants whose main function is to conduct sugars and other food materials from the leaves, where they are produced, to all other parts of the plant.

phosphor any substance that is phosphorescent, that is, gives out visible light when it is illuminated by a beam of electrons or ultraviolet light. The television screen is coated on the inside with phosphors that glow when beams of electrons strike them. Fluorescent lamp tubes are also phosphor-coated. Phosphors are also used in Day-Glo paints, and as optical brighteners in detergents.

phosphorescence type of luminescence in which a substance exposed to radiation emits light, this emission continuing after the radiation has been removed.

phosphorylation chemical addition of a phosphate group ($-PO_3^{2-}$) to a (organic) molecule. One of the most important biochemical phosphorylations is the addition of phosphate to ADP to form the energy-rich ATP. Phosphorylation involving light (as in ◊photosynthesis) is termed photophosphorylation.

photochemical reaction any chemical reaction in which light is produced or light initiates the reaction. Light can initiate reactions by exciting atoms or molecules and making them more reactive: the light energy becomes converted to chemical energy. Many photochemical reactions set up a ◊chain reaction and produce free radicals.

photoelectric effect transfer of energy from light rays falling onto a substance to the ◊electrons within the substance. If the ◊frequency, and hence the energy, of the radiation is high enough, it is possible to 'boil' electrons, then known as photo-electrons, out of the substance. Being charge-carriers, these electrons can constitute a photoelectric current.

photoelectric filtering means of measuring the ◊astronomical colour index of a star, involving colour filters on photoelectric cells to define the colour index between two set wavelengths. The filters correspond to the ◊UBV photometry system.

photoelectricity phenomenon whereby certain materials, such as ◊selenium, can produce electrical output if exposed to light.

photolysis chemical reaction that is driven by light or ultraviolet radiation. For example, the light reaction of ◊photosynthesis (the process by which green plants manufacture carbohydrates from carbon dioxide and water) is a photolytic reaction.

photometry measurement of the ◊magnitudes of celestial bodies, originally carried out by expertise of eye alone, but now generally making use of photographic or photoelectric apparatus.

photomultiplier device used in ◊photometry for the amplification of light by the release and acceleration of electrons from a sensitive surface. The result is a measurable electric current that is proportional to the intensity of received radiation.

photon in physics, the ◊elementary particle or 'package' (quantum) of energy in which light and other forms of electromagnetic radiation are emitted. The photon has both particle and wave properties; it has no charge, is considered massless but possesses momentum and energy. It is one of the gauge bosons, and is the carrier of the ◊electromagnetic force, one of the fundamental forces of nature.

photosphere visible surface of the Sun, which emits light and heat. About 300 km/200 mi deep, it consists of incandescent gas at a temperature of 5,800 K (5,530°C/9,980°F).

photosynthesis process by which green plants trap light energy from the Sun. This energy is used to drive a series of chemical reactions which lead to the formation of carbohydrates. The carbohydrates occur in the form of simple sugar, or glucose, which provides the basic food for both plants and animals. For photosynthesis to occur, the plant must possess ◊chlorophyll and must have a supply of carbon dioxide and water. Photosynthesis takes place inside ◊chloroplasts which are found mainly in the leaf cells of plants.

The by-product of photosynthesis, oxygen, is of great importance to all living organisms, and virtually all atmospheric oxygen has originated by photosynthesis.

phylogeny historical sequence of changes that occurs in a given species during the course of its evolution. It was once erroneously associated with ontogeny (the process of development of a living organism).

piezoelectric effect property of some crystals (for example, quartz) to develop an electromotive force or voltage across opposite faces when subjected to tension or compression, and, conversely, to expand or contract in size when subjected to an electromotive force. Piezoelectric crystal oscillators are used as frequency standards (for example, replacing balance wheels in watches), and for producing ultrasound.

pigeon-hole principle in mathematics, another name for Schubfachprinzip.

pig iron or *cast iron* the quality of iron produced in a ◊blast furnace. It contains around 4% carbon plus some other impurities.

pinocytosis ingestion of the contents of a vesicle by a cell (see ◊endocytosis).

pion or *pi meson* in physics, a subatomic particle with a neutral form (mass 135 MeV) and a positively charged form (mass 139 MeV). The charged pion decays into muons and neutrinos and the neutral form decays into gamma-ray photons. They belong to the hadron class of ◊elementary particles.

Pioneer probe any of a series of US Solar-System space probes 1958–78. The probes *Pioneer 4–9* went into solar orbit to monitor the Sun's activity during the 1960s and early 1970s. *Pioneer 5*, launched in 1960, was the first of a series to study the solar wind between the planets. *Pioneer 10*, launched March in 1972, was the first probe to reach Jupiter (December 1973) and to leave the Solar System in 1983. *Pioneer 11*, launched April 1973, passed Jupiter December 1974, and was the first probe to reach Saturn (September 1979), before also leaving the Solar System. NASA ceased to operate *Pioneer 10* in April 1997. The probe had functioned for 25 years and reached a distance of 10 billion km from the Sun. *Pioneer 11* ceased to function in 1995.

piston barrel-shaped device used in reciprocating engines (steam, petrol, diesel oil) to harness power. Pistons are driven up and down in cylinders by expanding steam or hot gases. They pass on their motion via a connecting rod and crank to a crankshaft, which turns the driving wheels. In a pump or compressor, the role of the piston is reversed, being used to move gases and liquids. See also ◊internal-combustion engine.

pitch in mechanics, the distance between the adjacent threads of a screw or bolt. When a screw is turned through one full turn it moves a distance equal to the pitch of its thread. A screw thread is a simple type of machine, acting like a rolled-up inclined plane, or ramp (as may be illustrated by rolling a long paper triangle around a pencil). A screw has a ◊mechanical advantage greater than one.

placenta organ that attaches the developing embryo or fetus to the uterus in placental mammals (mammals other than marsupials, platypuses, and echidnas). Composed of maternal and embryonic tissue, it links the blood supply of the embryo to the blood supply of the mother, allowing the exchange of oxygen, nutrients, and waste products. The two blood systems are not in direct contact, but are separated by thin membranes, with materials diffusing across from one system to the other. The placenta also produces hormones that maintain and regulate pregnancy. It is shed as part of the afterbirth.

Planck's quantum constant constant (symbol *h*) with a value of about 6.63×10^{-34} joule seconds, which is the fundamental unit of ◊spin angular momentum.

Planck's radiation law energy of ◊electromagnetic radiation of a certain ◊frequency is given by the product of the frequency and Planck's constant, *h*.

plane figure in geometry, a two-dimensional figure. All polygons are plane figures.

plane-polarized light light in which the electric and magnetic vibrations of the waves are restricted to a single plane, the plane of the magnetic vibration being at right angles to that of the electric one.

planetary nebula shell of gas thrown off by a star at the end of its life. Planetary nebulae have nothing to do with planets. They were named by William Herschel, who thought their rounded shape resembled the disc of a planet. After a star such as the Sun has expanded to become a ◊red giant, its outer layers are ejected into space to form a planetary nebula, leaving the core as a ◊white dwarf at the centre.

plankton small, often microscopic, forms of plant and animal life that live in the upper layers of fresh and salt water, and are an important source of food for larger animals. Marine plankton is concentrated in areas where rising currents bring mineral salts to the surface.

plasma in biology, the liquid component of the blood. It is a straw-coloured fluid, largely composed of water (around 90%), in which a number of substances are dissolved. These include a variety of proteins (around 7%) such as fibrinogen (important in blood clotting), inorganic mineral salts such as sodium and calcium, waste products such as urea, traces of ◊hormones, and ◊antibodies to defend against infection.

plasma in physics, an ionized gas produced at extremely high temperatures, as in the Sun and other stars, which contains positive and negative charges in equal numbers. It is a good electrical conductor. In thermonuclear reactions the plasma produced is confined through the use of magnetic fields.

plasmolysis in a plant cell, the shrinkage of the cell contents away from the cell wall as a result of ◊osmosis in which water diffuses out of the cell.

plastic any of the stable synthetic materials that are fluid at some stage in their manufacture, when they can be shaped, and that later set to rigid or semi-rigid solids. Plastics today are chiefly derived from petroleum. Most are polymers, made up of long chains of identical molecules.

plate tectonics theory formulated in the 1960s to explain the phenomena of ◊continental drift and seafloor spreading, and the formation of the major physical features of the Earth's surface. The Earth's outermost layer, the lithosphere, is regarded as a jigsaw puzzle of rigid major and minor plates that move relative to each other, probably under the influence of convection currents in the mantle beneath. At the margins of the plates, where they collide or move apart, major landforms such as mountains, ◊volcanoes, ocean trenches, and *ocean ridges* are created. The rate of plate movement is at most 15 cm/6 in per year.

platinum resistance thermometer thermometer that uses the change in the electrical ◊resistance of a platinum coil with temperature to allow measurements over a very wide range (over 1,300 degrees).

Platonic solid in geometry, another name for a regular ◊polyhedron, one of five possible three-dimensional figures with all its faces the same size and shape.

pluteus in echinoderms, an advanced larval stage characterized by bilateral symmetry.

pneumatics study and production of devices that rely on air ◊pressure for their operation.

point sets in geometry or topology, sets comprising some or all of the points of the space under study.

poisoning (of a catalyst) the reduction in effectiveness of a ◊catalyst as a result of its being contaminated by a reactant or a product of the reaction it catalyses. Although in theory a catalyst is unaffected by the reaction it catalyses, in practice particles ('poisons') accumulate on the surface of the catalyst and reduce its effectiveness.

Poisson's ratio ratio of the lateral ◊strain to the longitudinal strain in a wire held under tension.

polar body in ◊meiosis, any of three (haploid) egg nuclei that develop from a secondary oocyte (the fourth nucleus is the ovum); the three polar bodies degenerate.

polarimetry in astronomy, any technique for measuring the degree of polarization of radiation from stars, galaxies, and other objects.

Polaris or *Pole Star* or *North Star* bright star closest to the north celestial pole, and the brightest star in the constellation Ursa Minor. Its position is indicated by the 'pointers' in Ursa Major.

Polaris is a yellow supergiant about 500 light years away. It is also known as *Alpha Ursae Minoris*.

polariscope an instrument that enables the rotation of the plane of polarization of ◊polarized light to be determined.

polarized light light in which the electromagnetic vibrations take place in one particular plane. In ordinary (unpolarized) light, the electric fields vibrate in all planes perpendicular to the direction of propagation. After reflection from a polished surface or transmission through certain materials (such as Polaroid), the electric fields are confined to one direction, and the light is said to be *linearly polarized*. In *circularly polarized* and *elliptically polarized* light, the electric fields are confined to one direction, but the direction rotates as the light propagates. Polarized light is used to test the strength of sugar solutions, to measure stresses in transparent materials, and to prevent glare.

polar planimeter device invented by Swiss physicist Jakob Amsler-Laffon to measure area on a curved surface; it could be used to determine Fourier coefficients and was thus particularly valuable to ship-builders and railway engineers.

polybasic describing an ◊acid that has more than two atoms of replaceable acidic hydrogen in each of its molecules.

polyhedron in geometry, a solid figure with four or more plane faces. The more faces there are on a polyhedron, the more closely it approximates to a sphere. Knowledge of the properties of polyhedra is needed in crystallography and stereochemistry to determine the shapes of crystals and molecules.

polymer compound made up of a large long-chain or branching matrix composed of many repeated simple units (*monomers*) linked together by ◊polymerization. There are many polymers, both natural (cellulose, chitin, lignin) and synthetic (polyethylene and nylon, types of plastic). Synthetic polymers belong to two groups: thermosoftening and thermosetting (see ◊plastic).

polymerization chemical union of two or more (usually small) molecules of the same kind to form a new compound. *Addition polymerization* produces simple multiples of the same compound. *Condensation polymerization* joins molecules together with the elimination of water or another small molecule.

polysaccharide long-chain ◊carbohydrate made up of hundreds or thousands of linked simple sugars (monosaccharides) such as glucose and closely related molecules.

population genetics the branch of genetics that studies the way in which the frequencies of different ◊alleles (alternative forms of a gene) in populations of organisms change, as a result of natural selection and other processes.

population I stars younger stars, generally formed towards the edge of a ◊galaxy, of the dusty material in the spiral arms, including the heavy elements. The brightest of this population are hot, white stars.

population II stars older stars, generally formed towards the centre of a ◊galaxy, containing few heavier elements. The brightest of this population are red giants.

porism old-fashioned term for a conclusion or hypothesis following directly upon a statement or proposition.

porosity percentage of empty space existing within a material.

Portland cement widely used building material comprising chalk or limestone mixed with clay or shale, burnt in a kiln after being finely broken up and mixed together.

positron in physics, the antiparticle of the electron; an ◊elementary particle having the same mass as an electron but exhibiting a positive charge. The positron was discovered in 1932 by US physicist Carl Anderson at Caltech, USA, its existence having been predicted by the British physicist Paul Dirac in 1928.

potential difference (pd) difference in the electrical potential of two points, being equal to the electrical energy converted by a unit electric charge moving from one point to the other. The SI unit of potential difference is the volt (V). The potential difference between two points in a circuit is commonly referred to as voltage. See also ◊Ohm's law.

potential energy (PE) in physics, energy possessed by an object by virtue of its relative position or state (for example, as in a compressed spring or a muscle). It is contrasted with kinetic energy, the form of energy possessed by moving bodies. An object that has been raised up is described as having gravitational potential energy.

power in mathematics, that which is represented by an ◊exponent or index, denoted by a superior small numeral. A number or symbol raised to the power of 2 – that is, multiplied by itself – is said to be squared (for example, 3^2, x^2), and when raised to the power of 3, it is said to be cubed (for example, 2^3, y^3). Any number to the power zero always equals 1.

power series an infinite series of the general form:

$$a_0 + a_1x^1 + a_2x^2 + a_3x^3 + ... + a_nx^n + ...$$

This is called a power series in x. Examples of power series are the exponential series:

$$ex = 1 + x + x^2/2! + x^3/3! + ...$$

the logarithmic series, and the series for the trigonometric functions (sine, cosine, and tangent).

Poynting–Robertson effect interaction of dust particles in interplanetary space with solar radiation causing a loss in orbital velocity of the dust around the Sun. This causes the dust particles to spiral into the Sun, if the effect is unopposed. However, under certain circumstances, ◊radiation pressure is large enough to oppose the effect.

Precambrian in geology, the time from the formation of Earth (4.6 billion years ago) up to 570 million years ago. Its boundary with the succeeding Cambrian period marks the time when animals first developed hard outer parts (exoskeletons) and so left abundant fossil remains. It comprises about 85% of geological time and is divided into two periods: the Archaean, in which no life existed, and the Proterozoic, in which there was life in some form.

precession slow wobble of the Earth on its axis, like that of a spinning top. The gravitational pulls of the Sun and Moon on the Earth's equatorial bulge cause the Earth's axis to trace out a circle on the sky every 25,800 years. The position of the celestial poles (see ◊celestial sphere) is constantly changing owing to precession, as are the positions of the equinoxes (the points at which the celestial equator intersects the Sun's path around the sky). The *precession of the equinoxes* means that there is a gradual westward drift in the ecliptic – the path that the Sun appears to follow – and in the coordinates of objects on the celestial sphere.

precession of the equinoxes apparent movement per year of the two points in the sky representing the ◊equinoxes; 50.26″ in per year, also called the constant of precession. Precession is caused mainly by the gravitational effect of the Moon on the Earth's equatorial 'bulge'.

predicate calculus in logic, part of the theory of devising models involving deduction and the use of variables and negatives in systems of sentences; the term occurs commonly in ◊mathematical logic.

pre-operational describing a stage of human development between the ages of two and seven years in which a child learns to imitate and acquires language to describe concrete objects.

pressure in a fluid, the force that would act normally (at right angles) per unit surface area of a body immersed in the fluid. The SI unit of pressure is the pascal (Pa), equal to a pressure of one newton per square metre. In the atmosphere, the pressure declines with height from about 100 kPa at sea level to zero where the atmosphere fades into space. Pressure is commonly measured with a ◊barometer, manometer, or ◊Bourdon gauge. Other common units of pressure are the bar and the torr.

primary factors most reduced (lowest) form of numbers, which, when multiplied together, produce the principal numbers or expression.

prime number number that can be divided only by 1 and itself, that is, having no other factors. There is an infinite number of primes, the first ten of which are 2, 3, 5, 7, 11, 13, 17, 19, 23, and 29 (by definition, the number 1 is excluded from the set of prime numbers). The number 2 is the only even prime because all other even numbers have 2 as a factor.

Principia Mathematica title of two works: the first (full title ***Philosophiae Naturalis Principia Mathematica***), by Isaac Newton, published in 1687, was a compilation of mathematics combined with physics, and was a landmark in both disciplines; the second, by Bertrand Russell and Alfred North Whitehead, was an attempt to derive the foundations of mathematics, published 1910–13.

probability likelihood, or chance, that an event will occur, often expressed as odds, or in mathematics, numerically as a fraction or decimal.

In general, the probability that n particular events will happen out of a total of m possible events is n/m. A certainty has a probability of 1; an impossibility has a probability of 0. Empirical probability is defined as the number of successful events divided by the total possible number of events.

Procyon or ***Alpha Canis Minoris*** brightest star in the constellation Canis Minor and the eighth-brightest star in the night sky. Procyon is a white star 11.4 light years from the Sun, with a mass of 1.7 Suns. It has a ◊white dwarf companion that orbits it every 40 years.

producer gas gas used in furnaces and the generation of power formed by the partial combustion of coal, coke or anthracite in a blast of air and steam.

product result of multiplying one quantity by another.

projective geometry form of two- and three-dimensional geometry concerned with the geometrical properties that remain constant (invariant) under projection, that is, extended on a single plane, or projected from one plane onto another. Perspective – two-dimensional representation of three-dimensional reality – uses the basic theory of projective geometry.

proof in mathematics, a set of arguments used to deduce a mathematical theorem from a set of axioms.

proper motion gradual change in the position of a star that results from its motion in orbit around our Galaxy, the Milky Way. Proper motions are slight and undetectable to the naked eye, but can be accurately measured on telescopic photographs taken many years apart.

Barnard's Star is the star with the largest proper motion, 10.3 arc seconds per year.

prophage DNA of a nonvirulent ◊bacteriophage that has become linked with the bacterial host's DNA and which is replicated with it. See ◊lysogeny.

prophylaxis any measure taken to prevent disease, including exercise and ◊vaccination. Prophylactic (preventive) medicine is an aspect of public-health provision that is receiving increasing attention.

proprioceptor in biology, one of the sensory nerve endings that are located in muscles, tendons, and joints. They relay information on the position of the body and the state of muscle contraction.

protein complex, biologically important substance composed of amino acids joined by ◊peptide bonds. Proteins are essential to all living organisms. As ◊enzymes they regulate all aspects of metabolism. Structural proteins such as ***keratin*** and ***collagen*** make up the skin, claws, bones, tendons, and ligaments; ***muscle*** proteins produce movement; ***haemoglobin*** transports oxygen; and ***membrane*** proteins regulate the movement of substances into and out of cells. For humans, protein is an essential part of the diet, and is found in greatest quantity in soy beans and other grain legumes, meat, eggs, and cheese.

protein synthesis manufacture, within the cytoplasm of the cell, of the proteins an organism needs. The building blocks of proteins are ◊amino acids, of which there are 20 types. The pattern in which the amino acids are linked decides what kind of protein is produced. In turn it is the genetic code, contained within ◊DNA, that determines the precise order in which the amino acids are linked up during protein manufacture.

Interestingly, DNA is found only in the nucleus, yet protein synthesis occurs only in the cytoplasm. The information necessary for making the proteins is carried from the nucleus to the cytoplasm by another nucleic acid, ◊RNA.

Proterozoic eon of geological time, 3.5 billion to 570 million years ago, the second division of the Precambrian. It is defined as the time of simple life, since many rocks dating from this eon show traces of biological activity, and some contain the fossils of bacteria and algae.

proton (Greek 'first') in physics, a positively charged subatomic particle, a constituent of the nucleus of all atoms. It belongs to the baryon subclass of the hadrons. A proton is extremely long-lived, with a lifespan of at least 10^{32} years. It carries a unit positive charge equal to the negative charge of an ◊electron. Its mass is almost 1,836 times that of an electron, or 1.67×10^{-27} kg. Protons are composed of two up ◊quarks and one down quark held together by ◊gluons. The number of protons in the atom of an element is equal to the atomic number of that element.

proton–proton cycle process of ◊nuclear fusion by which relatively cooler stars produce and radiate energy; hotter stars commonly achieve the same result by means of the carbon–nitrogen cycle.

protoplanet early stage in the formation of a planet according to the theory by which planetary systems evolve through the condensation of gas clouds surrounding a young star. The theory is not, however, generally accepted.

protoplasm contents of a living cell. Strictly speaking it includes all the discrete structures (organelles) in a cell, but it is often used simply to mean the jellylike material in which these float. The contents of a cell outside the nucleus are called ◊cytoplasm.

protostar in astronomy, early formation of a star that has recently condensed out of an interstellar cloud and which is not yet hot enough for hydrogen burning to start. Protostars derive their energy from gravitational contraction.

prototype experimental version of a system, where the initial design can be tested and improved upon in the light of tests carried out.

protozoa group of single-celled organisms without rigid cell walls. Some, such as amoeba, ingest other cells, but most are saprotrophs or parasites. The group is polyphyletic (containing organisms which have different evolutionary origins).

Prout's hypothesis now defunct proposal that all the chemical ◊elements were made from the combination of different numbers of hydrogen ◊atoms.

psychoanalysis theory and treatment method for neuroses, developed by Sigmund Freud in the 1890s. Psychoanalysis asserts that the impact of early childhood sexuality and experiences, stored in the unconscious, can lead to the development of adult emotional problems. The main treatment method involves the free association of ideas, and their interpretation by patient and analyst, in order to discover these long-buried events and to grasp their significance to the patient, linking aspects of the patient's historical past with the present relationship to the analyst. Psychoanalytic treatment aims to free the patient from specific symptoms and from irrational inhibitions and anxieties.

psychosis or **psychotic disorder** general term for a serious mental disorder where the individual commonly loses contact with reality and may experience hallucinations (seeing or hearing things that do not exist) or delusions (fixed false beliefs). For example, in a paranoid psychosis, an individual may believe that others are plotting against him or her. A major type of psychosis is schizophrenia.

Ptolemaic model of the universe ◊geocentric model in which the Earth remained stationary as the other planets, the Sun, the Moon and the stars orbited it on their spheres. It was eventually replaced by the ◊Copernican model.

pulley simple ◊machine consisting of a system of one or more grooved wheels that enables a ◊mechanical advantage to be achieved, for example, to lift heavy objects.

pulmonary pertaining to the lungs.

pulsar celestial source that emits pulses of energy at regular intervals, ranging from a few seconds to a few thousandths of a second. Pulsars are thought to be rapidly rotating ◊neutron stars, which flash at radio and other wavelengths as they spin. They were discovered in 1967 by Jocelyn Bell-Burnell and Antony Hewish at the Mullard Radio Astronomy Observatory, Cambridge, England. By 1998 1,000 pulsars had been discovered since the initial identification in 1967.

pulsating nova or **recurrent nova** a ◊variable star, probably not a true ◊nova, in which the change between more and less luminous stages is extreme.

pulsating universe or **oscillating universe** theory that the universe constantly undergoes a ◊Big Bang, expands, gradually slows and stops, contracts, and gradually accelerates once more to a Big Bang. Alternative theories include an ever expanding universe and the ◊steady-state universe.

putrefaction decomposition of organic matter by micro-organisms.

pyrometer in physics, any instrument used for measuring high temperatures by means of the thermal radiation emitted by a hot object. In a **radiation pyrometer** the emitted radiation is detected by a sensor such as a thermocouple. In an **optical pyrometer** the colour of an electrically heated filament is matched visually to that of the emitted radiation. Pyrometers are especially useful for measuring the temperature of distant, moving or inaccessible objects.

pyrophoric finely powdered metals, or mixtures of metals and their oxides, which have a tendency to burst into flame, or oxidize when exposed to air.

Pythagoras' theorem in geometry, a theorem stating that in a right-angled triangle, the area of the square on the hypotenuse (the longest side) is equal to the sum of the areas of the squares drawn on the other two sides. If the hypotenuse is h units long and the lengths of the other sides are a and b, then $h^2 = a^2 + b^2$.

Q

quadrant type of early sextant, with which the observer's latitude could be calculated.

quadratic equation in mathematics, a polynomial equation of second degree (that is, an equation containing as its highest power the square of a variable, such as x^2). The general formula of such equations is:

$$ax^2 + bx + c = 0$$

in which a, b, and c are real numbers, and only the coefficient a cannot equal 0.

In coordinate geometry, a quadratic function represents a ◊parabola.

quadratic extension extension of a field to a larger field by adjoining the root of a quadratic equation, for example, the set of all $p + q\sqrt{2}$ with both p and q as rational numbers is a quadratic extension of the field of rationals.

quadrilateral plane (two-dimensional) figure with four straight sides. The following are all quadrilaterals, each with distinguishing properties: *square* with four equal angles and sides, four axes of symmetry; *rectangle* with four equal angles, opposite sides equal, two axes of symmetry; *rhombus* with four equal sides, two axes of symmetry; *parallelogram* with two pairs of parallel sides, rotational symmetry; *kite* with two pairs of adjacent equal sides and one axis of symmetry; and *trapezium* one pair of parallel sides.

qualitative analysis in chemistry, a procedure for determining the identity of the component(s) of a single substance or mixture. A series of simple reactions and tests can be carried out on a compound to determine the elements present.

quantitative analysis in chemistry, a procedure for determining the precise amount of a known component present in a single substance or mixture. A known amount of the substance is subjected to particular procedures.

Gravimetric analysis determines the mass of each constituent present; ◊*volumetric analysis* determines the concentration of a solution by ◊titration against a solution of known concentration.

quantum chromodynamics (QCD) in physics, a theory describing the interactions of ◊quarks, the ◊elementary particles that make up all hadrons (subatomic particles such as protons and neutrons). In quantum chromodynamics, quarks are considered to interact by exchanging particles called gluons, which carry the ◊strong nuclear force, and whose role is to 'glue' quarks together.

quantum electrodynamics (QED) in physics, a theory describing the interaction of charged subatomic particles within electric and magnetic fields. It combines quantum theory and ◊relativity, and considers charged particles to interact by the exchange of photons. QED is remarkable for the accuracy of its predictions; for example, it has been used to calculate the value of some physical quantities to an accuracy of ten decimal places, a feat equivalent to calculating the distance between New York and Los Angeles to within the thickness of a hair. The theory was developed by US physicists Richard Feynman and Julian Schwinger, and by Japanese physicist Sin-Itiro Tomonaga in 1948.

quantum mechanics branch of physics dealing with the interaction of matter and ◊radiation, the structure of the ◊atom, the motion of atomic particles, and with related phenomena (see ◊elementary particle and ◊quantum theory).

quantum number in physics, one of a set of four numbers that uniquely characterize an ◊electron and its state in an ◊atom. The *principal quantum number* n defines the electron's main energy level. The *orbital quantum number* l relates to its angular momentum. The *magnetic quantum number* m describes the energies of electrons in a magnetic field. The *spin quantum number* m_s gives the spin direction of the electron.

quantum physics branch of physics that takes into account the quantum nature of matter, energy, and radiation.

quantum theory general mathematical theory based on Max Planck's discovery that radiant energy is quantized, that is, emitted in discrete quanta ('packets') of energy. The original theory has been extended to interpret a wide range of physical phenomena; for example, quantum mechanics and wave mechanics are now extensively used to give quantitative accounts of the behaviour of small particles, such as electrons.

quark in physics, the ◊elementary particle that is the fundamental constituent of all hadrons (subatomic particle that experiences the strong nuclear force and divided into baryons, such as neutrons and protons, and mesons). Quarks have electric charges that are fractions of the electronic charge ($+\frac{2}{3}$ or $-\frac{1}{3}$ of the electronic charge). There are six types, or 'flavours': up, down, top, bottom, strange, and charmed, each of which has three varieties, or 'colours': red, green, and blue (visual colour is not meant, although the analogy is useful in many ways). To each quark there is an antiparticle, called an antiquark.

quartan fever type of fluctuating malarial fever that peaks every fourth day.

quartic to the power of four; it is occasionally replaced by the word 'biquadratic'.

quasar from *quasi-stellar object* or *QSO* one of the most distant extragalactic objects known, discovered in 1963. Quasars appear starlike, but each emits more energy than 100 giant galaxies. They are thought to be at the centre of galaxies, their brilliance emanating from the stars and gas falling towards an immense ◊black hole at their nucleus. Most quasars are found in elliptical galaxies.

Quaternary period of geological time that began 1.64 million years ago and is still in process. It is divided into the Pleistocene and Holocene epochs.

quaternary ammonium ion an ion in which the hydrogen atoms of the normal ammonium ion $(NH_4)^+$ have been replaced by organic ◊alkyl or ◊aryl radicals; it therefore has the formula $(NR_4)^+$.

quaternion one of an extended system of complex numbers, representable in the generalized form: $a + bi + cj + dk$ where a, b, c and d are real numbers, and in which i, j, and k are additional objects that multiply according to specific rules such that: $i^2 = j^2 = k^2 = -1$, $ij = -ji = k$, $jk = -kj = i$ and $ki = -ik = j$.

quintic to the power of five.

quotient result after dividing one quantity by another.

R

raceme in botany, a type of inflorescence.

racemic mixture mixture of equal quantities of two ◊enantiomorphs (isomers with mirror-image molecular structures). Because the ◊optical activity of each component exactly cancels that of the other, the racemic mixture as a whole is optically inactive.

radar acronym for *radio direction and ranging* device for locating objects in space, direction finding, and navigation by means of transmitted and reflected high-frequency radio waves.

radial pulsation periodic expansion and contraction of a star that may be merely an optical effect of recession.

radial velocity in astronomy, the velocity of an object, such as a star or galaxy, along the line of sight, moving towards or away from an observer. The amount of ◊Doppler shift (apparent change in wavelength) of the light reveals the object's velocity. If the object is approaching, the Doppler effect causes a blue shift in its light. That is, the wavelengths of light coming from the object appear to be shorter, tending toward the blue end of the ◊spectrum. If the object is receding, there is a ◊red shift, meaning the wavelengths appear to be longer, toward the red end of the spectrum.

radiant in astronomy, the point in the sky from which a ◊meteor shower appears to emanate.

radiant heat energy that is radiated by all warm or hot bodies. It belongs to the ◊infrared part of the electromagnetic ◊spectrum and causes heating when absorbed. Radiant heat is invisible and should not be confused with the red glow associated with very hot objects, which belongs to the visible part of the spectrum.

radiation in physics, emission of radiant energy as particles or waves – for example, heat, light, alpha particles, and beta particles (see ◊electromagnetic waves and ◊radioactivity). See also ◊atomic radiation.

radiative equilibrium in a star, represents an even process by which energy (heat) is transferred from the core to the outer surface without affecting the overall stability of the star.

radical in mathematics, operation principle in the extraction of roots; that is, square roots, cube roots, and so on.

radical in chemistry, a group of atoms forming part of a molecule, which acts as a unit and takes part in chemical reactions without disintegration, yet often cannot exist alone for any length of time; for example, the methyl radical $-CH_3$, or the carboxyl radical $-COOH$.

radio transmission of ◊electromagnetic radiation of ◊frequencies from about 10^4 hertz to 10^{11} hertz. Transmission of communication signals frequently involves the use of either amplitude or ◊frequency-modulated carrier waves.

radioactive decay process of disintegration undergone by the nuclei of radioactive elements, such as radium and various isotopes of uranium and the transuranic elements. This changes the element's atomic number, thus transmuting one element into another, and is accompanied by the emission of radiation. Alpha and beta decay are the most common forms.

radioactive fallout airborne radioactive material resulting from a natural phenomenon or from an artificial occurrence, such as the explosion of a nuclear bomb.

radioactivity spontaneous alteration of the nuclei of radioactive atoms, accompanied by the emission of radiation. It is the property exhibited by the radioactive ◊isotopes of stable elements and all isotopes of radioactive elements, and can be either natural or induced. See ◊radioactive decay.

radioimmunoassay (RIA) in medicine, technique for measuring small quantities of circulating hormones. The assay depends upon the ability of a hormone to inhibit the binding of the same hormone (which has been labelled with a radioactive isotope) to a specific antibody by competition for the binding sites.

radio interferometer type of radio telescope that relies on the use of two or more aerials at a distance from each other to provide a combination of signals from one source which can be analysed by computer. Such an analysis results in a resolution that is considerably better than that of a parabolic dish aerial by itself because of the greater effective diameter.

radioisotope contraction of *radioactive isotope* in physics, a naturally occurring or synthetic radioactive form of an element. Most radioisotopes are made by bombarding a stable element with neutrons in the core of a nuclear reactor (see ◊fission). The radiations given off by radioisotopes are easy to detect (hence their use as ◊tracers), can in some instances penetrate substantial thicknesses of materials, and have profound effects (such as genetic ◊mutation) on living matter.

radio map of the sky celestial chart depicting sources and intensities of radio emission.

radiometer device for the detection (and also measurement) of radiant ◊electromagnetic radiation.

radiomicrometer an extremely sensitive detector of infrared radiation.

radio scintillation ◊scintillation in received radio emission; the equivalent of 'twinkling' in visible light from the stars.

radiotherapy treatment of disease by ◊radiation from X-ray machines or radioactive sources. Radiation, which reduces the activity of dividing cells, is of special value for its effect on malignant tissues, certain nonmalignant tumours, and some diseases of the skin.

radio wave electromagnetic wave possessing a long wavelength (ranging from about 10^{-3} to 10^4 m) and a low frequency (from about 10^5 to 10^{11} Hz). Included in the radio-wave part of the spectrum are microwaves, used for both communications and for cooking; ultra high- and very high-frequency waves, used for television and FM (◊frequency modulation) radio communications; and short, medium, and long waves, used for AM (◊amplitude modulation) radio communications. Radio waves that are used for communications have all been modulated (see ◊modulation) to carry information. Certain astronomical objects emit radio waves, which may be detected and studied using radio telescopes.

radius a straight line from the centre of a circle to its circumference, or from the centre to the surface of a sphere.

radius vector in astronomy, an imaginary line connecting the centre of an orbiting body with the centre of the body (or point) that it is orbiting.

Raman effect in spectroscopy, the change in the ◊wavelength of light scattered by molecules.

Ranger spaceprobes series of nine US spaceprobes, only the final three of which were successful. All were meant to photograph the surface of the Moon before crashing onto it.

Rankine cycle cycle used in steam power plants, where water is introduced under ◊pressure into a boiler, evaporation taking place followed by expansion without loss of heat to end in condensation and a repeat of the cycle.

rare-earth element alternative name for ◊lanthanide.

ratchet wheel wheel with inclined teeth on its rim, used in gearing systems.

rational number in mathematics, any number that can be expressed as an exact fraction (with a denominator not equal to 0), that is, as $a \div b$ where a and b are integers; or an exact decimal. For example, $\frac{2}{1}$, $\frac{1}{4}$, $\frac{15}{4}$, $-\frac{3}{5}$ are all rational numbers, whereas π (which represents the constant 3.141592 ...) is not. Numbers such as π are called ◊irrational numbers.

Rayleigh–Jeans law formula giving the intensity of blackbody radiation at long ◊wavelengths for a radiator at a certain temperature. It is thus an approximation to Planck's full formula for the black-body intensity based on quantum concepts.

RDX or *cyclonite* or **hexogen** a very powerful explosive compound.

reaction in chemistry, the coming together of two or more atoms, ions, or molecules with the result that a chemical change takes place; that is, a change that occurs when two or more substances interact with each other, resulting in the production of different substances with different chemical compositions. The nature of the reaction is portrayed by a chemical equation.

real number in mathematics, any of the ◊rational numbers (which include the integers) or ◊irrational numbers. Real numbers exclude ◊imaginary numbers, found in ◊complex numbers of the general form $a + bi$ where $i = \sqrt{-1}$, although these do include a real component a.

reaper device used to collect crops such as wheat, while it grows in the field.

reciprocator device that uses a ◊piston moving cyclically within a system to carry out some task, such as pumping water.

rectifier in electrical engineering, a device used for obtaining one-directional current (DC) from an alternating source of supply (AC). (The process is necessary because almost all electrical power is generated, transmitted, and supplied as alternating current, but many devices, from television sets to electric motors, require direct current.) Types include plate rectifiers, thermionic ◊diodes, and ◊semiconductor diodes.

recursive in mathematics, a very general description of a function with natural numbers, as arguments, corresponding to the intuitive notion of computability. The basic recursive functions are $x + y$, xy, $f(x, y, z, ...) = x$, $g(x, y, z, ...) = y$, and a restricted form of the taking of a minimum.

red giant any large bright star with a cool surface. It is thought to represent a late stage in the evolution of a star like the Sun, as it runs out of hydrogen fuel at its centre and begins to burn heavier elements, such as helium, carbon, and silicon. Because of more complex nuclear reactions that then occur in the red giant's interior, it eventually becomes gravitationally unstable and begins to collapse and heat up. The result is either explosion of the star as a ◊supernova, leaving behind a ◊neutron star, or loss of mass by more gradual means to produce a ◊white dwarf.

red shift in astronomy, the lengthening of the wavelengths of light from an object as a result of the object's motion away from us. It is an example of the ◊Doppler effect. The red shift in light from galaxies is evidence that the universe is expanding.

reduction in chemistry, the gain of electrons, loss of oxygen, or gain of hydrogen by an atom, ion, or molecule during a chemical reaction.

reflecting telescope in astronomy, a telescope in which light is collected and brought to a focus by a concave mirror. ◊Cassegrain telescope and Newtonian telescope are examples.

reflection the throwing back or deflection of waves, such as ◊light or sound waves, when they hit a surface. The *law of reflection* states that the angle of incidence (the angle between the ray and a perpendicular line drawn to the surface) is equal to the angle of reflection (the angle between the reflected ray and a perpendicular to the surface).

reflection, laws of incident ray of light, the reflected ray of light, and the normal to the reflecting surface all lie in the same plane. Secondly, the angle between the incident ray and the normal is the same as that between the reflected ray and the normal to the surface.

reflex in animals, a very rapid involuntary response to a particular stimulus. It is controlled by the nervous system. A reflex involves only a few nerve cells, unlike the slower but more complex responses produced by the many processing nerve cells of the brain.

reflex action an involuntary response to a stimulus.

reflex arc route of nervous impulses from the point of stimulation, along ◊sensory nerve fibres to the central nervous system, and back along motor nerve fibres to the effector organ or muscle.

refracting telescope or *refractor* telescope that uses lenses to magnify and focus an image onto an eyepiece.

refraction the bending of a wave when it passes from one medium into another. It is the effect of the different speeds of wave propagation in two substances that have different densities. The amount of refraction depends on the densities of the media, the angle at which the wave strikes the surface of the second medium, and the amount of bending and change of velocity corresponding to the wave's frequency (dispersion). Refraction occurs with all types of progressive waves – ◊electromagnetic waves, sound waves, and water waves – and differs from ◊reflection, which involves no change in velocity.

refraction, laws of incident ray, the refracted ray and the normal to the surface between the two media at the point of incidence lie in the same plane. In addition, ◊Snell's law states that the ratio of the sines of the angles of incidence and refraction is equal to a constant. See ◊refractive index.

refractive index measure of the refraction of a ray of light as it passes from one transparent medium to another. If the angle of incidence is i and the angle of refraction is r, the ratio of the two refractive indices is given by $n_1/n_2 = \sin i/\sin r$. It is also equal to the speed of light in the first medium divided by the speed of light in the second, and it varies with the wavelength of the light.

refractive material materials able to stand very high temperature, such as brick and concrete.

refractometer device for determining the ◊refractive index of a substance.

refrigerator device that uses an external power source to absorb heat at a low temperature, and reject it at a higher one. This is made possible through the evaporation of special ◊fluids in the device's coils.

rejection immune response in the recipient of a tissue or organ transplant. If rejection does not respond to treatment, the donated tissue is destroyed. ◊Immunosuppressive drugs are used to try and prevent rejection.

relative atomic mass the mass of an atom relative to one-twelfth the mass of an atom of carbon-12. It depends primarily on the number of protons and neutrons in the atom, the electrons having negligible mass. If more than one ◊isotope of the element is present, the relative atomic mass is calculated by taking an average that takes account of the relative proportions of each isotope, resulting in values that are not whole numbers. The term *atomic weight,* although commonly used, is strictly speaking incorrect.

relative molecular mass the mass of a molecule, calculated relative to one-twelfth the mass of an atom of carbon-12. It is found by adding the relative atomic masses of the atoms that make up the molecule.

The term *molecular weight* is often used, but strictly this is incorrect.

relativity in physics, the theory of the relative rather than absolute character of motion and mass, and the interdependence of matter, time, and space, as developed by German-born US physicist Albert Einstein in two phases:

special theory of relativity (1905) Starting with the premises that (1) the laws of nature are the same for all observers in unaccelerated motion, and (2) the speed of light is independent of the motion of its source, Einstein arrived at some rather unexpected consequences. Intuitively familiar concepts, like mass, length, and time, had to be modified. For example, an object moving rapidly past the observer will appear to be both shorter and heavier than when it is at rest (that is, at rest relative to the observer), and a clock moving rapidly past the observer will appear to be running slower than when it is at rest. These predictions of relativity theory seem to be foreign to everyday experience merely because the changes are quite negligible at speeds less than about 1,500 km s^{-1}, and they only become appreciable at speeds approaching the speed of light.

general theory of relativity (1915) The geometrical properties of space-time were to be conceived as modified locally by the presence of a body with mass. A planet's orbit around the Sun (as observed in three-dimensional space) arises from its natural trajectory in modified space-time; there is no need to invoke, as Isaac Newton did, a force of ◊gravity coming from the Sun and acting on the planet. Einstein's general theory accounts for a peculiarity in the behaviour of the motion of the perihelion of the orbit of the planet Mercury that cannot be explained in Newton's theory. The new theory also said that light rays should bend when they pass by a massive object. The predicted bending of starlight was observed during the eclipse of the Sun 1919. A third corroboration is found in the shift towards the red in the spectra of the Sun and, in particular, of stars of great density – white dwarfs such as the companion of Sirius.

replication in biology, production of copies of the genetic material DNA; it occurs during cell division (◊mitosis and ◊meiosis). Most mutations are caused by mistakes during replication.

repressor substance a substance produced by a DNA regulator ◊gene. When the repressor is inactivated by an inducer, the DNA structural genes are freed for the synthesis of ◊messenger RNA.

resistance in physics, that property of a conductor that restricts the flow of electricity through it, associated with the conversion of electrical energy to heat; also the magnitude of this property. Resistance depends on many factors, such as the nature of the material, its temperature, dimensions, and thermal properties; degree of impurity; the nature and state of illumination of the surface; and the frequency and magnitude of the current. The SI unit of resistance is the ◊ohm.

$$\text{resistance} = \frac{\text{voltage}}{\text{current}}$$

This is known as ◊Ohm's law.

resolution of a telescope, the clarity of the final presentation to the observer (in image, radio picture or X-ray read-out).

resolving power ability of an optical device to discern two closely spaced light sources as independent entities.

resonance in chemistry, the concept that, in certain molecules, the electrons involved in linking the constituent atoms are not associated with a specific bond (or bonds) but oscillate between atoms. Thus such molecules are not represented by a single valence-bond structure but by two or more alternative structures; the molecule 'resonates' between these alternative structures – that is, its structure is a resonance hybrid of the alternatives. The best known example of resonance is benzene, which, according to Kekulé's original formulation, resonates between two forms in which the double and single bonds are transposed. In Robinson's later modification, the six carbon atoms are linked by single bonds and the extra electrons are distributed equally among the carbon atoms, this being represented diagrammatically by a circle within the hexagonal carbon ring.

respiration metabolic process in organisms in which food molecules are broken down to release energy. The cells of all living organisms need a continuous supply of energy, and in most plants and animals this is obtained by *aerobic* respiration. In this process, oxygen is used to break down the glucose molecules in food. This releases energy in the form of energy-carrying molecules (◊ATP), and produces carbon dioxide and water as by-products. Respiration sometimes occurs without oxygen, and this is called *anaerobic* respiration. In this case, the end products are energy and either lactose acid or ethanol (alcohol) and carbon dioxide; this process is termed ◊fermentation.

resting potential potential difference across a nerve or muscle membrane in the absence of a stimulus.

retaining wall structure, usually of concrete, forming the wall of a structure sunk below the level of the ground, that is, holding back the outer volume of earth surrounding the structure.

reticulo-endothelial system group of cells that exist in continual contact with the blood and lymph, that is, in the bone marrow, spleen, liver, and lymph nodes. They ingest bacteria, other foreign particles and dead tissue, and aid tissue repair.

retort glass vessel in the form of a glass bulb with an extended, fluted neck. Generally, any vessel in which a chemical reaction takes place.

retrograde in astronomy, the orbit or rotation of a planet or ◊satellite if the sense of rotation is opposite to the general sense of rotation of the Solar System. On the ◊celestial sphere, it refers to motion from east to west against the background of stars.

reversing layer lower ◊chromosphere of the Sun, a comparatively cool region in which radiation at certain wavelengths is absorbed from the continuous spectrum emitted from the Sun's ◊photosphere.

revolver pistol with a revolving magazine carrying the bullets and their charges, enabling five or six shots to be taken in succession before reloading.

Reynolds number number used in fluid mechanics to determine whether fluid flow in a particular situation (through a pipe or around an aircraft body or a fixed structure in the sea) will be turbulent or smooth. The Reynolds number is calculated using the flow velocity, density, and viscosity of the fluid, and the dimensions of the flow channel. It is named after British engineer Osborne Reynolds.

rhesus factor group of ◊antigens on the surface of red blood cells of humans which characterize the rhesus blood group system. Most individuals possess the main rhesus factor (Rh+), but those without this factor (Rh−) produce ◊antibodies if they come into contact with it. The name comes from rhesus monkeys, in whose blood rhesus factors were first found.

ribonucleic acid full name of ◊RNA.

ribosome in biology, the protein-making machinery of the cell. Ribosomes are located on the endoplasmic reticulum (ER) of eukaryotic cells, and are made of proteins and a special type of ◊RNA, ribosomal RNA. They receive messenger RNA (copied from the ◊DNA) and ◊amino acids, and 'translate' the messenger RNA by using its chemically coded instructions to link amino acids in a specific order, to make a strand of a particular protein.

Riemann geometry system of non-Euclidean geometry devised by Bernhard Riemann, developed primarily as ◊elliptic geometry, but then extended to ◊hyperbolic geometry.

Riemann hypothesis statement that has as yet not been proved (or disproved), that the ◊zeta function takes the value zero in the right-half plane of the ◊Argand diagram only for complex numbers of the form $\frac{1}{2} + ia$, where i = √−1 and a is real.

Riemann space non-Euclidean geometry, using n-dimensional coordinates $(x_1, ..., x_n)$ and calculating length according to the formula:

$$ds^2 = \Sigma g_{ij}{}^2\, dx^i dx^j$$

where ds is the limiting incremental length along a curve, dx^i is 'a limiting increment in the i coordinate', and i, j run through the values 1, 2, 3, ..., n.

Riemann surface in non-Euclidean geometry, a multi-connected many-sheeted surface that can be dissected by crosscuts into a singly connected surface. Such a representation of a complex algebraic function is used to study the 'behaviour' of other complex functions as they are mapped conformally (transformed) onto it. A Riemann surface has been described as topologically equivalent to a box with holes in it.

right ascension in astronomy, the coordinate on the ◊celestial sphere that corresponds to longitude on the surface of the Earth. It is measured in hours, minutes, and seconds

eastwards from the point where the Sun's path, the ecliptic, once a year intersects the celestial equator; this point is called the **vernal equinox**.

ring mathematical structure that constitutes a restricted form of field in which division might be unavailable.

rivet fixing device that pins together two sheets of material, usually metal, by insertion through a hole through the sheets, and expansion of the heads by striking with a hammer or other tool.

RNA abbreviation for **ribonucleic acid** nucleic acid involved in the process of translating the genetic material ◊DNA into proteins. It is usually single-stranded, unlike the double-stranded DNA, and consists of a large number of nucleotides strung together, each of which comprises the sugar ribose, a phosphate group, and one of four bases (uracil, cytosine, adenine, or guanine). RNA is copied from DNA by the formation of ◊base pairs, with uracil taking the place of thymine.

roll movement of any aircraft about the axis running down the centre of the aircraft.

root of an equation, a value that satisfies the equality. For example, $x = 0$ and $x = 5$ are roots of the equation $x^2 - 5x = 0$.

root in mathematics, a number which when multiplied by itself will equal a given number (the inverse of an ◊exponent or power). On a calculator, roots may be found by using the buttons marked $x^{\frac{1}{y}}$ or inv x^y. For example, the cubed root of 27 is found by pressing 27, then inv x^y, then 3.

rose symmetrical curve represented by the equation:

$$(x^2 + y^2)^3 = 4a^2x^2y^2$$

where a is constant.

rotation in geometry, a ◊transformation in which a figure is turned about a given point, known as the **centre of rotation**. A rotation of 180° is known as a half turn.

Royal Greenwich Observatory (RGO) originally one of the two UK national astronomical observatories run by the Particle Physics and Astronomy Research Council (PPARC). It was founded in 1675 at Greenwich, East London, to provide navigational information to sailors. After World War II it moved to Herstmonceux Castle in Sussex, where the 2.5-m/8.2-ft Isaac Newton Telescope (INT) was constructed in 1967. Following the relocation of the INT to the island of La Palma, in the Canary Islands, RGO was relocated to Cambridge in 1988–90. In 1998 the Cambridge site was closed and the RGO merged with the Royal Observatory Edinburgh to form a new Astronomy Technology Centre on the Edinburgh site.

RR Lyrae variable type of short-period ◊variable star. Spectrally classified as A to F giants, RR Lyrae variables were once called **cluster-Cepheids** (see ◊Cepheid variable).

rudder part of the tailplane of an aircraft that moves about a vertical axis perpendicular to the wings, controlling the yaw motion.

Rydberg constant in physics, a constant that relates atomic spectra to the ◊spectrum of hydrogen. Its value is 1.0977 x 10^7 per metre.

Rydberg's constant constant that relates the ◊wavelength of spectral lines in hydrogen-like elements to the inverse-squares of integers.

S

saccharide another name for a ◊sugar molecule.

salt in chemistry, any compound formed from an acid and a base through the replacement of all or part of the hydrogen in the acid by a metal or electropositive radical. *Common salt* is sodium chloride.

saltpetre former name for potassium nitrate (KNO_3), the compound used in making gunpowder (from about 1500). It occurs naturally, being deposited during dry periods in places with warm climates, such as India.

saponification in chemistry, the ◊hydrolysis (splitting) of an ◊ester by treatment with a strong alkali, resulting in the liberation of the alcohol from which the ester had been derived and a salt of the constituent fatty acid. The process is used in the manufacture of soap.

satellite any small body that orbits a larger one, either natural or artificial. Natural satellites that orbit planets are called moons. The first *artificial satellite, Sputnik 1,* was launched into orbit around the Earth by the USSR in 1957. Artificial satellites are used for scientific purposes, communications, weather forecasting, and military applications. The brightest artificial satellites can be seen by the naked eye.

saturated vapour pressure ◊pressure exerted by a ◊vapour that exists in equilibrium with its liquid.

scalar quantity in mathematics and science, a quantity that has magnitude but no direction, as distinct from a vector quantity, which has a direction as well as a magnitude. Temperature, mass, and volume are scalar quantities.

Schlieren photography means of photographing turbulences in fast-moving ◊fluids, through the change of ◊density and ◊refractive index that such turbulence produces.

Schmidt camera telescopic camera incorporating an internal corrective lens or plate that compensates for optical defects and chromatic faults in the main mirror. The system was invented by Estonian lens-maker Bernhard Schmidt.

Schrödinger's equation an equation that considers the ◊electron in terms of a wave of probability, and which enables the behaviour of the electron in atoms and electric potentials to be calculated, and also the spectra of atoms to be predicted. It is the basis of wave mechanics.

Schubfachprinzip or *pigeon-hole principle* principle that states that if in n boxes one distributes more than n objects, at least one box must contain more than one object. The principle is used in the logic of number theory.

Schwann cell in vertebrates, the neurilemma cell of myelinated peripheral nerve fibres, important in the manufacture of ◊myelin. On myelin-coated fibres a Schwann cell occurs between each pair of adjacent nodes.

scintillation in radioastronomy, a rapid oscillation in the detected intensity of radiation emitted by stellar radio sources, caused by disturbances in ionized gas at some point between the source and the Earth's surface (usually in the Earth's own upper atmosphere).

screw in construction, cylindrical or tapering piece of metal or plastic (or formerly wood) with a helical groove cut into it. Each turn of a screw moves it forward or backwards by a distance equal to the pitch (the spacing between neighbouring threads).

scuba acronym for *self-contained underwater breathing apparatus* another name for ◊aqualung.

seafloor spreading growth of the ocean ◊crust outwards (sideways) from ocean ridges. The concept of seafloor spreading has been combined with that of continental drift and incorporated into ◊plate tectonics.

secant in ◊trigonometry, the function of a given angle in a right-angled triangle, obtained by dividing the length of the hypotenuse (the longest side) by the length of the side adjacent to the angle. It is the reciprical of the cosine (sec = $\frac{1}{\cos}$).

second order of a differential equation, involving only first and second ◊derivatives. The term is occasionally used in algebraic contexts to mean 'of the second degree', that is, involving expressions raised to at most the power of two (squares).

secular in astronomy, gradual, taking aeons to accomplish.

secular acceleration of the Moon, of the Sun apparent acceleration of the Moon and Sun across the sky, caused by extremely gradual reduction in speed of the Earth's rotation (one 50-millionth of a second per day).

sedimentary rock rock formed by the accumulation and cementation of deposits that have been laid down by water, wind, ice, or gravity. Sedimentary rocks cover more than two-thirds of the Earth's surface and comprise three major categories: clastic, chemically precipitated, and organic (or biogenic). Clastic sediments are the largest group and are composed of fragments of pre-existing rocks; they include clays, sands, and gravels.

Chemical precipitates include some limestones and evaporated deposits such as gypsum and halite (rock salt). Coal, oil shale, and limestone made of fossil material are examples of organic sedimentary rocks.

Seebeck effect in physics, the generation of a voltage in a circuit containing two different metals, or semiconductors, by keeping the junctions between them at different temperatures. Discovered by the German physicist Thomas Seebeck (1770–1831), it is also called the thermoelectric effect, and is the basis of the thermocouple. It is the opposite of the Peltier effect (in which current flow causes a temperature difference between the junctions of different metals).

selenium (Greek *Selene* 'Moon') grey, nonmetallic element, symbol Se, atomic number 34, relative atomic mass 78.96. It belongs to the sulphur group and occurs in several allotropic forms that differ in their physical and chemical properties. It is an essential trace element in human nutrition.

Obtained from many sulphide ores and selenides, it is used as a red colouring for glass and enamel.

self-inductance or *self-induction* in physics, the creation of an electromotive force opposing the current.

self-pollination pollination of a plant by itself, whether intra- or interfloral.

semiconductor material with electrical conductivity intermediate between metals and insulators and used in a wide range of electronic devices. Certain crystalline materials, most notably silicon and germanium, have a small number of free electrons that have escaped from the bonds between the atoms. The atoms from which they have escaped possess vacancies, called holes, which are similarly able to move from atom to atom and can be regarded as positive charges. Current can be carried by both electrons (negative carriers) and holes (positive carriers). Such materials are known as ***intrinsic semiconductors***.

semipermeable membrane membrane that allows certain substances in solution, such as ◊crystalloids, to pass through it but is impervious to others, such as ◊colloids. Semipermeable membranes are used in ◊dialysis.

sensorimotor phase first stage in human mental development from birth to about two years of age in which reflex actions lead to an awareness of the permanence of objects.

sensory nerve an afferent nerve of the peripheral nervous system, made up of sensory neurons, which carries impulses to the central nervous system.

sepal part of a flower, usually green, that surrounds and protects the flower in bud. The sepals are derived from modified leaves, and are collectively known as the calyx.

sequence list of mathematical objects indexed by the natural numbers, following one another in some defined relationship (but with no mathematical operation implied). Sequences are said to increase (to higher values) or decrease (to lower), and may be finite (if the list terminates), convergent (to a limit) or divergent. If the values increase or decrease along the sequence, the sequence is said to be monotonic or monotone.

series sum of a list that constitutes a sequence. Series may be represented in an abbreviated form using the summation sign – for example, the series $a_1 + a_2 + a_3 + ... + a_n$ to infinity may be represented as:

$$\sum_{k=1}^{\infty} a_k$$

The word 'series' is for historical reasons occasionally misused to mean 'sequence', as in the Fibonacci series. Strictly speaking, however, a series is the limit of the sequence of partial sums.

servo mechanism mechanism that uses relatively low power to control the behaviour of a much larger output device in a proportionate way.

set or ***class*** in mathematics, any collection of defined things (elements), provided the elements are distinct and that there is a rule to decide whether an element is a member of a set. It is usually denoted by a capital letter and indicated by curly brackets {}.

sextic to the power of six.

shooting star another name for a ◊meteor.

shrapnel strictly, an artillery shell filled with small spheres with an explosive charge gives rise to shrapnel. It now also covers general fragments of metal produced from an exploding device. It is named after English artillery officer Henry Schrapnel.

shuttle device for carrying thread on a loom.

sidereal period orbital period of a planet around the Sun, or a moon around a planet, with reference to a background star.

The sidereal period of a planet is in effect a 'year'. A ◊synodic period is a full circle as seen from Earth.

sidereal time in astronomy, time measured by the rotation of the Earth with respect to the stars. A sidereal day is the time taken by the Earth to turn once with respect to the stars, namely 23 h 56 min 4 s. It is divided into sidereal hours, minutes, and seconds, each of which is proportionally shorter than the corresponding SI unit.

Siemens–Martin process another name for the open-hearth process.

sigma Σ ◊summation symbol.

sigma bond type of chemical bond in which an electron pair (regarded as being shared by the two atoms involved in the bond) occupies a molecular orbital situated between the two atoms; the orbital is located along a hypothetical line linking the atoms' nuclei.

silicon (Latin *silex* 'flint') brittle, nonmetallic element, symbol Si, atomic number 14, relative atomic mass 28.086. It is the second-most abundant element (after oxygen) in the Earth's crust and occurs in amorphous and crystalline forms. In nature it is found only in combination with other elements, chiefly with oxygen in silica (silicon dioxide, SiO_2) and the silicates. These form the mineral quartz, which makes up most sands, gravels, and beaches.

Silurian period of geological time 439–409 million years ago, the third period of the Palaeozoic era. Silurian sediments are mostly marine and consist of shales and limestone. Luxuriant reefs were built by coral-like organisms. The first land plants began to evolve during this period, and there were many ostracoderms (armoured jawless fishes). The first jawed fishes (called acanthodians) also appeared.

silver nitrate white, crystalline substance used in chemical analysis and inks.

simplex method in linear computer-programming, an algorithm designed to find the optimum solution in a finite number of steps.

sine in trigonometry, a function of an angle in a right-angled triangle which is defined as the ratio of the length of the side opposite the angle to the length of the hypotenuse (the longest side).

single phase electrical power transmission involving a single sinusoidally varying ◊potential difference.

singularity in astrophysics, the point in ◊space-time at which the known laws of physics break down. Singularity is predicted to exist at the centre of a black hole, where infinite gravitational forces compress the infalling mass of a collapsing star to infinite density. It is also thought, according to the Big Bang model of the origin of the universe, to be the point from which the expansion of the universe began.

Sirius or ***the Dog Star*** or ***Alpha Canis Majoris*** brightest star in the night sky, 8.6 light years from the Sun in the constellation Canis Major. Sirius is a white star with a mass 2.3 times that of the Sun, a diameter 1.8 times that of the Sun, and a true luminosity of 23 Suns. It is orbited every 50 years by a ◊white dwarf, Sirius B, also known as the Pup.

SI units (French *Système International d'Unités*) standard system of scientific units used by scientists worldwide.

Originally proposed in 1960, it replaces the m.k.s., c.g.s., and f.p.s. systems. It is based on seven basic units: the metre (m) for length, kilogram (kg) for mass, second (s) for time, ampere (A) for electrical current, kelvin (K) for temperature, mole (mol) for amount of substance, and candela (cd) for luminosity.

smelting processing a metallic ore in a furnace to produce the metal. Oxide ores such as iron ore are smelted with coke (carbon), which reduces the ore into metal and also provides fuel for the process.

smoke suspension of a solid in a gas; the solid is in the form of extremely small particles and the smoke may be a ◊colloid.

Snell's law of refraction in optics, the rule that when a ray of light passes from one medium to another, the sine of the angle of incidence divided by the sine of the angle of refraction is equal to the ratio of the indices of refraction in the two media. For a ray passing from medium 1 to medium 2:

$$\frac{n_2}{n_1} = \frac{\sin i}{\sin r}$$

where n_1 and n_2 are the refractive indices of the two media. The law was devised by the Dutch physicist Willebrord Snell.

soap mixture of the sodium salts of various ◊fatty acids: palmitic, stearic, and oleic acid. It is made by the action of sodium hydroxide (caustic soda) or potassium hydroxide (caustic potash) on fats of animal or vegetable origin. Soap makes grease and dirt disperse in water in a similar manner to a detergent.

sodium pump hypothetical mechanism that maintains the asymmetry of the ionic (concentration) balance across a nerve cell membrane, reflected in the cell's ◊resting potential.

sodium theory theory which proposes that the excitation of a nerve results from momentary changes in the selective permeability of a nerve cell membrane, which admits sodium and chloride ions into the cell and allows potassium ions to diffuse out. The ion movements briefly reverse the polarization of the membrane, resulting in an ◊action potential which constitutes the nerve impulse.

sodium thiosulphate correct chemical name for sodium hyposulphite (hypo), the substance used to fix photographic images after developing.

soft iron form of iron with a low carbon content that does not retain ◊magnetism once the current in a ◊coil surrounding it has been removed.

soil mechanics branch of engineering that studies the nature and properties of the soil. Soil is investigated during construction work to ensure that it has the mechanical properties necessary to support the foundations of dams, bridges, and roads.

solar constant mean radiation received from the Sun at the top level of Earth's atmosphere: 1.95 calories per sq cm per minute.

solar energy is produced by ◊nuclear fusion and comprises almost entirely ◊electromagnetic radiation (particularly in the form of light and heat); particles are also radiated forming the ◊solar wind.

solar flare sudden and dramatic release of a huge burst of ◊solar energy through a break in the Sun's ◊chromosphere in the region of a ◊sunspot. Effects on Earth include auroras, magnetic storms, and radio interference.

solar parallax ◊parallax of the Sun, now measured as 8.794 in.

solar prominence mass of hot hydrogen rising from the Sun's ◊chromosphere, best observed during a total ◊eclipse. Eruptive prominences are violent in force and may reach heights of 2,000,000 km/1,243,000 mi; quiescent prominences are relatively pacific but may last for months.

solar rotation is differential, the equatorial rotation taking less time than the polar by up to 9.4 Earth-days.

Solar System the Sun (a star) and all the bodies orbiting it: the nine planets (Mercury, Venus, Earth, Mars, Jupiter, Saturn, Uranus, Neptune, and Pluto), their moons, the asteroids, and the comets. The Sun contains 99.86% of the mass of the Solar System.

solar wind stream of atomic particles, mostly protons and electrons, from the Sun's corona, flowing outwards at speeds of between 300 kps/200 mps and 1,000 kps/600 mps.

solder an ◊alloy that is heated and used to join two metals together.

solenoid device consisting of a series of wires wound around a cylinder, which produces a magnetic field within the cylinder when a current flows through the wire windings. The intensity of the magnetic field depends directly on the number of turns of the wire.

solid in physics, a state of matter that holds its own shape (as opposed to a liquid, which takes up the shape of its container, or a gas, which totally fills its container). According to ◊kinetic theory, the atoms or molecules in a solid are not free to move but merely vibrate about fixed positions, such as those in crystal lattices.

solid-state physics study of materials in the solid state, investigating the magnetic, thermal, and electrical properties, for example.

solstice either of the days on which the Sun is farthest north or south of the celestial equator each year. The *summer solstice,* when the Sun is farthest north, occurs around 21 June; the *winter solstice* around 22 December.

soluble group notion introduced to extend theorems concerning commutative groups to a wider class of groups that, in an intuitive sense, can be constructed out of commutative 'pieces'. Given a group G the commutator subgroup C is introduced (generated by elements of the form $xyx^{-1}y^{-1}$); G can then be 'collapsed' to an Abelian group by a process that reduces C to the identity element; C is then collapsed in an identical fashion, and the process continually repeated. If the process, through a finite number of steps, eventually leads to a last group that is already commutative, G is said to be soluble.

solution two or more substances mixed to form a single, homogenous phase. One of the substances is the *solvent* and the others (*solutes)* are said to be dissolved in it.

solvent substance, usually a liquid, that will dissolve another substance (see ◊solution). Although the commonest solvent is water, in popular use the term refers to low-boiling-point organic liquids, which are harmful if used in a confined space. They can give rise to respiratory problems, liver damage, and neurological complaints.

somatic cell any cell in an organism, excluding the reproductive cells.

sound physiological sensation received by the ear, originating in a vibration that communicates itself as a pressure variation in the air and travels in every direction, spreading out as an expanding sphere. All sound waves in air travel with a speed dependent on the temperature; under ordinary conditions, this is about 330 m/1,070 ft per second. The pitch of the sound depends on the number of vibrations imposed on the air per second (◊frequency), but the speed is unaffected. The loudness of a sound is dependent primarily on the amplitude of the vibration of the air.

space collection of mathematical objects (referred to as points) with an associated structure resembling (or analogous to) the properties of the space of everyday experience.

space constant term characterizing the line in non-Euclidean geometry that relates the angle of parallelism of two lines – a concept formulated by Hungarian mathematician János Bolyai.

space-time in physics, combination of space and time used in the theory of ◊relativity. When developing relativity, Albert Einstein showed that time was in many respects like an extra dimension (or direction) to space. Space and time can thus be considered as entwined into a single entity, rather than two separate things.

spar beam running the length of a wing or tail-plane.

speciation formation and development of species.

specific heat capacity in physics, quantity of heat required to raise unit mass (1 kg) of a substance by one ◊kelvin (1 K). The unit of specific heat capacity in the SI system is the ◊joule per kilogram kelvin ($J kg^{-1} K^{-1}$).

spectral classification in astronomy, the classification of stars according to their surface temperature and ◊luminosity, as determined from their spectra. Stars are assigned a spectral type (or class) denoted by the letters O, B, A, F, G, K, and M, where O stars (about 40,000 K) are the hottest and M stars (about 3,000 K) are the coolest.

spectral line dark line visible in an absorption ◊spectrum, or one of the bright lines that make up an emission spectrum. Spectral lines are caused by the transference of an ◊electron in an atom from one energy level to another; strong lines are produced at levels at which such transference occurs easily, weak where it occurs with difficulty. ◊Ionization of certain elements can affect such transferences and cause problems in spectral analysis.

spectroheliograph device with which spectra of the various regions of the Sun are obtained and photographed.

spectroscope an instrument that produces a spectrum for study or analysis. An object that produces radiation, such as a heated substance, forms an emission spectrum (see also ◊absorption spectrum). Elements have characteristic spectra and spectroscopy is used in chemical analysis to identify the elements in a substance or mixture. Molecules or their constituent atoms or components of atoms can be made to absorb various types of energy in a characteristic way and give rise to such analytical techniques as infrared, ultraviolet, X-ray, and nuclear magnetic resonance spectroscopy. See also ◊mass spectroscope.

spectroscopy study of spectra (see ◊spectrum) associated with atoms or molecules in solid, liquid, or gaseous phase. Spectroscopy can be used to identify unknown compounds and is an invaluable tool in science, medicine, and industry (for example, in checking the purity of drugs).

spectrum plural *spectra* in physics, an arrangement of frequencies or wavelengths when electromagnetic radiations are separated into their constituent parts. Visible light is part of the ◊electromagnetic spectrum and most sources emit waves over a range of wavelengths that can be broken up or 'dispersed'; white light can be separated into red, orange, yellow, green, blue, indigo, and violet. The visible spectrum was first studied by Isaac Newton, who showed in 1672 how white light could be broken up into different colours.

speed of light speed at which light and other ◊electromagnetic waves travel through empty space. Its value is 299,792,458 m/186,281 mi per second. The speed of light is the highest speed possible, according to the theory of ◊relativity, and its value is independent of the motion of its source and of the observer. It is impossible to accelerate any material body to this speed because it would require an infinite amount of energy.

spherical aberration an optical error occurring when a lens or curved mirror does not bring all the incident rays of light to a sharp focus. See also ◊aberration.

spherical collapse initial stage in the collapse of a star, followed by gravitational collapse and finally ◊singularity.

spherical geometry system of non-Euclidean geometry devised by German mathematician Bernhard Riemann as an extension of ◊elliptic geometry and comprising two-dimensional geometry as effected on the outer surface of sphere.

spin in physics, the intrinsic ◊angular momentum of a subatomic particle, nucleus, atom, or molecule, which continues to exist even when the particle comes to rest. A particle in a specific energy state has a particular spin, just as it has a particular electric charge and mass. According to quantum theory, this is restricted to discrete and indivisible values, specified by a spin ◊quantum number. Because of its spin, a charged particle acts as a small magnet and is affected by magnetic fields.

spin-orbit interaction an interaction between ◊electrons orbiting a ◊nucleus in an ◊atom that arises from the magnetic field produced by the nucleus interacting with the spinning electron is to split the individual ◊spectral lines in a ◊spectrum into a number of components.

spiral nebula spiral ◊galaxy – not really a ◊nebula at all (although many do appear nebulous).

spirillium bacterium with a spiral shape (see ◊bacteria).

spore small reproductive or resting body, usually consisting of just one cell. Unlike a ◊gamete, it does not need to fuse with another cell in order to develop into a new organism. Spores are produced by the lower plants, most fungi, some bacteria, and certain protozoa. They are generally light and easily dispersed by wind movements.

Plant spores are haploid and are produced by the sporophyte, following ◊meiosis.

sporozoite protozoon of the class Sporozoa, such as the malarial parasite Plasmodium.

Sputnik (Russian 'fellow traveller') series of ten Soviet Earth-orbiting satellites. *Sputnik 1* was the first artificial satellite, launched 4 October 1957. It weighed 84 kg/185 lb, with a 58 cm/23 in diameter, and carried only a simple radio transmitter which allowed scientists to track it as it orbited Earth. It burned up in the atmosphere 92 days later. Sputniks were superseded in the early 1960s by the Cosmos series.

squaring the circle ancient Greek problem in geometrical construction, to describe a square of exactly the same area as a given circle, using ruler and compass only. German mathematician Ferdinand von Lindemann established that π was a ◊transcendental number; unable thus to be the root of an equation, it cannot be constructed by ruler and compass – and the problem is therefore not solvable.

squid acronym for *superconducting quantum interference device* device that makes use of the ◊Josephson effect to produce a highly sensitive magnetic field detection system, or an ultra-fast switching device for use in computers.

stain in chemistry, a coloured compound that will bind to other substances. Stains are used extensively in microbiology to colour microorganisms and in histochemistry to detect the presence and whereabouts in plant and animal tissue of substances such as fats, cellulose, and proteins.

standard deviation in statistics, a measure (symbol Σ or s) of the spread of data. The deviation (difference) of each of the data items from the mean is found, and their values squared. The mean value of these squares is then calculated. The standard deviation is the square root of this mean.

standard gauge distance between the steel rails on the majority of the world's railways; 4 ft 8 in/1.435 m.

Stark effect splitting of ◊spectral lines into a number of components by a strong electric field.

starlight energy (seen as light) produced by a star through ◊nuclear fusion.

statics branch of mechanics concerned with the behaviour of bodies at rest and forces in equilibrium, and distinguished from ◊dynamics.

steady-state theory in astronomy, a rival theory to that of the ◊Big Bang, which claims that the universe has no origin but is expanding because new matter is being created continuously throughout the universe. The theory was proposed in 1948 by Hermann Bondi, Thomas Gold, and Fred Hoyle, but was dealt a severe blow in 1964 by the discovery of cosmic background radiation (radiation left over from the formation of the universe) and is now largely rejected.

steam turbine ◊turbine that is powered by a jet of high-◊pressure steam.

steel alloy or mixture of iron and up to 1.7% carbon, sometimes with other elements, such as manganese, phosphorus, sulphur, and silicon. The USA, Russia, Ukraine, and Japan are the main steel producers. Steel has innumerable uses, including ship and car manufacture, skyscraper frames, and machinery of all kinds.

Stefan–Boltzmann law in physics, a law that relates the energy, E, radiated away from a perfect emitter (a ◊black body), to the temperature, T, of that body. It has the form $E = \sigma\, T^4$, where E is the energy radiated per unit area per second, T is the temperature, and σ is the **Stefan–Boltzmann constant**. Its value is 5.6705×10^{-8} W m^{-2} K^{-4}. The law was derived by Austrian physicists Joseph Stefan and Ludwig Boltzmann.

stellar of a star, of the stars.

stereochemistry branch of chemistry that is concerned with a study of the shapes of molecules.

stereoisomerism type of isomerism in which two or more substances differ only in the way that the atoms of their molecules are oriented in space.

stereoscope device that can produce the effect of three-dimensional images using only two-dimensional images, using the human brain to carry out the merging necessary.

steroid in biology, any of a group of cyclic, unsaturated alcohols (lipids without fatty acid components), which, like sterols, have a complex molecular structure consisting of four carbon rings. Steroids include the sex hormones, such as testosterone, the corticosteroid hormones produced by the adrenal gland, bile acids, and cholesterol.

The term is commonly used to refer to anabolic steroid. In medicine, synthetic steroids are used to treat a wide range of conditions.

stone common name for a calculus, a hard accretion of organic or inorganic salts that precipitate and grow in the kidneys, urinary tract or gall bladder. Calculi are often associated with, or cause, infection in the organs concerned.

strain in the science of materials, the extent to which a body is distorted when a deforming force (stress) is applied to it. It is a ratio of the extension or compression of that body (its length, area, or volume) to its original dimensions (see ◊Hooke's law). For example, linear strain is the ratio of the change in length of a body to its original length.

strangeness ◊quantum number assigned to certain unstable ◊elementary particles that decay much more slowly than was originally expected. Stable particles, such as ◊protons, have a strangeness quantum number of zero. Others, such as the ◊hyperons, have nonzero quantum numbers.

stratigraphy branch of geology that deals with the sequence of formation of ◊sedimentary rock layers and the conditions under which they were formed. Its basis was developed by English geologist William Smith. The basic principle of superimposition establishes that upper layers or deposits have accumulated later in time than the lower ones.

streamline line in a fluid such that the ◊tangent to it at every point gives the direction of flow, and its speed, at any instant.

streptococcus any one of a genus of round or oval Gram-positive bacteria that have a tendency to form pairs or chains. They are widely distributed in nature, living mainly as parasites in the bodies of animals and humans. Some are harmless, but others are implicated in a number of infections, including scarlet fever.

stress and strain in the science of materials, measures of the deforming force applied to a body (stress) and of the resulting change in its shape (◊strain). For a perfectly elastic material, stress is proportional to strain (◊Hooke's law).

Strömgren sphere or *H II zone* zone of ionized hydrogen gas that surrounds hot stars embedded in interstellar gas clouds.

strong nuclear force one of the four fundamental forces of nature, the other three being the electromagnetic force, gravity, and the weak nuclear force. The strong nuclear force was first described by Japanese physicist Hideki Yukawa in 1935. It is the strongest of all the forces, acts only over very small distances (within the nucleus of the atom), and is responsible for binding together ◊quarks to form hadrons, and for binding together protons and neutrons in the atomic nucleus. The particle that is the carrier of the strong nuclear force is the ◊gluon, of which there are eight kinds, each with zero mass and zero charge.

subarachnoid describing the fluid-filled region between the arachnoid membrane and the pia mater membrane which surround the brain and spinal cord.

substitution reaction in chemistry, the replacement of one atom or functional group in an organic molecule by another.

substrate in biochemistry, a compound or mixture of compounds acted on by an enzyme. The term also refers to a substance such as agar that provides the nutrients for the metabolism of microorganisms. Since the enzyme systems of microorganisms regulate their metabolism, the essential meaning is the same.

sugar or *sucrose* sweet, soluble, crystalline carbohydrate found in the pith of sugar cane and in sugar beet. It is a **disaccharide** sugar, each of its molecules being made up of two simple-sugar (**monosaccharide**) units: glucose and fructose. Sugar is easily digested and forms a major source of energy in humans, being used in cooking and in the food industry as a sweetener and, in high concentrations, as a preservative. A high consumption is associated with obesity and tooth decay. In the UK, sucrose may not be used in baby foods.

summation symbol sign (Σ) representing the sum taken over all instances that accompany the sign, indicated above and below it. Thus:

$$\sum_{i=1}^{n} a_i$$

means $a_1 + a_2 + a_3 + ... + a_n$. The symbol is the capital form of the Greek letter sigma.

sunspot dark patch on the surface of the Sun, actually an area of cooler gas, thought to be caused by strong magnetic fields that block the outward flow of heat to the Sun's surface. Sunspots consist of a dark central **umbra,** about 4,000 K (3,700°C/6,700°F), and a lighter surrounding **penumbra,** about 5,500 K (5,200°C/9,400°F). They last from several days to over a month, ranging in size from 2,000 km/1,250 mi to groups stretching for over 100,000 km/62,000 mi.

supercharger in internal-combustion engines, the use of a compressor to supply air or fuel–air mixtures at a high ◊pressure to the ◊piston cylinders; in aero engines, a device to maintain ground-level pressures in the engine inlet pipe when flying at high altitude.

supercharging heating of a liquid above its boiling point.

supercluster in astronomy, a grouping of several clusters of galaxies to form a structure about 100–300 million light years across. Our own Galaxy and its neighbours lie on the edge of the local supercluster of which the Virgo cluster is the dominant member.

superconductivity in physics, increase in electrical conductivity at low temperatures. The resistance of some metals and metallic compounds decreases uniformly with decreasing temperature until at a critical temperature (the superconducting point), within a few degrees of absolute zero (0 K/–273.15°C/–459.67°F), the resistance suddenly falls to zero. The phenomenon was discovered by Dutch scientist Heike Kamerlingh Onnes in 1911.

superego in Freudian psychology, the element of the human mind concerned with the ideal, responsible for ethics and self-imposed standards of behaviour. It is characterized as a form of conscience, restraining the ◊ego, and responsible for feelings of guilt when the moral code is broken.

superfluid fluid that flows without viscosity or friction and has a very high thermal conductivity. Liquid helium at temperatures below 2 K (–271°C/–456°F) is a superfluid: it shows unexpected behaviour; for instance, it flows uphill in apparent defiance of gravity and, if placed in a container, will flow up the sides and escape.

superheterodyne or **supersonic heterodyne** means of receiving radio transmissions involving the changing of the ◊frequency of the carrier wave to an intermediate frequency above the limit of audible sound by a heterodyne process. In this, the received wave is combined with a slightly different frequency wave produced within the receiver. Once the intermediate frequency has been formed, the combined waves are amplified and the signal taken off by a demodulator.

superior planet planet that is farther away from the Sun than the Earth is: that is, Mars, Jupiter, Saturn, Uranus, Neptune, and Pluto.

supernova explosive death of a star, which temporarily attains a brightness of 100 million Suns or more, so that it can shine as brilliantly as a small galaxy for a few days or weeks. Very approximately, it is thought that a supernova explodes in a large galaxy about once every 100 years. Many supernovae – astronomers estimate some 50% – remain undetected because of obscuring by interstellar dust.

supersonic speed speed greater than that at which sound travels, measured in ◊Mach numbers. In dry air at 0°C/32°F, sound travels at about 1,170 kph/727 mph, but decreases its speed with altitude until, at 12,000 m/39,000 ft, it is only 1,060 kph/658 mph.

supersynthesis radio interferometer system in which two synthesis aerials are used; one is static and utilizes the rotation of the Earth to provide a field of scan, the other is mobile.

surface area in mathematics, area of the outside surface of a solid.

surface tension in physics, the property that causes the surface of a liquid to behave as if it were covered with a weak elastic skin; this is why a needle can float on water. It is caused by the exposed surface's tendency to contract to the smallest possible area because of cohesive forces between ◊molecules at the surface. Allied phenomena include the formation of droplets, the concave profile of a meniscus, and the capillary action by which water soaks into a sponge.

surveying the accurate measuring of the Earth's crust, or of land features or buildings. It is used to establish boundaries, and to evaluate the topography for engineering work. The measurements used are both linear and angular, and geometry and trigonometry are applied in the calculations.

suspension bridge bridge in which the spanning roadway or railway is supported by a system of steel ropes suspended from two or more tall towers.

synapse junction between two nerve cells, or between a nerve cell and a muscle (a neuromuscular junction), across which a nerve impulse is transmitted. The two cells are separated by a narrow gap called the **synaptic cleft.** The gap is bridged by a chemical ◊neurotransmitter, released by the nerve impulse.

synchrotron particle ◊accelerator in which particles move, at increasing speed, around a hollow ring. The particles are guided around the ring by electromagnets, and accelerated by electric fields at points around the ring. Synchrotrons come in a wide range of sizes, the smallest being about 1m/3.3 ft across while the largest is 27 km/17 mi across. The Tevatron synchrotron at Fermilab is some 6 km/4 mi in circumference and accelerates protons and antiprotons to 1 TeV.

synchrotron radiation polarized form of ◊radiation produced by high-speed ◊electrons in a magnetic field; it is this radiation that is emitted by the Crab nebula (in Taurus).

syndrome in medicine, a set of signs and symptoms that always occur together, thus characterizing a particular condition or disorder.

synodic period time taken for a planet or moon to return to the same position in its orbit as seen from the Earth; that is, from one ◊opposition to the next. It differs from the ◊sidereal period because the Earth is moving in orbit around the Sun.

synthesis aerial radio interferometer system utilizing a number of small aerials to achieve the effect of an impossibly large single one.

systole in biology, the contraction of the heart. It alternates with diastole, the resting phase of the heart beat.

T

tangent in geometry, a straight line that touches a curve and gives the gradient of the curve at the point of contact. At a maximum, minimum, or point of inflection, the tangent to a curve has zero gradient. Also, in trigonometry, a function of an acute angle in a right-angled triangle, defined as the ratio of the length of the side opposite the angle to the length of the side adjacent to it; a way of expressing the gradient of a line.

tautomerism form of isomerism in which two interconvertible ◊isomers are in equilibrium. It is often specifically applied to an equilibrium between the keto ($-CH_2-C=O$) and enol ($-CH=C-OH$) forms of carbonyl compounds.

Taylor's theorem or *Brook Taylor's theorem* expands a function of x as an infinite power series in powers of x.

tensor calculus position in ordinary space usually requires specification of three coordinates, singly indexed, for example, x_1, x_2, x_3. In describing mathematical objects more complicated than position, a generalized type of coordinate system may be used: for example, x_{ijk} where i, j, k can each take values 1, 2 or 3. Tensor calculus is a systematized use of such awkward objects.

terminal velocity or *terminal speed* the maximum velocity that can be reached by a given object moving through a fluid (gas or liquid) under the action of an applied force. As the speed of the object increases so does the total magnitude of the forces resisting its motion. Terminal velocity is reached when the resistive forces exactly balance the applied force that has caused the object to accelerate; because there is now no resultant force, there can be no further acceleration.

terpene any of a class of organic compounds, originally derived from plant oils, that contain only carbon and hydrogen and are empirically regarded as derivatives of isoprene (C_5H_8). They are classified according to the number of isoprene units in the molecule – for example, monoterpenes contain two isoprene units and have the formula $C_{10}H_{16}$, sesquiterpenes contain three units ($C_{15}H_{24}$), and diterpenes contain four units ($C_{20}H_{32}$). Turpentine consists of a mixture of several monoterpenes. Rubber is a polyterpene with between 1,000 and 5,000 isoprene units.

tertian fever type of fluctuating malarial fever that peaks every third day.

Tertiary period of geological time 65–1.64 million years ago, divided into five epochs: Palaeocene, Eocene, Oligocene, Miocene, and Pliocene. During the Tertiary period, mammals took over all the ecological niches left vacant by the extinction of the dinosaurs, and became the prevalent land animals. The continents took on their present positions, and climatic and vegetation zones as we know them became established. Within the geological time column the Tertiary follows the Cretaceous period and is succeeded by the Quaternary period.

tesla SI unit (symbol T) of ◊magnetic flux density. One tesla represents a flux density of one ◊weber per square metre, or 10^4 gauss. It is named after the Croatian–born US physicist Nikola Tesla.

tesselation covering of a plane surface by regular congruent quadrilaterals in a side-by-side pattern; the first quadrilateral is derived by joining the mid-points of the sides of a given (regular or irregular) quadrilateral.

tetrahedron *plural tetrahedra* in geometry, a solid figure (◊polyhedron) with four triangular faces; that is, a pyramid on a triangular base. A regular tetrahedron has equilateral triangles as its faces.

theodolite device used in ◊surveying for measuring the relative angles and positions of objects, so that plans may be drawn up.

thermal column of warm air, which is of a lower ◊density than its surroundings, and contains rising currents of air.

thermal conductivity in physics, the ability of a substance to conduct heat. Good thermal conductors, like good electrical conductors, are generally materials with many free electrons (such as metals).

thermionic tube or *thermionic valve* an evacuated metal or glass container enclosing a system of electrodes. The ◊cathode emits ◊electrons when heated, and these are attracted to a positively charged ◊anode. Perforated grid electrodes within the tube can be used to control the electron current.

thermochemistry branch of chemistry that deals with the heat changes that accompany chemical reactions.

thermocouple device comprising two wires of different metals (such as copper and iron) joined, and with their other ends held at different temperatures. A small current is set up within the wire proportional to the size of the temperature difference between the two ends. This makes thermocouples useful in the determination of temperature.

thermodynamic equilibrium system is said to be in thermal ◊equilibrium if no heat flows between its component parts.

thermodynamics branch of physics dealing with the transformation of heat into and from other forms of energy. It is the basis of the study of the efficient working of engines, such as the steam and internal-combustion engines. The three laws of thermodynamics are: (1) energy can be neither created nor destroyed, heat and mechanical work being mutually convertible; (2) it is impossible for an unaided self-acting machine to convey heat from one body to another at a higher temperature; and (3) it is impossible by any procedure, no matter how idealized, to reduce any system to the ◊absolute zero of temperature (0 K/–273°C/–459°F) in a finite number of operations. Put into mathematical form, these laws have widespread applications in physics and chemistry.

thermopile instrument for measuring radiant heat, consisting of a number of thermocouples connected in series with alternate junctions exposed to the radiation. The current generated (measured by an ◊ammeter) is proportional to the radiation falling on the device.

thermoplastic or *thermosoftening plastic* type of ◊plastic that always softens on repeated heating. Thermoplastics include polyethylene (polyethene), polystyrene, nylon, and polyester.

theta functions four types of ◊elliptic function devised by German mathematician Carl Jacobi. Each function is defined as a Fourier series, and written θ₁, θ₂, θ₃, and θ₄; any θ can be converted by translation of the argument into another θ multiplied by a simple factor. (The quotient of any two θ is then periodic twice.)

thixotropy property of a substance that enables it to form a jellylike ◊colloid that reverts to a liquid on mechanical agitation. Nondrip paints are common thixotropic materials.

thread, Whitworth see ◊Whitworth standard.

three-body problem mathematical problem in astronomy, to describe the gravitational effects of three interacting celestial bodies on each other, and the shape of their orbits round each other.

thrust propulsive ◊pressure exerted by for example, a jet or rocket engine.

tide the rhythmic rise and fall of the sea level in the Earth's oceans and their inlets and estuaries due to the gravitational attraction of the Moon and, to a lesser extent, the Sun, affecting regions of the Earth unequally as it rotates. Water on the side of the Earth nearest the Moon feels the Moon's pull and accumulates directly below it producing high tide.

Titan in astronomy, the largest moon of the planet Saturn, with a diameter of 5,150 km/3,200 mi and a mean distance from Saturn of 1,222,000 km/759,000 mi. It was discovered in 1655 by Dutch mathematician and astronomer Christiaan Huygens, and is the second-largest moon in the Solar System (Ganymede, of Jupiter, is larger).

Titania fourth (known) moon out from Uranus, and probably its largest.

titration in analytical chemistry, a technique to find the concentration of one compound in a solution by determining how much of it will react with a known amount of another compound in solution.

TNT (abbreviation for **trinitrotoluene**) $CH_3C_6H_2(NO_2)_3$, a powerful high explosive. It is a yellow solid, prepared in several isomeric forms from toluene by using sulphuric and nitric acids.

tolerance in measurement, range in the physical dimensions of an object within which the true dimensions lie. Often expressed in the form of, for example, ± 3 mm for a length.

tolerance in medicine, gradual increase, when a drug is taken over a long period, of resistance to its effects in the patient. This means that more of the drug must be taken to achieve the desired effect.

tomography the technique of using X-rays or ultrasound waves to procure images of structures deep within the body for diagnostic purposes. In modern medical imaging there are several techniques, such as the CAT scan (computerized axial tomography).

topography the surface shape and composition of the landscape, comprising both natural and artificial features, and its study. Topographical features include the relief and contours of the land; the distribution of mountains, valleys, and human settlements; and the patterns of rivers, roads, and railways.

topology branch of geometry that deals with those properties of a figure that remain unchanged even when the figure is transformed (bent, stretched) – for example, when a square painted on a rubber sheet is deformed by distorting the sheet.

Topology has scientific applications, as in the study of turbulence in flowing fluids.

torque turning effect of force on an object. A turbine produces a torque that turns an electricity generator in a power station. Torque is measured by multiplying the force by its perpendicular distance from the turning point.

torus ring with a D-shaped cross-section used to contain ◊plasma in nuclear fusion reactors such as the Joint European Torus (JET) reactor.

total internal reflection the complete reflection of a beam of light that occurs from the surface of an optically 'less dense' material. For example, a beam from an underwater light source can be reflected from the surface of the water, rather than escaping through the surface. Total internal reflection can only happen if a light beam hits a surface at an angle greater than the critical angle for that particular pair of materials.

toxin any poison produced by another living organism (usually a bacterium) that can damage the living body. In vertebrates, toxins are broken down by ◊enzyme action, mainly in the liver.

tracer in science, a small quantity of a radioactive ◊isotope (form of an element) used to follow the path of a chemical reaction or a physical or biological process. The location (and possibly concentration) of the tracer is usually detected by using a Geiger–Muller counter.

trans- prefix used in ◊stereochemistry to indicate that two groups or substituents lie on opposite sides of the main axis or plane of a molecule (as opposed to *cis-*, which indicates that they are on the same side).

transcendental curve curve for which there is no representative algebraic equation; examples are logarithmic curves and trigonometric curves.

transcendental number ◊real number that is not an ◊algebraic number, and can therefore not be expressed as a root (solution) of an algebraic equation with integral coefficients; an example is ◊Euler's number (e).

transfer RNA (tRNA) a relatively small molecule of ribonucleic acid, the function of which is to carry ◊amino acids to ◊ribosomes where ◊protein synthesis occurs. Each amino acid is borne by a different tRNA molecule. tRNA is complementary to ◊messenger RNA (mRNA).

transfinite see ◊set theory.

transformation in mathematics, a mapping or ◊function, especially one which causes a change of shape or position in a geometric figure. Reflection, ◊rotation, enlargement, and translation are the main geometrical transformations.

transformation in genetics, the substitution of one section of ◊DNA by another. It requires at least two crossovers (or breaks) in the DNA and is a source of genetic variation.

transformer device in which, by electromagnetic induction, an alternating current (AC) of one voltage is transformed to another voltage, without change of ◊frequency. Transformers are widely used in electrical apparatus of all kinds, and in particular in power transmission where high voltages and low currents are utilized.

transistor solid-state electronic component, made of ◊semiconductor material, with three or more ◊electrodes, that can regulate a current passing through it. A transistor can act as an amplifier, oscillator, photocell, or switch, and (unlike earlier thermionic valves) usually operates on a very small amount of power. Transistors commonly consist of a tiny sandwich of germanium or ◊silicon, alternate layers having different electrical properties because they are impregnated with minute amounts of different impurities.

transit in astronomy, the passage of a smaller object across the visible disc of a larger one. Transits of the inferior planets occur when they pass directly between the Earth and the Sun, and are seen as tiny dark spots against the Sun's disc.

transition metal any of a group of metallic elements that have incomplete inner electron shells and exhibit variable valency – for example, cobalt, copper, iron, and molybdenum. They are excellent conductors of electricity, and generally form highly coloured compounds.

transuranic element or *transuranium element* chemical element with an atomic number of 93 or more – that is, with a greater number of protons in the nucleus than has uranium. All transuranic elements are radioactive. Neptunium and plutonium are found in nature; the others are synthesized in nuclear reactions.

transverse wave wave in which the displacement of the medium's particles is at right angles to the direction of travel of the wave motion.

Triassic period of geological time 245–208 million years ago, the first period of the Mesozoic era. The continents were fused together to form the world continent ◊Pangaea. Triassic sediments contain remains of early dinosaurs and other reptiles now extinct. By late Triassic times, the first mammals had evolved.

tribology study of ◊friction and similar surface effects.

trigonometry branch of mathematics that solves problems relating to plane and spherical triangles. Its principles are based on the fixed proportions of sides for a particular angle in a right-angled triangle, the simplest of which are known as the ◊sine, ◊cosine, and ◊tangent (so-called trigonometrical ratios). Trigonometry is of practical importance in navigation, surveying, and simple harmonic motion in physics.

trim in ◊aerodynamics, the slight actions on the controls needed to achieve stability in a particular mode of flight.

triode ◊thermionic valve consisting of an ◊anode, a ◊cathode and a grid.

tripeptide sequence of three ◊amino acids, often occurring in the biochemical synthesis or breakdown of ◊proteins.

Triton in astronomy, the largest of Neptune's moons. It has a diameter of 2,700 km/1,680 mi, and orbits Neptune every 5.88 days in a retrograde (east to west) direction. It takes the same time to rotate about its own axis as it does to make one revolution of Neptune.

trophoblast in medicine, the outer layer of the ovum that supplies nutrition to the embryo and attaches the ovum to the wall of the uterus.

trypanosomiasis any of several debilitating long-term diseases caused by a trypanosome (protozoan of the genus *Trypanosoma*). They include sleeping sickness in Africa, transmitted by the bites of tsetse flies, and Chagas's disease in Central and South America, spread by assassin bugs.

T Tauri variable another name for ◊nebular variable star.

turbine engine in which steam, water, gas, or air is made to spin a rotating shaft by pushing on angled blades, like a fan. Turbines are among the most powerful machines. Steam turbines are used to drive generators in power stations and ships' propellers; water turbines spin the generators in hydroelectric power plants; and gas turbines (as jet engines) power most aircraft and drive machines in industry.

turbofan an aero engine in which part of the power produced by the gas turbine engine is used to drive an intake fan inside a duct.

turboprop jet engine that derives its thrust partly from a jet of exhaust gases, but mainly from a propeller powered by a turbine in the jet exhaust. A turboprop typically has a twin-shaft rotor. One shaft carries the compressor and is spun by one turbine, while the other shaft carries a propeller and is spun by a second turbine.

turbulence irregular fluid (gas or liquid) flow, in which vortices and unpredictable fluctuations and motions occur. Streamlining reduces the turbulence of flow around an object, such as an aircraft, and reduces drag. Turbulent flow of a fluid occurs when the ◊Reynolds number is high.

twistor theory model of the universe proposed by English mathematician Roger Penrose, based on the application of complex numbers (involving the square root of –1) used in calculations in the microscopic world of atoms and quantum theory to the macroscopic ordinary world of physical laws and relativity. The result is an eight-dimensional concept of reality.

Tyndall effect scattering of light to produce a visible beam.

U

UBV photometry measurement of the ◊astronomical colour index of a star, utilizing the ultraviolet, blue and yellow visual images over two pre-set wavelengths obtained by ◊photoelectric filtering. Other standardized filter wavebands are also used.

ultrasonics branch of physics dealing with the theory and application of ultrasound: sound waves occurring at frequencies too high to be heard by the human ear (that is, above about 20 kHz).

ultrasound scanning or *ultrasonography* in medicine, the use of ultrasonic pressure waves to create a diagnostic image. It is a safe, noninvasive technique that often eliminates the need for exploratory surgery.

ultraviolet excess screening technique devised by English astronomer Martin Ryle and US astronomer Allan Sandage to measure the spectral red shift of suspected ◊quasars. It was this process that resulted in the discovery of quasars.

ultraviolet radiation electromagnetic radiation invisible to the human eye, of wavelengths from about 400 to 4 nm (where the ◊X-ray range begins). Physiologically, ultraviolet radiation is extremely powerful, producing sunburn and causing the formation of vitamin D in the skin.

umbra central region of a shadow that is totally dark because no light reaches it, and from which no part of the light source can be seen (compare ◊penumbra). In astronomy, it is a region of the Earth from which a complete ◊eclipse of the Sun or Moon can be seen.

uncertainty principle or *indeterminacy principle* in quantum mechanics, the principle that it is impossible to know with unlimited accuracy the position and momentum of a particle. The principle arises because in order to locate a particle exactly, an observer must bounce light (in the form of a ◊photon) off the particle, which must alter its position in an unpredictable way.

unconditioned reflex behavioural reflex or response that is natural and not acquired by training or conditioning.

unconditioned stimulus natural stimulus unassociated with behavioural training; it evokes a natural or unconditioned reflex or response (see ◊conditioned stimulus).

unified field theory in physics, the theory that attempts to explain the four fundamental forces (strong nuclear, weak nuclear, electromagnetic, and gravity) in terms of a single unified force.

uniformitarianism in geology, the principle that processes that can be seen to occur on the Earth's surface today are the same as those that have occurred throughout geological time. For example, desert sandstones containing sand-dune structures must have been formed under conditions similar to those present in deserts today. The principle was formulated by Scottish geologist James Hutton and expounded by Charles Lyell.

unit theory or *theory of units* in a field or ring, involves an element that possesses an inverse. In a field, every nonzero element is a unit; in a ring, 1 and −1 represent a unit.

universal set in set theory, with regard to a ◊mathematical structure, a set of objects in the structure. More generally, it represents the 'universe of discourse' appropriate to the discourse – for example, the set of vowels and the set of consonants are disjoint sets within the universal set comprising the alphabet.

urea cycle biochemical process discovered by German-born British biochemist Hans Adolf Krebs and Henseleit 1932, by which nitrogenous waste is converted into urea, which is easily excreted. When ◊proteins and ◊amino acids break down, ◊ammonia, which is highly toxic, is formed. Most of the ammonia is converted into glutamate, and becomes usable for the synthesis of more amino acids and proteins. Any excess is converted into the water-soluble compound, urea, which can be excreted as urine. Free ammonia, carbon dioxide, and ◊ATP react to form carbamyl phosphate. This compound then forms citrulline by reacting with the amino acid ornithine, which can then accept another amino group giving arginine. Arginine can then break down, giving urea, for excretion, and ornithine, which can take part in the cycle again.

V

vaccine any preparation of modified pathogens (viruses or bacteria) that is introduced into the body, usually either orally or by a hypodermic syringe, to induce the specific ◊antibody reaction that produces ◊immunity against a particular disease.

vacuole in biology, a fluid-filled, membrane-bound cavity inside a cell. It may be a reservoir for fluids that the cell will secrete to the outside, or may be filled with excretory products or essential nutrients that the cell needs to store. Plant cells usually have a large central vacuole containing sap (sugar and salts in solution) which serves both as a store of food and as a key factor in maintaining turgor. In amoebae (single-celled animals), vacuoles are the sites of digestion of engulfed food particles.

vacuum in general, a region completely empty of matter; in physics, any enclosure in which the gas pressure is considerably less than atmospheric pressure (101,325 pascals).

valency in chemistry, the measure of an element's ability to combine with other elements, expressed as the number of atoms of hydrogen (or any other standard univalent element) capable of uniting with (or replacing) its atoms. The number of electrons in the outermost shell of the atom dictates the combining ability of an element.

valve, thermionic see ◊thermionic valve.

vanadium silver-white, malleable and ductile, metallic element, symbol V, atomic number 23, relative atomic mass 50.942. It occurs in certain iron, lead, and uranium ores and is widely distributed in small quantities in igneous and sedimentary rocks. It is used to make steel alloys, to which it adds tensile strength.

Van Allen radiation belts two zones of charged particles around the Earth's magnetosphere, discovered in 1958 by US physicist James Van Allen. The atomic particles come from the Earth's upper atmosphere and the ◊solar wind, and are trapped by the Earth's magnetic field. The inner belt lies 1,000–5,000 km/620–3,100 mi above the Equator, and contains ◊protons and ◊electrons. The outer belt lies 15,000–25,000 km/9,300–15,500 mi above the Equator, but is lower around the magnetic poles. It contains mostly electrons from the solar wind.

van de Graaff generator electrostatic generator capable of producing a voltage of over a million volts. It consists of a continuous vertical conveyor belt that carries electrostatic charges (resulting from friction) up to a large hollow sphere supported on an insulated stand. The lower end of the belt is earthed, so that charge accumulates on the sphere. The size of the voltage built up in air depends on the radius of the sphere, but can be increased by enclosing the generator in an inert atmosphere, such as nitrogen.

van der Waals' law modified form of the gas laws that includes corrections for the non-ideal behaviour of real gases (the molecules of ideal gases occupy no space and exert no forces on each other). It is named after Dutch physicist J D van der Waals.

vapour one of the three states of matter (see also ◊solid and ◊liquid). The molecules in a vapour move randomly and are far apart, the distance between them, and therefore the volume of the vapour, being limited only by the walls of any vessel in which they might be contained. A vapour differs from a ◊gas only in that a vapour can be liquefied by increased pressure, whereas a gas cannot unless its temperature is lowered below its ◊critical temperature; it then becomes a vapour and may be liquefied.

vapour density density of a gas, expressed as the ◊mass of a given volume of the gas divided by the mass of an equal volume of a reference gas (such as hydrogen or air) at the same temperature and pressure. It is equal approximately to half the relative molecular weight (mass) of the gas.

vapour pressure pressure of a vapour given off by (evaporated from) a liquid or solid, caused by vibrating atoms or molecules continuously escaping from its surface. In an enclosed space, a maximum value is reached when the number of particles leaving the surface is in equilibrium with those returning to it; this is known as the **saturated vapour pressure** or **equilibrium vapour pressure**.

variable in mathematics, a changing quantity (one that can take various values), as opposed to a constant. For example, in the algebraic expression $y = 4x^3 + 2$, the variables are x and y, whereas 4 and 2 are constants.

variable star in astronomy, a star whose brightness changes, either regularly or irregularly, over a period ranging from a few hours to months or years. The ◊Cepheid variables regularly expand and contract in size every few days or weeks.

variance in statistics, the square of the ◊standard deviation, the measure of spread of data. Population and sample variance are denoted by Σ^2 or s^2, respectively. Variance provides a measure of the dispersion of a set of statistical results about the mean or average value.

variety in algebra, the set of solutions of a simultaneous system of equations with a fixed number of variables. In two dimensions, examples are a circle, an ellipse, and a parabola. In three dimensions, a variety is a surface, for example, the surface of a sphere.

vector space or **linear space** mathematical structure comprising two types of objects: vectors and scalars. Vectors can be added by themselves; scalars lengthen or shorten them (that is, scale the vector length up or down) and are commonly either real or complex numbers. In general, scalars of a vector space comprise a field. The prime example of a vector space is the collection of elementary vectors in the two- or three-dimensional space of everyday experience. (The operation of addition follows the parallelogram law: to add two vectors, complete the parallelogram defined by the two lines – the sum is given by the diagonal through the common origin.) Vector spaces provide a framework for the study of linear transformations – which can be represented by ◊matrices in finite-dimensional spaces – and are important in mathematical modelling of complicated systems (engineering, biological, and so on) where general transformations are approximated by linear ones, with recourse to the apparatus of differential calculus.

Vega or **Alpha Lyrae** brightest star in the constellation Lyra and the fifth-brightest star in the night sky. It is a blue-white star, 25 light years from the Sun, with a true luminosity 50 times that of the Sun.

Venn diagram in mathematics, a diagram representing a ◊set or sets and the logical relationships between them. The sets are drawn as circles. An area of overlap between two circles (sets) contains elements that are common to both sets, and thus represents a third set. Circles that do not overlap represent sets with no elements in common (disjoint sets). The method is named after the English logician John Venn.

vernal equinox see spring ◊equinox.

vernalization the stimulation of flowering by exposure to cold. Certain plants will not flower unless subjected to low temperatures during their development. For example, winter wheat will flower in summer only if planted in the previous autumn. However, by placing partially germinated seeds in low temperatures for several days, the cold requirement can be supplied artificially, allowing the wheat to be sown in the spring.

vernier device for taking readings on a graduated scale to a fraction of a division. It consists of a short divided scale that carries an index or pointer and is slid along a main scale. It was invented by French engineer Pierre Vernier.

vesicle small sac containing liquid. It is the medical term for a blister or elevation of the outer layer of the skin (epidermis) containing serous fluid.

vestigial organ in biology, an organ that remains in diminished form after it has ceased to have any significant function in the adult organism. In humans, the appendix is vestigial, having once had a digestive function in our ancestors.

Viking probes two US space probes to Mars, each one consisting of an orbiter and a lander. They were launched on 20 August and 9 September 1975. They transmitted colour pictures and analysed the soil.

virtual particle theory theory devised by English physicist Stephen Hawking to account for apparent thermal radiation from a black hole (from which not even light can escape). It supposes that space is full of 'virtual particles' in a particle–antiparticle relationship, being created out of 'nothing' and instantly destroying each other. At an ◊event horizon, however, one particle may be gravitationally drawn into the ◊singularity, and the other appear to radiate as heat.

virus infectious particle consisting of a core of nucleic acid (DNA or RNA) enclosed in a protein shell. Viruses are acellular and able to function and reproduce only if they can invade a living cell to use the cell's system to replicate themselves. In the process they may disrupt or alter the host cell's own DNA. The healthy human body reacts by producing an antiviral protein, interferon, which prevents the infection spreading to adjacent cells.

There are around 5,000 species of virus known to science (1998), though there may be as many as 0.5 million actually in existence.

viscosity in physics, the resistance of a fluid to flow, caused by its internal friction, which makes it resist flowing past a solid surface or other layers of the fluid. It applies to the motion of an object moving through a fluid as well as to the motion of a fluid passing by an object.

viscous force drag that occurs on an object placed in a viscous medium. For example, air causes a viscous force on an aircraft travelling through it. For two parallel layers of fluid close to each other, the viscous force is proportional to the difference in velocity between the two layers.

vision, persistence of see ◊persistence of vision.

vitalism the idea that living organisms derive their characteristic properties from a universal life force. In the 20th century, this view is associated with the French philosopher Henri Bergson.

vitamin any of various chemically unrelated organic compounds that are necessary in small quantities for the normal functioning of the human body. Many act as coenzymes, small molecules that enable ◊enzymes to function effectively. Vitamins must be supplied by the diet because the body cannot make them. They are normally present in adequate amounts in a balanced diet. Deficiency of a vitamin may lead to a metabolic disorder ('deficiency disease'), which can be remedied by sufficient intake of the vitamin. They are generally classified as *water-soluble* (B and C) or *fat-soluble* (A, D, E, and K).

volcano crack in the Earth's crust through which hot magma (molten rock) and gases well up. The magma is termed lava when it reaches the surface. A volcanic mountain, usually cone shaped with a crater on top, is formed around the opening, or vent, by the build-up of solidified lava and ashes (rock fragments). Most volcanoes arise on plate margins (see ◊plate tectonics), where the movements of plates generate magma or allow it to rise from the mantle beneath. However, a number are found far from plate-margin activity, on 'hot spots' where the Earth's crust is thin.

volt SI unit of electromotive force or electric potential, symbol V. A small battery has a potential of 1.5 volts, whilst a high-tension transmission line may carry up to 765,000 volts. The domestic electricity supply in the UK is 230 volts (lowered from 240 volts in 1995); it is 110 volts in the USA.

voltaic cell another name for an electric ◊cell.

volumetric analysis procedure used for determining the concentration of a solution. A known volume of a solution of unknown concentration is reacted with a solution of known concentration (standard). The standard solution is delivered from a burette so the volume added is known. This technique is known as ◊titration. Often an indicator is used to show when the correct proportions have reacted. This procedure is used for acid–base, redox, and certain other reactions involving solutions.

Voyager probes two US space probes. *Voyager 1*, launched on 5 September 1977, passed Jupiter in March 1979, and reached Saturn in November 1980. *Voyager 2* was launched earlier, on 20 August 1977, on a slower trajectory that took it past Jupiter in July 1979, Saturn in August 1981, Uranus in January 1986, and Neptune in August 1989. Like the ◊Pioneer probes, the *Voyagers* are on their way out of the Solar System; in August 1999, *Voyager 1* was 11.2 billion km/8.7 billion mi from Earth, and *Voyager 2* was 8.7 billion km/5.4 billion mi from Earth. Their tasks now include helping scientists to locate the position of the heliopause, the boundary at which the influence of the Sun gives way to the forces exerted by other stars.

vulcanization technique for hardening rubber by heating and chemically combining it with sulphur. The process also makes the rubber stronger and more elastic. If the sulphur content is increased to as much as 30%, the product is the inelastic solid known as ebonite. More expensive alternatives to sulphur, such as selenium and tellurium, are used to vulcanize rubber for specialized products such as vehicle tyres. The process was discovered accidentally by US inventor Charles Goodyear in 1839 and patented in 1844.

W

Wankel engine rotary petrol engine developed by the German engineer Felix Wankel in the 1950s. It operates according to the same stages as the ◊four-stroke petrol engine cycle, but these stages take place in different sectors of a figure-eight chamber in the space between the chamber walls and a triangular rotor. Three power strokes are produced for every turn of the rotor. The Wankel engine is simpler in construction than the four-stroke piston petrol engine, and produces rotary power directly (instead of via a crankshaft). Problems with rotor seals have prevented its widespread use.

warp threads in weaving stretched lengthwise across the fabric. Compare ◊weft.

water gas mixture of carbon monoxide and hydrogen gas, produced by passing steam over hot coke.

watt SI unit (symbol W) of power (the rate of expenditure or consumption of energy) defined as one joule per second. A light bulb, for example, may use 40, 60, 100, or 150 watts of power; an electric heater will use several kilowatts (thousands of watts). The watt is named after the Scottish engineer James Watt.

wave, electromagnetic see ◊electromagnetic wave.

wavefront line of points in a wave motion that are all of equal ◊phase.

wavelength the distance between successive crests of a wave. The wavelength of a light wave determines its colour; red light has a wavelength of about 700 nanometres, for example. The complete range of wavelengths of electromagnetic waves is called the electromagnetic ◊spectrum.

wave, longitudinal see ◊longitudinal wave.

wave mechanics branch of ◊quantum theory that derives the various properties of ◊atoms on the basis of every particle having an associated wave existing in a multidimensional space, representing probabilities of certain properties of the particles involved. ◊Schrödinger's equation is the basis of wave mechanics, which has been shown to be equivalent to ◊matrix mechanics.

wave, transverse see ◊transverse wave.

wax solid fatty substance of animal, vegetable, or mineral origin. Waxes are composed variously of ◊esters, ◊fatty acids, free ◊alcohols, and solid hydrocarbons.

weak nuclear force or *weak interaction* one of the four fundamental forces of nature, the other three being gravity, the electromagnetic force, and the strong force. It causes radioactive beta decay and other subatomic reactions. The particles that carry the weak force are called weakons (or intermediate vector bosons) and comprise the positively and negatively charged W particles and the neutral Z particle.

weber SI unit (symbol Wb) of ◊magnetic flux (the magnetic field strength multiplied by the area through which the field passes). It is named after German chemist Wilhelm Weber. One weber equals 10^8 maxwells.

weft threads across the width of the material to be formed by weaving.

welding joining pieces of metal (or nonmetal) at faces rendered plastic or liquid by heat or pressure (or both). The principal processes today are gas and arc welding, in which the heat from a gas flame or an electric arc melts the faces to be joined. Additional 'filler metal' is usually added to the joint.

Wheatstone bridge circuit that is divided into sections enabling the relative ◊resistances or devices placed in the sections to be deduced.

white blood cell or *leucocyte* one of a number of different cells that play a part in the body's defences and give immunity against disease. Some (neutrophils and macrophages) engulf invading microorganisms, others kill infected cells, while lymphocytes produce more specific immune responses. White blood cells are colourless, with clear or granulated cytoplasm, and are capable of independent amoeboid movement. They occur in the blood, lymph, and elsewhere in the body's tissues.

white dwarf small, hot star, the last stage in the life of a star such as the Sun. White dwarfs make up 10% of the stars in the Galaxy; most have a mass 60% of that of the Sun, but only 1% of the Sun's diameter, similar in size to the Earth. Most have surface temperatures of 8,000°C/14,400°F or more, hotter than the Sun. Yet, being so small, their overall luminosities may be less than 1% of that of the Sun. The Milky Way contains an estimated 50 billion white dwarfs.

Whitworth standard standard of screw thread used before the advent of the metric standard, in which the pitch of the ◊helix is standardized relative to the diameter of the bar on which the thread is cut.

Wien's law relationship between the intensity and frequency of black-body radiation at the high-frequency end of the ◊spectrum. Wien's displacement law relates the wave-length of maximum intensity to the temperature of the black body.

wind tunnel an enclosure that contains a large ◊turbine capable of sending air streams over any object (such as a model aircraft) whose ◊aerodynamic performance is to be assessed. Lift, drag, and airflow patterns are observed by the use of special cameras and sensitive instruments. Wind-tunnel testing is used to assess aerodynamic design, prior to full-scale construction.

work in physics, a measure of the result of transferring energy from one system to another to cause an object to move. Work should not be confused with energy (the capacity to do work, which is also measured in joules) or with power (the rate of doing work, measured in joules per second).

working fluid ◊fluid that is used in such a way that its internal energy is converted into external energy. One example is water in ◊hydroelectricity generation.

wrought iron fairly pure iron containing some beads of slag, widely used for construction work before the days of cheap steel. It is strong, tough, and easy to machine. It is made in a puddling furnace, invented by Henry Colt in England in 1784. Pig iron is remelted and heated strongly in air with iron ore, burning out the carbon in the metal, leaving relatively pure iron and a slag containing impurities. The resulting pasty metal is then hammered to remove as much of the remaining slag as possible. It is still used in fences and gratings.

X Y Z

X-ray band of electromagnetic radiation in the wavelength range 10^{-11} to 10^{-9} m (between gamma rays and ultraviolet radiation; see ◊electromagnetic waves). Applications of X-rays make use of their short wavelength (as in ◊X-ray diffraction) or their penetrating power (as in medical X-rays of internal body tissues). X-rays are dangerous and can cause cancer.

X-ray astronomy detection of X-rays from intensely hot gas in the universe. Such X-rays are prevented from reaching the Earth's surface by the atmosphere, so detectors must be placed in rockets and satellites. The first celestial X-ray source, Scorpius X-1, was discovered by a rocket flight in 1962.

X-ray diffraction method of studying the atomic and molecular structure of crystalline substances by using ◊X-rays. X-rays directed at such substances spread out as they pass through the crystals owing to ◊diffraction (the slight spreading of waves around the edge of an opaque object) of the rays around the atoms. By using measurements of the position and intensity of the diffracted waves, it is possible to calculate the shape and size of the atoms in the crystal. The method has been used to study substances such as ◊DNA that are found in living material.

xylem tissue found in vascular plants, whose main function is to conduct water and dissolved mineral nutrients from the roots to other parts of the plant. Xylem is composed of a number of different types of cell, and may include long, thin, usually dead cells known as tracheids; fibres (schlerenchyma); thin-walled parenchyma cells; and conducting vessels.

yarn thread that has been spun.

yeast one of various single-celled fungi that form masses of tiny round or oval cells by budding. When placed in a sugar solution the cells multiply and convert the sugar into alcohol and carbon dioxide. Yeasts are used as fermenting agents in baking, brewing, and the making of wine and spirits. Brewer's yeast (*Saccharomyces cerevisiae*) is a rich source of vitamin B.

ylem hypothetical primordial state of matter – neutrons and their decay products (protons and electrons) – that might have existed before the Big Bang. The term was taken from Aristotle and forms part of the alpha-beta-gamma theory.

Zeeman effect splitting of ◊spectral lines of a substance placed in an intense magnetic field.

zenith uppermost point of the celestial horizon, immediately above the observer; the nadir is below, diametrically opposite. See ◊celestial sphere.

zeta function function that may be represented as the value of the infinite series:

$$\zeta(s) = 1 + \frac{1}{2^s} + \frac{1}{3^s} + \frac{1}{4^s} + \ldots$$

where s is a complex number. The function was significant in Swiss mathematician Leonhard Euler's study of prime numbers. See also the ◊Riemann hypothesis.

zodiac zone of the heavens containing the paths of the Sun, Moon, and planets. When this was devised by the ancient Greeks, only five planets were known, making the zodiac about 16° wide. In astrology, the zodiac is divided into 12 signs, each 30° in extent: Aries, Taurus, Gemini, Cancer, Leo, Virgo, Libra, Scorpio, Sagittarius, Capricorn, Aquarius, and Pisces. These do not cover the same areas of sky as the astronomical constellations.

zodiacal light cone-shaped light sometimes seen extending from the Sun along the ◊ecliptic, visible after sunset or before sunrise. It is due to thinly spread dust particles in the central plane of the Solar System. It is very faint, and requires a dark, clear sky to be seen.

zone of avoidance apparent lack of distant ◊galaxies in the plane of our own Galaxy, now explained as being caused by optical interference of dust and interstellar debris on the rim of the Galaxy.

zygote ovum (egg) after fertilization but before it undergoes cleavage to begin embryonic development.

Index

Index

The index refers to the biographies in which the index entries appear. An index entry in uppercase indicates that the scientist has a biography in the book.